WATER INFORMATION CENTER, INC.

PERIODICALS

Water Newsletter

Research and Development News

Ground Water Newsletter

BOOKS

Geraghty and Miller   *Water Atlas of the United States*

Todd   *The Water Encyclopedia*

van der Leeden   *Ground Water — A Selected Bibliography*

Giefer and Todd   *Water Publications of State Agencies*

Soil Conservation Service   *Drainage of Agricultural Land*

Gray   *Handbook on the Principles of Hydrology*

National Water Commission   *Water Policies for the Future*

Publication of this book, which is a photographic reproduction of the text of the paperback edition issued by the U.S. Government Printing Office, has been undertaken to make this significant report available in an enduring casebound format for general and reference use.

Reprinted 1973 by Water Information Center, Inc., Water Research Building, Manhasset Isle, Port Washington, N.Y. 11050.

Library of Congress Catalog Card Number: 73-91106

ISBN: 0-912394-08-0

Printed in the United States of America

WATER

POLICIES

FOR THE

FUTURE

~~~~~~

**Final Report to the President
and to the Congress of the
United States by the
National Water Commission**

Published by
WATER INFORMATION CENTER INC.
Port Washington, N.Y.

NATIONAL WATER COMMISSION
800 N. Quincy Street
Arlington, Virginia 22203

June 14, 1973

The President
The White House

The Honorable
The Speaker of the House
of Representatives

The Honorable
The President of the
Senate

Dear Mr. President:

Dear Mr. Speaker:

Dear Mr. President:

The final report of the National Water Commission is presented herewith in accordance with the provisions of Public Law 90-515, approved September 26, 1968, which established the Commission.

The report contains the Commission's conclusions and recommendations on the policies which it believes the Nation should adopt at this point in its history for the efficient, equitable, and environmentally responsible management of its water resources.

The Commission has examined virtually the entire range of water resources problems facing the Nation, including the effects of water management on the Nation's economy and on its environment and how the differences between these two major objectives can be best resolved. The problems of reconciling Federal and State water law have been addressed, as have the problems of integrating ground water and surface water management. Each of the important purposes for which water is used has been studied, and appropriate policies have been drawn for improving both water-related programs and organizational arrangements. Ways in which existing water supplies can be used more efficiently and present supplies can be augmented have also been examined. Standards by which interbasin transfers of water and other kinds of water projects should be judged have been developed and ways in which water management decisionmaking can be improved have been formulated. The report considers the problems of acquiring basic water data and pursuing research so that management of the Nation's water resources can be more knowledgeably and effectively based. Finally, the financing of future water programs as well as the important question of how and by whom the cost of water programs should be paid are also addressed.

Accompanying the Commission's discussion and conclusions on these and other aspects of water resources are specific recommendations for action at the Federal, State, and local levels. Many of these recommendations would require enactment of new legislation. Some, however, could be accomplished by executive action alone or by action of State and local entities.

The Commission has had the cooperation of and extensive review and comments from all levels of government, from private organizations, and from interested citizens. For this and for the broad range of public participation incident to the preparation of this report, the Commission is grateful. It is particularly appreciative of the cooperation of the Water Resources Council and its constituent agencies for their helpful review and comments. Finally, the Commission acknowledges with gratitude the valuable work of its staff; the research and analysis of universities, firms, public agencies, and individuals who worked for the Commission under contract; and the advice and guidance received from the experts who served the Commission as consultants.

The Commission transmits its final report to you with the earnest hope that it will contribute importantly to the timely and wise solution of America's water resources problems.

Respectfully submitted,

Charles F. Luce
Chairman

Howell Appling, Jr.

James R. Ellis

Roger C. Ernst

Ray K. Linsley

James E. Murphy

Josiah Wheat

The Commission

Charles F. Luce, Chairman

Chairman of the Board of Trustees and Chief Executive Officer, Consolidated Edison Company of New York, Inc., since 1967. Native of Platteville, Wisconsin. BA, LLB, University of Wisconsin; Sterling Fellowship, Yale Law School. Law clerk to Mr. Justice Hugo L. Black for the Supreme Court term of 1943-44. Attorney, Bonneville Power Administration, Portland, Oregon. Private practice of law for 15 years in Walla Walla, Washington. During 1947-61, served as general counsel for the Confederated Tribes of the Umatilla Indian Reservation, Pendleton, Oregon. Appointed Bonneville Power Administrator in 1961. Member of U.S. negotiating team which concluded protocols to the Treaty with Canada for cooperative development of the Columbia River. In 1966 President Johnson appointed Mr. Luce Under Secretary of the Interior. Member, Board of Trustees of Columbia University in the City of New York; and of the Boards of Metropolitan Life Insurance Company, UAL, Inc., and United Airlines, Inc. Mr. Luce was appointed to the National Water Commission on October 9, 1968.

Howell Appling, Jr.

Founder and President, Independent Distributors, Inc., a wholesale farm equipment distribution firm in Portland, Oregon. Mr. Appling is an engineering graduate of Rice University; a former member of the State of Oregon Land Board; former Oregon Secretary of State; Director and former President, National Farm Equipment Wholesalers' Association; consultant to Oregon State University Agricultural Experiment Stations; Member, State of Oregon Investment Council; former member, State of Oregon Board of Control; former member, State of Oregon Banking Board; former water treatment engineer, Consolidated Chemical Industries, Inc., of Houston, Texas, and Baton Rouge, La. Mr. Appling was appointed April 9, 1969, to fill the place left vacant by Russell E. Train, who had resigned to become Under Secretary of the Interior.

James R. Ellis

Attorney and partner in the law firm of Preston, Thorgrimson, Ellis, Holman and Fletcher, Seattle, Washington; Member, Board of Regents, University of Washington, 1965 to date, President 1971-72; Trustee; The Ford Foundation, 1970 to date; Vice President and member of the Council, National Municipal League, 1968 to date; Member of the Council, Chairman of Emerging Issues Committee, past Chairman of Metropolitan Government Committee and American Institute of Planners Liaison Committee, Section of Local Government Law, American Bar Association; President, Forward Thrust, Inc., 1966 to date; President, Municipal League of Seattle and King County, 1962-64; Member, Washington State Planning Advisory Council, 1966-72; Member, Urban Transportation Advisory Council, U.S. Department of Transportation, 1970. Mr. Ellis was appointed to the National Water Commission on October 30, 1970.

Roger C. Ernst

Consultant, Arizona Public Service Company, and President, Central Arizona Water Conservation District. He also is a member of the Arizona State Water Quality Control Council and the Arizona Water Resources Council, and President of the Association on American Indian Affairs. Mr. Ernst was formerly State Land Commissioner, State Water commissioner, and State Engineer for Arizona. He was also formerly an Assistant Secretary of the Interior and served as General Manager of the Wellton-Mohawk Irrigation District, and Assistant to the General Manager of the Salt River Valley Water Users Association. He is a native of Colorado. Mr. Ernst was appointed to the National Water Commission on November 21, 1969.

Ray K. Linsley

Professor of Hydraulic Engineering, Stanford University. Also served as Executive Head, Department of Civil Engineering, Associate Dean, and Director of Program in Engineering-Economic Planning. Before joining the University, Mr. Linsley worked with the Tennessee Valley Authority and with the U.S. Weather Bureau. On leave from the University, he was Fulbright Professor at Imperial College of Science and Technology, London, England, and Staff Assistant, Office of Science and Technology, Washington, D.C. Mr. Linsley is consultant to various Federal agencies, State of California, World Meteorological Organization, UNESCO, and several foreign governments. He serves as President of Hydrocomp International and has authored several textbooks in hydrology and water resources engineering and numerous technical papers. He is a Registered Professional Engineer in California and Connecticut. Mr. Linsley has been a member of the National Water Commission since October 9, 1968.

James E. Murphy

Attorney and member of the law firm of Murphy, Robinson, Heckathorn, and Phillips, Kalispell, Montana. Native of Laredo, Missouri; Member of the Missouri House of Representatives, 1939-41. Wheat rancher and a Director of the Conrad National Bank of Kalispell, Montana, Member of the Columbia Interstate Compact Commission. Montana representative on the Pacific Northwest River Basins Commission from 1966 to 1969. Member of the Montana House of Representatives 1967-73, and Chairman of its Judiciary Committee. Co-author, Montana Water Conservancy District Act. Former member of the Republican National Committee for Montana. Mr. Murphy was appointed to the National Water Commission on October 30, 1970.

Josiah Wheat

Partner in the law firm of Wheat, Wheat and Stafford of Woodville, Texas; Legal Counsel, Texas Water Quality Board; Assistant General Counsel, Lower Neches Valley Authority; formerly Chairman of the Board and twice President, Texas Water Conservation Association; Past President, State Bar of Texas; Member, House of Delegates, American Bar Association; Fellow, American Bar Foundation; Member, Executive Committee, State Bar of Texas Section on Environmental Law; Member, American Bar Association Special Committee on Environmental Law; Past President, Deep East Texas Council of Governments. Mr. Wheat was appointed to the National Water Commission on November 21, 1969.

FORMER COMMISSIONERS

Samuel S. Baxter (October 9, 1968 — October 30, 1970)

Consulting Engineer; formerly Commissioner and Chief Engineer, Water Department, City of Philadelphia, Pennsylvania. Past National President, American Society of Civil Engineers, American Water Works Association, and American Public Works Association.

Frank C. Di Luzio (October 9, 1968 — November 21, 1969)

Civil Engineer, Special Assistant to the Governor of New Mexico, formerly Vice President, Edgerton, Germeshausen and Grier, Inc., and President, Reynolds Electrical and Engineering Company, Inc. Mr. Di Luzio was also an Assistant Secretary of the Interior and prior to his appointment to that office he was Director of the Office of Saline Water in that Department.

Clyde T. Ellis (October 9, 1968 — October 30, 1970)

Attorney, Member of the staff of the Senate Appropriations Committee. Formerly General Manager of the National Rural Electric Cooperative Association and before that a Representative from Arkansas in the Congress of the United States.

Russell E. Train (October 9, 1968 – January 20, 1969)

Attorney, Chairman of the Council on Environmental Quality, Executive Office of the President. Formerly Under Secretary of the Interior. Before that he was President, The Conservation Foundation, and a judge of the U.S. Tax Court.

Myron A. Wright (October 9, 1968 – November 21, 1969)

Civil Engineer, Executive Vice President, Exxon Corporation; Chairman of the Board and Chief Executive Officer, Exxon Company, U.S.A. (formerly Humble Oil and Refining Company). Past President of the Chamber of Commerce of the United States and the National Wildlife Federation, and a governor of the U.S. Postal Service.

APPRECIATION

The Commission wishes to take this opportunity to express its sincere appreciation to the members of the staff and its consultants who gave so unstintingly of their time and efforts to help the Commission, to the former members of the Commission who helped lay the ground work, and particularly to recognize the wisdom and perspicacity of Professor Abel Wolman who helped guide the Commission in the deliberations which led to this report.

The Commission pauses during its 44th Meeting on October 17, 1972, for this photo. 1. to r. Murphy, Appling, Ernst, Schad, Luce, James Ellis, Linsley, Wheat.

PROFESSIONAL STAFF*

Executive Director	Theodore M. Schad
Deputy Director	Howard L. Cook
Assistant Director-Programs	Ralph E. Fuhrman
Assistant Director-Administration	Robert N. Baker
Assistant to the Director	Florence Broussard
Editor-in-Chief	Myron B. Katz

Legal Division

Philip M. Glick, Legal Counsel
Charles J. Meyers
Ernst Liebman
John L. DeWeerdt
Richard L. Dewsnup
Gary L. Greer
William A. Hillhouse II

Engineering and Environmental Sciences Division

Victor A. Koelzer, Chief
Edwin B. Haycock
Alexander Bigler
Kenneth L. Bowden
John S. Gladwell
Jack D. Lackner
Thomas Scott
Richard Tucker
Robert E. Vincent

Social and Behavioral Sciences Division

Lyle E. Craine, Chief
  (June 1969 – August 1970)
Dean E. Mann, Chief
  (September 1970 – October 1971)
Gary Taylor
Harry R. Seymour
Frank Bollman
Helen Ingram
Ray M. Johns
Truman P. Price
John H. Stierna
Henry Vaux, Jr.
Ann S. Wilm

Forecast Division

Russell G. Thompson
M. Leon Hyatt

PRINCIPAL CONSULTANTS

Edward A. Ackerman**	Ralph W. Johnson
Harvey O. Banks	Gilbert F. White
Irving K. Fox	Edward Weinberg
Maynard M. Hufschmidt	Nathaniel Wollman

Abel Wolman

*Members of the staff who served for a year or more. See Appendix III for complete roster of staff members, with biographical sketches of principal staff members.
**Deceased

Water is one of several resources without which a Nation cannot satisfy the fundamental wants of its people or achieve the important national goals it sets for itself. Without water, life itself cannot be sustained. But this is true of other resources as well—sunlight, soil, air. Just as it cannot be established which blade of a scissors does the cutting, it cannot be determined which of several critical resources is most important to the Nation's welfare. Each is indispensable. Each must be husbanded and cared for, protected from overuse and misuse, in order that the people may prosper and civilization may flourish.

As with most other critical resources, the rate of use of water in the United States is rapidly increasing. Moreover, the Nation has experienced deterioration in the quality of its surface and ground water supplies. As the Nation's population expands, as it grows more industrialized and urbanized, competing demands upon water increase. To determine what policies the Nation should adopt at this point in its history so that its finite water resources yield the highest measure of utility to society is the mission of the National Water Commission and the purpose of this report. The Commission in carrying out its mission has sought to look forward, not backward. It has asked, and tried to answer, whether basic water policies of the past are suited for conditions of the present and the foreseeable future. In no way has the Commission attempted to pass judgment on the wisdom of past water policies for the times in which they were fashioned.

Background

The National Water Commission was established by an Act of Congress approved by the President on September 26, 1968. It stemmed from proposals for water developments in the Colorado River Basin which raised a number of fundamental questions as to the future policies for water resources development in the United States. Congress was asked in those proposals to authorize the Central Arizona Project in Arizona and New Mexico, to establish a Lower Colorado River Basin Development Fund, to authorize the Bridge Canyon and Marble Canyon dams affecting the Grand Canyon of the Colorado, and to authorize study of importation of water into the Colorado River basin from other regions of the country. The U.S. Bureau of the Budget, the predecessor of the present Office of Management and Budget, advised the Senate Committee on Interior and Insular Affairs in May 1965 that, although it had no objection to authorization of the Central Arizona Project and the Lower Colorado River Development Fund, many of the other proposals required further careful study. The Bureau pointed out that while the long-range water problems of the Lower Colorado River basin were serious, such problems were by no means limited to that area; they were becoming increasingly critical for other parts of the country as well.

Under these circumstances, concluded the Bureau, it would be appropriate to review water resource development problems and opportunities for the Nation as a whole, and the Bureau recommended establishment of a national water commission. "Only a national commission," it said, "can effectively assess the many common aspects of water problems that we face, and only such a commission can outline the consistent courses of action which must be followed if this Nation is to achieve the most efficient utilization of its precious water resources."

Several bills to establish a national water commission for these purposes were promptly introduced and considered by the Congress and its committees during the ensuing 3 years. On September 26, 1968, the President approved the National Water Commission Act.[1] The text of the Act is reproduced as Appendix I.

The National Water Commission Act

The duties of the Commission are stated in one long sentence, Section 3(a) of the National Water Commission Act, which says:

The Commission shall (1) review present and anticipated national water resource problems,

---

[1] P.L. 90-515, September 26, 1968, 82 Stat. 868, 42 USCA 1962a, note (1971 Supp.).

making such projections of water requirements as may be necessary and identifying alternative ways of meeting these requirements—giving consideration, among other things, to conservation and more efficient use of existing supplies, increased usability by reduction of pollution, innovations to encourage the highest economic use of water, interbasin transfers, and technological advances including, but not limited to, desalting, weather modification, and waste water purification and reuse; (2) consider economic and social consequences of water resource development, including, for example, the impact of water resource development on regional economic growth, on institutional arrangements, and on esthetic values affecting the quality of life of the American people; and (3) advise on such specific water resource matters as may be referred to it by the President and the Water Resources Council.

The Commission is composed of seven members appointed by the President and serving at his pleasure, with a chairman designated by the President. The Commissioners serve on a part-time basis, and have other continuing occupations. They are forbidden to hold any other position as officers or employees of the United States. The names and identification of the Commissioners appear on pages iv, v, and vi.

The Commission is required to consult with the Water Resources Council regarding its studies and to furnish proposed reports and recommendations to the Council for review and comment.

The Commission is authorized to make interim and final reports and to submit these reports simultaneously to the President and the Congress. The President is required to transmit the Commission's final report to the Congress together with such comments and recommendations for legislation as he deems appropriate.

The Commission is to terminate not later than September 26, 1973. Five million dollars was authorized to be appropriated for its work.

Earlier Water Study Commissions

The United States has made frequent use of congressional or presidential study commissions to examine difficult problems and to propose solutions. Since the turn of the century, at least 20 national commissions or similar groups have been established by Congress or the President to study water resources. The first was the Inland Waterways Commission established by President Theodore Roosevelt in 1907, and the last, until now, was the Senate Select Committee on National Water Resources established in 1959.[2]

Many of the recommendations of these earlier water study commissions were later enacted into law, although some were enacted only after they were subsequently endorsed by other commissions after many years had elapsed. For example, most of the main ideas embodied in the Water Resources Planning Act[3] in 1965 were repeatedly explored by many of these forerunner study groups and can be found in their recommendations many years earlier.

Role of the National Water Commission

The National Water Commission and its assignment differ from the previous water policy study commissions in several significant respects. The Commission is charged with studying virtually all water problems, programs, and policies in the context of their relationship to the total environment, including "esthetic values affecting the quality of life of the American people." This required the Commission to look at problems and policies of State and local entities as well as those of the Federal agencies.

Another distinguishing characteristic is that the members of the Commission are to be citizens who do not serve the Federal Government in any other capacity and thus have no commitment to any Federal agency or program. In establishing the Commission, the Congress emphasized this point, asking that it "exercise independent judgment"[4] and that it "carry on deliberations without restrictions or condition of limitations of any kind."[5]

---

[2] For a summary of the recommendations of all but the last of these earlier study groups, see U.S. CONGRESS, Senate Select Committee on National Water Resources (1959). Reviews of National Water Resources During the Past Fifty Years, Committee Print No. 2, 86th Congress, 1st Session. U.S. Government Printing Office, Washington, D.C.

[3] P.L. 89-80, July 22, 1965, 79 Stat. 245, 42 USCA 1962a (1971 Supp.).

[4] U.S. CONGRESS, Senate (1966). National Water Commission, Hearings before the Committee on Interior and Insular Affairs, 89th Congress, 2d Session, May 16 and 17, 1966. Sen. Henry M. Jackson quoted in a statement of Sen. Warren G. Magnuson. U.S. Government Printing Office, Washington, D.C. p. 9.

[5] U.S. CONGRESS, House of Representatives (1967). Colorado River Basin Project, Hearings before the Subcommittee on Irrigation and Reclamation of the Committee on Interior and Insular Affairs, 90th Congress, 1st Session, March 13, 14, 16, and 17, 1967. Representative Thomas S. Foley. U.S. Government Printing Office, Washington, D.C. p. 182.

Conduct of the Commission's Work

Members of the Commission were appointed on October 9, 1968, and funds to initiate the Commission's work were appropriated shortly thereafter. The Commission held its first meeting on November 21, 1968. The first members of the staff were appointed and began work on December 30, 1968, and the nucleus of the staff was assembled by the end of June 1969.

In preparing to carry out its assignment, the Commission first consulted with the Water Resources Council, then laid out a preliminary program of studies covering areas of water resources policy in which the development of background information appeared to be needed to form the basis for policy recommendations. In the summer and fall of 1969 this preliminary program was discussed with representatives of the major Federal agencies having responsibilities in the field of water resources, and, in a series of public conferences, with local, State, and regional officials, as well as private citizens and representatives of groups interested in national water policy. Following these conferences, the Commission approved a program of background studies covering 22 fields of interest related to water policy. Appropriations for the first full fiscal year of the Commission's work were made available in mid-December of 1969,[6] and work began on the background studies in January of 1970.

Meetings of the Commission have been held about once each month since November of 1968. The size of the Commission's staff ranged from 19 on June 30, 1969, to a maximum of 44 on June 30, 1971, including temporary, clerical, and administrative personnel. A list of the principal members of the staff is on p. vii, and more information is contained in Appendix III of this report. Numerous consultants were retained on a part-time basis and contracts for research studies to provide background information were awarded to various individuals, universities, consulting organizations, foundations, and other organizations. Information on consultants and contractors is also contained in Appendix III.

The Commission's regular staff was organized into three major groups: Engineering and Evironmental Sciences, Social and Behavioral Sciences, and Legal. In addition, an ad hoc Forecasting Unit functioned for a little over 1 year, and an Administrative Division handled clerical and administrative functions and served as liaison with the General Services Administration, which had statutory responsibility for financial and administrative services for the Commission. The Executive Director served as Secretary to the Commission.

Three interim reports have been made to the President and the Congress, on January 30, 1970, January 22, 1971, and March 2, 1972.[7] These were progress reports covering the Commission's activities for the preceding calendar year. They were printed along with the comments of the Water Resources Council, which had been furnished copies of the proposed reports as called for in the National Water Commission Act.

Throughout its existence the National Water Commission has endeavored to keep the public informed about its work, and copies of a review draft of the Commission's final report were made available to the public 90 days before any final decisions were made by the Commission. In addition, reports on the background studies undertaken as a part of the program of special studies have been released through the National Technical Information Service of the U.S. Department of Commerce, and comments were invited from those interested. Through March 1, 1973, more than 22,000 copies of some 60 such reports had been purchased. A complete list of the background study reports that have been released is included in Appendix II of this report.

A final series of regional public meetings was held in early 1973 at which the Commission received the views of interested parties on the review draft of its report. A total of 351 witnesses testified or filed statements at these meetings, and, in additon, several thousand individuals and organizations furnished written statements commenting on the review draft of the report. In important respects the Commission has modified its report in the light of the information and viewpoints presented at these public meetings.

Conclusion

The report that follows reflects the Commission's earnest effort to comply with the mandate given it by the National Water Commission Act. The report contains many recommendations for improvement of policies dealing with protection, development, and use of the Nation's water resources. The National Water Commission believes that adoption of these recommendations will lead the Nation to the utilization of its water resources in ways that will make an optimum contribution to the welfare of its citizens.

---

[6]P.L. 91-144, December 11, 1969, 83 Stat. 323, 336.

[7]U.S. NATIONAL WATER COMMISSION (1970, 1971, & 1972). Interim Reports Nos. 1, 2, & 3. U.S. Government Printing Office, Washington, D.C.

Contents

		Page
Letter of Transmittal		iii
The Commission		iv
The Staff		vii
Preface		ix
Table of Water Equivalents		xxi
Glossary		xxiii

CHAPTER 1   FORECASTING FUTURE DEMANDS FOR WATER 1

Water Requirements vs. Demand for Water 2
Alternative Futures 3
Water Quantity 4
Quality of Water 4
Water Uses 6
The Present Water Quantity Situation 8
The Future Water Situation 9
Alternative Futures 11
Conclusions 17

CHAPTER 2   WATER AND THE NATURAL ENVIRONMENT 19

Some Basic Ecological Principles 20
Environmental Effects of Reservoir Development 21
   Conclusions on Water Development Projects 26
Estuaries and the Coastal Zone 28
   Conclusions on Coastal Zones 32
   Recommendation 32
Channelization 32
   Conclusions on Channelization 35
   Recommendations 36

CHAPTER 3   WATER AND THE ECONOMY 39

The Value of Water 40
   Conclusions on Water Value 47
Regional Effects of Water Developments 48
   Conclusions on Regional Development 61

CHAPTER 4   WATER POLLUTION CONTROL 63

Commission Approach 63
The Importance of Clean Water 64

Sources of Pollution 64
What is Happening to Water Quality? 68
When is Water Polluted? 69
Adequacy of Technology 71
Costs 74
Strategies for Eliminating Pollution 76
Who Should Pay? 84
Who Should Regulate? 85
Improving the Effectiveness of Pollution Abatement Programs 86
Problems Not Solved by Improved Regulation 97
Pollution in Estuaries and the Coastal Zone 100
Pollution Problems of the Great Lakes 103
Recommendations 107

CHAPTER 5   IMPROVING WATER-RELATED PROGRAMS 111

Section A   Introduction 111
Section B   The Inland Waterway Program 113
The Program 113
Appraisal of the Program 114
Discussion 117
Recommendations 120
Section C   Food and Fiber Programs: Increasing Agricultural Production Through
Water Resource Development 121
Description of Federal Programs 122
Weaknesses of the Programs 128
Supply and Demand 130
Discussion 141
Conclusions 141
Recommendation 142
Section D   Acreage Limitations and Subsidies in Reclamation Programs .. 142
Present Status of Acreage Limitations 143
Subsidy in Reclamation Programs 145
The Problem 145
Discussion and Conclusions 147
Recommendations 148
Section E   Programs for Reducing Flood Losses 149
The Programs 150
Appraisal of Programs 154
Discussion 159
Conclusions 159
Recommendations 160
Section F   Municipal and Industrial Water Supply Programs 161
The Programs 162
Appraisal of Programs 165
Conclusions 169
Recommendations 170
Section G   Power Production – The Waste Heat Problem 171
Demand for Electric Generating Facilities 171
The Problem of Waste Heat Disposal 171
Cooling Water Requirements 172

Effects of Cooling Systems 175
Discussion of Problems 175
Conclusions 182
Recommendations 183
Section H   Erosion and Sedimentation Damage Control Programs 184
The Programs 184
Appraisal of Programs 186
Conclusions and Recommendations 187
Section I   Recreation at Reservoirs 187
Background 188
The Programs 190
Discussion 197
Conclusions 198
Recommendations 199
Section J   Improving Federal Water Programs From the Standpoint of Fish and Wildlife 200
Discussion 200
Conclusions 202
Recommendations 203

**CHAPTER 6   PROCEDURES FOR RESOLVING DIFFERENCES OVER ENVIRONMENTAL
AND DEVELOPMENTAL VALUES** 205

The Problem 205
Background 206
Possible Solutions 210
Conclusions 222
Recommendations 224

CHAPTER 7   MAKING BETTER USE OF EXISTING SUPPLIES 227

Section A   Introduction 227
Section B   Improving Ground Water Management 230
The Problem 232
Integrating Use of Surface Water and Ground Water Supplies 233
Ground Water Management 234
Ground Water Mining 238
Problems of Ground Water Pollution 243
Interstate Ground Water Aquifers 244
The Need for Information 245
Conclusions 246
Recommendations 247
Section C   Pricing as a Means of Motivating Better Use 247
The Problem 248
Discussion 248
Conclusions 259
Recommendations 259
Section D   Transfer of Water Rights Under Appropriation Doctrine 260
The Problem 260
Improving States' Water Rights Records 261
Simplification of Transfer Procedures 262
Legal Restraints and Prohibitions on Transfers of Water Rights 264

Evaluation of Federal Water Supply Projects 269

Conclusions 270

Recommendations 270

Section E   Improvements in State Water Laws to Provide Recognition for

Social Values in Water 271

The Lack of Legal Protection for Some Water Values 271

Public Access to Waters and Adjacent Shorelands 274

Coordinated Land and Water Management for Public Recreation 276

Conclusions 278

Recommendations 278

Section F   A Permit System for Riparian States 280

The Problem 281

Enactment of Permit System 281

Minimum Flow 287

Allocation of Water in Periods of Shortage 289

Transfer of Water Rights 292

Conclusions 293

Recommendations 293

Appendix to Section F – A Comparison of the Florida Water Resources Act

of 1972 With the Commission's Recommended Principles 294

Section G   Reducing Water Losses by Improved Efficiency 299

Water-Saving Practices 299

Conclusions 304

Recommendations 305

Section H   Reuse of Municipal and Industrial Wastewater 306

Reclaiming Wastewater 307

The Potential of Wastewater Reuse 311

Conclusions 314

Recommendations 314

CHAPTER 8   INTERBASIN TRANSFERS 317

The Problem 317

Legal Framework 318

Social and Environmental Considerations 319

Economic Considerations 319

Area-of-Origin Protection 323

Institutional Arrangements 329

Conclusions 329

Recommendations 331

CHAPTER 9   MEANS OF INCREASING WATER SUPPLY 335

Increasing Water Supply by Desalting 335

Conclusions on Desalting 345

Recommendations 346

Precipitation Augmentation 346

Conclusions on Precipitation Augmentation 351

Recommendations 351

Increasing Water Supply Through Land Management 351

Conclusions on Land Management 359

Recommendations 359

Overview of Potential Technology 359
    Conclusions on Potential Technology 362
Improving Technological Innovation 362

CHAPTER 10   BETTER DECISIONMAKING IN WATER MANAGEMENT 365

Water Resources Planning 365
The Role of the Public in Water Resources Planning 372
Evaluation as a Basis for Decisionmaking 379
    Recommendations 386
Authorization, Budgeting, and Appropriations 387
    Recommendations 394

CHAPTER 11   IMPROVING ORGANIZATIONAL ARRANGEMENTS 397

Section A   Introduction 397
Section B   Federal Coordination and Review 398
    The Water Resources Council 398
    An Independent Board of Review 406
Section C   New Functions for Federal Water Agencies 409
    Data-Gathering Services 410
    Engineering Services 410
    Technology Services 412
    Recommendations on New Functions 413
Section D   Organizations for Water Planning and Management For River Basins and Other Regions ... 414
    Intrastate Organizations 414
    Ad Hoc and Interagency Committees and River Basin Commissions for Planning ... 416
    Interstate and Federal-Interstate Water Compacts 418
    Federally Chartered Corporations for Multistate Water Management Activities ... 427
Section E   The Great Lakes 433
    Institutions 435
    Management 437

CHAPTER 12   WATER PROBLEMS OF METROPOLITAN AREAS 441

Water Management Problems 442
Institutional Arrangements 449
Federal-State-Local Cooperation 453
Conclusions 455
Recommendations 456

CHAPTER 13   FEDERAL-STATE JURISDICTION IN THE LAW OF WATERS 459

The Problem 460
Conforming Federal Uses to State Procedures 461
Reserved Rights 464
The Navigation Servitude and the Role of No Compensation 468
Eminent Domain Procedures 469
Sovereign Immunity: Suits by State Officials and Individuals 469
Conclusions 470
Recommendations 471

CHAPTER 14   INDIAN WATER RIGHTS 473

Background 473
Accepted Premises 476
Discussion and Recommendations 477
Conclusions 483

CHAPTER 15   PAYING THE COSTS OF WATER DEVELOPMENT PROJECTS 485

Present Federal Cost-Sharing Policies 485
Appraisal of Present Cost-Sharing Policies 490
Conclusions 494
Recommendations 497

CHAPTER 16   FINANCING WATER PROGRAMS 501

Capital Demands for Water Resources Development 501
Alternative Methods of Financing Water Developments 517
Recommendations 525

CHAPTER 17   BASIC DATA AND RESEARCH FOR FUTURE PROGRESS 527

Basic Data 527
    Conclusions on Basic Data 531
    Recommendations 531
Research 532
    Conclusions on Research 537
    Recommendations 537

APPENDIX I   The National Water Commission Act 539
APPENDIX II   Background Studies Undertaken for the National Water Commission ... 542
APPENDIX III   The Commission Staff and its Operations 555
APPENDIX IV   Acknowledgements 566
               Index 569

TABLES

Chapter 1   Forecasting Future Demands for Water
    1-1.–Water withdrawals for selected years and purposes 7
    1-2.–Recent trends in consumptive use of water 7
    1-3.–Streamflow compared with current withdrawals and consumption 9
    1-4.–Projected water use by purpose 11
    1-5.–Projected water use by region 12

Chapter 3   Water and the Economy
    3-1.–Proposed source of water supplies for selected potential new towns 60

Chapter 4   Water Pollution Control
    4-1.–Estimate of total costs of abatement of point-sources of pollution, 1973-83 ... 75

Chapter 5   Improving Water-Related Programs

5-1.–Status of lands in U.S. Army Corps of Engineers flood control
and major drainage programs as of December 1971 123

5-2.–Total acreage irrigated by Bureau of Reclamation water for selected years 126

5-3.–Acreages and values of crops grown on farms in Bureau of Reclamation
projects in 1969 128

5-4.–Major crops eligible for various Federal agricultural programs served
by Bureau of Reclamation project facilities–1969 129

5-5.–Farm value of major crops eligible for Federal agricultural programs
total and Bureau of Reclamation served acreage–1969 129

5-6.–Summary of alternative futures reviewed by the Commission for
agricultural water demands 131

5-7.–Forecasts of regional consumptive use of water in western water
resources regions for selected alternative futures in 2000 132

5-8.–Forecasts of national land use for selected alternative futures in year 2000 133

5-9.–Indications of prices received by farmers for selected commodities
under alternative futures in 2000 134

5-10.–Irrigation cost and annual repayment charge per acre, Missouri River
Basin Project 146

5-11.–Projected growth of utility electric generating capacity 173

5-12.–Heat characteristics of typical steam electric plants 174

5-13.–Electrical power generating technologies 178

5-14.–Selected basic information for Federal and federally assisted
reservoirs having Federal recreation facilities–1972 193

Chapter 7   Making Better Use of Existing Supplies

7-1.–Annualized marginal costs of sewage collection and treatment in
residential areas 250

7-2.–Summary of residential water use, Johns Hopkins Study 252

7-3.–Price effects on residential demands, 1963-65 253

7-4.–Current pricing policies of water utilities 254

7-5.–Approximate costs of secondary and advanced treatment (June 1967 Cost Levels) 310

Chapter 9   Means of Increasing Water Supply

9-1.–Potential annual increase in water supply from watershed land management 357

Chapter 10   Better Decisionmaking on Water Management

10-1.–Effect of different discount rates on the present worth of a future benefit
of one dollar 384

Chapter 12   Water Problems of Metropolitan Areas

12-1.–Estimated savings resulting from joint administration of water supply
and waste disposal 447

12-2.–Revenues, debt outstanding and ratios, city governments, United States,
selected years 450

Chapter 15   Paying the Costs of Water Development Projects

15-1.–Maximum Federal cost shares for construction agencies 491

15-2.–Maximum Federal cost shares for grant agencies 492

Chapter 16   Financing Water Programs

16-1.—Federal outlays by category and agency for water resources and related
developments 502

16-2.—Comparison of Federal outlays for water resources with those for other
Federal civil public works and the total U.S. budget 503

16-3.—Estimated historic Federal expenditures for water resources and related
activities 505

16-4.—Total historical expenditures for water resources development 506

16-5.—Projection of capital investment costs based on extrapolation of "needs"
in Framework Studies of WRC 507

16-6.—Pollution control costs under standards established under the 1965
Federal Water Pollution Control Act 508

16-7.—Survey results of estimated construction cost of sewage treatment facilities
planned for the period FY 1972-1976 509

16-8.—Projected cash outlays required in principal industries to meet water
quality standards established under the 1965 Act by 1976 510

16-9.—Estimated water pollution control expenditures: Current levels and
required to meet water quality standards established under the 1965 Act by 1980 511

16-10.—Index of pollution control investment costs related to level of abatement 512

16-11.—Total national costs for municipal and industrial treatment 512

16-12.—Estimated additional costs for municipal and industrial wastewater
management 513

16-13.—Estimated additional per capita costs for municipal wastewater
management, 1983 514

16-14.—Estimated capital costs for water pollution control 516

16-15.—Summary of annual capital demands on governments under various water
resources policies 517

16-16.—Government finances, revenue, direct expenditures, and debt
1960, 1965, 1970 519

16-17.—Sources of revenue–Federal, State, and local governments 520

16-18.—Indebtedness and debt transactions of State and local governments
1969-1970 521

16-19.—Gross outstanding debt of State and local governments selected periods,
1950-1970 522

GRAPHIC ILLUSTRATIONS

1-1.—Average annual precipitation 3

1-2.—Bar chart showing lowest annual runoff in the one driest year out of 20 as a
percentage of the mean annual runoff for that basin 5

1-3.—Water resources regions used in the first National Assessment 10

4-1.—Total control costs as a function of effluent control levels 76

5-1. Irrigation development in the 17 Western States, 1899-1969 127

11-1.—Map showing area covered by River Basin Commissions, Interagency Committees,
and Federal-State Compact Commissions 419

16-1.—10-year trend in Federal water resources expenditures 504

16-2.—Engineering News-Record Construction cost index (1913=100.0) 515

TABLE OF WATER EQUIVALENTS

1 cubic foot . . . 7.48 gallons .... 62.4 lbs. of water

1 acre-foot . . . 43,560 cubic feet .... 325,851 gallons
An acre-foot covers 1 acre of land 1 foot deep

1 cubic foot per second (cfs) .... 449 gallons per minute

1 cfs .... 646,317 gallons per day
For 24 hours .... 1.983 acre-feet
For 30 days .... 59.5 acre-feet
For 1 year .... 724 acre-feet

1 million gallons .... 3.07 acre-feet

1 million gallons per day (mgd) .... 1,120 acre-feet per year

1 mgd .... 1.55 cfs

Metric Equivalents

1 U.S. gallon .... 3.785 liters
A liter is a cubic decimeter, slightly more than a U.S. quart

1 liter .... 0.264 U.S. gallons

1 cubic foot .... 28.317 liters

1 cubic meter . . . 1,000 liters .... 35.315 cubic feet

1 million U.S. gallons .... 3,785.4 cubic meters

1 acre-foot .... 1,233.5 cubic meters

Glossary

Ability-to-pay principle — the pricing of goods or services on the basis of family income or some other measure of financial capability rather than on the basis of benefits received. (See benefits-received principle.)

Acre-foot — the quantity of water required to cover 1 acre to a depth of 1 foot; equal to 43,560 cubic feet or 325,851 gallons.

Alternative futures — a range of different future economic, social, and demographic patterns of development, each depending on a different set of assumptions with respect to public policies, life-styles, patterns of consumption, etc., and any one of which could materialize. Contrasts with a single projection of future population, production, water requirements, etc.

Appropriation (funds) — at the Federal level, the process whereby Congress enacts a statute permitting expenditure of funds, sometimes repeatedly over a period of several years, for construction of authorized projects or implementation of authorized programs.

Appropriation doctrine — the system of water law adopted by (and dominant in) most Western States. The basic tenets of the appropriation doctrine are (1) that a water right can be acquired only be diverting the water from a watercourse and applying it to a beneficial use and (2) in accordance with the date of acquisition, an earlier acquired water right shall have priority over other later acquired rights. The first in time of beneficial use is the first in right, and the right is maintained only by use. Water in excess of that needed to satisfy existing rights is viewed as unappropriated water, available for appropriation by diversion and application to a beneficial use. (See riparian doctrine.)

Aquifer — a saturated underground body of rock or similar material capable of storing water and transmitting it to wells or springs.

Area of origin — in the case of interbasin water transfers, the area exporting water.

Assimilative capacity — the ability of bodies of water to purify themselves after absorbing waste discharges or to dilute such wastes and thus render them innocuous.

Authorization — at the Federal level, the process whereby Congress enacts a statute approving construction of a project or implementation of a program, frequently specifying a maximum amount to be appropriated for the purpose (but not appropriating the required funds).

Benefit-cost analysis — comparison of the expected benefits of a water project with the anticipated costs of that project. Ordinarily, unless the computed benefits exceed the computed costs, the project is not considered feasible.

Benefits-received principle — the pricing of goods or services on the basis of benefits received by users; those who use a service pay for the service. (See ability-to-pay principle.)

Best known technology — for water pollution control is a shorthand term to describe those techniques and methods known by the NWC staff to be under consideration in the spring of 1972 when the Commission's estimates of cost of various pollution control measures were prepared. Does not necessarily bear any relationship to the term "best available technology" as used in the Federal Water Pollution Control Act Amendments of 1972.

Biochemical oxygen demand — the requirement for oxygen when organic matter decomposes in bodies of water; oxygen-demanding wastes lower dissolved oxygen levels in water which in turn can adversely affect aquatic life. Also called "BOD."

Biota — The flora and fauna of a region.

Conjunctive management – the situation where management of two or more water resources, such as a ground water aquifer and a surface water body, is integrated.

Consumptive use – water withdrawn from a supply which, because of absorption, transpiration, evaporation, or incorporation in a manufactured product, is not returned directly to a surface or ground water supply; hence, water which is lost for immediate further use. Also called "consumption."

Cost allocation – the apportionment of the costs of a multipurpose water project among the various purposes served.

Cost effectiveness – comparison of alternative ways to achieve a given objective in order to identify the least-cost way.

Cost-sharing – the assignment of the responsibility for paying the costs of a water project among two or more entities as for example among the Federal Government, a State government, and individual users.

Depletion – the withdrawal of water from surface or ground water reservoirs at a rate greater than the rate of replenishment.

Desalting – the technical process of converting sea water or brackish water to fresh water or otherwise more usable condition by removing dissolved solids. Also called "desalinization" and "desalination."

Discharge – the rate of flow of a spring, stream, canal, sewer, or conduit.

Discount rate – the interest rate used in evaluation of water (and other) projects for the purpose of calculating the present value of future benefits and future costs, or otherwise converting benefits and costs to a common time basis.

Diversion – see "withdrawal."

Divide – a ridge which separates two river basins or drainage basins.

Drainage basin – the land area from which water drains into a river, as for example the Columbia River Basin is all the land area which drains into the Columbia River. Also called "catchment area," "watershed," or "river basin."

Ecology – the study of the interrelationships of living organisms to one another and to their surroundings.

Ecosystem – recognizable, relatively homogeneous units, including contained organisms, their environment, and all of the interactions among them.

Effective economic demand – in an economic sense, demand for a product (good or service) is reflected by the quantities consumers will purchase at alternative price levels. With respect to a water project or program, effective economic demand is the willingness and ability of those who benefit to pay the full costs of the output of the project or program.

Effluent – the outflow of used water from a sewer, holding tank, industrial process, agricultural activity, etc.; sometimes treated, other times not.

Eminent domain – the right of a government to acquire private property for public use, even from an unwilling owner, upon payment of compensation to the owner; occasionally conferred upon private entities vested with a public interest such as utilities.

Estuary – the lower course of a river which flows to the sea and which is influenced by the tides; or an arm of the sea itself that extends inland to meet a river flowing to the sea; the reaches of a river into which sea water intrudes and mixes with fresh water from land drainage.

Eutrophication – overfertilization of a water body due to increases in mineral and organic nutrients, producing an abundance of plant life which uses up oxygen, sometimes creating an environment hostile to higher forms of marine animal life.

Evaluation – examination of a proposed water project to determine feasibility.

Evaporation – conversion of liquid water into water vapor; hence, the dissipation of water from water surfaces and the ground into the atmosphere.

Evapotranspiration — water dissipated to the atmosphere by evaporation from water surfaces and moist soil, and by plant transpiration.

External diseconomy — a harmful effect on one or more persons or firms which stems from the activity of other persons or firms; the activity yields private benefits or advantages to the individuals or firms engaged in it but results in social costs, disadvantages, or economic penalties to others; for example, where expansion of wood pulp production benefits a pulp mill but results in discharge of additional effluents into a stream harmful to recreationists and other users of the downstream water resource. Also called "externality."

Flood plain — the land area bordering a river which is subject to flooding.

Floodway — the riverbed and immediately adjacent lands needed to convey high velocity flood discharges.

Floodway fringe — lands immediately adjacent to floodways which are still subject to flooding but which are not needed for high velocity flood discharge and are flooded less frequently and for shorter durations than floodways.

Ground water — water that occurs beneath the land surface and completely fills all pore spaces of the rock material in which it occurs.

Ground water mining — the condition when withdrawals are made from an aquifer at rates in excess of net recharge; sooner or later the underground supply will be exhausted or the water table will drop below economic pump lifts.

Headgate — a device to control water flow, placed at the entrance to a pipeline, canal, or irrigation ditch; the point at which water is diverted from a river into an irrigation ditch.

Headwaters — the place where a river originates.

Humid region — an area of the country with ample rainfall, generally considered to be in excess of 20 inches annually.

Hydrologic cycle — the circulation of water from the sea, through the atmosphere, to the land; and thence (with many delays) back to the sea by overland and subterranean routes, or directly back into the atmosphere by evaporation and transpiration.

Instream use — use of water which does not require withdrawal or diversion from its natural watercourse. For example, the use of water for navigation, waste disposal, recreation, and support of fish and wildlife.

Interbasin transfer — the physical transfer of water from one watershed to another. On a large scale, the transfer of large quantities of water from one major river basin to another.

Interstate compact — in the case of water resources, agreements between two or more States for dealing with water resources problems involving more than one State and beyond the legal authority of one State alone to solve. Such agreements require the consent of Congress. The Federal Government may participate in some compacts, in which case the agreement is called a Federal-interstate compact.

Inverse condemnation — the act of taking property by governmental action prior to filing eminent domain proceedings. In such cases the property owner must file suit to recover compensation.

Joint costs — the costs of those parts of a water project which cannot be isolated as to a single purpose. For example the cost of a dam structure itself which simultaneously serves two or more purposes such as power production, flood control, and navigation. (See separable costs.)

Lacustrine — pertaining to lakes generally as distinguished from other bodies of water such as rivers, oceans, ground water aquifers, and estuaries.

Leaching — removal of salts and akali from soils by water which percolates through the soil.

Littoral rights — the water rights of landowners adjacent to lakes, equivalent to the riparian rights of landowners bordering a stream. (See riparian doctrine.)

Marginal cost pricing — charging a price for a good or service equal to the incremental cost of the last unit produced. Marginal cost pricing generally has the attribute of leading to the most efficient use of scarce resources. When marginal cost pricing does not prevail, efficiency can be improved by moving resources away from industries where prices are below marginal costs and into industries where prices are above marginal costs.

Mouth of a river — the point where a river empties into another river or into the sea.

Multiple use — in the case of water resources, development of a particular water resource to serve two or more purposes simultaneously.

No discharge policy — the policy which prohibits discharge of any harmful substance into a water body. Strictly applied, the policy would forbid discharges which are within the capacity of a water body to assimilate and render harmless.

Nonpoint-source — the diffuse discharge of waste into a water body which cannot be located as to specific source, as with sediment, certain agricultural chemicals, and acid mine drainage.

Nonreimbursable cost — a cost of a water project which will not be repaid out of project revenues but which will be borne instead by the construction or operating entity and funded by the government.

Once-through process — the withdrawal of water from a water body for use in cooling or processing and subsequent return of that water, usually at a higher temperature or other altered condition, into the same body of water from which it came. Contrasts with water recycling processes.

Pathogenic bacteria — bacteria capable of causing disease.

Peak pricing — the technique of pricing goods or services higher at times of peak demand and lower at times of reduced demand to discourage consumption "on peak" and encourage consumption "off peak," thus to make more efficient use of plant capacities.

Phreatophytes — (literally, "well plants") plants that send their roots down to the water table, or to the capillary fringe immediately above the water table;

some of which consume relatively large quantities of water.

Point-source — a specific site from which wastewater is discharged into a water body and which can be located as to source, as with effluent, treated or otherwise, from a municipal sewage system, outflow from an industrial plant, or runoff from an animal feedlot.

Precipitation — any form of rain or snow falling to the earth's surface.

Recycling process — in the case of water, the withdrawal of water for use in cooling or processing and the subsequent reconditioning and reuse of that same water over and over, usually with relatively small additions of "makeup" water required to compensate for losses through evaporation or otherwise.

Regulation (stream) — the artificial manipulation of the flow of a stream, as by the storage of water and its later release.

Reimbursable costs — those costs of a water project which are expected to be recovered, in whole or in part, usually from direct beneficiaries, and repaid to the funding entity.

Reservoir — a pond, lake, aquifer, or basin, either natural or artificial, in which water is stored, regulated, or controlled.

Residual — material or energy flow, the value of which is less than the cost of using it.

Return flow — the portion of withdrawn water that is not consumed by evapotranspiration and that returns instead to its source or to another body of water.

Riparian doctrine — the system of water law historically recognized by the Eastern States. The riparian doctrine protects landowners adjacent to lakes and streams from withdrawals or uses which unreasonably diminish water quantity or quality. Under the riparian doctrine, individuals have a right to make reasonable use of the stream waters flowing by lands they own so long as that use does not substantially diminish either the quantity or the quality of the water passing to landowners downstream. Where diversions or uses have been unreasonable, they either have been enjoined or riparian owners adversely affected have been compensated for interference with their rights. (See appropriation doctrine.)

River basin – see "drainage basin."

Runoff – the part of precipitation that appears in surface streams.

Sediment – soil or mineral material transported by water and deposited in streams or other bodies of water.

Separable costs – the costs of a water project which can be isolated and exclusively allocated to a single purpose. For eample, the costs of turbine generators at a hydroelectric plant. (See joint costs.)

Site-specific – phenomena which occur under certain conditions at a particular site but which would not necessarily occur at another site.

Sovereign immunity – the doctrine under which the Federal Government cannot be sued without its consent.

Standard metropolitan statistical area (SMSA) – an integrated economic and social unit with a large population nucleus. There are over 245 SMSA's in the United States. Each contains at least one central city with 50,000 inhabitants or more, or two adjoining cities constituting, for economic and social purposes, a single community with a com-bined population of at least 50,000, the smaller of which must have a population of at least 15,000. Each SMSA includes the county in which the central city is located, and adjacent counties that are metropolitan in character and economically and socially integrated with the county of the central city.

Storage – the impoundment in surface reservoirs or accumulation in underground reservoirs of water for later use or release.

Streamflow – the discharge in a surface stream course.

Sustained yield – in the case of ground water aquifers, the quantity of water which can be withdrawn annually without, over a period of years, depleting the available supply.

Transpiration – the process in which plant tissues give off water vapor to the atmosphere.

User charge – a charge made upon direct beneficiaries (users) of a water project, designed to recover part or all of the cost of the project.

Watershed – a geographic area which drains into a particular water body. (See drainage basin.)

Water table – the upper level of an underground water body.

Withdrawal – the diversion and removal of water from a natural watercourse. Also called "diversion."

Forecasting Future Demands
for Water

The United States is blessed with a bountiful supply of water, although it is not always in the right place at the right time nor of the right quality. Because of the general abundance of water, national water policy has evolved over most of the past century as if water had no cost and there were no limits to its availability. But as demands come close to and in some regions even exceed supplies of water, it becomes necessary to seek ways to increase efficiency in the use of water. At the same time, there is a great and proper national concern that water be used in ways compatible with its vital role in sustaining a healthful and esthetically pleasing natural environment.

To increase efficiency in water use and to protect and improve its quality, and to do these things at least cost and with equity to all parts of our country will, in the Commission's view, require major changes in present water policies and programs. The Commission is not unmindful of the important contributions to the Nation's development of its great water programs of the past such as navigation, flood control, hydroelectric power, and reclamation. But the Commission, in looking to the future, has been faced with the reality that conditions have changed since the policies for those programs were established. It has been compelled to conclude that these changed conditions call for new policies. No longer is it a national goal to stimulate settlement of the West. That goal has been accomplished; indeed, the Governor of one Western State has enunciated a policy of "visit us, but don't stay." Thus, a principal basis for policies of providing free land and cheap

~~~~~~~~~~~~~~~~~~~~~~~~~~~~

Traditional stream gaging methods are yielding satellite observations for measurement of water availability

irrigation water for Western farmers has disappeared. So, also, has the policy basis for toll-free improved inland waterways eroded with the development of alternative means of transport: heavy trucks traveling on a national highway system; pipelines carrying oil, gas, and coal; and a national rail network in financial difficulty. Among the many other changes in national goals noted by the Commission perhaps the most important of all is the desire to clean up our rivers and lakes and to preserve as much as possible of the rivers that have not yet been developed. As recently as a decade ago this did not seem a high priority national goal. But in the past 10 years repeated acts of the Congress, and of State and local legislative bodies, have attested to the emergence of this vital new national policy objective.

It is not the Commission's function, however, to decide what the Nation's social goals and objectives—and their relative priorities—should be. This is the job of the President, the Congress, and the State and local governments, working under our representative form of government. Programs to protect, develop, and use water require large public expenditures. Water programs are not the only social demands competing for limited capital resources. Housing, education, health care, aid to the indigent, transportation, energy, air pollution control, national security, law enforcement, and other social demands all seek a larger share of the Nation's resources. To recommend where water programs should fit into the overall priority list is beyond the scope of the Commission's assignment. Some of the Commission's recommendations will cost a great deal of money, especially its recommendations to improve the quality of the Nation's water, which if adopted will cost the United States Treasury more than all of the navigation, flood control, hydroelectric power, and irrigation projects undertaken by the Federal Government since the formation of the Union. The Commission hopes that its recommendations will be implemented with dispatch, but it is not prepared to say whether or not and the extent to which its recommendations regarding water should be given preference over the many other social demands upon the Nation's limited resources. Consequently, it has sought to recommend water policies of such nature that they can be readily adapted to whatever other policies and priorities are chosen to guide the Nation's future destiny.

Above all, the National Water Commission in its deliberations and in the discussion and recommendations of this report has sought to set a stage for rational decisionmaking. It has shied away from the temptation to apply simple but unrealistic solutions to difficult and complex problems, as appealing as that seems to be for many advocates of both water development and water quality programs. It has tried to point out that alternatives are available, and some of the consequences of alternative courses of action. Most importantly, it has attempted to fashion policies for management of the Nation's precious water resources that are both practical of achievement and responsive to the conditions the United States is likely to confront in the remaining decades of the 20th century.

Foremost among the policies that the Commission believes must be implemented if the Nation is to achieve wise and efficient use of its water resources is that direct beneficiaries of water facilities should be obliged to pay the cost of such facilities unless it can be demonstrated that user charges are impracticable and would frustrate important national purposes. User charges designed to recover all or a major portion of the costs of water-based services are the primary mechanism which the Commission believes will prevent distortion in the allocation of economic resources. Coincidentally, user charges will discourage construction of projects that unnecessarily change the environment and encourage conservation practices that help to protect the environment. User charges appear to offer the best assurance that, insofar as water programs are concerned, the United States will get its money's worth, and that natural economic advantages and consumer choices will be allowed to establish the pattern of production for the Nation's farms, factories, and waterways.

By advocating user charges the Commission does not imply opposition to Federal, State, or municipal investment in water resource development. Where interstate or international waters are involved, where multipurpose river basin developments are involved, or where there is an unwillingness or inability of non-Federal interests to fulfill a national need, the Federal Government should participate vigorously in water resource developments. At the State and local governmental level, where public interest or public preference calls for it, governmental participation will have to be substantial. What the Commission recommends against is not public investment but unjustified public subsidy which tends to reduce efficiency, distort the allocation of scarce resources, encourage construction of projects that are uneconomic, and promote the wasteful use of water. Who should finance, construct, and operate various water resources developments is one question. Who should pay for them is another. The Commission believes that even where a public agency is the proper entity to finance, build, and operate a water project, the direct beneficiaries should ordinarily be obliged to pay for the full costs of the facilities from which they benefit.

The Commission recommends the adoption of national policies which, within appropriate constraints of environmental protection and desired patterns of land use, will encourage the use of water in the most efficient and equitable way to meet the people's demands for goods and services. And insofar as appropriations of Federal tax dollars for water programs are concerned, the Commission recommends that they be vastly increased, but broadly redirected from projects to control or use water to projects for the improvement of water quality.

WATER REQUIREMENTS VS. DEMAND FOR WATER

A persistent tendency of water resources planning has been the issuance of single valued projections of water use into the future under a continuation of present policies, leading to astronomical estimates of future water requirements.[1]

The amount of water that is actually used in the future will depend in large measure on public policies that are adopted. The National Water Commission is convinced that there are few water "requirements," except for relatively small amounts for drinking, cleaning, fire fighting in municipalities, and similar other essential social and environmental purposes. But there are "demands" for water and water-related services that are affected by a whole host of other factors and policy decisions, some in fields far

---

[1] For the most recent manifestation of this, see U.S. WATER RESOURCES COUNCIL (1968). The Nation's Water Resources. U.S. Government Printing Office, Washington, D.C.

2

FIGURE 1. — Average annual precipitation

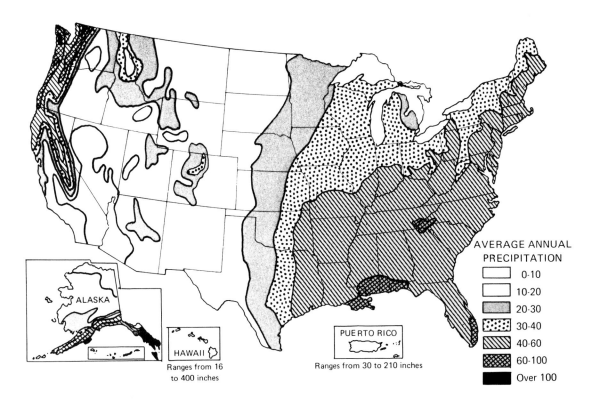

AVERAGE ANNUAL
PRECIPITATION

	0-10
	10-20
	20-30
	30-40
	40-60
	60-100
	Over 100

ALASKA

HAWAII
Ranges from 16
to 400 inches

PUERTO RICO
Ranges from 30 to 210 inches

Source: U.S. WATER RESOURCES COUNCIL (1968). The Nation's Water Resources. U.S. Government Printing Office, Washington, D. C. Part 3, Chapter 2, p. 2.

removed from what is generally considered to be water policy. For example, the invention of the kitchen garbage disposal unit greatly increased the load on municipal sewage treatment plants, and the decision to support the price of cotton led to vast increases in irrigated acreage on the High Plains of Texas.

ALTERNATIVE FUTURES

It is impractical, and in fact undesirable, to attempt to forecast precise levels of future water use on the basis of past water use. How much water will be used, where, and for what purposes will depend on the policies that are adopted. A range of "alternative futures" is possible, depending upon population levels and distribution, per capita energy consumption, rate of national income growth, technological development, water pricing policies, consumer habits and lifestyles, various governmental policies, and other variables.

Although the full range of possibilities should be considered in planning, development, and management of water resources, the Commission believes it is unrealistic to develop water policy on the basis of a "crisis scenario" such as a severe worldwide drought extending over many years. Rather than base national water policy on such speculation, it is better to provide for the possibility of the occurrence of such events by more direct measures, such as, for example, a national or even a world food bank. For this reason, the Commission did not try to encompass all possible alternative futures in its background studies, but selected for illustrative purposes only a reasonable number of possible combinations of policies for study, as referred to later.

In formulating a national water policy, two measurements of water must be considered, quantity and quality. The latter, of course, is a relative term depending on the use which is to be made of the water.

WATER QUANTITY

The source of all water available to the Nation is precipitation. Precipitation for the 48 contiguous States averages about 30 inches a year, enough for most purposes, but it is neither evenly nor regularly distributed. Annual precipitation varies from over 100 inches in coastal regions of the Pacific Northwest to less than 4 inches in parts of the Southwest (Figure 1-1). In Alaska, the normal annual precipitation ranges from about 5 inches in the extreme north to more than 200 inches at places along the southern panhandle. In Hawaii and Puerto Rico also there is great variability in precipitation from place to place.

Only a portion of the precipitation flows from the watershed into streams or ground water basins. The runoff from a watershed is more variable than precipitation because consumptive use in the watershed is satisfied before runoff occurs. Runoff also varies greatly within a given year and between years. Within a normal year, the ratio of maximum flow to minimum flow may be 500 to 1. Average annual runoff varies from near zero in the Great Salt Lake desert to more than 50 inches in the Olympic Peninsula. It exceeds 10 inches in the third of the country in which the climate is considered to be humid, and it is less than 1 inch in the third of the country considered to be arid.

Figure 1-2 shows, for each of the major water resources regions, the lowest annual runoff of the previous 20 years as a percentage of the mean annual runoff. In general, the lowest flow deviates least from the mean and therefore is most dependable in the Northwest, the Northeast, and the Southeast. The areas of greatest flow variability are the arid regions of the Southwest and North Central parts of the contiguous United States. But even in the humid areas a series of dry years may result in serious drought conditions such as occurred in the Northeast during the period 1961 to 1966.

The Nation's water programs have primarily emphasized measures to offset the variability in precipitation and streamflow and its effect upon water supplies. The variability in precipitation in many basins has made it necessary to seek a means of controlling and regulating the natural streamflows, both to reduce flooding during periods of high flow and to provide water for desired uses during periods of low flow or high withdrawals. Similarly, the differences in precipitation and runoff between areas have encouraged residents of relatively low-flow areas to seek water transfers from areas where flows were greater or the water was thought to be less fully used. In response, government—Federal, State, and local—and nongovernmental entities have made major investments in water control, storage, transfer, and distribution works.

QUALITY OF WATER

Quality determines the usability of water in any particular location. Over time, water quality in many of the Nation's streams and estuaries has deteriorated through the cumulative effects of two separate but often concurrent actions. The first, of great concern in most of the Western United States, is the concentration of dissolved solids in the streamflow. This concentration occurs because part of the water withdrawn for such uses as irrigation returns to the stream bearing dissolved material. When water is evaporated from reservoirs the salts remain and their concentration is increased. Finally, any diversion of flow leaves less water to dilute high salt concentrations due to natural causes, such as salt springs.

The Colorado River is an excellent example of quality deterioration caused by dissolved solids. Generally, flows in the headwaters of the Colorado River are of high quality, usually with less than 50 parts per million (p.p.m.) of dissolved solids, but the concentration increases progressively downstream from both natural and manmade causes. At Imperial Dam, in the Lower Colorado River Basin, the measured flows have had an average concentration of about 750 p.p.m. If present trends continue, it is estimated that the concentration will reach 1,250 p.p.m. by the year 2000, two and a half times the recommended maximum allowable concentration for municipal water supplies, and dangerously high for agricultural use.[2]

The second type of water quality deterioration is caused by the generation and disposal of residuals by both producers and consumers. Marketable goods are produced and residuals, the material and energy byproducts that are not incorporated into the

---

[2] U.S. BUREAU OF RECLAMATION (1972). Colorado River Water Quality Improvement Program. U.S. Government Printing Office, Washington, D.C. pp. 1, 43, 45.

VARIATION IN ANNUAL RUNOFF

FIGURE 2.— Bar chart showing lowest annual runoff in the one driest year out of 20 as a percentage of the mean annual runoff for that basin

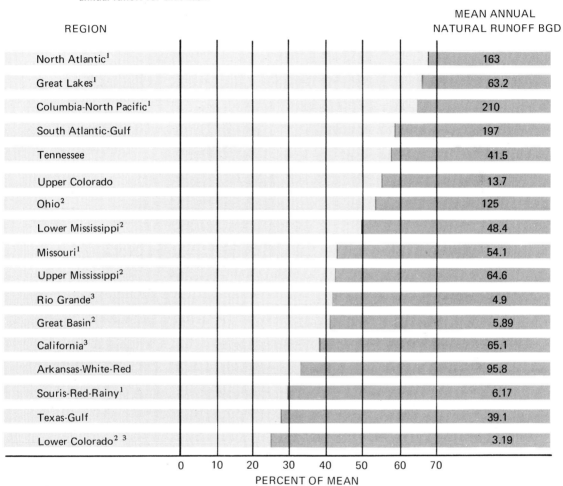

₁ Does not include runoff from Canada
₂ Does not include runoff derived from upstream regions
₃ Does not include runoff from Mexico

[1] Does not include runoff from Canada
[2] Does not include runoff derived from upstream regions
[3] Does not include runoff from Mexico

Source: U.S. WATER RESOURCES COUNCIL (1968). The Nation's Water Resources. U.S. Government Printing Office, Washington, D. C. Part 1, p. 23.

product, are frequently disposed of in water. Consumer use of goods results in wastes such as old automobile bodies, disposable bottles and cans, sewage, carbon monoxide, newspapers, and heat, all of which may end up in and pollute water. Many of these wastes are misplaced resources that can and should be put to use. Broadly speaking, all raw material and energy inputs to any system ultimately become residuals to be disposed of in a gaseous, liquid, or solid state, or as energy. When these residuals are disposed of in the Nation's streams they degrade water quality and may make the streamflow unsuitable for other purposes, or make treatment necessary before it can be used again. Water quality of streams in the vicinity of many of the Nation's largest metropolitan areas is diminished in this way.

Both concentration of dissolved solids and disposal of residual wastes are of increasing concern in the United States. The Commission's views on the problems of water quality are discussed in Chapter 4 of this report.

WATER USES

Water use consists of (1) intake uses, (2) onsite uses, and (3) instream or flow uses. Intake uses include water for domestic, agricultural, and industrial purposes—uses that actually remove water from its source. Onsite uses[3] consist mainly of water consumed by swamps, wetlands, evaporation from the surface of water bodies, natural vegetation, unirrigated crops, and wildlife. Flow uses include water for estuaries, navigation, waste dilution, hydroelectric power and also some fish and wildlife and recreational uses.

Water uses are measured in two ways, by amount withdrawn and by amount consumed. Water withdrawn is water diverted from its natural course for use, and may be returned later for further use. Water consumed is water that is incorporated into a product or lost to the atmosphere through evaporation and transpiration, and cannot be reused. Water consumption is the more important indicator, since some part of withdrawn water can usually be reused, although not always near the point where the first withdrawal takes place. Under certain circumstances, therefore, large water withdrawals over a short time period may become critical, adversely affecting onsite and instream uses.

---

[3]Some onsite uses deplete water supplies before they reach the streams, and therefore have never been measured as a part of the Nation's water supplies available for use.

Trends in Intake Water Use

Historic withdrawals and consumptive uses of water for major intake uses are summarized in Tables 1-1 and 1-2, respectively. As indicated in Table 1-1, current withdrawals for the purposes specified are over nine times greater than in the year 1900. The growth in these water withdrawals has been substantially greater than the growth in U.S. population over this same period: U.S. population increased about two and one-half times and water withdrawals per person have increased about three and one-half times.

Figures on total consumptive use of water for the important intake uses are available only for more recent years, as shown on Table 1-2, and the data are less reliable, because return flows are so much more difficult to measure than withdrawals. Consumptive uses may increase at a more rapid rate than withdrawals in the future if recycling of water becomes more common.

Although the data may not be very accurate, it is clear that the Nation's growing agricultural and increasingly industrialized economy has required larger and larger quantities of water to be withdrawn and consumed. Because this trend foretells difficult quantity and quality problems in many areas of the Nation, the Commission has explored alternatives for lessening this trend through various policy and procedural changes. (See particularly Chapter 7.)

Table 1-1 also indicates there has been a major change in the relative proportion of withdrawals of water used for irrigation and steam electric power production in recent years. The proportion of total withdrawals used for irrigation has been declining steadily since 1920 when 61 percent of all withdrawals were used for irrigation purposes. In contrast, there has been a steady increase in withdrawals for steam electric power production since 1910, but consumptive use for this purpose is still small, whereas it is high for irrigation.

Trends in Onsite and Flow Water Uses

Only sparse data on important onsite and flow or instream water uses are available. Nevertheless, these uses, including navigation, waste disposal, recreation, and conservation of fish and wildlife, have grown to great importance in our society. Unfortunately, these uses are not measured by the more conventional types of data collection and analysis. This is especially true of water use for esthetic purposes such as inspiration and relaxation, scenic drives, and for

TABLE 1-1.—Water withdrawals for selected years and purposes, United States including Puerto Rico.
(Billion gallons per day)

Year	Total Water Withdrawals	Irrigation	Purpose of Withdrawals			
			Public Water Utilities	Rural Domestic	Industrial and Miscellaneous	Steam Electric Utilities
1900	40	20	3	2.0	10	5
1910	66	39	5	2.2	14	6
1920	92	56	6	2.4	18	9
1930	110	60	8	2.9	21	18
1940	136	71	10	3.1	29	23
1950	200	110	14	3.6	37	40
1960	270	110	21	3.6	38	100
1970	370	130	27	4.5	47	170

Source: Withdrawals reported for 1900 to 1940 are taken from PICTON, Walter L (March 1960). Water Use in the United States, 1900-1980, prepared for U.S. Department of Commerce, Business and Defense Services Administration. U.S. Government Printing Office, Washington, D.C. p. 2. Withdrawals reported for 1950 to 1970 are taken from MURRAY, C Richard & REEVES, E. Bodette (1972). Estimated Use of Water in the United States in 1970, Geological Survey Circular 676. U.S. Geological Survey, Washington, D.C. p. 10.

TABLE 1-2.—Recent trends in consumptive use of water in the United States, including Puerto Rico.
(Intake Uses Only)
(Billion gallons per day)

Year	Total Consumptive Use	Irrigation	Purpose of Use			
			Public Water Supply	Rural Domestic	Self-Supplied Industrial and Miscellaneous	Steam Electric Utilities
1960	61	52	3.5	2.8	3.0	0.22
1965	77	66	5.2	3.2	3.8	0.41
1970	88	73	5.9	3.4	5.3	1.04

Source: Figures taken from MacKICHAN KA & KAMMERER JC (1961). Estimated Use of Water in the United States, 1960, Geological Survey Circular 456. MURRAY, C Richard (1968). Estimated Use of Water in the United States, 1965, Geological Survey Circular 556. MURRAY, C Richard & REEVES, E Bodette (1972). Estimated Use of Water in the United States in 1970, Geological Survey Circular 676. All published by U.S. Geological Survey, Washington, D.C. Estimates of consumptive use were not tabulated before 1960.

recreation purposes such as motorboating, sailing, and white water canoeing. Successful planning for and management of our water resources require that these uses be taken into account.

There are some indicators of the importance of flow and instream water use. For example, between 1950 and 1970, there was a fourfold increase in traffic moving on the Nation's inland waterways from 52 billion ton-miles to 204 billion ton-miles.[4] Between 1950 and 1970, the number of recreational boats is estimated to have increased from 3.5 to 8.8 million.[5] In 1965, some 42 million persons participated in recreational boating for a total of 265 million days.[6] Also in 1965, about 13 million recreation days were spent at waterfowl hunting and 42 million persons participated in fishing activities.[7] Obviously, these uses must be recognized as competitive and alternative uses of the Nation's fresh water resources, although some of the boating and fishing takes place on the oceans and estuaries.

THE PRESENT WATER QUANTITY SITUATION

Regional withdrawal and consumptive uses of water in 1970 are shown in Table 1-3 along with the water supply available in each region under four different availability criteria. Hence, it is possible to compare, for the Nation as a whole and for individual regions, water withdrawals and water consumption with mean annual runoff and with annual flows that have been available 50 percent, 90 percent, and 95 percent of the years. Comparison of the mean annual runoff with current consumptive use of water indicates that the present water quantity situation is very favorable for all regions except the Rio Grande, Lower Colorado, and Great Basin regions. Regional

[4]U.S. ARMY CORPS OF ENGINEERS (1951). Annual Report of the Chief of Engineers, volume I. U.S. Government Printing Office, Washington, D.C. and U.S. ARMY CORPS OF ENGINEERS (1972). Waterborne Commerce of the United States, Calendar Year 1970, Part 5, National Summaries. U.S. Army Engineer District, New Orleans, La. p. 32.

[5]BOATING INDUSTRY ASSOCIATIONS & NATIONAL ASSOCIATION OF ENGINE AND BOAT MANUFACTURERS (1972). Boating '71, A Statistical Report on America's Top Family Sport. Boating Industry Association, Chicago, Ill. p. 8.

[6]U.S. BUREAU OF THE CENSUS (1970). Statistical Abstract of the United States. U.S. Government Printing Office, Washington, D.C. p. 203.

[7]U.S. DEPARTMENT OF THE INTERIOR (1971). Selected Outdoor Recreation Statistics. U.S. Government Printing Office, Washington, D.C. pp. 39, 41, 109.

summaries, such as shown on Table 1-3, fail to disclose local shortages caused when water within a region is not available at the places where there is a demand for it. This is particularly true within regions such as the Columbia, Missouri, and Arkansas-White-Red, where the flow of water is from the arid portions to the humid portions, or where use of ground water exceeds recharge, such as in the High Plains of Texas and Central Arizona.

In most regions, annual flow available 50 percent of the years is nearly the same as the mean annual flow. Table 1-3 shows that the Lower Colorado region already uses more water than its available natural supply, and the Great Basin and Rio Grande regions use 60 percent or more of their average supplies. In 1 year out of 10, consumptive use in the latter two regions exceeds the runoff, but storage facilities permit carryover of flows to cover deficiencies. The Upper Colorado region, although it has adequate water, will run short at least 1 year out of 10 because of its compact obligation to deliver water to the Lower Colorado region, but large amounts of holdover storage are available. At flows available 95 percent of the years, the same three regions (Rio Grande, Lower Colorado, and Great Basin regions) would face unfavorable water supply-demand balances and the Upper Colorado, California, and Texas-Gulf regions become of concern.

These comparisons indicate that the six regions mentioned above would, in 1 year out of every 20, be the ones most susceptible to drought and water shortages if present policies are continued. Even at present, the Lower Colorado region faces severe water management problems. Consumptive use of water currently exceeding the natural supply is made possible through use of natural flows from outside the basin (runoff from the Upper Colorado region is allocated for use in the Lower Colorado region under the terms of the Colorado River Compact), repeated reuse of water, and mining of ground water. Large amounts of ground water also are being mined in the Texas-Gulf, Rio Grande, Arkansas-White-Red, and California regions.

In summary, two problems are evident. First, certain large and economically important regions of the Nation either already are or potentially could in the future be using water beyond their natural water resource. Steadily increasing municipal and industrial water requirements in these areas, and potentially others, combined with established and, in some places, expanding irrigation activities could place severe strains upon limited water resources. At the

TABLE 1-3.–Streamflow compared with current withdrawals and consumption.
(Billion gallons per day)

Region	Annual Flow Available[2]				Fresh Water Consumptive Use 1970[1]	Withdrawals 1970[1]
	Mean Annual Run-Off[2]	50% of the Years	90% of the Years	95% of the Years		
North Atlantic	163	163	123	112	1.8	55
South Atlantic-Gulf	197	188	131	116	3.3	35
Great Lakes	63.2	61.4	46.3	42.4	1.2	39
Ohio	125	125	80	67.5	.9	36
Tennessee	41.5	41.5	28.2	24.4	.24	7.9
Upper Mississippi	64.6	64.6	36.4	28.5	.8	16
Lower Mississippi	48.4	48.4	29.7	24.6	3.6	13
Souris-Red-Rainy	6.17	5.95	2.6	1.91	.07	.3
Missouri	54.1	53.7	29.9	23.9	12.0	24
Arkansas-White-Red	95.8	93.4	44.3	33.4	6.8	12
Texas-Gulf	39.1	37.5	15.8	11.4	6.2	21
Rio Grande	4.9	4.9	2.6	2.1	3.3	6.3
Upper Colorado	13.45	13.45	8.82	7.50	4.1	8.1
Lower Colorado	3.19	2.51	1.07	0.85	5.0	7.2
Great Basin	5.89	5.82	3.12	2.46	3.2	6.7
Columbia-North Pacific	210	210	154	138	11.0	30
California	65.1	64.1	33.8	25.6	22.0	48
Conterminous United States	1,201				87	365
Alaska	580				.02	.2
Hawaii	13.3				.8	2.7
Puerto Rico					.17	3.0
Total United States	1,794				88	371

[1] MURRAY, C Richard & REEVES, E Bodette (1972). Estimated Use of Water in the United States in 1970, Geological Survey Circular 676. U.S. Geological Survey, Washington, D.C. p. 17.

[2] U.S. WATER RESOURCES COUNCIL (1968). The Nation's Water Resources. U.S. Government Printing Office, Washington, D.C. p. 3-2-6.

same time, many areas are facing the growing problems of water quality deterioration.

Second, ground water in many areas is being mined or used at rates exceeding recharge. The economy of these areas is based upon the foundation of a temporary and dwindling water resource. In the major ground water-using areas, substitute supplies of water are not readily available and alternative water supplies can be obtained only at relatively high cost.

Both of these problems are viewed by the Commission as matters of major national concern and they receive further attention in this and later chapters.

THE FUTURE WATER SITUATION

A comprehensive effort at projecting future water uses was completed by the Water Resources Council

FIGURE 3. — Water resources regions used in the first National Assessment

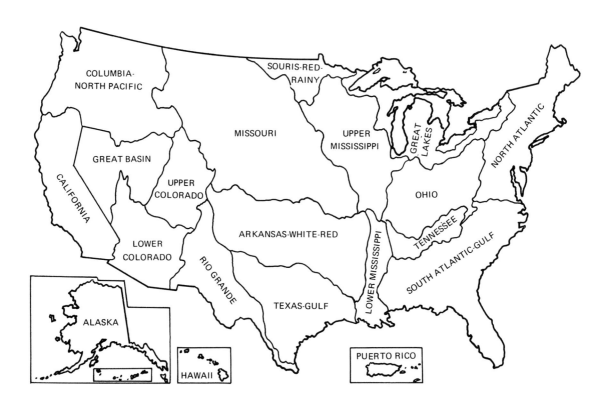

Source: U.S. WATER RESOURCES COUNCIL (1968). The Nation's Water Resources. U.S. Government Printing Office, Washington, D. C. Part 1, p. 5.

in 1968 and its report is commonly called the First National Assessment.[8] While time and changing circumstances have dated these projections, they do serve as a limited framework for studying the future water situation. The Water Resources Council is in the process of preparing an updated National Water Assessment that should be available in December 1975.

Projections of the First National Assessment are based largely on extensions of past trends, which may not continue, especially if the Nation adopts policies recommended in this report. National projections from the First National Assessment are summarized in Table 1-4. Table 1-5 summarizes the total

projected water uses for the regions of the United States shown in Figure 1-3.

The First National Assessment also included some indicators of onsite and flow uses of water. These uses were stated primarily in terms of specific activities and not in terms of water consumption, although estimates of flow requirements for navigation on major inland waterways and of water consumption by fish and waterfowl developments are included. Very large increases in these uses were projected for the future. The total traffic on inland waterways was projected to increase by 170 percent by the year 2000, on the assumptions that present policies would be continued and that the waterways would retain their current share of total intercity commerce. The First National Assessment also suggested that water-based recreation of all types could increase by about 170 percent between 1965 and

---

[8] U.S. WATER RESOURCES COUNCIL (1968). The Nation's Water Resources. U.S. Government Printing Office, Washington, D.C.

TABLE 1-4.—Projected water use, by purpose, United States[1]
(Billion gallons per day)

Type of Use	Projected Withdrawals			Projected Consumptive Use		
	1980	2000	2020	1980	2000	2020
Rural domestic	2.5	2.9	3.3	1.8	2.1	2.5
Municipal (public supplied)	33.6	50.7	74.3	10.6	16.5	24.6
Industrial (self-supplied)	75	127.4	210.8	6.1	10	15.6
Steam-electric power						
Fresh	134	259.2	410.6	1.7	4.6	8
Saline	59.3	211.2	503.5	.5	2	5.2
Agriculture						
Irrigation	135.9	149.8	161	81.6	90	96.9
Livestock	2.4	3.4	4.7	2.2	3.1	4.2
U.S. Total	442.6	804.6	1,368.1	104.4	128.2	157.1

[1] U.S. WATER RESOURCES COUNCIL (1968). The Nation's Water Resources. U.S. Government Printing Office, Washington, D.C. Part 1, p. 8.

2000. Fresh water sport fishing was projected to increase from 470 million man-days of activity in 1960 to 970 million man-days in the year 2000. If these projections are anywhere near what may be realized, these water-based activities must be given increased attention in future water planning.

ALTERNATIVE FUTURES

Most estimates of future demands for water and water-related activities have been based upon a single projection of the important variables affecting water requirements. Future water demands will depend, however, on a number of variables, including: (1) population, (2) the rate of national income growth, (3) per capita energy consumption, (4) factors affecting demands for food and fiber for domestic use and for export, including the lifestyles and eating habits of people, (5) government programs dealing with resource development and distribution, such as environmental protection goals and crop price support programs, (6) the rate of technological change, (7) recreational water uses, and (8) the price of water

to the various users. Any attempt to anticipate and identify future water resource problems should consider all of these and other factors which will influence water demands.

It is difficult, if not impossible, to attach values to or make a single or "best" estimate for many of these variables 50, 30, 20, or even 10 years in the future, and it is impossible to assign a single value or "best" estimate to these same variables at some future time period. Therefore, in formulating national water policy the Nation should not be bound by any particular projection or forecast of the future. Rather, the problems of meeting future water requirements should be investigated in terms of a range of possible outcomes, or alternative futures. Under this concept, alternative forecasts should be made to ascertain the effects of alternative courses of action. Such forecasts may have a powerful influence on the final choice of a course of action. For example, if the doubling of electric energy use every decade will require more cooling water than the Nation finds consistent with environmental goals, a policy of electric energy conservation may be selected; or if a

TABLE 1-5.—Projected water use by region (Billion gallons per day)						
	Projected Total Withdrawals			Projected Total Consumptive Use		
	1980	2000	2020	1980	2000	2020
North Atlantic	54.9	113.9	236.3	2.9	5.0	8.5
South Atlantic-Gulf	53.2	87.4	130.2	3.4	5.7	8.3
Great Lakes	47.9	96.6	191.0	1.9	3.2	5.5
Ohio	41.7	65.1	90.2	1.6	2.5	3.6
Tennessee	12.3	13.9	18.1	0.6	0.8	1.1
Upper Mississippi	14.8	30.6	41.3	1.1	1.8	2.6
Lower Mississippi	12.8	28.0	39.4	3.0	4.5	6.3
Souris-Red-Rainy	.9	2.0	2.8	0.2	0.5	0.5
Missouri	23.3	27.9	31.6	13.2	15.0	16.4
Arkansas-White-Red	17.3	25.3	31.6	8.5	10.6	12.3
Texas-Gulf	29.1	57.3	92.6	9.4	10.9	12.3
Rio Grande	8.3	9.5	11.7	4.7	5.0	5.5
Upper Colorado	5.7	6.6	6.7	2.7	3.1	3.1
Lower Colorado	8.5	8.4	8.9	4.1	4.6	5.3
Great Basin	7.1	7.6	7.8	3.3	3.6	3.8
Columbia-North Pacific	41.4	90.1	156.7	13.6	17.3	21.6
California	56.3	120.5	244.8	29.2	32.7	38.2
Alaska	0.5	0.9	4.2	0.1	0.1	0.2
Hawaii	2.7	4.7	8.6	0.7	1.0	1.4
Puerto Rico	4.0	8.3	13.7	0.4	0.5	0.6
U.S. Total	442.7	804.6	1,368.1	104.4	128.2	157.1

Source: U.S. WATER RESOURCES COUNCIL (1968). The Nation's Water Resources. U.S. Government Printing Office, Washington, D.C. Part 1, p. 24.

Note: Columns may not add due to rounding.

crop price support program that keeps farm land in humid areas out of production thereby stimulates a demand for interbasin water transfers to irrigate new land in dry areas, with undesirable environmental consequences, another type of crop price support technique may be selected.

Because it believes the concept of alternative futures should become a basic part of all future water resources planning and decisionmaking, the Commission asked its staff to analyze the effects of changes in policy, lifestyles, and technology on future demands for water and water-related services. These analyses were made not for the purpose of advocating any particular course of action, but to illustrate the very dramatic changes in water demands that can result from changes in various factors that, superficially, may appear to be only remotely related to water. Significantly, most of these factors are within the control of society, if it wishes to exercise such control.

Effects of Change on Future Demands for Water

The principal staff analysis had the objective of analyzing the effects of changes in policy and technology on future demands for water. Demand for water for cooling steam electric powerplants and in the petroleum refining industry, as well as residential water demand, were considered in the study, along with the preliminary results of Iowa State University model studies of demand for water for irrigated agriculture, which are discussed in Section C of Chapter 5. The analysis made use of an economic model developed in a study undertaken for Resources for the Future,[9] growing out of earlier work performed for the U.S. Senate Select Committee on National Water Resources.[10] The model evaluates the relationships among water quality and quantity and costs of future programs on the basis of several variations in future population and industrial activity, to indicate the range of choice open to the Nation in meeting future demands through combinations of waste treatment and water storage for dilution of wastes. The variables considered and the salient conclusions from the staff's investigation are briefly reported here.[11]

Variables Considered: The following variables were considered:

1. Four levels of population for the contiguous United States (264 million, 279 million, 299 million, and 318 million in the year 2000) and an assumed level of productivity (output per man-hour) of the labor force.[12]

2. Two assumptions were made regarding waste heat disposal: (a) that no temperature limitations are imposed on receiving waters at the point of discharge and (b) that no more than 5.4° F. increase in water temperatures at the point of discharge is permitted.[13]

3. Two assumptions were made concerning dissolved oxygen in fresh waters of the Nation: (a) that 4 milligrams (mg.) per liter would be maintained and (b) that 6 mg. per liter would be maintained.[13]

4. Two assumptions were made about sewage treatment: (a) that all wastewater discharges to coastal areas and estuaries would be given primary treatment and (b) that such treatment would be at a secondary level.[13]

In addition, the analysis incorporated the latest available information on demand for electric power from the Federal Power Commission studies, on water-use coefficients for steam electric power generation from the work of the Commission's Panel on Waste Heat,[14] on water use in the five major water-using industries, on advanced cooling methods and accelerated rates of recirculation of water in industry, and on agricultural demands for water from the Iowa State University model.

Conclusions from the Analysis: The analysis shows that the rate of growth of the population and the economy and the alternative water policies and water use technologies that are adopted would have very significant effects on future water demands. The following more specific conclusions with respect to water use in the year 2020 were reached in the study:[15]

1. Water withdrawals in the year 2020 may range from 570 billion gallons per day (b.g.d.) to 2,280 b.g.d. depending on the combination of variables that are assumed. In comparison, the Water Resources Council projected the total withdrawals at 1,368 b.g.d. under a continuation of policies and trends in effect in 1968 (see Tables 1-4 and 1-5).

2. Water consumption in the year 2020 may range from 150 to 250 b.g.d. in comparison to the Water Resources Council's projection of 157 b.g.d. (see Tables 1-4 and 1-5).

3. Greater recycling of industrial process water and recirculation of water used for cooling would significantly reduce water withdrawals in the Nation without any substantial total increase in water consumption. This would be particularly true for steam electric power generation where the studies indicate that water withdrawals would be four times greater in the year 2020 under a continuation of present technology than with substantially advanced technology which would increase consumptive use only about 1 percent.

[9] WOLLMAN, Nathaniel & BONEM, Gilbert W (1971). The Outlook for Water; Quality, Quantity, and National Growth. Published for Resources for the Future, Inc., by The Johns Hopkins Press, Baltimore, Md.

[10] U.S. CONGRESS, Senate Select Committee on National Water Resources (1960). Water Supply and Demand, Committee Print No. 32, 86th Congress, 2d Session. U.S. Government Printing Office, Washington, D.C.

[11] For details, see THOMPSON, Russell G et al. (1971). Forecasting Water Demands, prepared for the National Water Commission. National Technical Information Service, Springfield, Va., Accession No. PB 206 491.

[12] *Ibid.*, p. 291.

[13] These assumptions were from the Wollman-Bonem study.

[14] KRENKEL, Peter A et al. (1972). The Water Use and Management Aspects of Steam Electric Power Generation, prepared for the National Water Commission by the Commission's Consulting Panel on Waste Heat. National Technical Information Service, Springfield, Va., Accession No. PB 210 355.

[15] For more detail on the conclusions of this study, see THOMPSON, Russell G et al. (1971). Forecasting Water Demands, prepared for the National Water Commission. National Technical Information Service, Springfield, Va., Accession No. PB 206 491.

4. Water withdrawals for steam electric generation cooling purposes would be significantly affected by water quality standards. A limit on temperature increase in water at the point of discharge of no more than 5.4° F. could reduce withdrawals for this purpose about 75 percent from the levels forecast for the year 2020 based on extension of present trends.[16]

5. Increasing the water quality standard of dissolved oxygen from 4 to 6 mg. per liter for all fresh waters in the Nation, to reflect greater concern for environmental quality, would increase the cost of treating wastewaters about 50 percent.

Future Municipal Water Demands

Results of research[17] on methods of forecasting future demand for water for municipal purposes were also considered by the Commission as a part of its analysis of alternative futures. The studies showed a rather substantial variation in possible future demand for water in the four cities for which such demand was analyzed through the use of the model developed during the course of the study. The model took into account six factors: regulations, pricing policy, education campaigns, housing patterns, supply cost, and technology of demand. Using these, 96 possible outcomes were developed, showing possible variations in total water demand in the year 2000 of up to 29 percent under various combinations of these factors.

Of all the in-house uses of water, the study found that only toilet flushing appears to be excessive at present, and might offer some scope for reduction of demand through regulation. Use of water for lawn sprinkling was found in this and other studies[18] to be price sensitive, and probably excessive, so that use could be reduced through a combination of improved pricing and educational policies.

In view of the great possibilities for reduction in per capita water use, as well as total use, it would be

---

[16] But the temperature limit would require greater use of cooling towers, and an increase in consumptive use.

[17] For details, see WHITFORD, Peter W (1970). Forecasting Demand for Urban Water Supply, a dissertation submitted to the Department of Civil Engineering, Stanford University, Palo Alto, Calif.

[18] See, for example, HOWE, Charles W and LINAWEAVER, F Pierce, Jr (1967). The Impact of Price on Residential Water Demand and its Relation to System Design and Price Structure, in *Water Resources Research*, V. 3, pp. 13-32 and LINAWEAVER, F Pierce, Jr, GEYER, John C, and WOLFF, Jerome B (1967). A Study of Residential Water Use, prepared for the Technical Studies Program of the Federal Housing Administration, Department of Housing and Urban Development. U.S. Government Printing Office, Washington, D.C.

wasteful for municipalities to plan to meet future demands on the basis of a single valued projection of past trends.

Future Agricultural Water Demands

Much more detailed analyses of future demands for water for agricultural purposes were made because water used for irrigated agriculture is the dominant consumptive use of water in the United States, especially in the regions most likely to face water shortages in the future. In 1970, for example, irrigation accounted for 83 percent of all the water consumed offsite in the Nation (Table 1-2). For the year 2000, the Water Resources Council's projection indicates that agriculture (irrigation and livestock) still could account for about 73 percent of all water consumed offsite in the Nation (Table 1-4). The future agricultural demand for water depends on a number of variables, including: (1) food and fiber demand (domestic and export); (2) Federal policies adopted for control of farm production, resource development, and environmental quality; (3) the rate of technological advance; and (4) the price of water to the various users. It is also affected to a very great extent by the way other resources, such as capital required to implement modern technologies, fertilizer, and land, are used with and as a substitute for water.

In its search for answers to how these variables interact to influence demand for water for irrigated agriculture in the Western regions, the Commission contracted with Iowa State University for an analysis of how a series of alternative future policies would affect demands for land and water for agriculture. By going to Iowa State University, the Commission was able to take advantage of work done by that University for the Tennessee Valley Authority, in developing relationships between fertilizer use and crop production, and the Bureau of Reclamation, in developing relationships between water use and crop production.

The analysis[19] was made in a national context in which land and alternative technologies over the 48

---

[19] For details, see HEADY, Earl O et al., Iowa State University (1971). Agricultural Water Demands, prepared for the National Water Commission. National Technical Information Service, Springfield, Va., Accession No. PB 206 790; and MADSEN, Howard C et al., Iowa State University (1972). Alternative Demands for Water and Land for Agricultural Purposes, prepared for the National Water Commission. National Technical Information Service, Springfield, Va., Accession No. PB 211 444.

contiguous States were allowed to be used with, or substituted for, water in the nine Western basins in which demand for irrigation water is greatest. The effects of various combinations of alternative assumptions as to population level, farm policy, water price, level of exports, and rate of technological advance were analyzed by the use of a large-scale linear programing model. The results of the 1969 Census of Agriculture were not available at the time the studies were begun, so 1964 was used as the base year for the model forecasts.

A single year, 2000, was chosen for analysis because the research staff believed more could be learned by studying a wider range of possible outcomes for a single year than by studying a lesser number of alternatives over many years.

The study was not made for the purpose of suggesting that any of these alternatives be adopted as a goal for national policy, but to determine the availability of water and land and the resulting economic effects in terms of commodity prices should such conditions prevail in the year 2000.

Alternative Futures for Agriculture: Altogether, 11 possible alternative futures for agricultural water demands were analyzed. The alternatives were selected to illustrate a wide range of possible conditions that might possibly prevail in the year 2000. Three possible population levels were considered— 325 million, 300 million, and 280 million— corresponding roughly to the B, C, and D level projections of the U.S. Census Bureau at the time the study was initiated.

Nine of the 11 alternative futures assumed a free market for farm products because other types of farm programs are more difficult and costly to set up and evaluate in a linear programing model of the size and nature of that used in the analysis. The other two futures assumed an annual land retirement program similar to the wheat, feed grain, and cotton programs used during the 1960's.

To evaluate the possible effects of water pricing policy on use of water for irrigation, three alternative assumptions as to the future price of water for irrigation were considered in three of the studies, while the other eight assumed that present average prices for water would prevail.

At the time the studies were undertaken, crop production for foreign export had remained relatively constant through the decade of the 1960's, and the statistics for the latter part of the decade indicated a downturn in the acreage required to produce crops

for export. For this reason, eight of the alternative futures included an assumption that exports of agricultural products would be at the 1967-1969 level. In order to test the higher ranges of demand for agricultural products, however, one future combined a doubling of the 1967-1969 export demand with the 325 million assumption as to population.

The assumptions of the studies in regard to future advances in agricultural technology (crop yields) and changes in per capita food consumption were supplied by Iowa State University, based on its continuing studies of these factors. Since these called for an increase in per capita consumption of beef and veal in the year 2000 of 35 percent above current levels, the Commission asked that two of the alternative futures include an assumption that beef and veal consumption continue at current levels, with the increase in demand for protein met by substitution of vegetable protein, along the lines subsequently suggested in an article in the Wall Street Journal.[20]

The original study did not take into account the effects of agriculture on water quality, so the Commission requested that the final two alternative futures include assumptions that the use of nitrogen fertilizers be restricted, as a rough measure of what might happen if drastic measures to reduce pollution from nonpoint-sources were to be adopted.

Conclusions from the Analysis: The results of the study, based on conservative yield trends, indicate that U.S. agriculture would not be faced with aggregative strains on food-producing capacity and water supplies relative to needs in the year 2000 under any of the alternative futures considered. Under the assumptions of the study, even if irrigated area is not increased over the next 30 years (to the year 2000), capacity of American agriculture will be sufficiently large to meet the anticipated demands at reasonable prices. Projected food demands in the year 2000, according to the conclusions of the study, could be met by returning land idled under Government programs to production with the use of less irrigated land than at present. If more vegetable protein were consumed by people, instead of being fed to livestock, the demand for irrigation water would be reduced even further. Hence, in the event of potential

---

[20] Recent newspaper stories suggest that such substitutions may be imminent. See, for example, BRAND, David (1973). Battle for Survival, a news story quoting Aaron Altschuel, Professor of Nutrition, Georgetown University, Washington, D.C. The Wall Street Journal, February 7, 1973. Vol. LI, No. 26, pp. 1 and 12.

Food-producing capacity and water supplies through the year 2000 can be compatible

future water scarcities in the West, agriculture need not use more but actually could release a fairly large supply of water for industrial and urban uses. Finally, the study indicates that increasing the price of water for irrigation in the 17 Western States would create the potential for release of substantial quantities of water from agriculture for uses in other sectors and locations without putting pressure on the Nation's food supplies or export potentialities or having other than minimal effects on the cost of food to the Nation's consumers.[21]

---

[21] See HEADY, Earl O et al., Iowa State University (1971). Agricultural Water Demands, prepared for the National Water Commission. National Technical Information Service, Springfield, Va., Accession No. PB 206 790. pp. V-1 to V-3.

Other Possible Alternatives for Agriculture: Several reviewers of the Commission's draft report have suggested that the Commission should evaluate an alternative future incorporating assumptions that the recent surge in food exports, which increased the 1972 export level substantially above the 1967-1969 average, will continue and that the masses of world population will become dependent on the United States for their food supply. If at the same time the trend toward increasing crop yields in the United States were reversed and the rate of population growth in the United States increased, there might indeed be food shortages. Incorporation of such assumptions in a model study could undoubtedly lead to solutions which would call for vast increases in the amount of land required for crop production. Nevertheless, the Commission believes that for illustrative purposes the alternative futures considered in the Iowa State University studies provide a realistic range of alternatives. If the Nation decides to plan for greater crop production, such a decision should be based on thorough consideration of all of the possible options, looking to achieving greater production goals in the most efficient way possible. And if as a matter of national policy the Nation decides to increase its food export capability by a program of subsidizing the reclamation of land, a decision we do not recommend, it should do so in full awareness that the general taxpayer would be providing an indirect export subsidy for foodstuffs.

CONCLUSIONS

Water use is responsive to many variables in policy and technology as well as to rates of growth in the population and the economy which cannot be forecast with any assurance. Thus, any projection of the future need for water based only on past trends is quite likely to be wrong. What must be done is to study a variety of alternative futures in which the factors affecting water use are explicitly considered. The alternative futures discussed in this chapter indicate the wide ranges of policy choices, tradeoffs, and flexibility in water use that are available. The Commission believes that all policy planning activities should give consideration to a wide range of possible choices so that there is assurance that the selected course of action will, regardless of any future which can reasonably develop, be a sound decision for the Nation. In the words of René Dubos, "trend is not destiny."[22]

---

[22] DUBOS, René (1972). A God Within. Charles Scribner's Sons, New York, p. 291.

Water and the
Natural Environment

The environmental effects of water projects and water use are receiving increasing attention, in the press, in Congress, and in the courts. Stream channelization; flood control, hydroelectric power, and irrigation projects; and major industrial water uses such as the cooling of thermal powerplants are attacked on grounds ranging from their impact on fisheries and wildlife to their esthetic unsuitability and their alleged long-term effects upon the complex ecology of interrelated river and ocean systems.

The Nation has become more sophisticated in its understanding of ecological processes and painfully aware that past water uses and developments have produced some unpleasant and unforeseen results. For example, the invasion of the Great Lakes by sea lamprey through the Welland Canal;[1] increased salinity in the Colorado River as irrigation has increased and the flow has decreased; and the discovery that large bacterial populations, created by sewage enrichment of streams and lakes, can react as "environmental catalysts" with discharges of inorganic mercury to produce the highly toxic methyl mercury.[2]

[1] STEVENS, Harry K et al., Michigan State University (1972). Recycling and Ecosystem Response, prepared for the National Water Commission. National Technical Information Service, Springfield, Va., Accession No. 208 669. p. 69.

[2] BEETON, AM (1971). Man's effects on the Great Lakes, Ch. XIV in GOLDMAN, Charles R (1971). Environmental Quality and Water Development, prepared for the National Water Commission. National Technical Information Service, Springfield, Va., Accession No. PB 207 114.

Boating on scenic Lake Powell just above Aztec Canyon in southern Utah illustrates change in recreational and envrionmental values resulting from reservoir construction.

Yet at the same time the Nation has enjoyed environmental benefits from water projects: Glen Canyon undammed was beautiful, but so is Lake Powell; the C&O Canal and its adjacent lands offer recreation, charm, and a slice of history in metropolitan Washington, D.C.; water projects have opened new routes to natural treasures in backcountry and offer new fishing and recreational opportunities. Clearly, the environmental results of water use and development can be good as well as bad.

All projects alter the natural environment. The challenge is to choose well, to try to foresee the environmental consequences of proposed water uses and projects, to evaluate the costs and benefits of alternatives, and to act accordingly—which includes deciding not to develop when environmental and other costs outweigh the benefits. On the other hand, some environmental change is inevitable, not all of which will be necessarily bad. Even environmental enhancement by various pollution control techniques has associated environmental costs which must be considered. The Nation has gone astray, however, when it has permitted the use and development of waters without regard for ecological processes and the environmental values associated with natural water systems. It need not continue to do so.

In order to protect and achieve environmental quality, the Commission believes that it is necessary:

1. To understand and be able to predict the primary environmental effects which a particular water program, project, or use, and the alternatives to it, including no development, may produce.

2. To assess the secondary effects which are likely to be produced and the broader environmental costs and benefits which are likely to result.

3. To take environmental values and processes into account in selecting among alternatives, so as to accommodate those values or processes, or, where a conflict of values is necessarily present, to reach an

informed and balanced judgment as to what will best serve the public interest.[3]

SOME BASIC ECOLOGICAL PRINCIPLES[4]

To understand some of the basic environmental impacts caused by water developments and water uses, it is necessary to understand some basic ecological principles.

Ecology is "the study of the interrelationships of living organisms to one another and to their surroundings."[5] Interrelationship is the key concept, both within ecosystems and among them. Speaking generally, although they do not conform to strict, well-defined boundaries, ecosystems are recognizable, relatively homogeneous units, including the organisms, their environment, and all of the interactions among them. When one part of the ecosystem is affected it in turn affects the other, interrelated parts. However, ecosystems are not independent; they blend one into another, changing in space and over time, and interact. Ecologists speak of the "Law of the Holocoenotic Environment," that there is "complete interrelatedness and interdependency of all life and physical factors in the biosphere."[6]

Within each ecosystem each organism has its own ecological niche or role in the ecological process. If conditions permit, these niches will become increasingly specialized, creating a more diverse community. Developments within the ecosystem are subject to limiting factors—substances or conditions, biological or physical, that limit or reduce the functioning of an organism, species, population, biotic community, or ecosystem.

Ecosystems are powered largely by energy from the sun. Green plants, the primary producers, through the process of photosynthesis convert carbon dioxide and water into oxygen and organic chemical energy, which becomes the fuel for the food chain. The productivity of each level within the ecosystem depends upon the productivity of the primary producers. Another form of power is chemosynthesis, where organisms derive their energy from direct chemical transformations. Compared with photosynthesis, this is usually of minor importance in most aquatic ecosystems.

At each level about 10 percent of the energy is passed on through the food chain. The remainder is either metabolized by the organism for its own maintenance or passed on at death to decomposer organisms such as bacteria and fungi. These decomposers play a vital part in the ecosystem in converting organic material back into the nutrients needed by green plants, utilizing oxygen in the system. This is the process of natural recycling.[7]

Ecosystems are self-regulating, relying upon feedback mechanisms to maintain order. They react to stresses or to changes in input by striking new balances. For example, if additional energy is introduced into the system, such as that provided by organic sewage, primary production will increase, touching off further changes in production and consumption.

Ecosystems evolve, if permitted to do so, through orderly processes, sometimes over a long period of time. The process of change is referred to as succession. The early stages of succession are characterized by a relatively few small and simple organisms and by relatively low primary productivity, although it exceeds the demands upon it. As succession continues, the system becomes more complex. More production machinery (green plants) develops, but there are more consumers of the primary production and more of the energy generated by production is required for the maintenance of the producing organisms.

---

[3] See Chapter 6 for a discussion of the National Environmental Policy Act of 1969 (NEPA) and other procedures designed to produce this decision, and Chapter 10 on decisionmaking.

[4] The Commission's background reports for this section are GOLDMAN, Charles R (1971). Environmental Quality and Water Development, prepared for the National Water Commission. National Technical Information Service, Springfield, Va., Accession Nos. PB 207 113 & 207 114. STEVENS, Harry K et al., Michigan State University (1972). Recycling and Ecosystem Response, prepared for the National Water Commission. National Technical Information Service, Springfield, Va., Accession No. PB 208 669. For a helpful description of ecological principles, see THORNE ECOLOGICAL FOUNDATION (1971). Field Syllabus, Seminar on Environmental Arts and Sciences, Aspen, Colorado. Mimeo, The Foundation, Boulder, Colo.

[5] BORN, Steven M & YANGGEN, Douglas A (1972). Understanding Lakes and Lake Problems. Environmental Resources Unit, University of Wisconsin Extension, Madison. p. 12.

[6] THORNE ECOLOGICAL FOUNDATION (1971). Field Syllabus, Seminar on Environmental Arts and Sciences, Aspen, Colorado. Mimeo, The Foundation, Boulder, Colo.

[7] See generally, RICHERSON P & McEVOY J (1971). The measurement of environmental quality, Ch. VIII, in GOLDMAN, Charles R (1971). Environmental Quality and Water Development, prepared for the National Water Commission. National Technical Information Service, Springfield, Va., Accession No. PB 207 113.

Diversity is a characteristic of the increasingly complex ecosystem. In general, organisms tend to become larger and more complex. There are more species, and the increased competition among them results in specialization; the niches are defined more precisely to those in which particular organisms are best adapted to compete. This diversity is important for the resilience of an ecosystem. The more diverse ecosystem, with its wide variety of species adapted to particular niches, is better able to withstand stresses than are less diverse ecosystems. The stability of an ecosystem is directly related to its diversity and complexity. Factors which limit diversity, whether natural or manmade, reduce stability.

Succession continues until an equilibrium, or climax, is attained. At this point, diversity within the ecosystem is at a maximum permitted by the limiting factors of the environment, and the production of the ecosystem is balanced by the demands for energy within it. The ecosystem has reached its carrying capacity. However, it is not static; it is in a dynamic condition created by the interplay of physical, chemical, and biological forces and limitations. The dynamic character of ecosystems makes time an important dimension; changes, including those triggered by man's activities, may be subtle but can become critical over a long period.

ENVIRONMENTAL EFFECTS OF RESERVOIR DEVELOPMENT

All water projects and water uses have environmental repercussions. Reservoir development provides a good vehicle for discussing environmental impacts, to illustrate the problems generally, because of widespread interest in them and the controversies which they have generated. Consider the case of Hetch Hetchy in the early part of this century, where the issue was whether to dam a river within Yosemite National Park to provide water for San Francisco; or the more recent controversies over proposed dams on the Colorado River—Echo Park, Marble Canyon, and Bridge Canyon; or current issues such as the proposed Tocks Island and Gillham Dams and the future of the Middle Snake.

The purpose of this section is to suggest the range and magnitude of the potential environmental effects generated by impounding a stream, effects which the Commission believes must be investigated and evaluated in order to facilitate sound decisions about water resources. No attempt is made here to set out all possible environmental impacts, adverse or beneficial, which may be associated with reservoir construction and operation. Moreover, no attempt is made to predict what impacts a particular project will have, because the effects are site-specific (that is, they likely will vary from one site to another).

This section deals exclusively with the environmental effects of reservoir development, some good but many bad. It does not catalog or evaluate nonenvironmental effects of reservoirs, some bad but many good. Hence, the important social and economic values of hydroelectric generation, slack-water navigation, flood control, irrigation, municipal and industrial water supply, and recreation made possible by reservoir developments and discussed in detail elsewhere throughout this report are ignored here. This discussion of the environmental effects of reservoirs should not be construed to indicate that the Commission is either opposed to or invariably critical of reservoir developments.

The emphasis here on the relatively direct, primary environmental effects of reservoirs should not obscure an important point: reservoir development and use produce secondary effects which may have great environmental significance. For example, a hydroelectric project may require the mining and production of materials and the taking of land for long-distance transmission systems, which a fossil fueled electric plant at the load center would not—a secondary environmental cost—but it may also make an urban fossil plant unnecessary, conserving non-renewable fossil fuels and curtailing air pollution—secondary environmental benefits.

By the same token, the specification of possible adverse effects should not be taken as a general indictment of reservoirs. Many have produced net environmental benefits. However, historically emphasis has been placed upon assets. In order to make a balanced evaluation of the environmental effects of reservoir development, it is necessary to appreciate adverse impacts as well.

Effects in Terms of Ecological Processes

Reservoirs create new conditions for organisms, and ultimately, as adjustments are made, foster new ecosystems. Some of the organisms flooded are tolerant to inundation; others are not. Water currents, levels, temperatures, and other characteristics will change as a stream is converted to a lake. Within the reservoir the old stream ecosystem is replaced by a new lake-like one; below the dam there is still a stream, but here too conditions will be altered.

Yellowtail Dam's full reservoir backs up 71 river miles of the Bighorn Canyon in Montana and Wyoming

The predictable effect of a dam and reservoir is change of the organisms within the affected ecosystems. A possible effect is a loss of diversity and stability. If the conversion from a stream to a lake system diminishes the types of habitat available, as well it may, diversity will be reduced. Even if the changed conditions are as diverse as before, some of the previous niches may no longer exist. New and different ones may succeed them. Some species which live in a stream may not survive in a lake. Change, *per se,* is not necessarily bad, assuming equivalent diversity, since new organisms may thrive. However, it is important to be able to predict which organisms may live and which may die. It is possible that rare species will be lost or that keystone species (those upon which associated species depend for support) will be eliminated, triggering significant further change. New species may or may not be less desirable than the old, or they may prosper at the expense of some other desirable species.

A second possible effect is increased primary productivity in an impoundment. A reservoir may act as a "nutrient trap," holding nutrients which otherwise would have continued downstream, thereby increasing the nutrient content behind the dam, while decreasing it downstream. The impacts of this phenomenon will vary depending upon the characteristics of the reservoir, such as its depth and the ratio of inflow to storage, and of the stream. However, under some circumstances, the additional nutrients will accelerate eutrophication within the lake, stimulating the growth of algae, acquatic weeds, and bacteria. The upper levels of the food chain characteristically are unable to expand their feeding fast enough to keep pace with the increase of the primary producers. Further, many of the plants produced during advanced eutrophication may be inedible. When the plants die, they are used directly by the decomposers in large quantities, a process which requires substantial amounts of oxygen and may, in severe circumstances, deplete the oxygen available to sustain fish and other life in the lake.[8]

A similar effect may be created when a new reservoir inundates vegetation which cannot tolerate flooding. The decay of the dead vegetation may deplete dissolved oxygen, particularly in the depths, and produce hydrogen sulphide.

Effects Within the Impoundment

Inundation can produce serious effects on the area within the impoundment. Historic, archaeological, scenic, and other significant sites which may be within the impoundment will be flooded; existing land uses will be displaced. The vegetation which cannot tolerate inundation will be replaced in places by more tolerant vegetation, a change which may be important if the new species are more or less desirable than the old.

Inundation means a changed habitat for wildlife and other fauna, perhaps a critical loss for some species and a gain for others. Mitigation of any loss through the providing of other, comparable habitat may or may not be possible. At the same time, the reservoir provides new habitat for waterfowl and other lake-oriented species. Terrestrial insects may be eliminated within the impoundment, to be replaced by aquatic species. The change in habitat may also mean the loss of certain predator species, permitting other species to reproduce at an accelerated rate.

Inundation of a stretch of stream may alter recreational opportunities substantially.[9] Some of the more bitter recent fights over reservoirs have involved the proposed substitution of motor and sail boating and lake fishing for white water canoeing and stream fishing. Typically, the reservoir offers a greater water surface and total volume than the stream did, and the surrounding area can be developed to permit easier access. The likely upshot is that more people will use the reservoir than used the stream, that there will be more fish because of the increased acreage of water, and that people will enjoy new opportunities for water-based recreation. However, this may come at the expense of other important recreational assets. Recreational values cannot be measured solely in terms of increased user-days. Diversity is important for recreation, as it is for ecosystems. In some cases, impoundments increase diversity; in other cases they

reduce it. Providing lake recreation where none existed before may provide real net benefits. On the other hand, replacing a shrinking number of miles of high-quality streams with lakes can be a poor exchange, particularly if there is already other lake recreation available.

A reservoir can be expected to support a fishery different from the one in a stream. Deep lakes stratify in the summer, with a sun-warmed layer, the epilimnion, on top and a colder layer, the hypolimnion, below. The two are separated by a zone of rapidly changing temperature, the thermocline. As decaying organic matter consumes oxygen in the colder depths, the oxygen cannot be readily replenished by photosynthesis or by wind action. As a result, fish tend to live in the warmer epilimnion, but the waters there may be too warm to support some important game and commercial species of fish. Thus, the fish which live in a reservoir may not be of the same quality—either for recreational or for commercial fishing—as those which previously lived in the stream.

As a result of the reservoir's operation, its water level will fluctuate on a daily or a seasonal basis, the amount of drawdown varying with the size and shape of the reservoir and the purpose of the releases. Although the environmental effects will vary with the amount, rate, and pattern of releases, the reservoir drawdown will affect the habitat of flora and fauna, may interfere with recreation, and can produce ugly mud flats. Natural, unregulated streams fluctuate also, of course, sometimes with serious effects.

Effects Downstream

Dams are barriers to the upstream migration of anadromous fish. Various techniques are available to hatch fish below the dam or to transport fish over and around the dam and thus mitigate the effects of the barrier. However, fish ladders are sometimes unsuccessful. If the fish are transported successfully over the dam, the young downstream migrants sometimes are unable to find their way back through the nearly still waters of the reservoir. Where the project includes hydropower facilities, there can be significant fingerling mortality in downstream passage through the turbines.

The operation of a reservoir or series of reservoirs may have beneficial or detrimental impacts downstream. The water of the hypolimnion is typically much colder than the water downstream. Releases from this layer in significant amounts can shock the fishery below or can maintain a good cold water

---

[8] *Ibid.*

[9] See also Chapter 5, Section I, Water-Based Recreation, for a discussion of recreation at reservoirs.

fishery. By the same token, releases from the epilimnion may be too warm for some species. The temperature tolerance limits seem particularly important during spawning seasons. Releases from the hypolimnion are likely to be low in dissolved oxygen, which can have a detrimental effect downstream. These effects may be mitigated by the use of variable level discharges. Knowledge about potential effects is critical for the proper operation of the reservoir.[10]

Another environmental impact of reservoir operation which has received attention lately is the so-called "gas bubble disease" phenomenon. Waters flowing over a spillway entrain air which plunges to the depths in the stilling basin and dissolves, producing a supersaturation of the dissolved gases.

Along the Snake and Columbia Rivers, where hydroelectric dams stairstep downstream, the supersaturation is not relieved between dams. Fish extract the gases from the water through their gills, so that the dissolved gases enter the blood and tissues. Under lower water pressures, or higher temperatures, the dissolved gases attempt to return to a gaseous state and produce bubbles which can block the blood vessels of a fish.[11] Spillway modifications or more effective use of hydropower potential to reduce water flowing over spillways are expected to ameliorate the problem.

Effects of Altered Flows

A primary purpose of constructing a reservoir is to change the pattern of flows from that which existed before: capturing high flows to prevent floods or to store runoff for water supply, and later releasing the water at a controlled rate of flow to produce hydroelectric power or to augment natural low flows. These alterations in the timing and magnitude of flows offer significant benefits. However, they also have the potential for causing environmental disruption where particular levels or patterns of flow are important. Reservoir storage may lessen total flows downstream because of increased evaporation. As water in the reservoir evaporates, the remaining water—and discharges from it—are more saline. Furthermore, removal of water from the system, particularly high-quality water, leaves less flow to dilute and carry the salt load downstream.

Reservoirs almost always alter the pattern of sediment deposition downstream. One of the Commission's background studies points out that the effect of reservoirs may be either to diminish sediments downstream, where the reservoir traps upstream sediments, or to increase them, if before impoundment a river flushed out accumulated sediments downstream during times of high flow, but did not do so after regulation.[12] The altered sediment load downstream may affect the fishery, either improving or degrading it, and change the pattern of deposition at the mouth of the river. Sediment build-up within the reservoir may also produce important effects.

Effects of Changed Land Use

Some of the most significant environmental impacts associated with reservoirs may come from the changed land use patterns which the reservoir permits or encourages. For example, a flood control project may encourage people to build or to plant crops in the flood plain downstream, reducing the diversity and stability of that area. The lake created by the storage reservoir may act as a magnet for recreational, residential, or commercial development, which in turn increases pollution. Construction can cause sedimentation; development can increase runoff; increased recreational use may overcrowd the lake and the surrounding area.[13]

Water development tends to generate changed land uses, and these secondary developments themselves affect the natural environment. This relationship underscores the need to coordinate water resources planning with the planning for and regulation of land use and water quality, points which are developed at more length elsewhere in this report.[14]

[10] See generally, HAGAN RM & ROBERTS EB (1971). Ecological impacts of water storage and diversion projects, Ch. XI in GOLDMAN, Charles R (1971). Environmental Quality and Water Development, prepared for the National Water Commission. National Technical Information Service, Springfield, Va., Accession No. PB 207 113.

[11] SMITH HA Jr (Summer 1972). N_2 – Threat to Pacific Northwest Fisheries? Water Spectrum 4(2):41-47.

[12] HAGAN RM & ROBERTS EB (1971). Ecological impacts of water storage and diversion projects, Ch. XI in GOLDMAN, Charles R (1971). Environmental Quality and Water Development, prepared for the National Water Commission. National Technical Information Service, Springfield, Va., Accession No. PB 207 113.

[13] See generally, HENWOOD K (1971). Impact analysis and the planning process, Ch. IX in GOLDMAN, Charles R (1971). Environmental Quality and Water Development, prepared for the National Water Commission. National Technical Information Service, Springfield, Va., Accession No. PB 207 113.

[14] See Chapter 4 on water pollution and Chapter 10, Section B, on planning.

Esthetic Effects of Reservoir Development

Congress regarded esthetic values as important in establishing this Commission. The National Water Commission Act directs the Commission to "consider economic and social consequences of water resource development, including, for example, the impact of water resource development on . . . esthetic values affecting the quality of life of the American people; . . ."[15]

The Commission's background study on esthetic values[16] recognizes that an esthetic experience is in part a product of the observer's "state of mind" and the context of observation. However, esthetics also may be evaluated in terms of the environmental stimuli. Certain basic characteristics, such as vegetation patterns, land form definitions and the prominence of the waterscape, can be identified. These can be evaluated in terms of the presence or absence of certain attributes which produce high or low esthetic quality.

The study also suggests a classification of manmade elements and describes various ways in which development may be made most compatible with the esthetic characteristics of the land and water. Reservoirs, of course, offer certain esthetic advantages of their own, such as a visible increase in the amount of water in the landscape.

The Commission believes that the types of analysis suggested by the background study can be helpful in at least three situations:

1. Where the decision already has been made to construct a reservoir at a particular site, but consideration of esthetic factors can lead to a design which is tailored to the important characteristics of the setting.

2. Where a choice must be made between alternative sites for a reservoir, and the alternatives will have different esthetic impacts.

3. Where the choice to be made is among different types of projects which might meet a particular need (or whether there should be a project at all) and the esthetic characteristics of the area are significant.

This approach does not provide an answer for when esthetic values may be so significant as to outweigh other considerations or to make the difference on balance. It simply provides a basis for treating esthetics less subjectively, permitting some evaluation of how outstanding the esthetic characteristics of a site really are.[17] It remains for decision-makers to evaluate the esthetic considerations with other relevant considerations. However, the Commission believes that esthetic factors should be described as carefully and assessed as objectively as possible, by reference to standards such as those suggested in the background study. Furthermore, to identify assets of national or regional value, land and water resources planning should include identification of and recommendations for protection or rehabilitation of high quality esthetic settings.

Loss of Wildness[18]

For many who love a free-flowing, undeveloped river, no list of environmental impacts, or combination of impacts, such as that set out above, can capture the full loss when a previously undeveloped stream is dammed. To them, undeveloped streams are rare and valuable natural resources, worthy of protection for their own sake. They are examples of nature untouched by the works of man and some, at least, should be preserved that way as part of our heritage, for ourselves and for generations to come.

The Wild and Scenic Rivers Act of 1968 is responsive to this concern. It established a system of wild and scenic rivers to be protected from development or from land uses which would be incompatible with the existing primitive character of the area. The Act designated eight rivers as immediate components of the system, charged the Secretaries of the Interior and Agriculture with studying 27 more as expeditiously as possible, and provided for the possible inclusion of other rivers within the system. All Federal agencies are to consider the potential of river areas as wild, scenic, or recreational in "planning for the use and development of water and related land resources . . .".[19] The process is a slow one. A river

[15] *National Water Commission Act,* P.L. 90-515, September 26, 1968, 82 Stat. 868, 42 USCA 1962a note.

[16] LITTON, R Burton Jr et al. (1971). An Aesthetic Overview of the Role of Water in the Landscape, prepared for the National Water Commission. National Technical Information Service, Springfield, Va., Accession No. PB 207 315.

[17] See also, LEOPOLD, Luna B (1969). Quantitative Comparison of Some Aesthetic Factors Among Rivers, Geological Survey Circular 620. U.S. Geological Survey, Washington, D.C.

[18] See generally, NASH R (1971). Rivers and Americans: A century of conflicting priorities, Ch. IV in GOLDMAN, Charles R (1971). Environmental Quality and Water Development, prepared for the National Water Commission. National Technical Information Service, Springfield, Va., Accession No. PB 207 113.

[19] *Wild and Scenic Rivers Act,* P.L. 90-452, Section 5(d), October 2, 1968, 82 Stat. 910, 16 USCA 1276(d).

The Wild and Scenic Rivers Act of 1968 will protect scenic rivers, such as this, from incompatible use

may be added to the system only by the action of Congress or by the Secretary of the Interior's approval of a river corridor designated by a State legislature. Proposed additions to the system are subject to review by interested Federal agencies. In many instances, the Federal Government would be required to acquire fee title or scenic easements in the land corridor along the river to provide the management necessary to preserve the river's qualities.

The Wild and Scenic Rivers Act does not provide the sole vehicle for determining that the qualities of a particular river reach are such that a dam should not be built. Under the National Environmental Policy Act and the Federal Power Act, as interpreted by the courts, Federal licensing and construction agencies have an obligation, before licensing or constructing a dam, to consider whether that is the best use of the river or whether the river should be left in its natural state. They should decide how to act in light of all relevant factors, including the secondary environ-

mental costs and benefits of proceeding or of denying a license or foregoing a project. The existence of a mechanism by which Congress may designate certain rivers as wild or scenic should not relieve Federal agencies from this responsibility.[20]

CONCLUSIONS ON WATER DEVELOPMENT PROJECTS

Potential water resources programs and projects need to be approached carefully and analyzed comprehensively so they do not produce unexpected and environmentally unacceptable results.

Elsewhere, this report makes a number of recommendations directed toward the better planning and

[20] HILLHOUSE, William A & DeWEERDT, John L (1972). Legal Devices for Accommodating Water Resources Development and Environmental Values, prepared for the National Water Commission. National Technical Information Service, Springfield, Va., Accession No. PB 208 835. Chs. 1, 7.

evaluation of such programs and projects. These recommendations, designed to further sound projects and to eliminate unsound ones, are applicable to environmental considerations as well as to economic ones. Since the rationale for these recommendations is set out more fully in other chapters of this report, the discussion here is limited to ways in which these recommendations apply to environmental considerations.

1. **Develop an adequate data base.** The Commission has recommended an extensive, continuous program for collecting and organizing data on the condition of the Nation's waters.[21] Too little is known about their present characteristics and quality and additional information is needed to assist intelligent judgment about the levels of quality which should be sought and the measures needed to achieve them.

However, if the Nation is to have environmentally sound land and water development, it may not rely upon water quality data alone, important though that is. A broader data base is needed. The ecological processes and environmental attributes of potentially affected areas should be studied; wherever practicable, these studies should include the geology, soils, fisheries, climate, vegetation, historical and archeological resources, land uses, esthetics, and other relevant factors.

2. **Conduct further research into the environmental impacts of water resource development.** The Commission has identified this as one of the Nation's primary water research needs.[22] Too little is known about the environmental impacts, good and bad, of water projects. In particular, while our knowledge about ecological processes is expanding and becoming more sophisticated, there is a need for further work to improve the prediction of ecological effects of proposed water projects and of possible modifications or alternatives.

3. **Utilize planning techniques which are sensitive to ecological processes and environmental values.** Some imaginative techniques exist. The work of the Potomac Planning Task Force, assembled by The American Institute of Architects, provides an example.[23] The Task Force recommended an "environmental approach," starting with "the recog-

nition that nature contains intrinsic resources which may be utilized to our benefit but may not be overtaxed except at a cost."[24] They suggested gathering appropriate data on such natural resources as terrain, water, minerals, and vegetation; by analyzing this data, unique or scarce components of the landscape could be identified, as well as the most appropriate areas for different types of land and water use. The Task Force applied this approach to five major physiographic regions within the Potomac Basin and to the Washington metropolitan area.[25] Innovative approaches such as this, conducted with realistic consideration for the resulting plans' economic and political acceptability, offer promise.

A later section of this report deals with the role of the public in water resources planning.[26] While public participation serves to develop public preferences broadly, including economic preferences, one important function is to involve members of the public from the inception of planning in order to identify what they believe are the important elements of environmental quality, to broaden and deepen the planning agency's examination of environmental effects, to suggest alternatives which the agency might not consider under traditional approaches, and to educate both the public and the agency.

In some situations it is helpful and practical to construct and operate a model to simulate the effects which different actions will produce within the system modeled. For example, in Chapter 11, Section E, the Commission recommends increased Federal support for water quality models for the Great Lakes.

4. **Develop rigorously and present as clearly as practicable the environmental impacts associated with a proposed water resources project and the available alternatives.** The National Environmental Policy Act (NEPA) requires Federal agencies to describe the environmental impacts of major proposed actions, including those which cannot be avoided should the proposal be implemented, and to explore and describe alternatives to the proposed action.[27] The Commission believes that NEPA, if properly applied,

---

[21] See Chapter 17, Basic Data and Research.

[22] See Chapter 17.

[23] POTOMAC PLANNING TASK FORCE (1967). The Potomac, A Report on Its Imperiled Future and a Guide for its Orderly Development. U.S. Government Printing Office, Washington, D.C.

[24] *Ibid.,* p. 44.

[25] See also, McHARG IL & CLARKE MG (1971). Skippack Watershed and the Evansburg Project, Ch. XVI in GOLDMAN, Charles R (1971). Environmental Quality and Water Development, prepared for the National Water Commission. National Technical Information Service, Springfield, Va., Accession No. PB 207 114.

[26] Chapter 10, Section C.

[27] P.L. 91-190, January 1, 1970, 83 Stat. 852, 42 USCA 4321-47.

provides an important tool for planning and evaluating water resources programs and projects. However, too often an environmental impact statement submitted under NEPA reads like a justification for a particular project rather than a rigorous exploration of impacts and alternatives. Impact statements, and the analysis which they reflect, should help shape agency decisions, not simply justify them.[28]

NEPA, as interpreted by the courts, requires a "rather finely tuned and 'systematic' balancing analysis in each instance"—an assessment of the relative weight of environmental, economic, and other costs and benefits.[29] Accordingly, it is appropriate for development agencies to discuss the range of benefits which a proposed project may produce. However, an environmental impact statement which emphasizes the positive and talks primarily about the "environmental" benefits which a project may bring by providing additional water supply, flood protection, and water recreation, misses an important point. The environmental impact statement is supposed to be a tool for assessing and evaluating the impacts which a proposed project will have upon the natural environment, so that these may be considered along with other factors.[30] In order to serve this purpose, an environmental impact statement should describe in detail the nature and magnitude of the environmental impacts which a project and its alternatives may produce, good and bad, and the possible combined or synergistic effects with other existing or proposed developments and land uses. Beyond this, the Commission believes that an environmental impact statement is particularly helpful when it identifies and discusses measures which can be taken to mitigate the adverse environmental impacts of a proposed action, including measures which might be taken by another government agency.

5. **Reach a decision.** Even improved programs of data collection, research, planning, and analysis should not be expected always to produce definitive information on every possible environmental impact of a proposed project and its alternatives.

Some predicted consequences, good or bad, may remain as unproved possibilities, incapable of being established either as future fact or of being dismissed with certainty. Planners and decisionmakers must meet their responsibilities fully and fairly to evaluate the information which is available or reasonably attainable, but when they have done so, the time comes for judgment of probabilities and decision on the best information available.

6. **Monitor environmental consequences.** Once projects are completed, the environmental impacts should be monitored to obtain information which would provide a better basis for future decisions to protect the environment when water projects are undertaken.

ESTUARIES AND THE COASTAL ZONE

When the National Water Commission was created in 1968, a two and one-half year study of national oceanographic research and development authorized by Congress in 1966 was nearing completion by the Commission on Marine Science, Engineering and Resources. The designed overlap of the two commissions made it clear that Congress did not expect the National Water Commission to consider in any detail the problems of the oceans.[31] Therefore this report does not. Other recent Federal reports have discussed estuaries and the coastal zone in considerable detail.[32]

However, the Nation's estuaries and coastal zone, the areas where the rivers and oceans interact, are an

[28] See U.S. GENERAL ACCOUNTING OFFICE (1972). Improvements Needed in Federal Efforts to Implement the National Environmental Policy Act of 1969, Report to the Subcommittee on Fisheries and Wildlife Conservation, House Committee on Merchant Marine and Fisheries, by the Comptroller General of the United States, B-170186. General Accounting Office, Washington, D.C.

[29] *Calvert Cliffs' Coordinating Committee v. AEC*, 449 F.2d 1109, 1113 (D.C. Cir. 1971).

[30] See U.S. COUNCIL ON ENVIRONMENTAL QUALITY (May 1972). Memorandum to Federal Agencies on Procedures for Improving Environmental Impact Statements. Reprinted in Environment Reporter, Current Developments [Bureau of National Affairs, Inc., Washington, D.C.] 3(3):82-87.

[31] See U.S. COMMISSION ON MARINE SCIENCE, ENGINEERING AND RESOURCES (1969). Our Nation and the Sea: a Plan for National Action. U.S. Government Printing Office, Washington, D.C.

[32] See for example, U.S. DEPARTMENT OF THE INTERIOR (1970). National Estuary Study, House Document 91-286, Part II, 91st Congress, 2d Session, U.S. Government Printing Office, Washington, D.C.; U.S. DEPARTMENT OF THE INTERIOR (1970). The National Estuarine Pollution Study, Senate Document No. 91-58, 91st Congress, 2d Session. U.S. Government Printing Office, Washington, D.C.; U.S. NATIONAL ACADEMY OF SCIENCES/NATIONAL ACADEMY OF ENGINEERING (1970). Waste Management Concepts for the Coastal Zone. National Academy of Sciences/National Academy of Engineering, Washington, D.C.; U.S. COUNCIL ON ENVIRONMENTAL QUALITY (1970). Ocean Dumping, A National Policy. U.S. Government Printing Office, Washington, D.C.

integral part of our river systems. Development, preservation, or use of water in some parts of the system affects other parts, making it impossible to discuss national water policy meaningfully without considering the role of estuaries and the coastal zone. This section, then, discusses two matters which relate to planning sound water projects, water uses and related development: the impact of upstream development on estuaries and the impact of development within the coastal zone itself.[33]

Estuaries — The Rich Mixing Zones

The estuarine region—the intermediate zone between fresh water rivers and open ocean—is affected by the mass movements of each but possesses the exclusive character of neither. Traditionally, the term "estuary" applies to the lower reaches of a river into which sea water intrudes and mixes with fresh water from land drainage. In all estuarine systems the essential process is that of mixing, of the interchange between the waters of the ocean and fresh water from lands, with the fresh water inflow and tidal currents primarily determining the circulation patterns.

Productivity is an important attribute of estuaries and their associated marshlands. Rivers drop sediments rich in nutrients; and the interaction of the tidal wedge, pushing upstream from the sea, and of the downstream currents tends to hold waterborne nutrients in the estuaries. Tides and currents flush the marshes, bringing additional nutrients to the plants in intertidal areas; the shallow water permits good light penetration and provides excellent conditions for fixed plants growing in the estuaries; floating algae add their production. As a result, the estuarine region is the most biologically productive area known on earth.[34]

Oysters and crabs spend their lives within the marsh-estuarine ecosystem. Two-thirds of the commercial fish caught nationally spend an important part of their life cycle in estuaries whether spawning, nursing, foraging, living there, or just passing through. The estuarine regions also provide important habitat for waterfowl and wildlife.

The Coastal Zone — An Area with Competing Demands

The term "coastal zone" describes the part of the continent where the land meets the sea, including the estuaries, marshlands, and lands adjacent to the shoreline, and the adjacent sea.

The coastal zone is subject to multiple, frequently competing demands. Some require changes in the natural environment and ecology of the coastal zone; others require their preservation. The coastal zone is urbanized, industrialized, and densely populated.[35] It is at the heart of commerce, a medium for shipping and a place for harbors, a mecca for recreation and second homes, a logical site for powerplants and other installations which require large amounts of cooling water, and a disposal ground for wastes of varying character washed from upstream sources or discharged locally by municipalities and industries. It is a source of vast amounts of oil, gas, and other resources.[36] It is the primary supplier of the Nation's fish harvest and a potentially fertile field for aquaculture. It is also the location of delicately balanced estuarine ecosystems and a place where there still is some solitude and wilderness.

Upstream Development

The discussion earlier in this chapter of the potential environmental effects of reservoir development illustrates the types of impacts which upstream development may have. Where reservoirs intercept sediment, for example, the creation of productive delta land may be retarded or reversed or beaches may erode because of a reduction in the supply of sand. Erosion control, channel lining, and other steps to improve upstream conditions may have adverse effects on the estuaries and coastal zones.

Estuaries may suffer from major alterations of fresh water inflow, particularly where they accentuate natural fluctuations. Salt water intrusion may

---

[33] See Chapter 4 for discussion of estuarine pollution and ocean dumping.

[34] See KETCHUM, Bostwick H & TRIPP, Bruce W (1972). Pre-Publication Summary, A Summary of the Conclusions and Recommendations of the Coastal Zone Workshop, held in Woods Hole, Mass., from May 22 to June 3, 1972. Woods Hole Oceanographic Institute, Woods Hole, Mass.

[35] "The coastal counties contain only 15 percent of the land area of the United States, but within this area is concentrated 33 percent of the Nation's population, with about four-fifths of it living in primarily urban areas which form about 10 percent of the total estuarine zone area . . .

"The coastal counties have within their borders 40 percent of all manufacturing plants in the United States." U.S. DEPARTMENT OF THE INTERIOR (1970). The National Estuarine Pollution Study, Senate Document No. 91-58, 91st Congress, 2d Session. U.S. Government Printing Office, Washington, D.C. pp. 20-21.

[36] See THEOBALD PK et al. (1972). Energy Resources of the United States, Geological Survey Circular 650. U.S. Geological Survey, Washington, D.C.

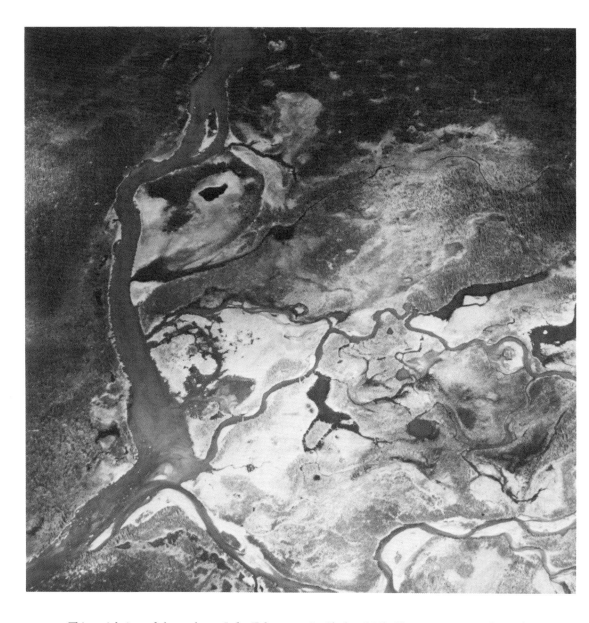

This aerial view of the outlet to Lake Telequance in Alaska vividly illustrates an estuarine region

reach farther upstream, increasing the salinity of the estuaries and decreasing the amount of mixing. This change may have an adverse impact upon estuarine ecosystems. For example, significant changes in the flow of fresh water from the Susquehanna River into the Chesapeake Bay could affect the Bay's oyster crop which thrives between certain salinity limits. On the other hand, natural fluctuations such as that experienced during hurricane Agnes in 1972 sometimes have a much greater effect than any manmade changes.

Rivers play an important role in many estuaries by flushing out collected nutrients, as well as by depositing nutrients from upstream. Diminished inflows from upstream developments, together with the addition of nutrients from man's activities, can upset the prevailing delicate balance. It has been suggested that smaller inflows may result in greater transparency, higher temperatures, and a longer retention time within the estuary. These conditions may cause eutrophication, with resulting damage to commercial and other fish species.[37] Larger inflows may also cause changes within estuaries.

Moreover, altered inflows may alter the ecology of marshlands which are associated with the estuaries, insofar as organisms there rely upon particular patterns of inundation and salinity.

Estuaries and the coastal zone are affected by land and water use throughout an associated river system. In turn, restrictions on the use of the coastal zone generate pressures to locate new uses upstream. Therefore, the coastal zone may not rationally be managed in isolation. It would not do to ban a particular use of a site on an estuary because of its anticipated adverse effects, if the banned project were then located upstream, with much the same harmful effect.

Speaking generally, comprehensive river basin planning has given too little attention to the effects of upstream water uses and development on the estuaries into which the rivers drain. There are examples of a broader approach, but comprehensive planning of this type is still in its infancy and carried out on a very restricted scale. Water resources development plans and projects prepared by river basin planning entities should include measures to protect the important characteristics of estuarine and coastal waters and of marshlands, and the costs of these measures should be borne by project beneficiaries where possible.

Coastal Zone Development

The Nation's estuaries and shorelands have been subjected to massive physical modification, threatening the ecological balance and the maintenance of high biological productivity which makes these areas so important.[38] This modification—dredging, filling, and development—may enhance valuable uses, but it also may damage estuarine ecosystems by altering circulation patterns and flows or by filling marshes and estuarine shallows. For example, ditching and diking can provide fresh water impoundments for waterfowl habitats in marshy backbay shorelands and open up fish access to wetland areas, but these operations also can alter conditions to the detriment of important species. Dredging and filling may improve navigation, boating, and water circulation by deepening watercourses, but may also destroy habitat and foraging areas, imposing a cost to be borne by fish and wildlife,[39] and can impair the capacity of an estuary to handle discharges from industries and municipalities. Natural forces also affect the ecological balance. For example, one-quarter of Maryland's annual "loss" of approximately 400 acres of coastal wetlands has been ascribed to natural erosion and succession.

Until very recently the primary Federal mechanism for controlling the physical modification of estuaries was the U.S. Army Corps of Engineers dredge and fill permit program under Section 10 of the Rivers and Harbors Act of 1899.[40] This Act was construed by the courts as authorizing the Corps of Engineers to deny a permit where the activity would harm fish and wildlife or cause other environmental damage.[41] Section 13 of the Rivers and Harbors Act of 1899 was the primary statutory basis for the Corps of Engineers' program to regulate water quality through discharge permits.

[37] See GOLDMAN CR (1971). Biological implications of reduced fresh-water flows on the San Francisco Bay-Delta System, pp. 109-124, in SECKLER, David [ed.], California Water, A Study in Resource Management. University of California Press, Berkeley.

[38] Coastal wetlands near population centers have been affected strikingly. The Department of the Interior found that 12,635 acres, or 29 percent of the Long Island wetlands existing in 1954, were developed between 1954 and 1964. U.S. DEPARTMENT OF THE INTERIOR (1970). National Estuary Study, House Document No. 91-286, Part II, 91st Congress, 2d Session. U.S. Government Printing Office, Washington, D.C. Volume 3, p. 32. Later studies concluded that an additional 4,400 acres of high tidal marsh were developed in Nassau and Suffolk counties since 1964. See O'CONNOR, Joel S & TERRY, Orville W (1972). The Marine Wetlands of Nassau and Suffolk Counties, New York, prepared in cooperation with the Nassau-Suffolk Regional Planning Board. Marine Sciences Research Center, State University of New York, Stony Brook, New York.

[39] Hedgpeth reports that the surface area of Boca Ciega Bay in Florida has been reduced by 20 percent since 1950 with the resultant estimated loss of fisheries worth about $1.5 million annually. See HEDGPETH JW (1971). Protection of environmental quality in estuaries, Ch. XIII in GOLDMAN, Charles R (1971). Environmental Quality and Water Development, prepared for the National Water Commission. National Technical Information Service, Springfield, Va., Accession No. PB 207 114. p. 8.

[40] Act of March 3, 1899, 30 Stat. 1151, 33 USCA 403.

[41] Zabel v. Tabb, 430 F.2d 199 (5th Cir. 1970), cert. denied, 401 U.S. 910 (1971); see also HILLHOUSE, William A II & DeWEERDT, John L (1972). Legal Devices for Accommodating Water Resources Development and Environmental Values, prepared for the National Water Commission. National Technical Information Service, Springfield, Va., Accession No. PB 208 835. Ch. 6.

Section 402 of the Federal Water Pollution Control Act, as amended in 1972, shifted responsibility for the issuance of permits for discharges to the Environmental Protection Agency (EPA) and to the States. Section 404 of that Act provides for a permit program, administered by the Corps of Engineers, for the discharge of dredged or fill material at specified disposal sites. These sites are to be determined applying guidelines developed by the Administrator of EPA in conjunction with the Secretary of the Army. The Administrator is empowered to prohibit specification of any area as a disposal site and to restrict the use of sites.

Additional controls on activities carried out in estuarine areas are provided by the Coastal Zone Management Act of 1972.[42] Under this Act, States will develop and administer management programs for their coastal zones, subject to the approval of the National Oceanic and Atmospheric Administration. Provision also is made for the establishment of estuarine sanctuaries. Federal agencies carrying out activities that affect the coastal zone must do so in a manner consistent with the State program to the maximum extent practicable. Federal agencies issuing permits or providing assistance for activities affecting the coastal zone also must take into account the State's management program.

CONCLUSIONS ON COASTAL ZONES

One of the major premises of this report is that water resources and water quality planning must be integrated with land use planning.[43] This is especially true in the coastal zone and in upstream areas where land use affects the estuaries. Decisions about where, whether, and how to dredge and fill, develop real estate, preserve natural systems, locate industries, and dispose of wastes determine to a large extent the possible uses and the environmental health of the waters and associated shorelands of the coastal zone. For this reason, planning for the coastal zones should be handled in coordination with general land use and water resources planning, as discussed in Chapter 10.

RECOMMENDATION

2-1. Water resources development plans and projects should include measures to protect the

estuarine and coastal waters and marshlands. The cost of measures required for such protection should be included in the joint costs of proposed projects and borne by the beneficiaries of the projects, except where Federal policy authorizes nonreimbursable allocations to be borne by the Federal Government for benefits of widespread or national scope that cannot be traced to particular beneficiaries.

CHANNELIZATION

During the regional conferences held in January and February 1973 to receive public comments on the review draft of this report, a number of witnesses urged that the National Water Commission give further attention to the environmental effects of channelization. The witnesses then went on to level considerable criticism against the programs of stream channelization conducted by the Soil Conservation Service of the U.S. Department of Agriculture and, to a lesser degree, by the U.S. Army Corps of Engineers and other water resource development agencies.

Channelization is not a water program objective. It is an engineering measure by the use of which various objectives, or combinations of objectives, may be achieved. These objectives include: *drainage* (that is, the reclamation of wetlands by lowering the level of the water table); *flood control* (through lowering flood stages by increasing the capacity of stream channels); *navigation* (by increasing the natural depth of some of the larger rivers); and *erosion control* (by the substitution of artificial channels for gullies or other eroding natural channels).

Since channelization, or channel rectification, is a measure used for a number of purposes, it is discussed at a number of points in this report. As a drainage improvement measure, it is mentioned in Section C of Chapter 5. Its use for reducing flood damages and for making possible more intensive use of flood plain lands subject to frequent flooding is referred to in both Section C and Section E of that chapter. Section H of the same chapter deals with erosion and sedimentation, and channelization is also mentioned in this context. And channelization for navigation would be covered under the principles enunciated in Section B of Chapter 5.

Since at least two other investigations of the effects of channelization were under way during preparation of this report, the National Water Commission did not attempt to duplicate the work being

---

[42] Public Law 92-583, 86 Stat. 1280, 16 USCA 1451 *et seq.*
[43] See Chapter 10.

Trees, shrubbery, and undergrowth in this natural channel help hold back flood waters

This concrete channel lacks esthetic beauty and requires frequent maintenance

done under these investigations, but made use of information developed.[44]

Principal Effects

It is not channelization in itself that has led to the widespread opposition to the use of this measure but rather its environmental consequences and the downstream effects. Actually, diversion, terrace outlet, and other channels provided as erosion control measures are rarely criticized, as they reduce erosion and, where necessary, are protected by vegetal or artificial linings.

When channelization is undertaken for the purpose of draining wetlands or reducing the frequency of flooding of wooded, brush-covered, or pastured flood plain lands, undeveloped lands are frequently converted to intensively cultivated croplands. This results in the loss of both valuable habitat for fish and wildlife and the esthetic values of a natural area.

Another consequence is the acceleration of erosion that results from many channelization projects. Excessive erosion is caused by failure to make proper provisions in the planning of such projects for bank protection and other measures required to stabilize the new channels. The usual reason for omitting these important ancillary measures is to reduce the cost of the channelization project. Since the necessity for reducing costs is most imperative for those projects undertaken to bring new lands into production (because the resulting increase in farm income must exceed project costs) it is normally channelization undertaken to drain wetlands or to decrease the frequency of flood overflow that gives rise to the most serious erosion problems. Had the erosion and sedimentation damages been added to the cost of such projects some of them would have failed to meet the test of economic justification.

Another consequence of channelization is the replacement of meandering natural streams by systems of straight ditches forming a severe and unattractive geometrical pattern. The esthetic value of the channelized flood plains are further decreased by the removal of trees and other vegetation, by the unsightly appearance of the raw ditch banks, by the muddy torrents that occur during storms, and, in some places, by the failure of the perennial flow that existed under natural conditions. Even in urban areas the installation of artificial channels for flood protection not infrequently meets with criticism because such channels, although more hydraulically efficient, are less pleasing to the eye than the natural channels they replace. In most cases, without expensive maintenance, the new channel will return to its original meandering course.

A further undesirable consequence of channel rectification in headwater valleys is an increase in the frequency and magnitude of downstream floods. This comes about because of the reduction of flood stages in the channelized reach, for any reduction in stage in upstream reaches decreases the temporary storage of flood waters in those reaches and thus increases peak flows in downstream reaches.

This leads also to lowering of ground water levels, by reducing the time available for infiltration of rain water which is speeded downstream by the artificially improved channels.

The foregoing paragraphs constitute a brief summary of the principal adverse effects of channelization projects. There are, of course, benefits resulting from channelization.

Fertile lands can be made available for crop production by drainage improvement and by reducing the frequency of flood overflow through channelization, and in the long run the resulting enhancement in the efficiency of the Nation's agricultural plant may be a desirable consequence.[45] Quite naturally, the owners of wetlands and of rural flood plain lands subject to frequent flooding are desirous of increasing their incomes by utilizing these lands for crop production, and it is nearly always increased farm income that makes possible the favorable ratio of benefits to costs that is necessary to obtain Federal assistance in planning and carrying out channelization projects. In urban areas subject to damage and

---

[44] For more detailed information on the subject of channelization, see U.S. CONGRESS, HOUSE OF REPRESENTATIVES (1971). Stream Channelization, Hearings before the Conservation and Natural Resources Subcommittee of the Committee on Government Operations, 92d Congress, 1st Session. Four volumes, June 3, 4, 9, 10, and 14, 1971. U.S. Government Printing Office, Washington, D.C. ARTHUR D. LITTLE, INC. (1972). Final Draft Report: Channel Modifications—An Environmental, Economic and Financial Assessment, prepared for the Council on Environmental Quality. Two volumes, March 31, 1972.

---

[45] As pointed out in Section C of Chapter 5, however, the Commission's background studies indicate that there is no immediate need for bringing new land into agricultural production, and this suggests that until such time as an increase in the Nation's agricultural land base is urgently needed, there is no need for the Federal Government to subsidize projects designed to increase production of crops that are in surplus or are price supported or involved in programs to take land out of production.

Failure to provide bank protection on this channel leads to excessive erosion

possible loss of life by floods there is an even more powerful incentive for seeking Federal assistance in increasing the capacity of stream channels. In some areas, drainage projects are desired in order to eliminate mosquitoes and other hazards to public health. The accrual of these and other beneficial effects to landowners and to nearby communities has created interest groups that oppose the efforts of the environmental interests to stop channelization activities.

CONCLUSIONS ON CHANNELIZATION

There can be no doubt that most channelization projects produce both beneficial and detrimental effects, just as do all other measures used in developing water resources. And as for all other types of water projects, the question to be answered is this: Are the benefits to the Nation sufficient to outweigh the total cost to the Nation, including the cost of the detrimental effects previously described? Channelization projects are similar to all other water projects in still another respect: For some of them the benefits exceed the costs and for others the reverse is true.

The evidence placed before the Commission makes it impossible to avoid the conclusion that in many cases insufficient weight has been given to the detrimental consequences of channelization, and particularly to losses not readily expressible in monetary terms. There appears to be a tendency fully to evaluate all benefits that would result from channelization projects, but to underestimate, or even to ignore, some operation and maintenance expenses and damages resulting from lowering of ground water tables, destruction of fish and wildlife habitat, increasing downstream sedimentation and flood damages, and loss of esthetic values. The work

This picture of the junction of the "old" and "new" channel of the Forked Deer River in Tennessee illustrates effect of channelization on a natural environment

accomplished during the past few years by the Water Resources Council in its development of principles, standards, and procedures for the evaluation of water projects has made it abundantly clear that in the past such evaluations have generally failed to consider all of the consequences of carrying out such projects.[46] It has also made it clear that there are many detrimental effects that must be added to the cost of such projects if a valid benefit to cost comparison is to be made. The Commission hopes that as the procedures being developed by the Council are perfected, and all Federal agencies are required to comply with them, the intensity of the channelization controversy will gradually wane.

The Commission also believes that as another means of insuring that future channelization projects are truly in the national interest, the direct benefici-

aries thereof should be required to assume any costs properly allocable to the purpose of increasing the value of private lands. This would serve to dampen the desire of landowners to make more intensive use of wetlands and of lands subject to frequent inundation.

The Commission urges, in Section E of Chapter 5 of this report, that the use of flood plain lands be regulated by the States or appropriate local governmental entities. If the recommendations of that section are implemented, the need for future channel improvement projects, particularly in urban areas, would be substantially reduced.

RECOMMENDATIONS

2-2. **All agencies responsible for planning and carrying out channelization projects should broaden and otherwise improve their evaluation procedures, making a special effort to reflect in the cost estimates damages caused by increased downstream flooding and sedimentation,**

---

[46] A recent court decision emphasizes the need for developing better information on the environmental effects of channelization before proceeding with authorized projects. See *Natural Resources Defense Council, Inc. v. Grant*, Civ. No. 754, E.D.N.C., February 5, 1973.

lowering of ground water levels, and loss of fish and wildlife habitat and esthetic values. The full cost of continuing maintenance should also be reflected.

2-3. All future proposals for channelization projects should be required to indicate the part of the cost thereof that is properly allocable to the purpose of increasing the value of lands in private ownership, and no such project should be approved unless and until an appropriate non-Federal entity has agreed to assume that part of the project cost.

2-4. In considering requests for funds to carry out previously authorized channelization plans, the Appropriations Committees of the Congress should require the submission, by both the agency that would be responsible for the use of these funds and the Council on Environmental Quality, of statements on the probable effects of the proposed undertaking on downstream flood and sedimentation problems, on ground water levels, on fish and wildlife habitat, and on esthetic and other noneconomic values and these Committees should provide for the funding of only those projects for which, in their opinion, the benefits are sufficient to justify both the monetary and nonmonetary costs to the Nation.

Chapter 3

Water and the Economy

Water is basic to our economic growth. No economic activity takes place without it. . .or with too much of it. But water generally has been very inexpensive and is often used very extravagantly. In this chapter, the great paradox of water, an indispensable but relatively inexpensive natural resource, is examined. Assessments are made of the economic value of water in serving the diverse purposes of society and of the role of water development in influencing where people will live and how their regions will develop.

The Commission has found that values of water are generally low in most of its present uses. However, as natural supplies become more fully utilized, competition between water uses is intensifying in an increasing number of areas. As a consequence, water values are increasing and new approaches to valuing water and water-related services are needed.

Water is a mobile resource that is used and reused within a stream system. Water may be used in the stream or withdrawn for use away from the stream, but most if not all water in the United States is now in use for one or more purposes, economic or environmental. A given use of water changes its characteristics of quantity, quality, location, and timing of flow within the hydrologic system and consequently its values for other uses. Therefore, it is concluded that water in a particular river or ground water basin must be valued in terms of all of its uses, economic and environmental, within the system. Assessments of various development and management

~~~~~~~~~~~~~~~~~~~~~~~~~~~~~~~~~~~

This river in Maine provides a natural transportation artery for pulp wood

Three types of powerplants at Parr, S.C. depend on water for energy production

proposals should be made in the context of the entire hydrologic system and all water uses contained therein.

Examination of the role of water development projects in influencing regional development and population distribution leads to the conclusion that while water developments have had very significant impacts in the past, their role in economic development diminishes as a higher level of economic development is attained. Under certain circumstances, water development projects still play a significant role in increasing economic activity and employment opportunities, but in most instances they are no longer the major determinant.

Every proposed water project should be carefully analyzed with respect to its economic characteristics and the area of its economic influence. Furthermore, since water alone does not produce regional development, it is appropriate for water projects to be considered as only one factor of a regional development program. It is apparent that under most conditions, water alone does not produce economic development; other more significant forces now control regional economic and population growth.

The Commission believes that in the future, policies for water development and use must be increasingly subordinated to other governmental policies, including land use, energy, environmental protection, and food and fiber production. Water development and conservation should be used to support these broader national policies.

There is a widespread and growing awareness of the need to improve land use throughout the country. Historically, water developments, both public and private, have had important impacts on land use through such purposes as navigation, irrigation, drainage, and flood control. Increasing recognition must now be given to the very important impacts of land use on water resources. This interrelationship was illustrated dramatically by the national controversy over location of the new Miami jetport in relation to water supply for the Everglades National Park. Many new facilities, such as subdivisions, shopping centers, factories, highways, electric generation stations, strip mines, and cattle feeding operations, have enormous potential impacts on the quantity, quality, location, and timing of flows within hydrologic systems. The Commission believes that proposed legislation, now being considered by the Congress, for Federal assistance for State land use planning could be of critical significance for the development and use of water resources. Greatly increased attention must also be given to the effective regulation of occupancy in flood plains, wetlands, and coastal areas.

Finally, the Commission believes that the self-purifying capacity of water bodies is a valuable national resource that has been widely abused. Within limits, water bodies can perform the valuable service of assimilating certain wastes and rendering them harmless. There is a need to develop a philosophy of controlling the use of assimilative capacity in such a way as to maintain desirable environmental standards. This will involve tradeoffs because wastes must be either recycled or disposed of in air, water, or landfill. While recycling of wastes is frequently a desirable goal, disposal needs will continue and selections of the disposal method will require judgments based on the economic and environmental facts of each situation. The self-purification capacity of a given stream varies with the quantity, quality, location, and timing of flow. Here is an obvious situation where land use regulation, influencing the location of new installations, will indirectly influence disposal of such wastes as heat and organic matter into the Nation's waterways.

THE VALUE OF WATER

Water is sometimes referred to as "our most valuable resource." It is necessary for life. Take water from an area and the basis for plant and animal life is gone, leaving a barren desert. It is not surprising that demands for water are often treated as "requirements" or "needs" that absolutely must be satisfied, regardless of cost.

Although it is true that life depends on water, society does not usually act as though water had value equal to life itself. The reason is that the supply of water far exceeds what is required to sustain human life. In practice, water is "used" extravagantly. Large quantities of water are polluted and made unfit for further use. The standard explanation for treating water so carelessly is that it costs too much to do otherwise—a reason that seems to contradict the idea that water is our most valuable resource. Obviously, water value is a complex subject.

Value Concepts

Value means, simply, the degree to which something is desirable, useful, or important. Since there is a limited supply of water in many areas, knowledge of its value in alternative uses is a prerequisite to selecting the most valuable uses from the range of choices that are available. Should water be diverted for irrigation or saved for fish? Should water be transferred from one basin to another or should it be left for uses where it originates? Should valuable labor and materials be put into water development projects or should these resources be employed in other uses—roads, schools, etc.? The answers ultimately depend on relative values.

Economic Values: Economic value has been the principal concept of value in our society. In a competitive economy, economic values are measured by market prices. When it is working well, the market pricing system reveals the value that goods and services have for people, and the value of the resources such as water used in the production of these goods and services. But for various reasons market prices are not always a good or complete measure of the true worth of an item. Distortions of economic values can result from undesirable distribution of income and from assorted market imperfections such as monoply power, lack of knowledge, hidden subsidies, etc. Futhermore, social and environmental factors are seldom reflected in or subject to market transactions, and hence often have inadequate economic value attached to them.

In the case of water these problems are often important. Various institutional arrangements have been employed to allocate water by nonmarket means. But this approach also has problems because choices are often made without the benefit of market prices that usually indicate economic value and assist decisionmaking.

Fortunately, it is possible to estimate economic values even though market prices are not available. Sometimes there are prices for the services of water that permit an estimate of the value of the water itself. In other situations, estimates can be made of values gained through use of water that are fairly comparable to market price evaluations. These estimated water values can be used for essentially the same purposes that market prices serve.

Evaluation Principles: The objective is to obtain values for water that are comparable to the price-based values that allocate other resources and products throughout the economy. The principle is to estimate value as the amount a user would be willing to pay for the water. His willingness to pay for the water reflects the desirability, usefulness, and importance of water to him.

Small amounts of water in some selected uses show very high willingness to pay (for example, household supplies for drinking and cooking). But, willingness to pay for additional water declines as the most essential uses are satisfied. If the quantity of water available is large enough, willingness to pay and value can decline to zero or even become negative. Beyond some quantity, more water has no value.

The difference in value between the most valuable use and the least valuable use explains the paradox of water being essential, but used as though it had very low value. It is essential and highly valuable only in quite small quantities. Its price is set not only on the basis of its essentiality, but on the basis of its abundance as well. In almost every part of the country so-called essential uses can be easily served with only a small fraction of available supplies. The uses that are competing and pressing against supplies generally are associated with lower water values (i.e., values for which there is much less willingness to pay). Allocation decisions revolve around these low-value uses and it is most important to know their values. The high-value uses will almost always be supplied through the market.

Most water is used by industries, agriculture, or public utilities to produce goods and services that people want. Very little water is used directly by consumers. Thus, the value of water is determined more by its contribution to production processes than by its direct value to consumers. The amount that any producer would be willing to pay for water is limited by the amount of profit he can make by using the water. A producer should always be willing to pay an amount for water up to the additional revenue he receives from the additional production obtained by its use, minus any other additional costs which the increased production imposes.[1] Another measure of the value of water to the producer is the additional costs he would incur if he used another process of production that eliminates or reduces water use. *In almost every use of water there is a way of accomplishing the same objective with less water, but at a higher cost.* Often the extra cost involved is not large.

Special Problems in Water Valuation

Evaluation always involves problems and water evaluation is no exception. Four of these problems in valuing water resources and water use are discussed below.

Measuring Water "Use": A consistent definition of "use" of water is essential for comparable measures of the value of water in different uses. But, defining water use is difficult because the users of water differ greatly in the way that they use water. Some uses have no measurable effect on the water and hence several users can use the same unit of water at the same time or in sequence—for example, fish, navigation, and recreation. Others, such as agricultural uses, consume much of the water that is used and it is not available for any subsequent uses.

The key to describing the way in which a user uses water is to look to the pattern of sequential and simultaneous uses. Each use of water needs to be described and measured in terms of the effect it has upon the capacity of the water to serve other purposes. On that basis, use of water involves not only the quantity of water being employed but also the effect that the use has upon quality of water, and upon the time and location of its availability to other potential uses.

Separating Out Value of Other Services: In many cases water has been stored for a period of time, conveyed for some distance, processed to improve its quality, and metered out to individual users. The value of this water actually includes two elements—value of the water resource itself and value of the service rendered by the agency that stores, conveys, processes, and delivers the water. To isolate the value

---

[1] For example, suppose a farmer's application of an extra acre-foot of irrigation water increases his crop production, which in turn increases his farm revenue by an additional $30. Suppose further that additional nonwater expenses which are required to cultivate, harvest, and market the extra production total $10. In these circumstances, an irrigator should be willing to pay up to, but no more than, $20 for the extra acre-foot of water.

of the water itself at the point of diversion from the natural supply, the costs involved in bringing it from the point of origin should be subtracted from the value of water at the point of use.

Choosing Accounting Perspective: The willingness to pay or value of water depends in part upon the point of view or accounting perspective of the individual making the evaluation. From the point of view of a private water user, water value is determined by its contribution to his net revenues or satisfaction. His perspective is narrow and the consequences of his use on other individuals often do not enter into his evaluation. A regional perspective would take into account all the returns that occur in the region. It may consider some effects that may not enter into the consideration of an individual firm, such as employment and economic activity induced in other sectors of the regional economy as a result of water development and use. From the national point of view, the goal is to increase net social income from use of all national resources. All benefits and costs should be taken into account. Induced employment or disemployment that occurs outside of a benefited region should be evaluated as well as the more apparent regional effects.

Different evaluation purposes may call for different accounting perspectives. Economists generally favor the national point of view where all effects, including those that are external to individuals or regions, are taken into account. Regional estimates of value consistently tend to be higher than national estimates because the beneficial economic effects of water resource projects are generally concentrated in a local region, whereas detrimental effects may occur in other regions of the Nation, and are hard to identify.

Recognizing Noncommercial Values: Much esthetic or social value is derived from water. Water provides enjoyment for people through recreation, scenic beauty, and the simple appreciation for nature. Although these are difficult to evaluate, they are undeniably desirable, useful, and important and thus valuable uses of water. Estimates of the economic value of water, including these difficult-to-evaluate benefits, can contribute much to better decisions about water management and use even where certain values can only be approximated or protected by placing limits on permissible changes in natural water systems, such as maintaining minimum streamflows.

Estimates of Water Value in Major Uses

A report prepared for the Commission by Colorado State University (CSU) contains estimates of water values in some of the major withdrawal and instream uses.[2] The values developed in the Colorado study are useful primarily because an attempt has been made to compare water uses on a consistent basis, permitting a comparison between *relative* values in various uses.[3]

The generally low values presented here reflect the generally abundant supplies of water that have been available for economic development in the United States to the present time. As demands for various water uses increase, more costly alternatives, such as recycling processes or improved irrigation techniques, will tend to reduce water use per unit of production and the values per unit of water in various uses can be expected to increase.

Crop Irrigation: Crop irrigation is one of the largest uses of water. Irrigation accounts for about 35 percent of total water withdrawals and about 83 percent of the water consumed in the United States. Over half of the water diverted for irrigation is consumed through evaporation and transpiration, and thus is not available for any subsequent use. The water that is not consumed may return to the system after considerable delay (a month or more for much of it) at a downstream location or in a ground water aquifer often some distance from the point of diversion and sometimes degraded in quality.

The value of irrigation water depends upon environmental conditions, the crop grown (high-valued vegetables and fruit, or low-valued forages and grains), the stage of growth of the crop, and the efficiency of water utilization on the farm. There are literally scores of estimates of irrigation water value resulting from many different studies. These studies have employed a variety of concepts and perspectives in evaluation, which means that all the estimates are

[2] YOUNG, Robert A & GRAY, S Lee, Colorado State University (1972). Economic Value of Water: Concepts and Empirical Estimates, prepared for the National Water Commission. National Technical Information Service, Springfield, Va., Accession No. PB 210 356.

[3] Some studies have taken an alternative approach and have related various measures of the value of output to the units of water consumed in each use. High values of production are related for such industries as printing and publishing or clothing manufacture. See, for example, WOLLMAN, Nathaniel, et al. (1962), The Value of Water in Alternative Uses, University of New Mexico Press, Albuquerque, N.M.

not strictly comparable. Nevertheless, there is considerable common ground among the studies. Most seek to estimate water value from the point of view of the private irrigator, that is, his theoretical willingness to pay for the water used. They commonly estimate the value of water delivered to the farmer's headgate rather than at point of diversion.

The CSU study indicates a value for irrigation water ranging from $15 to $40 per acre-foot at the farmer's headgate, with most estimates clustering around $20 per acre-foot. The higher values are generally for irrigation of higher-valued crops and for irrigation in the most arid areas or in areas with longer growing seasons. In the humid East, relatively small amounts of irrigation water are used, but it is mostly applied to high-value crops and has values in about the same range.

The value of irrigation water may often reflect some farm prices that are government supported. Without price supports the value estimates for water used for irrigating price supported crops would be lower.

Municipal Water Use: A large portion of water used by municipalities is returned to the natural water system soon after its use. Since most domestic and municipal water is used for washing (clothes, dishes, streets, etc.) and carrying away wastes, quality degradation can be serious unless the water is treated to reduce pollutants.

Water for municipal uses usually enjoys priority over other uses, perhaps because drinking water is essential to life. However, the amount required for drinking is so small that it is insignificant in determining the total value of water in municipal and domestic uses. Most water employed in municipal and domestic uses is not nearly as essential as drinking water and, as a result, is much less valuable.

Estimation of the value of water for municipal and domestic uses must proceed without benefit of the techniques that can be employed for valuing water for a production use. Nevertheless, there have been several studies of household demand.[4] In general, they support estimated values of around $100 per acre-foot for in-house uses and about $66 in the West and $16 in the East for lawn and garden irrigation.

These values include the costs incurred in delivery of water to the residential user.

Industrial Water Use: Withdrawals of water by industry account for more than one-half of all withdrawals. Most of this water is used for disposing of heat or other waste, and returned to the stream. Very little water is actually consumed by industry; therefore, use of water by industry primarily affects water quality. Ninety percent of water used by industry is for cooling (principally in steam electric generating plants).[5] Most of the remaining industrial uses are concentrated in five industries: food products, pulp and paper, chemicals, petroleum, and primary metals.

The most appropriate method for determining the value of water in industrial uses is to examine the cost of alternative processes that will produce the same product while using less water. Internal recycling of water is a primary alternative.

The costs of recycling are usually quite low. For cooling uses, recycling through a cooling tower (where heat is transmitted directly to the atmosphere) can be accomplished at costs ranging from $2.50 to $4.20 per acre-foot, with the higher costs occurring in warm or humid regions where the cooling process is less efficient. The value of water for once-through cooling (where warmed water is returned to the water body) thus can be no more than $2.50 to $4.20 per acre-foot, at the site of use. The value of the water at the point of diversion actually will be less than that by the amount of additional cost in delivering it from that point to the plant.

Water for process uses such as washing or carrying dissolved materials generally is more expensive to recycle and costs may vary greatly with the nature and extent of quality degradation occurring in the process. The mean value of recycling process-water in the five major water-using industries ranged from less than $5 to about $26 per acre-foot, with an average of $13. Scattered estimates in minor industries are largely consistent with findings for the major industries.

---

[4] See discussion summarizing the results of these studies in YOUNG, Robert A and GRAY, S Lee, Colorado State University (1972). Economic Value of Water: Concepts and Empirical Estimates, prepared for the National Water Commission. National Technical Information Service, Springfield, Va., Accession No. PB 210 356, pp. 184-198.

[5] MURRAY, C Richard & REEVES, E Bodette (1972). Estimated Use of Water in the United States in 1970, U.S. Geological Survey Circular 676. U.S. Geological Survey, Washington, D.C. p. 5. Also, for discussion of this subject see THOMPSON, Russell G, et al. (November 1971). Forecasting Water Demands, prepared for the National Water Commission. National Technical Information Service, Springfield, Va., Accession No. PB 206 491. pp. 145-191.

This cooling tower on the Susquehanna River permits recycling of powerplant condenser water

Costs of water supply for industry usually are less than 2 percent of production costs. In water-short areas, because water rights or purchased supplies may be more costly, industrial plants usually are designed to extensively recycle the water used. Thus, generally where water is more costly, the value in use will be higher and the amounts used by a typical plant will be less.

Waste Assimilation: Watercourses are used extensively to assimilate and transport waste materials, mainly in conjunction with municipal and industrial water use. In fact, many streams are now overused for this purpose. Nevertheless, if waste could not be disposed of in streams, it would have to be put somewhere else and there would be added disposal costs and potential environmental problems with land disposal or air pollution. Thus, when streams can be used to assimilate and transport waste materials, they provide a valuable service. However, use of streams for waste assimilation degrades the quality of the water and may reduce its usefulness for other purposes.

The best measure of the value of water for wasteload assimilation is the alternative cost of providing treatment for the effluent. A given quantity of water under given stream and weather conditions can only assimilate a certain amount of waste material without exceeding quality limits. A reduction in flow thus implies an increase in treatment level and treatment costs to stay within standards. The value of water can be estimated by the change in cost that would be associated with a change in flow.

Under minimum cost combinations of treatment and dilution, the change in cost associated with each additional acre-foot in flow of water would range from about 10-15 cents per acre-foot in the water-abundant Southeast and Pacific Northwest to about $6.50 per acre-foot in the arid Southwest.[6] These values will tend to increase over time as the required degree of treatment is raised to secondary and tertiary levels to meet water quality standards.

---

[6] Correspondence in the Commission's files from Robert A. Young and S. Lee Gray, January 4, 1973.

Navigation: A large river such as the Mississippi or lower Columbia can be used for navigation with little or no effect upon the water. Navigation's only requirement is that sufficient water be in the critical parts of the stream at the right time. In smaller streams, substantial regulation of flows may be required to facilitate navigation.

The value of water for navigation is the difference between the economic costs of water transport and those of the least-cost alternative mode of transportation. In the major waterways, the Ohio or the Mississippi, water no doubt has a positive value for navigation. However, for some waterways savings in costs are insufficient to cover the costs of constructing and operating navigation facilities. The value of water for navigation, on such waterways, when other costs are subtracted, would be zero or negative, although navigation projects might still be justified to achieve social purposes such as transportation diversification.

Hydropower Generation: Hydropower plants account for less than one-sixth of the total electric energy generated in the United States, and there are few undeveloped major hydro sites except pumped storage sites. Additional power generation will have to come largely from thermal generating plants. Nevertheless, in many streams water passes through one or more powerplants. It is an important use of water. Use of water for electric generation may have substantial impact on the timing of flows within the hydrologic system. Furthermore, the location of diversion points for nonpower, offstream uses may affect electric generation potentials and thereby the potential total value of water use from the system.

Hydropower may be valued by comparison with the lowest-cost alternative, usually power generation by comparably-owned steam plants. The value of the water for hydropower generation is the difference between the costs of producing the hydropower (including transmission) and the costs of the lowest-cost alternative (also including transmission). It will vary from site to site depending on such variables as differences in head (the distance water falls in turning turbines), transmission distances to load centers, the suitability of sites for hydropower construction, streamflow variations, storage, etc.

The value of water for hydropower generation was measured in a long-run perspective (using capital costs as well as operating costs) on the basis of the cost and efficiency characteristics of existing plants. In no case were regional values more than $1 per acre-foot and

in one region they dropped to only 14 cents per acre-foot. Short-run values (where the construction costs of existing generating plants and storage dams are ignored) ranged from $3.92 per acre-foot down to 43 cents per acre-foot. These values apply to the water at a typical hydropower site. In several river systems the same water may pass through a number of hydrosites before all its potential for generating electricity has been exhausted, thus multiplying the above values.

Recreation: Streams or other bodies of water are an important part of many recreation areas and serve a basic role in many recreational activities. But, as with other instream uses, it is difficult to define just how recreation "uses" the water. Many recreational uses are complementary to other uses, especially uses that require water impoundments. Often water is used for recreation in its natural setting and is not physically affected by being employed for recreation. Still, recreation does use water in a sense, when a certain volume of water must be retained in a lake, reservoir, or stream to support recreation activities, or where recreation use precludes or limits other uses. Water-based recreation itself can be a source of locally significant pollution. Some water may be consumed by evaporation while it is being held for recreation.

The value of water for recreation depends on a number of factors, including accessibility, setting, type of beach, and various aspects of quality. Value varies greatly from case to case, ranging in a few selected examples from a few cents per acre-foot of water to $150 per acre-foot of water in the recreation pool of a heavily-used reservoir. "The more typical range appears to lie in the area of $3 to $5 per acre-foot."[7]

Water Value in a Systems Context[8]

The value of water in alternative uses provides only a part of the information needed for decisions about water development and allocation. Because of the

[7] YOUNG, Robert A & GRAY, S Lee, Colorado State University (1972). Economic Value of Water: Concepts and Empirical Estimates, prepared for the National Water Commission. National Technical Information Service, Springfield, Va., Accession No. PB 210 356. p. 241.

[8] This material is based on a Commission study prepared at Washington State University in which the systems approach to valuation of water is demonstrated empirically for the Yakima, Columbia, and Susquehanna River basins. See BUTCHER, Walter R et al. (1972). National Water Commission. National Technical Information Service, Springfield, Va., Accession No. PB 210 357.

Water in lovely natural setting provides recreational opportunities

combinations of uses and reuses of water that are possible within a water system, it is equally as important to know how uses combine and interact in the total system. The possibility of using water more than once, either simultaneously or in sequence, means that the total value gained from use of a given unit of water may be several times greater than the value in any single use.

Since water usually stays in the system or returns to it, its condition when it leaves one use can be very important to other water uses. "Upstream" and "downstream" uses are commonly used to illustrate this relationship. An upstream industry, for example, withdraws water, uses it, and returns part of it, somewhat polluted, to the stream. The downstream user must operate with water reduced both in quality and quantity. The value of the water to the downstream uses may be reduced as a result. The gain in value from the upstream use is not free of some costs in the sense of reduced values elsewhere.

The return of water to the system after use raises all sorts of possibilities for getting additional value from the water in another use, at another time and

place in the system. Wise use of this natural recycling system is one of two key principles in obtaining the most value from the Nation's water resources. The other principle is to give preference to high-valued uses where other factors, including system effects, are equal.

Return flow and reuse are important factors in water system evaluation. Uses that have fast and complete return of the water can be located in the system so that the same physical unit of water is used many times over (if damaging pollution can be avoided in the process). Such a use pattern can generate large values for the water in the system even though each individual use of the water adds only small value per unit of water employed. Conversely, impressively high-valued uses that preclude the possibility of other uses in the total system limit value to less than might be achieved if several quick turn-around uses of lower value could occur throughout the system. Once the water is taken from the system by consumptive use, the possibility of gaining value from its use is also lost. In some pollution cases return water not only may be unfit for subsequent use but may also contaminate the other water in the system.

The siting and timing of uses takes on particular importance when water use is viewed in its system context. The importance of location is apparent when water is used for waste conveyance and dilution. The potential for making valuable use of the water is greater if pollution-sensitive uses can be located upstream of polluting uses. Thus, value in the system will be greatest when waste-releasing uses which prevent or impair other uses are located as far as possible down the stream, leaving as much of the stream as possible to be used by other potential users. (Obviously, pollution-sensitive uses of estuaries cannot be relocated to upstream sites. Hence, special care must be taken to protect estuaries from pollution.)

Value Comparisons for Water Allocation

Value estimates are useful only if they contribute to better decisions about how water should be allocated. In the relatively simple case of choosing an allocation among competing uses that have similar effects upon the water resource, a comparison of value per unit of water used indicates the direction allocation should take. As water becomes relatively scarcer, it will be more important to put it to its most valuable uses if net social gains are to be maximized. Implementation of water marketing and pricing procedures can help greatly in this situation in encouraging reallocation of water to its most valuable uses.

A more typical situation is one in which the choice must be made between uses that employ and affect water in very different ways. Comparison of values is more complex in this case. Private individuals and even individual cities and towns lack direct incentive to take into consideration effects of their use that occur elsewhere and affect others. Value determination must come from an integrated view of uses if comparisons of value are to result in choices that maximize system value.[9]

River basin planning efforts are one attempt to account for interdependencies in water systems. Planning for whole rivers and entire river basins, including all uses and related activities, has done much to fit together compatibly the several uses and demands on a river system. However, river basin planning agencies need to place greater emphasis on maximizing water value at the user or consumer level.

There is a need in river basin planning for a systematic procedure for evaluating the multitude of possible alternative combinations of developments and uses that could be fitted into a river system. This requires some form of systems analysis. Through simulation of possible choices in a model of a basin, systems analysis can provide important information on likely consequences before decisions on development are actually made. It could be described as a response and accounting system—the response portion referring to the way that components of the system are affected by various physical as well as economic changes.

Systems analysis of water values does not require that all uses of water be valued directly in monetary terms. Minimum streamflows or water required, for example, for maintenance of marshes and estuaries may be valued indirectly in terms of the economic values which are foregone as a result.[10] With such information, reasoned judgments may be made as to socially desirable actions.

CONCLUSIONS ON WATER VALUE

The comparison of water values in alternative uses will become increasingly important in the years ahead, as growing demands compete for limited natural supplies and values in use increase. The opportunities for net gains by better allocations will be much greater. Not only will efficiency in design of facilities be important, but also efficiency in allocation of the water itself. Economic values provide the best general indication of the basic worth of water if appropriate attention is given to protection of environmental values. Pricing policies, discussed in Chapter 7, can be most helpful in improving the allocation of water. A systems framework is important, as is appropriate measurement of values in use not only in terms of quantity but also quality and timing and location of return flows.

The Commission's conclusions can be summarized as follows:

1. In river basins where present and projected demands for water indicate some element of competition, the values of water in alternative uses (including environmental values) should be estimated as a part

[9] See Chapter 7, Making Better Use of Existing Supplies, and Chapter 11, Improving Organizational Arrangements.

[10] For example, if society decides on a minimum streamflow to protect some benefits such as those of marshes and estuaries, and if as a result other potential benefits are sacrificed, the social value of the benefits from the minimum streamflow must be at least as great as the value of the benefits foregone. Otherwise a rational society would not have made such a choice.

of planning studies and the resulting development plan should seek to maximize these values.

2. Water resources' should be analyzed as individual hydrologic systems taking into account the value of the various aspects of water uses including their impact on quantity, quality, timing, and location. Proposed diversions and instream uses should be analyzed in these same terms and evaluated on the basis of their effects on subsequent uses within the system.

3. Values of water for fish, wildlife, and esthetics cannot now be satisfactorily determined directly by economic evaluation. However, they can be indirectly determined by considering the economic values of uses in the hydrologic system with and without these uses. These "with and without" values should be determined so that informed judgments can be made on balancing of all uses within the hydrologic system. The value of the uses preserved must be judged to equal or exceed the value of alternative uses foregone.

REGIONAL EFFECTS OF WATER DEVELOPMENTS

Economic growth and prosperity of regions within the United States have long been important goals of Federal water resources development. Water resource development has also been viewed by some as a means to achieve a national policy of population distribution—primarily to encourage growth in small cities and towns, thus reducing the concentration of people in the Nation's great cities. This concern stems from the expectation that the Nation will continue to have large increases in population.[11]

During the national and regional conferences held by the Commission in 1969, however, a number of people questioned the effectiveness of water development as a stimulus to regional economic development under present conditions. Others expressed the view that more explicit recognition of regional economic and demographic effects of proposed water developments should be included in planning studies undertaken by Federal water agencies. It was argued that inclusion of these effects would permit responsible officials to evaluate proposed water developments in terms of their social consequences.

Disagreement exists as to whether water and water development merely permits growth or whether it can actually induce growth. It is acknowledged that no area can grow and prosper without adequate water supplies. This does not mean, however, that water alone can exert a controlling influence. Even in the arid West, where population growth has been rapid, household and industrial uses constitute only a very small fraction of consumptive water use.

The Commission has considered the opposing arguments, contracted for technical studies on this topic, and inspected a number of areas of the Nation. This section summarizes findings with respect to the past, present, and possible future role of Federal water resources development as a means of inducing population growth and redistribution and economic prosperity in regions of the United States.

The problem is to determine whether the development of water resources can increase income and employment and induce structural shifts in a region's economy that stimulate future economic growth.[12] Regional economic development is a complex economic and social phenomenon. It is not possible to make a categorical generalization of the role of water resource developments in inducing regional economic development. Presently available data and sophisticated computer models, while helpful, cannot show what would have happened in a region without a particular water development. For example, would California still have prospered without the huge Central Valley project? Might not other forms of development have induced more growth than has irrigated agriculture? Would the Upper Mississippi Valley have prospered more, as much, or less without the Upper Mississippi navigation channel? Will future growth in Florida and related coastal areas really be hindered without the Cross Florida Barge Canal?

While definitive answers to such questions do not exist, there are important principles and criteria that can be used to assess the regional development effects, if any, from proposed future water developments. The President and the Congress must make the

---

[11] The U.S. population totaled 200 million at the time the National Water Commission was established in 1968. Various official projections indicate America's population will exceed 300 million some time in the next century. U.S. COMMISSION ON POPULATION GROWTH AND THE AMERICAN FUTURE (1972). Population and the American Future. U.S. Government Printing Office, Washington, D.C. Ch. 1, p. 12.

[12] The concern in this chapter is with the distribution of population and economic activity among regions. There is little question that water developments, such as water and sewer lines or flood protection, can have a significant influence on the location of population and economic activity within a particular metropolitan area. See Chapter 12, Water Problems of Metropolitan Areas.

Shasta Dam, key feature of California's Central Valley Project

final judgment as to whether water development should be used for this purpose.

A closely interrelated issue is population dispersal. For a long period of time, arguments have been made for using water resources development to encourage population growth in the small cities, towns, and rural areas throughout the Nation. In the late 1890's, for example, George Maxwell, one of the early supporters of a Federal reclamation program, was convinced that irrigation could solve national social problems by decentralizing population from urban centers back to the land.[13] While the National Water Commission recognizes that in localized situations water development programs such as irrigation projects or navigation channels[14] have an impact on geographic distribution of population, and population distribution has a very definite impact on water resources, we are making no recommendations as to population distribution because the subject was covered exhaustively by the Commission on Popula-

[13]HAYS, Samuel P (1959). Conservation and the Gospel of Efficiency. Harvard University Press, Cambridge, Mass. p. 10.

[14]For discussion of this subject, see LEWIS, W Cris et al., Utah State University Foundation (1971). Regional Economic Development: The Role of Water, prepared for the National Water Commission. National Technical Information Service, Springfield, Va., Accession No. PB 206 372.

tion Growth and the American Future, which reported last year.[15]

To develop a proper perspective on water resources development as related to population distribution and regional economic development, the past, present, and possible future role of water resources development should be analyzed.

The Past

Historically, locations of bodies of water were important in determining where settlements were established. The development of water resources contributed to the economic activity that made growth and development possible. Water-powered mills, State canals, Federal river and harbor improvements, and the Federal reclamation program are examples of water developments that have, in years past, contributed to economic growth and development.[16] In 1950, the President's Water Resources Policy Commission said:

> Had it not been for the big and little reclamation projects, the West as we know it today would not exist, for impounded water alone makes possible not only agriculture, but the very life of the people in this vast semiarid region. . .
>
> . . . Federal reclamation projects have had much to do with development of the West.[17]

Over time, however, the importance of water location or water resource development for economic growth has diminished. Steam engines, internal combustion motors, and central station electric generation have substantially reduced and in many cases virtually eliminated the significance of onsite water power. The expansion of railroads and highways made water routes relatively less important. As regional per capita income grew, water-related basic industries produced proportionately less and less income, even though aggregate water use has continued to increase. Some cities that formerly depended on irrigation or waterway transportation (e.g., Phoenix, Salt Lake City, Detroit, and New York) attained sufficient size and economic diversity that their continued growth became more dependent on other factors. Thus, the relative importance of water development as an inducement to economic growth has tended to decline.

The Present

The Influence of Water Policies and Programs on Population Distribution: On the whole, water resource development does not appear to be an effective means to implement a national policy for the distribution of population. Under present and foreseeable future conditions in the United States, water programs and projects are unlikely to affect significantly net migration from region to region. Although water projects may encourage a clustering of workers and their families in certain irrigated or recreation areas, the number of people affected in this manner is likely to be relatively small. While it is true that irrigation projects may increase farm income and enhance prosperity of residents, even very large irrigation developments will not attract large populations because agriculture is not labor intensive. For example, the High Plains of Texas with about 15 percent of the Nation's irrigated land has only about one-third of 1 percent of the Nation's population. Industrial development offers greater hope of regional development because of the greater employment potential but, generally speaking, the need for Federal water projects is small.

The complex and powerful forces that create population growth or decline in specific areas involve many factors that are beyond the influence of water resource projects. For example, characteristics favorable to population growth of small communities include: (1) location near existing metropolitan areas; (2) some minimum concentration of population; (3) history of recent growth rather than decline; (4) an economic base which includes manufacturing as a

---

[15] The Commission on Population Growth and the American Future devoted about 30 percent of its published background studies to distributional aspects of the population issue. They found that although population concentration increases the intensity of certain urban problems, the origin of these problems is frequently technological and institutional in character. The Population Commission's report reflects a general deemphasis of population distribution as a panacea for urban problems. See U.S. COMMISSION ON POPULATION GROWTH AND THE AMERICAN FUTURE (1972). Population and the American Future. U.S. Government Printing Office, Washington, D.C.

[16] LEGLER, John B et al., Washington University (1971). A Historical Study of Water Resources Policy of the Federal Government, 1900-1970, prepared for the National Water Commission, Washington University, St. Louis, Mo. pp. 1-37.

[17] U.S. PRESIDENT'S WATER RESOURCES POLICY COMMISSION (1950). A Water Policy for the American People, Volume 1, General Report. U.S. Government Printing Office, Washington, D.C. pp. 152-153.

basis for growth; and (5) access to metropolitan areas via the Interstate Highway System.[18]

Although many of the Nation's metropolitan areas are located adjacent to a lake, river, or estuary because of the important historical role of water in economic growth, recent trends reveal that metropolitan areas located adjacent to water demonstrate no more growth potential than those not located close to water. The same trend is observable in growing nonmetropolitan communities; the greatest proportion have experienced significant growth by virtue of their location adjacent, not to water, but to a metropolitan area.[19]

Studies have also shown that investments in community water facilities do not directly influence population growth.[20] Investments in water resource developments to stimulate population growth in selected areas are not likely to be effective unless other ingredients of growth exist and are simultaneously developed. For example, Federal assistance for the construction of water and sewer facilities offers little real promise of influencing development and growth in communities not otherwise able to attract commercial enterprises.

The Influence of Water Development on Regional Economic Growth: The accomplishments of the reclamation program in fostering irrigated agriculture in the West[21] and the experiences of the Tennessee Valley where TVA activities stimulated growth and relative prosperity[22] have attracted proponents of water development to the view that water development by itself is an effective stimulus to economic growth. Contrasting views, however, have also been expressed. Various studies have concluded that an adequate supply of water was not a guarantee of growth, and further, that an apparent shortage of water was not necessarily an impediment to rapid economic growth.[23] It has also been shown that there are so many opportunities for water conservation and reuse that the physical availability of water, beyond some minimal amount, has very little influence on industrial location.[24]

The availability of an inexpensive supply of water, for example, is less important for most proposed new plant locations than other factors that have greater direct effects on costs and revenues, such as the cost and availability of labor and proximity of the site to markets and to raw materials. Even for industries that are major users of water (for processing, cooling, or transporting of products), other cost factors are usually of greater importance in location decisions.

However, it has been found that regional growth is stimulated by water developments in certain situations, even though water-related goods and services comprise a declining portion of the Nation's economic activity. This can be explained by the wide

---

[18] RIVKIN/CARSON, INC. (1971). Population Growth in Communities in Relation to Water Resources Policy, prepared for the National Water Commission. National Technical Information Service, Springfield, Va., Accession No. PB 205 248. pp. 7-19.

[19] *Ibid.*, pp. 6-17.

[20] The findings were as stated:

"The test results also show no correlation between (water) expenditures and population growth by location or size of county. Neither SMSA counties nor the most populous counties appear to be influenced in their rate of growth by water resource investment.

"On the other hand, the analysis shows that metropolitan location is correlated with growth, confirming the expectation that metropolitan counties and counties peripheral to them grow more rapidly than other counties, and they do so regardless of the intensity of water resource investment.

"Our tests, therefore, reject the hypothesis that water resources expenditures effect population growth."

These findings, based on data from 350 sample counties (or 11 percent of the more than 3,000 counties in the U.S.), were developed from an in-depth statistical analysis of selected community-oriented water programs. Expenditures for irrigation facilities were not included in the analysis. RIVKIN/CARSON, INC. (1971). Population Growth in Communities in Relation to Water Resources Policy, prepared for the National Water Commission. National Technical Information Service, Springfield, Va., Accession No. PB 205 248. pp. 68-73, 177-191.

[21] U.S. CONGRESS, House Committee on Interior and Insular Affairs (January 1959). Reclamation—Accomplishments and Contributions, a report by the Library of Congress Legislative Reference Service, prepared by Theodore M. Schad and John Kerr Rose, Committee Print No. 1, 86th Congress, 1st Session. U.S. Government Printing Office, Washington, D.C. pp. 28-36.

[22] GARRISON, Charles B (1971). Effect of Water Resources on Economic Growth in the Tennessee Valley Region. University of Tennessee, Knoxville. Also, WIEBE, Jacob E (1970). Effects of Investments in Water Resources on Regional Income and Employment. University Microfilms, Ann Arbor, Mich. (Unpublished Ph.D. dissertation at the University of Tennessee, published on request by University Microfilms.)

[23] For example, see HOWE CW (April 1968). Water resources and regional economic growth in the United States, 1950-1960. The Southern Economic Journal 34(4):477-489.

[24] KNEESE AV (October 1965). Economic and related problems in contemporary water resources management. Natural Resources Journal 5(2):236-258.

variance in effects from water projects—partly because of the widely differing economic characteristics of the regions in which developments are located. These effects are both short- and long-term in nature.

Short-Term Effects: Construction of water projects plays a role in providing short-term impacts on a region's economy. These short-run effects were recognized by the National Resources Planning Board when it urged that public works planning include "the objective of seeking through such work to stabilize employment and economic activity."[25] Subsequently, a large "shelf" of planned water projects was developed in anticipation of a postwar depression, which did not materialize.

The significance of water projects as a means of providing short-term employment opportunities was investigated by Haveman and Krutilla. They concluded:

> In considering water resource development as a stimulant for the economy, the policy maker must distinguish the several different kinds of projects. There are substantial differences in the structure of demands imposed upon the economy and each project type tends to stimulate quite different parts of the economy.[26]

For example, construction of the powerhouse at Beaver Dam in northwestern Arkansas had a ratio of material, equipment, and supply cost to onsite labor cost of 4.54 to 1. Therefore, much of the impact occurred at distant manufacturing locations rather than at the dam site. In contrast, the Painted Rock Dam in southwestern Arizona (a large earth-fill dam) had a ratio of 1.71 to 1, thus suggesting that much more impact occurred locally per dollar of direct labor cost.[27]

The extent of unemployed labor, especially in the industrial sector, is a useful measure of the short-term employment gains possible from constructing water development projects. The greater the unemploy-ment, the greater the possible gains. However, it should be recognized that there are serious problems in scheduling public works projects. A project planned to relieve unemployment will not likely be under construction until the economic recession which caused the unemployment is over.

Long-Term Effects: Short-term effects disappear rapidly as project construction is completed. The real measure of regional economic inducements from water development is how they influence long-term growth prospects. Studies of some specific water resource developments illustrate the fact that water developments vary widely in their discernible long-term effects on regional economic development.

Minidoka Project – The Minidoka irrigation project in Idaho produced $150 million of gross crop value in 1970. Since 1909, when the project began, cumulative gross value of crops produced on Minidoka's project lands has been $3.5 billion—third ranking Federal irrigation project in the Nation. Dominant crops are potatoes, alfalfa hay, and sugar beets. Idaho is the leading potato producer in the Nation, with Minidoka project lands producing one-third of the State total.[28]

Minidoka County is one of 16 counties, parts of which are included in the project. Even though this county has a predominantly rural population, a net population gain of 47 percent occurred during the 1950 to 1960 decade; half was due to net in-migration. Yet, 14 of the other counties in the project area experienced net out-migration in the same period. Between 1960 and 1970, Minidoka County had a 9 percent gain in population, while six of the remaining 15 counties had losses.[29]

In the absence of a "with-and-without" analysis it is difficult to say how these counties would have developed if there had not been a Minidoka project. Obviously, the Minidoka irrigation project has stimulated growth in southeast Idaho. However, the

[25] U.S. NATIONAL RESOURCES PLANNING BOARD (1941). Development of Resources and Stabilization of Employment in the United States, House Document No. 142, 77th Congress, 1st Session. U.S. Government Printing Office, Washington, D.C. p. 3.

[26] See HAVEMAN, Robert H & KRUTILLA, John V (1968). Unemployment, Idle Capacity, and the Evaluation of Public Expenditures: National and Regional Analyses. Published for Resources for the Future, Inc., by The Johns Hopkins Press, Baltimore, Md. p. 36.

[27] *Ibid.,* Table 6, pp. 20-21.

[28] U.S. BUREAU OF RECLAMATION (1971). Water and Land Resource Accomplishments 1970, 2 volumes. U.S. Government Printing Office, Washington, D.C.

[29] U.S. BUREAU OF THE CENSUS (1962). County and City Data Book 1962. U.S. Government Printing Office, Washington, D.C. pp. 83-93. and U.S. BUREAU OF THE CENSUS (June 28, 1971). Current Population Reports, Population Estimates and Projections, Components of Population Change by County: 1960 to 1970, Series P-25, No. 461. U.S. Department of Commerce, Washington, D.C.

effects of the project were not uniform among all areas within the project, and it is probable that irrigation development was not the sole cause of the changes that have taken place.

Tennessee River — The Tennessee River represents another case where major water resource developments have been undertaken by the Federal Government. Through the Tennessee Valley Authority (TVA), public investments have been made for hydro and steam electric power generation, navigation improvements, flood control facilities, fertilizer production, recreation facilities, and many types of research and development activities.

Private investment in plants along the Tennessee River has totaled more than $2 billion since 1933[30]—most of this occurred during the 1960's.[31] Waterfront industries now employ more than 38,000 workers. Most of this investment has been made by the chemical, primary metals, and pulp and paper industries. The chemical industry is a large user of water. Most of the chemical firms along the Tennessee River produce products that require large quantities of processing water and large quantities of power per dollar of value added. Many of the chemical products can be shipped in barges. These same general characteristics—large users of processing water and power relative to value added, and potential for barge use—apply also to the primary metals and pulp and paper industries.

Much of the industrial growth in the Tennessee Valley can be attributed to the *combination of* (1) large blocks of relatively low-cost power, (2) low-cost water supplies, (3) favorable market and resource locations, (4) availability of both rail and water transportation, (5) specific site characteristics, and (6) favorable national growth of specific industries (e.g., chemicals). Through multipurpose developments, TVA activities contributed to some but obviously not all of these factors.

Tucumcari Project[32] — Quay County, New Mexico, is the home of the Tucumcari Project, a moderate-sized irrigation development. About $3 million in crop value was produced in 1970 from 35,000 acres irrigated—or $89 per acre. Alfalfa hay is the principal crop grown and it is used to support the local livestock-based economy. Quay County lost 12 percent of its population during the 1950-60 decade, because of heavy out-migration, and suffered an 11 percent population loss from 1960 to 1970. The proportion of low-income families in Quay County exceeded the national average by 55 percent in 1960. Without irrigation water, there would have been little economic activity in the project area. But even with irrigation, economic growth has been limited.

Monongahela River — The Monongahela River waterway is used primarily to transport coal and lignite from upstream counties in Pennsylvania and West Virginia to Pittsburgh and other areas via the Ohio River. This waterway has been a large carrier of tonnage for the past 50 years. In 1969, a total of 40 million tons was shipped on the Monongahela River, about two-thirds more than on the Tennessee River.[33] However, the counties along the Monongahela have experienced substantial amounts of out-migration. Over 170,000 people left the Monongahela area during the 1950's.[34] Out-migration continued, at a slower rate, between 1960 and 1970. Per capita income grew at a modest rate, but remained below the national average.[35]

The contrast between the Monongahela region and the Tennessee Valley is reflected in the character of

---

[30] TENNESSEE VALLEY AUTHORITY (1971). Annual Report of the Tennessee Valley Authority, Volume I-Text, 1971. U.S. Government Printing Office, Washington, D.C. p. 13.

[31] About 62 percent of the $2 billion in private investment occurred during the 1961-71 decade, or about 30 years after TVA was established. Since 1950, annual increments of private investment along the waterway have generally been parallel to changes in national economic conditions. See TENNESSEE VALLEY AUTHORITY (1966). Navigation and Economic Growth, Tennessee River Experience. Tennessee Valley Authority, Knoxville, Tenn.

[32] Data found in: U.S. BUREAU OF RECLAMATION (1971). Water and Land Resource Accomplishments 1970, Statistical Appendix. U.S. Government Printing Office, Washington, D.C. p. 155. and U.S. BUREAU OF THE CENSUS (1962). County and City Data Book 1962. U.S. Government Printing Office, Washington, D.C. and U.S. BUREAU OF THE CENSUS (June 28, 1971). 1970 Census of Population, Advance Report, Final Population Counts, New Mexico PC(V1)-33, revised. U.S. Department of Commerce, Washington, D.C.

[33] U.S. ARMY CORPS OF ENGINEERS (1970). Waterborne Commerce of the United States, Calendar Year 1969, Part 2, Waterways and Harbors, Gulf Coast, Mississippi River System and Antilles, U.S. Army Engineer District, New Orleans, La. pp. 18, 26.

[34] U.S. BUREAU OF THE CENSUS (1962). County and City Data Book 1962. U.S. Government Printing Office, Washington, D.C. Monongahela service area includes Marion and Monongalia Counties, West Virginia, and Fayette and Greene Counties, Pennsylvania.

[35] Based on data prepared by the Bureau of Economic Analysis, U.S. Department of Commerce.

the river traffic. Coal amounts to 80 percent of the tonnage on the Monongahela River, but only 39 percent on the Tennessee. The Tennessee River carries chemical products, petroleum products, and agricultural commodities in addition to coal, reflecting the more diversified and growing economic base of the Tennessee Valley compared to the relatively specialized and slow-growth economy of the Monongahela area.[36] In the Monongahela River region, the ability of the waterway to foster economic growth is dependent on the demand for coal and on coal mining technology. The influence of the waterway may decline as development of unit trains becomes increasingly important as a substitute for water navigation. Hopes for sustained future growth depend more on the region's ability to diversify its economic base than on improvements in the waterway.

South-Central Arizona — Testimony on the review draft of the Commission's report at several regional conferences in early 1973 disclosed that notwithstanding substantial expansion in Federal and non-Federal irrigation projects, agriculture in many project areas continues to decline in relative economic importance. For example, in 1959, personal income from farming accounted for 7.9 percent of all personal income in Arizona; by 1971, although farm earnings had increased absolutely, they had declined to only 3.7 percent of the total. In the three counties of the Arizona Water Conservation District (which counties include the cities of Phoenix and Tucson), farm earnings represented 14.1 percent of total personal income in 1950 and, despite a modest absolute increase, only 3.1 percent in 1969.[37]

An Unanswered Question — Each of these illustrative cases leaves one nagging question unanswered: What would have happened without TVA, or without the Minidoka or Tucumcari Projects? The answers cannot be determined with confidence. At the present time, analytical problems seriously limit the

ability of planners, engineers, and economists to assess what would have happened without these water developments. Possibly, some of these areas would have prospered even without the developments. Some areas might have declined. Others may have experienced little real change.

One conclusion is clear: regions differ widely in the type of economic impact that can result from the development of their water resources. Because of this variability, it is necessary to identify the strategic factors that shape the role of water development in a region's future development.

Critical Factors That Determine Water Development Effect on Regional Economic Development: Four major factors determine the degree to which various types of water improvements may contribute to regional economic development. These factors are:

1. The extent of *demand* for water-related factors of production of goods and services, such as municipal and industrial water supply, irrigated land, water-based transportation and recreation, hydroelectric power, and flood-free land.

2. The availability of low-cost *substitutes* for water-related factors of production or alternatives, such as dryland agriculture, land-based transportation and recreation, nuclear or fossil-fuel generated energy using recycled cooling water, etc.

3. The region's *competitive advantage* or economic potential to supply water-related goods and services to national markets.

4. The capability of the region to *capitalize on developmental opportunities.*

Market Demand — The stronger the demand for production dependent on specific water-related goods and services, the greater the contribution a particular water development can make to regional growth. The derived demand for water developments depends on markets for the final goods and services produced. The factors affecting these markets include national population growth, industrial activity, exports, per capita use, and sensitivity of demands to price and income changes.

For example, as the Nation's population grows and as personal incomes rise, water projects with recreational facilities become more likely to stimulate regional growth—especially if such projects are near large urban areas where population growth is greatest. Lake Sidney Lanier in northern Georgia (created by Buford Dam) had nearly 12 million visitor-days of

[36] U.S. ARMY CORPS OF ENGINEERS (1970). Waterborne Commerce of the United States, Calendar Year 1969, Part 2, Waterways and Harbors, Gulf Coast, Mississippi River System and Antilles. U.S. Army Engineer District, New Orleans, La.

[37] FIRST NATIONAL BANK OF ARIZONA, Marketing Department (1971 & 1972). Arizona Total Personal Income by Major Sources, October 4, 1972 and Personal Income by Major Sources and Earnings by Broad Industrial Sector for Selected Counties, August 26, 1971. From data furnished by the U.S. Department of Commerce, Office of Business Economics.

recreation in 1970—among the highest in the Nation.[38] In this instance, the recreation demands of Atlanta's population stimulated local business activities related to the Federal water project.

Substitutes — The second major factor that determines the capability of water resource developments to induce growth is the degree to which other resources may be economically substituted for water-related resources. While it is possible to substitute dry land for irrigated land, rail or highway transportation for waterway transportation, and steam-generated electrical energy for hydroelectric power, the determining factor is the relative cost of the substitute.

Bulk commodities such as petroleum and coal products, the principal commodities shipped on inland waterways, can usually be shipped most economically by water transportation, although they are also shipped by other modes when water transportation is not available or when the per unit cost of an alternative is competitive with water transportation.[39] The importance of pipeline transportation as a substitute for water transportation has been particularly evident over the past quarter century.[40]

Irrigated land, especially under the favorable repayment terms for Federal irrigation projects, often has lower direct costs per unit of value produced than is available from nonirrigated land.

Substitutes must always be considered as a means of meeting demands for goods and services. Frequently, water-related goods and services have been cheaper than substitute nonwater-related goods and services—a factor that has tended to increase the significance of water development as an inducement of growth. But as low-cost substitutes for water services are developed, and as progressively higher-cost water projects are next in line for development, cost differentials tend to narrow and the growth inducements of water developments tend to diminish.

Competitive Advantage — The competitive advantage or relative potential of each region for supplying water-related goods and services is another important factor. A region's competitive advantage depends on three important attributes: (1) the resource base, such as mineral deposits, soil fertility, timber, labor supply, water supply, and proximity to markets; (2) public facilities, such as industrial parks, water and sewer systems, highways and airports, educational and cultural opportunities, etc.; and (3) the efficiency of firms in producing needed goods and services. These attributes are included in the package that industrial developers emphasize in promoting their location to prospective firms. They are important reasons for much of the industrial development along the Tennessee River, the Ohio River, and a few other major inland waterways. Navigation capacity, low-cost electrical energy, and water supply, although important, are merely components of the overall competitive advantages enjoyed by these areas.

Capitalizing on Development — The fourth major factor is the capacity of a region to capitalize on developmental opportunities. This capability is dependent on: (1) the region's economic base; (2) the laws and institutional arrangements, such as land use regulation and taxation, that serve as inducements or constraints to economic growth; and (3) the complementary development activities that are undertaken to reinforce the advantages of any particular water development.

A highly developed economic base will permit economic activities related to water development to be multiplied as private firms purchase supplies and services from other firms, and sell their products. Payette, Idaho, serves as an example where urban income in 1949 was estimated to be 123 percent of the value of crops grown. In this case, the urban income was generated indirectly from irrigation on Boise project land.[41] A more recent study concerned the impact of irrigated agriculture on Nebraska's economy. It demonstrated significant economic gains for the State's crop processors and their suppliers during 1963.[42] Had Nebraska's economic base lacked

---

[38] U.S. ARMY CORPS OF ENGINEERS, unpublished data provided the National Water Commission.

[39] One of the major arguments in support of inland navigation in the past was the competitive influence of waterway transportation in reducing rail rates.

[40] Pipelines now surpass inland water transportation in terms of ton-miles shipped. LEWIS, W Cris et al., Utah State University Foundation (1971). Regional Economic Development: The Role of Water, prepared for the National Water Commission. National Technical Information Service, Springfield, Va., Accession No. PB 206 372. pp. III 66-67.

[41] U.S. CONGRESS, House, Committee on Interior and Insular Affairs (1955). The Growth and Contribution of Federal Reclamation to an Expanding National Economy, prepared by the Bureau of Reclamation, October 1954. Committee Print No. 27, 83d Congress, 2d Session. U.S. Government Printing Office, Washington, D.C. p. 10.

[42] ROESLER, Theodore W et al., University of Nebraska (1968). The Economic Impact of Irrigated Agriculture on the Economy of Nebraska, prepared for the Bureau of Reclamation. Bureau of Business Research, Lincoln, Neb. p. 46.

Aerial view of spectacular Lake Powell, formed by the building of Glen Canyon Dam

a crop processing capability, these gains would have been diffused and dissipated so as not to contribute significantly to Nebraska's economic growth. In general, a project area's economic base determines the extent of the indirect or multiplier effects (usually called "secondary benefits").

Legal and institutional arrangements constitute a framework within which economic activities take place. Land use and business regulations vary with State and local jurisdictions. The structure and traditions of the financing organizations may also vary significantly and in turn shape the character of economic development responses to water development projects.

Finally, the simultaneous presence of complementary developmental activities reinforces the growth inducements provided by water projects. For example, fertilizer production at Muscle Shoals, Alabama, has tended to reinforce the growth potential created by other TVA facilities. Similarly, recreational developments financed by private investment or by State and Federal agencies can generate significant growth in tourist and recreation-related sectors of the region's economy, along with other water project benefits, as apparently was the case at Georgia's Lake Sidney Lanier, Minnesota's Leech Lake, and Utah's Lake Powell. The relationship of complementary development activities to water resources development was explicitly recognized in the Corps of Engineers report on water resources development in Appalachia.[43] There, planners estimated developmental benefits by assessing what would happen as a result of the entire package of development activities planned for Appalachia, including improvements in highways and education, for example, as well as water resource development.

In summary, four major factors determine the extent regional economic development is likely to result from proposed water developments. These factors provide a means for evaluating water developments, separating those that can contribute substantially to economic growth and development in a region from those that cannot. Hence, the Commission believes these factors should be evaluated where regional economic development is to be considered in project evaluation.

The Problem of Regional Offsets: When Federal water developments are used to encourage economic growth in certain regions, offsetting declines or reductions in the pace of growth may result in other regions.[44] This issue is illustrated by the charges that irrigation projects in the West have displaced farmers elsewhere in the Nation. The illustration often used is that cotton production on Western irrigation develop-

---

[43] The planning report was authorized in Section 206(a) of the *Appalachian Regional Development Act of 1965*, P.L. 89-4, March 9, 1965, 79 Stat 5, 15, 40 USCA App. Sec. 206(a), which states:

"The Secretary of the Army is hereby authorized and directed to prepare a comprehensive plan for the development and efficient utilization of the water and related resources of the Appalachian region, giving special attention to the need for an increase in the production of economic goods and services within the region as a means of expanding economic opportunities and thus enhancing the welfare of its people, which plan shall constitute an integral and harmonious component of the regional economic development program authorized by this Act."

The last phrase was the principal guide used in estimating benefits based on a combination of development activities rather than on water resources development alone. This was in contrast to then current procedures as described in Senate Document 97. U.S. CONGRESS, Senate (May 1962). Policies, Standards, and Procedures in the Formulation, Evaluation, and Review of Plans for Use and Development of Water and Related Land Resources, Senate Document No. 97, 87th Congress, 2d Session. U.S. Government Printing Office, Washington, D.C.

[44] LEWIS, W Cris et al., Utah State University Foundation (1971). Regional Economic Development: The Role of Water, prepared for the National Water Commission. National Technical Information Service, Springfield, Va., Accession No. PB 206 372. pp. III 86-90.

ments has led to displacement of production in the Southeast because the national market for cotton is limited.

If regional growth is due either to relocations of existing firms or to establishment of new firms that displace economic activity in other areas, offsets are generated. In planning water programs that are intended to induce regional economic growth, planners should attempt to distinguish new growth that would not otherwise occur elsewhere from growth that will produce adverse offsets in other areas.

Although adverse effects from regional offsets may be serious in some instances, it does not mean water resource developments that may generate regional offsets are to be invariably condemned. Relocation of private firms and the establishment of new firms occurs continually, with and without "special" inducements, and is usually due to opportunities for reducing costs. Firms also often relocate to take advantage of changing market situations. These adjustments to cost and revenue considerations are essential characteristics of a competitive economy and lead to increased economic efficiency. The net result of these adjustments is generally reflected by reduced market prices for the goods and services produced.

These gains in national efficiency may, however, adversely affect workers or businessmen who cannot or will not relocate. When such displacement occurs, Federal, State, and local governments may incur higher expenditures for worker relocation, retraining programs, or public assistance. These considerations make it imperative that the executive and the legislative branches carefully consider the equity as well as the efficiency aspects of regional offsets related to Federal water development programs.

Water resource developments have had and will continue to have regional offset implications, but their significance depends on a number of factors including, but not limited to, market demands for the goods and services made available as a result of water resource development.

Market demand is a dominant factor in determining the extent to which regional offsets will occur. Where market demand for the ultimate product is strong and growing, economic development in a water project area is not likely to generate substantial adverse effects elsewhere.

Conversely, regional offsets are likely to be high when firms, capitalizing on a water development, produce products for which demand is not growing or growing only slowly—for example, agricultural commodities such as cotton. In this case, there is a declining national demand for acreage on which to produce these crops. Regional offsets could be expected to be significant if major new irrigation projects are developed to produce agricultural products for which demand is weak.

The Future

Economic growth in the future will be shaped by basic market forces and governmental policies. Improved transportation and communication systems have strengthened the influence of nationwide and international markets and of Federal economic policies on economic growth in each of the Nation's component regions. Regional economic growth is increasingly dependent on the performance of the national economy.

The trend in the last few decades has been for regional per capita incomes to gravitate toward the national average. During the period from 1929 to 1970, national per capita income increased by more than 4.25 percent annually. However, regions such as the Southeast and Southwest grew at rates sufficiently higher to improve their per capita income levels from 52 and 67 percent, respectively, of the national average to 81 and 89 percent of the national average in 1970. At the same time, other regions that were well above the national average in 1929 grew at more modest rates.[45] The upward trend in regional incomes stems primarily from gains in national economic performance. The narrowing of regional differences stems primarily from the inclination of industry to gravitate toward areas of low wage rates and surplus labor and the inclination of workers to gravitate to areas of high wage rates and superior employment opportunities. Water projects cannot be credited with making more than a minor contribution to these national phenomena.

Obviously, as the Nation grows, industries will increase their investment in capital facilities to spur production of needed goods and services. The increased production will not occur randomly, but will occur in those areas capable of producing the

goods and services at the least cost. Thus, each region will share in increased economic activity in relation to its competitive advantage.[46] Many diverse areas share to some extent in national growth and prosperity—but not in a uniform pattern. The various regions of the Nation differ in their growth characteristics and stage of development, as well as in their rates of growth. Overall, however, fewer and fewer areas are completely isolated from the general trends in national prosperity. Thus, caution should be exercised in considering major new water programs for the specific purpose of promoting regional development.

Future Directions for Water Policy Related to Regional Development: The Commission discerns several ways for water resource development to contribute to regional economic growth in the future. The role water development can play, however, must always reflect a basic principle. Water must be increasingly viewed as a scarce resource, one to be developed for regional economic growth only when:

(a) *market demands* indicate that the goods and services that would be produced are needed by a growing economy,

(b) *substitutes* for water-related goods and services are not economically competitive in meeting these demands,

(c) the *competitive advantage* is favorable, and

(d) the region is willing and economically able to undertake *complementary development activities.*

Failure to recognize this fundamental principle will result either in (1) water developments poorly planned and ineffective for regional growth purposes or (2) significant economic losses in other regions as the water development merely relocates economic activities.

Management of Existing Water Developments — Consonant with this principle, the Commission believes that, in the future, increased emphasis must be placed on the management of *existing* water developments as a means of improving regional growth potential rather than relying as heavily as in the past on new projects. A number of existing waterways, for example, may have potential for further development of plant sites and barge terminal facilities that would be attractive to industrial firms, if other factors are

---

[45] U.S. DEPARTMENT OF COMMERCE, Office of Business Economics (May 1970). Personal income in metropolitan and nonmetropolitan areas. Survey of current Business 50(5):22-35. and U.S. DEPARTMENT OF COMMERCE, Office of Business Economics (August 1971). Regional and state income gains in 1970. Survey of Current Business 51(8):30-31.

[46] RIVKIN/CARSON, INC. (1971). Population Growth in Communities in Relation to Water Resources Policy, prepared for the National Water Commission. National Technical Information Service, Springfield, Va., Accession No. PB 205 248. pp. 35-36.

favorable. Use of water-saving techniques or an effective transfer mechanism for water rights in irrigation areas might enable some supplemental irrigation adjacent to existing project lands without new project development. If other factors suggest industrial development potential is favorable, protection and intensive development of a modest portion of a flood plain (provided that it is consistent with sound land use plans) should be employed rather than establishing flood protection projects covering entire flood plains.

Use of existing developments to achieve increased regional gains has the twofold advantage of being more efficient and reducing the otherwise long lead time required for project planning and construction.

New Developments — New water developments, of course, will be needed in the future. Most of these new projects will be sought in response to traditional water purposes such as flood protection or water supply. Many of these future developments will not produce significant regional gains as the relative importance of water developments as a stimulus for economic growth diminishes. Some will generate significant regional offsets unless market demands are increasing at a sufficiently rapid rate to absorb the goods and services produced.

Population Distribution Strategies and Their Relationship to Water Resources: In coming months and years, public debate on a national policy on population distribution is likely to increase. There are a number of possible strategies for population dispersal, among which the following are receiving considerable attention:

1. *Rural development* (sometimes referred to as rural industrialization, reversing rural-urban migration, rural areas development, area re-development, and the like).
2. Creation of *new towns* (sometimes referred to as planned communities) to absorb future increases in population.
3. Distribution of population in a network of *growth centers*.

Rural Development — The Federal role in rural development usually involves investment in public facilities including sewer and water grants and loans from the Economic Development Administration (EDA) and the Farmers Home Administration (FHA) in rural areas to assist them in attracting

industry and thus creating jobs.[47] The Federal assistance is directed towards nonmetropolitan areas. FHA, for example, is prohibited from providing financial assistance for water and sewer projects to areas "in any city or town which has a population in excess of ten thousand inhabitants . . ."[48]

The Nation's rural areas differ widely in terms of economic or resource characteristics. Timber-producing portions of the Pacific Northwest and Upper Great Lakes, for example, are quite distinct from the coal mining areas of the Appalachian Mountains or the Midwest's agricultural prairies, yet all are classified "rural." Each of these diverse rural areas has certain demands for water and sewer facilities, but the "needs" will vary depending on the anticipated water use and the life styles preferred by the area's residents. In areas where rural residents live in reasonably close proximity to each other, centralized water systems may be an efficient method of providing water for population growth. In other areas where residences are widely scattered, centralized water systems may be impractical.

The Commission does not see a need for initiation of new water programs to respond to potential population growth in rural areas. If the Nation chooses to adopt a rural development approach to population distribution, existing Federal water programs could be used to provide water and water-related services.

---

[47] The EDA program, which grew out of the area redevelopment program of a decade ago, is predicated on the assumption that water and sewer facilities provide jobs, reduce unemployment, and thus promote economic growth. The program generally serves nonmetropolitan areas, but grants and loans have been made to Chicago and Omaha. For an assessment of the EDA program, see the following: U.S. DEPARTMENT OF COMMERCE, Economic Development Administration (1967). Regional Economic Development in the United States, 3 vols. U.S. Government Printing Office, Washington, D.C. BOOZ, ALLEN & HAMILTON, INC., Washington, D.C. (1970). An Evaluation of the Business Loan Program of the Economic Development Administration, prepared for the Economic Development Administration. U.S. Department of Commerce, Washington, D.C. U.S. CONGRESS, House, Special Subcommittee on Economic Development Programs of the Committee on Public Works (1970). Evaluation of Economic Development Programs–Part II, 91st Congress, 2d Session. U.S. Government Printing Office, Washington, D.C.

[48] *Rural Development Act of 1972,* P.L. 92-419, Sec. 109, August 30, 1972, 86 Stat. 657, 659, 7 USCA Sec. 1926.

59

New Towns — New towns are not new.[49] About 3,000 years ago, the Greeks founded entirely new "settlements for purposes of colonization, commerce, and absorption of population increases in the city-states."[50] In the United States, a number of "new towns" have been developed. Reston (Virginia), Columbia (Maryland), and Jonathan (Minnesota) are recent examples of privately developed new towns established in an attempt to accommodate increased population in a desirable living environment.

Water is required for new towns just as numerous other resources and facilities are needed. The question, however, is whether a "special" water program is required.

Even though a location close to surface water may be a desirable feature, relatively few developers of proposed new towns intend to use specially developed surface water supplies. The distribution of proposed new communities by source of water supply is shown in Table 3-1.

Because 91 percent of the proposed new towns included in the sample are either within or on the periphery of a metropolitan center, water planners

may see the simple extension of municipal water lines as an attractive alternative to entirely new water projects. The Commission believes that water development for new towns should be viewed in the same way as water problems of other kinds of cities and towns.

Growth Centers — The Commission on Population Growth and the American Future has endorsed a "growth centers" strategy for aiding the normal transition of people from declining rural areas to urban places with job opportunities.[51] The growth centers concept focuses on existing communities that have demonstrated capabilities for further expansion in economic and population growth.

The growth centers approach requires identification of an economic base or growth nucleus that can provide jobs. While the characteristics of the required base might vary, it has generally been defined as a town or city having (1) some minimum initial concentration of people,[52] (2) a viable economic base, and (3) a favorable rate of growth. Government development funds are then channeled to these growth centers. For example, the Appalachian Regional Development Act authorizes investment of supplemental Federal grant funds for projects of various kinds in designated growth centers.[53] The theory is that growth centers have the greatest potential for development and are the areas most likely to produce a satisfactory return on Federal investment in terms of goals achieved.

The programs of EDA, under the Public Works and Economic Development Act of 1965,[54] make certain

---

TABLE 3-1. —Proposed source of water supplies for selected potential new towns

Water Source	Number of Communities	Percent Distribution
Ground Water Only	9	26
Surface Water Only	6	17
Extension of Municipal Water Lines Only	18	51
Combination of Sources[1]	2	6
	35	100

[1] One development anticipates using both ground and surface water supplies. The other anticipates temporary use of ground water until municipal lines are extended to reach this satellite new town.

Source: Sample of unnamed, proposed new towns seeking Federal financial assistance; provided by U.S. Department of Housing and Urban Development (1971). Letter and attachment dated July 26, 1971, from Samuel C. Jackson to Theodore M. Schad. On file, National Water Commission.

---

[49] New towns traditionally have been defined as preplanned, self-contained communities, established for specific purposes.

[50] CLAPP, James A (1971). New Towns and Urban Policy. Dunellen Publishing Co., Inc., New York. p. 16.

[51] U.S. COMMISSION ON POPULATION GROWTH AND THE AMERICAN FUTURE (1972). Population Growth and the American Future. U.S. Government Printing Office, Washington, D.C. Ch. 12.

[52] Various minimum size standards have been argued. See MORRISON, Peter A (1971). Dimensions of the Population Problem in the United States, prepared for the Commission on Population Growth and the American Future. RAND Corporation, Santa Monica, Calif. pp. 52-53. In a few cases 5,000 people may be a sufficient number to permit viable future growth, but in most cases 25,000 to 100,000 people may be needed. The Commission on Population Growth and the American Future uses 25,000 as the minimum population size for a growth center, although it suggests the desirability of some flexibility because of regional differences.

[53] Appalachian Regional Development Act of 1965, P.L. 89-4, March 9, 1965, 79 Stat. 5, 40 USCA App. Secs. 1-405.

[54] Public Works and Economic Development Act of 1965, P.L. 89-136, August 26, 1965, 79 Stat. 552, as amended 42 USCA Secs. 3121 et seq.

redevelopment areas and economic growth centers eligible for increased grant and loan assistance. Because the EDA program is generally aimed at assisting depressed areas, other criteria for eligibility such as high rates of unemployment and low income levels are considered along with optimum size to identify communities eligible for assistance. These criteria can be modified from program to program, however, to meet different purposes. Whereas Appalachian and EDA programs were primarily intended to benefit depressed areas, other criteria could be developed to identify appropriate centers of emerging growth to receive Federal assistance to accommodate future population increases.

If and when the Nation adopts a population-based growth center strategy, Federal water development programs could respond. Under existing assistance programs, water supply and sewage facility investments are generally treated separately from other developmental activities such as land use regulation, educational investments, transportation improvements, etc. They could all be coordinated around a central theme of community (or growth center) development.

Synthesis – It is likely that all three alternatives—rural development, new towns, and growth centers—will be used in some combination to affect population distribution. Regardless of the ultimate outcome, water resources should be planned and managed to respond to future changes in population and the response should be under terms that are most efficient and equitable from a national standpoint.

Water planning, undertaken jointly with planning for land use, housing, transportation, education, and industrial development, encourages efficiency in the construction and operation of water supply and sewage treatment facilities, especially when investments are staged at rates comparable to actual need.

Existing Federal water programs, established for purposes other than population distribution, have the potential for accommodating population dispersal objectives if the President or Congress so direct. The application of technologies in water reuse and recycling may help stretch limited water supplies and thereby assist likely areas of growth. Transfer of water use (for example, from irrigation to municipal and industrial uses) may offer some communities opportunities to meet water needs at costs far less than the development of new supplies.

CONCLUSIONS ON REGIONAL DEVELOPMENT

1.   While water resources projects have had very significant impacts on regional economic development and population distribution in the past, they are not usually the most efficient way to accomplish these objectives and their importance is diminishing.

2.   Under certain conditions, water development may be helpful as one of several ingredients necessary to encourage regional economic development and population growth, or to preserve existing development. However, water developments differ widely in the effects they induce. Congress, in making judgments as to whether water developments should be used to aid regional growth, should require evaluations of certain critical growth factors in order to enhance the effectiveness of developments and reduce offsetting losses in other regions. These factors include: market demands, availability of substitutes for water services, competitive advantage of the region, and the potential for capitalizing on growth opportunities.

3.   Federal water programs can be easily adjusted to support whatever population distribution policy the Nation adopts. However, water programs are not, in and of themselves, adequate to effectuate a national policy concerning where people will live. Water programs should continue to accommodate future population growth and economic well-being by responding to the pattern of interregional population distribution. In some instances water programs may influence desired population distribution provided other controlling conditions are favorable. Where Congress has determined that the growth of a particular area should be promoted in the national interest such programs may be used if they provide the most efficient way to achieve that growth.

POSTED
DANGER
CONTAMINATED WATER

Chapter 4

Water Pollution Control[1]

The development of the Nation has exacted a high price in the deteriorating quality of its water resources. Rivers, lakes, and coastal waters have been heavily damaged by the uncontrolled discharge of wastes; by polluted runoff from urban, agricultural, and mining development; and by accelerated siltation, erosion, and sedimentation.

Efforts to clean up water pollution have been impeded by basic disagreements over goals to be sought and strategies for water quality management. Complexities and costs have often been obscured by the rhetoric in which oversimplified solutions are advanced. As a basis for sound decisions about programs for water quality improvement, the American people need to know the facts about water pollution and to understand the costs and benefits of alternative strategies for managing water quality.

In this chapter, a range of possible pollution abatement programs is examined in the context of a total environment and a whole society. It is generally recognized that improved water quality will enhance the immediate environment, augment the useful supply of water, and reduce costs stemming from the use of polluted water. It is also necessary to recognize that matter can be altered but not destroyed and some processes which abate the pollution of water can impair other elements of the environment. The consumption of minerals and energy to construct and operate waste treatment systems can drain supplies of limited and nonrenewable resources. Many valid unmet needs compete for limited tax moneys and expenditures for water pollution abatement can impose heavy social costs in lost opportunities for the solution of social problems. Water quality management policies which do not recognize these facts

~~~~~~~~~~~~~~~~~

Polluted waters are off-limits for recreational and fish and wildlife use

cannot be sustained. The difficult and important task is to weigh the benefits and costs of each available alternative and to devise policies and systems which will improve these choices over time.

COMMISSION APPROACH

The Commission is convinced that a new ethic of conservation and reuse must replace the history of exponential growth in the production of wastes. Our 4-year study of water pollution has demonstrated the environmental truth of the aphorism "there is no such thing as a free lunch." The Nation can no longer rely on "cheap raw materials," "underpriced" water, and "free" waste disposal to achieve its national development goals.

It is increasingly evident that some wastes in our waters need never have been produced and represent, in effect, misplaced resources. If appropriate regulations are enforced and polluters are required to pay the cost of abating their pollution, the Commission believes that the amount of waste production will be minimized and the costs of its treatment will be more equitably shared.

The Commission believes that for the next decade the primary national water resource priority should shift from water development to water quality management to meet a high standard of water quality. Regulations and expenditures should be directed at the most effective site-specific pollution

[1] In preparing this chapter, the Commission relied on background information from HINES, N William (1971). Public Regulation of Water Quality in the United States, prepared for the National Water Commission. National Technical Information Service, Springfield, Va., Accession No. PB 208 309, and PANEL ON WATER POLLUTION CONTROL (1971). Water Pollution Control in the United States, prepared for the National Water Commission. National Technical Information Service, Springfield, Va., Accession No. PB 212 139.

abatement rather than uniform national requirements and absolute goals. National water quality goals should be set only after analysis of the effect which their achievement will have upon other national goals. A 10-year national financial commitment to achieve water quality standards is necessary because of the sheer magnitude of the long-accumulated backlog of work and the need to establish equity among the State and local governments which have been unevenly affected by prior Federal grant programs. At the end of this period, the Federal grant program should terminate and local and State agencies should operate and improve their systems and the users of such systems should pay the costs.

THE IMPORTANCE OF CLEAN WATER

In the past, wastes were discharged into waterways with little regard to the costs imposed on other users and on the public by the resulting decline in water quality. Limited only by the laws of public and private nuisance, these practices were not entirely satisfactory even in a frontier society with an abundance of clean water. Under today's increasing demands for high-quality water, unrestrained waste disposal leads to serious conflicts among potential water uses and occasions the loss of social and environmental values.

Projections of future water demands[2] in some regions of the United States make it clear that unless major new supplies of fresh water can be developed, increased reuse of existing water supplies will be essential to meet these demands. Reuse is possible because the great majority of users return water to its source after use; however, to rely on reuse to satisfy increasing demands, water returned must be of sufficiently high quality that its usability is not destroyed.

Impairment of water quality also seriously threatens in-place water uses. The maintenance of desirable fish and wildlife populations and the preservation of natural beauty require water of good quality. The demand for water-based recreation is increasing dramatically and requires clean water.

Water quality is impaired primarily by the use of the water as a receptor of wastes. Wastes may contain bacteria or viruses harmful to human health. The decomposition of organic wastes robs water of dissolved oxygen essential to support the life process of aquatic creatures. Salts, acids, phenols, alkalies, and other compounds present in industrial waste-

waters frequently degrade water for a wide range of uses. Various organic or inorganic chemicals reaching waters through direct discharges and through land runoff disrupt the delicate food chains of lower levels of life and ultimately may prove toxic to people. At the opposite extreme, chemical nutrients stimulate the growth of some aquatic organisms in nuisance quantities. Dissolved and suspended materials affect the color and turbidity of water and may congest watercourses as they are deposited. Heat added to water in industrial cooling processes may have deleterious effect on aquatic life, and reduces capacity to purify organic materials. Finally, the escape of radioactive material into water can pose a threat to all forms of life.

SOURCES OF POLLUTION

Pure water is a manufactured product. Natural water is not pure. Its quality is affected by a variety of geologic, hydrologic, and biologic factors. Natural impurities such as sediments, decaying vegetation, and wastes from wild animal populations impose measurable levels of contamination on many watercourses. Dissolved minerals rendered some of our surface and ground waters unfit for certain uses long before man appeared on the scene. But most of what we call pollution today results from disposal of the waste products of civilization. Controlling man-caused pollution is the central concern of this chapter.

Pollution sources are of two types: (1) waste discharges from identifiable points (point-sources) and (2) diffused wastes reaching water through land runoff, washout from the atmosphere, or other means (nonpoint-sources). The two differ in their amenability to control. Discrete point-sources may be controlled directly while nonpoint-sources are extremely difficult to control.

Point-Sources

Municipal Sewerage Systems: The sanitary wastes from an urban population of roughly 160 million people are systematically collected through sewers and subjected to some type of treatment before being discharged into water bodies. Municipal systems also collect and treat a significant portion of the Nation's industrial wastes. Municipal effluents contain large amounts of organic materials, dissolved minerals, and often contain residues from industrial wastes. In many places, municipal wastes do not receive adequate treatment. Even where secondary treatment

[2] See Chapter 1.

is provided, important nutrients and toxic materials escape removal. Some measure of the deficiencies in municipal waste control is provided by a comparison of the present value of existing municipal sewage treatment plants ($8.5 billion)[3] and the estimate of additional investments needed in such plants by 1985 ($15 billion) to meet water quality standards established under the Water Quality Act of 1965.[4]

Storm Water Runoff: A second source of water pollution attracting increasing attention is storm water runoff from urban areas. Urban land runoff is commonly collected in storm sewers and discharged into waterways. Frequently, storm water inlets connect directly with sanitary sewers. Where a combined storm and sanitary sewer system is used, heavy storm runoffs result in temporarily overloading or bypassing of local waste treatment plants so that raw or partially treated sewage is discharged into watercourses. Even where separate storm sewers are utilized, storm water poses a pollution threat. Accidental interconnections with sanitary sewers are common, and recent studies have revealed that the first "flush" of storm water often carries a pollution load of some constituents greater than that of raw sanitary sewage.[5] It should be noted that the early runoff from heavy rainfall on rural agricultural land and even on wilderness areas also transfers a heavy pollution load to watercourses.

Industrial Wastes: The total output of organic wastes from water-using industries in the United States is estimated to have a pollution strength three to four times greater than the domestic sewage handled by all municipalities combined,[6] and organic industrial wastes are growing at a rapid rate. In addition, industry effluents contain a variety of inorganic wastes which in their initial state, in degraded forms, and in compounds affect the usability of water in

diverse ways ranging from outright toxicity to harmless but unpleasant tastes. The rapid development of new synthetic chemicals promises new and more exotic types of production wastes for the future. In 1968, according to Federal agency studies, only 37 percent of the wastewater discharged by industry received any treatment whatsoever; and 7 percent of what was treated passed through municipal sewage plants.[7] One projection to the year 2000 shows that, unless process changes occur, there will be a sevenfold increase in the wastes of water-using industries.[8] Obviously, there will have to be changes in processing.

Discharge of heated industrial wastewater also affects water quality, and may have adverse effects on the biota. By far the largest discharger of waste heat is the electric power industry, which uses great quantities of water for cooling. Growth estimates lead to predictions of a six- to tenfold increase by the year 2000 in the discharge of heated water from powerplants. One commonly used method of reducing or eliminating the discharge of heat to watercourses is the installation of cooling towers; however, such installations increase consumptive use of water, require more energy,[9] and may affect air quality.

Animal Wastes From Commercial Feedlots: Steady increases in per capita meat consumption and continued population growth have caused agricultural technology to seek more efficient methods for producing meat animals. One result is the modern confined feeding operation in which large numbers of animals are scientifically fed and managed in tightly restricted quarters. Feedlots carrying more than 10,000 head of cattle or swine each are not unusual. Current estimates project continued expansion of confined feeding operations.

Unfortunately, animal waste management practices have not always kept pace with improved-efficiency

[3] U.S. ENVIRONMENTAL PROTECTION AGENCY (1972). The Economics of Clean Water, Vol. 1, Environmental Protection Agency, Washington, D.C. p. 120, assuming treatment plants represent 45 percent of total of costs given therein which also include interceptors, outfalls, and pumping plants.

[4] See Chapter 16, Financing Water Programs.

[5] BRYAN, Edward H (1970). Quality of Storm Water Drainage from Urban Land Areas in North Carolina. Report No. 37, Water Resources Research Institute, University of North Carolina, Raleigh, N.C.

[6] U.S. COUNCIL ON ENVIRONMENTAL QUALITY (1970). Environmental Quality, The First Annual Report of the Council on Environmental Quality. U.S. Government Printing Office, Washington, D.C. p. 32.

[7] U.S. ENVIRONMENTAL PROTECTION AGENCY (1972). The Economics of Clean Water, Vol. 1, Environmental Protection Agency, Washington, D.C. p. 17.

[8] U.S. NATIONAL ACADEMY OF SCIENCES-NATIONAL RESEARCH COUNCIL, Publication 1400. National Academy of Sciences-National Research Council, Washington, D.C. p. 12.

[9] See Chapter 5, Section G, for more complete discussion of waste heat problems. The Commission established a special panel to study this subject. See the report by the CONSULTING PANEL ON WASTE HEAT (May 1972). The Water Use and Management Aspects of Steam Electric Power Generation, prepared for the National Water Commission. National Technical Information Service, Springfield, Va., Accession No. PB 210 355.

Industrial and mine wastes degrade watercourses

feeding operations. In yesterday's small feedlot operation, manure was a valuable byproduct used to fertilize the land that produced the crops fed to the next generation of animals. Today, labor costs of spreading manure coupled with the availability of low-cost chemical fertilizers have converted this once-valuable byproduct into a waste disposal problem of sizable dimensions in some sections of the country.

Nonpoint-Sources

Sediment: Sediment is frequently found in natural water supplies. In excess quantities, it impairs recreation, interferes with aquatic species, increases the costs of water control projects, and increases the expense of water treatment for municipal and industrial purposes. Sediment, therefore, must be considered as a pollutant. In addition, eroding sediment transports pesticide residues and chemical nutrients from fields to waterways.[10]

---

[10] For more detailed discussion of erosion and sedimentation see Chapter 5, Section H.

Sediment in streams is a natural phenomenon—sediments were present in the Nation's waters long before the country was settled. Natural happenings such as lightning-caused forest fires can trigger accelerated erosion. Man's activities, such as urban construction, overgrazing, surface mining, or recreational activities, can have a similar result. The effects are more dramatic where soils are least protected by vegetative growth, as in the Southwestern United States, where streams have always carried heavy concentrations of sediment. Man's activity has, for the most part, increased sediment loads in streams of the populated areas of the country. Unprotected croplands, overgrazed pastures, strip mines, roadways, and clearing for urban construction all have increased the production of sediment over that occurring in nature. Agricultural development increases erosion rates four to nine times while urban construction may increase the erosion rate a hundredfold during the period of construction.

Agricultural Chemicals: Chemical fertilizers and pesticides can cause serious adverse effects if they reach waters in excessive quantities. Current evidence suggests that these chemicals are entering waters in increasing concentrations. Nitrogen and phosphorus, the two chief nutrients in agricultural fertilizers, directly stimulate and feed the growth of algae. A certain amount of algae is essential as food for other forms of aquatic life, but dense algae blooms reduce water quality by increasing turbidity and forming scum and floating mats. Heavy algae growth may compete with other aquatic life forms for dissolved oxygen. This algae growth can be reduced or eliminated by minimizing escape of chemicals from the fields through the use of good fertilizer application techniques. Phosphate fertilizer that reaches water is usually carried there by eroded soil particles, but nitrogen is soluble and is carried in the drainage.

While there are pesticide residues in many of the Nation's waterways, the level of pesticide concentrations in water is generally low. Because many of the persistent pesticides precipitate rapidly from water, low pesticide levels in water samples may not reflect accurately the availability of these compounds to aquatic flora and fauna. Bottom sediments frequently contain pesticide concentrations many times greater than the overlying water. Whether these pesticides are a cause of trouble depends on potential for scour, and on the aquatic life in the area.

Although the precise routes by which pesticides travel through the environment are not known, agriculture's role in their dissemination is generally acknowledged. Nearly a billion pounds of pesticides, of which agriculture uses slightly more than 50 percent,[11] are used in the United States each year. These totals, large as they are, are of little value in appraising water quality, because of the large variety in kinds, variations in persistence, and uncertainties in effects. As with phosphate fertilizers, eroding soil particles are suspected to be the major vehicles for transporting pesticides to waterways.

Mine Drainage: Drainage from active and abandoned mines pours harmful acids, minerals, and sediments from 11 million acres of mine land into streams and lakes in 31 States. It is impossible to document the amount of the damages, since many watercourses received such inflows under natural conditions. Mining operations for nearly 20 different minerals create wastes which diminish water quality, but coal mining is the biggest offender. Acids from coal mines account for a large share of the damages from mine drainage pollution, mostly in the Ohio River Basin.

A recent study of active mines revealed that over half of them pumped untreated wastewater directly from the mine into a nearby stream. Like feedlot wastes, drainage from active mines will respond to a point-source style of regulation based on collection and treatment of the wastewater prior to its discharge. The 90,000 or so abandoned mines which account for 60 percent of acid drainage are still another problem.[12] Data to show that the benefits from control measures undertaken to date are sufficient to justify the costs of such measures are not available.

Spills of Oil and Other Hazardous Substances: An estimated 10,000 spills of oil and other hazardous materials occur annually in or near navigable waters of the United States. Although damages from other hazardous substances spilled into waters can be just as significant as those caused by oil pollution, the volume of oil transported and used vests it with great potential for damage and makes it the major concern.

Most large oil spills come from vessels, pipelines, oil terminals, and bulk storage facilities. Two hundred thousand miles of pipelines carry annually more than a billion tons of oil and hazardous substances. These pipelines cross waterways and reservoirs and are subject to leakage.[13] Spills from this source are not frequent, but the hazard is increasing as the amount of exposure increases. In addition, disposal of used oil is beginning to be recognized as a matter of environmental concern, particularly since the tax incentives for re-refining used oil were eliminated.

Other Sources: Other nonpoint-sources of pollution, such as animal and vegetable residues washed from open lands, runoff from commercial and industrial sites, salting of highways for ice control, discharges of waste materials from vessels, and washout of residuals deposited in the atmosphere through man's activities, are also causing increasing environmental damage.

[11] U.S. COUNCIL ON ENVIRONMENTAL QUALITY (1970). Environmental Quality, First Annual Report of the Council on Environmental Quality, U.S. Government Printing Office, Washington, D.C. p. 131.

[12] U.S. DEPARTMENT OF THE INTERIOR, Federal Water Quality Administration (June 1970). Clean Water for the 1970's. U.S. Government Printing Office, Washington, D.C. p. 9.

[13] U.S. COUNCIL ON ENVIRONMENTAL QUALITY (1970). Environmental Quality, First Annual Report of the Council on Environmental Quality. U.S. Government Printing Office, Washington, D.C. p. 38.

Oil spills spread rapidly on water surfaces

WHAT IS HAPPENING TO WATER QUALITY?

One major impediment to an adequate assessment of water quality is that existing monitoring and surveillance programs are inadequate to provide the data base required for a comprehensive analysis of water quality conditions, except in a limited number of waterways. Even where extensive sampling programs have been instituted, little or no historical water quality data exist from which to make comparisons over a period of time. For these reasons, most assessments of water quality are highly subjective.

One method for assessing current status is by comparison with the past. The overall impression gathered from two recent studies of water quality conditions is that some deterioration has occurred over time but also some improvement has been shown. One study of long-term changes on selected waterways revealed cases of marked improvements in dissolved oxygen and a few other water quality indicators during the last 30-40 years, but a general increase in dissolved solids.[14] These findings are corroborated by a U.S. Council on Environmental Quality (CEQ) report which notes that while the total biochemical oxygen demand (BOD) loading of waters increased only slightly over a 10-year period (during which the production of potential BOD materials more than doubled), the discharge of other types of pollutants increased significantly.[15] It can be concluded from these reports that pollution control

[14] WOLMAN MG (November 26, 1971). The Nation's Rivers. Science 174(4012):905-918.
[15] U.S. COUNCIL ON ENVIRONMENTAL QUALITY (1971). Environmental Quality, The Second Annual Report of the Council on Environmental Quality, August 1971. U.S. Government Printing Office, Washington, D.C. p. 218.

efforts of the past decade have held even or gained somewhat on oxygen-demanding wastes, but have lost ground against some other pollutants. This is not surprising, as conventional waste treatment processes have been principally directed to reduction of oxygen demand.

A more recent study undertaken for the CEQ based on a sample of water quality stations and adjusted for variations in flow also shows a mixed picture of trends in water quality. In general, it shows that there has been a dramatic worsening in the concentration of phosphorus and nitrogen compounds and a slight increase in the total oxygen-demanding wastes.[16]

A more optimistic view is presented by responses received by the Commission staff to an inquiry concerning recent changes in water quality. Reports received from 30 States and three interstate agencies indicated that in the past several years both general improvements in water quality and specific instances of upgrading have overshadowed isolated situations of deterioration.[17]

A second method of assessment is to compare existing quality to stated objectives as expressed in water quality standards. EPA has recently made a systematic attempt to record such information.[18] An inventory of some 260,000 miles of streams and shorelines by that agency shows that almost 30 percent of the Nation's stream and shoreline miles are out of compliance with one or more criteria at least once a year. The study does not, however, permit a quantitative judgment as to losses or damages from pollution, because the comparison does not take account of the fact that failure to meet certain criteria 100 percent of the time may have little or no detrimental effect.

Notwithstanding uncertainties resulting from the lack of reliable data and the imprecision of evaluation procedures, the available reports contain a consistent theme of substantial noncompliance with existing standards. Decisive action is needed to achieve the Nation's stated water quality objectives.

[16] U.S. COUNCIL ON ENVIRONMENTAL QUALITY (1971). Environmental Quality, The Third Annual Report of the Council on Environmental Quality, August 1972. U.S. Government Printing Office, Washington, D.C. pp. 13-14.

[17] Correspondence in files of National Water Commission.

[18] U.S. ENVIRONMENTAL PROTECTION AGENCY (1972). The Economics of Clean Water, Vol. 1, Environmental Protection Agency, Washington, D.C. Part I.

WHEN IS WATER POLLUTED?

Pollution can be defined in alternative ways which have markedly different implications for the Nation's effort to improve water quality. One view of pollution is expressed in the Federal Water Pollution Control Act Amendments of 1972,[19] which defines "pollution" as "man-made or man-induced alteration of the chemical, physical, biological, and radiological integrity of water."[20] Thus, natural water quality appears to be regarded as a norm from which any deviation constitutes pollution. This is not a good standard on which to base the definition of pollution. In some places water is naturally toxic, naturally hot, naturally turbid, naturally radioactive, or naturally acid or alkaline. Some lakes are naturally choked with algae, and the eutrophication of lakes is a natural process in their aging. Oil seeps in large quantity occur in nature. Heavy sediment loads occur naturally in many flowing streams. Man-induced changes due to discharges of specific chemicals can actually improve the usefulness of water, for example, where wastes which contain lime neutralize the excess natural acidity of streams, or where nutrients are needed to support aquatic life. Conservation of marine species that are heavily used as a source of food for man may require replacement of nutrients in the marine environment to maintain the food chain.

If the purpose of the 1972 Act's definition of pollution were just to bring within the ambit of the control program all discharges of substances potentially harmful to water quality, its breadth of scope would be commendable. However, this all-encompassing definition does not merely expand the jurisdiction of the control program; it is an integral component of a water quality policy which is designed ultimately to prevent all use of water bodies for waste disposal. The 1972 Act establishes 1985 as a tentative target date for achievement of this "no discharge" goal.

Such a goal is unrealistic. Tolerance of foreign materials in water varies greatly among different water uses. The ranking of purposes for which water is used in terms of the quality levels required in natural watercourses might be represented as follows: (1) preservation of the natural environment, as in the

[19] Public Law 92-500, October 18, 1972, 86 Stat. 816, 33 USCA 1251-1376. Hereinafter referred to as the "1972 Act."

[20] Ibid., Section 502(19), 86 Stat. 887, 33 USCA 1362(19).

"wild river" program; (2) water contact sports, such as swimming and water-skiing; (3) use as a source of a potable domestic water supply;[21] (4) preservation of aquatic life; (5) noncontact recreational uses, such as boating; (6) agricultural use, such as irrigation and livestock watering; (7) industrial use; (8) navigation; (9) disposal and transport of wastes. Only use (1) requires natural water quality. In all other cases water quality different from that which would exist in nature will adequately support the desired uses. In fact, natural water itself often is unfit to satisfy important uses, and a requirement that all water discharged after use be distilled would not assure water of useful quality.

The Commission believes adoption of "no discharge" as a national goal for water quality management is no more sound than would be the establishment of a "no development" goal for controlling land use. First, the "no discharge" policy ignores the functional interrelationships among environmental resources and places man in absolute oppostion to natural processes of runoff and drainage. Second, the maximum degree of industrial or sewage treatment process changes cannot eliminate all wastes which are now discharged to water. Forbidding the disposal of these wastes in water inevitably will result in their disposal in the air or on land, but with no assurance that such disposal alternatives are either environmentally or economically preferable to disposal in water. Third, the no discharge policy assumes that restoration and preservation of natural water quality is of higher value than any other use of the resource. This assumption will not pass the tests commonly applied to determine how or whether resources should be used. The costs of achieving the social objective of pure water are so great that they surely will necessitate a cutback or postponement of other worthy domestic programs. An examination of relative priorities among social goals is in order. In the Commission's view, a reduction in waste disposal beyond that necessary to protect existing or anticipated future uses of receiving waters would create costs unrelated to any social benefit and would result in needless expenditures and a waste of other resources such as air, land, minerals, and energy. Absolutely pure water simply is not necessary for many uses, and these include uses such as recreation and fish propagation. Adoption of a no discharge

policy thus amounts to the imputation of an extravagant social value to an abstract concept of water purity; a value the Commission is convinced the American people would not endorse if the associated costs and effect on other resources were fully appreciated and the policy alternatives clearly understood.

The danger of setting the restoration of natural water quality as a national goal lies not merely in its conceptual unsoundness, but in its potential for doing long-term harm to the pollution control effort. Like other oversimplified solutions to complex social problems, this policy holds out a promise of "natural" water it cannot redeem. Water quality regulation which loses touch with the reasons people value water is hopelessly adrift and eventually will founder. When it does, the attendant loss of public confidence will make it more difficult to marshall public support to reestablish a program with rational objectives.

In the Commission's view, pollution should be defined in a functional and dynamic manner by saying that *water is polluted if it is not of sufficiently high quality to be suitable for the highest uses people wish to make of it at present or in the future.* Such uses should be determined by responsible public authorities. Under this approach, maintenance of natural water quality is necessary only where some use of the resource requires it.[22] This is not to say that the pollution control program ought to ignore any man-induced alteration of water quality. Rather, the goal of the control program should be to regulate those changes to achieve and maintain a quality sufficient to sustain the uses people wish to make of the water now or in the future.

It is this relative theory of pollution upon which was based the national water quality standards program introduced by the Water Quality Act of 1965.[23] This legislation fostered the establishment of receiving water standards for nearly all of the Nation's surface waters. In the 1965 Act, the congressional description of the water quality standards intended was somewhat lacking in detail; the Act simply provided that the standards shall be such as "to protect the public health or welfare, enhance the quality of water," and serve the purposes of the Act,

[21] Where water bodies are used as a source of domestic supplies without filtration, this use must be placed ahead of water contact sports in the ranking.

[22] For a more complete discussion of this philosophy, see U.S. CONGRESS, House of Representatives (1966), "Water Pollution Control," House Report No. 2021, 89th Congress, 2d Session. U.S. Government Printing Office, Washington, D.C.

[23] P.L. 89-234, October 2, 1965, 79 Stat. 903.

taking into consideration the "use and value [of the interstate waters] for public water supplies, propagation of fish and wildlife, recreational purposes, and agricultural, industrial, and other legitimate uses."[24] For this reason, several years were required to establish satisfactory standards and there has not been time for them to be fully implemented. Nevertheless, the Commission believes the concept of water quality standards provides the foundation for an effective national strategy for pollution control. Standards based on present and proposed water uses not only represent the most rational national water quality policy from a cost-benefit standpoint, they also permit maximum adaptability of national goals to local situations. Although refinements were clearly needed, particularly clarifications in matters of responsibility and treatment required, the State-Federal water quality standards program was proceeding in the right direction and should be restored as the basic framework for the national effort to clean up our waterways.

ADEQUACY OF TECHNOLOGY

The Commission does not believe that lack of adequate technology is a significant impediment to controlling most point-sources of pollution. In a separate section of this report,[25] the Commission has concluded that existing technology is capable of producing a finished municipal effluent suitable for all uses with the possible exception of direct human consumption. Less confidence is expressed with regard to the reuse of industrial wastes, but there, too, production process changes coordinated with existing treatment methods can produce a reusable effluent from most industries within the next decade. If the Commission's assessment of the capability of existing technology to produce effluents suitable for direct reuse is correct, discharges sufficient to satisfy adequate water quality standards are certainly attainable. The importance of discovering new treatment processes should not be minimized, but the Commission believes most water quality objectives can be achieved through creative application of known technology.

Adapting Technology to Special Problems

Land Disposal of Municipal and Industrial Wastes: Broad-scale land disposal of wastewater is attracting increasing interest in the United States as a substitute for conventional biological treatment. Although the dedication of marginal lands to the disposal of municipal and industrial effluents by filtration through the natural soils has been practiced in other countries, a project in Muskegon County, Michigan, represents the first attempt in the humid portion of the United States to use land disposal on a large scale for handling the wastewater from an urban population.[26] The Muskegon project, which is not yet operational, will spray-irrigate 6,000 acres of land having sandy soil, using the effluent from the system's biological treatment lagoons. Another 4,000 acres will be used for treatment and storage lagoons and a protective zone to isolate the project from neighboring lands. The capital cost of the project was estimated to be comparable to the cost of a conventional waste treatment system with similar capabilities, but the net operating costs are estimated by sponsors to be 50 percent lower. When the project is complete, it will handle the effluent from a population of 138,000.

The possibility of lower costs is not the sole attractive feature of land disposal. Not only does the land disposal system have a potential for reducing BOD without producing the amount of sludges which plague most conventional systems of waste treatment, it is expected to have advantages in the handling of dissolved solids. Sponsors of the Muskegon system claim that filtration through soil provides an effective means of removing, decomposing, recycling, or immobilizing some substances which now escape from most conventional treatment facilities. By using agricultural land as a "living filter," they claim, the nutrient value of such wastes can be reclaimed for agricultural production, rather than in the aquatic food chain.

Because the Muskegon system will disperse residuals and may be cheaper to operate than conventional municipal treatment methods, it is often cited to demonstrate the feasibility of a "no discharge" policy. In the Commission's view, land disposal is by no means a complete solution for the country's waste disposal problem. Many design and operational problems exist which are site-specific in nature. Michigan pollution control officials are concerned that the filtrate of the Muskegon drainage fields might contain undesirable concentrations of

---

[24] *Ibid.*, Section 5(c) (3).

[25] See Chapter 7, Section H, Reuse of Municipal and Industrial Wastewater.

[26] *See* DAVIS GW and DUNHAM A (1971). Wastewater Management Project, Muskegon County, Michigan, prepared for the National Water Commission. National Technical Information Service, Springfield, Va., Accession No. PB 208 310.

Sugar beet wastes killed these fish in Ohio

nitrates, chlorides, and other salts, just as do the return flows from irrigation projects in arid lands. Projecting the Muskegon approach to larger urban communities produces estimates of enormous land areas needed for waste disposal (448,000 acres in the case of Chicago and more than a million acres for New York City) which certainly would not be available nearby at reasonable cost. Obtaining public acceptance of large "sewer farms" may be difficult in particular locales. Land disposal is further site-specific in the sense that local soil and climatic conditions will affect both operating costs and system efficiency. In some areas, land disposal may be precluded by a need to return municipal effluents to the source of withdrawal to sustain the flow of streams or to satisfy vested water rights.

The Commission regards land disposal as an alternative treatment method, which should be evaluated along with other methods to determine which produces the desired results at least cost. At the moment, such evaluation is difficult because of lack of reliable information about large-scale land disposal. The Muskegon project is not yet operational and no experience has been gained on any other spray-irrigation system of comparable size. Land disposal is not a panacea through which a no discharge policy may be accomplished; however, it is sufficiently attractive to merit attention as an alternative which should be considered where suitable land is available at costs which make the technique economically competitive with other systems and where the waste-water is not required to be returned to the stream from which withdrawn.

Aquaculture: Techniques for increasing the useful productivity of bodies of water by the scientific application of treated wastes may also hold promise. Man removes food from the sea much as crops are grown on land and such removal requires the replacement of nutrients to permit harvest on a sustained yield basis. As waste treatment becomes more sophisticated it may improve the food production capability of water bodies through controlled management of nutrients. The 1972 Act contains appropriate recognition of the potential value of aquaculture projects by authorizing the approval of discharges which might otherwise be prohibited as pollutants.[27]

Storm Flow Treatment: The technology of handling the pollution associated with storm water overflows from combined sewers is an emerging one. For many years it was believed that the solution lay in dividing the combined systems into separate sanitary and storm systems. While this approach is effective on a selective basis, in other cities it is expensive and disruptive, and may not solve all of the problems. Inadvertent or intentional cross-connections between storm and sanitary systems have to be eliminated, sometimes at great expense, and the "first flush" of pollutants from the city streets still carries a significant pollution load. If large areas of rural land contribute to the stream, however, the contribution of urban storm flows may be so small as to be unimportant.

One solution is to store storm water runoff overflows, whether from combined systems or separate storm sewer systems, so that they may be released at controlled rates to undergo conventional treatment. The fact that most storm flows are discharged to waterways in developed metropolitan areas limits opportunities for storage in conventional impoundments created by dams. The most widely advocated approaches for storing storm waters have been construction of concrete holding tanks at each sewer outfall, or combination of adjacent outfalls, and excavation of large underground tunnels to which a number of sewers are connected. The latter approach is limited to areas of favorable geologic conditions, where there is no possibility of ground water contamination, conditions which probably occur under far less than half of the major cities in the United States. Studies in four major cities where favorable geological conditions were present showed

the deep tunnel approach to cost only one-fourth to one-half as much as sewer separation, and to be only about 60 to 85 percent as costly as holding tanks.[28] One segment of a system to implement such a program currently is being tested in Chicago.

Even with storage, it must be recognized that occasional storms, beyond the design capacity of the system, will cause overflows and discharge of untreated pollutants to the receiving stream. The design of the Chicago system will permit such an overflow about once in 5 years. However, such overflows ordinarily occur at times when the receiving stream has an unusually high flow, so that the pollution impact will be significantly lessened by dilution. For this reason, less costly measures, such as settling basins to collect the solid wastes, may provide all of the pollution abatement that is economically justified.

Other alternatives which demand attention are instream aeration of streams to provide oxygen for reduction of BOD, extending storm sewer outfalls into large bodies of receiving water some distance away from shore so that storm waters may be conveyed to points where they will not adversely affect water use, and insystem storage of peak combined flows so that they may be temporarily held and treated later.[29]

Feedlot Runoff Control: Promising strides are being made in the control of runoff from animal feedlots. Most States now require registration of feedlots where the size, animal density, proximity to a watercourse, or method of waste disposal is likely to cause water pollution problems. Where investigation reveals actual or potential pollution, control measures are required. Typically, the control consists of diversion structures to prevent surface drainage from passing through the feedlot, plus construction of retention structures to capture wastewater escaping from the feedlot proper. The control system usually includes procedures such as irrigation and landspreading for emptying the contents of the retention

[27] 1972 Act, Section 318(a), 86 Stat. 877, 33 USCA 1328(a).

[28] METROPOLITAN SANITARY DISTRICT OF GREATER CHICAGO, STATE OF ILLINOIS & CITY OF CHICAGO (January 1972). Development of a Flood and Pollution Control Plan for the Chicagoland Area— Evaluation Report of Alternative Systems. Metropolitan Sanitary District of Greater Chicago, Chicago, Ill. ROY F WESTON, INC (August 1970). Combined Sewer Overflow Abatement Alternatives – Washington, D.C. Roy F.

Weston, Inc., West Chester, Pa. SOUTHEAST WISCONSIN REGIONAL PLANNING COMMISSION (October 1971). A Comprehensive Plan for the Milwaukee River Watershed, Planning Report No. 13. Southeast Wisconsin Regional Planning Commission, Waukesha, Wisc.

[29] Computer regulation of combined sewer flows has demonstrated a capability for elimination of more than half of the peak period overflows at reasonable costs in Detroit, Minneapolis, and Seattle.

structures. For roofed or indoor feeding stations, land-spreading of wastes or lagooning are commonly used. Such collection and land disposal systems seem adequate to handle most feedlot waste problems. Another possible control strategy is the employment of land use regulation to restrict the siting of feedlots to areas where they will cause minimal environmental harm.

Control of Nonpoint-Sources

The methods for controlling nonpoint pollution sources are in a more primitive stage of development than the techniques for remedying point-sources. By and large, pollution caused by such processes as soil erosion, mineralization, land runoff, acid drainage, and oil spillage is not susceptible to control through conventional abatement methods; however, some nonpoint pollution is preventable by exercise of control over contributing elements or activities. For example, earthmoving in connection with construction is subject to stringent erosion control restrictions in some States, and the President has recommended Federal legislation to encourage extension of such controls to all States, with Federal enforcement if the States fail to act.[30] The President's recommendations were partially incorporated in the 1972 Act.[31] Similarly, pollution resulting from improper use of pesticides and fertilizers could be controlled by banning, restricting, or requiring more careful appreciation of potential pollutants. However, such direct regulation involves a difficult balancing of economic and environmental values. The 1972 Act wisely provides for studies of pesticide problems,[32] prohibits discharge of toxic chemical, biological, and radioactive wastes,[33] and provides for the establishment of toxic effluent standards.[34]

It is not so much that techniques are not known for direct control to minimize effects of other nonpoint-sources, such as soil erosion from agricultural land, as it is a matter of laissez faire land use policy. A landowner may be taken to court for permitting a field to grow up to noxious weeds or allowing his dog to destroy stock, but there are still many States in which no one has authority to do anything about it if the same landowner allows his topsoil to erode away into the public waters. The collective effect of this environmental impact is extremely serious not only to the landowners but to the public at large. Acceptable soil loss limits should be established and enforced by existing soil conservation or pollution control agencies, or by other State agencies capable of administering such a program.[35]

COSTS

Estimating the costs of pollution control measures needed to achieve compliance with specific water quality standards involves a compounding of uncertainties. The target is vague and it is moving. Under the circumstances, it is possible only to make order-of-magnitude estimates.

The Commission estimates that expenditures for water pollution control in the period 1973 to 1983 to meet existing approved water quality standards established under the 1965 Act 100 percent of the time would be about $206 billion in 1972 dollars, exclusive of the costs of controlling pollution from such nonpoint-sources as agricultural runoff and soil erosion, mine drainage, and watercraft wastes. This figure would cover the costs for new or replacement facilities and additional operating and maintenance costs for municipalities and industries; however, there are alternatives that can be considered for specific situations that may result in substantial reduction of costs.

Meeting the standards by 1983 would require expenditures of about $21 billion annually, which would be unprecedented in the Nation's pollution control history. This amount is about on the same order of magnitude as total annual expenditures for highways by Federal, State, and local governments. Moreover, the Federal cost of $126 billion would be 50 percent greater than the amount of all Federal expenditures on all water projects to date.[36] An undertaking of this magnitude would be required if point discharges are to meet water quality standards established under the 1965 Act 100 percent of the time. The Commission is not convinced, however, that the social and economic benefits of reaching 100 percent compliance will justify the added increment

[30] NIXON, Richard (1972). The President's 1972 Environmental Program. Weekly Compilation of Presidential Documents 8(7):218-227. February 14, 1972.

[31] 1972 Act, Section 304(e), 86 Stat. 852, 33 USCA 1314(e).

[32] Ibid., Section 104(l)(2), 86 Stat. 822, 33 USCA 1254(l)(2).

[33] Ibid., Section 301(f), 86 Stat. 846, 33 USCA 1311(f).

[34] Ibid., Section 307(a), 86 Stat. 856, 33 USCA 1317(a).

[35] The State of Iowa currently has such a program. See Iowa Code 467A.42-53 (1971).

[36] The Commission's staff estimated total Federal expenditures on all water projects to date to be $87.7 billion in 1972 dollars. See Table 16-4.

TABLE 4-1. – Estimate of total costs of abatement of point-sources of pollution, 1973-83[1]

Item	Expenditures Required (billions of dollars at 1972 price levels)	
	To Meet Water Quality Standards Established Under the 1965 Act 100% of the Time	To Achieve "Best Known Technology"
Municipal		
Collection sewers	$ 40	$ 40
Wastewater treatment plants	15	40
Storm water systems	113	234
Added operation & maintenance costs to 1983	16	38
TOTAL	$184	$352
Industrial		
Capital investment	$ 10	$ 49
Added operation & maintenance costs to 1983	12	59
TOTAL	$ 22	$108
TOTAL	$206	$460

[1] Summarized from Table 16-12, Chapter 16, and excluding costs of controlling waste heat and agricultural and other nonpoint-sources of pollution.

of costs required. It should be noted that more than half of the costs would be for control of pollution from storm water in urban areas, the economic or social value of which may vary greatly between different places. Before a 100 percent compliance program is undertaken, a careful analysis should be made to determine the usefulness of a uniform national storm water treatment program in comparison with its enormous costs and its adverse impacts on other resources.

As indicated in Table 4-1, the Commission estimates that implementation of a pollution abatement policy calling for the use of the "best known" technology for treatment of all municipal and industrial wastes by 1983 would require expenditures totaling about $460 billion through 1983. Implementation of a true "no discharge" policy if, in fact, such a policy could be implemented, would undoubtedly cost several times as much. For this massive investment, the Nation would realize only marginal gains in the uses that could be made of its waters. Some idea

of the cost of moving from the present water quality standards approach to a no discharge policy is provided by Figure 4-1 prepared by the U.S. Environmental Protection Agency, which shows how costs increase with great rapidity as the level of treatment increases. More than half of the costs of total pollution control would be expended to remove the last 1 percent of pollutants.

In controlling water pollution, benefits are subject to severely diminishing returns. As indicated on the graph, to clean up the last 1 percent of pollution involves a doubling of the very large costs of eliminating the first 99 percent. These enormous costs of achieving the no discharge goal must be viewed in terms of the sacrifices society would be obliged to make in other social demands such as housing, education, medical care, slum clearance, full employment, and price stability. Moreover, large amounts of scarce natural resources and energy would have to be expended to clean up the last increment of pollution. Finally, the expenditure of such additional

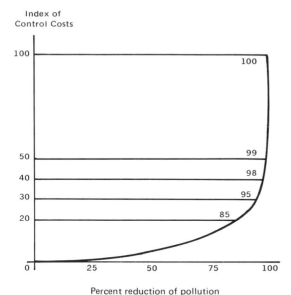

Figure 4-1.—Total control costs as a function of effluent control levels

Index of
Control Costs

Percent reduction of pollution

Source: U.S. ENVIRONMENTAL PROTECTION AGENCY (1972). The Economics of Clean Water, Vol. I. U.S. Government Printing Office, Washington, D.C. p. 151.

large amounts of resources to eliminate the last increment would probably have serious offsetting, adverse waste disposal impacts on the Nation's air and land. These adverse impacts on land and air may be far more damaging to the environment than the retention of the last 1 percent of water pollution, particularly in areas where the self-purifying capacity of water is great or where other uses of water are not adversely affected.

On the other hand, polluted water itself causes substantial economic costs. There are losses in income from the closing or curtailment of commercial and sport fisheries, costs to manufacturers of preprocessing excessively polluted waters for industrial purposes or of resorting to higher-cost processes because of polluted water, costs to municipalities and others of purifying water supplies to meet drinking water standards, and losses of potential recreation. There are also costs to society at large from ecological damage to lakes, rivers, estuaries, and other water bodies. Losses and costs associated with not abating pollution, while difficult to compute, are nevertheless very real, and must be taken into account in any

estimate of the benefits and the costs of meeting water quality standards.

The Commission commends the Congress for requiring studies of the environmental impact, and the economic and social costs and benefits of achieving the objectives of the 1972 Act,[37] and for authorizing a thorough study of all aspects of the 1983 goal of reducing waste discharges to whatever level is economically achievable with the best available technology.[38] It is unfortunate that such studies were not undertaken prior to enactment of the 1972 Act itself. We fear that the Nation has already become committed to an enormously costly water quality goal with negative environmental and social ramifications.

STRATEGIES FOR ELIMINATING POLLUTION

Unacceptable levels of pollution are encouraged when society does not require dischargers of wastes to include the costs of adequate waste disposal as a part of their cost of doing business. Because use of water as a waste receptor has been free, the polluter has been allowed to shift these costs to other water users who must accept them in the form of impairment of the quality of the resource. The economic essence of pollution control is the creation of mechanisms to correct the misallocation of waste disposal costs. The issue is how to do it.

Compelling payments by polluters to compensate parties injured by pollution is one technique for forcing the polluter to assume this cost of his economic activity, either by indemnifying injured parties or by modifying his activities to reduce or eliminate the pollution. The traditional method for compelling such payments has been the law suit to recover damages for private nuisance. This approach continues to have great utility in particular cases; however, its after-the-fact character combined with its cost make private litigation an insufficient framework on which to construct a general control program. The need for some form of broad-scale governmental action is commonly conceded.

Government may employ two different, but not mutually exclusive, strategies to produce the necessary reassignment of pollution costs. One

[37] 1972 Act, Section 305(b)(1)(D), 86 Stat. 854, 33 USCA 1315(b)(1)(D).

[38] *Ibid.,* Section 315, 86 Stat. 875, 33 USCA 1325, which establishes a National Study Commission and authorizes $15 million for a thorough study of the economic, social, and environmental effects of achieving or not achieving the effluent limitations and goals set forth in the 1972 Act.

approach is to use economic inducements to bring about desired changes in the disposal of wastes. Regulation, the other approach, involves the application of legal force and economic sanctions to compel compliance with established norms. Traditionally, Federal, State, and local governments have relied almost exclusively on a regulatory approach. Because the problem is economic in origin, economic inducements also deserve attention as a means of encouraging corrective action.

Of course, both economic sanctions and economic incentives will more effectively eliminate pollution when they are elements of a total strategy of water quality management developed as a part of overall land and water resource planning.

Economic Correctives

Some economists believe that correctly applied economic inducements are the best way to achieve prompt and lasting results in cleaning up pollution.[39] Under this philosophy, polluters could either be provided with incentive payments or subsidies to control their wastes or they can be charged for their pollution. Properly tailored, payments and charges are equally capable of correcting a pollution problem. The most important difference between the two is that payments spread the cost of pollution control measures among a broader group (the taxpaying public) while charges force the polluter to assume the costs, and pass them on to the consumers of his goods or services.

Subsidies: Historically, the payment approach to water pollution control has been used in a variety of forms, all of which involve partial subsidies. Examples of partial payments (subsidies) for pollution control include tax incentives such as investment credits and accelerated depreciation, research and development grants to industries, Small Business Administration loans to firms for pollution control equipment, and grants for municipal waste treatment plant construction. The Commission believes subsidies may be necessary for a short time to achieve prompt correction of a major backlog of need and to avoid serious hardships while doing so. Over the long term, however, the use of subsidies to achieve pollution abatement has three serious drawbacks. First, they are premised on an unsound and unfair policy; second, they do not promote economic efficiency;

and third, they do not always achieve the desired results.

Subsidies to stop polluting involve tacit recognition of a right to destroy the quality of water that does not exist if pollution is defined as an interference with the use of water by others. Federal subsidies for pollution abatement unfairly deflect pollution control costs from the consumers of the polluter's goods and services to the general taxpayer. This deflection is not only inequitable, it promotes uneconomic allocation of resources. Subsidizing pollution control expenditures gives benefited producers competitive advantage in pricing their products in the market,[40] and encourages overproduction of their products and underproduction of other nonpolluting products. Subsidies are also uneconomic in the sense that they provide a disincentive to search for nonpolluting least-cost alternatives. Finally, subsidies to industry do not induce changes in waste disposal practices unless the payment is large enough to make the performance desired less costly than other alternatives. Subsidies might, however, be justified in some instances to soften the impact of regulation and thus serve the limited purpose of accelerating changes which already have been mandated.

Construction Grants: The early Federal grant program to assist municipalities in the construction of waste treatment facilities has been an example of a subsidy program which consistently failed to achieve the anticipated water quality improvement objectives. The program was not funded sufficiently to be effective, limitations spelled out in the statutes produced serious inequities, and by frequent increases in grant percentages the program rewarded procrastinators. The 1972 Act attempted to remedy the funding deficiency by establishing higher grant levels financed with contract authority which would not be subject to the vagaries of annual appropriations acts. As pointed out earlier, however, less than half of the 1973 and 1974 authorization has been made available for allotment. The 1972 Act also attempted to remove prior inequities by authorizing reimbursement of a portion of the costs of facilities that had not received the full amount of Federal aid authorized

---

[39] For discussion of this point, see KRIER, JE (1971). The Pollution Problem and Legal Institutions: A Conceptual Overview, UCLA Law Rev. 18:429.

[40] Such a subsidy, on a State or local basis, may be justified as a means of regional self-help, to prevent an industry from moving elsewhere, with resultant economic losses to the region involved which would create a greater burden than the cost of the subsidy. The local tax credits provided by Washington State law is an example of such a program that has been successful.

under the earlier programs but reimbursement author-izations have not yet been fully implemented by appropriation or allocation.

The grant program is a necessary and main step to achieve a timely national water cleanup, but still suffers from the inequity of deflecting up to 75 percent of the capital cost of sewage interceptor and treatment facilities from local users to national taxpayers. Any construction grant program is con-trary to the principle that the cost of pollution control should be borne by the persons directly benefited by the goods or services produced by the activity causing pollution. Under the "polluter pay" principle espoused by the Commission, users of municipal sewers and waste treatment services should ultimately pay the full cost of controlling the pollution they create. The Federal grant program is necessary in order to achieve clean water on a national scale within a relatively short time, but the Commission believes that this program should be terminated at the earliest date consistent with the achievement of the national goal.

One rationalization of a continuing construction grant program financed by the Federal income tax holds that it would be a socially regressive allocation of costs to rely solely on user charges to support the financing of waste disposal facilities.[41] This, it is argued, would saddle lower income groups with a disproportionate share of the cost of cleaning up waters to make them available for recreational use by the more affluent. Funding obtained from the Fed-eral income tax is generally a less regressive source of payment than utility user charges. The Commission believes this fact has particular significance only when the heavy cost of catching up with generations of neglect is sought to be paid in a short time. Over the longer term, however, income redistribution and pollution abatement goals should be considered ob-jectively and independently. There is no adequate

reason why the actual cost of protecting the environ-ment against the harmful effects of human sewage should not be borne proportionally by all contribu-tors of wastes. Properly calculated, sewer charges to urban households for ordinary treatment processes should be a relatively small proportion of the average family's budget.[42] Those who are unable to pay should be assisted by adequate income maintenance programs rather than by burdening the pollution abatement program with income redistribution objec-tives.

Congress has not sought to justify construction grants on income redistribution grounds. The basis for such grants has been the pragmatic goal of getting the job done. Federal grants have been aimed at accelerating needed local action, but the program hasn't worked the way it was intended to.

Deficiencies in Prior Construction Grant Programs – A review of the 15-year history of the prior construc-tion grant programs indicates that some cities have delayed construction while waiting for Federal funds to become available or for grant percentages to increase. Progress on some facilities has been carried on at inefficient rates of construction because Federal funds have not been made available as promised. One General Accounting Office report observes that the majority of States are constructing waste treatment facilities "at a rate consistent with the availability of Federal funds."[43] An illustration which could be cited is the experience of the Ohio River Valley Water Sanitation Commission (ORSANCO) which came into being on June 30, 1948, the date the first Federal Water Pollution Control Act was approved. At that time, 1 percent of the sewage in the Ohio River Basin was treated. ORSANCO operated on the thesis that cities would take action if there were specific standards which could be publicly demonstrated as necessary to achieve ends. The standards permitted

---

[41] NADER TASK FORCE (1971). Water Wasteland, Nader Task Force Report on Water Pollution, David R. Zwick & Marcy Benstock [editors]. Center for the Study of Responsive Law, Washington, D.C. p. XVI-22.

[42] On the average, sewer charges are currently by far the lowest of all public service or utility fees, much less than the cost of water, electricity, or telephone service. See PANEL ON WATER POLLUTION CONTROL (1971). Water Pollution Control in the United States, prepared for the National Water Commission. National Technical Information Service, Springfield, Va., Accession No. PB 212 139. p. 74. The Commission recognizes that in some instances the adoption of its recommendations would

lead to substantial percentage increases in sewerage charges but, as indicated in the Panel report, they would still be far less than charges for other services. Only in the event that unnecessarily stringent requirements for municipal waste treatment were imposed would the resulting costs place a serious burden upon the average household.

[43] COMPTROLLER GENERAL OF THE UNITED STATES (1969). Examination Into the Effectiveness of the Con-struction Grant Program for Abating, Controlling, and Preventing Water Pollution, B-166506. U.S. General Accounting Office, Washington, D.C. p. 15.

alternatives – technical, administrative, and financial – to be adopted, and led to an understanding and acceptance of responsibility by local interests. By the time Federal grants became available in 1956, some 55 percent of the sewage was treated. Since then, however, progress has slowed as cities waited their turn for Federal grants.

A further example of the inadequacies of the prior construction grant program is evidenced by the response of the City of New York to a Federal lawsuit charging the City with violating water quality standards. In the public hearing the City pointed out that the Federal Government had provided only 3 to 4 percent of the funds for the City's treatment plant construction program, instead of the 55 percent promised in the law.[44]

A number of other deficiencies in the grant program can be cited. Like most such restricted-purpose programs, the Federal grant program has not stimulated the search for least-cost solutions, because it encourages municipalities to favor projects that will qualify for Federal funding rather than the most economic solutions. The 1972 Act further accentuates this problem by limiting the discretion of the Administrator of the Environmental Protection Agency to prescribe no less than secondary treatment for all municipal waste treatment.

Prior to the passage of the 1972 Act, some municipalities assisted by the construction grant program offered urban industries waste treatment services at unrealistically low costs.

Congress has attempted to eliminate this deficiency by requiring, as a precedent for any grant, that provision be made for industrial users of the treatment works to pay their proportionate share of operation and maintenance costs of the works plus the construction costs of the portion of the plant allocable to the treatment of their wastes to the extent attributable to the Federal share of the cost of construction.[45]

In summary, the construction grant program has had a mixed effect as an incentive to local action and in some cases has been implemented with uneconomic results. The Federal Water Pollution Control Act should be amended further and administered in such a way as to remedy these deficiencies.

---

[44]NEW YORK TIMES (August 30, 1972). City Blames U.S. for Dirty Water, Says Promises of Funds for Cleanup are Unfulfilled. p. 40.

[45]1972 Act, Section 204(b)(1), 86 Stat. 836, 33 USCA 1284(b)(1).

A Grant Program Terminating in 1983 — The demand for a cleanup of polluted waters on a national scale and at an early date can only be met by a Federal construction grant program which is adequately and reliably funded. The Federal grant program has also created too many inequities and expectations to be terminated summarily at this time. Therefore, the Commission believes that the program should be continued until the Nation has eliminated the present backlog of needed facilities and has fulfilled the reasonable expectations of communities currently relying on Federal funding, including reimbursements. The 1972 Act wisely attempted to restore equity to the Federal grant program by providing partial reimbursement for communities which acted early and at their own cost to clean up their waters. The Commission believes that Federal grant policy should encourage local governments to act promptly and should not reward procrastination. This policy can be implemented by appropriating money to finance the reimbursements, by setting a realizable goal for completion of the program, and by making a determination to cut off further grant eligibility thereafter.

The grant cutoff date must be related to the level of funding which the Congress and the President determine can be appropriated and spent to achieve the clean waters goal. The Commission urges that this goal be accomplished within 10 years if this can be done without impairing programs which the Congress finds more important to the national welfare. Any cutoff date will create some inequities but the Commission believes these will be outweighed by the benefits from putting the Nation's municipal waste disposal systems on a sound long-term economic and fiscal footing. The establishment of the grant cutoff date will provide an incentive for cities to expedite construction of treatment plants, so as to qualify for the grants, and will therefore result in a much more effective program. After the cutoff date, responsibility for construction, maintenance, operation, repair, replacement, and improvement of municipal sewage disposal systems should be borne by local government and paid for by user charges.

During the period the program continues, its effectiveness can be greatly enhanced if the historic unevenness of funding can be eliminated, so that States and municipalities can plan construction projects on a rational basis. Underfunding of grants impedes progress toward achieving the goals of the water quality standards program and cuts out much of the ground beneath enforcement proceedings against both industries and municipalities. The contract authority provisions of the 1972 Act could provide a basis for at least partially solving this problem, if adequate amounts are authorized and made available.

Federal policy on grants should specifically require that municipalities shall have established cost-based pricing of all future municipal waste collection and treatment services through local assessments and user charges by the time the cutoff date is reached. Full development of regional waste management systems should be encouraged where they can lead to better resource management, environmental protection, and economies of scale. Grant funds should not be disbursed to construct facilities which lack cost effectiveness from the standpoint of regional problem-solving.

The points enumerated above are addressed with varying effectiveness by the construction grant provisions of the 1972 Act. No cutoff date was established, but the Act provides a foundation for eventual termination of construction grants by requiring that each applicant for Federal grant funds adopt a charge system for all of its waste treatment service that will pay for replacement of facilities as well as for their operation and maintenance.[46]

Effluent Charges: An effluent charge is a direct charge for pollution which is permitted to be discharged into a natural watercourse. Effluent charges are designed to remedy the misallocation of resources which occurs when certain users are allowed to impose on others a part of the costs associated with their use.[47] Such external diseconomies are undesirable in an economy which is otherwise controlled by the marketplace, because they distort the prices of goods and services in which water use is a cost factor. Effluent charges are designed to remedy this defect by imposing a cost on polluters based on the harm caused by their wastes. If the charges are set correctly, they provide an incentive to waste producers to reduce their discharge of wastes or else indemnify society so substantially as to have it elect to suffer the pollution and enjoy the compensation. If society is dissatisfied with the compensation and the pollution continues, the charges should be set higher.

Several European nations have attempted to use or are considering using effluent charges along with other types of service charges to provide funds for managing water quality.[48] A system of effluent charges was authorized in 1969 in the State of Vermont to provide pollution-reduction incentives to dischargers who cannot comply with the terms of their discharge permits to change their processes, but the State has not yet been able to work out the details and put it into effect.[49]

To be effective, effluent charges would have to be set at levels required to bring about a reduction in discharge of pollutants sufficient to permit established water quality standards to be met. Such variable effluent charges present administrative problems and could in some cases permit costs to be inequitably imposed upon a downstream user of polluted waters. These problems may be avoided and the same results achieved by a system of regulations adequately enforced by injunctive relief and civil and criminal penalties. The Commission would be opposed to establishing effluent charges under circumstances where they might permit the destruction of the public usefulness of a body of water in exchange for the payment of a fee.

Assertions that effluent charges will result in better control of pollution are as yet unproved. Where roughly the same or better results, in terms of water quality improvement, can be achieved through regulation as through effluent charges, it is appropriate to continue our efforts to refine regulatory techniques.

User and Service Charges: A user charge is a charge for the discharge of pollutants into a waste disposal system. User charges have long provided the basis for revenue bond financing for many types of public facilities in most local communities. Municipal waste treatment, with its captive customers, is an ideal enterprise to put on a self-sustaining basis. Both amortized capital costs and operating costs are easily apportioned among consumers of the system's services through user charges, including assessments against new users to pay for their share of the cost of the facility which serves them. Such a public utility approach to municipal waste treatment is preferable under both economic and equity criteria and it is now

---

[46] *Ibid.*

[47] See generally KNEESE, Allen V & BOWER, Blair T (1968). Managing Water Quality: Economics, Technology, Institutions. Published for Resources for the Future, Inc., by The Johns Hopkins Press, Baltimore, Md.

[48] *Ibid.*

[49] U.S. ENVIRONMENTAL PROTECTION AGENCY Water Pollution Control Research Series (1972). Development of a State Effluent Charge System, Vermont Department of Water Resources, Project No. 16110 GNT 02/72.

Effluent charges would have to be set high enough to prevent environmental degradation

in practice in many cities where a user service charge reflects the cost of the services provided. This is the principle in the Ruhr Basin in Germany where a user charge for service provided is imposed to raise money for construction, operation, and maintenance of facilities, and in cities in the United States such as Philadelphia, Los Angeles, Detroit, and Baltimore. Some cities, such as Racine, Wisconsin, and East Chicago, Indiana, have legislative policy which encourages industrial connections and uses a four-point control to determine if industrial wastes are accepted for treatment: (1) it must be cheaper for the city to treat the wastewater than industry; (2) the wastewater must be compatible with the municipal waste in the treatment plant either with or without prior treatment; (3) monitoring controls and effective measures to prevent concentrated discharges (slugs) that might temporarily overload or bypass the treatment plant must be provided; and (4) industry must pay the added cost of the treatment.

Such variable pricing of municipal collection and treatment services to industrial dischargers based on volume and strength of wastes has proved to be an effective incentive to reducing industrial waste-loads.[50] The Commission believes this practice should be encouraged, with charges for effluents at such levels as to encourage dischargers to install pretreatment facilities or to change processes so as to reduce wastes which might overtax the capacity or are incompatible with the processes of the treatment plant. The Commission recognizes, however, that there are severe difficulties and high costs involved in administering any system of charges based on quality of effluents. Such a system requires a level of detailed information about waste discharges and their effects on other water uses that is still not completely available in many areas, and a very complex accounting system, to properly assess the charges.

---

[50] U.S. COUNCIL ON ENVIRONMENTAL QUALITY (1971). Environmental Quality, The Second Annual Report of the Council on Environmental Quality. U.S. Government Printing Office, Washington, D.C. p. 137.

Regulation

For the reasons stated above a practical and effective pollution abatement program must be based on a legal regulatory system which effectively prohibits dischargers from disposing of wastes which have received inadequate treatment. One writer has described legal regulation as "mutual coercion, mutually agreed upon."[51] For such a regulatory system to work, it must impose understandable and enforceable limitations on all dischargers and must find and penalize failure to comply with such limitations fairly but relentlessly. The power to regulate point-sources of water pollution is possessed by a multitude of local governments, by specialized agencies in all 50 States, by a handfull of interstate agencies, and by the Federal Government. Although for some years public regulation has been the prevalent means of attempting to cause dischargers to improve their performance in waste treatment, the basic ingredients for an effective system of legal regulation have only recently been created in most States and at the Federal level. For years Federal and interstate pollution control programs were not well designed to utilize coercive regulatory techniques. At the State and local level, the potential for strong enforcement has long existed, but in most areas only in the past few years has it been utilized effectively.

The history of pollution control in the United States reveals that public regulation has passed through a series of evolutionary stages. Public regulation started out as a strictly local enterprise in which agencies concerned with water supply, health, sanitation, and other related activities carried out modest programs within their own limited domains. In the early 1900's, as water pollution worsened and need for some centralized regulation became apparent, various State departments whose work involved water quality matters were given regulatory powers. When separate, uncoordinated regulation by several State agencies proved unequal to the task of handling the growing size and complexity of the pollution problem, the seeds were sown for development of the modern centralized State pollution control agency.

About this same time, State pollution control officials began to recognize that some problems on interstate and border waters were beyond their control because they originated in other States. Two regulatory responses appropriate for dealing with extra-State problems are voluntary arrangements among the several States and creation of a Federal authority. Both were proposed in the mid-1930's, but the use of interstate compacts developed ahead of Federal regulation. After an initial flowering, the interstate arrangement has failed to realize the hope of its advocates and has gradually faded in relative importance in the face of escalating Federal activity.

The Federal role, as created in the first legislation in 1948, was primarily a supportive one. Federal funds and technical assistance were applied to strengthen local, State, and interstate water quality programs. The States responded unevenly to the stimuli of Federal assistance and the threat of Federal intervention. Some States developed strong aggressive programs while others languished. When this style of Federal involvement did not produce desired results, the Federal Government embarked on a series of steps expanding Federal activity.

The first was the Federal involvement in financing municipal treatment plants under the 1956 amendments to the Federal Water Pollution Control Act. This program also proved to be inadequate and Congress adopted the Water Quality Act of 1965, which stepped up Federal financing and for the first time laid the framework for a coordinated national program of water quality regulation. Under the 1965 Act, the States were encouraged to create receiving water standards for all waters. The standards are intended to be sufficiently high to protect existing and future uses. Through regulations adopted in implementing the 1965 Act and conditions imposed in the disbursement of Federal funds, Federal administrators sought to create a corollary national policy of best practicable treatment of all wastes discharged to water. Both legislative and administrative actions placed severe strains on State-Federal relations in water quality control.[52]

Federal pressure coupled with an awakening of grassroots concern for environmental values unquestionably has acted to spur most State programs to greatly improved regulatory performance. Nevertheless, impatience with results being achieved has led to far-reaching Federal legislation which changes dramatically the pollution control role of the Federal Government.

---

[51] HARDIN G (1968). The Tragedy of the Commons. Science 162(3859):1243-1248, December 13, 1968.

[52] See U.S. CONGRESS, House, Committee on Public Works (1971). Water Pollution Control Legislation—1971 (Oversight of Existing Program), Serial 92-10, 92nd Congress, 1st Session. U.S. Government Printing Office, Washington, D.C. pp. 266, 400, 423, 435.

Improved Planning

Control of water pollution will increasingly be accomplished through continuous management of water quality within basins and other regional or metropolitan frameworks. Creation of such management systems heightens the need for comprehensive water quality planning. Without concerted planning effort, attainment of water quality goals will be delayed and costly.

One past deficiency with some water quality planning has been its narrow focus. This deficiency has manifested itself in several forms. First, the search for alternatives has sometimes been foreclosed by the arbitrary imposition of a single strategy or method of control. For example, a requirement that all point-sources of discharge within a basin employ secondary treatment processes precludes consideration of other alternatives for achieving the desired water quality at lower costs. A "no discharge" goal would likewise inhibit achievement of the least costly method of achieving water quality standards. To be fully effective, planning must include adequate and continuous monitoring of water quality and full consideration of all alternatives for achieving specific goals, including such approaches as regulatory changes, pricing techniques, regional systems, controlled use of the capacity of flowing water to purify itself, low flow augmentation, land use controls, as well as different methods and levels of waste treatment. The advantage of preserving the widest range of planning options is demonstrated in the Delaware estuary, where employment of a mix of alternative approaches led to the adoption of a plan to achieve the requisite quality level at two-thirds the estimated cost of uniform secondary treatment.

A second deficiency stems from the planning of water quality programs in isolation from related planning activities. Water quality planning should be a composite of water supply planning, other water resource planning, sewage disposal and storm water drainage planning, land use planning, and planning efforts of other environmental agencies handling air quality and solid waste problems.[53] Coordination of water quality planning with other types of planning is difficult, but failing to recognize and consider the interrelationships will retard the effectiveness of all affected programs. For example, the future likelihood of an extensive need to reuse treated wastewater makes important the integration of planning for wastewater treatment and municipal and industrial water supply. As another example, planning which fails to consider total environmental impacts in choosing waste disposal methods incurs the risk of diverting a waste from one medium where it causes slight environmental harm to another medium where its impact is severe. In an absolute sense, a "no discharge" goal for waterborne pollutants could represent an institutionalization of this failure.

For example, an arbitrary decision to eliminate discharge of waste material into watercourses will require tertiary or advanced waste treatment processes that will require more use of construction materials, more power and chemicals for operation, and more sludge that will have to be put somewhere. If it is burned, it may pollute the atmosphere. If it is placed on land, it may pollute ground water basins. The same problem arises if discharge of waste heat into watercourses is prohibited. Total recycling of cooling water through cooling towers or ponds will cause an evaporative loss twice that from cooling in the receiving water body. The increase in evaporative loss will cause a reduction in the flow of water downstream; thus, where maintenance of low flow is critical, the no discharge policy creates problems. Also, more power will be required for operation of the cooling towers, with greater depletion of fuel reserves, more solid wastes to be disposed of, and larger requirements for chemicals.[54] Thus, uniform policies to eliminate discharges into water without first determining their effect and the consequences of alternatives to reduce or eliminate the impact may very well, in fact, cause a much greater deterioration of the total environment.

One other deficiency in a few existing water quality plans has been a lack of coordination between planning activities and the information needs of pollution control programs. Long-range plans frequently do not provide adequate guidance in day-to-day regulatory activities or help with decisions as to the siting of plants. Large-scale and long-term planning efforts need to be continued and improved, but for the next few years extra emphasis should be placed on the development of immediate-impact plans for local basins or metropolitan areas.

Water quality planning has a long history of undersupport but the importance of better planning is beginning to be recognized in State and Federal budgets. A major investment is needed to assure that

---

[53] See Chapter 10 for discussion of this point.

[54] See Chapter 5, Section G.

adequate planning underlies the proposed acceleration in pollution control measures. To use planning moneys most effectively requires careful identification of rational planning units; renewed commitment to interagency coordination; development of a better system for the collection, storage, and retrieval of water quality data; the refinement of arrangements to receive public inputs; creation of procedures for periodic program assessment; and a number of other matters discussed in more detail in Chapter 10.

The 1972 Act attempts to cover all of these matters and more. It authorizes $300 million for grants to support the development of areawide waste treatment management plans in urban and other regions with substantial water quality problems[55] and $200 million for basin planning under the Water Resources Planning Act.[56] The areawide waste treatment management concept called for in the 1972 Act represents a laudable effort to overcome cost-effectiveness deficiencies encountered in the prior Federal construction grant program. Under the new arrangement, Federal waste treatment grants can go only to a designated waste treatment management agency which must have the capability to implement the approved plan for the area within its jurisdiction. Unfortunately, the 1972 Act succumbed to the temptation to prescribe the nature and form of local organization. Federal prescription of local agency form is unsound in concept and may serve to inhibit or warp desired areawide action. The form of intrastate planning and operating agencies should be determined by the States. Handling of interstate basin planning through the Water Resources Council as provided in the 1972 Act should assure integration with other water resources planning as recommended by the Commission.

WHO SHOULD PAY?

The total costs of eliminating water pollution are staggering. However, realization of the magnitude of overall costs should not obscure a fundamental issue that must be resolved. What is to be the formula for assessing costs among the citizenry? Until recently, Federal financing played a minor role in pollution control. Of total capital expenditures for public waste treatment facilities and sewers from the time records began to be kept through June 30, 1971 only $4.9 billion out of a total of $84 billion (adjusted to 1972

price levels) were financed by Federal funds.[57] In recent years, with increased public demand for clean water, the Federal Government has assumed a larger portion of the financing burden.

One solution to the problem of allocating the costs of waste treatment is to treat it as a collective one and to rely extensively on the Federal income tax system to provide the necessary funds. To the extent that the national interest is served and our common physical and mental well-being are at stake, this approach has some merit. Indeed, only Federal funding is capable of raising the large amounts needed to implement a nationwide clean up on a timely basis. National action also minimizes obstacles to investments in water quality projects which have been raised because of local fiscal constraints and political resistance. However, removing the investment burden from the local level has the disadvantage of blurring important cost-benefit decisions that are most squarely faced when both the benefits and costs accrue to an identifiable community or region, and decisionmakers know they are spending their own money and not someone else's. Also, the historical variability in Federal appropriations for the small portion of pollution control programs which have been borne by the Federal Government to date has impaired orderly development of the program. Appropriations lagged behind authorizations in two-thirds of the years since the Federal construction grant program was initiated in Fiscal Year 1957, and less than three-fourths of the $4.3 billion authorized through 1971 was appropriated. Futhermore, less than half of the contract authority authorized by the Congress in the 1972 Act[58] has been allocated by the Administrator. The legality of withholding these funds is being tested in the courts and the U.S. District Court in Washington, D.C. on May 8, 1973 ruled that impoundment is illegal.

An even more serious difficulty with the early Federal construction grant programs lies in the inequity of forcing taxpayers in communities which had acted on their own to remedy local pollution problems to help pay the costs for other communities which have been dilatory. This inequity will be remedied if the reimbursements authorized by the 1972 Act[59] are implemented.

---

[57] PANEL ON WATER POLLUTION CONTROL (1971). Water Pollution Control in the United States, prepared for the National Water Commission. National Technical Information Service, Springfield, Va., Accession No. PB 212 139. p. 17.

[58] Section 207, 86 Stat. 839, 33 USCA 1287.

[59] Section 206, 86 Stat. 838, 33 USCA 1286.

---

[55] 1972 Act, Section 208, 86 Stat. 839, 33 USCA 1288.

[56] Ibid., Section 209, 86 Stat. 843, 33 USCA 1289.

"Fish-eye" camera view of secondary clarifier at Des Moines, Iowa, sewage treatment plant

The most equitable and economically efficient association of cost with benefits over the long term will be produced by assigning the costs of preventing water pollution to those whose wastes cause pollution. Under such a "polluter pay" principle, industries and municipalities would be expected to assume the economic burden of controlling their wastes. Under our economic system, costs thus incurred will be passed along to consumers in the form of higher prices for goods and services.

Thus, the ultimate user of the products and services will pay the costs of preventing the pollution which his consumption would otherwise cause. In nearly all cases the "polluter pay" principle yields both the fairest and the least-cost results. Except in situations like the present backlog in municipal waste

treatment plant construction or cases where other social policies countervail against it, the Commission urges consistent application of this principle in distributing the costs of water quality management.

WHO SHOULD REGULATE?

Regulation involves several different types of governmental activity. The three clearest phases of regulation are policy formulation, translation of policies into programs, and program administration. All three need not be concentrated in one level of government, and they often are not so concentrated. Analysis of the current national effort in regulating pollution shows that the formulation of broad policy on national water quality has been largely taken over by the Federal Government. Under the 1972 Act, responsibility for general design of programs is also assumed by the Federal Government, but responsibility for implementation, planning, and program administration is assigned to the States. All responsibilities may be assumed by Federal authorities if the States do not perform them satisfactorily. Thus, on the surface it appears Congress did not intend the new water quality program to be a Federal undertaking, but rather intended a joint venture in which implementation of a national water quality policy is carried out by State and local agencies within federally established guidelines. However, at the moment, State and local decisionmaking is substantially constrained by the threat of duplicative Federal regulatory activity and the need to meet arduous conditions attached to Federal grant programs. The Commission believes the concept of shared responsibility is fundamentally sound, and that with modification to redirect program objectives and to reduce the opportunities for unilateral Federal action and thereby restore State and local initiative, it represents the best arrangement for achieving the widest range of social objectives.

Prior to the 1972 Act, the Federal Government had been assigned a role subsidiary to that of the States in the national program for water quality improvement. The Federal Government was expected to provide leadership and support necessary to assure competent State and local performance of their primary functions. In carrying out its responsibilities for research, financial assistance, and enforcement, the Federal agency was forced to search continuously for an optimal balance between offers of assistance, demands for performance, and assertions of Federal authority. Under such circumstances, it was unrealistic to expect a high degree of intergovernmental harmony; the best to be hoped for was creative tension. As noted earlier, the Commission believes this cooperative approach is sound and recommends its restoration. The arrangement is not without defects, but the major problems centered not in the concept but in its implementation by all levels of government.

There are valid reasons to support the cooperative approach to solution of the Nation's water quality problems. Although the problem of pollution is nationwide, conditions of pollution are local phenomena with local causes. The most noticeable effects of pollution are also primarily local although some of the most critical effects, such as those from heavy metals and certain types of pesticides, are cumulative and are felt over long distances. Marked differences in local water conditions and pollution sources render unproductive any regulatory scheme which pursues nationwide uniformity as a major program goal.

The regulatory approach needed is one with sufficient flexibility to allow adjustment of policies and programs to fit a wide variety of local situations. The effectiveness of such regulation is enhanced if the decisionmaker is familiar with the problems and the social and economic milieu in which they arise, and has freedom to select from various technical approaches that one which is most suitable for local conditions. Under such conditions, sound political theory supports the notion that the level of government closest to the problem should deal with it, if competent to do so.

State and local governments possess the competence to handle most water quality problems. While this competence has been underutilized in the past, largely because adverse effects of pollution are often felt downstream or out of State, public opinion and Federal pressures are leading to significant changes. Recent studies of State and local pollution control programs document a new resolve to regulate forcefully and comprehensively.[60] These studies belie assertions that State and local governments are unable to deal effectively with water quality problems. It appears that a satisfactory division of governmental responsibility for pollution control was developing prior to the 1972 Act. It would be unwise to implement the 1972 Act in such a way as to jeopardize the State-Federal partnership before it can be fairly tested.

IMPROVING THE EFFECTIVENESS OF POLLUTION ABATEMENT PROGRAMS

Federal Activities

Research: Federal preeminence in the organization, conduct, and funding of research and development of pollution control technology is considered desirable by many observers because of the commonality of

---

[60] HINES, N WILLIAM (1971). Public Regulation of Water Quality in the United States, prepared for the National Water Commission. National Technical Information Service, Springfield, Va., Accession No. PB 208 309; and COMPTROLLER GENERAL OF THE UNITED STATES (1972). Water Pollution Abatement Program: Assessment of Federal and State Enforcement Efforts, B-166506. U.S. General Accounting Office, Washington, D.C.

the problems. The performance of the present research program, however, has drawn some criticism,
and it is difficult to conclude that the money has
been well spent. Although the Federal agency has its
own network of laboratories, about two-thirds of the
$60 million annual water pollution control research
budget is spent on out-of-house research under grants
and contract. Emphasis has been on the application
of known technology to new purposes. Consequently,
few technological innovations have been produced by
the Federal research effort. In the past, the concentration on applied research was probably justified by
the need to encourage fuller utilization of proven
processes; however, accelerating demands for higher
levels of waste removal create a need for shifting
more research emphasis to the search for new
technology.

Financial Assistance: Federal financial assistance is
provided in the form of annual program grants to
State agencies, short-term grants to planning groups,
and construction grants to local communities to help
build public waste treatment plants. Program and
planning grants are authorized to be significantly
increased in the 1972 Act to keep pace with rising
costs and increased workloads. As discussed earlier,
the prior construction grant program was not successful, and the appropriations fell far short of the
authorizations. The 1972 Act authorizes much higher
grant levels, a larger Federal share, and allocation of
grants on the basis of need, but it is not adequate to
achieve the goals set forth in the Act. The National
Water Commission proposes achievable goals, adequate and equitable funding to accomplish such goals,
and an eventual transition from a Federal-State
subsidy program to one which allocates the costs of
pollution control to polluters through utility-type
charges which will facilitate economic efficiency.

Regulation: Before the 1972 Act, the Federal regulatory effort was concentrated primarily in three areas:
(a) general abatement proceedings, (b) establishment
and enforcement of water quality standards, and
(c) implementation of the Refuse Act permit program. The Federal agency also has special responsibilities in the control of spills of oil and other
hazardous substances and in the prevention of water
pollution from Federal installations. Except for the
Refuse Act suits, the Federal regulatory process was
handicapped by complicated procedures with lengthy
built-in delays. The 1972 Act dramatically expanded
and streamlined Federal regulatory activity.

The 1972 Act is by far the most complex and
comprehensive Federal entry into the field of environmental regulation. The water quality policy
announced in this Act represents a radical departure
from prior theory. In contrast to the traditional
regulatory purpose of preventing waste dischargers
from interfering with other beneficial water uses, the
newly established purpose of the control effort is to
eliminate all man-caused alteration of the chemical,
physical, biological, and radiological integrity of
water.

The mainspring of the statute is a system for
controlling point-sources of pollution through the
establishment and enforcement of increasingly more
stringent direct limitations on the quality of effluents. Effluent limitations are based primarily on
the technological and economic feasibility of waste
reduction rather than local water quality needs. The
water quality standards established in response to the
1965 Water Quality Act are retained as a floor under
the new effluent limitations and are expanded to
include all navigable waters.

Depending on the character of the discharge,
effluent limitations are required to be based on a
number of factors, including existing and subsequently established water quality standards and
federally established toxicity limits and pretreatment
standards. In addition, if adequate technology is
available and a favorable relationship exists between
economic and social costs and benefits, effluent
limitations must be set to attain or maintain an
overall water quality standard which provides for the
protection of public water supplies, agricultural and
industrial uses, and the protection of a balanced
population of shellfish, fish, and wildlife, and allows
recreational activities in and on the water. Achievement of this water quality goal is targeted for 1983.
New sources of pollution must immediately comply
with federally established performance standards
which reflect the greatest degree of effluent reduction
achievable by use of the best available demonstrated
control technology, processes, and operating
methods, including a no discharge standard where
practicable.[61]

Under the Act, effluent limitations are tightened in
a predetermined sequence. By 1977, all dischargers,
except publicly owned treatment facilities, are expected, at a minimum, to employ the best practicable

[61] 1972 Act, Section 306(a)(1), 86 Stat. 854, 33 USCA
1316(a) (1).

control technology currently available. If more stringent limitations are required to meet local water quality standards, they must be met. Publicly owned treatment works must use at least secondary treatment by 1977. The final upgrading benchmark mandated by the Act is 1983, by which time all dischargers, except publicly owned treatment works, are required to apply the best available technology economically achievable. By the same date, publicly owned treatment works must be employing the best practicable water treatment technology. The new Act does not, however, say how its stated goal of elimination of all discharges of pollutants by 1985 is to be achieved, and this is one of the great weaknesses of the Act.

A national pollutant discharge elimination system is created as the vehicle for implementing the new effluent-limitations approach. The Act makes unlawful the discharge into water of any pollutant without a discharge permit and then sets out detailed procedures for the operation of the permit program. Permits will set forth specific upper limits for each potentially polluting constituent of a discharger's waste stream. Where desired waste reduction cannot be accomplished immediately, the permit will establish an abatement schedule for the discharger. The permit will also require each discharger to perform such monitoring and reporting functions as are needed to check on his compliance with permit conditions.

The 1972 Act seeks to provide maximum opportunity for public participation in the pollution control effort by requiring public hearings at key points in the implementation of the permit system and by assuring that water quality information, discharge requirements, and monitoring data be made available to the public.

The Act contemplates that the permit program will be a joint Federal-State effort. Specific provision is made for a State-by-State delegation of responsibility for administering the national permit program. However, if a State will not or cannot carry out the objectives of the program, the Environmental Protection Agency (EPA) may administer the program directly. To receive the delegation, the States must demonstrate the capability to fully carry out the objectives of the national permit program as specified in the 1972 Act and as further developed in guidelines issued by EPA. Even though responsibility for administering the permit program is delegated, State processing of permits is subject to review by EPA and State permits may be vetoed on a permit-by-permit

basis if the Administrator believes it is necessary to achieve requirements of the 1972 Act or regulations issued thereunder.[62]

Prompt and tough enforcement procedures are set out to assure compliance with the new permit program and with other requirements under the Act. The enforcement process under the new permit system eliminates a longstanding deficiency in enforcement of pollution abatement laws by shifting to the polluter the burden of proving that his discharges are in conformance with the law. Upon finding a violation of the Act, Federal authorities are authorized to pursue alternative enforcement tactics. Civil relief may be sought immediately in the courts, or an order may be issued directing the polluter to comply with the Act, or a notice of violation may be served on the polluter. In the latter two cases, the affected State agency is also notified. Uncorrected violations may result in the imposition of civil penalties of up to $10,000 per day and criminal fines of up to $50,000 per day and jail terms of up to 2 years for repeated offenses.

Improvements Needed: The Commission believes that the 1972 Act represents a praiseworthy attempt by Congress to provide a more effective program of water quality control and enhancement. However, in the Commission's view, there are certain provisions of the Act, particularly with reference to goals, regulation, permit systems, grants, Federal-State relations, and accountability which must be revised or clarified if the laudable purpose outlined by the Congress is to be attained without disrupting ongoing successful water quality programs and without creating unnecessary economic and social hardships and environmental damage.

First, as was discussed earlier, the shift away from reliance on water quality standards and economic practicability as the bases for regulation should be reversed. The new Act's establishment of a no discharge goal to be achieved through application of the best available waste treatment technology is unsound in theory and will prove unworkable in practice. The Congress should revise this misconceived goal now and reaffirm its commitment to the water quality standards approach and economically practicable minimum treatment requirements.

Second, if the Congress intended the new national permit system to be operated by the States, as we believe it did, a longer time must be allowed and greater assistance provided to the States to facilitate

[62] *Ibid.*, Section 402(d), 86 Stat. 882, 33 USCA 1342(d).

Enforcement of new water pollution control laws should prevent this type of waste disposal

their acceptance of the delegation to administer the program. We cannot foresee all the ramifications of the current plan to begin operation of the permit program at the Federal level and later shift responsibility to the States, but it seems likely that both the public interest and regulated dischargers will suffer from the transition of an ongoing program. The Commission recommends a change in the legislative and administrative deadlines which create the present urgency to initiate the issuance of permits by EPA. The permit program should be implemented with all deliberate speed, but wherever possible the continuing responsibility for issuing and enforcing permits for the waters of each State should be fixed prior to commencement of permit issuance. Review of the stringent guidelines and detailed standards established under the 1972 Act and promulgated by EPA convinces the Commission that a workable delegation process could be modeled on the mechanism utilized under the 1965 Water Quality Act to establish water quality standards, with appropriate tightening to eliminate unnecessary delays.

Third, the experience in State-Federal relations gained in implementing the water quality standards program under the 1965 Act convinces the Commission it is undesirable to create, as does the 1972 Act,[63] an unqualified power to commence unilateral Federal enforcement procedures in respect to a program primarily administered by the States. A strong Federal enforcement capability is needed as a backstop to State regulation, but it should be invoked only after State enforcement authorities demonstrate that they are unable or unwilling to carry out the necessary enforcement action. Except for cases of emergency, notice to the affected State and expiration without corrective action of a short, but reasonable, time period should be made a prerequisite to initiation of Federal enforcement procedures.

Fourth, Federal grants for municipal pollution control facilities must be made available by the Congress and the President in amounts sufficient to

[63]*Ibid.,* Section 309(a)(3), 86 Stat. 859, 33 USCA 1319(a)(3).

achieve the national water quality goals. Water quality standards set pursuant to the policies recommended by this Commission cannot be achieved in the next 10 years with the level of funding authorized in the 1972 Act. The Congress substantially underestimated the cost of achieving the goals described in the 1972 Act and the executive impoundment of funds has further cut the congressionally authorized moneys by more than half. The result is a serious conflict between federally mandated requirements and Federal appropriations and allocations to meet those requirements. The waste treatment facilities which are needed will only be accomplished by a Federal grant program if the funding promised to perform Federal grant commitments is made available. If Federal financing continues to lag behind Federal promises, the grant program will become increasingly inequitable and local incentive will again be weakened.

Fifth, the 1972 Act suffers from absolute legislative mandates which do not give the Administrator of the Environmental Protection Agency the discretion necessary to adopt the flexible grant requirements needed to meet different local water and waste conditions. The Administrator should be authorized to encourage those local expenditures which will produce the greatest improvement in water quality and constitute the most effective use of limited funds. The uniform requirement for secondary treatment could cause clean water moneys which have been squeezed out of a tight budget to be expended for facilities with minimal impact upon the receiving waters while leaving raw sewage outlets without interception. An examination of the effectiveness of secondary treatment on the Missouri River by the General Accounting Office in 1971 pointed out the importance of applying those pollution abatement techniques which will do the most good.[64] The history of funding to date demonstrates that available moneys are seriously limited. Any realistic grant program operating under budget constraints should provide the most cost-effective solution for each situation.

Sixth, a basic issue which the 1972 Act fails to clarify is the matter of accountability. Stated simply, the issues are what level of government should be assigned responsibility for deciding to what degree

water quality will be protected and who should create and administer the regulatory programs necessary to achieve this protection. Imprecision in the assignment of these responsibilities and attendant misunderstandings have been a major reason for lack of progress to date. The 1972 Act speaks ambiguously to these questions; the Commission believes they should be faced squarely and resolved once and for all, as discussed hereinafter under the heading "Permits".

Finally, the 1972 Act sets a 1983 standard for effluent limitations of "best available technology economically achievable." If this means the same thing as the 1977 standard of "best practicable control technology currently available," it should be deleted as unnecessary. If "best available" is intended to mean that discharges can be required to install new pollution control facilities each time a technological advance is made, the provision should be applicable only when receiving water quality standards require it. A moving effluent standard not related to the achievement of desired water quality will unnecessarily increase costs paid by consumers and could discourage producers from making necessary major investments in water pollution abatement facilities which require many years to amortize.

Interstate Agencies

The presence and performance of interstate agencies created to handle water quality management in waters which cross State lines is a noteworthy facet of the total picture of governmental activity. The theoretical attractiveness of using regional agencies to control water quality throughout an entire watershed or basin is recognized, and such agencies have been created for several major basins. As presently constituted and operated, however, interstate pollution control agencies play a much less important role in the water quality regulation than do local, State, and Federal agencies. Elsewhere in this report specific recommendations are made for the improvement of such interstate agencies.[65]

State Programs

State programs have undergone dramatic changes in the past 10 years. Although universal adoption of water quality standards has provided a common denominator among State programs, substantial variety exists in the development of such key

---

[64] COMPTROLLER GENERAL OF THE UNITED STATES (1972). Alternatives to Secondary Sewage Treatment Offer Greater Improvements in Missouri River Water Quality, B-125042. U.S. General Accounting Office, Washington, D.C.

[65] See Chapter 11.

program elements as administrative structure, financing, standards, permits, information gathering, enforcement, control of nonpoint-sources, and planning. In some cases, variations reflect a justifiable concern for local hydrologic and economic factors. Too often the differences among States are symptomatic of shortcomings in their regulatory programs. Reviews of the water quality programs of nearly one-third of the States lead to the conclusions which follow.[66]

Administrative Structure: The structure and organization of State programs are undergoing significant changes. In a number of instances reorganization has not resulted in functional change because the same policies and personnel are dominant in the new structure. In most States responsibility for the water quality program is now assigned either to a separate agency created expressly for that purpose or to a special agency created within an established department. A trend is observable in the direction of making water quality regulation a function of a comprehensive State environmental protection agency, which has responsibility for control of air quality, water quality, and solid waste disposal. This theoretically permits coordination of pollution abatement programs, and should eliminate programs which merely transfer pollutants from one medium to another. It does not always succeed. The Federal effort to achieve this coordination through establishment of the Environmental Protection Agency (EPA) has not yet been successful.

In the Commission's view, State water quality programs should be made a functional component of an environmental resources program capable of coordinating resource allocation and management with the full range of environmental protection activities. The State program should be capable of administration by metropolitan or regional water quality agencies, if such decentralization is practical. However, coordinating, review, and preemptive powers should be retained at the State level to assure satisfactory statewide administration.

Financing: State expenditures for administration of pollution control programs have increased sharply in recent years, but in many States the control agency

still lacks the resources to mount a full-scale attack on water quality problems. Increasing emphasis on planning, surveillance, and enforcement, which demand large numbers of people, requires greater commitments of funds than are presently provided by State governments. On the horizon lie even larger financial requirements to cope effectively with nonpoint-sources; until nonpoint-sources are controlled, water quality objectives will not be achieved. State legislatures must be prepared to provide the necessary resources for effective programs if the present primacy of State regulation is to continue as a viable policy.

Standards: All States have established receiving water standards for interstate waters and nearly all States apply comparable standards to the rest of their surface waters. Most States make some use of general effluent standards as well, principally through limitations on discharges.

A major advantage of the approach to water quality standards contained in the 1965 Act is its capability for adaptation of standards to a wide variety of local needs and conditions. This value should not be lost through misguided desires for nationwide, or even statewide, uniformity in standards. Uniform effluent standards or treatment requirements, and nondegradation policies are clearly contrary to the situation-specific theory of standard setting, and it is doubtful whether a specific set of water quality criteria for designated uses can serve effectively as more than a guideline to be adjusted for local conditions. Uniformity should exist in the policies and procedures under which standards are established, but not in the standards themselves. Uniform national water quality criteria for designated water uses should not be established until more scientific knowledge becomes available regarding geographic and ecologic variation. An exception to this general rule needs to be made, however, to apply a total ban on discharges of toxic materials. For standards to be in the public interest, there must be a determination that there is a favorable relationship between the economic, social, and environmental costs of achieving them, including any economic or social dislocation in the affected communities or industries, and the economic, social, and environmental benefits to be obtained. To the extent waters of high quality should be protected, this should be accomplished within the standards framework by designating them for uses which guarantee protection of existing quality. The Commission recommends

[66]See HINES, N William (1971). Public Regulation of Water Quality in the United States, prepared for the National Water Commission. National Technical Information Service, Springfield, Va., Accession No. PB 208 309.

development of use designations which serve to protect high-quality water.

Full provision should be made for public participation in the determination of protected water uses and in the establishment and review of quality standards. Local and regional interests should have paramount responsibility in the designation of water uses, but broad national interests must be recognized in cases where unique areas need to be protected through high-use classifications, such as preservation of wild rivers. Standards should be periodically reviewed.

The water quality standards have provided a focus which has had a salutory effect on control programs, even though they have not yet been fully implemented. Creation of the standards forced States to articulate program goals with respect to water quality. Development of such goals is an essential element of meaningful planning and is a prerequisite to consistent administration of other facets of a comprehensive control program. Standards simplify the enforcement process by replacing the vagaries of "pollution" with an objective measuring stick for determining diminished water quality. Standards provide a framework for the development of stream surveillance programs and serve as a touchstone for such systematic pollution prevention activities as waste discharge permits. Finally, standards serve as a baseline against which to measure progress in water quality improvement.

Refinement of use designations and upgrading of specific quality standards are clearly needed in many areas. Nevertheless, based on the staff review of programs in nine States[67] and the General Accounting Office report which covers six additional States,[68] the Commission believes present receiving water standards are capable of protecting adequately most reasonable present and future uses. Failure in implementation is the major impediment to achievement of the water quality goals represented by the current standards. To remedy this defect, the Commission recommends implementation of receiving water standards through a comprehensive waste discharge permit system.

Permits: Advocates of a "no discharge" policy claim the water quality standards program created by the 1965 Act failed to produce desired results because the concept of relating discharge requirements to receiving water standards is administratively impractical. It is urged that by basing individual effluent limitations on the best available control technology economically achievable, which, it is apparently assumed, is more easily discovered and applied, the proposed system will free the administrators from the heavy burden of translating water quality standards into effluent limitations.

In the view of the Commission, the pronouncement that the water quality standards approach of the 1965 Act is inadequate is premature.[69] Although it represented a milestone in the evolution of the national program, the 1965 Act was deficient in not providing the blueprint for a completely developed water quality standards program. The concept of the 1965 Act was sound, but the legislative design for implementation of the Act's policy was so vague that years have been wasted trying to assemble this puzzle, which was missing key pieces. By failing to set time limits for review and approval of procedures for translation of receiving water standards into specific discharge limitations, the Act neglected an essential implementation step. This gap has already been filled by most States through the adoption of permit systems, under which State agencies regularly impose effluent limitations or treatment requirements consistent with approved water quality standards. Where comprehensive permit systems are used to implement quality standards, and where the Federal agency approved the standards, regulation under the 1965 Act is going forward and improved water quality is resulting.

It is frequently contended that effluent limitations based on technological feasibility would be easier to establish than effluent limitations based on water quality standards in the receiving waters because administrators would not have to determine how much, if any, waste can safely be discharged consistent with the standards set for the particular receiving water before deciding what limitations can be imposed. Limitations based on what is technically feasible, however, completely ignore the economic impact and practicability of the restrictions, the impact on other resources, and the effects on both the individual discharger and on society as a whole.

[67] *Ibid.*, p. 254.

[68] COMPTROLLER GENERAL OF THE UNITED STATES (1972). Water Pollution Abatement Program: Assessment of Federal and State Enforcement Efforts, B-166506. U.S. General Accounting Office, Washington, D.C. pp. 18-27.

[69] U.S. CONGRESS, Senate, Committee on Public Works (1971). Federal Water Pollution Control Act Amendments of 1971, 92d Congress, 1st Session, Senate Report No. 92-414. U.S. Government Printing Office, Washington, D.C. p. 7.

That which is technologically achievable may be wholly unnecessary to protect the uses made of the body of water, may be completely beyond the means of the city or the industry involved, and may cause untold waste of other, more critical resources. For these reasons, the Commission believes the policy calling for uniform effluent limitations[70] should be rejected.

A permit system based on achieving a given quality of receiving water presupposes the technological ability to predict the effect of waste discharges on the quality of water under varying conditions. Scientifically-based predictive models for making such calculations are available, but further development is needed to make them more readily usable. Recent progress toward development of usable models has been very rapid, as the scientific community has responded to the massive environmental interest and expenditures in recent years. The experience of States having successful permit systems suggests that, while determining permissible wasteloading is a significant task, it is well within their information and manpower capabilities. The present state of knowledge is adequate to take initial steps involved in issuing permits based on existing standards; greater precision in the establishment of permit terms can be attained as information improves.

Overall, determining acceptable wasteloading is not as demanding of administrative skill as is establishing permit conditions dischargers will accept as fair and feasible. Thus, because the difficult problems associated with meeting requirements for practicability and technological feasibility are present under both systems, along with the full assortment of followthrough problems, the differences in administrative efficiency do not appear to be an overriding factor.

The Commission concludes that basing discharge limitations on applicable water quality standards is feasible. Such an approach is preferred because it provides superior safeguards against both underprotection and overprotection of water quality.

At the time the 1972 Act was passed, 47 States utilized some form of permit system, but few States have developed this regulatory technique to its full potential. Discharge permits should be required for every existing or potential[71] point-source of pollution to all waters in the State, including ground water. Permits should contain limitations requiring sufficient removal or control of wastes to assure compliance with standards set for local receiving waters, and a time frame for compliance which sets priorities and reflects capacity for financing not only water pollution abatement but air pollution control and solid waste disposal as well, so that overall environmental quality improvement is taken into account. Permit procedures should provide full opportunity for public participation and provide effective review avenues to aggrieved parties. Waste discharge limitations should be stated in terms of concentrations and maximum amounts per unit of time, and should be related to seasonal variations in flow and receiving water characteristics.

Where it is necessary to allocate the capacity of receiving waters to purify wastes, the permit agency should seek to develop an equitable allocation of that capacity among affected permittees and no "grandfather" rights should be recognized. If insufficient data exist to execute such a policy, a best practicable treatment standard will have to be employed which includes consideration of such factors for the specific discharging entity as cost, age of plant, social, economic, and physical environmental impacts, and engineering aspects of the application of various types of control techniques or process changes. In addition, consideration should be given to possible alternatives or supplementary programs such as instream treatment to achieve quality objectives as readily and at the lowest cost possible.

Surveillance and monitoring procedures at control points along the rivers should be adequate to detect immediately any violations of quality standards. Immediate attention should then be given to monitoring the point-sources and determining responsibility for the violation. Enforcement measures should be stiff enough to insure prompt correction. Permit duration should be limited to guarantee reexamination at reasonable intervals, and the terms and conditions of permits should be upgraded to take account of technological advances. An annual permit fee is advocated to help defray costs incurred in checking on dischargers' performance of permit conditions. Programs for the training and certification of waste treatment plant operators should be provided which are sufficient to assure competent operation of facilities in accordance with the terms of the permits.

While the 1972 Act contemplates that the permit program will be a joint Federal-State effort and that the States will operate the new system and continue to have and exercise the primary responsibility for

[70] 1972 Act, Section 301(b)(2)(A), 86 Stat. 845, 33 USCA 1311(b)(2)(A).
[71] For example, storage pits for oil or other potential pollutants which might leak or overflow into nearby water bodies if not properly constructed.

93

regulation and enforcement under the national policy, the EPA requirements thus far made known and the delay in approving State programs would seem to indicate a contrary intent. So detailed are the matters with which that agency appears to be concerning itself that it will be difficult, if not impossible, for a State to administer its own program and EPA does not have, and is not likely to have, the manpower or budget to take over the State permit programs. However, the 1972 Act itself, by its provisions, would require judgments to be made at the Federal level which would be better left to the States. For example, the Act sets the qualifications for members of State water quality boards, allows local officials to fractionalize the State program by setting their own standards, allows the Regional Administrator to veto individual permits and imposes other detailed requirements that involve the EPA in the day-to-day operation of the State program. It appears to the Commission this is not the proper role to be played by the national government, would be inefficient, and is not desirable. The Federal Government should set the national goals and policy and should look to the States for results only. As many decisions as possible as to how those results will be obtained should be left to the States.

Information Collection: In only a few States are information collection and processing programs adequately developed. Such programs are essential to effective regulation and must be financed at a level sufficient to permit continuous review and interpretation of data and evaluation of the effectiveness of plans. A technical competency is required which can only be developed by providing sufficient funds for the programs on a continuing basis not subject to year-to-year fluctuations. If the permit system is to perform its functions, the control agency must provide effective review of self-reported information and conduct a vigorous monitoring and inspection program. To keep costs down as well as to prevent being inundated with unused data, there must be a two-stage monitoring—the first limited to a few parameters which would reflect changes and indicate the need for second-stage monitoring, which should be a comprehensive analysis to define responsibility.

State officials should have authority to enter and inspect the premises in which an effluent source is located or in which records are required to be kept under the terms of a permit. Systematic surveys are needed to detect unreported point-sources and to determine the extent and type of pollution resulting from nonpoint-sources. A comprehensive surveillance network should be maintained to monitor water quality in place. This last point is the crux of an effective program; it defines success or failure, and pinpoints the areas where more attention is needed. It provides the basis for comparison of the effectiveness of alternative programs, and thus it is essential to have valid data competently and completely interpreted, and not limited to data for specific enforcement actions. Thus, the function should be carried on by an independent agency, such as the U.S. Geological Survey, which is not involved in either policing or regulation.

The Federal Government, in cooperation with State and interstate agencies, has been attempting to develop a strategy for monitoring and a national data collection, storage, and retrieval program. The efforts to date have not yet resulted in a design which enables State, interstate, and local governments to utilize the system for their own management purposes. The Commission believes that one agency, preferably the U.S. Geological Survey because of its competence in the organization and operation of joint Federal-State programs for the collection and analysis of data, should be given responsibility for developing water quality data programs. Data to be collected should include information on instream quality of water and such other information as is necessary to revise standards, monitor compliance, and fully evaluate the status and progress of water pollution control programs. The pattern for Federal-State cooperation should encourage local responsibility for monitoring and should be generally similar to that used in the national streamflow data program. States should collect data on effluents and instream quality as necessary to monitor permits, while Federal-State cooperative effort should be expended to maintain records of quality at principal streamflow stations. Many States already require industry to report new processes, products, and types of wastes, so that control agencies could anticipate problems associated with new pollutants in effluents or intended for widespread application. All States should have such requirements, including an ongoing program of technology assessment.

Enforcement Procedures: For most of its history, State pollution regulation was premised largely on an unfortunate analogy to nuisance law. This approach encouraged the view that regulatory objectives were substantially achieved when the polluter had been identified and his liability established. This view of the enforcement function fostered endless delays in obtaining abatement of pollution. While the polluter negotiated with agency engineers concerning corrective measures, his pollution continued, having become legitimized. In a sense, by its subjection to regulation. Most States now recognize that the critical phase of regulation begins as soon as a violation is determined.

Subjection of all point-sources of pollution to permit limitations creates a framework which will make possible more direct administrative enforcement techniques. Information suggesting violation of permit conditions should, in theory, trigger a simple and swift administrative procedure to determine and rectify discharger noncompliance. As time passes, this will become more of a reality, but at present there is a confusion of laws and regulations in a number of enforcement agencies, not always coordinated.

Many States now have a streamlined administrative enforcement procedure under which the pollution control agency may hold hearings, issue emergency abatement orders, and revoke permits on grounds of noncompliance where there is a threat of irreparable harm from discharges. In some States the procedures need amplification and the right of the alleged polluter to appeal such determinations to the courts should be preserved. Once the data collection and monitoring programs recommended herein become effective, there should be less need for reliance on court action.

The advantages of the more direct enforcement procedures available within a permit framework have not yet been realized in most States where efforts must still be concentrated on those enforcement activities designed to bring dischargers under permit. Policies and practices carried forward from an earlier era of more leisurely regulation undermine both enforcement efforts and permit administration. Furthermore, with the increased role of the Federal Government in recent years, it is easy for States to sit back and let Federal agencies take the initiative in enforcement.

A substantial measure of voluntary compliance is critical to the success of the regulatory effort. Past State reluctance to employ coercive techniques in dealing with overt recalcitrance acted as a disincentive to dischargers to agree to and implement needed pollution control actions. This difficulty is fast disappearing. Recognizing that some dischargers face real problems in compliance, agencies should demand information adequate to distinguish inability from recalcitrance.

To obtain voluntary compliance, it is necessary that the enforcement program present a credible threat that noncompliance will result in decisive action and meaningful sanctions. It is also essential to have reasonable goals and time schedules. Compliance procedures should be streamlined and unfruitful negotiation reduced by the adoption and publication of specific guidelines for enforcement procedures. Statutes should provide effective sanctions, which attach to the initial violation and escalate with repeated violations; these should bear some relation to the damages and not be so punitive as to discourage the courts from applying them.

In addition, if a State agency having responsibility for public health and safety does not have express powers to deal summarily with emergency situations which endanger human health or safety, State statutes should be enacted to confer such powers.

Perhaps more important than better sanctions is demonstration of a willingness to wield whatever stick is available swiftly and forcefully. Some State officials with responsibility for enforcement have been unwilling to act against powerful local interests, and have been content to let Federal officials take the responsibility for acting against polluters, a responsibility which some zealous Federal officials have been eager to grasp. Improved performance by State officials will require a combination of more intelligent use of statutory powers and policy directives, based on realistic water quality standards and a realistic time frame for meeting them, expansion of the professional pool from which program administrators are drawn, development of reliable Federal cooperation and mobilization of public opinion to influence and support administrative recognition of environmental values.

Local Government

Municipal governments have primary responsibility for the construction and operation of waste treatment facilities to control sanitary sewage and industrial wastes discharged into municipal sewers. Although good progress has been made in providing treatment for municipal wastewater, there is still much to be done. Deficiencies in performance of municipal government responsibilities lie chiefly in the areas of organizational efficiency and operating practices.

Organizational Efficiency: Intramural jealousies among neighboring communities often act to promote inefficiencies in the planning of collection

Municipal sewage treatment is primarily the responsibility of local governments

systems and to stifle realization of economies of scale in the construction of regional treatment plants. Coordinated metropolitan and regional waste management is essential to achieving cost effectiveness in waste treatment systems and in protection of water quality from pollutants from all sources.[72] The Commission strongly supports current efforts to systematize metropolitan and regional water quality planning so as to control pollution in the most efficient way. Areawide waste treatment management plans created in response to the requirements of the 1972 Act should prove to be a powerful force for rational water quality management, if suitable organizations can be developed under State law for waste treatment management.

Waste treatment planning should recognize that even though collection of wastewater from a large area into a single treatment plant will fix responsibility for facility planning, operation, and monitoring, in some instances a single large plant can be less desirable than building a number of plants at various points. With dispersal of plants it may be possible to achieve water quality standards in the receiving waters with a lower degree of treatment and at a lower cost than at a single large plant.

Responsibility for Construction: From time to time suggestions have been made that authority for regional waste management systems be placed in the Federal Government, which would design and construct regional systems to combat pollution. Such suggestions appear to be based on the opinion that efficiency would be promoted, and that existing Federal construction agencies which are running out of work have the competence to undertake regional waste management.

The Commission finds no evidence that the design and construction of waste disposal systems would be better performed by Federal construction agencies. Local government has demonstrated the capability to design and construct the most sophisticated systems when adequate financing is available. Uniform design is neither practical nor desirable. Decentralized responsibility for construction provides lower administrative costs and encourages variation in systems and methods, compatibility with local conditions, and cost effectiveness competition between areas.

---

[72] See Chapter 12 for a more complete discussion of this subject.

Local policymakers will be making land-use decisions which affect the design criteria of sewerage systems. Local sewerage agencies will be responsible for meeting water quality standards, levying user charges, and producing environmentally and socially acceptable projects. A large Federal planning, engineering, and construction organization is not necessary to achieve adequate local water supply and sewage disposal facilities and should not be created or maintained in the absence of such necessity.

Operating Practices: The prevalence of industrial discharges in municipal wastewater can create serious problems in the operation of a municipal treatment plant. Many materials, in high concentrations or discharged to sewers in batches or surges, can retard or destroy biological waste removal processes; heavy organic wastes can overload treatment capacity. Excessive quantities of flow such as storm water or flushing water can hydraulically overload the plant and reduce its efficiency. Carefully prepared and sternly enforced pretreatment contracts or regulations are required to prevent these interruptions of effective plant operation. The frequently employed practice of designing a municipal treatment plant without a prior detailed survey of expected connections and then being compelled to adopt an ordinance prohibiting the connections so as to protect the plant should be discouraged.

A second operating problem lies in securing and retaining adequately trained personnel to manage and maintain community treatment facilities. Local officials have frequently failed to take enough responsibility for assuring competent operation of a municipal wastewater treatment plant, with the result that a plant which is adequate in all other respects regularly produces an unsatisfactory effluent. Municipalities should support strong State programs for training and certification of treatment plant operators and provide a rate of compensation commensurate with achieving full benefits from their significant investment in treatment facilities.

Suburban and Rural Units: Nonurban local governments also have important regulatory responsibilities in protecting water quality. Creative exercise of county land-use control powers can prevent improper waste management practices in rural residential subdevelopments, construction projects, landfills, and mining and manufacturing sites. Drainage districts, soil conservation districts, small watershed districts, and the like could play major roles in controlling runoff from land under cultivation or opened in connection with construction projects. But generally, such rural special districts have failed to adopt water quality improvement as a program goal. Because control of open land runoff is such a critical component of a successful water quality program, the Commission urges careful examination of the opportunities for agencies of local governments to achieve specific water quality objectives by soil conservation, land use, and surface water control methods.

If existing local government units are not capable of mounting effective programs to control sources of water pollution lying in the nonurban areas, effort must be directed at organizing and implementing new institutional arrangements for bringing such pollution under control. Several States are currently experimenting with innovative regional agencies which might be adaptable to this purpose.[73]

PROBLEMS NOT SOLVED BY IMPROVED REGULATION

Disposal of Residues

Improvement of regulatory law cannot change the fundamental law of the conservation of matter. Production changes can lead to improved performance in industrial waste management by eliminating some wastes or recapturing them as valuable by-products, but until new processes are developed further, much pollution control will continue to involve the capture and removal of pollutants from wastewater discharges. Thus, disposing of the residues of waste treatment will continue to be a problem with serious environmental impacts.

Until technology can find ways to use these residues, planning for their handling and disposal essentially involves a search for lesser evils. Matter which will pollute fresh water may also cause environmental harm if dumped into oceans, expelled into the atmosphere through incineration, spread on land, or buried in landfills. What is needed in each case is a careful search for the method of disposing of residues with the least overall environmental impact, recognizing local conditions and the interrelationships among air, land, and water resources.

The sludge disposal program of Chicago offers an example for cities unable to rely on ocean dumping.

[73] See UNIVERSITY OF IOWA (April 1971). Contemporary Studies Project: Impact of Local Governmental Units on Water Quality Control, Iowa Law Review 56(4):804-929.

Sludge from Chicago's treatment plants accumulates at the rate of 900 tons per day. For years the sludge was stored in lagoons until almost 5 million tons accumulated and all storage areas were filled. After several false steps, Chicago now is implementing two programs for land disposal of these sludges. One program involves the movement of the stored sludge by rail to an agricultural area in central Illinois where it is applied to croplands. The second program involves disposal of current sludge production; it is being transported by barge and pipeline to an area near Peoria, where it is spread on strip-mined land, in an effort to reclaim the land. The Chicago experience should provide important information to other cities faced with a conflict among environmental concern, economics, and local resistance to residual disposal sites.

Much earlier, the City of Milwaukee found a market for some of the residuals from its sewage treatment plant by processing the sludge from the plant into fertilizer which has been marketed commercially for many years under the trade name Milorganite. In its new plant, however, the City has omitted the fertilizer production process because the sewage to be handled had lower concentrations of nitrogen and phosphorus, the essential ingredients for fertilizer. The commercial market for this type of fertilizer is probably very limited, because the material is not competitive with lower-cost mineral fertilizers. Sludge is available free at many sewage treatment plants all over the country, but there are few takers.

It is the Commission's view that the Nation must move toward reuse of sludge from waste treatment processes, because of the massive volumes involved and the need to conserve resources. The full extent to which land disposal of sludge can be used is highly site-specific—its applicability will depend on the individual situation. The most critical requirement is land, which will not always be available.

Achieving Cost Effectiveness

Only through cost effectiveness and environmental impact studies can the Nation find an answer to the question of how clean can waterways be kept, and relate the pollution abatement program to other aspects of the national economy. The strategy of regulation should focus resources first on correcting problems that will have the greatest impact in improving water quality. For example, priorities in regulatory attention should be based on the seriousness of the problems requiring attack, and not, as has too often been the case in the past, on the susceptibility of problems to easy administrative solution, or on the reduction of all problems to a uniform and conventional solution. Because water quality improvement occurs over time, and sometimes over space, deliberate planning is required to assure that the allocation of available resources produces maximum incremental gains. The areawide waste management requirements of the 1972 Act could provide an important push for improved cost effectiveness in expenditures under the construction grant program; however, the uniform secondary treatment requirement of this Act may cause ill-timed or unnecessary expenditures.

A major concern of cost effectiveness relates to achieving the maximum water quality improvement for each dollar spent on pollution control facilities, particularly in the Federal grant programs which local officials frequently look upon as windfalls. Under a control program where appropriate water quality standards are set and enforced, and where costs are allocated on a "polluter pay" principle, identification and application of least-cost solutions will be a natural objective of the industry or municipality disposing of wastes.

Alternative methods of achieving water quality standards must also be considered in relation to the overall environment and those methods which achieve water quality improvement at the expense of other environmental values should be reexamined. Again, there is no simple answer to this problem, for unless a coordinated water-air-land appraisal is completed, the least-cost solution for water may well result in environmental harm to other resources of more serious and longer-term significance.

The best way to achieve cost effectiveness and at the same time minimize environmental impact is to eliminate restrictions on the range of alternatives open to decisionmakers searching for least-cost, optimum-effect pollution control methods. Up until now, most of these restrictions have been administrative in origin so could be changed without difficulty, but the 1972 Act will dramatically limit choices unless the concept of uniform method and the goal of no discharge are abandoned.

Economic Dislocations

Recent studies of 11 selected industries predict that minor, though not insignificant, economic dislocations will result from the full implementation of existing water quality standards.[74] The analysis, however, was predicted on a full-employment economy and increasing prices of goods concurrent with construction costs. No analysis has been made on the impact of requirements which would be imposed by the 1972 Act. Those requirements will necessarily increase cost and local area impact. Added costs of treatment will be reflected in higher prices for products produced in such a way as to use water for waste disposal that may put some products at a competitive disadvantage in relation to domestic substitutes and foreign imports. Such competitive shifts plus the inability of marginal industries to afford necessary pollution control investments will cause some plant closings. In some cases, firms forced to close will already have been in serious economic jeopardy due to other economic factors. Thus, one effect of tougher pollution regulation will be to accelerate the closing of operations which would eventually have closed anyway. These plant closings, of course, will have serious local impacts, but may not significantly disrupt the overall national economy if the Nation enjoys prosperity, so that new jobs can be found for displaced workers. Over the period studied (1972-1976), the number of jobs which will be lost through plant closings caused by increased pollution regulation would be substantial, but the study estimates that this loss of jobs will be offset by jobs created in pollution control industries and services so that the net effect would be to increase the unemployment rate by only 0.1 to 0.2 percentage points (from an assumed baseline unemployment rate of 4.6 percent).[75] The Commission doubts that this report adequately reflects the fact that most of the costs of pollution control are in skilled services or the construction industry, whereas the jobs to be lost through plant closings are those of semiskilled or unskilled production workers. On the basis of these studies, therefore, the Commission concludes that economic dislocations which will occur as the result of the tightening of pollution regulation under the 1985 "no discharge" goal of the 1972 Act will cause serious local area problems which will require special programs to ameliorate economic losses. The Nation will not really have an adequate appraisal of this impact until the National Study Commission established under the 1972 Act[76] completes its $15 million study.

Qualified Manpower

The congressional decree of rapidly accelerating program requirements to meet water quality goals will be efficiently met only if competent personnel are available to plan, administer, and operate the required programs and facilities, both public and private. There is a need to upgrade the technical competence of personnel now in water pollution control programs and to recruit better trained personnel into expanding programs. In the area of municipal wastewater treatment, three trends result in a need for trained manpower: more treatment plants, higher levels of treatment and, in selected areas, reclamation of wastewater requiring higher levels of operational control.[77]

The Environmental Protection Agency estimates that approximately 12,700 additional employees will be required to man wastewater treatment facilities proposed for construction during the 1972 to 1976 period. Of these, 16 percent are for professional positions, 65 percent for operators and maintenance workers, and the remaining 19 percent are for administrative support.[78] In addition, there is a need to improve the skills of present personnel through inservice training.

It appears that additional effort will be necessary to provide adequate trained manpower for the efficient functioning of the Nation's water pollution control programs. The Commission believes this should be accomplished by providing training opportunities for potential workers and inservice training for personnel currently employed, particularly in the subprofessional categories. It will be necessary, of course, that salaries in the field be competitive to attract a sufficient number of competent trainees.

The Environmental Protection Agency administers a broad education and training program in water pollution control including programs of undergraduate and graduate training, grants for professional manpower and technicians, training programs for

[74] U.S. COUNCIL ON ENVIRONMENTAL QUALITY, DEPARTMENT OF COMMERCE, & ENVIRONMENTAL PROTECTION AGENCY (March 1972). The Economic Impact of Pollution Control, A Summary of Recent Studies. U.S. Government Printing Office, Washington, D.C. p. 3.

[75] Ibid., p. 13.

[76] 1972 Act, Section 315, 86 Stat. 875, 33 USCA 1325.

[77] See Chapter 7, Section H, for the Commission's discussion of this subject.

[78] U.S. ENVIRONMENTAL PROTECTION AGENCY (1972). The Economics of Clean Water, Washington, D.C. p. 146.

local wastewater treatment plant operators, direct training courses at regional facilities, and support of periodic short courses at regional, State, and local levels.

Education and training programs usually suffer from low visibility in the competition of the budget process at all levels of government. However, the Commission believes it is the height of fiscal folly to authorize the expenditure of billions of dollars for water pollution control programs without priority attention to the manpower resources needed to run them efficiently. The 1972 Act authorizes such programs[79] but funds must be provided to implement them if they are to be effective.

POLLUTION IN ESTUARIES AND THE COASTAL ZONE

Water pollution is a prominent and pressing problem in the management of coastal-zone waters. Coastal waters, estuaries, and the open ocean have been the natural recipient of most of man's liquid-borne waste materials as well as some atmospheric-borne[80] and solid wastes. When major watercourses enter estuaries, some of the pollutants dissipate into the sea, but some concentrate sluggishly in the estuaries. Thus, a plotting of water quality gradients in coastal areas often will show that the pollution is concentrated primarily in the poorly flushed, finger-like, subestuaries near major urban areas. It can be shown, for example, that the amounts of nutrients discharged to the Hudson estuary are five to ten times greater than its capacity to assimilate and recycle them.[81] Furthermore, although the open ocean is vast, its ability to assimilate the wastes reaching it has limits.

Microbiological pollution of coastal waters associated with the discharge of raw sewage is cause for concern. Estuarine waters receiving primary treated sewerage effluents have been shown to contain bacterial pathogens. Enteric viruses of human origin

have been isolated also from shellfish inhabiting these waters. Sewage polluted water leads to the closing of oyster beds to commercial harvesting; it is reported than one-fifth of the U.S.'s 10,000,000 acres of near-shore shellfish grounds have been closed because of pollution.[82] Reductions in fishery resource populations and severe restrictions on their consumption by the public are a threat to the commercial fishing industry. Furthermore, the ability of finfish and shellfish to accumulate substances disposed of into streams and coastal waters to a much higher concentration than that in the surrounding waters requires that the human risk involved in such food sources be determined.

A report of the National Academy of Sciences suggests that coastal zone ecosystems are being subjected to pollution-caused stress which is extremely severe, and might be irreversible.[83] This stress cannot now be fully quantified, although Federal and State agencies are actively studying some of the complex effects of wastes on marine biota, including the effects of bacterial and viral pathogens, heavy metals, pesticides, organometallic compounds and parasite protozoa, sewage sludges, and heated discharges.

Unfortunately, some of the toxic pollutants are not subject to casual observation and may not even be suspected; moreover, some basic pollution damage, such as reduced productivity of certain marine organisms, may be very difficult to detect. Although the impact of particular types of pollution is not fully known, it is clear that the types of wastes discussed in the following paragraphs contribute to the pollution of the coastal zone.

Liquid Wastes

The volume of industrial and municipal liquid wastes being discharged into the waters of the coastal zone is substantial. In 1968, over 8 billion gallons of municipal wastes in the coastal counties and nearly

---

[79] 1972 Act, Sections 104(g), 109, and 111, 86 Stat. 821, 829, 831, 33 USCA 1254(g), 1259, 1261.

[80] A recent study indicates that atmospheric washout may be a primary contributor of heavy metals to the seas, sometimes contributing more than the rivers do. See U.S. NATIONAL ACADEMY OF SCIENCES (1972). Marine Environmental Quality, Suggested Research Programs for Understanding Man's Effect on the Oceans. National Academy of Sciences, Washington, D.C. Table 3, p. 12.

[81] U.S. NATIONAL ACADEMY OF SCIENCES (1972). Marine Environmental Quality, National Academy of Sciences, Washington, D.C. p. 10.

[82] *Ibid.*, p. 23.

[83] All [biological] communities are fragile in the sense that they are susceptible to stresses that are not part of their historic experience. Many of the substances entering the sea today as wastes are clearly not part of this experience. Depending on the level of stress they impose, such substances can reduce population sizes, exterminate species, and even eliminate· entire biotas. See U.S. NATIONAL ACADEMY OF SCIENCES/NATIONAL ACADEMY OF ENGINEERING (1970). Wastes Management Concepts for the Coastal Zone. National Academy of Sciences/National Academy of Engineering, Washington, D.C., especially Chapter 5, Biological Effect.

22 billion gallons of industrial wastes in the coastal States were discharged daily. Municipal wastes include substantial amounts of industrial wastes, which add to their complexity. The National Estuarine Pollution Study reported that only about half of the municipal wastes received secondary treatment. The exact nature of all these discharges and their effect on the marine ecosystems is not known and needs to be monitored.

Solid Wastes

The use of the estuarine shoreline for refuse dumps and landfills results in considerable debris getting into the water; water leaching through these dumps can pollute the estuaries. Spoil disposal from dredging activities is another form of solid waste material that contributes to estuarine degradation.[84]

Industrial Use of Cooling Water

Powerplants are the major users of water in the estuarine zone. In 1950, 22 percent of the Nation's powerplants were in the coastal zone; it is anticipated that in the late 1970's over 30 percent of the plants will be located there,[85] emphasizing the necessity to find suitable sites. The subject of siting powerplants and other water-using enterprises is discussed in Chapter 6.

Heat sometimes has a deleterious effect on the aquatic environment, and the quantity of water used for cooling can create critical problems for some marine organisms. The screens which cover the intake pipes of the cooling system for thermal electric plants as well as the system itself sometimes cause mortality by capturing zooplankton, larval, and juvenile life forms. On the other hand, the warm water releases promoted the growth of some species, and have actually improved fishing, but in some instances sudden shutdown of the plant has caused increased mortality in fish species attracted by the warm water.

Sedimentation

The natural process of sedimentation is modified and in many instances intensified by man's activities. Increasing the influx or altering the composition of substances and accelerating their deposition in es-

tuarine and coastal waters can be detrimental to navigation, recreation, and propagation of fishery resources. Restricting the movement of sand through estuaries, however, may deprive nearby beaches of needed replenishment and cause erosion.

Ocean Dumping

In 1968, almost 62 million tons of wastes (dredge spoils, industrial wastes, sewage sludge, construction and demolition debris, refuse, explosives, and miscellaneous other wastes) were known to have been dumped into the sea off the United States coasts, including areas beyond the coastal zone. Dredging spoils made by far the largest contribution, some 52,200,000 tons, to this total.[86] Some of the wastes dumped are hazardous to public health, harmful to marine life, and esthetically unattractive.

The tonnage of wastes dumped at sea increased fourfold from 1949 to 1968. Of the 250 known disposal sites, 50 percent are off the Atlantic Coast, 28 percent are off the Pacific Coast, and 22 percent are in the Gulf of Mexico.[87] Only partial figures are available since 1968, but one study reports that ocean dumping off the Pacific Coast (excluding dredging spoils which contributed 8,320,000 tons in 1968, explosives, and radioactive wastes) has declined from 1,007,500 tons in 1968 to 23,860 tons in 1971.[88]

Whatever the magnitude of present ocean dumping, increasing demands for waste disposal sites, together with concern over the possible environmental effects, make it a live, current subject. Legislation has been enacted to forbid the dumping of any radiological, chemical, or biological warfare agent or high-level radioactive waste and to require a permit from the Environmental Protection Agency or the Secretary of the Army for the dumping of any other waste.[89]

---

[84] U.S. DEPARTMENT OF THE INTERIOR (March 1970). The National Estuarine Pollution Study, 91st Congress, 2d Session, Senate Document No. 91-58. U.S. Government Printing Office, Washington, D.C. p. 33.

[85] Ibid.

[86] SMITH, David D & BROWN, Robert P, Applied Oceanographic Division, Dillingham Corporation, La Jolla, Calif. (1971). Ocean Disposal of Barge-Delivered Liquid and Solid Wastes from U.S. Coastal Cities. U.S. Environmental Protection Agency, Washington, D.C. p. 21, Table 4.

[87] U.S. COUNCIL ON ENVIRONMENTAL QUALITY (1970). Ocean Dumping, A National Policy. U.S. Government Printing Office, Washington, D.C. p. 1.

[88] See BROWN, Robert P & SHENTON, Edward H (1971). Evaluating Waste Disposal at Sea − The Critical Role of Information Management. Paper presented at the 7th Annual Conference of the Marine Technology Society, Washington, D.C. August 16-18, 1971. Table 1, p. 4.

[89] Marine Protection, Research, and Sanctuaries Act of 1972, P.L. 92-532, Title I, October 23, 1972, 86 Stat. 1052, 33 USCA 1401-1421.

Spoil from dredging operations can damage fish and wildlife resources

The new legislation is largely a product of a study of ocean dumping made by the Council on Environmental Quality, *Ocean Dumping – A National Policy (1970)*. Much of the discussion during congressional hearings on the legislation focused on which dumped wastes would be forbidden or phased out under the standards provided in the bills, since the Council on Environmental Quality had recommended that dumping of a number of types of wastes, including digested and undigested sewage sludge, should be stopped and no new dumping allowed.[90]

The National Water Commission agrees that ocean dumping of toxic materials should be stopped, and that all ocean dumping should be subject to regulation. The Commission cannot, however, endorse a blanket ban on all dumping of sludge and relatively harmless industrial wastes because of its concern over the alternatives for disposal of these residues. The Commission believes that, given the current state of knowledge, a case-by-case analysis of available waste disposal alternatives, including ocean dumping, and their economic, social, and environmental effects is needed before decisions are made. In some instances, ocean dumping of sludge may prove to be the most attractive alternative; the nutrients contained in sludge may provide valuable nourishment for the marine ecosystems. Likewise, the use of old automobile bodies to form fishing reefs has provided valuable fish habitat. Intelligent administration of the 1972 legislation[91] should permit continuation of ocean dumping when it is the most efficient means of waste disposal.

[90] U.S. COUNCIL ON ENVIRONMENTAL QUALITY (1970). Ocean Dumping – A National Policy. U.S. Government Printing Office, Washington, D.C. p. vi.

[91] 1972 Act, Section 403, 86 Stat. 883, 33 USCA 1343.

POLLUTION PROBLEMS OF THE
GREAT LAKES[92]

The changes that have occurred in the Great Lakes as a result of pollution have been cited as a striking example of the misuse of one of the major water resources of North America. Dramatic changes in the biota and increased productivity of Lake Erie, often erroneously referred to as the "death of Lake Erie," are cited repeatedly as the dire consequences of pollution. Yet, as recently as the early 1950's many people, including some in the scientific community, believed that the Great Lakes were too large to be seriously affected by man's activities. Pollution of tributaries, bays, harbors, and some inshore waters was evident, but the possibility that a body of water covering almost 10,000 square miles, such as Lake Erie, could be undergoing measurable changes was not recognized until late in the 1950's. Nevertheless, it has been well documented that all of the Great Lakes, except Lake Superior, have undergone significant changes in quality of their environments and nature of their biota.

Present use of Lake Superior for disposal of taconite iron ore waste has generated concern that this lake may also be subjected to significant quality changes, and legal action has been taken in an attempt to stop the practice.

Nature of Pollution

The Great Lakes have been used as a receptacle for wastes, liquid and solid, discharged by industries, municipalities, individual homes, and ships, or deposited as dredging spoil. Many industries and municipalities do not discharge directly into the Lakes, but the tributaries carry the effluent there. Most of the water withdrawn for municipal and industrial uses from the Lakes is returned at lower quality. Treatment removes many pathogens and toxic materials, but fails to remove nutrients, such as nitrogen and phosphorus, and various other chemicals. Unlike rivers, whose currents flush out these waste deposits, the Lakes act like sinks. Wastes tend to settle in the relatively quiet waters and accumulate on the bottom. Some discharges are significantly warmer than the receiving waters, which is not beneficial to the cold water fish that once thrived in the Lakes.

The U.S. Army Corps of Engineers dredges about 10 million cubic yards of sediments yearly and commercial interests another 2 million cubic yards to maintain depths of navigable waterways. The dredged material from the harbors of industrial cities contains polluted materials, including agricultural sediments from upstream, which may be toxic to aquatic life and have a high oxygen demand. Dredging is not in itself a new source of pollution, since the dredged material is already in the Lakes, but the moving of the material releases buried nutrients and produces highly visible and odoriferous results which dramatize the pollution problems. In response to criticism of the practice of dumping spoil into offshore waters, the Corps developed an interim plan of diked disposal for polluted sediments. This evoked criticism because the diked areas include marshes and lagoons from which nutrients continue to enrich lake waters. Marshes play an important role in straining nutrients from land wash and for that reason, as well as for providing a source of food for the lake fish, should be preserved. For example, the filling of the "Black Swamp" in the area of Toledo is considered to be one of the principal reasons for the algal blooms in western Lake Erie. The swamp had strained the nutrients from the Maumee River drainage. The needed long-term solution, however, is pollution abatement in the rivers to prevent the offensive material from reaching the lake in the first place, and selection of inlake disposal areas where the dredged spoil material can be buried by sand on the lake bottom.

Present Environmental Quality of the Great Lakes

Water quality in most of the Great Lakes is better than a casual reading of the newspapers would lead one to believe, although there are areas of very poor quality. Dissolved oxygen content of even the deepest waters remains near saturation throughout the year, except in Lake Erie and southern Green Bay. The coliform content is usually low in most open lake waters, and the 5-day biochemical oxygen demand is usually less than 1 p.p.m. In general, the open waters of all the Lakes are of good to excellent quality.

The suspended microscopic plants and animals comprising the planktonic community are the same

[92] The background studies for this section of the Commission's report are: BEETON AM (1971). Man's effect on the Great Lakes, Ch. XIV in GOLDMAN, Charles R (1971). Environmental Quality and Water Development, prepared for the National Water Commission. National Technical Information Service, Springfield, Va., Accession No. PB 207 114; and KELNHOFER, Guy T (1972). Preserving the Great Lakes, prepared for the National Water Commission. National Technical Information Service, Springfield, Va., Accession No. PB 211 442.

species found in other large, deep lakes of the Northern Hemisphere. Many of them are cosmopolitan in distribution. Diatoms are probably the most important components of the algal communities, although green and blue-green algae become very abundant at times, especially in the nearshore waters, in bays and harbors, and in Lake Erie, areas that have been influenced most by enrichment.

Most areas of Lakes Huron and Superior are nutrient poor, as evidenced by the high transparency, high dissolved-oxygen content, low total dissolved solids content, and nature of the biota.[93] The offshore waters (greater than 19 miles from shore) of Lake Michigan also have a high dissolved-oxygen content and relatively high transparency, but the concentrations of dissolved solids are higher. Portions of Lake Erie have high phosphorus concentrations, low transparency, an annual oxygen depletion in the bottom waters, abundant plankton, and high productivity.[94] Lake Ontario receives nutrient rich waters from Lake Erie, but its great depth apparently does not permit full utilization of the nutrients by the algae. Lake Ontario has a greater chemical content than Lake Erie, but much of the biota consists of those organisms which are also important in Lakes Huron and Superior.

The Eutrophication Problem: Many of the changes which have taken place in Lakes Erie, Michigan, and Ontario indicate accelerated eutrophication, i.e., nutrient enrichment. Increases in nitrogen and phosphorus, and decreases in dissolved oxygen content, are accepted indices of eutrophication. Most of the alterations in the biota have considerable significance as indices of eutrophication also. Changes in species composition and increased abundance of plankton, and decline and disappearance of salmonoid fishes, have occurred in a number of small lakes undergoing eutrophication.

It appears that many of the important changes in the Great Lakes are those taking place in the sediments due to the entrance of tremendous amounts of nutrients and organics. Major changes in the characteristics of the lake bottoms and extensive depletion of dissolved oxygen offer evidence of change in the sediments. The oxygen demand of Lake Erie sediments is about three times that of Lake Michigan sediments and at least ten times that of Lake Huron sediments. Changes in the fish population of Lake Erie may be closely related to changes in the sediments, since all Great Lakes fishes, except sheepshead, have eggs that settle and hatch on the bottom.

Recent studies of Lake Michigan have demonstrated that it is unrealistic to assume that the entire volume of the Lakes is available for dispersion and dilution of domestic and industrial wastes. Inshore and offshore waters of Lake Michigan have pronounced differences in concentrations of major nutrients, especially in the vicinity of urban centers and along the east shore where most of the major tributaries enter the Lake.[95] The inshore environments are deteriorating at a much faster rate, with greater concentrations of ammonia, nitrate, organic-N, and soluble phosphate. The abundance of algae inshore reflects the differences in nutrients. The response is not limited, however, to increased algae growth. The species composition of inshore areas and in bays differs from offshore, with eutrophic species common in the inshore zone of many areas.

Similar inshore-offshore differences have been demonstrated for Lakes Erie and Ontario. Thus, it is the shallow water environments that are first altered, and they are of the greatest importance for water supply, waste disposal, fish production, and recreation.

Man's Impact on the Fisheries: The decreased abundance of some species of fish can be attributed to intensive fishing. In early years, the huge lake sturgeon were caught and purposely destroyed to eliminate them from fishing grounds, since their large size damaged gear used to capture other species.[96] Over 8 million pounds were caught in 1879, 5 million pounds in 1890, and 106,000 pounds by 1925. Only 41,000 pounds were taken throughout the Great Lakes in 1969.[97] The sturgeon has been protected since 1929, but its numbers have not increased, since

[93] BEETON AM (1965). Eutrophication of the St. Lawrence Great Lakes. Limnology and Oceanography 10(2):240-254.

[94] BEETON AM (1969). Changes in the environment and biota of the Great Lakes, pp. 150-187 in NATIONAL ACADEMY OF SCIENCES, Eutrophication: Causes, Consequences, Correctives. National Academy of Sciences, Washington, D.C.

[95] U.S. FEDERAL WATER POLLUTION CONTROL ADMINISTRATION (1968). Lake Michigan Basin, Physical and Chemical Conditions.

[96] SMITH SM (1968). Species succession and fishery exploitation in the Great Lakes. Journal of Fisheries Research Board of Canada 25(4):667-693.

[97] U.S. DEPARTMENT OF COMMERCE (1970). Great Lakes Fisheries 1969, Annual Summary, C.F.S. No. 5474.

many of the rivers and shallow areas otherwise suitable for the species are severely polluted.

Construction of the Welland Canal opened the upper Lakes to the predatory sea lamprey. The sea lamprey attaches to other fish with its sucker-like mouth and feeds on the blood of its victims. A lamprey destroys at least 20 pounds of fish during its life, and the lake trout is especially vulnerable to its predation. Once spawning populations of the lamprey were established, the lake trout fishery collapsed. The annual lake trout catch was around 10 million pounds in Lakes Huron and Michigan during the 1930's; less than 1 million pounds were caught in these Lakes by 1949. The sea lamprey has now been controlled in Lake Superior and the lake trout catch, which previously had fallen spectacularly, is now recovering.

Changes in the drainage basin of Lake Ontario, e.g., damming and siltation of streams, made many of the streams unsuitable for stream-spawning fish, such as the Atlantic salmon. The salmon ascended various streams tributary to Lake Ontario in the pioneer days, but rapidly declined in abundance and had almost disappeared by 1880.[98]

Several developments between 1900 and 1970 were especially important to later changes in the Great Lakes. Several exotic species were introduced; for example, smelt, carp, and alewife, which competed for food and thus replaced the natural species. Also, the introduction of nylon nets undoubtedly had an effect in removing smaller fish and thus accelerating the effects of intensive fishing. The attempt to establish uniform fishing regulations was unsuccessful, and overfishing of many stocks continued. The sharp increase in industry and in the population in the region was also of major importance. Major urban centers were developing rapidly and sewerage systems were expanded to carry waste to the Lakes, under the assumption that the large volume of water in the Lakes would dilute any pollutants to concentrations harmless to the fisheries.

Future Prospects

Some of the changes in the Great Lakes, such as increases in chemical content, increased abundance of plankton, and changes in the characteristics of the lake bottoms, have been subtle, and were not recognized until lake conditions were substantially altered. Lake Erie has shown the greatest changes in the environment and biota. Increases in the chemical content and abundance of plankton in Lake Ontario closely parallel changes in Lake Erie.

The effect of a rapidly increasing population is beginning to show in Lake Michigan, although changes have been more gradual than in Lake Erie and probably will continue to be more gradual, because the volume of Lake Michigan is much greater than that of Lake Erie. The extent of change in Lake Michigan might have been much greater if the Chicago Sanitary Canal had not been constructed to divert wastes from Chicago away from Lake Michigan. The long-term outlook for Lake Michigan is not encouraging, since the net addition and flow-through of water is small and most of the major tributaries are seriously polluted.

The possibility of improving conditions in Lake Erie is somewhat better, since high-quality Lake Huron water enters the Lake via the St. Clair and Detroit Rivers. Abatement of the pollution discharged into the Lake or its tributaries should eventually lead to improvement of conditions in Lake Erie, since it is theoretically possible to exchange the entire volume of the Lake in about 3 years.

Municipalities contribute major inputs of phosphorus to the Lakes, as shown by data from the International Joint Commission report on pollution of Lakes Erie and Ontario.[99] Ten percent of the total phosphorus comes from direct discharge into Lake Erie. Municipalities also contribute about 55 percent of the phosphorus inputs from tributaries to Lake Erie. Together, municipal and industrial wastes account for about 75 percent of the estimated total phosphorus input to Lake Erie and Lake Ontario, and it is estimated that up to 50 percent of the phosphorus in municipal wastewaters comes from detergents. Even larger amounts probably come from runoff from agricultural lands. This ever-increasing discharge of nutrients is a major factor in accelerated eutrophication of the Lakes. The problem is compounded since large amounts of nutrients are retained or stored in the Lake, especially in the sediments.

As pointed out previously, pollution flows directly into inshore areas, bays, and harbors. The critical

[98] International Board of Inquiry for the Great Lakes Fisheries (1943). Report and Supplement. U.S. Government Printing Office, Washington, D.C. p. 18.

[99] INTERNATIONAL LAKE ERIE WATER POLLUTION BOARD & INTERNATIONAL LAKE ONTARIO-ST. LAWRENCE RIVER WATER POLLUTION BOARD (1969). Pollution of Lake Erie, Lake Ontario and the International Section of the St. Lawrence River, report to the International Joint Commission. International Joint Commission United States – Canada, Washington, D.C. pp. 47-49.

Untreated storm water pollutes watercourse near Chicago

areas now adversely affected are Green Bay, southern Lake Michigan, Saginaw Bay, the shores of the Detroit River, western Lake Erie, southern shore of Lake Erie, and western Lake Ontario. The intensive pollution abatement programs now being mounted in these critical areas will undoubtedly be a major step towards improving conditions throughout the Great Lakes.

The Great Lakes, as interstate waters, are subject to the Nation's water quality programs. All of the Great Lakes States have established receiving water standards within their jurisdictions under the provisions of the 1965 Act. The States have their own water quality programs, based upon State law, as well. In addition, the recently created Great Lakes Water Quality Board, created under the Great Lakes

Water Quality Agreement between the United States and Canada, will provide further impetus toward achievement of water quality standards under which the quality of the Great Lakes will be improved.

The complexities of the Great Lakes, including the differing conditions within each Lake and the interrelationships among the Lakes, makes the setting of intelligent water quality and discharge standards extremely difficult. An enormous investment will be required to install and operate municipal and industrial treatment facilities in order to meet particular water quality standards in the Great Lakes basin. It is imperative, therefore, that the standards be grounded firmly on facts and biological understanding and not on uninformed speculation. They must be precise and tailored to the wide variation of conditions in the Lakes, including flow regimens and other physical influences on fisheries, beaches, and algal growth. The National Water Commission is not convinced that the present standards have been based on an adequate understanding of the operation of the Lakes and of the effects which may result from the use of a particular standard. Elsewhere in this report the Commission recommends increased Federal support for research and collection of environmental data which will improve the predictive and analytical abilities of our standard-setting entities, and enable better predictions to be made of the impact of standard setting.[100] Studies[101] and demonstration projects[102] authorized by the 1972 Act should provide the necessary information, if the Act is properly implemented.

RECOMMENDATIONS

4-1. The Nation's water pollution control policy should be based on the principles that (1) water is polluted when its quality has been altered by the activities of man to such a degree that reasonable present and prospective uses as designated by public authorities are impaired, and that (2) the objective of pollution control should be to protect the designated uses. The 1972 Act should be revised to restore these policies.

4-2. Receiving water standards should be established under the principles stated in 4-1, above, for all State waters, including ground waters. Standards should be sufficiently high to protect all existing uses and all reasonably foreseeable future uses, but should also take into account the economic, social, and environmental costs of achieving them.

4-3. A national water pollution abatement program sufficient to achieve the approved water quality standards should be accomplished in 10 years. To achieve this goal Federal construction grants at the percentages prescribed in the 1972 Act should be authorized and allocated to qualifying State and local governments at levels which will assure the completion of all necessary projects, and the reim-

bursement for projects which have not received the full amount of aid under prior programs. The Federal grant program should terminate upon the achievement of the national cleanup goal.

4-4. Increased research and development should be undertaken: (1) on alternative methods for waste treatment and disposal, with particular attention to methods which make productive use of the nutrient value of wastes, including further demonstration projects to test the utility of land disposal and aquaculture techniques under varying local conditions and different composition of wastes; (2) on the impacts which alternative water pollution abatement processes may have upon other environmental elements such as air and land; and (3) on the development and improvement of techniques for controlling nonpoint pollution sources.

4-5. The 1972 Act should be amended to give the EPA Administrator the flexibility to approve grants for alternatives to either conventional treatment processes or uniform treatment requirements when such alternatives can reasonably be expected to produce equal or better receiving water quality for the expenditure of a lesser amount of Federal funds.

4-6. Federal grants to municipalities during the national cleanup period should be made contingent upon adoption by the municipality of schedules of service charges which will provide, after the grant program is terminated, for full recovery of capital and operating costs of the system, exclusive of those costs which will have been financed with Federal or State grants. Charges should be based on the costs which users impose on the system.

4-7. The following steps should be taken under the 1972 Act:

a. Accomplishment of an expanded program of planning of regional water quality management for the entire country, coordinated with planning under the Water Resources Planning Act.

b. Appropriation of necessary funds for grants to States and interstate agencies of 50 percent of the cost of carrying out this planning.

c. Periodic national program evaluations to measure progress in water quality improvement, made in conjunction with the

---

[100] See Chapter 17.

[101] 1972 Act, Section 104(f), 86 Stat. 820, 33 USCA 1254(f).

[102] *Ibid.,* Section 108, 86 Stat. 828, 33 USCA 1258.

periodic assessments of water supplies by the Water Resources Council and the annual reports of the Council on Environmental Quality.

4-8. Regional or metropolitan waste management agencies organized under State authorization should be charged with planning and implementing programs for collection and disposal of waterborne wastes. Such agencies should provide for local or State decisionmaking with regard to techniques for meeting standards, financing the program, and enforcement. The 1972 Act should be amended to delete requirements for Federal control over the organizational form of such agencies, leaving the form of local government up to the States.

4-9. Water quality standards should be implemented through a national waste discharge permit system, administered by State authorities under Federal guidelines. The 1972 Act should be implemented by EPA in a manner which will maximize the opportunity for early State assumption of responsibility for the issuance and enforcement of permits. Discharge limitations should be based on local receiving water standards, taking into account the self-purifying capacity of natural water bodies. Such capacity should be allocated, with appropriate safety factors, to existing discharges, conservation and recreation reserves, and a reserve for future discharges in accordance with applicable land use and comprehensive water quality plans.

4-10. Permits issued under the national permit system should place dischargers in compliance with Section 13 of the Refuse Act.

4-11. The States should have primary responsibility for information collection systems, but the Federal Government should have responsibility for developing, in cooperation with the States, both a national stream surveillance system and a uniform data collection, storage, and retrieval program, under the direction of the U.S. Geological Survey.

4-12. Except in the event of default in performance as determined through preestablished procedures, States should have primary responsibility for definition and implementation of water quality standards, including the time frame for implementation, and for regulatory and enforcement actions, including the issuance and administration of the permit system. Federal agencies should avoid taking actions which interfere with or supersede legitimate State and local functions in the implementation of the Nation's pollution control program.

4-13. The Congress should obtain greatly improved information on the cost effectiveness of Federal water quality programs, looking toward providing assurance as to: (1) costs to the Nation of achieving alternative levels of water quality improvement, (2) beneficial effects to be realized through the programs, (3) probability of proposed programs achieving objectives, and (4) priorities for the abatement of pollution from alternative sources in various regional and local areas.

4-14. Present education and training programs should be continued and expanded as needed to meet manpower requirements. However, the level and composition of education and training programs should be justified on the basis of periodic surveys of the manpower needs for water pollution control programs of State and local governments.

4-15. Study of alternative methods of disposing of residues should continue, so as to provide data to guide future decisions. This should include a comprehensive survey by the National Oceanic and Atmospheric Administration to determine the extent of pollution throughout the coastal zone and adjacent oceanic areas and the Great Lakes.

4-16. Estuarine and lacustrine research programs of the Federal Government and of State agencies should seek improved bases for the establishment of water quality standards for estuarine and coastal waters and for the Great Lakes.

Improving Water-Related Programs

Introduction

In this chapter the Commission briefly describes and appraises the principal Federal water programs and offers its recommendations for their improvement. These programs came into being over a period of a century and a half during which fundamental changes took place, not only in the Nation's water problems, but also in the American people's concept of the proper role of their Federal Government. For many years after the adoption of the Constitution it was generally held that the Federal Government was without power to undertake "internal improvements," other than improvements in aid of navigation; and even this limited power was not finally established until 1824 when the Supreme Court held that the Commerce Clause of the Constitution had vested the Federal Congress with power over navigation within all of the States.[1] In that same year, appropriations were made for removing some minor obstructions to navigation from the Ohio and Mississippi Rivers. Additional navigation improvements were authorized by subsequent Congresses. Not until the 20th century did the Federal Government accept major responsibility for water resources development for other purposes. In 1902, the Congress utilized the Property Clause of the Constitution as a base for the Reclamation Act.[2] Fifteen years later, after great

floods on the Mississippi, the Congress for the first time accepted a limited responsibility for flood control.[3] But it was not until 1936 that it authorized a nationwide flood control program.[4] Thereafter, the scope of Federal responsibilities broadened with great rapidity, as will be evident from the subsequent discussion of the present Federal water programs.

These programs came into being one at a time as the American people reached a consensus that a problem existed and that it would be proper for the Federal Government to play a part in solving that problem. But throughout the almost two centuries in which this was taking place the Nation was growing, new demands were evolving, and the people's concept of the role of the Federal Government was changing. It is not surprising, therefore, that some of the basic policies underlying these programs are inconsistent; and, in many respects, anachronistic when viewed in the light of what has happened since they were established.

The Federal program to make the inland waterways navigable had its beginnings in an era when the young Nation had practically no transportation system for bringing the products of the border regions to its cities, or to its coastal harbors for export. Navigable waterways were essential if those regions were to be settled, become productive, and thus make the Nation stronger and its people more prosperous. There being but few settlers in the undeveloped hinterlands, it was obvious that if the waterways were to be built the Nation as a whole would have to bear

---

[1] *Gibbons v. Ogden*, 22 U.S. 1 (1824).

[2] *Act of June 17, 1902*, P.L. 161, 57th Congress, 32 Stat. 388.

~~~~~~~~~~~~~~~~~~~~~~~~~~~~~

Increased recreational use adds a new dimension to water development

---

[3] Federal assistance for the control of floods on the Mississippi and Sacramento Rivers was authorized by the *Act of March 1, 1917*, P.L. 367, 64th Congress, 39 Stat. 948. The Mississippi authorization was broadened by the *Act of May 15, 1928*, P.L. 391, 70th Congress, 45 Stat. 534.

[4] *Act of June 22, 1936*, P.L. 738, 74th Congress, 49 Stat. 1570.

the cost. Today, the regions served are highly developed and the beneficiaries of new waterways are in a position to help pay for them. Moreover, the Nation has a nationwide transportation system providing alternatives to waterway transportation. The problem is no longer one of developing the only practicable means of transporting goods, but of developing the most efficient combination of transportation modes.

The Federal Reclamation Program came into being when many were seeking homes on the land, and in an era still strongly influenced by the American dream of a great unified Nation extending from the Atlantic to the Pacific. Today, farming is highly mechanized, the United States has an agricultural plant capable of producing food and fiber in excess of the Nation's needs, and the movement of people is from the land to the cities.

When it was authorized, the nationwide Federal flood control program was an expression of the desire of the majority to help their unfortunate fellow citizens in those cities that had developed from early settlements on river banks which had grown beyond the point at which a new start was economically feasible. This humanitarian motivation was reinforced by the need for a program of public works to get people back to work in the depths of a great depression. Very few could foresee that this program would be continued long beyond the time when the major flood problems that inspired it had either been solved or could be addressed more effectively in alternative ways. Probably none could foresee that today the Federal Government would be building works to increase the value of agricultural lands in river bottoms, and even to provide protection for the narrow flood plains of the smallest creeks; problems of such small magnitude that they can easily be solved by local entities, or in some instances, by the States. Today, the major problem requiring solution is not one of stopping damages already being experienced, but of keeping more flood problems from developing. The Nation has had little success in this, as is shown by the fact that flood damages continue to increase despite the billions spent for protective works.

The major water problems of today were of little consequence when the Nation decided to assume responsibility for navigation improvements, reclamation, and flood control. Today, the United States is faced with a tremendous problem of pollution control. The great majority of its citizens live in cities, and the water problems of the urban areas cry out for attention. Recreation has become one of the most important uses of water resources. The people of the United States give far greater weight to environmental and esthetic values than they did when many of the water policies still in effect were enacted into law. In short, present conditions and needs differ greatly from those that existed when the Nation's most costly water programs were, for reasons good and sufficient at the time, brought into being. This Commission concluded early in its life that it had no more important task than that of reappraising existing policies and programs in the light of changed conditions and needs, and of distilling from the results of these appraisals guidelines for bringing the water policies and programs of the United States into consonance with the needs of the Nation in the remaining decades of the 20th century.

The long-term trend, beginning with the justly celebrated "Conservation Crusade" of the present century, has been toward comprehensive multiple-purpose programs for major river basins. This trend has been accelerated by the enactment of the Water Resources Planning Act of 1965,[5] and there can be no doubt that when Congress enacted this law, it took a long step in the right direction. But it failed to modernize the policies that govern the components of the comprehensive programs contemplated by the Act. The navigation component is still planned and carried out under policies designed to meet conditions and demands existing in a nation just beginning to expand into vast undeveloped regions. Those components that increase the productive capacity of the Nation's agricultural plant are governed by policies fashioned during a period in which no one dreamed that there would be a time when the Federal Government would be forced to establish programs to *reduce* the production of food and fiber. Some flood control projects, undertaken under policies initially intended to rescue already imperiled people and property, are being used to make possible more intensive use of flood plain lands. The prospect of future flood protection at little or not direct cost to landowners is encouraging them to develop flood plain lands. Thus, policies that were intended to put an end to flood losses tend to create new flood problems faster than the Nation can solve its old ones. These are evidence that the Nation has not kept its water policies and programs up to date. It indicates that the kinds of programs the Water

---

[5] P.L. 89-80, July 22, 1965, 79 Stat. 244, as amended, 42 USCA 1962 *et seq.*

Resources Planning Act was intended to bring into being cannot be attained unless the legislation underlying the component programs is brought into consonance with a single set of rational principles and modified to meet changed conditions and demands. The recommendations advanced in the succeeding sections of this chapter are proposed to achieve these ends.

Section B

The Inland Waterway Program[6]

THE PROGRAM

The inland waterway program of the Federal Government had its beginning in 1824 when a small appropriation was made to the U.S. Army Corps of Engineers to remove a few snags and sandbars that were interfering with navigation on the Mississippi and Ohio Rivers. Over the ensuing years, many rivers were improved by deepening them or by the construction of systems of locks. The United States now has more than 25,000 miles of commercially navigable waterways. More than 15,000 miles of these waterways have depths of 9 feet or more, and almost 9,000 miles have a depth of 12 feet or more. Of special importance is the system of waterways in the Mississippi River Basin which encompasses almost 9,000 miles of federally improved waterways extending from the Gulf of Mexico to the upper reaches of the Mississippi and Ohio Rivers, to established ports well up on the Arkansas, Tennessee, Cumberland, and Missouri Rivers, and up the Illinois River to connect with Lake Michigan. The Gulf Intracoastal Waterway is another heavily used component of the waterway system of the United States.[7]

Commercial traffic on the inland waterway system, exclusive of the Great Lakes, totaled about 204 billion ton-miles in 1970, which is more than four times the traffic carried by the waterways in 1950. About 36 percent of the tonnage moving over the inland waterways in 1970 was petroleum and petroleum products. Bituminous coal and lignite made up about 21 percent of the tonnage, and grains, grain products, and soybeans about 5 percent.[8] The use of the inland waterways for recreation is increasing rapidly and congestion is becoming a serious problem where recreational craft wish to pass through locks.

During recent years, the inland waterway system has carried about 10 percent of the Nation's total intercity traffic, while about 6 percent of that total has moved on the Great Lakes, 44 percent by rail, 20 percent by trucks, and another 20 percent by oil

---

[6] At the time the National Water Commission was created, the Congress was awaiting completion of the studies and report of the U.S. Commission on Marine Science, Engineering, and Resources, created under Public Law 89-454 of the 89th Congress to study the problems and develop new policies for the ocean resources adjacent to the United States. This made it evident to the National Water Commission that the Congress did not intend it to duplicate the work of the Marine Commission and make recommendations as to policies governing ocean shipping, foreign commerce, and maritime problems. Hence, the recommendations in this section are not intended to apply to deep-draft vessels operating on the Great Lakes, on the lower reaches of major rivers used by such vessels, on the entrance channels to deep-draft harbors, or on the oceans. The Commission recognizes that, with the development of new type barges and cargo containers, an increasing amount of cargo will move from inland shallow-draft waters into foreign commerce without being unloaded at coastal harbors and reloaded into oceangoing vessels. In time this change of technology conceivably may require that new national policies be adopted for both inland and ocean shipping. But for the foreseeable future, the Commission believes that the traditional distinction between inland waterway and ocean shipping can be observed, and that as a practical matter the self-supporting policies which it recommends for inland waterway transportation can be implemented even though some cargo which originates at inland ports may move directly into foreign commerce. Should a fuel tax be imposed as suggested by the Commission, it can be allocated between taxable and nontaxable uses and refunded to the taxpayer in the same manner as the tax on gasoline purchased for on-farm use.

---

[7] BLOOD, Dwight M (1972). Inland Waterway Transport Policy in the U.S., prepared for the National Water Commission. National Technical Information Service, Springfield, Va., Accession No. PB 208 668. pp. II-1 to II-3.

[8] U.S. ARMY CORPS OF ENGINEERS (1972). Waterborne Commerce of the United States, Calendar Year 1970, Part 5, National Summaries. U.S. Army Engineer District, New Orleans, La. And U.S. ARMY CORPS OF ENGINEERS (1951). Annual Report of the Chief of Engineers, Volume I. U.S. Government Printing Office, Washington, D.C.

pipeline. The proportion of the total traffic carried by inland waterways has increased from about 4 percent in 1950 to 10 percent in recent years.

Federal expenditures for the improvement of the inland waterway system had totaled $3.2 billion[9] by June 30, 1971. The cost to the Federal Government of operating and maintaining the system has been running over $80 million annually. Under present policies, the Federal Government usually bears the full construction cost of improving waterways for commercial use, but non-Federal interests are required to provide lands, easements, rights-of-way, and spoil areas and provide and maintain public terminal and transfer facilities.

In 1970, there were 1,849 transportation companies operating on the inland and coastal waterways. Only 141 of these were subject to regulation by the Interstate Commerce Commission. The 1,849 companies operated almost 24,000 vessels of which about three-fourths are unpowered barges.[10] The largest barges now in use have a capacity of 3,000 tons, a load that would fill 55 average sized railroad freight cars or 30 of the big new ones. Barges are joined into "tows" which are generally pushed[11] by diesel-powered towboats. Towboats with powerplants of 4,000 horsepower are fairly common. Such a vessel can handle up to 20,000 tons of freight in a single tow. Towboats with powerplants of 8,500 horsepower have proven practicable on the Mississippi River. Average charges to shippers of moving bulk commodities on the waterways are said to be about 3 mills per ton-mile[12] and average transportation savings over alternative means of transportation have been estimated by the Corps of Engineers to average 5 mills per ton-mile.[13]

Since the beginning of the Federal program in 1824, the Corps of Engineers has been responsible for its planning and execution. In the early years of the Nation, States undertook the construction of waterways. One of the most famous, as well as the most successful, of the State projects was the Erie Canal built by the State of New York. Later, it was rebuilt as the State Barge Canal and is still in operation.[14] However, the other State canal projects have been abandoned or replaced by Federal waterways.

From the beginning of the Federal program, there has been a strong demand for waterway projects in the belief that the "low cost" transportation thus permitted would stimulate economic development in the less developed regions of the Nation. The construction of waterways has also been used as a means of forcing reductions in railroad freight rates. For these and other reasons, many parts of the country still seek projects to make their rivers more navigable. The Corps of Engineers has made reports on a number of potential waterways and the Congress has authorized the construction of an additional 2,351 miles of waterway, the cost of which is presently estimated at $4.6 billion. Other possible waterways not authorized, but supported by the regions that would be benefited, would have an aggregate length of 2,514 miles and, according to preliminary estimates, would cost about $5 billion.[15]

During recent years, a counterforce has come into play in the form of an increased public interest in the impact of waterway construction on the environment. This force has resulted in the stoppage of construction work on one project, the Cross-Florida Barge Canal Project, and in the future it may be much more difficult to obtain authorizations or appropriations for new waterway projects than has been the case in the past.

APPRAISAL OF THE PROGRAM

The Federal inland waterway program has been appraised by many study commissions and similar bodies since its beginning almost a century and a half ago. The National Water Commission has reviewed the findings of the principal previous studies, as well as the results of an independent study made for it by

---

[9] Not converted to present dollars. Information furnished by Corps of Engineers.

[10] BLOOD, Dwight M (1972). Inland Waterway Transport Policy in the U.S., prepared for the National Water Commission. National Technical Information Service, Springfield, Va., Accession No. PB 208 668. pp. II-10, II-13.

[11] Except on the Gulf Intracoastal Waterway where they are pulled.

[12] AMERICAN WATERWAYS OPERATORS (1973). Statement of Braxton Carr, President, at Washington Conference, National Water Commission, February 9, 1973.

[13] U.S. CONGRESS, Senate Committee on Public Works (1955). Hearings on Flood Control, Rivers and Harbors, and Miscellaneous Projects, S. 414, S. 524, and S. 1069, 84th Congress, 1st Session. Statement of Lt. Gen. Samuel D. Sturgis, Chief of Engineers, April 18, 1955. p. 31.

[14] The State of New York is seeking Federal participation in the operation, maintenance, rehabilitation, and improvement of the State Barge Canal. It is also considering legislation to impose user charges on the carriers using this waterway.

[15] Information on potential waterways furnished by U.S. Army Corps of Engineers.

Professor Dwight M. Blood of the University of Wyoming.[16] There is no need to repeat all of the findings of these reports here, since the reports are readily available. The principal deficiencies pointed out in these reviews may be briefly stated as follows:

First, a major weakness of the present program stems from deficiencies in the procedures by which it is determined whether or not a proposed waterway project would result in a justified addition to the national transportation system.

Second, a major weakness of the legislative policies governing the present program is that they do not require beneficiaries to share in the cost of constructing, operating, and maintaining Federal waterway projects.

Third, the inland waterway system is inescapably an element of the national transportation system. Yet, the waterways are not planned, evaluated, or regulated as a part of the national transportation system.

Deficiency in Evaluation Procedures

This deficiency is serious, but calling attention to its existence should not be interpreted as an attempt to cast doubt upon the economic justification of waterway improvement as such. Some of the existing waterways have undoubtedly reduced the real cost of transportation to the Nation by amounts greatly exceeding the costs of providing them. For example, there can be no doubt but that the improvement of the mainstem of the Ohio River has been a sound investment for the Nation. But there is a tendency to conclude that because some waterways have contributed greatly to the prosperity of a region or the Nation, all waterways are, or will be, justified. This is a very old mistake. The success of the Erie Canal, built by the State of New York early in the last century, brought on a great demand for similar waterways in other States. Many of the waterways built by the States and private enterprise turned out to be financial failures. Modern economics has provided much more reliable methods for predicting what effect a contemplated waterway project would have upon the national income. Yet, projects are still undertaken that could not pass the test of an unbiased economic evaluation.

Deficiency in the Present Cost-Sharing Policy

The Federal waterway improvement program had its beginnings when the major reason for providing transportation facilities–then limited to waterways and roads–was to induce the settlement and economic development of regions that were essentially uninhabited. This was an overriding national purpose. When a region to be served by a waterway had few people living in it, there was no way for local beneficiaries to assume any part of the cost of improvements and it was in the national interest for the Federal Government to bear these costs. As time passed, other means of transportation were developed, and the regions served by waterways increased in population and affluence. The national purpose of pushing back the frontier and developing underdeveloped regions was achieved. Eventually, railways, highways, and pipelines were developed, and improving technology made the waterways a highly efficient and competitive mode of transport, the costs of which can easily be paid by the direct beneficiaries. However, the policy of Federal assumption of practically all costs which had been established during the formative period of the Nation's economic growth has never been adjusted to take into account the present competitive situation in the Nation's transportation system. New waterway projects serving highly developed regions are still being installed entirely at Federal expense, paid for from the general revenues. Commercial users of inland waterways pay no Federal fuel tax, nor any lockage fees or other form of remuneration for the cost of providing and maintaining the waterways. A change in the policy governing the division of the cost of waterway projects between the public Treasury and those who directly benefit from the low-cost transportation facilities is long overdue. The lack of an equitable cost-sharing policy is a major weakness of the present waterway program.

Failure to Treat Waterways as Elements of a National Transportation System

The third major defect stems from the fact that to date the United States has failed to develop a really effective national transportation policy, and hence has not achieved a national transportation system that meets the transportation demands of the United States at least cost to the public as a whole. The present situation is well characterized in a report,[17]

[16]BLOOD, Dwight M (1972). Inland Waterway Transport Policy in the U.S., prepared for the National Water Commission. National Technical Information Service, Springfield, Va., Accession No. PB 208 668.

[17]U.S. DEPARTMENT OF COMMERCE (March 1960). Federal Transportation Policy and Programs. U.S. Government Printing Office, Washington, D.C.

Inland waterways provide low cost transportation for bulk commodities

issued by the Department of Commerce in 1960, in the following words:

> National transportation is presently out of balance. It is less a national system than a loose grouping of individual industries. We have built a vast network of highways, railways, inland waterways and seaports, airways and airports, and pipelines, with little attention to conflict among these expanding networks. Economic regulation has been administered in rigid compartments although many basic problems are common to many areas of transportation. Total capacity is not closely geared to total need.

Although the remedy lies in the development of an effective national transportation policy, it is impossible to separate water policy and transportation policy insofar as inland waterways are concerned. A *water* commission is not in a position to deal with this problem in its entirety. Nevertheless, it is appropriate for this Commission to call attention to the fact that the national transportation system can never attain optimum efficiency until its waterways become an integral component of that system, and are utilized in such a way as to minimize the total cost to the Nation of meeting its transportation needs. It is also appropriate for this Commission to point out that when waterway user charges are imposed, as recommended in this report, and institutional arrangements require that the rates charged by other modes of transportation realistically reflect economic costs, freight which can move on the waterways at the least real cost to the Nation will be encouraged to move by water. Finally, it is proper for this Commission to emphasize the importance of initiating a vigorous effort to achieve the goal of an efficient and fully coordinated national transportation system, and as a first step to improve the data base for such an effort.

DISCUSSION

The Commission's review of the three areas of deficiency leads to consideration of remedies which would modernize the Nation's waterway policies by improving evaluation procedures, promoting more equitable cost-sharing arrangements, and lead to better utilization of waterways as elements of a national transportation system.

Improving Evaluation Procedures

First, there is an urgent need to improve the procedures by which the decision is reached that a particular waterway project should be added to the national transportation system. This subject is treated broadly in Chapter 10 of this report in the section on evaluation. However, the problem of evaluating waterway projects is rendered unique by the fact that the Congress has, for this one type of water project, enacted into law certain procedures for determining the desirability of the construction of a contemplated waterway. This it did by including in Section 7 of the Department of Transportation Act of 1966 a provision requiring a determination of the probable effect of the waterway on the cost of transportation *to shippers*.[18] While there can be no objection to requiring the report on a waterway to show the potential savings to shippers, this is not a measure of the economic benefits of a waterway. From the standpoint of the Nation, a waterway project is justified only if it will reduce the economic–i.e., "real"–cost *to the Nation* of providing the transport services in question, and if the benefits derived exceed these costs. An estimate of the savings to shippers is of little value in determining whether a proposed waterway should be built, for a number of reasons not the least of which is that these so-called savings may be wiped out after the investment is made if the competing mode–such as a railroad–reduces its rates. This is not true of reductions in economic costs. They represent the value of the resources, including labor, required to provide the transportation service, and hence do not change if rates change. It follows that a comparison of economic costs must be made to determine whether the construction of a waterway would reduce the real cost to the Nation of providing needed transportation services.

It is the view of this Commission that it would be desirable for reports on potential waterway projects to show both the "savings to shippers" as required by Section 7 of P.L. 89-670, and a comparison of the true economic costs of transportation by the waterway and by the least-cost alternative mode–rail, truck, pipeline, or combinations thereof– and the associated benefits. The Congress and the public would then know three things: (1) what shippers might save, either by shifting their shipments to the waterway or as a result of the competing mode reducing its charges; (2) what "real" savings would accrue to the Nation if the waterway were constructed; and (3) whether construction of the waterway is economically sound. Unfortunately, and in the opinion of the Commission unnecessarily, Section 7

---

[18] P.L. 89-670, October 15, 1966, Sec. 7, 80 Stat. 931, 942, 49 USCA 1656.

has been interpreted as requiring the executive branch to confine its analysis to a determination of the first figure. The law does not prevent the executive branch from applying any test of desirability that it considers essential to determining whether or not a project is in the national interest. The Commission believes the economic test should be included in any future evaluation of a proposed navigation project and that Congress should amend Section 7 to *require* that an economic evaluation be made in addition to the estimation of the savings to shippers.

Improving Cost-Sharing Policy

As indicated previously, there is no longer any rational justification for assumption by the Federal Treasury of the entire cost of constructing, operating, and maintaining navigable waterways. Once this is accepted, the problem becomes one of deciding what share of the cost should be borne by non-Federal interests, and what is the best way to collect that share. Many who have advocated cost-sharing have proposed that the carriers operating on Federal waterways be required to pay tolls, or user charges. Others have suggested a fuel tax.[19] Another means, less frequently proposed, would be to require the carriers to maintain a record of their use of Federal waterways, probably in terms of ton-miles, and periodically to submit a report somewhat like an income tax return, along with a payment of whatever tax might be due for the number of units of use reported.

After considering these approaches, the Commission arrived at the conclusion that for *existing* waterways recovery of construction costs already incurred is impractical and that the most practicable system for recovering future operation and maintenance costs would be a combination of a fuel tax and lockage charges. The fuel tax should be paid both by commercial and pleasure craft. The lockage charges might be collected as lockage fees at each passage through the lock of a commercial vessel and by sale of annual lock permits to recreational vessels and other small craft. An alternative for commercial vessels would be for the lockmaster to record their passage and bill each company on a monthly or quarterly basis. It appears to be the view of some representatives of inland waterway shipping interests that if user charges are imposed they should be

uniform on all segments of interconnected waterways, such as the Mississippi River and its tributaries. The Commission believes this would be feasible.

At the hearings on its draft report, Commission members repeatedly asked witnesses who represented inland waterway interests what distinction they saw between on the one hand, trucks which must pay user charges in the form of license fees, toll charges, and fuel taxes and, on the other hand, barge tows which pay no such user charges. Some witnesses replied that trucks carry a different kind of cargo than barges, typically a higher-value cargo. Most asserted that trucks do not pay 100 percent of the cost of the highways they use; that passenger car owners and general taxpayers pay part of the cost. In view of the Commission's recommendations as to the charges to be collected from users of existing improved waterways—which would apply to recreational as well as commercial craft, and would not in fact reimburse the Federal Government for 100 percent of the costs of improving the waterways—the Commission regards these attempted distinctions as being without any real difference. Furthermore, the user charges that are collected by Federal and State governments in the form of fuel taxes do pay 100 percent of the costs of constructing and operating the Federal interstate highway system, and proposals to divert a portion of the revenues from these charges to mass transit subsidies are being seriously considered.

It is the view of the Commission that for waterways built in the future, the entire cost—construction costs as well as operation and maintenance costs—should be borne by the direct beneficiaries of the project. It would not, however, be desirable to require the repayment of the construction costs of new waterways in the form of user charges as this could result in the user charges for the new waterways being several times larger than those collected on the old waterways. A preferable system would be one under which the user charge collected on a new waterway would be the same as the charge for a comparable old waterway in the same region, and which would require that an appropriate non-Federal entity[20] or a Federal or Federal-State corporation[21] agree, in advance, to repay the construction cost, with interest, in installments over a period of years, in

---

[19] Presidents Kennedy, Johnson, and Nixon have supported fuel tax legislation, but the Congress has not seen fit to enact such legislation.

[20] Perhaps a State, or an interstate compact commission, where more than one State should contribute.

[21] Patterned after the St. Lawrence Seaway Development Corporation, perhaps, or similar to the Delaware River Basin Commission or a federally chartered regional corporation as discussed in Chapter 11 of this report.

a manner similar to that in which non-Federal entities presently reimburse the Federal Treasury for capacity provided in Federal reservoirs for the storage of water to be used for municipal and industrial supply. The costs of operating and maintaining the new waterways would, under such a scheme, be covered by the fuel taxes and user charges collected from the users of all components of the waterway system.

The cost to the Federal Government of operating and maintaining the shallow-draft inland waterways averaged about $73 million annually for the 5-year period 1968-1972, inclusive.[22] The commercial traffic on these same waterways during this 5-year period amounted to something less than 200 billion ton-miles. Had a user charge system to recover the entire cost of operating and maintaining these waterways been in effect during that period, the user charge per ton-mile should not have amounted to more than about 0.4 mil ($.0004) per ton-mile of commercial traffic, since recreational traffic would also bear part of the cost.[23] Although numerous statements were made at the Commission's regional conferences to the effect that user charges would seriously reduce or even eliminate the use of inland waterways, no solid evidence was offered in support of such statements. On the contrary, testimony as to the wide disparity in favor of water rates over rail and truck rates suggested that for the principal waterways traffic would not be diverted by user charges such as those recommended by the Commission.

In summary, the Commission believes that:

(1) For existing, or "old," waterways, the aim should be to recover, through a combination of fuel taxes and lockage charges, a progressively increasing annual total that would, by the end of 10 years, and indefinitely thereafter, be sufficient to cover the entire Federal annual expenditure for operation and maintenance. No attempt should be made to recover any part of the sunk construction cost.

(2) For "new" waterways, it would be desirable for the Federal Government to require that in advance of construction an appropriate entity other than the Federal Treasury agree to repay the construction cost, with interest, over a specified period of years. Costs of operating and maintaining the new waterways should be collected from the users, the same as for existing waterways.

There are a number of reasons for requiring future costs of waterways to be paid by the users rather than the Federal taxpayers. One of these reasons has already been mentioned: If non-Federal interests agree to repay the first cost of a waterway, the Congress and the public can be sure that those urging the project are sincere in believing that it is justified. Thus, cost-sharing requirements would be effective in eliminating political pressures from a group seeking a project for no other reason than that they expect it to be paid for by the Federal Treasury.

Another reason for requiring cost-sharing is that it is essential to prevent the inequity that results when those who benefit substantially from the construction of a public work pay no more of its cost than those who receive no benefits whatsoever, and who may even be adversely affected because they reside in a region that will be placed at a disadvantage by a project that stimulates the economy of a competing region.

User charges on waterways can also help eliminate inequities between different modes of transportation that result from uneven Federal policies. The railroads believe it is inequitable to require them to compete with carriers who pay nothing for the use of waterways provided at public expense. The problems involved in imposition of user charges to correct this inequity are complicated by the deficiencies in present laws governing the regulation of transportation rates. The principal objective of regulation should be to achieve a national transportation system that meets the Nation's transportation needs at least cost. To assure that this goal be achieved, it is essential that waterways be used to transport freight that can move by water at a lesser real cost to the Nation than by any other mode of transportation. But present regulation by the Interstate Commerce Commission does not always prevent competing modes from reducing their rates below cost for the purpose of diverting from the waterways traffic that could move at a lesser real cost by that mode. For

---

[22] Data provided by the U.S. Army Corps of Engineers. The amount shown does not include the cost of operating and maintaining those lower reaches of major rivers that are used by deep-draft vessels. The annual operation and maintenance costs for these deep-draft sections averaged about $13.5 million for the 5-year period 1968-1972.

[23] Information furnished the Commission by Professor Marvin Barloon of Case Western Reserve University suggests that from 15 to 20 percent of the marine fuel consumption in the Mississippi River and tributaries and Gulf coastal waterways might be for pleasure boat operation. (Letter dated February 21, 1973, to Commissioner James R. Ellis.)

this reason, the Commission believes that when the Congress imposes user charges on waterways it must also make possible such regulation of rates as may be necessary to insure that each mode of transport is used to the best advantage of the Nation as a whole. Regulation should require that all rates be compensatory, and filed with at least 30 days notice, to preserve rate stability, but otherwise should promote, rather than stifle, competition among various modes.

Better Utilization of Waterways as Elements of a National Transportation System

The foregoing leads directly into the third deficiency mentioned which presents a problem that lies somewhat outside the proper sphere of interest of the National Water Commission, since it involves both transportation and water policies. Nevertheless, the Commission believes it has an obligation to recommend that provisions be made at an early date for a vigorous attempt to determine the changes in national transportation policy that will insure that waterways shall be used most effectively and equitably as an important element of the national transportation system. The complex problems involved cannot be solved by simply requiring carriers to pay for the use of the public waterways.

Pending the development of a better solution to this problem than any that has been previously proposed, two courses of action should be pursued: (1) The Congress should seek to assure that the Nation's great investments in waterways shall be used—to the extent that their use is economically justified—by requiring that the rates charged by other modes of public transportation be so regulated that the imposition of user charges would not have the effect of shifting to these other modes any traffic that can move at lesser real cost by water; and (2) the executive branch should take steps to make available a more adequate data base to those who must ultimately find an answer to the difficult and complex problem of bringing into existence the best possible national transportation system.

The Commission recognizes the concerns expressed by knowledgeable witnesses at the hearings on its review report to the effect that inland water carriers could not expect fair treatment if they were placed under the regulatory jurisdiction of the same Federal agency that regulates rail and truck carriers. Simply stated, the water carriers fear that the agency would be pro-railroad or pro-truck. If such fears proved well-founded, the Commission's recommendation that waterways be treated as part of a national

transportation system would be frustrated. However, the Commission believes that the Congress by setting up and overseeing the right kind of transportation regulatory agency could provide reasonable assurances that such agency would not favor one form of transportation over another, but allow each to carry that cargo which from the standpoint of the national interest it carries best. If Congress does not create such a body, it cannot establish and enforce a rational national transportation policy.

RECOMMENDATIONS

5-1. **Any report proposing a Federal inland waterway project should provide an estimate of the true economic cost and benefit to the Nation of providing the contemplated transportation service, and a comparison thereof with the true economic cost of providing this service by the least-cost alternative means. This should be in addition to the estimate presently required by Section 7 of the Department of Transportation Act of 1966.**

5-2. **Legislation should be enacted to require non-Federal interests to bear an appropriate share of the cost of Federal inland waterway projects. Such legislation should require: (a) that carriers and pleasure craft using inland waterways be required to pay user charges such that the total collections on all Federal waterways would be sufficient to cover Federal expenditures for operation and maintenance of the entire system; (b) that within the bounds of administrative practicability the user charges should consist of a uniform tax on all fuels used by vessels operating on the inland waterways, plus lockage charges at rates sufficient to repay the cost of operating and maintaining the locks within integral segments of the total waterway system; (c) that charges be imposed gradually over a 10-year period and increased progressively so that by the end of that period they will be sufficient to recover annually the entire cost of operating and maintaining the Federal inland waterway system; and (d) that as a condition for Federal construction of future inland waterway projects responsible federally chartered or non-Federal entities be required to enter into agreements to repay the construction costs, including interest, over a specified period of years unless the Congress determines that a particular waterway will result in national defense benefits sufficient to**

120

justify assumption of a part of the cost by the Federal Government.

5-3. Any legislation requiring the payment of waterway user charges should also authorize and direct the Federal transportation regulatory agencies to regulate rates for all competing modes of transportation in such a way as to encourage the use of the waterways for any traffic that could move by that mode at the least economic cost to the Nation.

5-4. The Department of Transportation should broaden and intensify its efforts to improve national transportation policy. It should develop a plan for such administrative and legislative actions as may be required to bring into being an integrated national transportation system in which all modes of transportation, including inland waterways, are utilized in such a way as to reduce to a practical minimum the cost to the Nation of meeting the demands for transportation. To prepare the way for the development of such an integrated and efficient national transportation system, the Department of Transportation should develop and submit to the President and the Congress recommendations designed to provide the data base that will be needed to achieve the objective of this recommendation.

~~~~~~~~~~~~~~~~~~~~~~~~~~~~~ *Section C*

Food and Fiber Programs:[24] Increasing Agricultural Production Through Water Resource Development

The Federal Government has a number of water resources development programs that increase the number of acres in the Nation's agricultural land base or that increase the productivity of the agricultural land now farmed. These programs encompass three principal activities: supplying irrigation water, protecting agricultural land from floods, and draining land for agricultural use. The issue to be faced in this section is whether these programs should be continued at present levels, expanded, or reduced.

The Commission has made no attempt to evaluate the farm price support programs of the Federal Government, even though the size and nature of those programs may affect the demand for water and land. Land retirement programs and acreage allotments, for example, encourage intensive farming on land remaining in production, with heavy inputs of water and fertilizer. Production quotas, on the other hand, would tend to discourage intensive farming. The alternative futures analyzed in the study[25] of future demands for water and land for agriculture included alternative hypotheses as to future farm policies. The Commission's mandate, however, does not extend to an evaluation of farm price support programs and no recommendations on them are made.[26]

In the balance of this section, there follows a brief description of the programs and an inquiry into present and future demand for agricultural production and the adequacy of present and future resources to meet the demand.

[24] This discussion excludes problems of forest products on which the Commission has made no study and expresses no opinion. The discussion also excludes measures unrelated to water resources that are aimed at increasing agricultural production, such as research and extension programs.

[25] HEADY, Earl O et al., Iowa State University (1971). Agricultural Water Demands, prepared for the National Water Commission. National Technical Information Service, Springfield, Va., Accession No. PB 206 790; and MADSEN, Howard C et al., Iowa State University (1972). Alternative Demands for Water and Land for Agricultural Purposes, prepared for the National Water Commission.

National Technical Information Service, Springfield Va., Accession No. PB 211 444.

[26] Recent developments suggest a trend toward the free market policies assumed in 9 of the 11 alternative futures analyzed in the Iowa State University studies. The Department of Agriculture has reduced the acreage set aside in the land retirement program for 1973, and in testimony before the Agriculture Appropriations Subcommittee of the House Committee on Appropriations on February 21, 1973, Secretary of Agriculture Earl L. Butz announced that the Administration intended to propose modifications in the domestic farm programs to move agriculture toward greater independence and greater reliance on the marketplace.

DESCRIPTION OF FEDERAL PROGRAMS

Three departments of the Federal Government are responsible for the principal water supply, flood control, and drainage programs. The Bureau of Reclamation of the U.S. Department of the Interior is principally concerned with irrigation in the 17 Western States. It supplies raw, arid land with irrigation water, thereby bringing new land into agricultural production, and it provides supplemental irrigation water for lands already in cultivation, thereby maintaining or increasing their productivity. The U.S. Army Corps of Engineers provides flood control and drainage for land presently being cropped as well as for potential cropland. The Corps also furnishes some irrigation water. The U.S. Department of Agriculture has two agencies engaged in water control programs. The Soil Conservation Service (SCS), operating under Public Law 566 of the 83rd Congress, provides flood protection and drainage for small, upstream watersheds. Some irrigation water is supplied from these projects. The Department's Agricultural Stabilization and Conservation Service (ASCS) has an extensive program of financial assistance for drainage of agricultural land to enhance its productivity. The extent of the increase in farm productivity resulting from drainage and flood protection programs is not easily documented, since neither the Corps of Engineers nor the Agriculture Department publish such data. On the basis of the acreage involved, it is likely that the Department of Agriculture's program has the largest impact on crop production, followed by the Corps of Engineers and Bureau of Reclamation programs, in that order. Programs of other agencies, such as the Tennessee Valley Authority and the International Boundary and Water Commission, have a much lesser effect and are not discussed herein, but the same policies adopted for the major programs should be extended to them.

Department of Agriculture Programs

Some conception of the magnitude of the Department of Agriculture programs is revealed by gross expenditures and other operational data. The Agricultural Conservation Program of ASCS and predecessor agencies in the 35 years of operation between 1935 and 1970 disbursed $6.7 billion on land and water conservation measures, improving the drainage on more than 52 million acres and assisting construction of some 80,000 small irrigation reservoirs and

over 2 million ponds and pits providing water for agricultural use.[27]

The small watershed program of the SCS under Public Law 566 has led to authorization for the installation of more than 1,000 projects (as of June 30, 1971) at a cost of about $2.3 billion. These projects deal with watersheds totaling roughly 66 million acres, but no estimate of the agricultural land benefited or the crops which will be produced on those lands is available in a form useful for making policy recommendations. Stream channeling for drainage and flood protection is part of the small watershed program, and estimates indicate that more than 20,000 miles of streams will be altered. Some 6,000 miles of channel alterations have already been completed at a cost of $166.5 million.[28] In January 1972, slightly under 3,000 applications for grants under the program were pending for a like number of small watersheds embracing 227 million acres.[29]

Corps of Engineers Programs

Flood Control and Drainage: The nature of the flood control program of the Corps of Engineers results in the protection of large amounts of agricultural lands surrounding urban and suburban developed areas. In addition, large areas of low-lying lands have been reclaimed through Corps of Engineers flood control and major drainage projects, particularly in the valley of the lower Mississippi River and its tributaries, and in Central and Southern Florida. The Corps of Engineers does not publish data that permit an analysis of the costs per acre of draining or protecting arable land from floods, nor does it publish data on the incremental amount of agricultural production that results from its flood control and drainage projects. Gross figures on land suitable for agriculture that has been or will be protected by Corps flood

---

[27] U.S. DEPARTMENT OF AGRICULTURE, Agricultural Stabilization and Conservation Service (October 1971). Agricultural Conservation Program, Practice Accomplishments by States, 35 Year Summary, 1936 Through 1970. U.S. Department of Agriculture, Washington, D.C. pp. 97-99, 111, 112, 166-168, and 179-181.

[28] The Commission's views on channelization are contained in Chapter 2.

[29] U.S. DEPARTMENT OF AGRICULTURE (March 1972). Inventory of Benefits, Costs, and Other Data for P.L. 566 Watershed Work Plans. A staff report on Project Plans approved to July 1971 under Public Law 566 of the 83d Congress. Compiled by the Natural Resources Economics Division, Economic Research Service, for the Soil Conservation Service. U.S. Department of Agriculture, Washington, D.C.

control projects are presented in Table 5-1. A total of 53.6 million acres of land are benefited by projects completed or under construction, and another 36.7 million may be benefited by future work.

TABLE 5-1.–Status of lands in U.S. Army Corps of Engineers flood control and major drainage programs as of December 1971

Status	Completed Or Under Construction	Future Work[1]	Total
Agricultural	(Millions of Acres)		
Cleared and suitable for agriculture	29.6	19.6	49.2
Suitable for agriculture when cleared	6.3	6.4	12.7
Not suitable for agriculture	8.1	4.3	12.4
Not classified	9.6	6.4	16.0
Total	53.6	36.7	90.3
Drainage			
No drainage problem	23.7	11.5	35.2
Drainage works provided	12.7	11.1	23.8
Drainage required	17.2	14.1	31.3
Total	53.6	36.7	90.3

[1] Includes projects authorized but not started and future work.

Source: U.S. ARMY, Office of Chief of Engineers, Policy Programs and Legislative Branch, Policy and Analysis Division, Washington, D.C. (1972). Communication of February 15, 1972, to National Water Commission.

Works already completed or now under construction would allow 6.3 million acres of land not presently cultivated to be added to the agricultural land base when it is cleared. Moreover, the productivity of 12.7 million acres has already been enhanced by the building of drainage works. It is also likely that some portion, perhaps a large one, of the 29.6 million acres cleared and suitable for agriculture are not now being cultivated but could be brought into production if demand warranted it.[30] Some indication of the actual effect of this program is provided by a report issued by the Department of Agriculture which indicates that the Corps' flood control program in the lower Mississippi valley contributed to the clearing of 4.1 million acres of land in the period 1950-1969, land which was largely devoted to the growing of soybeans.[31] At its New Orleans conference, the Commission was told that the channel clearing and straightening under this program had worsened flood problems downstream by speeding up the flow of water, requiring the construction of additional protective works to provide protection against higher flood stages.

Recent Projects: In the absence of detailed data from the Corps of Engineers, the staff reviewed the project reports submitted to the 91st Congress by the Corps, which formed the basis for projects which were authorized in the Flood Control Act of 1970,[32] and therefore indicate the nature of the future Corps programs. The projects having agricultural flood control or drainage benefits can be divided into two groups. The first group is composed of projects devoted almost entirely to producing agricultural benefits. The second group consists of projects which, though devoted in part to agriculture, have substantial urban, recreational, and other components.

There are five almost entirely agricultural projects. When completed, these projects would add 237,570 acres of cropland and improve 133,925 additional acres at a total cost of $37 million. The largest single project is along the Red River downstream from Alexandria, Louisiana, in Eastern Rapides and South-Central Avoyelles Parishes, Louisiana. The project would provide flood control and drainage to protect 206,000 acres from overflow. Some farming is presently taking place on about one-third of the land but it is subject to flooding four or more times per year. The added land would support soybeans, pasture,

[30] A large portion of this 29.6 million acres falls within the 36.4 acres that either have no drainage problem or have been provided drainage works.

[31] U.S. DEPARTMENT OF AGRICULTURE, Economic Research Service (October 1971). Land Use Change in the Southern Mississippi Alluvial Valley, 1950-69, Agricultural Economic Report No. 215. U.S. Department of Agriculture, Washington, D.C. pp. 5, 6, 11.

[32] P.L. 91-611, December 31, 1970, Title II, 84 Stat. 1818, 1825.

cotton, and corn. "The recommended project would have a significant impact on regional development. . .by permanently making its land resource more productive." In the benefit-cost evaluation, the increased agricultural production provides all but $50,000 of the estimated $3,364,000 of benefits. The cost of the project is $25.9 million, composed of $9.4 million from SCS and $16.5 million from the Corps.[33]

The other four projects in this first group are the following:

1. Steele Bayou, Yazoo River: The project would permit more intensive farming on 96,000 acres, and add 29,000 acres presently wooded but suitable for agriculture when cleared. Cost: $4 million.[34]

2. Posten Bayou, Arkansas: Improvements to interior drainage network and new outlet to Red River should "assure greatly expanded production from some 12,500 acres of fertile farm lands and make possible the conversion of additional marginal woodlands into productive agricultural lands." Project would permit conversion of 2,570 acres of woodlands to cropland. Cost: $2 million.[35]

3. Fort Chartres and Ivy Landing Drainage District No. 5 and Stringtown Drainage and Levee District No. 4, Illinois:[36] Construction of three pumping stations, new drainage ditches, and rehabilitation of existing ditches. Project area contains 18,700 acres of highly productive bottomland, 95 percent of which is cultivated. Flooding occurs practically every year. Seventy-five percent of $281,100 annual benefits are crop damage prevention.

Some small wooded areas will be converted to cropland. Cost: $2.4 million.

4. Western Tennessee Tributaries, Tennessee and Kentucky:[37] Construction of two pumping stations and improvement of channels. Total cleared acreage: 7,425. Practically all tillable land is in cultivation. Flooding occurs nearly every year. Primary problem is crop production losses. Benefits to farmers would largely be from higher crop yields. Cost: $2.7 million.

The second group of Corps projects, consisting of those with substantial nonagricultural components, contains six projects. Their aggregate total cost is $282 million. Agricultural benefits account for varying shares of the total benefits set forth in each proposal. The following four proposals identify significant agricultural benefits:

1. Sabine River and Tributaries, Texas and Louisiana:[38] Three multiple-purpose dam and reservoir projects, local flood protection, and extension of an authorized commercial navigation channel. Estimated average annual flood damages on the Sabine River under 1964 conditions are approximately $2.4 million of which 40 percent are agricultural losses. Total improved agricultural land in the flood plain is 47,998 acres. Approximately 952,900 acres of land are subject to flooding. Average annual benefits from the project include $3.7 million damage prevention and $.2 million improved agricultural efficiency. Water requirements and supply for irrigation in the basin are included in the project. Cost: $191.8 million.

2. Sheyenne River, North Dakota:[39] Multiple-purpose reservoir. Agriculture is the basic industry of the basin. Forest losses are likely in the areas downstream from the proposed dam. "Once these areas are protected from flooding, timber would be cleared for agricultural use." Average annual agricultural benefits of $181,900 account for 12 percent of

[33] U.S. DEPARTMENT OF THE ARMY, Chief of Engineers (1971). Eastern Rapides and South-Central Avoyelles Parishes, Louisiana, Senate Document No. 91-113, 91st Congress, 2d Session. U.S. Government Printing Office, Washington, D.C. pp. 5, 6, 93.

[34] U.S. DEPARTMENT OF THE ARMY, Chief of Engineers (1970). Steele Bayou, Yazoo River (Lower Tributaries), Mississippi, Senate Document No. 91-74, 91st Congress, 2d Session. U.S. Government Printing Office, Washington, D.C.

[35] U.S. DEPARTMENT OF THE ARMY, Chief of Engineers (1970). Posten Bayou, Arkansas, House Document No. 91-318, 91st Congress, 2d Session. U.S. Government Printing Office, Washington, D.C. pp. viii, xviii.

[36] U.S. DEPARTMENT OF THE ARMY, Chief of Engineers (1970). Fort Chartres and Ivy Landing Drainage District No. 5 and Stringtown Drainage and Levee District No. 4, Illinois, House Document No. 91-412, 91st Congress, 2d Session. U.S. Government Printing Office, Washington, D.C. pp. 4, 40, 37.

[37] U.S. DEPARTMENT OF THE ARMY, Chief of Engineers (1970). Western Tennessee Tributaries, Tennessee and Kentucky, House Document No. 91-414, 91st Congress, 2d Session. U.S. Government Printing Office, Washington, D.C. pp. 17, 19, 5, xvi.

[38] U.S. DEPARTMENT OF THE ARMY, Chief of Engineers (1971). Sabine River and Tributaries, Texas and Louisiana, House Document No. 91-429, 91st Congress, 2d Session. U.S. Government Printing Office, Washington, D.C. pp. 279, 189, 91, 114, 84.

[39] U.S. DEPARTMENT OF THE ARMY, Chief of Engineers (1970). Sheyenne River, North Dakota, House Document No. 91-330, 91st Congress, 2d Session. U.S. Government Printing Office, Washington, D.C. pp. 21, xvii, xv.

total average annual benefits. Total cost: $20 million. Twelve percent of total cost: $2.4 million.

3. Souris River, North Dakota:[40] Reservoir for flood control and channel improvement. Agriculture is the principal occupation of the basin; farms comprise 85 percent of the land. Average annual agriculture benefits from the project of $53,300 comprise 1 percent of total average annual benefits. Total cost: $34 million. One percent of total cost: $.34 million.

4. Running Water Draw, Plainview, Texas:[41] Channel improvements, outlet channels, underground flood conduits, and diversion works. Economy of the area is centered around irrigated agriculture. Increased land use affecting about 1,810 acres will result from the project. Twelve percent of average annual benefits are due to increased land use. Flood damages along Running Water Draw and in playa lakes areas are 95 percent urban and 5 percent agricultural. Eighty-eight percent of average annual benefits are due to flood control; 4.4 percent is due to control of agricultural flood damage. Total cost: $5.8 million. 16.4 percent of total cost: $.95 million.

Irrigation: The Corps of Engineers has no single-purpose irrigation projects, but provides additional capacity in some of its reservoirs for storage of irrigation water. In the 17 Western States, the Bureau of Reclamation is responsible for marketing this water under Section 8 of the Flood Control Act of 1944.[42] Considerable controversy has arisen over the application of this provision of law, particularly on the Missouri and Columbia Rivers, where irrigation pumpers who would otherwise have had to divert from a free-flowing stream can now pump from a reservoir. It appears equitable to expect the pumpers to reimburse the Federal Government for the benefits received as a result of reduced pumping head and more dependable water supply, but they should not have to pay a portion of the costs of the reservoirs unless they have storage space allocated for their use.

In the Eastern States, the Corps of Engineers usually requires irrigation water users to make a contribution of half the portion of the costs of multiple-purpose projects allocated to irrigation, in lieu of the interest-free repayment provisions of the Federal reclamation laws. The largest Corps project having irrigation as a purpose is the Central and Southern Florida project, where over a million acres of agricultural land are being reclaimed by a project authorized in 1948. A recent report[43] on an addition to that project authorized in the Flood Control Act of 1968[44] recommended construction of an inter-related system of canals, levees, pumping stations, and structures necessary to supply irrigation water, maintain optimum water levels, and remove flood waters in Martin County, Florida, and is an example of a recently authorized Corps of Engineers project which is primarily for irrigation. Annual benefits of the project are stated to be as follows:

Purpose	Dollars	Percent
Flood Damages Prevented	720,000	5
Increased Land Use	4,747,900	33
Irrigation	8,799,000	62
Recreation	13,000	—
Total	14,279,900	100

Total costs of the project were estimated to be $15,470,900 and the benefit cost ratio is stated to be 15.3 to 1.[45]

The cost allocation, based on allocating to flood control the cost of an alternative plan to provide the same flood control benefits but with the irrigation and recreation features omitted, was computed as follows:

Purpose	Cost Allocation	Percent
Flood Control	$8,136,700	53
Irrigation	7,234,200	47
Recreation	100,000	—
Total	$15,470,900	100

[40] U.S. DEPARTMENT OF THE ARMY, Chief of Engineers (1970). Souris River, North Dakota, House Document No. 91-321, 91st Congress, 2d Session. U.S. Government Printing Office, Washington, D. C. pp. 19, 67.

[41] U.S. DEPARTMENT OF THE ARMY, Chief of Engineers (1969). Running Water Draw, Plainview, Texas, House Document No. 91-192, 91st Congress, 1st Session. U.S. Government Printing Office, Washington, D.C. pp. 4, 8, 29.

[42] P.L. 534, December 22, 1944, 78th Congress, 58 Stat. 887, 890, 43 USCA 390b.

[43] U.S. ARMY CORPS OF ENGINEERS, Jacksonville District (1967). Survey-Review Report on Central and Southern Florida Project, Martin County, Florida. Jacksonville, Fla. (Portions of the report published later as Senate Document No. 101, 90th Congress. U.S. Government Printing Office, Washington, D.C.)

[44] P.L. 90-483, August 13, 1968, Title II, 82 Stat. 731, 740-741

[45] Survey-Review Report. p. 25.

Federal share of the costs is to be $8,072,500, with local interests required to assume the balance of the cost, consisting of providing all lands, easements, and rights-of-way, assuming the costs of new highway bridges and alterations to utilities, and making a cash contribution estimated at $5,266,000 prior to construction. In addition, the local interests are required to operate and maintain the project features after completion.

With provision of adequate flood control and irrigation facilities, it is considered by the Corps of Engineers that citrus fruits will become the dominant agricultural industry by the year 2020 using 79,400 of the 85,500 acres benefited by the project, an increase of 59,700 acres over that planted in citrus in 1965. The value of the crops to be produced is obviously high enough to support full repayment of the project costs.

Bureau of Reclamation Program

The Bureau of Reclamation maintains excellent statistics on the amount of land irrigated through its projects, the nature and value of the crops grown, and the expenditures incurred for construction and operation. Table 5-2 shows the acreage irrigated by Bureau projects for selected years.

In 1969, the total[46] of 8.6 million acres served by Bureau of Reclamation projects was slightly more than one-fifth of the total of 39.1 million acres irrigated in the Nation in 1969, 89 percent of which (34.8 million acres) were located in the 17 Western Reclamation States.[47] The average increase in land served by Bureau of Reclamation projects during the 20-year period 1950 to 1969 was 175,000 acres per year. Figure 5-1 shows the relationship between Federal and non-Federal irrigation in the 17 Reclamation States. Between 1949 and 1959, non-Federal irrigated acreage increased about 33 percent, while Federal irrigated acreage increased a little over 40 percent. In the next decade, non-Federal irrigation in those States increased by only 7 percent as Federal irrigation rose by 26 percent. Since 1939, the increase in non-Federal irrigation in the 17 Reclamation States has been due largely to the use of ground water, a negligible source of supply for Federal projects. Expressed as a percentage of all irrigated land in the Reclamation States, Federal irrigation accounted for 21 percent in 1949, for 22 percent in 1959, and for 25 percent in 1969.

Table 5-3 gives acreage and value of principal crops grown in Bureau projects for the year 1969.

It can be calculated from Table 5-3 that about 23 percent of reclamation land produces hay with an average annual gross return of $106.50 per acre. Barley and corn are grown on about 13 percent of reclamation land and produce annual gross revenues around $100 per acre. Thus, 36 percent of the land irrigated by Bureau project water produces crops whose gross value, without deducting costs of labor, equipment, fertilizer, and pesticides, averages about $100 an acre. On the other hand, fruits and nuts account for 7 percent of reclamation land and have an annual gross return around $660 per acre; vegetables account for 9 percent of the land and have an annual gross return of approximately $600 per acre. Thus, only 16 percent of reclamation land is used for high-value crops.

TABLE 5-2.—Total acreage irrigated by Bureau of Reclamation water for selected years	
Year	Irrigated Acreage
1906	22,300
1910	473,423
1920	2,205,420
1930	2,790,856
1940	3,391,070
1945	4,162,588
1950	5,077,186
1955	6,261,761
1960	6,899,711
1965	8,012,021
1969	8,575,761
1971	8,833,998

Source: U.S. BUREAU OF RECLAMATION (1972). Federal Reclamation Projects, Water & Land Resource Accomplishments 1971. U.S. Government Printing Office, Washington, D.C. Table 5, p. 64.

[46] Use of Bureau of Reclamation statistics for 1949, 1959, and 1969 permits comparisons to be made with U.S. Census Bureau Censuses of Agriculture.

[47] U.S. BUREAU OF THE CENSUS (May 1972). 1969 Census of Agriculture—County Data (by state and for the United States). Issued on a State by State Basis. U.S. Department of Commerce, Washington, D.C. Another 600,000 acres in the West were irrigated with Bureau of Indian Affairs water. See U.S. BUREAU OF INDIAN AFFAIRS, Division of Economic Development (undated). Irrigation Land Data, Calendar Year 1969. Memo, Bureau of Indian Affairs, Washington, D.C.

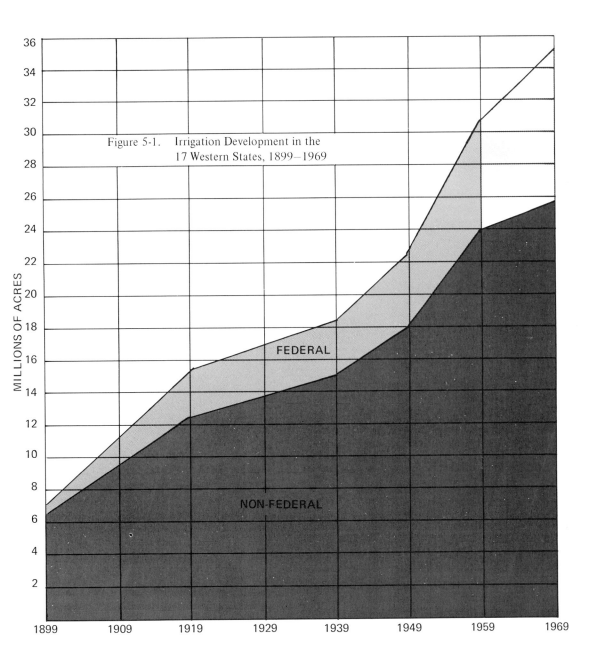

Figure 5-1.   Irrigation Development in the
              17 Western States, 1899–1969

FEDERAL

NON-FEDERAL

MILLIONS OF ACRES

36
34
32
30
28
26
24
22
20
18
16
14
12
10
8
6
4
2

1899   1909   1919   1929   1939   1949   1959   1969

Source: U.S. DEPARTMENT OF COMMERCE, Bureau of the Census. Adapted from Figure 1.2, Earl O. Heady,
       Howard C. Madsen, Kenneth J. Nicol, Stanley H. Hargrove, Future Water and Land Use Effect of
       Selected Public Agricultural and Irrigation Policies on Water Demand and Land Use, p. I-32.

TABLE 5-3.—Acreages and values of crops grown on farms in Bureau of Reclamation projects in 1969		
	Total Acreage Harvested on Farms in Bur. of Reclamation Projects (acres)	Gross Crop Value for Farms in Bur. of Reclam. Projects (dollars)
Wheat	374,317	25,709,921
Barley	617,209	46,952,959
Corn	455,156	52,347,501
Oats	114,502	6,053,908
Rice	190,485	50,453,415
Sorghum	242,317	20,967,682
All Hay	1,997,483	213,275,585
Beans, Dry Edible	320,913	44,821,334
Cotton	569,018	104,530,488
Sugar Beets	586,774	139,885,503
Vegetables	746,679	450,283,840
Fruits and Nuts	606,474	402,068,630
Potatoes	309,582	136,798,334

Source: U.S. BUREAU OF RECLAMATION (1970). Federal Reclamation Projects, Water & Land Resource Accomplishments, 1969. U.S. Government Printing Office, Washington, D.C. Table 3, pp 43-44.

As of June 30, 1971, projects were authorized, but not yet constructed, to provide a full water supply for the irrigation of 552,000 acres of land and a supplemental water supply for another 1.6 million irrigable acres, 1.2 million acres of which are located in the Central Arizona Project.[48]

Statistics compiled by the Bureau of Reclamation for June 30, 1971, showed that the total construction cost of all authorized Bureau of Reclamation projects was $12.1 billion, of which $6.2 billion was tentatively allocated to irrigation. The Bureau expects to secure repayment contracts for about $2.1 billion, and through June 30, 1970, only about $266 million had actually been repaid on matured repayment contracts and $268 million from special sources, such as contributions and advances and water service contracts.[49]

---

[48] BOLLMAN, Frank H et al. (July 1972). A Summary Appraisal of Farm Productive Capacity, Part III, Status of Irrigated Agriculture. Unpublished memo, National Water Commission, Arlington, Va. pp. 49, 50. Based on U.S. Bureau of Reclamation figures.

[49] U.S. BUREAU OF RECLAMATION (1972). Statistical Report of the Commissioner, Statistical and Financial Appendix, Schedules I, II, and III. pp. 79-83.

WEAKNESSES OF THE PROGRAMS

A primary weakness of the Federal water resources development projects is that they have been heavily subsidized by the Federal Government; that is, by all the taxpayers of the Nation, to provide benefits for a few. The water users on some modern Federal Reclamation projects, for example, repay no more than 10 percent of the construction costs attributable to irrigation, the remaining cost being borne by the Federal Government in three ways: by not requiring the water users to reimburse the Treasury for the interest on the capital advanced for project construction, by permitting power revenues and sometimes other nonirrigation revenues to be credited toward irrigation reimbursement, and by alocating an unduly large part of the costs to nonreimbursable purposes.

As another example, flood control projects undertaken by the Corps of Engineers and the Soil Conservation Service often make it possible for landowners to receive large windfall benefits by enabling them to convert woodlands or pasture lands to croplands. As explained in Chapter 15, in some instances beneficiaries receive these windfalls at little or no cost to themselves, particularly in the lower Mississippi River and Tributaries project, where the Federal Government pays the full cost of constructing, operating, and maintaining the project. Finally, water projects that result in large increases in the production of certain commodities have been undertaken with little or no consideration of the demand for those commodities.

Still another major weakness of present procedures for deciding whether a water project should be undertaken is found in the evaluation procedures used.[50] Of particular importance is the value assigned various crops in evaluating benefits of contemplated projects. Because of the price-support programs utilized by the United States to maintain farm income, prevailing prices received by farmers for supported crops should not be used in making an economic evaluation of a water project that will further increase the production of these price-supported commodities. Often in the past the prices used in evaluation of such water projects were not adjusted for price supports. For this reason alone it seems certain that some water projects that have been undertaken in the past have not been economically sound. In 1966, the Water Resources Council established price standards for project evaluation which

---

[50] See Chapter 10 for the Commission's discussion of evaluation procedures.

reject use of prevailing prices received by farmers for supported crops. Instead, the standards require use of "adjusted normalized" prices which are supposed to correct for the impact of price-support subsidies.

One of the great controversies in water policy has been the role of Bureau of Reclamation irrigation development in producing "surplus" crops. The Commission has been unable to determine the exact impact of the Reclamation program on crop surpluses; however, nearly 37 percent of the acreage served by Bureau of Reclamation project facilities produced crops eligible for Federal price support programs in 1969. (Table 5-4.) In terms of the value of major price-supported crops, Bureau-served projects account for significant production of only sugar beets, barley, rice, and cotton (Table 5-5), and for only 4.2 percent of the total value of all crops eligible for price supports. There is no way, short of a massive field investigation of the operations of individual farmers, to determine exactly how much of the production from Federal reclamation projects is paid for in part through the price-support program.

TABLE 5-4.—Major crops eligible for various Federal agricultural programs served by Bureau of Reclamation project facilities—1969

Crop	Reclamation Project Acreage	Percent of Total Reclamation Project Acreage
Wheat	374,317	4.36
Corn	455,156	5.31
Cotton	569,018	6.64
Sorghum	242,317	2.83
Barley	617,209	7.19
Oats	114,502	1.34
Rye	2,291	.03
Sugar Beets	586,774	6.84
Rice	190,485	2.22
	3,152,069	36.76

Source: U.S. BUREAU OF RECLAMATION (1971). Summary Report of the Commissioner, Bureau of Reclamation 1970, Statistical and Financial Appendix, Parts I, II, & III. U.S. Government Printing Office, Washington, D.C. p. 115.

It is obvious, however, that agricultural price-support and supply-control programs encourage farmers to use irrigation water on crops with acreage allotments just as they have stimulated increased use

TABLE 5-5.—Farm value of major crops eligible for Federal agricultural programs total and Bureau of Reclamation served acreage—1969

Crop	Total National (millions of dollars)	Reclamation Served (millions of dollars)	Reclamation Proportion (%)
Wheat	1,816	26	1.4
Corn (grain)	5,290	52	1.0
Cotton (lint)	1,055	105	10.0
Sorghum (grain)	791	21	2.7
Barley	369	47	12.7
Oats	565	6	1.1
Rice	450	50	11.1
Sugar Beets	353	140	39.7
Total	10,689	447	4.2

Sources: U.S. BUREAU OF RECLAMATION (1971). Summary Report of the Commissioner, Bureau of Reclamation 1970, Statistical and Financial Appendix, Parts I, II, & III. U.S. Government Printing Office, Washington, D.C. p. 115. and U.S. DEPARTMENT OF AGRICULTURE (1971). Agricultural Statistics 1971. U.S. Government Printing Office, Washington, D.C. p. 459.

of fertilizers and other measures which increase productivity. Elsewhere in this report, measures are advocated that will facilitate transfers of water to its most productive uses.[51] The Commission also recommends that irrigation users served by new Federal projects pay the full costs of water supply.[52] These changes may result in more or less irrigation water use, but the resulting total costs to society will be lower because they will improve efficiency in the use of water and related resources.

When irrigators receive water on a subsidized basis, incentives to use water carefully and efficiently are often removed. Where water is priced substantially below cost, it will be to the advantage of irrigators to be lavish in its use and neglectful of programs to stretch supplies and improve the productivity of water.

The assertion that the price of irrigation water is often substantially below the cost and, as a result, uneconomic projects are sometimes advanced was

[51] See Chapter 7.

[52] See Chapter 15.

confirmed at the Commission's public conferences held in January 1973. For example, a spokesman for the Pacific Northwest Waterways Association told the Commission that application of full-cost pricing to one Federal Reclamation project presently under construction (the Manson Unit in the State of Washington) would increase annual water charges to irrigators from $32.50 per acre to $414.00 per acre. Subsequently, at the same conference, the President of the Washington State Reclamation Association (who is also manager of the South Columbia Basin Irrigation District) testified that annual gross crop receipts on the nearby Columbia Basin Project were about $218 per irrigated acre. Even if future specialized crop production on the Manson Unit produces many times that amount of gross crop receipts, it is doubtful that the value of the crops plus the increased business profits generated in processing and marketing them could support the $414 full-cost annual charge per acre for water alone, plus the additional costs of bringing orchards into production.

Bureau of Reclamation figures show that total capital costs of the Manson Unit project, including costs of the Federal Columbia River Power System to furnish pumping power but excluding any interest component, will be $16,624,000 to provide a full water supply to 2,052 acres and a supplemental supply to 4,003 acres. The interest-free irrigation cost to develop the Manson Unit will be $2,746 per acre. Of the total interest-free $16,624,000 cost, only $3,855,000 will be repaid by irrigators; the balance will be covered by power revenues.

SUPPLY AND DEMAND

The answer to the question whether or not the water resources development programs described herein should be continued at present levels, expanded, or reduced depends in part upon future food and fiber demands. Those demands will be a function of four variables:

(1) population levels;
(2) income levels, lifestyles, and eating habits;
(3) export and import levels; and
(4) food prices.

The domestic supply available to meet future food and fiber demands is also a function of four variables:

(1) the resource base, including the arable land base and water supply;
(2) technological, scientific, and managerial advances affecting agriculture;
(3) governmental policies relating to control of supply and to restrictions on the use of

fertilizers and other inputs that increase production; and

(4) resource and product prices.

In recent years the Department of Agriculture, the Bureau of Reclamation, and the Tennessee Valley Authority have attempted to make model studies to develop relationships among and between these variables. The Tennessee Valley Authority, because of its role in fertilizer production, undertook studies of the relationships between fertilizer application and crop production. The Bureau of Reclamation is developing such relationships between water use and crop production. In order to take advantage of the work underway for these agencies at the Iowa State University, the National Water Commission contracted with the University for analyses of the demand for land and water for crop production under 11 different sets of hypotheses, or alternative futures. The full results of the analyses are contained in two reports[53] prepared for the Commission and are summarized briefly here. They serve to confirm the Commission's conclusions that the Nation's land and water resources are adequate to meet future needs at least through the year 2000 if they are used in ways which avoid waste and inefficiency.

Alternative Futures for Agriculture

Eleven possible alternative futures for agricultural water demands were analyzed. The assumptions on which they are based are summarized in Table 5-6. The alternatives were selected to encompass a wide range of possible alternative futures.

The 11 forecast models or alternative futures analyzed can be considered in four general groups. The first (Futures A, B, C, and D) defines alternative futures in terms of conventional sets of assumptions dealing with population, farm policies, exports, technology, etc. The second (Futures A1, A2, and A3) incorporates alternative prices of water. The third (Futures G and H) provides for continuing per capita beef and veal consumption at present levels (116.7 pounds per capita per annum) and for substituting vegetable proteins for the 26 percent increase in per

[53] For details, see HEADY, Earl O et al., Iowa State University (1971). Agricultural Water Demands, prepared for the National Water Commission. National Technical Information Service, Springfield, Va., Accession No. PB 206 790; and MADSEN, Howard C et al., Iowa State University (1972). Alternative Demands for Water and Land for Agricultural Purposes, prepared for the National Water Commission. National Technical Information Service, Springfield, Va., Accession No. PB 211 444.

TABLE 5-6.–Summary of alternative futures reviewed by the Commission for agricultural water demands

Alternative Future	Farm Policy	Population	Water Price	Exports[4]	Technology
Future A	free market	300 million[1]	present	1967-69 average	trend
Future A1	free market	300 million	$15.00/A.F.	1967-69 average	trend
Future A2	free market	300 million	$22.50/A.F.	1967-69 average	trend
Future A3	free market	300 million	$30.00/A.F.	1967-69 average	trend
Future B	free market	280 million[2]	present	1967-69 average	trend
Future C	annual land retirement	280 million	present	1967-69 average	trend
Future D	free market	325 million[3]	present	double the 1967-69 average	advanced
Future G	free market with beef consumption held at present per capita levels	300 million	present	1967-69 average	trend
Future H	annual land retirement with beef consumption held at present per capita levels	300 million	present	1967-69 average	trend
Future I	free market with 110 pound nitrogen limitation	280 million	present	1967-69 average	trend
Future J	free market with 50 pound nitrogen limitation	280 million	present	1967-69 average	trend

[1] This is the C population level of the Department of Commerce.
[2] This is the D population level of the Department of Commerce.
[3] This is the B population level of the Department of Commerce.
[4] Imports of beef and veal, lamb and mutton, and dairy products are assumed to equal average 1967-69 per capita levels in 2000.

capita beef and veal consumption in 2000 assumed in all of the other alternative futures. Finally, the fourth (Futures I and J) incorporates an assumption of a restriction on the rate of application of nitrogen fertilizer in agriculture as one possible step that might be taken to improve environmental quality.

The forecasts of agricultural water demands deal with water use only in the nine Western basins where the largest consumptive use of water is for irrigation and where over 90 percent of the currently irrigated land is located. Water use in the East was not considered because it appears that demands for water for agriculture will not be controlling outside of the Western basins. Selected results from seven of the alternative futures are presented in tabular form (Tables 5-7, 5-8, and 5-9). Regional consumptive use of water in the 9 Western basins is presented in Table 5-7. National summaries of land use for major types

of crops, excluding forest products, are shown in Table 5-8, and resulting national average farm prices for each of the alternative futures are presented in Table 5-9. These results are described briefly in the following paragraphs.

300 Million Population: Four of the alternative futures analyzed are based on a population of 300 million and a free market in U.S. agriculture in 2000.[54] Under the assumptions of these models, crop production would be allocated and land and water could be used among areas and regions so that the national production pattern is most efficient, and no

[54] Detailed results of these analyses are given in HEADY, Earl O et al., Iowa State University (1971). Agricultural Water Demands, prepared for the National Water Commission. National Technical Information Service, Springfield, Va., Accession No. PB 206 790. Part IV.

TABLE 5-7.—Forecasts of regional consumptive use of water in western water resources regions for selected alternative futures in 2000
(Billion gallons per day)

River Basin	Total 1970[1]	Future A		Future A3		Future B		Future C		Future D		Future G		Future J	
		Agri-culture	Total[2]	Agri-culture	Total[2]	Agri-culture	Total[2]	Agri-culture	Total[2]	Agri-culture	Total[2]	Agri-culture	Total[2]	Agri-culture	Total[2]
Missouri	12.0	10.2	13.3	2.7	5.8	9.9	13.0	10.8	13.8	11.2	14.4	8.8	12.0	10.5	13.5
Arkansas-White-Red	6.8	4.2	5.5	3.0	4.3	4.1	5.3	3.4	4.6	4.2	5.6	3.8	5.1	3.7	4.9
Texas-Gulf	6.2	3.9	11.0	3.3	10.3	3.5	10.1	3.8	10.5	4.0	11.7	3.5	10.6	3.9	10.5
Rio Grande	3.3	2.5	3.1	1.3	1.9	2.0	2.5	3.1	3.6	3.0	3.6	1.9	2.4	2.5	3.0
Upper Colorado	4.1	2.4	2.9	0.1	0.6	2.1	2.6	2.7	3.2	2.9	3.5	2.0	2.6	2.3	2.8
Lower Colorado	5.0	2.2	4.4	1.0	3.3	2.2	4.4	3.3	5.5	2.0	4.3	2.1	4.3	3.2	5.4
Great Basin	3.2	1.9	3.2	0.6	1.9	1.9	3.2	1.9	3.2	1.9	3.2	1.3	2.5	2.0	3.2
Columbia-North Pacific	11.0	12.1	13.6	3.6	5.1	11.3	12.7	12.3	13.7	12.1	13.7	10.9	12.4	11.8	13.2
California-South Pacific	22.0	21.4	29.9	12.9	21.3	20.4	28.4	20.2	28.2	21.0	30.1	16.1	24.6	20.8	28.8
Western Basins	73.6	60.8	86.9	28.5	54.5	57.4	82.2	61.5	86.3	62.3	90.1	50.4	76.5	60.7	85.3

[1] MURRAY, C Richard & REEVES, E Bodette (1972). Estimated Use of Water in the United States in 1970, Geological Survey, Geological Survey Circular 676. U.S. Geological Survey, Washington, D.C. p. 17.

[2] Includes agriculture, rural domestic, municipal, self-supplied industrial, recreation, and thermal electric power. Also included are onsite consumptive uses, the forecast export to Mexico, depletion of the Upper Milk River by Canada, and transfer of water from the Missouri river basin into the Souris-Red-Rainy river basin.

TABLE 5-8.—Forecasts of national land use for selected alternative futures in year 2000, in millions of acres

Land Use	1964 Level[1]	1969 Level[2]	Year 2000 Level[3]						
			Future A	Future A3	Future B	Future C	Future D	Future G	Future J
Dryland annual crops	176.4	n.a.	189.5	187.7	177.3	188.0	219.2	172.9	209.2
Dryland tame hay & silages	57.2	n.a.	99.1	115.5	77.8	70.2	80.2	40.6	83.0
Dryland wild hay & silages	921.2	n.a.	938.5	938.8	936.8	938.8	938.4	934.8	938.5
Total dryland	1,154.8	1,024.2	1,227.1	1,242.0	1,191.9	1,197.0	1,237.8	1,148.3	1,230.7
Irrigated annual crops	13.3	n.a.	6.1	4.1	6.1	8.9	8.1	7.0	6.1
Irrigated tame hay & silages	7.5	n.a.	10.9	2.3	9.8	10.1	10.1	6.6	10.4
Irrigated wild hay, pasture, fruits, nuts, etc.	10.5	n.a.	10.2	6.0	10.1	10.2	10.4	10.2	10.2
Total irrigated[4]	31.3	34.8	27.2	12.4	26.0	29.2	28.6	23.8	26.7
Unused cropland & hayland	n.a.	n.a.	16.4	12.5	51.0	44.9	4.5	95.0	13.4
Unused wild hay & pasture land	n.a.	n.a.	11.2	10.9	12.9	10.9	11.3	14.9	11.2
Total unused land[5]	55.5	58.0	27.6	23.4	63.9	55.8	15.8	109.9	24.6
Cropland shifted[6]	n.a.	n.a.	49.3	52.1	42.8	2.1	21.0	19.0	31.3

[1] U.S. BUREAU OF THE CENSUS (1967). U.S. Census of Agriculture, 1964, Volume I, Statistics for States and Counties. U.S. Government Printing Office, Washington, D.C.
[2] U.S. BUREAU OF THE CENSUS (1972). U.S. Census of Agriculture, 1969, Volume I, Statistics for States and Counties. U.S. Government Printing Office, Washington, D.C.
[3] HEADY, Earl O et al., Iowa State University (1971). Agricultural Water Demands, prepared for the National Water Commission. National Technical Information Service, Springfield, Va., Accession No. PB 206 790. Part IV; and MADSEN, Howard C et al., Iowa State University (1972). Alternative Demands for Water and Land for Agricultural Purposes, prepared for the National Water Commission. National Technical Information Service, Springfield, Va., Accession No. PB 211 444. pp. 34,61.
[4] 17 Western States only.
[5] Land either currently used for crop production or currently in Federal land retirement programs that would not be needed for crop production in 2000.
[6] Land either currently used for annual crops production or currently in land retirement programs but used for tame hay production in 2000.

133

TABLE 5-9.—Indications of prices received by farmers for selected commodities under alternative futures in 2000

Item[1]	Actual 1969[2]	Future A[4]	Future A3	Future B[4]	Future C	Future D	Future G[4]	Future J[4]
Crop prices								
Corn (dol./bu.)	1.12	1.10	1.21	0.93	1.38	1.58	0.89	1.40
Wheat (dol./bu.)	1.24	1.49	1.65	1.22	1.93	2.26	1.16	1.79
Soybeans (dol./bu.)	2.33	2.25	2.58	1.78	2.89	3.81	1.67	2.42
Cotton (dol./bu.)	0.21	0.14	0.16	0.14	0.23	0.20	0.14	0.21
Hay (dol./ton)	25.00	25.01	28.22	21.10	39.40	33.46	18.35	26.06
Livestock-products								
Cattle & calves (cents/lb)	26.20	33.90	37.07	29.93	46.62	37.57	27.33	35.82
Milk (dol./cwt)	5.46	3.41	3.53	3.22	3.77	4.39	3.20	3.65

[1] All prices for 2000 are measured in 1970 equivalent dollars and do not take into account inflations from 1970 to 2000.
[2] U.S. DEPARTMENT OF AGRICULTURE, STATISTICAL REPORTING SERVICE (1970). Agricultural Prices: 1969 Annual Summary, Washington, D.C., Pr. 1-3(70).
[3] HEADY, Earl O et al., Iowa State University (1971). Agricultural Water Demands, prepared for the National Water Commission. National Technical Information Service, Springfield, Va., Accession No. PB 206 790.
[4] MADSEN, Howard C et al., Iowa State University (1972). Alternative Demands for Water and Land for Agricultural Purposes, prepared for the National Water Commission. National Technical Information Service, Springfield, Va., Accession No. PB 211 444. pp. 35, 62.

restraints, such as land retirement, would be placed on geographic and land-water substitutions.[55]

Under Future A, with 300 million people and present prices of water in year 2000, total consumptive use of water in the Western water resource regions would increase 19 percent over the 1970 level (Table 5-7), but there still would be a surplus of water for the West as a whole.

Under this future, only a part of the Texas-Gulf river basin might face a water deficit because of the large municipal and industrial water requirements forecast for that region in 2000.[56] Other regions of

---

[55] Water available in 2000 is based on mean annual runoff and reservoirs constructed estimated as of 1980 adjusted for reservoir evaporation. For the nine Western river basins, a total of 213.7 million gallons per day of water is estimated to be available for withdrawals and consumptive use in 2000.

[56] Water consumption in agriculture can vary as the amount and location of irrigated agriculture and livestock production respond to conditions under each forecast model. Withdrawals and consumptive use of water for nonagricultural purposes were assumed for the purposes of these models to be fixed on a per capita basis, and the studies do not, therefore, show how the demands would respond to changes in the price and availability of water or to changes in the policies governing their use.

water scarcity would include the lower rainfall areas of the Nation and those areas that currently are mining ground water—the Southwestern United States and the Great Plains area, including parts of the States of Kansas, Nebraska, Oklahoma, and Texas.

The irrigated croplands in the Western States are among the most productive in the Nation. Currently, around 35 million acres of land are irrigated in the 17 Western States. The model study for Future A shows that if land now idle under government programs would be allowed to return to production, it could be substituted for water on irrigated land. Because the idle lands are not as productive,[57] larger acreages would be required, but the food and fiber needs of the Nation could be met even if the amount of land irrigated in the Western States had to be reduced because of an increase in nonagricultural water requirements. Even with the increased food and fiber

---

[57] Recent studies by the Department of Agriculture contain estimates that diverted lands were only 80 to 90 percent as productive as the cropland remaining in production. U.S. DEPARTMENT OF AGRICULTURE (1969). Productivity of Diverted Land, by P. Weisgerber, Economic Research Service, Washington, D.C.

demands of this Future, 16.4 million acres of cropland and hayland would remain unused. An additional 11.2 million acres of other lands also would be unused.[58]

The term unused refers to land either currently used for crop production or currently in Federal land retirement programs that would not be needed to meet food and fiber demands, domestic and export. Obviously, this acreage could serve nonagricultural purposes.

With the continued excess supply capacity for U.S. agriculture in the year 2000, indicated under Future A of the study, farm commodity prices would not be likely to rise to high real levels (Table 5-9). In general, farm prices for most commodities under Future A would be near 1969 levels. The study indicates that even if there is somewhat reduced acreage of irrigated land in the year 2000, the problems of agriculture nationally promise to continue to be problems of excess production capacity and low prices.

Effects of Increasing Water Price: To evaluate the possible effects of water pricing policy on water allocation and the potential substitution of dryland farming for irrigated farming, analyses of water demand were made under assumptions that the average price of water for irrigation would be $15, $22.50, and $30 per acre-foot consumed, compared with the present $6 average price[59] on Federal reclamation projects. These analyses (Alternative Futures A1, A2, and A3)[60] were made as variations of the basic Future A. Obviously, there will be no change in the price of water delivered under existing contracts, but it is likely that future water supplies will be more costly and may well reach the levels chosen for these studies by the year 2000. In some areas, irrigators are already paying more than $30 per acre-foot for water used to grow high-value crops. Future A3 of the study indicates that at $30 per

acre-foot demand for water in the Western water resource regions by the year 2000 would be 32 billion gallons per day less than for Future A, and about 19 billion gallons a day less than at present (Table 5-7). With the assumed higher water price, the Nation could meet the food and fiber demands forecast under Future A3 and release additional water for other uses, should the need arise. Farm prices under Future A3, however, would show only modest increases over Future A (Table 5-9).

280 Million Population: If present trends continue, a lower population than 300 million is highly probable in the year 2000, and therefore two alternative futures, Future B and Future C, assuming a population of 280 million were included in the study. The first, Future B, is a free market solution similar to Future A except for a lower population. The second, Future C, incorporates the lower population with an annual land retirement program similar to the wheat, feed grain, and cotton programs used during the decade 1961-1970.

As might be expected, the study shows that the annual water consumption in the Western regions under Future B would be 6.5 percent less than under Future A (Table 5-7). Fewer regions would face potential water problems under Future B than under Future A, but the available water supply would be exhausted in the Southwest, Southern California, Nebraska, Northern Kansas, and in the High Plains areas of Oklahoma and Texas.[61]

The study indicates that with a population of only 280 million in the year 2000, the surplus capacity of agriculture would exceed that under Future A and would approach that of the 1961-1970 period, when an average of 56 million acres of cropland were idle annually under Federal supply control programs. More water would be available for irrigation in the West because of the lower municipal and industrial water requirements under the 280 million population. While a reduced population growth is suggested by some as a necessary future means to retain environmental quality, the lower food demand would imply a long-run continuation of price and income problems for the agricultural sector (Table 5-9). With nearly 64 million acres of land not needed to meet food and fiber demands for the 280 million population in 2000, capacity would exist to alter land and water use for agriculture so that this sector need not add to environmental deterioration even under a population considerably greater than at the present (Table 5-8).

---

[58] Other lands are wild hay and pasture lands.

[59] HEADY Earl O et al., Iowa State University (1971). Agricultural Water Demands, prepared for the National Water Commission. National Technical Information Service, Springfield, Va., Accession No. PB 206 790. Page III-18 shows prices paid by farmers on Bureau of Reclamation projects ranging from less than $1.00 in some high mountain areas to over $50.00 per acre-foot consumed in some Southern California coastal areas.

[60] For more details on these futures, see HEADY, Earl O et al., Iowa State University (1971). Agricultural Water Demands, prepared for the National Water Commission. National Technical Information Service, Springfield, Va., Accession No. PB 206 790.

[61] *Ibid.*

Future C is the same as Future B except for the assumption that the Nation will continue to pay for holding 45 million acres of cropland out of production in the year 2000 to control crop output. The program simulated would be similar to the annual wheat, feed grain, and cotton programs used during the 1961-1970 decade and would not allow land uses and crop production to be fully allocated among regions so as to achieve the most economical production as determined by a free market. Under these assumptions, the model shows some land retirement would result in all regions of the Nation.

The annual land retirement program permits substitutions of water in the Western States for land in States east of the Missouri River, but also leads to some substitution of water in the West for dryfarmed land in the West. This was exactly the nature and outcome of agricultural and water policies of the 1960's decade: (1) to achieve farm price and income goals the supply of land for crops was reduced by payments that diverted it from producing food and (2) public investments were used to increase the supply of water for food production.

Higher Demands for Food and Fiber in the Year 2000: To show the effects of very substantially increased demands for food and fiber on demand for water and land for agricultural purposes, the assumptions underlying Future D consisted of a population of 325 million in the year 2000, doubling of the 1967-1969 level of agricultural exports in the year 2000, and advanced technology to improve production potentials, particularly in the livestock industry.[62] Dryland crop production yields for principal crops were assumed to reach about 108 bushels per acre for corn, 40 bushels per acre for wheat, and 81.2 bushels per acre for grain sorghum,[63] compared to 84, 31, and 55, respectively, in 1969.[64] Also, agriculture in the Southeast in 2000 was assumed to approach levels of productivity and costs achieved in the Corn Belt.

With the increased food and fiber demands under these assumptions, water consumption would be 2-1/2 percent higher than under Future A (Table 5-7). Water for consumptive use in both agriculture and municipal and industrial uses would be higher and, thus, total water consumption would be greater than under any of the other alternative futures considered. A greater number of regions would be water-scarce and additional pressures would be placed on available water supplies in the Western basins, but the study indicates that the increased production of food and fiber could be achieved even if the total amount of land irrigated in the Western regions had to be reduced by 6.3 million acres because of the demands for water for other purposes. The higher food and fiber demands forecast under Future D of the study would still leave 4.5 million acres of cropland and hayland unused (Table 5-8). Including the wild hay and pasture land unused, only 15.8 million acres would not be in production.

The high food and fiber demands under Future D would result in relatively high levels for farm prices (Table 5-9). Thus, consumer food costs also would increase substantially compared with levels implied by the earlier forecast models reviewed. The high farm prices indicated to result under Future D would provide incentives for new lands to be brought into production either through irrigation, drainage, or other forms of land reclamation. Recent studies indicate that from 49 to 150 million acres of new lands, exclusive of those held in current land retirement programs, could be farmed if the need arises.[65] According to one study, 33 million acres of this additional land could be used for major field crops such as soybeans, corn, rice, and cotton.[66] Under the higher farm prices of Future D, much of this land would start to enter intensive production.

Should conditions of Future D be realized in the year 2000, the study indicates that food and fiber demands still could be satisfied through investments to speed the rate of technological advance and by farming new lands. Also, even at the higher level of

[62] For complete details on this model, *ibid.*, Appendix M.

[63] *Ibid.*, p. M-17. All projection studies utilize a number of assumptions. One of the most critical in considering land use is continuing improvement in crop yields. The assumptions of yield improvement in these studies are solidly based on several decades of past performance and are believed to be conservative when compared with actual experience on many well managed farms.

[64] See U.S. DEPARTMENT OF AGRICULTURE (1971). Agricultural Statistics for 1969. U.S. Government Printing Office, Washington, D.C.

[65] U.S. DEPARTMENT OF AGRICULTURE (1971). Exploring our cropland potential. The Farm Index 10(9):11. and UPCHURCH LM (1967). The capacity of the United States to supply food for developing countries, Ch. 14 in IOWA STATE UNIVERSITY CENTER FOR AGRICULTURAL ECONOMIC DEVELOPMENT. Alternatives for Balancing World Food Production and Needs. Iowa State University Press, Ames. pp. 215-223.

[66] U.S. DEPARTMENT OF AGRICULTURE (1971). Exploring our cropland potential. The Farm Index 10(9):11.

Irrigated lettuce provides high crop returns on lands near Blythe, California

water consumption posed by Future D, the study shows that there would still be enough water for the needs of the West as a whole. Thus, the study suggests that the water problem of the future, even with substantially higher food and fiber demands than at present, is not one of outright water shortage.

Eating Habits of Consumers and the Demand for Water: The previously discussed alternative futures were based on conventional assumptions as to the level of population, exports of farm products, Federal farm policies, and rate of technological advance. One set of alternative futures examined the outcomes under a pricing system for water allocation in 2000. The Commission also had a separate study[67] made of alternative futures incorporating possible changes in

[67] MADSEN, Howard C et al., Iowa State University (1972). Alternative Demands for Water and Land for Agricultural Purposes, prepared for the National Water Commission. National Technical Information Service, Springfield, Va., Accession No. PB 211 444.

the lifestyles or eating habits of consumers and a possible restriction on the use of fertilizer to reflect national concern with environmental quality.

In recent decades, many substitutions by consumers have affected resource use and food prices. In the area of food and beverages, vegetable fats have replaced animal fats as margarine has been substituted for butter. Synthetic sweeteners have replaced ordinary sugar in tea, coffee, and carbonated beverages, and synthetic juices have come to serve as replacements for citrus. Consumers also have substituted synthetic materials for clothing, affecting the demand for natural fibers. The possibility that vegetable proteins might be substituted for a part of the greatly increased demand for animal proteins assumed in the first seven model studies led the Commission to request analysis of alternative futures in which per capita consumption of beef and veal would be assumed to continue at current levels (116.7 pounds per capita per annum) and the increased demands for protein (projected to reach 157.7 pounds in the other

137

studies) would be met by substituting vegetable proteins.

Two possible alternative futures were investigated under these assumptions (Future G and Future H, Table 5-6), both based on 300 million population. Under Future G, a free market was assumed, but Future H contains the assumption that government supply control programs similar to those used over the past decade would be continued in 2000 in attempts to control excess supply and raise farm prices.[68]

The regional consumptive use of water under Future G is shown in Table 5-7. The national summary of land requirements and of farm commodity prices are shown in Tables 5-8 and 5-9, respectively. Data summarized on the tables show that such a substitution, if made by consumers, would free up substantial amounts of water and land in the year 2000, with 95 million acres of cropland and hayland not required for agricultural purposes.

The reason that the substitution of vegetable protein for animal protein in the diet would require far less land and water is, very simply, that cattle and other meat animals are very inefficient converters of plant to animal protein. Beef cattle require many pounds of plant protein to produce one pound of meat protein.[69] If human beings consume the vegetable protein directly, instead of through the beef cycle, they increase their efficiency of food utilization several times.

Quality of the Environment and the Demand for Water: Recent studies[70] indicate that pollution caused by runoff from agricultural land may have a deleterious effect on water quality, since water soluble nitrogen fertilizers are sometimes carried into the streams and underground water basins by runoff and deep percolation. In an effort to determine the effect on water use if measures to reduce such pollution are adopted, the Commission had an analysis made of two alternative futures under

assumptions that restrictions would be placed on the use of nitrogen fertilizers. Such restrictions would obviously increase the demand for water and land resources.

Two specific limitations on nitrogen fertilizers used in agriculture were considered in the study—110 pounds per acre per year (about the present level of use) and 50 pounds per acre per year. The inclusion in the study of these alternative futures is not a suggestion by the Commission that these levels of restriction be adopted as national policy, but is for the purpose of forecasting demands for agricultural water and land should such limitations be imposed. Other than for the nitrogen fertilizer restriction, the forecast models for Futures I and J[71] are just like Future B with a population of 280 million (Table 5-6). Only the results of Future J are shown in the tables.

With nitrogen fertilizer application restricted to a maximum of 50 pounds per acre in the year 2000, the most restrictive of the two models, water consumption would increase by nearly 4 percent over Future B (Table 5-7). There would be an equivalent reduction in the total water surplus in the Western basins and additional regions would face potential water problems. With the 50-pound fertilizer limitation, the entire Southwestern United States would be water-scarce.

The reduction in crop yields with the 50-pound limitation on the use of nitrogen fertilizer is forecast to result in a substantial increase in the crop acreages required to meet demands for food and fiber (Table 5-8). Both dryland and irrigated acreages of crops would be higher, although the greatest change would occur in dryland acreages. The total acreage of crops would be nearly 40 million acres more than under Future B and would be even higher than under Future A (with 300 million population). The large increase in crop acreages under this alternative future would decrease unused cropland and hayland by nearly 38 million acres, but nearly 25 million acres of land would still be unused (Table 5-8). In addition, crop prices would be substantially higher than under Future B (Table 5-9).

---

[68] For further details on these two forecast models, *ibid.*

[69] In a recent article in the Wall Street Journal, Volume LI No. 26, February 7, 1973, pp. 1 & 12, David Brand quotes food scientists as saying that it takes 100 pounds of plant protein to produce less than 5 pounds of edible meat protein.

[70] See for example, U.S. COUNCIL ON ENVIRONMENTAL QUALITY (1972). Environmental Quality, The Third Annual Report of the Council on Environmental Quality, U.S. Government Printing Office, Washington, D.C. p. 16.

[71] For the methods and procedures followed under these assumptions, see MADSEN, Howard C et al., Iowa State University (1972). Alternative Demands for Water and Land for Agricultural Purposes, prepared for the National Water Commission. National Technical Information Service, Springfield, Va., Accession No. PB 211 444.

Projection of Past Trends in Agriculture

Another useful way to look at the future is to compare it with the past. In general, over the last 50 years, more and more food has been grown on fewer and fewer acres and with less and less labor. Thirty years ago, one farmer fed 13 persons;[72] in 1971, each farmer fed 48.2 persons.[73] In 1949, 334.4 million acres of cropland were harvested;[74] 20 years later, the figure had dropped to 273 million acres, an average decline of 3.5 million acres a year.[75] In the same period, population increased 36 percent (from 149.8 million to 203.2 million)[76] and farm output increased 40 percent.[77] Thus, a comparison of the facts of the past with the forecasts obtained from the analyses of alternative futures is consistent with the thesis that agricultural land availability will not limit food and fiber supply.

OBERS Projections: Projection of past trends has led some of the Federal agencies involved in water resources planning to the conclusion that there will be an increase in irrigated acreage in the future. A recent report[78] prepared for the Water Resources Council to serve as a basis for regional water resources planning under the Water Resources Planning Act projects harvested irrigated cropland at 39.8 million acres in the year 2000,[79] considerably above the acreage indicated in the Iowa State University studies to be required to meet demands. The OBERS projections are single-valued projections based on assumptions that U.S. population will reach 306.8 million by the year 2000, and that there will be no policy or program changes of an unusual or unforeseen nature. The report states that

> The projections are in no sense a goal, an assigned share, or a constraint on a region's economic activity. They carry no connotation as to desirability or undesirability. Especially, they should not constrain the planner in considering alternative levels of growth which might be achieved through more or less resource development.[80]

The agricultural projection system used in the report is based largely on the extension of historical trends.[81] Yield projections are based on general assumptions that research leading to increases in crop yields will continue to increase, but at a dampened rate, and that implementation of current knowledge and technologies will lag, but that there will be more extensive use of fertilizers and pesticides, improved varieties, and improved management practices.[82]

Since they are a single-valued set of projections, the OBERS projections do not consider the possibility of substituting land for water and other possible alternative futures covered in the Iowa State University analyses. But they do provide another possible alternative future that should be considered as a possibility, a future that would apparently continue the policy of maintaining surplus or reserve capacity in the Nation's agricultural plant.

Findings of Other Studies

Most other studies corroborate the proposition that the Nation's agricultural land base is adequate to meet future food and fiber demands without Federal water resource development programs to enlarge the base or its productivity. The National Advisory

[72] U.S. DEPARTMENT OF AGRICULTURE (1958). Agricultural Statistics 1957. U. S. Government Printing Office, Washington, D.C. p. 556.

[73] U.S. DEPARTMENT OF AGRICULTURE, Economic Research Service (June 1972). 1972 Changes in Farm Production and Efficiency, A Summary Report, ERS Statistical Bulletin No. 233, U.S. Department of Agriculture, Washington, D.C. p. 29.

[74] U.S. DEPARTMENT OF AGRICULTURE (1971). Agricultural Statistics 1971. U.S. Government Printing Office, Washington, D.C. Table 626, p. 436.

[75] U.S. BUREAU OF THE CENSUS (May 1972). 1969 Census of Agriculture–County Data (United States). Issued on a State by State basis. U.S. Department of Commerce, Washington, D.C. p. 1.

[76] U.S. BUREAU OF THE CENSUS (July 1970). Statistical Abstract of the United States 1970, 91st Annual Edition. U.S. Government Printing Office, Washington, D.C. Table 2, p. 5.

[77] KRAUSE OE (1971). Farm production capacity can meet our needs, pp. 278-284 in U.S. DEPARTMENT OF AGRICULTURE. A Good Life for More People, The Yearbook of Agriculture 1971, House Document No. 29, 92d Congress, 1st Session. U.S. Government Printing Office, Washington, D.C.

[78] U.S. DEPARTMENT OF COMMERCE, Bureau of Economic Analysis–U.S. DEPARTMENT OF AGRICULTURE, Economic Research Service (1973). 1972 OBERS Projections of Regional Economic Activity in the U.S., prepared for the U.S. Water Resources Council. U.S. Government Printing Office, Washington, D.C. 5 volumes.

[79] *Ibid.*, Table 6, p. 43.

[80] *Ibid.*, p. 7

[81] *Ibid.*, p. 29.

[82] *Ibid.*, p. 31.

Commission on Food and Fiber,[83] reporting in 1967, concluded:

> Reclamation and land development projects paid for by public investment have significantly increased farm production in the past three decades, during which agriculture was plagued with overproduction and surpluses. Clearly, it is unsound policy to invest public funds in new farm capacity at a time when the overriding problem is too much capacity.

The Commission recommends that public funds for agricultural reclamation, irrigation, drainage and development projects should be justified on the basis of whether they represent the cheapest means of getting additional farm production—if needed.[84]

The National Advisory Commission on Rural Poverty was even more specific, recommending:

> That land development programs of the Bureau of Reclamation, the Soil Conservation Service, and other Federal agencies be discontinued, and that no more public money be invested in developing privately owned farmland until the nation needs more land for producing the desired output of food and fiber products. Exceptions should be made where land development offers the only feasible escape from poverty for Indians and other specific groups of rural poor people.[85]

A recent official publication of the U.S. Department of Agriculture summarized a comprehensive land and water study by natural resources experts in the Department's Economic Research Service (ERS) which adds further support to the assertion that the Nation's land base will be adequate to meet future food and fiber demand.[86] The study points out that acreage actually used for crops has been decreasing at an average of 2 million acres a year since 1950 and that the increase in idle cropland is a result of a 50 percent increase in cropland productivity since 1950.

Analyzing trends in population, production, and land use, and projecting changes to the year 2000, ERS concludes agriculture will have no difficulty meeting the country's needs for food and fiber (excluding forestry products).[87]

Under assumptions used, including a U.S. population projection of 308 million for the year 2000 which is decidedly high based on present trends, the report says:

> ...the domestic use of farm products is expected to rise 55 percent in the next 30 years, allowing for the projected population increase plus a small gain in per capita food consumption. With land development following recent trends, ERS projects that by the year 2000 there will be a 3-percent (additional) decrease in land in farms.[88]

The reduction in farmland contemplated amounts to 34 million acres, a little over 3 percent of the more than 1 billion acres of land in farms in 1969. It includes 1-1/2 million fewer acres of cropland.

There are, of course, other views, based on the adoption of other assumptions. A committee of the National Academy of Sciences assumed a U.S. population in the year 2000 between 300 and 340 million, a world population between 6 and 7 billion (nearly double the present level), the risk of world famine and the likelihood of increased American food exports, and it accordingly recommended:

> *That the efficiency and capacity of agricultural productivity, both in the United States and abroad be increased to the maximum levels possible.* This is necessary not only to assure national food reserves, but also to help those countries in need. Overproduction, as well as underproduction, of perishable products must be controlled, for it is evidence of poor national management and vitiates the improvement of farm production and management. The Department of Agriculture has been working in these directions for a long time, in collaboration with the Department of State and the United Nations. The effort should be continued, improved, and intensified.[89]

---

[83] Created by Executive Order No. 11256, November 4, 1965.

[84] U.S. NATIONAL ADVISORY COMMISSION ON FOOD AND FIBER (1967). Food and Fiber for the Future. U.S. Government Printing Office, Washington, D.C. p. 21.

[85] PRESIDENT'S NATIONAL ADVISORY COMMISSION ON RURAL POVERTY (September 1967). The People Left Behind. U.S. Government Printing Office, Washington, D.C. p. 138.

[86] U.S. DEPARTMENT OF AGRICULTURE (1972). Farmland: Are we running out? The Farm Index. December 1972. pp. 8-10.

[87] *Ibid.*

[88] *Ibid.*

[89] U.S. NATIONAL ACADEMY OF SCIENCES, Committee on Resources and Man (1969). Resources and Man, A study and Recommendations. W. H. Freeman and Company, San Francisco, Calif. p. 13.

But the dominant theme of the studies of American agriculture is overproduction accompanied by a depressed agricultural economy.[90]

DISCUSSION

At each of the hearings on the Commission's draft report, witnesses representing groups that would continue the national programs of subsidies to bring new farm lands into production urged upon the Commission the possibility that a national food shortage may lie ahead. They pointed to the very recent dramatic increases in food exports to Russia, China, and India. They suggested that this sharp upward trend of exports might continue. They pointed also to the example of the corn blight of 1970, and foresaw that the high-yielding hybrid grains might suffer catastrophic destruction through uncontrollable diseases, or that the droughts of the mid-1930's might reoccur. They questioned whether agricultural technology would continue to improve at the rates assumed in the Iowa State University forecasts, and similar forecasts of the National Advisory Commission on Food and Fiber and the National Adivsory Commission on Rural Poverty. In other respects too, for example, the possibility of even more severe limits upon the use of chemicals in agriculture than assumed in the Iowa study, these witnesses questioned the accuracy of the Commission's forecast that the Nation already has adequate agricultural production capacity to meet the needs of the next 30 years.

Any forecast can, of course, err. Neither this nor any other Commission has the gift of prophecy. We do not know whether any of the alternative futures used in the Iowa State University studies will materialize. But the Commission believes the assumptions which underlie them are not unreasonable. In the Commission's view it would be highly imprudent to conclude, as a matter of national policy, that we should continue to subsidize the bringing into production of new farm lands on the basis of speculations of food shortage that might arise because farm technology may falter; or because blights and droughts of catastrophic proportion may occur; or because other nations such as Russia and China may become dependent upon the United States for food supply.

If our Nation, or the United Nations, concludes that food shortages may be caused by sudden and catastrophic events, whether climatic or biologic, the Commission believes the proper policy to guard against this disaster would be a national or world program for food storage. A World Food Bank would make sense for many reasons, not the least of which would be its symbolizing the dependence of nations upon each other, the "One World" of Wendell Wilkie. If there is to be a national or world catastrophe that causes food shortages, the addition of a few million more acres of farm land will not prevent it. And if for whatever reason there should arise a need for more farm land in the United States to meet an unexpectedly rapid increase in exports of farm products, the sensible way to meet such need would be to allow a free and unsubsidized market to do so in the most economic manner. That might or might not involve bringing new land under irrigation or draining and protecting new land from floods. It should depend on what at the time proves to be the least-cost method of increasing farm production. The cost, in any event, should not be borne by the taxpayers, but should be incorporated into the price of the crops exported, so that the United States will no longer be buying imports at today's prices and selling exports at prices of the 1940's and 1950's.

CONCLUSIONS

Land reclamation measures such as irrigation and drainage of new land, protection of existing and potential cropland from floods, and provision of supplemental irrigation water for existing croplands have added to the excess productive capacity of U.S. agriculture and have thereby contributed to the high costs of crop price support and land retirement programs. If the assumptions used in the Iowa State University studies are reasonable, and we believe that they are, there appears to be adequate productive capacity in the Nation's agriculture to meet food and fiber demand under various alternative futures at least until the year 2000. In such case there would be no need in the next 30 years to continue federally subsidized water resource development programs to increase the agricultural land base of the country, but where the Federal Government has executed contracts to complete water projects already begun, such projects should of course be completed.

Even if none of the alternative futures assumed in the Iowa State University studies adequately project

[90] See for example, CLAWSON, Marion M et al. (1960). Land for the Future. Published for Resources for the Future by The John Hopkins Press, Baltimore, Md.; JOHNSON, Glenn L & QUANCE, C Leroy (1972). The Overproduction Trap in U.S. Agriculture. Published for Resources for the Future by The Johns Hopkins Press, Baltimore, Md.

the actual supply and demand for food and fiber for the year 2000, there is still no justification for subsidizing reclamation projects. If, for example, export demand for food and fiber greatly exceeds the amount contemplated in any of the alternative futures considered, that demand should nevertheless be satisfied in the most efficient way. Efficiency in agriculture, as in many other sectors of the economy, is more often than not distorted by subsidies. The discipline of the marketplace should be relied upon to insure that, consistent with environmental constraints, food is produced in the least-cost way. That may or may not entail more land under irrigation than at present. But the decision should not be distorted by the influence of subsidies.

If the demand for such high-value, specialty crops as fruits, nuts, and vegetables should increase so as to require the use of additional land, the demand can be met by the private sector in a number of ways without Federal subsidy, for example, by shifting land presently in use for production of low-value crops to production of high-value crops.

Even if the United States should embark upon large-scale aid programs to supply food to the rest of the world, the reclamation of farm lands should pay its own way. Any subsidies in the price of exported food found advisable for reasons of foreign or domestic policy should be straightforward (e.g., direct appropriations to the Department of State to purchase food in the open market) so that whatever

food is produced is obtained in the most efficient least-cost way.

The adoption of the Commission's recommendations on cost-sharing (Chapter 15), which would require identifiable beneficiaries or owners of benefited property to repay their respective shares of the full costs of irrigation, drainage, and flood control projects, and the recommendations on project evaluation as a basis for decisionmaking (Chapter 10), which would require that consideration be given to both the positive and negative effects of proposed projects on all regions, would serve to limit public support for those projects and programs which would not contribute significantly to the development of viable economies and qualify environments in the Nation's water resource regions.

The Commission is aware that its recommendations would lead to a reduction in new starts on projects by the Federal water agencies. The future role of these agencies is considered in Chapter 11, Section C.

RECOMMENDATION

5-5. **Legislation should be enacted to require full repayment of costs of Federal water resource development projects that result in increases in production of food and fiber in accordance with the principles set forth in Chapter 15 of this report.**

~~~~~~~~~~~~~~~~~~~~~~~~~~~~~~~ *Section D*

Acreage Limitations and Subsidies in Reclamation Programs[91]

National farm policy has sought creation of an agricultural community of independent, self-reliant, and self-sufficient farmers. This goal rested essentially on what has been called the Agrarian Myth, epitomized in Thomas Jefferson's belief that the Nation's welfare depended on the civic virtue produced

by such an agrarian society.[92] The distribution of public land in 160-acre blocks free of charge to homesteaders reflected this goal. The acreage limitation (originally 160 acres) in reclamation law also reflects this goal. The 1902 Reclamation Act said in effect that Government assistance in securing irrigation water would be available to farmers owning not more than 160 acres.[93] At the same time, the

---

[91] The background and operation of the acreage limitation described in this section are taken largely from HOGAN, Harry J (1972). The Acreage Limitation in the Federal Reclamation Program, prepared for the National Water Commission. National Technical Information Service, Springfield, Va., Accession No. PB 211 840. This study is referred to hereafter as HOGAN.

---

[92] HOGAN. p. 24 *et seq.*

[93] *Reclamation Act of 1902*, P.L. 161, June 17, 1902, Sections 3, 5, 57th Congress, 32 Stat. 388, 389, 43 USCA 431, 434.

reclamation farmer remained subject to market forces, which over the years have led him to enlarge his farm and, therefore, to seek means of avoiding the acreage limitation.

PRESENT STATUS OF ACREAGE LIMITATIONS

The original acreage limitation appeared in Section 5 of the 1902 Act, but the currently prevailing general rule was adopted in the 1926 Omnibus Adjustment Act, Section 46, which provided that water delivery contracts, which formerly had been entered into with individual farmers, would be executed only with public irrigation districts. The statute then stated, in effect, that the owners of irrigable lands in excess of 160 acres were required to dispose of these lands before they could receive water from a Federal project.[94]

By later amendment of this general provision, by special legislation for specific projects, and by administrative action, the acreage limitation now has the following status:

1. Some districts are completely exempted from the limitation. The Northern Colorado Water Conservancy District, which embraces six counties and receives 230,000 acre-feet per year of supplemental water, obtained its exemption by legislation.[95] The Imperial Irrigation District in southeastern California obtained exemption by a ruling of the Secretary of the Interior, later confirmed in court.[96]

2. The Small Reclamation Projects Act of 1956[97] has been construed to grant an exemption. On irrigation projects qualifying for Federal loans interest is payable on construction costs allocable to excess acreage, hence the acreage limitation was thought not to be applicable.[98]

3. By a 1956 amendment to Section 46 of the 1926 Act, excess lands acquired by mortgage foreclosure, inheritance, or devise may receive reclamation water for 5 years.[99]

4. Some landowners and districts obtained exemption when water under U.S. Bureau of Reclamation (Bureau) control is declared to be natural flow, in which the landowners or districts had rights antedating the construction of the project. The most notable example of this exemption is found in the Sacramento River Diverter contracts executed in connection with the Shasta Dam project in Northern California.[100]

5. Similarly, land irrigated by reclamation water percolating to ground water aquifers may be exempt, on the theory that the delivery of such water is "unavoidable." "Unavoidable delivery" clauses now appear in the California Central Valley Project contracts.[101]

6. The Bureau may not seek to trace reclamation water through the wholesaler to the ultimate user, who can thereby avoid the acreage limitation. This is the case with the Metropolitan Water District (MWD) of Southern California, whose reclamation water supply is described as municipal and industrial water. In fact, however, some of the water is used directly for agriculture and some replaces water that is used for agriculture.[102]

7. Irrigators may receive a *de facto* exemption for protracted periods of time during contract negotiations. In the Sacramento Diverter situation, Shasta Dam went into operation in 1944, but the contracts were not signed until 1963 and did not take effect until 1964, 20 years after the project went into operation.[103] Under the 1926 Omnibus Act, the acreage limitation does not take effect for another 10 years, that is, until 1974. (In connection with the Shasta Dam project, the Bureau has yet to reach agreement with Delta water users further downstream on the Sacramento River.)

8. It has been recently suggested by a Federal District Court that the acreage limitation expires

[94] *Act of May 24, 1926*, P.L. 284, Section 46, 69th Congress, 44 Stat. 636, 649, as amended, 43 USCA 423e.

[95] *Act of June 16, 1938*, P.L. 665, 75th Congress, 52 Stat. 764, 43 USCA 386.

[96] Letter dated February 24, 1933, from the Secretary of the Interior to the Imperial Irrigation District, conferred the immunity. In an opinion dated December 31, 1964 (M-36657), (71 S.D. 496), the Solicitor of the Department of the Interior overturned the ruling and held that the acreage limitation applied. In subsequent litigation, the U.S. District Court, So. District, California, ruled on January 5, 1971, that the limitation did not apply. The Department did not appeal. *United States v. Imperial Irrigation Dist.*, 322 F. Supp. 11 (S.D.Cal. 1971).

[97] P.L. 984, August 6, 1956, 84th Congress, 70 Stat. 1044, as amended, 43 USCA 422a to 422k-1.

[98] HOGAN. p. 76

[99] *Act of July 11, 1956*, P.L. 690, 84th Congress, 70 Stat. 524, 43 USCA 423e.

[100] HOGAN. pp. 72, 130-136.

[101] HOGAN. p. 72.

[102] HOGAN. p. 73. It should be noted, however, that the price of MDW's municipal and industrial water is higher than that of water identified as irrigation water in other Bureau contracts.

[103] HOGAN. p. 74.

Siphon tubes take water from farm ditch into crop rows in California's Central Valley

when the contracting irrigation district makes full payment of its contractual repayment obligation for reimbursable capital costs allocable to irrigation.[104] The case is now on appeal, and the issues are quite complex, involving the interpretation of a succession of reclamation laws and a number of conflicting opinions by Interior Department Solicitors. The trial court found it to be a fact, however, that the Department had an administrative practice of releasing the limitation upon payment of the contract obligation.

9. By administrative regulation, the 1926 Act has been interpreted to give owners of excess irrigation project lands 10 years in which to sell excess land (or to suffer exercise of the power of sale conferred on the Secretary).

The foregoing list enumerates exceptions to the limitation, either temporary or permanent. In addition, there are techniques available to ameliorate the effects of the limitation when it has been applied.

The Agrarian Myth hypothesized a family farm that was (a) family owned, (b) family run, and (c) family occupied.[105] The 1902 Act required ownership and (somewhat loosely) residence but not family operation. By 1926, family residence was dropped from the statutory law, leaving ownership as the only element that mattered. The excess land law has come to mean that no single individual can have beneficial ownership of more than 160 acres of irrigated land in any given reclamation project. Thus, a husband and wife with two minor children can operate 640 acres—the parents' 320 acres in cotenancy or community property and the children's interest in individual ownership (outright or in trust) in 160 acres each. A farmer and his wife may own 320 acres in every irrigation district in the West. A corporation may own 160 acres in each reclamation project. A joint venture may own and operate as a single unit a farm composed of as many 160-acre parcels as there are partners in the firm: 10 partners—1,600 acres irrigated by reclamation water. The farm family of four described above may add as much land as it wishes to its 640 acres by leasing from neighbors, so long as no single ownership exceeds 160 acres. A corporation may *operate* as many acres as it wishes, so long as it does not *own* more than 160.[106]

In short, where the acreage limitation has not been lifted by exemption, its effect is not to control the size of farm operating units but to regulate the benefits accruing from subsidized irrigation by limiting beneficial ownership to 160 acres.

---

[104] *United States v. Tulare Lake Canal Co.*, No. 2483-Civil, Federal District Court, Eastern Dist., Calif. Opinion entered and judgment filed March 15, 1972. See the memorandum and order in *United States v. Tulare Lake Canal Co.*, 340 F. Supp. 1185 (E.D.Cal. 1972) (alternative holding).

[105] HOGAN. pp. 6-7.

[106] The foregoing description of the operation of the acreage limitation is taken from HOGAN, pp. 77-97.

SUBSIDY IN RECLAMATION PROGRAMS

Irrigation subsidy is the difference between the costs of irrigation projects, including irrigation components of multipurpose projects, and the amount that beneficiaries repay. The principal elements of the subsidy are (1) interest-free, long-term loans, (2) payment of irrigation costs by electric power revenues and by revenues from the sale of municipal and industrial water, and (3) allocation, to an unwarranted extent, of joint costs of multiple-purpose projects to nonirrigation features.

The interest-free loan is the largest component of the subsidy. Reclamation farmers are allowed an initial development period of 10 years in which no capital charges are payable; thereafter, they are supposed to repay the capital charges in annual installments spread over 40 years, at no interest charge. The magnitude of the subsidy can be expressed in several ways. For example, if the irrigation cost per acre (i.e., the part of project costs allocated to irrigation) is treated as a capital obligation that never has to be repaid, and if the farmer's annual repayment charge is regarded as a perpetual return on that investment, the rate of return on the Government's investment will be extraordinarily low. In 22 units of the Missouri River Basin Project, the return rate by such calculation exceeds 1 percent in the case of only one unit (where the rate is 1.65 percent). The other 21 units have rates ranging from a low of zero percent (five units) to a high of 0.90 percent. Table 5-10 presents data for 22 units.[107]

Another way of describing the interest subsidy is to suppose that the annual repayment charge is paid to retire a fixed-term obligation at the end of a 40-year period at a given rate of interest. If the rate of interest is fixed at 6 percent,[108] the amount of principal thus repaid is also very small. In Table 5-10, for example, the first unit (Ainsworth) has an annual irrigation charge of $5.77 per acre, which is to be paid for 40 years (disregarding the 10-year development period). Such a payment at 6 percent interest would repay a principal amount of $86.84 per acre when the cost allocated to irrigation is $753 per acre. Similarly, in the Angostura unit, the annual irrigation charge of $1.84 per acre would repay a principal amount of $27.69, when the amount allocated to irrigation is $1,174. In other words, at 6 percent

interest, the irrigator in Ainsworth is repaying about 12 percent of the irrigation cost allocation and in Angostura less than 3 percent.

Table 5-10 also suggests the magnitude of the subsidy reclamation farmers receive from power revenues, sales of municipal and industrial water, and other assistance. The difference between the figures in the column headed "Project Construction Cost Allocated to Irrigation" and the column headed "Irrigation Repayment Obligation" is made up by nonirrigation revenues assigned to assist payment of the irrigation component of project costs. It will be noted that in the Angostura unit the ratio of irrigator payments to total project costs allocated to irrigation is about 1 to 9. In the aggregate, as of 1970, power payments alone are expected to account for $5 billion of the $7.9 billion reimbursable by irrigation.[109]

Another practice which may contribute to the subsidy is the allocation of multipurpose project costs to such nonreimbursable features as flood control and recreation. There is room for debate on the extent of the subsidy, for it can be contended that present allocations of joint and separable costs properly represent the benefits generated or costs incurred by each of the several purposes of any given project. The Comptroller General, however, has been critical of cost allocations on a number of Bureau of Reclamation and U.S. Army Corps of Engineers projects.[110] Suffice it to say that since irrigation, municipal, and industrial water supplies are at least partially reimbursable and since navigation, flood control, recreation, and water quality improvement features are not, there is some incentive for beneficiaries who must pay to exaggerate the benefits of nonreimbursable components of projects.

THE PROBLEM

The acreage limitation of the reclamation program has served two basic purposes: (1) to justify Federal support of subsidized irrigated agriculture as a means of promoting the "family farm" and (2) to apportion to some degree the windfall gains from the subsidies among a larger number of beneficiaries. The Nation faces two questions: (1) whether to continue the subsidized support of irrigation in future programs and (2) whether to lift the acreage limitation as applied to present subsidized irrigation programs.

[107] HOGAN, pp. 240-242.

[108] Six percent interest is about the middle of the range of rates that public and private utilities have been paying in recent years. See HOGAN, pp. 245-247.

[109] HOGAN. p. 234.

[110] HOGAN. p. 232.

	TABLE 5-10.—Irrigation cost and annual repayment charge per acre, Missouri River Basin Project			
Project Units	Project Construction Cost Allocated to Irrigation Per Acre[a] (dollars)	Irrigation Repayment Obligation Per Acre[b] (dollars)	Annual Irrigator Construction Repayment Charge Per Acre (dollars)	Rate of Return (percent)
Ainsworth	753	286	$5.77	0.77
Almena	1,213	183	4.20	0.35
Angostura	1,174	132	1.84	0.16
Bostwick	748	221	4.62	0.62
Cedar Bluff	1,267	189	4.09	0.32
Crow Creek Pump	362	62	0	0
Dickinson	656	15	0	0
East Bench	401	96	0	0
Farwell	693	237	4.38	0.63
Fort Clark	603	52	1.48	0.25
Frenchman-Cambridge	921	162	3.71	0.40
Garrison Diversion	959	77	1.20	0.13
Glen Elder	258	0	0	0
Glendo	109	79	1.80	1.65
Hanover Bluff	885	153	1.10	0.12
Heart Butte	162	91	1.45	0.90
Kirwin	1,052	179	5.12	0.49
Oahe	1,083	176	3.20	0.30
Rapid Valley	192	0	0	0
Sargent	561	205	4.73	0.84
Savage	451	101	3.00	0.67
Webster	1,209	228	4.78	0.40

[a] These figures are the construction costs per acre allocated to the irrigation component of the project. Interest is not payable on these costs allocated to irrigation, even though other sources of revenue than irrigators' payments are used to discharge much of the obligation (e.g., power revenues).

[b] These figures are the repayment obligation per acre that the contracting irrigation district assumes in the water delivery contract. The difference between costs allocated to irrigation and the district's repayment obligation is made up from other revenues (e.g., power revenues).

Source: U.S. BUREAU OF RECLAMATION (1971). Summary Report of the Commissioner, Bureau of Reclamation 1970, Statistical & Financial Appendix, Part IV. U.S. Government Printing Office, Washington, D.C. pp. 159-227.

The Commission takes the position generally that direct beneficiaries should ordinarily pay the full costs of water development projects, including payment of interest on capital invested.[111] The question then arises whether or not irrigated agriculture should be excepted from that recommendation. To state the question in a different form: Can subsidies to irrigated farms be justified either on the historic basis of promoting the family farm or on the basis of modern circumstances? If the answer generally is

"No," then reclamation farmers, like other water users, should be required to pay their full share of the costs of a water development project. If those costs are paid, there will be no private windfall gains and therefore no need to impose an acreage limitation to achieve their wider distribution.

A conclusion that the Nation should not subsidize reclamation programs in the future and therefore should abandon the acreage limitation in reclamation projects built hereafter does not answer the question of what should be done with existing projects, where a subsidy has already been granted on a contractual

[111] See Chapter 15.

basis and the acreage limitation imposed. Even if the family farm rationale for subsidization of irrigation can no longer be supported, the question remains of the windfall gains that might be conferred if the limitation were lifted on existing projects.

DISCUSSION AND CONCLUSIONS

Future Reclamation Programs

The Federal reclamation program has by no means guaranteed family farms owned, operated, and occupied by farm families. In fact, family occupancy was an ambiguous requirement at best, early erased by an administrative ruling requiring only that the owner live within 50 miles of the farm,[112] hardly a commuting distance in 1910. Family operation was never required, although in 1902 it might have been thought to be natural. In any event, at the present time a large amount of irrigated acreage in Bureau projects is owned by persons who do not farm the land but lease it out for others to cultivate.[113] What remains of the concept of the family farm is ownership, and ownership only. Where the limitation applies, it means that no one person may receive reclamation water for more than 160 acres of land that he owns in any one irrigation district.

As thus construed and applied, the acreage limitation has little to do with the nature of rural life or the mode of farming. Reclamation farm families seem to adopt about the same lifestyle and farming patterns as nonreclamation farm families. In California, the Commission was told many reclamation farmers as well as nonreclamation farmers tend to live in town and commute to the farms. Sizes of farms are about the same within any given irrigation district, whether or not the farms are subject to the acreage limitation.[114] When differences exist between reclamation and nonreclamation farms, they are found in the nature of the landholding patterns. The reclamation farmer must lease excess acreage; the nonreclamation farmer can buy as much land as he chooses. But in scale of operations, capital investment, and all other aspects of farm operations, the reclamation farmer and his nonreclamation counterpart are indistinguishable.

[112] Reclamation Service Regulations, May 31, 1910; 38 L.D. 637.

[113] See HOGAN, pp. 110-122.

[114] In fact, in five counties of the California San Joaquin Valley, the average size of a reclamation farm operation is larger than the average size of all farm operations, in some cases by sizable amounts. See HOGAN, pp. 119-120.

In summary, the Commission finds no evidence that Federal support of the subsidized reclamation farm and imposition of the acreage limitation have produced cultural patterns any different from those found in comparable nonreclamation farming communities.

The Commission finds, on the other hand, that to continue subsidization of new irrigation projects does have disadvantages for the Nation.[115] The most serious is the expansion of the productive capacity of the Nation's agricultural plant when there is a surplus of many crops—a surplus that is expected to continue in the future.[116] Reclamation projects add to that surplus, to the detriment of farmers already in business and at high cost to the taxpayer.[117] Not only must the taxpayer pay a large portion of the costs of bringing new land into production, but he must also pay for farm price-support programs, the costs of which go up as farm production of supported crops increases. Howe and Easter have estimated that of the annual payments to farmers under the 1964 and 1966 price support program between $83 million and $179 million could be directly attributed to lands brought under Bureau of Reclamation water service during the 1944-1964 period.[118]

It is doubtful that taxpayers as consumers benefit greatly from these price-support expenditures or from subsidizing irrigation projects. For those crops which come under farm price-support programs, prices at the food store will be as high as they would otherwise be. But with greater production from subsidized irrigation, more tax funds will be required (1) to

[115] See Chapter 5, Section C.

[116] See Chapter 5, Section C. Fruits, nuts, and vegetables are not in surplus, but only 15 percent of reclamation land is devoted to those crops.

[117] HOWE Charles W & EASTER, K William (1971). Interbasin Transfers of Water. Published for Resources for the Future, Inc. by The John Hopkins Press, Baltimore, Md. pp. 140-141. The authors estimate that the 3.3 million acres of additional irrigated cropland developed by the Bureau in the period 1944-1964 displaced from 5 to 18 million acres elsewhere in the country. This amounts to something between 8 and 20 percent of the 66 million-acre decline in harvested cropland in the 20-year period.

[118] HOWE Charles W & EASTER, K William (1971). Interbasin Transfers of Water. Published for Resources for the Future, Inc. by The Johns Hopkins Press, Baltimore, Md. p. 143. Additional calculations for cotton indicate that price support and land retirement payments cost the Federal Treasury between $201 and $468 per year per acre of reclamation irrigated cotton. See pp. 146, 148-154.

maintain price-support levels and (2) to underwrite the irrigation subsidy.

For crops which are not under price-support programs but which are grown on reclamation project lands, food store prices will probably be lower, but not by much because the price received by farmers represents only a fraction of the retail price of food and subsidized irrigation accounts for only a fraction of total agricultural production.[119] In many cases, the combined social costs of producing subsidized products (i.e., the price paid by consumers *plus* the subsidy paid by taxpayers) exceed the costs which would otherwise prevail in the absence of the subsidy.

The Commission concludes that subsidization of new irrigation projects is not justified on either social or economic grounds. Reclamation farms differ little from nonreclamation farms, but federally subsidized irrigation does increase farm surpluses, increasing the costs of price-support programs and disadvantaging farmers in other parts of the country. Direct beneficiaries of Federal irrigation developments should, therefore, be compelled to pay in full the costs of projects allocated to irrigation in conformity to the general principle of full-cost repayment proposed for other water development projects elsewhere in this report.

If full repayment of irrigation costs is required of benefited irrigators, no reason is perceived for subjecting them to an acreage limitation. No subsidy has been conferred and no windfall gains will be obtained. In fact, there appear to be good reasons not to impose a limitation. As a general proposition, restraints on citizen behavior should be avoided unless good cause is shown for limiting freedom of choice. Moreover, arbitrary rules restricting economic choice are likely to cause misallocation of resources. The average size of the American farm has been on the increase as economies of scale are achieved with improved technology.[120] An acreage limitation runs counter to this trend and could produce one of two undesirable consequences: (1) Economic pressures would be such that evasion of the law would occur or (2) the law would be enforced despite the economic pressures but at the cost of a less efficient irrigation

industry. Accordingly, the Commission concludes that the 160-acre limitation should be eliminated in future reclamation programs if direct beneficiaries pay in full the costs of projects allocated to irrigation.

Existing Reclamation Programs

The reasons for eliminating the acreage limitation in future programs offer little guidance for handling the problem under present programs. There is little evidence that farm efficiency now suffers from the limitation, since various business arrangements allow the farming entrepreneur to put together an operating farm of the size he deems optimal. Costs are incurred (1) to set up arrangements satisfactory to the administrators in the Bureau of Reclamation and (2) to litigate the legality of the arrangements.

There are those who would urge that the 160-acre limitation be given real teeth as a means of restraining large-scale corporate farming. The Commission does not believe the acreage limitation is adequate to the job if indeed it is desirable to do such a job in the first instance. The Bureau of Reclamation serves almost 9 million acres out of a harvested cropland base of 273 million acres, and a significant part of the reclamation land is not subject to the acreage limitation. Even assuming the doubtful legality of applying the limitation to operating size instead of applying it merely to ownership, the effect on land tenure and corporate farming would seem to be miniscule.

There are others who would urge outright abolition of the limitation.[121] They, however, have not always faced up to the question of the reclamation subsidy and the relation of the limitation to it. It would not do to abolish the limitation if the effect would be to confer large windfall gains on reclamation farmers.

It is the Commission's opinion that any lifting of the acreage limitation on existing reclamation projects should be accompanied by an increase in the price of reclamation water reflecting more accurately the real cost of obtaining the water and delivering it to the farmer.

RECOMMENDATIONS

5-6. **Subsidization of new irrigation projects should be discontinued. Direct beneficiaries of Federal**

---

[119] Thus a general change in technology affecting all farm production could have a far greater impact on food prices than will a change in output of irrigated agriculture which contributes only 20 percent of total farm output.

[120] Between 1935 and 1972, average farm size in the United States increased from 155 to 394 acres. This same trend has occurred also in the 17 Western Reclamation States.

[121] GOVERNOR'S TASK FORCE ON THE ACREAGE LIMITATION PROBLEM (January 4, 1968). Report of the Governor's Task Force on the Acreage Limitation Problem. Department of Water Resources and Department of Agriculture, State of California, Sacramento.

irrigation developments should pay in full the costs of new projects allocated to irrigation.

5-7. Congress should abolish the 160-acre limitation in reclamation projects constructed in the future; provided, however, that direct project beneficiaries pay the full costs of the projects allocated to irrigation.

5-8. With respect to existing reclamation projects, Congress should enact legislation authorizing four distinct ways in which the acreage limitation may be lifted.

    a. Any irrigation district should be able to make a lump-sum payment of the balance remaining due on a contractual obligation incurred for irrigation and receive an exemption from the acreage limitation.[122]

    b. Any irrigation district should be able to pay interest on the balance remaining due on a contractual repayment obligation incurred for irrigation and receive an exemption from the acreage limitation.

    c. Any landowner who has executed a recordable contract to sell excess acreage should be able to retain that excess acreage by making such lump-sum payment or by paying such interest assigned to all the land he owns within a project, including his original 160 acres. Project costs should be apportioned on an acreage basis.

    d. Any landowner who wishes to acquire excess acreage should be able to do so and receive reclamation water if he makes such lump-sum payment or pays such interest as is assigned to all the land he will own within a project, including his original 160 acres.

These four proposals would not fully recapture the subsidy granted to irrigation water. Those parts of the subsidy consisting of assistance from power revenues and from overallocation to such nonreimbursable benefits as flood control and recreation will not be recaptured. But in view of the fact that under existing, binding legal arrangements, operators of farms containing excess acreage may receive reclamation water without recapture of the subsidy, the proposals are thought to go as far towards recapture as is practicable.

~~~~~~ *Section E*

Programs for Reducing Flood Losses

The annual flood damage in the United States has been roughly estimated to average $1 billion.[123] There is also a toll in human life, even though a high degree of flood protection has been provided, at great cost, for most cities located in major river valleys. Relatively small cities, like Rapid City, South Dakota, are, however, still vulnerable, as was demonstrated when a flood of great magnitude struck that community in June 1972, taking 237 lives and causing damage estimated to be in excess of $1 billion.[124] In that same month, Hurricane Agnes resulted in at least 122 deaths at scattered points over a five-State area.[125] During the period 1955 through 1969 the loss of life in the United States attributed to floods averaged 83 per year.[126] Despite the more than $8 billion that the Federal Government has spent in its attempt to reduce those losses, the total loss continues to grow. The conclusion is inescapable: the Nation should improve its programs for dealing with flood problems.

There are a number of measures that can be used to mitigate flood damages. Flood plain areas where people and property are already concentrated may be given full or partial protection by construction of engineering works such as reservoirs, levees, channel improvements, and bypasses. The Nation has invested

---

[122] A Federal district court has adopted this proposition as the existing law, but the case has been appealed.

[123] TASK FORCE ON FEDERAL FLOOD CONTROL POLICY (August 1966). A Unified National Program for Managing Flood Losses, House Document No. 465, 89th Congress, 2d Session. U.S. Government Printing Office, Washington, D.C. p. 3.

[124] Unpublished data compiled by the American Red Cross.

[125] GENERAL ADJUSTMENT BUREAU, INC (1972). Nature's Destructive Forces. General Adjustment Bureau, New York.

[126] U.S. NATIONAL OCEANIC AND ATMOSPHERIC ADMINISTRATION. Climatological Data, National Summary, 1970.

billions of dollars in such works since the Federal Government began its efforts to bring floods under control; first in the Lower Mississippi Valley in 1918 and throughout the Nation in 1936. When it became clear that new flood problems were being created faster than the old ones were being eliminated, other measures began to receive serious attention. These included the regulation of flood plain use to prevent their development in such a way that excessive damage will occur when floods strike, and to require that any structures that are built on the flood plain shall be designed so that they suffer little damage in time of flood. The latter measure, sometimes referred to as "flood-proofing," finds favor where lands suitable for development are limited.

Flood losses can also be reduced by warning occupants of the threatened area of the flood wave descending upon them and helping them to evacuate the area expected to be inundated. The use of this technique is dependent upon flood forecasting and the Federal Government provides a flood warning service through the National Weather Service. In predicting flood stages on the major streams, a rather high degree of reliability has been attained and warning times are long enough to permit removal of property to locations where it will not be damaged. Flash floods from small drainage areas, particularly in mountainous areas, cannot always be predicted far enough in advance to make it possible to protect movable property. This can result in disasters such as that visited upon Rapid City in 1972. Flash flood warnings can, at best, save lives if they are heeded. Rapid City, for example, had about 5 hours advance warning of the flood, but lacked an effective community action program.

When floods occur, Federal, State, local, and private organizations cooperate in carrying out flood emergency programs. Overall coordination is provided by the Office of Emergency Preparedness, and tax relief and disaster relief loans and grants are provided when the President declares the flooded area to be a disaster area.

All of the measures mentioned above should be considered in developing a plan for mitigating flood losses in a particular area, and the plan should be tailored to the unique needs of that area. In general, the objective should be to arrive at the best combination of measures.

THE PROGRAMS

The principal programs through which the Federal Government attempts to reduce the drain on the economy and the human suffering that result from floods are, in brief:

1. The "flood control" activities of the Corps of Engineers of the United States Army which are carried out primarily under the authorities made available to that agency by the Flood Control Act of 1936,[127] and a great body of additional amendatory and supplementary legislation.

2. The program of the Soil Conservation Service of the U.S. Department of Agriculture under the authorities of the Watershed Protection and Flood Prevention Act of 1954,[128] as amended, often informally referred to as the "small watershed program."

3. The program of the Tennessee Valley Authority,[129] one purpose of which is to reduce flood damages.

4. The Federal Reclamation Program administered by the Bureau of Reclamation of the U.S. Department of the Interior pursuant to legislation[130] which makes it possible to provide flood control capacity in the multiple-purpose reservoirs of Federal Reclamation Projects.

5. A flood insurance program[131] directed by the Federal Insurance Administration of the U.S. Department of Housing and Urban Development and carried out by a pool of insurance companies.

Program of the Corps of Engineers

The legislative base for this program is a series of "Flood Control Acts," the first of which was enacted in 1936. Previous to that Act there was no nation-wide flood control program, although the Federal

[127] P.L. 738, June 22, 1936, 74th Congress, 49 Stat. 1570.

[128] P.L. 566, August 4, 1954, 83d Congress, 68 Stat. 666, as amended, 16 USCA 1001-1008.

[129] Carried out under the *Tennessee Valley Authority Act of 1933*, P.L. 17, May 18, 1933, 73d Congress, 48 Stat. 58, as amended, 16 USCA 831 *et seq.*

[130] *Reclamation Project Act of 1939*, P.L. 260, August 4, 1939, Section 9, 76th Congress, 53 Stat. 1187, 1193-1196, as amended, 43 USCA 485h.

[131] Authorized by the *National Flood Insurance Act of 1968*, P.L. 90-448 Title XIII, 82 Stat. 476, 572 (codified, as amended, in pertinent part at 42 USCA 4001 *et seq.*). The earlier *Federal Flood Insurance Act of 1956*, P.L. 1016, August 7, 1956, 84th Congress, 70 Stat. 1078, was not utilized because of difficulties foreseen and the burden that it would have placed on the Federal Treasury.

Government had, under legislation enacted in 1917[132] and 1928[133] accepted responsibility for controlling floods of the Lower Mississippi River, and had also undertaken some flood control work on the Sacramento River[132] and in the Florida Everglades.[134] The 1936 Act was the first of a series and the resulting body of legislation is known collectively as the "Flood Control Acts." The designation can be misleading to the uninitiated because this large body of law makes it possible for the Corps of Engineers (Corps) to undertake projects and activities serving a multiplicity of purposes other than flood control, including—but not limited to—the drainage of wetlands,[135] the generation of power, and the provision of water supply. Of particular importance from the standpoint of reducing future flood losses is the Flood Control Act of 1960, Section 206 of which authorized the Corps to provide the States and local governmental entities with the information they need to regulate the use of flood plain lands. This authorization made it possible for the Corps to establish a Flood Plain Management Service, and in this way to give impetus to the use of nonstructural measures for dealing with the Nation's flood problems.[136]

The authorities provided the Corps by the earlier Flood Control Acts enabled it to propose projects for protecting against floods in rivers and streams, but not against overflows resulting from abnormally high levels of the oceans or lakes. As damages caused by such overflows increased, the Congress broadened the flood control legislation to make it possible for the Corps to provide protection against floods induced by hurricanes.[137]

Since the beginning of the flood control program of the Corps of Engineers in 1918, the Congress has appropriated a total of more than $8 billion[138] for the construction of engineering works such as dams, levees, and enlarged channels.

The cost-sharing policies applicable to this program are discussed in Chapter 15 of this report. In brief, the Federal Government assumes the full cost— construction and operation and maintenance—of providing protection by major reservoirs, while for local protection projects, such as levees and channel improvements, non-Federal interests must provide lands, easements, and rights-of-way, and must also maintain and operate the works after completion. On the average, the value of lands, easements, and rights-of-way amount to about 20 percent of the first cost of the local protection projects that have been installed. For hurricane protection projects, non-Federal interests are required to assume at least 30 percent of the first cost and all of the cost of operation and maintenance.

Since the authorization of the flood plain management program by the Flood Control Act of 1960 a slow, but continuous, trend toward greater reliance on flood plain regulation has become evident. By the end of Fiscal Year 1970, flood plain information had been furnished some 1,300 communities. The number of communities taking any positive action as a result of receiving flood plain information is not known.

Program of the Soil Conservation Service

The enactment of the Watershed Protection and Flood Prevention Act of 1954[139] and subsequent amendments thereto has enabled the Soil Conservation Service (SCS) to carry out, within headwater watersheds, a program of flood damage reduction by the construction of engineering works similar to, but smaller than, those installed by the Corps of Engineers to reduce flood damages in downstream valleys. Although similar in nature to the flood control

---

[132] *Act of March 1, 1917*, P.L. 367, 64th Congress, 39 Stat. 948.

[133] *Act of May 15, 1928*, P.L. 391, 70th Congress, 45 Stat. 534.

[134] *Act of July 3, 1930*, P.L. 520, 71st Congress, 46 Stat. 918, 925.

[135] See Section C of this chapter.

[136] P.L. 86-645, July 14, 1960, Section 206, 74 Stat. 480, 500, as amended, 33 USCA 709a.

[137] In the *Act of June 15, 1955*, P.L. 71, 84th Congress, 69 Stat. 132, Congress authorized a survey of the Eastern and Southern seaboard to determine methods of preventing and mitigating harm from hurricanes. Subsequently Congress adopted the procedure of authorizing individual projects for hurricane protection. Earlier Congress had directed the Corps to undertake shore protection works, but these works are not elements of the flood control program.

[138] Actual appropriations, not converted to present dollars. This is an updating of the cost figure appearing in House Document No. 465, 89th Congress, 2d Session.

[139] P.L. 566, August 4, 1954, 83d Congress, 68 Stat. 666, as amended, 16 USCA 1001 *et seq.* The Flood Control Act of 1936 had authorized the Department of Agriculture to propose land treatment plans for the reduction of floods in major river basins, but the surveys made pursuant to this authority revealed that land treatment alone does not substantially reduce large floods on major rivers, and this finding led the Soil Conservation Service to seek authority to deal with floods in upstream valleys by the construction of engineering works.

Development on flood plains invites flood damages

program of the Corps, the Public Law 566 program differs in that local organizations, such as Soil Conservation Districts, sponsor the construction of the works and agree to assume responsibility for them after they are constructed.

Although initiated as a program to reduce flood damages along headwater streams, amendments to Public Law 566 make it possible for "watershed projects" to serve a multiplicity of purposes, including reclamation by irrigation and drainage,[140] municipal and industrial water supply, recreation, streamflow regulation, and fish and wildlife enhancement.

As of the end of Fiscal Year 1972, the engineering works installed, or to be installed, under approved watershed plans included some 7,000 reservoirs and 21,000 miles of improved channel.[141] The total estimated cost of these structures will amount to approximately $2 billion. An inventory[142] made by the SCS has led it to conclude that the work accomplished or planned to date meets about 10

---

[140] See Section C of this chapter.

[141] The channel improvement work under this program constitutes the major component of the work discussed on channelization in Chapter 2 of this report.

[142] U.S. DEPARTMENT OF AGRICULTURE (1967). Statistical Bulletin No. 461, 1967.

percent of the total "needs" of the United States. This would indicate that the Public Law 566 program might ultimately result in an expenditure of $20 billion for the construction of headwater engineering works. To date, about three-fourths of the cost of such structures has been borne by the Federal Government.

In 1968, the Soil Conservation Service initiated a program under which it provides for headwater streams reports similar to those provided by the Flood Plain Information Service of the Corps of Engineers. Reports for 18 communities are expected to be completed by the end of Fiscal Year 1972. The recently enacted Rural Development Act of 1972[143] provides specific authority for this activity.

In compliance with provisions of Public Law 566, the Soil Conservation Service pays 100 percent of that part of the construction cost of works which is allocable to flood control, but the non-Federal organizations provide lands, easements, and rights-of-way and agree to operate the works.

Program of the Tennessee Valley Authority

The Tennessee Valley Authority (TVA) was created in 1933 as a regional resource development agency.[144] Among its assignments was the construction of dams and reservoirs in the Tennessee River and its tributaries to promote navigation and to control destructive flood waters in the Tennessee and lower Ohio and Mississippi Basins. In addition to achieving the above benefits, all the major dams in the Tennessee River and its tributaries contain powerhouses and produce electricity. Tributary storage is primarily responsible for reducing flood levels upstream from Chattanooga in the eastern part of the basin. The lower and western end of the basin is connected to the Cumberland River at Barkley Canal which permits combined use of both reservoir systems for control of releases during flood stages on the lower Ohio and Mississippi Rivers. Significant flood control contributions to localized areas in the Tennessee Valley are made by smaller TVA dams and reservoirs and by urban channel improvements.

A community flood damage prevention program, begun by TVA in 1953, outlines local flood situations and assists communities in preparing new or revised flood plain provisions for inclusion in zoning ordinances and subdivision regulations.

Program of the Bureau of Reclamation

The Reclamation Project Act of 1939[145] authorized the inclusion in Bureau of Reclamation reservoirs of capacity to be used for the reduction of flood flows. About $700 million of construction costs have been tentatively allocated to flood control under this authority, all of which is borne by the Federal Government.[146]

The Flood Insurance Program of the U.S. Department of Housing and Urban Development

Under the National Flood Insurance Program authorized in 1968,[147] the Federal Insurance Administration of the Department of Housing and Urban Development (HUD) can make available, through the insurance industry, subsidized flood insurance for any properties that are in existence at the time that the Administration delineates the flood hazard area in which they are located. Properties built subsequently are required to pay "actuarial" rates; that is, rates high enough to cover the average loss that might be expected over a long period of time.

Other Programs

Other programs intended to result in reductions in flood losses are:

1. A cooperative program of the Corps of Engineers, the U.S. Geological Survey, and the National Oceanic and Atmospheric Administration (NOAA) through which maps of flood plains are prepared for inclusion in Flood Plain Information Reports prepared by the Corps of Engineers, and which are also used by the SCS, the TVA, and the Federal Insurance Administration.

2. The National Weather Service of NOAA operates 12 River Forecast Centers that issue flood warnings that have been of great value to cities located on larger streams, but of limited value to communities or areas subject to flash floods on small streams.

3. Flood emergency programs to minimize losses of life and property when major floods occur.

---

[143] P.L. 92-419, August 30, 1972, 75 Stat. 307.

[144] *Tennessee Valley Authority Act of 1933*, P.L. 17, May 18, 1933, 73d Congress, 48 Stat. 58, as amended, 16 USCA 831 *et seq.*

[145] *Reclamation Project Act of 1939*, P.L. 260, August 4, 1939, Section 9, 76th Congress, 53 Stat. 1187, 1193-1196, as amended, 43 USCA 485h.

[146] U.S. BUREAU OF RECLAMATION (1972). Statistical Report of the Commissioner. Appendix II, p. 81.

[147] *National Flood Insurance Act of 1968*, P.L. 90-448, August 1, 1968, Title XIII, 82 Stat. 476, 572 (codified, as amended, in pertinent part at 42 USCA 4001 *et seq.*).

Through these programs the Corps of Engineers and the Department of Agriculture work with local authorities, the American Red Cross, and other organizations to reduce the impact of such floods, under the overall coordination of the Office of Emergency Preparedness. The latter organization also encourages communities to develop flood emergency plans so that they will be prepared to act quickly and efficiently in the event a flood emergency should arise. It has also encouraged States to enact "Disaster Acts" that will improve the machinery available when any type of disaster strikes.

APPRAISAL OF PROGRAMS

The National Water Commission has made a systematic effort to appraise the programs previously described, giving special attention to the possibilities for improving them. Its principal findings are briefly presented in the following paragraphs.

There is need for a change in the way the Nation looks at its flood problem. It is natural for the general public to think that the way to solve the flood problem is to build levees, reservoirs, and other engineering works. This was particularly true after the series of spectacular floods such as those that preceded the enactment of the Flood Control Act of 1936. Moreover, it is natural for Congress, in the aftermath of such disasters, to turn to such visible means of control. Undoubtedly, the construction of engineering works has greatly reduced the flood losses that the Nation would otherwise have suffered, and it is certain that many such works have resulted in benefits far exceeding their costs. As many have pointed out, however, the flood problem has grown despite the billions spent for protective measures.[148] The extensive damages from the 1972 Hurricane Agnes floods in communities such as Wilkes-Barre, Pennsylvania, already having Federal flood control projects suggests that such projects give occupants of flood plains a false sense of security, since no flood control project can prevent damages from the maximum possible flood.

In the mid-1940's, the more perceptive observers of the situation began to call attention to the fact that protecting people and property already in the flood plains was not enough, that something must be done to stop the rapid development of flood plain land and the consequent creation of additional flood problems.[149] This obviously sensible notion eventually gained supporters and Section 206 of the Flood Control Act of 1960 referred to earlier made it possible for the Corps of Engineers to establish its Flood Plain Management Service.[150] This was an important step forward. But other steps must follow until there is a fundamental reorientation in the way the people of the United States think about their flood problem, and until the Congress, the agencies responsible for programs affecting the Nation's flood plains, and the public at large agree that the goal to be attained is the best use of flood plain lands. One of the steps in this direction must, of course, be the attainment of a consensus on what is meant by "best use." It is the view of this Commission that from the standpoint of the Nation the best use of any parcel of flood plain land is that which makes the greatest net contribution to the welfare of the people of the United States, taking into account intangible, as well as material, contributions.

More attention should be given alternatives and to finding the best combination thereof. Although planners generally accept the idea that all feasible alternatives should be given full and equitable consideration, and that their objective should be to find the best combination of measures, the Federal agencies have not been particularly successful in putting the concept into effect. This is especially true when a group of agencies attempts to formulate a comprehensive regional plan and finds that the inclusion therein of measures that one agency would install would require omission of those that another agency would like to carry out. Too often the final plan turns out to be no more than a poorly coordinated conglomerate of the plans favored by the individual agencies. The Water Resources Council is making a serious attempt to improve Federal planning procedures to alleviate this problem. The Council is

---

[148] For a brief history of the Nation's efforts to solve the flood problem, see AREY, David F & BAUMANN, Duane D, University of Pittsburgh, Pittsburgh, Pa. (1971). Alternative Adjustments to Natural Hazards, prepared for the National Water Commission. National Technical Information Service, Springfield, Va., Accession No. PB 211 922.

[149] WHITE, Gilbert Fowler (1945). Human Adjustment to Floods. University of Chicago, Chicago, Ill.

[150] P.L. 86-645, Section 206, July 14, 1960, 74 Stat. 480, 500, as amended, 33 USCA 709a. Even earlier, the Tennessee Valley Authority and the U.S. Geological Survey had assisted local entities with arrangements for regulating the use of flood plain lands.

handicapped by the fact that the legislative authorities under which the various Federal agencies work constitute a poorly coordinated assemblage of laws enacted at intervals over a long period of years during which planning concepts changed radically.

There is a need for strengthening programs that promote better use of flood plain lands. Response to Section 206 of the Flood Control Act of 1960, under which the Corps of Engineers established its Flood Plain Management Service, has exceeded in both magnitude and public approbation that expected by the supporters of the legislation. Because it was viewed as an experiment, Section 206 placed a limit upon the amount that could be spent in any one year. Although this limit has since been increased, the requests for services have continued to outrun the capacity of the Corps of Engineers to meet the demand. In view of the general approval of the program, and since small expenditures for this service may obviate great expenditures for flood protection in the future, it would appear desirable to remove this limitation. The Appropriations Committees will, of course, see to it that the appropriation for any particular year does not exceed a justifiable level.

Another retarding factor is the insufficiency of funds for the preparation of flood plain maps through the joint program of the U.S. Geological Survey, the National Oceanic and Atmospheric Administration, and the Corps of Engineers. This deficiency also holds back the Flood Insurance Programs of HUD.

Flood plain management plans should be broadened. The flood plain management plans being provided under the authorities of Section 206 are of great value to communities wishing to regulate the use of their flood plain lands. The Commission is of the opinion, however, that they would be of still greater value if they were accompanied by the results of a study of both the lands subject to flooding and the surrounding uplands. Among other things, this study should provide a comparison of the cost *to the Nation* of using the flood plain lands for various purposes, with the cost of using, for those same purposes, alternative lands not subject to overflow. In addition, the reports on such studies should provide information on the environmental and social implications of developing, or not developing, such lands.

Progress toward the goal of making optimum use of flood plain regulation should be speeded up by offering financial assistance to the States. The cooperation of the States is absolutely essential if the objectives of the Flood Plain Management Program are to be achieved. Even where the Federal Government is able to provide flood hazard maps only the States, or governmental subdivisions thereof, can exercise the police power required to control land use. It is becoming increasingly evident that if flood hazard maps for all flood plains in the Nation must be made by the Federal agencies presently engaged in that activity, progress in bringing the Nation's flood plains under regulation will be disastrously slow. Moreover, if flood insurance is to be made available to flood plain occupants throughout the Nation, and if the agencies responsible for the administration of Federal grant, loan, or mortgage insurance programs are to comply with Executive Order No. 11296,[151] the agencies concerned must have early access to at least preliminary flood hazard determinations in all flood plain areas in which their services are demanded. For all of these reasons, it is essential, in the opinion of the Commission, that all States develop effective organizations and programs, either statewide or regional, to promote wise use of flood plain lands. The Federal Government should assist the States in this because the savings, in the form of reductions in future flood damages and expenditures for flood protection measures and disaster relief, will far exceed the cost of establishing and maintaining such non-Federal organizations and programs.

There is a need for public acquisition of flood plain land to control flood plain use. It has been declared by some that the present programs for controlling flood plain use are deficient in that they make no provision for public acquisition of lands subject to frequent overflow. They point out that in some instances the Federal Government would, in the long run, save money were it to acquire such lands. While an economically valid argument might be made that Federal acquisition of certain flood plain lands would be justified, the establishment of a program for this purpose could lead to a great increase in the landholdings of the Federal Government. This Commission doubts the wisdom of adding to the already large proportion of the Nation's lands that is owned by the Federal Government. Yet, it cannot be denied that certain flood plain areas, particularly areas of critical environmental concern, would be of greater value to the Nation if they were used for parks or

---

[151] This Executive Order requires these agencies to evaluate flood hazards in connection with grants, loans, or mortgage insurance for buildings, structures, roads, or other facilities in order to minimize future flood damages, or Federal expenditures for flood protection and disaster relief. Federal Register 31(155):10663-10664. August 11, 1966.

similar purposes. Where this is found to be the case, it would be consistent with good public policy for the States, or other non-Federal entities, to acquire the land and for the Federal Government to assume a part of the acquisition cost. Federal contributions toward such acquisition should be made through programs other than those established to develop water resources. For example, assistance in acquiring lands for recreational purposes could appropriately be made available from the Land and Water Conservation Fund.[152]

Federal agencies fail to give adequate consideration to the flood hazard in carrying out programs affecting the flood plain. When, in 1966, President Johnson transmitted to Congress the Report of a Task Force on Federal Flood Control Policy[153] he also issued Executive Order No. 11296.[154] This Order requires the agencies responsible for a wide range of Federal programs affecting, or capable of affecting, the use of flood plain lands, to take the flood hazard into account in their administration of those programs. Unfortunately, this is not being done. At the Washington conference on the review draft of this report, representatives of the State of Pennsylvania pointed out that Small Business Administration loans had been made for rebuilding on the flood plains. Since Executive Order No. 11296 did not achieve the results expected of it, the Bureau of the Budget in 1968 requested the Water Resources Council to assist in the development of guidelines for the application of the Executive Order. This resulted in the preparation of "Proposed Flood Hazard Evaluation Guidelines for the Federal Executive Agencies." It was first issued in preliminary form and, after extensive review, issued in final form in April 1972 for the guidance of the executive agencies. The guidelines should make Executive Order No. 11296 more effective, but until flood plain maps and management plans become available for all of the flood plain areas in which agencies operate, a considerable degree of uncertainty will continue to exist as to the hazard on any particular part of a particular flood plain. When a flood plain management plan has been developed for any area, and this plan has been approved by both the State and the Federal Government, then all Federal agencies should be required to comply with it.

There is a need for improvement in the procedures for preparing plans for flood loss reduction and flood plain management. Soon after the release of the Report of the Task Force on Federal Flood Control Policy, the Bureau of the Budget called upon the Water Resources Council to develop procedures for implementing the recommendations of the Task Force. This, and several other developments, led the Council to undertake a number of studies. As a result of these studies, the Council has issued several documents having important implications for plan formulation. One of these sets forth proposed "Principles and Standards for Planning Water and Land Resources." Another outlines a "Unified National Program for Flood Plain Management." Neither of these reports has been placed in final form. Both will have important implications for future plan formulation. The National Water Commission is of the opinion that, when completed, these reports will help to improve plans and correct some of the deficiencies mentioned above. Nevertheless, it believes that further work is necessary and that in the course of this work the recommendations at the end of this section should be given full consideration.

There is a need for considerable strengthening of the present program for providing flood forecasts. A recent report by the Office of Emergency Preparedness (OEP) evaluates present provisions for the prediction of floods and the issuance of warnings.[155] Particular attention is called to the deficiencies of the flash flood prediction and warning system. OEP also offers recommendations for correcting present inadequacies. As the recommendations to follow will show, the National Water Commission agrees that the present system requires strengthening.

There is need for intensification and unification of basic data collection. The Task Force on Federal Flood Control Policy offered a number of recommendations on data collection designed to provide better information on floods and flood problems. The Water Resources Council has gone part of the way in implementing these recommendations, and the established basic data collection programs of the Federal

---

[152] See *Land and Water Conservation Fund Act of 1965*, P.L. 88-578, Section 5, September 3, 1964, 78 Stat. 897, 900 as amended, 16 USCA 460*l*-8.

[153] Entitled "A Unified National Program for Managing Flood Losses" and printed as House Document No. 465, 89th Congress, 2d Session.

[154] Evaluation of Flood Hazard in Locating Federally Owned or Financed Buildings, Roads, and Other Facilities, and in Disposing of Federal Lands and Properties. Federal Register 31(155):10663-10664. August 11, 1966.

[155] U.S. OFFICE OF EMERGENCY PREPAREDNESS (January 1972). Disaster Preparedness, Report to the Congress. 3 volumes. U.S. Government Printing Office, Washington, D.C.

and State agencies continue. Many of those responsible for planning and carrying out programs to reduce flood losses have said that the existing data base is inadequate.

The role that flood insurance should play in a unified national program for reducing flood losses is not yet clear and there is need for an independent study of present flood insurance legislation and activities. As indicated previously, this is a new program authorized in 1968 by Public Law 90-448. As of June 1972 when the Nation suffered a series of disastrous floods about 93,000 policies had been sold to a potential market that had previously been estimated as 2 to 3 million property owners.[156] In other words, less than 5 percent of those eligible had purchased insurance. After the great floods caused by Hurricane Agnes it was discovered that an insignificant proportion of the losses suffered would be covered by insurance payments. For example, in Wilkes-Barre, Pennsylvania, one of the hardest hit communities, only two policies had been purchased. By December 1972, the number of policies in effect had increased to 125,000.[157]

Considerable doubt has been expressed concerning the wisdom of the high degree of subsidization that is being used to develop a market for flood insurance, as well as of the practicability of withholding, as required by present law, emergency relief from those who could have covered their losses by insurance. After the great floods of June 1972, the Federal Government reduced further the already highly subsidized rates for flood insurance by 37-1/2 percent, and deferred the date at which it would make available unsubsidized insurance. In addition, it has been pointed out that insurance can do nothing to reduce damages to existing property, and thus cannot stop this large and continuing drain upon the Nation's economy.

When the Task Force on Federal Flood Control Policy considered flood insurance as one of the alternative means of coping with the flood problem, it pointed out that " . . . if misapplied an insurance program could aggravate rather than ameliorate the flood problem."[158] In the light of this danger, and of the experience during recent floods, there would appear to be an urgent need for the independent study recommended by this Commission.

On the credit side of the ledger, it must be said that the law authorizing the National Flood Insurance Program requires that land-use regulations be put into effect before flood insurance may be made available to those subject to damage. This feature of the program provides an effective incentive for better utilization of flood plain lands. Wise use of flood-prone lands is also furthered by the fact that people are made aware of the flood hazard in areas in which flood insurance is offered. Some have expressed the view that if the flood insurance program is to become effective, the purchase of flood insurance must be made mandatory, and the Department of Housing and Urban Development has moved in this direction by proposing legislation that would prohibit financial assistance in the acquisition of flood plain property or for construction on flood plain lands—either through Federal agencies or lending institutions over which the Federal Government has any supervisory control—unless the property or the contemplated improvement is covered by flood insurance. Others propose abandonment of Federal programs under which disaster relief is made available to victims of major floods as a means of compelling flood plain occupants to buy flood insurance.

There is need for extensive reforms in the programs under which engineering works are constructed for the purpose of reducing flood losses. This Commission's appraisal of the programs through which the Corps of Engineers and the Soil Conservation Service provide flood protection by means of reservoirs, levees, and other engineering works has revealed the same deficiencies found by earlier Commissions.[159] Needed reforms of special importance are:

1. A change in the basic cost-sharing policies to (a) eliminate the unconscionable windfall gains accruing to some landowners when protection provided at no expense to them results in large increases in the value of their lands, (b) provide for uniformity in the policies governing the programs of different agencies,

[156] GENERAL ADJUSTMENT BUREAU, INC (1972). Destruction and Devastation: The Floods of June 1972.

[157] Information provided by the Federal Insurance Administration.

[158] TASK FORCE ON FEDERAL FLOOD CONTROL POLICY (August 1966). A Unified National Program for Managing Flood Losses, House Document No. 465, 89th Congress, 2d Session. U.S. Government Printing Office, Washington, D.C. p. 38.

[159] For example, see TASK GROUP ON FLOOD CONTROL (1955). Report of the Task Group on Flood Control, in TASK FORCE ON WATER RESOURCES AND POWER, Report on Water Resources and Power, volume II, prepared for the Commission on Organization of the Executive Branch of the Government. U.S. Government Printing Office, Washington, D.C.

and (c) equalize cost-sharing for the different means of providing protection.[160]

2. Improvement in the economic evaluation of proposed flood control projects and programs, including elimination of the practice of including in the benefit-cost analysis benefits for protection of improvements not yet constructed.

3. The addition to the conditions that must be met by local interests of a requirement that they agree to regulate the use of flood plain lands to the extent necessary (a) to obviate the need for additional protective works and (b) to minimize losses in the event of a flood larger than that which the proposed works can control.

4. Imposition of a requirement that costs of works needed to protect downstream interests from increased flood heights caused by or resulting from upstream channelization or drainage works be included as a cost of the upstream project.

Insufficient attention is being given the need for reducing losses resulting from storm runoff originating in urban areas. It has been called to the attention of the Commission that losses resulting from flood runoff originating in urban areas are increasing within what might be called a "no man's land" lying between the problem area covered by the Federal flood control programs and the problem area within which the cities have generally assumed responsibility by providing storm sewer systems. The authorities of the Federal Flood Control Acts have, with a few exceptions, been utilized only in those instances in which the flood waters originated almost entirely on lands not under the jurisdiction of municipal governments.

The Commission is satisfied that this is indeed a serious class of flood problems. But it is not convinced the vast powers and resources of the Federal Government must be exercised to cope with problems the solution to which appears to be well within the capabilities of municipal governments or other local entities established for the purpose. The Commission favors, therefore, continued adherence to the policy that any engineering works required to reduce losses resulting from flood runoff originating wholly, or largely, within an urban area should be designed, constructed, and maintained by a local entity. However, to the extent that flood plain maps delineating flood hazard zones are required by the local entity to enable it to regulate the use of lands subject to flooding, the agencies—Federal, State, or regional—that prepare such maps elsewhere in the region should have the authority to assist the local entity in those instances in which this would reduce the cost of the work.

In many instances, the flood losses occasioned by urban storm runoff result in large part from the deposition of eroded material. There is, therefore, an intimate relationship between the problem dealt with here and the problems of erosion and sedimentation discussed in Section H of this chapter. But whether the problem stems primarily from erosion and deposition, or from damage by water, the Commission is of the opinion that the primary responsibility for its solution should be left with a local entity.

Means must be devised for coordinating water planning and land-use planning. The Congress has under consideration legislation to establish a national land-use policy[161] and to authorize a program of land-use planning to be carried out primarily by the States. In the event such a program is brought into being, there will be an urgent need for coordination between the land-use plans developed thereunder and plans developed for use in regulating the Nation's flood plains. There is not at present a legislative base for such coordination, nor are existing organizational arrangements capable of providing the necessary coordination.

Appraisal by Task Force on Federal Flood Control Policy

In 1966, the Bureau of the Budget invited Dr. Gilbert F. White[162] to chair a "Task Force on Federal Flood Control Policy," made up primarily of representatives of the Federal agencies most concerned. This Task Force submitted a report entitled "A Unified National Program for Managing Flood Losses," which the President transmitted to the Congress with his commendation.[163] The National

---

[160] This is needed to thwart efforts by local interests to force adoption of plans not most desirable from the standpoint of the Nation in order to minimize the non-Federal share of the cost; for example, efforts to obtain protection by reservoirs because under present policies the Federal Government bears the entire cost of reservoir protection.

[161] Representative of the legislation under consideration were S.632 and S.992 of the 92d Congress.

[162] At that time Chairman, Department of Geography, University of Chicago; presently Director, Institute of Behavioral Sciences, University of Colorado.

[163] The Congress had this report printed as House Document No. 465, 89th Congress, August 1966.

Water Commission has reviewed this report and is of the opinion that it presents an excellent appraisal of the complex of activities discussed in this section.

This Commission's appraisal of these activities parallels that of the Task Force in many important respects, although the report of such a highly specialized Task Force naturally deals with many details not covered in this report. However, the discussion of major issues by the Task Force augments and reinforces a number of the points made in this Commission's appraisal. For this reason, and also because of the general excellence of the Task Force report, the National Water Commission considers it an important complement to its own report, and required reading for those having a particular interest in the Nation's flood problem.

DISCUSSION

The reforms in cost-sharing proposed by the Commission in this report will require the identification of beneficiaries and the assessment of project costs against them. During the regional conferences held by the Commission in January and February of 1973, a number of participants expressed the view that it would be wholly impracticable to identify the direct beneficiaries of flood protection projects, and to assess the costs on the basis of benefits received. The Commission's recommendations are based primarily upon its understanding of the following two points: (1) in order to justify a Federal flood control project it is necessary to demonstrate that benefits exceed costs and that since this requires estimation of the benefits accruing to all parts of the flood plain, all of the information required to identify beneficiaries and assess costs will be available for every project for which a proper economic evaluation has been made; and (2) for many years drainage districts and other public improvement districts in the United States have been successfully solving assessment problems that are more complex than those stemming from the construction of most flood control works. At the conference held in Washington, D.C., the Commission's confidence in the conclusions it had reached was strengthened by the more direct evidence provided by the General Manager of the Miami Conservancy District, who appeared to tell the remarkable story of how, beginning in 1915, the people of the Miami River Basin undertook—with no Federal assistance—to provide flood protection for the City of Dayton, Ohio, and other valley communities; an undertaking that has cost them, to date, more than

$90 million.[164] When questioned, the General Manager assured the Commission that, "You *can* identify the beneficiaries." He warned, however, that "You have to *want* to do it first."

The point was also made at the regional conferences on the review draft that in some instances floods and flood damages in the lower reaches of a stream are increased because of upstream activities. Examples mentioned were the conversion of land in forest or grass cover to cropland, and the enlargement of channels for the purpose of reducing flood damages or draining wetlands. Since in many instances these adverse downstream effects result from Federal projects or activities undertaken with Federal assistance, witnesses urged that the United States should be responsible for preventing the damages. Undoubtedly, upstream flood control works which speed up the flow of water toward the lower reaches of the river can increase the downstream damages and necessitate higher levees and increased flood protection downstream. Such damages, or the costs of mitigating them, should be included as a part of the cost of the upstream project and recovered from the beneficiaries thereof when it is constructed.

CONCLUSIONS

The United States has made heroic efforts to protect the lives and property of those who live on flood plain lands, and to maintain the flow of wealth that results from the use of these lands. Citizens in all parts of the Nation have been content to see billions of dollars spent to help fellow citizens subject to loss of life or fortune. But, throughout the many years that this benevolent effort has been under way, other individuals have been busily developing other flood plain areas in such ways that the initial goal of rescuing those unfortunate enough to be endangered by floods has become less and less attainable. Obviously, there must be a drastic change in the Nation's attitudes and programs. In the foregoing appraisal, this Commission has attempted to focus attention upon the main deficiencies of the present programs.

The rectification of the deficiencies mentioned will require concerted action by the Congress, the President, and the agencies involved. The Water Resources Council, if strengthened in the ways suggested in this

---

[164] The story of The Miami Conservancy District, including a discussion of assessments, will be found in: MORGAN, Arthur E (1951). The Miami Conservancy District. McGraw-Hill Book Company, New York. 504 pp.

report, will be able to exert a powerful influence in implementing the recommendations offered by this Commission. But over and above the official actions called for by these recommendations, there is a need for a better understanding by the public at large of the basic nature of the flood problem, and in particular, an understanding that the ultimate goal of all public flood control programs should be the *best* use of the Nation's flood plain lands.

RECOMMENDATIONS

5-9. Flood plain lands should be treated as an important resource and should be managed so as to make the maximum net contribution to national welfare, keeping in mind (a) that the material wealth of a nation is not enhanced by development of any tract of land subject to flood overflow unless the net value of the resulting production exceeds the costs of development plus the flood losses (or the cost of preventing such losses) and (b) that any nonmaterial values sacrificed through development must also be counted as a cost.

5-10. In formulating plans for flood loss reduction full and equitable consideration should be given to all practicable alternative measures for achieving that goal, with a view to finding the best combination of such measures, using the evaluation principles recommended in Chapter 10 of this report.

5-11. The present trend toward greater use of flood plain regulation as a means of reducing future flood damages, or of reducing future costs for protective measures, should be strengthened by the following Federal actions to encourage wise use of flood plains:

    a. Enactment of legislation to authorize the Water Resources Council to make Federal grants to the States to be used for mapping flood plains, determining flood hazards, making flood plain management plans, establishing State standards for flood plain regulation activities, and assisting local governmental entities in carrying out flood plain management programs; these grants not to exceed 50 percent of the amount expended by the States for such purposes.

    b. Amendment of Section 206 of the Flood Control Act of 1960 to require that reports prepared thereunder provide, in addition to flood hazard information,

    (1) a comparison of the cost of creating values by further development of the flood plain lands with the cost of creating these same values by available alternative measures (such as development of nearby uplands) and (2) a delineation of those flood plain areas that could be of greater value to the Nation if used for open spaces (such as city parks).

    c. Removal of present legislative limitations upon the amounts that can be appropriated for flood plain management studies in any one year.

    d. Increasing the funds available for carrying out the cooperative flood plain mapping program of the U.S. Geological Survey, the National Oceanic and Atmospheric Administration, and the Corps of Engineers.

5-12. Existing programs, such as the Land and Water Conservation Fund and urban park grants through which Federal assistance may be extended to State and local entities to encourage the establishment of parks and other open spaces, should be utilized to the fullest practicable extent to encourage public acquisition of those flood plain lands for which the best use is found to be for recreational or open space purposes.

5-13. The requirements of Executive Order No. 11296 should be strictly observed by the Federal agencies to which the order applies, and in particular those agencies should refrain from making any grants or loans, or from insuring any loans, that would be used for construction in flood plains or for the reconstruction of structures that have been seriously damaged by floods, unless adequate provisions have been made to prevent the repetition of such damages by flood-proofing or other means.

5-14. Executive Order No. 11296 should be amended to require that all Federal programs within areas covered by a flood plain management plan shall comply with such plan provided it has been approved by the entity representing the community affected, by the responsible State organization, and by the Corps of Engineers or other appropriate Federal agency.

5-15. The Water Resources Council should promulgate guidelines at the earliest practicable date to govern the formulation of flood loss reduction and flood plain management plans to be used in future water resources planning.

5-16. The flood forecasting program of the Federal Government should be substantially strengthened by organizational changes along the lines recommended in Chapter 11 of this report and more adequate financing should be provided.

5-17. Communities located in areas subject to flash floods should develop a community action plan to permit prompt response to a flood threat whenever it develops. Communities should develop methods of flood forecasting based on rainfall information from upstream watersheds and should use automatic warning devices where they are found to be feasible.

5-18. The Water Resources Council should develop a plan for a unified national program for the collection of basic data on floods and flood damages as recommended by the Task Force on Federal Flood Control Policy as set forth in House Document No. 465, 89th Congress, to be implemented, to the extent possible, by executive order, and if necessary by legislation to be proposed by the President.

5-19. The General Accounting Office, or other appropriate independent agency, should make an appraisal of the flood insurance program being carried out by the Department of Housing and Urban Development under the authority of the National Flood Insurance Act of 1968.

5-20. Future Federal or federally assisted projects, including structural measures for the control of floods, should comply with the following provisions:

a. The share of the cost of the project to be borne by non-Federal interests should be in accord with the cost-sharing principles recommended in Chapter 15 of this report.

b. The Federal agency proposing the work, or proposing a Federal contribution thereto, should demonstrate by an evaluation in consonance with the principles recommended in Chapter 10 of this report that the sum of all beneficial effects would exceed the sum of all costs, with due consideration being given both material and nonmaterial benefits and costs.

c. The State or a responsible local governmental entity should agree to regulate the use of flood plain lands to the extent necessary to prevent further developments that would (1) make necessary the installation of additional protective works or (2) be subject to substantial damage in the event of a flood exceeding the magnitude of the design flood.

5-21. Any Federal legislation to authorize a program of land-use planning should include special provisions for the coordination of any plans made under that program with flood plain management plans made by the States and the Federal water resources planning agencies.

Section F

Municipal and Industrial Water Supply Programs

From the earliest days of the Nation, cities and industries have provided their own water supplies. In general, there is no reason why they should not continue to do so. For many years this was recognized by the Congress and several laws contain statements to the effect that the Federal Government will confine itself to an ancillary role in this field.[165] The Water Supply Act of 1958[166] made it possible to increase the capacity of major Federal reservoirs, constructed primarily for purposes other than the provision of water supply, in order to store water for municipal and industrial (M&I) purposes. This did not add to the Federal responsibility for M&I water as

[165] For example, the Water Supply Act of 1958 contains the following: "It is hereby declared to be the policy of the Congress to recognize the primary responsibilities of the States and local interests in developing water supplies for domestic, municipal, industrial, and other purposes..."

[166] P.L. 85-500, July 3, 1958, Title III, 72 Stat. 297, 319, as amended, 43 USCA 390b.

non-Federal interests were required to assume the full cost of the added capacity.

In recent years, a tendency for increasing the Federal role in the provision of M&I water is emerging. For example, the Rural Development Act of 1972 authorizes the Secretary of Agriculture to bear up to one-half the costs of reservoir storage capacity for present M&I water supply needs.[167] This Act also permits agencies of the U.S. Department of Agriculture to provide grants and loans for the installation of community water supply facilities in communities having a population of up to 10,000, a substantial increase over the previous limit. Moreover, the Act permits these agencies to provide grants and loans for water supply facilities of private business enterprises located within cities with a population up to 50,000, or in the urban areas surrounding such cities.

Earlier, the Congress had authorized programs under which grants and loans are made to cities for the purpose of assisting them to meet their expanding needs for M&I water, and to rural communities for the same purpose.[168] The assistance to the cities is made available through the U.S. Department of Housing and Urban Development. The assistance to the rural communities is provided through the programs of the Department of Agriculture, and especially the program of the Farmers Home Administration.

It is evident that the process of abandoning the traditional policy of local responsibility for providing M&I water supplies is already rather far advanced. The Federal policies and programs concerned with water supply would seem to be in just such a period of flux as the Nation's pollution control policies and programs have but recently passed through. As will be brought out subsequently, this Commission finds rather widespread concern among State and local public officials that the present trend will eventually result in as high a degree of Federal domination in the water supply field as has already materialized in the field of pollution control. From this situation stems the principal problem to be dealt with in this section.

Other, less significant, problems stem from the needs for: (1) better coordination between plans for comprehensive river basin development and plans for supplying water to urban areas; (2) more efficient use of water in urban areas; (3) better coordination of the wide array of Federal grants and loans available to aid cities in meeting their water supply requirements; and (4) acceleration of certain types of research.

THE PROGRAMS

Storage in Federal Reservoirs

Various legislative attempts to make possible the use of Federal reservoirs to supply M&I water culminated in the Water Supply Act of 1958[169] which established a uniform policy governing the programs of both the U.S. Army Corps of Engineers and the U.S. Bureau of Reclamation. Under this policy, these agencies may provide additional capacity for M&I water in reservoirs to be constructed primarily for other purposes, on condition that non-Federal interests agree to pay the costs allocable to the provision of such water. Payments on costs incurred for the purpose of meeting anticipated future demands need not begin until the additional capacity provided is actually used, but the amount on which payment may be thus deferred cannot exceed 30 percent of the total estimated cost of the reservoir. The non-Federal entity must start to pay interest on the cost of capacity provided for future use after 10 years, even if it has not started to use this capacity by that time. A 1963 Act[170] provides that the local interests may continue to use the storage capacity covered by a contract so long as they meet certain specified requirements.

Storage Capacity in Soil Conservation Service Reservoirs

The Soil Conservation Service (SCS) has authority to include additional capacity in reservoirs constructed pursuant to Public Law 566[171] for the provision of M&I water. Up to the time of enactment of the Rural Development Act of 1972, repayment of the full cost of such additional capacity was required under conditions generally similar to those applicable to Corps of Engineers and Bureau of Reclamation

[167] P.L. 92-419, August 30, 1972, Sections 201(f), 301, 86 Stat. 657, 668, 669 (amending Section 4 of the *Watershed Protection and Flood Prevention Act of 1954*, as amended, 16 USCA 1004, and Section 32(e) of Title III of the *Bankhead-Jones Farm Tenant Act*, as amended, 7 USCA 1011).

[168] See subsequent descriptions of these programs.

[169] P.L. 85-500, July 3, 1958, Title III, 72 Stat. 279, 319, as amended, 43 USCA 390b.

[170] *Act of October 16, 1963*, P.L. 88-140, 77 Stat. 249, 43 USCA 390c-390f.

[171] *Watershed Protection and Flood Prevention Act of 1954*, P.L. 566, 83d Congress, August 4, 1954, 68 Stat. 666, as amended, 16 USCA 1001 *et seq.*

reservoir projects. As previously mentioned, however, the Federal Government may now bear up to one-half of the costs of reservoir storage for present M&I water supply needs.

Loans and Grants to Cities

The U.S. Department of Housing and Urban Development (HUD) is authorized to assist cities to provide municipal water supplies by:
(1) Making grants, under Section 701 of the Housing Act of 1954,[172] for the preparation of comprehensive plans for urban development including water supply facilities. These grants are limited to cities of less than 50,000 population and to certain other specified areas.
(2) Making grants, under the Housing and Urban Development Act of 1965,[173] for the construction of water facilities. Grants may amount to 50 percent of the cost generally, and under certain circumstances, up to 90 percent for communities of less than 10,000.
(3) Under the Housing Amendments of 1955,[174] HUD may make loans to communities for the planning and construction of public works, including M&I water supply facilities.
(4) HUD also has programs of technical assistance, grants and loans for urban renewal, new communities, and demonstrations, including the water supply aspects thereof.

Federal Assistance for Rural Water Supplies

The Farmers Home Administration (FHA) of the Department of Agriculture assists communities in rural areas to provide themselves with central water supplies under the provisions of the Consolidated Farmers Home Administration Act of 1961,[175] as amended. Grants of up to 50 percent of the construction cost of water facilities may be made. Although the FHA can provide loans for water supply facilities only in those instances in which private capital cannot be obtained, so many applications comply with the requirements of the law that the demand has been about double the amount of available funds. However, the Rural Development Act of 1972 has tripled the amount that can be appropriated for grants for water and waste disposal facilities.

Rural communities in areas designated as economically depressed can obtain additional assistance from the Economic Development Administration of the U.S. Department of Commerce.

Regional Plans and Water Supply

The Water Resources Planning Act of 1965 authorized the formulation of comprehensive plans for major river basins or other regions. Municipal and industrial water supply needs are to be taken into account in the preparation of these plans. Provisions are made in the law for the participation in plan formulation of the agencies responsible for carrying out the water programs of the Federal Government and for participation by the States, local governmental entities, and private enterprise. The Act provides for financial assistance to the States to enable them to play a more effective role in plan preparation. It also provides for coordination by the Water Resources Council.

In addition to authorizing the preparation of comprehensive regional plans, the Congress has also authorized the preparation of a regional water supply plan for the Northeastern United States by the Corps of Engineers with the cooperation of Federal, State, and local agencies.[176] The justification for this type of planning effort is, according to the authorizing legislation, "that assuring adequate supplies of water for the great metropolitan centers of the United States has become a problem of such magnitude that the welfare and prosperity of this country require the Federal Government to assist in the solution of water supply problems." This planning effort was coordinated with the North Atlantic Regional Water

---

[172] P.L. 560, August 2, 1954, Section 701, 83d Congress, 68 Stat. 590, 640, as amended, 40 USCA 461.

[173] P.L. 89-117, August 10, 1965, Section 702, 79 Stat. 451, 491, as amended, 42 USCA 3102.

[174] P.L. 345, August 11, 1955, Title II, 84th Congress. 69 Stat. 635, 642, as amended, 42 USCA 1492.

[175] P.L. 87-128, August 8, 1961, Section 306, 75 Stat. 294, 307, as amended, 7 USCA 1926. This Act was renamed the Consolidated Farm and Rural Development Act and amended by the Rural Development Act of 1972, P.L. 92-419, August 30, 1972, 86 Stat. 654, to permit FHA to make loans and grants for water supply facilities serving communities of up to 10,000 people, and to make loans and grants for water supply facilities for areas outside the boundaries of cities having a population of 50,000 or more and their adjacent urbanizing areas.

[176] *Act of October 27, 1965*, P.L. 89-298, Section 101, 79 Stat. 1073, 42 USCA 1962d-4. The Northeastern Water Supply Study (often referred to as NEWS) is separate from, but coordinated with, the North Atlantic Regional Water Resources Study.

Modern newsprint plant draws water from Chickamauga Lake in the Tennessee Valley

Resources Study[177] made under the general direction of a Coordinating Committee of 24 members in accordance with guidelines established by the Water Resources Council.

Provisions for Coordination of Water Supply Construction Grants

Because of the overlapping of responsibility among the Federal programs providing loans and grants, the Office of Management and Budget requested the Federal agencies most concerned to establish a coordinating committee. This committee is made up of representatives of the Department of Housing and Urban Development, the Economic Development Administration, the Environmental Protection Agency, and the Farmers Home Administration. Under the procedures established, any one of these agencies receiving an application for a grant refers it to the other agencies represented on the committee and subsequently a determination is made of the agency in the best position to serve the applicant.

The Office of Management and Budget has also initiated an Integrated Grant Application (IGA) Program which enables public agencies to apply for a number of Federal assistance grants by the submission of a single application. This application is processed by a task force of concerned Federal and State agencies under the auspices of a Federal Regional Council and the grant finally approved is

---

[177] This study also was authorized by P.L. 89-298, Section 208, 79 Stat. 1073, 1085-1086. A report on this study has been completed and is under review by the Water Resources Council.

made by the Federal agency agreed upon. So far, this mechanism has dealt only with applications for planning grants, but the intent is that· ultimately construction grants will be processed in a similar manner.

Federal Assistance in Emergencies

In the event a serious drought reduces available municipal and industrial water supplies to the point that local authorities call for emergency assistance, all agencies—Federal, State, and local—generally join in working out a plan of action and in putting it into effect. Such plans must be tailored to the circumstances existing at the particular time and place. The local entities, of course, are responsible for carrying out the needed emergency conservation measures. The Office of Civil Defense of the Department of Defense stands ready to loan emergency water supply equipment. Where feasible, the agencies responsible for Federal reservoirs modify the operation of those reservoirs. In general, however, there can be no standardized procedure for dealing with drought emergencies.

Federal Research

The Environmental Protection Agency provides an important service through the research work of its Division of Water Supply. The results of this work are intended to provide a sound basis for the establishment of standards for potable water supply and methods of monitoring the quality of supply. Research has also been initiated on the difficult problems that will confront the Nation when, in the not too distant future, it will become necessary to rely upon renovated wastewaters as a major source of industrial supply, and in some instances, of municipal supply.

APPRAISAL OF PROGRAMS

A Commission expected to show how present programs might be improved must find, and call attention to, the deficiencies of these programs. For this reason, the result of this appraisal is, in large part, a list of shortcomings. But, to provide perspective, a background statement is needed.

Background

As with other uses of water, municipal and industrial uses are increasing. The increases are attributable to the same factors which affect many other resources and which are recited over and over in assessments of the future. For example, population growth, increasing urbanization, expanding industrial production, and increasing per capita income.

Excluding the large amounts of water used by the electric power industry for cooling thermal power-plants, municipal and industrial water in metropolitan areas can be looked at, in terms of withdrawals, as about evenly divided between industrial purposes and municipal purposes. Municipal water supply systems provide water for domestic purposes, commercial uses, fire protection, street flushing, lawn and garden irrigation, and in many cities for industrial use. In addition, much water is lost from such systems by leakage. Most industrial water is self-supplied and is used by a relatively small number of firms in five major industries—food, paper, chemicals, petroleum, and metals. Most water for rural domestic use is also self-supplied.

Estimates furnished by the American Water Works Association indicate that there are about 30,000 water utilities in the United States, of which about 5,900 are investor-owned. The latter serve about 30,000,000 people. The total number of persons receiving water through municipal systems, including investor-owned systems, has been estimated to be 175,000,000. More precise figures will result from an inventory now being made by the Environmental Protection Agency.

City Supplies: Meeting demands for municipal and industrial water is essentially an urban problem, with an estimated 70 to 80 percent of municipal and industrial withdrawals occurring within metropolitan environs. The problems of meeting M&I water demand cannot be isolated from the major problems encountered in effectively providing other services to meet the Nation's growing urban needs. All of the economic, social, institutional, technical, and environmental problems of urban growth require attention.

The Nation has the basic water resources to meet the expected doubling of municipal and the quadrupling of industrial (self-supplied) withdrawals by the year 2020.[178] What it may not always have is the willingness or in some cases the ability to make the institutional arrangements needed to manage the resource in order that these demands are met effectively.

Some water shortages are now apparent and others are likely to develop in certain regions and local areas.

[178] Derived from projections made by the Water Resources Council and published in The Nation's Water Resources (1968).

165

M&I water supply shortages stem from (1) storage and distribution systems that have insufficient capacities to meet peak demands, (2) deterioration in the quality of the source of supply, (3) lag in developing and applying water and wastewater treatment and water supply augmentation technologies, and (4) lag in planning, constructing, and operating major water supply projects. Some shortages result from wasteful use of the available supply, especially in cities that do not meter deliveries.

Some cities have access to reserves of high-quality surface or ground water adequate to meet their needs for the foreseeable future. Other cities, to avoid shortages, must either expand their water supply systems or institute measures (such as full cost pricing) to reduce per capita demand, reduce water wastage, or deliberately control their growth. The most difficult municipal water supply problem in the future will be that of maintaining the quality of water supply in the face of increasing use and reuse of water for many purposes.

Protection of public health was the original justification for intervention by the Federal Government in water quality problems. Substantial progress was made early in this century in developing water treatment methods which were highly successful in eradicating disease and sickness caused by contaminated water supplies.

In 1969, almost a thousand representative public water supply systems were surveyed by the Bureau of Water Hygiene[179] in the U.S. Environmental Health Service. Included in the survey were eight large urban areas across the country and one complete State (Vermont). Of the approximately 17-1/2 million people in this sampling, about 15-1/2 million were drinking water that was safe and of good quality. Most of those people lived in cities having a population of 100,000 or more. The remaining 2 million people, residing in both large and small communities, were drinking water of inferior quality; that is, water that, although safe, had a bad taste, odor, appearance, or other quality characteristic that made it less desirable for household use and human consumption than the water supplied the other 89 percent of those included in the sample.[180]

These results are considered by many to be reasonably representative of the current quality status of the M&I water supplies of the United States. They do not suggest that there is a need for asserting Federal control over the quality of drinking water; however, the Environmental Protection Agency reports that State and local water quality control programs are not providing adequate regulation of quality at local water supply systems because of deficiencies in planning, training, and enforcement activities.[181]

Rural Supplies: A survey made by the Farmers Home Administration in 1970 indicated that there are more than 17,000 rural communities that have no central water system, and that of those communities that already have such systems, there are more than 14,000 having facilities needing improvement or enlargement. The estimated cost of all needed work amounted to about $4.2 billion.[182] However, this amount includes the estimated cost of providing sewers as well as water supply facilities.

Some Major Shortcomings

The principal results of the Commission's appraisal of present Federal programs may be summarized as follows:

There is need for a comprehensive restatement of policy to govern the role of the Federal agencies in meeting the Nation's needs for municipal and industrial water supplies. The Water Supply Act of 1958,[183] states that it is "the policy of Congress to recognize the primary responsibility of the States and local interests in developing water supplies for domestic, municipal, industrial, and other purposes." Similar language is found in other laws. Yet, in the legislation authorizing the programs previously discussed, the Congress has created an almost bewildering array of Federal subsidies for the purpose of shifting much of the responsibility for, and the costs of, M&I water supplies to the Federal Government. In addition, the Commission finds that an

---

[179] Now a part of the Water Supply Division of the U.S. Environmental Protection Agency.

[180] WATER QUALITY OFFICE, Water Hygiene Division, Environmental Protection Agency (April 1971). Community Water Supply Study: Significance of National Findings. Reprint, previously printed as Bureau of Water Hygiene, USPHS, report dated July 1970. Environmental Protection Agency, Washington, D.C.

[181] BUREAU OF NATIONAL AFFAIRS (March 24, 1972). Federal standards not broad enough to cover community supply problems. Environment Reporter, Current Developments 2(47):1428-1429.

[182] U.S. FARMERS HOME ADMINISTRATION, Department of Agriculture (July 30, 1970). Summary of Water and Sewer Needs Inventory. Unpublished mimeo, Farmers Home Administration, Washington, D.C.

[183] P.L. 85-500, July 3, 1958, Title III, 72 Stat. 279, 319, as amended, 43 USCA 390b.

increasing number of State and local officials believe that certain Federal agencies fully intend that the Federal Government shall become as dominant in the water supply field as it has become in the field of pollution control, and they point out that it was but 25 years ago that in enacting the first of the major Federal Water Pollution Control Acts[184] the Congress said "it is hereby declared to be the policy of Congress to recognize, preserve, and protect the primary responsibilities and rights of the States in controlling water pollution." These State and local officials fear that eventually the previously quoted language of the Water Supply Act of 1958 will have no more force and effect in limiting Federal intervention in M&I water supply than did the language of the Water Pollution Control Act of 1948 in limiting the Federal intervention in pollution control. Moreover, these non-Federal officials, as well as many of the experts that have appeared before this Commission, are of the opinion that the States, local entities, and private enterprise are competent to meet the water supply needs of the cities with relatively little Federal intervention. For example, the American Water Works Association has issued a formal policy statement[185] in which appears the following:

> The responsibility for water resources projects, of which public and industrial water supplies are a primary consideration, should rest with that echelon of government or of private interests closest to those people benefited. This broad management responsibility includes sponsoring, planning, development, financing, ownership, operation, and maintenance. The cost of such projects should be borne proportionately by those who are benefited.

The National Water Commission finds itself in full agreement with the position taken by the American Water Works Association. It has seen no evidence that would lead it to believe that the design and construction of local water supply systems would be better performed by Federal construction agencies. Local government has demonstrated the capability to design and construct the most sophisticated systems when adequate financing is available. Uniform design is neither practical nor desirable. Decentralized

responsibility for design and construction makes for lower administrative costs, insures adaptation of plans to local conditions, capabilities, and desires, encourages cost-effectiveness competition between areas, and imparts a sense of local pride and responsibility. In addition, local assumption of responsibility for water supply can strengthen the power of a local government over land-use decisions. Finally, when a community must meet its own needs for water supply, it is much more likely to require that the water users pay the full cost of providing the service. The advantages of managing water systems as self-sustaining, utility-type enterprises are detailed in Section C of Chapter 7 of this report.

There is also a need for bringing existing laws into consonance with such a restated expression of Federal policy. After a clear and unequivocal policy is established by law, all existing legislation authorizing Federal activities having to do with M&I water supply should be brought into line with that policy. The legislative changes necessary to accomplish this can best be determined by the agencies of the executive branch and this Commission would suggest that after the Congress establishes such a policy it request the President to have prepared, for its use, a report indicating the extent to which existing legislation would have to be amended to bring it into consonance with that policy.

There is a need for better coordination between plans prepared to guide the development of metropolitan regions and cities and the comprehensive water plans being developed for river basins and regions. The Federal water agencies and the States are rapidly proceeding with the development of comprehensive plans for major river basins, or other regions, under the authorities of the Water Resources Planning Act of 1965,[186] and a number of other authorities. At the same time, most large cities have found it desirable to prepare broad plans to guide their future development. In some instances, organizations that have been established for large metropolitan regions containing a number of municipalities have formulated or are formulating comprehensive urban plans for these regions.[187] The National Water Commission is of the opinion that both types of planning should continue. But it is also of the opinion that the coordination between the end products of the two should be improved. In particular, the

---

[184] *Water Pollution Control Act*, P.L. 845, June 30, 1948, 80th Congress, 62 Stat. 1155.

[185] AMERICAN WATER WORKS ASSOCIATION (November 1971). Statements of policy on public water supply matters. Journal American Water Works Association 63(11):43-55. Part II.

[186] P.L. 89-80, July 22, 1965, 79 Stat. 244, as amended, 42 USCA 1962 *et seq.*

[187] The problem of planning for metropolitan areas is dealt with in some detail in Chapter 12 of this report.

Commission finds that municipal and industrial water supply needs have not been adequately considered in comprehensive framework studies conducted under the provisions of the Water Resources Planning Act of 1965.

An examination of several framework plans by HUD resulted in the finding that the relation of water use to the planned use of urban land resources had been largely ignored. A preliminary critique of the M&I water supply appendix of the Columbia-North Pacific Region Comprehensive Framework Study, prepared for HUD, revealed several deficiencies, including inadequate study of, and attention to, M&I water supply needs.[188] In another HUD evaluation of a framework study—that for the Pacific Southwest Region—other planning deficiencies were cited, one being that the study did not cover metropolitan areas at all. Instead, the areal scope of the study appeared to run up only to the fringes of metropolitan areas.[189] It appears that Type I Framework studies of water and related land use tend to focus on rural areas where the old line water and agricultural agencies have traditionally operated. Apparently, insufficient effort has been made to coordinate with, or lend support to, metropolitan and areawide planning agencies.

While these problems may contribute to serious deficiencies because municipal and industrial water supply is not adequately considered in Federal, State, and local planning activities, they do not require changes in legislation or in funding levels. For the most part, Federal planning assistance programs provide ample opportunity for conducting adequate and properly coordinated water supply planning.

There is a need for coordinating the planning of new small water supply systems in suburban areas with the central system for the metropolitan area. As a metropolitan area expands, many small systems are installed in the fringe area which are destined eventually to become components of the major system serving the previously developed areas.

Particularly around many of the smaller central cities has there been a reluctance to annex the fringe communities[190] and this has resulted in an increase in the number of small communities seeking assistance from the Farmers Home Administration to install small systems to meet their own needs. This is one of the reasons for including in Chapter 12 of this report a recommendation designed to improve institutional arrangements for managing metropolitan area water services.

There is also a need for providing in comprehensive river basin plans for better coordination of withdrawals of water by self-supplying industries. Much of the water used by industry never passes through a public water supply system, but is withdrawn from and returned to the streams by the individual industries. Practically all cooling water for thermal powerplants is self-supplied in this sense. It has been estimated that within metropolitan areas about half of the water used by industries is self-supplied. The magnitudes of such withdrawals are often so great that provisions should be made in both comprehensive river basin plans and metropolitan regional plans to insure that the effects of the withdrawals are taken into account and that an appropriate amount of water is available to meet the demands of the self-supplied industries. In some instances, such planning will result in the finding that certain industries should be located elsewhere. The recommendations of Chapter 11 of this report can improve plans for metropolitan regions in this respect and the recommendations of Chapter 10 can do the same for comprehensive river basin plans. States, and subdivisions of States, can be powerful factors in the solution of such problems by the exercise of their latent administrative powers. In the West, where careful management of the relatively small supply is essential, it has long been accepted practice to control industrial withdrawals through administrators, water boards, or other management entities. In the East, there is an increasing use of permit systems by the States.

In some urban areas a considerable proportion of the water withdrawn is wasted and conservation programs should be set in motion. In planning to meet future demands for municipal and industrial water, full consideration should be given to the possibilities for reducing water withdrawals by

[188] NORTHAM, Ray M (October 12, 1971). Summary of Major Points Identified in a Review of the Columbia - North Pacific Region Comprehensive Framework Study, prepared for the Department of Housing and Urban Development, Contract No. H-1551. HUD Region X, Seattle, Wash. p. 14.

[189] WARNE, William E (October 1971). Comparative Review, Analysis, and Evaluation of the Pacific Southwest's Water Resources Study, Part I, prepared for the Department of Housing and Urban Development, Contract No. H-1595. HUD Region IX, San Francisco, Calif. Chapter VII.

[190] The reverse situation is also found. Fringe communities will resist annexation unless the advantages, as they see them, outweigh the disadvantages.

metering, by the imposition of pricing systems that encourage more efficient use of water, by changes in building codes, by reducing leakage, and by other measures, as an alternative to increasing the supply, or as a means for minimizing the necessary increase. The possibilities for making better use of existing supplies are discussed in Chapter 7 of this report.

There is a need for better coordination of the Federal grant and loan programs. As previously mentioned, an Integrated Grant Application Program has been established, but to date this has dealt only with applications for planning grants. It is the opinion of the Commission that, if grants for construction are to be continued, early action should be taken to broaden this program so that such grants may be brought under some degree of coordination; or, as an alternative, that some other means be developed to provide better coordination and administration of the many programs through which Federal financial assistance may flow to communities desiring to provide or improve water supply systems.

The research now under way does not adequately meet modern needs. Leaders in the water supply industry have assured this Commission that there is a real need for the improvement of the Federal research program previously described. They point out that the protection of public health is of overriding importance and that for this reason precedence should be given to two fields of research. One is to provide the fundamental data needed to establish safe standards for water for human consumption, and to develop practicable methods of monitoring the quality of such water. Of comparable importance is the research needed in the development of methods for treating wastewaters, including municipal sewage, to make it suitable for industrial use, and, when the need arises, for human consumption.[191] These water supply experts also point out that a great deal more should be learned about the effectiveness of present treatment methods in rendering safe for human consumption wastewaters containing viruses and pathogenic bacteria. They also report that there is an urgent need for studies of the build-up of chemicals and other agents under repeated recycling of wastewater. Much has been said that leaves the general public with the impression that the advanced waste treatment practices presently in use can be depended upon to produce water safe for consumption by man. Experts in whom this Commission has confidence express the view that the research accomplished to

date does not provide an adequate basis for such a conclusion.

CONCLUSIONS

The foregoing appraisal of the Federal programs presents a list of deficiencies that may be taken as the conclusions of this Commission as to reforms needed. These need not be repeated here. However, the studies it has made to evaluate future needs for municipal and industrial water, and its investigations of metropolitan problems on a broad front, have led the Commission to a few general conclusions which influenced the formulation of the recommendations which follow. These general conclusions are briefly stated in the following paragraphs.

It seems certain that population growth, increasing per capita use, migration of people to urban areas, and expanding economic activity will strain many existing municipal and industrial water supply systems in the years to come. Effective planning followed by effective implementation measures will be required if serious shortages of water service for the Nation's cities are to be avoided. In the more water-scarce and rapidly growing areas, competition for water supplies will mount and improved water husbandry will become increasingly necessary.

Studies made for and by the Commission have led it to conclude that while Federal assistance to rural communities in the form of water facilities grants and loans is beneficial to these rural communities, their influence upon population distribution is limited.[192] Such assistance alone will not materially affect or reverse the flow of population from rural to urban areas, a trend which is beyond the ability of water facilities significantly to influence.

A further conclusion of the Commission is that problems of drinking water quality and safety of service have been demonstrated on a national basis, that this justifies the promulgation of Federal drinking water standards, and that the Federal standards should be implemented primarily by the States. A related conclusion is that present research and development programs should be strengthened.

Finally, the Commission reached the conclusion that there is a considerable element of inequity in the policies that presently govern the programs through which grants and low-cost loans are made available to

---

[191] The subject of reuse is treated in some detail in Chapter 7 of this report.

[192] See in particular: RIVKIN/CARSON, INC (1971). Population Growth in Communities in Relation to Water Resources Policy, prepared for the National Water Commission. National Technical Information Service, Springfield, Va., Accession No. PB 205 248.

communities. Under these programs, communities that have been conscientious in planning and diligent in building water supply facilities will be unable to demonstrate an urgent need for assistance and for this reason will be denied grant funds. Other less conscientious communities that have been derelict and as a result find themselves with inadequate supplies will be able to demonstrate urgent need and, accordingly, will be awarded grants. Because grant funds derive from the general fund of the Treasury, the taxpayers at large are obliged to subsidize, and thus reward, communities which in the past have not made adequate expenditures for water supply facilities. On the other hand, those communities (and their taxpayer-residents) that have taken seriously their obligations to provide themselves with adequate water supply facilities, and who have made the necessary sacrifices to do so, are penalized; they pay the taxes but do not share in the benefits. This is certainly not calculated to instill in the Nation's communities a resolve to provide for themselves those services which are appropriately a local community's responsibility and which, in the absence of extenuating circumstances, should not be subsidized.

The Commission believes that subsidies are only justified if they serve some compelling social purpose; where society benefits but where conventional markets and pricing mechanisms do not adequately reflect those benefits, the Commission believes that a general rule to follow is this: direct beneficiaries of water projects who can be identified and reached should ordinarily be obliged to pay all project costs which are allocated to the purpose from which they benefit.[193]

RECOMMENDATIONS

5-22. A national policy should be developed and enacted into law to clearly delineate the role to be played by the Federal Government in the provision of water for municipal and industrial use:

a. Primary responsibility for the provision of municipal and industrial water supplies should remain with non-Federal public entities and private enterprise.

b. Agencies of the executive branch should encourage cities and other non-Federal public entities to operate their water systems on a utility basis, the revenues of which should be sufficient to cover all costs.

c. Except for water used on interstate carriers, the responsibility for enforcing any drinking water standards established by the Federal Government should be discharged by the States and their political subdivisions.

5-23. All existing legislative Acts authorizing any Federal agency to assist non-Federal entities to plan or construct projects for supplying municipal and industrial water should be amended to eliminate any inconsistencies with the national policy that would result from the previous recommendation.

5-24. The agencies responsible for preparation of comprehensive river basin or other regional water plans, and the agencies responsible for urban planning, should jointly develop more effective means of cooperation and coordination, as recommended hereinafter in Chapters 10 and 11.

5-25. City governments and metropolitan regional entities should develop and put into effect water conservation plans designed to reduce waste and make more efficient use of their present municipal and industrial supplies.

5-26. Present means for the coordination of grant and loan programs should be made more effective, and as an initial step in this direction, the Integrated Grant Application Program should be broadened to encompass grants and loans for construction.

5-27. Research essential for the development of better drinking water standards, and of improved means for testing water supplies for compliance with those standards, should be accelerated, along with research for the purpose of improving methods of renovating wastewaters for direct human consumption as detailed hereinafter in Section H of Chapter 7.

---

[193] See Chapter 15 of this report for a discussion of cost-sharing.

Power Production — the Waste Heat Problem

Through the 1940's, the power-related water problem attracting most attention in the United States derived from the decision of the Federal Government to generate power at the dams it had constructed primarily for purposes other than power production. This precipitated some of the most violent debates in the history of Federal water policy development. The Commission considered the historic power issues, including private versus public development of sites, power marketing, the preference clause, headwater benefits, power partnership, and relicensing or takeover of Federal Power Commission licensed projects at the expiration of the license period.[194] Although these issues, in the minds of some, are not resolved, the Commission does not believe they rank in critical importance with the issues involved in the disposal of waste heat from thermal electric power production, which looms as one of the most crucial problems of the future water use.

Accordingly, this section addresses those problems which arise because thermal electric powerplants do not convert all of the heat generated from fuel into electricity. The "waste heat" is released through different kinds of cooling systems, most of which use significant amounts of water; some requiring diversions of very large quantities, and others consuming significant amounts. In the most-used, once-through cooling system, the heated water is discharged into the Nation's rivers, lakes, and coastal waters. In other water cooling systems, the heat is discharged into the atmosphere. All of the systems affect the natural environment and may affect other water uses. Therefore, the magnitude of the demand for cooling water and the effects of alternative ways of releasing the heat are important issues of national water policy.

DEMAND FOR ELECTRIC GENERATING FACILITIES

In the United States, with a growing population and, more significantly, an even greater growth in per capita energy consumption,[195] electrical energy demands will continue to grow, even if not at the present rate of doubling every 10 years. It has been pointed out that "... even assuming near zero population growth, a drop to one half the present rate of growth in individual wealth, and a corresponding 50 percent reduction in the current rate of increase in power use in the next decade, U.S. consumption of electricity will *still* triple by 1990."[196]

Perhaps the most broadly-based forecast of future electrical energy requirements was made by the U.S. Federal Power Commission and is shown in Table 5-11. It is regarded by the Commission as representative of the most probable conditions likely to be realized for the next 20 years and is used to indicate future powerplant siting requirements.

THE PROBLEM OF WASTE HEAT DISPOSAL

The projections of Table 5-11 indicate that increasing power demands will be met in large part by the construction of thermal plants. At the same time, the pattern of future site development apparently will tend toward larger thermal powerplants than has been the case in the past. The FPC has estimated that approximately 395 new sites will be needed by 1990 for large plants (160 nuclear and 140 fossil fuel).[197] Many of these plants will exceed 1,000 megawatts in size. Although generally more efficient and more economical than smaller plants, larger-sized plants heighten the potential waste heat problem because they are larger point-sources of heat, raising the possibility that some local waters will not be able to support the increased consumptive losses or assimilate the heat without auxiliary cooling methods.

[194]PRICE, Truman P (February 1971). Hydroelectric Power Policy, prepared for the National Water Commission. National Technical Information Service, Springfield, Va., Accession No. PB 204 052.

[195]LANDSBERG HH (June 1970). A disposable feast. Resources Newsletter, Resources for the Future, Inc. [Washington, D.C.] 34:1.

[196]LEES, Lester et al. (September 1, 1971). People, Power, Pollution, Environmental and Public Interest Aspects of Electric Power Plant Siting, EQL Report No. 1. California Institute of Technology, Environmental Quality Laboratory, Pasadena. p. 5.

[197]U.S. FEDERAL POWER COMMISSION (1972). The 1970 National Power Survey. U.S. Government Printing Office, Washington, D.C. p. I-18-7.

Table 5-11. – Projected growth of utility electric generating capacity

(thousands of megawatts)

Type of Plant	1970 (actual)		1980		1990	
	Capacity	% of Total Generation	Capacity	% of Total Generation	Capacity	% of Total Generation
Hydroelectric-conventional	51.6	16.4	68	9.4	82	5.4
Hydroelectric-pumped storage	3.6	0.3	27	0.8	70	1
Fossil steam	259.1	80.5	390	60.9	558	43.5
Gas-turbine and diesel	19.2	1.4	40	0.9	75	0.8
Nuclear	6.5	1.4	140	28	475	49.3
TOTALS	340	100	665	100	1,260	100

Notes: (1) The projections are premised on an average gross reserve margin of 20%.
(2) Since different types of plants are operated at different capacity factors, this capacity breakdown is not directly representative of share of kilowatt-hour production. For example, since nuclear plants are customarily used in baseload service and therefore operate at comparatively high capacity factors, nuclear power's contribution to total electricity production would be higher than its capacity share.

Source: U.S. FEDERAL POWER COMMISSION (1972). The 1970 National Power Survey. U.S. Government Printing Office, Washington, D.C. pp. I-18-29.

COOLING WATER REQUIREMENTS

The peak electrical energy demand in many regions has shifted from winter to summer largely because of the increase in air conditioning loads. Summer is generally the period of lower river flows, higher water temperatures, and decreased waste assimilative capacity, a combination of factors which tends to exacerbate the waste heat problem.

The type of generating facility, the plant heat rate (i.e., efficiency), the inlet water temperature, the design temperature rise across the condenser, and the type of cooling method used are the important factors involved in determining the total quantity of heat that will be released and the quantity of cooling water needed.

Table 5-12 presents a comparison of the heat characteristics and cooling water requirements of typical thermal powerplants. It shows that 58 to 67 percent of the heat energy required for thermal generation of electricity is nonproductive (i.e., it is rejected to the biosphere as waste heat). In fossil fuel plants, a small portion of this nonproductive heat is discharged directly to the air through the boiler and stack but most of it is released to water through the condenser cooling system. In a nuclear plant, however, there are minimal stack and in-plant losses, leaving nearly all the waste heat to be discharged through the condenser cooling system.

The development of more light water reactor capacity will increase waste heat discharges and cooling water requirements. The heat discharges indicated in Table 5-12 are representative of the steam electric powerplants which will be constructed between now and the end of the century. Although breeder reactors, which are not expected to be in commercial operation before the late 1980's at the earliest, will increase efficiency of nuclear plants, the increase will still not be significantly beyond the 40 percent efficiency that represents the upper end of the current range.

The central problem is how to release heat without causing undesirable environmental impacts. In some situations, the heat may be put to beneficial use, as discussed later in this section. However, typically, the problem is one of dissipating the heat added to the water used for condenser cooling, either by discharging it directly to a water body or to the atmosphere through an auxiliary cooling system.

A number of cooling methods are available, including once-through or run-of-river systems, cooling ponds or canals, and cooling towers. Once-through cooling systems take water from a source such as a river, ocean, or lake, pass it across the condenser, and discharge it at a higher temperature to the same body of water from which it came. Cooling ponds are impoundments constructed specifically to hold and recycle cooling water and allow it to dissipate heat to the air. The most common types of cooling towers are those in which cooling water is cycled through the tower where it is cooled through evaporation. Another type of cooling tower, not in common use, is the dry or closed-cycle tower where no evaporation takes place. Here, cooling water is kept in a closed system and heat is dissipated to the air as in an automobile radiator.

A once-through cooling system imposes tremendous diversion demands. For example, a 1,000 megawatt light water reactor (33 percent efficient) requires 1,900 c.f.s. or 1,375,600 acre-feet per year for a 15° F. water temperature rise across the condenser.[198] In 1970, steam electric utilities accounted for 45.9 percent of the water diverted in the United States, and that percentage may increase sharply in the future.[199]

Cooling towers and cooling ponds recycle water and therefore divert only a small fraction of the water withdrawn in comparable once-through cooling systems, but an evaporative cooling process consumes considerably more water, a significant consideration in cooling system design, especially in water-short areas. Consumptive losses are on the order of 1 percent of condenser flows for once-through cooling, 1-1/2 percent for cooling ponds, and approximately 2 percent for evaporative cooling towers and spray ponds. For example, for a 1,000 megawatt light water reactor, consumptive losses for each of the three systems would approximate 18, 27, and 36 cubic feet per second (13,000, 20,000, and 26,000 acre-feet per year), respectively.

During its meetings in Southern California and the Delaware River Basin, the Commission was told that there would be insufficient cooling capacity available in fresh water streams in those areas to provide water cooling for powerplants required to meet all projected loads in the future.

Consumptive losses for the dry cooling tower, the costliest of cooling methods, are negligible.

---

[198] A modern 1,000 megawatt fossil fuel plant with a once-through system would require approximately 1,150 c.f.s. (832,600 acre-feet per year) at full capacity.

[199] See Chapter 1 of this report.

TABLE 5-12.— Heat characteristics of typical steam electric plants[1]

(heat values in B.t.u. per kw.-hr.)

Plant Type	Thermal Efficiency (Percent)	Required Input per kw-hr (Heat rate)	Total Waste Heat (Required input minus kw-hr heat equivalent)[2]	=	Lost to Boiler Stack[3] (etc.)	+	Heat Discharged to the Condenser	Cooling Water Requirement (Cubic feet per second per megawatt, of capacity)[4]
Fossil fuel	33	10,500	7,100	=	1,600	+	5,500	1.6
Fossil fuel (recent)	40	8,600	5,200	=	1,300	+	3,900	1.15
Light water reactor	33	10,500	7,100	=	500	+	6,600	1.9
Breeder reactor	42	8,200	4,800	=	300	+	4,500	1.35

[1] Not using cooling towers.
[2] The heat equivalent of one kilowatt-hour of electricity (kw.-hr.) is 3,413 British thermal units (B.t.u.).
[3] Approximately 10 to 15 percent of required input for fossil fuel.
Approximately 3 to 5 percent of required input for nuclear.
[4] Based on an inlet temperature in the 70° s F. and a temperature rise across the condenser of 15° F.

Source: KRENKEL, Peter A et al. (May 1972). The Water Use and Management Aspects of Steam Electric Power Generation, prepared for the National Water Commission by the Commission's Consulting Panel on Waste Heat. National Technical Information Service, Springfield, Va., Accession No. PB 210 355.

EFFECTS OF COOLING SYSTEMS

The discharge of heat to a body of water can cause a number of effects—beneficial, detrimental, or insignificant—depending to a great extent on the desired uses of the receiving waters. In navigable waters, the addition of heat in the winter could lengthen the shipping season by elimination of lock jamming, and by shortening the period of ice cover in shipping lanes. Discharge of heat in colder waters could also be beneficial in promoting the growth of fish.

The greatest potential impact of heat discharge to water, however, is on aquatic life. The net effect of heat is to decrease the dissolved oxygen content of the receiving water. Discharges of large quantities of heat relative to the assimilative capacity of the receiving waters could have serious effects on the associated ecosystems. Temperature changes have a direct effect on metabolism, reproductive cycles, behavior, digestion, respiration rates, and other factors. Mortality can occur when temperature tolerances are exceeded and from too rapid changes in temperature. Since fish are at the apex of the aquatic food pyramid, any drastic change in any part of the pyramid will be reflected in changed fish population or species diversity or both.

It should be noted that not all water temperature changes are manmade. Indeed, in many areas water temperatures fluctuate naturally and more rapidly over wider temperature ranges than man-induced temperature changes, depending on variations in season, in streamflow, and other factors.

Chlorine is sometimes added to prevent fouling of the condenser in once-through cooling systems. In the operation of cooling towers, a number of chemicals are used to prevent or reduce wood deterioration, biological growths, corrosion, scaling, and general fouling. These chemicals, as well as others occurring naturally in water, tend to become concentrated by evaporation and are released to water bodies in what is termed blowdown. Metal loss from corrosion, and the mechanical and hydraulic effects of intake and discharge facilities can also have detrimental environmental effects. Ordinarily, however, these adverse effects can be reduced or eliminated by proper engineering design and site selection.

Cooling tower discharges have caused vapor plumes, fog, precipitation, and icing, primarily because of inadequate consideration of climatological and meteorological factors in plant location and cooling tower design. Severe problems are likely if powerplants are located in areas of high smog and air pollution potential, especially in small valleys where there is a propensity for stagnation of overhead air masses. However, adequate investigation and proper siting should minimize these adverse impacts.

Another possible adverse effect, especially in densely populated areas, is the release of large quantities of heat to the atmosphere.[200] Man affects the climatic conditions of the earth by the release of heat and materials into the air. Especially in high heat release areas, these releases can change the opacity of the atmosphere.[201] Measurable climatic modifications include, among other things, increases in mean air temperature, in precipitation, and in cloud cover. Resources development policy needs to consider fully the long-range implications of these modifications.

Where cooling ponds are used, they must be quite large, up to 10 to 20 square miles in area. They are often enclosed by dikes, and in many cases require energy for pumping water into the cooling pond.

It is important to recognize that actions taken to deny the use of water as an interim medium of thermal release will increase the total rejection of thermal energy, because auxiliary cooling methods such as cooling towers reduce overall plant efficiency and therefore require higher heat inputs for equivalent electrical energy output.

DISCUSSION OF PROBLEMS

Diffusion of Waste Heat

Waste heat is different from other residuals which can be collected, concentrated, and disposed of under controlled conditions, yet it must be dispersed in such a way as to minimize adverse effects on the environment. The capacity of water to absorb and dissipate heat is a valuable resource which, under many conditions, can be safely used. Using water bodies to accept waste heat provides two major benefits: (1) water as a dilution, dispersion, and dissipation medium is four and one-half times more efficient than air on a weight basis and 42 times more efficient on a volume basis and (2) the improved efficiency of the cooling process reduces the alloca-

[200] JASKE RT et al. (November 1970). Heat rejection requirements of the U.S. Chemical Engineering Progress 66(11):17-22.

[201] LANDSBERG HE (December 1970). Man-made climatic changes. Science 170(3964):1265-1274.

Cooling tower on Trojan Nuclear Plant prevents discharge of heat into the Columbia River

tion of resources and the production of energy otherwise required for this function.

Towers and ponds also use water to convey heat away from the condensers, but discharge the waste heat directly to the atmosphere. While these systems prevent heat from being injected into water bodies, they are costly, require additional electric energy to operate (which in turn requires additional generating capacity), and require additional land.

However, use of water bodies also involves costs which place a limit on their use. Sound resource management policy requires a balancing of values, an assessment of the benefits and costs of the cooling alternatives in order to decide which is the most appropriate for the particular situation. The decision as to which cooling method to employ in any given situation should be made on the basis of system capital and operation and maintenance costs, the availability of water for diversion and consumption, the natural resources required, impacts on other uses and total environmental effects. Rigid environmental standards which do not permit the use of water to absorb waste heat, even where the environmental costs of once-through cooling are minimal, would deny the opportunity to make a rational evaluation.[202] Precluding consideration of one alternative and its associated set of costs or benefits is not the kind of rational decisionmaking which must

---

[202] WRIGHT, James H (August 1971). Testimony before the Public Hearing to Consider Revising Thermal Standards for Lake Michigan to Conform with the Recommendations of the Lake Michigan Enforcement Conference. Department of Natural Resources, State of Wisconsin.

be employed if the Nation's total resource base is to be most effectively managed and used.

Powerplant Siting and Water and Related Land Resources Planning[203]

Since thermal powerplant siting can have significant impacts on the Nation's water and related land resources, the Commission believes that river basin commissions and other planners should give greater attention in water resources planning to potential sites and to the effects which powerplant siting and operation may have upon other water and land uses within the basin.[204] This would provide a much needed tie between water resources and land-use planning. The Water Resources Council should assist field planning entities by providing additional policy and procedural guidance. It would be appropriate for the Council to establish a work group of agency and industry representatives to address this issue.

A number of new possibilities for future thermal powerplant siting exist. Proposals for floating power-plants, powerplants constructed on manmade islands on the continental shelf, and underwater plants resting on the ocean floor are under consideration. Potential advantages of ocean siting include dispersion of heated discharges by ocean currents and their diffusion into the large volumes of water available, no demand on fresh water sources, and perhaps improved conditions for fish as the upwelling of heated water pushes nutrient-laden lower layers to the surface. Siting alternatives of this type deserve special attention for the intermediate and long term.

Combinations of concepts offer possibilities deserving exploration. For example, waste treatment plant effluent might be used as a partial water source with ultimate cooling water disposal through deep ocean outfalls or through pump-back as in pumped-storage developments. The Commission believes innovative combinations should be given early study and evaluation. Many of the siting alternatives are presently in the category of possibilities; it is important that their probabilities of success be assessed. A coordinated research and development effort is necessary to provide these assessments and

should include technical, economic, environmental, and social considerations.

Potential and Developing Technologies

New technological developments, especially in power generation, may ameliorate the waste heat problem in the long term. Unfortunately, these can be expected to have little effect on plant systems put into operation through the year 1990 because of the time lags between development on a proven research basis and commercial availability and between commerical availability and widespread use. The first time lag relates to proving technical and economic feasibility; the second involves developmental, regulatory, licensing, and construction activities and their associated lead times.

Generation: Increasing generation efficiency is an important key to reducing or eliminating waste heat problems. The Commission's Consulting Panel on Waste Heat estimated the most probable share of the Nation's total generating capacity in the year 2000 for each method of generation, the time when each new generation technology will first come into practical use under present and under accelerated research and development, and the expected thermal efficiency of each technology. These estimates appear in Table 5-13 and indicate that nearly two-thirds of the Nation's generating capacity in the year 2000 will be comprised of systems presently in widespread use.

The nuclear breeder is expected to be the next generation technology to be developed for wide-spread use. Under present planning assumptions, the thermal energy of a breeder reactor is to be converted to electrical energy using conventional (steam turbine) Rankine cycle technology. However, efficiencies using this technology are limited because the limitations of metals involved preclude obtaining steam temperatures much in excess of 1050° F., the equivalent of an available fossil fuel steam plant. Since the primary thrust of breeder development has been to provide a large bulk heat source, the supporting research into power technology using advanced cycles of higher efficiency has not been accorded the degree of attention which the Commission believes is warranted. Greater emphasis should be placed on achieving the goal of higher efficiency by developing the supporting technology for advanced cycles and, if possible, an early replacement of the Rankine cycle. The breeder reactor, however, will produce large amounts of radioactive

---

[203] See Chapter 6 of this report for a discussion of recommended improvements in the procedures which govern powerplant siting.

[204] The New England River Basins Commission has prepared a plan for a siting program that appears to constitute a first step in this direction.

TABLE 5-13.—Electrical Power Generating Technologies

Method of Generation	Fuel Used	Average Thermal Efficiency of Plants Built in 1990-2000 Period[1]	Heat Discharge to Condenser Cooling Water BTU/KWH	Date First Major Unit Could be in Operation Present R&D Funding	Accelerated R&D Funding	Expected % of Total Capacity Year 2000
PRESENT SYSTEMS						
Hydroelectric (Conventional & pumped storage)	Water	--	-0-	SOA		5
Fossil Fuel[2]	Coal, Oil, Gas	∼ 42%	3,900	SOA		10-20
Shale Oil, Coal Gasification & Coal Liquification (new fossil fuel)	Oil & Gas	42%	3,900	1995	1985	10-15
Internal Comb. Eng.	Oil	25-35%	-0-	SOA		<1
Gas Turbine	Gas, Oil	20-30%	-0-	SOA		<1
Topping G.T. w/Waste Heat Boiler	Gas, Oil	40%		SOA		<1
Light Water Reactors	Uranium & Thorium	∼33%	6,600	SOA		30 - 40
DEVELOPING SYSTEMS FOR THE SHORT TERM (1970-2000)						
Gas Cooled Reactors	Uranium & Thorium	∼40%	4,800	SOA		10 - 20
Nuclear Breeders	Uranium & Thorium	38-42%	4,500	1990	1985	10 - 15
Fuel Cells[3]	Partially Oxidized Coal, Oil & Gas	60%	-0-	1985	1980	<5
EGD (Electrogasdynamics)	Nat. or Manu. Gas	40-55%	-0-	Never	1990	<5
MHD	Fossil or Nuclear	55%	-0-	Never	1990	
MHD Topping Cycles	Fossil or Nuclear	60%	1,700	Never	1990	
Geothermal	Geothermal Energy	20-30%		SOA		<1
DEVELOPING SYSTEMS FOR THE LONG TERM (After 2000)						
Thermoelectricity	Any Heat	10-15%		Indefinite		0
Thermionic	Any Heat	10-30%		Indefinite		0
Fusion	Hydrogen or Helium (seawater)	75-95%	Small	Never	2010	0
Solar	Sun's Energy	14-25%		Never	1990	<1

SOA - State of the Art
[1] Where SOA, the efficiency given reflects the Panel's estimate of improvements in state of the art technology.
[2] Conventional fossil fuel, excluding shale oil, coal liquification and gasification
[3] Not Central Station

Source: KRENKEL, Feter A et al. (May 1972). The Water Use and Management Aspects of Steam Electric Power Generation, prepared for the National Water Commission by the Commission's Consulting Panel on Waste Heat. National Technical Information Service, Springfield, Va., Accession No. PB 210 355. p. 25.

material and will greatly multiply safety problems in handling, transport, and disposal of this material.

The fuel cell represents a potential revolutionary change in future power systems. It is a device which converts the chemical energy in gaseous fuels directly to electrical energy, thereby avoiding some of the efficiency limitations imposed on heat engines by the second law of thermodynamics and making it possible to discharge waste heat directly to the atmosphere. The fuel cell is not a large central station generation method. Rather, it lends itself to unique possibilities of distributing generating capacity within urban areas. Units presently contemplated for commercial use in the late 1970's will generate 26,000 kw. The Commission believes the present developmental effort on the various types of fuel cell and supporting gas fuel supply research, though substantial, is inadequate; an accelerated research and development program is warranted and would be in the national interest. Of particular interest is the possibility of producing with nuclear reactors the hydrogen used as fuel in the fuel cells.

Magnetohydrodynamics (MHD) is another promising technology. Instead of a solid conductor rotating in a magnetic field, a jet of high-temperature, high-velocity ionized gas is forced through a magnetic field. By placing electrodes in this hot gas stream, direct current at relatively high voltages can be obtained. MHD can be used as a topping cycle for conventional steam generation systems or by itself; either way, the efficiency is 40-50 percent greater than with present fossil fuel plants and would therefore have a significant effect in reducing heat rejection. A number of developmental problems remain, however, so that MHD probably will not be a large contributor to the Nation's generating capacity during the present century.

Fusion power appears to be the promising technology for more efficient generation in the long term. It may be able to reduce waste heat discharges from the present 60-70 percent to a range of 5-25 percent of the total heat generated. Even with an expanded research and development program, however, fusion is not expected to be a major contributor to central station technology before 2010.

Solar power and geothermal power are two other potential sources which have the advantage of being renewable and relatively free of environmental problems but, like fusion, will require very large research and development expenditures to demonstrate commercial feasibility.

The Commission recommends a greatly expanded research and development program to develop more efficient generation systems as a long-term solution, recognizing that it is unlikely that such new technologies will significantly reduce waste heat discharges until after the turn of the century.

Cooling: The potential for reducing heat discharge to water bodies through new cooling systems technologies generally rests in improvements to systems already developed or under development. Major design breakthroughs in lowering the cost of dry tower cooling, while unlikely based on current assessment, would be of great significance. Dry towers produce negligible consumptive loss of water and no heat discharge to water. Unfortunately, present dry tower designs range from $18-$32 per kilowatt in capital cost (as opposed to $2-$5 per kw. for once-through systems, $4-$9 per kw. for cooling ponds, and $5-$13 per kw. for wet cooling towers). Moreover, dry cooling towers are quite costly to operate and maintain, especially since they reduce a powerplant's average annual electrical energy output from 6 to 8 percent (and require the construction of 12 to 16 percent additional installed capacity).[205,206]

Beneficial-Use Technology: If waste heat can be put to beneficial use, it may become an asset. A number of possibilities are being investigated, ranging from its use in aquaculture, mariculture, and agriculture to airport defogging and deicing, deicing of shipping lanes, extending recreation seasons, acceleration of sewage treatment, space-heating and air-conditioning, and industrial processes. However, cooling water is discharged in large volumes at a relatively low temperature on a continual basis. These characteristics make it very difficult for existing systems to use the heat. To solve the waste heat problem, beneficial uses must either (1) reduce adverse effects on the water environment or (2) provide an economic gain or payout to help allay the cost of necessary special cooling systems. Beneficial

[205] U.S. FEDERAL POWER COMMISSION (1972). The 1970 National Power Survey. U.S. Government Printing Office, Washington, D.C. p. I-10-8.

[206] For example, providing dry tower cooling for each new thermal electric power generating plant constructed through 1990 would require the construction of additional installed capacity equivalent to about 40 3,000 megawatt powerplants just to provide electrical energy to operate the dry cooling facilities.

uses of waste heat should be looked upon as a possible help in reducing heat discharge to water bodies, but they cannot be counted on to provide any significant relief from the waste heat problem in the near term except on a localized basis. For the longer term, the possibilities appear more attractive. Continued research and development may achieve breakthroughs which could completely change the economic feasibility of some uses. Of the presently identified uses, agriculture, aquaculture, space-heating, and air-conditioning hold the greatest promise for the future, and should be the focus of future research and development activities.

Waste heat appears to have significant potential for use as an integral part of an urban energy center. However, such use might require close-in siting of future powerplants which, in the case of nuclear plants, for example, may present problems.

The potential for beneficial-use technology suggests the need for an expanded view of energy as a resource and for an emphasis on more efficient use of energy and the byproducts of its generation. Possibilities exist for amalgamating the location and operation of thermal powerplants with the operation of industrial plants, the production of agricultural commodities, the mining and processing of minerals, the extraction of salt from saline water, and the operation of other commercial ventures. Developments of this type can seldom be "add on" processes. For greatest efficiency they must be completely engineered on an integrated basis at the outset.

Transmission: New transmission technologies could allow much greater flexibility in siting. For instance, these technologies may make it possible to locate powerplants economically where water supplies are abundant, even at long distances from load centers.

In addition to underground transmission, the development of such things as superconductivity, SF_6 gas-cooled transmission, and the combined cryogenic electrical and liquified gas concept would be significant breakthroughs in allowing greater flexibility in siting. An accelerated research and development program on transmission technologies is warranted.

Energy Conservation: Faced with projected great increases in the number and size of powerplants and the total production of electrical energy, many people are asking, "Do we need all this power?" "Are we making the most efficient use of what we have now?"

Present uses of electrical energy are not nearly as efficient as is practically possible. For instance, the development of more efficient energy-consuming appliances and stricter requirements for insulation in building construction could conserve energy. At present, however, there is no national policy of energy conservation to guide energy development and use. Energy conservation will not alone solve the problems of waste heat, but it should be a national objective because of the potential benefits, including conservation of fuel resources, reduction in air pollution, fewer new generation facilities, and, of specific concern to this Commission, reduction in the energy impacts on the Nation's water resources.

It must be recognized that minimum electrical energy use does not necessarily mean optimum net benefits to society or optimum use of resources. Nevertheless, energy consumption should be considered in the design of buildings, industrial processes, and energy-consuming products to take into account the long-term total costs, including social and environmental costs, of electric power production. The Federal Government has the opportunity to influence the efficiency of energy use. Federal agencies should give greater attention to more efficient energy use as a first step toward a national policy of energy conservation.

Information Collection

A systematic approach will be required to develop solutions for the complex problems outlined. Chapter 4 of this report discusses generally the Nation's need to improve the collection and usability of water quality information. However, important elements of such an approach toward waste heat merit brief discussion here.

Information Storage and Retrieval: A great deal of study has been done to determine the effects of heat on aquatic systems, and a number of basic relationships are known. At present, however, it is extremely difficult to organize the wealth of available information into a usable and readily retrievable form. Furthermore, there is no orderly feedback mechanism whereby priority research needs are communicated to those who are doing the research. An information and retrieval center, or centers, are needed to become clearinghouses for information exchange in this area.[207]

---

[207] See Chapter 17 for specific recommendations on this and subsequent information collection elements.

180

Standardization: A review of testing methods, environmental survey procedures, and regulatory criteria reveals a lack of standardization of sampling and measurement technology in determining temperature effects on biota. Such standardization would prove valuable for those in research, in the utility industry, and in the regulatory agencies, as a means of assuring a common base in setting criteria and standards. It would also be of particular value in establishing an information system such as discussed above.

Modeling: An important aspect of powerplant site evaluation is the need to assess the probable impact of alternative cooling systems on the water resource. Simulation and predictive modeling techniques, while still in the embryonic stages of development, show significant promise for describing thermal life support system interaction and the processes governing heat movement in aquatic systems. Continued development and refinement of modeling techniques should be supported with a view to their leading to (1) better definition of possible problems during the planning phase before powerplants are designed and constructed and (2) better selection and design of heat discharge systems to mitigate adverse environmental impacts.

Pre- and Post-Operational Studies: Another important aspect in assessing the possible impact of heat on the water environment is the opportunity to learn from actual experience gained in powerplant operation. This can be most meaningful if carried out through a regularized process of pre- and post-operational investigations and monitoring studies correlated with the predictive modeling mentioned earlier. Actual effects could then be compared with those predicted and refinement of modeling techniques can be made which in turn would lead to better plant designs and aid in assessing effects of future sites and condenser cooling alternatives.

Temperature Standards

In setting temperature criteria, a range of factors such as temperature rise, temperature tolerances, total heat input, mixing zones and passageways, exposure time, seasonal variability, and geographical and hydrologic characteristics must be considered. Either indiscriminate heat discharge or total prohibition of heat discharge is an unwise policy for this Nation to follow. The question is how much temperature rise or heat input to allow in any specific

water area. Unfortunately, this question has no single answer applicable everywhere and for all time because of the great variability in both ecosystem response and the desired uses of water bodies.

The best possible information should be available to facilitate rational decisionmaking. Accordingly, temperature criteria should be based upon coordinated research programs, a recognition of geographical, hydrological, and seasonal differences, and the diversity of ecological systems. A Federal program is needed (1) to establish for ecologically representative aquatic systems in the U.S. the sublethal and lethal temperature levels for aquatic life, taking into account such things as acclimatizations, seasonal patterns, and duration of exposure, and (2) to aid in the establishment of a national policy on temperature criteria, including guidelines on which to base judgment. Both should be subject to constant review and modification as more definitive information becomes available.

Research and Development

In addition to research for the purpose of determining environmental impact and for setting environmental standards, a great deal of additional research and development is needed in the following areas:

1. More effective chemical and mechanical processes in the operation of cooling systems.
2. Early assessment of new siting alternatives.
3. Power generation technology.
4. Cooling system technology.
5. Transmission technology.
6. Beneficial and multiple-use technology.

Programs are under way to provide more money for research and development, which is essential because current industry and government funding levels are inadequate. The Research and Development Goals Task Force to the Electric Research Council reported in 1971 that a $30 billion commitment over the next 29 years would be required to achieve the research and development goals which the task force identified, approximately double the then existing level of combined expenditures of government, manufacturers, and utilities.[208] The electric utility industry recently has increased its support of research

---

[208] ELECTRIC RESEARCH COUNCIL, R&D GOALS TASK FORCE (June 1971). Electric Utilities Industry Research and Development Goals Through the Year 2000, Report of the R&D Goals Task Force to the Electric Research Council. ERC Pub. No. 1-71. Electric Research Council, New York, N.Y. p. 2.

and development, but the Commission concurs with a U.S. Office of Science and Technology finding that the general level of research and development by electric utilities is below an appropriate level for an industry of its size.[209] It is important that electric power utilities devote a reasonable portion of their revenues to research and development. At the same time, regulatory commissions at the Federal and State level should take positive action to assure that the utility industry can recover research and development expenses in its rates.

One approach to funding which merits consideration is the establishment of an energy/environment research and development fund, funded through imposition of a surcharge or tax on all energy consumers. This has been the subject of proposed Federal legislation. The Electric Research Council, recently incorporated as the Electric Power Research Institute, Inc., supports a similar approach. Plans are under way for participating investor owned utilities to seek rate relief for an assessment of 1/10 mill per kilowatt-hour on electric generation. If this program is agreed to by regulatory bodies and implemented, approximately $137 million per year will be available by 1974 for research and development.[210] Similar assessments by publicly owned systems would increase the total to approximately $177 million a year. Coupled with increased Federal support of energy research and development and additional spending by individual utilities, this would provide a needed thrust forward.

The research and development identified above will be of great significance in a number of ways: fuel and energy conservation, improved air quality, improved esthetics, and improved land use, in addition to a reduced impact of energy generation on water resources. Since water is only one factor, funding and management for needed research should be designed within a much broader context than is within the charge of this Commission. The Commission is aware of the large number of studies, conferences, hearings,

[209] U.S. OFFICE OF SCIENCE AND TECHNOLOGY, Energy Policy Staff (August 1970). Electric Power and the Environment. U.S. Government Printing Office, Washington, D.C. pp. 42-44.

[210] HARRIS, Shearon (March 15, 1972). Testimony, pp. 76-105 in U.S. CONGRESS, Senate, Committee on Commerce, Energy Research and Development, Hearings, 92d Congress, 2d Session, Serial No. 92-62. U.S. Government Printing Office, Washington, D.C. Other proposals vary in the amount of the assessment; most are in the range of $150-$300 million in additional research and development funds annually.

legislative proposals, and calls for a comprehensive national energy policy and a coordinated energy research and development program. It supports the general thrust of these proposals and urges the early implementation of a broad policy and a diversified program of research and development in energy generation and related matters.

CONCLUSIONS

Demand for electrical energy in the foreseeable future will continue to increase even if not at the present rate of doubling every 10 years. Major reductions in electrical energy use are unlikely, especially in the near term. Hence, reduced electrical energy requirements cannot be counted on to provide relief from the need for more powerplants or from the waste heat problem during this period. Reducing the rate of expansion in electrical energy usage would, however, reduce somewhat the need for additional generating facilities and would yield a number of other benefits.

Present electrical energy-using equipment and appliances are far from the most efficient possible, even under present technology. Most present-day building construction and appliance manufacturing companies employ designs with a low first cost and with resultant high energy consumption, as opposed to a higher first cost and a subsequently lower long-term energy usage. The Federal Government has the opportunity to influence the more efficient use of energy through widely diversified federally supported research and development programs, and in the design of federally supported and financed facilities and facilities designed primarily for the use of the Government. This influence should be used as the first step in the development of a national policy of energy conservation.

Two perspectives are needed in addressing the issue of siting future steam electric powerplants. One perspective must deal with the near to intermediate term, during which powerplants must be planned, designed, constructed, and operated using currently proven and available technology. This period is expected to include much of the remaining part of the 20th century. The second perspective must deal with that period beyond the turn of the century when current and future research and development efforts might have a significant impact on the means of energy generation. This later period, though less predictable, should provide greater flexibility of choice among more alternative courses of action.

Waste heat can be dispersed to the biosphere in various ways, all of which must be considered in the establishment of policies concerning environmental quality. In order to assess adequately the total environmental impact of heat release, it is necessary first to assess the alternative controlled release mechanisms in terms of their overall environmental impact, including local concentration effects.

The ability of water to absorb heat is a valuable natural resource which, under many conditions, can have high utility in diluting, dispersing, and dissipating waste heat. However, for protecting various uses of water, such as providing habitat for aquatic life, there must be a limit to the use of water for this purpose. Where heat input will adversely affect important aquatic life or other environmental values, permissible heat inputs will have to be allocated among the various heat contributors (who might then have to resort to auxiliary cooling methods).

While a great deal of information is available on the effects of heat additions on the aquatic ecology, there is need for:

1. a data center and retrieval system whereby information concerning thermal effects is readily available;
2. an efficient feedback of research needs;
3. standardization of sampling, measuring, and research techniques;
4. continual assessment of predictive modeling technology; and
5. a regularized system of pre- and post-operational monitoring studies to determine the environmental effects of plant operation.

Temperature standards should be based on an adequate recognition of geographical, hydrological, and seasonal differences and the diversity of ecological systems. A systematic, flexible, and well-financed environmental research program is needed to provide the kinds of information on which rational standards may be set and on which informed decisionmaking may be based, in particular with respect to the effects of temperature and temperature change on aquatic life.

Water resources planning studies should be broadened in focus to include greater consideration of sites for steam electric power generation and their possible effects on the water environment.

New technologies are not expected to have a significant impact in providing relief from the waste heat problem in the near term. For the intermediate and longer term, however, a number of technological possibilities in the areas of generation, cooling,

transmission, beneficial-use and multiple-use systems, and new siting alternatives could mitigate significantly the adverse effects of powerplant operation on water resources. An accelerated research and development program is a necessity if the Nation is to meet the demands for electrical energy and a quality environment in a timely and orderly manner.

RECOMMENDATIONS

5-28. The President and the Congress should develop and implement a national policy of energy conservation. As an immediate step in this direction, the President should issue an executive order directing the agencies of the Federal Government to give greater consideration to reducing energy requirements in their own activities, such as housing, transportation, defense, and environment, and to exercise such influence as they may have over non-Federal interests to further the Federal policy.

5-29. Appropriate Federal agencies and power utilities should undertake a greatly expanded research and development program with the following objectives:

   a. To develop more efficient and environmentally compatible means of generating electrical energy (including fuel cell, MHD, the breeder reactor, advanced power cycles, nuclear fusion, goethermal, and solar energy).

   b. To develop more effective means of managing large quantities of waste heat discharge and for dealing with problems arising as a result of cooling system operation.

   c. To develop and assess new siting alternatives in order to increase siting options (including the development of better means of electric power transmission).

   d. To develop means of combining electrical power generation with other processes in multiple-use systems as well as means of beneficially using waste heat discharge with a view to more efficient total energy use.

5-30. Federal water pollution control legislation should recognize the capacity of receiving waters to absorb heat as a valuable resource.

5-31. The water and related land resources planning studies undertaken under the Water Resources

Planning Act should, in cooperation with private interests, be broadened to provide more attention to potential powerplant sites and the effects which powerplant siting and operation may have upon other land and water uses. The Water Resources Council, assisted by a work group made up of representatives from industry, Federal and State agencies, and the general public should provide policy and procedural direction.

Erosion and Sedimentation Damage Control Programs

In rural areas the erosion of agricultural lands reduces their productivity by carrying away fertile top soil, by making some areas unusable as a result of gully formation, and by destroying rich bottomlands by bank erosion and, in some instances, by the deposition of the eroded material. The eroded material carried by rivers in flood increases flood losses when it is deposited in places from which it must be removed, as from highways and flooded buildings. And the soil particles eroded from rural lands carry with them nutrients—particularly some of the excess nutrients placed on farmlands in the form of fertilizers—and other agricultural chemicals that are recorded as pollutants when the streams are monitored for conformance with water quality standards. There is, therefore, a close relationship and a considerable degree of interdependence between the erosion and sedimentation problem, the flood loss problem, and the pollution problem.

In urban areas, material eroded from lands on which buildings and street systems are under construction is frequently deposited on developed areas at lower elevations, and the cost of removing the sediment from streets and drainage systems can be substantial. The urban erosion and sedimentation problem and the problem of reducing flood losses resulting from storm runoff originating within urban areas—which is discussed in Section E of this chapter—are related. The same runoff that causes soil to erode carries it to lower levels where much of the sediment is deposited, and in doing so increases the flood losses previously mentioned. Moreover, it is the first flush of urban flood runoff that carries pollutants into stream systems and which, as explained in Chapter 4, will require vast expenditures for treatment if presently contemplated quality standards are to be met at all times. In short, in urban areas as in rural areas, the problems of erosion,

sedimentation, reduction of flood losses, and the pollution of streams are interrelated.

Because water is the causative factor in the erosion and sedimentation problem, as well as in the related problems, Federal erosion control activities are discussed in this report.

THE PROGRAMS

Programs of the Soil Conservation Service

The Soil Conservation Service (SCS) of the U.S. Department of Agriculture administers two nationwide programs that decrease damages caused by water erosion. One of these is carried out under Public Law 46,[211] the Act that established the SCS; the other, under the Watershed Protection and Flood Prevention Act,[212] as amended. The latter program is sometimes referred to as the "Small Watershed Program," and sometimes as the "Public Law 566 Program." Through the Public Law 46 program the SCS, by providing technical assistance, encourages farmers to adopt soil-conserving practices such as contour cultivation, terracing, crop rotations, conversion of steep lands to pasture or woodland, and the installation of gully control structures. This involves working out with each farmer a plan for the best use of his land. This assistance is given in cooperation with a Soil Conservation District established under State law. There are over 3,000 soil conservation districts in the United States, and these encompass almost 2 billion acres of land and 99 percent of the farms in the United States. Through the Public Law 566 program the SCS assists local organizations (usually Soil Conservation Districts) to install works such as

[211] *Act of April 27, 1935*, P.L. 46, 74th Congress, 49 Stat. 163, as amended, 16 USCA 590a-590f.

[212] P.L. 566, August 4, 1954, 83d Congress, 68 Stat. 666, as amended, 16 USCA 1001 *et seq.*

reservoirs, levees, channels, grade stabilization structures, and bank protection measures. The reservoirs are intended to reduce flood damages along headwater streams, provide irrigation water, store water for municipal use, provide for streamflow regulation, serve as recreational facilities, and enhance the fish and wildlife resource. The channel improvements reclaim wetlands, in addition to reducing flood losses in the adjacent areas. Such improvements may also have adverse effects upon the fish and wildlife resource, and may increase downstream flooding.[213]

Plans for entire watersheds are carried out by the local organizations with technical and financial assistance provided by the SCS and other agencies of the Department of Agriculture. In general, soil erosion control measures are applied to the lands of the watersheds in the same way as they are to other lands in Soil Conservation Districts. From the standpoint of alleviating sedimentation damages, the most effective of the measures installed through the Public Law 566 program are the bank protection measures, the grade stabilization and gully control structures and, in certain watersheds, debris basins. Recent legislation[214] authorizes the Secretary of Agriculture to assist farmers and communities in rural areas to install pollution control measures. This should make it possible for the Department of Agriculture to deal with erosion control as a multiple-purpose measure for reducing the rate at which nutrients are carried to the stream system, as well as a means for preserving soil fertility and reducing sediment damages.

A recent development has been the decision of some States to broaden the missions of the Soil Conservation Districts to enable them to assist in the alleviation of erosion and sedimentation problems in urban areas. Since these Districts utilize the technical assistance of the SCS, this development has had the effect in some places of bringing that agency into urban areas. Also, the recently enacted Rural Development Act of 1972 will give the SCS a more important role in urban areas.

Program of the Agricultural Stabilization and Conservation Service (ASCS)

Through its Rural Environmental Assistance Program (REAP) this agency, also in the Department of Agriculture, assists farmers to install soil conservation measures by paying a part of the cost thereof, generally on a 50-50 basis. The ASCS is also responsible for the Long-Term Land Retirement Programs. These programs result in the shifting of considerable land into soil conserving uses and thus help alleviate erosion and sedimentation problems.

Program of the Tennessee Valley Authority(TVA)

One of the purposes of the comprehensive program of TVA is the reduction of soil erosion on private lands through the encouragement of better farm and forestry practices.

Programs of the U.S. Army Corps of Engineers

The Corps of Engineers through its Civil Works Program installs bank protection measures to stop land destruction and in some cases to reduce the rate of sedimentation of downstream channels and reservoirs.

Programs for Management of Federal Lands

The Forest Service of the Department of Agriculture, and the Bureau of Land Management and the National Park Service of the Department of the Interior, administer very large areas of public land. Management practices on these public lands are such that soil erosion, and thus the discharge of sediment into stream systems, are held at as low a level as the agencies having jurisdiction find it practicable to achieve with the authorities and funds available to them. To the extent practicable, the Bureau of Indian Affairs of the Department of the Interior assists Indians and Alaskan natives to use and manage their lands in a manner consistent with the principles of resource conservation, and in this way contributes to the alleviation of erosion and sediment problems.

Program of the Environmental Protection Agency (EPA)

This agency is interested in erosion and sediment from the standpoint of pollution control and has recommended[215] amendment of the Federal Water Pollution Control Act by the addition of a new Title (the Sedimentation Control Act) that would authorize the Administrator of EPA to "promulgate guidelines for the effective control of sedimentation from land-disturbing activities, including clearing,

---

[213] Channelization is discussed in more detail in Chapter 2.

[214] *The Rural Development Act of 1972*, P.L. 92-419, August 30, 1972, 86 Stat. 657.

[215] Letter February 8, 1972, from EPA Administrator to the Speaker of the House and the President of the Senate, submitting a draft of the proposed legislation.

Mud flats at upper end of Canyon Ferry Lake collect sediments from upstream erosion

grading, transporting, and filling land," excepting lands used for agriculture and forestry and lands that would be protected by a proposed Mined Areas Protection Act. This legislative proposal is obviously intended to alleviate erosion and sediment problems in urban areas.

APPRAISAL OF PROGRAMS

In the rural areas of the Nation the programs briefly described above appear to have been fairly effective in persuading landowners to adopt erosion control measures. Nevertheless, an inventory of conservation "needs" made by the SCS, in cooperation with other agencies, in 1967 resulted in a finding that almost two-thirds of the present cropland should have more intensive treatment.[216] This indicates that it may be many years before erosion has been reduced

[216] U.S. DEPARTMENT OF AGRICULTURE (1971). Basic Statistics—National Inventory of Soil and Water Conservation Needs, 1967, Statistical Bulletin No. 461. U.S. Government Printing Office, Washington, D.C.

to the lowest level that is economically feasible to achieve. But there appears to be general agreement that in those areas in which a comprehensive program of soil conservation measures has been put into effect the discharge of eroded material into the stream system has been strikingly reduced. In the long run, therefore, there should be a substantial reduction in the erosion from rural lands and a consequent reduction in sediment damages. However, the degree to which downstream sediment damages may be decreased will be limited by the fact that when less eroded material enters a river the capacity of the river to erode its banks and bed increases.

On urban lands, the erosion and sedimentation problems can be serious during periods when much construction is under way and thereafter until vegetal cover is established. As indicated previously, however, there appears to be a desire for Federal programs to assist the cities in dealing with these problems, and both the EPA and the SCS have indicated a willingness to provide such assistance. In those urban areas in which serious erosion and sedimentation problems are being experienced, it would appear that the local governmental entities are not making effective use of their regulatory powers, and it is not evident to this Commission that there is any real need for Federal subsidies to achieve adequate erosion control in urban areas.

CONCLUSIONS

The Federal programs that have been initiated over the years for the purpose of decreasing soil losses in .rural areas have been relatively successful in achieving their objective. This Commission has not detected a need for a change in their basic nature, or for the diversion of any larger proportion of the national income to this purpose. Undoubtedly, however, the newer national goal of improving the quality of the Nation's rivers will have the effect, over a period of time, of according preference to those measures most effective in reducing the quantities of nutrients that reach the streams. It may also have the effect of increasing Federal expenditures in some areas and decreasing them in others, depending upon the demand for water quality improvement in the various parts of the Nation.

The Commission understands that erosion and sedimentation problems in urban areas are becoming progressively more serious. Undoubtedly, much eroded material may be washed from raw construction sites and undoubtedly this is causing considerable damage in some cities. But this Commission fails to see the necessity for the Federal Government establishing a program for the purpose of solving a problem that the local governmental entities can themselves virtually eliminate by regulating those actions of landowners and builders that create such problems.

The attention of the Commission has also been called to the fact that the first flush of storm runoff from urban areas can carry a considerable load of pollutants into the streams. There is much evidence that this is true. It is not evident, however, that dangerous pollutants are carried by material eroded from raw construction sites. And even if in some instances this should be true, it does not alter the fact that the local governmental entities have the power to put a stop to excessive erosion from lands under their jurisdiction without calling upon the Federal Government for help. The Commission is compelled, therefore, to take the same position with respect to erosion in urban areas that it took—in Section E of this chapter—with respect to the closely related problem of reducing those flood losses that result from storm runoff originating within urban areas.

RECOMMENDATIONS

5-32.   **Special attention should be given in the planning and carrying out of soil conservation and other programs that can bring about a reduction in the surface runoff and erosion originating on rural lands, to those measures capable of decreasing the amounts of harmful pollutants entering the stream system including, but not limited to, such pollutants as pesticides, animal and human wastes originating on feedlots and farmsteads, and nutrients applied to the land in the form of inorganic fertilizers. Activities such as channelization of streams which may augment sedimentation should be avoided.**

5-33.   **Primary responsibility for the reduction of damages resulting from urban erosion and sedimentation should remain with local governmental entities, and Federal assistance should be limited to the provision of technical advice.**

~~~~~~~~~~~~~~~~~~~~~~~~~~~~~~~~~~~~~~ *Section I*

Recreation at Reservoirs

This section is concerned primarily with outdoor recreation at Federal reservoirs, focusing on issues arising from Public Law 89-72, the Federal Water Project Recreation Act. Omitted from consideration, except by incidental reference, is the role of the private and non-Federal public sectors. Also omitted is consideration of nonwater-based recreation, and recreation on or bordering the Nation's coastal shorelines, Great Lakes, and natural lakes and ponds. The problem of public access to these waters is discussed in Section E of Chapter 7 as is also the preservation of minimum flows for recreation.

Esthetic and environmental values other than recreation, pollution abatement, and fish and wildlife are treated elsewhere in the Commission's report.

Concentration of the Commission's attention on recreation at reservoirs does not mean it considers other forms of water-based recreation unimportant or to merit lower priority. It merely reflects the fact that the Commission's role is to deal with water problems and water policy—not recreation in general. The value of white water boating, stream fishing, and wild areas is undisputed. These values should be taken fully into account in evaluating proposals for reservoir projects and in the designation of wild and scenic rivers.

BACKGROUND

Outdoor recreation has experienced a phenomenal boom in the past two decades. This results mostly from the general increase in leisure time for the average American, improved mobility, and a generally prosperous economy. Recreation can be a family activity, it is generally healthy, and it need not be costly.

The manufacture of goods, transportation of persons and supplies, provision of facilities, and consumption spending for outdoor recreation have been estimated to place it among the top 10 major economic activities of the Nation. The Federal Government spends about $1 billion per year on outdoor recreation. One-half of the pickup trucks sold in 1972 were recreation vehicles. There has been an unprecedented boom in boats and small motorized vehicles such as motorcycles, minibikes, and snowmobiles. Resort hotels, trailers, motor homes, and campers are heavily oriented to outdoor recreation.

Water is a great magnet—about half of all outdoor recreation is water-oriented. Three-fourths of the Federal share of the Land and Water Conservation Fund and two-thirds of the State share of such funds have been water-oriented.[217]

The Nation's recreational water potential is very great. One-third of the 60,000 miles of coastal shoreline of the 48 contiguous States has recreation potential although only 1 percent is publicly owned. There is considerable recreation potential for the 5 to 6 thousand miles of Great Lakes shoreline, the 45,000 square miles of the Nation's 100,000 other fresh water lakes, the 2 million small ponds, the 2 to 3 million miles of streams and rivers, the 20,000 islands, and the 56,000 shoreline miles in reservoirs of the U.S. Army Corps of Engineers, the U.S. Bureau of Reclamation, and the Tennessee Valley Authority.

Outdoor Recreation Resources Review Commission

The National Water Commission has drawn heavily upon the work of the Outdoor Recreation Resources Review Commission (ORRRC), a congressionally authorized Commission which reported in January 1962. Its report, "Outdoor Recreation for America," and its 27 separate study reports is the most exhaustive analysis available of recreation in the United States.[218]

The ORRRC report dwelt at length on water (emphasizing it as a key factor in recreation supply), the needs for water, and the important role played by inland waters, coastal and Great Lakes shorelines, and Federal impoundments. The report contained five major recommendations and about 50 more detailed ones, including two on Federal impoundments.

With respect to Federal impoundments, the Commission recommended: "(1) Outdoor recreation should be considered as an important purpose of Federal multipurpose water resource developments, and thus guaranteed full consideration in the planning, design, construction, and operation of projects. . . .Existing developments should be reviewed under these criteria. . . . (2) Reservoir planning should provide for acquisition of adequate shoreline lands for public access and use."

[217] U.S. DEPARTMENT OF THE INTERIOR, BUREAU OF OUTDOOR RECREATION (undated). The 1965 Nationwide Inventory of Publicly-Owned Recreation Areas and an Assessment of Private Recreation Enterprises. Bureau of Outdoor Recreation, Washington, D.C.

U.S. BUREAU OF OUTDOOR RECREATION (undated). The 1965 Survey of Outdoor Recreation Activities. U.S. Government Printing Office, Washington, D.C.

U.S. BUREAU OF OUTDOOR RECREATION (1971). Selected Outdoor Recreation Statistics. U.S. Government Printing Office, Washington, D.C.

U.S. BUREAU OF OUTDOOR RECREATION (1972). The 1970 Survey of Outdoor Recreation Activities. U.S. Government Printing Office, Washington, D.C.

[218] U.S. OUTDOOR RECREATION RESOURCES REVIEW COMMISSION (1962). Outdoor Recreation for America. U.S. Government Printing Office, Washington, D. C. (Also, 27 separately published study reports, especially No. 4 - Shoreline Recreation Resources; No. 7 - Sport Fishing Today and Tomorrow; No. 10 - Water for Recreation - Values and Opportunities; and No. 26 - Prospective Demands for Recreation.)

The Nationwide Outdoor Recreation Plan

This plan was directed by P.L. 88-29 to be prepared at 5-year intervals by the Secretary of the Interior, with the first one due in 1968.[219] The plan is required to be submitted by the President to the Congress. Delegation for preparation was initially made to the Bureau of Outdoor Recreation and is now placed in the Office of Economic Analysis of the Department of the Interior. The first plan has yet to be sent to Congress. The draft of the report without recommendations was made available to the Commission staff. It considers water-based recreation at length, although does not specifically focus on it. The plan is now scheduled for publication in 1973.

Congressional Actions

Congress has given muscle to the recommendations of the Outdoor Recreation Resources Review Commission, has enacted more legislation and appropriated more funds for outdoor recreation in the past 10 years than in the preceding 50, and has given reality to the assertion that outdoor recreation is now a major economic and social phenomenon of the Nation.

Some major recent recreation enactments which indicate the importance Congress attaches to outdoor recreation include the following:

1. **P.L. 88-29.**[220] An Act to promote the coordination and development of outdoor recreation programs. This is generally known as the Organic Act for the Bureau of Outdoor Recreation. In it are found not only the directive to prepare the Nationwide Outdoor Recreation Plan, but also a national policy for outdoor recreation, as well as authorities for technical assistance to the private sector and to promote Federal coordination.

2. **P.L. 88-578.**[221] Amended several times, this Act provides grants-in-aid to States and local governments for outdoor recreation land acquisition and development, and direct acquisition aid principally to the National Park Service and Forest Service. Admission and user fee provisions are included. There flows annually into the fund $300 million, mainly from offshore oil royalties.

Appropriations for Fiscal Years 1965-1973, inclusive, have been:

	Million $	Percent
Federal	721	43
States	940	57
Total	1,661	100

About three-fourths of the Federal funds and two-thirds of the State and local funds have gone to water-oriented recreation. The paramount purpose is to acquire recreation lands and waters where the need is greatest, and to do this before such lands are committed to nonrecreation uses or priced out of reach. About 35 percent of the total State portion of the funds has gone to local governments through the States, including about 10 percent to major metropolitan areas or control cities.

3. **National Recreation Areas, Seashores, Lakeshores, and Rivers.** There are 29 such areas, each designated by statute, all but three of which are water-oriented. They include nine seashores, four lakeshores, three rivers, and the remainder involve seven Bureau of Reclamation reservoirs, and one municipal utility reservoir. Six are administered in whole or in part by the Forest Service, and the remainder by the National Park Service.

4. **National Park System.** About 100 new units have been added to the National Park system in recent years, including seven national parks, such as the Redwood, North Cascades, Voyageurs, and Canyonlands. Many of these new units, as well as older parks, have extensive water-based recreation opportunities.

5. **P.L. 90-542.**[222] This Act provides for a National Wild and Scenic River System. Eight rivers were established as components of the system by the basic Act, with the door open to add others later. The Lower St. Croix recently has been added (P.L. 92-560).

6. **P.L. 90-543.**[223] This Act created a national system of recreation and scenic trails. The Appalachian and Pacific Crest trails were established and 14 additional trails were designated to be studied for suitability.

---

[219] *Act of May 28, 1963*, P.L. 88-29, 77 Stat. 49, as amended, 16 USCA 760*l* to 460*l*-3.

[220] *Ibid.*

[221] *Land and Water Conservation Fund Act*, P.L. 88-578, September 3, 1964, 78 Stat 897, as amended, 16 USCA 460*l*-4 to 460*l*-11.

[222] *Wild and Scenic Rivers Act*, P.L. 90-542. October 2, 1968, 82. Stat. 906, as amended, 16 USCA 1271-1287.

[223] *National Trails System Act*, P.L. 90-543, October 2, 1968, 82 Stat. 919, 16 USCA 1241-1249.

7. **P.L. 92-347.**[224] This Act establishes a system of admission and special recreation use fees, including the Golden Eagle passport. Criteria for establishing fees are spelled out. The Senate Committee report states: "...the committee rejects the policy recently adopted by some federal agencies requiring federal fees to be at the same level as state, local or commercial fees for comparable facilities in a given area. This policy would, in effect, permit non-Federal operators to fix the level of federal fees and could undermine the establishment of a fair and uniform fee system...."[225]

8. **P.L. 88-577.**[226] This Act establishes a national system of wilderness areas.

9. **P.L. 89-72.**[227] This Act bears directly on recreation at Federal multipurpose water resource projects and is discussed under "Federal Reservoirs."

THE PROGRAMS

The Bureau of Outdoor Recreation

The Bureau of Outdoor Recreation in the Department of the Interior administers the Land and Water Conservation Fund. It has made numerous special studies of recreation areas, rivers, seashores, lakeshores, trails, parks, and islands, a number of which have resulted in enabling legislation.

The Outdoor Recreation Resources Review Commission strongly emphasized the private non-Federal role: "...individual initiative and private enterprise should continue to be the most important force in outdoor recreation,... Government....should also stimulate commercial development, which can be particularly effective in providing facilities and service where demand is sufficient to return a profit."[228] Nevertheless, the Bureau has done little to provide

technical assistance to private interests in such fields as research, financial aids, consulting advice, or equipment development as authorized under P.L. 88-29.

Also, the Bureau is ineffective in promoting coordination of Federal activities relating to outdoor recreation. The Secretary has authority only to "promote," not to require, coordination.

House Report 92-586 concluded that: (1) BOR did not vigorously exercise its responsibility to advise the Soil Conservation Service (SCS) on recreation values and the need for public access at reservoir projects financially aided by SCS and (2) BOR was excluded from discussions between the Corps and Reclamation concerning the 1971 Corps revision of the 1962 Corps-Reclamation joint reservoir land acquisition policy.[229]

Initially, the BOR was active in coordination, serving as staff to the President's Recreation Advisory Council, established in 1962, and consisting of the Secretaries of Interior, Agriculture, Defense, Commerce, and Health, Education and Welfare and the Administrator of the Housing and Home Finance Agency, the predecessor to the Department of Housing and Urban Development. Subsequently, the Chairman of the Tennessee Valley Authority and Administrator of the General Services Administration were added. The Director of the Bureau of Outdoor Recreation reported directly to the Council (not through the Secretary of the Interior) and served as its Executive Director.

The Council issued a series of seven major policy guidelines, which were binding on the member departments and agencies.[230] Circulars 2 and 5 define the Federal role and guidelines for Federal investment

[224] *Act of July 11, 1972*, P.L. 92-347, 86 Stat. 459, 16 USCA 460*l*-6a.

[225] U.S. CONGRESS, Senate, Committee on Interior and Insular Affairs (1971). Golden Eagle Passport, Senate Report No. 92-490, 92d Congress, 1st Session. U.S. Government Printing Office, Washington, D.C. p. 3.

[226] *Wilderness Act*, P.L. 88-577, September 3, 1964, 78 Stat. 890, 16 USCA 1131-1136.

[227] *Federal Water Project Recreation Act*, P.L. 89-72, July 9, 1965, 79 Stat. 213, as amended, 16 USCA 460*l*-12 to 460*l*-22.

[228] U.S. OUTDOOR RECREATION RESOURCES REVIEW COMMISSION (1962). Outdoor Recreation for America. U.S. Government Printing Office, Washington, D.C.

[229] U.S. CONGRESS, House, Committee on Government Operations (1971). Public Access to Reservoirs to Meet Growing Recreation Demands, House Report No. 92-586, 92d Congress, 1st Session. U.S. Government Printing Office, Washington, D.C.

[230] PRESIDENT'S RECREATION ADVISORY COUNCIL. *Circ. 1*: Federal Executive Branch Policy Governing the Selection, Establishment, and Administration of National Recreation Areas. 8 pp. 1963. *Circ. 2*: General Policy Guidelines for Outdoor Recreation. 15 pp. 1964. *Circ. 3*: Policy Governing the Water Pollution and Public Health Aspects of Outdoor Recreation. 10 pp 1964. *Circ. 4*: A National Program of Scenic Roads and Parkways. 7 pp. 1964. *Circ. 5*: Guides for Federal Outdoor Recreation Investment. 3 pp. 1965. *Circ. 6*: Federal Executive Policy Governing the Reporting of Recreation Use of Federal Recreation Areas. 5 pp. 1965. *Circ. 7*: Non-Federal Management of Recreational Facilities on Federal Lands and Waters. 9 pp. 1965.

Bureau of Reclamation lakes are heavily used for recreational boating

in outdoor recreation. Among other things, they state that: (1) Primary priority for Federal investment shall be assigned to projects to be acquired and developed in conjunction with bodies of water. Reservoirs are specifically mentioned. (2) Outdoor recreation shall be one of the primary purposes in planning multipurpose water resource developments and an equitable share of the cost shall be allocated to recreation.

The importance of controlling pollution of Federal waters for recreation purposes, encouraging recreational use of Federal waters, and eligibility of Federal reservoirs for national recreation area status also are covered in the policy mandates.

In addition, the Council resolved several jurisdictional conflicts over what agencies should administer recreation at Federal reservoirs. For example, it assigned to the Forest Service responsibility for both the Corps of Engineers' Allegheny Reservoir and the Bureau of Reclamation's Flaming Gorge.

In recent years, the President's Recreation Advisory Council has been allowed to lapse, and the Bureau of Outdoor Recreation's coordination functions largely have ceased. Yet, in 1970, eight

Federal departments, 55 Federal bureaus or their equivalent, and 41 independent Federal agencies, commissions, and councils were responsible for 262 Federal outdoor recreation programs, many of which dealt with water.[231]

Federal Reservoirs

Eight Federal agencies are involved: the Corps of Engineers, Bureau of Reclamation, Tennessee Valley Authority (TVA), Forest Service, Bureau of Sport Fisheries and Wildlife, National Park Service, International Boundary and Water Commission (United States and Mexico), and Soil Conservation Service (SCS).

The Corps, Reclamation, and TVA are the three main Federal reservoir agencies. The Forest Service, Bureau of Sport Fisheries and Wildlife, and the National Park Service are resource management agencies, which have assigned to them part or all of the recreation responsibilities at 44 Corps and 53 Reclamation reservoirs. Two TVA reservoirs have public recreation administered in part by the Bureau of Sport Fisheries and Wildlife.

The International Boundary Commission is responsible for two reservoirs on the Rio Grande. The National Park Service handles the public recreation at one, and the State of Texas at the other. The SCS is discussed subsequently under "Land Management Agencies."

Table 5-14 summarizes selected statistics for the eight Federal agencies and indicates the number of reservoirs having public recreation facilities, area, visitations, expenditures, and fee collections. Data are not wholly comparable between agencies as partially explained by footnotes and are estimated with varying reliability. Hence, totals cannot be drawn.

About 675 Federal and 111 federally assisted reservoirs have public recreation facilities. These reservoirs involve about 16.8 million acres of land and water, about 56,000 miles of shoreline, and had an estimated 409 million recreation visits in 1972.

Combining the agencies, it has been estimated that visitations will increase one-third within the next 8 years, a doubling of operations and maintenance funds will be needed, and expenditures for capital improvements should increase by 25 times to meet policy standards for quantity and quality which the Federal Government has adopted.

TVA does not exclusively administer public recreation at any of its reservoirs, but shares it wholly or in part with local public or private bodies and in two instances with the Bureau of Sport Fisheries and Wildlife. TVA does administer a special recreation and environmental education area located between TVA's Kentucky Lake and the Corps' Lake Barkley, known as the "Land-Between-the-Lakes."[232]

The Federal reservoir and associated agencies are guided by a variety of statutes and guidelines resulting in different policies and priorities.[233]

Construction Agencies

Section 1 of P.L. 89-72, the Federal Water Project Recreation Act, reads:

> ... it is the policy of the Congress ... that ... in investigating and planning any Federal navigation, flood control, reclamation, hydro-electric, or multiple-purpose water resource project, full consideration shall be given to opportunities, if any, which the project affords for outdoor recreation . . . .

In addition the Act also provided that: (1) non-Federal bodies must agree to administer recreation,

[232] TENNESSEE VALLEY AUTHORITY (1970). Recreation. TVA, Division of Reservoir Properties, Knoxville, Tenn. p. 9.

[233] Some of the more important are the following: the *Flood Control Act of 1944*, P.L. 534, Section 4, December 22, 1944. 78th Congress, 58 Stat. 887, 889, as amended, 16 USCA 460d; the *Fish and Wildlife Coordination Act*, P.L. 85-624, August 12, 1958, 72 Stat. 563, as amended, 16 USCA 661 *et seq.*; the *Multiple-Use Sustained Yield Act*, P.L. 86-517, June 12, 1960, 74 Stat. 215, 16 USCA 528-531; the *Tennessee Valley Authority Act of 1933*, P.L. 17, May 18, 1933, 73d Congress, 48 Stat. 58, as amended, 16 USCA 831 *et seq.*; the *Park Service Organic Act*, P.L. 235, August 24, 1916, 64th Congress, 39 Stat. 535, as supplemented, 16 USCA 1 *et. seq.*; the *Watershed Protection and Flood Prevention Act*, P.L. 566, August 4, 1954, 83d Congress, 68 Stat. 666, as amended, 16 USCA 1001-1008; the *Land and Water Conservation Fund Act*, P.L. 88-578, September, 1964, 78 Stat. 897, as amended, 16 USCA 460*l*-4 to 460*l*-11; the *Federal Water Project Recreation Act*, P.L. 89-72, July 9, 1965, 79 Stat. 213, as amended, 16 USCA 460*l*-12 to 460*l*-22; Senate Document 97, 87th Congress (1962), and its Supplement No. 1 of 1964 relating to standards for evaluating recreation benefits; the seven Recreation Advisory Council circulars previously discussed; and some 29 individual national recreation area, lakeshore, river, and seashore acts, some 35 to 50 individual recreation acts affecting the Forest Service, and a memorandum of agreement of August 1964 between the Secretary of the Army and the Secretary of Agriculture.

[231] U.S. BUREAU OF OUTDOOR RECREATION (1970). Federal Outdoor Recreation Programs and Recreation-Related Environmental Programs. U.S. Government Printing Office, Washington, D.C.

TABLE 5-14. — Selected basic information for Federal and federally assisted reservoirs having Federal recreation facilities 1972[1]

Agency	Reservoirs (number)	Water and Associated Land Areas (thousand acres)	Estimated Visitation (thousand years)	Estimated Federal Recreation Expenditures		Estimated Federal Recreation Fee Collections (thousand $)
				Capital Improvements (thousand $)	Maintenance & Operations (thousand $)	
1. Corps of Engineers	390	10,977	330,000[2]	7,600	15,000	400
2. Bureau of Reclamation	245	5,889	56,000[2]	3,000	5,550	250
3. Tennessee Valley Authority	40	852	16,600	2,357	1,991	127
4. Forest Service	151[3]	814[4]	28,800[5]	1,885	7,439	1,589
5. National Park Service	12[6]	3,508	13,306	10,032	7,145	261
6. Bureau of Sport Fisheries and Wildlife	53[7]	2,457	11,000	1,038	1,358	106[8]
7. Soil Conservation Service	111[9]	64	6,225	23,000[10]	None[11]	None[11]
8. International Boundary and Water Commission, United States and Mexico	2[12]	--	--	--	--	--

[1] Data are only indicative due to lack of comparability and overlap in estimation.
[2] Includes visits at areas managed and reported by other Federal agencies at Corps and Reclamation projects.
[3] Includes Federal and other public impoundments at which Forest Service manages recreation areas. Remaining data for Forest Service apply only to Forest Service facilities. The Forest Service administers portions or all recreation at 29 Corps, 26 Reclamation and 96 other public or publicly assisted reservoirs.
[4] Includes only water area of public impoundments. To include all national forest land surrounding such impoundments would add millions of acres.
[5] Estimated by *doubling* visitor days to approximate visits.
[6] Includes 11 Reclamation reservoirs and one reservoir of the International Boundary Commission.
[7] Includes portions of 14 Corps, 17 Reclamation, and two TVA reservoirs.
[8] For 1971.
[9] There are 6,350 federally assisted reservoirs under the SCS small watershed program, but only 111 have Federal recreation cost-sharing. In addition, 186 have been authorized, but not constructed, with recreation to be included.
[10] Includes recreation component of structures.
[11] Recreation improvements and fees handled wholly by local public sponsors.
[12] Data for one included in National Park Service estimates. Recreation on the other is handled by State of Texas and thus omitted.

pay one-half the separable costs allocated to recreation, and all the maintenance, operation and replacement recreation costs for projects authorized after July 9, 1965; (2) lacking such agreement at the time of authorization, the Federal agency can build and finance only minimum recreation facilities for health and safety, plus acquire potential recreation land and hold it for 10 years pending negotiation of the required cost-sharing agreement; (3) at the end of 10 years and still lacking such agreement, the acquired land must be disposed of. In addition, Section 7, which applies to Reclamation, and an administrative agreement between the Army and OMB applicable to the Corps, prevent or limit upgrading or new facilities at projects authorized or constructed prior to the Federal Water Project Recreation Act.

Of 101 Corps projects authorized since enactment of the Act, only three have cost-sharing agreements. In 1970, Reclamation had 15 agreements. TVA is exempt.

User Charges: Admission and user fees have been in effect in varying degree at numerous Federal recreation areas at Federal reservoirs since the Land and Water Conservation Fund first took effect in 1965.[234] The fee system under the Fund Act has not worked well. Collections have underrun projections; there has been little consistency between agencies, especially in designating areas and length of charge season; the honor system has failed; there has been no central coordinating authority; collection costs per dollar of receipts have varied greatly between agencies from minimal to equaling or exceeding receipts. Moreover, willingness to try to make a fee system work has varied by agency, and local public opposition to Federal recreation fees has varied.[235]

In general, the fee system since 1965 can be classed as a failure and disappointment. Congress has responded by amending the Fund Act several times, the most recent being P.L. 92-347 of July 11, 1972.[236] Under this Act, admission fees are charged only at designated units of the national park system and national recreation areas administered by the Forest Service, the theory being that admission fees are practical in these instances because of limited access and only a few entrance points.

---

[234] The National Park Service has charged entrance fees for selected units of the national park system for many years.

[235] U.S. DEPARTMENT OF THE INTERIOR (1971). Federal Recreation Fees. Volume II. A report to the Congress by the Secretary of the Interior. 121 pp., illus.

[236] *Act of July 11, 1972* 86 Stat. 459, 16 USCA 4601-6a.

Otherwise, Congress has provided only for a user fee system applicable to all Federal agencies providing specialized recreation sites, facilities, or services. Each agency, however, prescribes its own rules and regulations. This leaves uncoordinated the designation of areas and length of charge season.

Agencies are directed in the Act to consider several criteria in establishing fees: (1) direct and indirect cost to the government; (2) benefits to the recipient; (3) the public policy or interest served; (4) the comparable recreation fees charged by non-Federal public agencies; (5) the economic and administrative feasibility of fee collection; and (6) other pertinent factors. Relation of fees to operation and maintenance (O&M) costs is omitted, as is comparability with private fees for comparable facilities. The latter was rejected on the grounds that it would enable private commercial recreation operators to control the Federal fee structure.

In 1972, user charges collected for the use of special services at Federal reservoirs averaged only about 7 percent of the O&M costs charged to recreation, summarized below from Table 5-14.

Agency	User Fees (thousand $)	Operation & Maintenance (thousand $)
Corps of Engineers	400	15,000
Forest Service	1,589	7,439
Reclamation	250	5,550
Bureau Sport-Fisheries & Wildlife	106	1,358
National Park Service	261	7,145
Tennessee Valley Authority	127	1,991
Soil Conservation Service	0	0
Total	2,733	38,483

There are numerous reasons for the inability of agencies to collect a larger percentage of O&M costs, including relatively few areas designated for fee collection, shortness of season, and the cost of collecting fees at a large number of access ports. The figures suggest that the agencies' estimates of visitor days of use of recreation facilities must be vastly overstated, or it would be possible to collect a larger percentage of the costs.

Financing Recreational Development: Funds for recreational development of Federal reservoirs seem

194

generally to be inadequate to develop the full potential. Low priority attaches to recreation within the construction agencies themselves, the Office of Management and Budget (OMB) and, to a lesser extent, the Congress. At top levels within the agencies, requests for funds for recreation rather than for other programs are often cut to bring total agency budget requests within prescribed ceilings.

Requests often are cut again at the OMB level. OMB seems to take the general position that the Corps, Reclamation, and TVA are not recreation resource management agencies, and consequently believes that as much recreation as possible at their reservoirs should be handled by non-Federal public bodies, private concessionaires, or recognized Federal recreation resource management agencies such as the Forest Service and National Park Service.

The Corps has the greatest need for additional funds for recreation development, assuming 100 new reservoirs will be added to its system within the next 10 years. Presently, 390 are operative and 598 are authorized. All come under the Federal Water Project Recreation Act by law or administrative interpretation. The following tabulation shows 1970 Corps expenditures for recreation, contrasted to the average annual expenditures estimated by some recreation experts as needed to adequately provide for recreation over the next 10 years assuming development at all reservoirs:

Item	1970 Expenditure (million $)	Average Annual Needs Next 10 Years (million $)
Construction	21.0	50.0
Postconstruction development at existing reservoirs	6.5	100.0
Operation and Maintenance	13.2	50.0
Total	40.7	200.0

Reclamation is estimated to need a fivefold increase in capital improvement expenditures, a sixfold increase in operation and maintenance expenditures, and about $20 million for additional land acquisition.

Cost-sharing for Recreation: The cost-sharing provisions of the Federal Water Project Recreation Act affect only the Corps and Reclamation. TVA, the SCS small watershed program, national recreation areas, national forests, and Federal lands classified for retention in Federal ownership are exempted. The philosophy behind the provisions is to require both local administration and cost-sharing by local public bodies for recreational facilities considered local in character.

Reluctance of State and local bodies to share in Federal reservoir recreation costs is due to Federal agency control, shortage of local financial resources for recreation purposes, distortion of local recreational programs which can be caused by financing such major projects as those of the Corps, reluctance of local bodies to finance recreation for use by people outside their respective taxing jurisdictions, a desire to have projects taken over by exempted Federal agencies such as the Forest Service, unwillingness to spend local money on Federal land that must remain in Federal ownership, and, of course, to the fact that Federal reservoirs are not always prime recreational assets. Many local agencies also know that a major attraction of the Federal reservoirs is the fishing potential, which is usually extremely good immediately after the reservoir is first filled because of the large amount of nutrient provided by decaying vegetation covered by the water. Often, after a period of years the fishing potential drops rather dramatically and if a new reservoir is built in the vicinity many of the fishermen will transfer their activities to the new site.

Deficiencies in Administration: The construction agencies basically are just that—construction-oriented. There are a few competent and dedicated resource or recreation-management personnel, but they have little influence on policy and do not occupy the top positions. Fundamentally, these construction agencies are managers of neither people nor resources, both of which are essential ingredients of successful recreation administration.

Within the Corps, for example, several basic management problems are apparent, including inadequate recreation planning and inadequate coordination between construction and land acquisition; lax administration of existing facilities; inadequate facilities, lack of interpretive facilities, and lax enforcement of regulations.[237]

[237] CRAFTS, Edward C (1970). How to Meet Public Recreation Needs at Corps of Engineers Reservoirs, prepared for Corps of Engineers contract DACW 73-70-C-0038. The Corps, Washington, D.C.

Land Management Agencies

The three main land management agencies involved in recreation management at Federal reservoirs—namely, the Forest Service, Bureau of Sport Fisheries and Wildlife, and National Park Service—become involved because some reservoirs occur wholly or partly within lands under their administration, and they are requested to assume recreation responsibilities by the reservoir agencies under standing memoranda of agreement, or they are assigned such responsibilities by Congress if lands surrounding a reservoir are declared to be a national recreation area. The Forest Service is the most deeply involved in terms of number of reservoirs, water area, visitations, maintenance and operation, and fee collections (Table 5-14). The National Park Service exceeds in terms of recent capital improvements.

The following summarizes the number of construction agency reservoirs administered in whole or in part by the land agencies:

Administering Agency	Construction Agency			
	Corps of Engineers	Bureau of Reclamation	Tenn. Valley Auth.	Inter- national Boundary Comm.
Forest Service	29	26	-	-
National Park Service	1	10	-	1
Bureau of Sport Fisheries & Wildlife	14	17	2	-
Total	44	53	2	1

In addition, the Forest Service administers recreation at 87 State and local, eight SCS, one Bureau of Indian Affairs, and a number of small private reservoirs in the national forests. About 15 percent of total national forest recreation use is reservoir-oriented; about 50 percent is water-oriented.

Recreation reservoir problems of land agencies are minor compared to those of the construction agencies because: (1) recreation is recognized as a primary high-priority function of the land agencies, not only by the agencies themselves, but also by OMB and Congress· (2) the land agencies are better staffed with recreation resource professionals, some of whom occupy key policy positions in the agencies; (3)

budgeting for recreation receives high priority; (4) legislative authorities are generally adequate; (5) cost-sharing requirements are less troublesome because they enjoy congressional recognition of being "national" in purpose; (6) recreation funding generally is more adequate; and (7) the land agencies have a more receptive philosophy on recreation fees and apply them more successfully.

The Soil Conservation Service (SCS) merits brief special mention. Basically, it is a land conservation agency; but in connection with the P.L. 566 program[238] it is also a reservoir construction agency. There are 1,067 SCS projects containing 6,350 reservoirs, averaging 10 acres of water surface and 27 acres of land and water each.

P.L. 566 reservoirs are not included generally in the term "Federal Reservoirs." They occupy a special category of "Federally Assisted Reservoirs," even though Federal dollars may pay all construction costs allocated to flood prevention. Projects must be sponsored by a local public body, usually a conservation district which obtains title or easement to the land, owns the structure, and operates the project. Not more than 50 percent of the costs of dam construction, basic facilities, or land rights allocated to public recreation can be federally borne. If there is Federal assistance for recreation facilities, public access must be provided.[239] All recreation O&M costs and fees, if any, are handled by the local sponsor.

Despite the small size of the SCS reservoirs, this reservoir system holds substantial public recreation potential. Only 111 or about 2 percent of the 6,350 P.L. 566 reservoirs have received Federal recreation funds. One difficulty is that private landowners, who may have given the local sponsors an easement for the reservoir, may not want the public crossing their land;

[238] P.L. 566, August 4, 1954, 83d Congress, 68 Stat. 666, as amended, 16 USCA 1001-1008.

[239] U.S. SOIL CONSERVATION SERVICE (January 1972). Multiple-Purpose Watershed Projects Under Public Law 566. PA-575. U.S. Government Printing Office, Washington, D.C.

NATIONAL ASSOCIATION OF SOIL AND WATER CONSERVATION DISTRICTS, now the National Association of Conservation Districts (undated). Accelerating America's Watershed Program. National Association of Soil and Water Conservation Districts, Washington, D.C.

U.S. SOIL CONSERVATION SERVICE (April 7, 1972). Public Access at Reservoir Sites in PL-566, Flood Prevention, and RC&D Projects. Watersheds MEMORANDUM-119; Resource Conservation & Development Memorandum-10.

such permission is a necessary prerequisite to obtaining Federal assistance in recreation.

House Report 92-586 of October 12, 1971, by the Government Operations Committee, dealing with public access to reservoirs to meet growing recreation needs concluded: (a) thousands of reservoir lakes in upper watershed projects financed by the SCS have substantial recreational potential; (b) the SCS has failed to provide land rights to insure public recreation access, discourages public recreational use of such reservoir lakes, and thus is in violation of the national outdoor recreation policy of P.L. 88-29; (c) P.L. 566, as amended, provides adequate authority to require sponsoring local organizations to provide public access at reservoir lakes financed by SCS which have . . . recreational values; and (d) SCS has failed to apply its nondiscrimination regulations to recreational developments added by private land developers at SCS reservoir lakes.[240]

Islands for Recreation

One glaring omission in water-based recreation legislation is lack of authorization to recognize unique recreation and environmental values offered by the Nation's islands. There are 20,700 coastal and inland islands 10 acres or larger covering 7.7 million acres within the 48 contiguous States and the outer islands of Hawaii, Puerto Rico, and the Virgin Islands, excluding the three New York islands (Manhattan, Staten, and Long). In addition, Alaska alone has 5,700 more islands covering 21.1 million acres.[241]

DISCUSSION

The background on recreation at Federal water projects poses a number of difficult questions. Among these are questions such as: "Why have local interests not participated in the cost-sharing opportunities under Public Law 88-29?" "What is needed to make user fee collections more nearly equivalent to operation and maintenance costs of the recreational facilities?" "How can one decide which Federal reservoirs should be developed for recreational purposes?"

It seems plausible to start with the premise that the recreational potential of the various Federal reservoirs is not equal. Some reservoirs are unsuited for recreation because of large drawdowns, poor accessibility, lack of local demand, and unfavorable topographic situations at the reservoir site. Some reservoirs are located in areas where water recreational opportunities are scarce, others are located where such opportunities are abundant. One reason for lack of response of local entities to the cost-sharing opportunities of Federal reservoirs is undoubtedly the fact that they have more attractive recreational opportunities to develop with their money. What is clearly needed is a rational basis for decision as to which reservoirs offer important recreational potentials which should be captured.

A further clear difficulty in the planning and management of recreational facilities at Federal reservoirs is the lack of adequately qualified recreational personnel in the offices of the construction agencies.

The development of recreational potential of Federal reservoirs could probably be considerably enhanced if each construction agency would develop a well informed and adequate staff, perhaps located at a central office, but available to all field offices for planning in connection with those reservoirs considered to be important recreational possibilities. It would be the function of this staff to decide which reservoirs are of high potential, what land acquisition is required at these reservoirs, what facilities are needed, and what management capability is necessary to achieve the benefits of the reservoir.

Under restrictive land acquistion and generous public land disposal policies of the past, adequate land for public recreation access or development is frequently unavailable except when reservoirs are located within Federal land reservations. The Federal Water Project Recreation Act also includes certain land acquisition restrictions.

Under Executive Order No. 11508, the General Services Administration is surveying all Federal real estate and reporting as excess, property it judges to be underutilized or unutilized.[242] Lands of the National Park Service, Forest Service, and Bureau of Land Management are exempt. This Executive Order could well be amended to exclude potential recreation development or access sites bordering Federal reservoirs based on careful studies by the recreation

[240] U.S. CONGRESS, House, Committee on Government Operations (1971). Public Access to Reservoirs to Meet Growing Recreation Demands, House Report No. 92-586, 92d Congress, 1st Session. U.S. Government Printing Office, Washington, D.C.

[241] CRAFTS, EC (December 1970). Islands in time. American Forests 76(12):15-19, 54-58; U.S. BUREAU OF OUTDOOR RECREATION (1970). Islands of America. 95 pp. illus.

[242] Providing for the identification of unneeded Federal real property. Federal Register 35(30):2855. February 12, 1970.

planners indicating those lands which are of high potential for recreation.

The whole problem of recreation at the Federal reservoirs is further confounded by inadequacies of data. Federal agencies claim a total annual visitation of over 400 million, which represents on the average two visits for every citizen in the United States each year. If the number were accurate and a user charge could be collected for every visit, a charge of 10 cents per visitor would cover the present operation and maintenance cost for recreation facilities at all Federal reservoirs. Obviously, the figure must be in error but the reasons for this are unknown. It is probably the compounding of estimates from a large number of sources that leads to this extraordinarily high number.

This compounding of error in the estimates of recreational use has another impact on Federal reservoirs in the planning phase. It seems entirely possible that the estimates for Federal reservoir recreational use made during the planning stages are excessive except possibly for the most attractive reservoirs. This leads to excessive expectations of recreational use on many reservoirs and leads to the conclusion that lack of interest in some Federal reservoirs is the result of some fault in the system, whereas in fact it may simply be a result of overexpectations. Clearly, it is necessary that a program of adequate data collection be instituted so that the number of visitations at existing reservoirs is accurately known, and the nature of the visitation is adequately defined. It is important to know whether a visitor is merely driving past a reservoir because it happens to be on the route which he is following to some other destination, whether the visitors are from local sources coming for a few hours for picnicking and fishing, or whether the visitors are campers planning to stay for several days or more. It would appear appropriate to suggest that the Bureau of Outdoor Recreation be instructed to develop procedures to provide adequate and consistent data on recreational use of Federal reservoirs and that these procedures be employed by all Federal agencies.

Even though estimates of visitation of Federal reservoirs may be high, there seems little reason to believe that it would not be possible to collect user fees sufficient to meet O&M expenses and quite possibly to cover some of the capital investment costs of recreation facilities. What appears to be needed is careful planning of recreational facilities and access roads so that the collection can be achieved efficiently, and adequate staffing of the recreational facilities so that there is manpower to collect the fees at least during those periods of the year when the use is high enough to warrant the effort. Finally, of course, a reasonable and equitable scale of fees needs to be established for each facility. Use of launching ramps, picnic areas, and campgrounds should certainly be susceptible to fee collection. Where marinas are provided, rental rates for marina mooring should be adequate to cover the costs incurred in providing the mooring. There are a relatively large number of private recreational enterprises in the United States which apparently are able to make a financial success of their operation on the basis of user fees, and the statistics on reservoir-based recreation suggest that operation and maintenance expenses can at least be recovered by appropriate fees at Federal projects. Here again, however, the construction agencies need adequate staff for proper planning of the recreational facilities and sufficient funding to provide the necessary staff for maintenance and regulation of facility use and collection of user fees. Thus, some initial pump priming may be necessary by the Congress in order to get the recreational program off dead center.

CONCLUSIONS

Outdoor recreation in general and water-based recreation in particular have become major national economic and social activities. Water is an important outdoor recreation resource and is the focal point of half or more of all outdoor recreation. Recreation is becoming a progessively more important service which water provides for people. Although some Federal reservoirs are even more intensively used by recreationists on peak user days than many national parks, the 56,000 miles of shoreline in Federal reservoirs possess substantial undeveloped recreation potential which should be developed for public recreation use.

Some Federal impoundments are overused and others underdeveloped with respect to water-based recreation. Some are either close to population centers or in arid areas where natural water resources are scarce. Not all Federal reservoirs, however, are ideal recreational sites because of topography, location, drawdowns, and other problems. What is urgently needed is a careful assessment of existing and proposed reservoirs to identify those which are prime recreational sites and a program of achieving the necessary recreational development at these prime sites.

Congress, especially during the last decade, has declared a national policy and enacted a strong legislative base for outdoor recreation, about half of which is water-oriented. In addition, through numerous acts, Congress has directed special attention to recreation at Federal and federally assisted reservoirs. The Commission endorses the present policies of Federal outdoor recreation investment in projects related to reservoirs and other water bodies.

The Secretary of the Interior should utilize to the fullest his authorities in P.L. 88-29 to provide technical assistance to the private sector, particularly in developing water-based recreation facilities.

The problems of the Federal agencies concerned with the development of recreation at Federal reservoirs appear to result largely from inadequate staff with the proper expertise to develop good recreational plans at existing or proposed reservoirs. This shortage is made worse because efforts are dispersed over all reservoirs rather than over those reservoirs which show the highest recreation potential. Finally, there is inadequate staff on site for management of the facilities, collection of user fees, and other necessary on-site functions.

RECOMMENDATIONS

5-34. Each construction agency should develop a central staff with the necessary expertise in recreation planning. This staff should be responsible for deciding which Federal reservoirs have important recreational potential deserving of development and should provide the plans necessary for effective development and management of these sites.

5-35. For those reservoirs considered to be prime recreational sites the construction agencies should procure the necessary recreational lands as part of the overall land acquisition program.

5-36. Executive Order No. 11508 should be amended to exclude from declaration as excess, lands at Federal reservoirs which have potential for recreation development or access sites within 20 years. Construction agencies should be authorized and funds provided them not only to retain such land as now owned, but also to acquire additional land as needed if such land meets the criterion of potential value for recreation within a 20-year period. Such lands should be classified for retention in Federal ownership.

5-37. Recreation admission and user fees should be charged at all Federal reservoirs where revenues can be expected to exceed the costs of collection. In addition to implementing the criteria already enacted into law with respect to admission and recreation use fees, charges should be related to fees charged for nearby comparable private facilities and to that portion of operation and maintenance costs attributable to the specialized facility for which a user fee is assessed with the objective of having the amount collected from fees equal the O&M cost for that particular facility.

5-38. The Bureau of Outdoor Recreation should devise a system of data collection which will provide accurate information on visitation at existing reservoirs and on the nature and purpose of these visits. The system should be used by all agencies managing recreation facilities at reservoirs and should be designed to provide a base which can be useful in estimating recreation requirements and benefits of future reservoirs.

5-39. In evaluating the recreational benefits of proposed reservoirs full consideration should be given to the recreational opportunities in free-stream fishing, white water boating, and other benefits foregone if the reservoir is constructed. The Nation should match its program of reservoir construction with a program of stream protection for the purpose of obtaining an effective mix of water-based recreational opportunity.

5-40. Those agencies responsible for the administration of recreational facilities at existing Federal reservoirs should make a careful study of the financing required to place these facilities in proper condition, and to staff the project with the people necessary to properly manage, maintain, and collect user fees at these sites.

5-41. A national policy to protect and manage islands or portions thereof which possess unique environmental and recreational values should be developed. Legislation should be enacted to create a national system of Federal and State islands to supplement other national and State conservation systems of parks, forests, recreation areas, wild and scenic rivers, trails, seashores, lakeshores, and wilderness areas. Financing of such a system should be authorized under the Land and Water Conservation Fund Act.

Improving Federal Water Programs from the Standpoint of Fish and Wildlife

There is widespread public awareness of the importance of fish and wildlife values, and the vital role which fresh and marine waters play in providing habitat and sustaining desired levels of wildlife populations. Developments which cause water quality to deteriorate or which drain, dredge, or otherwise alter habitat and feeding and spawning areas have resulted in substantial damage to the Nation's fish and wildlife resources.

In years past, water development projects and water-related activities, on both State and Federal levels, often went forward with little regard for the damage caused to fish and wildlife resources. Thousands of miles of natural stream channels were relocated or altered; some streams were dried up; estuaries and marshes suffered from drainage and landfill operations; and estuarine habitat essential for shellfish and other species was destroyed by dredging and channel deepening. Water quality deterioration and water temperature alteration have also adversely affected fish and wildlife resources in both marine and fresh waters.

The basic need, in the view of the Commission, is to assure that fish and wildlife values receive full consideration and reasonable protection in all water resource activities where potential damage to those values could occur. There is an important distinction between the damage already sustained by fish and wildlife values, populations, and habitat, and the adequacy of present legislation to prevent further damages under future projects. In many instances, past damage cannot be repaired; in some instances, such as in the improvement of water quality, it can.[243] The most important problem, however, is one of examining Federal and State legislation to determine whether there are sufficient statutory safeguards to assure that future projects affecting water will not be constructed until there has been a fair and adequate consideration of the fish and wildlife resource. The problem is to establish whether or not there is adequate legislation available to insure that unreasonable or unnecessary damage from careless assessment or reckless disregard be avoided.

DISCUSSION

Federal legislation requires that fish and wildlife values must be considered in advance of any water project construction licensed or funded by the Federal Government. The Fish and Wildlife Coordination Act now requires that fish and wildlife receive "equal consideration" with other project purposes, provides for enhancing these values where possible, and authorizes compensatory wildlife features where some damage is inevitable.[244]

Most Federal agencies with water project responsibilities are covered by the Coordination Act (the Tennessee Valley Authority is specifically exempted). Moreover, all Federal agencies and licensees of the Government are within the purview of the National Environmental Policy Act (NEPA) which requires that an environmental impact study be made and a statement filed with the U.S. Council on Environmental Quality (CEQ) before projects are constructed.[245] Since fish and wildlife values are part of the environmental considerations, they must be evaluated in the required impact statement, and alternative proposals must be considered, including the alternative of not building a project at all.

Since NEPA was enacted only 3 years ago, and since some litigation is still pending to seek clarification of the full range of the Act, it is too early to tell what the shortcomings, if any, of that Act might be with respect to fish and wildlife resources. To the extent that the Act might require amendment, that determination can best be made in light of further judicial interpretation, in the experience of agencies in complying with it, and in the evaluation by the body politic of the extent to which the Act achieves its purposes in ways which are acceptable to society.

There are, however, many activities which affect waters important to fish and wildlife but which are

---

[243] See Chapter 4 for the Commission's views on water pollution control.

[244] *Fish and Wildlife Coordination Act*, P.L. 85-624, August 12, 1958, 72 Stat. 563, as amended, 16 USCA 661 *et seq.*

[245] *National Environmental Policy Act of 1969*, P.L. 91-190, January 1, 1970, 83 Stat. 852, 42 USCA 4321 *et seq.*

Ducks find nesting place in Shawnee National Forest, Illinois

beyond the reach of the Coordination Act and NEPA. Among these are non-Federal activities with respect to non-navigable inland waters. Fish and wildlife values are vulnerable, at least from the standpoint of Federal protection, in non-navigable waters to the extent that water-related activities are conducted by those who are not required to obtain Federal licenses or permits. As an illustration, dredging and channel alteration is controlled through permits issued by the U.S. Army Corps of Engineers, but those permits are only required when the waters are navigable in interstate or foreign commerce, and no application for the Corps permit need be filed for those activities in other inland waters. The channel improvement work under way in those waters with the assistance of the Soil Conservation Service is under attack by environmental interests as a "channelization" program that results in major damages to the fish and wildlife resources.

Since the States historically have been viewed as having regulatory jurisdiction over waters which are not navigable in interstate or foreign commerce, the Commission believes that the States should enact statutes which would provide adequate measures of protection to fish and wildlife values. Some States have already accomplished this, but many have not.

CONCLUSIONS

Fish and wildlife values have suffered damage as a result of water-related activities. The present protections afforded by the Fish and Wildlife Coordination Act and the National Environmental Policy Act seem to be adequate to prevent unreasonable or unnecessary damage to these resources under future projects constructed or licensed by the Federal Government. While there has been some complaint that fish and wildlife interests have not been considered at the initial stages of water project planning, the Coordination Act requires those values to be considered as part of the planning process. Failure to treat fish and wildlife on an equal basis with other project purposes is violative of that Act. Moreover, the U.S. Water Resources Council is in a position to require coordinated planning of fish and wildlife interests along with other project purposes in the river basin planning program conducted under the Water Resources Planning Act.

The Commission believes that joint participation of fish and wildlife agencies in project planning should begin at the initial stages of such planning; fish and wildlife agencies should not have to react to initial design plans of projects already formulated but rather should sit in on the initial development of those plans at the inception of project planning. This is what the Coordination Act requires and is the direction in which joint planning has been moving. The Coordination Act already provides that fish and wildlife be made a project purpose and planning objective the same as all other purposes and objectives. The Commission believes that this kind of coordinated planning, with early and active fish and wildlife agency participation, should be continued and, if necessary, strengthened. Without passing judgment on the validity of complaints that fish and wildlife have not been considered at the early stages of project planning, the Commission believes that the Water Resources Council should be able to require that the intent of the Coordination Act is satisfied in the planning undertaken under the aegis of the Council.

The Commission does not believe that final plans for a Federal water project which do not meet with the enthusiastic endorsement of fish and wildlife interests are necessarily inappropriate or that fish and wildlife purposes have perforce been inadequately taken into account. There will be occasions where conflicting views will not be susceptible to reconciliation, where the position of one interest will be irreconcilably at odds with that of another. No amount of legislation can compel enthusiastic acceptance of project plans by fish and wildlife interests when they believe such plans to be defective. What is required is the mechanism to assure fair and honest consideration of all views and all project purposes on a fully participating and coordinated basis. Where disagreements cannot be satisfactorily resolved, the conflicting viewpoints should be transmitted to the Congress for resolution at the time the project is being considered for authorization. The Commission believes that the Water Resources Council has an important supervisory and coordination role to play in this arena. Not only must it insure that fish and wildlife receive proper attention along with other project purposes at the time of project plan formulation, but it can act as a mediator to help resolve opposing views before conflicts are put before Congress.

Much of the controversy over fish and wildlife problems associated with proposed water projects and water-related activities stems from insufficient knowledge about the prospects for damage from such projects and activities. Too little is known. Fish and wildlife interests are understandably reluctant to endorse project plans when there is doubt about the impact of the proposed project upon fish and wildlife values. Where such doubts exist, it is the natural inclination of fish and wildlife interests to resolve the uncertainties in favor of opposition to projects. An obvious way to reduce doubts and permit everyone to proceed with greater assurance and certainty is to gain additional knowledge. This can best be done through carefully designed research into the impact of projects and water-related activities upon fish and wildlife values.

Some water-related activities are beyond the coverage of the Fish and Wildlife Coordination Act and NEPA, particularly non-Federal projects on non-navigable inland waters. Since the States have jurisdiction over these waters, adequate measures to protect fish and wildlife should be provided by State statutes to fill this void where it is not already filled.

RECOMMENDATIONS

5-42. The Fish and Wildlife Coordination Act requires that fish and wildlife conservation receive equal consideration and be coordinated with other features of water resource development programs. To the extent that observance of this statutory requirement is breached, the Coordination Act should be more rigorously applied. The Water Resources Council should supervise and coordinate Federal water project planning to assure that fish and wildlife values receive equal consideration with other project purposes, as required by the Coordination Act.

5-43. More research should be undertaken to resolve uncertainties about the prospective impacts of water resources projects upon fish and wildlife values. Systematic pre- and post-construction assessment of the impact of federally funded or licensed projects upon fish and wildlife and the efficacy of protection facilities should be undertaken in order to displace conjecture with well-documented facts.

5-44. On nonnavigable inland waters, where many activities such as dredging and channel alteration are beyond the scope of Federal law, the States should provide statutory protection for fish and wildlife values. In particular, State statutes should provide that fish and wildlife be made a project purpose and receive equal consideration with other project purposes, comparable to the provisions of the Fish and Wildlife Coordination Act applicable to Federal projects.

Chapter 6

Procedures for Resolving Differences Over Environmental and Developmental Values[1]

The general subject of the needs and mechanisms for balancing developmental and environmental values pervades discussion of the Nation's water policies. Every proposed water project or use, public or private, has an impact upon the environment and raises a series of questions such as:

— What are the important environmental values involved?
— What are the important values associated with development?
— Is there an accommodation which will produce the values associated with development while protecting the values associated with the natural environment?
— If not, what balance among competing values will best serve the public interest?

These questions are addressed throughout the Commission's report. This chapter focuses on procedures for accommodating important developmental and environmental values where possible, and where it is not possible, procedures for resolving issues among the conflicting values with respect to Federal water resources projects and non-Federal water-related projects which require a Federal license or

permit. The basic question addressed here is this: What procedures can be used to identify important environmental and developmental values and limitations—to give them proper weight, so as to reach a sound accommodation of values or a balance among them—without an unacceptable cost in delay and frustration of needed projects?

THE PROBLEM

The Nation's record of taking ecological processes and environmental values into account in water development and use has been unsatisfactory.[2] While a number of projects have been planned and executed with a careful regard for environmental values, a significant number—including both governmental projects and nongovernmental projects which require licenses or permits—have not been. Too many of these projects have caused unnecessary damage, leaving the Nation environmentally poorer. Furthermore, in some cases, of which the Cross-Florida Barge Canal is an extreme but graphic example, the cost of modifying or abandoning a project to mitigate unacceptable environmental damage has resulted in a financial loss as well.

Chapter 2 points out that the Nation cannot afford to build or sanction water projects without taking environmental concerns fully into account. However, as that and other chapters affirm, water projects can offer a number of economic and social benefits. The Commission believes that careful planning frequently can accommodate important developmental and environmental values into a harmonious solution. However, where the values necessarily conflict, the Nation needs procedures for striking a balance which best serves the public interest fairly and promptly in order to avoid the social, economic, and environmental costs which attend delay in reaching needed decisions.

[1] The background studies for this chapter are GOLDMAN, Charles R (1971). Environmental Quality and Water Development, prepared for the National Water Commission. National Technical Information Service, Springfield, Va., Accession Nos. PB 207 113 & 207 114, and HILLHOUSE, William A II & DeWEERDT, John L (1972). Legal Devices for Accommodating Water Resources Development and Environmental Values, prepared for the National Water Commission. National Technical Information Service, Springfield, Va., Accession No. PB 208 835.

America's environmental values are threatened by increased development

[2] See Chapters 2 and 4 of this report.

The primary legislative response thus far has been the National Environmental Policy Act (NEPA).[3] The Commission considers an institutional arrangement a good one if it develops the information which a politically responsible decisionmaker needs to make a full, fair, and expeditious evaluation of relevant issues and to strike an appropriate balance among the relevant factors. Judged in this light, NEPA is a major breakthrough. It requires consideration of environmental as well as developmental values and puts this burden initially upon the project or licensing agency. NEPA requires the utilization of expert advice from other agencies, accommodation of public views, and consideration of alternatives. It is designed (1) to make agencies more sensitive toward environmental values and the need for an appropriate balancing of values, in the early stages of the planning process, and (2) to develop useful information on all relevant factors for the ultimate decisionmaker.[4]

The Commission applauds the thrust of these requirements which should help produce soundly conceived projects, especially in the long run. NEPA does much to meet previous deficiencies in taking environmental values into account. The Commission recommends hereafter some additional measures, supplementing NEPA, to improve this process further.

Certain requirements of NEPA are adding significantly to delays before there is a final decision whether a project may proceed.[5] Delays at any point before a project is put into operation can be costly. The Commission recognizes the value of time spent in careful project formulation and evaluation; this is essential if the Nation is to have sound water projects and to avoid unsound ones. The source of concern is nonproductive delays, particularly at later stages of project evolution, which might be avoided with improved procedures.

The timing of a delay is frequently critical. For example, delay when a project is under construction

or delay which blocks the operation of a completed project can be especially serious. When the public interest requires some decision on a particular project, such as an industrial installation or a water supply project, and the expeditious pursuit of alternatives if the project is unacceptable, unexpected or an unexpectedly prolonged delay is disruptive. This type of crisis situation, irritated by delay, may encourage unsound decisions, simply to resolve the matter and end the delay.

Environmental review is not the only culprit in instances of delay.[6] Furthermore, NEPA is a new statute and the problems of devising appropriate procedures to comply with it may be transitional. The threat of litigation has encouraged agencies to act, so that the long-term effect should be better procedures and better projects, which should not be subject to all of the delays attending projects which have not taken environmental processes and values adequately into account.

The Commission is concerned that present arrangements for environmental review under NEPA and other statutes present inherent possibilities for delay which, in instances of critical timing, may be unacceptable. Accordingly, the Commission recommends certain new procedures to expedite environmental review.

BACKGROUND

Requirements for environmental review apply to nearly all water-related projects and uses. However, the impact of these requirements has fallen most strikingly upon Federal public works projects, several of which have been enjoined in court for failure to

---

[3] P.L. 91-190, January 1, 1970, 83 Stat. 852, 42 USCA 4321-47.

[4] See generally, HILLHOUSE, William A II & DeWEERDT, John L (1972). Legal Devices for Accommodating Water Resources Development and Environmental Values, prepared for the National Water Commission. National Technical Information Service, Springfield, Va., Accession No. PB 208 835, Ch. 2. For a summary of needed improvements in impact analysis see GOLDMAN, Charles R (1971). Environmental Quality and Water Development, prepared for the National Water Commission. National Technical Information Service, Springfield, Va., Accession No. PB 207 113. Summary, pp. 16-17.

[5] See, e.g., letters to the Council on Environmental Quality, from the Tennessee Valley Authority (April 5, 1972), the Soil Conservation Service (April 11, 1972), the Corps of Engineers (April 12, 1972), the Atomic Energy Commission (April 13, 1972), and the Federal Power Commission (April 21, 1972), responding to Russell Train's request that the agencies identify delays resulting from compliance with NEPA. The letters are published in U.S. CONGRESS, Senate (1972). Joint Hearings before the Committee on Public Works and The Committee on Interior and Insular Affairs, United States Senate, 92d Congress, 2d Session, on the Operation of the National Environmental Policy Act of 1969, Serial No. 92-H32. U.S. Government Printing Office, Washington, D.C.

[6] See, e.g., statement of John N. Nassikas, Chairman, Federal Power Commission, before the Senate Committee on Commerce, June 1, 1972. Appendix CC states that nearly three-fourths of the large fossil-fueled and nuclear electric plants installed 1966-71 were delayed, but that labor-related and equipment problems caused the majority of these delays.

comply with statutes,[7] and upon private projects which require several licenses or permits before they may proceed.

Non-Federal Projects Requiring Licenses

Because of the multiple points at which some governmental approval is required, private projects must run a gauntlet of environmental reviews, and therefore provide a good vehicle for discussion of current environmental requirements, the benefits and delays which these requirements may cause, and recommendations for change. The following discussion uses electric powerplants as a primary example, since they are subject to regulation at multiple levels of government, raise obvious environmental issues with respect to their location and operation, and have excited a great deal of public controversy. However, other types of private, water-related developments face comparable environmental regulation and raise the same kinds of issues.

An electric utility, applying for the necessary licenses and permits to construct and operate a large powerplant, may expect to have repeated environmental reviews of different aspects of its proposed plant. Overall, the process is often uncoordinated, overlapping, and noncomprehensive.

State and Local Requirements: NEPA applies only to actions of the Federal Government. However, a range of State, regional, and local agencies may impose requirements of their own for powerplant siting. It would be misleading to suggest that each of these agencies imposes environmental requirements, but many do. It also would be misleading to suggest that obtaining a permit poses a problem in each case, but where a utility must have all of such permits, a single denial may frustrate the project. This situation may encourage opponents of a project to fight it in every possible forum, raising some issues repeatedly.

Significantly, present arrangements do not guarantee that environmental values will be systematically and carefully considered. Most States do not provide a comprehensive review of the effects of a proposed powerplant site on air, land, and water; or evaluate the relative environmental impact of alternative sites.[8]

Consideration of Water Quality: The Federal Water Pollution Control Act Amendments of 1972 require State or Federal discharge permits, limiting the composition of the effluent which an entity may discharge, if any. Such permits may issue only after an opportunity for public hearing and are to be based upon guidelines developed by the Environmental Protection Agency.[9] In addition, if there is any discharge into navigable waters, the State must certify that the discharge will comply with the effluent limitations and other standards required under the Federal Water Pollution Control Act Amendments of 1972 before a Federal license or permit to construct or operate facilities may issue.[10]

Calvert Cliffs Coordinating Committee v. AEC,[11] interpreting NEPA prior to the passage of these Amendments, had required the Atomic Energy Commission (AEC) to give independent consideration to stringent discharge limitations even though a State had certified that its water quality standards would be met by the proposed operation. The 1972 Amendments now provide that NEPA shall not be interpreted to authorize a licensing agency to review effluent limitations established under the new Act or to impose different effluent limitations as a prerequisite to the issuance of a license.[12]

The 1972 Amendments also provide that unless a new source of discharge is involved, the Environmental Protection Agency need not file an environmental impact statement before a discharge permit is issued.[13] This provision appears to be directed at the decision in *Kalur v. Resor*,[14] which held that NEPA

---

[8] See Summary of NARUC Questionnaire in Appendix E, in Statement of John N. Nassikas, Chairman, Federal Power Commission, before Senate Committee on Commerce, June 1, 1972.

[9] P.L. 92-500, Section 402, October 18, 1972, 86 Stat. 816, 880, 33 USCA 1342.

[10] *Ibid.*, Section 401, 86 Stat. 877, 33 USCA 1341.

[11] 449 F.2d 1109 (D.C. Cir. 1971).

[12] *Federal Water Pollution Control Act Amendments of 1972*, P.L. 92-500, Section 511(c) (2), October 18, 1972, 86 Stat. 816, 893, 33 USCA 1371(c) (2).

[13] *Ibid.*, Section 511(c) (1), 86 Stat. 893, 33 USCA 1371(c) (1).

[14] 335 F.Supp. 1 (D.D.C. 1971).

---

[7] See, *e.g., Environmental Defense Fund v. Corps of Engineers,* 324 F.Supp. 878 (D.D.C. 1971) (Cross-Florida Barge Canal); *Environmental Defense Fund v. Corps of Engineers,* 325 F.Supp. 749 (E.D. Ark. 1971), injunction released after the filing of an adequate environmental impact statement, 342 F.Supp. 1211 (1972) (Gillham Dam); *Environmental Defense Fund v. Tennessee Valley Authority,* 339 F.Supp. 806 (E.D. Tenn. 1972) (Tellico Project); and *Natural Resources Defense Council v. Grant,* 341 F.Supp. 356 (E.D. N.C. 1972) (SCS Chicod Creek Project).

did not exempt the Refuse Act Permit Program[15] from the environmental impact statement requirement, delaying action on the large number of pending discharge permit applications for existing sources.

While the 1972 Amendments deal with some previously existing sources of delay in resolving water quality matters, the new requirements are complex and may present other possibilities for delay. For example, Section 208 of the new Act requires areawide waste management plans for "each area within the State which, as a result of urban-industrial concentrations or other factors, has substantial water quality control problems." These plans, among other things, must provide for a program to regulate "the location, modification, and construction of any facilities within such area which may result in any discharge in such area. . . ." Once the plan has been approved, discharge permits may not be issued for point-sources which are in conflict with it.

Federal Licensing Proceedings: When a utility applies to the Federal Power Commission (FPC) or the Atomic Energy Commission (AEC) for a license to construct a powerplant, it may anticipate that the proceedings will take longer than they would have before enactment of NEPA. At least in the case of the AEC, NEPA has expanded the range of the agency's required environmental considerations before it may issue a license. The AEC must now take environmental values into account, balance the economic and technical benefits of the proposed action against the environmental costs, and consider alternatives which would change the balance of values.

Before the passage of NEPA the Federal Power Act had been interpreted to require broad consideration of environmental values.[16] Now, however, after passage of NEPA, the FPC staff must spend additional time preparing environmental impact statements. This task is complicated by *Greene County Planning Board v. FPC,*[17] which requires the FPC staff to prepare and circulate its own environmental impact statement before the licensing hearing, rather than simply circulating the environmental material submitted by the applicant.

Licensing hearings themselves are time consuming and, with increased public interest in environmental values, applicants may anticipate more contested proceedings and a large number of potential intervenors.

Proceedings before the Atomic Energy Commission involve special problems of delay because the AEC requires an operating license as well as a construction permit. Delay in reaching a decision on the operating license can be costly since if construction is completed the plant would stand idle until the license is issued. In order to minimize delay, the AEC has supported provisions for a fuller consideration of issues at the construction stage, with the operating license hearing limited to changes in technology since construction licensing.[18]

Environmental review presents additional problems for those powerplants which were initiated, but not licensed to operate, before NEPA. *Calvert Cliffs Coordinating Committee v. AEC*[19] held that the AEC must subject these plants to relatively immediate environmental scrutiny and may not delay such review until the utility applies for an operating license. The AEC responded to the *Calvert Cliffs* decision by promulgating regulations which required some immediate review, but permitted a utility to operate a new plant on an interim, partial basis in order to test the facility before the AEC completed a full NEPA review.[20] However, these provisions were struck down as inadequate by a Federal District Court in *Izaak Walton League v. Schlesinger* (the *Quad Cities* case),[21] which held that the AEC should have completed its NEPA review and the environmental impact statement process before it permitted even interim operation. The effect of the decision may have been mitigated by Public Law 92-307, authorizing temporary operating licenses after suffi-

---

[15] See 33 CFR Section 209.131, implementing 33 USCA 401 *et seq.* The Federal Water Pollution Control Act Amendments of 1972 supersede the Refuse Act Permit Program (RAPP), providing that permits under the 1899 Refuse Act shall be treated as permits under the new Act and that pending applications under RAPP shall be treated as applications for discharge permits under Section 402 of the new Act.

[16] See *Udall v. Federal Power Commission*, 387 U.S. 428 (1967).

[17] 455 F.2d 412.

[18] SCHLESINGER, James R, Chairman, U.S. Atomic Energy Commission (1972). Statement, pp. 68-110, in U.S. CONGRESS, Joint Committee on Atomic Energy, H.R. 13731 and H.R. 13732, to Amend the Atomic Energy Act of 1954 Regarding the Licensing of Nuclear Facilities, Part I, Hearings, 92d Congress, 2d Session, U.S. Government Printing Office, Washington, D.C.

[19] 449 F.2d 1109 (D.C. Cir. 1971).

[20] See U.S. ATOMIC ENERGY COMMISSION, Licensing of Production and Utilization Facilities, Implementation of National Environmental Policy Act of 1969. In Federal Register 36(175):18071-18076. September 9, 1971.

[21] 337 F.Supp. 287 (D.D.C. 1971).

cient environmental review, where necessary to insure an adequate power supply.

Additional Responsibilities of Federal Licensing Agencies:

Planning Requirements — A licensing agency's responsibility is not limited to providing a simple yes or no response to a single project proposed by the applicant. This is particularly true with respect to the Federal Power Commission, which has the obligation under the Federal Power Act to license a project only if it is best adapted to a comprehensive plan for the development of the waterway.[22] The FPC addresses these planning responsibilities in the licensing hearing. Before any specific project can be licensed, the FPC must decide whether any project—or none—is appropriate, what hydro and nonhydro development options are available, what hydro sites exist, and which of the possible hydro projects would foreclose other development options. This process can be extremely time consuming.

An adversary licensing hearing is only one approach toward exercising this planning responsibility. An alternative would be to develop a comprehensive plan independently. Proponents of the adversary process argue that the options are developed sharply for consideration only when the underlying assumptions may be cross-examined in a quasi-judicial proceeding. However, proponents of separate, pre-licensing planning argue that adversary hearings tend to focus too narrowly on the pros and cons of a particular application and do not guarantee the kind of comprehensive view which is necessary for planning.

Consideration of Alternatives — All Federal licensing agencies are required by NEPA to consider alternatives to major proposed actions and to describe those alternatives in environmental impact statements. The FPC had been required to consider alternatives before NEPA was enacted, as part of its planning responsibility under the Federal Power Act.[23] However, NEPA imposed additional requirements on agencies such as the AEC. In order to comply with NEPA, the AEC now should consider coal-fired and other alternatives to a nuclear plant, as well as the alternative of no plant at all. *Natural Resources Defense Council v. Morton,*[24] involving the Department of the Interior's offshore oil leasing program, apparently requires the Federal agencies to develop alternatives beyond their licensing jurisdiction, in no way limiting the inquiry except by saying that agencies need consider only "reasonable" alternatives.

This situation produces a dual problem. First, an agency such as the AEC must develop a record upon and evaluate a number of alternatives. Second, if it should determine that a nonnuclear alternative is preferable to the proposed nuclear plant, it lacks the jurisdiction to implement its decision with a license or by ordering construction of the preferred alternative. All that it will have done is to develop information which may be of use to some other agency.

Related Federal Permits: An electric utility, like other enterprises, frequently must obtain permits from one or more Federal agencies in addition to the one which will license its projects. A discharge permit provides one example. Moreover, if an enterprise is located on a navigable waterway from which it plans to divert water, it needs a permit from the Corps of Engineers for structures in the water. NEPA applies to permits for structures which may have a significant environmental impact, so that the Corps may be obliged to evaluate the environmental impact before issuing a permit.[25]

Litigation: The Commission recognizes that in some ways litigation is better suited to producing expeditious decisions than are other institutional arrangements.[26] For example, a project may languish in a legislature for years, and an administrative proceeding may range over a number of time-consuming issues. By comparison, a court may zero in on critical issues

---

[22] P.L. 333, 74th Congress, August 26, 1935, 49 Stat. 842, 16 USCA 803(a).

[23] See *Udall v. Federal Power Commission,* 387 U.S. 428 (1967); *Scenic Hudson Preservation Conf. v. Federal Power Commission,* 354 F.2d 608 (2d Cir. 1965), cert. denied, 384 U.S. 941 (1966).

[24] 458 F.2d 827 (D.C. Cir. 1972).

[25] See *Zabel v. Tabb* 430 F.2d 199 (5th Cir. 1970); see generally, HILLHOUSE, William A II & DeWEERDT, John L (1972). Legal Devices for Accommodating Water Resources Development and Environmental Values, prepared for the National Water Commission. National Technical Information Service, Springfield, Va., Accession No. PB 208 835. Ch. 6.

[26] See generally, THOMPSON, Grant P (1972). Courts and Water: The Role of the Judicial Process, prepared for the National Water Commission. National Technical Information Service, Springfield, Va., Accession No. PB 211 974.

framed by the pleadings and produce a relatively prompt result. However, repeated or poorly-timed opportunities for litigation can interfere with decisionmaking and exact heavy social costs. The advantages of judicial scrutiny, as an institutional check on the administrative process, must be preserved, but it should be structured to yield timely decisions.

One of the disturbing aspects of litigation is the possibility of multiple, separate appeals from the various proceedings. A party may prevail in one forum only to be frustrated in another, even though the issues in the two proceedings are much the same.

A second disturbing aspect of litigation is the possibility of circumventing the usual agency proceedings, and appeals therefrom, by bringing a collateral attack in court. Thus, in the *Quad Cities* case,[27] the plaintiffs did not wait for the AEC to rule upon the utility's application for an interim license, then attempt to appeal from that decision, if adverse. Instead, the plaintiffs argued in a Federal District Court that the AEC could not even consider whether to grant an interim operating license until it had filed an environmental impact statement. While only a Court of Appeals could have reviewed a decision by the AEC, the District Court acted to determine whether the AEC was following the procedures required by law and held that this determination need not be delayed until the AEC had acted. The *Quad Cities* plaintiffs were able to cite unusual circumstances to justify their collateral attack. However, the Court's reasoning might be extended to other circumstances as well.

A third, and perhaps the most disturbing, possibility is that the threat of litigation may encourage a decision in order to avoid further delay, rather than a decision on the merits. Consider the example of an electric utility which has completed construction of a nuclear powerplant and has an operating license from the AEC, or of any industry which has completed a new installation and received a discharge permit. The costs of the plant, and perhaps demands for service, militate for putting the plant into operation as soon as possible after administrative approval. A lengthy judicial challenge at this point may threaten delay and costs sufficient to force the utility to concede to opponents' positions, justified or not, without testing them in court.

A single timely judicial review can provide a valuable check as to whether the licensing agency properly applied governing law; but the possibilities of multiple appeal, of collateral attack, and of litigation when a plant is ready to begin operating are disruptive.

Federal Water Resources Projects

This discussion has dealt at length with non-Federal water-related projects because of the multiple permit and licensing requirements which are unique to them. Federal projects and the obstacles which they face are described in considerable detail elsewhere in this report.[28] Long before NEPA, Federal projects faced a long process of planning, review, evaluation, consensus building, authorization, and funding.[29] NEPA requires agencies to develop projects more carefully and may result in some proposed projects being dropped entirely as unsound. The Commission believes that NEPA review, supplemented by the measures recommended in this report, rarely will cause serious delays in authorization and funding for sound Federal water projects.

Once a project has been funded and construction begins, environmental reviews can create more serious problems of delay. In some cases, environmental review may lead to the conclusion that a project is undesirable and may prevent the expenditure of more money on a bad project. However, stopping a project at this stage, even temporarily, may also seriously upset expectations and add new social costs to the project. Moreover, if the project is stopped by a court or by the executive, the purpose of Congress in approving the project may be frustrated.

Accordingly, with public works projects as with licensing, timing is a critical problem of delay. An orderly set of procedures can permit a careful, early evaluation of all relevant factors, so that the critical decisions are not deferred until a time when any delay is seen as disruptive.

POSSIBLE SOLUTIONS

It follows from the discussion above that the Nation's choices are not limited to either accepting public or nonpublic projects without consideration of environmental values, on the one hand, or providing such consideration at the expense of badly needed

---

[27] *Izaak Walton League v. Schlesinger,* 337 F.Supp. 287 (D.D.C. 1971).

[28] See, *e.g.,* Chapter 10.

[29] See generally, ALLEE, David & INGRAM, Helen (1972). Authorization and Appropriation Processes for Water Resource Development, prepared for the National Water Commission. National Technical Information Service, Springfield, Va., Accession No. PB 212 140.

projects, on the other. However, the Nation will be required to decide which environmental and developmental values are most important and to strike a balance where an accommodation of all important values is impossible.

In the short term, there may be examples of significant disruption, especially where a project was initiated before the passage of NEPA (signed into law on January 1, 1970), yet now must comply with environmental requirements. In particular instances, Congress may want to provide emergency interim relief where important national goals are jeopardized by delays created by the environmental review process and where the administrative process does not offer an adequate remedy. These are transitional problems and will likely be associated with specific situations so that congressional relief should be limited and tailored closely to fit the individual facts. The Commission believes, however, especially for the long term, that projects may be developed and evaluated so as to identify important values, present alternatives, and strike a sound accommodation or balance without unacceptably disruptive delay.

Non-Federal Projects Requiring Licenses

Prelicense Planning: As noted above, the FPC has planning responsibilities and, under present arrangements, it pursues them in the context of a licensing hearing. The process is initiated by an applicant who presents a specific project, expecting acceptance or rejection upon defined standards. That project, and alternatives, are evaluated in an adversary proceeding, commonly with formal intervention required as a prerequisite to participation.

The licensing proceedings for the hydro development of the Middle Snake River demonstrate how long this combined planning and licensing may take.[30] Competing applicants first applied for a license in 1955. After extended FPC hearings and judicial review in the Federal Court of Appeals and the U.S. Supreme Court, the FPC was directed to reconsider the matter. Most recently, in 1971, an FPC hearing examiner decided that dams should be licensed at Mountain Sheep and Pleasant Valley. That decision is subject to review by the FPC and by the courts and would be displaced if Congress chooses to preserve the reach of the river involved. Therefore, as of this writing, 18 years after initial application, it has not been finally determined whether some hydro facility will be located on that reach of the Middle Snake River. There was no lack of a comprehensive plan for the Snake River when application for a license was first made in 1955. The Corps of Engineers had submitted such a plan to Congress in 1948. Much of the delay came from extended proceedings on whether a project should be built by Federal or non-Federal entities or by one or another of competing non-Federal entities. And in recent years, the question of development versus preservation of a scenic reach of the river has become the dominant issue.

The threshold question is whether comprehensive development of the area would be accomplished if a particular kind of project were included in the development plan; in other words asking whether the particular kind of project unduly impairs environmental values or forecloses desirable development options. The answers to such questions constitute prelicense planning and when used by developers to guide project formulation will increase the prospects that a project will be licensed.

Plant Siting: Certain proposed Federal legislation[31] and recently enacted State legislation[32] provide for prelicensing arrangements to determine where plants may be located and to resolve State and local environmental questions in a single proceeding. The legislation is directed specifically at powerplant siting, but the Commission believes that the basic principles apply to other water users who may need governmental approval for location of plants and face a maze of State and local land use, pollution, and other environmental reviews. If these matters can be resolved conclusively through a relatively early siting proceeding, subsequent licensing proceedings can be greatly simplified and expedited.

Siting legislation typically addresses the issues of (1) early public disclosure of potential sites by the developer, (2) early authoritative determination of site suitability, and (3) consolidated review of project proposals.

---

[30] See HILLHOUSE, William A II & DeWEERDT, John L (1972). Legal Devices for Accommodating Water Resources Development and Environmental Values, prepared for the National Water Commission. National Technical Information Service, Springfield, Va., Accession No. PB 208 835. Ch. 7.

[31] See, *e.g.,* H.R. 5277 (S. 1684), proposed Power Plant Siting Act of 1971, March 1, 1971, 92d Congress, 1st Session, and H.R. 11066, proposed Electric Power Supply and Environmental Protection Act, October 4, 1971, 92d Congress, 1st Session.

[32] See, *e.g.,* Washington Revised Code. Ch. 80.50.

Site Identification — Under the Nixon Administration's powerplant siting proposal,[33] developers would have to file annually their proposals for plant sites 10 to 15 years before the start of construction. The Commission believes that this is a desirable requirement, which could be applied to other major installations as well. Such an arrangement should improve prospects for accommodating developmental and environmental values since it would allow time— before the crisis when a facility arguably must be built to serve immediate needs—to explore site and design alternatives. It also should permit greater opportunity for public participation in the planning process, thereby perhaps resolving or narrowing potential disputes at the outset.

The Commission recognizes that a company's early disclosure of potential plant sites may result in land speculation, driving up acquisition costs. Furthermore, once a site has been identified as being potentially suited for a plant, it is important to prevent that use from being precluded by other development, except by a conscious planning decision. Both of these points underscore the need for an early determination of site suitability on which the developer may act.

Determination of Site Suitability — Under the Administration's approach, proposed powerplant sites would be subjected to mandatory public hearings before a State or interstate certifying agency 5 years prior to scheduled construction to determine "whether or not construction of any plant at the proposed site would unduly impair important environmental values."

Five years in advance of construction does not seem too early to address a number of issues. Once the siting agency has information on what kind of plant is contemplated for each proposed site, it would be possible to examine what environmental and developmental options would be foreclosed if the site is used for the particular type of plant. In appropriate cases, it also should permit conditions to be imposed on the use of the site, so that an appropriate plant may be built without sacrificing other important values.

---

[33]H.R. 5277 (S. 1684), proposed Power Plant Siting Act of 1971, March 1, 1971, 92d Congress, 1st Session. This is based on a report prepared by the Energy Policy Staff, Office of Science and Technology in cooperation with several other Federal agencies. See U.S. OFFICE OF SCIENCE AND TECHNOLOGY, Energy Policy Staff (August 1970). Electric Power and the Environment. U.S. Government Printing Office, Washington, D.C.

The advance determination of site suitability should promote a sound balancing of values with respect to plant siting; the certifying agency could examine the various factors relevant to siting without the pressure of having to meet an immediate need. If the agency denied use of the site for a powerplant, or for a particular kind of powerplant, the utility still would have an opportunity to develop alternative sites.

In addition, each siting agency should consider potentially acceptable plant sites on its own initiative, so as to identify the most appropriate sites within its jurisdiction. This type of procedure could be expected to produce an inventory of suitable sites, although some might be suitable only for particular kinds of plants, or only if certain requirements were met.

Since a determination of site suitability is a land use decision, analogous to zoning, it seems proper to proceed through the use of one or more legislative hearings. While the Commission appreciates the argument that issues tend to be presented more clearly and facts more concretely in an adversary proceeding, the flexibility of legislative hearings makes the latter approach preferable. Judicial review of the suitability determination could be limited accordingly.

Consolidated Certification Proceedings — So far as powerplants are concerned, only hydroelectric projects are presently subject to comprehensive, single agency review. As noted above, a utility wishing to construct a thermal powerplant must obtain approval from a number of agencies at different levels of government. Other enterprises may face a similar situation.

The numerous forums required for approval of a powerplant at the State and local level, in combination with the multiple Federal licenses or permits which may be required, offer risks of unnecessary delay, duplication, and possible frustration of basically sound projects, without assuring careful consideration of environmental values. No one should be happy with this situation. Consumers want a reliable source of power; conservationists want protection for the environment; utility representatives are interested in overcoming delays when their projects are held up in the licensing process.

Under the Administration's approach at least 2 years prior to scheduled construction a proposed powerplant site would be subject to certification by a single State or interstate certifying agency, which would be authorized to issue a certificate if it found:

Licensing agencies require cooling tower at Trojan Nuclear Plant on the banks of the Columbia River

. . .after having considered available alternatives, that the use of the site. . .will not unduly impair important environmental values and will be reasonably necessary to meet electric power needs, or otherwise to deny such certificates if the applicant fails to conform with the requirements of this Act.[34]

The certifying agency would be required to respect various criteria for balancing values that would be promulgated by a Federal agency designated by the President, and certification would not relieve the applicant from obtaining any other required Federal permits.

The "one stop" certification process of resolving as many licensing requirements as possible in a single proceeding seems to be a valuable mechanism. It should avoid much of the delay and duplication inherent in present State and local procedures and provide for assessing the relevant issues in a single, authoritative proceeding. By consolidating a number of separate proceedings, it has the further advantage

of eliminating the possibility of judicial appeals from different decisions.

The Administration's proposal provides one of several possible answers to a fundamental question concerning powerplants, and perhaps certain other types of installations as well: What are the respective interests of the States, regions, and the Federal Government in siting decisons? The answer provided in the Administration's proposal seems to be that the States have a sufficient interest, perhaps because land use decisions traditionally have been a State province, so that they should make the decisions; but that the Federal Government also has an interest which requires the States to follow federally imposed criteria.

How are federally imposed criteria justified? It might be argued that the Federal interest is the same as the States' if both want reliable power and a quality environment. Under this line of argument it might follow that there is no need for the Federal Government to preempt the decision by imposing criteria to govern the balancing. There may be a special Federal interest in obtaining prompt power-plant siting decisions because of interrelated power

---

[34] H.R. 5277, proposed Power Plant Siting Act of 1971, March 1, 1971, 92d Congress, 1st Session. Section 7.

needs in different areas, but if this were the extent of the Federal interest, it would be sufficient to require the States to act within a certain time and, if they do not, for the Federal Government then to preempt the decision. However, the Federal interest may extend further. Powerplants may be sited miles from the load center, such as the Four Corners powerplants designed to serve the Pacific Southwest. If a particular State is hostile to powerplants, perhaps because the power primarily will serve customers in other States, desirable sites may be foreclosed. By the same token, if a given State is overly receptive to powerplants, environmental assets with a significance transcending the State's boundaries, such as pure or wild streams or clean air, may be threatened. Finally, the Federal Government may have an interest in seeing that power needs are met adequately on a rational, coordinated basis nationwide. These kinds of Federal interests would require that the Federal Government have the opportunity for the final say with respect to siting of all types of electric powerplants, regardless of the fuel used.

The arrangement of State action pursuant to Federal criteria has precedent in the regulation of air and water pollution, but is not the only mechanism to strike a balance between Federal and State interests with respect to powerplant siting. Obvious alternatives are to have a certification proceeding at the State (or regional) level and again at the Federal; to have the State proceeding determinative, unless challenged, in which case a Federal agency would review the decision; to have a joint determination in the first instance, utilizing a board with Federal and State representatives; or to have the Federal Government preempt the field. The Commission's recommendation is to authorize State or joint Federal-State siting and licensing decisions under certain conditions, as stated more fully in Recommendation 6-4 at the end of this chapter.

Proceedings Before Licensing Agencies: Even if certain issues are resolved or limited by prelicensing site determination, the licensing proceedings for electric power facilities still offer possibilities of unnecessary delay.

Delays During Hearings — A hearing examiner may limit delays during hearings through a variety of techniques, many of them already used by licensing agencies. For example, a hearing examiner may limit the number of intervenors where a particular interest is adequately represented by those who already are

parties.[35] Licensing agencies may provide opportunities for interested persons to make limited appearances, perhaps by submitting written statements, without becoming formal parties. Both the Atomic Energy Commission and the Federal Power Commission utilize such techniques.[36] Agencies may use prehearing conferences to facilitate the later presentation of evidence by (1) settling peripheral and procedural issues, (2) defining the issues to be addressed at the hearing, and (3) setting reasonable limits on the amount and scope of direct testimony and cross-examination so as to eliminate repetitive matter. Where parties have similar interests on particular issues, the hearing examiner may require those parties to make a unified presentation and limit the number of attorneys who will cross-examine in the parties' common interest.[37]

Some agencies require direct testimony to be presented in writing and to be circulated in advance to all parties.[38] This technique also appears to offer opportunities for expediting proceedings, especially if combined with an early definition of the issues.

The Possibility of Legislative Hearings — In some situations a legislative hearing is both appropriate and attractive. By using a legislative hearing, the licensing agency may develop information without rigid formalities and without cross-examination and other procedural restrictions characteristic of quasi-judicial procedures. The agency can make its decision without being limited strictly to the record developed in the hearing. Therefore, use of legislative hearings often means a shorter hearing and, perhaps, an earlier administrative decision.

However, the use of legislative hearings, without taking additional measures, will not necessarily

---

[35] *Cf.* 18 CFR Section 1.8(b) (FPC); see, also, 10 CFR Section 2.714 (AEC) (Atomic Energy Commission, Rules and Regulations, Restructuring of Facility License Application Review and Hearing Processes. Federal Register 37(146):15127-15143. July 28, 1972. p. 15132).

[36] 10 CFR Section 2.715 (AEC); 18 CFR Section 1.10 (FPC).

[37] See 10 CFR Section 2.715a (AEC) (Atomic Energy Commission, Rules and Regulations, Restructuring of Facility License Application Review and Hearing Processes. Federal Register 37(146):15127-15143. July 28, 1972. p. 15132); 18 CFR Section 1.8(g) (FPC).

[38] See, *e.g.,* 10 CFR Section 2.743 (AEC) (Atomic Energy Commission, Rules and Regulations, Restructuring of Facility License Application Review and Hearing Processes. Federal Register 37(146):15127-15143. July 28, 1972. p. 15134); 18 CFR Section 1.26 (FPC).

shorten materially the time before a final decision results. Unless appeal is precluded, an agency's decision after a legislative hearing is subject to judicial review. Although review may be limited to an examination of whether the licensing agency acted arbitrarily or capriciously, the fact of appeal means a delay, and that delay may not be shorter than if the court were applying a "substantial evidence" test of review. Moreover, even if Congress were to preclude judicial review, the possibility would remain that litigants would seek to challenge the agency's action by bringing a suit for an injunction in a Federal District Court. So long as the licensing agency is required to act pursuant to defined statutory standards in deciding whether or not to issue a license, there is a question whether the agency has followed those standards, and those who are dissatisfied with the agency's action—whether they be opponents of the project or an applicant whose application was denied—may attempt to take that question to court.

One alternative, of course, is for Congress to make the decision of the licensing agency final, free from judicial scrutiny either on appeal or in a collateral proceeding. However, the Commission believes that the public interest would not be served by insulating the actions of licensing agencies from judicial scrutiny. A preferable approach, referring to the example of an AEC operating license, is to determine as many issues as possible well before a plant is constructed, so that the issues to be faced upon an application for an operating license, when delay may be most critical, are strictly limited. For all new projects, the AEC must conduct a full NEPA review before issuing a construction permit. Therefore, any additional environmental review at the operating license stage should be limited to those questions raised by intervening circumstances since construction was licensed.[39] Insofar as disputed issues are decided at the operating license stage, Congress could provide for an expedited review in a Federal Court of Appeals.

Consideration of Alternatives — The discussion above noted that Federal licensing agencies have the obligation under NEPA and the Federal Power Act, as construed by judicial decisions, to consider a relatively open-ended range of "alternatives," limited only by what is "reasonable." The Commission recognizes the value of assessing alternatives to a proposed course of action, but submits that the

public interest is best served if these are developed and evaluated, to the maximum extent feasible, before a specific project is ready for licensing. During the planning process there is flexibility to consider a range of alternatives without the constraints of heavy investment in a particular project and demands for immediate licensing. Broad alternatives, such as the possibility of a different rate structure, should be considered, but in an appropriate industry-wide proceeding, rather than in the process for licensing particular projects. Similarly, other broad issues of national policy, such as the possibilities and ramifications of importing fuels, should be addressed elsewhere.

The arrangements suggested earlier in this chapter provide a means for addressing different site alternatives. If a siting agency, pursuant to appropriate procedural limitations, concludes that a plant is justified at a particular site as a matter of sound land and water use, the licensing agency should be able to accept it as determined that the proposed plant would be consistent with a comprehensive plan for development of the waterway. If the planning process addresses itself to alternative site possibilities and to possible alternative uses of sites, so that the inventory of approved sites reflects a judgment that they are the best suited for particular plants, and the process adequately protects Federal interests, the licensing agency should not need to consider sites other than those identified in the inventory.

If a licensing agency is to choose objectively from among the reasonable alternatives, the choice may not be easy. For example, in the case of a choice between an atomic and a hydro project, both of which require Federal licenses, development of information about the alternatives will require expertise. A similar situation may exist with respect to fossil-fueled plants, which are licensed at the State level under present arrangements. A variety of possibilities for reaching a choice among alternatives is available.

The AEC and the FPC might be left with their respective jurisdictions, but with reciprocal participation in hearings before one agency by the staff of the other. While information on atomic and hydro alternatives would be developed, if expertise is necessary to develop information on fossil plants and neither the AEC nor the FPC has sufficient expertise, the staff of a State utility commission would have to be included.

Such an arrangement may present two problems. First, either for lack of expertise or because of a development mission, a particular licensing agency

---

[39] See 10 CFR Part 50, Appendix D.

may not make a sound choice among alternative fuels. Conversely, it may be that, given the present three forums (AEC, FPC, and State commissions) for licensing available alternatives, each may decide an alternative it cannot license is best, resulting in no project being licensed. If either or both of these problems are significant, alternative solutions include a joint hearing by the AEC and FPC, perhaps joined by a State utilities commission, on the issue of the optimal power source; extension of the consolidated site certification procedure, discussed above, to determine the choice of fuels; determination of the best type of plant by a board representing Federal and State interests; or creation by Congress of a single Federal power entity, combining the jurisdictions of the AEC and the FPC and perhaps asserting jurisdiction over powerplants using coal, oil, or gas.

The Commission believes that the existing arrangement under which a licensing agency is directed to consider a range of alternatives, even though it may lack jurisdiction to license the alternative which is best on balance, is unsatisfactory. Furthermore, the broader questions of how far Federal agencies, whether licensing or project agencies, must go under NEPA in identifying, developing, and evaluating alternatives, are troubling. The subject transcends water policy. However, Congress has held oversight hearings on the administration of NEPA.[40] The Commission endorses this practice and recommends that Congress hold hearings on the problems of alternatives described here.

Integration of NEPA into Licensing Proceedings — A licensing agency may be subject to collateral attack for alleged failure to comply with NEPA requirements. Under present arrangements, some environmental issues are considered in licensing hearings, but those hearings do not necessarily embrace all of the issues which might be raised about the adequacy of the licensing agency's environmental impact statement and NEPA review. Separate NEPA procedures, decisions, and appeals are employed and cause delays. If the licensing decision is to reflect a balance of all values and to produce a desirable degree of finality, it should contain a resolution of the NEPA issues. Therefore, the Commission believes that the NEPA procedures should be integrated with licensing procedures.[41]

The *Calvert Cliffs*[42] decision makes it clear that a licensing agency's responsibilities under NEPA go beyond those of an umpire; the agency has the affirmative duty to explore the NEPA issues at the licensing hearing. *Greene County Planning Board v. FPC*[43] requires the agency to prepare its own NEPA statement for publication and circulation before the licensing hearing commences. Therefore, the opportunity exists to combine the licensing hearing procedures with the NEPA process without adding unduly to present procedural requirements.[44]

Agencies commonly accept written comments on the impact statement from members of the public. The Commission endorses this practice, since the public has a significant role to play, both in identifying issues and developing information. Furthermore, the Commission recommends that members of the public also be given an opportunity to comment orally on the impact statement before the licensing hearing begins. Written and oral comments raising issues or developing information will aid the staff, applicant, and intervenors in the licensing proceeding. Licensing hearings should commence only after there has been sufficient time for public review of and comment on the environmental impact statement.

Since the licensing agency has an affirmative responsibility to explore NEPA issues, it is incumbent upon the agency staff to examine comments received from the public and from other Federal, State, and local agencies; to explore the issues raised and, if necessary, to develop information on these issues for the licensing hearing record. The hearing examiner should be given the opportunity independently to review the balance struck by the staff in the prehearing statement, rather than merely providing the agency itself with the comments of the public and

[40] See, *e.g.*, U.S. CONGRESS, House of Representatives (1972). Administration of the National Environmental Policy Act — 1972, Hearings before the Subcommittee on Fisheries and Wildlife Conservation, Committee on Merchant Marine and Fisheries, House of Representatives on NEPA Oversight, Serial No. 92-94, 92d Congress, 2d Session. U.S. Government Printing Office, Washington, D.C.

[41] See the procedures of the AEC, at 10 CFR Part 50, Appendix D.

[42] 449 F.2d 1109 (D.C. Cir. 1971); see HILLHOUSE, William A II & DeWEERDT, John L (1972). Legal Devices for Accommodating Water Resources Development and Environmental Values, prepared for the National Water Commission. National Technical Information Service, Springfield, Va., Accession No. PB 208 835. Ch. 8.

[43] 455 F.2d 412 (2d Cir. 1972).

[44] On December 18, 1972, the FPC issued an order (Order No. 415-C) amending the Commission's regulations to comply with the Greene County decision.

Federal, State, and local agencies. The comments, however, should be included in the hearing record.

Having before him the outside comments and the information developed by the participants and having assured adequate exploration of the matters raised in the comments, the hearing examiner should be able to issue his initial decision, simultaneously resolving both the licensing and NEPA issues in his opinion. Those who presented comments and those who participated in the hearing should have an opportunity to take exceptions to the initial decision, for purposes of appeal to the licensing agency. That agency, reviewing the record and the exceptions, would determine whether the balance struck was appropriate and the record was adequate. The final decision and the environmental impact statement would be subject to appeal in a Court of Appeals. Collateral attack upon the impact statement should be precluded.

Related Federal Permits: A utility or other enterprise which must obtain several Federal permits or licenses may be required to meet similar or identical issues in different proceedings before different agencies. NEPA might be construed to require each Federal agency to make an independent environmental review of the situation, although probably only one environmental impact statement need be filed.[45]

The Commission believes that when an issue has been authoritatively determined by one Federal agency, that issue should not be subject to consideration *de novo* by another Federal agency. One way to avoid the possibility of duplicating review would be by designating one Federal agency which now considers whether to issue a permit with respect to some aspect of a project and which is the agency required to make the most comprehensive examination, as the "lead agency" for purposes of environmental review. Once the lead agency had determined a particular issue, other Federal agencies would be required to accept that determination for purposes of their permits.[46]

A second alternative, at least for electric powerplants, is to provide for a consolidated proceeding at the Federal level, much as the Administration's siting bill would provide at the State level. The entity so constituted might be given jurisdiction over all Federal issues with respect to the licensing of powerplants (*i.e.*, assume all such jurisdiction now vested in the AEC, FPC, EPA, and Corps of Engineers), or it might be limited only to those issues which now are addressed by more than one Federal agency. In either case, the entity would not have a development or an environmental protection mission, but would make an independent determination in the public interest, a factor which makes this second alternative attractive. Neither alternative would preclude judicial review, but both would minimize the possibility of separate appeals from Federal licensing and permit decisions.

Federal Public Works Projects

Federal water projects proceed through several stages from inception to implementation—staff planning, agency review, executive review by other Federal agencies with an interest, and, finally, congressional action. Each stage provides important opportunities for resolving differences over environmental and developmental values.

Planning: Opportunities for accommodation should be explored at the earliest stages in the planning of Federal water projects while flexibility still exists and before proponents have expended so much money, time, and prestige that their positions are virtually set in concrete.

Too often in the past, however, a project has emerged from planning without full consideration of important environmental and developmental values and possible alternatives which might have permitted a sound accommodation between the two. Such an accommodation often is possible. The Delaware River Basin Commission found an accommodation at Tocks Island permitting private utilities to have a pumped storage project without using Sunfish Pond.[47] The Corps of Engineers proposed an alternative alignment for the Cross-Florida Barge Canal, although very late in the game, which might have saved reaches of the Oklawaha River.[48]

[45] See U.S. COUNCIL ON ENVIRONMENTAL QUALITY (1971). Statements on proposed Federal actions affecting the environment. Federal Register 36(79):7724-7729, April 23, 1971.

[46] The Federal Water Pollution Control Act Amendments of 1972 take essentially this approach for effluent limitations.

[47] HILLHOUSE, William A II & DeWEERDT, John L (1972). Legal Devices for Accommodating Water Resources Development and Environmental Values, prepared for the National Water Commission. National Technical Information Service, Springfield, Va., Accession No. PB 208 835. Ch. 4.

[48] *Ibid.*, Ch. 5.

Several recent developments suggest that planning may develop alternatives and promote accommodation more successfully in the future than it has in the past. Among these are the directions for comprehensive river basin planning under the Water Resources Planning Act;[49] the NEPA requirements that planning be interdisciplinary and include alternatives;[50] section 122 of the River and Harbor and Flood Control Act of 1970, requiring the Corps of Engineers to promulgate guidelines "to assure that possible adverse economic, social and environmental effects" are fully considered and that "final decisions on the project are made in the best over all public interest. . . .";[51] the proposed principles, standards, and procedures suggested by the Water Resources Council;[52] and proposed legislation which would require Federal water projects to be coordinated with State land use regulations.[53] One of the Commission's background studies argues powerfully that the Nation should go further in these new directions to include aspects of the social and natural environment in the planning and evaluation of proposed water development projects.[54] The Commission agrees that the planning process should be modified to include identification and balancing of values.

NEPA is designed to improve agency planning by requiring project agencies to consider expected environmental effects of a proposed project and the available alternatives. However, a construction agency can still be expected to pursue its development mission aggressively. For example, the statutory mandate of the Bureau of Reclamation emphasizes repayment and economic and engineering feasibility.[55] While NEPA requires improved quality and scope in the information which construction agencies develop, there is need for an independent, environmentally-oriented input into the planning process, as well as for improved environmental analysis by the agency itself.

Several of the Federal construction agencies have experimented with techniques to introduce public concerns and preferences from the inception of the planning process. Chapter 10 of this report applauds that effort, but suggests further steps which should be taken.[56] The Commission believes that those recommendations, if implemented, would generate information producing better projects and a better informed citizenry.

Agency Review: Before NEPA, the processes for project review—whether within the agency, by comment from sister agencies, or by members of the public—were not geared to produce a full consideration of environmental impacts. Project agencies were relatively free to shape their projects as seemed best to them so far as environmental aspects were concerned.[57] NEPA and other recent requirements have improved the review process, but the Commission believes that there is room for further improvement.

NEPA requires the project agency to circulate an environmental impact statement to other Federal agencies "which [have] jurisdiction by law or special expertise with respect to any environmental impact involved" for comment.[58] These comments are available to Congress. However, the process is subject to limitations. For example, a commenting agency cannot be expected to make a comprehensive review of every project described in NEPA statements; due to constraints of time and mission the commenting agency must limit its consideration and the depth and detail of its comments.

Agency review is also subject to special constraints when the reviewing agency is a member of the same department as the project agency.[59] The competing

[49] P.L. 89-80, July 22, 1965, 79 Stat. 244, as amended, 42 USCA 1962 *et seq.*

[50] P.L. 91-190, January 1, 1970, 83 Stat. 853, 42 USCA 4332.

[51] P.L. 91-611, December 31, 1970, 84 Stat. 1818.

[52] Federal Register 36(245):24144-24194, Part II, December 21, 1971.

[53] See, *e.g.,* S. 632, proposed Land and Water Resources Planning Act of 1971, 92d Congress, 1st Session.

[54] GOLDMAN, Charles R (1971). Environmental Quality and Water Development, prepared for the National Water Commission. National Technical Information Service, Springfield, Va., Accession No. PB 207 113. pp. 53-58.

[55] See 43 Stat. 702, 43 USCA 412; 53 Stat. 1193, 43 USCA 485h.

[56] See, also, GOLDMAN, Charles R (1971). Environmental Quality and Water Development, prepared for the National Water Commission. National Technical Information Service, Springfield, Va., Accession No. PB 207 113. pp. 52-53.

[57] The *Fish and Wildlife Coordination Act* (P.L. 85-624, August 12, 1958, 72 Stat. 564, 16 USCA 661-666c), for example, requires project agencies only to "consult with" the Fish and Wildlife Service and State wildlife agencies.

[58] P.L. 91-190, January 1, 1970, 83 Stat. 853, 42 USCA 4332.

[59] See HILLHOUSE, William A II & DeWEERDT, John L (1972). Legal Devices for Accommodating Water Resources Development and Environmental Values, prepared

values may be thrashed out in-house, away from public view, so that a single, departmental position emerges, effectively silencing competing positions. Only an independent agency, pursuing an environmental protection mission, can be expected to develop environmental considerations fully, to impress their importance upon the project agency, and to make them available to Congress.

To some extent the Council on Environmental Quality (CEQ) and the Environmental Protection Agency (EPA) both perform this function. The CEQ reviews environmental impact statements for particular projects and, if it believes that a statement is deficient, may attempt to persuade the project agency to do further work. The CEQ can be extremely persuasive, particularly when it enjoys access to the Office of Management and Budget and to the President, and some projects have not seen the light of day after CEQ review. However, the CEQ does not make its comments public, since it believes that this would be inconsistent with its role as an advisor to the President.[60]

The Clean Air Act requires the EPA to comment in writing, and to make its comments available to the public, on the environmental impact of certain matters falling within its jurisdiction.[61] This provision has considerable promise, although so far it has not been exercised extensively.[62] The Commission would like to see thorough EPA reviews of the potential environmental effects of proposed water projects developed for informed administrative, congressional, and public consideration. The Commission also would like to see the agency review process supplemented by the use of environmental advocates, as recommended later in this chapter.

NEPA apparently contemplates that members of the public may comment upon environmental impact statements, for it provides that such statements shall be made available to the public. Comments accompany the proposed Federal action through the review process and are available to Congress. However, Federal agencies could improve the procedures by which they obtain and evaluate public comments.[63]

Those who believe that a project proposal fails to comply with the requirements of NEPA should be given full opportunity to make their views known to the project agency either by commenting in writing on a draft NEPA statement or by participating in an agency hearing designed to solicit views as to why the proposal may not comply with NEPA. After receiving these public comments, the agency should prepare its final environmental impact statement, which should be a detailed document setting out the points which the agency had considered (including those raised in the NEPA comments), how it had resolved them, and the planning techniques which it had utilized.

Adopting these procedures, as some Federal agencies already have, would seem to offer several advantages. It could (1) give the project agency an opportunity to reconsider its environmental analysis in the light of possible objections and to make any changes which it believed were desirable; (2) produce more thorough environmental impact statements, providing Congress with better information about a proposed project; and (3) provide the basis for determination at an early stage whether the project agency complied with the procedural requirements of NEPA, a possibility discussed later in this chapter.

Executive Review: The Commission believes that Executive review of projects can be improved. Several alternatives for improvement are available.

Environmental Veto — The Commission believes that it would be inadvisable to give an environmental agency veto power over proposed Federal water projects which that agency concludes fail to protect

for the National Water Commission. National Technical Information Service, Springfield, Va., Accession No. PB 208 835, Ch. 3; FOX IK (1971). Some political aspects of the relationship between large scale interbasin water transfers, and EIPPER AW (1971). The role of the technical expert in decisionmaking, Chapters XXIII & XXI in GOLDMAN, Charles R, Environmental Quality and Water Development, prepared for the National Water Commission. National Technical Information Service, Springfield, Va., Accession No. PB 207 114.

[60] TRAIN, Russell (1970). Testimony of Russell Train on Administration of the National Environmental Policy Act, Part I, Hearings before the Subcommittee on Fisheries and Wildlife Conservation of the Committee on Merchant Marine and Fisheries, 91st Congress, 2d Session, Serial No. 91-41. U.S. Government Printing Office, Washington, D.C. pp. 69, 56, 57.

[61] P.L. 91-604, December 31, 1970, 84 Stat. 1709, 42 USCA 1857h-7.

[62] COMPTROLLER GENERAL OF THE UNITED STATES (1972). Improvements Needed in Federal Efforts to Implement the National Environmental Policy Act of 1969, Report to the Subcommittee on Fisheries and Wildlife Conservation, Committee on Merchant Marine and Fisheries, House of Representatives. U.S. General Accounting Office, Washington, D.C.

[63] *Ibid.*

some level of environmental quality, irrespective of potential developmental values. If important values conflict, they should be balanced according to their merits case by case.

NEPA reflects an "action forcing" and "full disclosure" philosophy; better decisions should result if project agencies broaden their consideration to include the environmental effects of proposed projects, develop possible alternatives permitting an accommodation of values, subject their planning to critical scrutiny by expert agencies and by the general public, and develop a full record on projects which go to Congress so that the Congress may make an informed decision in light of all relevant considerations. The Commission endorses this philosophy and concludes that an "environmental czar," an agency with a limited mandate and power to veto particular projects without exposing them to a full balancing process, is undesirable.

Project Analysis — Under present arrangements, Congress is entitled to receive a report from a project agency with respect to a particular proposed Federal water project and to authorize the project even though the executive branch of the Federal Government may oppose it. Similarly, Congress is free to appropriate funds for a project not included in the President's proposed annual budgets. However, the ultimate decisionmaking power which vests in Congress does not preclude the executive branch from analyzing projects from an environmental as well as economic viewpoint. The executive is properly concerned with what projects will be authorized or funded each year, and its position, based on careful analysis, could be expected to be persuasive with Congress.

The present executive branch review of projects, particularly at the annual budget stage, is not as effective as it might be. The Office of Management and Budget disclaims the expertise to review the environmental aspects of projects which an agency wants to include in the budget. The Council on Environmental Quality reviewed the Cross-Florida Barge Canal and argued successfully to the President that the project should be stopped. However, the CEQ appears to have become involved in that particular project only because of its magnitude and controversial nature. A more systematic environmental review of proposed projects appears desirable.

Board of Review — Later in this report the Commission recommends a top-level board of review

which would evaluate Federal water projects prior to authorization.[64] One of the functions of such a board of review would be to take a broad look at particular plans and projects in light of interrelated national needs and policies. The board of review should address itself explicitly, although not necessarily exclusively, to the environmental and developmental aspects of projects. The board of review would hold hearings and meet with interested parties to gather information relevant to its deliberations; this will assure that it has adequate information about the developmental aspects of proposed projects. The Commission recommends that it utilize an environmental advocate or some other appropriate device to assure that it gives full consideration to the environmental aspects as well.

Congressional Action: While innovative planning, development of differing views, and careful review all will tend to produce Federal water project proposals which strike a sound balance among values, there will remain situations in which important national values conflict and a final resolution must be made. The Commission believes that Congress is the appropriate entity to make this resolution.

The Central Arizona Project demonstrates the need for Congress to continue its role as the ultimate balancer of values with respect to Federal water projects.[65] The controversy over the proposed Bridge Canyon and Marble Canyon Dams appeared to require a choice between important national values: an improved power and water supply for the Pacific Southwest or protection of the Grand Canyon National Park and National Monument. Congress was clearly the proper forum for the balancing and resolution of those competing values. Broad matters of policy were involved that went beyond technical questions on which expertise could be determinative. Widespread public participation and development of positions were appropriate. Congress has the authority to weigh varying national objectives, is politically responsible for its decisions, and represents the public

---

[64] See Chapter 11.

[65] See HILLHOUSE, William A II & DeWEERDT, John L (1972). Legal Devices for Accommodating Water Resources Development and Environmental Values, prepared for the National Water Commission. National Technical Information Service, Springfield, Va., Accession No. PB 208 835. Ch. 3. GOLDMAN, Charles R (1971). Environmental Quality and Water Development, prepared for the National Water Commission. National Technical Information Service, Springfield, Va., Accession No. PB 207 113. p. 40.

generally. Its resolution of the value questions produced a high degree of finalty.

The Central Arizona Project also underscores the flexibility which Congress has to resolve conflicts by a range of alternatives transcending any one agency's jurisdiction. For example, one of the main arguments made for the two dams on the Colorado River was the need to finance augmentation of the water supply. Congress was able to respond to this perceived need, in a way which an administrative agency could not, by making the Mexican Treaty obligation a national one, so that the Federal Government will bear the cost of providing the required water for Mexico.[66]

In the future, a number of projects may be developed from regional, interagency, and intergovernmental planning efforts. As land use planning expands, water projects may also be coordinated with State and local land use determinations. These developments are welcome. Trial balances among environmental and developmental values should be struck and tested as the planning proceeds, but Congress, with its broad, national perspective, will continue to play the essential role of striking the final balance.

It is most important that the key issues which Congress is asked to decide be sharpened and that Congress is provided with all the information needed to make those decisions. The procedures previously suggested in this chapter, together with current procedures under NEPA, should help accomplish this. However, Congress need not rely upon those procedures alone and may wish to take additional measures. One such measure is an environmental advocate.

Use of an Environmental Advocate — In the past, environmental values have not always been presented fully to Congress. Today, when environmental values are publicly popular and organized environmental groups seek to present their views to Congress, this deficiency is less likely, particularly when controversial projects are under consideration. Nevertheless, Congress might profitably use an environmental advocate to focus attention on important environmental matters and to present arguments from an environmental viewpoint. Congress could designate the EPA to act as such as environmental advocate. Alternatively, if Congress were concerned that an executive agency might be subject to competing pressures within the executive branch, despite its mission, or that EPA's other responsibilities make it an inappropriate agency to act, Congress could employ an advocate directly responsible to it.

If Congress uses an advocate, some members of the general public may find it unnecessary to testify if they would feel that their interests were adequately protected by the advocate. However, use of an environmental advocate should not supplant all testimony by interested individuals and groups. Public witnesses have served a valuable role in identifying issues and suggesting alternatives, and the Commission believes that it is desirable to encourage their continued participation in congressional hearings.

The Possibility of Obtaining Final Decisions: NEPA directs project agencies to comply with certain mandatory procedures. A project agency must carefully consider the environmental impacts of proposed projects and the alternatives which are available, then file an environmental impact statement detailing this consideration. If the agency fails to file an impact statement[67] or files a statement which does not reflect an adequate consideration of the environmental impacts and alternatives,[68] it is subject to an injunction until it complies with NEPA, even if a project is already under construction.

NEPA has been interpreted to apply to major Federal actions even though they arise from programs initiated before the passage of the Act. The Council on Environmental Quality guidelines provide that:

Where it is not practicable to reassess the basic course of action, it is still important that further incremental major actions be shaped so as to minimize adverse environmental consequences. It is also important in further action that account be taken of environmental consequences not fully evaluated at the outset of the project or program.[69]

Congressional authorization of the project, *per se*, has not proved a defense in these cases. A Federal district court specifically rejected the Government's

---

[66] *Colorado River Basin Project Act*, P.L. 90-537, September 30, 1968, 82 Stat. 887, 43 USCA 1512.

[67] See, *e.g.*, *Natural Resources Defense Council v. Grant*, 341 F.Supp. 356 (E.D. N.C. 1972) (SCS Chicod Creek Project) and *Environmental Defense Fund v. Tennessee Valley Authority*, 339 F.Supp. 806 (E.D. Tenn. 1972) (Tellico Project).

[68] See, *e.g.*, *Environmental Defense Fund v. Corps of Engineers*, 325 F.Supp. 749 (E.D. Ark. 1971), injunction released, 342 F.Supp. 1211 (E.D. Ark. 1972) (Gillham Dam).

[69] Federal Register 36(79):7724-7729, April 23, 1971.

argument on this point in issuing a temporary injunction against further construction of the Corps of Engineers' Gillham Dam.[70] The U.S. Court of Appeals for the District of Columbia has pointed out that Congress may authorize a project, in this case a nuclear test, and appropriate funds for it on the assumption that the project agency would comply with all applicable legal requirements and, therefore, that the action of Congress need not be read as a judgment that all such requirements had been or would be met.[71]

The Commission recognizes that the courts have distinguished carefully between enforcing the procedural requirements of NEPA—that the project agency perform a careful evaluation of the environmental impacts and alternatives—and judging the merits of an authorized project. The Gillham Dam litigation is a good case in point. After the project was enjoined initially, the Corps of Engineers filed a new, considerably more detailed impact statement. The Court found the statement adequate and lifted the injunction, declining to substitute its judgment of the project's merits for that of Congress.[72]

The careful analysis which NEPA requires is healthy, and in the absence of congressional action, the Commission believes that courts have acted properly in enforcing this requirement. Nonetheless, it is disturbing when issues of a project's fundamental compliance with NEPA are raised—and resolved—after construction has begun and people have shaped their decisions in reliance on the project. To avoid dislocation and waste, the issues of NEPA compliance should be faced and resolved as soon as there is sufficient information to do so.

Future Projects — Under the procedures recommended in this chapter, Congress will be in a position to make an informed, dispositive determination of an agency's compliance with NEPA at the same time it considers the merits of a proposed project. The possible environmental effects of the project will have been developed through the project agency's environmental impact statement, the comments of sister agencies, public comments, the evaluation of the board of review, and congressional hearings utilizing an environmental advocate. All interested parties will have had an opportunity to express their views in one way or another. Consequently, the Commission believes that congressional authorization of a project in the future should dispose of all questions of whether it was conceived and developed in accordance with NEPA, and recommends that legislation authorizing projects so provide.

Projects Authorized Before the Passage of NEPA — The Commission does not recommend a blanket exclusion of all authorized projects from the coverage of NEPA. There may be important incremental steps at which evaluation of alternatives and the choice of a more environmentally sound course of action is possible. However, Congress should reserve for itself the decision whether to review the fundamental premises of an authorized project and should assume responsibility for any such review. Executive or judicial termination of an authorized project on the basis that it is fundamentally unsound environmentally presents difficult separation of powers questions.[73] If Congress reassesses a project and determines that it should proceed, perhaps in appropriating funds after considering the possible environmental impacts of the project, the decision is made by the same entity which authorized the project to proceed in the first instance. Congress may scrutinize current projects in the light of the existing stage of construction and the available alternatives. The question for Congress would not be the narrow one of whether the law had been complied with, but would be whether, in light of all considerations, the project should proceed and, if so, how.

CONCLUSIONS

1. The Nation's record of taking important environmental values into account in the planning, evaluation, licensing, and construction of water resource projects has not been completely satisfactory. In the past, developmental values have tended to predominate.

2. The National Environmental Policy Act does much to meet previous deficiencies in taking environmental values into account and in striking a sound accommodation or balance among developmental and

---

[70] 325 F.Supp. 749, 762 (E.D. Ark. 1972).

[71] *Committee for Nuclear Responsibility v. Seaborg*, 463 F.2d 783 (D.C. Cir. 1971); *cf. D.C. Federation of Civic Associations v. Volpe*, 459 F.2d 1231 (D.C. Cir. 1971) (Three Sisters Bridge case).

[72] *Environmental Defense Fund v. Corps of Engineers*, 342 F.Supp. 1211 (E.D. Ark. 1972).

[73] *Cf.* BENNETT, Charles (March 23, 1971). Statement, pp. 34-83 in U.S. CONGRESS, Senate, Subcommittee on Separation of Powers of Committee on the Judiciary (1971), Executive Impoundment of Appropriated Funds, Hearings, 92d Congress, 1st Session. U.S. Government Printing Office, Washington, D.C.

America needs to preserve its environmental values

environmental values. However, the process could be improved by the adoption of additional measures supplementing NEPA.

3. Environmental review requirements, particularly under NEPA, have created uncertainties and delays. Delays, especially when a project is under construction or completed, can be costly and disruptive. The Commission is concerned that there are inherent possibilities for delay at critical junctures under present arrangements for environmental review and concludes that certain measures are needed to expedite that review.

4. Careful planning frequently can accommodate important developmental and environmental values in a harmonious solution.

5. Difficult choices must sometimes be made among important environmental and developmental values in particular cases where all such values cannot be accommodated, but it is possible to achieve a sound balancing of values, without unacceptable delay, through the use of appropriate procedures.

6. In considering a proposed water project or use, developmental values should not be sought irrespective of environmental values which will have to be foregone as a result; nor should any single level of environmental quality be protected irrespective of potential developmental values. Where important environmental and developmental values conflict and cannot be reconciled, the attainment of one must be viewed as a sacrifice of the other. Sometimes it will

be rational to make substantial environmental sacrifices; other times it may not be worth even a small sacrifice. Only if the social benefits to be gained outweigh the social costs to be sacrificed should a proposed project or use be sanctioned.

7. Present arrangements with respect to non-Federal projects which require licenses and permits could be improved by the measures set forth in Recommendation 6-1.

8. Congress should continue to make the choice where important development and environmental values conflict with respect to proposed water projects requiring Federal authorization and funding, rather than delegate that responsibility to an executive balancing agency or to an agency with veto power over projects believed to be environmentally unsound.

9. Present arrangements for achieving an accommodation or a balance among important developmental and environmental values with respect to Federal water resources projects could be improved by the measures set forth in Recommendation 6-2.

RECOMMENDATIONS

6-1. The following measures should be adopted with respect to non-Federal projects which require licenses or permits to utilize the Nation's waters:

a. **Planning and licensing responsibilities should be separated by the use of pre-licensing planning.**

b. **Siting questions should be resolved and State and local environmental requirements satisfied by:**

 (1) **Long-range planning for plant sites, with notice to the public and an** opportunity for the public to participate in the planning.

 (2) **An authoritative determination of the suitability or nonsuitability of a proposed site, in light of environmental and developmental values, well before the planned date of construction.**

 (3) **A single certification proceeding capable of balancing values and resolving all questions of State and local law relevant to the siting of a particular proposed plant.**

c. **Delays during licensing hearings should be limited by limiting the number of inter-** venors, **by allowing written statements, by prehearing conferences to settle side issues and limit testimony, by allowing for unified presentation by parties with similar interests, by circulating direct testimony in advance, by legislative-type hearings, or by some combination of these devices.**

d. **NEPA review should be integrated into Federal licensing proceedings by the following measures:**

 (1) **The staff environmental impact statement should be submitted for comments and notice of its availability should be provided at the time the notice of the licensing hearing is given.**

 (2) **Licensing agencies should accept and encourage oral and written comments from the public on matters discussed in the staff environmental impact statement.**

 (3) **Licensing hearings should commence only after a period of time sufficient for public review of and comment on the staff environmental impact statement.**

 (4) **Comments on the environmental impact statement received from the public, and from Federal, State, and local agencies, should be submitted for the hearing record to permit the hearing examiner to assess whether the staff has developed an adequate evidentiary record with respect to the NEPA issues.**

 (5) **The hearing examiner's decision should determine both the licensing and the NEPA issues, subject to review by the licensing agency and appeal of the agency's decision.**

e. Federal licensing agencies should be authorized to rely upon proper determination by a State or interstate site planning agency that development at an approved site is consistent with a comprehensive plan, in order to limit the scope of alternatives to be considered during the licensing proceeding. Where the site planning agency makes a comprehensive examination of alternative site possibilities and evaluates the environmental and developmental attributes associated with them,

Congress should authorize Federal licensing agencies to limit their consideration of sites to those approved by the site planning agency.

f. Licensing agencies' responsibility to consider alternatives should be united with the authority to license the alternative judged best.

g. Federal licensing and permit requirements should be consolidated so that issues which now are addressed by several Federal agencies shall be resolved in a single agency proceeding. Congress might designate one agency presently required to examine a proposed project as the lead agency to determine such issues, or provide for a consolidated proceeding before an entity constituted so as to assure a balanced approach, with the competence and responsibility to assess all relevant factors.

6-2. The following measures should be adopted to improve the accommodation or balancing of important environmental and developmental values associated with Federal water resources projects:

a. Better environmental information should be introduced into water resources planning through improved techniques of public participation and agency environmental analysis.

b. The public comment process under NEPA should be developed by encouraging written comments, or oral presentations in a hearing held by the project agency, on draft environmental impact statements, and by requiring project agencies to respond to such comments in preparing final environmental impact statements.

c. The proposed Board of Review, utilizing an environmental advocate or some other effective device, should examine the development agency's compliance with environmental requirements and the proposed balance among environmental and developmental values.

d. An environmental advocate should be employed by Congress to assure that important environmental matters are brought to its attention before it acts on a project.

e. Congress should determine the adequacy of a project's fundamental compliance with environmental requirements, including NEPA.

6-3. Congress should hold hearings on the issues raised by the NEPA requirement that Federal agencies consider alternative courses of action. These hearings should address the question of how far Federal agencies must go in identifying, developing, and evaluating alternatives; the appropriate procedures for this consideration; and the means of uniting the responsibility to consider alternatives with the power to implement the alternative judged best.

6-4. Congress should authorize Federal agencies having authority to determine, license, or approve the selection of a site for a powerplant or other water-using industrial plant affecting both State and Federal interests to enter into agreements with those States and interstate agencies meeting federally prescribed standards and criteria embodied in regulations to be promulgated for the purpose of enabling State and interstate agencies to establish their eligibility. Under the agreements an eligible State or interstate agency could be authorized to hold public hearings either independently or jointly with the Federal agency to consider siting or licensing proposals, or both, and make final determinations in accordance with applicable Federal and State laws and regulations and such additional guidelines as might be included in the agreements.

Making Better Use
of Existing Supplies

Introduction

This chapter, in sections lettered A through H for ease of reference, deals with improvement in the practices, procedures, and laws relating to existing water use. The purpose of the recommended changes is to secure greater productivity, in both monetary and nonmonetary terms, from existing water supplies. Thus, the recommendations relate both to measures that would contribute to economic growth and to measures that would enhance the recreational and esthetic value of water. "Existing supplies" means water supplies presently in use, whether the uses are instream (i.e., confined to the water body itself), direct surface diversions, or withdrawals from surface or ground water storage.

The chapter begins with ground water (Section B), for the problems associated with its management are widespread and the savings that could be achieved are large since the volume of water involved is large. The Commission concludes that a uniform national ground water law is not desirable because of the great variety in aquifer characteristics, in legal regimes allocating the resource, and in the economic and social milieu in which the uses take place. But ground water management represents a national problem, acute in some parts of the country and emerging in others. Recommendations are addressed to the States for improving ground water use, primarily by providing for integrated administration and management of surface and ground water supplies by agencies fully empowered to effectuate conjunctive use. Steps are recommended to prevent premature exhaustion of supplies through ground water mining. It is suggested that the Federal Government examine

~~~~~~~~~~~~~~~~~~~~~~~~~~~~~~~~~~~~~~~

Orchard irrigation, Salt River Project, Arizona

State ground water management programs before authorizing additional water development projects. The Commission is also concerned about ground water pollution, not because ground water quality is now bad, but because deterioration is occurring and the effects are long term and sometimes irreversible. The Federal approach to surface water quality should apply also to ground water, in that the States should set standards acceptable to the Federal Government on discharges reaching ground water reservoirs. Lastly, the section recognizes that the need for information to accomplish these objectives is great and that additional funding should be provided the U.S. Geological Survey to conduct investigations.

Section C discusses pricing as a means of achieving better use of water. Pricing means user charges that reflect the costs of the water and the supply system. The Commission concurs in the great weight of current thinking that holds that water is not ordinarily a free good but is usually a scarce and valuable resource for which there is competition. At a minimum, users should pay the costs of supplying the water, and the price to each user should reflect the extra cost of serving him—a concept called "incremental or marginal cost pricing." Of course, it is not administratively feasible to fix a different price for each user—but users can be classified in groups, and incremental costs for enlarging and extending the system can be charged to those users benefiting from the added system components.

It is the Commission's belief that an economically sound system of user charges for water services will conserve water supplies, retard premature investment in water development projects, reduce financial burdens now borne by those who do not benefit from the services, and allocate water more efficiently among competing users. To accomplish these objectives, it is recommended that Federal assistance be conditioned on cost-based pricing of water supply.

Free bargaining in water *rights* is another means of allocating the resource more efficiently. However, a large amount of water in the West, especially relatively low-value agricultural water, cannot be freely bargained over. It is held under vested legal rights by the users, or is held by the U.S. Bureau of Reclamation and is furnished the user under long-term contracts that would be difficult to amend with pricing provisions. That water, nevertheless, is often capable of being reallocated to more valuable uses by operation of market forces if legal obstacles to water rights transfers are removed. Section D describes those obstacles and proposes changes in laws and procedures for their removal. Three principal categories of changes are proposed:

(1) State water rights records should be improved to reflect actual, existing uses, uses not on the record should be required to file, "paper rights" not in use should be terminated.

(2) The legal and administrative procedures for effecting a water right transfer should be simplified.

(3) Legal restraints and uncertainties on the power to make transfers should be removed; in the case of Bureau of Reclamation water, the user should be free to make a transfer without Bureau consent if the works have been paid for; if the works have not been paid for, the Bureau should be required to consent to the transfer if that portion of the outstanding loan allocable to the water transferred is paid off or is refinanced in accordance with then-prevailing Federal repayment policies governing municipal and industrial water supply. In the case of non-Federal water, State law should be changed to allow individual users as well as public districts to make transfers, without restrictions on service areas. All transfers, of course, would continue to be restricted by the rule that the transfer may not injure the rights of others.

Section E draws attention to the failure of State law in many instances to recognize and give legal protection to instream water values, such as fish and wildlife, recreation, and esthetics. Related to the problem of recreation is public access to water bodies. Because of the great variety in State laws and the diversity of approaches available to protect instream values, the Commission has not proposed a model law. Instead, it has drawn attention to the problems and proposed alternate routes to solutions. Reference is made to a number of apparently successful efforts recently initiated by States. Specifically, Section E notes five different legislative actions aimed at protecting instream values:

(1) reserving portions of streams from development and setting them aside as "wild rivers;"

(2) authorizing a public agency to file for and acquire rights in unappropriated water;

(3) setting minimum streamflows and lake levels;

(4) establishing environmental criteria for the granting of permits to use water;

(5) forbidding the alteration of watercourses without State consent.

A State considering legislation to protect instream values should at the same time review its law on public access to water bodies. The law is extremely complicated and much of it must be decided by the courts, for it involves Federal and State land titles, the concept of navigability, and the somewhat obscure doctrine of the public trust, which traces its history back to the Tudor Period of England. Nevertheless, legislatures can contribute by reviewing the law on public access, by providing for co-ordination of State water use plans with State recreational plans, and by appropriating funds for the policing and maintenance of public beaches, lake shores, and river banks.

Section F adopts the premise that better use of existing water supplies can be made in the Eastern riparian States if they would adopt a comprehensive permit system, on a basin-by-basin basis, as competition for water use sharpens. That premise is supported by drawing attention to the need that planners and investors—public and private—have for certainty in water rights and administration and to the greater effectiveness of administrative agencies, rather than courts, in protecting instream values and other public interests. The Commission's recommendations build on the thinking, incorporated in recent legislation, that use of all water, both ground water and surface water, should be comprehended by the permit system; water uses both before and after enactment of necessary permit system legislation should be regulated; minimum flows and public values should be protected; and the record system should be comprehensive and detailed. The section seeks to advance current thinking by setting out specific, somewhat detailed provisions for allocation of water in periods of shortage and by providing for private bargaining for the transfer of water rights permits to higher uses. A balance is sought to be struck between certainty for users and flexibility for public purposes by providing that the term of a permit should reflect the amortization period of the associated investment and that permits should be renewed unless the water is needed for a public purpose.

Reduction of physical losses of water by better husbandry is considered in Section G. The greatest savings can be effected in the agricultural area, which accounts for about 83 percent of the Nation's consumptive use of water, but worthwhile savings can also be accomplished in municipal and industrial use.

The section recommends that several measures be taken in the West, where most agricultural water is consumed. These same measures can be applied in the East, under a permit statute, when water supply becomes short. In the West, an appropriative right is defined in terms of, and is measured by, beneficial use. There is no right to use an amount in excess of what is deemed beneficial. State water agencies should strengthen the administration of water rights to enforce the beneficial use concept and to reduce waste, and Congress should have reports on waste prevention when considering projects for additional water supply. It would also be desirable for the Western States to quantify the "duty of water," that is, the amount of water reasonably necessary to irrigate specified crops in designated farming regions. Similar quantification should be applied to conveyance losses in canals used to move water to the point of use.

Under Western law it will be necessary to provide incentives other than legal compulsion to achieve additional savings from such practices as lining canals and ditches, switching to sprinkler irrigation, managing surface and ground water conjunctively, selecting more protected reservoir sites, and improving techniques in scheduling the time and amount of irrigation water deliveries. The traditional incentive for saving—that the benefits accrue to those who save—is absent under the laws of some States, which hold in effect that any savings which are achieved belong to the stream for use by others. Without overlooking the problems of quantification and protection of property rights of other users, the Commission recommends that the States encourage water-savings practices by allowing use of salvaged water on other land of the salvor or by allowing him to sell such salvaged water for use by others.

The most effective means of reducing water consumption by municipalities and industries is a sound pricing system coupled with individual metering. Many cities have a pricing system exactly the opposite of what would save water: the more water that is used, the cheaper the rate.

Many industries are supplied through municipal systems. Incentives to make those uses more efficient can be inaugurated through the adoption of a cost-based pricing system. Other industries are self-suppliers, and States should seriously consider user withdrawal charges in such cases; in the East this could be part of the enactment of a comprehensive water rights permit system of regulation.

The Nation can also make better use of existing water supplies if municipal and industrial wastewater is reused in accordance with a comprehensive waste treatment and reuse plan—a topic discussed in Section H. While supply conditions in the Nation at large will not require society to face soon the complex technical and psychological problem of reuse for domestic purposes, significant water savings can be achieved from reuse for industrial and recreational purposes. Costs are a factor, of course, and the economics of reuse will vary from place to place depending on circumstances. However, as the Nation moves toward higher water quality, the move should be accompanied by careful consideration of greater reuse of existing supplies.

Another obvious way to make better use of existing water supplies is to provide for adapting existing projects to changing needs. Reservoirs built for irrigation, for example, might well be adapted for use to supply municipal and industrial water needs as demands for those purposes grow. In many instances, the changeover will result easily, through the working of the market. For some reservoirs, however, particularly those constructed by the Federal Government, the terms of the original authorization are such that no transfer of use is possible without legislative reauthorization. The need for this and recommendations for periodic review of project authorizations is discussed in the introductory portion of Chapter 5.

The emphasis of this chapter is on developed water resources—that is, existing supplies of water already in use. But closely related is further development of indigenous supplies. One traditional means of putting an indigenous supply to better use is streamflow (or river) regulation by means of dams and reservoirs. There is no doubt that streamflow regulation will continue to be an attractive alternative for putting water supplies to better use, and that multipurpose dams will be built in the future when they are economically desirable and environmentally acceptable.

Development of streamflow regulation tends to be a gradual process with dams being constructed sequentially as demand develops. This staged process of regulation can be disrupted by preemption of reservoir sites by incompatible development, such as highway construction and urbanization. A study prepared by the Corps of Engineers at the request of the Commission states that of 132 Corps projects now authorized but as yet unbuilt, 35 are on sites threatened by preemption. A parallel study by the Bureau of Reclamation states that six sites, out of 63 authorized projects, are similarly threatened. Similar preemption threatens unauthorized project sites.

It does not follow, of course, that the preemption of a reservoir site by other uses is necessarily a misallocation of resources. It is quite possible that other uses of the site are more productive. The problem is that present policy does not adequately recognize and deal with the matter. Congress should authorize advance acquisition of those high-priority reservoir sites which (1) are potentially highly desirable to meet future water demands, (2) have no use more valuable than for water storage, and (3) are in danger of preemption. To implement this policy, Congress should direct the planning and construction agencies to prepare requests for the acquisition of sites meeting these criteria.

Simply acquiring a reservoir site prior to project planning, as useful as that is as a means of reducing windfall benefits and insuring against preemption of sites for uses which are not the highest and best, should not mean that society is irrevocably committed to use of a particular site for a particular purpose. Resale of reservoir sites or aqueduct rights-of-way, held for future water development, should be encouraged whenever superior alternatives appear or it is clear the sites will not be developed for the intended purpose.

~~~~~~ *Section B*

Improving Ground Water Management[1]

All water that exists below the surface of the earth in the interstices of soil and rocks may be called subsurface water; "that part of subsurface water in interstices completely saturated with water is called groundwater."[2] Of practical concern is that portion of ground water that can be extracted by wells or that forms the base flow of surface streams. There is misinformation, misunderstanding, and mysticism about ground water that credits it with occurrence in underground rivers, pools, and veins, and that separates "percolating" underground water from "underground streams." With a few exceptions, such as in some limestone formations, ground water does not occur in pools or channels of the kinds thus called to mind; it is found in interstices of porous and permeable subsurface formations.

How much water is this? The ground water supply in storage to a depth of one-half mile within the 48 contiguous States has been estimated at 180 billion acre-feet. In contrast, the larger lakes of North America contain about 27 billion acre-feet. Natural annual recharge may average more than 1 billion acre-feet. While this estimate of recharge may be liberal, it indicates the general magnitude of annual recharge compared to ground water in storage. On the basis of the above estimates, the volume of ground water in storage to a depth of one-half mile is roughly equivalent to the total of all recharge during the last 160 years.[3]

The total amount of ground water in storage which is usable with present technology is said to approximate 10 years' annual precipitation or 35 years' annual surface runoff—some 46 billion acre-feet.[4] Ground water supplies about 22 percent of the water withdrawn for use in the country, and this percentage

---

[1] This section is based in part on two background studies prepared for the National Water Commission: MACK, Leslie E (1971). Ground Water Management. National Technical Information Service, Springfield, Va., Accession No. PB 201 536. CORKER, Charles E (1971). Ground Water Law, Management and Administration. National Technical Information Service, Springfield, Va., Accession No. PB 205 527.

[2] WALTON WC (1970). Groundwater Resource Evaluation. McGraw-Hill Book Co., New York.

[3] NACE RL (1960). Water Management, Agriculture, and Ground-Water Supplies, Circular 415. U.S. Geological Survey, Washington, D.C. p. 3.

[4] CROSBY JW III (1971). A layman's guide to ground water hydrology, ch. II in CORKER, Charles E, Ground Water Law, Management and Administration, prepared for the National Water Commission. National Technical Information Service, Springfield, Va., Accession No. PB 205 527. p. 52.

is likely to increase because of increasing demands and the wide availability of ground water.[5] Between one-third and one-half of the coterminous United States is underlain by ground water areas capable of yielding 50 gallons per minute or more to wells.

The great increase in the use of ground water for irrigation, commencing in the late 1930's, is attributable in part to technological advances. Inexpensive energy became available to most farms to power irrigation pumps. The Southern High Plains of Texas provide a dramatic example of the consequences. This area covers about 25,000 square miles overlying the Ogallala Formation, an aquifer with minimal recharge in this region. In 1937, some 600 irrigation wells had been drilled in the area.[6] By 1969, the number of wells had increased to 55,000, irrigating approximately 4 million acres of land with an annual withdrawal rate of about 5 million acre-feet.[7] Parallel developments occurred in some other parts of the country. In the decade 1950-1960, wells in Maricopa County, Arizona, were pumping about 2 million acre-feet of water a year, lowering the water table in some places by as much as 150 feet during the 10-year period.[8] While there seems to be no nationwide overdraft on ground water aquifers, local overdrafts are experienced across the country, from New York, New Jersey, and Florida to California.

Several characteristics of ground water warrant its prudent management. Because of its slow movement through aquifers, it may be thought of as water in storage. The reservoir is readily accessible in many parts of the country, often where surface supplies are becoming scarce and costly to use. It loses little water to evaporation, it requires no construction of dams to provide the storage capacity, and the water is often of good quality. All of these advantages can be offset by misuse of the resource. Thus, from the national standpoint, proper management of ground water is an important element in a water conservation and development program.

In the Eastern and Midwestern portions of the country, ground water law is judge-made law, deriving from the English common-law rule of "absolute ownership."[9] Each landowner was allowed to pump water from wells on overlying land without restriction. Damage inflicted on neighbors was not compensable. The "American rule" modified the common law only slightly; it required the use to be "reasonable" and gave protection to injured neighbors for uses deemed unreasonable, such as outright waste or, in some jurisdictions, use away from the overlying land. Interpretation of the American rule varies from State-to-State and from case-to-case, since the resolution of each controversy is *ad hoc*. To generalize to the extent possible, the Anglo-American ground water law conferred a privilege on landowners to pump ground water as they saw fit, restrained only by a vague rule of reason that prohibited extreme conduct injurious to others. Pumping that caused a permanent lowering of the water table was not actionable under the common law.

In some Western States, the common law of ground water has been significantly modified. Responding to continuously falling water tables and to the prospect of exhaustion of aquifers, Western courts and legislatures have adapted the prior appropriation system to ground water (i.e., a water right is acquired by withdrawing water and applying it to a beneficial use). The operation of appropriation law on ground water is similar in some respects to its operation on surface water, and is different in other respects. When a court or administrator deems that there is no more surface water available for use, the stream is closed to further appropriations. Similarly, an overdrawn aquifer may be closed to additional pumpers.

The appropriation law of surface water and ground water may differ, however. When surface supplies are short, each user is shut down in inverse chronological order of the date of his right. Thus, a late priority gets surface water in wet years and does not in dry years. When a ground water aquifer is overdrawn, established pumpers are usually permitted to

---

[5] U.S. WATER RESOURCES COUNCIL (1968). The Nation's Water Resources. U.S. Government Printing Office, Washington, D.C. p. 3-2-7. See also McGUINNESS CL (January 1965). Ground water – a key resource. Ground Water 3(1):24-29.

[6] McGUINNESS CL (1963). The Role of Ground Water in the National Water Situation, U.S. Geological Survey Water Supply Paper 1800. U.S. Government Printing Office, Washington, D.C. p. 843.

[7] TEXAS WATER DEVELOPMENT BOARD (1971). Inventories of Irrigation in Texas 1958, 1964, and 1969, Report 127. Texas Water Development Board, Austin, Tex. Table 1.

[8] McGUINNESS CL (1963). op. cit. p. 149.

[9] This discussion is based on CORKER, Charles E (1971). Ground Water Law, Management and Administration, prepared for the National Water Commission. National Technical Information Service, Springfield, Va., Accession No. PB 205 527. pp. 98-127.

continue pumping in the amounts historically withdrawn. The consequence may be a continual lowering of the water table. Thus, while surface water appropriation serves to allocate a short supply, ground water appropriation law does not necessarily do so. Courts have stated that in such circumstances junior pumpers may be forced to pay the increased costs of senior pumpers, but decrees to this effect are hard to find.

Only a few States have squarely faced the broader social problems caused by ground water mining. The California Supreme Court confected a rule that required pro rata cutbacks in pumping when an aquifer is overdrawn.[10] The New Mexico legislature empowered the State Engineer to declare overdrawn aquifers to be critical ground water areas and impose drilling restrictions therein. Under this statutory authority the State Engineer has reserved one-third of the water in overdrawn aquifers from present use and has set a life of 40 years for the balance of the supply. He administers drilling permits so as to apportion the available two-thirds of supply over the 40-year period.[11]

THE PROBLEM

The three principal problems of ground water law, management, and administration are: (1) integrating management of surface water and ground water, (2) depletion of ground water aquifers at rates exceeding recharge (often referred to as the "mining" of ground water), and (3) impairment of ground water quality. Lesser, though important, problems are also considered: accelerating collection of ground water data together with fuller and more meaningful interpretation of it, aquifer protection, and subsidence. The Commission does not propose a uniform Federal law for ground water, but a number of measures that the States should adopt without delay are proposed and it is recommended that Federal financial assistance be tied to satisfactory performance by the States in ground water management and administration.

Where ground water law is applied to adjudicate private disputes over well interference, there is no need for uniform legislation or for Federal concern. Each State should be free to allocate the burdens and

benefits of ground water use as it sees fit, as there is no significant national impact from one decision or another. In such disputes, the States should consider employing the flexible powers of the equity court to achieve least-cost physical solutions.

However, at least one consequence of the operation of ground water laws and decisions is of national concern. It is the mining of ground water. The Federal concern here arises not so much from the fact that the resource may be ultimately depleted, although that is a problem, but from the fact that the depletion is unplanned, and the future is not provided for. As disaster approaches, the Federal Government is likely to be implored to step in with a rescue project, commonly conceived as one to furnish a supplementary water supply at taxpayers' expense to save an established economy, an economy that became established in the first place by imprudent overuse of ground water. The principles that should govern a rescue project of this sort are discussed in Chapter 8 in connection with interbasin transfers of water; means for avoiding doomsday are considered in this section.

This section also considers the integrated use of surface water and ground water and the management of these often interrelated sources of supply in conjunction with one another. Federal legislation on these topics is not proposed because the problems cannot be solved most effectively by a single, national approach. The management of ground water depends on the characteristics of the aquifer systems, on the availability of indigenous surface supplies, on the feasibility of importing water, and on the legal regimes presently applicable to the resource. Thus, each State will have to design ground water and surface water management schemes to suit its own physical and institutional peculiarities. Nevertheless, the Commission urges immediate and concentrated attention to ground water administration and management in the numerous States where ground water pumping is on the increase.

DISCUSSION

The discussion hereinafter covers several of the important aspects of ground water management: the reasons why use of surface water and ground water should be integrated; the need for ground water management; the problems of, and proposed solutions to, ground water mining, ground water pollution, and interstate ground water aquifers; and, finally, the need for more and better information.

---

[10] *Pasadena v. Alhambra,* 33 Cal. 2d 908, 207 P. 2d 17 (1949).

[11] See, for example, *Mathers v. Texaco,* 77 N.M. 239, 421 P. 2d 771 (1966).

Integrating Use of Surface Water and Ground Water Supplies

Two aspects of integration are considered. First, the need for integration of the two water supplies—surface and ground—should be understood. Second, heavy use of ground water can adversely affect surface water supplies and this, too, must be understood.

The Need for Integration: Ground water is often naturally interrelated with surface water: ground water feeds springs and surface streams, and surface water charges ground water reservoirs. Nevertheless, there persists in the laws of many States myths (long ago abandoned by hydrologists) that ground water is separate from and unrelated to surface water.[12]

Recommendation No. 7-1: State laws should recognize and take account of the substantial interrelation of surface water and ground water. Rights in both sources of supply should be integrated, and uses should be administered and managed conjunctively. There should not be separate codifications of surface water law and ground water law; the law of waters should be a single, integrated body of jurisprudence.

Discussion — As a consequence of the faulty perception of hydrology that ground water is separate from and unrelated to surface water, different legal regimes were applied to surface water and ground water, and only recently and in only a few water-short Western States has an effort been made to coordinate the administration of the integrated surface water—ground water supply. As Colorado and New Mexico have discovered, when the coordination effort comes late—after an economy has been developed in reliance on two different legal systems for one interrelated supply—achieving coordinated administration is very difficult. The problem in those two States is that surface water users generally came first, followed by ground water users pumping from aquifers interdependent with the surface stream. Over time, depletion of the underground aquifer reduced surface flow so that senior surface users were deprived of water by junior pumpers. Untangling this confusion has been a persistent problem in parts of the West. The next portion of this section discusses

some possible means of improving the situation where the problem has already become acute, but the recommendation here is addressed to the States in which the problem lies in the future and there is still opportunity to avoid it by present action.

To effectuate Recommendation 7-1, the States will have to proceed along a variety of paths, because the evolution of their laws has taken different directions. States that have an appropriation system for surface rights may wish to adapt that system to ground water uses, as has occurred in several Western States. Such States, as is recommended later, should also institute management schemes for the common resource. States adhering to the riparian system of water rights may find it desirable to adopt a statutory permit system encompassing surface and ground water and modifying the common law theretofore applicable.[13] Proposals for a statutory permit system for these States will be found in Section F of this chapter.

Overdrafts Affecting Surface Supplies:

Recommendation No. 7-2: Where surface and ground water supplies are interrelated and where it is hydrologically indicated, maximum use of the combined resource should be accomplished by laws and regulations authorizing or requiring users to substitute one source of supply for the other.

Discussion — In several Western States, notably Arizona, Colorado, and New Mexico, heavy use of ground water has caused reduced flows in rivers that form the source of supply for surface water

---

[12] CORKER, Charles E (1971). Ground Water Law, Management and Administration, prepared for the National Water Commission. National Technical Information Service, Springfield, Va., Accession No. PB 205 527. p. 147.

[13] The system of water law adopted by most Western States is known as the law of appropriation. The basic tenets of that system are that (1) a water right can be acquired only by diverting the water from the watercourse and applying it to a beneficial use and (2) in accordance with the date of acquisition, an earlier acquired water right shall have priority over later acquired water rights. Water in excess of that needed to satisfy existing rights is viewed as unappropriated water, available for appropriation by diversion and application of the water to a beneficial use. The process of appropriation can continue until all of the water in a stream is subject to rights of use through withdrawals from the stream.

Riparian water rights, characteristic of the Eastern States, protect adjacent landowners from withdrawals or uses which unreasonably diminish water quantity or quality. Where diversions or uses have been unreasonable, either they have been enjoined or riparian owners adversely affected have been compensated for interference with their rights. The concern of riparian law has been one of protecting private, rather than public, rights in lakes and streams.

appropriators with much earlier priorities. Serious difficulties arise in attempting to identify particular pumpers who are responsible and to determine the amounts by which each is depleting the surface stream. It may be equally difficult to identify the surface rights that have been injured, since the stream may have been losing water to ground water diversions over extended periods of time.

The objective, in situations such as these, is to integrate ground water and surface water uses. Suppose, for example, that the combined supply of ground and surface water would satisfy the demand of all appropriators—surface and underground, senior and junior—but that the surface supply alone would not satisfy surface diverters. If so, it would be undesirable to close wells so as to guarantee surface appropriators their full supply at the surface. Instead, the owners of rights to divert water from one source should be encouraged and, where the occasion warrants, required to take their supply from the other source. If senior surface appropriators in this illustration could thus be supplied from time to time from underground diversions, there might be no need to close interfering wells at times when the combined resource is adequate for all but when the surface streamflows are too low.

Where alternate points of diversion exist, as, for example, where a surface water user also owns a well that could supply his needs if he were authorized to use it, laws should be enacted and administrative regulations promulgated to foster conjunctive use. In this illustration, a regulation might authorize use of the well to take water normally taken from the stream. Where an administrator finds it necessary or desirable, a regulation might require use of the well. Water pumped from the well could be charged against the user's surface entitlement. Of course, where such alternative facilities do not exist or would be costly to install, a program of management to shift the cost of conjunctive use from individual users to all users may be called for.

Ground Water Management

Recommendations 7-1 and 7-2 urge the States to regulate both surface and ground water uses because complex problems of conjunctive use are beyond the reach of private law doctrines. Just as one kind of regulation, described above, may promote conjunctive use of privately-owned water rights, another kind of regulation—in the form of management by a public agency—may also help make optimum use of the combined resource. This kind of management may involve allocating the supply of ground water and surface water not only to the production of goods but to esthetic and recreational uses as well. Managers, properly directed, should take the necessary steps to protect, conserve, and in some instances augment the supply to assure its optimum use.

Recommendation No. 7-3: The Commission recommends that States in which ground water is an important source of supply commence conjunctive management of surface water (including imported water) and ground water through public management agencies.

Discussion — At least two modes of organization are available for ground water management. That most commonly encountered is the single regulatory agency, at the State level, having jurisdiction over the entire State and empowered to declare ground water basins to be in critical condition under prescribed statutory standards. New Mexico is an example of this approach. The other mode, examples of which are found in California, is to create a public management district embracing the critical aquifer. The Commission expresses no strong preference for one form of organization over the other. The form of organization should depend on the problems encountered—hydrological, institutional, and legal. In general, however, the more comprehensive the management needs to be, the more appropriate is the district form of organization, subject to oversight by the State Engineer.

The managing agency, State or local, will face certain operational choices. It must determine whether water extraction is (1) to be permitted to exhaust the supply or (2) to be limited to water available on a "sustained yield" basis at determined or determinable pump lifts. It can thus chart a course somewhere between complete depletion and full preservation. Similarly, it may decide whether and under what circumstances to permit new uses in a basin, whether or not to limit those new uses to the available recharge, whether to prolong or shorten the life of the aquifer. For example, for a designated basin it may be possible to establish an economically optimum useful life and then, giving due regard for annual withdrawals and annual recharge, to prohibit new wells that would exhaust the resource before the end of the time period so designated.

Different management tools can be used in different circumstances. Where a basin has already

234

undergone adjudication and many private rights have been decreed, management may amount to little more than administration of the decreed rights and regulation of new withdrawals. On the other hand, the management agency might use economic tools in lieu of, or in addition to, regulatory ones. A water management agency having the power to impose pump charges would be able to introduce incentives to affect decisions of water users in the interest of the best use and conservation of the resource. Through taxing or pricing mechanisms a management agency may, in effect, efficiently ration ground and surface water.

An illustration is provided by the management scheme employed by the Orange County Water District in Southern California. The District can buy imported water from the Metropolitan Water District of Southern California. Ground water is also available, but sole reliance on it would cause an overdraft, as it has in the past. Each year the Orange County Water District determines how much of the water demand shall be supplied from ground water and how much from imported water. The determination of the amount of ground water withdrawal is based in part on the quantity in storage in the aquifer and the anticipated recharge, including artificial recharge.

Suppose in a given year that the District decides to meet demand with 60 percent ground water and 40 percent surface water; these percentages establish each user's "fair share" of basin supply. Then the District establishes the cost differential between pumped water and imported water. Suppose imported water costs $14 per acre-foot more than pumped water. If a water user takes a total of 100 acre-feet of water during the year, pumping 60 percent and taking imported water for the other 40 percent, he pays no special charge,[14] although he has, of course, paid a premium of $14 per acre-foot for the imported water. If the user takes the full 100 acre-feet in ground water, he must pay a Basin Equity Assessment of $14 per acre-foot on 40 of the 100 acre-feet that he pumped. If another user takes his 100 acre-feet all in imported water (paying the $14 per acre-foot premium on the total imported), the District will credit him with $14 per acre-foot for the 60 acre-feet he could have pumped from the aquifer. As a consequence, all water users in the District pay approximately the same price per acre-foot for water no matter what the source, and all water users pay part of the costs for importing water even though some may use no part of it.[15] Even in the absence of a supply of imported water, a similar pricing system can be used to apportion withdrawals between indigenous surface supply and ground water supply.

The question of responsibility for organizing a water management agency with broad powers to effect conjunctive use must be resolved. Despite the success of the Orange County Water District, experience elsewhere (for example, in Colorado) suggests that little is accomplished if formation of the district is left to the local users. There is a reluctance to grant to such an agency the taxing and other powers essential for comprehensive, conjunctive management.[16] Therefore, the Commission recommends that the power to create and oversee the work of local water management agencies be vested in State administrative officers generally charged with the administration of natural resources—the State department of natural resources, the State engineer, or other appropriate State officers.

Recommendation No. 7-4: The States should adopt legislation authorizing the establishment of water management agencies with powers to manage surface water and ground water supplies conjunctively; to issue revenue bonds and collect pump taxes and diversion charges; to buy and sell water and water rights and real property necessary for recharge programs; to store water in aquifers, create salt water barriers and reclaim or treat water; to extract water; to sue in its own name and as representative of its members for the protection of the aquifer from damage, and to be sued for damages caused by its operations, such as surface subsidence.

---

[14] There are various other charges and taxes in the Orange County District; here there is reference only to the equalization charge, called the Basin Equity Assessment.

[15] The District also buys imported water from MWD for artificial recharge. Those purchases are financed by taxes and other water charges.

[16] The comprehensive management system found in Orange County is encountered infrequently elsewhere. Other States experiencing substantial overdrafts have achieved some success in regulating withdrawals by a quota system (e.g., New Mexico). Still others have attempted regulation but for a variety of reasons it has failed to curtail drilling (e.g., Arizona). In the Texas High Plains, an effort is made to limit ground water withdrawals by prohibiting runoff of tail water from the farm. Wastewater ponds collect the excess water which is then used for irrigation. Thus, pumping is limited, to the extent the regulation and its enforcement are effective, to the amount that can be used on the farm. This regulation does not, of course, restrict the drilling of more wells and the irrigation of more land; all it does is prevent waste.

Discussion − A full range of powers for effective management would include the following:

(a) **Financial Powers.** The management agency should have the power to issue revenue bonds and to levy pump taxes and diversion charges. The power to impose charges on the use of water within the district is vital if the agency is to be able to enforce rational choices between surface and ground water use where both are available and physically accessible to users.

It might be questioned whether a pump tax could be levied in districts where there are outstanding adjudicated water rights. The Commission believes the imposition of a pump tax is valid and that the courts would so hold. Water rights, like other kinds of property, are subject to taxation. A water right is no more than the right to the use of a quantity of water, and if a right-holder's use is fulfilled on terms substantially approximating those to which he is accustomed, he is unlikely to obtain legal relief because he is taxed for its use. Where the rights vary in value owing to differences in priority, the tax structure could and should take these differences into account.

A precedent exists in the Orange County Water District, where all pumpers, new or old, are charged for withdrawals.[17] Precedents also exist in the regulation of oil and gas, where production controls have been established to deal with the common pool problem and to support prices. Looking at the pump tax from the broad standpoint of regulatory power under the Federal Constitution, it is observed that one user's ground water pumping in a limited recharge aquifer necessarily increases the costs of all pumpers and eventually exhausts the resource. The objectives of the pump tax are (1) to apportion those increased costs among the pumpers equitably and (2) prolong the life of the resource. These objectives are clearly within the police power of the State, and the means employed to achieve the objectives−the pump tax−is rationally connected to them. The Commission believes, therefore, that pump taxes will withstand constitutional challenge.[18]

(b) **Acquisition and Alienation of Property.** The water management agency should be able to acquire water and water rights and real property for such purposes as spreading water for aquifer recharge. The agency should have power to buy and sell water and water rights and to export water out of the district when it is economically feasible to do so (when, for example, the return on water exported out of the district is greater than the return on that same water used within the district).

(c) **Operations.** The agency should be empowered to store water either underground or in surface reservoirs; to extract water; to create barriers against saline or other low-quality water intrusion; and to reclaim and treat water.

(d) **Litigation.** The agency should be authorized to represent all landowners and water right owners in representative suits with respect to water rights and water quality within its jurisdiction, to sue in its own name to enjoin or to obtain damages for activities injurious to ground water or to the storage capacity of the aquifer.

With this range of powers available to it, a water management agency should be able to perform comprehensive management functions within its territorial jurisdiction.

Aquifer Protection: While it is customary to think of the ground water in an aquifer as a natural resource, it is perhaps less obvious, but equally true, that the aquifer itself−its water-carrying, water-storing capacity−is an important resource to be protected.

Recommendation No. 7-5: The States should adopt laws and regulations to protect ground water aquifers from injury and should authorize enforcement both by individual property owners who are damaged and by public officials and management districts charged with the responsibility of managing aquifers.

Discussion − There are a number of ways in which the aquifer's important characteristics−its capacity to store water of good quality, its transmissivity, and its capability of being recharged−may be damaged or even destroyed. Activities that might harm the aquifer may or may not involve withdrawing water from it for use. Miners may intentionally drain an aquifer in order to remove rocks and minerals. Such highway and building construction activities as blasting and excavation, and gravel pit operations, may damage an aquifer. Development may seal off the recharge zone of an aquifer, as, where a surface

---

[17] *Orange County Water Dist. v. Farnsworth,* 138 Cal. App. 2d 518, 292 P. 2d 927 (Cal. Dist. Ct. of Appeals, 1956, sustained the constitutionality of a pump tax imposed under the authority of Section 44 of Cal. Stat. 1953, Ch. 770. The pump tax was levied as a replenishment assessment to pay for imported water to recharge an overdrawn aquifer.)

[18] State constitutions may, however, contain specific prohibitions that will require amendment.

Discharge from irrigation well, Rio Grande Project, New Mexico

area is covered with a layer of impervious materials, or, the weight of overlying structures produces compaction of the aquifer or its recharge zone.

Private remedies are generally available for aquifer damage of the types described, and these should be retained. Such remedies make relief available to owners of property rights where a public agency fails to act. Moreover, private property owners should be able to obtain compensation for wrongful damage to the aquifer measured by the loss they have suffered. Nevertheless, the Commission believes that statutory, publicly administered laws and regulations should also be available to prevent injury to aquifers. In the event of conflict between private plaintiffs and public officials over the conduct of litigation involving aquifer damage, control of the litigation can be given to the public official.

The importance of protecting underground aquifers from irremediable injury dictates the enactment of State legislation to permit regulation of those activities most likely to be harmful. Initially, permits should be required for all potentially dangerous or harmful activities on or below the surface. There should be continuous monitoring of the effects of activities that might reasonably affect water-bearing formations. As greater knowledge is acquired, regulations can be made more precise.

Subsidence: Just as it may happen that surface activities may seal or compact an aquifer, interfering with recharge, it may also occur that withdrawals of water from the formation may remove essential support of the surface resulting in collapse or subsidence of the surface and interference with surface uses attended by damage to structures located there.

The laws of most States make owners or possessors of mineral or other subsurface estates liable to owners or possessors of the surface estate for failure to provide subjacent (i.e., underlying) support. It is not clear that users of water from an aquifer would be similarly liable to owner-occupants of the surface for subsidence, since liability in the case of mineral operations usually is based on the legal relationship between the surface and subsurface owners. Uncertainties that exist in State law with respect to the duties of well owners to the owners of surface estates should be resolved. Where management of the aquifer has been charged to a public agency, the agency should be required to respond in the event damage from subsidence occurs. Recommendation 7-4 provides that water management agencies should be

subject to suit for damages caused by their operations. Revenues from the pump tax may be used to provide a fund from which injured persons might be compensated.

Reports on Management:

Recommendation No. 7-6: Any Federal agency seeking authorization of a Federal water project for an area having a usable ground water aquifer should describe and evaluate the ground water management programs in the area.

Discussion — Congress should be apprised of the status of ground water management programs in areas in which the desirability of authorizing Federal water projects is under consideration. Federal agency reports on proposed water projects should contain appropriate descriptions and evaluations of such ground water management programs so the Congress can judge whether or not and the extent to which progress in effective conjunctive management of ground water and surface water is being made and, thus, the extent to which that option is adequately considered as an alternative to proposed Federal projects.

Ground Water Mining

Ground water mining occurs when withdrawals are made from an aquifer at rates in excess of net recharge. The problem becomes serious when this practice continues on a sustained basis over time: ground water tables decline, making the pumping of water more and more expensive; compaction may occur in the aquifer, adversely affecting storage capacity and transmissivity; and quality may be threatened by salt water intrusion. Ground water mining may occur in aquifer systems having ample recharge as well as those having negligible recharge. In recharge aquifers, mining results from withdrawals substantially in excess of net recharge. In aquifers with little or no recharge, virtually any withdrawal constitutes mining and sustained withdrawals will, in due course, exhaust the supply or lower water tables below economic pump lifts. A prime example of ground water mining in an aquifer system with negligible recharge is found in the Ogallala Formation in the High Plains of Texas, an area that also has limited surface water resources.

The Southern High Plains of West Texas comprise all or part of 28 contiguous counties south of the

Canadian River and bordering New Mexico. Most of the irrigated acreage has been developed since World War II. The population of the area has increased in the major towns and cities during this period and is now over 600,000.[19] The area is heavily dependent on irrigation. Pumpage from 1953 to 1961 averaged 5 million acre-feet annually, compared to estimates of annual recharge of only 100,000 to 350,000 acre-feet.[20] As a result, the resource is being rapidly depleted. Precipitous declines in agricultural production are forecast by 1990, with cotton production reduced to 65 percent of that in 1966 and grain sorghums to 20 percent. These could be offset to some degree by a return to dryland farming. By 2015, irrigated acreage, without other sources of water, is projected to decline from 4 million acres at present to 125,000 acres, water pumpage from 4.1 million to 95,000 acre-feet annually, and value of agricultural production from $430 million to $128 million per year.[21] With less than 2½ percent of the present irrigation water, it is expected that output will be 30 percent of the present value. While one may argue about the specifics of the forecasts, there is little argument about the general prospects for the future.

A similar situation is developing in other portions of the Ogallala Formation, which extends as far north as the Platte River and underlies portions of New Mexico, Oklahoma, Eastern Colorado, Western Kansas, and Nebraska. In the Texas Northern High Plains (the 10 counties of the Panhandle north of the Canadian River), irrigated acreage increased from 317,000 acres to 1,144,000 acres, and pumpage from 363,000 acre-feet to 1,378,000 acre-feet during the period 1958-1969.[22] In Kansas, it is reported that 10,000 new wells were drilled in the Ogallala Formation between 1965 and 1971.[23]

[19] U.S. BUREAU OF THE CENSUS (January 1971). 1970 Census of Population, Advance Report, PC(VI)-45, Texas. U.S. Government Printing Office, Washington, D.C. Table 1.

[20] HUGHES, William F & HARMAN, Wyatte L (1969). Projected Economic Life of Water Resources, Subdivision Number 1, High Plains Underground Water Reservoir, Technical Monograph 6. Texas A&M University, College Station, Tex.

[21] Ibid., p. 5.

[22] TEXAS WATER DEVELOPMENT BOARD (1971). Inventories of Irrigation in Texas 1958, 1964, and 1969, Report 127. Texas Water Development Board, Austin, Tex. Table 1.

[23] KRAUSE, Keith, Executive Director, Kansas State Water Resources Board, Topeka (February 8, 1972). Personal communication.

Mining ground water is not inherently wrong. It is wrong, however, when the water is mined out without taking account of the future value of the water and the storage capacity of the reservoir. If a ground water aquifer were entirely unrelated to other aquifers and to surface water bodies, and if it were entirely owned by one person or organization, society could leave the decision to mine or not to mine to the owner. Presumably, the owner would seek to balance benefits from present production against anticipated benefits from future production in such a way as to maximize economic return from the resource over time as in the case of any other type of mining. The owner's self-interest would ordinarily coincide with society's interest. But ground water reservoirs are often associated with surface supplies and with other aquifers and are rarely in a single ownership. Accordingly, ground water reservoirs often suffer from the mismanagement associated with other "common pool" resources, namely, excessive use leading to premature exhaustion.

Common pool resources are those in which the right to make use of the resource without charge is shared with others. In the most aggravated cases there is no limit on the amount each may take. Since the resource is not priced, there is no incentive on the part of any user to reduce consumption today in order to save for tomorrow. Anyone who foregoes present consumption to preserve future supply runs the risk that another will take the resource for present use. In short, there is no incentive to save for tomorrow even though all may agree that prices may be substantially higher (and therefore the resource more valuable) in the future or that excessive use today lowers prices below long-run profit maximizing levels. Examples include unregulated commercial fishing and oil production, as well as ground water pumping. The social consequences are twofold: the resource may be consumed at a rate faster than is desirable and economies dependent on the resource may wither and die prematurely. The Nation should be concerned with both.

Although the classic cases of misallocation of common pool resources involve uses that are neither priced nor limited in quantity, placing a restriction on the number of new wells that can be drilled and the amount of water that can be pumped from old wells does not solve all the problems. So long as the withdrawal of water is not priced (i.e., is available without cost to the user), each pumper has an incentive to take the maximum he is allowed to pump, since any "prudent" saving on his part does not necessarily accrue to his account. Moreover, denial of entry of new pumpers may have the effect of allocating the water to present-day, low-value uses, freezing out newer, more valuable uses.

Pump Taxes: In theory, one good way to deal with the problem is to operate ground water reservoirs as if they were in a single ownership, to the extent that may be possible. In practice, this means creating a management district whose officers seek to maximize combined net revenues over time. The district could adopt a pricing system for the withdrawal of water by imposing a pump tax on each acre-foot extracted. The amount of the tax should be determined by estimating the future value of the water and charging a price for present withdrawals equal to the future value discounted to present value. For example, if the district estimates the value of water 20 years from now to be $50 an acre-foot and if it adopts a discount rate of 7 percent, the pump tax on present withdrawals would be $13 an acre-foot ($13 placed at 7 percent interest for 20 years grows in value to $50). Those pumpers whose present uses produce revenues equal to or greater than the pump tax and other costs will continue to pump. Present uses of lesser value will be discontinued and the resource saved for future, more valuable uses.

If a full-scale pricing system like the one described were to be put into effect, a transition period of gradual full implementation might have to be provided, to allow for adjustment to the new system. The Commission believes that adoption of this pricing system will not have serious dislocation effects. It will lead rather to more efficient and more conservative use of water, to cultivation of higher-value crops, and only gradually to the phasing out of marginal farms. The latter may produce some dislocation, but that must be compared with the present situation of unregulated or partially regulated pumping, which results in excessive and uneconomic withdrawals, premature exhaustion of the aquifer, and unavailability of water for future users.

The question often arises in discussions of pump taxes of where the proceeds should go. To achieve economically efficient use of the resource, the theoretically correct answer is that it does not matter where the proceeds go so long as they do not go back to the user in proportion to the amount of water he has used. But some better practical answers can be given. One appropriate disposition would be to purchase the pumping rights of users who say they cannot afford the pump charges. Another appropriate

use would be the creation of a development fund for planning and constructing a project to import water where economically feasible or for developing an alternative economic base less dependent on large uses of water.

If a full-scale pricing system on underground water, as described, is thought to be too great a departure from orthodoxy, the use of a more modest pump tax to achieve less-than-ideal goals of conservation and economic efficiency may be desirable.

For example, a district managing an aquifer which has little or no recharge could arbitrarily determine a period of use for the aquifer, say 40 years. This will certainly be easier than attempting to accurately forecast the future value of water. The period of use may or may not be economically optimum. The district would then determine annually the amount of water that should be withdrawn in each succeeding year, taking account of recharge, if any, to achieve the 40-year aquifer life span. Next it would set a pump charge at a level which would encourage district members in any particular year to pump all the water scheduled for availability that year, no more and no less. If greater amounts are pumped, the pump charge was set too low and should be raised; if lesser amounts are pumped, the pump charge was set too high and should be lowered.

Trial and error should establish with fair accuracy the correct level of pump charges necessary in any year to extend the life of the aquifer to the desired terminal date. As conditions change over time and the value to users of pumped water shifts, the level of pump charges can be appropriately manipulated from one year to the next so that the desired period of use of the aquifer is realized.

Because of diminishing returns, as more and more water is used in a given year, each additional acre-foot pumped that year will yield progressively less value to the user. The first units of water, naturally, are the most productive and return the most extra revenue. Any additional water is relegated to progressively less efficient use. The pump charge per acre-foot remains constant but the extra revenue derived from each extra unit of water gets progressively less as more and more water is used. Each user will pump water until the value to him from the last acre-foot pumped (the extra crop revenue attributable to that acre-foot of water) just equals the pump charge (plus, of course, any other costs of pumping, which may be considerable). Thereafter he will stop pumping. If during a pumping season, the last acre-foot pumped is more valuable to him than the pump charge on that acre-foot plus other pumping costs, he will pump more. Why not? The cost for that acre-foot of water is less than the extra revenue which is expected to be obtained from its application to the land. If, on the other hand, the last acre-foot pumped is less valuable than the pump charge and other costs on that acre-foot, he will pump less. No sensible user will pump an extra acre-foot of water the cost of which exceeds the extra return attributable to it.

Economists correctly argue that this process results in an efficient allocation of the scarce water resource. All users pay the same pump charge. Each user pumps water to the point where the value to him of the last acre-foot pumped is equal to the pump charge and associated costs. For some users (those who are most efficient, whose lands are highly productive), this may be a large amount of water. For others (those who are less efficient), the break-even point where value of water to the user equals the pump charge and associated costs will be reached quickly after only relatively small amounts of water are pumped and used. In this way, the amount of water scheduled for availability during a year will be apportioned to users so that the value of agricultural production in the district from that given amount of water is maximized. Those who can use the water most profitably will use more than those whose use is marginal. This is what is meant by efficient allocation of the water resource. Returns to society from the given amount of available water are maximized.[24]

Failure to charge a price for water, to levy a pump tax, or to institute some other effective method of regulation will result in a less-than-optimum allocation of the water. Free water means too much will be pumped, some of what is pumped will be used wastefully, perhaps on land which is only marginally productive, and the life of the aquifer will be prematurely terminated. Rationing water on the basis of so many acre-feet per acre of farm land and prohibiting its sale and transfer means a low-productivity farm of a given size will receive the same amount of water as a high-productivity farm of the same size; too much water will be used on the former and not enough on the latter. By pricing water as a scarce resource (e.g., levying a pump tax or by allowing water to be freely sold from one user to another) it will be rationed out efficiently so that production in the district will be maximized each year for the set amount of water scheduled as available that year.

Quota Restrictions: An alternate means of regulating withdrawals is the quota system. One example is prior appropriation, whereby new pumpers are excluded from the aquifer and historic pumpers are limited to their historic use.[25] The quota system will not yield good economic results, however, unless pumping rights are freely transferable. Since under the quota system there is no entry by new, higher-valued uses, and since the present allocation is based on historic

---

[24] An illustration of how this efficiency mechanism works may be useful. Suppose that two 1,000-acre cotton farms use a common pool of underground water for irrigation. Suppose further that each farm, being of equal size, is allotted the same amount of water—100 acre-feet each. With 100 acre-feet of water, Farm A with fertile soil is capable of producing 1,500 bales of cotton. With an identical amount of irrigation water, Farm B with less fertile soil produces only 1,000 bales of cotton. Without a pricing mechanism on irrigation water and without transferability of water by sale, this situation could persist indefinitely. With a pricing system, however, Farm A is liable to bid water away from Farm B. For Farm A, being more productive than Farm B, the extra revenue from the application of extra acre-feet of water continues to exceed the extra cost long after that break-even point is reached by Farm B. As a result, suppose half of the water to which Farm B is entitled is sold instead to Farm A. Farm A will then end up with 150 acre-feet of irrigation water and Farm B will be left with 50 acre-feet. What are the results? Because of diminishing returns (technically because of diminishing marginal-physical-product of water, which is the same thing), the 50 percent increase in irrigation water for Farm A will probably not increase Farm A's cotton production by as much as 50 percent.

The increase will be something less. Suppose, because of the 50 percent additional irrigation water, Farm A's production increases from 1,500 bales to 2,000 bales (a 33-1/3 percent increase). For the same reason (diminishing returns) that Farm A's output did not increase by 50 percent because of a 50 percent increase in irrigation water, Farm B's output will probably not decrease by as much as 50 percent because of its 50 percent decrease in irrigation water. Suppose, as a result of 50 percent less water, Farm B's production decreases from 1,000 to 667 bales (a 33-1/3 percent decrease). Before the reallocation, the combined production of Farms A and B was 2,500 bales. After reallocation, the combined production of Farms A and B, with the same 200 acre-feet of water, is 2,667. Because it has been more efficiently allocated, entirely as a result of pricing, the same 200 acre-feet of water has been able to provide a net increase in society's cotton production of 167 bales. QED.

[25] The California Supreme Court, operating under a mixed system of appropriation law, reasonable use rules, and prescriptive rights, ordered percentage cutbacks in withdrawals by all users, where it concluded that the overdraft on an aquifer was too great. *Pasadena v. Alhambra*, 33 Cal. 2d 908, 207 P. 2d 17 (1949).

use without regard to value in use, the more efficient user has no source of additional supply except to buy it from an existing user. Therefore, in the interest of efficient allocation of water, restrictions on transfers in States employing the quota system should be abolished.

Whether a State employs a pump tax or a quota system or some other effective means for regulating ground water withdrawals, the regulator must fix the life of the aquifer if withdrawals persistently exceed recharge. This decision should be based on the relative benefits from producing water today as compared to producing water in the future. The calculations should be reviewed periodically as the economy changes, with the withdrawal rate increasing or decreasing as forecasts change. A region with a growing water demand and expensive alternative sources of supplemental supply should adopt a slower rate of withdrawal than a region with a static or declining demand.

As has been shown, however, some high growth areas are depleting their ground water at rapid rates. There are at least two reasons: (1) the common pool phenomenon is at work, because the regulation of withdrawals is inadequate, and (2) there often is an expectation that subsidized surface water will be imported to the region in the future.

Recommendation No. 7-7: Where ground water mining is occurring, the States themselves (or local management agencies) should immediately institute regulation of ground water withdrawal and conjunctive management of ground water and surface water, where the latter source of supply is available. Regulation and management can include levying of pump taxes, or implementation of quota restrictions with freely transferable pumping rights, or some other means, and should have as its purpose conservation and prudent use of the water resource. It can also include artificial recharge, improving infiltration capacity, and other management activities. It should take account of the value of present uses as compared to the estimated value of future uses, the desirability of preserving some ground water for future use irrespective of estimated future value, and such effects on the aquifer system from rapid depletion as loss of storage capacity and reduced transmissivity.

Recommendation No. 7-8: The President should issue an executive order directing Federal agencies charged with responsibility of water resource planning and development to include in all pertinent studies and
project proposals a description of the ground water resource, whether or not ground water is being mined and, if so, the regulatory and management regime applicable to it, together with an evaluation of that regime.

Recommendation No. 7-9: Congress should scrutinize closely the economic justification for water supply projects designed to supply supplementary water to areas that have mined ground water and should examine the circumstances giving rise to the project proposal including the presence or absence of ground water regulation and management, and their operation.

Discussion – The Commission believes that ground water mining is a national problem because of the misallocation of resources resulting from excessive pumping and because the Federal Government is likely to be called upon as the agency of first resort for a rescue operation. The Commission does not believe, however, that the Congress should enact a comprehensive Federal ground water law regulating withdrawal. Rather, Congress should assist States and local regions to obtain the information necessary to make sound decisions, it should declare a policy of supporting water development projects only when they are economically sound, and it should implement this policy by close scrutiny of proposed "rescue projects," examining not only the economics of project proposals but also conservation and management practices applied to ground water and surface water by the region to benefit from the project.

The Commission has given extended thought to the role of the Federal Government in discouraging ground water mining and promoting prudent aquifer management. One possibility is preemptive Federal regulation. The Commission rejects this alternative because it does not think the problem is capable of a single solution and questions the likelihood of a Federal agency developing multiple solutions adaptable to a variety of local conditions. Moreover, the Commission believes that the States and local units of government are as capable of weighing present values of ground water use against estimated future values as a Federal agency, provided they have adequate information.

Clearly, the Federal Government has a direct financial interest in ground water mining when a region suffering from overdraft seeks a rescue operation. Chapter 8 on interbasin transfers deals specifically with the criteria that should govern Federal assistance to water resource projects. It is recommended that Congress require a water project to meet the following conditions: (1) that it be the least-cost alternative source of water to serve the given purposes; (2) that the value of the water in the new uses exceed the value in the old uses plus the costs of construction; and (3) that the productivity of the investment in the project be compared to productivity of alternative investments. It could be argued that if these conditions are met, it really makes no difference whether the project is designed to rescue an overdrawn aquifer system or to provide a supply for an area to be brought under irrigation for the first time. Satisfaction of these conditions, however, is a guaranty that the project is economically sound.

The difficulty of this hypothesis is that the economic criteria cannot be applied with mathematical certainty. All figures supplied in response to the criteria are subject to a range of accuracy and involve a good deal of judgment. Moreover, since the purpose of a rescue project is to save a declining economy, there may be a temptation to shade the figures in favor of the project and even to loosen or dispense with the criteria.

The Commission believes, therefore, that Congress should be as fully informed as possible of all the circumstances surrounding proposed water development projects. If a proposal is for a project to rescue an overdrawn aquifer, Congress should know that fact and should know also what steps, if any, the region has taken to conserve its ground water. Congress should scrutinize closely project proposals for areas mining ground water that have not instituted conservation regimes and prudent management practices as described earlier.

Problems of Ground Water Pollution

Because they are more lasting, the effects of ground water pollution can be more significant than the effects of surface water pollution, yet, paradoxically, less attention has been paid to it and less is known about it. There is a great variety in the sources of ground water pollution. Some are obvious, such as waste disposal wells into which toxic substances are intentionally injected. Others are unintended by-products of other activities: oil and gas operations which permit the seepage of petroleum or salt water into fresh water strata; agricultural operations which permit introduction of excess applications of ferti-

lizers and pesticides into the ground water; use of salt on roadways to remove snow and ice which results in percolation of saline water into fresh water aquifers; human wastes which reach ground water reservoirs creating health hazards from viral infections. In some instances, the effect on ground water quality from polluted surface water runoff is not known since long periods of time often elapse between cause and effect and since some purification occurs in the meantime.[26] A Senate Committee has reported that ground water quality is deteriorating, but that ground water pollution has not yet reached dangerous levels.[27] Ground water pollution has long-term and sometimes irreversible effects; the consequence of aquifer pollution may be to place greater demands on other sources of water. The Commission believes that the subject is of national concern.

Recommendation No. 7-10: Funds should be granted to the U.S. Geological Survey to increase its study of ground water pollution, the causes thereof, and the relationship between surface water pollution and ground water pollution. The USGS should monitor ground water quality, giving priority to aquifers threatened by impairment of quality.

Recommendation No. 7-11: The States should regulate the drilling, completion, operation, and abandonment of wells for the purpose of protecting ground water quality. Well drillers should be licensed, permits should be required before drilling is permitted, and drilling and completion reports (including well logs where appropriate) should be required.

Recommendation No. 7-12: The regulation of ground water quality by the States should be the responsibility of the same agencies that regulate surface water quality.

Recommendation No. 7-13: A State agency should be responsible for identifying the adverse effects on ground water quality resulting from land use, and the States, or governmental subdivisions thereof, should

---

[26] The reader is referred to Chapter 4 on the control of water pollution.

[27] U.S. CONGRESS, Senate (1971). Federal Water Pollution Control Act Amendments of 1971, Report of the Committee on Public Works, U.S. Senate, together with Supplemental Views to Accompany S. 2770. 92d Congress, 1st Session, Senate Report No. 92-414. U.S. Government Printing Office, Washington, D.C. p. 73.

regulate land use among other purposes so as to control or eliminate such adverse effects.[28]

Recommendation No. 7-14: Any report on a water supply project proposed by a Federal agency should contain a full description of the quality of the local ground water, its suitability for use, the deterioration that has occurred in the last 20 years (if data are available), the ground water quality control program applicable in the area, and its adequacy.

Recommendation No. 7-15: Federal legislation on control of surface water pollution should be expanded to include ground water pollution, and the regulatory regime and enforcement techniques at the Federal level should be the same for both surface and ground water.[29]

Discussion — Just as regulation of withdrawal and use should embrace both ground and surface water, regulation of waste discharge should also cover the two. Not only are sources of supply often interrelated but the expertise bearing on surface water quality will also bear on ground water quality. The agency that regulates one should regulate the other. Adequate protection of aquifers will require some specialized techniques of regulation, relating to the supervision of drilling, operation, and completion of wells. For example, a shallow well for domestic water supply might routinely be drilled within 90 days of notice to the agency if disapproval is not forthcoming. At the opposite extreme, no waste disposal well should be permitted until the agency determines the risk of harm to the aquifer and concludes that the benefit outweighs the risk.

In addition to regulation of well drilling through licensing and drilling permits, other means of regulation are likely to become necessary as knowledge increases about the effect of polluted surface runoff on ground water quality. For example, land use controls will become progressively more important because of the potential detrimental effects of septic tanks, evaporation pits, sanitary land fills, and excavation. Continuous monitoring of ground water quality and scientific investigation of the relation of surface operations to ground water quality are necessary to develop effective techniques and sound criteria for additional regulation.

Interstate Ground Water Aquifers

The focus of the discussion thus far has been on problems of management of intrastate aquifers. The same problems can arise in interstate aquifer systems, and their solution is more complicated since two or more sovereignties are involved. Where a common pool extends beneath two or more States, excessive pumping in State A may lower the water table in State B, increasing pumping costs of B's residents or interfering with senior surface water rights in State B. Pollution of an interstate aquifer in State A may spread to State B. Adoption of the regulatory and management measures recommended in this section should prevent some controversies from arising and may postpone others. Ultimately, however, two or more States overlying a common aquifer in which long-term withdrawals exceed recharge face controversies over their respective shares of the supply.

At present there is virtually no law available to resolve such controversies. The United States Supreme Court has never adjudicated an interstate ground water aquifer. The Special Master in *Arizona v. California*[30] indicated in a draft opinion that he was prepared to enjoin additional pumping in New Mexico where its effect would be to deplete the surface flow available to senior Arizona priorities, but the matter was disposed of by consent decree. It seems clear that a full-scale judicial apportionment of an interstate aquifer would be a very burdensome undertaking, requiring the tribunal to make difficult findings of fact and to propound conclusions of law unassisted by prior precedents.

Under these circumstances, the Commission believes the States would be well advised to enter into agreements for the regulation and management of interstate aquifers. The measures recommended here for intrastate aquifers are equally applicable to interstate aquifers. The States could implement those measures either by interstate compact or by

---

[28] This particular recommendation is neutral with respect to proposals for Federal land use planning and regulation; it pertains only to State and local regulation.

[29] This recommendation is not intended to suggest that surface stream standards and ground water standards should be identical. Because ground water is often slow to recharge, it frequently has less assimilative capacity than surface water; hence, ground water standards might properly be stricter than surface water standards. What is intended is that Federal pollution control embrace both surface water and ground water and that the same agency administer both, using the same regulatory techniques.

[30] *Arizona v. California*, 373 U.S. 546 (1963). The Special Master's report is on file in the Supreme Court but is not otherwise generally available.

reciprocal legislation. If appropriate legislation for aquifer regulation and management existed in each overlying State, interstate cooperation might be achieved by administrative agreements reached by the officials of the two States responsible for ground water administration.[31]

The Need for Information

Whoever has the task of allocating and distributing ground water to various users for various purposes must first face a central and pervasive problem: the prediction of how much, where, and when water will be available; of what quality it will consist; of how long it will last if it is to be mined; and the effects of development and utilization of the resource. Since many ground water basins are supplied from surface water, difficulties in forecasting supplies include those associated with predicting surface flows together with those of predicting the movement of water beneath the surface of the earth. Data about particular sources of ground water are relatively difficult to obtain, costly, and usually less precise than comparable data about the water that is visible at the earth's surface.

Not only is there a need for more data and analysis, there is also a pressing need to translate such data into terms that are readily understood by persons who must make water management decisions. The translations must comprehend not only facts of hydrology but also of geology, law, economics, and public administration.

Because failure to determine ground water supplies accurately is potentially disastrous, additional work in charting available supplies and rates of replenishment is called for.

Recommendation No. 7-16: The U.S. Geological Survey should make continuing intensive investigation of significant aquifer systems giving priority to those with falling water tables and deteriorating water quality. The investigations should seek to determine:

a. aquifer boundaries, thickness, saturation, and transmissivity;
b. the suitability of overlying land and wells for artificial recharge programs;
c. depth of water, quality and temperature of water;
d. the storage capacity at various ground water levels;

e. the source of pollutants found in the aquifer;
f. natural discharge from the aquifer, principal withdrawals, sources and amounts of recharge, anticipated yields, and the effect of pumping on surface supplies;
g. the extent of past ground water mining and the estimated economic life of the aquifer under various assumptions as to rates of withdrawal; and
h. the susceptibility of the aquifer to operation and management on a "sustained yield" basis.

Recommendation No. 7-17: Federal appropriations for the Federal-State cooperative study programs should be increased to meet the amount of matching funds available from the States.

Recommendation No. 7-18: The U.S. Geological Survey (USGS) should report the results of these investigations to the Congress, the Water Resources Council, the Office of Management and Budget, the Environmental Protection Agency, the Governors, State engineers (or their equivalents), and State water quality control agencies of the affected States, and local officials, including city councils, county officials, and local water management officials.

Recommendation No. 7-19: On the basis of data received from the USGS, the Water Resources Council should formulate recommendations for improved ground water management practices and transmit its recommendations to appropriate Federal, State, and local officials.

Recommendation No. 7-20: Federal and State courts should be empowered to obtain the services of the USGS in water litigation for water supply and quality investigations, and these services should be available at cost, subject to the availability of personnel and other resources to conduct the investigations.

Discussion — The USGS is the Federal agency principally responsible for ground water research. It has investigated and surveyed ground water resources for many decades. Early emphasis was on the location, boundary description, and calculation of the depth of overlying land down to water of major aquifers. Developing needs have led to more detailed research describing the quality and quantity of the available ground water, the suitability of overlying land and wells for artificial recharge, the potentiality of wells, and the effect of subsurface waste disposal on the aquifer. This research has required the location

---

[31] CORKER, Charles E (1971). Ground Water Law, Management and Administration, prepared for the National Water Commission. National Technical Information Service, Springfield, Va., Accession No. PB 205 527.

and measurement of natural discharges and artificial withdrawals and the determination of physical characteristics of the aquifer including thickness, saturation, permeability, transmissivity, and geological composition. Ground water research has been closely related to surface water research in field work, and the ground water-surface water system has been recognized as a single resource.

Studies are initiated by Congress, by the USGS itself, by the USGS at the request of other Federal agencies, and by the States under a matching funds, cooperative program. The intensity and detail of the studies vary greatly. Availability of data and the needs of cooperating States are largely responsible for the variability. Since the cost of in-depth exploratory drilling programs is generally high, the USGS relies heavily on core samples, water samples, and pumpage and water level records provided by private well users. These data are supplemented by USGS investigations and by projections based on geological data. Extensive use has been made of digital and analog computer models in some areas to describe aquifers and to predict future water supply, given changing pumpage and recharge rates. Unfortunately, extensive data and models are available only for selected aquifers.

Due primarily to insufficient funding and the relatively recent emergence of scientific ground water research methods, ground water research remains behind surface water research in meeting current information needs. The USGS recently reported that only 40 percent of the national need for ground water resource appraisal is currently being met. Only 20 percent of the needed intensive systems studies have been conducted. In some instances the lack of Federal funds has prevented the making of studies under the cooperative program, even though the States were prepared to pay their share of the costs.

Ground water data are available in USGS or cooperating State publications. Much of the information remains very technical and not readily understood by people of nontechnical backgrounds who must make water management decisions.

CONCLUSIONS

Approximately one-fifth of America's present water withdrawals are derived from ground water. The ground water share of the Nation's water requirements is expected to increase because of increasing demands and the wide availability of ground water.

Ground water is often interrelated with surface water and the ways in which one is managed can often affect the other. Accordingly, ground water and surface water laws should be integrated and the two sources of supply should be managed on an interchangeable and coordinated basis where applicable.

Management can be undertaken by a statewide agency or at the local level by a water management district. Goals of optimum use can be achieved either by regulatory directives or by economic incentives. To be effective, water management agencies must be empowered with sufficient authority to get the job done—to insure that the combined ground-surface water supply is used efficiently and the aquifer protected from damage or premature depletion. It is most important that water management agencies have regulatory power, as well as the power to levy pump taxes or other kinds of charges on ground water withdrawals and that pumpers have the right to transfer water allotments.

So that Congress can judge the adequacy with which the States and localities are managing their ground water and surface water resources conjunctively, Federal agencies proposing Federal water projects should report on such ground water management programs.

In some parts of the country, ground water is being withdrawn faster than it is being recharged. This is called ground water mining and, although it is not necessarily undesirable, when done recklessly and without considering future prospects, it can result in serious economic repercussions. Mining water from a common pool which underlies numerous discrete land ownerships is particularly harmful because normal economic mechanisms which provide incentives to consider future consequences may not be operating.

A good way to insure that ground water is not inappropriately mined is to calculate its future value (properly discounted) and to charge users accordingly by means of a uniform pump tax. If the value of pumped water to a user exceeds the discounted-future-value charge, he will pump; otherwise he will not. Because of difficulties in accurately estimating future values, a pump tax can be set at a level to extend the life of a ground water aquifer to some date in the future which is conceived as the "appropriate" period of use for the aquifer. Another alternative is to set quota restrictions on the amount of water each user can withdraw based on historic use of each user. To assure efficient allocation of the water, however, pumped water should be freely transferable by sale from one user to another.

Although it has not received as much attention as surface water pollution, ground water pollution may be more significant. Because surface water and ground water are so often interrelated and because the same water quality control expertise must often be applied to both, the agencies which monitor and enforce surface water pollution controls should be responsible for ground water pollution abatement as well, at both the Federal and State levels.

Another problem stems from the fact that one ground water pool may underlie two or more States. Little law has been developed for the regulation and management of such interstate aquifers. It is clear that interstate aquifers should be managed and regulated in the same fashion as intrastate aquifers. To do so, it is desirable that States enter into arrangements with one another to permit appropriate management and regulation of interstate aquifers.

Finally, it is apparent that there is a deficiency in the amount of technical data and other information about ground water resources, information which is needed to make sound decisions with regard to regulation and management. Fortunately, the U.S.

Geological Survey has substantial experience in making ground water investigations. Its investigations should be expanded to fill in the gaps of present knowledge needed for effective and efficient management of ground water supplies. The information developed by these investigations should be transmitted, together with interpretations, to appropriate Federal, State, and local agencies and officials.

RECOMMENDATIONS

To effect the desired improvement in management of the Nation's ground water resources, and in light of the above conclusions, the Commission has developed 20 specific recommendations which are spelled out in detail in the body of this section. The first two call for better integration of ground and surface water use. Then follow four recommendations on ground water management, three on ground water mining, and six on pollution of aquifers. The final five recommendations propose improvements in ground water information systems.

Section C

Pricing As A Means Of Motivating Better Use[32]

In the past, water has been generally so abundant, relative to the demand for it, that it was available virtually for the taking. Today, however, this is no longer the case. Water has become a resource that is relatively scarce. The land, labor, and capital resources needed to convey water to places of useful application and to collect and treat wastewater are also scarce.

If a resource is scarce, it behooves society to apportion its use in such a way as to obtain the maximum beneficial return. The limited supply of usable water should be allocated among the uses where it will be most productive. The pricing

mechanism is a powerful and remarkably effective way to do this. By charging a price for water and water-related services, the scarce water resource will be shifted to its most productive uses, where it has maximum utility for society.

The more units one consumes of any commodity, the less useful is the last unit consumed. As any one user "consumes" more and more water, the value to him of the last water used becomes lower and lower. When a price tag is attached to water, each user will continue to use more and more water until the value to him of the last unit used is reduced to the point where it equals the price he is charged for water. Thereafter, he will stop using water.

Those whose use of water yields a utility or value in excess of the cost to them of the additional water will use more; those whose use of water costs them more than the utility or value they obtain will use less. Thus, water use will be shifted to where it is most productive in terms of aggregate utility or value to society.

[32] This section is based in part on DAVIS, Robert K & HANKE, Steve H, George Washington University (1971). Pricing and Efficiency in Water Resource Management, prepared for the National Water Commission. National Technical Information Service, Springfield, Va., Accession No. PB 209 083.

While other means might be employed to motivate better use of existing and future supplies of water such as elaborate rationing mechanisms, nothing is as comprehensive and as effective as the pricing mechanism.

THE PROBLEM

Systems of pricing and user charges are employed for a number of purposes including the provision of revenues to recover costs of supply, allocation of financial burdens to direct beneficiaries, and provision of incentives to insure that the value of the services of water is at least equal to the cost of supply, thereby avoiding overinvestment in water developments.

The primary concern here is with the potentials for pricing water to provide incentives for improved utilization of water. This section discusses the principles of pricing, obstacles to greater use of pricing systems, and potentials for increasing efficiency of use through the administrative pricing of municipal, industrial, and irrigation water supplies and municipal sewerage services. The basic principles of pricing discussed in this section apply to all uses of water. The Commission's specific recommendations as to pricing policies for navigation, recreation, and other water uses are discussed in their respective sections of this report.

DISCUSSION

Allocation by Pricing

The general function of prices in the economy is to allocate resources among various production and consumption activities. Given the limits on national resources—water, land, labor, minerals, capital goods, etc.—output of one commodity can increase only if resources are diverted to it from production of something else. Consumers may benefit from almost any increase in a commodity output; but the crucial question is whether they benefit by more than the cost of foregone alternative products and services that must be given up because of diverted resources. One role of prices is to reflect these costs to consumers and thus provide an incentive for them to increase consumption only if real benefits exceed real costs. Another role of prices is to inform the producer of the consumer's relative desire for a commodity and hence indicate the extent to which resources should be devoted to expanding its production. Prices thus

serve two functions: to allocate consumption and to induce production of the desired level of supply.

The purpose of prices is to provide checks and balances on consumption and production activities so that value gained from expansions of output will be greater than the value of the alternative opportunities that must be foregone to make the expansion possible. Prices can play this role not only in the marketing of private goods, but also in regulating the consumption of certain commodities produced by governments. Pricing is potentially a powerful tool for the efficient allocation of water and water-related services.

Valuing Water Resources: Water is a mobile resource typically used and reused until it is "lost," usually through evaporation or into the sea. The perspective needed for proper evaluation of a given amount of water is the entire flow or hydrologic system. The same unit of water may be used for a number of uses within the stream including, for example, hydro-power, recreation, fish production, waste dilution, and navigation. Or the water may be diverted from the stream to be used for metropolitan, industrial, or agricultural uses. These diversions may return to the stream diminished in quantity or degraded in quality. Occasionally, they may even be improved in quality for subsequent uses. In any event, they are often changed in time of flow and in location from the original diversion. Substantial interdependencies among water uses should be fully recognized in the management of water supply.[33]

The evaluation of water should give full recognition to the effect that each use has on subsequent uses. Reducing the quality, delaying flows, or diverting water to a different location makes it potentially less useful to others. These are just as much measures of use as is the more obvious "use" of a quantity of water. Ideally, water uses would be priced on the basis of how much of the "usefulness" is "taken out" of the water. A use that diverts water, uses it, and returns it quickly in good condition to the same point in the stream would be charged little. A diversion with long conveyance and return far downstream would pay more, as would uses that degrade quality or divert at critical times but return

---

[33] YOUNG, Robert A & GRAY, S Lee, Colorado State University (1972). The Economic Value of Water: Concepts and Empirical Estimates, prepared for the National Water Commission. National Technical Information Service, Springfield, Va., Accession No. PB 210 356.

flow to the stream only after delay to a less-desirable location.

Such a comprehensive pricing system is far from a practical reality at this time, although there are elements of such a system in use in scattered locations.[34] For this reason, efficient use of water, in hydrologic systems where sequential uses occur, requires regulation of uses within a legal and administrative framework. The competitive market is not constituted to account for optimum utilization of water in such cases because the economic effects extend beyond the buyers and sellers involved. Nevertheless, the use of pricing systems within established legal and administrative frameworks will greatly enhance the efficiency of water use, as will the reform of present legal systems to provide for the free exchange of water rights under specific conditions.[35]

Principles of an Effective Pricing System

In order for prices to properly serve their allocative function in consumption and production, they must be equal to costs of supplying the product. This equality of prices to costs must be true at the margin. The price should equal the cost of the last unit supplied. This is the principle of incremental or marginal cost pricing. Pricing on any other basis, specifically at less than incremental cost, causes consumers to use more than would be justified on the basis of the principle that benefits gained from use should be greater than costs for *each* unit.

Incremental cost pricing means that the price of a product should be equal to the cost of the last unit used. Production of an extra unit of output that is priced at a level below the extra cost of its production leads to an inefficient use of resources. It means that the value of the extra unit to the consumer (i.e., the price) is less than the value of the resources that go into its production. Too much of the product is being produced and consumed which in turn means that too much of society's scarce resources are tied up in its production and, accordingly, too little is available for the production of other goods and services.[36]

Efficiency can be improved by establishing a different set of prices for a variety of different conditions. For example, water supply systems are characteristically subject to strong peak demands. Prices at times of peak demand should reflect the costs of providing this little used but costly peaking capacity. Similarly, prices to users farthest from the source of supply should reflect the increasing costs of conveyance to them. And prices to users at higher elevations should reflect added costs of pumping.[37] In this way expensive and uneconomic uses will be discouraged in favor of more efficient use. Table 7-1 demonstrates that there is an enormous variation in the costs per user in water supply and sewage collection systems depending on distance of the user from the plant and the population density of the area served.

Incremental cost pricing alone may not produce sufficient revenues to cover all costs. For some industries, such as water utilities, incremental costs (the extra cost involved in the production of an extra unit of output) are constantly falling as production expands (until full capacity is reached). This results from the large proportion of fixed costs associated with investments in reservoirs and distribution facilities and means that setting price equal to incremental cost may result in a price which is less than the average cost per unit. At such a price, total revenues will fail to fully cover total costs. In some cases, public districts raise the additional revenues from property taxes. A preferred solution is to raise all revenues required through a two-part pricing system. The first part is a fixed charge or assessment on the user to cover the revenue deficit. The second part is a price or toll paid by each user based on the

---

[34] Pollution taxes in the Ruhr Valley are an oft-cited example of charging for quality degradation. See Chapter 7 in KNEESE, Allen V (1964). The Economics of Regional Water Quality Management. Published for Resources for the Future, Inc., by The Johns Hopkins Press, Baltimore, Md. The concept of water prices varying by peak demands is incorporated in water supply contracts of the California Department of Water Resources.

[35] See Chapter 7, Section D, Transfer of Water Rights Under Appropriation Doctrine.

[36] When the condition prevails all around that prices of various products are equal to their respective marginal costs, the economy is using its scarce resources in the most efficient way. If this condition does not prevail, efficiency can be increased by moving resources away from industries where prices are below marginal costs and into industries where prices are greater than marginal costs.

[37] The concept of water prices varying by peak demands, distance conveyed, and pumping costs are all incorporated into the water supply contracts of the California Department of Water Resources. See STATE OF CALIFORNIA, Department of Water Resources (1963). The California State Water Project in 1963, Bulletin No. 132-63. The Resources Agency of California, Sacramento. pp. 149-155.

TABLE 7-1.—Annualized marginal costs of sewage collection and treatment in residential areas

Density (People/ acre)	Cost Category	Distance From Treatment Plant (Miles)					
		5	10	15	20	25	30
		(1957-59 dollars per capita)					
0.4	Collection	33.60	33.60	33.60	33.60	33.60	33.60
	Transmission	122.50	246.00	368.00	495.00	613.00	736.00
	Treatment	2.07	2.07	2.07	2.07	2.07	2.07
	Total	158.17	281.67	403.67	530.67	648.67	771.67
1	Collection	14.59	14.59	14.59	14.59	14.59	14.59
	Transmission	49.00	98.10	147.20	196.30	245.40	294.50
	Treatment	2.07	2.07	2.07	2.07	2.07	2.07
	Total	64.66	114.76	163.86	212.96	262.06	311.16
4	Collection	6.46	6.46	6.46	6.46	6.46	6.46
	Transmission	14.50	29.00	43.50	58.00	72.50	87.00
	Treatment	2.07	2.07	2.07	2.07	2.07	2.07
	Total	23.03	37.53	52.03	66.53	81.03	95.53
16	Collection	4.86	4.86	4.86	4.86	4.86	4.86
	Transmission	4.60	9.25	13.90	19.55	24.20	28.85
	Treatment	2.07	2.07	2.07	2.07	2.07	2.07
	Total	11.53	16.18	20.83	26.48	31.13	35.78
64	Collection	1.22	1.22	1.22	1.22	1.22	1.22
	Transmission	1.95	3.90	5.85	7.80	9.75	11.70
	Treatment	2.07	2.07	2.07	2.07	2.07	2.07
	Total	5.24	7.19	9.14	11.09	13.04	14.99
128	Collection	0.62	0.62	0.62	0.62	0.62	0.62
	Transmission	1.40	2.80	4.20	5.60	7.00	8.40
	Treatment	2.07	2.07	2.07	2.07	2.07	2.07
	Total	4.09	5.49	6.89	8.29	9.69	11.09
256	Collection	0.27	0.27	0.27	0.27	0.27	0.27
	Transmission	1.15	2.30	3.45	4.60	5.75	6.90
	Treatment	2.07	2.07	2.07	2.07	2.07	2.07
	Total	3.49	4.64	5.79	6.94	8.09	9.24
512	Collection	0.16	0.16	0.16	0.16	0.16	0.16
	Transmission	0.80	1.70	2.60	3.50	4.40	5.30
	Treatment	2.07	2.07	2.07	2.07	2.07	2.07
	Total	3.03	3.93	4.83	5.73	6.63	7.53

Source: DOWNING, Paul B. (1969). The Economics of Urban Sewage Disposal. Frederick A. Praeger, Publishers, New York. Table 29, p. 102.

incremental cost of the service provided. If a water utility system is worth building, it is worth being utilized well. That is what incremental cost pricing implies. Together, the two charges should be set sufficiently high to fully recover from users all costs of the utility service.[38]

The most common method of full cost recovery is to price according to average costs per unit. If total costs of providing water to a community are $100,000 a month and an average of 10 million cubic feet of water is delivered to users each month, the average cost per unit of water delivered is 1 cent; a price of 1 cent per cubic foot would fully recover all costs. Average cost pricing is easily understood but, as this discussion of incremental cost pricing suggests, it leads to the overcharging of some users and the undercharging of others.

Except where cost differentials are insufficient to justify the added administrative burden of billing a number of different rates, rates should differ among different classes of users according to the incremental cost of serving each class. Application of detailed incremental cost pricing could involve enormous problems of computation and resistance from water users because of complication and misunderstanding. Obviously, different prices based on different times of use or on distance from source should be imposed by establishing a limited, rather than a large, number of price classes in order to be administratively feasible and understandable to users.

Users should also be reasonably certain as to the pricing situation they face. This means that although the price structure may have a schedule of different prices for different incremental cost situations, the overall price structure itself should not be changed frequently. To illustrate, prices for residential water might be set to change seasonally or even monthly to reflect changes in incremental cost. Such price fluctuations will be understood by the user who understands time-based price changes at his neighborhood movie theater or for his long distance telephone calls. The uncertainty to be avoided is frequent or abrupt changes—more often than every 3 to 5 years—in the overall pricing structure.

Present Status of Pricing Systems

Present water pricing is far from the ideal desired for an effective pricing system. Pricing by public agencies is typically based on revenue considerations. The primary aim is fiscal balance and smooth customer relations. Pricing to provide efficient checks and balances on resource allocation is not given very high priority. Pricing is commonly below the cost of amortizing and operating a diversion and delivery system. Funds are sought elsewhere to make up the difference.

Self-supplied users who account for about 80 percent of all water withdrawals (57 percent by industry, mostly for cooling, 21 percent for self-supplied irrigators, and 1 percent for rural supplies other than irrigation)[39] usually pay no price, as such. However, they do generally bear the full costs of their own diversion and delivery systems and thus have, in effect, an internal price equal to costs of obtaining supply. Neither public nor self-supplied users pay for the opportunity cost (resource value) of water. Users of water, public or private, are now typically awarded a right to divert and use water free of charge and need give no heed to values that some other use of the water might yield.[40] Furthermore, only infrequently do means exist for sale of water rights to bring about a reallocation to higher-valued uses. As a result, withdrawals from the natural water system are not always allocated to the uses that will yield the highest return.

[39] MURRAY, C Richard & REEVES, E Bodette (1972). Estimated Use of Water in the United States in 1970. U.S. Geological Survey Circular 676. U.S. Department of the Interior, Washington, D.C. pp. 4-8 and U.S. DEPARTMENT OF AGRICULTURE, Economic Research Service (1968). Major Uses of Land and Water in the United States with Special Reference to Agriculture, Summary for 1964. Agricultural Economic Report No. 149. U.S. Department of Agriculture, Washington, D.C. pp. 40-43.

[40] Pump taxes have been imposed in Southern California (see Chapter 7, Section B) and some State permit statutes authorize the imposition of withdrawal charges (see Chapter 7, Section F). In Great Britain, river basin authorities have recently been authorized to impose charges that vary according to the nature of the source, time of year, purpose of use, and the location, quantity, and quality of effluent disposal. CRAINE, Lyle C (1969). Water Management Innovations in England. Published for Resources for the Future, Inc., by The Johns Hopkins Press, Baltimore, Md. p. 74. In Canada, a number of provinces levy charges for various water uses. TINNEY ER & O'RIORDAN J (May-June 1971). Water as a consumer commodity. Journal of Soil and Water Conservation 26(3):102-106.

[38] For additional discussion on this problem, see LOEHMAN, Edna and WHINSTON, Andrew (1971). A new theory of pricing and decisionmaking for public investment. Research sponsored by Resources for the Future, Inc., and the Office of Water Resources Research. The Bell Journal of Economics and Management Science, Vol. 2, No. 2, Autumn 1971. pp. 606-625.

The ability to apply refined pricing systems to the total supply is now limited. Pricing of self-supplied water to reflect opportunity costs of water would require legislation that not only adopts a policy in favor of pricing but also establishes entities to levy and collect charges.[41] Nevertheless, existing municipal and industrial supplies controlled by a water service agency can be subjected to improved pricing policies and water developed in the future for any purpose can be also.

Pricing Municipal Water Supplies

Costs of municipal water supplies are increasing as cities must go farther for new water sources and as low-density suburban areas requiring expensive distribution facilities are brought into the supply systems.

Influence of Pricing on Municipal Water Use: There is strong evidence that metering and pricing have substantial impacts on water use. Introduction of metering, for example, reduced water use by 36 percent in Boulder, Colorado.[42] Reductions ranging from 20 to 50 percent have been achieved in other areas by metering.[43] Metering does two things. First, users are made aware of the extent of their water use. Second, water charges are, in effect, changed from a flat-rate system of pricing to rates based on incremental use. Both the information and the financial incentive are important in achieving reduction in water use.[44]

The effect of pricing on water use is highly dependent on local conditions, including the pattern of water use. Studies show, for example, that a 10 percent increase in price may effect a reduction in overall use as great as 12 percent or as little as zero change. In Chicago, a recent study showed that price changes had no significant impact on use in the central city but did significantly affect suburban

use.[45] The reductions that are achieved may not be long-term, for as real incomes rise consumption may start to rise again. Nevertheless, the need for expanding supply is postponed for a while.

Response to price changes varies with the type of water use. A 1964 survey of urban areas over 25,000 population indicated a weighted average water use pattern of 42 percent residential use, 21 percent commercial, 20 percent industrial, and 17 percent public uses such as public institutions, street cleaning,

TABLE 7-2.—Summary of residential water use, Johns Hopkins Study

Type of Study Area	Average Annual Use	Average Maximum Daily Use
	(gallons per day per dwelling unit)	
Metered public water and public sewers		
West (10 areas)	458	979
East (13 areas)	310	786
Metered public water and septic tanks		
(5 areas)	245	726
Flat-rate public water and public sewers		
(8 areas)	692	2,354
Apartment Areas		
(5 areas)	191	368
All 41 study areas	398	1,096

Source: LINAWEAVER FP Jr et al. (1967). A Study of Residential Water Use, HUD TS-12, prepared for Techical Studies Program, Federal Housing Administration, U.S. Department of Housing and Urban Development. U.S. Government Printing Office, Washington, D.C.

---

[41] See Chapter 7, Section B, on ground water management for a discussion of pump charges.

[42] HANKE SH (October 1970). Demand for water under dynamic conditions. Water Resources Research 6(5):1253-61.

[43] WHITFORD, Peter W (1970). Forecasting Demand for Urban Water Supply, Report EEP-36. Stanford University, Palo Alto, Calif.

[44] The additional reductions will be made primarily by residential users, since most industrial and large commercial customers are already metered, even when householders are not.

[45] Lack of significant impacts in Chicago was attributed to the large proportion of water users not under direct billing plus the generally low level of prices which varied from 8 to 22 cents per 1,000 gallons in the 1951-61 period. See WONG ST (February 1972). A model on municipal water demand: A case study of Northeastern Illinois. Land Economics 48(1):34-44.

etc.[46] Commercial establishments, including laundries and car washes, are ordinarily responsive to prices charged. Pricing response for manufacturing water use is highly variable depending on the industry and plant design. Since the major component of industrial use is for cooling purposes, a low-value use, higher prices would probably have a significant impact. Residential water use is extremely important in most metropolitan areas because it is not only a major use but is generally the greatest contributor to peak demands on the supply system. Table 7-2 indicates that residential use, primarily lawn sprinkling, may be many times greater on the peak summer day than the average through the year.

Residential water use may be divided into in-house or domestic use and lawn sprinkling. The most comprehensive study of price effects on residential use was carried out by a Johns Hopkins University study group in the early 1960's.[47] Price effects, as Table 7-3 indicates, were found to vary by type of use, and by region of the country.

TABLE 7-3.–Price effects on residential demands 1963-65	
Use	Use Response to a 10 Percent Increase in Price
Domestic	– 2%
Sprinkling	– 11%
West	– 7%
East	– 16%

These data indicate that while the effect of price on use within a household may be expected to be modest, there is a significant effect on sprinkling uses, particularly in the East. Hanke found that the metering effect in Boulder resulted in (1) significant reductions in the amount of water used, (2) increased attention to water leakage, and (3) even a reduction in the area of yard sprinkled.[48]

As noted in Table 7-2, water use in apartments is lower than in detached homes. Similarly, seasonal variations due to sprinkling demands are less for apartments. Therefore, increases in water prices will have much less impact on the use of established apartment areas. However, there is some evidence that increasing water rates increases consideration of modified water-using equipment, such as toilets, showers, and washing machines, that use less water than the unmodified versions.[49] The installation of meters and significant increases in water prices can be expected to lead to some water-savings practices through the installation of water-saving equipment and improved maintenance programs.

There is widespread practice of using "declining block" water pricing in metropolitan areas; larger users pay less per unit of water as they use more. This practice of promotional pricing can encourage inefficient water use. For example, in some areas "declining block" pricing policy actually permits suburban users to pay less per unit of water for lawn sprinkling at times when they are burdening the supply system with the most costly peak demands. In such a situation, prices are lowest when incremental costs are highest.

The installation of meters and the use of cost-based pricing policies will lead to (1) more efficient use of presently developed water supplies and (2) the deferral of increasingly costly investments for development of new supplies. In El Paso, Texas, for example, low water prices were responsible for 35 percent of water deliveries being used for lawn and garden irrigation. In recognition of this fact and of declining ground water supplies, the El Paso water utility has recently raised summer water rates and launched an innovative program of awards for low water-using landscaping.[50]

[46] HITTMAN ASSOCIATES, INC. (1970). Price, Demand, Cost and Revenue in Urban Water Utilities, HIT-474. Hittman Associates, Inc., Columbia, Md.

[47] The Johns Hopkins residential water use project produced a large number of papers and reports. See, for example, HOWE CW & LINAWEAVER FP Jr (1967). The impact of price on residential water demand and its relation to system design and price structure. Water Resources Research 3(1):13-32.

[48] HANKE SH (October 1970). Demand for water under dynamic conditions. Water Resources Research 6(5):1253-61.

[49] See, for example, GRUBISICH, Thomas (December 9, 1971). Water-saving devices flow onto market. Washington Post. K1, K10. Some developers and managers of apartments were installing water-saving devices following combined water and sewer bill increases of up to 50 percent, with more increases expected. However, a Commission study by Resources for the Future, Inc., anticipated very modest savings in in-house water use under projected residential pricing policies. HOWE, Charles W et al., Resources for the Future, Inc. (1971). Future Water Demands, prepared for the National Water Commission. National Technical Information Service, Springfield, Va., Accession No. PB 197 877. p. 9.

[50] HICKERSON, John T, General Manager, El Paso Water Utilities, Public Service Board, El Paso, Texas (1972). Correspondence dated April 10, 1972, with National Water Commission.

TABLE 7-4.–Current pricing policies of water utilities			
Current Policies	Yes	No	No Response
1. Water utility is expected to be self-supporting	219	1	0
2. Present rate structure promotes:			
Location of new firms	172	37	11
Lawn sprinkling	140	64	16
Air conditioning	122	80	18
Recreational use	142	62	16
Other	30	13	177
3. Extension of water service used to:			
Force annexation	112	94	14
Extension of other municipal services	66	130	24
4. Utility provides:			
Contributions to general fund of local government	124	90	6
Tax contributions	55	147	18
5. Utility provides:			
Free fire services	143	75	2
Free water to local government	86	133	1
Free water to other facilities	11	204	5

Source: FRISTOE, Charles W et al., U.S. Office of Water Resources Research and University of Florida (1971). Applied Criteria for Municipal Water Rate Structures. National Technical Information Service, Springfield, Va., Accession No. PB 202 013. p. 116.

Objectives of Urban Water Utilities: There is a widespread movement to make urban water utilities financially self-supporting and to upgrade management practices. This desirable trend is reinforced by the efforts of national organizations such as the American Water Works Association.

It does not follow, however, that a policy of financial self-support will necessarily lead to adoption of appropriate pricing policies. A survey carried out by researchers at the University of Florida indicates that while the 200 responding utility managers were in fact overwhelmingly committed to a policy of financial self-support (see Table 7-4), their utilities were also managed to pursue a variety of policies including promotion of industrial water use, provision

of free fire services, contributions to general government revenues, etc.

Water utilities are public service enterprises. Their regulation by various politically elected and appointed officials may be aimed at accomplishing a number of objectives and only incidentally concerned with conserving and efficiently using water supplies. For example, even though it may be an inefficient use of water supplies, the majority of utilities surveyed indicated that their rate structures promoted lawn sprinkling. The promotion of large green lawns may be a valid community objective. The policy issue involved in such low-value local uses is whether other uses of the water that may as a result be foregone are more valuable than large, green lawns. The local community must ask how much is this objective costing and who is bearing the financial burden involved?

The Commission urges all water utilities to review their present pricing policies and to consider the use of cost-based pricing. In areas with acute water shortages, it may be desirable for State or regional water supply entities to require pricing policies of community water utilities that lead to high, rather than low, value uses of water. Cost-based pricing of water supplied to local utilities is one policy that should be used to encourage more efficient and conserving use of scarce water supplies.

Pricing Sewerage Service: Just as pricing provides a way to induce efficient use of municipal water supplies, pricing may also be employed to improve the management of municipal sewage wastes. That is, pricing may be used to efficiently allocate municipal treatment capacity and the assimilation capacity of the water bodies receiving treated effluent.

The practice of including sewerage system charges in water billings provides an incentive for reduced water use which may result in reduced discharges of water into the collection system. Reduction of discharges into the sewer system, in turn, may very significantly reduce the costs of waste treatment.

Pricing of sewerage services for domestic waste would probably have some impact on the amount of sewered waste material if it provides incentives for household treatment, such as installation of on-site waste disposal systems. However, monitoring of waste disposal from the individual household is not now economically feasible.

Industrial waste disposal presents a different situation. Industrial users of municipal systems are more readily susceptible to charges because they are fewer in number relative to other users and because, unlike domestic users, their waste-producing processes can often be subject to substantial changes if cost incentives exist. For example, industries can reduce waste discharges through process changes and more intensive internal control as well as through on-site treatment. Although there are great variations from city to city, approximately one-half of the wastes treated in municipal plants on a nationwide basis are from industrial sources.

Some industrial wastes impose particularly severe costs on municipal systems because they produce toxins that interfere with the biological processes of treatment plants. Aside from differences in technical requirements for treating industrial and domestic wastes, there are significant differences in the economics of waste treatment for municipal and industrial operations. The greater concentration and volume of manufacturing wastes result in lower unit investment costs for treatment. However, operating costs for industrial waste treatment are higher than municipal operating costs—averaging twice as much per unit of installed capacity. Because of differing technical requirements and cost structures, the commonly supposed economics of combining industrial and domestic wastes may be nonexistent in particular instances.[51]

It is apparent that in most cases industry does not carry an appropriate share of costs for the use of municipal waste treatment facilities. The most common methods of municipal sewerage system finance (e.g., property tax, flat monthly rates, charge based on water consumed) bear little or no relationship to the burden of waste a user places on the treatment system. The one method which appears to offer the most efficient and equitable division of cost among different users, while at the same time providing appropriate deterrents to waste production, is a system of user charges based on the volume and strength of wastes contributed.

Some case examples illustrate that towns which have imposed sewage charges on industry for the use of public waste treatment plants have experienced reductions of wasteloads.[52]

Otsego, Michigan: The town's waste treatment plant was severely overloaded. The principal cause was one major industrial operation, which was supplying a load of 1,500 pounds of biochemical oxygen demand (BOD) per day. [In 1965] the city commission decided to charge the company for all expenses for treating wastes from the industry above 500 pounds [of BOD] per day, the amount for which the plant was designed. The first monthly billing of the firm after the initiation of the surcharge was based on an estimated BOD load of 900 pounds per day, down from the 1,500 pounds before the tax. For the second thirty-day billing period, the firm's BOD load was down to about 733 pounds per day. For the third, 500 pounds per day. Thus, in three months, the

[51] DAVIS, Robert K & HANKE, Steve H, George Washington University (1971). Pricing and Efficiency in Water Resource Management, prepared for the National Water Commission. National Technical Information Service, Springfield, Va., Accession No. PB 209 083. p. 93.

[52] Ibid., pp. 94-95.

effluent charge had led to a 66 percent reduction in the amount of untreated wastes released by the plant.

Springfield, Missouri: Faced with sharply rising waste loads in 1962, Springfield decided to apply a surcharge on industrial waste discharges above the normal strength of sewage. Each [industrial] plant discharging sewage above the permissible concentration was notified of the amount of the prospective surcharge, and of the fact that the city would review the assessment whenever a plant made operational changes. Even before the first billing, some plants began to take action. A packing plant that faced an assessment of about $1,400 per month modified its production processes and ended up with a sewer bill of only $225 per month. Many other industries in the town took similar corrective action and reduced their charges substantially.

Philadelphia, Pennsylvania: This city recently instituted a surcharge for wastewater . . . in excess of normal wastewater. The charge affixed is one and one-half cents ($.015) a pound for pollutants received into the wastewater system in excess of 350 milligrams per liter of BOD *or* in excess of 400 milligrams per liter of suspended solids *or* both. Customers subject to the surcharge are required to conduct measurement and sample analysis of their sewage discharge and to maintain the records necessary for calculation of the surcharge. Preliminary results from this new policy suggest a substantial response to the charge in due course.

It appears that user charges levied on industrial users of municipal waste treatment systems offer promise not only of fairly distributing waste treatment costs but of radically reducing the quantities of industrial waste discharged and of reducing the costs and complexities of municipal plant operations.

Pricing Irrigation Water

Agriculture, in contrast to manufacturing and most other uses, consumes a large part of its water withdrawals. This means that there is less return flow to the water source from agriculture than from most other uses, and therefore less water available for reuse. About 83 percent of all water consumption is due to irrigation, and about 60 percent of irrigated acreage is self-supplied, the remainder being supplied by Federal, State, and local water agencies and by private and mutual water companies. The value in use of irrigation water tends to be low, typically in the range of $5 to $25 per acre-foot. This means the extra crop revenue (net of other expenses) which is attributable to the application of an acre-foot of water is only $5 to $25. Unless this value in use increases, it would never be worthwhile for an irrigator to spend more for water unless he is raising a very high-value crop. Use of self-supplied water is, of course, not priced, and use of water supplied by an agency is rarely priced on the basis of incremental cost.

Among the responses that could be expected from irrigators to higher water prices would be to reallocate water use to crops returning higher values per unit of water used, to use more intensive management practices, and to shift to more conserving irrigation technologies, for example, sprinkler rather than gravity-flow irrigation. Information on the actual effect of increased prices is relatively scarce. Ground water pumping provides some data on the response of irrigators to changing costs but even those data are somewhat clouded because of improving pumping technology and relatively declining energy costs in recent years.

As for surface water, studies indicate that a 10 percent increase in irrigation water price may result in a 6 to 7 percent reduction in water use.[53] A simulation study prepared for the Commission computed effects of various water prices on irrigated farm production under particular assumptions for the year 2000.[54] As irrigation water prices went up (and the model allocated crop production to nonirrigated areas), the quantity of irrigation water demanded in the 17 Western States became progressively smaller. For example, with a price of $30 per acre-foot *consumed* (10 cents per 1,000 gallons), estimated withdrawals for irrigation declined by more than half.

It seems clear from the studies cited that demand for irrigation water is responsive to changes in price

[53] BAIN, Joe S et al. (1966). Northern California's Water Industry. Published for Resources for the Future, Inc., by The Johns Hopkins Press, Baltimore, Md. and HEDGES, Trimble R & MOORE, Charles V (1962). Economics of On-Farm Irrigation Water Availability and Costs, and Related Farm Adjustments, Giannini Foundation Research Report No. 257. Giannini Foundation of Agricultural Economics, University of California, Berkeley.

[54] HEADY EO et al., Iowa State University (1972). Agricultural Water Demands, prepared for the National Water Commission. National Technical Information Service, Springfield, Va., Accession No. PB 206 790. The model referred to assumed a population of 300 million and removal of Federal program restraints, allowing allocation of agricultural production to the most efficient producing areas.

and that greater efficiency could be attained in irrigation water use by adoption of a pricing system. At present, however, efficient water use is *not* the objective of most water supply agencies. Restrained legally and institutionally from gaining economic benefit by selling water to more productive users,[55] individual farmers and irrigation districts may seek only to have the available water supply delivered at the lowest possible price to the user. Many districts do not even measure the amount of water delivered to users.

Major changes in these patterns of behavior are not likely to occur until economic incentives arise for making more efficient use of water. But even under present legal and institutional arrangements, some incentives exist for making better use of water, and pricing could be an effective tool to accomplish that objective. For example, in cases where a district is supplying surface water and the farmer controls his own irrigation pumps for ground water, the district may wish to manage surface and ground water use conjunctively, although it controls only the surface supply. The district may wish to distribute surface supplies early in the irrigation season and to utilize the irrigators' pumping capacity later in the irrigation season. In order to encourage use of surface supplies in the early season and ground water later, prices or tolls for surface delivery must first be set below, and then later above, the variable costs of pump operation.[56] Thus, irrigation use of particular supplies can be effectively controlled by pricing policy but the lack of complete control over both surface and ground water would prevent pricing of the surface water at a full incremental cost level.[57] Other local conditions might produce other instances where pricing could be effectively employed to accomplish specific local objectives. If a district were perennially short of water, a pricing policy could embody a concept of "standard irrigation efficiency" based on district averages. Irrigators using more water than the "standard," suitably adjusted for soil conditions, crops, and other variables, might be required to pay a surcharge for the excess use.

The U.S. Bureau of Reclamation, which provides some 8.5 million acres with full or supplemental water supplies, should consider pricing as a means of encouraging better use of water. Under present practice, the Bureau enters into long-term contracts for water deliveries at prices based on estimates of irrigators' ability to pay. The central objective of the Federal reclamation program has been the promotion of irrigation-based agricultural communities, not the efficient use of water. This policy is reflected in the ability-to-pay criterion for the pricing of water to irrigation districts. There is substantial potential for more efficient use of Bureau-supplied water through a shift to a cost-based pricing approach, at least on new irrigation projects.[58] Incremental cost pricing would provide a powerful incentive for efficient use of irrigation water, particularly in the more arid areas of the West. It would also stimulate the development of new technologies leading to still more efficient use.

The Ability to Pay Issue

There is some public opposition to the use of pricing and user charges by government agencies. One reason is that such charges are visible to the user; government revenue raising seems to be more palatable when it is less visible. The high visibility of prices, of course, is exactly the reason they are effective in improving the allocation of resources.

The second and more substantive issue is the assertion that user charges and prices are regressive and thus discriminate against lower income families. That is, payments for water-related services would represent a larger portion of a poor family's income than a rich family's income. Therefore, the argument is that water and water-related services, so often provided by a governmental entity, should be financed out of general tax revenues. For example, one proposal would be for the Federal Government to finance or provide tax credits for domestic waste treatment because it would then be supported by the progressive income tax rather than more regressive local taxes or user charges.[59]

In the first place, it is not at all clear that implementation of incremental cost-based pricing practices, as advocated here, results in increasing the

---

[55] On such restraints, see Chapter 7, Section D.

[56] Any financial deficit which results can be covered by land assessment.

[57] See TAYLOR, Gary C (1967). Economic Planning of Water Supply Systems, Giannini Foundation Research Report No. 291. Giannini Foundation of Agricultural Economics, University of California, Berkeley, p. 74.

---

[58] The Commission has not studied the legal feasibility of increasing prices for water presently supplied under long-term contracts.

[59] URBAN SYSTEMS RESEARCH AND ENGINEERING, INC. (1971). Metropolitan Water Management, Case Studies and National Policy Implications, prepared for the National Water Commission. National Technical Information Service, Springfield, Va., Accession No. PB 199 493. p. 12.

Furrow irrigation from gated surface pipe permits close control of water deliveries

relative burden on the lower income families. The lawn sprinkling situation provides an important illustration. Owners of homes on large lots, generally in wealthier suburban neighborhoods, should pay the full costs of their water services. Davis and Hanke found in their study of the Washington metropolitan area that application of incremental cost pricing would reduce the cost for the inner city resident while increasing the cost to the suburban user. In Boulder, Colorado, the *cost* of supplying sewer and water services to new homes is $1,450 per home while the *charge* is only $600. The difference is made up by revenues from established residents, frequently less affluent than the new home residents.[60]

In any event, nonwater utilities do not ordinarily give special rates to low income customers. And ability to pay does not enter into the conventional market. A pound of sugar is priced the same in the store for the millionaire as for the pauper. If the

objective is income redistribution, the stratified pricing of goods and services in selected industries such as water or sewerage utilities is hopelessly unsatisfactory. A more appropriate device might be the tax structure or welfare payments.

The strongest argument in support of cost-based pricing and user charges is that by encouraging efficiency in use they improve resource allocation and prevent premature investment for expansion of facilities. The entire society is made better off. However, there is room for compromise. Efficiency in allocation of municipal water supply would not be seriously reduced by providing for the sale of minimum amounts of services at less than cost. For example, in-house requirements for drinking, cooking, sanitation, and bathing might be subject to less-than-cost prices. Additional use, presumably for less essential purposes, could be subject to pricing that fully recovers the associated incremental costs. The Commission is not advocating this less-than-cost pricing policy, because it thinks that water policy is a very inexact and inefficient way to improve the

[60] HOWE, Charles, Professor of Economics, University of Colorado. Boulder (1971). Correspondence dated November 18, 1971, with the National Water Commission.

economic well-being of the poor. It seems appropriate that the issue of income distribution should be resolved through reforms in tax structures or welfare transfer expenditures while systems of pricing and user charges should be employed to encourage prudent use of water resources.

CONCLUSIONS

Pricing is becoming increasingly important. As water demands increase, use will press more heavily on the given natural supplies, costs of diversion and delivery will increase, and competition and inter-action among uses will be more intense. Pricing, including allowance for the value of the resource itself, can help to bring about better use of the Nation's water resources.

As valuable as pricing of water can be toward motivating better use, it cannot be relied upon exclusively to achieve always the highest and best use from an overall social standpoint. It should not, for example, be allowed to lead to improper land use. Land use planning should set constraints on the use of both land and related water so that when water pricing is implemented, the resulting use from a social standpoint is indeed the highest and best. Likewise, pricing cannot be relied on to preserve environmental quality, and water quality standards will have to be established outside the pricing mechanism.[61]

A uniform nationwide system of prices, surface water diversion charges, and pumping taxes would also be inappropriate. The structure of user prices or withdrawal charges imposed should vary from area to area and from situation to situation depending on conditions (e.g., large unused system capacity versus full utilization of existing capacity).

In some areas, the costs of providing water services are comparatively low and provide a temptation to set prices that yield revenues in excess of costs. This may be true for many municipalities that are financially pinched and look upon water service facilities as a means of raising revenues for unrelated municipal purposes. The Commission disapproves of setting water supply and sewerage charges at levels which not only fully recover costs but also return additional "excess" revenues for nonwater purposes. The purpose of pricing water and water-related services is to encourage more prudent and efficient use of water, not to raise revenues beyond that required to cover costs.

The Commission recognizes that provision of water supply and sewerage services benefits affected properties. These benefits from construction of water supply and sewerage facilities become capitalized into the value of the properties served. Hence, the Commission concludes there is justification for imposing a combination of charges and assessments to recover costs. It may be appropriate, for example, to (1) levy a special assessment based on front-footage or acreage of benefited property to recover construction costs of a water or sewerage system and simultaneously diminish unintended windfalls to property owners, and (2) charge a price per unit to recover operation and maintenance expenses.

The Commission concludes that systems of pricing and user charges that recover the full costs of water services directly from users will conserve water supplies, discourage premature investment in water development projects, reduce financial burdens now borne by nonusers, and, most importantly, make the use of scarce resources more efficient.

RECOMMENDATIONS

7-21. Water management agencies should review their metering and pricing policies. Wherever economically justified, meters should be installed and water deliveries measured. Where feasible, water and sewerage charges should be based on two considerations:
   a. the costs that users impose upon the system, and
   b. the costs imposed on society from the loss of the use of the resource for other purposes.
   Provision should also be made for recovery of unintended windfall benefits conferred upon affected properties by construction of facilities.

7-22. Where water is a scarce resource, States should investigate the legal and institutional feasibility of imposing withdrawal charges on self-suppliers of water diverting from surface and ground water sources as a means of improving efficiency in the use of water.

7-23. All Federal agencies that supply water to users should adopt a uniform policy of cost-based pricing in all future water supply contracts, and, wherever practicable, extend that policy to classes of users who are not now charged.

---

[61] For the Commission's views on pollution abatement, see Chapter 4.

Transfer of Water Rights Under
Appropriation Doctrine[62]

As the Nation's population and its economic activities expand, greater and greater demands are made on its relatively fixed supply of water. Water, once so abundant as to be considered a virtually free good, is increasingly viewed as a scarce resource.

Along with growing demands on the Nation's water supply have come far-reaching changes in conditions throughout the land. Agrarian activities have become comparatively less important in the economic scheme of things. New technologies have given rise to changes in the ways in which food and fiber are produced on the Nation's farms. Migration from rural to urban areas has intensified. Land use patterns have become dramatically rearranged.

Water supply should be adaptable to these changing conditions. Since it is in limited supply, it should be deployed in such a fashion as to yield the highest return to social well-being. That cannot be done, of course, unless the disposition of water is sufficiently unfettered to permit it to be allocated where it will do the most good. Immutably fixing ancient allocations of water in a world where change is a transcendent characteristic is almost guaranteed to make those allocations inconsistent with contemporary requirements, to say nothing of future needs.

Unfortunately, some legal and other institutional arrangements do just that; they lock into concrete a pattern of water use which at one time may have been appropriate but which no longer is. Ways must be found to do some unlocking. The Nation must encourage changes in both the purposes and places of water use in order to achieve the best utilization of its water supplies. In other words, water supplies should be freed to be transferred to places of highest and best use.

THE PROBLEM

The law of most Western States authorizes the owner of a water right to sell the right to another, who in turn is then permitted to transfer the right to a different place of use or to a different kind of use. The transfer must be made in accordance with State administrative procedures which are designed to protect other water users from adverse effects from the transfer.[63]

The sale of water rights is fairly common in some Western States. Unfortunately, legal and institutional obstacles obstruct the smooth operation of the transfer process in much of the West. If these obstacles were removed and the transfer of water rights made more feasible and facile, it would be expected that high-value users, such as cities and industries, would purchase water rights from low-value users, such as some agricultural owners of water rights. This reallocation process, operating in a framework of voluntary action in response to traditional economic incentives, would increase the benefits gained from the use of water and would tend to delay or make unnecessary the construction of new sources of supply.

The necessity of processing each water rights transfer through an administrative proceeding, the fact that no two water rights are identical, and the fact that there are few buyers and sellers, will prevent the development of a market in water rights comparable to the auction market of a stock or commodity exchange. Nevertheless, it is reasonable to assume that removal of legal and institutional obstacles will significantly increase the number of transfers which will be made.

The principal opportunity for reallocation of water through voluntary transfers would seem to be from relatively low-value agricultural uses to higher-value municipal and industrial uses. Several studies show wide disparities in the value of water among these alternative uses. One study, for example, concluded that "there are in excess of one million acre feet of water being utilized in the Imperial Valley alone

---

[62] This section is based in large measure on two background studies prepared for the National Water Commission: MEYERS, Charles J & POSNER, Richard A (1971). Market Transfers of Water Rights. National Technical Information Service, Springfield, Va., Accession No. PB 202 620, and DEWSNUP, Richard L & MEYERS, Charles J (1971). Improvement of State Water Records. National Technical Information Service, Springfield, Va., Accession No. PB 202 618

[63] Transfer of water rights in riparian jurisdictions is discussed in Chapter 7, Section F.

whose direct value in use is less than $10 per acre-foot." This compares with public investment in additional water supplies 'for Southern California at costs of around $100 per acre-foot.[64] Another study concludes that "a fairly large supply" of irrigation water will be available for transfer to more valuable uses at least through the year 2000.[65] A 1959 study of the South Platte Basin of Colorado showed a low rental price of water of $2.50 per acre-foot in the early season and a high of $8 in the late season.[66] Still other studies show wide ranges of disparities in values of water uses between agricultural and industrial use.[67]

Whatever might be the precise figures for any particular area, it seems inescapable that a considerable volume of water in the West is devoted to low-value agricultural uses at a time when there·exists industrial and urban demand at substantially higher prices. It is desirable to permit the reallocation of the low-value water where a willing seller and a willing buyer desire to do so, where the transfer can be made without violating overall land use plans, and where the rights of others are not impaired by the transaction.

Sales of water rights which are taking place at present demonstrate that voluntary reallocation of water to more valuable uses will occur when legal and institutional barriers can be overcome.[68] The purpose of this section is to identify and describe these barriers and to find methods of removing them.

DISCUSSION

In order to facilitate voluntary transfers of water rights, a number of changes in both State and Federal laws will be required. The changes can be grouped into three general categories:

(1) Improvement of State water rights records.
(2) Simplification of procedures for transferring water rights.
(3) Modification of certain laws that restrain or prohibit transfers.

Improving States' Water Rights Records

One requisite for facilitating voluntary transfers of water rights is a record system which identifies existing rights so that prospective buyers can know what it is that can be sold. In the Western appropriation system, this identification requires description not only of what a prospective seller owns, but also the relationship of the seller's right to other rights on the stream. Water rights records are inadequate for this purpose in many Western States because there exist (a) legally enforceable water rights that do not appear on the record and (b) invalid "paper" rights that appear on the record but are legally unenforceable.[69]

Two pieces of State legislation are required to eliminate these defects. The principles of this proposed legislation are stated in the following two recommendations.

Recommendation No. 7-24: Any water right not properly recorded 5 years from the effective date of the statute should lose its priority and should receive water only after all properly recorded water rights have been served.

Discussion — Not only would this statute facilitate sales of water rights by encouraging the recordation of all claims to the use of water, it would reduce the adjudication costs for determining the validity and priority of old claims in the future. In the 21st century, such adjudications for 19th century claims

[64] HOWE, Charles W et al., Resources for the Future, Inc. (1971). Future Water Demands, prepared for the National Water Commission. National Technical Information Service, Springfield, Va., Accession No. PB 197 877. p. 84.

[65] HEADY, Earl O et al., Iowa State University (1971). Agricultural Water Demands, prepared for the National Water Commission. National Technical Information Service, Springfield, Va., Accession No. PB 207 790. p. V-7.

[66] ANDERSON RL (1961). (1959 Study dealing with South Platte Basin of Colorado). Agricultural Economics Research 13:57.

[67] NATIONAL ACADEMY OF SCIENCES (1968). Water and Choice in the Colorado Basin, A Report by the Committee on Water of the National Research Council, Publication 1689. National Academy of Sciences, Washington, D.C. p. 71. Also, BROWN G Jr & McGUIRE CB (1967). A socially optimum pricing policy for a public water agency. Water Resources Research 3(1):33-43, and WOLLMAN, Nathaniel et al. (1962). The Value of Water in Alternative Uses. The University of New Mexico Press. Albuquerque, N.M.

[68] A number of cities in Colorado are actively engaged in programs of acquiring irrigation water rights and transferring them to municipal use. To a lesser extent, transfers of this type are also occurring in Oregon, New Mexico, and Arizona.

[69] Another source of uncertainty is the Federal reserved right for Indian reservations and other Federal establishments. Clarification and recordation of these rights are recommended in Chapters 13 and 14.

would otherwise be dependent on evidence difficult to obtain and usually unreliable.

Recommendation No. 7-25: The State engineer or any party with an interest should be permitted to apply in an administrative proceeding for the cancellation of any water right of record on grounds of abandonment or forfeiture. No such proceeding should affect a purchaser of such water right unless a notice of *lis pendens* (litigation pending) has been filed in the appropriate records office prior to the date the purchase agreement is entered into. The few States not having forfeiture statues should enact them as part of this law.

Discussion — A number of States have forfeiture statutes, and the doctrine of abandonment appears to be part of the common law of all States. The difference between forfeiture and abandonment is intent. Forfeiture usually results from nonuse for a consecutive number of years; intent is not required by the statutes. Abandonment can result from nonuse for any period of time but, unlike forfeiture, intent to relinquish the right must be proved. Though some have argued that forfeiture statutes encourage waste by inducing the appropriator to apply water when he does not need it (thereby avoiding application of the forfeiture statute), the Commission believes that on balance these statutes serve the useful purpose of providing a mechanism for eliminating stale claims from the record. However, in order to encourage transfers of water rights, purchasers of rights that might be subject to attack on grounds of forfeiture are protected if the contract for purchase was entered into before the forfeiture proceeding was recorded.

Simplification of Transfer Procedures

The second group of proposed changes relates to procedures for changes in points of diversion, places of use, and nature of use. Western law uniformly requires some sort of proceeding before an owner of a water right can change its place or nature of use. The proceeding serves a necessary purpose—determination of the effect of a proposed change on junior appropriators. No change can be made without protection of these junior users and their rights. Protection is usually accomplished by limiting the amount of water that can be transferred to the amount consumptively used by the transferor. In other words, the seller cannot sell all the water he has a right to divert but only that portion of the water he

diverts which he has a right to consume (i.e., that does not return to the stream). (Occasionally, in lieu of prohibiting changes which adversely affect junior appropriators, payment of compensation is allowed.)

A simplified illustration may help explain the transfer process. Farmer F owns an early appropriative right that entitles him to divert 1,000 acre-feet of water during the irrigation season. Not all of this water is consumed by raising crops. Let us assume that 60 percent (600 acre-feet) is lost by evaporation and consumed by crops, and that 40 percent (400 acre-feet) returns to the stream and is subsequently diverted by junior appropriators. F enters into a contract to sell the consumptive use portion of his water right to municipality M which plans to take the water out of the basin. A transfer proceeding must be held to determine the facts assumed above, after which an order allowing transfer from F to M of 600 acre-feet may be entered.

Several changes in the procedures regulating transfers would improve this process and they are embraced in Recommendations 7-26, 7-27, and 7-28. A change in substantive law is included in Recommendation 7-29.

Recommendation No. 7-26: All transfer proceedings should commence as administrative proceedings before the State engineer (or the equivalent water administration agency), who should be charged with the duty of making an independent determination of the adverse effect of the proposed change on junior appropriators. This determination may be based on his own investigations (given in a report to the parties), or on evidence presented by the parties, or both. The determination should be subject to judicial review but should be sustained if supported by substantial evidence.

Discussion — Most Western States follow this procedure at present, but some do not. Whatever may be said of the administrative process in other contexts, it is clear that the State engineer who administers the distribution of water is more likely than a court of general jurisdiction to have the necessary expertise to determine reliably and expeditiously the streamflow effects of a transfer.

Recommendation No. 7-27: An application for a transfer of a water right should be denied if the transfer would have the effect of substantially degrading stream quality below the water quality standards existing at the time the application is made.

Discussion — This provision seeks to balance environmental claims, economic efficiency, and private property rights. Reference to the hypothetical transfer from farmer *F* to city *M* may help clarify the point. Farmer *F* has historically diverted 1,000 acre-feet of water at his headgate, consuming 600 acre-feet and returning 400 acre-feet to the stream. City *M* proposes to transfer the 600 acre-feet of consumptive use to its municipal system in another basin. Since junior rights in the 400 acre-feet of return flow are protected, the transfer would be permitted under Western law.

Under some circumstances, the transfer could nevertheless have an adverse effect on environmental values. Suppose the city proposes to take the 600 acre-feet at a new point of diversion 10 miles upstream from the old point of diversion, thus diminishing streamflow between the new point of diversion and the old. If water quality standards in that reach of the river had been set to promote fish culture, and if they would be violated as a result of the transfer, then the State engineer should deny the application or reduce the amount of water permitted to be transferred. The recommendation proposes that transfers which do not violate *existing* quality standards would be permitted. It should also be noted that the use of the water by the purchaser after the transfer will be subject to valid police power regulations aimed at protecting environmental quality, or promoting other social objectives.

Recommendation No. 7-28: When it appears that the effect on junior appropriators from a change in point of diversion, or place or nature of use will be difficult to determine in advance of making the transfer, the State engineer should be authorized to issue a conditional order allowing the transfer, subject to further proceedings to modify the order so as to prevent such harm as might be proved in later proceedings. If it appears in the later proceedings that the harm sustained by the protesting junior appropriators is slight compared to the value in use after the change, the State engineer may deny specific relief, and transfer the case to the district court for the recovery of damages, including costs and reasonable attorneys' fees, by junior appropriators who have sustained harm.

Discussion — Further improvement in transfer procedures can be made by adopting the Colorado practice of allowing transfers but subjecting them to future modification after the effect on junior appro-priators has been observed. Under the practice generally prevailing at the present time, the decisionmaker is handicapped by being required to decide prospectively and speculatively the probable future effect of a transfer on junior appropriators. Such effects are sometimes both problematical and relatively insignificant.

In addition to providing for flexibility, Recommendation 7-28 provides for compensation as an alternative remedy where the value of the new use is substantially greater than the value of the old use. While this provision could be characterized as permitting "private eminent domain," it is in fact but a modest departure from the current rules of Western law which allow private condemnation of rights-of-way for canals and water pipelines and which also permit condemnation by a preferred use of an inferior use.[70] This proposal enlarges the class of preferred uses from specifically named uses (e.g., municipal) to any new use substantially more valuable than the old ones. It is in accord with recommendations made in 1955 by the President's Advisory Committee on Water Resources Policy.[71]

So much for procedural changes. A final recommendation on State recordkeeping and water rights administration involves a change in the substantive law as well. It will be recalled that in the transfer from *F* to *M*, described above, *F* had a right to divert 1,000 acre-feet but was permitted to transfer only his consumptive use of 600 acre-feet because the law properly protected junior appropriators who had made investments in reliance on the return flow from *F's* diversion. After *M* has bought and paid for the 600 acre-feet and obtained the necessary transfer order, it will run the water through its municipal system and is likely to have a return flow as high as 70 percent. What rights should *M* have in this 420 acre-feet? The Commission believes that *M's* property interest in this water should be protected if the return flow can be adequately identified. There is no reason to give a new, free supply of water to users below *M's* outfall, where those users had no previous reliance on the new supply and have not paid for it. Rather, *M* should be entitled to use the full supply it purchased as its needs arise. The following recommendation proposes both a recording provision to identify return

[70] *Clark v. Nash*, 198 U.S. 361 (1905). *Kaiser Steel Corp. v. W. S. Ranch Co.*, 81 N.M. 414, 467 P. 2d 986 (1970).
[71] PRESIDENTIAL ADVISORY COMMITTEE ON WATER RESOURCES POLICY (1955). Water Resources Policy, House Document 315, 84th Congress, 2d Session. U.S. Government Printing Office, Washington, D.C. Section V.

flow from transferred uses and a substantive rule to clarify property rights.

Recommendation No. 7-29: After the effective date of the statute, all orders allowing the transfer of a water right should specify the new point of diversion, the amount of the new diversion in volume and rate of flow, the place and nature of the new use, its consumptive use, and, where feasible, the amount of return flow from the new use, and the point of its reentry into the system. Where the transfer order contains these specifications, the full amount of the water that has been permitted to be transferred should be the property of the new owner, including the return flow from the new owner's new use. Until the new owner fully uses or sells the return flow from the new use, other water users should be permitted to make interim use of such return flow, but the new owner should have the right to recapture the return flow when he (or his assignee) has a beneficial use for it and when it can be identified and segregated from other sources of supply and this should be stated in any State permit authorizing such interim use.

Discussion — Vesting title to the return flow in the purchaser of a transferred water right is merely a clarification of the existing law in some States. Where a city or other user develops a supply of imported water, the return flow therefrom should be the property of the importer.[72] Once the new owner's return flow is clearly identified as a new source of water under the recording provision, there is little reason to give it to others free of charge.

Legal Restraints and Prohibitions on Transfers of Water Rights

The third category of change to facilitate voluntary transfer of water rights involves the repeal of laws that forbid transfer, and the clarification of laws that obscure the power of water rights holders to make transfers. Both Federal and State law would be affected.

Substantive Changes in the Federal Law: In 1970, the U.S. Bureau of Reclamation supplied 25.6 million acre-feet of water for irrigation use in the West and an additional 2 million acre-feet for municipal, industrial, and other nonagricultural uses. The irrigation

water was provided for 140,500 farms with a total of 8,570,000 irrigated acres.[73]

Despite the size of these deliveries, the law is far from clear about the nature of the title the Bureau has to this water. This uncertainty as to title, the nature of the water right, and the transferability thereof deter the reallocation of reclamation water from agricultural use to other, often higher-valued uses.

A brief review of Reclamation Law may help put the problem in perspective. Apparently, the original 1902 Reclamation Act contemplated that water rights would be held by the individual irrigators, subject to a 10-year repayment obligation. But the inability of individual irrigators generally to discharge their debts led, in 1926, to a statutory requirement that repayment contracts be executed by irrigation (or conservancy) districts. It apparently became the practice for the Bureau to apply for and hold the water right, with the understanding that upon full repayment the right would pass to the district. Under the 1939 Act, so-called "9(e) contracts" are authorized whereby the irrigators pay operating costs and only such share of construction costs as the Secretary of the Interior finds them able to pay. When, if ever, the water right passes to the district is uncertain. Finally, in some projects, as for example the Boulder Canyon Project on the Colorado River, no State filings at all were made by the Bureau.

Further confusion exists with respect to the present purposes of reclamation activities. It seems indisputable that in 1902 the policy objective was to develop the West with family farms of 160-acre size each. Section 5 of the Act provided that "No right to the use of water for land in private ownership shall be sold for a tract exceeding one hundred and sixty acres . . . and no such sale shall be made to any landowner unless he be an actual bona fide resident on such land . . . ."[74] The acreage limitation is still in force, more or less, but the residency requirement has frequently been disregarded.[75] (If Congress should decide to retain the acreage limitation for irrigation water, transfer of Bureau of Reclamation water rights from one farmer to another would also be subject to the limitation. But the limitation would

---

[72] See, for example, *Stevens v. Oakdale Irrigation District,* 13 Cal. 2d 343, 90 P. 2d 58 (1939), and *Los Angeles v. Glendale,* 23 Cal. 2d 68, 142 P. 2d 289 (1943).

[73] U.S. BUREAU OF RECLAMATION (1971). Water & Land Resource Accomplishments, 1970. U.S. Government Printing Office, Washington, D.C. p. 1.

[74] *The Reclamation Act of 1902,* 57th Congress, P.L. 161, June 17, 1902, 32 Stat. 388, 43 USCA 431.

[75] See Chapter 5, Section D, on Acreage Limitations and Subsidies in Reclamation Programs.

Irrigation diversion dam and headgate structure

not affect the transfer of Bureau water rights from irrigation use to municipal and industrial use, the usual transfer expected to occur under the recommendations of this section.)

Over the years, the Bureau of Reclamation's programs have been expanded beyond the fostering of family farms. The Bureau now furnishes power from hydroelectric projects and will soon furnish power from a fossil fuel steamplant, it provides municipal and industrial water, and, in some parts of the West, it services national parks, monuments, recreation areas, wildlife refuges, and so forth. In short, the mission of the Bureau of Reclamation is much broader now than it was originally.

It is the Commission's view that apart from the acreage limitation question, the legitimate interests of the Bureau of Reclamation (and the people of the United States) in present-day use of project water are the following:

(1) Project water should be available for transfer to its highest and best use; and

(2) Repayment of outstanding loans should not be jeopardized by water transfers.

In order to encourage these two objectives, the Commission makes the following three recommendations. The first two, Recommendations 7-30 and 7-31, deal with construction costs; the third, Recommendation 7-32, deals with operation and maintenance costs.

Recommendation No. 7-30: Congress should declare a national policy of permitting the transfer of water

rights to more valuable uses through voluntary agreements and through the exercise of eminent domain powers as authorized by law. To that end, Congress should authorize the transfer of water rights, under which water is furnished to others by Federal agencies, without the consent of the Federal agency supplying the water provided, however, that the agency certifies that the financial obligations for the *construction* of the works have been repaid, and further subject to the provision of Recommendation 7-32 with respect to operation and maintenance costs.

Discussion – The Federal Government has no financial interest in paid-out projects unless it retains operation and maintenance responsibility. The Government does have an interest in facilitating transfer of water from less to more productive uses. This recommendation advances the Federal interest in efficiency by reducing the costs of transfer in two ways: (1) It permits the complex legal question of the Government's ownership of water rights to be by-passed; blanket consent to the transfer is granted if the Government has no further financial claims against the water users. The question of who has the power to make the transfer then becomes a question of State law. (2) It avoids unnecessary negotiation costs in obtaining the consent of the Federal agency where the Government has no financial interest in the water.

The recommendation reflects the Commission's position that the United States should not use its legal position to prevent transfers of water from irrigation use to more valuable uses. The Commission believes that whatever interest the Federal Government may have in continued support of irrigation, is, in the case of water transfers, outweighed by the national interest in more productive use of water.

Moreover, except in the case of condemnation, the water users themselves still decide whether to continue irrigation or to sell to other users. Neither this nor any other recommendation would *require* a transfer; the recommendations *permit* the transfer if the water users desire to make it and if the Federal Government's financial interests are protected.

Regarding the question of subsidies and windfall gains, if the project has already been paid out, the subsidy granted to the original water user will have already been capitalized and will be recovered by him in any transfer, whether to a new use or to a similar use.[76]

Recommendation No. 7-31: Where a Federal agency is supplying water to users who have not repaid all the *construction* costs required to be repaid by water delivery contracts, the Federal agency should consent to the transfer of water rights in such supply if the United States is paid, by either the old or new owner, a lump sum equal to the amount of outstanding construction costs allocable to the quantity of water transferred. Even in the absence of a lump-sum payment, the Federal agency should consent to such transfer if the new owner assumes the contractual repayment obligations allocable to the quantity of water transferred and if interest is paid on the amount from the date of the transfer at the rate specified for federally assisted municipal and industrial water supply as of the date of such transfer. This provision, too, is subject to Recommendation 7-32 on operation and maintenance costs.

Discussion – This recommendation protects the Federal financial interest by requiring repayment of the unpaid balance of the construction costs allocable to the amount of water transferred, plus interest, if lump-sum payment is not made. The requirement

---

[76] For example, suppose the real cost of developing irrigation water were $10 per acre-foot but the farmer paid only $6 per acre-foot; he is subsidized to the tune of $4 per acre-foot. If the value in use to the farmer is also (coincidentally) $10 per acre-foot, that is the least he would be willing to sell it for. If the value to a municipal or industrial purchaser is $20 per acre-foot, a bargain will be struck by the farmer-seller and the industry-purchaser somewhere between $10 and $20 per acre-foot. Suppose the price agreed on is $15 per acre-foot. Not all of the $9 difference between what the farmer paid for the water ($6) and what he sells it for ($15) is a windfall profit attributable to the irrigation subsidy. Only $4 per acre-foot, the difference between what it cost to bring

water to the farmer and what he paid for it, is a gain from the subsidy. The remaining $5 per acre-foot represents an increase in value of the water resource in an alternate (and higher) use. Another farmer who paid the full $10 per acre-foot costs for developing his water supply would also make the same $5 gain in a sale to the same purchaser. The gain from the subsidy, then, is the difference between the $6 charge for water and the $10 real cost, which every subsidized farmer receives, even when he sells to another farmer. Historically, no effort has been made to recover this subsidy, and the administrative costs of doing so would be extremely high, if not prohibitive.

that the new owner pay interest at prevailing Federal water development rates is justified by several considerations. Resource allocation is apt to be distorted if purchasers of water can acquire a supply at the zero or unrealistically low (i.e., subsidized) interest rates which have been accorded irrigators. The real cost of water bought on credit is the cost of the capital to acquire it. For the Federal Government to subsidize a municipality's acquisition of a water supply could result in the purchase of an excessive amount of water and its use for purposes no more productive than the former uses. Moreover, charging interest on what is essentially a loan to the water purchaser will discourage promotion of projects ostensibly for interest-free irrigation but actually intended to be transferred to municipal and industrial users on subsidized (noninterest-bearing loan) bases. Lastly, since it is contemplated that most transfers will be made to municipalities, the interest requirement will result in all municipalities being treated alike, avoiding favored treatment to those who may be located near an irrigation project.

Recommendation No. 7-32: Where a proposed transfer of water rights threatens to impair the ability of a person or organization to pay *operation and mainte-nance* **costs when such person or organization is obligated by contract with a Federal agency to pay such costs, the new owner should have the right to assume an obligation to pay annually to such agency that portion of such operation and maintenance costs allocable to the quantity of water transferred.**

Discussion — The transfer of water rights for use in large quantities outside project boundaries may impair the ability of the remaining water users to pay annual operation and maintenance costs. This recommendation seeks to satisfy the Federal interest and yet provide definite rules that will facilitate transfers. By law, the share of operation and maintenance charges will be fixed by the ratio of transferred water to total water supply.

All three of these recommendations would affect Federal reclamation law which consists of two classes of statutes: (1) general legislation governing the relationship between the Bureau of Reclamation and the individuals or entities that receive reclamation water and (2) specific statutes authorizing particular projects, some provisions of which may depart from general principles.

The principal pieces of legislation of the first type include the following:[77]

(1) The 1902 Act (32 Stat. 388), which contemplated issuance of water right certificates to individual water users after repayment of construction costs in a 10-year period.

(2) The Warren Act of 1911 (36 Stat. 925), providing for contracts for delivery of surplus project water to individuals or irrigation organizations outside project boundaries.

(3) The 1922 Act (42 Stat. 541), authorizing contracts with irrigation districts in lieu of water right applications from individual users.

(4) The 1926 Omnibus Adjustment Act (44 Stat. 636), requiring contracts to be with irrigation districts rather than with individual users and extending the repayment period to 40 years.

(5) The Reclamation Project Act of 1939 (53 Stat. 1187), which designated the 40-year construction cost repayment contract as a 9(d) contract and authorized a new form of water service contract, the 9(e) contract, which could have a term for any period up to 40 years at water charges that would "in the Secretary's judgment . . . produce revenues at least sufficient to cover an appropriate share of the annual operation and maintenance cost and an appropriate share of such fixed charges as the Secretary deems proper . . . . " A 10-year development period was added to the 40-year repayment period.

(6) In 1956, Public Law 643, 84th Congress (70 Stat. 483), removed some of the ambiguities of the 9(e) contracts by providing for renewal of the contracts, by crediting excess operation and maintenance charges against construction costs, and by allowing conversion to 9(d) contracts when remaining construction charges could be recovered within a fixed term (usually 40 years).

(7) The Water Supply Act of 1958, Public Law 85-500 (72 Stat. 319), authorizing inclusion of storage capacity in Bureau of Reclamation reservoirs for present and anticipated future

---

[77] A full description of Reclamation law may be found in U.S. CONGRESS, Senate (1964). Reclamation Repayment Contracts, A Compilation together with Explanatory Notes on Basic Features of Several Types of Contracts Most Frequently Entered Into, prepared by the Bureau of Reclamation, Senate Document 92, 88th Congress, 2d Session. U.S. Government Printing Office, Washington, D.C.

demand for municipal and industrial water supply.

Each of these statutes modified to some degree the practices and procedures followed under earlier statutes. Recommendations 7-30, 7-31, and 7-32 contemplate enactments of this general nature, declaring a national policy of permitting the transfer of reclamation water in order to facilitate the reallocation of the resource to more productive uses. The legislation recommended would constrain such transfers only to the extent necessary to protect the Federal financial interest or to accomplish other Federal objectives such as the excess land limitation, if that policy should be continued. Thus, the legislation implementing these recommendations should provide generally that the " . . . Act shall be a supplement to the Federal reclamation laws,"[78] and that it amends or repeals any laws inconsistent with it. Since the recommended legislation would create no new burdens on holders of reclamation water rights or water delivery contracts, but rather confers benefits on them, no question of its validity should arise.

Substantive Changes in State Law: The substantive law of the States will also require change if voluntary transfers of water rights are to be facilitated. Two classes of problems exist:

(1) Uncertainty exists about who owns certain kinds of water rights and, therefore, about who has the power of disposition over them.

(2) Even where there are no such uncertainties, legal restrictions have been placed on the power of individuals and organizations to make water transfers.

Uncertainties Over Ownership and Power of Disposition – The first category of State law problems involves the uncertainty of water rights ownership, particularly acute in the case of Bureau of Reclamation projects, but also troublesome with respect to projects built and operated by State or local agencies. The Commission believes there are two ways to cut the Gordian knot: (1) by allowing individual water users to apply for transfer orders under the standard State procedures for changes in point of diversion, or place or nature of use, and (2) by authorizing irrigation districts upon a vote of the members to apply for transfer orders in accordance with the standard State procedures. To achieve these objectives, States should enact legislation as described in Recommendations 7-33 and 7-34.

Recommendation No. 7-33: Any user of water who has a contract for the use of such water, or whose right to the use is transferable with a parcel of land upon the sale of such land, should be entitled to sell his right to use such water and to apply for a change in the place or nature of use of such water in accordance with the law and procedures governing changes in points of diversion, nature, and place of use of water rights. In such proceeding, the applicant should not be required to prove ownership of an appropriation or permit right but should be allowed to transfer whatever right or privilege he may have, subject to the rule that such transfer shall not injure the rights of other water uses.

Discussion – This recommendation builds on Recommendations 7-30, 7-31, and 7-32 in seeking to simplify the transfer of water furnished by the Bureau of Reclamation to an irrigation district and then to the ultimate consumer, usually a farmer. Rather than trying to sort out a complex legal situation regarding title, the proposed statute deals functionally with the ultimate beneficiary of the water supply and allows him to make agreements for the sale of the water. Concomitantly, it allows him to institute proceedings (along with the purchaser) for an order changing the place or nature of use. The general provision making such transfers subject to the vested rights of others takes care of two problems— the reliance of others on return flow (the usual problem of water transfers) and the special problem of any financial obligation that might exist under the contract between the user and either the irrigation district or a State or Federal agency. The administrative agency that handles water rights transfers can impose the necessary conditions to protect these interests.

Recommendation No. 7-34: Upon the vote of a majority of the members of an irrigation district entitled to vote for members of the governing board, the district may enter into a contract for the sale of the water, or any portion thereof, to which it is legally entitled by contract or otherwise, and for its delivery to a purchaser at such place and for such nature of use as the purchaser shall designate, subject to the provisions of law regarding changes in the point of diversion, place, and nature of use. Except where individual users have voluntarily transferred

---

[78] This language is taken from Section 5 of Public Law 84-643, July 2, 1956, 70 Stat. 483, 43 USCA 485 h, the 1956 Act clarifying Section 9(e) contracts.

their right to the use of water to the district, the diminution of supply available for use by members of the district by virtue of the transfer should be shared *pro rata* on the basis of average use over the 5 years preceding the date of the contract of sale. Without proof of more than a legal right to receive water, the district may apply for a change in the point of diversion, or in the place or nature of use, and a transfer of such right should be allowed, subject to the rule that the transfer shall not injure vested rights of others.

Discussion — This recommendation rounds out the quintet of proposals designed primarily to enhance the marketability of the lower-valued portion of the large volume of irrigation water administered by the Bureau of Reclamation. Recommendations 7-30, 7-31, and 7-32 remove Federal restrictions on the transfer of project water, except for conditions regarded as necessary to protect the Federal purse. Those recommendations throw back onto State law the burden of determining who can make water transfers.

One mode of resolving the question of who can make water transfers would be an attempt to unravel "title" to the water right, but that would be a complex and expensive exercise. It therefore seems preferable to specify the actions that water users may take to sell their rights to receive water. In essence, Recommendation 7-33 allows a project water user to sell his water if he can meet the standard applicable to all other water users, namely that the transfer does not injure vested rights of others.

Recommendation 7-34 deals with the public irrigation district, allowing it to sell upon a majority vote of its members. This provision is desirable because it permits a prospective purchaser of large quantities of water to deal with an entity rather than with numerous individual users, thus reducing the costs of the transaction and making it less cumbersome. Protection is afforded district members by requiring resulting water shortages to be pro-rated. More efficient farmers can make up their shortages by purchases from less efficient farmers in the same project. The recommendation contemplates that the district itself will seek to buy individual rights prior to consummating a transfer. So much for uncertainties over ownership and powers of disposition.

Restrictions on Powers of Transfer — The second category of State law problems consists of restrictions on the legal power of clearly recognized owners of

specifically defined rights to make transfers. One such restriction, found in the law of only a few States at the present time, makes an appropriative water right "appurtenant" to the land (i.e., not subject to separate sale and use apart from the original tract of land benefiting from the right). Another restriction denies the power of irrigation districts to provide water outside district boundaries. The Commission believes that these restrictions, and others of like nature, would be impliedly repealed under the provisions of Recommendations 7-33 and 7-34. However, to make the matter entirely certain, the following recommendation is proposed.

Recommendation No. 7-35: Each State having the appropriation system of water rights should provide for an administrative procedure for the transfer of such rights by changes in point of diversion, place of use, and nature of use. Protection should be provided for the vested rights of other water users. Any person or organization having the right to use water should be entitled to transfer such right, and all statutes, judicial decisions, and administrative regulations to the contrary should be repealed.

Evaluation of Federal Water Supply Projects

The legal and institutional reforms proposed here give promise of adding flexibility to the utilization of water resources. Elsewhere the Commission recommends that alternative sources of water be examined and evaluated in any proposal for construction of a project to provide a new or supplemental water supply. One such alternative, as this section repeatedly suggests, is the reallocation of water from existing, low-value uses to the higher-value uses which a proposed project might otherwise serve.[79] The Commission believes that this alternative should be considered in evaluation of any proposed Federal water project and, accordingly, makes the following recommendation.

Recommendation No. 7-36: Every report on a proposed water supply project submitted to Congress should include a study of existing developed water

---

[79] Section 8 of the 1902 Reclamation Act provided: "...the right to the use of water acquired under the provisions of this Act shall be appurtenant to the land irrigated...." In view of the numerous amendments to the Reclamation law since 1902, it is not clear that this provision still has force. If it does, it is the intent of the Commission to repeal it by the legislation proposed in Recommendations 7-30 and 7-31.

supplies in the general area of the project, the value of the water as presently utilized in the region, the estimated value in use of the supply to be developed by the projects, and the legal and economic feasibility of meeting the demand for the new supply by the transfer of water rights from the old uses to the proposed new uses. The report should contain a description of the water rights transfer law, procedures, and institutions, and an evaluation thereof in accordance with the recommendations set forth in this section.

CONCLUSIONS

Where resources are scarce, society cannot have all of everything it would like. Where scarce resources are diverted excessively into the production of certain things, it is done at the sacrifice of producing other things. Having too much of one thing means not having enough of another. To maximize returns to society, it is desirable that an optimum balance be struck.

In a mixed economic system as America's, where heavy reliance is placed on private action, the price mechanism of the marketplace is used to strike the balance. Goods and services in great demand command high prices and return large profits. The resources used in their production receive high returns and are bid away from alternate uses. On the other hand, products for which demand is poor or supply excessive receive low prices. Their producers suffer losses instead of profits. The resources associated with their production receive low returns and, where substitutability is possible, get bid away from production of relatively unwanted goods and services into the production of goods and services in greater demand. In this way, benefits to society are maximized. This is what is meant by the term "economic efficiency."

The Commission believes that much of the Nation's water supply, being a scarce resource, should be responsive to this kind of pricing mechanism so that it will not be inefficiently utilized for the production of things in superabundance but will be diverted instead into the production of things society craves more. Unfortunately, because of existing State and Federal laws and administrative procedures, there are impediments to the transfer of water rights from low-value uses to higher-value uses. This section has identified

those impediments and has developed a set of recommendations designed to eliminate them or to reduce their adverse effect.

The Commission believes that implementation of its recommendations will facilitate voluntary agreements for the sale of water rights and for their reallocation to more valuable uses. If these recommendations are adopted and put into effect, the Commission believes it likely that construction of new water supply projects can be postponed in some areas for considerable lengths of time, that an economic incentive will be provided for saving water (since the amount saved will be able to be sold), that water will be put to better use so as to maximize the economic yield to society, and that, accordingly, the allocation of resources will be made more efficient.

RECOMMENDATIONS

Thirteen recommendations have been developed and described in detail in this section. The first two recommendations are designed to improve State water rights records, thus providing more and better information. The next four recommendations seek to simplify water transfer proceedings and, therefore, make them less expensive; and to give to purchasers of water the rights to the return flow generated by their new use thus to enable all of the transferred water to be put to more valuable uses. The next six recommendations are calculated to remove the uncertainties and complexities in Federal and State law concerning title to water rights. In effect, they will empower the actual user of water to make a sale of his water right so long as the rights of creditors, including the Federal Government, and of other water users are protected. Finally, the last recommendation urges that before any federally financed water supply project is submitted to Congress, there will be a report on the legal, institutional, economic, and physical feasibility of satisfying demand by the alternative of reallocating existing water supplies to new uses through the transfer of water rights.

In short, adoption of these recommendations will remove a number of significant impediments to the transfer of water rights. The Commission believes that the removal of these impediments will encourage such transfers and encourage greater efficiency and effectiveness in the use of the Nation's water resources.

Improvements In State Water Laws To Provide Recognition For Social Values In Water[80]

State laws creating and protecting rights to the use and enjoyment of water fail to give adequate recognition to social (that is, noneconomic) values in water.[81] This omission derives in the West from the law of appropriation, which embodied the social preference during the period of its formulation for economic development over protection of such social values as esthetics, recreation, and fish and wildlife propagation. In the East, where the law of riparian rights prevails, some greater protection of these values is possible since riparian landowners are entitled to a reasonable streamflow in competition with those who would divert the stream to economic uses. But even in the East, the protection of social values lies in the hands of private citizens and not with public authorities, for riparian rights are private rights, not public rights.

The Commission believes that State laws should be improved to provide greater protection of social values in water. Specifically, legal rights should be created in the public for such social uses as esthetics, recreation, fish and wildlife propagation, and legislation should be enacted to make water surfaces, beaches, and shorelines accessible to the public for recreational use.

---

[80] This section is based in large measure on two studies conducted by the legal staff of the National Water Commission: DEWSNUP, Richard L (1971). Legal Protection of Instream Water Values. National Technical Information Service, Springfield, Va., Accession No. PB 205 003, and DEWSNUP, Richard L (1971). Public Access Rights in Waters and Shorelands. National Technical Information Service, Springfield, Va., Accession No. PB 205 247.

[81] Use of water for economic purposes serves an important social purpose. Economic use is also a social use. To facilitate this discussion, however, a distinction is made between economic and social values. As used here, economic uses and values refer to those activities which produce goods and services normally priced and sold in the marketplace. Social uses and values, as used here, exclude such market-oriented activities. The distinction is made solely for purposes of discussion and does not imply that economic activity serves no socially useful purpose.

DISCUSSION

The Lack of Legal Protection for Some Water Values

There are a number of defects in present State statutes which are, in large measure, responsible for some water values receiving favored protection at the expense of other water values which have been more or less ignored. A background of those legal deficiencies and some of the problems they create is useful. Also useful for purposes of remedying these defects is an abbreviated catalog of State legislative action, much of it quite recent, employed to help redress the balance.

Legal Doctrines: The system of water law adopted by most Western States is known as the law of appropriation. The basic tenets of that system are that (1) a water right can be acquired only by the acquiring party diverting the water from the watercourse and applying it to a beneficial use and (2) in accordance with the date of acquisition, an earlier acquired water right shall have priority over other later acquired water rights. Water in excess of that needed to satisfy existing rights is viewed as unappropriated water, available for appropriation by diversion and application of the water to a beneficial use. The process of appropriation can continue until all of the water in a stream is subject to rights of use through withdrawals from the stream.

Riparian water rights, characteristic of the Eastern States, protect adjacent landowners from withdrawals or uses which unreasonably diminish water quantity or quality. Where diversions or uses have been unreasonable, they either have been enjoined or riparian owners adversely affected have been compensated for interference with their rights. The concern of riparian law has been one of protecting private, rather than public, rights in streams and lakes.

Specific Problems: Appropriation doctrines of the West made it virtually impossible (1) to preserve instream values or (2) to acquire a water right

271

pursuant to a diversion if the intended use was not for an economic purpose. Appropriators could divert water out of a stream, imperiling instream values; and the only kind of diversions allowed were those which served traditional economic purposes. Hence, neither instream values nor out-of-stream, noneconomic values could be protected. Some examples may assist understanding.

Since rights could be acquired only by diverting water from a stream, there was no legal way to protect beautiful waterfalls relied on by a resort to attract guests. Such natural waterfalls are instream values.

When a public agency claimed that a water right had been acquired by the public through long use of a stream as a fishery, the claim was denied in favor of new diversions from the stream.

Where water was released from a reservoir to sustain water quality, the released water was sometimes diverted for use by others, thus impairing water quality and frustrating the purpose of the release.

Even when a diversion was made from the stream, a water right could not be recognized unless the use qualified as "beneficial." But, since State statutes generally seemed to equate beneficial use with economic use, diversion of water for the purpose of developing a waterfowl marsh or some other "noneconomic" use would not qualify, and no water right for such purposes could be acquired.

The problems in the Eastern States have been of a different nature. The major challenge facing the Eastern States is to achieve a better balance between public use and private use of the water resource. Economic development and social purposes can both be served, and riparian rights can be protected if Eastern State laws continue to recognize private riparian rights but only to the extent of a minimum flow of reasonable quality, adequate to serve reasonable riparian (private) needs and interests. In some instances the public interest in water quality might be transcendent, in which case attention will have to be given to ways of acquiring public rights of access and use in certain waters where no such rights now exist but where the public need is overriding.

Examples of State Legislative Action: A number of States are seeking ways to reform their water laws to provide protection for social values of water. Existing water uses under appropriation rights in the Western States, validly acquired and in good standing under State law, cannot be taken from the owners in the name of State legislative reform, unless procedures of

constitutional due process are followed and just compensation is paid. The legal reforms thus far adopted by the Western States, where the law of appropriation controls, have made no effort to deny water uses under existing rights, but have concentrated instead on preserving and protecting social values only in those waters which thus far remain unappropriated. In some cases, that is not much. In other cases, however, there are substantial waters remaining unappropriated.

Opposition can be expected in State legislatures to proposals which appear to restrict future water appropriations for economic development. Such opposition is justified to the extent that legislation is proposed which tips the scales excessively in favor of "social" values at the expense of economic development, just as critics are presently justified in pointing out the excessive dominance of economic development objectives over noneconomic social objectives. What should be sought is a fair balance of water uses covering the full spectrum of public interests.

The legislative reforms catalogued below illustrate a wide range of courses of action. Some reforms might be well suited to the needs of one State but ill suited to the needs of another. Each State will have to evaluate the utility of these statutes in light of its own problems, circumstances, and administrative structure.

Direct Legislative Reservation or Appropriation of Waters – In 1970, Oklahoma demonstrated the most direct approach by enacting a statute similar to the Federal Wild and Scenic Rivers Act, which declares that certain specified streams and rivers are set aside and reserved for scenic, recreational, wildlife, and related uses.[82] While State agencies are involved in the administration and management of the river areas to protect public rights and regulate public use, the reservation (or appropriation) of the rivers is accomplished by the statute, without any subsequent administrative hearings, debates, determinations, or other procedures. The merits of such legislation for each particular river or stream (or stretch of river or stream) are evaluated in State legislative committee hearings and debated on the floor of the legislature prior to enactment.

Legislative Authorization of Administrative Filings for Water Rights – Montana enacted a statute in 1969 which identified 10 major trout streams of that

---

[82] Oklahoma Stat., 82 Sections 1451-59 (1971).

State and authorized the State Fish and Game Department to file on the amount of water needed to sustain the trout fishery.[83] Under the statute, such a filing does not forever foreclose further appropriations and withdrawals for new economic uses, but it does protect the minimum flow from further depletions by appropriation unless an applicant can convince the State district court that a proposed withdrawal will be more beneficial than the use of the water to sustain the fishery.

Administrative Reservation of Minimum Stream-flows — The State of Washington enacted a statute in 1969 which authorizes the State Department of Water Resources to establish minimum flows or levels for streams and lakes to protect fish and wildlife resources and recreation and esthetic values, and to preserve water quality.[84] Minimum streamflows or lake levels are to be established whenever it appears to the Department that such action is in the public interest. The statute requires coordination among the State agencies having pertinent water resource responsibilities, and sets forth procedures for public notice and hearings before such minimum flows are determined.

Criteria to Guide the State Engineer in Reviewing Water Applications — Nearly all Western States provide by statute for new water rights to be acquired through the filing of written applications with the State water rights administrator (often called the State engineer). The administrator is required to review the application and either approve or reject it, or, in a proper case, impose limitations on the manner or duration of the use. In so doing, he is guided by a number of statutory criteria. The most common criteria are that there must be unappropriated water sufficient to satisfy the application, and the proposed use must not interfere with or impair existing rights. In 1971, Utah enacted a statute which added a new criterion—it requires the State engineer to reject an application which will have an unreasonable adverse impact on recreation or environmental values of the watercourse.[85]

Protection of Natural Stream Beds from Alteration — Much difficulty has arisen when highway plans have contemplated altering, relocating, channelizing,

or encasing a natural stream. The conflict usually is between minimizing construction costs for the highway, on the one hand, and maintaining the natural stream environment for its esthetic, recreational, and fishery values, on the other.

In 1963, Montana enacted a statute providing for stream bed protection, which has served as a model for a number of statutes enacted by other States.[86] The Montana statute provides that no State agency or political subdivision, including, of course, the State Highway Department, shall alter any natural stream bed without first obtaining the approval of the State Fish and Game Commission. In the event of a dispute, machinery for arbitration is provided.

Public and Private Rights in Water Diverted or Reserved for Social Uses — Most States now permit diversions for maintaining offstream fisheries and waterfowl management areas, even by private applicants, but have not yet authorized diversions by private persons to create purely esthetic amenities. Such uses should have legal recognition, but approval of a particular application should be dependent upon the facts and circumstances surrounding the proposal and should take into account the alternative uses for the water sought to be appropriated.

Some have argued that private persons should be awarded water "rights" in the social values of natural streams.[87] The Commission notes that preservation of important natural stream values will simultaneously protect private as well as public interests in those values no matter in whose name the values are protected. For example, if a proprietor develops a resort adjacent to scenic waterfalls, he will be vitally interested in the preservation of the falls. But that interest will be protected as effectively through a reservation by the State of sufficient water to sustain the falls as by granting a private water right to the proprietor. The only material difference would be that all members of the public, including the proprietor and his guests, would be the designated beneficiaries of the right rather than the proprietor and his guests alone. To this extent, then, private interests are protected through public rights which safeguard instream values.

The Commission believes the public interest is better served through procedures such as the one just

---

[83] Rev. Codes of Montana Ann., 89-801(2) (1947 Rep. Vol. 6, Part 1).

[84] Rev. Code of Washington, 90.22.010 and 90.22.020.

[85] Utah Code Ann. (1953), Section 73-3-8.

[86] Rev. Codes of Montana Ann., Sections 26-1501 *et seq.* (1947 Rep. Vol. 2, Part 2).

[87] In the Eastern States, where the doctrine of riparian rights prevails, private rights to instream social values are recognized.

illustrated than by awarding water rights for the social values of natural streams to private individuals. The latter course of action would result in a number of private individuals holding water "rights" to natural stream values, and would raise difficult and complex questions. For example, could the public be denied enjoyment of instream social values by the private water right owners? Could such owners sell and transfer their private rights to these social values? Would these rights descend to the heirs of the owners?

Summary — Six different legislative actions have been identified for the States to undertake in order to optimize the use of water resources for "social" as well as for conventional economic purposes. First, States can enact statutes to set aside and reserve certain waters for scenic, recreation, wildlife, and related uses. Second, States can legislatively authorize a State agency to file for and acquire rights in unappropriated water for social purposes. Third, States can authorize an appropriate State agency to establish minimum streamflows or lake levels for social purposes. Fourth, States can establish statutory criteria, including an environmental criterion, to guide State water administrators in approving or rejecting applications for unappropriated water. Fifth, States can forbid State and local governmental agencies from altering watercourses without first obtaining approval from an appropriate State agency. And, finally, States under the appropriation doctrine can simultaneously protect both public and private social values in waters by public reservation of sufficient water to safeguard the desired stream values.

Public Access to Waters and Adjacent Shorelands

Many socioeconomic and technological changes in American life have combined to intensify national demand for recreation. Increasing productivity, resulting in more leisure time and income, combined with a growing population stimulate recreation demand. In addition, increased urbanization, greater transportation capabilities, higher levels of educational attainment, timesaving and laborsaving household appliances, and an evolving lifestyle favoring outdoor recreation all add to the growing demand for recreation.

Increasing demand for recreation manifests itself in a number of ways, not the least of which is a significant surge in public demand for water-related recreational opportunities. Hence, the question of public access to waters and adjacent shorelands is gaining increasing importance.

Basis for Public Rights in Shorelands: Rights of public access to and use of waters and shorelands are rooted in the common law of England. There, the rights of the Crown and Parliament over waters and shorelands were qualified—these rights were "sovereign" subject to public uses for navigation and fishing. The public uses were recognized as public rights, and are often referred to in judicial decisions as a "public trust" which must be protected.

In America, the 13 original States succeeded to all of the rights of both the English King and Parliament with respect to navigable waters, their beds, and adjacent shores—but still subject to the public trust (public use for navigation and fishing). When these States formed the Federal Union and adopted the Constitution, they retained their ownership interest in navigable waters and shorelands. As additional States were subsequently admitted to the Union, they were accorded "equal footing" with the original States, including State ownership rights over navigable waters and shorelands.

In England, the legal test of navigability—and thus the measure of the public trust—was whether waters were affected by the ebb and flow of the tide. The U.S. Supreme Court rejected the English tidal test of navigability, and adopted instead a test of navigability-in-fact, which means that all waters, whether coastal or inland, are subject to the public trust if they are capable of supporting navigation.

A distinction must be made between ownership of waters, on the one hand, and public trust and rights of public use in waters, on the other. Federal court decisions determine the legal test of navigability to establish which waters and shorelands are *owned* by the States. Each State is free to declare its own legal test of navigability for the purpose of establishing the public trust and rights of public use of waters. Thus, if a State declares that floating logs for timber operations or floating pleasure craft are forms of navigation, then all waters within the State capable of such uses, whether owned by the State or not, will be subject to public access and use. On the other hand, if a State declares that a body of water must be capable of supporting commercial vessels transporting cargo and passengers, then fewer waters, even though owned by the State, will be navigable, and the public trust with respect to waters will be correspondingly restricted.

As a general proposition, there are no public trust rights in nonnavigable waters. States, of course, have police power over private property, including waters where there are no public access or public ownership rights. For example, States may regulate conduct on private waters, or prosecute for crimes committed thereon, or promulgate zoning regulations to govern development in or adjacent to such waters. But police power authority offers no basis for declaring public rights of use; private rights in nonnavigable waters and in the shores, beds, and banks of nonnavigable waters cannot be diminished through police power regulation to provide public access. Nor, for that matter, can such private rights in those *lands* be diminished through a new test of navigability which includes waters previously deemed nonnavigable. State legal tests of navigability are important, however, because they are a critical measure of public rights of access and use (as contrasted to ownership) of *waters*, and such public rights of use can be extended to *waters* previously considered nonnavigable.[88]

The Submerged Lands Act: Aside from the original 13 States and Texas, all other States were carved out of Federal territory and thus derive their *ownership* interest in navigable waters and in their beds and shorelands under the test of navigability laid down by the Federal courts. As pointed out above, State ownership accrues by virtue of the doctrine of constitutional equal footing.

Many lakes and streams occupy a questionable status with regard to their navigability—they are shallow enough or small enough to raise doubts as to whether they meet the Federal test of navigability for purposes of State ownership. Ordinarily, this would be a legal question to be resolved by the Federal courts, but some clarification is given by the Submerged Lands Act.[89] That Act granted to the Coastal States the submerged lands within 3 miles of the seacoast, and also sought to clarify State interest in inland navigable waters. The legislative history of the Act shows that, exclusive of the Great Lakes, ownership of approximately 29 million acres of the beds and shorelands of inland waters was confirmed in the States for purposes of title and administra-

tion.[90] The Senate Committee Report[91] cited a Census Bureau publication to show where the inland navigable waters covered by the Act were located.[92]

In a great number of cases where the navigability of a body of water is unclear, reference to the Census Bureau publication will help to clarify the question and thus to clarify public use rights as well, because Congress assumed the waters listed in that publication to be navigable. While this can be no more than a legal presumption as to the existence of the public trust (the Submerged Lands Act applies only if the waters were navigable at the date of statehood), that Census Bureau publication will be a valuable aid to the States in resolving rights of public use.

One caveat is important. For purposes of the Submerged Lands Act, the question of navigability is always resolved under the test laid down by the Federal courts; individual State tests of navigability are not applicable. The State tests of navigability can properly be applied to *waters* whether owned by the State or not, to impress the public trust upon them, but cannot be applied to beds and shorelands which are held either in Federal or private ownership.

Many of the legal questions relating to navigability and the public trust are extremely complicated and must be resolved by the judiciary. It is this very complexity and uncertainty which have caused the States to be hesitant about moving forward to resolve questions of public access and use of many waters which have a high value for that purpose.

Problems of the Shoreland Boundaries: Ocean beach areas subject to the public trust of access and use are those covered by the ebb and flow of the tide, measured to the line of the average high tides.[93] On inland waters, the shorelands include the area between the water's edge and the ordinary high water mark. Most inland bodies of water experience some seasonal fluctuation, and when the water level reaches its ordinary high cycle the area is usually inundated for a long enough period to prevent the growth of vegetation, and so the vegetation line usually designates the ordinary high water mark.

[88] DEWSNUP, Richard L (1971). Public Access Rights in Waters and Shorelands, prepared for the National Water Commission. National Technical Information Service, Springfield, Va., Accession No. PB 205 247. p. 47.

[89] *Submerged Lands Act* P L. 31, 83rd Congress, May 22, 1953, 67 Stat. 29, 43 USCA 1301 *et seq.*

[90] U.S. CONGRESS, Senate, Committee on Interior and Insular Affairs (1953). Submerged Lands Act, Senate Report No. 133, 83d Congress, 1st Session. U.S. Government Printing Office, Washington, D.C.

[91] *Ibid.,* p. 77, Appendix G.

[92] U.S. BUREAU OF THE CENSUS (1942). Areas of the United States, 1940. U.S. Government Printing Office, Washington, D.C.

[93] See *Borax Consolidated, Ltd. v. City of Los Angeles,* 296 U.S. 10 (1935).

Clearly, the landward boundary line of inland shores and ocean beaches is of extreme importance for public recreational use. The beach area immediately above the boundary line is commonly referred to as the dry-sand area, because the tide does not ebb and flow over it. These boundary lines change when natural forces or events cause erosion, or when sediments are deposited to form accretions, or when waters gradually recede permanently exposing dry lands that were previously water-covered.

Courts are often presented with difficult legal questions concerning ownership and public access rights in the dry-sand areas of the beach. The U.S. Supreme Court has said that ownership questions must be resolved by Federal law when the upland is owned by the United States or derived from Federal patents,[94] but State courts have applied State law when the question was simply one of public access easements and not one of ownership. For example, the Oregon court has held that dry-sand beach areas within that State are subject to public access rights, even though privately owned, by virtue of customary public use predating statehood.[95] California's court held that, under State law, 5 years of continuous public use of beach areas in private ownership will result in public access rights by virtue of an implied dedication to public use by the owner.[96] These decisions result in public rights of recreational use in areas of critical recreational importance, and they give State legislatures and administrative agencies an excellent opportunity to regulate public use, license concessionaires, provide sanitation facilities, and otherwise enhance the public recreational potential.

Opportunitites for State Action: Public recreational rights in waters and shorelands are largely dependent upon the initiative and aggressiveness of the States. State legislation cannot diminish either Federal or private ownership interests, but in areas clouded with uncertainty, the courts have shown an inclination to be persuaded by State statutes declaring public access rights.

Beyond the concept of the public trust, some States have declared public rights in nonnavigable waters by virtue of the "public" nature of water itself. Some States have defined riparian rights rather narrowly in order to sustain broader public use of waters. Others have said that even when a State sells or conveys shorelands to private ownership, a right of public use survives.

Since State statutes and legal doctrines vary, the extent of public use of waters and shorelands varies. For example, virtually all waters in Minnesota are navigable and subject to public use under the laws of that State.[97] Virginia, on the other hand, utilizes a more restrictive test of navigability,[98] a test which prohibits public uses on the Jackson River even though the Corps of Engineers is constructing a dam and contemplates reservoir releases which had been designed—in cooperation with the Virginia Fish and Game Department—to serve public recreational use on the River below the dam.

As can be seen, statutes and legal doctrines vary from State to State. Nevertheless, opportunitites for enhancing public recreational use of waters and shorelands are available to, and await action by, the individual States.

Coordinated Land and Water Management for Public Recreation

Many States have statewide water plans. States also have statewide outdoor recreation plans. Since water and recreation are often closely linked, these plans should be coordinated within each State so that there is a systematic and sensible approach to public recreation for water-related values. Potentials can better be assessed and priorities weighed through such coordination, and there can be a conscious and deliberate effort to ascertain and protect public rights. The wetlands illustrate one example where important resources have actually been in State ownership and subject to public trust rights, but where drainage and development have caused much damage because some States simply were not aware of what they owned and what the public rights were.

Evaluation of Recreation Potentials: Coordinated planning assumes that in any water project funded or controlled by State agencies or subordinate units of State government, the recreational potential will be fully evaluated—including use of reservoirs, streams and access along the shores and banks. Minimum streamflows might be established in light, not only of fishery or water quality considerations, but also of downstream and other potential uses. In short,

[94] *Hughes v. State of Washington*, 389 U.S. 290 (1967).

[95] *State ex. rel. Thorton v. Hay*, 462 P.2d 671, Oregon (1969).

[96] *Gion v. City of Santa Cruz* and *Dietz v. King*, 2 Cal. 3d 29, 465 P.2d 50 (1970).

[97] *Lamprey v. Metcalf*, 52 Minn. 181, 53 N.W. 1139 (1893).

[98] *Boerner v. McCallister*, 197 Va. 169, 89 S.E.2d 2 (1955).

Big Surf Recreational Development, Salt River Project, Arizona

coordinated planning should make possible the formulation of comprehensive water project plans in which recreation is given full and equitable consideration as a purpose of water resource development.

Acquisition of Public Access: In many instances, rights of public access to and use of water and water facilities will have to be acquired, either by negotiated purchase or by eminent domain, where no public rights exist. State legislatures should grant State agencies the power of eminent domain for this purpose, to be exercised where the public need is substantial and where the State agency is prepared to supervise public use to assure reasonable sanitation and conduct, and to prevent unnecessary annoyances to the owners of water facilities or adjacent lands.

Zoning: Statewide planning might also preserve some social values of water through the promulgation of zoning regulations to assure that construction and development in waters and adjacent lands do not impair the public interest in recreation and scenic and esthetic values. This is particularly important in connection with lakes and ponds located within or near metropolitan areas, where the amenities of such waters have public importance. Zoning regulations can be promulgated even though there are no public rights in the lands or the waters, so long as such regulations do not deny the landowners reasonable use of their property.

These and similar considerations illustrate the need for coordinated statewide planning and ways in which such coordinated planning can meet public recreational demand and preserve the public interest in fish, wildlife, scenic, esthetic, and environmental values of water and associated land resources.

Incentives for State Action

Those State agencies responsible for management of fish, game, wildlife, recreation, and water resources should present persuasive cases to State legislatures for authorization and funding of improved statewide management and planning. Private fish and wildlife groups and environmental organizations can certainly be expected to lend their support in legislative committee hearings.

Once coordinated planning is authorized and implemented, the appropriate agency or agencies might well report periodically to the legislature, setting forth proposed legislation needed to bring about desirable reforms and requesting funds sufficient to carry out programs and acquire necessary facilities.

Federal financial incentives to encourage the States to bring about needed reforms quickly are desirable. At present, Congress provides funds, through the U.S. Water Resources Council, to assist the States in water resource planning. Funds also are made available to the States from the Land and Water Conservation Fund, administered by the U.S. Bureau of Outdoor Recreation, for the purpose of planning and acquiring outdoor recreation rights and facilities. The Commission believes that these funds should continue to be made available to the States, but that the two programs be coordinated more closely on the Federal level so as to require higher levels of coordination on the State level.

CONCLUSIONS

State laws in many instances are inadequate to protect important social uses of water. Historically, the problem in the Eastern States has been that rights of "social" use of nonnavigable waters have been recognized only in private riparian landowners, with no public rights of either access or use. In Western States, the problem is that water has been diverted from streams to such an extent that instream values which should have been protected have been largely impaired, and in some cases, destroyed.

The Commission finds that certain legal reforms at the State level are necessary in order to realize optimum use of water resources in the public interest. Some States have taken an aggressive lead in revising

their water statutes to recognize social values of waters, and they are to be commended.

The Commission recognizes that the States have different legal systems and doctrines, and that no single uniform statute will serve all States equally well. However, the public need for optimum use of water resources for recreation, quality improvement, scenic, and esthetic purposes, as well as for conventional economic values, is clear. Legal reforms are needed to accomplish that result.

The courses of action available to a particular State will, in large measure, depend upon the laws and organizational structure for water conservation and use within the State. Many problems deserve attention, including protection of natural stream channels from unreasonable alteration or relocation; securing public access to some waters, beaches, shorelands, and wetlands; requiring public access rights to reservoirs or similar water facilities as a condition of public financing of water projects by State and local agencies; zoning ordinances to protect against development adjacent to water which would unreasonably detract from public use or natural amenities; and a broader test of navigability under State laws to extend public rights of use in more watercourses.

The Commission does not believe that every private water development should necessarily be made available for public recreation use. Many privately owned water facilities will have only nominal value for public recreation purposes or there may be adequate alternatives available. However when privately owned water developments have exceptional recreational potential, a strong case can be made for provision of public access for recreation or for public purchase and development for that purpose.

The Commission commends those States that have taken steps to provide effective protection for non economic social uses of water, and encourages the remaining States to review their water laws and enact appropriate legislation without delay

RECOMMENDATIONS

Beyond urging the States to proceed energetically to revise their water statutes so as to recognize social values of water, the Commission advances the following specific recommendations:

7-37.   State property rules relating to water should authorize water rights to be acquired for all social uses, noneconomic as well as economic In particular, recreation, scenic, esthetic water quality, fisheries, and similar instream values are kinds of social uses, heretofore neglected, which require protection. As these values, and rights in them, are recognized and protected in natural lakes and streams, their benefits should be clearly mandated for general public use, particularly when they are uniquely suited to such uses.

7-38. Private social uses of water, for such purposes as boating, swimming, fish culture, and general recreation, should be authorized in appropriation States when water is diverted from natural watercourses for that purpose—but such rights should be granted only after a review is made to ascertain that such use will not constitute a substantial impairment of natural instream values susceptible to public use.

7-39. Public rights should be secured through State legislation authorizing administrative withdrawal or public reservation of sufficient unappropriated water needed for minimum streamflows in order to maintain scenic values, water quality, fishery resources, and the natural stream environment in those watercourses, or parts thereof, that have primary value for these purposes.

7-40. State legislatures can and should liberalize their tests of navigability for purposes of the public trust, thus bringing more waters (as distinguished from shorelands) within the ambit of public use. States should take steps to assure public use of beds and shorelands of all navigable inland waters covered by the Submerged Lands Act which have a potential for such public use.

7-41. Statewide outdoor recreation plans should include a review of beaches and shorelands to ascertain those areas that are in public ownership or subject to rights of public use; and, where public rights exist, measures should be taken to assure that public access is protected and public use regulated.

7-42. Where wetlands are administratively or judicially determined to be State owned and have primary value for waterfowl propagation or other wildlife purposes, they should ordinarily be reserved or otherwise protected from drainage operations and developments which would destroy or substantially impair such values.

7-43. Where there are no presently existing public rights of access and use of streams, lakes, and storage reservoirs, and where such areas are particularly valuable for public recreational use, the States should endeavor to purchase access easements for public use. In the Eastern States, these access easements ordinarily will be acquired in nonnavigable lakes and streams; whereas, in the Western States such easements more likely will be acquired in irrigation reservoirs and similar facilities that were constructed earlier for other purposes, are privately owned and operated, but which have important potential for fishing, boating, and related recreational pursuits.

7-44. If access easements for public recreational use cannot be acquired by negotiation and purchase, then the States should authorize eminent domain to be exercised on a selective basis, as justified by public need.

7-45. Whether easements for public access are acquired by negotiated purchase or condemnation, the Commission believes adequate provision should be made to assure that public use does not become unregulated public abuse. Those enjoying public access should be prevented from engaging in annoying conduct, littering, or other abuses which would detract from enjoyment of the area by other members of the public or interfere with the rights of adjacent landowners. An appropriate State agency should be charged with the specific responsibility of supervising public use of areas where access easements are acquired, including the installation of restroom facilities, providing garbage or refuse containers, and policing such public use areas with reasonable frequency and thoroughness.

7-46. To assure that public use is properly controlled, or to assure that adjacent landowners are protected if public use is not properly controlled, the States should consider (1) authorizing compensation to landowners in the event they suffer damages from public misconduct, (2) creating buffer zones between areas open to use by the public and privately owned adjacent lands, and (3) including conditions or restrictions within access easements to provide reasonable landowner protection—and making these provisions specifically enforceable by the landowners.

A Permit System For Riparian States

Nearly all of the States east of the Mississippi River follow the riparian law of water rights. The key features of the riparian doctrine as set forth in the textbooks are:

(1) the place where water may be put to use is restricted;

(2) a riparian landowner has a legal privilege to make use of water at any time, subject only to the limitation that the use be reasonable;[99] and

(3) the water supply is shared in times of shortage.

Some of the Eastern States have permit systems, although few go far in regulating water uses. Riparian States, especially those without permit systems, usually lack an adequate recordkeeping system as well. As a consequence of the riparian rules and the absence of records, the public planner and private investor are confronted with several uncertainties in water resource development:

(1) What is the existing demand on supply?

(2) What is potential demand on supply?

(3) What security will present development have in the future?

(4) What kind of private, consensual arrangements can be made to safeguard supply?

These uncertainties have not yet caused serious problems in the East, for water supplies have been abundant. But if demand increases as some projections indicate,[100] greater stability will be required, as some Eastern States have already realized. In those States, the response has been enactment of permit legislation.

It is the purpose of this section to put forth a set of principles to assist State legislatures in formulating permit systems for riparian jurisdictions. The Commission does not recommend the immediate adoption of permit statutes by all Eastern States. Any change in the law has some costs; a fully developed permit system with extensive recordkeeping and provisions for allocation of water would have high costs relative to the value of much of the water being regulated.

States would be well advised to proceed on a basin-by-basin basis, applying the permit system to those areas experiencing the sharpest competition for water supply. Thus, the system proposed contemplates the enactment of general enabling legislation to be implemented from time to time by administrative action as the need arises.

THE PROBLEM

As noted, a number of riparian States have more or less comprehensive permit statutes on the books at the present time. In addition, the National Conference of Commissioners on Uniform Laws promulgated a Model Water Use Act in 1958 and the U.S. Office of Water Resources Research provided support for the preparation of a Model Water Code in 1970. Both pieces of draft legislation are more elaborate than that proposed here: the instant proposal does not deal with water pollution control, weather modification, flood control planning, institutional arrangements, and other such matters covered elsewhere in the report.

This section has the limited purpose of setting forth principles applicable to a system of regulated withdrawals of water for municipal, industrial, and agricultural use in a riparian jurisdiction while simultaneously providing protection within the system for instream values having importance to riparian landowners and to the public. In limiting the scope of the section, it is not intended to minimize the need for States to coordinate other programs with the type of permit system described here. For example, it will be particularly important for States to make any permit program consistent with their water quality programs particularly in the setting of minimum flows.

In view of the Commission's assertion that no crisis in water use exists generally in the humid East and that a number of permit statutes for riparian jurisdictions have been proposed and enacted, it is a fair question to ask why the Commission writes on this subject. The answer is twofold. First, it is desirable that the riparian States direct attention to regulation of water withdrawals before a crisis arises. When competition for water supply intensifies, the court-administered riparian legal system of allocation will not be adequate to meet social needs. It is ponderous,

---

[99] Another way of stating this proposition is that the riparian right is not lost by nonuse.

[100] U.S. WATER RESOURCES COUNCIL (1968). The Nation's Water Resources. U.S. Government Printing Office, Washington, D.C. Table 1-2, p. 1-24.

expensive, and uncertain in result. In time, most riparian jurisdictions are likely to require a system of water allocation that facilitates development by providing security of investment while protecting social and environmental values of instream uses. Second, the permit system designed differs somewhat in approach and emphasis from the systems heretofore proposed or adopted. The basic approach is to establish minimim flows to protect such social and ecological values as esthetics, recreation, and the biosphere. The water remaining is subject to development for use in producing goods and services. The Commission would rely more on market forces to reallocate water to more valuable uses, and less on administrative allocation. Thus, it seeks to give permittees certainty in legal tenure and as much certainty in physical supply as the nature of the resource allows—for the twin purposes of encouraging original investment in the quantity of water committed to development and of facilitating the transfer of water to more productive uses by means of buying and selling water rights permits.

The basic features of the Commission design are the following:

1. The permit system should apply to withdrawals existing at the time the legislation is enacted as well as to future withdrawals.
2. The permit system should apply to withdrawals of ground water as well as surface water, whether or not the supplies are interrelated.
3. Any person or organization should be eligible to apply for and receive a permit for use of water at any location. Riparian restrictions on who may use water at what locations should be abolished.
4. The following information should be contained in each permit:
   (a) the source of supply,
   (b) the point of diversion or well location,
   (c) the place of use,
   (d) the nature of use,
   (e) the volume of the withdrawal and of consumptive use, on an annual or seasonal basis, as may be appropriate,
   (f) the rate of withdrawal,
   (g) the times of use, and
   (h) if practicably ascertainable, the amount of return flow and the point at which it reenters the hydrologic system.
5. After enactment of the legislation, no new withdrawal should be allowed unless a permit has been issued; all existing withdrawals should be subject to termination unless a permit has been obtained for them within a stated period of time (e.g., 5 years).
6. Permits granted for withdrawals of water, from either surface bodies or underground aquifers, should be subject to cancellation for prolonged nonuse and to modification for prolonged underuse.
7. Appropriate State administrative agencies should be delegated authority to establish and maintain minimum flows for surface streams, and minimum water levels for lakes, to promote the public health, safety, and welfare, to safeguard private investment made in reliance on streamflow and lake levels, and to protect the public interest in fish, wildlife, recreational, esthetic, and ecological values.
8. Water should be allocated in periods of shortage as follows:
   (a) Water users who initiated their withdrawals after enactment of the permit system should be curtailed in inverse order of the date of their permits.
   (b) Water users whose withdrawals antedate enactment of the permit system should be curtailed only when supply is insufficient after all postenactment permit holders have been curtailed; the available supply should be pro rated among preenactment permittees according to volume of use.
   (c) Preenactment permittees should be curtailed when necessary to preserve essential minimum flows.
9. Permits should be made transferable to facilitate private bargaining for the reallocation of water to more productive uses, subject to administrative restrictions to protect the interests of other permittees and the public interest in minimum streamflow.

DISCUSSION

Enactment of Permit System — Relation to Prior Law

Constitutionality: The first four features of the proposed permit system can be summarized as follows: the system would apply to all water uses, those made both before and after enactment of the statute, whether the source be surface water or ground water. The question arises whether the proposal is so radical a departure from present law that it is politically infeasible or constitutionally abhorrent. The Commission believes the answer is "No." Permit systems have been adopted in 11 Midwestern and Eastern States that formerly applied riparian law: Florida,[101] Indiana,[102] Iowa,[103] Kansas,[104] Maryland,[105] Minnesota,[106] Mississippi,[107] Nebraska,[108] New Jersey,[109] South Dakota,[110] and Wisconsin.[111] In addition, three Pacific Coast States now have permit systems, although their prior law had in it strong elements of riparianism.[112] The number of permit statutes should dispel doubts of political feasibility where the problem of water use is perceived to be significant, and the fact that none of these statutes has fallen before a constitutional attack ought to give some assurance of validity. Under the system here proposed, existing withdrawals would be confirmed in right and shortages pro rated as the orthodox riparian law requires, subject only to the requirement that they be placed on record and that they be curtailed to preserve minimum flow—both requirements justifiable under the police power[113] and probably under the public trust to preserve navigation, fisheries, and recreation.[114]

Perhaps more controversial is the requirement that new uses obtain a permit before initiation. The riparian law of surface water and the common law of ground water both hold that a riparian or overlying landowner has a privilege of withdrawing water despite the adverse effect the withdrawal may have on others. This privilege is modified by the proposed system in two respects: a permit is required and protection is given to withdrawals earlier in time. In extreme drought a later permittee is shut down in order to supply water to an earlier user. Theoretically, the prior law would have allowed all users to obtain some water, although a study shows that, in fact, the prior user was often protected under the riparian doctrine.[115]

The Commission believes that legislation restricting unused riparian rights, as described herein, would be valid under the 14th amendment of the Federal Constitution, although the issue is not wholly free from doubt. That amendment forbids States from depriving a person of property without due process of law. For State legislation to be declared in violation of the amendment, the court must find that property is affected and that the effect is a taking rather than a regulation. Thus, the nature of the interest invaded and the seriousness of the invasion must be judged in relation to the objective of the legislation and the reasonableness of the means of achieving the objective. The interest invaded under the proposed legislation is the privilege of making use of water any time in the future. This is a privilege of highly uncertain value, for it depends on the economic value of the future use *and* on the future actions of all other riparian landowners along the stream, all of whom have the same privilege and therefore the power to reduce the supply available for use.

The objective of the legislation abolishing unused riparian rights is to protect existing investments in the resource, preserve some amount of water for public purposes, and allocate the remaining supply according

[101] Florida Stat. Ann., Sections 373.081 *et seq.*

[102] 6 Burns Indiana Stats. Ann., Sections 27-1401 *et seq.*

[103] Iowa Code Ann., Ch. 455A.

[104] Kansas Stat. Ann., Sections 82a-701 *et seq.*

[105] Ann. Code of Maryland, Art. 96A, Sections 10 *et seq.*

[106] Minnesota Stat., Sections 105.37 *et seq.*

[107] Mississippi Code (1942) Ann. (1972 Supp.), Sections 5956-01 *et seq.*

[108] Rev. Stat. Nebraska (Re-issue of 1968), Sections 46-201 *et seq.*, 46-233 *et seq.*, Const. Art. XV Sections 4-6.

[109] New Jersey Stat. Ann., Sections 58:1-2 *et seq.* (surface water), 58:4A (ground water).

[110] South Dakota Comp. Laws Ann. (1967), Sections 46-1-1 *et seq.*

[111] Wisconsin Stat., Section 30.18 (1971).

[112] See Oregon Rev. Stat., Sections 537.110 *et seq.*; Rev. Code Washington, Sections 90.03.010, 90.03.250; California Water Code, Sections 1200 *et seq.* California Const., Art. 14, Section 3.

[113] All property is held subject to reasonable regulation by the State exercising its police power. Regulation of the use of water resources is allowable under the general welfare aspect of the police power. Many of the statutes noted above have been upheld by the courts on this basis.

[114] The public trust protects public rights of navigation and incidents thereto including fishing, hunting, and recreation. The doctrine derives from the English common law which preserved public rights in waters affected by the ebb and flow of the tide. The trust arises wherever there has been State ownership of the underlying beds, but may also be imposed when there is State ownership of the water itself. Title to the beds of streams "navigable in fact" at the time of statehood were held by the States, and any private use of these waters is subject to limitation by the rights of the public. Some States have gone beyond the Federal test of navigability and have declared public rights in waters meeting a "sawlog" or "pleasure boat" test of navigability. Public rights in these waters are based in a public trust originating in the State ownership of the water resource and in the exercise of the police power.

[115] DAVIS, Clifford (1971). Riparian Water Law, A Functional Analysis, prepared for the National Water Commission. National Technical Information Service, Springfield, Va., Accession No. PB 205 004. pp 44-48.

to a system that will promote public and private planning and investment by enhancing the security of the rights created under the system.

The means employed by the statute are rationally adapted to the end: all water rights are required to appear on the records; definite rules for allocating a scarce supply are adopted; an effort is required from the administrative agency to limit rights of withdrawal to available supply; and permission to make future withdrawals pursuant to permit is granted until the safe supply is exhausted.

In the light of the zoning cases,[116] the proposed permit statute is likely to survive constitutional challenge in the U.S. Supreme Court. Although it deprives a riparian or overlying landowner of a privilege, the privilege is highly contingent, and the offsetting gain—to landowners and to society as a whole—is a permit system that provides information for decisionmaking and certainty for investment, thus promoting productive use of resources.

Moreover, in testing the proposed statute against the 14th amendment it must be recalled that a portion of the unused riparian right is always preserved for the riparian landowner, because minimum flows are established and protected. It is true that the complaining riparian landowner cannot himself withdraw that water; nevertheless, the element of riparian law that provides for streamflows at reasonable levels is carried forward into the proposed new law. Furthermore, the riparian owner who chooses to initiate a use has an equal chance with others under the proposed statute to obtain a permit and withdraw water. This chance lasts as long as the supply dedicated to development lasts.

While the prospects are good that the U.S. Supreme Court would uphold the proposed statute, State supreme courts may have trouble with prior restrictive decisions interpreting due process provisions of State constitutions. In those States, it may aid the case for constitutionality to include in the statute a provision allowing riparian landowners to exercise their unused riparian rights within a stated period of time, which might be the same period allowed for existing users to record their existing uses. Such riparians would have to apply for permits just as all other users do, but they would be allowed a period of grace in which to initiate a withdrawal. The advantage of the period of grace is that it allows

riparian landowners contemplating a use in the near future to initiate that use and receive the superior, more secure right that preenactment users receive. The constitutionality of the statute abolishing unused riparian rights may perhaps be made secure by the period of grace provision, because the expectations of riparian landowners of making withdrawals in the near future are not impaired by the statute. Concommitantly, the expectations that *are* impaired are less concrete, less valuable, and hence less deserving of constitutional protection.

A quite different constitutional question may be disposed of summarily—the power of a State to apply its permit system to an interstate stream. The Supreme Court has established that States having territorial jurisdiction over an interstate stream must share the supply. As Mr. Justice Holmes put it: "A river is more than an amenity, it is a treasure. It offers a necessity of life that must be rationed among those who have power over it."[117] Implementing this principle, the Court, speaking through Mr. Justice Brandeis, held that the apportionment of an interstate stream ". . .is binding upon the citizens of each State and all water claimants, even where the State had granted the water rights before. . ." the apportionment.[118] Thus, every permittee of one State receives his permit subject to a claim for equitable apportionment of the supply by another State. The effect of an apportionment may be to reduce the supply on which the permittee relies—a circumstance to be treated like any other shortage in supply, under the allocation scheme devised for scarcity.

Permit Applications: The information required for the granting of permits comprehends the data that planners and investors need for water resource development and that administrators need to regulate withdrawals. If permits cover all withdrawals, the aggregate information provided by the permits gives a reasonably full picture of the demand side of the supply-demand equation. When this information is supplemented with runoff and streamflow data for surface water bodies, and with such ground water data as amount in storage, amount of recharge, and depth to water, development and administration of water resources can proceed on a knowledgeable basis. It is particularly important under the proposed

---

[116] See, *e.g., Consolidated Rock Products Co. v. City of Los Angeles,* 20 Cal. Rptr. 638, 370 P.2d 342 (1962), appeal dismissed 371 U.S. 36 (1962).

[117] *New Jersey v. New York,* 283 U.S. 336, at 342 (1931).

[118] *Hinderlider v. LaPlata River & Cherry Creek Ditch Co.,* 304 U.S. 92, at 106 (1938).

permit system to determine the amount of consumptive use, and thus the amount of return flow, when the permit is issued. This information becomes important when the permit is transferred, for ordinarily only the consumptive use will be transferable, since other users may be dependent on return flow.

An example may help clarify the nature and utility of the information contained in the permit. Suppose that an Illinois farmer has been withdrawing water for irrigation of his farm for a number of years before enactment of the permit system.[119] His application for a permit would contain the following information:

(a) Source of supply: South Fork Sangamon River

(b) Point of diversion: [Surveyor's description of location of diversion point], NW Quarter, Section 21, Twp. 21 North, Range 21 East, Christian County, Ill.

(c) Place of use: S 1/2 NW Quarter, Section 21, etc.

(d) Nature of use: Irrigation of crops

(e) Volume of withdrawal and consumptive use: 400 acre-feet withdrawal; 150 acre-feet consumptive use; June, July, August annually

(f) Rate of flow diverted: Maximum of 3 cubic feet per second

(g) Times of use: June, July, and August, from time to time as needed to supplement rainfall

(h) Return flow; point of reentry: 250 acre-feet return flow; 90 percent returns to stream within 1,000 yards from point of diversion.

As noted, it is not costless to obtain this kind of information. The State administrative agency should be given discretion to exempt inconsequential uses from the permit system altogether and to waive particular information requirements where the cost of obtaining the information is disproportionate to the value of the water.

Any applicant for a permit, whether an existing user or one who desires to initiate a use after passage of the statute, would be required to furnish the information listed with supporting surveys and engineering data. The permit agency should have power to investigate the facts on its own motion and so should other users who might be affected by the granting of a permit. In case either the permit agency or another user wishes to oppose the granting of the permit or the terms thereof, there should be an administrative hearing to determine the facts, and the order issuing from the hearing should be subject to judicial review.

The permit agency should have authority to limit the amount of water to be withdrawn and consumed to the amount reasonably necessary to accomplish the purposes for which the permit is granted. The agency should not be given the power to limit or reject applications on the broad basis of whether they "serve the public interest." While the statutes of a number of Western States contain such a provision—as does the proposed Model Water Code—the Commission believes that the standard is too vague to be meaningful and accordingly opens the door to arbitrary action by administrators. If a State legislature chooses to enact standards which would limit the issuance of permits, these should be sufficiently clear and precise to prevent administrative abuse. Applications for withdrawals should ordinarily be granted, for the expense of preparing the information in the application and the cost of the works to divert the water is a sufficient guaranty that the use is (or will be) productive. If more valuable uses emerge later, they can be supplied by transfers from less valuable uses.

The permit statute should provide for temporary permits, obtainable when a project is initiated, for large-scale projects requiring time to plan, to finance and, in the case of public works, to be authorized. These temporary permits would be replaced by final permits after the project is completed. The statute could contain maximum time periods in which the work must be commenced or completed, or the agency could be given discretion to set such a time period, the exercise to be based on the size of the project and the delays it faces as compared to the barrier to other development erected by long-term reservations of water.

If the State has or is developing a State water plan, the agency should be authorized to determine whether the application is in conformity with the plan, but again it is important not to delay development for long periods of time because the plan contemplates eventual development of the water resource in some other manner. In short, State water planners should not be permitted to reserve water indefinitely any more than others should.

A permit statute could incorporate a pricing system if the State desired. The subject is fully discussed in Chapter 7, Section C. Only two points need be added. First, imposing charges for water withdrawal will tend to reduce the necessity of close

---

[119] Although the case is hypothetical, Illinois, which has no permit system, was chosen to lend verisimilitude to the illustration.

Spruce Knob Lake in the Monongahela National Forest, West Virginia

examination of the amount of water a permittee should be allowed to withdraw and consume, for if the user charge properly reflects the opportunity cost of the water,[120] excessive use will be discouraged. Second, there may be constitutional objections to imposing charges on uses that antedate the permit statute, although the objections might be overcome if the charge is characterized as a tax. As to new uses, no objection seems valid, for if it is constitutional to abolish unused riparian rights and require permits for new uses, it is constitutional to impose user charges on the new uses.

Cancellation of Permits: The Commission recommends that the riparian permit system follow the appropriation permit system in providing for the cancellation of permits for nonuse and in reducing the quantities permitted to be withdrawn where there has been an extended period of underuse. California,[121] Arizona,[122] Nevada,[123] New Mexico,[124] Utah,[125] Wyoming,[126] Kansas,[127] Mississippi,[128] and Iowa[129] have statutes that permit cancellation of water rights for 4 or 5 years of continuous nonuse. Use in lesser quantities than the permit specifies may result in reduction of the right, under either a forfeiture statute[130] or the beneficial use doctrine which limits the right to the amount of water put to actual, beneficial use.[131]

It may be argued that forfeiture statutes are counterproductive in encouraging wasteful use of

[120] That is, the value of the water in alternative uses that are foregone.

[121] California Water Code, Sections 1241, 1675.

[122] Arizona Rev. Stat. Ann., Section 45-101(c).

[123] Nevada Rev. Stat., Sections 533.060, 534.090.

[124] New Mexico Stat. (1953) Ann., Section 75-5-26.

[125] Utah Code Ann. (1953), Section 73-1-4.

[126] Wyoming Stats. (1957), Section 41-47.

[127] Kansas Stat. Ann., Section 82a-718.

[128] Mississippi Code (1942) Ann. (1972 Supp.), Section 5956-06.

[129] Iowa Code Ann., Section 455A.29.

[130] See *Rocky Ford Irr. Co. v. Kents Lake Reservoir Co.,* 104 Utah 202, 135 P.2d 108 (1943), rehearing denied.

[131] *Green v. Chaffee Ditch Co.,* 150 Colo. 191, 371 P.2d 775 (1962).

water in order to preserve the right. This practice may occur from time to time—in violation of antiwaste regulations—but on balance, the Commission believes that forfeiture statutes promote good resource allocation by making provision for the elimination of paper rights from the records, thus making the records more reliable and planning and development more secure.

Two constitutional objections to forfeiture statutes may be suggested. It could be argued that the addition of a forfeiture statute to a permit system theretofore lacking this feature is a retroactive change in the nature of the property right. If this argument were to be made, it would probably be rejected on the rationale that the regulation is prospective in that water rights holders have advance notice of the consequences of nonuse. The other constitutional challenge will be based on the riparian rule that water rights are not lost by nonuse. However, if the permit system requires present and future users to acquire permits, it abolishes unused riparian rights. The forfeiture statute implements the general scheme of maintaining accurate records of all uses. Thus, the forfeiture provision stands or falls with the rest of the statute.

In the West, the forfeiture period is 4 or 5 consecutive years of nonuse. This may be too short in the East. A precise period of time for forfeitures is not proposed, but the period should not be too long. If an excessive period of nonuse is tolerated, when a drought comes the latent rights will be revived at the very time when there is no water to supply them. On the other hand, if the period is too short they may be lost in a wet cycle of years because there was no occasion to use them.

Duration of Permits: The Commission has given serious attention to the length of time a permit should run. The Model Water Use Act would limit the term to 50 years.[132] The Model Water Code suggests a maximum period of 20 years, except for municipalities requiring more time for debt retirement.[133] The Iowa statute specifies 10 years for agricultural permits.[134]

The argument for a limited term instead of a perpetual term rests on the idea that the State should be empowered to recapture the resource at some future point in time and reallocate it to other uses. While the argument has some merits, it also has some defects. The period of time becomes crucial, for if it

is too short, development will be deterred since the investment cannot be recovered in the time allowed. This problem can be solved if discretion is granted to the permit agency to fix the term according to amortization requirements—*and* if the agency exercises its discretion wisely.

There is also implicit in the recapture proposal the notion that the State agency can somehow reallocate the resource better than the market can. It is not transparently clear why this should be so. Presumably, upon expiration of a permit, there would be no more water available for reallocation by the permit agency than there was for transfer by sales transactions before the permit expired. This is true because both the permit agency and the private sector can transfer only the consumptive use—not the amount withdrawn—when other permittees have rights in return flow.[135] The transferable consumptive use is as available for reallocation through operation of market forces as it is by administrative determination. If the permit agency makes its determination on the basis of economic efficiency, it is seeking to do indirectly what outright bargain and sale does directly. In short, there is good reason to suppose that bargaining will produce better economic results than administrative allocation will. It follows, then, that limiting the term of a permit is not necessary to achieve reallocation of the resource to more productive uses and, in fact, may impair it.

On the other hand, the limited term permit may be supported on the ground that it promotes flexibility in reallocating water to *nonmonetary* uses when permits expire. For example, if the public prefers higher minimum flows than the permit agency has initially established, the expiration of term permits

---

[132] *Model Water Use Act,* Section 406.

[133] Model Water Code, Section 2.06.

[134] Iowa Code Ann., Section 455A.20.

[135] Protection of rights in return flow is fully considered in Chapter 7, Section D. The existing and proposed permit statutes do not seem to recognize that expiration of a permit does not liberate all water withdrawn pursuant to the permit. But a simple illustration will make this point. Suppose *A* receives a 20-year permit for withdrawal of 5,000 acre-feet, of which 40 percent is consumed (2,000 acre-feet) and the remaining 3,000 acre-feet is returned to the stream. In the 19th year of *A's* permit, *B* is given a permit to withdraw 3,000 acre-feet, which is made up entirely of *A's* return flow. If the State permit agency can recapture the full 5,000 acre-feet upon the expiration of *A's* permit, *B* has been given a permit for 1 year only. Yet, existing statutes containing time limitations seem to contemplate that each permittee will have the same term—20 years in this illustrative case. And if this were not the fact, the water resource would not be put to its most productive use, since many developers in *B's* position could not invest in a 1-year permit.

will enable the change to be made without expenditure by the State. If perpetual permits were issued, additional minimum flow would have to be purchased. There may be some advantage in adopting a system that requires such purchase, for it tells us whether the public is willing to pay the real costs of higher minimum flows. But many think the public interest is imperfectly expressed by the use of such an economic approach.

Still another approach is available. The permit might be limited in time to a fixed period or to a variable period depending on amortization requirements, but subject to automatic renewal for a similar period unless the permit agency found that the water was required for a higher public purpose. This approach would protect existing uses, which may be expected to continue to be productive even though the investment has been amortized, while providing the attractive aspects of flexibility associated with a term permit. It also avoids a criticism sometimes leveled at perpetual term permits, namely, that the holder of the permit, who obtained it without cost, gains windfall profits when a public agency is forced to buy or condemn the perpetual right for a higher public purpose. Higher public purpose would be defined narrowly as supplying municipal water demand or protecting vital instream values through increase in minimum flow. Before denying permit renewal, the permit agency should be required to hold a hearing and state its reasons for reallocating the water to a higher public purpose, and its order should be subject to judicial review.

The Commission has concluded that, as among (1) perpetual permits, (2) limited term permits, and (3) limited term permits with automatic renewal except for water to be reallocated to a higher public purpose, the last is the best choice. It strikes a balance between the security needed for private investment and the flexibility desired for public purposes.[136]

Minimum Flow

The Commission recommends that the permit statute delegate authority to an administrative agency to establish minimum flows for surface streams and minimum water levels for lakes, in order to promote public health, safety, and welfare, to safeguard

private investment made in reliance on continuing streamflows and lake levels, and to protect the public interest in fish, wildlife, recreational, esthetic, and ecological values. Two classes of interest in issue here are: the public interest historically accounted for by the public trust doctrine and the private interest of riparian landowners who have made investments (e.g., a country home, a fishing resort) in reliance on instream values. The setting of minimum flows protects both of these interests by limiting the amount of water that can be withdrawn pursuant to permit.

At least five States have general enabling statutes for setting minimum streamflows and lake levels. They are Florida,[137] Iowa,[138] Mississippi,[139] New Jersey,[140] and Washington.[141] Under these statutes, various criteria are used to determine the minimum flow or lake level but there is a uniform policy of denying permits for withdrawals that would infringe upon the established minimums. In addition to the type of statute just described, a number of States have "wild rivers" legislation or similar laws that preserve designated streams or reaches thereof from development.[142]

Establishment of minimum flows is recommended on two bases:

(a) Flows which should be preserved under average conditions of supply (desirable flows); and

(b) Flows which must be preserved under all conditions (essential flows).

The essential flows would include those needed for the protection of human health and safety and other

---

[136] Commissioner Ernst believes that the term should be perpetual in order to give greater security to investment and to avoid inefficient use toward the end of a limited term.

[137] Florida Stat. Ann., Sections 373.081(7), (8), 373.141.

[138] Iowa Code Ann., Sections 455A.1, 455A.22.

[139] Mississippi Code (1942) Ann. (1972 Supp.), Sections 5956-02(i), (j), 5956-04.

[140] New Jersey Stat. Ann., Sections 58:1-35, 58:1-40.

[141] Rev. Code Washington, Section 90.22.010.

[142] Oklahoma preserves certain free-flowing and scenic rivers under authority of the Oklahoma Scenic Rivers Act. Wisconsin protects the flow of designated streams under its Wild Rivers Act. In Oregon, the waters of designated streams have been withdrawn from appropriation to preserve scenic and recreational resources. Washington restricts withdrawals from specified stretches of the Columbia River to protect fish. In accordance with enabling legislation, the Governor of Idaho has appropriated waters from several lakes to be held in trust for the people of the State to preserve scenic and recreational qualities. In Montana, the State Fish and Game Commission is authorized to appropriate water of designated trout streams to preserve a minimum flow necessary to protect fish and wildlife.

flows which are so valuable that they should be preserved in all circumstances, even though this requires the curtailing of private uses. The desirable flows would protect values which are important to the public, but not so important that they could not bear a portion of the shortage in times of low flow. Desirable flows would vary according to the time of the year and the location at which the flows are to be protected.

No attempt is made to specify all the considerations that should go into the determination of minimum flows or the administrative procedures that should be employed. Historical flows will have great significance as will prepermit uses. As to the latter, even essential minimum flow will have to take account of historic uses, for they could not be substantially impaired without raising constitutional questions of the taking of private property without just compensation. This is not to say that historic uses cannot be curtailed for short periods in cases of emergency produced by extreme drought. But serious constitutional questions would arise if the minimum flow were set so high that historic uses would be regularly curtailed in periods of normal low flow.

The two-level approach is somewhat different from that taken by many States which protect minimum flow levels. A number of States base the flow to be preserved on some historic level of flow, such as the average of the minimum daily flows during each of the 5 lowest years in the period of the preceding 20 years.[143] That approach has the advantages of protecting all instream values during a period of low flow and of being related to an ascertainable, historic amount. However, there seems to be little reason to assume that the entire historic low flow is always necessary to protect instream values and to prohibit all withdrawals when flows are at a historic low level. Whether the prohibition of withdrawals is desirable depends upon their effect on important public and private values. Accordingly, it is recommended that minimum flows be established on the basis of an assessment of flows required to protect instream values.

It will be essential for State legislatures to provide standards for determining what values are to be so preserved and under what circumstances. Furthermore, it may be desirable for States to use special panels, acting in accordance with the statutory standards, to determine the minimum flows. The determination is likely to be one in which there is broad public interest and the body making the determination should be one which may be expected to be responsive to the various dimensions of that interest. This body could be expected to act in a legislative fashion, liberally utilizing public hearings and other devices for generating information about the flows needed to protect instream values. Perhaps it should be required to articulate the alternatives and their social, environmental, and other consequences before it reaches its decisions.[144]

Presumably, specialized State agencies, such as the fish and game and pollution control agencies, would make significant contributions. If the State had a mechanism for identifying and preserving wild and scenic rivers, the minimum flow procedures should be coordinated with that mechanism. Furthermore, in setting minimum flows for particular reaches of a river, the panel should be cognizant of water requirements elsewhere on the river so that its determinations would be consistent with conditions throughout the river basin.

Ideally, minimum flows should be determined for an area before permits were issued by the permit agency for new uses, since this information would be helpful to public and private planners in deciding whether to invest in water supply. Some States might choose to set minimum flows even for areas in which a permit system was not yet required. This course of action would provide the advantage of protecting important public values at an early stage, before they might be threatened by private diversions.

The standards for determining minimum lake levels might be different in some cases from those used to determine minimum streamflows. If the lake is one to which the public has access, the public values to be protected are similar to those in a river, and the same standards might apply. However, in other instances, the public interest will be quite limited, and less important than the interest of private lakeside owners. For example, if one party wants to make a diversion from a small lake which is entirely surrounded by private cottages, the issue is more whether a certain lake level should be preserved to protect the interests of the surrounding landowners than whether a public interest should be protected.

---

[143] See Mississippi Code (1942) Ann. (1972 Supp.), Section 5956-02(i); New Jersey Stat. Ann., Section 58:1-35; Florida Stat. Ann., Section 373.081(7).

[144] This is similar to the approach to decisionmaking required by the *National Environmental Policy Act of 1969* (NEPA), P.L. 91-190, January 1, 1970, 83 Stat. 852, 42 USCA 4331 *et seq.*

Private litigation has arisen over lake levels,[145] and it appears that the courts have used a rule of reason to set minimum levels, designed to protect the interests of the surrounding landowners while permitting some diversion.[146]

The best way to deal with this conflict may be in the context of a permit application. As soon as any party applies for a diversion from a lake, the issue is raised as to whether the interests of littoral owners will be protected. The permit agency should take evidence on the particular facts of the competing interests in the lake and determine an appropriate minimum level. Once a minimum has been set, it will be necessary in times of short supply to enforce it by regulating competing diversions.

After providing procedures for setting streamflow and lake level minimums, the statute must attend to their enforcement. Both public officials and private citizens should be permitted to bring actions. The State is the proper plaintiff in public actions, which might embrace administrative cease and desist orders enforceable by fines and physical actions to shut down illegal withdrawals. Private suits should be maintainable by any person having an interest in the minimum flows or lake levels. Those persons would include littoral owners, fishermen (if the violation threatens injury to fish), and recreationists. It should not be necessary for the private citizen to proceed first through the permit agency, although that course should be open to him, too. Since the minimum flows and lake levels are to be fixed precisely, and since the rules for allocating water in periods of shortage are to be clear, definite, and nondiscretionary, the private plaintiff should have recourse to the courts in the first instance if he so chooses.

The permit statute should also provide for regulation of pumping from ground water aquifers. The subject is not discussed extensively in this section, since it is treated in Chapter 7, Section B. Briefly, the administrative agency should have power to establish well-spacing patterns to prevent well interference, to restrict pumping to protect the storage capacity of the aquifer and to prolong the period of time of its use, and to regulate land and water use to protect ground water quality. In addition, the statute should confer authority on the administrative agency to require initiation of comprehensive management prac-

tices for all water sources where circumstances warrant. The legislation should also authorize the voluntary formation of water management districts upon local initiative.

Allocation of Water in Periods of Shortage

The allocation scheme which the Commission proposes has three parts:

1. Postenactment permittees would be shut down in order to supply preenactment permittees and to maintain desirable minimum flows. Within the class of postenactment permittees, uses would be shut down in inverse order of the dates of their permits: the last to receive a permit would be the first to be shut off.

2. If insufficient water then remained to supply all preenactment permittees and to maintain desirable minimum flows, (1) desirable minimum flows would be reduced and (2) the available supply would be shared *pro rata* by the preenactment permittees.

3. In extreme emergency, preenactment permittees would be shut down to preserve essential minimum flows.

The purpose of these provisions is to define in advance the rules which will be applied to allocate the water supply in times of shortage, so that investors and planners can gage the relative reliability of various water rights. Some water users require a firm supply of water at all times, and they need to know the rules of the game so they may acquire firm water rights to protect themselves in time of shortage. Clear allocation rules would encourage the transfer of water rights to their highest economic use.

Some riparian States which have adopted permit systems have chosen not to provide a scheme for allocation in times of shortage.[147] Other statutes provide authority for a water management agency to adopt contingency plans, to be implemented only in times of shortage.[148] However, advance definition of

---

[145] See, *e.g., Taylor v. Tampa Coal Co.,* 46 So.2d 392 (Fla. 1950); *Harris v. Brooks,* 225 Ark. 436, 283 S.W.2d 129 (1955); and *Hoover v. Crane,* 362 Mich. 36, 106 N.W.2d 563 (1960).

[146] *Harris v. Brooks,* 225 Ark. 436, 283 S.W.2d 129 (1955).

[147] See New Jersey Stat. Ann., Sections 58:1-2 *et seq.;* Florida Stat. Ann., Sections 373.01 *et seq.;* and Minnesota Stat. (1971), Sections 105.37 *et seq.*

[148] In Iowa the water commissioner is authorized to temporarily suspend any diversions under a permit if there is a declared emergency. Under the Model Water Use Act (1958), Sections 501, 502, the commission regulates allocation in times of shortage. Preserved uses (those vested before adoption of the permit system) are preferred to permitted uses. In addition, the commission may rotate uses, suspend less beneficial uses, or apportion water between uses. The Model Water Code (1970), Section 2.09, empowers local governing boards to formulate plans for allocation in times of shortage. The plans are to be published in advance of emergency conditions.

the rules of allocation is preferable to either alternative. If the permit statute says nothing about allocation, parties are left to the rules which may have evolved under common law and to an emergency allocation by the courts, perhaps at a critical time when it will be difficult for users to purchase an additional supply. In fact, there are few common-law cases dealing with the allocation of shortages, so that the water user lacks predictability about the reliability of his right if the statute is silent.[149] While an emergency allocation scheme may have the advantage of flexibility, it has the disadvantages of having to be created in a time of crisis and of creating uncertainty for all water users.

Under the recommended arrangement, uses initiated after the adoption of a permit system would be shut down before prepermit uses were curtailed or desirable minimum flows invaded. State power to adopt such an arrangement seems clear if, as is argued, the State can abolish unused riparian rights. After the abolition, new rights could properly be subject to new rules, whatever the rule of allocation may have been at common law. However, States which already have adopted permit systems and rules relevant to allocation may encounter obstacles in attempting to change those rules, at least with respect to existing uses. For example, a State arrangement might require all permittees to share a shortage, irrespective of when their uses were initiated.

Where it is permissible under State law, there are distinct advantages to protecting prepermit uses as a class, while curtailing later uses. Such an arrangement provides certainty for existing uses, which should enhance the marketability of prepermit rights and their reallocation through bargain and sale to the highest economic use. The arrangement protects the investments of existing users while warning future users that their rights may be subject to curtailment in times of shortage. This arrangement works to limit the shifting of water from an existing use to a new use without payment. It also serves to protect existing riparian users against future withdrawals for nonriparian uses, allowing the extension of the permit system to nonriparian uses without upsetting riparian investments.

This protection for existing, prepermit uses appears to be consistent with the few cases in which courts

have been called upon to resolve conflicts between diverters who seek water for different uses. According to the Commission's background study,[150] these cases tend to protect existing uses under the rubric that it is not reasonable for a new use to displace an existing use and its accompanying investment.

As a practical matter, States which already have adopted permit systems may come out much the same way as recommended here, if the permit agency refuses to permit a new use unless it is confident that there is an adequate supply for all prior uses.

Just as there are advantages to protecting prepermit users as a class, there are advantages to applying a rule of priority to allocate water among postpermit users. Again, each permittee has more certainty if he knows that his right will be protected according to the date of his right. He may make a rational calculation of the relative reliability of a new water right or of an existing right which he might purchase.

Some States may choose to allocate shortages proportionately among postpermit users, especially if this presently is the rule of law in such States. Arguably, a rule of proportional sharing encourages efficient water use, since all must reduce their withdrawals during a time of shortage, and arguably it also encourages flexible private arrangements, such as rotation in water use. However, in some situations a rule of priority actually would provide more flexibility for private allocation arrangements (such as where some, but not all, water users agree to rotate use of the available supply), and a priority system may make it easier for a water user to obtain a firm supply by contractual arrangements with other water users. On balance, the Commission recommends a rule of priority for postenactment permits, but recognizes that some States may prefer to employ proportional sharing among postpermit users in time of shortage, having previously adopted that rule.

The next question that arises under the proposed allocation system is the relationship between preenactment permit claims and desirable minimum flow. The competition between the two would arise in this fashion: despite the fact that all postenactment uses have been shut down, the available supply may still be insufficient to satisfy preenactment permits in full. The scheme proposed here provides for an invasion of *desirable* minimum flow. (*Essential* minimum flow would never be subject to impairment, except by Nature.) Since desirable minimum flow has

[149] DAVIS, Clifford (1971). Riparian Water Law, A Functional Analysis, prepared for the National Water Commission. National Technical Information Service, Springfield, Va., Accession No. PB 205 004. p. 40.

[150] *Ibid.*, pp. 43, 45.

been established to protect amenities, it follows that amenities can share the burden of the short supply. The formula for sharing the shortage ought to be determined in advance so that users needing a larger supply could make arrangements for purchasing it. While a specific formula is not proposed, it is recommended that it reflect a judgment on the relative importance of desirable minimum flow and prepermit uses, with respect to that supply which is in excess of inviolate essential minimum flow.

An example may help illustrate the operation of the allocative scheme: Suppose that a severe drought has struck and that postenactment permits have already been shut off, leaving streamflow at 500 cubic feet per second (c.f.s.). Essential minimum flow has been established at 200 c.f.s. and desirable minimum flow at 400 c.f.s. Preenactment permit demand is 300 c.f.s. If the prepermit demand were fully satisfied, the flow would exactly equal essential minimum flow.[151] And if desirable minimum flow were fully preserved, only 100 c.f.s. would be left to satisfy the prepermit demand of 300 c.f.s.[152] Under the Commission's proposed allocation system, part of the 200 c.f.s. increment allocated to desirable minimum flow which is over and above what is allocated to essential minimum flow would be invaded to assure that more than 100 c.f.s. is supplied to prepermit users. If supply is allocated proportionally between the respective demands of 200 additional c.f.s. to maintain desirable minimum flow and 300 c.f.s. for prepermit users, the result would be an allocation of two-fifths of the available flow in excess of essential minimum flow or 120 c.f.s. to desirable minimum flow (resulting in a streamflow of 320 c.f.s.) and of three-fifths or 180 c.f.s. to prepermit uses, an invasion of desirable minimum flow of 80 c.f.s. Of course, other formulae could be employed and may well be preferred. However, some definite formula should be adopted by the permit agency in advance and it ought to reflect an assessment of the relative values of the withdrawals protected by permits and the instream uses protected by desirable minimum flow standards.

This proposal differs from the approach several States have taken. Some States have adopted minimum flows, which they would preserve against all diversions in times of shortage.[153] It is hard to justify halting all withdrawals in order to protect all public values associated with instream uses. For example, it may be more desirable to protect a valuable industrial withdrawal during a 2- or 3-month drought than to preserve a level of flow providing a beautiful view or public recreation. For this reason, it is recommended that minimum flows be set at two levels—those which are desirable under average supply conditions and those which are essential under all conditions. Essential minimum flows should be set as low as public health and safety will permit. Their purpose is not to protect recreation or scenic beauty in times of drought but to serve such vital functions as preventing contamination of public water supplies (as by salt water intrusion) or long-term or irreversible damage to the ecosystem. The constitutionality of curtailing preenactment uses for these purposes in times of emergency is beyond question. Not only does the riparian system itself contemplate preservation of a reasonable volume of flow, the police power justifies temporary prohibition of use in cases of public danger.

Similarly, a statutory scheme providing for the temporary reduction in the amount of use by preenactment permittees in order to preserve a portion of the desirable minimum flow is quite likely to be sustained on its face as a valid exercise of the police power in the regulation of riparian rights that gave rise to no justified expectation of certain receipt of quantities of water historically withdrawn for use. But any particular application of the statute may raise a constitutional issue if minimum flows are set so high as to regularly interfere with historic uses under conditions of average low flow.

In allocating water within the class of prepermit users, the same alternatives of proportional reduction or reduction by priority, and the same supporting arguments, are available as with postpermit users. However, where prepermit State law provided proportional reduction as the standard for allocation among users, States will face political and legal difficulties in converting to a priority standard. Under the arrangements recommended here, prepermit rights should be given the same status they had before enactment of the statute. This would seem to be the preferable arrangement in view of the expectations generated by the prior law.

---

[151] Essential minimum flow of 200 c.f.s. *plus* withdrawal of 300 c.f.s. *equals* supply of 500 c.f.s.

[152] *Deducting* desirable minimum flow of 400 c.f.s. from supply of 500 c.f.s. *leaves* 100 c.f.s. to supply a prepermit demand of 300 c.f.s.

[153] See Iowa Code Ann., Section 455A.22; New Jersey Stat. Ann., Section 58:1-40; Florida Stat. Ann., Section 373.141; Rev. Code of Washington, Section 90.22.010.

Ground water presents special problems. Since aquifers and surface streams frequently are hydrologically interrelated, it is important to apply the same general standards to both. However, those standards may need to be applied somewhat differently, and more flexibly, to ground water. In administering ground water uses vis-a-vis surface uses, the regulator must realize that the impact of ground water withdrawals upon surface supplies may not be felt for some period of time, and then may be spread over an additional period. Furthermore, in administering ground water uses vis-a-vis each other, the regulator must take into account the physical characteristics of particular aquifers. For example, well interference, and therefore well-spacing, may be heavily influenced by aquifer characteristics. In addition, States properly may be concerned with ground water levels and with the rates at which ground water is withdrawn and recharged. In short, the regulation of ground water uses calls more for flexible management than for the application of rigid rules.

Transfer of Water Rights

The permit statute should provide for the transferability of water rights subject to necessary restrictions to protect other permittees and to prevent infringement of desirable minimum flow. To implement this general principle, the statute should specifically abolish the rule of riparian law that limits use of water to riparian land and the rule that forbids the sale of water rights separately from riparian land. The statute should provide that where the interests of other permittees are not injured and desirable minimum flows are not adversely affected, a permittee for a consumptive use may transfer his permit to another for the same amount of consumptive use on different land or for a different purpose. Permits for nonconsumptive uses should also be transferable, but only to another nonconsumptive use and only if there is no adverse effect on other permittees and on desirable minimum flow.

The purpose of these recommendations is the one which runs throughout this section: to encourage the allocation of water to the highest and best economic use through the bargaining process. Present arrangements outside of the arid West offer little or nothing by way of mechanisms to facilitate the transfer of water rights. This is true in riparian States which have adopted permit systems, as well as in those which have not. In fact, the existing law in many States tends to discourage transfers by limiting water use to

riparian lands, at least where there may be injury to riparians if the water is used elsewhere.[154] The restriction may increase the water supply for riparians, but it frustrates the reallocation of water to higher economic uses, which will often require the use of water on nonriparian lands. Under the arrangements proposed here, important interests of riparians, as well as of the general public, are protected by the minimum flow provisions. Existing water users are protected from injury which a transfer might cause by imposition of appropriate conditions and limitations upon the transfer.[155] Therefore, there seems to be no reason for precluding transfers away from riparian lands.

Some permit systems frustrate private transfers by making permits terminable at any time by administrative action and the water reallocable by administrative determination.[156] Under such arrangements, an existing water user may have his supply terminated and his expectations disrupted, although some statutes would provide him with compensation.[157] This kind of administrative allocation is subject to possible abuse. It deters investment, even where compensation is provided, because it deprives the investor of certainty. There is no reason to conclude on principle that administrative reallocation will foster more productive use of water than will market reallocation. However, term permits, by which water can be reallocated to a public purpose at the end of the term, are recommended. If a governmental entity desires to obtain existing water rights prior to the expiration of the term and is unable to do so by negotiated purchase, eminent domain purchase is available. The permit agency should have power to extend terms when a permit is transferred. This power would permit transfer to a more valuable use requiring a longer time for amortization than remains for the permit being sold.

While market principles should govern the reallocation of water rights, an administrative mechanism is

---

[154] The majority rule is that riparian rights may not be exercised on nonriparian land. The minority rule permits use on nonriparian land provided that downstream riparians are not injured.

[155] See Chapter 7, Section D.

[156] See Iowa Code Ann., Section 455A.20; New Jersey Stat. Ann., Section 58:1-44.

[157] Under the Model Water Use Act (1958), Section 410, the commission may force the sale of a permit if there is an application for a more beneficial use (as determined by the commission) when there is no other supply available and the new user is willing to make reasonable payment to the owner of the permit.

necessary to facilitate such transfers and to protect the rights of other permittees and the public. Transfer procedures are discussed fully in Chapter 7, Section D. In general, the permit agency should conduct transfer proceedings to determine whether a transfer of a permit would injure other permittees or interfere with desirable minimum flows. Additional environmental values could also be considered in the proceeding. Agency determinations should be subject to judicial review to assure due process, correct errors of law, and determine whether findings of fact are supported by substantial evidence.

Ground water again presents special problems because of the physical characteristics of aquifers, but the analytical standards for transfers would still apply. It may be difficult to transfer ground water rights, at least if a significant distance is involved, because of the difficulty of determining injury in the complex context of an interrelated stream and aquifer, with numerous withdrawals. However, in the case of replacement wells—new wells drilled near old wells that have silted up or gone out of production for other reasons—a simplified procedure could properly be adopted. The replacement well is merely a substitute for the original permitted withdrawal, is located in essentially the same place, and is subject to the same permit conditions.

CONCLUSIONS

This section sets forth principles the Commission believes to be sound guides in the formulation of a permit statute to regulate withdrawal of water for municipal, industrial, agricultural, and other beneficial use in States that follow the riparian doctrine of water rights. The proposed permit system departs from model codes and statutes currently in force by placing greater reliance on market forces to reallocate water to more productive economic uses. It also differs in establishing two levels of minimum streamflow: (1) essential minimum flow that cannot be impaired by man's withdrawals and (2) desirable minimum flow that would not be subject to diminution by permits issued after the statute took effect but could be invaded in periods of drought to supply prepermit uses.

The Commission does not recommend the immediate enactment of a permit statute in every State not presently having one. It costs money to acquire the information required to operate a permit system properly, and those costs should not be incurred until scarcity and competition warrant the expense. However, it is not too early for legislatures to begin examination of their State's water situation, for it is highly desirable to establish a clear and definite legal system of water rights before an emergency arises. There is merit in early enactment of a permit statute that may be applied on a basin-by-basin basis, as the need arises.

RECOMMENDATIONS

The essential elements of the permit system which the Commission recommends for consideration by the riparian States are the following:

7-47. Permits should be required for all withdrawals of water, whether the use was initiated before or after enactment of the statute and whether the source of supply is surface water or ground water. Exceptions can be made for withdrawals of inconsequential amounts of water. Upon application filed within 5 years of the effective date of the act, a permit shall be issued for any use initiated prior to the enactment of the statute.

7-48. There should be no restrictions on who may apply for a permit or on the location where water may be used.

7-49. Permits should contain full information on (a) source of supply, (b) point of diversion or well location, (c) place, nature, and time of use, (d) volume and rate of withdrawal, and (e) amounts of consumptive use and return flow, and, if practically ascertainable, point of reentry to the hydrologic system of return flow.

7-50. Permits should be subject to cancellation after a specific period of nonuse.

7-51. Permits may be limited in time, but the initial period should be long enough for the permittee to amortize his investment comfortably, and renewal of the permit should be automatic unless the permit agency finds the water is necessary for a higher public purpose.

7-52. An administrative agency should be delegated authority to establish minimum streamflows and lake levels in accordance with standards that include consideration of (a) public health, (b) ecological values, (c) recreational use, (d) esthetics (including private investment in scenic values), and (e) alternate values of the water in municipal, industrial, and agricultural use.

7-53. Definite rules for allocating water in periods of shortage should be adopted before shortages occur. States should consider an allocation system (a) that would make all permits for uses initiated after enactment of the statute subordinate to permits for uses initiated before the statute and (b) that would distribute water to poststatute uses in order of temporal priority.

The statute might also provide that, subject to the preservation of essential streamflows and lake levels, prestatute uses would share available supply *pro rata* in times of shortage.

7-54. Permits should be freely transferable to promote the reallocation of water to more productive uses, subject to the restriction that a transfer should not injure other permittees or impair minimum streamflow or lake levels.

~~~~~~~~~~~~~~~~~~~~~~~~~~~~~~~~~~~~~~ *Section F*

Appendix: A Comparsion of the Florida Water Resources Act of 1972 With the Commission's Recommended Principles

Reproduced below, with commentary, are portions of the Florida Water Resources Act of 1972, Fla. Laws Ch. 72-299, approved April 24, 1972. At the time of this writing, the Florida law was the most recent and most comprehensive statute to be enacted by a riparian jurisdiction. The statute is in six parts, of which portions of Parts I, II, and III are reproduced, appending to significant sections of the law the Commission's commentary comparing them with the principles suggested in the preceding section of this chapter.

Part I declares general policy, sets forth definitions, delegates power to administer the statute to the Department of Natural Resources, directs the Department to prepare a State water use plan, and creates five water management districts.

Part II contains the basic permit legislation for withdrawal and use of water, and it receives the most attention.

Part III regulates the drilling, operation, and abandonment of water wells.

Part IV regulates the construction and operation of surface water reservoirs.

Part V deals with finance and taxation and Part VI with amendment and repeal of prior legislation.

Of Part I, only Section 2, the Declaration of Policy, is reproduced below; the other sections of interest are summarized.

Section 2. Declaration of policy.—

(1) The waters in the state are among its basic resources. Such waters have not heretofore been conserved or fully controlled to realize their full beneficial use.

(2) It is further declared to be the policy of the legislature to provide for the management of water and related land resources; to promote the conservation, development, and proper utilization of surface and ground water; to develop and regulate dams, impounds, reservoirs, and other works, and to provide water storage for beneficial purposes; to prevent damage from floods, soil erosion and excessive drainage; to preserve natural resources, fish and wildlife; to promote recreational development, protect public lands, assist in maintaining the navigability of rivers and harbors; and to otherwise promote the health, safety and general welfare of the people of this state.

(3) The legislature recognizes that the water resources problems of the state vary from region to region, both in magnitude and complexity. It is therefore the intent of the legislature to vest in the department of natural resources or its successor agency the power and responsibility to accomplish the conservation, protection, management and control of the waters of the state with sufficient flexibility and discretion to accomplish these ends through delegation of appropriate powers to the various water management districts. The department may exercise any power herein authorized to be exercised by a

water management district; however, to the greatest extent practicable such power should be delegated to the governing board of a water management district.

Section 3 contains definitions. Section 4 states specifically that all waters of the State are subject to regulation. Section 5 prescribes the powers and duties of the Department of Natural Resources. These are quite extensive, and the section is recommended to other States as a model.[158] Section 6 directs the Department to prepare a State water plan and sets forth the elements to be in its formulation. This provision, too, is recommended as a model for other States.

In one respect, however, Section 6, when considered with the rest of the statute, seems incomplete. The State water plan has no force of law; it may be considered when issuing use permits and promulgating rules for allocation in times of shortage, but it is not binding on the Department. Yet, the principal treatment of minimum flows and minimum lake levels appearing in the Florida statute is found in subsection (7) of Section 6, under which those minimums are merely elements to be considered in formulation of the plan. Nothing in the statute specifically gives streamflow and lake level minimums the force of law, although this result may eventually come to pass through interpretation of the "public interest" standard for granting permits. This point is discussed further in the comments on Part II of the statute.

A most useful set of provisions in Part I commences with Section 12; these provide for the division of the State into five water management districts following the boundaries of the natural river basins of the State. The Department may delegate to the governing board of each district power to administer the permit requirements of the other parts of the statute and to perform certain other responsibilities of the Department. Moreover, under Section 18, the districts have in their own right full power of ground water management, very similar to those recommended by the Commission in Chapter 7, Section B.

PART II – PERMITTING OF CONSUMPTIVE USES OF WATER

Section 1. Implementation of program for regulating the consumptive use of water.—The department may implement a program for the issuance of permits authorizing the consumptive use of particular quantities of water, or may authorize the governing board of a water management district to implement such a program. No such program shall be implemented or discontinued except after public notice and hearing. A hearing may be called by the department or by the governing board, upon its own initiative, upon petition from the board of county commissioners or boards of county commissioners of any combination of counties wholly or partly within the area proposed to be subject to the regulations provided herein, or upon petition signed by twenty-five percent (25%) of the registered voters of any territory proposed to be subject to the regulations provided herein, according to the most recent list of registered voters as disclosed by the records of the office of the supervisor of elections of the counties affected. Notice of public hearing on the proposed implementation of these regulations shall be published at least once a week for two weeks in a newspaper of general circulation in the area to be affected by such regulations, the last notice appearing no less than ten (10) days prior to the date of the public hearing. Upon implementation, the provisions of this part shall apply.

Comment: The Commission has recommended a similar provision whereby the permit system would be instituted on a basin-by-basin basis as the need for regulation arises.

Section 2. Permits required.—
(1) After the effective date of the implementation of these regulations in an area, no person shall make any withdrawal, diversion, impoundment, or consumptive use of water without obtaining a permit from the governing board or the department. However, no permit shall be required for domestic consumption of water by individual users.

(2) In the event that any person shall file a complaint with the governing board or the department that any other person is making a diversion, withdrawal, impoundment, or consumptive use of water not expressly exempted under the provisions of this act and without a permit to do so, the governing board or the department shall cause an investigation to be

---

[158] For some States, Subsection (9) providing for an annual conference on water resources may be superfluous.

made and if the facts stated in the complaint are verified the governing board or the department shall order the discontinuance of the use.

Comment: Subsection (1) above covers the withdrawal of all water, whether for consumptive or nonconsumptive use, except for the specific exemption of individual users for domestic consumption. The Commission similarly recommended that the permit system comprehend all water, whether surface or ground water, and all users, whether the uses were initiated before or after enactment of the statute. The Commission did not specifically exempt individual domestic uses, but did provide for exemption of "inconsequential uses," which could comprehend small individual domestic uses as well as other insignificant uses.

The Commission did not discuss enforcement, but it endorses Subsection (2) above.

Section 3. Conditions for a permit.—

(1)   To obtain a permit pursuant to the provisions of this act, the applicant must establish that the proposed use of water (a) is a reasonable-beneficial use as defined in Part I, Section 3(5), and (b) will not interfere with any presently existing legal use of water and (c) is consistent with the public interest.

(2)   The governing board or the department may authorize the holder of a use permit to transport and use ground or surface water beyond over-lying land or outside the watershed from which it is taken if the governing board or department determines that such transport and use is consistent with the public interest.

(3)   The governing board or the department by regulation may reserve from use by permit applicants water in such locations and quantities and for such seasons of the year as in its judgment may be required for the protection of fish and wildlife or the public health and safety. Such reservations shall be subject to periodic review and revision in the light of changed conditions; provided, however, that all presently-existing legal uses of water shall be protected.

Comment: Subsection (1) of Section 3 establishes three conditions for the issuance of a permit, two of which are repetitious. Condition (a) requires a "reasonable-beneficial use" as defined in Part I, Section 3 (5), which states the definition as "...the use of water in such quantity as is necessary for economic and efficient utilization, for a purpose and in a manner which is both reasonable and consistent with the public interest." Condition (c) requires the use to be "consistent with the public interest." "Public interest," on the other hand, is nowhere defined. The Commission has indicated its reluctance to recommend delegation of broad authority to administrative agencies under such vague standards as the public interest. It is the Commission's view that establishment of desirable and essential minimum flows protects the public interest and that permits should be issued upon application if minimum flows are not adversely affected thereby. The Commission supports condition (b), that permits not be granted for uses that would interfere with prior uses, but the recommended technique for achieving that result is to establish a priority system in periods of shortage for permits issued after the statute takes effect.

The Commission's recommendation is in accord with subsection (2) in abolishing restrictions on place of use but, again, it avoids the vague standard "consistent with the public interest."

Subsection (3) apparently deals with minimum streamflows and minimum lake levels, although those terms are not used here and there is no cross-reference to their use in Part I, Section 6 (7) (a)-(c). The Commission's recommendation would set "desirable minimum flow"—which postenactment permits could not impair—on broader bases than "protection of fish and wildlife or the public health and safety." Curiously, the Florida statute itself in the section using the term "minimum flow" [Part I, Section 6 (7) (a)] also employs a broader definition, being "the limit at which further withdrawals would be significantly harmful to the water resources or ecology of the area." However, the similarities between the Florida statute and the Commission's proposals are far greater than the differences. Both propose to protect minimum flows by limiting permitted new uses of water in excess of the minimum flow. The recognition of such minimums is a key point the Commission would emphasize to other States.

Section 4. Existing uses.—

(1)   All existing uses of water, unless otherwise exempted from regulation by the provisions of this act, may be continued after adoption of this permit system only with a permit issued as provided herein.

(2) The governing board or the department shall issue an initial permit for the continuation of all uses in existence before the effective date of implementation of this part if the existing use is a reasonable-beneficial use as defined in Part I, Section 3 (5) of this act and is allowable under the common law of this state.

(3) Application for permit under the provisions of (2) above must be made within a period of two (2) years from the effective date of implementation of this Part. Failure to apply within this period shall create a conclusive presumption of abandonment of the use and the user if he desires to revive the use must apply for a permit under the provision of Section 5 of this part.

Comment: As previously noted, the Commission's proposed permit system would require existing uses to obtain permits. The Florida statute allows 2 years; the Commission has not specified a time period but gave an example of 5 years. Local conditions will dictate the appropriate time period, but 2 years may be a little short in many States.

Section 5 which is not reproduced here, states the contents of a permit application regarding such matters as place, nature, and volume of use. The Commission's recommendations are generally similar and somewhat more detailed, especially as to return flow.

Section 6, also not reproduced here, deals with competing applications and provides that the board or department shall "approve or modify the applications which best serve the public interest." The Commission did not address itself to the issue of competing applications but expresses reservations on the standard adopted by the Florida statute. If the public interest in environmental values is otherwise provided for, as it is under the Commission's proposals, competition between applications could be resolved on the basis of priority in time of application, as it is in most Western States. Applications should be transferable, so that a later, more valuable use could buy out a prior, less valuable use. Alternatively, the permit agency could be required to grant the permit to the economically more valuable use.

Section 7. Duration of permits.—

(1) Permits may be granted for any period of time not exceeding twenty (20) years. The governing board or the department may base duration of permits on a reasonable system of classification according to source of supply, type of use or both.

(2) The governing board or the department may authorize a permit of duration of up to fifty (50) years in the case of a municipality or other governmental body or of a public works or public service corporation where such a period is required to provide for the retirement of bonds for the construction of waterworks and waste disposal facilities.

Comment: The Commission perceived both advantages and drawbacks in limiting the duration of permits and concluded that the permit term should be long enough to comfortably amortize the permit applicant's investment. The Commission also recommended that permits be renewed unless the water was needed for a public purpose. The Florida statute is more restrictive and subject to criticism in that it discourages investment in private projects that require longer than 20 years to amortize.

Section 8, which is not reproduced here, provides for modification and renewal of permits. The same procedures and standards apply to renewal of permits as to their first issuance.

Section 9 provides for revocation of permits for false statements in an application, for violation of permit terms, and for violation of the statute (1 year maximum suspension in the latter case). It also provides:

(4) For nonuse of the water supply allowed by the permit for a period of two (2) years or more, the governing board or the department may revoke the permit permanently and in whole unless the user can prove that his nonuse was due to extreme hardship caused by factors beyond his control.

Comment: Section 9 (4) has its counterpart in the Commission's permit system, but the Commission refrained from specifying a definite period of time for the forfeiture. Two years appears to be fairly short, at least by Western standards where the periods run 4 and 5 years.

Section 10 deals with "declaration of water shortage or emergency." It is long and only the essential provisions are summarized here. The statute contemplates the formulation by the management district board or by the department of a plan for allocating water in periods of shortage. No standards or guidelines are furnished other than directions to "adopt a reasonable system of permit classification according to source of water supply, method of extraction or diversion, use of water, or a combination thereof." Allocation of water in times of shortage is then made pursuant to the plan. The statute also contemplates that "an emergency condition. . .[may exist] due to a water shortage." This condition is one that goes beyond that anticipated in the plan and allows the board or department to issue orders requiring immediate compliance without prior hearing.

Comment: The Commission's permit system differs somewhat from the Florida statute in providing in advance more definite allocation rules for periods of shortage. Postenactment permits (i.e., those granted for uses initiated after the permit system becomes applicable to the basin) are shut down in inverse order of permit date to supply earlier permittees and to preserve desirable minimum flow. If the supply is still insufficient to satisfy all preenactment permittees and desirable minimum flow, the desirable flow is reduced on some basis specified by statute or regulation in advance, and the remaining supply is shared proportionally by the preenactment permittees. In cases of extreme drought, even preenactment uses can be temporarily curtailed to preserve essential minimum flow.

Part III of the Florida statute is entitled "Regulation of Wells." Section 1 contains definitions, Section 2 requires compliance with the statute and the regulations issued thereunder, Section 3 grants rulemaking power, and Section 4 contains the heart of the system as follows:

Section 4. Prior permission and notification.—

(1) Taking into consideration other applicable state laws, in any geographical area where the department determines such permission to be reasonably necessary to protect the groundwater resources, prior permission shall be obtained from the department for each of the following:

(a) The construction of any water well;

(b) The repair of any water well; or

(c) The abandonment of any water well;

Provided that in any area where undue hardship might arise by reason of such requirement, prior permission will not be required.

(2) The department shall be notified of any of the following whenever prior permission is not required:

(a) The construction of any water well;

(b) The repair of any water well; or

(c) The abandonment of any water well.

Comment: The Commission's statement of principles does not go into detail on well regulation, but the requirement that a permit be issued for withdrawal of ground water contemplates regulation of the sort specified by the Florida statute. The permit recommended by the Commission contains conditions relating to source of supply, well location, place and nature of use, volume and rate of withdrawal, and amount and place of reentry of return flow to the hydrologic system. In addition, Chapter 7, Section B, contains 20 recommendations relating to ground water administration and management, most of which are applicable to a comprehensive water control act in States where ground water is a significant source of supply.

The remaining Sections of Part III of the Florida law relate to licensing of well drillers (which the Commission recommends also in Chapter 7, Section B), exemptions of small wells, fees, and enforcement.

Summary – The Florida statute appears in general to be a carefully considered, comprehensive scheme for planning and regulating water resource development. It relies too heavily, however, on administrative discretion in resource allocation under the vaguest possible standard of an undefined "public interest." It also fails to make any provision for the voluntary transfer of permits. The Commission's recommended principles seek to provide greater certainty in the allocation process, to reduce administrative discretion to a narrow ambit, and to allow market forces to reallocate water to more valuable uses. Under the Commission's proposals, some water would be withdrawn from economic exploitation—the water designated as desirable and essential minimum streamflows and as minimum lake levels. The remaining water would be subject to use at any location upon application. Reallocation of water to higher uses through voluntary transfer of permits would be facilitated by a complete record system and by definite rules of allocation in periods of shortage. Original investment and voluntary transfer to new uses would also be promoted by fixing the term of the permit or its renewal at a period long enough to recover investment.

Reducing Water Losses by Improved Efficiency[159]

One means of making more efficient use of available water supplies is to reduce losses in existing systems. These losses occur from evaporation, leakage in storage and transmission systems, and careless use of water by the ultimate recipients, whether they be farmers, householders, or manufacturers. Not all losses can be eliminated, and not all those capable of being reduced should be, since the value of the water saved should exceed the costs of saving it. Nevertheless, improved water conservation practices give promise of significant savings at acceptable costs.

It is important, however, not to claim too much for water-saving practices. Not all water that is lost from a storage and delivery system or from extravagant uses is lost to the hydrologic system. Leakage from reservoirs and seepage from canals may feed surface flow or ground water aquifers. Excessive use by farmers and householders may generate return flow that also reaches streams and aquifers. Even the water consumed by salt cedars, cottonwood trees, and other phreatophytes does not necessarily go to waste, for it may support vegetation pleasing to the eye of some and useful as habitat for wildlife.

DISCUSSION

Water-Saving Practices

Practices which can yield important water savings can be classified into three areas—agricultural, urban, and industrial.

Agricultural Use: The greatest potential, as well as the greatest need, for water savings is in the irrigated areas of the West. Irrigation of crops accounts for over 80 percent of consumptive uses of water, most of which occurs in the arid and semiarid West.[160] There, irrigation water is almost always used pursuant either to water rights acquired under appropriation law or to long-term water delivery contracts executed in connection with reclamation projects. As such, the right of the irrigator to use water is vested, and the opportunities for reducing water use are consequently limited. For example, while pricing policies might be effective to encourage frugality of use among urban householders who simply purchase water service subject to rate changes, such policies have limited applicability to existing irrigation rights.[161]

Limiting Water Use to the Water Right — When the early water rights were acquired in the West, water was plentiful and little attention was given to the amounts claimed. Later, many water rights administrators concluded that some of the early water rights had been acquired by speculators for later sale and were grossly excessive, covering far more water than ever could be beneficially used by the appropriators. In some instances the excess water claimed was diverted from natural watercourses and allowed to run to waste to avoid forfeiture of the water right through nonuse.[162]

---

[159] This section is based in large part on independent research and analysis by the National Water Commission staff. It is also based in part on another report prepared for the Commission: DEWSNUP, Richard L (1971). Legal Aspects of Water Salvage. National Technical Information Service, Springfield, Va., Accession No. PB 205 005. See also BAGLEY, Jay M et al., Utah State University Foundation (1971). Extending the Utility of Non-Urban Water Supplies. National Technical Information Service, Springfield, Va., Accession No. PB 207 115.

[160] HOWE, Charles W et al., Resources for the Future, Inc. (1971). Future Water Demands, prepared for the National Water Commission. National Technical Information Service, Springfield, Va., Accession No. PB 197 877. p. 100.

[161] It is probably true that if present subsidies were removed from irrigation water under future Federal reclamation projects, so that the actual cost of delivered water was passed on to the irrigator, then there would be a much lower quantity of water demanded for irrigation under those projects. But since the immediate concern is one of finding ways to save water under existing agricultural projects and practices, where rights to use water are already vested (and, in the case of water delivery contracts, where water prices are fixed), the relevant inquiry at this point is how to reduce irrigation water use without impairing these existing rights.

[162] In some cases, it appears that excessive and wasteful amounts of claimed water were dignified by early court decrees, where appropriators would bring suits against each other and then reach agreement as to the amounts of water each was entitled to, and stipulate to a decree to be entered by the court. See *Allen v. Petrick*, 69 Mont. 373, 377; 222 P. 451 (1924).

No appropriation State recognizes as valid any part of a water right which is in excess of the water reasonably needed and actually used. Beneficial need to satisfy the purpose of the use is the limit of any water right, and any unreasonable diversion or application of water is unlawful and can be enjoined by the[163] administrator. Likewise, the administrator can require replacement or repair of defective headgates or diverting works which permit excessive leaks or water losses, and he can require improvements to be made in ditches and other transmission facilities to prevent unreasonable transmission losses. By rigorous monitoring, State water administrators can limit the amount of water use to the water right and thereby effect some savings.

Quantifying Use Under Water Rights — It will be difficult, however, for an administrator to ascertain what is an excessive or unreasonable, and therefore illegal, use. Litigation on a case-by-case basis is not feasible. Uncertainties can be better resolved by an administrative promulgation of specific standards or limits for water use for specified areas, depending on the nature of the soil, climate, crop, and related factors. This is, in effect, a quantification of beneficial need, commonly referred to as the "duty" of the water. It is expressed either in a number of acre-feet of water per acre per year or a rate of flow in cubic feet per second (c.f.s.) for a prescribed number of acres. While some States provide for a statewide duty of water by statute, others follow the preferable procedure of authorizing the administrator to set the "duty" as a result of field investigations.

A similar quantification can be provided for water transmission losses by establishing a standard of reasonableness to limit losses from seepage and evapotranspiration. The allowable water loss in transmission facilities is commonly calculated · as some amount of water per mile of ditch from the stream to the place of use. This method of quantification has been accomplished most effectively as a part of general adjudications of water rights. Unfortunately, many States have made little progress with such adjudications because insufficient funds have been allocated for hydrographic surveys of lands irrigated and water diverted.

No one knows the amount of irrigation water presently being diverted in excess of reasonable need or the amount lost by inefficient transmission facilities. It could be substantial. But it is clear that State administrators, given sufficient funds and staff, could monitor irrigation uses, quantify limits of use under water rights, and prevent any such excessive losses.

Ways to Improve Irrigation Efficiency — If excessive irrigation uses are discontinued, and if inefficient diverting works and transmission facilities are brought up to a reasonable standard, then the law requires no greater measure of efficiency. This does not mean that further levels of efficiency are not practicable or desirable; it simply means that further water-savings practices must be brought about by inducing irrigators to make improvements which they are under no legal compulsion to make. First, some of the steps that can be taken are considered and then the means of inducing irrigators to take them are considered.

Extensive programs have been under way for some time in many areas to line canals and laterals with concrete, plastic membranes, or other materials which prevent seepage and transpiration by ditch-bank vegetation. Some farmers have achieved more efficient application by converting from surface flooding to trickle irrigation by small transmission lines or to pressure sprinklers. Extensive tests by a University of Nebraska research team indicate that "every-other-row irrigation" (placing water in alternate furrows, leaving a dry furrow between each two watered furrows) can save a substantial amount of work and water without reducing crop yields.[164]

Where irrigation districts and other water users' organizations join forces, it is possible to realize other types of water savings. Frequently, surface supplies yielded in years of high runoff can be used to recharge underground basins, and the water can be subsequently withdrawn as needed. Underground storage can also be used to reduce or eliminate evaporation that otherwise would occur through

---

[163]Circumstances vary so much from area to area that no satisfactory definition of "reasonableness" has been devised; specific limits on use come from some form of quantification. But it will not be easy. "What may be a reasonable beneficial use, where water is present in excess of all needs, would not be a reasonable beneficial use in an area of great scarcity and great need. What is a beneficial use at one time may, because of changed conditions, become a waste of water at a later time." *Tulare Irrig. Dist. v. Lindsay-Strathmore Irrig. Dist.*, 2 Cal.2d 489, 567; 45 P.2d 972, 1007 (1935). See also HUTCHINS WA (1967). Background and modern developments in state water rights law. Water and Water Rights 1:86-87.

[164]MILLIGAN, Tom (1973). Should I irrigate only every other row? (based on work done by Bob Mulliner and Paul Fischbach, University of Nebraska). Irrigation Age, March 1973, pp. 16-18.

storage in surface reservoirs. Joint efforts can sometimes effect location of deeper storage reservoirs in mountain canyons on the higher reaches of streams (thus reducing evaporation by exposing proportionately smaller surface areas) as an alternative to shallower reservoirs sited at lower elevations.[165]

Where irrigation rights on streams prevent efficient application of water in periods of low flow, or where the rights call for smaller quantities than needed for efficient application, schedules of "rotation" can be implemented by irrigators operating in concert. Use of the stream can be rotated from user to user to allow greater volumes for shorter periods of time, increasing the efficiency of each use. Each irrigator is allowed a water "turn" equivalent to his water right, even though the amount and time of delivery is different from the pattern of use called for by the individual water rights.[166]

A higher degree of efficiency can be realized through storage facilities where waters controlled by direct flow rights can be impounded and later released on call so that the irrigator receives the amount of water to which he is entitled at the time needed and not at some other time. This has significant advantages over direct flow withdrawals where the amount diverted under direct flow rights might be excessive to the needs of one moment and deficient at other times, or when weather conditions might make irrigation unnecessary. Also, programs for phreatophyte eradication can, in some areas, result in substantial reductions in transpiration losses, and the water thus saved captured for use.[167] The environmental effects of eradication programs must be assessed in advance.

A number of rather sophisticated improvements in farm management practices might further reduce

---

[165]Monomolecular films were once viewed as having an important potential for reducing reservoir evaporation losses, but experimental results have been disappointing. The films are difficult to maintain. At "even moderate wind velocities, they can be destroyed by small organisms, and they increase water temperature, which in turn tends to promote evaporation rather than diminish it." NATIONAL ACADEMY OF SCIENCES (1968). Water and Choice in the Colorado Basin, A Report by the Committee on Water of the National Research Council, Publication 1689. National Academy of Sciences, Washington, D.C.

[166]Where significant water savings will result, or where efficiency will be materially improved, courts have imposed systems of rotation despite protests of nonconsenting appropriators. *Crawford v. Lehi Irrig. Co.,* 10 Utah 2d 165, 350 P.2d 147 (1960).

[167]Various estimates have been made of phreatophyte consumption. The following extract is typical of reports made a number of years ago:

"Along many of the river valleys of the West, saltcedars and other generally worthless vegetation (willows, cottonwoods, mesquite, greasewood, and certain reeds and weeds) have crowded onto river bottom land to such an extent that they now cover nearly 16 million acres and discharge into the atmosphere an estimated 20 to 25 million acre-feet of water annually. These plants, having their roots in the ground water, have first call on available water supplies, leaving for man only that which they cannot use. Losses are particularly acute in the water shortage States of Arizona and New Mexico, where the warmer climate leads to greater consumption of water, particularly by the saltcedars. Elimination of the consumptive waste from these plants provides an excellent opportunity for increasing the usefulness of available water supplies.

"...Federal and State agencies are...carrying on experiments and studies to determine ways and means whereby water lost through evaporation and transpiration can be salvaged for beneficial use. Estimates of possible savings in water through eradication and control range as high as 25 percent of present loss, or 6 million acre-feet annually, but additional research into the most economical methods for eradication and control is needed." U.S. CONGRESS, Senate, Select Committee on National Water Resources (1961). Report of the Committee Pursuant to S. Res. 48, Senate Report No. 29, 86th Congress, 1st Session. U.S. Government Printing Office, Washington, D.C. pp. 108-109.

More recent publications reveal conflicts which arise when proposals are made to remove phreatophytes:

"A case in point is Arizona, where Federal agencies are studying or proposing the removal of phreatophytes—deep rooted vegetation—from the banks of many rivers in the state. The main purpose of the removal is to conserve water in that arid state. . . .

"Bitterly opposing the phreatophyte removal projects, some of which are already under way, are conservationists and wildlife proponents who say that the riverbank vegetation is the only major wildlife habitat in the arid state. Remove it, they say, and the adverse effects on wildlife will be devastating and sometimes irreversible. Some also mention indications, somewhat less supported by scientific evidence, that the effects on fisheries may be equally detrimental. . . .

"The dove, quail, grey hawk and black-bellied tree duck are some of the birds affected, according to Arizona Game and Fish Department. Other types of wildlife are also affected, of course, including deer and javelina. Although waterfowl do not use the plant cover directly, it forms sanctuaries for ducks and geese using the Pacific Flyway. . . ." GILLULY RH (March 13, 1971). Wildlife versus Irrigation. Science News 99:184.

water use, and bring use efficiency well above the present estimated average of 45 percent. In several areas, data processing techniques are being used to schedule times and amounts of irrigation use. Even where high individual farm efficiencies have already been achieved and available supply is closely matched with consumptive needs (including leaching requirements), there is opportunity for further improvements in efficiency by modifications in cropping pattern to obtain more production per unit of water consumed. There are also opportunities for increasing yields without additional water by using better crop varieties, fertilizer, and moisture control.

The practices mentioned above are illustrative of the ways in which water use can be reduced or crop yields increased in irrigated areas. Yet, it is one thing to identify ways of improving irrigation efficiency and another to put them into practice. The primary incentive for an irrigator to make more frugal use of his water is the assurance that he will be entitled to use of the water he saves. Unfortunately, this is not now the case in some States. Vestiges of the appurtenance doctrine still remain, i.e., the irrigator is limited in his water use to the parcel of land for which the right was initially acquired. Where this is so, the irrigator has little incentive to improve the efficiency of his application or to reduce losses in his transmission facilities.[168] So long as his present water right yields sufficient water for his original tract, he will not make improvements to save water that he cannot use elsewhere or sell to others. It would be an important step forward if the States would review their water law doctrines and remove legal impediments to water-savings practices. In addition, the States should establish procedures for acquisition of rights in salvaged water. If irrigators do not desire to use water they save, they should be allowed to sell it, so that an incentive is created for improving efficiency when the value of water exceeds the cost of saving it.

Where irrigators are charged either a flat rate for all units of water used or progressively lower rates per unit as more and more units of water are used, there is an incentive toward excessive use. Reversing this policy (i.e., charging progressively higher rates as greater quantities of water are used) would create additional incentives to improve efficiency of use.

The Federal Government can add to the incentives for instituting water-savings practices by requiring project planning reports to evaluate the irrigation efficiency in the project area. If water supply can be increased by improving efficiency, this should be evaluated as an alternative to new project construction.

Urban Use: Wise use of urban water supplies not only conserves water for use by more consumers, but it saves the cost of developing and treating new potable supplies and reduces the volume of sewage water which must be treated. A number of opportunities exist to improve efficiency in urban water use.

Leaks, Valves, and Meters — Municipal water supplies are now depleted to some extent by leaks in the distribution system and by defective connections, valves, and fixtures, particularly in older systems.[169] Control programs which detect and correct significant leaks are clearly desirable.

Many cities do not meter water use by individual consumers and accordingly have no way of measuring water use and charging for the amount consumed. Without such charges there is no financial incentive for consumers to avoid excessive use. While it might not be feasible for all cities to install meters in all existing residences and other housing developments, it is advisable for each city not having meters to review the benefits which might be derived from such installation.[170]

Most cities would probably benefit from the installation of meters in all new water connections. Experience has shown that meter installations result in reduced water use. There is also some evidence that subsequent per capita use over the long run remains close to the reduced level, so long as individual

---

[168] *Salt River Valley Water Users' Association v. Kovacovich,* 3 Ariz. App. 28, 411 P.2d 201 (1966). An irrigator reduced transmission losses by eradicating weeds along his ditch and by lining it. The court refused to allow use of the water thus salvaged on other land owned by the irrigator although there was no proof that other users would be injured.

[169] HOWE, Charles W et al., Resources for the Future, Inc. (1971). Future Water Demands, prepared for the National Water Commission. National Technical Information Service, Springfield, Va., Accession No. PB 197 877. pp. 31-43.

[170] See Chapter 7, Section C, for further discussion of pricing municipal water.

consumption is measured and charges are imposed for the amount of water consumed.[171]

Pricing Policies – Most cities assess a flat charge for the first units of water consumed, and then assess progressively lower charges per unit as more water is consumed. The result is that the more water used, the cheaper the average unit price becomes; hence, there is little incentive to avoid excessive use. If the pricing policy were reversed, so that higher charges per unit were assessed as more units were consumed, there would be a financial penalty for excessive consumption and an incentive for individual conservation. Efficiency would also be improved by pricing policies which charged more at times of peak demand and less at times of slack demand.

Moreover, there should be no subsidy. Municipalities should charge high enough rates for water consumption and for sewage disposal to amortize at least the municipal share of investment in the facilities required to provide those services, and to pay all operation and maintenance costs.

Because of a large accumulated backlog of unbuilt but urgently needed sewage treatment facilities throughout the country, the Commission recognizes the desirability for substantial Federal assistance grants to construct sewage disposal facilities. Over the long run, however, the Commission believes that the guiding principle should be that municipal water users pay the full costs of both water supply and sewage disposal.[172]

Fixtures and Appliances – Plumbing fixtures have been designed to reduce water use without causing inconvenience to the consumer. These are on the market and are not unduly expensive. Shower, lavatory, and sink fittings with built-in flow regulators and valves can reduce water use. It has been estimated that the average shower requires 35 to 40 gallons of water, and that automatic flow regulation would reduce this use by about 50 percent. Toilet fixtures are available which reduce the amount of water used for each flush by more than one-half (from about 8 gallons to less than 4), an important savings, inasmuch as toilets account for about 45 percent of all the water used in the average household. Dishwashers and clothes washers are being redesigned to reduce substantially the rinse waters now required. And garbage disposal units are being developed which do not use water as now required by most kitchen disposal units. As a general observation, recent studies have shown that appliances and fixtures now available can reduce total water use in the average household by as much as 35 percent, and savings for commercial and business establishments can be as high as 50 percent.[173]

If water and sewage charges do not prove to be adequate incentives to encourage consumers to install water-saving appliances and fixtures, cities might well consider revising their municipal plumbing codes to require installation of certain of these devices for all new construction, or whenever specified appliances or fixtures are replaced in existing households.

Sequencing Uses and Reducing Peak Loads – As a part of municipal water management an effort should be made to arrange a sequence of uses and reuses where possible, since treated residential effluent might adequately serve certain industrial requirements as well as irrigation of parks and golf courses. Further, sprinkling irrigation of parks and golf courses, as well as private lawns and gardens, could profitably be scheduled for offpeak nighttime periods. This utilizes system capacity during periods of low use, rather than at times of heavy user demand, an efficiency which might permit postponement or avoidance of new investments in additional reservoir or pipeline capacity.

Public Relations Programs to Stress Wise Use – Finally, by means of a public relations program, cities should encourage consumers to exercise intelligence in water use, rather than emphasize the availability of

---

[171] Some have hypothesized that reduced water use, which follows a switchover from flat rates to metered charges, is short-lived; that subsequent consumption levels gradually rise to approximate the level of use prior to meter installation. This has not been proved. The experience of Boulder, Colorado, illustrates the reverse. There, meter installation caused average domestic use to drop 36 percent and lawn sprinkling more than 50 percent (corrected for weather conditions). Subsequent water consumption over a 6-year period revealed no significant return to the higher pre-meter level of use. Only 1.7 percent of householders interviewed said meters had given them no incentive to reduce their water use. HANKE SH & BOLAND JJ (November 1971). Water requirements or water demands? Journal American Water Works Association 63(11):677-681.

[172] See Chapter 7, Section C, Pricing as a Means of Motivating Better Use.

[173] GRUBISICH, Thomas (December 9, 1971). Water-saving devices flow onto market. Washington Post. pp. K-1, K-10.

Side-roll sprinkler system irrigation

water to perform household chores. Consumers may be expected to respond once they are made aware of the water charges they pay and of the costs of developing new supplies and installing additional sewage treatment facilities.

Industrial Use: Consumptive use of water by industry is small relative to consumption by agriculture and municipalities. While industrial *withdrawals* (excluding thermal electric cooling and mining) exceed municipal withdrawals by 50 percent, industrial *consumption* is about half of municipal. Thus, the savings in industrial water use are not likely to be large in absolute terms. Nevertheless, where there is scarcity, some saving practices may be economically

justified. For example, recent technological advances have permitted the steel industry to reduce water requirements by 90 percent in water-short areas. Perhaps the greatest saving can be achieved by reuse of cooling water, which accounts for about 67 percent of all industrial withdrawals. That subject is discussed in the next section.

CONCLUSIONS

Substantial savings can be made through improved efficiency in the use of water for irrigation. The Commission was impressed by the University of Arizona's demonstration of trickle irrigation in an enclosed environment system at Puerto Penasco, on the Gulf of California in Sonora, Mexico. This is a costly system, but it can show the way toward vast improvements in irrigation water use in the future. Other and less exotic opportunities for improved efficiency abound. For example, a statement submitted to the Commission by the Utah-Idaho Sugar Company at its public conference in Spokane indicates that that company achieved substantial reductions in water use when it switched in the early 1960's from gravity-flow irrigation to sprinkler irrigation on its Osgood Project in Southeastern Idaho. The U-I Osgood Project consists of approximately 6,000 acres of irrigated land and is not a Federal Reclamation project. Prior to the change to sprinkler irrigation, the Commission was told, the project had been "water hungry." After the change, which included squaring up fields and other modernizations, an additional 1,000 acres of land could be put under irrigation and the usage of water per acre for irrigating crops was cut in half.

It must not be assumed, however, that all irrigation water in excess of consumptive use is lost to the system. In many cases, perhaps most cases, the water is returned to the streams as streamflow or serves to recharge ground water. Some excess water is needed in almost all irrigated areas to leach salts from the soil. But in those cases where the return flow reaches the ocean or a saline lake, either as surface or ground water, improved efficiency can save water for other uses.

In most cases, what is lost through poor efficiency is water in storage which may prove a useful reserve against subsequent drought, or the value of the water by reason of location, timing, or quality. The return flows will occur farther downstream where there may be less favorable options for use. The return flows will occur later—sometimes several months later—when the water may be less valuable. The return flows will also contain more salts which may diminish their utility. Finally, if the excess water is added to the ground water, costs will be incurred in pumping it to the surface for use. Thus, while improved efficiency may not "save" large quantities of water, it may protect the value of the water. Each basin poses its own special conditions and the values gained from better management must be determined by a study of each basin.

The Commission believes that a number of useful steps can be taken to achieve water savings and has prepared specific recommendations on irrigation and municipal use.

RECOMMENDATIONS

Irrigation Use

7-55. The States in water-short regions should enforce existing laws to limit water use to beneficial need, and thus prevent wasteful application of water and unreasonable transmission losses.

7-56. The appropriation States should quantify "beneficial need" and "reasonable efficiency" for particular areas in order to reduce water waste.

7-57. States in water-short areas should adopt doctrines and procedures to encourage voluntary actions to improve efficiency of water use. Specifically, rights should be created in salvaged water, and the rights should be freely transferable to other uses and users, subject only to the limitation that rights of others should not be injured.

7-58. Irrigation water rate structures should be designed to encourage efficient, rather than excessive, water use.

7-59. Water supply projects should not be authorized by the Congress until evaluations are made with respect to the efficiency of use of presently developed supplies in proposed project areas, and until a report is made on the prospects and desirability of satisfying existing shortages in any particular area by water-savings practices in lieu of further project development.

Urban Use

7-60. Effective leak control programs should be instituted and meters to measure individual water use should be installed by water supply agencies in urban areas.

7-61. Water prices and sewer charges for individual service should be set at levels which fully cover the costs of amortizing and operating the facilities necessary to provide these services, and a municipal water supply rate structure should be adopted which encourages intelligent, rather than excessive, water use.

7-62. Amendments to plumbing codes should be adopted, requiring the installation of water-saving fixtures and appliances in all new construction, and whenever existing water-using appliances or fixtures are replaced.

7-63. The water supply should be managed to accommodate sequential uses of water, such as using effluent from treatment plants for irrigating parks and golf courses and for industrial use within the area; and irrigation uses should be timed to coincide with low water-demand periods to conserve reservoir and pipeline capacity.

7-64. A public relations program should be conducted to encourage wise water use, pointing out to consumers the benefits to the city and its inhabitants to be realized through conserving the water supply.

〜〜〜〜〜〜〜〜〜〜〜〜〜〜〜〜〜〜〜〜〜〜〜〜〜〜〜〜〜〜〜〜*Section H*

Reuse of Municiple and Industrial Wastewater

The National Water Commission Act requires consideration of reuse of wastewater as one of the alternative means of meeting future water demands. The potential usefulness of reuse is illustrated by the U.S. Water Resources Council's projections on withdrawals and returns. For example, in 1980 it is projected that municipalities will withdraw 34 billion gallons per day (b.g.d.) and return 23 b.g.d., or about 68 percent. Industry (not including mining and thermal-electric cooling uses) is expected in that year to withdraw 55 b.g.d. and return 50 b.g.d., or about 91 percent.[174] While the absolute quantity of withdrawals is expected to increase substantially by the year 2000, the percentage of returns from withdrawals remains about the same for both municipalities and industries.

This section considers the technological, economic, and managerial problems of reuse. It should be recognized at the outset that reuse occurs at the present time and that the discussion is directed toward its expansion. One-third of the Nation's population currently depends on municipal withdrawals from streams containing, on the average, 1 gallon of previously used water out of 30 gallons of flow. In some cases, as much as 1 gallon out of 5 of municipal water supply has been used before.[175] Ordinarily, these supplies have received only conventional purification treatment.

DISCUSSION

The rate at which the Nation will move toward greater reuse of wastewater depends on advances in treatment technology, costs, and the indirect consequences of more stringent water pollution controls. Present treatment technology is already adequate to permit reuses of municipal effluents for purposes not involving human consumption. In several localities, municipal wastewater is being treated and recycled directly into a system for reuse for industrial, recreational, and ground water recharge purposes. With respect to industrial effluents, many of the changes in treatment which would be required for direct reuse of such wastewater for industrial purposes will be required in any event by higher water quality standards. Direct reuse of industrial effluents will become progressively more attractive, therefore, not because the objective is reuse but because pollution control will produce that spillover benefit.

In the absence of compulsion, however, the controlling factor in direct reuse of wastewater for industrial purposes, naturally enough, is the cost of alternative sources of supply. At present, most alternative sources of water are less costly than either direct or indirect reuse.[176] There has thus been little economic incentive to bring about a higher degree of reuse. However, as costs of alternative supplies rise or as quality of wastewater improves, direct industrial reuse should increase materially. When it does, much

---

[174]U.S. WATER RESOURCES COUNCIL (1968). The Nation's Water Resources. U.S. Government Printing Office, Washington, D.C. pp. 4-1, 4-2-4.

[175]GAVIS, Jerome (1971). Wastewater Reuse, prepared for the National Water Commission. National Technical Information Service, Springfield, Va., Accession No. PB 201 535. p. 1.

[176]Direct reuse, as indicated, is made by the first user, who recycles the water through the same system after suitable treatment. Indirect reuse occurs when effluent is discharged into a water body by the first user, diluted by natural forces, and then withdrawn, treated (if necessary), and used by others.

of the water supply which industry would otherwise use, can be released for other purposes, including human consumption, thus, in effect, increasing the supply of water available for potable use.

The prospects for direct reuse of municipal effluent for human consumption depend both upon technology and public acceptance. Existing treatment technology can produce water that meets current Federal drinking water standards in terms of physical, chemical, and bacteriological criteria. However, those standards were not designed for application to municipal wastewater effluents that are recycled and reused again by human beings. They do not take into account possible toxic ingredients sometimes found in wastewater. As a result, some public health groups are concerned about (1) possible viral hazards and (2) trace amounts of new chemicals for which possible adverse health effects are not now predictable. These concerns stem both from the unpredictability of effects of reuse for human consumption and from the great difficulty of proper monitoring and operation of waste treatment facilities. At present, most sewage treatment plants are susceptible to breakdown. Presumably, proper design for contingencies, similar to those for water treatment plants, will be necessary if direct reuse for human consumption is to become a reality.[177] If and when these public health concerns are mitigated by further research, large-scale direct reuse of wastewater for human consumption will become a distinct possibility.

Reclaiming Wastewater

Types of Treatment: The treatment of wastewater for reuse may differ depending on whether the reuse is for industrial or municipal purposes. Moreover, the treatment of wastewater from industrial plants is highly situation-oriented, being dependent on the manufacturing processes used. For some industrial plants, the municipal treatment techniques are satisfactory. For other industrial plants, technology must be improved or industrial processes changed to meet water quality standards now in effect or soon to be imposed.

Treatment of municipal wastewater usually involves sequential phases, each designed to remove specific types of pollutants. Three phases will be described: primary treatment, secondary treatment, and advanced treatment.[178]

Primary treatment consists of ordinary sedimentation. This process of allowing materials to settle to the bottom of wastewater removes about 90 percent of settleable solids in raw sewage and from 40 to 70 percent of suspended solids.

Secondary treatment oxidizes organic matter in sewage through bacterial action. The most common methods are the "trickling filter" and "activated sludge" processes which typically reduce suspended solids to from 10 to 20 percent of the original amount. These processes can be designed to remove 90 percent of biodegradable organics (which, unless removed, consume large quantities of oxygen), 60 percent of nonbiodegradable organics, 50 percent of the nitrogen compounds, 30 percent of the phosphorous compounds, and over 99 percent of pathogenic (disease-producing) bacteria and viruses.

Advanced waste treatment, which for the purpose of this report is defined to include all types of treatment above secondary, removes one or more of the following impurities which usually remain in effluent after secondary treatment:

(a) The remaining suspended and colloidal solids.

(b) Plant nutrients, principally phosphorous and nitrogen compounds.

(c) Organic matter, such as pesticides and the products of bacterial metabolism that are resistent to biological treatment.

(d) Dissolved mineral matter.

No advanced treatment process has yet been devised to remove all contaminants in a single step at reasonable costs. Several desalting processes remove most pollutants except some of the pathogenic organisms, but currently these processes are not competitive in cost with other treatment processes. Moreover, some desalting processes have additional problems such as fouling with biological slime. One "desalting" technique, the reverse osmosis process, offers some hope of becoming competitive if the membranes, through which wastewaters in this process are forced, are sufficiently improved.[179]

[177] JOPLING WF et al. (October 1971). Fitness needs for wastewater reclamation plants. Journal American Water Works Association 63(10):626-629.

[178] FAIR GM et al. (1968). Water and Wastewater Engineering. John Wiley & Sons, Inc., New York. pp. 36-6, 36-7.

[179] GAVIS, Jerome (1971). Wastewater Reuse, prepared for the National Water Commission. National Technical Information Service, Springfield, Va., Accession No. PB 201 535. p. 45. See generally Chapter 9, Section B, of this report on Desalting.

Trickling filter at secondary treatment plant, Des Moines, Iowa

The current state of the art of advanced waste-water treatment has been based largely on further treatment of effluent from conventional secondary treatment plants; however, only 43 percent of the Nation's population is currently served by secondary treatment facilities.[180] Accordingly, most water pollution control programs have assumed that the next appropriate step is extension of secondary treatment and the addition of advanced treatment processes to known secondary treatment processes rather than devising new processes for combining secondary and advanced treatment.

Costs of Treatment:[181] The advanced treatment processes described below would have to be em-

[180] U.S. FEDERAL WATER QUALITY ADMINISTRATION (1970). Municipal Waste Facilities in the United States. Statistical Summary, 1968 Inventory, FWQA Publication No. CWT-6. U.S. Government Printing Office, Washington, D.C. p. 35.

[181] Based on GAVIS, Jerome (1971). Wastewater Reuse, prepared for the National Water Commission. National Technical Information Service, Springfield, Va., Accession No. PB 201 535.

ployed if large-scale reuse is contemplated in areas which already have secondary treatment facilities.

Solids — The residual solids that remain in wastewater after secondary treatment can be removed by any of several filtration methods at the relatively low cost of from 1 to 2 cents per 1,000 gallons. Filtration would also remove biodegradable organic impurities.

Nutrients — Phosphorous compounds can be satisfactorily reduced by chemical processes at a cost of about 14 cents per 1,000 gallons for a plant of 10 million gallons per day (m.g.d.) and for 8-1/2 cents per 1,000 gallons in a 100 m.g.d. plant (including debt service in both instances). Remaining suspended solids are removed at the same time.

The need for removal of nitrogen compounds is not established, and the state of the art for such removal is not yet well developed. Indications are that removal of nitrogen compounds could increase nutrient removal costs by 40 percent.

Recent laboratory investigations indicate the possibility of removing nutrients at the primary treatment step by adding chemical processes at that time, and then moving on to a secondary treatment process. Overall costs would probably be considerably less than by following the conventional treatment processes in normal succession.[182]

Nonbiodegradable Organics — These organic materials, including some that degrade very slowly, can be reduced to the very low concentrations present in natural water supplies through adsorption (adhesion of substances to a surface) by activated carbon. The cost range approximates 10 cents to 7 cents per 1,000 gallons for a 10 m.g.d. and a 100 m.g.d. plant, respectively.

Minerals — Characteristically, on a once-through basis, about 350 parts per million (p.p.m.) of dissolved minerals are added to municipal water supplies between initial intake and ultimate discharge. Thus, in continuous recycling, removal of this increment will be necessary once in each cycle in order to limit dissolved minerals to the maximum 500 p.p.m. recommended by the U.S. Public Health Service's drinking water standards. This can be done by the process of electrodialysis for a cost estimated to be in the order of 12 cents per 1,000 gallons for a 10

m.g.d. plant.[183] The reverse osmosis process can also be used to remove minerals.

Pathogens and Viruses — Pathogenic bacteria can be removed from wastewater safely by chlorination at a cost of less than 1 cent per 1,000 gallons. Viruses are removed in large part by secondary and advanced treatment processes but there is argument as to the degree of hazard remaining after such treatment. Most scientists counsel caution. They assert it has not yet been proven that treatment processes render wastewater free from viral hazard. On the other hand, some sanitary engineers and health officials believe that it may be impossible to "prove" the absence of every conceivable hazard in any source of water supply. They express the opinion that the risk of virological hazard in reuse of wastewater that has undergone advanced treatment is so low as not to merit any significant public health concern. However, until further research settles the difference of opinion, prudence suggests that direct reuse of municipal wastewater for domestic consumption be avoided.

Table 7-5 shows approximate 1967 costs of the various stages of secondary and advanced waste treatment, based on a variety of sources. The costs presented are believed to represent the best estimates available. They are necessarily generalized—both capital and unit treatment costs will vary widely in different parts of the country and in specific situations, depending particularly on the concentration of pollutants in the influent and the proportion of pollutants removed.

Table 7-5 demonstrates very significant economies of scale in secondary and advanced waste treatment (i.e., unit cost reductions which are associated with increasing sizes of treatment plants). The use of large-sized treatment plants, possibly serving several communities within a single regional system, will greatly reduce the per unit costs of water reclamation if collection and transmission costs are not excessive.

Net Costs for Reuse: The treatment cost estimates for reuse described above and in Table 7-5 are gross rather than net figures. In reality, the economic potential of reuse is enhanced by recognizing that advanced wastewater treatment simultaneously accomplishes two purposes: (1) it reduces water pollution and (2) it increases the usefulness of exist-

---

[182] SCHMID LA & McKINNEY RE (July 1969). Phosphate removal by a lime-biological treatment scheme. Journal Water Pollution Control Federation 41(7):1259-1276.

[183] BRUNNER CA (October 1967). Pilot-plant experiences in demineralization of secondary effluent using electrodialysis. Journal Water Pollution Control Federation 39(10):R1.

TABLE 7-5.–Approximate costs of secondary and advanced treatment[1]
(June, 1967 Cost Levels)

Costs of Advanced Treatment Processes in Addition to Costs of Secondary Treatment

Capacity of Plant (m.g.d.)	Secondary Treatment[3]		Nutrient removal (including suspended solids)[a 2 3]		Removal of nutrients plus nonbiodegradable organics[2]		Removal of nutrients & nonbiodegradable organic plus demineralization[b 2]	
	Capital Costs ($Million)	Total Unit Treatment Costs[c] (¢/1000 gal)	Capital Costs ($Million)	Total Unit Treatment Costs[c] (¢/1000 gal)	Capital Costs ($Million)	Total Unit Treatment Costs[c] (¢/1000 gal)	Capital Costs ($Million)	Total Unit Treatment Costs[c] (¢/1000 gal)
1	0.54	19	0.43	26.8	0.81	58	–	–
10	3.2	11	1.8	14.0	3.4	24	6.8	36
100	20	6.5	10.9	8.6	26	15.6	–	–

[a]Costs based on air stripping. If biological nitrification-dentrification is required, as is presently indicated, the costs would undoubtedly be greater. Costs of this process are not currently available, but some researchers have expressed the view that its use could raise the total cost of nutrient removal by as much as 40 percent.

[b]Based on assumed mineral concentration of 850 p.p.m. in effluent, reduced to 500 p.p.m. (drinking water standard), thus providing for one cycle of reuse. Costs of brine disposal, which may be substantial, are not included in above demineralization costs because of variability between sites.

[c]Includes operation and maintenance and interest and amortization on capital investment (at 4.5 percent interest over 25 years for comparative purposes only; not intended as a recommendation for financing assumption).

Sources of Cost Data:
[1] GAVIS, Jerome (1971). Wastewater Reuse, prepared for the National Water Commission. PB 201 535, National Technical Information Service, Springfield, Va.

[2] SMITH, Robert & McMICHAEL, Walter F (1969). Cost and Performance Estimates for Tertiary Wastewater Treating Processes, prepared for the Federal Water Pollution Control Administration. Report No. TWRC-9, Robert A. Taft Water Research Center, Cincinnati, 0.

[3] SMITH R (September 1968). Cost of conventional and advanced treatment of wastewater. Journal Water Pollution Control Federation 40(9):1546-1574.

ing water supplies for reuse. To the extent that the first purpose is required anyway, the incremental or marginal costs of the second purpose are significantly reduced.

Interestingly enough, current support for waste treatment is derived more from the public's attitude toward water pollution (because of its offensive nature esthetically and its impairment to aquatic life and recreational opportunities) than from the desire to conserve water supplies by reuse. The spillover benefit of increasing the usefulness of available water resources from water cleanup programs has not yet been fully recognized. Yet in the long run, increased use of reclaimed water could prove to be the greatest benefit to be derived from wastewater treatment.

Many municipalities and industries are currently under administrative or judicial orders to undertake specific levels of wastewater treatment to meet water quality standards. The Nation has made serious and substantial commitments for some of the necessary expenditures. The result in many instances will be effluents which approach the quality of an alternative fresh water supply. If the "no discharge" goal of the 1972 amendments to the Federal Water Pollution Control Act is achieved the quality of the effluent discharge would exceed that of most "natural" water supplies. Even with far less stringent requirements, however, the opportunity exists to combine the national commitment for pollution control with whatever additional treatment may be necessary to make effluents suitable for reuse.

What then would be the net cost of waste treatment for reuse? Many of the processes used in waste treatment for reuse are also used, to varying degrees, in the treatment of alternative sources of water supply with which reuse must be compared. Hence, the net costs of treatment for reuse, when compared with other alternatives, could be appreciably different from, and probably less than the total cost of treatment shown in Table 7-5. If the alternative supply source also includes treatment, as often it does, the cost of such treatment would be common to both the alternative and to reuse, and would serve to reduce cost differences between the two. Also, of course, any costs of conveyance to bring both the reuse supply and the alternative source to a common point for distribution must be included.

The true direct net cost of treatment for reuse can be expressed as follows:

(1) The cost of advanced treatment to make wastewater suitable for reuse,

(2) *minus* the cost of pollution control treatment measures otherwise necessary to achieve water quality standards,

(3) *minus* the cost of water treatment of the supply being considered as an alternative to reuse,

(4) *plus* or *minus* the difference in conveyance costs between the reusable supply and its alternative, including allowance for the cost of separate supply lines if reuse is contemplated for industrial water supply only.

The Potential of Wastewater Reuse

The projections made by the Water Resources Council indicate that future withdrawals of water by municipal and manufacturing users will increase significantly above present levels and, since only a portion of the water withdrawn is actually consumed, future returns of used water to water bodies will also increase markedly. To the extent that water supplies are limited, the desirability of reuse will expand. Some observations regarding the potential of reuse in helping to meet the Nation's water requirements will provide perspective:[184]

(a) By 1980, continuous reuse by manufacturers of only 20 percent of the projected total of 73 billion gallons per day (b.g.d.) of municipal and manufacturing effluents would completely satisfy the projected 1965-1980 increase in water withdrawals for manufacturing (15 b.g.d.), without development of any additional industrial water supply. Reuse by industry of an additional 14 percent of municipal and manufacturing effluents in 1980 would release enough potable water from manufacturing use to meet the 1965-1980 growth in municipal water withdrawal needs as well.

(b) By 2020, industrial reuse of 54 percent of total municipal and manufacturing effluents would meet the entire projected increase in industrial water withdrawals.

(c) By 2020, projected growth in municipal withdrawals could be met by a reuse of an additional 33 percent of municipal and manufacturing effluents. Adding this to the 54 percent referred to in (b) above would involve a total reuse of 87 percent of municipal and manufacturing effluents and obviate the need for any additional water supply. To accomplish this, some of the growth in municipal use would have to be supplied by reuse of municipal wastewater and, therefore, would depend upon solution of possible public health problems previously mentioned.[185]

---

[185] It is important to note that the potential reuse specified in (a) and (b) is not dependent upon resolving health problems (except to the extent that some industries, such as the food industry, produce products directly or indirectly associated with consumption by humans).

Another possibility that is seriously advocated is for dual water supply systems. One system would provide conventional supplies for uses involving human consumption and the second would supply treated effluents for all other uses. Estimates have been made that acceptable dual systems might be provided to new urban areas for about 20 percent higher cost than for a single supply system. See OKUN DA & McJUNKIN FE (1971). Feasibility of Dual Water Supply Systems, paper presented at the 7th Annual American Water Resources Association Meeting, October 1971. Unpublished. If proven to be justified, such systems would allow a vast increase in direct reuse without the health concerns expressed previously. Using such dual supply systems, the increases in both industrial and municipal withdrawals by 2020, as estimated by the Water Resources Council, could be fully supplied without direct reuse for human consumption.

---

[184] Figures are based on U.S. WATER RESOURCES COUNCIL (1968). The Nation's Water Resources. U.S. Government Printing Office, Washington, D.C. pp. 4-1, 4-2-5.

It should be emphasized that the degrees of reuse indicated above are simply illustrative, representing relatively crude estimates rather than precise conclusions. The Water Resources Council places considerable qualification on the accuracy of its projections. Also, the projections of water use represent national totals; it must be cautioned that future growth in uses might be at locations where reuse of effluents will be difficult or impossible. Further, over two-thirds of industrial use is expected to continue to be self-supplied (with the remainder obtained from general municipal supplies).

The physical accomplishment of reuse will be dependent on the location of effluent discharge and the location of reuse. (The extent of reuse will depend also on the pricing policies adopted, both with respect to withdrawals and with respect to discharges.) The degree of difficulty involved will vary widely from one locality and situation to another. Thus, it should be understood that the degree of reuse suggested in the observations above would not necessarily be in fact the best water management alternative.

Some Examples: After secondary treatment, some reuse of municipal effluents for industrial purposes presently occurs, primarily for cooling water. The Bethlehem Steel plant in Baltimore uses 125 m.g.d. of municipal effluent. The City of Colorado Springs treats about 5 m.g.d. (one-third of its wastewater) and sells it for industrial use. This has relieved pressures on the municipal supply and permitted delay of costly interbasin transfers of water. The City of Denver has large-scale plans for reuse. As a first phase, Denver proposes to reclaim 10 m.g.d. for industrial reuse by 1974. By 1986, 100 m.g.d. of reclaimed water is expected to be available. By the year 2000, or soon thereafter, Denver expects to supply 25 percent of its water needs by reuse.

Advanced waste treatment for reuse will greatly increase the sludge disposal problem. However, the problem will probably be no greater than would occur from the combined effects of (1) a conventional water supply treatment plant and (2) an alternative waste treatment plant needed for pollution control.

Considerable potential also exists for wastewater reuse for recreational and ground water recharge purposes, with appropriate controls. Secondary-treated municipal effluent with some degree of advanced treatment provides water for several artificial lakes and a swimming pool at Santee, California.

Other similar projects are planned. At the Whittier Narrows municipal treatment plant in California, secondary effluent is allowed to filter through percolating beds to recharge ground water aquifers. At Bay Park, Long Island, injection wells are recharged with secondary-treated effluent that has been subjected to some advanced treatment, in order to reduce sea water intrusion.

Again, a word of caution. Ground water recharge by subsurface injection of treated wastewater should be accomplished only with careful controls. This is necessary to insure noncontamination of present or potential drinking water supplies and to prevent other possible damage to the environment.

Reuse Prospects for Human Consumption: The previous discussion highlighted the considerable potential that exists for reuse of treated municipal and industrial effluents for industrial, recreational, and ground water recharge purposes. In general, decisions regarding direct reuse for municipal purposes need not be made for some time. In many instances, additional usable water for municipal purposes can be obtained by diverting present supplies from industry. Prospects for such diversions will be improved to the extent that industries reuse existing municipal and industrial wastewater.

Ultimately, however, decisions regarding direct reuse for human consumption will be necessary. The issues involved in reaching such decisions are complex. Comparisons of alternatives on the basis of economics will be needed. Such comparisons should include consideration not only of conventional water supplies but of other alternatives as well, including the dual water supply systems alluded to earlier. It will also be necessary to conduct the research, assemble the data, and establish the criteria and standards which will be needed by public health officials to assure that reuse of treated wastewater for intimate human contact is safe.

As indicated earlier, large-scale indirect reuse of previously used water for municipal purposes (including human consumption) already occurs in the United States. Despite this fact, public officials frequently go to great lengths to avoid such "indirect" reuse for human consumption. Although the public has not always been made aware of the alternatives, it has frequently responded to the call of public officials by agreeing to pay more for so-called "pure" natural supplies. New York City, for instance, has consistently chosen more costly supplies from the Catskill Mountains, even though many observers contend that plentiful lower-cost resources available in the Hudson River could have been made potable.

There has been an even greater reluctance, understandably, to accept direct recycling of treated wastewater for human consumption. Two emergency instances during the 1930's where virtually direct reuse for potable water supply was practiced are frequently cited. The City of Chanute, Kansas, reused sewage effluent, diluted as much as possible by a low river flow, for a period of about 2 months. Ottumwa, Iowa, also used water during a similar period, of which one-third to one-half was effluent from the City of Des Moines.[186] There were no known adverse health problems in either instance, even though advanced waste treatment was not used.[187]

Of more significance is the experimental arrangement by Windhoek, the capital of South West Africa (Namibia), a metropolitan area with a population of 84,000. During favorable periods when chlorine demand of the wastewaters is not too high, Windhoek recycles one-third of its effluent for direct reuse as potable water supply. Prior to this reuse, the effluent is subjected to advanced treatment in a 1 m.g.d. plant. Direct reuse at Windhoek represents the only feasible method of meeting expanding water requirements of that area. Public acceptance has been very good.[188]

Sewage Effluent-Irrigation Water Exchange: In and around some urban areas in arid parts of the country, water is pumped from ground water aquifers not only for domestic and industrial use but often for irrigation as well. Concurrently, disposal of municipal wastewater must be accomplished through treatment and discharge in watercourses or elsewhere. Studies of the economic, technical, legal, and environmental feasibility of combining these operations so that the two purposes can be served conjunctively have been made.[189] Opportunities for such conjunctive use were brought to the attention of the Commission in statements presented at regional public conferences held in early 1973 for discussion of the review draft of this report.

It is technically feasible and can make good economic sense to transfer water now utilized for irrigation to municipal use in exchange for treated sewage effluent. In effect, irrigation water would first be cycled through municipal systems prior to reuse on farms. Where water supplies are not abundant and conditions are otherwise favorable, such a system in which sewage effluent would be exchanged for ground water used for irrigation could substantially increase the efficiency of use and convert municipal effluent into a valuable water resource.

In such a water exchange, modestly treated sewage effluent, which is an inferior water resource for domestic use, would be allocated without further treatment to the irrigation of field and forage crops not intended for direct human consumption. An equivalent or equal-value amount of pumped ground water of high quality presently used for irrigation would be allocated instead to the municipal system (a portion of which would reappear at the sewage treatment plant for reuse on irrigated farms). Not only would water supplies be reused and conserved but the sewage disposal problem which can contribute to an excessive concentration of nitrate in an otherwise potable ground water aquifer is solved or ameliorated.

This exchange system might be applicable to many metropolitan areas in or near which crops are being irrigated. Some investigators state that in many cases the savings in advanced treatment and disposal, and the value of nutrients to irrigators would offset the cost of conveying the exchanged waters, even over considerable distances.[190]

[186] U.S. CONGRESS, Senate, Select Committee on National Water Resources (1960). Water Resources Activities in the United States: Present and Prospective Means for Improved Reuse of Water, pursuant to S. Res. 48, 86th Congress, 2d Session, Committee Print No. 30. U.S. Government Printing Office, Washington, D.C. p. 3.

[187] Less widely cited is the fact that, while these instances had public acceptance for general water supply, many citizens chose to use bottled water from other sources for drinking purposes. HANEY PD (February 1969). Water reuse for public supply. Journal American Water Works Association 61(3):73-78.

[188] STANDER GJ, Director, National Institute for Water Research, Pretoria South Africa (April 1970). Personal communication.

[189] See, for example, CLUFF, CB, DeCOOK, KJ & MATLOCK, WG (1971). Technical and institutional aspects of sewage effluent-irrigation water exchange, Tucson region. Water Resources Bulletin, 7:4, Journal of the American Water Resources Association, Urbana, Illinois, August 1971, pp. 726-739. And CAMPBELL, George W (1971). Desert water exchange between town and country. Arizona Agri-File. Cooperative Extension Service, University of Arizona, Tucson, June 1971.

[190] CLUFF, CB & DeCOOK, KJ (1973). Communication to the National Water Commission from the Water Resources Research Center, University of Arizona, Tucson. January 16, 1973.

CONCLUSIONS

The potential for reuse of treated municipal and industrial wastewater is considerable; the prospects are encouraging. The technology of reuse already provides important savings. Extension of the technology can be expected to yield significant gains in water conservation. The subject merits careful and serious consideration.

Table 7-5 indicates that after secondary treatment municipal wastewater can be brought to the chemical equivalent of drinking water quality at a cost of about 36 cents per 1,000 gallons for a 10 m.g.d. plant. This is a relatively high cost even in areas of the country where water is scarce. However, the actual net cost of treating for reuse could be much less because of pollution control requirements that will be imposed anyway and also because some of the advanced treatment processes involved probably will be required for any alternative supply sources as well.

This suggests that the future of advanced waste treatment, insofar as conserving water resources by reuse is concerned, is very real but that the degree of its employment will vary from one situation to another depending on location, needs of the time, and type of use. Industrial direct reuse can proceed on the basis of present technology, as can ground water recharge and recreation use. Ultimately, potable supplies from wastewater could be and probably will be made available for direct reuse.

Treatment up to and including the secondary phase, or even including the relatively inexpensive step of removing suspended solids, will be adequate for many industrial uses and for such uses as golf course irrigation. In these cases, the costs above the requirements for pollution control will be very small. Reuse may have to be accompanied by some demineralization in those cases where dilution with other supplies fails to produce a supply adequate to the needs of particular uses.

Removal of nutrients and suspended solids from wastewater has been utilized to provide water for recreational boating and fishing. Disinfection added to this procedure will provide water that can be used in contact with humans (in such sports as swimming and water-skiing), provided research leads health officials to conclude there are no significant health hazards.

The present procedure of a continuum of treatment steps, from lower to higher levels of treatment in sequence, is a logical outgrowth of existing technology. However, it is not the only, nor will it

necessarily be the best, course to pursue. Recent experimental work in which parts of primary, secondary, and advanced treatment are combined offers considerable promise for the future. Although this combined-phase technology has already been developed and seems ready for full-scale operations, it has not yet been incorporated into a full-scale plant.

RECOMMENDATIONS

7-65. The potential for reuse of wastewaters should occupy a prominent spot in future planning for overall water resources utilization.

7-66. The Commission believes that direct reuse of water for industrial purposes and that indirect reuse for purposes of human consumption will increase. Where feasible, such indirect reuse should be minimized by limiting wastewater reuse to processes that do not involve human consumption. This will have the effect of releasing for human consumption potable water now being used by industry. However, previously demonstrated successes in protection of public health in instances where municipal water supplies are derived from indirect reuse suggests that increases in such indirect reuse for human consumption should not be discouraged.

7-67. In regions where a high-quality source of water is used for irrigation of cropped fields or recreation turf areas such as golf courses and a source of treated municipal wastewater is available, arrangements for water exchange should be considered. Nutrient-rich municipal wastewater could be used for irrigation and exchanged for high-quality water which could be used for domestic and industrial use.

7-68. Direct reuse of water for human consumption should be deferred until it is demonstrated that virological and other possible contamination does not present a significant health hazard. Further knowledge on this subject is necessary, and the Commission endorses the research program recommended by the American Water Works Association, as follows:[191]

"1. Identify the full range of contaminants possibly present in treated wastewaters,

---

[191] AMERICAN WATER WORKS ASSOCIATION (October 1971). On the use of reclaimed wastewaters as a public water-supply source, AWWA policy statement. Journal American Water Works Association 63(10):609.

which might affect the safety of public health, the palatability of the water, and the range of concentrations.

"2. Determine the degree to which these contaminants are removed by various types and levels of treatment.

"3. Determine the long-range physiological effects of continued use of reclaimed wastewaters, with various levels of treatment, as the partial or sole source of drinking water.

"4. Define the parameters, testing procedures, analytical methodology, allowable limits, and monitoring systems that should be employed with respect to the use of reclaimed wastewaters for public water-supply purposes.

"5. Develop greater capability and reliability of treatment processes and equip-ment to produce reclaimed water of reasonably uniform quality, in view of the extreme variability in the characteristics of untreated wastewaters.

"6. Improve the capabilities of operational personnel."

The Commission also recommends that research focus on advanced treatment processes that incorporate or replace secondary treatment, on other methods of reducing the cost of advanced treatment, and on the practicability of installing and operating dual water supply systems—one for human consumption and the other for manufacturing purposes.

7-69. The net cost of treatment of water for reuse should be compared with the costs of such alternative sources of water as desalting and interbasin transfers before any such alternative is adopted.

Interbasin Transfers[1]

An interbasin transfer is one of many means of satisfying an increased demand for water in areas of limited supply. Physical transfer of water from one watershed to another has been a common means of augmenting supply. For example, part of New York City's municipal supply comes from the Delaware Basin, Denver's from the Colorado River Basin (across the Continental Divide), and Los Angeles's from the Great Basin, the Colorado Basin, and the Sacramento Basin. Similarly, agricultural water has been imported, for example, from the Colorado River Basin into the South Platte and Arkansas Basins in the State of Colorado. In California, the rivers flowing out of the Sierra Nevada have been rerouted to the more arid parts of the Central Valley. And part of the flow of the San Juan River in the Colorado Basin has been diverted to the Chama River, a tributary of the Rio Grande.

Proposals abound for more interbasin transfers in the future, on an even grander scale. A number of plans have been devised for transferring water from the Columbia River system in the Pacific Northwest to the Colorado River system in the Southwest. One such plan would transport 2.4 million acre-feet annually from the Snake River in Idaho at a cost estimated in 1963 at $1.4 billion;[2] another would divert 15 million acre-feet annually from the mainstream of the Columbia above The Dalles, at a cost of $12.8 billion in 1964 dollars.[3] The Texas Water Plan of 1968 would divert from the Mississippi and East Texas Rivers 17 million acre-feet for delivery as far west as New Mexico at an estimated cost in excess of $10 billion. An engineering consulting firm sketched out a plan in 1964 for tapping Alaskan and Canadian rivers of 110 million acre-feet annually for delivery to the Great Basin, Lake Superior, Texas, and Mexico, at a cost roughly estimated at $100 billion.

THE PROBLEM

The Commission's charge under the National Water Commission Act is to identify "alternative ways of meeting these [future water] requirements—giving consideration, among other things, to . . . interbasin transfers. . ."[4] The focus here is on large-scale, interstate, interbasin transfers in which the Federal Government has an interest both as manager of navigable waters and as potential financier, builder, and operator of the project.

By definition, an interbasin water transfer requires the physical transportation of water out of one river basin and into another. The water one area gains from an interbasin transfer, another area loses. Both the area of export and the area of import have something at stake.

Consider first the area of export. Since water is a precious natural resource and since it is difficult to foretell the quantity of water which may be put to

---

[1] This chapter is based in part on the following background studies prepared for the National Water Commission: FOX IK (1971). Some political aspects of the relationship between large scale interbasin water transfers and environmental quality, Ch. XXII in GOLDMAN, Charles R Environmental Quality and Water Development. National Technical Information Service, Springfield, Va., Accession No. PB 207 114. JOHNSON, Ralph W (1971). Law of Interbasin Transfers. National Technical Information Service, Springfield, Va., Accession No. PB 202 619. MANN, Dean E (1972). Interbasin Water Transfers, A Political and Institutional Analysis. National Technical Information Service, Springfield, Va., Accession No. PB 208 303.

~~~~~~~~~~~~~~~~~~~~~~~~~~~~~~~~

Friant-Kern Canal moves water from the Kings River Basin to the Kern River Basin

---

[2] About $2.1 billion in 1972 dollars.

[3] About $18.6 billion in 1972 dollars.

[4] *The National Water Commission Act,* P.L. 90-515, Section 3(a), September 26, 1968, 82 Stat. 868, 42 USCA 1962a note.

beneficial use in the future, areas with surplus waters today are understandably apprehensive about irrevocably committing their present surpluses for export to other areas.

Areas of water shortage, on the other hand, look with longing at areas with water surpluses where large amounts appear to flow more or less unused to the sea. The intensity of desire is amplified at the prospect that part of the expensive water transmission works required to effect interbasin transfers might be built by the Federal Government at the expense of the general taxpayer so that imported water can be delivered at prices below the costs of delivery.

With one area (the area of origin) alarmed about the possibilities of relinquishing a presently surplus but potentially useful supply of water and another area enthusiastic about relieving acute water shortages (perhaps at a price which fails to recover all costs), it is understandable why the topic of interbasin transfers generates passion and no small number of problems.

It is these problems—legal, economic, social, and environmental—to which this chapter addresses itself. To properly evaluate interbasin transfers it is necessary to examine the legal framework in which they may be undertaken, the ways of protecting areas of origin, the economics of such transfers, their social and environmental implications, the criteria which should be used to plan and evaluate them, and the institutional arrangements needed to insure that Congress, the ultimate decisionmaker, has before it accurate and unadorned facts as to the social and economic benefits and costs of proposed interbasin transfers.

DISCUSSION

Legal Framework

Under the Commerce Clause of the Constitution, Congress has the ultimate authority over the navigable streams of the Nation. It seems clear that congressional power extends to any body of water that would be considered a suitable source for an interstate, interbasin transfer. Congress has power both to forbid and to require a transfer. The power to prohibit has been clear at least since 1899 when the U.S. Supreme Court in *United States v. Rio Grande Dam and Irr. Co.*[5] upheld the 1890 Rivers and

Harbors Act,[6] which prohibited the creation of obstacles to the navigable capacity of waters subject to the jurisdiction of the United States. The power to order a transfer was confirmed in 1963 by *Arizona v. California*[7] in which the Supreme Court construed and held constitutional the Boulder Canyon Project Act[8] (under which Hoover Dam was built) to authorize the Secretary of the Interior to impound 30 million acre-feet of water and deliver it pursuant to contract on Federal terms irrespective of State law. Among other contracts upheld by the decision was that between the Secretary and the Metropolitan Water District of Southern California (which embraces the City of Los Angeles) providing for an interbasin transfer of Colorado River water.

It is true that the Supreme Court has not yet considered (for Congress has not yet authorized) a transfer from a river basin in one State to a different basin in another State where the source river does not cross or form the border of the two States. However, if Congress should authorize such a transfer, it is likely that the Supreme Court would uphold it, and would do so regardless of the lack of consent of the State of origin.[9]

The questions to be addressed, then, are not those of congressional power, of separation of powers of the legislative and judicial branches, or of distribution of power between the Federal Government and the States. The questions are only those of policy about *how*, if it has a mind to, Congress should exercise its power.

---

[5] *United States, v. Rio Grande Dam and Irr. Co.,* 174 U.S. 690 (1899).

[6] *Rivers and Harbors Appropriation Act of 1890,* September 19, 1890, c. 907 Section 10, 26 Stat. 426, 454, 33 USCA Section 403 note.

[7] *Arizona v. California,* 373 U.S. 546 (1963).

[8] *Act of December 21, 1928,* P.L. 642, 70th Congress, 45 Stat. 1057, as amended, 43 USCA 617.

[9] In commenting on the inapplicability of the Court-created doctrine of "equitable apportionment" in *Arizona v. California,* Mr. Justice Black stated: "It is true that the Court has used the doctrine of equitable apportionment to decide river controversies between States. But in those cases Congress had not made any statutory apportionment. In this case, we have decided that Congress has provided its own method for allocating among the Lower Basin States the mainstream water to which they are entitled under the Compact. Where Congress has so exercised its constitutional power over waters, courts have no power to substitute their own notions of an 'equitable apportionment' for the apportionment chosen by Congress." 373 U.S. at 565-66 (footnote omitted).

Social and Environmental Considerations

There is no difference in kind between interbasin transfers and any other water development project, so far as social, environmental, or economic values are concerned. But there is a difference in degree where the interbasin transfer is a large-scale project diverting water from one State to another. The investment is usually bigger, the effect on the environment is usually greater, and concern in the area of origin is usually more acute.

It is unlikely that any major interbasin transfer will be proposed that will require for its supply the condemnation of vested water rights (i.e., water which at present is legally diverted for private beneficial use). The cost of indemnification and political opposition will probably preclude it. But there are large volumes of water, not subject to private rights, serving purposes desired by the public— or at least parts of the public—which could be a practical source of supply for interbasin transfers. The public purposes served by these potentially transferable supplies include fish and game propagation, maintenance of ecological balance, water-based recreation, and scenic amenities.

The Commission recognizes and values efforts to quantify these public preferences but doubts that during the useful life of this report acceptable numbers can be developed. For the present and the foreseeable future, it appears that social preferences regarding water amenities will be expressed through the political process. Some seek to develop water resources; others seek to preserve water from being diverted, consumed, or degraded. These desires will be expressed in political action, as they have been in the past, and, as a result, some portion of the Nation's water resources will be precluded from developmental use.[10] The Commission does not presume to offer suggestions about how much water this should be. The people will decide that question through their elected representatives. It need only be noted that the ultimate authority resides in Congress, whose power over water is as broad as the Commerce Clause itself.

Thus, when the economic criteria that should govern an interbasin transfer are discussed in the next section, water which society has decided should be precluded from developmental activity is not considered. What is considered is water that remains

available for producing goods and services in the economic sector.

The political process has already produced substantive and procedural laws on environmental protection. Water quality legislation is an example of the former, the National Environmental Policy Act of the latter. Existing environmental policies and the Commission's recommendations for further environmental legislation, discussed in other chapters, are as fully applicable to interbasin transfers—no more and no less—as to other forms of water development, except for the admonition that the environmental evaluation of a major interbasin transfer should be prepared with special care in view of the potentially greater environmental impact implicit in development of larger projects.

Economic Considerations

The economics of interbasin transfers should be considered from both national and regional points of view. With respect to national economic development, the economic criteria which should govern planning and evaluation of interbasin transfers should be explored. With respect to regional economic development, an assessment should be made, among other things, of the use of interbasin transfers as a means of economic rescue for areas whose use of water is depleting underground supplies.

National Economic Development: Water resources are an important factor in economic production. Abundant water supplies of suitable quality are a vital component for much of the Nation's industrial and agricultural production. The central economic issue with respect to nonlabor resources, including water, is not only whether they are being fully employed but whether they are being employed in their most productive uses, where they can yield the greatest return to society.

Whether or not water resources are being allocated to their most productive uses and whether or not the allocation mechanism is sufficiently flexible as to be capable of adjustment to the most productive uses of tomorrow are important considerations.

Water differs from other resources in that to a large extent its allocation among different uses is made outside a market price system. Legal and administrative institutions, based more often than not on tradition rather than economic efficiency, play a basic role in water allocation. Therefore, public policy must be relied upon to be a major determinant in the flexible allocation of water resources to achieve

---

[10] For example, the *Wild and Scenic Rivers Act,* P.L. 90-542, October 2, 1968, 82 Stat. 906, as amended, 16 USCA 1271 *et seq.*

319

improved patterns of productive uses. Public incentive systems such as regulation, pricing, cost-sharing, and taxation can and do play important roles in this process.

Major interbasin transfers of water supplies are one potential means for moving water from low-value uses to more productive uses. From an economic standpoint it does not matter whether water is moved from one point in a basin to another or from one basin to another. In either event, what is sought is increased net productivity of water; that alone is the economic test to be satisfied.

The economic criteria for assessing interbasin transfer proposals with respect to their impact on national economic growth are no different from those which should be used to evaluate any other water resource project. Those criteria are simple to state but not always easy to apply. First, the interbasin transfer proposal should be the least-cost source of water supply to serve the purposes at hand. Second, the value of the water in its new uses should be greater than the value of water in its old uses plus the costs of transfer. In other words, benefits (appropriately reduced to reflect foregone future use in the area of origin) should exceed costs. Third, Congress as the decisionmaker should compare the anticipated net economic gain from a proposed transfer project with that of alternative investment opportunities by way of making judgments about priorities in public spending. In the case of interbasin transfers, adherence to these criteria is especially important because of the large sums of money involved.[11] Each criterion bears closer examination.

"Least-cost source of water supply," the first criterion, implies that the agency evaluating an interbasin transfer proposal should examine alternative sources of supply to serve the same purposes and calculate the costs thereof on the same basis that the interbasin transfer costs are calculated. This is called cost-effectiveness analysis. The benefits to be obtained are held fixed. The only question is to identify the least-cost way of securing those benefits. Limitations on construction agency authority (for example, lack of authority to manage ground water) should not restrict the evaluation. All alternative sources of water should be evaluated and compared. Costs of foregone future uses in the area of origin and the environmental costs should be included in the evalua-tion. Two basic points of the "least-cost alternative" criterion are that (1) the calculation of costs of alternatives should be made on one, uniform, consistent basis and (2) all social costs should be included in the evaluation.[12]

The second criterion requires that benefits exceed costs, that the value of the interbasin transfer water in the new uses in the importing region be greater than the value of the water in the old uses (including instream uses) in the exporting region, *plus* the costs of constructing and operating the transfer project. Applying this criterion may be difficult. Construction costs must be estimated, values of the new uses must be projected into an uncertain future, and values in the old uses often must be imputed, since most instream uses are not priced.

The Columbia River furnishes an example of the problem of imputed values: a single acre-foot of water in that stream could successively generate electric power, assimilate waste material, float commercial vessels and pleasure craft, support fish life, and provide scenic amenities. Placing accurate numerical figures on each use is difficult. Not all the estimated values will enjoy the same degree of precision. But precise or imprecise, difficult or easy, estimating such values is desirable in order to gain some intelligent notion of the full social costs and benefits of a proposed transfer. Failure to make such estimates means that project evaluators will not be taking into account the full consequences of a proposed project but will be proceeding instead on the basis of intuition (which may differ markedly from evaluator to evaluator).

The same problem exists on the receiving end of the transfer. Values must be imputed to nonpriced benefits. Moreover, benefits that are priced must be priced correctly. For example, it overstates benefits to base the value of additonal agricultural production on prices generated by Federal price support programs. Such prices are maintained high by substantial Federal farm subsidies. To remain effective, such subsidies would have to be increased further if more subsidized crops are produced. Furthermore, benefits must also be reduced by losses resulting from diminished production in other regions attributable to increased production in the importing region.

[11] BEATTIE, Bruce R et al. (1971). Economic Consequences of Interbasin Water Transfer, Technical Bulletin 116. Agricultural Experiment Station, Oregon State University, Corvallis, Ore.

[12] It is especially important in comparing costs to use the same rate of interest for all alternatives. See ECKSTEIN, Otto (1958). Water-Resource Development, The Economics of Project Evaluation. Harvard University Press, Cambridge, Mass. p. 242.

There is the further difficulty of long-term projections. Since any major transfer project may take a decade or longer to build and since projections of demand must precede evaluation of the proposal, it will not be uncommon for the demand projections for the first few years of water delivery to be based on a future 20 to 30 years distant. Projections of demand over the life of many projects may well be 100 years away. Forecasts for such distant time periods are unreliable. In just 11 years (between 1960 and 1971), demand projections for Feather River water by the Metropolitan Water District of Southern California were revised downward so substantially that what was estimated to be required by 1990 was later estimated as not required until 2020, 30 years further into the future. Meanwhile, an investment of nearly $2 billion is frozen into facilities that may not be fully used for 50 years.

The point should be emphasized that once a large-scale interbasin transfer is undertaken, a long-term commitment of large sums of capital to a relatively inflexible scheme of resource allocation is required. With changing consumer preferences, developing technology, and uncertain population growth and distribution, the Nation should proceed with extreme caution before entering upon such enterprises.

In addition to the imprecision of imputed values for unpriced uses and the unreliability of long-range projections, the period of time elapsing between authorization of large projects and their completion presents additional problems with respect to estimates of construction costs. Original estimates, on which project authorization is based, can become outdated. One reason is inflation, but if prices are rising more or less uniformly throughout the economy, this will not significantly affect cost-benefit analyses, since increases in costs should be more or less offset by increases in the value of benefits.

Other reasons are more significant. Because of shifts in supply or demand, real costs may increase without commensurate increase in project benefits. Moreover, modification in project design may occur between project authorization and construction. Whatever the reasons, the record on estimating project construction costs has not been good. For example, in 1937 the Bureau of Reclamation estimated the costs of the Colorado-Big Thompson interbasin transfer project at $44 million. When completed after World War II, the project cost was almost four times the original estimate—$161.6 million.[13]

To summarize the discussion of the second criterion: an interbasin transfer should produce benefits from the new uses of the water that exceed the losses from present and future foregone uses in the area of origin and that exceed the costs of the project as well. Applying this criterion may be difficult, because the foregone uses include both present and prospective uses whose value must often be simulated, since they are not priced. However, the difficulties in making these calculations can be avoided in those cases where the values of the new uses do not even exceed full construction, operation, and maintenance costs, plus interest. At least some—perhaps many—interbasin project proposals will not be able to meet that standard.

The third criterion proposes that Congress make a comparison between the net economic gain anticipated from the transfer project and the gain that might be realized from other investments. Consciously applying this criterion may be very difficult, for a vast array of alternative investment opportunities will exist. But this kind of comparison is done implicitly every time Congress appropriates money. It is desirable, therefore, that it be done consciously so that account is taken of the fact that other investment opportunities, and the net benefits associated therewith, are foregone if a transfer project is built.

The three economic criteria set out here are generally applicable to all investments—whether in water or other resources and whether by government or private firms. The difference comes in the means for generating the information necessary to apply the criteria. For example, in water resource development there are seldom arms-length transactions between willing buyers and willing sellers to establish the value of instream uses of water in an area of origin. Consequently, resort must be made to some technique for simulating the marketplace in order to

[13]HARTMAN, LM & SEASTONE, Don (1970). Water Transfers: Economic Efficiency and Alternative Institutions. Published for Resources for the Future, Inc., by The Johns Hopkins Press, Baltimore, Md. p. 48. The Bureau had contracted with the water users of the Colorado-Big Thompson project for their repayment of project costs on the basis of the original 1937 cost estimates. The beneficiary district agreed to repay one-half of the construction costs, without interest, up to a maximum of $25 million. Thus, at the maximum, the water users will pay about 15 percent of the actual project costs without interest, a far cry from the 50 percent project cost repayment from water users originally contemplated at the time of authorization. (Remaining reimbursable costs are to come from Missouri River Basin Project power revenues.)

estimate these nonpriced values. The difficulty of the task should not relieve project planners and evaluators from the obligation of applying all three criteria in developing and evaluating an interbasin transfer proposal.

Regional Economic Development: Obviously, at any point in time, the economic production of the Nation is the sum of the production of its constituent regions. However, economic development in one particular region may take place at the expense of growth in other regions. This may be in the national interest if, as a result, resources are more productively employed than formerly. It is possible, however, for economic gains in one region to be completely offset by losses in other regions. While such transfers of production may be in the interest of the benefited region, they contribute little or nothing to national economic growth.[14]

Any reallocation of water requires a comparison on a with and without basis which is not limited to the benefited area. In considering an interbasin transfer from Region A to Region B, it is important to evaluate the increased benefits that the water will generate in Region B together with the resulting disbenefits to Region A and to other regions as well.

It is clear with respect to agriculture, for example, that there is a national market with relatively limited potential for expanded exports. With the exception of a few high-value specialty crops, the expansion of production in one region will often be accompanied by offsets in production in other regions. This contributes to the national economy only if the new production is more efficient than the displaced production.

The current major interbasin transfer proposals appear to be designed primarily to serve one or more of the following objectives:

1. To preserve an agricultural economy or to expand agricultural production.
2. To ameliorate water quality problems.
3. To improve navigation and power production (Great Lakes).[15]

Each of these uses has a relatively low value per unit use of water. However, each use would presumably increase the competitive production advantages of the importing region in relation to, and in some cases at the expense of, other regions.

In many areas, economic growth has been based upon exploitation of a resource in fixed supply, such as minerals, virgin timber, or ground water. As the fixed supply diminishes, the economy involved has been compelled to adjust. In some parts of the West, for example, economic development has sometimes been based on ground water withdrawals that exceed recharge. As the ground water is depleted, new supplies must be imported, different economic activities found, or a significant proportion of the community must migrate to new locations. Such areas may be eager candidates for importation of water from interbasin transfers.[16]

The need for adjustment to changing conditions is pervasive throughout the economy and the ability to adjust at a reasonable rate is one of the strengths of the national economy. For example, the national average farm population decline in the 1960's was 4 percent annually,[17] forcing many rural communities to adapt their economy to a lower population. A similar gradual decline may be necessary in areas such as the high plains of Texas and New Mexico as ground water levels decline, unless efforts are successfully made to shift the economy, to the extent possible, to less water dependent activities. If an interbasin transfer project to serve this area meets the criteria discussed earlier, there is no reason why it should not be undertaken for the purpose of preserving the economy. If the criteria cannot be met, however, a region that is mining its ground water can slow down the rate of depletion and thus lengthen the period of adjustment, by restricting the amount of acreage (particularly new acreage) allowed to be irrigated from ground water sources and by adopting water pricing and other techniques which provide incentives for more efficient use of the ground water resource.[18]

There are, of course, numerous areas where depletion of an element essential to the local economy may make assistance of some sort necessary if social disruption and economic hardship and loss are to be

[14] See the discussion in Chapter 3 on the use of water to induce regional economic development.

[15] FOX, Irving K (1968). Some Political Aspects of Large Scale Interbasin Transfers, paper presented at the Annual Meeting of the American Association for the Advancement of Science, Dallas, Texas, December 30, 1968. Mimeo. p. 7.

[16] See Chapter 7, Section B, on Improving Ground Water Management.

[17] See U.S. DEPARTMENT OF AGRICULTURE (1971). Agricultural Statistics 1971. U.S. Government Printing Office, Washington, D.C. p. 454.

[18] Again see Chapter 7, Section B, on Improving Ground Water Management.

avoided. However, water programs are not always the best or cheapest assistance that can be rendered. In any event, Congress must, in each instance, determine whether there is a need for Federal assistance and, if there is, the amount and nature to be rendered.

Area-of-Origin Protection

Area-of-origin protection means provision of safeguards for areas exporting water. These safeguards may range from absolute prohibition of exports to pecuniary compensation, with a number of other protective devices in between. The definition of an area of origin varies considerably also, although reference to some type of hydrologic unit such as a river basin is fairly common.

Area-of-origin protection is peculiarly associated with water. Other resources are not similarly treated, probably because they are priced in conventional markets. For coal, oil, copper, timber, and other natural resources, the area of origin receives its "protection" in the form of taxes and revenues from the "export" of the resource. In the absence of a pricing system for the export of water, area-of-origin interests have resorted to the political process to obtain "in kind" protection, that is, enactment of laws reserving water for the area's "ultimate requirements" or providing for recapture in the event of future need. As a consequence of this approach, safeguards for a water exporting area have usually been tied to future or potential water development in the area.

Present Forms of Area-of-Origin Protection: The most pervasive form of area-of-origin protection was established by courts when they developed the riparian doctrine of water rights. Riparian water rights, characteristic of the Eastern States, protect landowners adjacent to lakes and streams from withdrawals or uses which unreasonably diminish water quantity or quality. Where diversions or uses have been unreasonable, they have either been enjoined or riparian owners adversely affected have been compensated for interference with their rights. The concern of riparian law has been one of protecting private, rather than public, rights in lakes and streams.

An early formulation forbade any use of water except on land contiguous to the stream, and in addition forbade use of water outside the watershed even though the parcel was contiguous to the stream but lay in two watersheds. This rule has since been undercut in some States by decisions that deny relief against transbasin diversions where the plaintiff riparian landowner cannot establish pecuniary damages. New York, however, has expanded the area-of-origin protection of riparian law in respect to transbasin diversions by the City of New York. A State statute provides that when the City takes water from a distant basin it must pay compensation not only for the value of the property, buildings, and equipment taken but also for all business losses and loss of income, both to riparians whose property is actually taken and to nearby nonriparians adversely affected.[19]

The western appropriation system has no such built-in protection for areas of origin. Under that system, the first person who diverts water from a stream and puts it to beneficial use acquires a legal right to continue such use, *regardless* of whether the use is inside or outside the basin of origin. Over the years some Western States have modified the prior appropriation doctrine by adopting statutory protections for areas of origin. California has been the scene of the most intense controversies, first during the Owens Valley dispute[20] in the early part of this century and later during the debate on the California State Water Project in the 1950's. One California area-of-origin statute prohibits the release of any State-appropriated water "necessary for the development of" a county of origin.[21] Another gives the watershed of origin a prior right in "all the water reasonably required to adequately supply the beneficial needs of the watershed."[22] Although this statute is said to provide a right of recapture, such right has never been exercised, and its effectiveness has been questioned.[23]

Colorado has a statute requiring contemporaneous construction of compensatory storage dams in the area of origin so that such area will be no worse off because of the diversion.[24] Some analysts charge that

[19] See *Van Etten v. City of New York,* 226 N.Y. 483, 124 N.E. 201 (1919). For a general discussion of the New York law see SAX, Joseph (1968). Water Law, Planning & Policy: Cases & Commentary. Bobbs-Merrill Company, Inc., New York.

[20] This experience is described in NADEAU, Remi A (1950). The Water Seekers. Doubleday & Company, Inc., Garden City, N.Y.; and in COOPER, Erwin (1968). Aqueduct Empire. Arthur H. Clark Co., Glendale, Cal.

[21] California Water Code, Sec. 10505 (West Supp. 1967).

[22] California Water Code, Sec. 11460 (West Supp. 1967); see also Secs. 11461, 11463.

[23] California Attorney General (1957). Report of the Attorney General's Committee of Water Lawyers on County of Origin Problems. State of California, Sacramento.

[24] Colorado Rev. Stat. Ann., Sec. 150-5-13(2)(d) (1963).

Ruedi Dam provides replacement storage for western slope below Fryingpan–Arkansas diversion

this requirement causes economic waste because the area of origin may not be prepared to use the compensatory storage for many years.[25] Texas prohibits its Water Development Board from planning a diversion of water from a basin of origin if the water will be needed to supply the reasonable future requirements of that region for the next 50 years.[26] An Oklahoma statute directs the State Water Resources Board to reserve to the area of origin sufficient water to take care of its present and reasonable future needs.[27]

States can also provide for the protection of areas of origin in interstate compacts. For example, in the Colorado River Compact the Upper Colorado River Basin States sought to reserve 7.5 million acre-feet of system water for future use.[28]

In recent years, when Congress was actively considering authorization of a study of a Columbia River diversion to the Southwest the area-of-origin protection issue emerged as a focal point of conflict and a variety of proposals were put forward to resolve it. After lengthy debates and numerous amendments, the following area-of-origin protections were incorporated in the Colorado River Basin Project (CRBP) Act of 1968:[29]

[25] See BEISE, CJ (June 1950). Compensatory storage. Rocky Mountain Law Review 22:453 [Now University of Colorado Law Review].

[26] Texas Water Code Annotated (Vernon) Sections 11.102. See also Sections 5.085(a), 5.085(b).

[27] H.J.R. No. 502, Title viii, [1957] Okla. Laws 670, referred to as a note in Oklahoma Rev. Code Ann. tit. 82 Sec. 1078 (1970).

[28] Colorado River Compact, Congressional Record 70:324 (1928), consented to by Congress in the *Boulder Canyon Project Act of 1928,* P.L. 642, 70th Congress, December 21, 1928, 45 Stat. 1057, 1064, 43 USCA 617.

[29] *Colorado River Basin Project Act,* P.L. 90-537, Section 203, September 30, 1968, 82 Stat. 885, 887, 43 USCA 1513.

1. "All requirements, present or future, for water . . . [in the area of origin] shall have a priority of right in perpetuity to the use of the waters of that river basin, for all purposes . . . "

2. Areas of origin would be given a financial guarantee, supported by a development fund, to assure a supply of water "adequate to satisfy their ultimate requirements at prices to users not adversely affected by the exportation . . . "

There may be less to these safeguards than meets the eye. Taking the protections in order, the first, alluding to water in the area of origin, has obvious uncertainties because of definitional problems. What is meant by present and future requirements? Is this phrase to be defined in physical or economic terms? How far into the "future" are extrapolations to be made? No criteria are provided for determining the requirements of the area of origin. Moreover, because this guarantee is statutory rather than constitutional, Congress can change its mind and convert this "perpetual" right into a temporary right. Before such a right in perpetuity could actually be exercised, further congressional action would be required. No Federal institutional machinery has been created to handle the administration of claims arising out of this right, leaving critical questions about implementation unanswered. How does an area of origin exercise its prior right? Who, other than Congress, could authorize a different use of the water? If Congress is the essential decisionmaker, is the right in perpetuity merely a right to petition Congress and plead a special case?

The second protection mentioned, a financial guarantee supported by a development fund, appears to be only slightly more workable. It must have adequate funding if it is to be even minimally effective, and the CRBP Act does not appear to provide that source of funding. Again, there is the problem of ambiguity. How much water is "adequate" to meet the area of origin's "ultimate requirement at prices to users not adversely affected by the exportation" of water to the Colorado River system? Does the word "ultimate" refer to time, to amount, or to both? How can anyone intelligently estimate at some distant future date what the price of a given unit of water might have been if no diversion had occurred?

The area-of-origin protections in the CRBP Act are deficient not only because of these ambiguities but also because no machinery has been provided to resolve the questions they pose. Would the States of origin decide or would Congress decide (1) whether ultimate requirements are being adequately met and (2) what the price of water would have been if no diversion had occurred? Who initiates inquiries into these questions? What if no price for the water is involved, but instead the people of the States of origin believe they are losing potential recreational or wildlife uses, which are generally not priced?

An earlier version of the CRBP also included a so-called "veto" provision, whereby a State of origin would have the power to bar the Secretary of the Interior from transmitting a favorable recommendation on a given project to Congress unless the exporting State approved the project. This veto provision was little more than a structured way of allowing the area-of-origin States to voice their opposition to a given project. Disapproval of the project by one or more area-of-origin States could not stop Congress from authorizing the project, nor could it prevent the Secretary from transmitting the plan to Congress. It would only stop him from stamping his formal approval on the project when transmitting it to Congress.

In summary, it is the Commission's conclusion that the "in kind" type of area-of-origin protection exemplified by the State and Federal legislation just discussed is unworkable and that other means should be explored.

Economic and Political Analysis: Earlier it was recommended that an interbasin transfer should be approved only if (a) the transfer is the least-cost source of water supply, (b) the value of the water in its new uses will be greater than the value of the water in its old uses plus the transporting costs, and (c) the net productivity of the transfer has been compared with that of alternative investment opportunities. If these criteria are satisfied, an interbasin transfer will necessarily add to the national economy. On the other hand, area-of-origin protection of the historic "in kind" type would often inhibit national economic growth. For example, a right in the area of origin to recapture water in the future would (if the importer believes the right will be enforced) deter investment in transbasin transfer facilities, because of the insecurity of future supply. A right in the area of origin to restrict exports to "surplus" water (defined as that in excess of ultimate future requirements) may make a sub-optimal quantity of water available for transfer.

The Commission believes that cash payments to the area of origin may prove to be the most effective means of protection. From the standpoint of efficient resource allocation alone, however, compensation is not required to be paid to the area of origin either for vested rights or for instream uses not the subject of vested rights, since by hypothesis the new uses in the importing region are more valuable than the old instream uses in the area of origin. Compensation or other protection for the area of origin is nevertheless desirable. The Nation's political and economic system is based on private ownership of property. The Constitution forbids legislation seeking to effect uncompensated transfers of private property from one group to another. In the private sector of the economy, a firm that believes it has a more valuable use for a resource than the present user must buy the resource.

It is true, however, that the water that will ordinarily be the subject of an interbasin transfer proposal is not "owned" in the conventional sense and accordingly is not capable of being sold. Interbasin transfer proposals in the West deal principally with unappropriated water. Both the Federal and the State governments have legislative power over the resource, but neither is an owner in the traditional sense empowered to make a conventional sale. Theoretically the Congress could order an out-of-State transfer of unappropriated water without incurring liability under the fifth amendment, but the theory collides with the political fact that the area of origin has a congressional delegation that must be overridden before the transfer can be authorized. As a practical matter, the United States and the State of origin must come to terms with each other. If the water to be transferred is from an interstate stream, the situation is more complex. Each State has a right to an "equitable share" that can be quantified only by adjudication, by interstate compact, or by congressional action. If protracted litigation is to be avoided, the States of the basin must also come to terms with each other as well as with the United States.

The situation in the East, where the riparian system of law prevails, is also complicated, partly for the same reasons and partly for different ones. The questions of interstate stream rights and of Federal-State relations are the same. In addition, there is the question of the property rights of riparian proprietors: Does every landowner along a stream have a legal cause of action for a transbasin diversion, so that either he must consent or the right must be condemned? If only those riparian owners who will be damaged by the transfer have a cause of action, how

is damage to be determined and how will the costs of transfer be determined in advance of construction and operation of the project?

In view of these legal and political constraints, is it possible to effectuate an economically sound interbasin transfer and yet avoid uneconomic "in kind" area-of-origin protection? The Commission believes that it is, by providing means for compensating the area of origin for its losses. Two institutional devices for arranging an interstate, interbasin transfer and concomitant protection of the area of origin are suggested. The first is the Federal-interstate compact. In this kind of arrangement the exporting States and the importing States could agree on the volume of water to be transferred, the compensation to be paid, and the apportionment of the compensation among the exporting States if more than one is affected. The Federal Government should be a party to the compact for it will nearly always have its navigation interest to protect and will often have other interests such as power production, irrigation projects, and reserved rights to look after.

The Commission has considered urging on Congress the adoption of a statement of policy that no interstate, interbasin transfer will be considered prior to an agreement among the affected States by compact. The Commission has concluded against the recommendation. In the first place, Federal claims must be resolved before any interstate, interbasin transfer can be agreed upon. The Congress has the ultimate authority to resolve these claims. Thus, to say to the States that they must reach compact agreement before coming to Congress is to require them to bargain in the dark. Secondly, even if a compact bargain is achieved, it may have to be renegotiated when the compact comes on for approval by the Congress. Not only are the previously mentioned Federal claims subject to congressional review but also the question of Federal financing must be settled, and the financial arrangements determined by Congress are likely to affect the bargain made by the States. Lastly, requiring compact agreement before an interbasin transfer is proposed to Congress gives any State in the area of origin a veto over the transfer. Yet some transfers may deserve authorization because they contribute to national economic development; one State should not be permitted to block such development.

The discussion above is not intended to denigrate interstate compacts. It is desirable for exporting States and importing States to resolve their differences in advance of congressional consideration of an interbasin transfer, so far as they are able to do so. But experience leads the Commission to believe that many issues will have to be negotiated in and resolved by Congress,[30] and accordingly it does not recommend compact agreement as an essential prerequisite to congressional consideration of interbasin transfer proposals.

Instead, the Commission recommends a second institutional device, a procedure for framing the issues in a debate on compensation. The agency charged with evaluating interbasin transfer proposals is required, under the economic criteria established earlier, to determine the value of the area-of-origin uses to be curtailed by the transfer. This determination should be transmitted to the area of origin and to the importing area for comment. After an appropriate period of time, the agency determinations (as revised in the light of the comments), and such reports and data as the affected areas care to submit, should be forwarded to Congress for its consideration. The Congress would make the final determination of the dollar amount of the opportunity losses that will be suffered by the area of origin because of the interbasin transfer. This amount of money would be paid to the area of origin *as part of the project costs;* the Federal Government would make the payments either as the losses occurred or in a single lump-sum, present-worth payment and would recover the costs from the importing entity, as part of total, true project costs.[31]

Obviously, a mighty contention would arise in Congress over the dollar amount of the area of origin's losses, and the figure adopted would likely be a compromise reflecting the political power of the contending forces. But that is precisely what will occur in any contest over an interbasin transfer; the difference under this proposal is that Congress will be debating an appropriate issue, namely, the compensation the area of origin ought to receive for its prospective losses. Instead of focusing the political contest on such imponderable questions as "ultimate requirements" and rights to recapture (how much and when), the contest will be centered on the economically sound question, how much should the area of origin be compensated for giving up a portion of its water resource.

In fixing the amount of compensation the area of origin is to receive, Congress will also have to decide how the compensation is to be divided where two or more States occupy the area of origin. Once again, this settlement will represent a political compromise but the study evaluating the project will provide information on the net losses to be suffered by each State (or portions thereof) in the area of origin. Such information should serve at least as the starting point of debate. As to the division of payments within each State, while Congress may have constitutional power to determine the allocation, it is preferable to award the compensation to the State and leave it to the State legislature to make an allocation, if it chooses.

The proposals made here may appear on first reading to be naive. But it should be recalled that major development of any interstate stream requires a political determination of which State is to receive what benefits. The Colorado River Storage Project Act is an excellent example.[32] While the five States of the Upper Colorado River Basin—Arizona, Colorado, New Mexico, Utah, and Wyoming—reached agreement by compact apportioning the stream, it was Congress which apportioned the Federal benefits by deciding on the location of projects and their magnitude. Similarly, the Colorado River Basin Project Act of 1968 was principally concerned with the authorization of the $1 billion Central Arizona Project, but the Act also authorized seven more projects on the Colorado River and its tributaries in Utah, New Mexico, and Colorado.[33] Even with unrealistically low interest rates, these projects had benefit-cost ratios, as calculated by the Bureau of Reclamation, barely in excess of unity; that is, they were hardly economically feasible.

The point the Commission seeks to make is neither naive nor cynical. The political process of the United States produces bargaining between interest groups on the distribution of Federal funds. Water projects are one example of the operation of this process. Any

---

[30] A major interbasin transfer, from the Colorado River to Los Angeles, contributed to a water allocation controversy between Arizona and California that had to be resolved by Congress. California claimed the right to take 4.6 million acre-feet from the River; Arizona contended that California should be limited to 4.2 million acre-feet. The two States could not agree and the Boulder Canyon Project was held up for 6 years until Congress resolved the dispute by fixing the California limitation at 4.4 million acre-feet. See *Arizona v. California,* 373 U.S. 546 (1963).

[31] In accordance with the Conclusions and Recommendations of Chapter 15, the Commission believes that beneficiaries of interbasin transfers should pay the full costs of the projects.

[32] *Colorado River Storage Project Act,* P.L. 485, 84th Congress, April 11, 1956, 70 Stat. 105, 43 USCA 620 *et seq.*

[33] *Colorado River Basin Project Act,* P.L. 90-537, September 30, 1968, 82 Stat. 885, 43 USCA 1501 *et seq.*

interbasin transfer proposal will be the occasion for such bargaining. The Commission's recommendation seeks to direct the bargaining away from area-of-origin protection of the "in kind" and "compensating-storage" type toward consideration of the question that would dominate the decision in a private transaction: what is the water worth to the seller and what is it worth to the buyer?

The analogy of interstate, interbasin transfers to private sales transactions is by no means perfect and may be thought to be too far removed from reality to be useful. After all, the seller-State may not calculate gain as a private seller would. The buyer-State may distribute the benefits and burdens of the project in such a manner that a citizen would view the project differently as a voter than he would as a private buyer. And the price is not the result of arms-length bargaining between the parties; in the end, it is imposed by an outsider, the Congress. Nevertheless, if it is conceded that some time, some place, an interbasin transfer proposal is in the national interest because national economic productivity is thereby enhanced, and if it is further conceded that the decision will be the product of the political process as it operates in Congress, it seems desirable to focus the attention of decisionmakers on the correct issues of economic policy inherent in interbasin transfer proposals.

Relation of Economic Criteria to Area-of-Origin Compensation: To recapitulate, the Commission recommends here and elsewhere in this report that all water resource projects be planned and evaluated in accordance with three economic criteria: (1) that the project be the least-cost alternative; (2) that it produce benefits in the new uses greater than the sum of the costs of construction, operation, and maintenance, and, in the case of interbasin transfers, the net opportunity costs of foregone uses in the area of origin, all discounted to a common time basis; and (3) that the net productivity of the project be compared to that of alternative investment opportunities.

The Commission also recommends that the direct beneficiaries of a project pay the full costs of the project, which include not only the construction, operation, and maintenance costs plus interest at market rates prevailing at the time of construction, but also, in the case of interbasin transfers, the net losses suffered by the area of origin because of the export of water.

Ordinarily, the importing State or States would be the principal—and sometimes the exclusive—beneficiaries of a Federal interbasin transfer project. Even for benefits such as fish and game, recreation, and scenic beauty, the States in which the benefits are generated should be required to repay their share of costs. The Federal Government should be required to assume nonreimbursable costs only when benefits cannot be allocated to individual States. In the Commission's view, most benefits would be assignable to States or subdivisions thereof and hence most costs would be reimbursable.

The Commission believes that importing States, in turn, should not confer inappropriate State subsidies on ultimate direct beneficiaries. Instead, wherever practicable, individual beneficiaries should be assessed in proportion to the project costs attributable to each. A beneficiary located at a high elevation far from the project water source where additional project pumping costs would be required to deliver water should pay more than a beneficiary located closer at lower elevations. Failure to assess costs in this fashion will lead to inefficient allocation of the water resource.

It might be questioned whether both sets of requirements are necessary. If the beneficiaries pay the full costs of the transfer, why require the planning and evaluating agencies to apply the three economic criteria recommended here? The answer lies in the fact that an interstate, interbasin transfer is not the result of an arms-length bargain between two parties who generate their own information as to benefits and costs. Such a transfer results from the action of a third party, the United States, which plans, authorizes, constructs, and operates the project. The agencies that generate the data on which the repayment obligations are based must have standards for planning projects and computing benefit and cost data. Those standards should embrace sound economic principles no matter who pays the project costs.

Similarly, repayment of total project costs by the beneficiaries should be required even though the economic criteria are satisfied and the project would appear to contribute to national economic development. This conclusion is based on two reasons: First, beneficiaries of public works programs aimed at increasing production should, as a matter of equity, pay the costs of the project unless some compelling social purpose justified their receiving a subsidy. Second, requiring beneficiaries to pay provides an additional check on the accuracy of benefit and cost

San Luis Canal facilitates interbasin transfer of water on California Water Project

figures obtained by indirect simulation of the marketplace. Project beneficiaries will not be willing to pay for fictitious benefits and there is little incentive to claim unrealistically low costs for a project when its direct beneficiaries will be obliged to pay for the actual costs that materialize.

For these reasons, the Commission recommends (1) that planning and evaluating agencies be instructed to adhere to the economic criteria set forth here *and* (2) that beneficiaries be required to pay the full costs of interbasin transfers.

Institutional Arrangements

The preceding discussion sets forth criteria for evaluating an interbasin transfer proposal. Congress will, of course, make the ultimate decision on authorizing any proposed project, but Congress will need assistance in the preparation and interpretation of information relating to satisfaction of the criteria.

The Commission recommends in Chapter 11 that federally funded water development proposals in general be subjected to review by an independent Board of Review. There is no reason to treat interbasin water transfers differently. The Board of Review will have a full understanding of the economic criteria set forth for evaluating interbasin transfers and will be expert in analyzing the data submitted by construction agencies and others in satisfaction of the criteria, since the process is the same for all water development projects, whether or not they involve transfers from one basin to another.

CONCLUSIONS

Proposals for physical transfers of water from one watershed to another abound. As economic demand for water increases, as available water supplies in areas of shortage shrink, as technological capability improves, and as national income grows, the feasibility

329

of interbasin transfers increases and the scale of proposals grows larger.

Congress has the power either to prohibit or to require an interstate, interbasin transfer. The ultimate decisions as to criteria for design, construction, review, benefited areas, repayment, protection for areas of origin, environmental safeguards, and other aspects of such interbasin transfers are all Congress's to make.

Sound economic criteria should govern the disposition of water which is available for economically useful purposes. The Commission concludes that proposed interbasin transfers should be planned and evaluated in accordance with three economic criteria.

First, a proposed project should be the least-cost way of securing a given supply of water. Second, the benefits generated by the transfer in the receiving area should exceed the full costs of the transfer *plus* the net benefits which that same water would have generated in the area of origin.[34] And third, the net productivity of the project should be compared to that of alternative investment opportunities.

Direct beneficiaries of an interbasin transfer who can be identified and reached should ordinarily be obligated to repay with interest the full project costs allocable to the purposes from which they benefit, including compensation to the area of origin for the costs of foregone opportunities occasioned by the water transfer. If these economic standards and repayment criteria are met, interbasin transfers will make an optimum contribution to the Nation's economic well-being; water will be employed in its most productive uses and the cause of economic efficiency will be served.

In computing benefits of an interbasin transfer, consideration should be given not only to the foregone opportunities which will be suffered in the exporting area, but to resulting offsets in other regions as well. If an interbasin transfer increases production in an importing area which, in turn, results in reduced production elsewhere in the Nation or requires larger farm subsidies than would otherwise have to be paid, net benefits will be reduced and the feasibility of many proposed interbasin transfers will be lessened.

Unless it is economically feasible, interbasin transfers should not be undertaken to rescue areas which are mining ground water, that is, which are depleting ground water reserves by pumping in excess of recharge.

In the final analysis, it is Congress which must exercise decisionmaking responsibilities with respect to interbasin transfers. The economic criteria which the Commission advances cannot and should not be binding on Congress. They are intended only to assist Congress in making its decisions. Congress can, if it chooses, reject interbasin transfers that appear sound and authorize transfers that do not. Whatever it does, however, Congress should have available to it project evaluations based on the criteria recommended here so that the decisions it makes will be made with full awareness of the social and economic consequences.

Because there is no market mechanism for pricing the export of water resources from one basin to another, some means must be devised to protect areas of origin from losses they may suffer as a result of water exports. The Commission concludes that "in kind" area-of-origin protections which limit exports to "surplus" waters, or seek compensating storage, or provide for recapture, or attempt to predict "ultimate requirements," "adequate supply to meet beneficial needs," and other equally ethereal concepts, are inappropriate. Such "in kind" protections are certain to produce excessive and unnecessary controversy and, even worse, they are likely to produce bad economic results as well. The Commission concludes that area-of-origin protection should be based on the anticipated losses suffered by the exporting region. The debate on area-of-origin protection which will accompany consideration of any major interbasin transfer should focus on compensating the area of origin for losses resulting from the transfer. The indemnification which is fixed as appropriate com-

---

[34] Economic evaluation requires that benefits from potential uses, as well as from existing uses, in the area of origin be compared to benefits from the new uses in the receiving area. In practice, such a comparison will often be difficult. But where there are prospective uses in the area of origin of a concrete nature and with a near-term prospect, the net benefits from such prospective uses should be added to the equation; that is, benefits in the receiving area should be greater than project costs plus net benefits from such prospective uses in the area of origin.

To illustrate, suppose a proposed interbasin transfer project will generate $10 million of annual benefits in the receiving area. To build and operate the works necessary to transfer the water to its users will cost $8 million annually. Additionally, the transfer will preclude development of a project in the area of origin which would have annual benefits of $4 million and annual costs of $3 million. Under the rule established here, the proposed transfer would be judged economically feasible since the benefits in the receiving area ($10 million) exceed both the costs of the transfer ($8 million) and the net benefits foregone in the area of origin ($4 million - $3 million = $1 million). In other words, $10 million > $8 million + $1 million; therefore, the project is feasible.

330

pensation to areas of origin should properly be included in project costs and be subject to full recovery from beneficiaries the same as other project costs.

Finally, the Commission concludes that existing institutional arrangements for development of water projects in general and interbasin transfers in particular are unsatisfactory. At present, the Federal agencies responsible for the design, construction, and operation of water resource projects, primarily the Corps of Engineers and the Bureau of Reclamation, are also responsible for evaluating those projects. Questions about the objectivity of the evaluation necessarily arise, for the appearance of impartiality is lacking, whatever the facts may be.

The Commission sees no reason why water resources planning functions now vested with the design and construction agencies and with other planning entities should not remain where they are. What is desired is to separate project evaluation, on the one hand, from planning, design, construction, and operation, on the other, so that Congress and the public can have the benefit of impartial evaluations. The Commission concludes that the best way to do this is to vest the project evaluation function in the hands of an independent Board of Review. If this is done, existing legislation prohibiting the study of interbasin transfers can properly be repealed.

RECOMMENDATIONS

8-1.   As part of an act repealing existing laws which prohibit the study of interbasin transfers, Congress should declare the following economic criteria to be applicable to the planning and evaluation of interbasin transfer proposals by Federal agencies:

a.   An interbasin transfer proposal should be the least-cost source of water supply to serve a given purpose, and all feasible alternative sources of supply should be examined and evaluated on the same basis. In comparing alternatives, due attention should be given to projected technological developments.

b.   The value of the water in the new uses should exceed the aggregate of the value of the water in the uses to which it would have been put had it not been exported, plus the costs of constructing and operating the interbasin transfer project.

c.   The net economic gains anticipated to accrue from the transfer project should be stated and compared to the gains that might be expected to accrue from alternative investment opportunities.

d.   An increase in regional economic development attributable to a proposed interbasin transfer should not alone serve to justify the proposal. The project should result in national economic development, that is, in net economic gains in benefited areas which more than offset resulting net economic losses in other areas of the country.

8-2.   Directly affected States should seek to reach agreement among themselves and with the Federal Government by Federal-interstate compact prior to submitting an interstate, interbasin transfer proposal to Congress.

8-3.   It should be the national policy to require the direct beneficiaries who are identifiable to pay the full reimbursable costs of an interstate, interbasin transfer project, including compensation to the area of origin for the present worth of the net benefits foregone as a result of the export of water. To effectuate this policy, Congress should enact legislation which embraces the following principles:

a.   The beneficiaries of a project should pay the total reimbursable costs of construction as those costs ultimately materialize, plus the reimbursable operation and maintenance costs. The repayment period should not exceed the economic life of the project works, and interest should be charged on the unrepaid investment at a rate not lower than the cost to the Federal Government of long-term borrowing at the time of construction. Some project costs, such as costs of construction in and compensation to the area of origin, should be allocated among benefited State and local governments in proportion to the benefits each receives. Other project costs, such as costs of canals, aqueducts and pumping in receiving areas, should be allocated to each benefited State and local government in proportion to the actual expenses incurred in bringing water to each (i.e., areas farthest from the area of origin or at higher elevations requiring additonal pumping should be obliged to bear a proportionately greater share of such costs). In turn,

Flatiron penstocks, Colorado-Big Thompson interbasin transfer

benefited State and local governments should assess individual direct beneficiaries in proportion to the project costs attributable to each. Since benefited localities can be easily identified it is expected that virtually all costs of an interstate, interbasin transfer will be reimbursable. Costs should be deemed nonreimbursable only when they cannot be properly assigned to States or subdivisions thereof.

b. Areas of origin should receive monetary compensation for net losses incurred as a result of the transfer. The amount of such compensation will be determined by Congress after consideration of estimates furnished by the area of origin, the beneficiaries of the project, and the Federal agencies involved in the planning and evaluation of the project. Direct beneficiaries of the project who are identifiable should be required to pay their share of these costs as part of the reimbursable costs of the project.

8-4. Evaluation of an interstate, interbasin transfer proposal in accordance with the criteria set forth here should be the responsibility of the independent Board of Review recommended in Chapter 11, Section B.

8-5. All interbasin transfer proposals should be carefully evaluated in accordance with environmental legislation in force at the time the proposal is made.

Means of Increasing
Water Supply

In the past, studies of water supply have been directed almost exclusively at controlling and distributing the existing streamflow or ground water supply to increase its utility and make it available to serve the growing demands for water in a particular region. In some areas, however, control of the existing supply has been pushed to or near the physical limit and pressures are building for works to transfer water from one river basin to another. Perhaps in recognition of these pressures and in the belief that there may be alternatives which could delay or eliminate the necessity for such transfers, the National Water Commission Act specifically directs the National Water Commission to consider alternative ways of meeting future water requirements, including those which might come about through technical advances.

In compliance with its legislative mandate, the Commission undertook two types of studies. The first was a detailed state-of-the-art examination of three specific possible means of increasing water supply for which research and development is fairly well advanced. These are desalting, precipitation augmentation, and land management. These three technologies are discussed in detail in the next three sections of this chapter. The second was an overview of potential future technological advances including those which would have the effect of increasing water supply. The results of the overview analysis dealing with potential means of increasing water supply are presented in Section E of this chapter.

INCREASING WATER SUPPLY BY DESALTING[1]

Sea water, which has a concentration of 35,000 parts per million (p.p.m.) of dissolved solids, and brackish water, which contains much less dissolved solids than sea water but which still is too concentrated for drinking or irrigation, are found in or near many places where fresh water supplies are limited but in great demand. Until recently, however, it was not technically feasible to convert meaningful amounts of sea water or brackish water into fresh water. But some 20 years of research and development, largely financed by the Federal Government, has greatly changed that picture. Today, the technology for large-scale desalting is at hand. What remains unsolved, however, at least in many areas of potential application, is economic feasibility.

In view of the investment which has been made in desalting research and development and of the obligation to consider alternative means of meeting future water requirements, the Commission has sought to ascertain to what extent in the future the Nation will be able to depend upon desalting as a source of water supply.

To appraise the likely future role of desalting, the Commission arranged for a state-of-the-art analysis. The analysis was directed toward appraising how close the Nation is to financially feasible desalting, considering present costs and possibilities for future cost reductions; the probable future markets for desalted water in view of the indicated costs of production; and the effect of noneconomic problems associated with desalting, such as adverse environmental impact. Finally, desalting was weighed in a general way against the alternative means of increasing water supplies.

State of the Art[2]

After 20 years of research, the mechanics of the most important desalting processes are reasonably

---

[1] This section is based largely on KOELZER, Victor A (1972). Desalting, prepared for the National Water Commission. National Technical Information Service, Springfield, Va. Accession No. PB 209 942.

~~~~~~~~~~~~~~~~~~~~~~~~~~~~~~~~~

Multistage flash distillation plant at Freeport, Texas

[2] This section includes information taken from U.S. OFFICE OF SALINE WATER (1971). Desalting Plants Inventory Report No. 3. Office of Saline Water, Washington, D.C., and O'MEARA JW (February 4, 1972). Statement of J.W. O'Meara, Director, Office of Saline Water, U.S. Department of the Interior, before the House Subcommittee on Irrigation and Reclamation. Mimeo, Office of Saline Water, Washington, D.C.

well understood. Worldwide use of desalting in small-sized plants in selected situations is fairly extensive. But the capacity of desalting plants is expanding rapidly, at a rate of 18 percent per year for the 10-year period 1961-1971. In 1970, 33 plants were placed in operation throughout the world, with a combined capacity of 59.7 million gallons per day (m.g.d.) and an average capacity of 1.8 m.g.d. The existing installations in the world, as of January 1, 1971, were as follows:

Process	No. of Plants[a]	World Plant Capacity (m.g.d.)	Percent of World Capacity
Distillation	688	290.4	95.5
Crystallization	3	0.3	0.1
Membrane	54	13.6	4.4
Total	745	304.3	100.0

[a]Of these, 64 had a capacity of 1 m.g.d. or more.

The U.S. and its territories had a total of 321 plants each having a capacity of 25,000 gallons per day (g.p.d.) or more, with a total combined capability of 54.8 m.g.d. The largest plant in operation anywhere in the world has a capacity of 30 m.g.d. It is the plant in Kuwait which began operating in 1972. A plant of this size is sufficient to supply municipal and industrial water for a population of 150,000 (assuming water requirements of 200 gallons per capita per day). The next largest is a 7.65 m.g.d. plant located at Terneuzen, Netherlands. A contract has been awarded for a 48 m.g.d. distillation plant in Hong Kong. The largest desalting plant in the U.S. is located in Key West, Florida. It has a capacity of 2.6 m.g.d. A sea water distillation module capable of producing 3 m.g.d. is now under construction in California's Orange County. Since January 1971, the estimated additional capacity placed in operation or under contract would increase the world total to about 440 m.g.d. Of this total, 14 m.g.d. is by the electrodialysis process, 12 m.g.d. is by reverse osmosis, and the rest is by distillation.[3]

Plants outside the U.S. are located primarily in the Middle East (Kuwait, Israel, and Saudi Arabia), the Caribbean, Latin America, and Europe (Netherlands, Spain, and the USSR). Much of present and future installed capacity is or will be sited outside the U.S.

A variety of processes are used in desalting.[4] As indicated above, distillation processes furnish most (nearly 95 percent) of the existing world capacity. About two-thirds of the capacity of the distillation plants use the multistage flash (MSF) process. However, about half of the distillation plants (mostly smaller plants representing only a small fraction of total capacity) utilize the now obsolete submerged-tube distillation process.

Currently, distillation is used almost exclusively for desalting sea water. Membrane processes, on the other hand, are used only for desalting brackish water, although recent research has indicated promise for application of the membrane process to desalting sea water as well. Crystallization processes, primarily freezing, probably are limited to small plants of 5 m.g.d. or less.

Extensive study has been made of dual-purpose plants (in which heat is used both for power generation and for desalting). The conceptual technology of dual-purpose nuclear plants has had considerable attention and appears to be sound. However, the only dual-purpose plants that have been built—a 2.5 m.g.d. plant at St. Thomas in the Virgin Islands, a 5 m.g.d. plant at Jidda, Saudi Arabia,[5] and the 7.5 m.g.d. plant at Rosarito Beach (Tijuana), Mexico[6]—are not large enough to demonstrate large-plant feasibility.

Costs of Desalting

Desalting costs have been significantly reduced in recent years. In 1952, when the U.S. Office of Saline Water (OSW) was established, the costs of desalting water in a few land-based plants ranged upward from $7 per 1,000 gallons in terms of current dollars.[7] Costs have now been reduced to about $1.00 per 1,000 gallons in sea water conversion plants and about 50 cents per 1,000 gallons in brackish water plants. Costs quoted for desalted water usually are at

---

[3] Data based on communication with the U.S. Office of Saline Water, Washington, D.C. (October 1972).

[4] Descriptions of desalting processes are included in a report by the Office of Saline Water. See U.S. OFFICE OF SALINE WATER (1968). The A-B-Seas of Desalting. U.S. Government Printing Office, Washington, D.C.

[5] U.S. OFFICE OF SALINE WATER (1972). Saline Water Conversion Summary Report, 1971-1972. U.S. Government Printing Office, Washington, D.C. p. 5.

[6] U.S. OFFICE OF SALINE WATER (1970). Desalting Plants Inventory Report No. 3. U.S. Government Printing Office, Washington, D.C. p. 11.

[7] U.S. OFFICE OF SALINE WATER (1972). Saline Water Conversion Summary Report 1971-1972. U.S. Government Printing Office, Washington, D.C. p. 1.

the plant boundary. Since most plants are at or near sea level, additional costs may be necessary for pumping to the place of use. At present, long-range projected desalting costs are on the order of 25-35 cents per 1,000 gallons at the plant (based on 1972 dollars) for large sea water desalting plants and less for brackish water plants.[8] The considerable spread between present costs and this goal emphasizes the fact that economic feasibility of desalting for many applications has not yet been proven and that efforts to reduce costs relative to alternative sources must be continued if desalting is to become a significant source of water supply. Many of the low prices that have been quoted for future desalting assume low interest rates, dual-purpose technology, large plants, and/or negligible brine disposal costs. The rapidly rising cost of energy will be a severely negative influence in achieving reductions in the cost of desalting.

Possibilities for Cost Reduction

Through Improved Desalting Technology: Advancements in desalting technology will take place, but unless and until a basic breakthrough occurs, totally unforeseen today, they are apt to be limited to gradual design improvements. The development of a longer-lived and more effective membrane for reverse osmosis particularly seems to offer the prospect of a large reduction in costs. Recent progress on the reverse osmosis process for both brackish and sea water applications has been highly encouraging.[9]

Through Reduction in Cost of Energy: While the energy requirements of the various processes differ rather widely, all desalting techniques require relatively large quantities of energy. With the exception of solar processes (which are not highly promising for installations of appreciable size), this energy must be supplied either by steam or by electricity. Among other factors, the minimum energy requirement depends on the salinity of the water to be treated. Lower salinity waters—up to 10,000 p.p.m.—are amenable to desalting with one of the membrane processes. Reverse osmosis and electrodialysis may be operated at very low energy consumption by operating at low pressure on the one hand or low current density on the other. Such operation, however, would sacrifice plant output and thus would involve a tradeoff of capital investment (the desalting facility) for low energy consumption.

Higher salinity waters—10,000 to 50,000 p.p.m.—can be desalted by one of the distillation processes. Tradeoff of capital investment for low energy consumption is also possible. That is, high efficiency plants—the Clair Engle demonstration plant at Chula Vista, California, for example—require heavy capital investment for construction of additional heat recovery stages. Energy usage at this plant is about 40 times the theoretical minimum (2.65 kw.-hr. per 1,000 gallons). Thus, if the energy rate is 5 mills per kw.-hr. the energy costs alone would still be about 13 cents per 1,000 gallons, or $43 per acre-foot. To this, of course, must be added the annual debt service on the capital cost of the desalting plant, as well as operating and maintenance costs, which together presently represent about 50 percent of production costs in most plants.

The implications of high energy use and resultant cost are evident. (The relationship between cost and demand for desalting is suggested in the subsequent discussion of markets for desalting.) They have caused desalting scientists to focus as much or more attention on the reduction of energy costs as on the basic desalting processes. There are only two ways in which energy costs can be reduced: (1) by reducing the cost of obtaining energy or (2) by more efficient use of the energy, for example, by combining power generation with desalting.

One potential means of reducing the cost of obtaining energy is by reducing the cost of producing steam for distillation or of power for other processes. The power industry appears to have already taken advantage of most of the possible economies of scale. With the rapid increase in fossil fuel cost, the industry is moving rapidly toward nuclear fueled plants for which projected steam costs are expected to remain relatively stable and lower than from fossil sources. A principal relatively near-term hope for reducing the cost of energy (steam or electricity) is in the use of breeder reactors in nuclear powerplants. Some experts forecast that, by the year 2000, the breeder reactor will produce energy at about 60 percent of present costs.[10] Others, however, suggest that such reductions involve consistently optimistic assumptions.[11]

---

[8] *Ibid.*, p. 45.

[9] Informal advice from OSW based upon recent laboratory results with sea water.

[10] STATE OF CALIFORNIA, Department of Water Resources (1969). Desalting—State of the Art, State of California Bulletin No. 134-69. State of California, Sacramento. p. 26.

[11] CLAWSON M et al. (June 6, 1969). Desalted water for agriculture; Is it economic? Science 164:1141-1148.

This reverse osmosis unit produces 27,000 gallons of high-quality water per day from brackish sources

Another possibility for reducing energy costs is to operate desalting plants on offpeak energy. A plant could operate under a contract for interruptible power with the power utility having the right to drop the load of the plant when an emergency occurs which requires use of reserves. For some desalting processes it would even appear possible to substitute a carefully controlled load-shedding system for spinning reserve, thereby effecting further economies in the cost of energy. This does not necessarily require that the plant operate only at nights or on weekends. Indeed, a desalting plant served by interruptible power might in some circumstances operate nearly 100 percent of the time. Similarly, dual-purpose power production-distillation plants may be operated on a basis of partially interruptible steam to take advantage of low-cost steam which might be available on this basis. It must be appreciated that desalting

plants operating on an interruptible basis cannot be relied upon as a firm water supply unless adequately backed up by storage or an alternative source.

Under such operation it should be possible to obtain energy at essentially the cost of fuel. This implies an energy charge but no capacity charge. However, because this kind of desalting operation would use plant facilities which are normally held in reserve, and because the economics of power system operation usually places the older and less efficient, as well as less pollution-free, plants in the reserve and peaking operation positions, desalting on an interruptible energy basis would more often than not involve, directly or indirectly, use of higher-cost plants.

Through More Efficient Use of Energy: The potential for using part of the heat from a nuclear or fossil fueled power generating plant for desalting probably represents a more promising method of reducing the near-term net cost of energy for desalting by distillation. Experience with such "dual-purpose" desalting plants is limited to the 2.5 m.g.d. plant in the Virgin Islands, a 5 m.g.d. plant recently placed in operation in Saudi Arabia, and the 7.5 m.g.d. installation at Rosarito Beach. Conceptual designs have been developed for large-scale dual-purpose plants at Bolsa Island and Diablo Canyon in California and for a plant in Israel.

The proposed dual-purpose Bolsa Island Project was not built because of a significant increase in estimated cost. While this increase was reflected in a rise in the indicated cost of the fresh water product from 22 to 37 cents per 1,000 gallons, the primary reason for not proceeding with plant construction was the increase in costs associated with the nuclear power production facilities which experienced even higher percentage increases.[12] Apparently, the Diablo Canyon desalting project was not recommended for early construction as a large-scale prototype plant because of indicated water costs and required Federal investment. Still large-scale, dual-purpose plants in the 50 to 100 m.g.d. capacity range offer promise for reducing costs and the technology for them needs to be developed.

Through Geothermal Plants: Geothermal development represents a special form of dual-purpose technology. By utilizing hot brine generated by heat beneath the earth's surface, both a water supply and power production can be obtained. Desalting of the brine, of course, is required if it is to be a source of water supply. However, because the source usually is at high temperatures (varying from 150° to 700°F.), the external energy that must be introduced is low. When the pressurized brine is tapped by a deep well, it flashes into a mixture of steam and hot saline water that flows to the surface.

Power generation using geothermal energy is feasible by itself in certain circumstances.[13] There are currently 728,000 kilowatts of installed geothermal power capacity in the world, half of it in Italy. Most such geothermal powerplants do not produce usable water as a byproduct. At the Cerro Prieto geothermal powerplant in Mexico, however, a desalting plant also supplies 38,000 g.p.d. for construction workers.[14]

The principal potential for combined geothermal power-desalting plants in the U.S. is in the Imperial Valley of Southern California. The Bureau of Reclamation of the U.S. Department of the Interior has recently completed a preliminary investigation of the geothermal potential of the Imperial Valley in cooperation with the Office of Saline Water (OSW), and has proposed a more detailed investigative program.[15] The Bureau estimates that a total of 1.1 billion acre-feet of brine is available, capable of providing as much as 2.5 million acre-feet of desalted water annually. To prevent land subsidence, the water withdrawn would need to be replaced by other wastewater or by sea water. Very preliminary estimates place delivered water costs at 30 to 45 cents per 1,000 gallons ($100 to $150 per acre-foot) and electrical energy costs at 3 to 5 mills per kw.-hr.

The Bureau and OSW propose a 3-stage study, as follows:

Stage 1: A 7-year research and development period, to obtain physical data necessary for determining the extent and potential of the geothermal resource and to build pilot and prototype plants to provide operating data. A total of $16 million for the 7 years is indicated to be required. (As a prelude to this, the Bureau and OSW are now cooperating on an 8,000-foot well drilled in the Imperial Valley in 1972. Well construction is by the Bureau, with OSW providing and operating a portable desalting plant.)[16]

Stage 2: A demonstration of large-scale development, to provide 100,000 acre-feet of desalted water annually and 400-500 megawatts of power. Replacement fluids would be from the Salton Sea, the Wellton-Mohawk Drain, or from ground water.

Stage 3: The program would provide for delivering up to 2.5 million acre-feet of water annually and

[12] STATE OF CALIFORNIA, Department of Water Resources (1969). Desalting—State of the Art, State of California Bulletin No. 134-69. State of California, Sacramento. pp. 41-43.

[13] STATE OF CALIFORNIA, Department of Water Resources (1970). Water for California—The California Water Plan Outlook in 1970, State of California Bulletin No. 160-70. State of California, Sacramento. pp. 88-91.

[14] ANONYMOUS (May 6, 1971). Geothermal resources gather a head of steam. Engineering News-Record 186(18):30-35.

[15] U.S. BUREAU OF RECLAMATION (1972). Geothermal Resource Investigations, Imperial Valley, California; Developmental Concepts, Bureau of Reclamation, Office of Saline Water, Washington, D.C. pp. iii, 55.

[16] U.S. BUREAU OF RECLAMATION (February 1972). Reclamation Report Cites Water, Power Potential in Geothermal Development, News Release 4523-72. U.S. Department of the Interior, Washington, D.C.

producing about 10,000 megawatts of power. A sea water source for replacement fluids would be required.

Obviously, this is a long-range program. The first stage alone would span 7 years. The Commission believes that the geothermal potential is well worth investigating, at least to the point where valid comparisons can be made with other alternatives for providing additional water supply to the area.

While the Commission has no basis for judging the details of the proposed program, it endorses the need, the objectives, and the general outline of stage 1. The question is raised, however, as to whether stages 2 and 3 should be Federal programs; no overriding requirement is seen for such a determination. The Commission suggests that the possibility of non-Federal development be given full consideration at the time stages 2 and 3 are undertaken.

Through Economies of Scale: Desalting plants offer some opportunity for reduction in unit costs through increases in size. There is an economic breakpoint beyond which the cost of incremental capacity becomes approximately constant. This is about 100 m.g.d. for distillation and about 10 m.g.d. for reverse osmosis. On the other hand, conventional sources of water supply, which are alternatives to desalting and which do not involve significant energy inputs, do offer substantial opportunities for economies of scale—a dam, a reservoir, a pipeline, or even a treatment plant usually become significantly less expensive per unit for supply as its size is increased. At the same time, many projects for conventional water supply will involve long-distance transfers, substantial investment for capacity not immediately required, and significant environmental and social questions; thus, they involve other kinds of costs.

Through Staged Construction: There are advantages accruing to desalting, derived from its flexibility to adapt to stage construction. Since desalting plants can be built in modules, they can be scheduled to meet increases in uses, as such uses grow. Conventional water supply sources usually require investment in large single increments of capacity, often resulting in unused capacity for many years. Such unused capacity is costly, because interest and other fixed costs must be paid whether capacity is fully utilized or not. Even more important, perhaps, are the smaller incremental requirements for capital investments associated with desalting and the better cash flow to meet

debt service during the initial stages of amortization of a capital investment.

Other Applications of Desalting Technology

The potential exists to use desalting facilities in roles other than that of a purely water supply function.

These include desalting of contaminated surface or ground water or of wastewater and industrial discharges high in dissolved solids and relatively undesirable for municipal or industrial uses. Considerable opportunity exists for using desalting plants to improve such water supplies. With increasingly stringent discharge criteria, the use of desalting as a means of meeting clean water standards will likely attract more attention in the future.

Where other sources of high quality water are not available, desalted water can be mixed with brackish water for municipal and industrial use. In effect, this augments the usable water supply. Thus, if brackish water has a salinity content of 1,000 p.p.m. and the usable quality limit is considered to be about 500 p.p.m., the usable volume of desalted water can, in effect, be doubled by blending it with brackish water. This approach has been considered in a number of areas including California, Utah, South Dakota, and elsewhere. It could be applicable wherever a supply of brackish water is economically available. In Utah, for example, the cost of a blended water supply by this method, delivered to the municipality, was estimated to vary from 19 cents to 33 cents per 1,000 gallons ($63 to $108 per acre-foot), depending upon the desalting process used and the source of the feed and blending water.[17]

Reuse of treated wastewater will be of increasing importance in the future. Where mineral buildup through reuse is a problem it may be desirable to utilize desalting for its removal. While in any instance chemical precipitation or dilution with high-quality water may be attractive alternatives, the potential for desalting in connection with wastewater reuse could be significant. This potential has had very little attention in the research investigations of the saline water program but now is receiving increasing attention. It may become an area of early major application for desalting.

---

[17] HAYCOCK, Edwin B et al. (1968). Utah Desalting Study, Preliminary Assessment of Desalting and Electric Power and Process Steam Production for the Wasatch Front Area. Utah Department of Natural Resources, U.S. Office of Saline Water, and U.S. Atomic Energy Commission, Salt Lake City, Utah. pp. 7, 149.

Forced circulation vapor-compression plant at Roswell, New Mexico

Desalting may be used as a means of treating point-sources of some kinds of pollution. For example, the Office of Saline Water and the Bureau of Reclamation have undertaken a program for the control of salinity on the Colorado River. Under this program detailed study will be given to the potential for using desalting to control pollution by dissolved solids from mineralized springs or other point-sources and from irrigation return flow.

Desalting and conventional water supply systems may be operated conjunctively. Under this approach, assuming a source of feed water, a desalting plant would be operated on an intermittent or interim basis to supplement natural or regulated surface supplies. The ability of a desalting plant to be operated as needed makes it adaptable to such a function. It would be used during seasonal peaks, periods of drought, or when the capacity of reservoirs or other water supply facilities had been reached, because of expanding requirements, but before additional facilities were constructed. In effect, this would stretch conventional water supplies and their associated facilities. The economics of this approach do not seem to have been thoroughly explored. However, conventional water supply sources have a much higher ratio of fixed capital costs to variable operational costs—on the order of 75 percent capital cost to 25 percent variable operational cost—compared with a corresponding ratio of about 40 percent to 60 percent for desalting plants. This might give desalting some advantage over conventional sources as an intermittent source of supply because the significantly smaller capital investment in facilities used only periodically may result in lower unit costs for the standby capacity. However, capital cost per unit of production will often be higher for desalting than for conventional sources of supply, particularly when ground water is a possible alternative. The use of desalting as a water supply source, in any instance, should be reviewed in terms of its impact upon the total water system economics as compared to alternative sources meeting the same needs.

Environmental Problems

Disposal of waste products from desalting plants can be a difficult problem under some circumstances. The volume of brine effluent from a sea water conversion plant typically is about 50 percent of the total volume treated. The effluent from a 10 m.g.d. plant will contain about 2,000 tons of salt residue daily. Where discharge can be made to the sea, disposal problems will be relatively minor, but the impact on the local ecology will still need to be investigated. Where disposal is inland, the problem will be much greater. Possible inland disposal methods include evaporation ponds, transport by conduit to the ocean or other salt water body, deep well injection, or central stockpiling of dry salts. Each disposal method has disadvantages, some from the viewpoint of costs, others from the viewpoint of possible environmental effects. The market for most of the salts is limited, so recovery and disposal through sale will not be practical in most instances.

Desalting plants can add to local environmental problems by discharge of waste heat from (a) producing the additional power necessary to desalt and (b) the heat in the plant effluent when a distillation process is used. While these heat discharges could be significant locally, they would represent small values in national totals. Significantly less heat will be discharged when power production and desalting are combined into a single dual-purpose plant.[18]

Probable Markets for Desalting

The future market for desalting will depend upon the interaction of a number of factors. Costs of production to be attained in the future will be significant as will the costs of any potential alternative. But other factors such as institutional and social considerations also will be important. In 1971, the Office of Saline Water analyzed in a preliminary way the potential market by the year 2020 for desalting under different assumptions regarding population growth, availability of alternative sources of water supply, water quality requirements, the degree of water recycling, and other factors.[19] That study indicated a wide range in the potential for desalting depending upon the particular set of assumptions. For example, a baseline projection of 7.7 b.g.d. was found if future water demands are about equal to the projections of the First National Assessment, discussed in Chapter 1, and if technology continues to improve and costs continue to decline. On the other hand, if costs were to remain constant at present levels and alternative water sources were available, the desalting demand would be relatively small at 1.1 b.g.d. If no further water importation projects were permitted, the study suggested a desalting demand of 40 b.g.d. A number of other projections keyed to different possible factors fell within these two extremes.

The study also indicated that the demand for desalting is highly sensitive to cost differences. The tabulation below based upon operating a 100 m.g.d. plant, with costs adjusted to a 1972 level, indicates the effect of different costs on the demand for desalting.[20]

Assumed desalting costs in 2020 (cents per 1,000 gallons)	Desalting capacity justified in 2020 (b.g.d.)
42	2.5
36	4.1
30	7.8
24	15.7
16.6	31.8

As indicated earlier, these cost figures, especially at the lower end of the spectrum, may have to assume

[18]STATE OF CALIFORNIA, Department of Water Resources (1969). Desalting—State of the Art, State of California Bulletin No. 134-69, State of California, Sacramento, p. 33.

[19]U.S. OFFICE OF SALINE WATER (June 24, 1971). Briefing Session for the Desalting Industry. U.S. Department of the Interior, Washington, D.C.

[20]Ibid., p. 21.

low interest rates or other favorable conditions in order to be achieved.

Markets for Municipal Use: Much of the future market will be for small- and medium-sized plants, up to 10 m.g.d., to serve small communities, industries, and remote developments in arid areas. Applications may develop, as well, for medium-sized plants, of 10 to 50 m.g.d., as increments to the water supply for medium or large cities. In special situations, costs could be competitive.

Still larger plants in the 50 to 250 m.g.d. range could serve the needs of large cities or regional municipal supply systems. Costs may be competitive with alternative sources of water in arid areas near the coast, such as Southern California, or in areas of brackish water, such as Utah. However, extending known technology to this size of plant, probably involving dual-purpose operations, is a step into the unknown.

Desalting may serve not only as a means of supplying water for municipal and industrial uses, but also for improving the quality of existing supplies. Moreover, some 1,200 communities in the United States currently have water rates to the consumer in excess of 75 cents per 1,000 gallons for the first 10,000 gallons used per month.[21] Future costs of conventional water supplies for these and other communities will certainly be higher than present costs. The increasing concerns about the effects water development will have upon the environment, institutional constraints, and competition from other types of water use all will add to the difficulty of developing conventional water sources in the future. Desalting may have application in areas having these types of problems even prior to the time that costs are reduced and desalted water becomes more nearly competitive with that from other sources.

Markets for Irrigation Use: The forecasts of water cost for plants in the large 50 to 260 m.g.d. size range, using existing technology ($80 to $180 per acre-foot), would seem to rule out irrigation use of desalted water when compared strictly on a cost-per-acre-foot basis. However, studies have demonstrated that this kind of comparison is not altogether valid—the utility of an acre-foot of desalted water

(which is more or less pure) cannot be equated to that of an acre-foot of natural water (which usually contains some salt).[22] If water of very good quality such as that obtainable by distillation were used for irrigation, water use could be limited essentially to that required for the plant's growth. With such water, a high level of management could be combined with the most modern agricultural technology and specialized plants to create a very productive agriculture. This potential probably will not be realized at present desalting costs.

There appears to be a limited opportunity for growing specialized crops in enclosed environment systems with desalted water.[23] A multipurpose experimental plant at Puerto Penasco, Baja California, in Mexico has been sponsored jointly by the Universities of Sonora and Arizona. The plant combines a 2,400 g.p.d. power-desalting plant with air-inflated plastic greenhouses to grow vegetables under controlled environment conditions. Since water evaporated or transpired by the plants is not lost to the atmosphere and there are no other water losses, consumptive use is about one-tenth of that common in field irrigation. A 5-acre plant of this type is now in commercial operation in the Shiekdom of Abu Dhabi, in the Middle East. A similar 5-acre commercial plant is now under construction on an Indian reservation near Yuma, Arizona.

Other technological innovations, on much larger scales, have been investigated in more theoretical terms. Of particular interest is a large-scale agro-industrial combination grouped around nuclear energy centers studied by the U.S. Atomic Energy Commission's Oak Ridge National Laboratory and by Texas A&M. This complex would provide electric energy and desalted water, and process steam and raw materials for a variety of industries. It also would provide desalted water for irrigation.

There are many questions to be answered before desalting for irrigation use occurs; certainly, significant irrigation use is not justified with present or immediately foreseen technology. Nevertheless, it is too early to write off the possibility of future

[21] AMERICAN CITY MAGAZINE, Pittsfield, Mass. (1971). Nationwide Study of High Municipal Water Rates, Research and Development Progress Report No. 719, prepared for U.S. Office of Saline Water. U.S. Government Printing Office, Washington, D.C. p. 4.

[22] U.S. OFFICE OF SALINE WATER (1969). Value of Desalted Water for Irrigation, Research and Development Progress Report No. 489, U.S. Government Printing Office, Washington, D.C.

[23] HODGES, Carl N & HODGE, Carle O (1969). Power, Water and Food for Desert Coasts: An Integrated System for Providing Them. Paper presented at 66th Annual Meeting, American Society for Horticultural Science, Pullman, Washington.

irrigation use for specialized crops and situations. It should be recognized, however, that even very limited use for irrigation would represent a large desalting investment—about 10,000 irrigated acres alone would require the entire present 55 m.g.d. desalting capacity of the U.S. At half the delivery requirement of Colorado River water, costs of desalted water using existing nuclear technology would still be equivalent to $40 to $90 per acre-foot, greatly in excess of the $2 to $10 per acre-foot average price of irrigation water (which usually includes substantial subsidies) and even in excess of the estimate value added by irrigation of specialized crops in Arizona, computed as being $27 to $36 per acre-foot.[24]

Application of Desalting Technology

Desalting plants capable of contributing significantly to a resolution of metropolitan area or regional water problems must be substantially larger than any operating today. While research and laboratory tests on desalting processes and pilot plants are important steps in research and development, a final step, the prototype stage, also is important to prove and demonstrate a major new technology such as desalting. The Saline Water Conversion Act of 1971[25] authorized and directed the Secretary of the Interior to report to the President and Congress within 1 year his recommendations as to the best opportunity for the early construction of a prototype desalting plant. The Act defines prototype as, ". . .a full-size, first-of-a-kind production plant used for the development, study, and demonstration of full-sized technology, plant operation, and process economics."

While the Secretary, in response to that directive, reported in 1972 that a desalting plant site meeting all of the requirements had not been satisfactorily identified, the need remains for prototype experience.

It appears highly likely that solutions to the inevitable problems that accompany scaleup in plant size can only be obtained in reasonable time with Federal assistance. In addition to questions related to plant design, purchasing, managing, and operating desalting plants involve considerations needing attention. Early answers to questions about the actual cost of such plants are important to the Federal Govern-

ment if it is to judiciously appraise the costs, the environmental and social impacts, and the suitability of desalting as an alternative to other large-scale water development projects (such as interbasin transfers of water) that involve Federal funding. The Atomic Energy Commission characterized the role of a prototype desalting plant as being similar to that of the Shippingport nuclear power generating plant of the 1950's which demonstrated the practicability of such plants and which was supported by Federal funds.[26]

Hence, the Commission believes that the Federal Government should provide assistance in the construction of a large prototype desalting plant for research and development purposes. To the extent that other entities secure benefits from such a research and development effort, they should be obliged to share in its costs to the equivalent of what they would otherwise have had to pay for the benefits they receive.

Large desalting plants will be constructed of individual desalting modules or units having a capacity of perhaps 20 to 40 m.g.d. each for plants using the distillation process. Membrane processes, on the other hand, do not require as large a unit module size. Units of 10,000 to 100,000 g.p.d. capacities using the reverse osmosis process can be added in modular fashion to make up plants of over 100 m.g.d. total capacity. From a purely technical viewpoint, while a single module would provide adequate data on the problems involved in scaleup from the smaller pilot plants, such a single module could not demonstrate all of the problems or take advantage of the opportunities encountered in a full-size plant operation. As indicated earlier, for example, the least cost of production for a distillation plant will be reached at about 100 m.g.d. Moreover, a prototype plant should be designed for and capable of helping to meet an existing water problem which could require a plant capable of a dependable output.

Depending on the circumstances, then, it may be appropriate for the prototype plant to consist of two or more modules. This matter will need to be weighed when the particular prototype plant is under consideration.

[24] NATIONAL ACADEMY OF SCIENCES (1968). Water and Choice in the Colorado Basin, A Report by the Committee on Water of the National Research Council. Publication 1689. NAS, Washington, D.C.

[25] P.L. 92-60, July 29, 1971, 85 Stat. 159, 42 USCA 1959 *et seq.*

[26] U.S. CONGRESS, Senate, Committee on Interior and Insular Affairs (1971). Saline Water Conversion Program, Hearings before the Subcommittee on Water and Power Resources, on S. 716 and S. 991, 92nd Congress, 1st Session. U.S. Government Printing Office, Washington, D.C. p. 141.

The Commission appreciates the fact that prototype experience with a single process using water from one source may not be transferable fully to plants using other feed water sources or desalting processes and that other prototype plants may be desirable. This is a matter which will need to be considered in the light of experience with the initial prototype plant and of the results of the continuing research and development program.

CONCLUSIONS ON DESALTING

Because of increasing future water demands and relatively fixed natural supplies of water, it is likely that desalting will play a significant future role in the United States. This applies especially to the use of smaller desalting plants, less than 10 million gallons per day (m.g.d.) capacity, in areas where other supplies are costly, where there are natural supplies of brackish water, where existing supplies need to be upgraded, or where point-sources of dissolved solids can be treated. There probably will be significant opportunities also for plants of up to 50 m.g.d. or larger as an incremental supply or for intermittent and conjunctive operation with existing surface and ground water sources. Large plants in the 50 to 250 m.g.d. range offer promise for desalting sea water primarily at this time through dual-purpose technology (e.g., desalting and power production), but the extent of this potential cannot be established without prototype experience. Still larger dual-purpose power generation and desalting plants up to 1,000 m.g.d. in size have been considered and analyzed for irrigation and industrial purposes, but they involve still greater uncertainties. Desalting projects using energy from outside sources are becoming less and less attractive as the cost of energy increases. They are only really attractive when they utilize or make possible the more efficient use of waste heat that might otherwise be lost, or a source of natural heat such as geothermal or solar energy.

There are certain policy matters relating to the future course of the Federal effort in any national desalting program. The first is whether the basic desalting processes are sufficiently developed so that private industry can assume most of the future research and development costs for small-sized plants. Many of the processes are now in commercial production and the Commission believes that desalting research and development is far enough advanced to eliminate the most important design, construction, and operational risks for desalting plants smaller than 10 m.g.d. using the distillation process but that important improvements in the reverse osmosis and freezing processes may occur and research in these areas should continue.

The Commission believes that federally sponsored research and development on small desalting plants (less than 10 m.g.d.), except for the reverse osmosis and freezing processes and for other processes needed in connection with large plant development, should be gradually eliminated over a 3-year period. The Federal research and development effort should be continued with respect to development of larger desalting plants and multipurpose desalting plants.

The second policy matter concerns the magnitude of the Federal Government's desalting research program as that program relates to other Federal research programs. In recent years, the U.S. Office of Saline Water (OSW) program has been on the order of $27 million annually. About half of this was for demonstration purposes. The OSW program has been about double that of the Office of Water Resources Research (OWRR) (also in the U.S. Department of the Interior) and about four times the Bureau of Reclamation's program of research in precipitation modification. The level of funding for research and demonstration by OSW appears appropriate. Any disparity between OSW and OWRR with respect to available funds would seem to reflect a deficiency for OWRR rather than an excess of funding for desalting.

Third, there should be some reshaping of the desalting program. There is need for more study relating to the application of desalting to other supply sources—desalting for interim use or in staged developments and for conjunctive uses. There also is need to give detailed study to the use of interruptible energy for desalting purposes. Applications of desalting to environment improvement will play an increasingly important role as wastewater criteria become more severe. Research and development to improve the capability to meet these requirements should continue.

A fourth matter is that of the proposed prototype program. While the Commission endorses the concept of Federal assistance for a large prototype desalting plant for research and development, it has some apprehension that the precedent might be used to justify Federal funds for other large plants to follow. While it is possible that future developments in carefully selected instances where private capital will not be made available might justify some Federal support, the Commission's endorsement at this time is limited to one large prototype plant.

RECOMMENDATIONS

9-1. **The basic research and development program of the Federal Government for desalting plants in the size range up to 10 m.g.d. should be largely phased out within the next 3 years. The Federal Government should retain a research and development interest in small desalting plants only for the freezing and reverse osmosis processes and for other processes not commercially proven which will be needed to foster development of large plants. The research and development program for larger desalting plants and for multipurpose applications should continue to be federally supported.**

9-2. **The Federal Government should provide a grant to aid in the construction and operation of one large prototype desalting plant when the technology has been developed adequately and where there is a clear requirement for the water produced. The amount of such Federal assistance should be limited to the residual uncovered costs of the project after power supply and water supply entities which will be direct beneficiaries of the project have contributed amounts equivalent to the lowest cost alternative power and water supplies which they would otherwise be obliged to pay for in the absence of the prototype facility.**

PRECIPITATION AUGMENTATION

In recent years, through scientific inquiry and experimentation, the prospects for successful modification of rainfall and snowfall patterns have begun to look promising.

Still, a certain amount of criticism and controversy surrounds the subject of precipitation augmentation. Many of the witnesses at the Commission's regional conferences in early 1973 urged the Commission to withdraw support of precipitation augmentation because of possible adverse environmental impacts. It is the purpose of this section to analyze the state of the art, to consider future prospects and implications, and to suggest the way in which appropriate public policy should be formulated in order to extract optimum public benefits from the new knowledge as it develops.

The discussion is limited to the subject of modifying precipitation for the purpose of increasing usable water supplies. It does not deal with other weather modification efforts designed to affect natural climatic forces—preventing hurricanes, suppressing hail, or dispersing fog. Hence the title "Precipitation Augmentation" rather than "Weather Modification."

The problem, essentially, is to appraise the extent to which precipitation augmentation can be relied upon as an effective and economical means of increasing usable water supplies. This appraisal, to be most meaningful, needs to be made in steps. First of all, an evaluation of the effectiveness of cloud seeding, the principal method for stimulating precipitation, needs to be made. Second, it is important to convert knowledge about effective cloud seeding into knowledge about whether or not and the extent to which an increase in precipitation can be channeled into a usable water supply. Third, the costs involved must be identified and compared with the benefits from precipitation augmentation efforts; costs of a social or environmental nature as well as economic costs should be taken into account. Fourth, precipitation augmentation programs need to be examined from the viewpoint of their ability to yield information needed for predicting the different direct and indirect effects. And, finally, examination of the legal and institutional implications of precipitation augmentation is necessary in order to define the potential liabilities and remedies, and the appropriate regulatory mechanisms needed to assure maximum net benefits to society.

Brief History[27]

The most common basis for precipitation augmentation is cloud seeding. The theory behind cloud seeding is that under certain conditions, air containing a great deal of moisture will not yield precipitation, or as much precipitation as might possibly occur, because of the absence of nuclei—microscopically small particles of dust, crystal, or chemical droplets. By implanting such particles artificially in supersaturated clouds, rainfall can be stimulated.

Precipitation augmentation through cloud seeding has been practiced for about 25 years. Although the theoretical basis for such modification was established in the 1930's, it was not until 1946 that laboratory experiments with silver iodide crystals established the probability of its effectiveness. By 1952, cloud seeding programs had been attempted over more than 10 percent of the land area of the United States.

[27] Based on LACKNER, Jack D (1971). Precipitation Modification, prepared for the National Water Commission. National Technical Information Service, Springfield, Va., Accession No. PB 201 534. pp. II-16 to II-21.

Silver iodide generator on Bridger Ridge north of Bozeman, Montana

A period of retrenchment set in shortly thereafter, as the need for evaluation of cloud seeding became apparent. By 1956, cloud seeding activities had been reduced to about one-fourth of the 1952 peak and thereafter stabilized at this level until about 1962, when they began a slow but steady increase.

Recent emphasis has been upon basic and applied research sponsored primarily by the National Science Foundation and the Bureau of Reclamation, U.S. Department of the Interior. Federal funding for this research in Fiscal Year 1972 was about $8.4 million annually, which included extensive experimental operations by the Bureau of Reclamation in the Colorado River Basin. Other Federal research includes that of the National Oceanic and Atmospheric Administration in the U.S. Department of Commerce.[28]

[28] U.S. FEDERAL COUNCIL FOR SCIENCE AND TECHNOLOGY, Interdepartmental Committee for Atmospheric Sciences (May 1972). National Atmospheric Sciences Program, Fiscal Year 1973, ICAS 16-FY73. Executive Office of the President, Washington, D.C. p. 93.

Appraisal of Precipitation Augmentation

The processes and potentials of precipitation augmentation are not all completely understood. Consequently, at the present stage of the technology it is difficult to predict with confidence the results of all types of cloud seeding. In the past, uncertainty about results and about resulting side effects has been a principal restraint in the formulation of policy on precipitation augmentation. Total failures are fairly easy to identify. If neither rain nor snow is produced after cloud seeding, the effort failed. If, however, cloud seeding is followed by precipitation, it has not always been easy to prove that the precipitation would not have occurred anyway in the absence of the seeding. Recent advances in knowledge of the processes involved, however, have been quite significant and suggest that a reasonable and useful appraisal can be attempted.

Effectiveness of Cloud Seeding: Experiments to increase precipitation have yielded results ranging from precipitation increases of as high as 200 percent for some individual storms, to slight decreases in the amount of precipitation which otherwise would have been expected. On the basis of these results, it has become apparent that precipitation can be increased under some sets of circumstances but not under others. Until recently, however, the wide range of results seemed to be inexplicable.

The most significant advance in recent technology has been the development of mathematical models which explain the effects of seeding and which can be used, in a limited number of cases, to predict likely precipitation changes with some degree of confidence. This prediction capability varies with the three types of cloud systems, described below as orographic, convective, and cyclonic.

The most promising precipitation augmentation results have been obtained from "orographic" cloud systems, where mountain ranges force moisture-laden air upward to form clouds. Orographic precipitation is the predominant form in the Western United States, where most precipitation accumulates during the winter season at higher elevations as snow. In the Colorado River Basin, for example, orographic cloud systems provide a very high percentage of the annual precipitation. The conditions necessary to increase precipitation from such clouds have been reasonably well established. The resulting average annual increases in precipitation, under existing techniques, may range from zero up to about 20 percent.

The Bureau of Reclamation estimates that a cloud seeding program for a 14,300-square mile area of the Colorado River Basin could increase precipitation about 15 percent, which would yield approximately 1,870,000 acre-feet of increased net annual runoff.[29] This estimate was based on some generalized assumptions that certain losses normally experienced after precipitation but before runoff, as well as some losses due to resulting increased vegetation, would occur. The estimate is useful for the purpose for which it was intended—as a preproject estimate for pilot investigations. However, it has not yet been proven by actual experience.

Precipitation augmentation is more complex for "convective" type clouds, which frequently are associated with thunderstorms and cover relatively small areas. These clouds are formed by the lifting of air resulting from heating at the earth's surface. Although these cloud systems occur throughout the Nation, they provide the primary summertime precipitation for the extensive agricultural areas of the Midwest, as well as for the high plains east of the Rocky Mountains. Experiments have demonstrated that seeding convective clouds may increase precipitation. The magnitude of increases, however, cannot yet be predicted with assurance.

Relatively few modification experiments have been conducted on "cyclonic" storms, in which the lifting action stems from the interaction of cold and warm air masses. These storm systems occur over large areas of the United States and provide major precipitation to all areas, especially to areas east of the Rocky Mountains. The documented results of the few precipitation augmentation tests conducted on cyclonic cloud systems have been inconclusive.

Effect on Usable Water Supply: Increases in average precipitation do not necessarily produce proportional increases in usable water supply, for several reasons. First, there is not a linear relationship between precipitation and runoff. That is to say, 1 inch of additional precipitation in a given season does not yield the same incremental additions to usable water supply as an earlier or a later inch of precipitation, depending on, among other things, the amount of precipitation which has already occurred in that season.

Secondly, although research data are limited, most investigators conclude that opportunities to increase precipitation in drought periods, when increases in water supply are disproportionately valuable, are less frequent than in wet periods, when water supply increases carry less utility. This disproportion between the effects in wet and dry periods can result in making some of the increased supply during wet periods unusable unless there is sufficient storage capacity available to hold water from wet to dry periods. For streams with a high degree of storage regulation, such as the Colorado River, any augmentation of flows is likely to be usable.

Vegetal cover of marginal value may expand as a result of increased precipitation. Unless such increases are controlled through land management techniques, such expanded vegetation can reduce the usable water yield from precipitation augmentation.

Disappointingly little attention has been directed toward the relationships between precipitation augmentation and usable water supply. Simulation models that have been developed recently hold considerable promise in evaluating some of these

[29] U.S. BUREAU OF RECLAMATION (1971). Project Skywater Atmospheric Water Resources Program. U.S. Government Printing Office, Washington, D.C.

relationships.[30] There has also been inadequate attention to the determination of the precipitation increases that are possible during critical drought periods, as well as the degree to which storage capacity can be utilized to make more fully usable the increases in average runoff that might result.

Costs: Estimates of costs of precipitation augmentation are cited in several investigative studies. Costs ranging from $1.00 to $2.30 per acre-foot of additional runoff are cited.[31] However, these represent only the direct capital and operation costs, and do not include any indirect economic, environmental, or ecological costs related to side effects. Some side effects may be beneficial, others may be harmful; hence, indirectly related costs may be negative or positive. Also, most of the present cost estimates are derived from planning reports. As such, they represent expectations rather than actual operational performances. Moreover, the question of usability must be taken into account since it is not at all certain that an acre-foot of runoff is necessarily equivalent to an acre-foot of usable water. Therefore, the cost estimates cited must be considered to be only approximate and are probably too low.

Economic, Environmental, and Ecological Effects: Determining the economic, environmental, and ecological consequences of modifying precipitation is even more complex than evaluating the augmentation to usable supply. While the direct benefits of precipitation augmentation are susceptible to relatively simple economic analysis, the "side effects"—those external to the intended purpose of the augmentation effort—are much more difficult to analyze. For example, even within the target areas of these efforts, it is possible simultaneously to have both beneficial and adverse effects (e.g., rainfall coming at a particular time could be highly beneficial to one crop but detrimental to another).

Ecological research to date indicates that catastrophic ecological impacts should not be expected. Sustained precipitation augmentation could bring about some alteration in the structure of plant and animal communities through shifts in rates of reproduction, growth, and mortality of weather-sensitive species. For example, while unmanageable outbreaks of weeds or insects are highly unlikely, big game animals could be affected adversely by increased snowpack. On the other hand, increased precipitation might lead to superior browse for big game animals.

In any event, ecological changes would require several years to occur, and, due to the relatively small incremental change in precipitation expected, may be very difficult to identify and measure. Experimental modification efforts should include careful monitoring of ecological changes, particularly the long-term and cumulative effects.

Cloud seeding may affect precipitation many miles downwind from target areas. There have been some studies that provide evidence of increasing precipitation as much as 100 to 200 miles distant from target areas. There apparently is no evidence thus far of any decreases peripheral to the target areas. Explanations of these effects have been postulated, but the causal links between cloud seeding and downwind effects have not been definitively established.

Floods, as well as droughts, have been blamed on augmentation efforts but such claims have not yet been proven. Analysis of simulated increases in precipitation, particularly in arid areas, indicates that flood peaks may be substantially heightened by relatively modest increases in precipitation, as low as 10 percent, for example. Future research should focus attention on this subject.

There have been a number of legal actions initiated as a result of presumed side effects from cloud seeding but, because of difficulty of proof, no damage judgments have been entered.

---

[30] LUMB AM & LINSLEY RK (1971). Hydrologic consequences of rainfall augmentation. Journal of the Hydraulics Division, Proceedings of the American Society of Civil Engineers 97(HY 7):1065-80.

[31] U.S. BUREAU OF RECLAMATION (1971). Colorado River Basin Pilot Project, Cloud Seeding Research in the San Juan Mountains. Bureau of Reclamation, Denver, Colo. and AUBERT EJ et al. (1969). The Utilization of the Atmospheric Water Resources in the Connecticut River Basin: An Essay, TRC Report 7494-352, prepared for the U.S. Bureau of Reclamation, contract 14-06-D-6569. Travelers Research Corporation, Hartford, Conn. p. iii.

Operational Status: Descriptive mathematical models of precipitation from orographic cloud systems are now sufficiently advanced to predict, at least in a limited number of cases, the effect of cloud seeding on precipitation. However, economic, environmental, ecological, and other side effects cannot yet be predicted reliably because of limitations in knowledge and practical experience. Predictive capabilities for convective cloud systems are considerably less accurate. At the present time, the effects of seeding cyclonic systems cannot be predicted at all.

Aerial view of cloud seeding operation near Payson, Arizona

The present state of knowledge might suggest that cloud seeding be limited to experimental programs for the time being. The Bureau of Reclamation project for the Upper Colorado Basin, for example, fits this category, and should soon supply much needed preoperational data to guide future operations. Yet, there are certain existing non-Federal operational projects which have merit, do not appear to cause undue damage, and yield significant operational data. Realism suggests that such operations be allowed to continue unless and until the need to impose additional regulation becomes apparent.

Legal and Institutional Implications: No significant body of common law has been found adaptable for the control of precipitation augmentation. A few cases that have reached the courts demonstrate that traditional tort and property rules are not fully satisfactory for solving the unique problems posed by precipitation augmentation.

State legislation shows a marked lack of uniformity: (a) at least one State completely prohibits cloud seeding, (b) some require licensing and regulation of operators, (c) some attempt to establish strict liability for modification activities, and (d) some provide no regulation whatever.

While substantial congressional interest has been demonstrated, Federal legislation has been limited largely to authorizations for weather modification research and development, including precipitation augmentation. However, in December 1971, Congress enacted a Weather Modification Reporting Act which provides that no person may engage in weather modification activity in the United States unless he submits reports on such activity to the Secretary of Commerce.[32] It also contains enforcement and penalty provisions. The legislation itself does not require reporting by Federal agencies. No other regulatory or policy legislation has been enacted.

Rules for implementing the Weather Modification Reporting Act were adopted in October 1972.[33] These rules require an initial report defining the purpose, size, and location; describing equipment, seeding agents, and techniques; and showing other related information to be provided to the Administrator, National Oceanic and Atmospheric Administration, before commencing any weather modification project or activity. During the project, interim reports are to be presented and at its conclusion a

---

[32] *Weather Modification Reporting Act,* P.L. 92-205, December 18, 1971, 85 Stat. 735, 15 USCA 330 *et seq.*

[33] U.S. NATIONAL OCEANIC AND ATMOSPHERIC ADMINISTRATION (1972). Maintaining records and submitting reports on weather modification activities. Federal Register 37(208):22977, October 27, 1972.

final report is to be prepared and submitted. These reports are to include specific data such as number of days of field operations, number of seeding missions, amount of seeding agent used, and similar data. The regulations also require maintenance and retention of adequate records.

The potential impact on downwind areas and the possibility of other side effects probably will lead to interstate involvements, calling for some type of Federal regulation. Ultimately, a Federal policy to regulate cloud seeding operations that have any potential for interstate influence will be required because of such interstate aspects. However, it does not seem wise to develop or implement specific policies until the processes of precipitation augmentation and their side effects are understood more thoroughly. Substantial understanding is rapidly becoming available through the research program of the Bureau of Reclamation and other research efforts. The processes should be adequately understood to permit policy formulation by or before completion of the Bureau of Reclamation's present research program scheduled for 1977. Until then, operational regulation should be limited to that provided by State and local entities. When the understanding of processes and side effects permits, Congress should address itself to appropriate legislation which would identify the Federal role and establish such Federal policy as may be needed in applying and regulating this imminently emerging technology for the benefit of society.

CONCLUSIONS ON PRECIPITATION AUGMENTATION

The Commission concludes that precipitation augmentation has potential as a technique for increasing future water supplies. The technique will probably be limited initially to certain areas of the Nation and to certain times of the year. But there is insufficient information at present to develop a comprehensive national policy with respect to this technology.

RECOMMENDATIONS

9-3. Research on precipitation augmentation should continue with emphasis not only on increasing rainfall and snowfall propitiously, but also on means of determining the effect on usable water supplies and on downwind and side effects, particularly those having economic, environmental, or ecological consequences.

9-4. Development of comprehensive Federal policy on precipitation augmentation should wait until results of current research develop better information on (1) operational capability, (2) side effects, and (3) the extent of regulation needed. When adequate research results are available, Congress should consider regulatory and other policy legislation.

9-5. The Act of December 18, 1971, under which the Secretary of Commerce has promulgated rules and regulations for reporting on all weather modification activities should be made applicable to Federal agencies. This could be accomplished by an executive order.

INCREASING WATER SUPPLY THROUGH LAND MANAGEMENT

The manner in which a watershed is managed can affect the amount and quality of water available for use. Four land management techniques hold potential for increasing the useful supply of water: (1) vegetation management in forest and brush areas, (2) phreatophyte control along river banks, (3) snowpack management in forest and alpine areas, and (4) water harvesting by treatment of soil surface to increase the collection of precipitation.

Experiments conducted in the United States since 1909 indicate that water yield can be increased by altering the amount and kind of vegetation on a forested watershed. Moreover, forest cutting patterns also can affect water yield.

Phreatophytes, deep-rooted vegetation growing along the banks of canals and rivers, present a unique circumstance. They exist in the shallow water-table environment along the banks of streams, in the flood plains, and in the delta areas at the heads of reservoirs. Because their root systems connect directly to the water table, and because they often receive large quantities of advective energy from adjacent dry areas, they consume great quantities of water. Phreatophyte control has been the subject of research efforts since 1940.

Nearly 40 years ago, the possibility of increasing water yield by snowpack management was suggested. A range of techniques, including snow fencing, can affect the timing and the amount of snowmelt runoff.

When managers of water resources undertake investigations of the various options open to them for augmenting water supplies, their catalog of alternatives should include land management techniques. For some situations, increasing water supply through land management might be the best way to proceed. Under certain circumstances, these techniques carry

Decreasing forest undergrowth increases usable water supplies

with them only nominal adverse side effects and, occasionally, beneficial side effects which should certainly not be overlooked. An important objective of this section is to explore the potentials of land management techniques so that they will be taken into account properly by water managers and, where appropriate, implemented—either alone or in conjunction with other water augmentation methods.

Before initiation of land management to increase usable water, a number of factors must be considered. First, it must be understood that increasing supplies of water is not the only objective of land management. In some situations it may be a relatively minor benefit resulting more or less incidentally from the comprehensive management of land and, where conflicts in multiobjective resource management programs occur, improving usable water supplies may

have to be subordinated to other more beneficial objectives.

Second, land management techniques to increase water supplies must not be viewed in isolation. They are but one of several approaches to increasing the amount of water available for use. In considering the array of alternative techniques, it is clear that one need not operate in a particular area on an exclusive basis. On the contrary, as different technologies evolve, it will probably be desirable to combine one or more techniques so they may operate in concert with one another, particularly when the simultaneous action of separate techniques working together have greater combined effect than the sum of their individual effects in isolation.

Land management techniques themselves have to be explored and the magnitudes of their respective water-augmenting potentials examined to give some perspective to the problem. Each of the four techniques identified will have implications not only from a water supply standpoint but from a comprehensive land management standpoint as well, and this, too, must be considered. The differences in opportunities between privately owned land and public lands are also of importance.

Managing Forests and Brushland to Increase Water Supplies

Forests, brush, and range lands are important sources of the Nation's water supply. Commercial and noncommercial forests occupy approximately one-third of the total land area of the United States, receive about one-half the total precipitation, and yield about 65 percent of the Nation's total streamflow. Of the annual precipitation of the Nation, amounting to an average of 30 inches, forest lands receive 42 inches compared with 24 inches on all other lands. Forest lands yield 17 inches of annual runoff compared to 4 inches from other lands.[34]

Because vegetation affects the quality and quantity of water yield from a watershed, management practices can be applied to improve the useful water supply. Vegetation impacts upon the water supply in a number of ways. It intercepts rain and snowfall which are evaporated from the surface of leaves and needles. It draws moisture from the soil and releases it into the atmosphere by transpiration. Through the beneficial effects of its roots, its leaves, and other residue, it may facilitate infiltration of precipitation into the soil. And it tends to shade the soil and reduce wind velocity, thus reducing evaporation from the soil surface.

The net loss of water through evaporation and transpiration from the vegetative cover on a watershed varies with the amount and kind of vegetation present, and, in forested areas, with the forest cutting practices employed. By altering the amount and kind of vegetation and the forest cutting practices, water yield can be affected.

Harvesting timber tends to increase runoff. Experiments with total forest cover removal have resulted in first-year increases in runoff ranging from 1.3 to 18.0 inches.[35] Partial removal of vegetative cover produces smaller increases and, in some cases, no increase at all. Generally, forest management which involves harvesting all of the trees in selected areas tends to produce greater increases in runoff than is produced by comparable reductions in vegetative cover by harvesting timber on an individual tree selection basis. In the East, most of the increased water yield occurs during the growing season; in the West, during the winter and spring. Data indicate a steady decline in increased annual water yield after the first year of vegetative cover removal. The rate of decline depends upon the rate of revegetation.

Conversion of one type of vegetal cover to another in forests and brushlands has produced mixed results. In the East, a conversion from hardwoods to eastern white pine may reduce water yield, while conversion of hardwoods to grass tends to increase water yield. In the Southwest, conversion from trees to grass, on moist sites, has significantly increased runoff. Similarly, in the West, substituting grasses for chaparral has been found to increase water runoff.[36]

Managing Streambanks, Canalbanks, and Flood Plains to Increase Water Supplies

Experimental data suggest that where rainfall is relatively plentiful, removing riparian vegetation (i.e., vegetation which grows on the banks of rivers or lakes) produces no greater water yield increase than does the removal of similar quantities of vegetation elsewhere on a watershed. The situation is different where precipitation is low. In the arid and semiarid areas of the Southwest, phreatophytes occupy about 16 million acres of land. These plants inflict significant drafts upon ground water and reduce the flow of streams and discharges of springs. In some cases, this vegetation invades stream channels, reduces channel capacity, and thereby tends to increase flood stages. However, its removal may result in higher flood stages downstream.

Many Federal, State, and local agencies have undertaken phreatophyte research and control programs. Data from some programs now being implemented indicate the extent to which available water supplies might be increased by reducing the consumption of water by phreatophytes. It is estimated that removal of 6,000 acres of saltcedar and mesquite, two common phreatophytes, along the Rio Grande River will produce an annual increase of about 14,000

[34] SOPPER, William E (1971). Watershed Management, prepared for the National Water Commission. National Technical Information Service, Springfield, Va., Accession No. PB 206 370. p. 2.

[35] *Ibid.*, p. 17.

[36] HIBBERT AR (February 1971). Increases in streamflow after converting chaparral to grass. Water Resources Research 7(1):71-80.

acre-feet of water for use. Along the Gila River in Southern Arizona, 11,200 acres of phreatophytes are estimated to consume about 40,000 acre-feet of water annually.[37] Phreatophytes often provide very important wildlife habitat, particularly in the Southwest, and their removal increasingly is being opposed by sportsmen and conservation groups. Otherwise, the plants usually are of only limited value.

In managing streambanks to increase water supplies, a distinction should be made between phreatophytes which constitute native vegetation and those which represent invasion of a non-indigenous species as a result of overgrazing or other land management practices. A distinction should also be made between phreatophytes which line the banks of natural watercourses and those which have grown up along the banks of canals, irrigation ditches, and other manmade watercourses and impoundments. Finally, tradeoffs should be evaluated. If the efficiency of an irrigation project is threatened by a proliferation of phreatophytes which line artificial canals, which are not native vegetation, and which, if allowed to remain uncontrolled, would bring pressures to bear for additional and otherwise unnecessary supplementary irrigation works to offset the reduction in efficiency, it may be more sensible and involve less cost (economic and environmental) to control those phreatophytes than build additional irrigation works. The ensuing discussion in this section on Balancing Conflicting Interests describes the factors which should be considered in evaluating phreatophyte control programs.

Managing Snowpack to Increase Water Supplies

Particularly in the West, alpine and commercial timber snowpack zones yield a major portion of the water runoff. In Colorado, for example, the alpine area produces an estimated 20 percent of the State's water runoff, but comprises only about 3-1/2 percent of the State's land area. In California, 51 percent of the total runoff yield is produced in the snowpack of the State's commercial timber and alpine zones.[38]

The amount of usable water yielded from snowpacks is a function of the amount of snow accumulated and the rate and timing of melt. Sunshine, temperature, and wind, as they are influenced by topography, are important factors that influence the distribution and melting of the snowpack. In many cases, manmade barriers can affect the distribution of snow. Accumulating snow in deeper packs as a result of barriers tends to prolong the period of snowmelt runoff. Snow fences may accumulate as much as 50 acre-feet of water per mile of fence. Costs for additional water yield from snow fencing in the Rocky Mountains are currently estimated at about $23 per acre-foot.

In forest areas, the watershed can be managed to affect snow accumulation and melt. Openings in the forest tend to trap snow, and wind currents redistribute it into the forest where the shade provided by the trees protects it from the sun. Moreover, studies have shown that in forest openings the maximum snow accumulation was on the downhill side where cold air draining downhill was restrained by the trees, thus reducing winter snowmelt. The redistribution of snowpack resulting from the creation of openings in the forest also tends to produce increased streamflows. This is probably because (1) some water, formerly used to replace soil moisture consumed by vegetation, is available for streamflow instead, (2) reducing vegetation decreases interception; snow on foliage evaporates more rapidly than snow on the ground (lower albedo of the snow-foliage mix and exposure to wind movement), (3) more snow is deposited in openings where soil moisture deficits are least, and (4) snow in an opening is exposed to evaporation for a shorter time. Moreover, once the snow in an opening begins to melt, it melts more rapidly than snow in the forest, reducing the opportunity for evaporation and transpiration losses.[39]

It is possible to manage forest areas to increase snow accumulation, or delay or advance melt, for the purpose of regulating the amount of water yield and the timing of delivery. Generally, reducing forest vegetation tends to facilitate greater snowpack accumulation. Snow accumulation in clearcut areas tends to be greater than in areas selectively cut. Stripcutting, however, tends to result in greater accumulations than clearcutting large areas.

The timing of snowpack melt is also affected by cutting practices. Particularly in some areas of the West, uncut forests provide more water from snow-

[37] SOPPER, William E (1971). Watershed Management, prepared for the National Water Commission. National Technical Information Service, Springfield, Va., Accession No. PB 206 370. p. 88.

[38] Ibid., p. 56.

[39] HOOVER MD (1969). Water yield improvement for the timber snow zone of the Central Rocky Mountain area, pp. 111-116 in MEIMAN, James R [ed.] Proceedings of the Workshop on Snow and Ice Hydrology, at Colorado State University, August 18-22, 1969. U.S./IHD Snow and Ice Work Group, c/o Colorado State University, Fort Collins, Colo.

Winter snowpack can be managed to increase usable water supplies

melt later in the year than do large clearcut areas. Selectively cut areas, however, tend to provide runoff from snowpack melt which is stretched out over even longer periods than that produced from uncut forests. Generally, snowmelt is more rapid as wider strips of timber are cut.

Managing Soil Surfaces to Increase Water Supplies

Water harvesting as a means of increasing water supplies was brought to the attention of the Commission during our visit to the Agricultural Research Service, and more recently through testimony on the review draft of this report at regional public conferences held in early 1973. Water harvesting is the term most commonly used in referring to the treating or waterproofing of a land surface to increase the collection of precipitation. It is most applicable to land areas not covered with brush or trees and thus does not involve conventional notions of vegetation management. Desert shrubland, for example, can be made into a productive watershed through application of water harvesting techniques. In the Tucson, Arizona, area an average of over 300,000 gallons per acre per year of high-quality water can be obtained through water harvesting.[40]

Research over the last several years on specialized construction equipment, on different types of catchment areas (e.g., graveled plastic catchments, sodium treated catchments, and compacted earth catchments), and on storage methods has reduced the cost of treatment of water harvesting catchments to a point where, in many areas, the water produced is economically competitive with water from other sources. This is particularly true when small volumes of high quality water are wanted for livestock, domestic, or industrial purposes, and where ground water is either not available or of poor quality.

Experimentation is also under way to develop dual-purpose water harvesting systems which will combine water harvesting with production of specialized crops such as grapes.[41] Experimentation indicates that the precipitation harvested (and stored) from 1 acre of land in a 12-inch per year rainfall area in the Sonoran Desert in Northwest Mexico and Southwest United States will support 1 acre of lettuce if the water is applied as needed with trickle irrigation. Under this system, 2 acres of land would be needed to grow 1 acre of lettuce.

Dual-purpose water harvesting systems may offer a solution of what to do with farm land when ground water is exhausted in those areas where ground water use for irrigation exceeds annual recharge. Additional research will be needed to further reduce costs of water harvesting systems, including development of efficient storage facilities without which water harvesting systems are incomplete.

Potential for Increasing Water Supplies

A recent estimate places the potential increase in water supply from watershed land management activities at approximately 9 million acre-feet annually for the 48 contiguous States combined, as shown in Table 9-1.

The estimates shown in Table 9-1 are the product of one of many possible sets of assumptions; they provide a working notion of the potential for increasing annual water supplies by land management techniques. As can be seen, in some cases the quantities of water involved and the associated costs make watershed land management an attractive technique for increasing water supplies. The estimates exclude national parks, designated wilderness areas and areas whose physical characteristics preclude use of these land management techniques. The management programs contemplated in Table 9-1 assume strip or block cutting in commercial forests at higher elevations for snowpack accumulation, even-aged management at the lower elevations, conversion of chaparral and pinon-juniper to grasses and forbs, and conversion of selected areas of phreatophytes to shallow-rooted vegetation.

Balancing Conflicting Interests

Land management to attain some increase in water supply can be accomplished without lowering water quality, degrading the watershed, or deteriorating the forest environment. But in planning the use of land management techniques to increase water supplies, balances must be struck.

The measures that would be contemplated in a land management program such as that assumed for Table 9-1 are not comparable to single-purpose experimental measures designed to test the maximum extent to which land management might increase water supply. That kind of single-objective program, while maximizing water supplies, would occasion other costs which could be unacceptably high. Experimental measures designed to maximize runoff from forest areas, if applied in a large-scale management program, would mean great loss in timber production. In contrast, increased water yield achieved from the multiobjective management program assumed in Table 9-1 would assure sustained-yield timber operations. Specialized cutting practices, particularly for snowpack management, will add comparatively minor

[40] CLUFF, C Brent & DUTT, Gordon R (1973). Communication to the National Water Commission from the Water Resources Research Center, University of Arizona, Tucson. January 16, 1973.

[41] CLUFF, CB et al. (July 1972). Development of Economic Water Systems for Increasing Water Supply, Phase II. Research funded by the State of Arizona and the U.S. Office of Water Resources Research. The University of Arizona, Tucson.

Area and Source		Potential Annual Increase Under Present Forest Conditions (1,000 acre-feet)		Direct Financial Cost per Acre-Foot
TABLE 9-1.—Potential annual increase in water supply from watershed land management				
Northeast (New England, Middle Atlantic, Great Lakes, and Central States) Commercial forests		2,350		$ 2.18
Southeast (South Atlantic and Gulf States) Commercial forests		2,750		2.64
Eastern United States	Total	5,100	Avge.	$ 2.42
Pacific Northwest (Eastern portions of Oregon and Washington) Commercial forests		160		3.17
California (excluding North Coast) Commercial forests'		130		2.13
Phreatophyte areas		10		10.50
Chaparral		410		20.45
Woodlands-grasses		370		45.00
Northern Rocky Mountains (Idaho, Montana, W. South Dakota, and Wyoming) Commercial forests		1,000		.89
Other		40		90.00
Southern Rocky Mountains (Arizona, Colorado, Nevada, New Mexico, and Utah) Commercial forests		530		1.07
Phreatophyte areas		900		14.00
Chaparral		290		18.00
Other		300		128.00
Western United States	Total	4,140	Avge.	$ 21.42
48 Contiguous United States	Total	9,240		

Source: SOPPER, William E. (1971). Watershed Management, prepared for the National Water Commission, National Technical Information Service, Springfield, Va. Accession No. PB 206 370, pp. 106-107. After a report by IC Reigner, RC Maloney & EG Dunford (1969).

Note: This estimate illustrates one of several possible potentials of land management to increase water supply. The Commission is aware of, and commends to the readers' attention, other estimates such as those of the Senate Select Committee on National Water Resources, Committee Print No. 21, 86th Cong. 2d Session (1960), and those appearing in the Comprehensive Framework Studies of the various regions of the Nation.

ncrements to timber cutting costs. Numerous experiments conducted by the Forest Service confirm that soil erosion and consequent water quality effects are primarily a product of the logging practice employed, particularly with respect to road construction. Where roads are located on limited grades, away from streams, and with appropriate drainage structures, erosion is not significant. Immediate stand regeneration and other treatment measures also will eliminate unacceptable rates of erosion. Soil nutrient levels, after timber is properly removed, are neither drastically nor irreversibly depleted.

The presence or absence of vegetative cover on a watershed affects not only the hydrologic cycle, but other systems as well. Wildlife habitat and recreation opportunities may depend upon the presence of vegetative cover.

Timber cutting practices designed to increase run-off and snowpack accumulation, such as those assumed in Table 9-1, need not harm, and may even improve, habitat for many species of wildlife but may be undesirable for others. For example, Forest Service data indicate that timber cutting in patches and narrow strips improves the forest edge effect and the growth of forage, increasing the wildlife carrying capacity of an area. It is possible to convert vegetative cover from one type to another and simultaneously give appropriate consideration to recreation values. A management program for the East Sycamore watershed in Arizona (part of the Salt River Project), for example, includes treatment and conversion in areas originally so thick with chaparral as to be impassable. Clearing patches and converting them to grasses can create new recreation opportunities for hikers and campers. A Forest Service analysis of this particular management program indicates that clearing and converting small areas may simultaneously increase water yield and improve wildlife habitat in the area.

Treatment of riparian areas presents particular problems. Experiments report stream temperature increases resulting from streambank vegetation removal ranging from $3°$ to $18°F$. Such temperature increases may have important fishery implications, harming some species and benefiting others. Data also disclose that high water temperatures are rapidly reduced when a stream passes through an area shaded by vegetation. Where high stream temperatures are undesirable, retaining riparian vegetation may be indicated, notwithstanding the adverse impact such a decision may have on the quantity of usable water supply.

Another factor to be considered is that in some areas, the Southwest for example, phreatophytes provide cover and nesting areas for resident and migratory game species, most notably doves. Moreover, in some areas, the existing configuration of vegetation supports species of birds identified as rare or endangered such as the Mexican duck, gray hawk, and green kingfisher.[42]

Federal and State agencies have conducted studies to discover the elements of a satisfactory environment for the species of wildlife present in given areas. Doves, for example, seem to prefer dense thickets of mature saltcedar; large blocks of saltcedar are preferred over narrow strips or small patches. Saltbush, by contrast, has little value for dove nesting but does provide cover for other small game birds and animals. In view of the importance of phreatophytes to wildlife, selective clearing appears to be indicated. Thus, by selecting the amount and kind of vegetation, and the sizes of the areas treated, a management program could be developed which strikes an appropriate balance between water yield and wildlife and other values.

Water harvesting is a way of converting otherwise unusable or marginal land resources into water resources. Nevertheless, such techniques will change natural soil and vegetative conditions and can be expected to encounter problems of public acceptance. The tradeoffs involved, however, should be realistically assessed. In some sections of the Nation water harvesting may be the only way that additional water can be economically developed at acceptable environmental costs, particularly when compared with alternative ways of augmenting water supplies.

Effect of Ownership on Land Management

Legal and institutional arrangements may make some kinds of land management techniques to increase water supply more or less difficult to implement depending on whether lands are held in private or public ownership.

Managing Privately Owned Lands: More than half of the Nation's forest land is privately owned. Theoretically, private landowners seek to maximize their return; if it is to their economic benefit to develop additional water supplies, it is likely they will do so.

In some instances, land management measures will serve to provide a year-round source of water where before streamflow was intermittent. In other instances, means of capturing the additional supply will be necessary if it is to be utilized effectively. In either event, cooperative programs, such as those sponsored by the Soil Conservation Service under the Small Watershed Program, might be adapted so as to encourage private landowners to apply land management practices to increase water supply.[43]

---

[42] BRISTOW B (1968). Statement by Arizona Game and Fish Department on phreatophyte clearing projects, pp. 41-43 in 12th Annual Arizona Watershed Symposium Proceedings, Phoenix, Arizona, September 18, 1968. State of Arizona Land Department, Phoenix, Ariz.

[43] The Small Watershed Program is carried on under the provisions of the *Watershed Protection and Flood Prevention Act*, P.L. 83-566, August 4, 1954, 68 Stat. 666, as amended, 16 USCA 1001, *et seq.*

In some instances, there may be little incentive for a private landowner to alter management practices if he himself has no need for additional water or if conditions do not permit his harvesting the increased water supply. To encourage practices which will increase the available supply of water to others, financial inducements may be necessary. Generally, State water laws will not permit vesting of ownership of water in a landowner if he intends merely to sell the developed supply to other beneficial users. To overcome this obstacle, short of amending State water laws, local water agencies may find it economically feasible to finance some land management practices of private landowners.[44]

Managing Publicly Owned Lands: Lands held in public ownership present greater opportunities for applying land management practices to increase water supplies. Moreover, these opportunities exist where the need for water is often greatest.

National forests occupy 21 percent of the total land area in the 11 Western States and yield approximately 55 percent of the streamflow.[45] These lands are managed under concepts of multiple use and sustained yield.[46] Land management techniques that include water yield as an objective are consistent with these national forest multiobjective concepts. Presently, the Forest Service is carrying on a number of projects which include land management for this purpose. Projects of particular value are under way in Arizona, California, Colorado, and Utah and others are planned.

CONCLUSIONS ON LAND MANAGEMENT

A practical potential exists for increasing or otherwise improving water supplies by application of appropriate land management techniques. Adroit management of land resources can, in some cases, simultaneously yield increased water supplies (because of less evapotranspiration) and increased usefulness of supplies (by delaying or stretching out runoff) without harmful environmental effects. The Commission concludes, however, that increasing water yield is inappropriate where it requires eradication of native vegetation and threatens the extinction of endangered species of wildlife.

RECOMMENDATIONS

9-6.   The Congress and the President should direct Federal agencies having land management responsibilities to give adequate consideration to water yield as an objective of multiobjective land management plans.

9-7.   Local non-Federal water management agencies, whose constituents would benefit from an increase in water supplies derived from land management practices, or public and private landowners who would benefit, should finance the additional cost of those management practices which are attributable to the water supply objective.

OVERVIEW OF POTENTIAL TECHNOLOGY

New sources of fresh water may be obtained through developments which alter the hydrologic cycle in controlled ways, developments which create fresh water from salty or polluted water, or developments which transfer and store water. Each of these offers the opportunity for using new or improved technology, if such technology is available.

At the request of the Commission, the National Academy of Sciences (NAS) established a Committee on Technologies and Water to explore potential technological advances and their possible impact on water supply and water use. This section presents key portions of the findings of that Committee in regard to potential water increasing technologies.[47]

A number of potential water increasing technologies not now generally under study were identified and discussed by the Committee. These technologies have in no way been proven to be either technically or economically feasible; yet, on the basis of considered judgment, they were thought by the NAS Committee to have sufficient promise to merit attention in the future. Application of any of these technologies depends upon research and development

---

[44] See Chapter 7, Sections D and E, for a discussion of State water laws.

[45] SOPPER, William E (1971). Watershed Management, prepared for the National Water Commission. National Technical Information Service, Springfield, Va., Accession No. PB 206 370. p. 3.

[46] As required under the *Multiple-Use Sustained Yield Act of 1960,* P.L. 86-516, June 12, 1960, 74 Stat. 215, 16 USCA 528-531.

[47] U.S. NATIONAL ACADEMY OF SCIENCES, Committee on Technologies and Water (1971). Potential Technological Advances and Their Impact on Anticipated Water Requirements, prepared for the National Water Commission. National Technical Information Service, Springfield, Va., Accession No. PB 204 053.

being specifically directed toward making them operable. Some of the technologies are thought to be physically feasible now and others, even with a research and development program, would require a considerable period of effort, perhaps 10 to 30 years or longer in some cases, before they could be made technically feasible.

The following technologies for increasing water supply are presented without evaluation by the Commission as to practicality or desirability. They are presented here as illustrations of what some serious scientists, picked by the National Academy of Sciences, consider worthy of future investigation.

Compact Water Desalting Units for Residential Use

Although most of the desalting development effort has been concentrated on larger-scale facilities for communities and cities, as discussed in earlier sections of this chapter, there is some opportunity for using individual household-size units in situations where saline water might be distributed to family units or where dwellings are located in rural areas having only saline water sources. Rural use is considered the more likely because it would usually be more economical to have a large central desalting facility in a municipal system than to distribute salt water to each household with its own small purification unit. An exception might be the situation in which only saline water would be distributed throughout the community, each residential unit then purifying only the small fraction of the water needed for drinking and cooking. Under that circumstance, sanitary uses could be met by the saline supply. Some home desalting units are already in use, and it may be expected that during the next 10 to 30 years, there will be increased application of such units.

Long-Term Seasonal Precipitation Forecasting

Normal water supply, planning and management decisions, as well as flood forecasting, could be improved by accurate longer-range precipitation forecasting. Arid region agricultural programs could be modified to suit expected conditions. Such forecasts would provide a basis for guiding water use, appraising its seasonal availability, and making reservoir management decisions. The impact of this technology could affect water use patterns and planning trends, particularly along the western margin of affected continents.

Numerous technological breakthroughs will be needed before successful long-term forecasting can be achieved. The Global Atmospheric Research Program now under way among the nations of the world is expected to provide methods for predicting general atmospheric circulation. The progress being made suggests that within the next decade or so useful forecasts applicable to water management may be available.

Augmenting Fog Drip

When low-lying clouds or fog intercept the earth's surface, condensation of water occurs, and the ground and covering surfaces become wet. Such interception occurs naturally in several places in the world, including the famous Green Belt in the desert-like climate of coastal Peru and the coniferous forests along the coastal shores and mountains of California and Oregon.

The prototype planting of Norfolk Island Pine on a cloud swept ridge on the island of Lanai in Hawaii suggests that vegetation management might augment the water received as fog drip. Other development possibilities using fog drip include planting crops under trees so the crops could utilize drip water, or using impervious surfaces under trees to collect fog drip water for delivery to crops.

Artificial Ice Fields

Water may be stored as artificial glaciers by creating masses of ice to meet the demand for water in seasons when normal streamflow is low but water demand is high. Such ice fields could be created by utilizing the cold winter air to freeze water removed from storage in reservoirs or diverted from streams.

The water yield from mountainous watersheds in the Western United States does not coincide with the peak demand seasons. Year to year holdover of water in reservoirs utilizes space which might serve to store additional water if a means of auxiliary storage of reservoir water could be devised. One such method would be to release the water from reservoirs on winter nights and spray it on shaded terraces or northern slopes. The water would freeze as it fell forming an ice field. In the late spring and early summer this ice would melt slowly, supplying additional water for downstream use when streamflows are low. Such accumulations of ice occur naturally under waterfalls.

Deliberate Snow/Ice Avalanching

Water can be stored in deep snowpiles by deliberately avalanching selected snowfields. Snow in hese deep piles would melt slowly and yield water ate in the spring to meet increased water demands or eplenish reservoir storage.

As much as 10 to 15 percent of some high mountain areas consist of avalanche paths, some of which do not avalanche with any consistency. It may be possible deliberately to induce avalanching repeatedly at selected sites, resulting in massive amounts of snow piled up at downhill terminal sites.

Advantage could be taken of the reduced area of large amounts of snow at the terminal site by applying snowmelt retardants to further delay the melt and prolong the water yield. The prospect of delivering prolonged yields of cold water from such snowpiles may make the technique locally feasible in offsetting adverse thermal quality in streams.

Melting Ice Caps to Create Lakes

There are sufficiently large enclosed basins of ice of considerable depth, which, if melted, would create lakes for water storage. In theory, a nuclear plant generating electrical energy might be installed in a polar region where waste heat could be released for melting ice, thereby avoiding the adverse effects of thermal pollution. If economically feasible, the electric power could be transmitted to a locally situated electroprocess industry such as an aluminum reduction plant or, by displacement, be transmitted over great distances, and the water conveyed to storage in reservoirs on land to increase the fresh water supply.

Iceberg Towing

Iceberg towing would involve capturing or quarrying floating icebergs and towing them to a suitable offshore point where they could be broken up into manageable pieces (perhaps by means of explosives). The fragments would be hauled onshore and the bulk ice would then be granulated and utilized either for cooling large thermal powerplants or large central air conditioning plants, such as the New York subway system. Water from the melted ice would be added to the municipal supply. In a humid area, the melting slush would theoretically condense additional moisture from the air, to augment water yield.

Iceberg towing might be significant for certain large cities, particularly Boston, New York, and Philadelphia in the East, and possibly the Los Angeles Basin. From an economic standpoint, the "cooling" value of the ice may exceed its value as a fresh water source.

Collapsible Bladders for Transport of Liquids

Petroleum products can be transported through waterways and the sea by using large watertight bags or bladders fabricated from strong sheet materials of reinforced synthetic rubber or some types of plastic films. The folded or rolled empty bladder would be moved to the point of loading, partially immersed in the waterway, loaded with the liquid to be transported, and then towed by ship to its destination. It could then be pumped out, collapsed, and returned for reuse. Quantities exceeding 100,000 gallons could be readily transported in this way.

The same method also could be used for transporting fresh water. Very large bladders could be loaded at the fresh water source, perhaps at a river mouth, and towed to cities or to industrial users located on tidewater or navigable inland watercourses where fresh water supplies are scarce. Water towing may provide a water source competitive with desalted water, or with water transported over very long distances by pipeline.

Undersea Aqueducts

Large quantities of fresh water could be transmitted for long distances to serve coastal cities and adjacent inland areas using undersea aqueducts. Since fresh water has a lower density than salt water, salt water will support a bouyant fresh water aqueduct. Foundation problems are thereby limited to the relatively simple problem of holding down the aqueduct. The density of the sea water also reduces the strength required to withstand the pressures needed to produce flow. In principle, a large-diameter, flexible or semirigid plastic pipe could be laid from a specially designed vessel. The pipe would lead from a pumping station near the mouth of a river, such as the Rogue or the Columbia, along the coast on the continental shelf to its destination. Additional pumping stations could be provided along the route as required. On the basis of materials needed, such an aqueduct should be relatively inexpensive to construct.

An extension of undersea aqueduct technology could permit drawing deep cold ocean water for cooling purposes. A further application could be the controlled updraft of nutrient-rich deep ocean waters to produce major new fisheries.

Offshore Reservoirs

Large fresh water reservoirs could be created in ocean water near major centers of water use, utilizing

361

techniques similar to those for undersea aqueducts. Offshore underwater reservoirs could provide a means for coastal cities with combined sewers to hold flood discharges in a sanitary, inoffensive, nonpolluting way until they could be processed through a waste treatment plant. Elsewhere, they could be used for temporary storage of fully reclaimed effluent from waste treatment systems until these waters could be recycled. The use of such reservoirs as terminals for undersea aqueducts would be possible in cases where reservoir sites are inadequate or land is too costly for this purpose.

Offshore reservoirs might take two forms, depending on whether the ocean surface could be reserved for the exclusive use of the reservoirs or not. If such reservation is possible and enforceable, the fresh water reservoir could be floating but made of material denser than sea water so that it would sink to the bottom when not in use and float when filled.

A submerged fresh water reservoir would require sufficient ballasting (perhaps with sand) to hold it down when completely filled and should be located so as not to interfere with ocean surface uses.

CONCLUSIONS ON POTENTIAL TECHNOLOGY

Each of the technologies identified above by the National Academy of Sciences' Committee on Technologies and Water would have to be carefully investigated for possible adverse environmental effects and should only be undertaken if the net benefits appear substantial, if the technology is the least-cost alternative, and if environmental standards can be satisfied.

In addition to these potential technologies for increasing water supply which have been suggested by the National Academy of Sciences, the investigation of potential technologies for decreasing water demand may also yield significant benefits. Application of research to ways in which industrial and other processes can be changed in order to effect substantial reductions in the amount of water required per unit of output or per unit of raw material processed could yield significant economic and environmental benefits by reducing the total quantity of water necessary to produce the quantity of goods and services demanded by society.

IMPROVING TECHNOLOGICAL INNOVATION

In the preceding portion of this chapter attention was directed to some dozen different water technologies which, if found to be feasible, could assist in meeting the Nation's future water demands. And there may be others. But the current program of research and development and technology assessment is not providing a comprehensive basis for determining the feasibility of these technologies or of those relating to water use which are potentially of comparable importance.

Thus, even though considerable sums are being spent on research and development in water technology and its adaption to practical situations, the Nation still is not able to make judgments regarding the potential utility of one technology as against others because all have not been studied adequately. Rather, some have been studied in depth while others have had little, if any, attention. And there is nothing to indicate that the technologies receiving the greatest attention are in fact the ones most likely to be successful or, if successful, the ones which will be most effective in increasing water supplies.

Nor is there evidence that the opportunities afforded by new technologies are being adequately appraised and incorporated into water resource planning programs. In fact, the opposite appears more commonly to be the rule. Water planning usually has reflected a conservative position toward technology. That is, planning is done within the framework of existing technology and does not as a rule presume the availability of new technologies. This is all the more remarkable since planning entities regularly anticipate economic and other changes which will affect the demand for water development. Measures which would help alleviate these difficulties are discussed in the following paragraphs.

Imbalance in Research and Development Programs

Of the dozen technologies discussed in this chapter, only one, desalting, has had a long-term sustained research and development program. It dates from 1952. The Office of Saline Water in the U.S. Department of the Interior was established specifically to direct research in this important area, largely through contracts with industry and research organizations. The indicated present and future reduction in desalting costs and the existence of technology adapted to differing conditions attest to the success of this highly specialized approach.

Research and development in weather modification and the more narrowly defined field of precipitation augmentation also have extended over a long period but on a much more intermittent basis with many participating research entities. It is only in the last few years that serious, well funded research in precipitation augmentation has been initiated by the Federal Government. In contrast to desalting, the entire program is not directed by a single agency.

Study of land management to increase water supply has been carried on over a lengthy period also, but usually as part of a broader program of land management for multiple purposes. In recent years, however, some studies have been undertaken for the specific purpose of increasing water supply. A number of Federal agencies, as well as States, are conducting land management studies.

The other technologies discussed in this chapter and other technologies relating to improved water use are receiving either no research and development attention or limited and very preliminary study, usually supported by general programs of research grants.

Imbalance in Planning Programs

The Nation, at both the State and Federal levels, has been and is conducting extensive studies relating to future water demands and how those demands are to be satisfied. Yet almost without exception those studies are based upon very conservative positions regarding technology, and water supply works being built or planned are basically unchanged from those planned almost a century earlier.

Research and development, if properly directed, could have a profound effect on future plans. Thus, planning programs should incorporate technology assessment as a significant part of the program not only to take advantage of new technologies, but also to identify opportunities for developing such technologies.

Proposed Office of Water Technology

From its examination of the research being done with respect to new water supply technology, as well as that relating to water use, the Commission has concluded that there is a pressing need for a U.S. Office of Water Technology (OWT) to direct an effective, balanced research and development program and to assist planning agencies in technology assessment and innovation.

The Office of Water Technology would provide the management for a concerted effort to develop and introduce new or improved technology into the water supplying and water using areas. The new OWT would include the program of the Office of Saline Water, the weather modification activities of the National Oceanic and Atmospheric Administration, the precipitation augmentation and geothermal research and development programs of the Bureau of Reclamation, the water research activities of the Environmental Protection Agency, and the program of the Office of Water Resources Research. As has been done so effectively by the Office of Saline Water, research and development activities should be accomplished primarily under contract with industry and non-Federal research organizations.

The principal role of the OWT should be to manage the program and make it an effective adjunct to ongoing water supplying and water using activities. It should do this by three distinct activities: (1) carrying on a systematic examination of technological trends to forecast the direction of technological developments, both those in the water field and those in related fields, which will impinge on water supplying and water using activities; (2) providing assistance to planning agencies so that they in turn may draw their plans so as to take advantage of technologies that are favorable and to minimize the adverse effects of others; and (3) budgeting and carrying forward a broadly conceived and balanced research and development program.[48]

---

[48] The Commission's recommendation regarding establishment of an Office of Water Technology is presented in Chapter 11.

Better Decisionmaking
in Water Management

This chapter explores the decisionmaking processes that are involved in water management. These processes contribute not only to formulation of water projects and programs, but also to the planning and management of the use and conservation of water resources at local and State as well as at the Federal levels.

Decisions to act, whether they are legislative or executive, Federal or local, discretionary or ministerial, seldom come about spontaneously or effortlessly. A decision to construct (or not to construct) a water development project of certain specifications, in a given place, for specified reasons, and at certain costs is typically the last in a chain of choices or acts. The advancing stages by which thoughts become plans, plans are translated into proposals for action, and action is executed form the thread of this chapter. The thread leads through water resources planning and project evaluation, legislative authorization, budgeting, and appropriation of funds.

At the outset this chapter examines the proper role of water resource planning in the decisionmaking process. Then, the contributions and limitations of public participation in the planning process are considered, and several recommendations are made, including one for a public advocate who may appear in a representative capacity in proceedings where significant and unrepresented public interests are involved.

Next, the chapter takes up the problem of evaluation of water resources development proposals. Evaluation is an integral step in the planning process. Traditionally, water development proposals have had to be justified on the ground that they will contribute to national economic efficiency or development. Today, there is growing recognition of a need to

include other standards of value in deciding what is a good public water resources investment. The section on evaluation concludes with a description of a highly quantitative tool of policy: the discount rate. The use and the effects of the use of discounting to measure the present value of future benefits and costs of public investments are discussed in such manner as to demonstrate the very great significance of the selection of a rate of discount in determining which projects and programs are selected for authorization.

The final section, entitled "Authorization, Budgeting and Appropriations," examines procedures through which plans of development are translated into legislative authority, are scheduled for implementation and, finally, are financed.

WATER RESOURCES PLANNING

Water resources planning is carried out at every level of government as well as by private industry. Planning is not decisionmaking but it is the prelude to informed decisionmaking. A considerable portion of the Nation's water planning is done in urban areas by city water and sewer departments, sanitary districts, and drainage and flood control districts. In rural areas, local water planning is being done by such agencies as soil conservation districts, watershed districts, and irrigation associations. Some States now have statewide water plans. In many States there are intrastate basin planning organizations, taking many forms, from irrigation districts to river basin authorities. In Wisconsin, for example, where the State constitution prohibited the State from undertaking projects of internal improvement, a private corporation was granted a charter for the development and management of one of the State's major river basins.

Water resources planning by Federal agencies evolved as a resource development activity. Navigation, hydroelectric power, irrigation, drainage, flood protection, reclamation, and similar types of improvements constructed with Federal funds have had to be planned and coordinated. The planning was designed largely to make the Nation's water resources either more productive, or, as in the case of flood control, less destructive to existing enterprises.

Some planning of this kind will continue to be done in the future, but most of the economic projects of this type have already been built. A more pressing need for the future is for planning for other purposes such as for joint or coordinated management of existing multipurpose water facilities by Federal, State, and local governments, for improved water quality in the Nation's streams and lakes, and for better local and non-Federal use of water and related land resources, as, for example, where it may be necessary to locate, license, and regulate the use of land for industrial, commercial, or residential purposes, or where it is necessary to coordinate the planning of metropolitan water and sewage treatment facilities with planning for land use in the areas to be served.

There is usually no "best" plan in any objective sense. In any given situation, the number of the alternative combinations of actions that might be taken is usually very large and the full range of their consequences is difficult to determine with any precision. Most of the development problems for which plans are drawn can be solved in a number of ways.

Planning for development, in most instances, involves many factors that are not always easy to quantify. Proposed developments usually affect some values which the planners may not know how to measure. Rather than recommend a specific planning solution, the planner should describe the major alternative courses of action, lay out the probable adverse and beneficial consequences of each choice, and submit the results to the elected decisionmakers for their determination.

Deficiencies in Planning

From its hearings, meetings, and studies and from professional planners, utility managers, water users, and others interested in and affected by planning, the Commission has been able to collect and consider both the strengths and weaknesses of the kind of planning that is being done today for the development, regulation, and use of the Nation's water resources. Most frequently voiced are criticisms that (1) water planning is not adequately integrated with

planning for the land uses that water developments are expected to serve; (2) while much attention has been devoted to planning for large river systems, too little effort is made to relate that planning to the needs of metropolitan areas; (3) plans have taken too little account of the environmental consequences and water quality planning has been conducted apart from water planning in general; (4) plans often do not reflect the interest of the general public, large segments of which have little voice in it; (5) planning, especially that required of the States as a condition of future Federal assistance, is expensive and time consuming out of proportion to the States' need for it and the benefits that result from it; (6) plans, particularly river basin plans, tend to avoid setting priorities and to proceed unrealistically with early action proposals that would ultimately cost substantially more than is likely to be spent for the area involved; (7) in the absence of national priorities, planning leads to development conflicts among regions of the Nation; (8) planning is too rigid in its adherence to long-range forecasts in a world of rapid social, economic, and technological change; and (9) planning tends to bury in the arithmetic of benefit-cost analysis important issues that must be decided on a nonquantitative and judgmental basis.

Each of these charges deserves serious reflection and consideration. Many of them are discussed in later sections of this chapter or elsewhere in the report. Those selected for discussion here reflect the Commission's considered conviction that large-scale Federal water developments will not play as dominant a role in future water resources planning as in the past. The most important challenges to planners in the future are those associated with local, non-Federal uses of water and land: water supply and wastewater treatment for growing metropolitan areas; management and regulation of use of water for local commercial, industrial, and residential development; water for recreation; water quality and pollution control; and powerplant siting and licensing.

Integrating Water Planning with Planning for Land Use and for Other Purposes

Water planning sometimes appears to be an end in itself. Water planners, operating apart from other functional planning agencies, often work without any first-hand knowledge of the needs and intentions of those who are planning for such things as land use, transportation, housing, and industrial development. Important decisions about land use may be con-

Use of land and water in upstream areas affects estuaries and coastal zones

strained or thwarted by independently-conceived water resource developments.

Land use planning and water resources planning should be integrated. Water resources planning is important, but it is only one aspect of overall resources planning to satisfy human wants. An example of the relationship between water and land planning is found in their mutual concern for flood damage reduction. Flood damages follow when lands used for carrying flood flows are occupied by buildings and other types of improvements. Land use plans made without the involvement of the water planner may permit the extension of residential and industrial buildings onto the flood plain; may permit flood storage areas, such as swamps, to be drained

and filled; and may approve the use of the flood plain for channel-constricting uses, such as filling for site improvement or for the disposal of solid waste materials.

Water planners, on the other hand, sometimes proceed without the involvement of the land use planners, for example, in the construction of reservoirs in rural areas. Such reservoirs frequently become recreation magnets for urban residents living in municipalities a considerable distance away. The recreation attraction of the reservoir sets in motion a land development process which will have a significant impact on local service demands and on local tax revenues. Rural governments in the vicinity of the reservoir site are not often equipped to manage the land development, traffic, law enforcement, and sanitation problems that follow in the wake of such water developments.

The uses of land and water in upstream areas may directly or indirectly affect downstream estuaries and coastal zones. Similarly, land uses in the coastal zones themselves may affect the uses of water there. Hence, both water and land use planning for upstream and for coastal zones need to be developed in conjunction with each other. Land use plans prepared and implemented by the States should, where appropriate, provide for developing and protecting the important characteristics of estuaries and coastal waters as a part of an overall effort to coordinate land use planning with water resource planning.[1]

How lands are to be used will in large measure determine where and how much water will be demanded and for what purposes. For example, decisions made in preparing land use plans for industrial parks, powerplant sites, irrigated agriculture, commercial development and other water-using purposes will determine whether or not, how, and the extent to which water resources will have to be developed to serve the intended uses. Similarly, a decision to license or not to license a thermal powerplant at a given site may in turn rest upon the availability of adequate sources and receiving bodies for cooling water and may influence plans for development of water resources for that site and for other adjacent and nearby lands. Just as the Federal Power Commission and the Atomic Energy Commission are now called to engage in planning as part of their licensing missions, State and local licensing and permit granting authorities will have to enter into planning (including, whether they realize it or not, water planning) in order to fulfill their duties in the future.

Those whose principal function is to plan and manage water resources operate under dual constraints. First, like the miner who must mine where the ore is, they must live with the kinds of physical constraints that confront all who deal with natural resources. For water planners these constraints can usually be overcome, but only at a cost. These costs, both monetary and nonmonetary, must be made known to those who plan for other kinds of development as well as to those who decide whether to undertake the water project. Second, because they plan for the development and management of a resource that serves other functions like housing, industrial development, recreation, and agriculture, water planners must operate within a framework of demands that may be continually shifting. Water supplies that are adequate for today's rural town may be inadequate for tomorrow's suburb. A different treatment of wastewater will be required when farmlands become residential tracts and water which was used for irrigation is transferred to municipal or industrial use. To meet these changes, water development plans must not only be tailored to satisfy immediate and foreseeable projected demands but also should be flexible enough to allow for conversions to the demands of the more distant future.

While representation of transportation and other interests on water resource planning bodies does help to reduce the risks of inadvertent conflicts, it does not wholly answer the need for coordinating water planning with planning for other functions. The problem is, in part, one of devising arrangements which will allow for joint scheduling of different but interrelated planning programs, arrangements which would make possible the joint consideration, within a common time frame, of the areas of mutual concern.

States that receive grants for water planning under Title III of the 1965 Water Resources Planning Act are required to coordinate that planning with all the other Federal, State, and local planning being done in their States. There has been little attention to this requirement by the States and no guidelines exist which would direct them to take specific, verifiable actions to effect such coordination. This is an area where leadership and action by the Water Resources Council is necessary, and it is an appropriate function of that body to outline and enforce procedures to accomplish this purpose in its administration of the grant program.

Bills introduced in the Congress[2] would establish grant programs to enhance State land use planning capabilities. Some of these bills would create a Land and Water Resources Council. Others would place a program of improving State land use planning in the Department of the Interior.

Even though land use planning by itself is beyond the Commission's statutory mandate, the strong interrelationships between water and land use planning suggest that it is appropriate for the Commission to urge the President and the Congress, in

---

[1] See Chapter 2 for a discussion of estuaries and the coastal zones.

[2] S. 632, proposed Land and Water Resources Planning Act of 1971, February 6, 1971, 92d Congress, 1st Session; see also S. 992, proposed National Land Use Policy Act of 1971, February 25, 1971, 92d Congress, 1st Session.

considering any legislation on the Federal role in land use planning, to make adequate provision for coordinating that Federal effort with water resources planning at local, State, and Federal levels. The chairman of the Water Resources Council should be a member of any coordinating body implementing any national land use policy legislation.

Recommendation No. 10-1: If Congress enacts legislation to establish a program of Federal grants to States for improving State land use planning, it should make adequate provision in that legislation for the coordination of water and land use planning at the State, Federal, and local levels, and should encourage the use of coordinating institutions, such as the Title II river basin commissions, where they exist.

Intrastate Water Planning and Management

Intrastate planning organizations play important roles in the water planning programs of many States. Some have the authority not only to plan but also to finance, construct, and operate facilities. The Miami Conservancy District in Ohio is an example of a multipurpose intrastate agency that has made a significant contribution to its area. Begun in 1914 in response to a devastating flood, it has constructed and locally financed five detention dams and many other local improvements.[3] In more recent years it has acquired important pollution control functions.

The Wisconsin Valley Improvement Company, owned by six paper mills and four power utilities, was granted a charter in 1907 to develop the Wisconsin River, which has a drainage area of almost 12,000 square miles.[4] The Corporation is regulated by the State, which approves its plans for building and financing works, establishes minimum and maximum water levels, and approves semiannual toll charges.

In Texas, the Lower Colorado River Authority (LCRA) is an example of the type of intrastate basin agency developed by that State to manage its waters. Created in 1934, it is one of the first of the local river authorities established in Texas. Since then, a number of others have been formed, including the Central and Upper Colorado River Authorities. The LCRA has installed six dams and reservoirs above Austin. These are operated as a system to provide flood storage, generate electricity, provide water supply, and offer recreation opportunities.

Similar types of intrastate water planning and management organizations exist in various parts of the United States. Their number is large and their programs differ in size, complexity, and breadth of purpose. They represent a local, pragmatic, and action-oriented approach to a water management need that was both obvious and urgent to residents and officials in their areas. Since most of these intrastate bodies were created to serve a specific local purpose, the purposes of each do not often encompass a full range of water interests. Thus, their authority may not allow them to deal with such important water concerns as ground water management, recreation, fish and wildlife propagation, or water quality. Problems are often not dealt with as logical wholes and there are no established mechanisms for integrating the planning of these organizations with one another and with many of the Federal, State, and local planning agencies.

These are limitations, however, which could be removed. The scope of these organizations' functions could be broadened as needed to allow them to forge more comprehensive water management programs. The States, where necessary, could give these intrastate water planning and management agencies better guidance on how their local planning and development programs affect and are affected by one another and by those of the Federal and State agencies with related water interests. The upgrading and strengthening of these types of intrastate bodies is worthy of attention because they can be effective, independent, and economical.

The Federal water planning interest, which focuses largely on multistate and international river basins, is also affected adversely when local and State water planning organizations fail to plan for the management of water resources in which there is a Federal interest. The volume, quality, and the dependability of the supply in the main stems of the larger rivers are affected in important ways by the kinds of resource use and development policies which are established in the upstream watersheds usually under State or local control. It would, therefore, also advance the Federal water interests to encourage and assist local and State governments to do a better job of building effective intrastate basin planning organizations in their areas to achieve better local management of their water and related land resources.

---

[3] BOOZ, ALLEN & HAMILTON, INC (1971). Analysis of Managerial, Financial and Regulatory Functions of Regional Water Resources Authorities and Other Institutional Arrangements. U.S. Office of Water Resources Research, Washington, D.C. p.36.

[4] *Ibid.*, p. 53.

369

Recommendation No. 10-2: The Water Resources Planning Act of 1965 should be amended to open the present program of water resources planning grants not only to the States, but to local, intrastate planning entities as well.

New Organizations for Metropolitan Areawide Water Planning

Because the majority of the population today lives in cities and metropolitan areas, a more urban orientation for water planning agencies is needed. Today, in many parts of the United States, planning entities with such an orientation are needed to provide better ways of developing and using water resources. They are needed especially in some of the heavily urbanized areas where competition for the use of a limited water supply is growing rapidly. The multijurisdictional character of rivers flowing through many of our larger urban areas makes it impractical for individual cities or counties to plan independently for their use. These rivers constitute a valuable local resource which must be used both simultaneously and sequentially by a large and growing number of public and private users.

A planning organization resembling or modeled after a river basin planning commission is an appropriate mechanism for bringing together in one place the necessary information about the water resource: information about the character, scope, and timing of the demands that are being placed on that resource by different user groups, and information about the nature, the extent, and timing of the future changes that can be anticipated in the supply and demand situation on the river. In such a forum, the principal users can negotiate with one another and develop a collective strategy for the river, one which will permit each of them to use his allocated share of the resource with reasonable security and, at the same time, commit him to abide by procedural rules and use regulations which are designed to accommodate new users and protect the rights of all the other users of the river.

Urban interests have not, however, been able to develop or promote their special views within the federally dominated multistate river basin planning commissions created under the Water Resources Planning Act. Ordinarily the multistate basin planning groups are not organized to provide direct representation of urban interests. The plans prepared by these kinds of river basin commissions may include flood control and navigation features which are designed in part to serve groups living in urban areas. On the whole, however, planning gives no special attention to the internal water needs of urban areas and fails to properly recognize nonutility types of urban water uses. As a result, plans are not often geared to the water problems and concerns of the average urban resident. To meet these urban needs, a more localized type of water planning is required, one conducted closer to the site of the problems and involving the participation of those who are intimately familiar with the full scope of urban interests and the local political and economic constraints of the metropolitan communities. This localized planning must be conducted by an entity having authority to deal with problems whose solution may involve other areas outside the local basin or metropolitan planning area, particularly where those areas may be wholly or partly located in different States.

The kind of intensive planning and management called for in metropolitan areas is seldom either necessary or workable on the scale of the larger, multistate river basins where the water interests are usually more numerous as well as more diffuse; where the issues are not often as clear cut; and where the demand-supply situation tends to be less tightly constrained. It would be useful, therefore, to have the Water Resources Council and the Federal-State river basin planning commissions identify smaller geographic planning areas both within and outside the jurisdiction of existing river basin commissions where more intensive water planning and management can serve metropolitan areas.

Where Federal interests are not involved directly, State and local governments should be encouraged to proceed on their own to establish intrastate planning bodies. The adoption of State laws for intrastate basin or metropolitan planning commissions or authorities, as in Texas and Wisconsin, would be helpful; State legislation could not only establish criteria for their creation but also provide advance authorization and specify funding sources for them.[5]

Where there is a distinct Federal interest in a small basin or metropolitan planning area because of the interstate or international dimensions of its water problems, a new Federal-State-local river basin organization could be created by amendment of the Water Resources Planning Act to authorize Federal participation in a new type of planning organization. The membership, geographic scope, authority, functions, financing, operating rules, and duration of each of

---

[5] See Chapter 11 for a more complete discussion of organizations for water resources planning and management.

these commissions would have to be tailored to meet the particular problems of the area and to make full use of the resources and powers of the participating States and local governmental units.

Recommendation No. 10-3: The Water Resources Planning Act of 1965 should be amended to provide for the establishment of Federal-State-local planning organizations for areas where there is a distinct Federal interest and where such organizations may be needed to provide more intensive and continuing attention to the water management needs of smaller basins or metropolitan planning areas.

Integrating Water Quality Planning With Water Resources Planning

Considerable progress has been made in getting the various water agencies to work together in joint planning programs. Those representing fish and game, forestry, agriculture, navigation, power development, and so on are beginning to find ways to accommodate their separate interests in the formulation of multipurpose water development plans. Until recently, planning for water quality has been conspicuously missing from this family of water concerns. Water quality planning has been assigned to the U.S. Environmental Protection Agency (EPA), an independent entity. Under administrative rules laid down by EPA, basin plans for water quality had to be prepared by States as a condition for the approval of Federal construction grants for sewage treatment works.[6] There was no requirement for a direct tie between these water quality plans and water resource planning conducted by the States or under the auspices of Federal-State river basin planning commissions. An unnatural separation of water quality planning from water resource planning, generally, was promoted by this arrangement.

The 1972 Amendments to the Federal Water Pollution Control Act[7] contain a number of provisions which if properly administered will permit combining water quality planning with water resources planning. One section of the Act requires development of areawide waste treatment management plans for areas which, by virtue of urban-industrial concen-

trations and other factors, have substantial water quality control problems.[8] The plans are to be made by area waste treatment management agencies designated by the Governors, and participation of the U.S. Army Corps of Engineers is authorized.

Other provisions of the Act require the President, through the Water Resources Council, to prepare comprehensive regional or river basin plans for all basins in the United States by 1980. The sum of $200 million is authorized to be appropriated for this purpose.[9] At the same time the States are required to have and to maintain continuing planning processes which result in plans which incorporate all elements of any applicable areawide waste treatment management plans and applicable basin plans prepared under the guidance of the Water Resources Council.[10] In addition, grants are authorized of up to 50 percent of the administrative expenses of qualified planning agencies capable of developing basin water quality control plans which, among other things, are to be developed in cooperation with and consistent with comprehensive plans prepared by the Water Resources Council.[11]

These provisions of the 1972 Amendments should make it possible to end the separation of water quality planning from water resource planning by bringing State water quality plans into phase with the comprehensive water resource plans for river basins being developed by the Water Resources Council, and by making local waste treatment plans one of the building blocks of State water quality plans.

The Water Resources Planning Act

In the Water Resources Planning Act of 1965, the Congress set out a policy "to encourage the conservation, development, and utilization of water and related land resources of the United States on a comprehensive and coordinated basis..."[12] Congress sought to achieve the "coordinated planning ... through the establishment of a water resources council and river basin commissions, and by providing financial assistance ... to increase State participation in such planning."[13] To date, seven river basin

[6] U.S. ENVIRONMENTAL PROTECTION AGENCY (January 1971). Guidelines for Water Quality Management Planning. Environmental Protection Agency, Washington, D.C.

[7] *Federal Water Pollution Control Act Amendments of 1972*, P.L. 92-500, October 18, 1972, 86 Stat. 816.

[8] *Ibid.,* Section 208, 86 Stat. 839, 33 USCA 1288.

[9] *Ibid.,* Section 209, 86 Stat. 843, 33 USCA 1289.

[10] *Ibid.,* Section 303(e)(3)(B), 86 Stat. 850, 33 USCA 1313(e)(3)(B).

[11] *Ibid.,* Section 102(c)(2)(D), 86 Stat. 818, 33 USCA 1252(c)(2)(D).

[12] P.L. 89-80, July 22, 1965, 79 Stat. 244, 42 USCA 1962.

[13] *Water Resources Planning Act*, P.L. 89-80, July 22, 1965, 79 Stat. 244, 42 USCA 1962.

commissions have been established under Title II of that Act. Despite the policy declarations of Congress, which indicated that the Water Resources Council and the river basin commissions are to coordinate Federal water planning activities, Congress has not used these bodies as the single point of coordination for all water-related planning.

The U.S. Department of Housing and Urban Development (HUD) administers a flood insurance program, pursuant to the National Flood Insurance Act of 1968,[14] and, through grant programs authorized under Section 701 of the Housing Act of 1954,[15] as amended, engages in water and related planning activities in municipalities, counties, multicounty development districts, and States. Like the water quality planning heretofore done under EPA grants, these programs need not be planned in coordination with established river basin commissions. The Tennessee Valley Authority (TVA) and the Federal-State compact commissions, such as the Delaware River Basin Commission, also do not conduct their planning activities under the auspices of the Water Resources Council. The U.S. Army Corps of Engineers carries on many water planning studies, such as the Northeastern U.S. Water Supply study,[16] which are conducted independently of other planning efforts of river basin commissions that are coordinated by the Water Resources Council. The Bureau of Reclamation has been charged with lead agency responsibilities in the multiagency Westwide Study,[17] which is preparing an 11-State water plan. The river basin commissions and the Water Resources Council are merely participants along with other State and Federal agencies having an interest in the planning. The Act authorizing the Westwide Study, although passed three years after the Water Resources Planning Act, assigned the responsibility for this interdepartmental and intergovernmental water study to the Secretary of the Interior.

In addition, the Congress has never given to the States the amount of money it authorized in the 1965 Act for their participation in the river basin commissions, $5 million annually for ten years.

Beginning with $1,875,000 in FY 1967, the appropriation was increased to $2,375,000 in FY 1970, and was held at $3.6 million in fiscal years 1972 and 1973. One consequence of this underfunding has been lackluster performance of the States as basin commission members. Another is the failure of the basin commissions to incorporate the views and secure the cooperation of local governments and private interests in the river basin planning. Thus, congressional authorizations for special planning studies and failure to support the Planning Act with adequate funding have not permitted the river basin commissions and the Water Resources Council to develop fully their potential as effective planning and coordinating bodies.

Recommendation No. 10-4: In appropriating funds for future water resources and water quality planning, Congress should provide for coordination with the plans and programs of the established Federal-State river basin commissions and the Water Resources Council. Congress should appropriate larger amounts under the Water Resources Planning Act for support of State water planning.

THE ROLE OF THE PUBLIC IN WATER RESOURCES PLANNING

In many of its conferences held throughout the country, the Commission detected concern about the Nation's water policies and practices, and evidence of increasing desire on the part of many "publics"[18] to participate in the planning processes of water resource agencies. Much of this heightened interest in public participation reflects an upsurge in interest in environmental quality, but all phases of water resource activities, not just environmental aspects, should be open to public review and should be influenced by public reactions.

Public participation should not be a one-way street. It should not only be a way of ascertaining different views, it should also provide those whose interests may be affected an opportunity to learn about decisions being made.

---

[14] Title XIII, P.L. 90-448, August 1, 1968, 82 Stat. 572, 42 USCA 4001.

[15] P.L. 83-560, August 2, 1954, 69 Stat. 640, 40 USCA 461.

[16] *Act of October 27, 1965,* Title I, P.L. 89-298, 79 Stat. 1073, 42 USCA 1962d-4.

[17] Authorized in the *Colorado River Basin Project Act* in 1968. P.L. 90-537, September 30, 1968, 82 Stat. 885, 43 USCA 1511.

[18] For the purpose of this chapter, a "public" refers to an individual or a group not having governmental decisionmaking authority. "Public participation" refers to activities of such individuals or groups in trying to influence decisionmaking. This section deals with public participation in water resources planning carried out by single government agencies and by interagency enterprises, and also in licensing procedures for private and other nonFederal water resource or related projects.

Some publics' views are vocally expressed and easy to detect; others, no less important, may be faint and easily overlooked. The problem is to identify important viewpoints and insure that they are adequately expressed and properly considered. It is important, however, to find a way to insure that expression and consideration of public viewpoints do not improperly impede the decisionmaking process.

Determining the role which public participation should play in water resource planning requires discovering (1) the limitations which are inherent in public participation; (2) the requirements which must be met to insure adequate participation; (3) how that participation should be structured (a) in Federal water resource planning, (b) in planning for non-Federal projects, and (c) in licensing proceedings; and (4) how excessive and damaging delays which might attend public participation in licensing proceedings can be avoided.

Limitations Upon Public Participation

The effectiveness of public participation in water resources planning is subject to certain constraints. Some constraints are appropriate, others are not. The first constraint, and an appropriate one at that, is imposed by our system of representative government. Public participation does not transfer the authority and duty for making decisions from those entrusted by law with that responsibility to those who are eager to participate. While it is desirable for planning agencies to encourage public participation, that does not diminish their responsibility to perform the duties assigned them by law. Secondly, even for those who are aware of the opportunities and who want to participate, limitations imposed by time and money may be disabling. Such publics may be at a significant disadvantage when pitted against others who have adequate funds, technical expertise, and political knowledge to advance their views. A third constraint is that those who feel that the planning agency always has its mind made up may be reluctant to participate in resources planning. Similarly, planning agencies may be reluctant to invite public participation if they believe some participants are always opposed to proffered proposals.

Nevertheless, a study conducted for the Commission indicates that in a significant number of cases public participation in the planning process reduces misapprehension, softens what might otherwise be hardened viewpoints, and facilitates the resolution of differences.[19] Polarized views constrain public involvement, but by providing opportunities for articulation of these diverse strongly held views, public involvement evidently can make for easier resolution of conflicts.

A fourth constraint is that publics are usually likely to participate in planning only if they perceive that their interests are affected substantially. When the impact of a proposed water project upon the public at large is diffused, even though the overall social impact may be substantial, individual publics may not be roused to participate.

Requirements for Adequate Public Participation

A public can be assured of the opportunity to have its views considered only if adequate procedures are provided. Public participation has its greatest effect in the formative stages of planning. Unfortunately, this is a point at which interest in participation is often low. In general, however, several basic requirements for adequate public participation can be identified:

(1) Notice must be provided to inform the publics of the planning activity and of the opportunities for participation, at the start.

(2) Forums must be provided to have the views of publics heard *throughout* the planning process, especially at or immediately preceding important decision stages. This should include the opportunity to propose and react to alternatives as the planning process evolves.

(3) Information must be made available to interested publics so that their participation can be informed, responsible, and substantive.

(4) Planners and decisionmakers must be able to assimilate public inputs and place them in perspective with all of the other information which must be taken into account in planning and decisionmaking.

(5) Decisions should be made openly by duly constituted officials.

[19] WARNER, Katharine P (1971). Public Participation in Water Resources Planning, prepared for the National Water Commission. National Technical Information Service, Springfield, Va., Accession No. PB 204 245. pp. 127-129. Compare, PETERSON MS (1971). Case description: Morrison Creek Stream Group Basin, California, Ch. XXVII in GOLDMAN, Charles R (1971). Environmental Quality and Water Development, volume II, prepared for the National Water Commission. National Technical Information Service, Springfield, Va., Accession No. PB 207 114.

(6) Schedules and deadlines should be set and kept to avoid unnecessary delays and to permit expeditious decisions.

Although there may be no single optimum planning process for all projects and programs, a process can be designed for most planning which will allow for adequate public participation. The points at which the public should have access to the planning process are outlined below.

Access Points for Public Participation in the Water Resource Planning Process[20]

1. Planning agency communication with publics concerning initial contemplation of study, proposed scope of study, and opportunities for public participation.
2. Identification of study goals and objectives.
3. Evaluation of resources; their availability and capability of meeting needs.
4. Formulation and evaluation of alternative plans.
5. Assessment of plans in light of costs and benefits in achieving originally hypothesized goals and objectives; and, as a result, reassessment of original goals and objectives.
6. Reformulation and evaluation of alternative plans.
7. Recommendation of a plan.
8. Review of the plan.

Water resources planning tends to proceed from identification of goals and objectives, through examination of the setting, consideration of alternatives, calculation of benefits and costs, and reassessment, to recommendation and review. Publics should have opportunities to contribute at each step. "Opportunity" is the key word throughout. Whatever procedures are adopted, they should be flexible enough to allow for innovation and adaptability to assure public participation which might not otherwise develop. Adoption of the following recommendation would strengthen public participation and lead eventually to better decisionmaking.

Recommendation No. 10-5: As provided in the Water Resources Planning Act, the Water Resources Council (WRC) with the approval of the President should:

a. **Direct Federal water resources planning agencies to adopt procedures and issue appropriate directives and guidelines to field entities to provide opportunities for broad public participation in water planning activities from the inception of the planning process on.**
b. **Monitor public participation in interagency planning by reviewing the adequacy of provisions for public participation.**

The WRC is the appropriate entity to direct Federal agencies to provide for public participation in water resources planning in which the Federal Government is involved and it is the appropriate entity to coordinate provisions for public participation in Federal interagency planning. It should not, however, prescribe specific, detailed public participation procedures, but should, instead, impose minimum requirements leaving to individual agencies responsibility for adopting, revising, and refining the necessary rules and procedures.

Until recently, public participation in water resources planning has emphasized public hearings. Generally, hearings were held at the beginning of a planning effort when general views of interested publics were solicited. Then, typically, there was a lapse in further public participation until after plan formulation was essentially completed, whereupon the plan was unveiled, usually to a group of people drawn from those residing in the area affected by the proposed project. Public hearings of this type are reactive in nature. The public is presented with a proposal on which to comment; a *fait accompli*, often with little if any opportunity to participate in its development or to view the alternatives which were considered by the technical planning staff.

Many of the newer public participation techniques are responsive to a desire by various publics to be more actively involved. Such techniques have attempted to escape dependence on those who always show up and are more or less adequately represented by local interests and articulate individuals. New techniques seek a broader representation and, hence, a broader consideration of public values and social needs. This is not to suggest that old voices should not be heard; but there is good reason why new voices, particularly voices of those who are seldom if ever noted, should be heard.

Some agencies have held public meetings, workshops, and technical briefings throughout affected areas and, chaired by local organizations, have developed explanatory brochures, and have explored issues

---

[20] These steps correspond closely to those enunciated by the U.S. Water Resources Council in its Proposed Principles and Standards for Planning Water and Related Land Resources (December 21, 1971). Federal Register 36(245):24144-24194, part II.

Congressional field hearings provide check on adequacy of public participation in planning

with public participants. Other agencies have created citizen review committees whose effectiveness tends to vary depending on the stage of the study in which participation is first introduced; the earlier the stage, the more effective seems to be a review committee's efforts.[21]

Recommendation 10-5 is limited to the WRC and to Federal agencies but it should be implicitly extended, to the extent applicable, to non-Federal water planning agencies. Non-Federal water planning activities, including the planning activities of State agencies and commissions created by interstate compacts, should

be similarly structured to insure adoption of adequate and effective public participation procedures.

Recommendation No. 10-6: As a prerequisite to project authorization, Congress should require Federal water resource agencies to report to it on public participation with respect to particular projects, showing compliance with agency public participation procedures, describing the questions considered and the viewpoints expressed, and providing supporting information for the decisions reached on controverted points.

The report to Congress recommended here would provide information for Congress on the issues which participating publics felt were important and on the ways in which an agency dealt with these in its planning. The report would also permit Congress a

[21] NEW ENGLAND RIVER BASINS COMMISSION (1971). Report of the Citizens Review Committee on the Connecticut River Basin Comprehensive Water and Related Land Resources Investigation to the New England River Basins Commission. New England River Basins Commission, Boston, Mass.

check on the adequacy of an agency's public participation regulations, on the WRC's guidelines, and on the extent of compliance with both. If it wishes, Congress can always augment an agency's public participation procedures by seeking additional testimony from public witnesses on specific issues in order to assure that all views are adequately considered.

Recommendation No. 10-7: Water resources planning agencies should structure their planning procedures so as to proceed promptly to resolution of issues and to conclusions, even though consensus is impossible, by scheduling the timing of public participation and defining the issues to be addressed. Agencies should not place excessive or sole reliance on formal proceedings, but should supplement the formal proceedings both before and after recommendations are made with informal meetings with interests affected by the proposal.

Public participation is vital; it is also an expensive, time-consuming process requiring significant commitments of an agency's planning budget and staff time. On controversial projects, there is always the possibility that hearings will become lengthy restatements of conflicting views long after it has become clear that consensus is impossible. That does not mean that some views should be ignored or inadequately explored in the name of efficiency. But lack of consensus should not impede the completion of reports. Informal discussions with both proponents and opponents of proposed projects can lead to better public response. Once fair and full consideration has been given to competing views, it is important that the planners draw their conclusions. The reports to Congress on public participation efforts will make the conflicting views known to Congress and that body may make an informed decision.

Recommendation No. 10-8: Water resources planning agencies should help compensate for the lack of resources of some participating publics (a) by providing timely, well-publicized information with respect to (1) opportunities to participate, (2) alternative courses of action, (3) the course of action favored by the planning agency, (4) benefits and costs, and (5) other relevant factors; (b) by scheduling at least one public hearing in the area of the proposed project; and (c) by making basic data, reports and other background information readily available to the public.

It has been suggested that limited financial, technical, and manpower resources available to many publics warrant government funding of participation by various publics in the planning process. The Commission has considered this possibility, but has rejected it. Access to agency background material, adequate notice, opportunities for participation at or before decisive stages in the planning cycle, full disclosure of material facts, hearings at or near the project site, and congressional review of public participation should be sufficient to overcome disparities in resources among various publics and between them and the planning agencies. The administrative problems of identifying those publics who should receive participation grants and of distributing such funds equitably make public funding inadvisable.

Licensing Proceedings for Non-Federal Projects

Many non-Federal projects are subject to licensing requirements with respect to their use of water. For example, under the Rivers and Harbors Act of 1899, all persons who discharged "refuse" into navigable waters or their tributaries had to obtain a permit from the U.S. Army Corps of Engineers.[22] Under the 1972 Amendments to the Federal Water Pollution Control Act, applicants for Federal licenses or permits to conduct any activity which may result in any discharges into navigable waters are to provide the licensing or permitting agency with certification from the State (after public notice and, where appropriate, after public hearings) that the discharge will meet applicable effluent limitations and Federal performance standards for discharge sources. Certification with respect to construction of a facility will with certain exceptions, fulfill the requirement with respect to any other Federal license or permit required for the operation of the facility, as well.[23] Permits are required from the Corps of Engineers for the discharge of dredged or fill material into the navigable waters at specified disposal sites,[24] and from EPA for the disposal of sewage sludge.[25]

Except for hydroelectric powerplants, which under several court decisions are subject only to the jurisdiction of the Federal Power Commission, a

[22] *Rivers and Harbors Appropriation Act of 1899,* March 3 1899, 30 Stat. 1151, 33 USCA 407.

[23] P.L. 92-500, October 18, 1972, Section 401, 86 Stat. 816 877, 33 USCA 1341.

[24] *Ibid.,* Section 404, 86 Stat. 884, 33 USCA 1344.

[25] *Ibid.,* Section 405, 86 Stat. 884, 33 USCA 1345.

variety of permits must be obtained from local, State, and Federal governmental agencies before any construction is undertaken which affects a water body.

Some of these licensing arrangements recognize that the public has an interest in the siting and use of water-related facilities and provide for public hearings or other opportunities for publics to be heard with respect to whether or not and under what conditions a particular license should be issued. However, these arrangements do not always operate to give interested publics an opportunity to express their views in the critical early planning stages, before a specific proposed project has been submitted by the non-Federal developer for the required permits.

Several bills introduced in the 92d Congress with respect to powerplant siting are of interest.[26] Although these bills deal with powerplant siting, their principles can be extended to other water-related activities as well. The primary thrust of this proposed legislation is to consolidate the many present licensing requirements into as few proceedings as possible, providing a procedure in which relevant factors may be considered and in which early disclosure of plant siting plans make early public participation possible.[27] This is desirable.

Recommendation No. 10-9: Federal and State governments should require advance public disclosure, as soon as feasible, in the prelicense planning of major non-Federal projects expected to have an impact on water resources (i.e., where a permit eventually will be required for the water use and where issuance of the permit is subject to a determination that it will serve the public interest).

The public has a legitimate interest in the use of water resources, especially the navigable streams and lakes which historically have been impressed with a public trust. Where this interest is recognized by legislation requiring a permit, as where it must be established that the public interest is served before a permit can be issued, it is appropriate to advise the public of a proposed use as far in advance as possible and to encourage the private entity responsible for planning and development of the resource to consider the views of interested publics.

It is not always feasible or desirable for private concerns to disclose their plans prematurely. For example, premature disclosure might impede the acquisition of necessary interests in real property by fostering artificial land speculation or, where the power of eminent domain is unavailable, by encouraging property owners to hold out for unreasonable prices. However, disclosure should be made as soon as feasible in order to inform the public about the expected water use and to give them an opportunity to express their views where it will count most, in the early stages of planning.

Public Participation in Planning for Non-Federal Projects

Under present arrangements, some Federal licensing agencies must engage in planning as part of their licensing mission. The Federal Power Commission, for example, is required to satisfy itself that a hydroelectric project "will be best adapted to a comprehensive plan for improving or developing a waterway or waterways for the use or benefit of interstate or foreign commerce, for the improvement and utilization of water power developments, and for other beneficial public uses, including recreational purposes; . . . ." and is authorized to require the modification of projects to accomplish this.[28] The Atomic Energy Commission evaluates proposed sites for nuclear powerplants to determine whether they meet the public interest in various ways, including health and safety.[29]

These agencies have formal procedures for interested persons to intervene in licensing proceedings and to participate as parties. However, under these procedures there is a question whether the views of all interested publics will be presented to the agencies as they engage in the planning which their licensing procedures require. For one thing, some planning decisions are made before a hearing is scheduled and before the public has an opportunity to participate effectively. This problem should be met by encouraging public intervention at an earlier stage in the planning process. In most situations it can also be tackled effectively by providing for public participation in land use planning and zoning, which can

---

[26] For example, the proposed Power Plant Siting Act of 1971, H.R. 5277, 92d Congress, 1st Session (1971); the proposed Electric Power Supply and Environmental Protection Act, H.R. 11066, 92d Congress, 1st Session (1971).

[27] See Chapter 6 on balancing environmental and developmental values for a discussion of H.R. 5277 and H.R. 11066.

[28] *Federal Power Act,* P.L. 74-333, August 26, 1935, 49 Stat. 842, 16 USCA 803.

[29] U.S. ATOMIC ENERGY COMMISSION, Regulations, 10 CFR 100.

often have a more important bearing on the siting of water-using facilities than planning which is associated with licensing.

There is still a lingering problem regarding public participation. Even when an agency's rules are adequate with respect to who may appear as formal parties and when they may appear, there is doubt whether certain segments of the public, who may be vitally affected by an agency's decision and who should be heard from, are likely to be represented before the agency at all.

Environmental issues and the viewpoints of those emphasizing environmental quality usually appear to be adequately developed in both AEC and FPC licensing proceedings, even though "environmentalists" may not always agree with the decisions rendered. Environmental organizations frequently appear as formal parties, present evidence in support of their positions, and cross-examine with respect to differing positions. Furthermore, and this is most important, the legislation under which Federal licensing agencies operate has been interpreted to impose an affirmative obligation upon them to develop and explore environmental issues.[30]

Other segments of the public who could be greatly affected by a licensing decision are not as well represented nor are they assisted as much by judicial decisions which require the licensing agencies specifically to take their interests into account. For example, certain classes of power consumers neither participate in hearings before Federal licensing agencies nor are they represented there by the agencies' staffs. Something should be done to insure that the voices of affected interests who would otherwise not be heard get heard.

Even environmental interests, which usually are adequately represented in "big" cases, may not be adequately represented in other licensing proceedings particularly non-Federal proceedings where NEPA does not apply. Several States have responded to this problem by designating an assistant attorney general to appear in appropriate cases as an advocate of the public's interest in environmental quality.[31]

The public advocate arrangement can be extended to encompass other values which should also be represented and it can be tailored to fit the requirements of particular licensing proceedings. It can serve to supplement direct public participation by providing an advocate for important interests which

licensing agencies should consider and, perhaps most important, it can offer representation for classes of interests which otherwise might not be represented at all.

Recommendation No. 10-10: Where conditions indicate, licensing agencies should seek to develop the interests of all those publics who are affected by agencies' decisions. Where it is determined that some publics are not adequately represented in licensing proceedings, licensing agencies should use independent public advocates to represent such interests, including environmental and consumer interests.

In seeking to expand public participation before licensing agencies, the use of one or more public advocates is preferable to amending licensing acts to require each licensing agency itself to consider specified interests. There is merit in leaving an agency with a broad standard which will permit it to take a variety of previously unrepresented or under-represented interests into account as they emerge. Amending organic acts by specifying particular interests to be considered might prejudice other interests not specified.

The task of representing otherwise inadequately represented publics should not be left to agencies' regular staffs. An agency's staff must develop a position on how it believes the agency should act on an application before it. A public advocate should be independent, free to represent a particular interest regardless of the position which a licensing agency's staff takes or the position which the agency ultimately accepts.

The Problems of Delay

The Commission recognizes that problems of delay may be especially serious in licensing proceedings of water or water-related projects, particularly where an applicant must obtain licenses from different agencies, and that encouraging representatives of the public to participate in these licensing proceedings may tend to increase the risks of damaging and unproductive delay. Society's interests are not well

---

[30] See Chapter 6 on balancing environmental and developmental values.

[31] See, for example, Washington Revised Code, Chapter 80.50, under which a "counsel for the environment" is appointed for powerplant certification proceedings; and Wisconsin's Chapter 75, Laws of 1967, Section 25(9), which provides for a "public intervenor" in proceedings where protection is needed for "public rights" in water such as a determination whether or not a permit for a dam should be issued.

served if a licensing agency is forced to act precipitately in a context of a crisis, inflamed by delays, or if a license applicant is forced to change its plans or project proposals, not on the merits, but simply to avoid further delay. The objective should be to accommodate interests of the publics and rights of the parties in order to produce a sound result in licensing proceedings, and to do so expeditiously.[32]

Three things can be done to help solve the problems of delay. The Commission believes, first, that it is essential to *identify disputed issues well in advance* of the time a particular facility may be required. The problem of delay is most serious when the applicant must meet a relatively immediate need and alternatives are severely limited by time pressures. Recommendation 10-9, calling for early public disclosure, is responsive to this concern.

Second, the Commission endorses the concept of extensive informal *prelicensing planning* to determine acceptable sites for industrial facilities and other projects requiring licenses, in the context of comprehensive land use and water resources planning. Such prelicensing land use planning would tend to resolve a number of issues, thereby limiting those which must be decided in a licensing proceeding.

Third, the Commission endorses the concept of consolidating required licenses into a *single proceeding* where possible. Consolidation or "one-step licensing" offers a mechanism for balancing competing values in a single proceeding, as discussed elsewhere in this report.[33] Furthermore, it offers obvious potential savings of time. Not only can proceedings be consolidated so that only a single presentation need be made, .but the possibility of separate appeals from numerous licensing decisions is eliminated.

EVALUATION AS A BASIS FOR DECISIONMAKING

In water resources planning, "evaluation" is simply a systematic method to test the desirability of undertaking any given water resources program or project. The principles and standards of measurement used in evaluation in large measure determine the future direction and pace of the Nation's water development.

In recent years, there has been a broadening of the traditional objectives of water resources development. In addition to the objective of developing the Nation's water resources to increase national economic output and efficiency, the list of other legitimate national objectives—some that may be economic in part, like regional development, and others that have to do with what are ordinarily considered noneconomic values such as scenery, fish and wildlife, and recreation—has been continually augmented.[34]

With the addition of new objectives, water resource planners must identify, measure, and weigh water values for a society increasingly concerned with the nonmarket as well as the "economic" consequences of water programs and projects. At the same time water quality control measures must also be evaluated.

Evaluation of Alternative Courses of Action

One of the major deficiencies in the current evaluation process is its continuing failure to encompass a sufficient number of feasible alternatives within a plan for developing the water resources or controlling the water quality of a given area. The evaluator's vision and his prerogative usually do not extend beyond locating and designing construction projects.

Alternatives which might solve a given problem may be outside the mission of his agency. For instance, the exploration of alternatives for additional municipal water supplies may neglect the role of pricing and metering in reducing consumption, the possibilities for reuse of wastewater, or upgrading the quality of potential local sources of supply. Cost-sharing arrangements may influence local beneficiaries to opt for a particular engineering project which may be an inferior alternative (because it costs more or yields fewer benefits or both) but which requires smaller payments from direct beneficiaries. In such cases management alternatives of development or no development, or development at a different location, or at a different time do not readily enter the screening.

---

[32] Improved procedures to minimize delays in licensing proceedings are discussed in detail in Chapter 6 on balancing environmental and developmental values.

[33] See Chapter 6 on balancing environmental and developmental values.

---

[34] The histories of major water development programs—the Reclamation Act of 1902, the Flood Control Act, and the Tennessee Valley Act—substantiate that executive and legislative policymakers have not been concerned solely with national economic development. Redistribution of income to different regions or classes of water users has been another principal objective.

Urban flood control projects require close coordination with rail and highway transportation facilities

The context within which alternatives are analyzed is important. The scope of water evaluation should not be restricted to or made to coincide with the jurisdiction of a particular water agency. Its authority simply may not extend to the type of alternatives which exist at the policy level where the political decisionmaker normally operates.

The Dominance of Benefit-Cost Analysis

The Flood Control Act of 1936 approved Federal investment and participation by the Corps of Engineers in flood control projects "... if the benefits to whomsoever they may accrue are in excess of the estimated costs, and if the lives and social security of people are otherwise adversely affected."[35] Since

---

[35] *Act of June 22, 1936,* P.L. 74-738, 49 Stat. 1570, 33 USCA 701a.

1936 economic analysis of water resources development, generally, has come to revolve around the so-called benefit-cost ratio, for which a gain in "national economic efficiency" requires a ratio of project benefits to project costs that is greater than one-to-one.

The methodology of this market-oriented water resources evaluation system has been continually improved to provide a rational basis for calculating in monetary terms the costs and benefits of water resources projects. The objective of national economic efficiency has been accommodated fairly easily within an assessment of the expected economic benefits of a project: power, irrigation water, navigation, or economic damages averted by controlling floods. Moreover, benefit-cost analysis has been extended to other agencies and has made evaluation procedures relatively uniform among them. It has also allowed limited comparisons to be made between the programs of different agencies.

Nevertheless, despite the refinement of benefit-cost analysis, it does not always supply a sufficient guide to the worth of a water resources project or program. Adverse effects of projects are seldom treated adequately; for example, increased flood heights downstream caused by upstream channelization or drainage projects are rarely considered. Furthermore, a ratio of dollar benefits to dollar costs cannot readily or appropriately place a precise value on the accepted "nonmonetary" objectives of water resources projects and programs.

In the calculation of monetary project benefits and costs, it is not always easy to account for the indirect effects, both positive and negative, or to assess the social impact of programs of water planning and development. Increase in national income—the net gain in market value of the goods and services from water resources development—is a contributor to national well-being, but it is not the only index of the social effects of development. Gains to a particular locality or region, monetary or nonmonetary, cannot always be equated with gains to the Nation. For example, changes in the distribution of wealth among regions can be an important effect of a water project or program. As a result of a decision to provide some type of water service in one region rather than in another, there may be offsetting losses in the "other" region. The redistributional effects need to be catalogued to show at different points in time the projected effects of the development.

Environmental changes that may occur as a result of project development should also be exhibited in the evaluation of a project or program. Many environmental effects can be quantified and can have dollar values attached. Crude indicators, such as miles of free flowing stream, can be provided. It might be shown, for example, that a particular project would inundate 50 miles of the last remaining 100 miles of spawning gravels accessible to an anadromous fish run, and that that adverse effect can be valued as a real cost or disbenefit. Project impacts upon ecosystems are likely to occur not only in the first phase of construction but will continue throughout the life of the project, and beyond. A time profile of expected environmental changes showing, for example, what wild rivers will be flowing or how many natural spawning areas may remain in 10, 20, or 50 years' time if all plans proceed as projected is useful information to include in an evaluation if the Nation is to preserve its options as it plans for development.

At the same time, conscious effort has to be made to avoid the temptation to achieve false precision in evaluation. It is folly to attempt to convert all economic, social, and environmental effects into a common unit. Dollar values—however appropriate to measure economic effects—may be worse than meaningless to measure noneconomic ones. They may be deceptive as well. A good safeguard against false precision is to quantify the quantifiable, and separate the nonquantifiable, leaving its evaluation in the plain, textual terms on which it must ultimately be assessed by decisionmakers. Environmental, social, ethical, and other human factors not readily or appropriately valued by the market can never be realistically weighed in the calculation of benefits and costs.

Criticism of the misuse of the national income or efficiency criteria (benefit-cost analysis) in the evaluation of water resources development should not, however, be allowed to detract from its usefulness in the decision process. These criticisms, properly construed, do not argue against analytical methods (which are being continually improved). They do argue against abuse of the methods and against slavish adherence to the notion that all water resource projects can be evaluated with exquisite mathematical precision.

Notwithstanding the importance of benefit-cost analysis, it is not everything nor should it necessarily be controlling. Rigorous analysis provides decisionmakers with information on the consequences of alternative decisions. It does not make those decisions. For a variety of reasons, not the least of which is that the future is not susceptible to precise forecasting, important social and political considerations, in addition to benefit-cost analysis, must also be taken into account by decisionmakers.

The Efficacy of Effective Demand in Evaluation

The first task of evaluation should be to establish whether an effective demand exists for the particular outputs or services of a water project or program. Evaluation can answer a searching first question: Is there an effective demand for the "services" of a particular water development? (It can answer others as well, such as: What benefits does society forfeit by undertaking development of a project?) Effective demand, demonstrated where the users of a water project or service signify a willingness to pay for the service or output to be provided, is the one sure measure of the economic benefits that will be obtained from a water resources project or program.

Benefits exist because there is a demand, not because a certain quantity can be supplied. The demand for more irrigation water does not stem from a simple desire for additional acres of irrigated land. The demand for irrigation water is derived from consumers' demand for food and fiber, the final goods produced from irrigation water. The first question to be asked, therefore, when considering the likely worth of an irrigation project is: Is there an effective demand for the food and fiber which can be produced by the irrigated project?

If consumers are willing to pay the full costs for food and fiber produced by water from an irrigation project, including of course the full cost of delivering the water to the irrigator, then it is safe to assume that irrigators, in turn, will have an effective derived demand for irrigation water. It is of fundamental importance in exploring the economic and social worth of a project to ascertain the willingness and ability of users to bear the costs of the project.

Evaluation in a Context of Multiobjective Planning

In December 1971, the Water Resources Council, after prolonged review by the Office of Management and Budget, published proposed principles and standards for evaluation of proposed water projects and programs in the light of three principal national objectives: national economic development, regional economic development, and environmental quality.[36] The classification of project and program benefits in accordance with their contribution to national income and economic development, the basic ingredient in computing the benefit-cost ratio, has been retained. Treatment of regional development as a national objective has been put on a narrower basis. Only where Congress has specified that regional development is to be considered an objective, as it has, for example, in Appalachia and in several other economic development regions, would regional development benefits be allowed to be taken into consideration in evaluating a Federal water resources investment.

Under the proposed principles and standards, environmental effects are also to be weighed. Project effects which relate to the quality of life will be exhibited in the project statement but the benefits will not be included in the benefit-cost ratio.

The proposed principles and standards represent a constructive step forward in the evolution of the evaluation process. They dispose of much of the previous criticism that the justifications for water development projects have been too narrowly conceived. Objectives other than national economic development are explicitly recognized as inherent and legitimate considerations in water resources development decisions. The methods devised to measure the contribution of a water resource development to these objectives can usefully exhibit both monetary and nonmonetary effects.

The proposed principles and standards have not yet been approved. Controversy over an appropriate discount rate (hereinafter discussed) may delay their implementation.[37] However, the Water Resources Council has sought professional opinion and has taken extensive testimony on its draft proposal, and consequently is in a position to make necessary refinements. When this has been done, the principles and standards should be approved.

Multiobjective planning has yet to be successfully fashioned and implemented in the field. Intelligent application of the principles and standards will require the design of specific procedures. In the River and Harbor Act of 1970 Congress directed the Secretary of the Army to promulgate guidelines designed "to assure that possible adverse economic, social, and environmental effects relating to any proposed project have been fully considered in developing such a project."[38] On July 10, 1972, the Corps of Engineers prepared "Proposed Guidelines for Assessment of Social, Economic and Environmental Effects of Civil Works Projects,"[39] directing its reporting officers to use the guidelines to identify and evaluate in a systematic way all significant project effects, both "beneficial" and "adverse," but

---

[36] U.S. WATER RESOURCES COUNCIL (December 21, 1971). Proposed principles and standards for planning water and related land resources. Federal Register 36(245):24144-24194, Part II.

[37] H.R. 16832, proposed Flood Control Act of 1972, 92d Congress, 2d Session, would have continued in force through December 1973 the evaluation standards now used.

[38] P.L. 91-611, December 31, 1970, Section 122, 84 Stat. 1818, 1823.

[39] See Federal Register 37(145):15013, July 27, 1972.

particularly those adverse effects specified in the 1970 River and Harbor Act.[40]

Noting that the assessment of project effects parallels and is concurrent with project formulation, the Guidelines summarized the sequence of tasks that should be used to assess project effects. Included are steps that call for the making of a projection of "without project" conditions throughout the economic time span of a proposed project, and making "with project" projections identifying "causative factors" and tracing their effects for each alternative. All signficiant effects of a project are to be identified and assessed. An illustrative list includes specific effects for each of three classifications: (1) social effects, (2) economic effects, and (3) environmental factors. Under social effects are items such as noise, displacement of people, archeologic remains, historic structures, educational and leisure opportunities, community cohesion, and institutional relationships. Under economic effects are included, among others, the familiar national economic development, as well as local government finances, land use, desirable regional growth, and real income distribution. Environmental factors include physical and hydrological factors and pollution related to air, water, land, animals, plants, and ecosystems.

Whatever form of multiple-objective planning is finally adopted, the implementation of proposed evaluation principles and standards by planning staffs of water resources agencies will entail significant changes in planning procedures and in present levels of expertise. There are a number of ways the required exhibits might be designed to include all significant effects to show market, nonmarket, and simulated market effects by locality or region, *viz*, the impact zone, the contiguous region, and the rest of the Nation, and by occupation or income class or by user group. The pioneering phase will require continuous and close monitoring of specific procedures during and after they have been put into operation. In this phase, the Water Resources Council should establish appropriate arrangements for guiding Federal and State agencies in the development of the recommended system of evaluation.

The Discount Rate

The evaluation process is concerned with the future uses of water and their likely contribution to social welfare over time. The relative importance of future benefits have, therefore, to be evaluated. The expected time stream of future benefits is associated with an expected time stream of future costs, for apart from the initial investment in the relatively short construction phase, there are usually continuing operation and maintenance expenditures over time.

For water resources projects, benefits and costs accrue at different dates. Net gain is not merely the simple sum of all the gains over the life of the project minus all the costs over the same period. What is essentially an opportunity cost has to be accounted for. This is accomplished by converting each stream – benefits and costs – to its present value. For this, a rate of interest called the discount rate is used.

The discount rate is based on the concept that capital invested in water projects would yield returns over the years if instead it were invested for some other purpose, and that this foregone earning potential should be taken into account by discounting those benefits of a project that do not accrue until the later years of its life. The discount rate seeks to express the future benefits of a project in terms of present values.

The present value of gains minus the present value of costs equals the present net worth of the project. The present value of benefits and the present value of costs can be converted to "average annual equivalents." The ratio of average annual benefits to average annual costs is the benefit-cost ratio. Projects are adjudged economically feasible when the benefit-cost ratio is 1:1 or greater. The interest rate used in discounting future benefits of water projects significantly affects the resulting benefit-cost ratio; hence, the strategic importance of the discount rate in shaping future water resources programs.

Project costs are largely incurred during the construction period early in the life of the project. As the discount rate is increased, the present value of benefits accruing in later years is greatly reduced. The effect of increasing the discount rate on reducing the present worth of future benefits is illustrated in Table 10-1.

---

[40] Section 122 of the River and Harbor Act specified that possible adverse economic, social, and environmental effects relating to any proposed Corps project be fully considered in developing the project, including: air, noise, and water pollution; destruction or disruption of manmade or natural resources, esthetic values, community cohesion and the availability of public facilities and services; adverse employment effects and tax and property value losses; injurious displacement of people, businesses and farms; and disruption of desirable community and regional growth.

TABLE 10-1.—Effect of different discount rates on the present worth of a future benefit of one dollar					
	3%	5%	8%	10%	12%
		(cents)			
50 years hence	23.0	8.0	2.0	0.90	0.40
75 years hence	11.0	2.6	0.3	0.08	0.02

Source: BARISH, Norman N (1962). Economic Analysis for Engineering and Managerial Decisionmaking. McGraw Hill Co., Inc., New York. Appendix Tables, pp. 688, 692, 693, 694, 695.

The implications of increasing the discount rate for water resource development are stated as follows by proponents of long-range river development.

The adoption of higher discount rates means that smaller, less costly projects having substantial benefits in the near future will be favored over large multi-purpose projects having benefits slowly building up over a period of years. Generally urban water supply and urban flood control projects will get priority while river basin programs will be adversely affected. Discount rates of 7 percent or more would likely jeopardize most river navigation projects since potential benefits from such projects do not usually reach anticipated levels until the second or third decade of project life. Traffic on a new waterway simply does not develop its full potential overnight. This is the type of project which is generally viewed as contributing to economic development of entire regions and it is long-range projects of this type which would be hardest hit as the discount rate advances.[41]

Since long-deferred benefits are discounted over a longer period of time, and hence, more heavily, the effect of a higher discount rate is to favor those projects which offer benefits in the immediate future as opposed to projects designed to last 50 to 100 years. It also tends to favor projects with relatively small initial costs. The relatively short-term projects are favored over long-term projects.

At the planning level, the choice of interest rate has considerable influence on the design that is selected. The choice of a relatively high interest rate "has the effect of eliminating the least productive of the proposed investment opportunities and conserving the limited funds to use in the most productive places."[42]

Different kinds of social programs may therefore result from using different discount rates. The use of low discount rates favors long-term capital intensive projects, benefits from which come largely in the more distant future. A high discount rate favors government investments from which yields are obtainable earlier.

The Joint Economic Committee sums up the situation: "If we need more expenditure on education now — better books and better teachers — a reduction in the discount rate would not provide them. It would only stimulate the construction of durable school buildings, the long-term investment portion of educational expenditure."[43]

For the design and evaluation of public water projects, the choice of the discount rate is one of the most significant and important problems for resolution. Many economists believe that the rate of discount should be selected so as to insure that capital channeled into public activities earns as bountiful a return as it would elsewhere. "...[T]he allocation of billions of dollars of public expenditures ... hang[s] on the resolution of the social discount rate."[44]

[41] Criteria News, National Waterways Conference, Inc., Issue No. 41, April 23, 1971. pp. 1-2. For a discussion of the techniques used in discounting anticipated values to present worth or in converting those values to average annual equivalents, see GRANT, Eugene L (1950). Principles of Engineering Economy, 3d Edition. The Ronald Press Co., New York, pp. 35-41.

[42] LINSLEY, Ray K & FRANZINI, Joseph B (1964). Water Resources Engineering. McGraw-Hill Book Company, New York. p. 366. The authors also emphasize, "It should also be noted that, for long-lived assets, a large difference in estimated life has less effect on annual cost than a moderate difference in interest rate. For example, assume a given life estimate is increased from 45 to 100 yrs and at the same time the interest rate used is increased from 3 to 4 percent; the increase of annual cost due to the higher interest rate is greater than the reduction of annual cost due to the estimate of longer life."

[43] U.S. CONGRESS, Joint Economic Committee (1968). Economic Analysis of Public Investment Decisions: Interest Rate Policy and Discounting Analysis, Report of the Subcommittee on Economy in Government. U.S. Government Printing Office, Washington, D.C. p. 11.

[44] HAVEMAN RH (1968). The opportunity cost of displaced private spending and the social discount rate, in WESTERN AGRICULTURAL ECONOMICS RESEARCH COUNCIL, Committee on the Economics of Water Resources Development, Conference Proceedings, December 17-18, 1968. Western Agricultural Economics Research Council, Denver, Colo. pp. 51-70.

Up to mid-1968, the interest rate used by Federal water resources agencies in project formulation approximated the average rate of interest payable by the Treasury on outstanding long-term marketable securities (15 years or more at original issue).[45] This is the interest rate which the Government pays on its long-term Treasury bonds and is determined by the rate of interest for such securities prevailing *at the time of issue*. Since most outstanding long-term Treasury bonds were issued long ago when interest rates were low, the resulting average rate of interest payable is relatively low. This so-called "coupon" rate at present is in the vicinity of 3-1/2 percent, about half the rate of 7 percent proposed by the Water Resources Council as the discount rate to apply to water resources projects "for the next five years."[46]

The "coupon rate" was endorsed by the Green Book (May 1950),[47] the Bureau of the Budget Circular A-47 (December 1952)[48] and the Presidential Advisory Committee on Water Resources Policy, (December 1955).[49] The coupon rate was also the rate defined in the Water Supply Act of 1958 for repayment purposes, and is determined annually by the Treasury in accordance with that law.[50] Legislation introduced in the 92nd Congress proposed a return to the coupon rate.[51]

A discount rate approximating the coupon rate was also endorsed in Senate Document 97 and under its formula the interest rate remained at 3-1/4 percent for a number of years. In mid-1968, under pressure from the Bureau of the Budget, the Water Resources Council was prompted to switch from the "coupon rate" of 3-1/4 percent to the "yield rate," then 4-5/8

percent, and, except for FY 1973, the rate for Federal water projects has been going up by 1/4 percent every year since. Unlike the coupon rate which is determined by interest rates prevailing at the time of issue, the yield rate is based on the interest rate which those bonds commanded in the market in the preceding fiscal year, rates which presently are higher than they were years ago.

Discount Rates Applying to Federal Water Projects	
Fiscal Year	Rate Percent
1963	3-1/4
1964	3-1/4
1965	3-1/4
1966	3-1/4
1967	3-1/4
1968	3-1/4
1969	4-5/8
1970	4-7/8
1971	5-1/8
1972	5-3/8
1973	5-1/2

In the fall of 1972 the yield rate stood at 5.7 percent but it can fluctuate from day to day as the money market dictates.

The Water Resources Council in December 1971 proposed that the discount rate which applied to Federal water resources projects be established in

---

[45] Agencies in the past have employed different rates to evaluate projects. In the 1950's the Bureau of Reclamation employed 2-1/2 percent while the Corps of Engineers used a rate of 3 percent.

[46] U.S. WATER RESOURCES COUNCIL (1971). Proposed principles and standards for planning water and related land resources. Federal Register 36(245):24193, Part II.

[47] U.S. FEDERAL INTER-AGENCY RIVER BASIN COMMITTEE (December 21, 1971). Subcommittee on Benefits and Costs (May 1950). Proposed Practices for Economic Analysis of River Basin Projects. U.S. Government Printing Office, Washington, D.C. p. 24.

[48] U.S. BUREAU OF THE BUDGET (December 31, 1952). Reports and Budget Estimates Relating to Federal Programs and Projects for Conservation, Development, or Use of Water and Related Land Resources, Circular A-47. Bureau of the Budget, Washington, D.C. Section 15, p. 14.

[49] PRESIDENT'S ADVISORY COMMITTEE ON WATER RESOURCES POLICY (December 22, 1955). Water

Resources Policy. U.S. Government Printing Office, Washington, D.C. p. 27.

[50] P.L. 85-500, July 3, 1958, 72 Stat. 319, 43 USCA 390b.

[51] S. 2612, 92d Congress, 1st Session, "National Water and Related Land Resources Policy Act" introduced by Senator Jennings Randolph joined by Senator Henry M. Jackson, and referred to the Senate Committee on Interior and Insular Affairs on September 29, 1971, in Section 10 proposes: "The interest rate to be used in plan formulation and evaluation for discounting future benefits and computing costs, or otherwise converting benefits and costs to a common time basis shall be based upon the average rate of interest payable by the Treasury on interest-bearing marketable securities of the United States outstanding at the end of the fiscal year preceding such computation which, upon original issue, had terms to maturity of 15 years or more. Where the average rate so calculated is not a multiple of one-eighth of 1 percent, the rate of interest shall be the multiple of one-eighth of 1 percent next lower than such average rate."

accordance with the following concept: The opportunity cost of all Federal investment activities, including water resource projects, is recognized to be the real rate of return on non-Federal investments. The best approximation to the conceptually correct rate is the average rate of return on private investment in physical assets, including all specific taxes on capital or the earnings of capital and excluding the rate of general inflation, weighted by the proportion of private investment in each major sector. The average rate of return on non-Federal investments is estimated at 10 percent.

Recognizing both the objective of subsidizing water resource projects and the objective of an efficient combination among and between Federal and non-Federal investment activities, the discount rate to be established on approval of the proposed principles and standards is 7 percent for the next five years.[52]

At the present time, economists are not in agreement that the opportunity cost of capital in the private sector is a valid or relevant concept for Federal investment in the public sector. Some believe that individual private decisions tend to be persistently and systematically biased in favor of present or near-term considerations and against long-term prospects; that in the aggregate, individuals in their private decisions concern themselves excessively with today and inadequately with tomorrow; that as individuals with finite life spans they do not plan sufficiently for future generations. As a result, it is argued, in the division of national income current consumption is greater than it should be and savings are correspondingly less. This reduced level of capital formation which stems from inadequate concern for futurity results in relatively high interest rates.[53] Investment in long-term projects that do not yield all of their benefits until some distant future date get short shrift (because, unless they are very attractive investment opportunities, tying up capital in projects which do not pay off for a long time can be painful when that capital could be earning a high rate of return invested elsewhere). Public enterprise is uniquely qualified to place long-term benefits in perspective. The argument against use of a high

discount rate based on the opportunity cost of capital in the private sector holds that public investment should be a countervailing force to offset the private bias against the long-term future; that use of a relatively low discount rate in water resources project evaluation encourages investment in socially useful projects which should be built but which, in the absence of a lower discount rate, would not be judged feasible.

The selection of the discount rate to be used in discounting future benefits and costs from water resources projects, in the final analysis, will constitute a social and political judgment. The appropriate rate should evolve from a fully informed political process which recognizes fiscal and budgetary considerations as well as national aims, preferences, and values about benefits that should accrue to future generations from the development of the Nation's water resources. Consequently, the political process has to be conducted with an awareness of the operational significance of the discount rate to shape the future level of Federal investment and the type of Federal water resource development which is to be undertaken. To this end, separate analyses under different discount rates—the coupon rate, the yield rate, and a rate reflecting the opportunity cost of non-Federal capital—might be made for all projects.

The Commission believes that the rate at which capital is available for relatively riskless investment in Government bonds should be the discount rate, since the higher opportunity cost of capital includes a factor for risk which is not present in Government projects.

RECOMMENDATIONS

10-11.   **The President should approve the substance of the principles and standards of multiple-objective planning, as proposed by the Water Resources Council, with the exceptions noted below with respect to the discount rate and the principle of effective economic demand.**

10-12.   **The principles and standards which are adopted for the evaluation of Federal water resources projects should include the principle that benefits for water resources development projects be derived by applying the concept of effective economic demand. This principle and the procedures it entails for implementation should be included as an amendment to the principles and standards proposed by the Water Resources Council. Care should be taken that the information**

[52] U.S. WATER RESOURCES COUNCIL (1971). Proposed principles and standards for planning water and related land resources. Federal Register 36(245):24144-24194, Part II, December 21, 1971.

[53] Other things equal, interest rates vary inversely with savings. The lesser the savings, the higher the interest rate, and vice versa.

used in the evaluation of water resources projects reveals fully (1) both the positive and negative effects of proposed projects upon all local interests and (2) any important positive and negative effects upon other regions.

10-13. The discount rate for evaluation of water resources projects should be established by the Treasury Department based on the average yield rates of outstanding long-term Treasury obligations. The discount rate should remain constant for a period of five years and then be recomputed.

AUTHORIZATION, BUDGETING, AND APPROPRIATIONS

The authorization, budgeting, and appropriation processes translate water resources plans into programs and projects. Congress exercises its power to approve and finance water resource development in two stages: authorization and appropriation. In the interval between the authorization of a program or project and the appropriation of funds for it, Federal agencies prepare schedules for its implementation. These schedules are transmitted as budget requests to Congress for action in the annual appropriation acts. These separate steps by which water resource programs and projects are conceived and executed by separate branches of government should be closely linked together if the Nation's water resources are to be efficiently managed, and its public funds effectively spent.

In the future a larger share of water resources projects may be financed by States and local governments than in the past, particularly if the Federal Government continues to implement revenue sharing on an increasingly broad front. Although many of the Commission's recommendations touching Federal planning, public participation, authorization of projects, budgeting procedures, and appropriations practices are not strictly applicable to decisionmaking at State and local levels, the general principles that should guide decisionmaking are adaptable with modifications at non-Federal levels of government as well as at the Federal level.

Water resources planning over the years has aimed at better coordination of the different types and levels of planning, both among Federal agencies and between Federal and non-Federal planners. Comprehensive planning on a regional or river basin scale by planning commissions has been authorized both in

the Water Resources Planning Act[54] and elsewhere. Complementary refinements in authorization, budgeting, and appropriations have not yet effectively linked each of these successive steps to the planning process and to each other.

In authorizing new projects and programs for developing water resources, the Congress has not always made full use of comprehensive river basin and regional plans. The authorization of aid to local agencies in meeting national objectives prescribed for them is not always implemented in a timely schedule by appropriation of needed funds. Failure of Congress or the President to make funds available for certain grant programs has led to large backlogs of grant-supported projects. Local administrators then avoid making commitments until the grant funds are in hand.

Budgeting procedures neither reflect nor promote the regional and the long-term nature of water resources development. Appropriations of funds for Federal construction projects that are made annually on an incremental basis unnecessarily subject the completion of projects to uncertainty and increase their total cost by spreading construction over a longer period of time than the most economical construction schedules sometimes call for. A growing backlog of projects authorized under obsolete planning and evaluative criteria and obsolete discount rates overburdens the appropriations process and permits start of construction of projects even though they may no longer measure up to current principles and standards for evaluating the worth of Federal investments in water resource development.

From Plans to Authorizations

Federal funds for water resources development are authorized both directly for Federal construction projects and indirectly to support programs of assistance to State and local agencies. For Federal projects specific project plans are prepared by one of the major Federal construction agencies—for example, the U.S. Bureau of Reclamation (Bureau), the U.S. Army Corps of Engineers (Corps), or the U.S. Soil Conservation Service (SCS). The plans are submitted to Congress for its approval, which is given in the form of an act approving the project and authorizing the appropriation of funds for it at a future time. In some instances, authority to approve project plans is delegated to the head of a department

---

[54] P.L. 89-80, July 22, 1965, 79 Stat. 244, 42 USCA 1962 *et seq.* (1964 Supp.).

Local officials use Soil Conservation Service Land Resources Unit map for planning

or agency, subject to veto by resolution of the appropriate congressional committee.

Congress also authorizes grants, loans, or other Federal assistance to be made to States or local agencies in accordance with the general outline of legislation authorizing specific programs. Federal assistance programs of this sort in the water resources field are now administered by the U.S. Department of Housing and Urban Development[55] (HUD), the U.S. Environmental Protection Agency[56] (EPA), the U.S. Farmers Home Administration[57] (FHA), and the U.S.

Department of Commerce's Economic Development Administration[58] (EDA).

Federal Construction Projects: Modern planning and evaluation techniques may lead to project selection on the basis of comprehensive river basin or regional plans based on principles and standards that take into account a multitude of criteria –economic, social, and environmental –at national and regional, as well as at local levels. Nevertheless, even though comprehensive plans for the development of river basins are routinely submitted to Congress, Federal water project proposals have not always arisen from or been considered in the context of a comprehensive basinwide or regional development plan. On the contrary, projects have often been presented and considered individually. Initiative for them has often been

[55] *Housing and Urban Development Act of 1965,* Title VII, August 10, 1965, P.L. 89-117, 79 Stat. 489, as amended, 42 USCA 3102.

[56] *Federal Water Pollution Control Act,* Section 201, P.L. 92-500, 86 Stat. 816, 833, 33 USCA 1281.

[57] *Act of August 8, 1961,* Title III, P.L. 87-128, 75 Stat. 307, as amended, 7 USCA 1921 *et seq.*

[58] *Act of August 26, 1965,* Title I, P.L. 89-136, 79 Stat. 552, 42 USCA 3121 *et seq.*

generated locally by those interested in obtaining major Federal expenditures in their local areas and by the Federal agencies to which fall the mission of constructing the projects: the Corps, the Bureau, and the SCS.[59] Congressional committees have usually followed the practice of examining projects one at a time.

Congressional politics and behavior lend themselves to particularized and fragmented decisionmaking in project authorizations. When an individual Representative or Senator perceives a local stake in the authorization of a project or project survey, he can often command considerable resources in producing congressional action. Mutual respect for a colleague's constituency affairs and his acknowledged superior insight into what may be best for his district or State inhibit congressional resistance at this stage. With the aid of tacit rules of mutual noninterference and accommodation, Congressmen have ordinarily been able to obtain authorization for local projects wherever there is substantial local support for them.

There is no single congressional committee in either house that might consider legislation to implement all the facets of a comprehensive river basin or regional development plan. Primary responsibility for the great bulk of congressional water business rests with six substantive committees—three in each body—and the two Appropriations Committees.[60] Bills for authorizations are considered by the committee identified with the Federal agency or program that the proposed project would involve, while the Appropriations Committee of each body handles the appropriations bills for water projects and programs through various subcommittees with responsibilities which partially, though not exactly, parallel those of the substantive committees.[61]

These facts have given rise to criticism that the congressional committee structure itself fosters overlapping and duplication of functions and abets

confusion and conflict among Federal agencies.[62] Nevertheless, there are few instances of real conflicts or failure of coordination between committees themselves.

Congressional committees occasionally work more or less jointly, even though the several committees routinely deal independently with related subject matter that arises within their separate jurisdictions. When a basin plan with various proposals for small watershed improvements, flood control structures, water quality improvement, municipal and industrial water supply, and regional waste treatment facilities is presented for authorization as a package, the several committees with jurisdiction should be able to coordinate their activities.

States have legal authority under the 1944 Flood Control Act[63] to review all Corps and Bureau projects. Where a State's interest can be perceived and the State is united behind a project, it can, of course, inform its congressional delegation. But the States are, by and large, too far removed from the authorization process to wield great influence. Interest varies from State to State. Sustained interest on the part of State officials comes only, as a rule, when State officials see water as a key to economic development.[64] Water projects planned and substantially financed by Federal money tend to be looked on as Federal largesse. There is reluctance on the part of State officials to look critically on them when they cannot be exchanged for more needed programs, and there is no mechanism whereby a water project might be traded for Federal help on a highway, airport, or schools.

Traditional decision processes may be changing. Public support for water development projects today seems less certain in the eyes of most legislators. The environmental issue has made the average development project less attractive as a constituency-pleasing device than it once was.

Fading with solid local support for large Federal water development projects is the climate of noninterference and absence of contention that has

[59] ELY, Northcutt (1971). Authorization of Federal Water Projects, prepared for the National Water Commission. National Technical Information Service, Springfield, Va., Accession No. PB 206 096. p. 113.

[60] ALLEE, David J & INGRAM, Helen M, Cornell University (1972). Authorization and Appropriation Processes for Water Resource Development, prepared for the National Water Commission. National Technical Information Service, Springfield, Va., Accession No. PB 212 140. pp. 4-7.

[61] SCHAD TM & BOSWELL EM (October 1968). Congressional handling of water resources. Water Resources Research 4(5):849-863.

[62] Ibid., p. 852.

[63] Act of December 22, 1944, P.L. 534, 78th Congress, 58 Stat. 887, 33 USCA 701-1(a). See ALLEE, David J & INGRAM, Helen M, Cornell University (1972). Authorization and Appropriation Processes for Water Resource Development, prepared for the National Water Commission. National Technical Information Service, Springfield, Va., Accession No. PB 212 140. p. 3-2.

[64] ALLEE, David J & INGRAM, Helen M, (1972), op. cit., p. 3-2.

characterized congressional water politics. Old procedures designed to reduce conflict are being replaced by rules and procedures deliberately calculated to bring issues into the open: for example, the changes in committee rules authorized by the Legislative Reorganization Act of 1970,[65] the filing requirements of the National Environmental Policy Act of 1969[66] (NEPA), and the multiobjective planning and project formulation advocated in the Water Resources Council's proposed principles and standards.[67]

River basin and regional planning in the future may contribute more concretely to program and project authorization than it has in the past. Experience in river basin planning under the Water Resources Planning Act and other legislation to draw together Federal and State plans for resource development and land use may ultimately produce river basin or regional plans of tangible usefulness to Congress.

Regional development plans comprehending not only water resources development projects, but also projects and programs to improve transportation, health services, educational facilities, and economic development have been tried. The 1965 Appalachian Regional Development Act directed the Secretary of the Army to prepare a comprehensive plan for developing and using water and related resources of the region within the framework of the overall economic development program authorized for the Appalachian region.

The plan was prepared and reported by the Office of Appalachian Studies, a group specially formed within the Corps of Engineers. Working under experimental conditions the Office of Appalachian Studies used projections of population, employment, and income as developmental benchmarks or targets that regional development efforts might reasonably be expected to achieve. Projections for economic subregions were converted into water development targets for growth centers within water subregions.

The major conclusion reached by those who took part in the Appalachian water planning experiment—that economic and social results are best achieved by well designed packages of total development ef-

forts[68]—points to the desirability of considering water development proposals in the future not merely as parts of comprehensive water plans, but in the larger context of overall regional or river basin development.

Federal Grant and Loan Programs: Congress's approach to Federal grant and loan programs has been somewhat different from that taken in the Federal construction programs. Congress has established policy guidelines in legislation authorizing grant and loan programs and has permitted administrative implementation of the programs, within authorized funding levels, to work out the details. Periodic congressional review of overall programs has been deemed sufficient to determine whether their objectives are being achieved at State and local level and whether the programs are adequate to meet changing needs. In the sewage treatment facilities grant program, however, the Administration has seldom recommended and the Congress has seldom appropriated the full amount of grants authorized. Local administrators have become wary of making commitments to construct needed projects, because they are not assured of receiving funds when needed. As local agencies delay action while awaiting funds, inflation increases costs. In order to alleviate this situation the use of the "contract authority" device conferring considerable financial discretion on administrators has been enacted for the EPA waste treatment grant program in the Federal Water Pollution Control Act Amendments of 1972.[69]

When contract authority is conferred in an authorization act, the Federal agency upon whom it is conferred is empowered to obligate the United States to make payments of grant funds up to the amount authorized, without waiting for an appropriation for the program. Title II of the 1972 Act provides contract authority to the Administrator of the Environmental Protection Agency (EPA) for a program of grants for construction of waste treatment works up to $18 billion over a three-year period. The Administrator of EPA, who is charged with administering the grant program, need not await annual appropriations for each of the years for which funds have been authorized. Instead, under the terms of the

[65] P.L. 91-510, October 26, 1970, 84 Stat. 1140, 2 USCA 190a.

[66] P.L. 91-190, January 1, 1970, 83 Stat. 852, 42 USCA 4432.

[67] U.S. WATER RESOURCES COUNCIL (1971). Proposed principles and standards for planning water and related land resources. Federal Register 36(245):24144, Part II, December 21, 1971.

[68] U.S. DEPARTMENT OF THE ARMY, Corps of Engineers, Office of Appalachian Studies (1969). Development of Water Resources in Appalachia. U.S. Government Printing Office, Washington, D.C. p. I-11-10.

[69] P.L. 92-500, October 18, 1972, 86 Stat. 816.

Act, his approval of applications for grants for construction of treatment works "shall be deemed a contractual obligation of the United States for the payment of its proportional contribution to such project."[70]

Contract authority thus helps guarantee the orderly and sequential funding that is necessary for grantees to contract for the necessary steps in the stages of project construction: (1) feasibility studies, (2) planning, (3) preliminary engineering, (4) acquisition of land, and (5) construction.

By involving Congress in a broad sense and leaving specifics to the agencies that administer Federal assistance programs, the use of contract authority achieves an appropriate division between policy-making and administration. Congress can be relieved of difficult project-by-project choices in the decision of which the vast majority of Congressmen have no essential interest and in which those who do have an interest are forced into trading positions. Opportunities can be taken to make use of those State capabilities for resource planning that have improved since enactment of the Water Resources Planning Act. Allowing projects to be generated out of State and regional planning efforts permits proposals initiated in localities to be decided at a governmental level close to the localities. The effects of a project upon population, income, employment, and the environment have their greatest incidence at the local level and State and local officials may be able to judge most accurately whether or not a project is desirable.[71]

Close attention to detail in monitoring the economic, social, and environmental features of specific proposals to be financed with Federal assistance can, if deemed desirable by the Congress, still be accomplished by (1) specifying guidelines for administering given kinds of projects in legislation authorizing grant programs, (2) vesting responsibility for developing evaluative criteria in the executive branch, for example, in the Water Resources Council or the Office of Management and Budget, and (3) requiring close scrutiny of grant programs by an independent board of review located in the executive branch of the Government.[72]

[70] *Ibid.,* Section 203(a), 86 Stat. 835, 33 USCA 1283(a).

ALLEE, David J & INGRAM, Helen M, Cornell University (1972), op. cit., p. 4-72.

See Chapter 11 for recommendations for an independent board of review for federally funded water development proposals.

Budgeting

The President's annual budget requests for the appropriation of funds for specific water resources programs are the means of implementing projects authorized by the Congress. Just as there should be links between planning and authorization, the budgeting process should also be phased with planning and authorization to achieve the maximum benefits from river basin planning and the most efficient use of public funds in putting plans and authorizations into practice. To this end the agency responsible for budgeting, the Office of Management and Budget (OMB), acts both to review proposals for authorization of programs and projects and—after congressional authorization has occurred—to guide or stage their implementation through its review of annual budget requests.

The Evolution of Budgeting and Its Relationship to Planning: Three major roles for the Federal budget have been identified: financial control, managerial control, and strategic planning.[73] Since the budget is cast in terms of the congressionally established appropriations procedure, and since appropriations are made to agencies for specific types of expenditures, different kinds of classifications of expenditures in the budget documents are important to display information for analysis, both by Congress and by the Executive, of how funds are allocated among various kinds of activities and of how they are allocated with respect to performance of the agencies' objectives.

Strategic planning as a budget function is concerned with specifying objectives, choosing among alternative programs to achieve those objectives, and then allocating resources among the programs. Strategic planning brings into the budgetary process those decisions about program objectives, specifications, and levels of funding which are taken as given in financial and management control functions. Some years ago the Bureau of the Budget, the predecessor of the OMB, established a "summer preview" calling for each major agency to submit to the Bureau a five-year financial program, together with a discussion and analysis of program issues considered by the agency to be important in subsequent budget discussions. The introduction of the Planning, Programming, and Budgeting System (PPBS) in 1965

[73] SCHULTZE, Charles L (1968). The Politics and Economics of Public Spending. The Brookings Institution, Washington, D.C. Ch. 1.

expanded and elaborated on this concept. Program budgeting under PPBS calls for the grouping of activities and costs of related programs into broad categories appropriate to strategic planning. These categories are usually quite different from categories appropriate to the control or management functions of budgeting.[74]

Long-term Regional Budget Classifications: Grouping budget data into regional sets can relate Federal spending with priorities established in regional development plans. Similarly, budget analyses that show the longer term consequences of project planning and new construction starts, will offer dollar measurement of alternative future water resource development programs for entire regions.

The integration of water resources planning with budgeting, if it is to be achieved, requires use of a common geographic unit for analysis and decision in both processes. Twenty major water resources regions of the Nation are the focus of long-range planning coordinated by the Water Resources Council. Present budgeting of the expenditures of the different Federal agencies for the hundreds of individual projects they undertake obscures the regional planning focus, even while making implicit, if unintended, regional allocations of resources. For example, if funds appropriated to the Corps of Engineers over two recent years are summarized by water resources region, the regional allocations that result appear to assign a priority to the Arkansas-White-Red Region which is twice that assigned to the Missouri Region, and a priority to the Columbia-North Pacific Region which is six times that assigned to the Great Lakes Region.[75] The Commission has found little evidence that long-range water resource planning efforts affect the allocation of funds and resources among geographic regions in such a way as to take interregional needs and conditions into account.

The Commission believes that the 20 major regions used by the Water Resources Council should be incorporated into the water resource budgeting process so that the relative needs and priorities for regions are related one to another. In this connection, the Commission shares the concern expressed recently by the Joint Economic Committee about the scarcity of regional data in the Federal budget:

The current budget document provides no information on the regional impacts of Federal spending. Without such, the Congress is seriously hindered in developing consistent national policy for regional objectives.

Moreover, because program expenditures are not broken down regionally, the priorities of localities and regions cannot influence the mix of Federal appropriations. Insofar as many Federal budgets—including those for hospital construction, pollution control, and highways, for example—are decided nationally the choice offered the locality or region is a take-the-gift-or-leave-it choice. The region is given no chance to say: 'Highway project x is of relatively low priority to us, while hospital project y is far more important.' Consequently, the ability of the Federal Government to respond to the need of localities and regions, as the people there see these needs, is decreased. Substantial gains would result from the formation of a regional breakdown for major portions of the budget.[76]

The strategic planning role of short-term budgeting must be made to include consideration of long-term plans, tradeoffs, and alternatives for each region. Once past levels of water expenditures have been reviewed, and a range of possible and practical future funding levels has been considered, budgeting priorities for water planning regions should then be recommended for each of a variety of alternative criteria. As an illustration, regional allocation criteria like those used by the Corps of Engineers in formulating the five-year civil works water resource program might establish alternatives for regional allocations of Federal water development funds for all Federal agencies under a given level of funding under one or more of the following criteria:

Regional water needs—Regions having the highest level of projected water resource needs would receive the most funds.

Federal income taxes paid—Regions paying the greatest amount in Federal income taxes would receive the most funds.

Population—Regions having the greatest number of people would receive the most funds.

[74] *Ibid.,* p. 25.

[75] Communication from the U.S. Army Corps of Engineers to the National Water Commission.

[76] U.S. CONGRESS, Joint Economic Committee (1970) Economic Analysis and the Efficiency of Government Report of the Subcommittee on Economy in Government 91st Congress 2d Session. U.S. Government Printing Office, Washington, D.C. p. 19.

Population and per capita income–For two regions having the same population, the one having the lower per capita income would receive the greater amount of funds.

Efficiency–Regions in which proposed projects have the highest benefit-cost ratio or greatest net benefits would receive the most funds.

The use of each criterion would provide a yardstick for measuring and displaying how regional allocations might be made to achieve regional parity within each criterion's specific frame of reference. National objectives, of course, cannot be so singularly measured. In practice, some combination of one or more regional criteria might, however, contribute to the determination of allocations of funds among regions.

Appropriations

Once a Federal water resources project has been authorized and funds for its construction have been recommended by the President in his budget, it is brought to life by the appropriation by Congress of funds for a new construction start. Typically, new construction starts are initiated by the appropriation of a sum that is relatively small in relation to the total estimated ultimate cost of the project. An example is the Frying Pan-Arkansas Project, estimated when construction was initiated to cost a total of $166,525,000 for which a new start appropriation of only $1,830,000 was appropriated in FY 1964. Budget requests for the next four years were for $6, $10, $18, and $21 millions, respectively.

A single project initiated in this fashion with a small appropriation may attract little notice in the overall budget request, even though the estimated ultimate total cost may be very substantial and the budgetary commitment to the project, once started, may be strong. Many projects begun simultaneously with small appropriations may represent very large budget commitments for the future. Incremental annual funding of the continuation of a project in progress tends to minimize the apparent magnitude of each project in the total construction program. Moreover, funding a project's prosecution to completion through annual incremental appropriations may subject it to delay and uncertainty for reasons external to the merits of the project. In some cases, annual appropriations have failed to keep up with increases of costs as a result of inflation or of intervening design changes. For example, four years after the first appropriation for it in 1964, the Frying Pan-Arkansas Project was estimated, in the FY 1968 Budget, to cost a total of $180,556,000, of which $37,399,000 had already been incurred and $142,413,000 would be required after June 30, 1967 to complete the project.

Five years later, despite the fact that an additional $77,474,000 had been spent, the FY 1973 Budget shows that the total projected costs of the project had increased to $296,485,000, and a balance of $180,648,000 would still be required to complete the project after June 30, 1972. Other examples could be cited showing that under the present system the rate of construction is not sufficient to keep up with inflationary cost increases or that substantial design changes are made during construction, or both. Forward funding of construction projects by appropriating sums at the time of new starts that, so far as then can be ascertained, will be sufficient to see the project through to completion would call attention to the full cost of the project at the time the decision is made and would permit a more efficient construction schedule. In order to avoid letting the construction agencies build up backlogs of appropriated funds, these funds could be handled in the same way as permanent, indefinite, appropriations are handled, with certification each year as to the amount required included as a part of the budgetary process.

The Authorization Backlog: Some observers maintain that the most important water resources decisions are made in selecting which of the many authorized projects are to be put in the budget as new starts.[77] The choices of these projects are made after authorization, during the annual appropriations process. Here, the phenomenon of the authorization backlog enters and plays a leading role.

The authorization backlog, that is, the list of projects that have been authorized but for which funds have not been appropriated, exists in part because many more projects have been authorized than can be promptly funded under the current levels of water development spending of less than 1 percent of the total annual Federal budget. The total cost of the backlog of projects of the Corps, Bureau, and SCS, authorized but unfunded, is estimated to be about $15 billion. The trend has been for the backlog to grow in recent years.

---

[77] ALLEE, David J & INGRAM, Helen M, Cornell University (1972). Authorization and Appropriation Processes for Water Resource Development, prepared for the National Water Commission. National Technical Information Service, Springfield, Va., Accession No. PB 212 140. pp. 5-15 to 5-25.

Because so many projects have been selected for authorization, some are likely never to be funded. Selecting projects from the backlog to be put in the annual budget for funding involves exercising options not necessarily best made at the budgeting stage or by appropriations committees. Consequently, the choices may be made on the basis of essentially budgetary and nonsubstantive criteria such as the size of the budget commitment represented by a project, how it fits into the current geographical spread of projects, its continuing political and local support, and the number of other projects readied for construction at the time. The passage of considerable time between project authorization and the first appropriation for construction may be attended by the occurrence of events and the development of new information that, had they been known at the time of authorization, might have affected the decision to authorize the project.

Projects authorized 10 or more years ago may have been economically attractive at the then prevailing project evaluation discount rates, but may prove unattractive at the rates in force at the time of the first appropriation for new construction. For example, most of the Corps' new construction starts in FY 1972 were originally authorized under a discount rate of 3¼ percent. The discount rate in FY 1973 was 5½ percent.

With respect to new projects, Congress might deal with the problem in the future by limiting the term of the authorization for particular projects so that authorization will lapse in the event funds are not appropriated within a specified term. A project authorization might, for example, be given a 5- or a 7-year term. In such case the project, if not started within that period, would require new authorization.

A different problem is presented with respect to existing authorizations that are awaiting funds. A simple approach might be simply to deauthorize all projects of more than 8 or 10 years' standing. Another approach would be to require any project which has been authorized for a given number of years to be reevaluated in light of present principles and standards before any funds could be appropriated for new construction.

RECOMMENDATIONS

10-14. Comprehensive river basin and regional development plans should be used as the basis for authorization and appropriation of funds for individual projects and programs within regions. The same geographic regions should be used as a basis for decision in both the water resources planning and in the budgeting processes—the major water resource regions of the Nation used by the Water Resources Council in the National Assessments.

10-15. The procedure for appropriating construction funds annually for ongoing water resources projects should be replaced by procedure whereby a permanent appropriation of the estimated total construction cost of each project is made at the time construction of the project is to begin.

10-16. Where grant programs are authorized to assist State and local entities in meeting national objectives, appropriate Federal program administrators should be given contract authority to obligate the United States, in advance of appropriations necessary, to pay the full authorized Federal share of the cost of meeting such objectives.

10-17. Each water agency should each year formulate a five-year program including a continuation of existing projects and new construction projects for submission to the Office of Management and Budget. The President should formulate and recommend to the Congress five-year national budget allocations for the total Federal water program. In his budget recommendations to Congress, the President should emphasize regions as well as individual water projects and organizational accounts.

10-18. Water resource programs, projects, or separable units thereof, which have been authorized for a period of ten years or longer and on which construction starts have not been made, should be deauthorized by Congress. No funds should be appropriated to start any project or program authorized for more than five years until it has been reevaluated and found feasible under principles and standards in force at the time of the proposed appropriation.

Improving Organizational Arrangements

~~~~~~~~~~~ *Section A*

Introduction

This chapter of the Commission's report examines a number of organizational arrangements for the planning, development, and management of the Nation's water and related land resources and makes recommendations for improving them. It is in five sections, which for ease of reference are lettered A through E.

In Section B, the Commission discusses the U.S. Water Resources Council. The Council's major tasks are to coordinate the water activities of the various Federal agencies among themselves and with the States, to review river basin plans for major river basins throughout the Nation, and to assure that Federal water policies and programs are adequate to meet the Nation's water needs. The Commission concludes that while the Council has accomplished many things, it generally has been unable to review and coordinate the policies and programs of the Federal agencies, to confront difficult policy issues and resolve them, and to resolve interagency conflicts. A policymaking component, with an ability to enforce decisions when consensus cannot be reached, should be built into the Council mechanism. The Commission recommends that the Council be placed within the Executive Office of the President and have an independent, full-time, presidentially appointed Chairman reporting to the President.

Other recommendations for improving the Council include central funding through the Council of planning studies by interagency committees and river basin commissions; extending the duration of the program of grants to the States for water planning;

~~~~~~~~~~~~~~~~~~~~~~~~~~~~

Water interrelationships require close coordination on all levels

coordination of grant applications from various agencies of a State seeking funds from various Federal agencies for water resources planning and programs; coordinating Federal participation in the negotiation and administration of water compacts; and revising the statutory membership of the Council.

In a separate heading under Section B, the need for an independent board of review in the Federal Government to examine federally funded water development proposals, river basin plans, and water development grant programs is discussed. The Commission recommends that such a review board be established.

Section C covers possible new functions for certain of the Federal water agencies. Recommendations are made that the functions of the National Oceanic and Atmospheric Administration and the United States Geological Survey be combined into a new agency in the Department of the Interior, and that a new Office of Water Technology also be established in Interior. Recommendations are also made for changing the engineering design and construction activities of the Soil Conservation Service, the Bureau of Reclamation, and the Army Corps of Engineers.

The chapter then turns to an examination of various organizations for water planning and management for river basins and other regions (Section D). First, various intrastate arrangements are discussed, particularly the Texas river authorities. The Commission concludes that these authorities have been an important force in developing the water resources of Texas, and that other States should consider using them for entire river basins or subbasins where other governmental entities are inadequate. The Gulf Coast Waste Disposal Authority in Texas appears to be an especially useful mechanism for attacking problems of water pollution on an intrastate regional basis.

Section D then examines certain multistate arrangements for river basins, including ad hoc and interagency committees and river basin commissions for planning, and interstate and Federal-interstate compact commissions. The Commission recommends the Federal-interstate compact as the preferred institutional arrangement for water resources planning and management in multistate regions. Nevertheless, it recognizes that the traditions, institutions, politics, and water problems of various portions of the United States vary greatly, that organizational arrangements which work well in one region may not work elsewhere, and that in each case the selection of an organizational arrangement for water resources planning and management must be appropriate to the circumstances.

As between the river basin planning commissions and the ad hoc and interagency committees for planning, the river basin commissions are preferred. Unless another entity for basin planning and implementation is substituted for a river basin commission, a commission should, after initial completion of its plan, (1) keep the plan up to date, (2) continue the coordination of planning efforts, and (3) reestablish and revise priorities in the light of changing circumstances.

Interstate and Federal-interstate compacts, if they affect a national or Federal interest, require the consent of Congress. Such compacts have been widely used for water resources management. The Commission encourages their continued use and makes a number of recommendations for improving them. There are certain kinds of water compacts, such as administrative agreements, agreements for local planning and zoning, and for interstate metropolitan water management, to which Congress should grant advance consent. The presence of a Federal representative should be required during negotiations of future water compacts so that the States involved may be better apprised of the Federal interest in the compact. Future water compacts should clearly state the role of the compact commission with respect to existing Federal agencies and programs, especially with regard to project construction, water quality, and regulatory functions. Finally, Congress should enact legislation granting the Federal district courts original jurisdiction over any case or controversy arising under an interstate water compact, and waiving the sovereign immunity of the United States to permit the United States to be made a party defendant in such a suit.

The final portion of Section D explores the possible uses of a federally chartered corporation, a type of organization that has not yet been utilized for water management. Such a corporation appears to have a variety of uses, particularly in conjunction with an interstate or Federal-interstate compact or a river basin commission. A regional corporation, because of its flexibility and relative isolation from political control and responsibility, lends itself best to operational tasks rather than planning or regulatory activities intended to be binding upon outside parties. Federally chartered corporations may be able to play important roles in facilitating joint efforts by local government units of two or more States sharing a waterway to handle such limited functions as water treatment and supply.

Section E discusses institutional arrangements for the Great Lakes. Recommendations are made to establish a task force for negotiating a Federal-interstate compact for the Great Lakes and to analyze the impact of alternative management strategies on the Lakes.

~~~~~~~~~~~~~~~~~~~~~~~~~~~~~~~~~~~~~~~ *Section B*

Federal Coordination and Review

THE WATER RESOURCES COUNCIL[1]

In 1965 Congress passed the Water Resources Planning Act,[2] by which Congress sought to coordinate the various water policies and programs of the Federal agencies and the State governments in a more comprehensive way than had been attempted in the past. The task of coordinating as well as appraising water policies and programs, and planning for the conservation and development of the Nation's water resources, was given to a newly created Water Resources Council, consisting of the Secretaries of Agriculture, Army, Interior, and Health, Education, and Welfare, and the Chairman of the Federal Power Commission.

The Water Resources Planning Act has two major goals. The first is the development of water and

---

[1] This section is based upon LIEBMAN, Ernst (1972). The Water Resources Council, prepared for the National Water Commission. National Technical Information Service, Springfield, Va., Accession No. PB211 443.

[2] *Water Resources Planning Act*, P.L. 89-80, July 22, 1965, 79 Stat. 244, 42 USCA 1962, *et seq.*

related land resource plans for the major river basins of the Nation. Such plans are to be developed jointly by interested Federal agencies, States, localities, and private groups through the device of a river basin commission, if it can be established. The President has directed the Council to develop such plans through existing Federal-State interagency or ad hoc committees in areas where commissions have not been established.[3] A second major goal of the Act is to coordinate Federal water policies and programs and assess their adequacy to meet water requirements and demands throughout the Nation.

In the early 1960's, the President requested the Secretaries of Army, Interior, Agriculture, and Health, Education and Welfare to review existing water resources development standards and make recommendations to him. The four Secretaries formed an ad hoc Water Resources Council and established an Interdepartmental Staff Committee which produced a statement of "Policies, Standards and Procedures in the Formulation, Evaluation, and Review of Plans For Use and Development of Water and Related Land Resources," later printed as Senate Document 97 of the 86th Congress.

When the Water Resources Planning Act became law on July 22, 1965, the President's ad hoc Water Resources Council, with the addition of the Chairman of the Federal Power Commission, became the statutory Council. The members of the Interdepartmental Staff Committee, representing the members of the ad hoc Council, formed a body known as the Council of Representatives (COR), which became the key working group of the Council. The chairman of the Committee became the Council's first Executive Director.

In 1967, the Secretary of the Department of Transportation became a statutory member of the Council on matters pertaining to navigation features of water resource projects. Regulations of the Council provide for associate members and observers. Associate members include the Secretary of Commerce, the Secretary of Housing and Urban Development, and the Administrator of the Environmental Protection Agency. Their concurrence in Council decisions is not required. Observers include the Attorney General, the Chairman of the Council on Environmental Quality, the Director of the Office of Management and Budget, and the Chairman of the seven river basin commissions established under Title II of the Act.

Under Council regulations, the members or their "designees" are to meet at least four times a year. Members decide issues by majority vote, except that decisions affecting the authority or responsibility of a member can be made only with his concurrence.

The bulk of the Council's work is carried out through a number of groups other than the members: the COR, the staff, task forces, and various technical, advisory, and field committees. It has been the COR, however, that has generally thrashed out issues and made the majority of the decisions for the members. Certain decisions are reserved solely for the members, although the COR first considers these issues and makes recommendations to the members.

Major Activities of the Council

Shortly after the Council was created, the President abolished the Interagency Committee on Water Resources (ICWR) which had been established in 1954 to coordinate Federal water resources activities and develop river basin plans. He placed its field subcommittees under the Council.

Under Title II of the Act, the establishment of Federal-State river basin commissions for planning was given top priority by the Council.[4] By October of 1972, seven river basin commissions had been established for New England, the Great Lakes, the Pacific Northwest, the Souris-Red-Rainy, the Ohio, the Missouri, and the Upper Mississippi basins. The area encompassed by each Commission is indicated on Figure 11-1, on page 419.

The Water Resources Planning Act requires the Council to prepare biennially, or less frequently as the Council may determine, an assessment of the adequacy of water supplies necessary to meet the water needs of the various regions of the United States. The Council published its first such assessment in late 1968.

In 1961, the Senate Select Committee on National Water Resources recommended that the executive branch develop by 1970 comprehensive plans for all the major river basins of the Nation. The President's ad hoc Water Resources Council began the planning program which initially called for 18 framework studies encompassing the Nation by 1970 and 16 more detailed subbasin studies. In 1965, the statutory Water Resources Council inherited this program. One framework study (Ohio River Basin) was completed in 1971; eleven more are to be completed in 1973. Of

---

[3] The Federal-State ad hoc and interagency committees are discussed in Section D of this chapter.

[4] The river basin commissions are discussed in detail in Section D of this chapter.

the subbasin studies, eight have been completed and seven more are to be completed in 1973.[5]

Title III of the Water Resources Planning Act established a program of grants to States for the purpose of increasing their capabilities in water resources planning. Five million dollars per year for 10 years was authorized. Between 1967 and 1972, Congress appropriated approximately $16 million of the $30 million that was authorized.[6]

The Water Resources Planning Act requires the Council to establish with the approval of the President principles, standards, and procedures for Federal participants in the preparation of comprehensive regional or river basin plans and for the formulation and evaluation of Federal water and related land resources projects. Senate Document No. 97, issued May 15, 1962, and the supplements thereto, now comprise the applicable principles, standards, and procedures. In 1968, the Council began a reappraisal of evaluation practices used in water planning. Proposed new principles and standards were published in the Federal Register on December 21, 1971. Hearings concerning them have been held, but as of March 1973 the final version had not yet been published.

The discount rate to be used in the evaluation of water and related land resource projects has been a sharp issue between the proponents and opponents of an expanded water development program. In 1968, the President decided that the formula calculated under Senate Document No. 97 produced a rate (3-1/4 percent) that was unrealistically low, and he instructed the Council to develop a more appropriate formula, which it did. For FY 1973, the rate stood at 5-1/2 percent. Under the proposed principles and standards, the rate would be set at 7 percent for the next 5 years.[7]

The Council engages in a number of activities to help reduce losses from flooding. It published a

uniform technique for determining floodflow frequencies, "flood hazard evaluation guidelines for federal executive agencies," a set of model State statutes and city and county ordinances, together with a commentary and a legal analysis, for use by States and local governments in regulating the use and occupancy of land in flood plains, and a draft version of a national unified flood control program.

To some extent, the Council has become involved in water compacts.[8] In 1968, after the Federal representative to the Delaware River Basin Compact had come to the Council for guidance concerning his vote on the Tocks Island pumped storage project, the Council proposed to expand its role by executive order to include supervisory and coordinating responsibilities over water compacts, but its plans were thwarted by the Bureau of the Budget. The Council did, however, play a major role in developing a coordinated Federal position on the consent legislation for the Federal-interstate compact for the Susquehanna basin, modeled on the Delaware compact. The Council succeeded in harmonizing the various Federal agency views and developing a set of reservations to the compact which were incorporated in the consent legislation. The Council may have to play this coordinating role again since similar Federal-interstate compacts have been proposed for the Potomac, the Hudson, and the Great Lakes.

Discussion of the Council's Role

Five statutory duties are explicitly given to the Council by the Water Resources Planning Act: (1) preparing the national assessment of water supply and demand; (2) developing principles, standards, and procedures for project formulation and evaluation; (3) establishing and maintaining liaison with river basin commissions; (4) making grants to States for water planning; and (5) encouraging and reviewing river basin plans.

A first national assessment was prepared in 1968 and a second is scheduled for 1975. Guiding, supervising, and coordinating the assessments, involving hundreds of people and dozens of Federal and State agencies, seems to be a task particularly suited to an interagency group such as the Council.

New principles and standards have been proposed, although the task has taken the Council a long time. They appear to be an important step toward pro-

[5] The *Federal Water Pollution Control Act Amendments of 1972*, P.L. 92-500, October 18, 1972, 86 Stat. 843, Section 209, authorized $200,000,000 to be appropriated to the Water Resources Council for the preparation of feasibility plans for all basins of the United States by January 1, 1980.

[6] U.S. CONGRESS, House, Committee on Appropriations (1972). Hearings before the Subcommittee on Public Works, 92d Congress, 2d Session, Public Works for Water, Pollution Control and Power Development and Atomic Energy Commission. Part 3.

[7] A discussion of the discount rate and the Commission's recommendation for the future appear in Chapter 10 of this report.

[8] The subject of Interstate and Federal-Interstate Compacts is treated in Section D of this chapter.

viding that all effects of plans and projects, beneficial and adverse, monetary and nonmonetary, are displayed in surveys and project reports for decision-makers. Procedures for implementing the principles and standards have not yet been developed.

The Planning Act encourages the Council to establish river basin commissions throughout the United States. With seven river basin commissions having been established, covering all or part of 32 States, the Council has carried out this function as rapidly as possible.

The grant program under Title III has been carried out by the Council to the limit of the congressional appropriations. State water planning has been augmented, the number of technically qualified people in State water planning has increased substantially, and State water programs are farther ahead than they would have been without the grants.

The requirements of the Act that the Title III program of grants to States be coordinated with the planning assistance programs of other Federal agencies has not been done very well by the Council. Nevertheless, the Council's development of a consolidated grant application procedure is a beginning. Under that procedure, water agencies of a State seeking Federal funds from various Federal agencies will submit a single application to the Federal Government through the Council.

The Planning Act requires that a State, as a condition of receiving a Title III grant, have a comprehensive water and related land resource planning program which provides for coordination with all Federal, State, and local agencies and nongovernmental entities having responsibilities in affected fields and for coordination between State comprehensive water resource planning and other statewide planning programs. The Council has done very little to determine how well this condition is being met by the States, nor has the Council helped the States to meet the condition effectively.

While the goal of the Senate Select Committee and President Kennedy to have comprehensive plans for all of the major river basins completed by 1970 has not been achieved, the lag has been due largely to budgetary restrictions. Nevertheless, the Council has reviewed and commented on a number of studies and forwarded them to Congress.

While one major goal of the Act is the development of river basin plans, another is to insure that Federal water policies and programs, river basin plans, and coordinating mechanisms are adequate to meet "requirements" throughout the Nation. To fulfill this second goal, Section 102(b) of the Water Resources Planning Act requires the Council to:

> maintain a continuing study of the relation of regional or river basin plans and programs to the requirements of larger regions of the Nation and of the adequacy of administrative and statutory means for the coordination of the water and related land resources policies and programs of the several Federal agencies; it shall appraise the adequacy of existing and proposed policies and programs to meet such requirements; and it shall make recommendations to the President with respect to Federal policies and programs.

Generally, these functions have not been carried out by the Council. To some extent, this is due to the fact that the Council has always had a limited budget and a professional staff of less than 20 persons. Just keeping up with the enormous task of preparing information, analyses, and recommendations for COR and Council meetings absorbs most of the staff's time.

The Council did appraise the adequacy of the administrative and statutory means for coordinating Federal participation in interstate water compact negotiation and administration, and the Council worked out a proposed solution, but it was not acceptable to the Bureau of the Budget and was not implemented. The Council also reviewed the Federal-interstate compact for the Susquehanna River Basin when it was proposed, and it coordinated and developed a Federal position on that compact which culminated in a series of reservations which were adopted by the Congress.

In the area of flood hazards, the Council reviewed Federal agency activities and issued proposed flood hazard guidelines for the Federal executive agencies. It reviewed various policies and programs of States and localities with regard to the flood hazard, and published model State statutes and ordinances, together with other legal materials, to stimulate flood plain regulation by States and localities. But by February 1973 it had not yet developed in final form a unified national program of flood plain management, even though it had been repeatedly requested to do so by the Office of Management and Budget (OMB), the successor agency to the Bureau of the Budget, because the President was asked by Congress to develop such a program by December 1, 1970.[9]

---

[9] *National Flood Insurance Act of 1968*, P.L. 90-448, Title XIII, August 1, 1968, 82 Stat. 572, 42 USCA 4001(c) (2), and Historical Note thereunder.

The Water Resources Council met on October 15, 1971, to discuss the new principles and standards, formation of new river basin commissions, and consolidated grant application procedures. Present were (seated, l to r, Deputy Administrator Robert W. Fri, EPA; Deputy Under Secretary Charles J. Orlebeke, HUD; Assistant Director Donald B. Rice, OMB; Assistant Secretary Thomas K. Cowden, USDA; Chairman John N. Nassikas, FPC; Assistant Secretary James R. Smith, Interior; Secretary of the Interior Rogers C. B. Morton (Chairman); Director W. Don Maughan, WRC; Chairman Russell E. Train, CEQ; Under Secretary Kenneth E. Belieu, Army; Assistant Secretary Merlin K. DuVal, HEW; Administrator Robert M. White, NOAA, Commerce; Assistant Attorney General Shiro Kashiwa, Justice; Under Secretary James M. Beggs, DOT; (standing) Executive Secretary P. T. Steucke, WRC.

The Council has been involved in the problems, policies, and programs of the coastal zones and estuaries, as well as in designations of wild and scenic rivers. It published a study of alternative institutional arrangements for river basins, and made various other technical studies. But on several occasions when the staff has attempted to tackle tough issues involving policies and programs, the COR or the Council members have shied away. Examples include the Council's failure to resolve any cost-sharing issues, taking a year to raise the discount rate, and the delay in developing a unified national program for flood plain regulation. When President Kennedy established his ad hoc Water Resources Council in 1961 pending passage of the Water Resources Planning Act, he asked it specifically to work on such topics as cost allocation, reimbursement, and cost-sharing, but the Council has not developed policies in these areas. The Commission has not found a single instance where the

Council made recommendations to the President on its own initiative[10] with respect to Federal policies and programs, although that is a mandate of the Act. From a review of the record, the Commission concludes that the Council has not carried out very well the mandates of Section 102(b) of the Water Resources Planning Act.

There are a number of reasons why the Council has plunged deeply into the planning arena and avoided policy and program issues. To a large extent, the answer lies in the inherent limitations of the Council mechanism.

Development of the elements of the planning program was given top staff priority early in the history of the Council. It was particularly easy for the staff and the members of the COR to concentrate on

[10] As explained earlier, the Council's recommendations to the President in December 1968 to raise the discount rate were submitted at the President's request.

planning activities, since most of them had been associated with planning in one form or another prior to their association with the Council. Also, at the time the Council came into existence, there were a number of ongoing river basin studies being conducted by interagency and ad hoc committees under the general direction of the Interagency Committee on Water Resources (ICWR). When the President transferred the functions of ICWR to the Council, the Council had to keep those planning efforts going. Finally, the member agencies of the Council and their constituencies generally stood to gain from the planning program, but in an immediate sense they had much to lose from pursuing the examination and resolution of controversial programs and policy issues which might result in fewer projects and programs for an agency.

The Council's director cannot readily resolve different issues or move the Council staff and COR to study policies and programs that might prove detrimental to any member agency. The director is essentially an employee of the chairman of the Council, who has been the Secretary of the Interior from the Council's inception. Unlike the member departments and agencies of the Council, the director and the Council itself have no independent political constituency. Aside from his persuasive powers and his power to put issues on the agenda of the COR, the director cannot force a resolution of issues.

There is now no policymaking component in the Council with a presidential and national point of view. That the chairman of the council has always been chosen from the members of the Council and has traditionally been the Secretary of the Interior has also posed problems. There is a basic potential divergence of interest between the position of chairman of the Council and the position of Secretary of a department. The conflicts between the Council's planning program and the Westwide Study of the Bureau of Reclamation for 11 Western States illustrate the awkward position of the Secretary of the Interior as head of Interior and chairman of the Council.

The Council has been criticized for operating on the basis of consensus, and it is true that the consensus rule limits what the Council can achieve. But the consensus rule has the virtue that when agreement is reached by the members, decisions are likely to be implemented. Examples include the development of a Federal position on the Susquehanna River Basin Compact, the flood hazard guidelines for Federal agencies to implement Executive Order 11296, and the model State statutes and ordinances for flood plain regulation. Critics of the Council, expecting it to resolve and implement controversial policies, often forget the consensual nature of the entire statutory arrangement. The Act requires that the Council make an assessment, develop principles and standards, maintain continuous studies, review and comment on plans, make recommendations to the President—these are not implementing and enforcement powers.

Conclusions and Recommendations on the Water Resources Council

The Water Resources Council has become an important and useful mechanism. However, a number of improvements need to be made to help it carry out the mandates and achieve the goals of the Water Resources Planning Act. The Council seems most weak in its ability to review the policies and programs of the Federal agencies, to confront policy questions and resolve them, and to resolve interagency conflicts. The Council needs a policymaking component, with an ability to enforce decisions when consensus cannot be reached. Implementation of the following two recommendations through appropriate legislation would help to build this policymaking component into the Council mechanism.

Recommendation No. 11-1: The Water Resources Council should have an independent, full-time chairman; he should be on the White House Staff and report directly to the President; the Council should be placed within the Executive Office of the President.

Recommendation No. 11-2: Each Water Resources Council member should be represented by a qualified employee from the member's department or agency; the representative should serve on the Council of Representatives and should report within his department or agency directly to the Water Resources Council member or to his alternate.

First, an independent and full-time chairman on the White House Staff, with his own staff and with presidential support, should be able to inject a national and presidential viewpoint into Council matters. Adequate presidential support for the independent chairman is a key ingredient. The independent chairman should be in charge of the Council's budget and not need to have the budget

403

approved by the other Council members, although he might wish to consult them. He should be able to innovate, attack the controversial problems, resolve interagency conflicts, and keep mission-oriented agencies in the COR from dominating Council activities and from limiting efforts in controversial areas. He could direct the submission of issues to the President for decision when necessary. His power to do so probably would mean that the power would not need to be used frequently, and the President thus should not be overburdened with water resource matters. A full-time, independent chairman would not have to devote most of his energies to other matters as the present and past chairmen have had to do. He would give continuity to the Council despite changes in cabinet officers. He would avoid the competing interests between the present chairman's dual roles as head of the Council and of a separate department of the government. In addition, an independent chairman would provide convenient support for members of the Council against pressures from bureaus in their agencies when such bureaus feel affected adversely by a Council decision. He would also provide liaison between the White House and presidentially appointed river basin commission chairmen.

An independent chairman on the White House Staff would be more influential with the Office of Management and Budget (OMB) in the area of water policy. OMB for many years has played, and will certainly continue to play, an important role in water resources policy. Executive Order 9384 of October 4, 1943, charged the Bureau of the Budget with the review of plans and projects for public works.[11] In many respects OMB, its successor agency, duplicates and oversees many of the functions of the Council. OMB often has spurred the Council to face policy issues that it otherwise might not have tackled, e.g., to increase the discount rate and to formulate a unified national flood protection program. On the other hand, OMB has sometimes effectively vetoed useful Council decisions, such as the Council's decision that it should coordinate Federal negotiators and representatives on interstate water compacts. There has been no chairman consistently willing and able to speak directly to the President on water policy matters when OMB has vetoed a Council position. The chairman of the Council should be able to do this. OMB is too much concerned with political and budgetary considerations to permit it effectively to be the water policymaker in the executive branch.

The second effect of these recommendations would be to strengthen the links between the President, the Council members, and the members of the COR. The alternate of a member should be able to speak for the member and his entire department or agency. An assistant secretary or person of equivalent status, with major responsibilities for water resources matters in his department or agency, seems to be required. Since the COR is a key working group of the Council, it must be composed of able persons, each of whom is close enough to his member to adequately represent him on the COR. The representative should approach problems from a national perspective. In many instances today the representative on the COR is not in close contact with either the member or his alternate. Upgrading the COR representative, freeing him to devote substantially full time to Council activities, and having him report to the member or his alternate appears to be a way to solve this problem.

The policymaking component of the Council staff should be strengthened with additional qualified personnel so that this component may devote full time to policy issues, develop positions, and make recommendations. Strengthened policymaking should also help to improve the planning program. Having the staff report to the independent chairman will keep it independent of the COR and strengthen the chairman.

Recommendation No. 11-3: Federal appropriations for all resources planning studies being conducted under the auspices of the Water Resources Council should be made to the Council, and the Council made responsible for assigning studies and apportioning funds.

The present system of financing river basin studies is not satisfactory. Federal moneys for river basin planning go to the participating Federal agencies rather than to the entity making the study. The appropriated moneys may never become part of the study budget; agencies may use their funds to insure that their projects are in the plan; shifting of funds as changes occur is difficult; the agency with the money may not be the best entity to do the planning, and central direction of the river basin planning effort by a responsible body or person is made more difficult. A more central administration of the river basin planning moneys by a Council, revised as set forth in

[11] Submission of reports to facilitate budgeting activities of the Federal Government. Federal Register 8(10):13782-13783. October 8, 1943.

Recommendations 11-1 and 11-2 above, should produce better plans. The provision in Section 209 of the Federal Water Pollution Control Act Amendments of 1972 for Council financing of Level B plans is an important step in this direction.

Recommendation No. 11-4: The grant program in Title III of the Water Resources Planning Act should be extended for at least 5 years beyond the statutory expiration date, and the present statutory ceiling of $5 million per year should be removed.

The program of Federal grants to States for augmented water planning has been beneficial, but the amounts granted have not been sufficient to adequately build up State capabilities. From 1965, when the Water Resources Planning Act was passed, until 1972 only about half of the moneys authorized by the Act were appropriated by Congress for the State grant program. The States' participation in the Council's comprehensive planning program in many cases has been that of reacting to federally conceived plans. The States should take a more active part in planning for conservation and use of the Nation's water resources. Increasing grants to States under Title III and extending the grant program for 5 more years, through FY 1981, would help achieve this goal.

Recommendation No. 11-5: All applications emanating in any single year from various agencies of a particular State seeking Federal funds for water and related land resource planning and programs should be consolidated into a single grant application and submitted to the Water Resources Council for coordination of the applications for funds from the various appropriate Federal agencies.

The President, by Executive Order 11647 issued on February 12, 1972, established Federal Regional Councils to coordinate the grant programs of the Federal human resource agencies (Labor; Housing and Urban Development (HUD); Health, Education and Welfare (HEW); Transportation; Office of Economic Opportunity (OEO); Environmental Protection Agency (EPA); and the Law Enforcement Assistance Administration). No such councils have been established to coordinate grants to States from the various Federal agencies for water planning and programs.

At present, States apply to many Federal agencies for water planning and program grants. A Federal agency to whom an application is made often is unaware of grants being made by or sought from other Federal agencies for water resources purposes. There is no overview of all of the Federal grants for water purposes to a particular State and no unified Federal judgment as to whether the grants sought are the best combination from both the national and the State points of view. The Water Resources Council coordinated a consolidated application from the State of Ohio and documented its experience.[12] Its report suggests the need for further consideration of the general problem of grant coordination, and particularly the role of the integrated Grant Application Program discussed under Municipal and Industrial Water in Chapter 5 of this report. An executive order or other appropriate directive should be issued requiring the consolidated grant application approach from States seeking Federal funds for water resources planning and programs.

Recommendation No. 11-6: The Water Resources Planning Act should be amended to make the Secretary of Commerce, the Secretary of Housing and Urban Development, the Administrator of the Environmental Protection Agency, and the Chairman of the Atomic Energy Commission statutory members of the Water Resources Council; and to eliminate statutory membership for the Secretary of Health, Education and Welfare.

In 1969, the members of the Water Resources Council approved a proposal to add the Secretaries of Commerce and HUD, and the Administrator of EPA to the Council as full statutory members. Legislation was drafted for this purpose but was not forwarded by the Administration to the Congress, apparently because it seemed inconsistent with proposed Administration legislation to reorganize the executive branch. Today, the Secretaries of Commerce and HUD and the Administrator of EPA are nonstatutory associate members of the Council; they cannot vote and their roles are essentially advisory.

Each of these agencies has been given substantial water resources reponsibilities since enactment of the Water Resources Planning Act in 1965. The Department of Commerce now has statutory responsibilities for certain marine resources affairs and for fostering industrial expansion and economic development involving substantial use of water resources.

---

[12] U.S. WATER RESOURCES COUNCIL (1972). Ohio Consolidated Grant, Analytical Report. National Technical Information Service, Springfield, Va., Accession No. PB 209 148.

The Department of Housing and Urban Development plans for urban population centers and provides a link between urban planning and comprehensive river basin planning. Its administration of the flood insurance program, established pursuant to the Housing and Urban Development Act of 1968, requires coordination with flood damage prevention programs, for which the Council has major responsibilities.

The continued expanded use of nuclear power, the role of nuclear power in regional powerplant siting and river basin planning, and the licensing of nuclear powerplants all involve consideration of impacts on water resources. The Atomic Energy Commission has direct programatic interest in the problem of waste heat disposal connected with nuclear generation of electric energy. During the past 2 years, the AEC has become a full member of several river basin commissions and is participating actively in the development of comprehensive river basin plans.

EPA now has the major responsibilities for water quality, a function that must receive adequate planning and coordination by the Council. The water quality function was vested in HEW at the time the Water Resources Planning Act was passed in 1965. While HEW today has some water-related responsibilities, particularly in the field of public health, those responsibilities do not seem to justify continued statutory membership in the Council for HEW, which could hereafter participate in Council affairs as an associate member. There is some virtue in not having the statutory membership of the Council grow too large, and thus only those departments and agencies with major water responsibilities should have statutory membership.

The Water Resources Planning Act should be amended to achieve the ends of this recommendation. If and when a Department of Natural Resources is established, Congress at that time can review the Water Resources Planning Act to see what other amendments to that Act would then be appropriate. Full membership now in the Council for the Secretaries of Commerce and HUD, for the Administrator of EPA, and for the Chairman of AEC should better enable the Council and those agencies to carry out their statutory responsibilities.

Recommendation No. 11-7: Congress should enact appropriate legislation giving to the chairman of the reconstituted Water Resources Council the responsibility for coordinating Federal participation in the negotiation and administration of river basin compacts of the Delaware and Susquehanna types, and water management compacts of the Ohio River Valley water sanitation compact type.

There is a need to provide a focal point within the Federal Government for coordination of the Federal interest in interstate and Federal-interstate compacts dealing with water and related land resources. An independent chairman of the Water Resources Council, which is charged by Congress to encourage the development of water and related land resources on a comprehensive and coordinated basis, would be the appropriate person on the White House Staff to have the responsibility for performing that function.

The independent chairman of the Council should maintain and distribute to appropriate Federal officers and agencies current information relating to water compact negotiations and administration which may affect Federal interests. He should provide appropriate information, advice, and assistance to States in the negotiation and drafting of water compacts. He should assist Federal representatives to compact negotiations in obtaining information, advice, and support from other Federal agencies; he should help develop a coordinated Federal position on all substantive issues that arise in the course of negotiations for the guidance of the Federal representative; and he should submit to the President his views and recommendations, as well as those of the Council, on any water compact presented to Congress for approval.

The chairman of the Council should also provide guidance to Federal representatives on compact commissions whether they serve a limited role as on the Ohio River Valley Water Sanitation Commission or the highly important role of Federal representative to a Federal-interstate compact of the Delaware and Susquehanna variety. Federal representatives in the administration of the water compacts should report to the President through the chairman of the Water Resources Council.

AN INDEPENDENT BOARD OF REVIEW

During the last few decades, a number of studies have been made of the way the Federal Government processes water development proposals which Federal agencies present to Congress for approval and funding. The studies were concerned with whether the project proposals of the water construction agencies were soundly conceived and whether they represented reasonably beneficial investments of Federal tax receipts.

The (First Hoover) Commission on Reorganization of the Executive Branch of the Government, created in 1947, had several recommendations on this subject.[13] The main report of the Commission called for a Board of Impartial Analysis for Engineering and Architectural Projects. The Board was to report to the President and Congress on the public and economic values of project proposals of the Department of the Interior. Another function of the proposed Board was to review previously authorized projects to determine whether they should be built or discontinued. Board members, outstanding in their knowledge of the water resources field, would be appointed by the President and become part of his Office. Subsequent study commissions came to generally similar conclusions about the need for a board to review water development proposals.[14]

The Need for Independent Review

The earlier study commissions recommended an independent board of review because they found many examples where the Federal water agencies had underestimated the costs and overestimated the benefits of projects they had proposed for authorization.[15] The study commissions were consistent in their conclusions that an independent board of review was needed because the water resource projects they examined did not always have economic justifications which would stand up under critical scrutiny. They found that neither the Bureau of the Budget (BOB) nor Congress had sufficient staff resources to make detailed, in-depth reviews of the many complicated water project proposals that they were being asked to approve. Nor did they think that BOB could be unbiased in reviewing projects, because of BOB's overriding commitment to carrying out the President's budgetary policies and its service relation to the Chief Executive. The study commissions found that the President and Congress were forced to make decisions on the basis of information which was often inaccurate, misleading, and inadequate. The projects, moreover, were so complex that they could be evaluated only by persons who were highly skilled and were free to devote sufficient time to do the work properly. Testimony received by the National Water Commission in its regional conferences indicated that these problems still exist.

The Commission does not find it surprising that Federal construction agencies tend to color their calculations with self-interest in making project evaluations. These tendencies cannot be checked by an interagency coordination process in which all the participants are equal and each is in control of his own separate program. The member agencies will only be critical of those features of another member's proposals which might threaten the performance of their own programs and projects.

Functions of a Review Board

The Commission agrees that an independent review board is needed in order to keep a check on the project evaluation biases of the Federal construction agencies. In addition, there are a number of other tasks of equal value which such a review board should perform to assist the President and Congress in making their decisions about the water resource investments. The board should:

(1)   Highlight the policy issues involved in those plans and projects which affect other national sectors, e.g., food and fiber production, transportation, and energy production;

(2)   Consider the economic efficiency of investing in water developments versus the alternative investment opportunities that may be available for achieving the same national and regional objectives;

[13] COMMISSION ON REORGANIZATION OF THE EXECUTIVE BRANCH OF THE GOVERNMENT (1949). Department of the Interior, House Document No. 122, 81st Congress, 1st Session. U.S. Government Printing Office, Washington, D.C. pp. 2-4.

[14] PRESIDENT'S WATER RESOURCES POLICY COMMISSION (1950). A Water Policy for the American People, 3 vols. U.S. Government Printing Office, Washington, D.C. Vol. 1, p. 3.
COMMISSION ON ORGANIZATION OF THE EXECUTIVE BRANCH OF THE GOVERNMENT (Second Hoover Commission) (1955). Report on Water Resources and Power, House Document No. 208, 84th Congress, 1st Session. U.S. Government Printing Office, Washington, D.C. Vols. I, II, pp. 38-39.
COMMISSION ON INTERGOVERNMENTAL RELATIONS (1955). Report to the President for Transmittal to Congress. U.S. Government Printing Office, Washington, D.C. pp. 241-247.
PRESIDENTIAL ADVISORY COMMITTEE ON WATER RESOURCES POLICY (1955). Report of the President's Advisory Committee on Water Resources Policy, House Document No. 315, 84th Congress, 2d Session. U.S. Government Printing Office, Washington, D.C.

[15] See, for example, COMMISSION ON ORGANIZATION OF THE EXECUTIVE BRANCH OF THE GOVERNMENT (Second Hoover Commission) (1955). Report on Water Resources and Power, House Document No. 208, 84th Congress, 1st Session. U.S. Government Printing Office, Washington, D.C. Vols. I, II, pp. 19-25, 127, 130, 134, 138.

(3) Examine the income distribution effects of Federal investments in water resource projects;

(4) Make certain that an adequate evaluation has been made of the principal alternative ways of dealing with the water needs of regions and communities;

(5) Determine the extent to which both the organized and unorganized interest groups of a region are aware of the proposed developments and of their likely effects, and the extent to which these interests have participated in the plan formulation process;

(6) Evaluate the effectiveness, propriety, and current need for the Federal aid programs of the water resource development agencies;

(7) Appraise the valuation given to the environmental and other intangible costs of proposed developments, and the risks entailed in the cumulative effects of tolerable amounts of certain kinds of environmental damages.

If the review board is to assess fully the relevant policy issues involved, it should evaluate not only project proposals but also river basin plans and grant programs. The river basin plans are the context within which the individual projects must be considered and evaluated, where the intents and purposes of the regional development agencies are displayed, and where interregional conflicts become apparent and the need for national policy guidance becomes acutely evident. One of the functions of a review board would be to make interregional comparisons in an effort to uncover the interrelationships and inter-dependencies among the different basin plans. A board could point out for the consideration of the President and the Congress where the incompatibilities exist between basin plans and how the water developments proposed in one region are likely to affect the water development prospects of another region.

The grant programs may constitute the largest part of the water resource development investments of the Federal Government, particularly since Congress passed legislation in October 1972 to authorize the Environmental Protection Agency to make grants of $5 billion in 1973, escalating in annual increments of $1 billion to a total of $7 billion for 1975, largely for municipal sewage treatment facility grants. If there is to be a review of the Federal Government's expenditures in all significant water resource development activities, clearly the grant program should receive its appropriate share of attention.

While it would not be appropriate for the review board to pass judgment on individual grant applications, although it may wish to examine the merits of a selected number of the larger projects funded under a grant program, the board should review the grant programs to determine how well they perform as instruments of national policy. The board should report to the President and the Congress its assessment of the grant programs at the time of the requests for annual appropriations for the grant administering agencies. Under this procedure, the grant programs would be under a continuing reappraisal conducted on an annual basis.

Procedures for the Review Board

It would be necessary for the review board to have the authority to conduct investigations and hold hearings. To minimize its staff, the board could rely on the sponsoring agencies to furnish the data it would require to make its evaluation of the agency's project proposal and plan. When it found questionable features which could lead to an adverse finding on a project proposal or plan, it would be appropriate for it to meet with the Federal, State, and local sponsors of that plan and its opponents, to discuss the board's findings, to request additional substantiating data that may be needed, and to hear any evidence which may have been overlooked. If the sponsors would not choose to withdraw or modify a proposal which the board found reason to criticize, the board could then proceed to forward the proposal, along with a record of its meeting with the sponsors and a copy of its evaluation.

If the review board, in the course of its reviews, should find that a water plan or project is likely to have unwanted effects upon other national sectors (food, energy, transportation, etc.), it would call them to the attention of the President and the Congress. It would not be the responsibility of a review board to recommend how these national policy issues should be resolved, since these are not technical questions. Instead, it would alert the political leadership to these issues and to those types of pending investment proposals where policy direction must be provided to avoid unnecessary conflict and waste.

Location, Organization, and Membership of a Review Board

Some of the study commissions that proposed a review board would attach it to the Office of the

President. The objective was to give the review board's findings more influence in the decisions of the executive branch by associating those findings with the prestige and power of the President. However, there does not appear to be adequate justification for placing such a review body in the Office of the President. From the standpoint of executive branch responsibilities, it is important only that it be given a strategic place in the project review process so that its comments on and evaluation of water development proposals can be made to Congress and the President before those proposals are acted upon. This would be true even if a Department of Natural Resources were established into which many of the Federal water agencies would be combined.

The review board should be structured as an independent agency; nominally within the executive branch but insulated from presidential politics by appointments which extend beyond the term of the President. A provision which would prohibit more than, say, four out of seven members to be selected from one particular political party would be an additional device to secure the board's independence of action. The review board would function free of any entanglements with the special interests of operating departments. By standing apart from the President's Office as an independent organization, there would be less opportunity to question the objectivity of a review board's actions when it is dealing with those water development proposals which the President may have cause to favor for personal or party reasons.

The chairman of the board of review should be the same person who serves as the independent chairman of the reconstituted Water Resources Council. Such a dual role was previously held by the President's Science Advisor who was simultaneously chairman of the Federal Council on Science and Technology and chairman of the President's Science Advisory Committee. By being a member of the executive office staff and of the Water Resources Council, the chairman will bring important assets to the board. The danger of compromising the board's independence by the dual chairmanships can be minimized if care is taken to maintain a complete separation between the work of the board and the Council.

Selection of the members should be made by the President with confirmation by the Senate. A system of staggered appointments with a maximum term length of about 6 years would seem to be desirable. A review board of five to seven members would be enough to conduct the board's business, would permit a mix of professional skills to be used, and would provide enough choice to allow for a balanced geographic representation on the board. In creating such a board, the Congress should be prepared to provide a level of funding which would permit the board to handle its workload with diligence and competence and to hire a competent staff.

Recommendation on a Board of Review

Recommendation No. 11-8: Legislation should be enacted to establish an independent board of review to examine federally funded water development proposals, river basin plans, and water development grant programs and to advise the President and the Congress on their need, feasibility, and utility. The chairman of the board of review should be the same person who serves as the independent chairman of the reconstituted Water Resources Council.

Section C

New Functions for Federal Water Agencies

A number of problems involving duplicative, unnecessary, or unintegrated functions of certain Federal agencies in the water resources field have been called to the attention of the National Water Commission. In this section, the Commission deals with three areas in which the functions of Federal water agencies need to be modified to keep up with changes in water programs which lie ahead or to more efficiently manage existing functions. The first involves duplication in certain of the programs through which the Federal Government collects and distributes basic water data. A second area is based on the fact that three Federal agencies—the Army Corps of Engineers, the Bureau of Reclamation of the U.S. Department of the Interior, and the Soil Conservation Service of the U.S. Department of Agriculture—all perform similar engineering functions in the water field. A third area involves the scattering of water technology functions among various Federal agencies.

DATA-GATHERING SERVICES

The National Oceanic and Atmospheric Administration (NOAA), among its other duties, collects data on climatological phenomena, including rainfall, and on floods and flood damages. It also issues flood warnings and flood and water supply forecasts. The U.S. Geological Survey (USGS) collects data on streamflow (including floodflows), ground water, and water quality. It also maps flood plains and investigates a variety of water problems. If the two agencies were to be merged and operated as a single agency, better coordination of complementary data programs would enhance their usefulness, and a consolidation of data archives would be of much benefit to potential data users.

The Soil Conservation Service now operates a network of snow survey sites in the Western United States and prepares and issues water supply forecasts. The Geological Survey collects snow survey data in the Eastern United States, and the National Weather Service prepares and issues water supply forecasts. It would seem desirable to consolidate the Soil Conservation Service snow survey functions in the newly formed agency which would combine NOAA and the Geological Survey.

ENGINEERING SERVICES

Major Federal water projects are designed and constructed by the Corps of Engineers and the Bureau of Reclamation. A third Federal engineering organization was created by the Soil Conservation Service to administer the Watershed Protection and Flood Prevention Program authorized in 1954 by Public Law 566.[16] Under this program, the Soil Conservation Service designs, supervises the construction of, and for some purposes assumes a large proportion of the cost of engineering works serving many of the same purposes as the major water projects constructed by the Bureau of Reclamation and the Corps of Engineers.

Various commissions and study groups in the past have questioned the need for three separate Federal

engineering service agencies for designing water projects. A review of their reports reveals four general approaches:

1. A majority of the previous study groups proposed preservation of the main features of the existing organization, and the establishment of machinery to achieve better coordination of the existing programs. The Senate Select Committee on National Water Resources was the latest of the groups to support this approach. Its report was an important reason for the enactment of the Water Resources Planning Act of 1965, and the establishment of the approach now in use.

2. Other studies, such as that of the "First Hoover" Commission, led to recommendations which proposed the establishment of a "Water Development Service" in the Department of the Interior, into which would be gathered all Federal agencies responsible for engineering, design, and construction of water resources projects.

3. A few study groups suggested that most of the Federal agencies concerned with natural resources be transferred to a new "Department of Natural Resources." The latest such proposal was that of the "Ash" Council (1970). Moreover, a minority of the "First Hoover" Commission (1949), as well as a task force of that Commission, made a similar recommendation.

4. One task force of the "First Hoover" Commission proposed that all Federal engineering construction programs be consolidated in a "Department of Works." This proposal, like that of the task force suggesting a Department of Natural Resources, was rejected by the Commission itself.

In approaching the question of whether the engineering functions of the Corps, the Bureau of Reclamation, and the Soil Conservation Service (SCS) should be consolidated, a threshold question should first be answered: Is it necessary for the Federal Government to provide engineering services for all of the water projects the Federal agencies now design and construct? The Commission believes the answer to this question is "No." Changing and emerging roles of these agencies argue against consolidation. Many of the functions of these agencies can be performed by non-Federal governmental entities. States, municipalities, interstate compact commissions, and entities such as conservancy, irrigation, or drainage districts can be given the responsibility for the design and construction of many of the engineering works that the Federal engineering agencies are now building or helping non-Federal organizations to build.

---

[16] *Watershed Protection and Flood Prevention Act*, P.L. 83-566, August 4, 1954, 68 Stat. 666, 16 USCA 1001-1007.

410

Soil and Water Conservation District Supervisors review goals and progress on water conservation activities

The Soil Conservation Service (SCS)

The SCS engineering organization was created for the purpose of designing and supervising the construction of the engineering works installed at Public Law 566 projects. The engineering services required in the installation of such works can be provided by non-Federal organizations at a local level as it already is in some areas; the Department of Agriculture need not provide such services.

SCS provides conservation engineering services in connection with programs other than those involving the construction of projects under P.L. 566. These services, virtually unique to SCS because of the specialized expertise in soil-water-plant relationships that they involve, are not likely to be easily obtainable outside SCS at the State and local levels and should continue to be provided by SCS in support of soil and plant management aspects of land use for erosion control and water conservation functions.

The Bureau of Reclamation

Commission studies of future needs for food and fiber, of the various ways in which these needs may be met, and of the relative cost of expanding the Nation's agricultural plant by bringing more land under irrigation or by other means lead to the conclusion that the Federal reclamation program, to the extent that it is used to increase the capacity of the Nation's agricultural plant, can be tapered off gradually. For the foreseeable future, any needed increases in food and fiber production can probably be met at less cost by non-Federal action than by the construction of major engineering works by the Federal Government. But in the water-short regions of the West, there is a growing need for a water management program that will insure the best use of the available supplies. Unless and until management entities are established for the Western river basins, as recommended elsewhere in this report, the Bureau of

411

Reclamation probably will be in the best position to serve as the management entity for most of these basins. The Bureau should continue to have the responsibility for operation and maintenance of existing Federal reclamation projects until they are turned over to the water users, but its primary mission should be to help achieve efficiency of irrigation for water conservation. That agency also should continue to represent the Federal Government during the payout period of Federal reclamation projects. The Commission foresees a gradual conversion of the Bureau of Reclamation from an agency mainly concerned with the design and construction of major engineering works to an agency mainly concerned with water system management in the Western regions.

The Commission has sufficient confidence in this forecast of the future of the Federal reclamation program to conclude that it would not be in the national interest to recommend a consolidation, at this time, of the Bureau of Reclamation and the Corps of Engineers. It would seem more sensible to permit the Bureau to complete the Federal reclamation projects now under way, while gradually converting itself to the type of management agency that will be needed in the future. This would avoid the sudden dislocations, the confusion, and the substantial waste that would result from the transfer of the engineering elements of the Bureau of Reclamation to a new agency.

The Corps of Engineers

The Corps of Engineers should continue to design, construct, operate, and maintain navigation projects and major flood control projects that exceed the capability of non-Federal entities. It should not continue to be involved, however, in small projects unrelated to navigation which could be as well handled by local interests. For example, the Commission does not believe that the Corps should be involved with local flood control on small streams, with municipal and industrial water supply and wastewater systems, or with local small craft harbors where such functions can be handled by local interests. This type of project should be a local responsibility.

The Corps, like the Bureau of Reclamation, is not likely to continue to exist as an agency specializing in the construction of great engineering works; it seems virtually certain that in the future the United States will need relatively few major navigation, flood control, or water power projects. In the years ahead "management" entities will probably be established in many of the Nation's river basins to perform many of the functions that have previously been performed through the nationwide Federal programs. The Delaware River Basin Commission is a precursor of the kind of management entities that are likely to evolve. Such entities should gradually be able to take over responsibility for the design and construction of most of the engineering works required for the solution of the internal water problems of the medium-sized basins for which they will probably be established, leaving to the Corps of Engineers only the relatively few very large and complex works that will be required to meet the needs of large basins.

For all of these reasons, it appears that the major project construction segment of the Corps of Engineers program will taper off in much the same way as will that segment of the Bureau of Reclamation program. Here again the Commission foresees a gradual shift to a very different kind of program involving such activities, for example, as operation and maintenance of completed projects where this function is not taken over by local interests, emergency flood planning, and dissemination to States, municipalities, and other local entities of information needed for regulation of flood plain lands.

TECHNOLOGY SERVICES

Currently, there is no central agency in the Federal Government concerned with broad research objectives directed toward advancing technology in the entire water resources field. Water technology research functions are now scattered among various Federal agencies, such as the Office of Saline Water, the National Oceanic and Atmospheric Administration (NOAA), the Environmental Protection Agency, and the various water construction agencies. In addition, the Office of Water Resources Research in the Department of the Interior makes grants and contracts and disseminates information concerning the results of water resources research.

The research of many agencies concerned with water resources is directed toward specific objectives. There is a need for a single Federal Office of Water Technology to undertake broader studies of technological trends and to undertake research in the field of all possible technological advances in the water resources field.

An Office of Water Technology should be established in the U.S. Department of the Interior to serve the water research needs of all Federal agencies. It should combine the functions of the existing Office of Water Resources Research, the Office of Saline Water, the weather modification activities of NOAA, the weather modification and geothermal steam programs of the U.S. Bureau of Reclamation, the water research activities of the Environmental Protection Agency, and should concern itself with a range of other alternative water technologies including wastewater reuse. One role of the Office of Water Technology should be to maintain a continuing state-of-the-art and technology assessment of known and possible future water technologies. It should emphasize technology related to the development of new sources of water and more efficient use of existing sources. It should provide technology services also to those involved in developing plans and strategies for the management and use of the Nation's water resources.

RECOMMENDATIONS ON NEW FUNCTIONS

11-9. Legislation should be enacted to establish in the Department of the Interior an agency made up of the National Oceanic and Atmospheric Administration and the United States Geological Survey, and to assign to the new agency responsibility for the collection and distribution of basic data on the Nation's water resources. The fisheries functions of NOAA should be merged with the Fish and Wildlife Service of the Department of the Interior, and the coastal zone management functions should be handled as a part of the overall land planning functions of the Federal Government.

11-10. The Watershed Protection and Flood Prevention Act of 1954 should be amended so that the Department of Agriculture no longer performs engineering functions under that Act, such as design of reservoirs and channels for flood control or land drainage, that may be readily provided by non-Federal organizations at the local level.

11-11. The Bureau of Reclamation should continue to bear responsibility for the construction of Federal reclamation projects until such time as projects under construction or under repayment contract are completed. While this is being accomplished, its engineering design and construction activities should be gradually phased out. It should progressively strengthen its capability as a water management entity, and eventually its principal responsibility, in addition to operating works retained under Federal control, should be that of improving the efficiency of water use in the water-short regions.

11-12. The Civil Works Program of the Corps of Engineers should be modified to: (a) limit the agency to design and construct only those engineering works that cannot as efficiently be provided by States, by interstate regional commission, or by conservancy, drainage, port, irrigation, or similar local districts; and (b) increase the emphasis placed upon the nonstructural segments of its programs, such as that segment through which it provides States, municipalities, and other non-Federal public entities with information they need to make more efficient use of flood plain lands.

11-13. An Office of Water Technology should be established in the Department of the Interior, combining the functions of the existing Office of Water Resources Research, the Office of Saline Water, the weather modification activities of NOAA, the weather modification and geothermal programs of the U.S. Bureau of Reclamation, and the research on wastewater reuse technology of the Environmental Protection Agency. Although it would be placed for administrative purposes under the jurisdiction of the Secretary of the Interior, the Office of Water Technology should be given a charter broad enough to meet research needs other than those of the Department of the Interior.

Organizations for Water Planning and Management for River Basins and Other Regions

Various regional organizational arrangements for water planning and management are assessed in this section, including (1) certain intrastate arrangements, such as State-created authorities for river basins or portions thereof; (2) Federal-State river basin coordinating committees and commissions for planning; (3) interstate and Federal-interstate compact commissions; and (4) Federal-State regional government corporations. These arrangements are not mutually exclusive; combinations of them may be quite useful in solving water problems, especially of an interstate nature. The final section of this chapter discusses institutional improvements for the Great Lakes.

INTRASTATE ORGANIZATIONS

Early Organizational Arrangements

There are a few rivers in the United States over which State-created entities exercise various degrees of planning, operational, and regulatory powers entirely within a State. One of the earliest of such intrastate organizational arrangements is the Wisconsin Valley Improvement Company, a corporation formed in 1907 under a charter from the State of Wisconsin. It is owned by six paper mills and four power utilities, and operates power dams and reservoirs on the Wisconsin River to supply water for hydroelectric power and for the pulp and paper industries.

Another early intrastate organizational arrangement is the Miami Conservancy District (MCD), established in 1914 by the Ohio legislature for the Miami River Basin in Ohio as a result of a 1913 flood that devastated the Miami Valley and the City of Dayton. Originally created as a single-purpose flood control district, MCD since 1953 has created a subdistrict to provide water supply, regulate streamflows, conserve water, and develop a regional water quality program. Two other subdistricts have been formed, one to construct channel improvements, the other to serve as a local cooperating agency for a Soil Conservation Service project.

The Texas River Authorities

Texas has a number of active river authorities, some of which have been operating for more than 40

years.[17] Many of them have fairly extensive regulatory and project construction powers. The authorities implement one or more of the following purposes: flood control, hydroelectric power, water supply, navigation, wastewater and sewage disposal, water pollution control, conservation and reclamation, drainage, recreation, and underground water conservation. Many of the authorities perform coordinating functions with Federal and other State entities, much like river basin commissions established under Title II of the Water Resources Planning Act.[18] A number of the authorities work closely with Councils of Government and other local governmental bodies in their areas, including water districts. All of the authorities may issue bonds to finance their projects. Two have taxing powers.

The Sabine River Authority of Texas was created in 1949. It is linked to the Sabine River Authority of Louisiana by an interstate compact, which apportioned the water of the Sabine River between the States and which provided for a permanent compact administration to develop, conserve, and utilize the waters of the Sabine River and its tributaries. The multipurpose Toledo Bend Project on the Sabine River was constructed and now operates through the compact mechanism. This combination of the use of State river authorities with an interstate compact commission is somewhat unusual, but there is no reason why it cannot be used elsewhere, particularly on rivers traversing or flowing between two or more States.

Water pollution control has become an important activity of the Texas river authorities. They may finance water quality projects, plan pollution abatement programs, build and operate sewage treatment

---

[17] Brazos River Authority (created in 1929), the Lower Neches Valley Authority (1933), the Guadalupe-Blanco River Authority (1933), the Lower Colorado River Authority (1934), the Central Colorado River Authority (1935), the San Antonio River Authority (1937), the San Jacinto River Authority (1937), the Upper Guadalupe River Authority (1939), the Sabine River Authority (1949), the Trinity River Authority (1955), and the Red River Authority (1959).
[18] *Water Resources Planning Act*, P.L. 89-80, July 22, 1965, 79 Stat. 244, 42 USCA 1962, *et seq.*

plants or contract with any public agency to treat sewage, enforce antipollution laws, and direct the operations of a regional waste treatment system which the Texas Water Quality Board has ordered to be created.

The Texas river authorities have been a major force in developing the water resources of Texas. Practically all of this development has been through means of revenue bonds without burdening the public treasury. The independent financial base of the authorities, through their ability to issue revenue bonds, levy service charges, and in two cases, to levy taxes, has enabled them to act effectively. The authorities often have difficulties engaging in activities which do not produce revenues, even though the authorities may desire and have power to undertake these activities. The limitation of a river authority's activities to those which produce revenues may be inevitable if it cannot levy taxes and does not receive tax dollars from the State legislature or Federal or State grants for projects and programs.

Problems may develop when a river authority has jurisdiction which is not coextensive with a basin. While most of the Texas authorities have basinwide territorial jurisdiction, several do not. Where no single regional agency has authority over an entire basin, there is no single regional agency viewing water problems on a basinwide basis, and it is difficult to develop and administer basinwide programs.

The Gulf Coast Waste Disposal Authority

In the summer of 1969, the Texas legislature created a new antipollution agency, The Gulf Coast Waste Disposal Authority (GCWDA), to meet the water quality needs in the Galveston Bay area which lies along the gulf coast between main river basins outside river authority boundaries. The GCWDA is unique among pollution control agencies, and as a prototype may have a significant impact upon regional pollution control throughout the United States as well as in Texas. The GCWDA has broad financing, planning, operational, and enforcement powers. It may construct, operate, or sell waste treatment facilities; contract with owners of other systems for GCWDA operation of the other's plants, or for treatment of wastes of GCWDA facilities; regulate solid waste disposal, septic tank usage, and disposal of waste from aircraft; sue to enforce Water Quality Board permit limitations; and make and enforce its own regulations.

Conclusions on Intrastate Arrangements

The experience of Ohio with the Miami Conservancy District and the Texas experience with its river authorities indicate that such organizations, especially if they are granted broad powers and have an independent financial base, can be useful institutional arrangements in planning and developing the water resources of intrastate river basins, particularly in conjunction with regional land use planning. Such organizations would appear to be especially useful in intrastate basins or subbasins which do not have entities planning or developing the water resources of the area. They would also be useful as integrating devices in intrastate basins or subbasins where water resources activities are fragmented among a number of existing local entities.

The Texas experience indicates that if river authorities do not have territorial jurisdiction generally coextensive with a river basin, the resulting fragmentation in authority may not produce optimum solutions to basin problems. On the other hand, river authorities for subbasins can be useful devices, particularly if there is an effective coordinating mechanism with river authorities in other parts of the basin. Contractual arrangements between intrastate river authorities can provide that coordinating mechanism. On interstate streams, interstate compacts may provide that coordination. State river authorities for subbasins of a river flowing between two or more States, when linked together by an interstate or Federal-interstate water compact commission, would appear to be useful organizational arrangements for water resources planning and development.

State river authorities appear to be useful mechanisms for attacking problems of water pollution on an intrastate regional basis. They can make water quality plans for a region and construct regional waste disposal systems. The Gulf Coast Waste Disposal Authority appears to hold much promise, particularly for coastal areas outside of the boundaries of river authorities.

Recommendation on Intrastate Arrangements

Recommendation No. 11-14: States should consider the use of river basin authorities, similar to the Texas river authorities, in the planning and management of their water resources for river basins or portions thereof lying within the State, particularly in areas not already included within the territory of existing effective entities. States should also consider the use of such river basin authorities in combination with an

interstate compact commission for rivers flowing between or among two or more States.

AD HOC AND INTERAGENCY COMMITTEES AND RIVER BASIN COMMISSIONS FOR PLANNING[19]

In the 1940's the Federal Government began to establish various committees, composed of representatives from Federal agencies and the States, for multipurpose river basin planning. These committees evolved from the experience of the Nation with the Federal natural resources planning organizations of the 1930's and with the Tennessee Valley Authority (TVA).[20]

Interagency and Ad Hoc Coordinating Committees

In August of 1939, the Army Chief of Engineers, the Commissioner of Reclamation, and the Land Use Coordinator of the Department of Agriculture concluded a "Tripartite Agreement" to provide for consultation between the parties in the preparation of river basin surveys. In 1943, the Tripartite Agreement was replaced by a new agreement between the Departments of Interior, Agriculture, Army, and the Federal Power Commission, establishing the Federal-Interagency River Basin Committee (FIARBC), which attempted to continue the coordination function that earlier had been carried out by the National Resources Planning Board. FIABRC set up regional interagency committees for specific basins: the Missouri in 1945, the Columbia in 1946, the Pacific Southwest in 1948, and the Arkansas-White-Red and the New York-New England basins in 1950. All the regional committees included representatives of the affected States.

The ability of FIARBC to achieve coordination between agency programs was limited in several ways.

The Committee had no statutory standing and no budget. The authority, power, and financial discretion of the constituent agencies remained with the agencies to be exercised individually by them. As a result, FIARBC's decisions were advisory only, and implementation of decisions depended upon the voluntary cooperation and individual consent of its member agencies. In addition, the ability of the member agencies to cooperate in effectuating a Committee decision with which it might agree was frequently limited by statutory provisions relating to the agencies' powers and duties.

The regional interagency committees chartered in the 1940's and 1950's generally provided forums for the various member agencies where each agency could communicate its planning program to the other agencies. Eventually, if plans were able to be reconciled and unanimous agreement obtained, the committee would "layer" these separate plans into an overall river basin plan. The interagency committees traditionally operated without offices or staff. Relations with State and local governments were informal and tenuous.

One of the difficulties with the regional committees was that they were not able to reconcile separate agency plans and policies. Often the committees were brought into existence only after conflicting project proposals of the separate agencies were already in existence, as in the Missouri and Columbia basins, or after one agency had completed extensive planning in the basin, but before a rival agency had begun, as in the Arkansas-White-Red basin.

After passage of the Water Resources Planning Act in 1965, the President on March 29, 1966, abolished FIARBC's successor, the Interagency Committee on Water Resources, and placed its existing subcommittees and the field committees under the Water Resources Council.

River Basin Commissions

The difficulties encountered in the interagency and ad hoc coordinating committees established for water resources planning in the 1940's and 1950's led to a search for a better water planning mechanism. Proposals were made to establish river basin commissions combining Federal, State, and private interests. When legislation was introduced in 1961 to establish a Water Resources Council, it contained a procedure for the establishment of river basin commissions throughout the Nation, except that it was not intended that commissions would be established in

---

[19] This section is based on part on HART, Gary W (1971). Institutions for Water Planning, prepared for the National Water Commission. National Technical Information Service, Springfield, Va., Accession No. PB 204 244, and INGRAM, Helen (1971). The New England River Basins Commission, A Case Study, prepared for the National Water Commission. National Technical Information Service, Springfield, Va., Accession No. PB 204 375.

[20] For a more detailed discussion of the national planning organizations of the 1930's, see U.S. DEPARTMENT OF AGRICULTURE, Economic Research Service (1972). A History of Federal Water Resources Programs, 1800-1960, prepared by Beatrice H. Holmes, Miscellaneous Publication No. 1233. U.S. Department of Agriculture, Washington, D.C. pp. 13-16, 18.

the areas covered by TVA or the Delaware River Basin Compact Commission.

Under Title II of the Water Resources Planning Act of 1965, the President by executive order establishes a river basin commission upon written request of the Water Resources Council or a State. The concurrence of the Council and at least one-half of the States in the basin or basins involved is an essential condition to establishment, with two exceptions: in the Upper Colorado and Columbia basins, three of the four States in each basin must concur.

Each commission is to serve as the principal agency for the coordination of Federal, State, interstate, local, and private water development plans for the basin; to prepare and keep up to date a comprehensive coordinated joint plan, including an evaluation of all reasonable alternatives and recommendations for individual projects; to establish priorities for the collection of basic data, for planning, and for construction of projects; and to undertake studies necessary for preparing the plan and for carrying out the broad policy goals of the Water Resources Planning Act.

A commission is to submit to the Water Resources Council for transmission to the President and by him to the Congress and the governors and the legislatures of the participating States "a comprehensive, coordinated, joint plan, or any major portion thereof or necessary revisions thereof, for water and related land resources development in the area, river basin, or group of river basins for which such commission was established."[2][1]

An independent Federal chairman and staff provide each of the river basin commissions with a focal point and an identity. The chairman is appointed by the President and cannot be a member of any Federal agency. All members of a commission except the chairman are delegates from and salaried by some other organization. Each of the Federal agencies with a substantial interest in the river basin is entitled to a member as is each of the States. Interstate and international joint commissions in the basin may also have representatives.

Voting provisions give each member a means to protect individual interests. According to the Act, every reasonable endeavor shall be made to arrive at a consensus on all the issues. If consensus cannot be reached, then each member is to be afforded an opportunity to report and record his individual views.

The chairman records the position of the Federal members while the vice chairman, an officer elected by the States, acts upon the instructions of the State members. Where there is controversy, there are no means whereby one side can carry the day by winning a majority vote among river basin commission members. As a practical matter, rarely, if at all, are dissenting views recorded. Bargaining takes place and an agreement is either worked out or the issue is deferred. River basin commissions are thus designed to achieve coordination without centralization of authority.

The salary of the chairman is borne by the Federal Government, while the remainder of the river basin commission's expenses are apportioned among Federal and State members as the commission decides. Provisions are made for advances by the Federal Government to commissions against State appropriations for which delay is anticipated because of later legislative sessions.

Congress placed limits upon the extent of a commission's activities. Authority was limited to planning—not regulation, construction, or management—and the Act states that the authority of river basin commissions cannot be construed to limit the authority already held by States or Federal agencies.

Even when carrying out their planning functions, river basin commissions are limited in what they can do. They operate administratively on small budgets. Neither Congress nor the member States appropriate money to the river basin commission for planning. Instead, Congress appropriates money directly to the member Federal agencies, and the States appropriate planning moneys to the member State agencies. The financial control over the river basin commission planning effort thus resides in the member agencies.

Member Federal agencies, States, and interstate agencies often pursue their water goals without using the river basin commission. In fact, only partial and often defensive inducements exist for members to associate themselves actively with the work of the commission. Likewise, only weak incentives exist for persons and entities making decisions on water and related land resource questions to turn toward river basin commissions for information and advice.

The resources available to the chairman and his staff give them much flexibility but not much authority. A commission can become involved in a wide range of resource and environmental questions on the basis of the Planning Act and the responsibilities of the commission membership. There is great latitude permitted in responding to invitations

---

[1] *Water Resources Planning Act,* P.L. 89-80, July 22, 1965, 79 Stat. 249, 42 USCA 1962b-4.

tendered by Governors or others for a commission to take up an issue. The commissions have resources to study or recommend. However, the commission has no way to enforce its decisions. There are few resources at the command of a chairman to reward those who work through a river basin commission and penalize those who do not. He is dependent upon his State and Federal membership for funding. At the same time, he cannot direct the flow of funds to others at work on projects related to a commission mission. The gingerly way in which some commissions have treated ongoing studies under the leadership of a Federal agency testifies to the inability of the commissions to challenge an established force in water development in the region.

Since a number of separate entities are involved in water resource decisionmaking in a region covered by a river basin commission, and the power of those separate entities remains undiminished, river basin commissions can act only as facilitators and provide a framework for bargaining. Under certain conditions, it is likely that river basin commissions can perform the role of linking various interests together more strongly. An able chairman may become influential in a river basin commission. In areas where there is a widely shared, regional view of water resources, then there may be a greater tendency to work through a river basin commission. It is likely that a river basin commission may perform its role more strongly where it does not need to compete with one dominant water development agency which has control over decisions.

Conclusions

River basin commissions are to be preferred over interagency and ad hoc committees for water and related land resource planning and should be encouraged as regional planning entities for water and related land resources. The commissions are new and unique regional institutions, and should be given a chance to develop joint coordinated comprehensive plans for their regions.

Recommendations on Interagency Committees and River Basin Commissions

11-15.   **The planning of water and related land resources in the United States for major interstate river basins should be done by Federal-interstate compact commissions or by river basin commissions established under Title II of the Water Resources Planning Act**

rather than by ad hoc or interagency coordinating committees.

11-16.   **The interests of important local units of government, particularly entities comprising large metropolitan regions in the area of a river basin commission's jurisdiction, should be reflected more fully in the deliberations of river basin commissions and Federal-interstate compact commissions.**

11-17.   **After completion of its comprehensive coordinated joint plan, a river basin commission should be continued in order to (1) update and revise the plan, (2) continue the coordination of planning efforts, and (3) reestablish and revise priorities.**

INTERSTATE AND FEDERAL-INTERSTATE WATER COMPACTS[22]

Agreements between States are useful devices for dealing with water resources problems involving areas larger than one State and beyond the legal authority of any one State to solve. Such agreements, or "compacts," require the consent of Congress if a national or Federal interest is affected by the compact.[23]

The earliest use of interstate compacts in the water resources field occurred under the Articles of Confederation, when such agreements were employed to deal with boundary problems and navigation and fishing rights in interstate waters. They generally were not used for any other water-related purposes until 1922 when the Colorado River Compact was agreed upon to allocate water rights among the Colorado River Basin States. The next half century spawned over 30 compacts dealing with assorted water problems in a variety of ways. In this same period, the Supreme Court encouraged their use in interstate disputes over water rights and pollution. Similarly, Congress indicated that it would look favorably upon compacts dealing with flood control and water quality.

Existing water compacts may be grouped into four general categories: (1) water allocation compacts; (2) pollution control compacts; (3) flood control and

---

[22] This section is based largely on MUYS, Jerome C (1971) Interstate Water Compacts, prepared for the National Water Commission. National. Technical Information Service, Springfield, Va., Accession No. PB 202 998.

[23] Article I, section 10, clause 3, of the U.S. Constitution provides that "No State shall, without the Consent of Congress, . . .enter into any Agreement or Compact with another State or with a foreign Power."

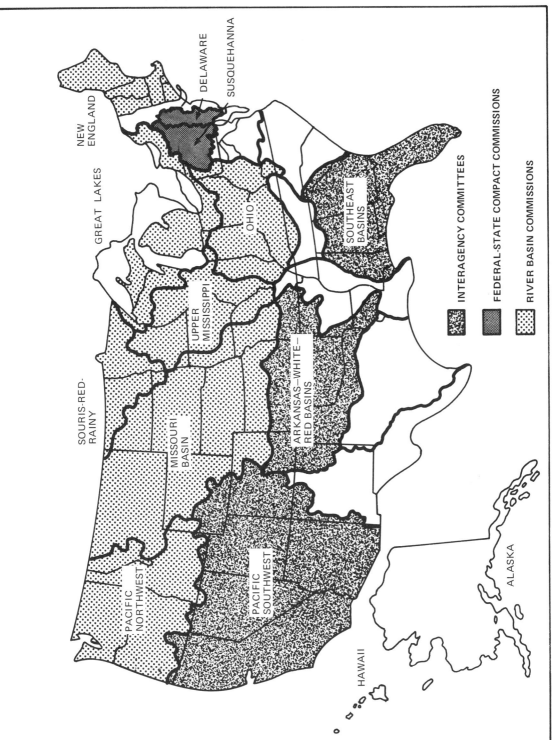

NEW ENGLAND

GREAT LAKES

DELAWARE

SUSQUEHANNA

SOUTHEAST BASINS

SOURIS-RED-RAINY

OHIO

UPPER MISSISSIPPI

MISSOURI BASIN

ARKANSAS—WHITE—RED BASINS

PACIFIC NORTHWEST

PACIFIC SOUTHWEST

ALASKA

HAWAII

INTERAGENCY COMMITTEES

FEDERAL-STATE COMPACT COMMISSIONS

RIVER BASIN COMMISSIONS

Figure 11-1. Map showing area covered by River Basin Commissions, Interagency Committees, and Federal-State Compact Commissions

planning compacts; and (4) comprehensive regulatory and project development compacts.

Water Allocation Compacts

The first interstate compact to allocate the waters of an interstate stream was negotiated in 1922 by the Colorado River Basin States. Subsequently, 18 additional compacts were established to apportion the waters of interstate streams. The general purpose of all water allocation compacts has been to accomplish an equitable apportionment of the water of interstate streams so that development of those rivers might proceed unmarred by continuing controversy among neighboring States over their relative rights in the common stream. The various compacts have taken a number of different approaches to allocating water rights to the signatory States. Whatever the allocation formula, existing uses and rights are usually protected. About half of the compacts expressly provide that the allocations are to include all Federal uses. Such provisions can be significant in the Western States because of extensive Federal land holdings and water use projects constructed under the Reclamation Act.

Pollution Control Compacts

The Supreme Court, Congress, and commentators have consistently viewed pollution control on interstate streams as a problem particularly susceptible to solution through the device of the interstate compact. In its 1921 decision in the interstate litigation between New York and New Jersey over pollution of the Hudson River, the Supreme Court expressed its view that the cooperative attack on pollution through interstate agreement was a more positive approach to such problems than adversary litigation. New York, New Jersey, and Connecticut subsequently entered into the Tri-State Compact in 1935 to deal with water quality problems in New York Harbor. Since that time, there have been at least 10 additional compacts which deal in various ways with interstate water pollution, ranging from simple bilateral agreements, such as that between California and Oregon on the Klamath River, to such multilateral treaties as the Ohio River Valley Water Sanitation Compact among eight States of the Ohio River Basin. The powers that may be exercised by the commissions created by these compacts span the spectrum from the Potomac River Commission's carefully circumscribed authority to study, report on, and recommend remedial actions on the pollution problems of that basin to the broad water quality standard-setting and enforcement powers of the Delaware and Susquehanna River Basin Commissions.

The five oldest water pollution compacts, the New York Harbor, Ohio River, Tennessee River, Potomac River, and New England agreements, were originally single-purpose compacts concerned only with pollution. More recent compacts encompass a more comprehensive approach to water problems, of which water quality control is just one aspect. At least one of the earlier compacts—the Potomac River Basin Compact—was subsequently amended, its authorized activities being broadened to include water and associated land resources as well as water pollution abatement.

All of the water pollution compacts provide for the creation of an administrative agency to implement the compact objectives. The first compact in this field, the New York Harbor compact, granted a broad water quality standard-setting and enforcement authority, a pattern that was followed on the Ohio River a few years later. However, both compacts contain a limitation on the interstate commission's enforcement authority, amounting to a veto over enforcement action; an enforcement order requires concurrence by a majority of the commissioners of the affected State. Subsequent compacts on the Potomac, Arkansas, Great Lakes, and in New England initially permitted those compact commissions to make recommendations only regarding pollution abatement. The Klamath River compact in 1957 blended the two approaches. It authorized the compact commission to establish standards which, if violated and the aggrieved State complains, are the basis for recommended improvement measures by the commission and for commission enforcement action if the recommendations are not followed. The recent experiments with the Federal-interstate compacts on the Delaware and Susquehanna return to the broader kinds of regulatory power originally conferred on the New York Harbor Commission in 1935, but without veto provisions.

Flood Control and Planning Compacts

There are a handful of compacts which deal principally with certain flood control aspects of water resources management—the Red River of the North compact, three compacts on the Connecticut, Merrimack, and Thames Rivers in New England, and the Wheeling Creek compact between Pennsylvania and West Virginia. Most of these compacts emerged from the Federal flood control program in the 1930's and were designed to promote cooperative State action in a national flood control program.

The authority conferred upon the Great Lakes Commission by the Great Lakes Basin Compact is perhaps the most limited in the water resources field. The compact creates the Great Lakes Commission to serve essentially an advisory function concerning the water resources of the Great Lakes Basin.

Comprehensive Regulatory and Project Development Compacts — The Federal-Interstate Compact

Over the past 50 years there has been a growing recognition of the need to better coordinate water resource planning and programs within the Federal establishment and between the Federal Government and the States. When compacts were proposed for this purpose, it was felt generally by the States that some way had to be found to make the United States a full partner in the compact in order to restrict its authority and its general inclination to "go it alone" in a basin. Thus, in 1953, the Missouri Basin Survey Commission unanimously agreed on the need for a regional coordinating and operating agency for that basin, but there were divergent points of view as to what kind of institutional arrangement would best meet the basin's needs. The Commission majority endorsed a federally created commission appointed by the President with broad powers to plan and implement a basinwide water resources program, while a three-member minority argued for a commission created under a "State-Federal" compact to which the States and the Federal Government would belong. Nothing came of either recommendation.

A subsequent effort by the New England States at a Federal-interstate compact in the late 1950's fared better among the States but failed to receive congressional consent, largely because of constitutional and other objections from the executive branch. However, concurrent with the unsuccessful efforts for a New England Federal-interstate compact, a more sweeping proposal emerged on the Delaware and received congressional consent in September 1961.

The Delaware River Basin Compact grew out of several decades of litigation among the basin States over the apportionment of the waters of that stream system and unsuccessful attempts to resolve the controversy by interstate compact. In the late 1950's, after a comprehensive study of various institutional approaches to the region's interstate water problems, the Delaware River Basin States reached agreement that a single, administrative entity was essential for the development plan and for the coordination of Federal, State, local, and private interests. To implement those objectives, the States speedily reached agreement on and ratified a compact creating the Delaware River Basin Commission (DRBC), comprised of the Governors of the basin States and a Federal representative appointed by the President. Congress consented to the compact with certain reservations.

The Delaware Compact reflects a significant departure from traditional compact usage in two respects: (1) the United States is a signatory party with the States and (2) extremely broad powers are granted to the compact commission.[24]

The DRBC is charged with formulating a "comprehensive plan" for the development and use of the basin's waters, and is endowed with broad planning, regulatory, and project construction powers to aid in implementing the basin plan.

To assure that development projects in the basin are in general conformity with the comprehensive plan, the compact confers a "licensing" power on the DRBC, providing that "no project having a substantial effect on the water resources of the basin shall hereafter be undertaken by any person, corporation or governmental authority unless it shall have been first submitted to and approved by the commission." The Commission is directed to approve any project which it finds "would not substantially impair or conflict with the comprehensive plan," and a project not meeting that standard may be either disapproved or approved subject to modification to make it consistent with the plan.

In addition to its comprehensive licensing authority, the DRBC is granted broad regulatory powers. Reinforcing that regulatory authority, the compact confers generous powers on the Commission to construct, develop, operate, and maintain "all projects, facilities, properties, activities and services, determined by the commission to be necessary, convenient or useful" for the purposes of the compact.

All of the grants of authority are to be exercised in consonance with "the purpose of the signatory parties to preserve and utilize. . .existing offices and

---

[24] Delaware River Basin Compact (1961). In U.S. CONGRESS, House (1968). Documents on the Use and Control of the Waters of Interstate and International Streams, House Document No. 319, 90th Congress, 2d Session. U.S. Government Printing Office, Washington, D.C. pp. 95-176.

agencies of government to the extent not inconsistent with the compact, and. . .to utilize. . .such offices and agencies. . .to the fullest extent it finds feasible and advantageous."

A unique feature of the compact is the conferral upon the DRBC of the power to allocate the waters of the basin among the signatory States in accordance with the doctrine of equitable apportionment. This provision for administrative allocation of interstate waters was designed as an alternative to (1) what was considered to be the relatively inflexible apportionments made by the traditional water allocation compacts and (2) litigation in the United States Supreme Court, where the basin States had already been on several occasions. This allocation power, as well as all other DRBC authority, may not be used to affect adversely the rights and obligations of the States under a 1954 Supreme Court decree, other than by unanimous agreement. The DRBC's power to make interstate allocations of water is supplemented by its authority to regulate withdrawals and diversions of surface and ground waters in certain situations.

The Commission has very broad financing authority. However, it does not have the power to tax and is specifically precluded from pledging the credit of any signatory party, or of any county or municipality, or to impose any obligation for the payment of the DRBC bonds upon any of those governmental entities.

The heart of the compact is the constraint which Commission approval of the comprehensive plan places on the water resources programs of the signatory parties. All Federal, State, local, and private water project planners are required to conform their projects to the DRBC's comprehensive plan. Since the content of the comprehensive plan is determined by majority vote of the DRBC, Congress has provided in the legislation consenting to the compact that the Federal Government need not shape its projects to a plan with which it is not in agreement. However, the consent legislation provides that "whenever a comprehensive plan, or any part or revision thereof, has been adopted with the concurrence of the member appointed by the President, the exercise of any powers conferred by law on any officer, agency or instrumentality of the United States with regard to water and related land resources in the Delaware River Basin shall not substantially conflict with any such portion of such comprehensive plan." The President may also "suspend, modify or delete" any provision of the comprehensive plan affecting Federal interests

when he "shall find that the national interest so requires."[25]

Public hearings are required as a precondition to almost all important Commission actions, and all DRBC meetings are required to be open to the public. In addition, the Commission is authorized, but not directed, to establish advisory committees representing a broad spectrum of water resource interest groups.

Although the executive branch in 1961 only reluctantly and conditionally endorsed the Delaware compact and stated that it should not be considered a precedent for other river basins, in fact the compact has had precedential effect. A similar compact was negotiated for the Susquehanna River and approved in 1970. Similar proposals are under consideration for the Hudson and Potomac Rivers, as well as the Great Lakes. The proposed compact for the Potomac River Basin has been approved by the States of Maryland and Virginia and needs approval only by the remaining States of Pennsylvania and West Virginia before going to Congress for approval of participation by the District of Columbia and the Federal Government.

The Federal-interstate compacts on the Delaware and the Susquehanna, providing broad powers for comprehensive regulation and project development of a river basin, appear to have great potential for solving major water and related land resource problems on a regional basis. The compact for the Susquehanna (1970) is so recent that no evaluation of the activities of the Susquehanna River Basin Commission can be made. But in the Delaware over a decade of experience there with the Federal-interstate compact provides some insight into the utility of this mechanism.

In the 12 years of its existence, the DRBC has achieved some important results. It successfully managed an emergency water situation in the Delaware basin during the 1965-67 Northeast drought. In July of 1964, it expanded its water supply jurisdiction to include the management of ground waters in the basin. It has approved for inclusion in its comprehensive plan several multipurpose water projects to augment water supplies. It has assumed responsibilities for repaying the costs of non-Federal water supply features in certain Federal reservoirs, apportioning among the States the costs that the

---

[25] *Act of September 27, 1961*, P.L. 87-328, 75 Stat. 688. Section 15.1(s)1.

States shall bear in meeting the non-Federal payment of the water supply costs of the projects.

In the field of water pollution control, the DRBC has established basinwide water quality regulations and abatement schedules for most of the major waste dischargers in the basin which account for 90 percent of the waste discharged into the river. In the Tocks Island, Darby Creek, and Gloucester-Salem areas, the DRBC has encouraged regional solutions to sewage disposal. It has financed a demonstration project to prove the feasibility of regional waste management, thus implementing a Commission policy adopted in 1968 to encourage the use of regional water pollution control facilities. Its pollution control standards and waste discharge allocations have upgraded sewage treatment along the main stream of the Delaware River and have helped guide industrial development. The DRBC's power to mandate regional waste treatment could result in substantial reorganization of waste treatment systems along the River.

The DRBC has endorsed the implementation of several Federal and State flood control projects. It has cooperated with the U.S. Geological Survey and the Corps of Engineers in encouraging flood plain mapping studies so that municipalities may adopt flood plain zoning ordinances and thus become eligible for Federal flood insurance. It has also encouraged the formation of watershed associations throughout the basin.

In recent years, the DRBC has begun to regulate the conditions for powerplant construction within the basin. It subjected the hydroelectric features of the Tocks Island project to conditions protecting the environment. It barred the use of Sunfish Pond for pumping water to supply hydroelectric power, and it required that the reservoir construction be done with a minimum of disruption to the area's natural environment. In April 1971, the DRBC indicated that all electric power projects of 100,000 kw. or more would be approved only after the utility companies prepared siting studies analyzing the effects of the site on the water resources of the basin. The DRBC also has reviewed several nuclear powerplant proposals.

In the field of recreation, the DRBC's efforts have centered around the development of the Delaware Water Gap National Recreational Area in the northern part of the basin. The park has been approved as part of the DRBC's comprehensive plan. Tocks Island has been endorsed as the major water recreation project within it. In 1971, the DRBC resolved that the upper branch of the Delaware River be included in the

National Scenic and Wild Rivers System. The DRBC and the Bureau of Outdoor Recreation of the Department of the Interior have discussed joint recreational plans for the region.

The Delaware Compact authorizes the Commission to review all projects which have a substantial effect on the water resources of the basin. Over 1,000 projects have been reviewed; most of them have been included in the comprehensive basin plan. The plan, based largely on the 1958 Corps of Engineers plan for the basin, has been continuously updated and implemented. The DRBC has endorsed a number of Federal, State, and local water resources projects. During the past 10 years, approximately 30 multipurpose Federal-State or wholly federally sponsored river management projects have been implemented. In addition, three proposed projects have been approved for construction and 17 others endorsed but not yet finally approved.

The DRBC has issued statements of policy, criteria, and standards setting forth the conditions under which the DRBC will grant approval of projects and policies. These statements play a regulatory role in setting the conditions with which Federal, State, and local agencies must comply in administering their water resource projects.

The DRBC has also maintained close working relationships with Federal, State, and local agencies. Each of the four member States has reorganized its respective water departments into environmental control agencies, and the DRBC works closely with them, particularly in the area of pollution control surveillance. The DRBC maintains a concurrent project review with the Delaware Valley Regional Planning Commission. As a matter of routine it notifies all county planning commissions, HUD certified areawide bodies, and concerned municipalities of its project review agenda.

Finally, the DRBC has been a useful mechanism for allowing the public to participate in the planning of projects in the basin and in providing a basinwide point of view for balancing diverse values and exploring various alternatives to proposed projects.[26]

---

[26] For more details of the activities of the DRBC, see U.S. ADVISORY COMMISSION ON INTERGOVERNMENTAL RELATIONS (1972). Multistate Regionalism, A-39. U.S. Government Printing Office, Washington, D.C. pp. 95-96, 99-108, 111-120.

Evaluation of the Compact Approach to Regional Water Problems

Perhaps the chief advantage of the compact approach to river basin management is its adaptability to the particular needs of a basin. Since a compact must be the product of agreement among the States, it can be shaped to meet any problems the States desire, in accordance with the particular regional philosophy of appropriate intergovernmental relations. Thus, it can be targeted on a single problem, such as water quality management, or may seek comprehensive, multipurpose goals. Similarly, it may create a permanent administrative entity and endow it with such powers, narrow or sweeping, as the participating States deem necessary or appropriate to accomplish their regional objectives, so long as they are consistent with broad national water resource goals.

The States may confer a wide range of powers on a compact agency which are generally adequate to deal with most interstate water problems. Indeed, it seems likely that a compact commission may be endowed with powers that the member States might not exercise independently, although the law on this point has yet to be clearly stated by the Supreme Court. The express conferral of Federal powers on a compact entity by congressional consent legislation may well cure any defects in the States' authority, and the participation by the United States as a signatory party, thereby clearly making the compact commission a Federal instrumentality, would put the question beyond doubt.

An often-voiced criticism of the compact approach to regional water resources management is that compacts require an exceedingly long time to negotiate and effectuate by State ratification and congressional consent. Although the record of the various kinds of water compacts is uneven on this score, there is substantial evidence to support the conclusion that the compact approach is not inherently more cumbersome and time consuming in its creation and change than other institutional approaches to comparable water resource problems. If there are delays in creation of compacts, the reasons are often due to specific policy controversies rather than the use of the compact mechanism. The more recent experience with the Delaware and Susquehanna compacts demonstrate that even such highly complex agreements can be negotiated and approved with impressive swiftness.

In order to minimize the delays and hazards attendant upon compact amendment and the accompanying need for new congressional consent, States should confer a broader range of powers on compact commissions. If the States are reluctant to grant certain powers to the compact agency unconditionally, then appropriate limitations on their use may be fashioned. Similarly, it seems desirable to permit some leeway for certain kinds of changes in a compact without the need for new ratification by the State legislatures and consent by Congress.

Consideration should be given by compact negotiators to provide for weighted representation on compact commissions, as opposed to the traditional equality among States which has characterized voting rights on compact commissions. Even though the States stand more or less on an equal plane in the Federal Union, they may have widely disparate interests in some river basins by virtue of geography, population, natural resources, and other factors. Although it obviously would be difficult to devise an acceptable formula, there appears to be some merit in recent proposals for proportional representation on compact commissions to reflect differing degrees of a State's interest in a particular river basin.

Recommendations on Interstate Compacts

The thrust of our recommendations in this section is for the greater utilization of the compact approach for dealing with regional water problems other than through federally directed and dominated programs.

Recommendation No. 11-18: The Federal-interstate compact is recommended as the preferred institutional arrangement for water resources planning and management in multistate regions.

The advent of the Federal-interstate compact and its record on the Delaware has shown that disparate Federal, State, and local elements of water resources policy can be forged into a promising comprehensive, cooperative, and consciously directed regional program. While there are some jurisdictional and other problems which remain to be fully worked out, the approach justifies endorsement for other regions where the States may consider it appropriate. It merits particular consideration in the Western public land States, where the Federal Government's dominant role as landowner and water master makes the goals of the Federal-interstate compact particularly relevant.

Recommendation No. 11-19: Congress should enact legislation granting advance consent to a limited class of water compacts not having a significant impact on Federal interests. Such compacts should be submitted to Congress to become effective 90 days thereafter unless, within the 90-day period, Congress denies its consent.

The Constitution does not specify when or in what manner the requisite congressional consent to an interstate compact must be given. The Supreme Court has held that the critical question is whether "Congress, by some positive act, in relation to such agreement, [has] signified the consent of that body to its validity."[27] Consent may be express or implied and may be evidenced either before or after an agreement is reached by the compacting States.

Congress could expedite the ability of States to enter into agreements involving water resources by granting advance consent to a limited class of compacts, thus removing the necessity for subsequent congressional consent. One such class of compacts involves what might be called "administrative agreements," which are designed primarily to bring about efficiencies in water resources management. An example would be an agreement among several States to contract jointly with the U.S. Geological Survey to establish certain stream-gaging stations on an interstate stream and to provide the resulting data to the parties to the agreement. The substance of such an arrangement is that the States are simply taking joint action in the interests of economy and efficiency, all within the scope of their individual powers. There is no objective to exercise their joint sovereignty to accomplish a regional purpose outside of their individual sovereign rights and responsibilities.

Another category might include agreements for local planning or zoning of interstate areas. These agreements could prove useful for developing land use controls on an interstate regional basis, particularly with regard to flood plains, wetlands, wild and scenic rivers, estuarine zones, and areas of natural beauty.

A third category might include advance consent for compacts for management of multistate metropolitan water systems.[28]

There is a virtue in having such agreements subject to a veto by Congress before they take effect so that the involved States themselves do not decide whether

Federal interests are affected. As an added safeguard with respect to any compact consented to in advance, Congress should screen such a compact by requiring that it be submitted to Congress, to become effective 90 days thereafter, unless within that period Congress denies its consent. In the event Congress failed to act within the 90-day period but later determined that the compact should not remain in effect, Congress, of course, could deny its consent to the compact.

Recommendation No. 11-20: Any interstate water compact granting broad project construction or regulatory authority to a compact commission should state the roles of the compact commission and of existing State and Federal agencies with regard to project construction, water quality, and other regulatory functions.

Project Construction and Regulatory Functions: The Delaware and the Susquehanna Compacts give a preference to existing State and Federal agencies in the construction of projects; the compact commission can only act when the State or Federal agencies are unable or unwilling to do so, or agree that a particular project is appropriate for commission action. However, if there is to be more meaningful State and regional action in the water resources field, the better practice would be to have compacts state that the individual member States and the compact commission, in that order, should construct needed projects, with Federal construction a last resort.

Consent legislation for the Delaware Compact did not address the issue of the relationship between the DRBC and State or Federal regulatory agencies. The consent legislation for the Susquehanna Compact made some attempt at clarification, but the language is ambiguous. Compacts giving regulatory functions to compact commissions should make clear who prevails in the case of any conflict between the exercise of authority by Federal or State regulatory commissions and by compact commissions. As a general rule, in case of any conflict the compact commission should prevail unless there are special reasons to the contrary.

Water Quality Regulation – Federal legislation since 1948 has encouraged compacts between States for the prevention and control of water pollution. Yet, even after recent sweeping revisions in the program by Congress, no guidance has been given to the States as to the kinds of provisions which should

---

[7] *Green v. Biddle,* 21 U.S. (8 Wheat.) 1, 86 (1823).

[8] See Recommendation 12-5 in Chapter 12.

be contained in compacts dealing with water quality.[29] The Commission recommends that interstate compacts dealing with water quality contain provisions covering the following matters:

(a) The compact agency should have broad authority to act as the joint agent of the member States in the establishment and enforcement of water quality standards and to receive grants for administering programs to prevent, reduce, and eliminate water pollution.

(b) The compact agency should preempt the member States' standard-setting authority only to the extent that the compact agency standards must be the minimal standards throughout the basin. The States should remain free to establish individually more stringent standards. Thus, States eager to develop high standards of water quality management need not fear that joint action by compact will commit them to a "least common denominator" level of interstate standards.

(c) The Federal standard-setting authority of the Environmental Protection Agency should bear the same relationship to a compact commission as it does to the member States; i.e., it should be held in reserve to be utilized only if the compact agency fails to establish adequate standards in a timely fashion.

(d) With respect to violations of established standards, the compact agency should possess the full arsenal of enforcement powers. It should be permitted to defer to the enforcement agencies of the member States for a reasonable period, but should be directed to move in its own right upon request of the affected State or upon the expiration of a specified, reasonably short period within which a State has failed, in the commission's judgment, to move expeditiously or effectively against a violation. In the same pattern, Federal authority should be exercised only upon request of the compact agency or if the compact agency has failed to respond expeditiously or effectively to an Environmental Protection Agency request for enforcement action.

(e) Compact agency decisions should be rendered by a majority vote. The practice of some compacts to afford the affected State a veto over enforcement action against it should be clearly prohibited. Provision should be made for tie breaking by arbitration or otherwise.

(f) Participation by the United States as a signatory party should be sanctioned.

Recommendation No. 11-21: Congress should enact legislation (1) granting the Federal district courts original jurisdiction over any case or controversy arising under an interstate water compact and (2) waiving the sovereign immunity of the United States and permitting the United States to be made a party defendant in such a suit.

Since an interstate compact is considered to be a law of each of the compacting States, actions thereunder may be challenged just as any other State action. The Supreme Court has held that the construction of such a compact sanctioned by Congress presents a Federal question appropriate for Supreme Court review. What is not clear, however, is whether compact questions also meet the general Federal question jurisdictional standards for United States district courts. There is a split of authority, but most courts have answered the question in the negative. Consequently, general references in compacts providing for judicial review of compact questions or enforcement of compact commission orders in courts of "competent jurisdiction" probably do not confer such jurisdiction. What is required is a specific grant of subject matter jurisdiction, such as that contained in the Delaware River Basin Compact consent legislation:

> The United States district courts shall have original jurisdiction of all cases or controversies arising under the Compact, and this Act and any case or controversy so arising initiated in a State Court shall be removable to the appropriate United States district court in the manner provided by § 1446, Title 28 U.S.C. . . . .[30]

Another major problem in a suit involving water compacts is that the Federal interests in the subject matter may be so significant as to make the United States an indispensable party, in which event the failure of the United States to consent to be joined may effectively block relief. Congress should enact legislation waiving the sovereign immunity of the United States and permitting the United States to be made a party defendant in such a suit.

---

[29] See Section 103 of the *Water Pollution Control Act Amendments of 1972,* P.L. 92-500, October 18, 1972, 86 Stat. 816, 818, 33 USCA 1253.

[30] *Act of September 27, 1961,* P.L. 87-328, 75 Stat. 688, Section 15.1(p).

FEDERALLY CHARTERED CORPORATIONS FOR MULTISTATE WATER MANAGEMENT ACTIVITIES[31]

In recent years, Congress has turned increasingly to the Federal corporation to perform complex financial or operational tasks for the Federal Government. Initially, such corporations were owned and operated by the Federal Government without contributions from or control by States, localities, or private interests. In the last decade a series of hybrid corporations has emerged. They have been chartered by the Federal Government, and have been subject to some degree of continuing Federal control. They have not had direct participation or control by private stockholders, nor have they been accorded the status of Federal agencies.[32]

The question addressed in this section of the Commission's report is whether the corporate mechanism is useful as a substitute for or supplement to regional multistate waterway commissions and Federal-interstate compacts through which governmental water resource planning, operations, and regulation have largely been conducted.

The Tennessee Valley Authority (TVA) is a singular example of a Federal corporation performing major functions in this area. But it has never been duplicated in the United States despite efforts to do so. It does not appear to be either advisable or feasible in the foreseeable future to establish additional federally owned and operated regional water resource corporations of the scope and type of TVA. However, there may be isolated situations in which federally owned and operated water resource projects of a self-supporting nature can be organized more feasibly as a Federal corporation than as a branch of another government department or agency.

For essentially the same reasons that the government corporation has proven its usefulness for handling particular types of financing and operational tasks in the Federal sphere, it would appear that corporations could also be utilized at the State level. In a sense, this has already been accomplished by many States through the establishment of special "municipal corporations" to perform tasks not lending themselves to the boundaries of the States' more conventional political subdivisions.

In the water resource field, there are a number of existing examples of special State authorities through which a number of participating county or municipal bodies perform planning, regulatory, and in some instances operational functions of mutual interest.[33] These special State authorities normally have been restricted to governmental entities; there has been only limited resort to the States' general powers to charter nongovernmental corporations, even of a nonprofit character. One example of this latter type of State activity, however, is the Wisconsin Valley Improvement Company, a private, nonprofit corporation chartered by the State of Wisconsin in 1907, to insure adequate water supply and maximize the utilization of the hydroelectric generating capacity of the Wisconsin River. There would appear to be a role for State established corporations in situations where the cooperation of two or more governmental or private entities within a single State is required for optimum water management and the Federal interest in the specific project is not sufficient to require its participation in, or control over, the operations of any such intrastate corporation.

The potential utility of the Federal Government's power to charter corporations as an aid to interstate water management is, however, a matter to which little previous consideration has been given. The Commission has canvassed the legal and policy questions inherent in having the Federal Government charter various types of water management corporations in order to evaluate the extent to which such corporations might be a useful alternative to the establishment of other types of public or quasi-public water management agencies.

General Considerations

Participation by Non-Federal Entities in Federally Chartered Corporations: The examples of Comsat and the other federally chartered corporations indicate that such an entity may have a majority of its board

---

[31] This section of the report is based upon SOLOMON, Richard A (1971). The Federal-State Regional Corporation, prepared for the National Water Commission. National Technical Information Service, Springfield, Va., Accession No. PB 202 997.

[32] The initial endeavor of this type was the Communications Satellite Corporation (Comsat), 47 USCA 701 *et seq.* It has now been followed in the operational area by the National Railroad Passenger Corporation, Public Law 91-518, approved October 30, 1970, and in the financial area by the corporation established by the *National Housing Partnership Act,* 42 USCA 3931 *et seq.* See also the Corporation for Public Broadcasting, 47 USCA 396 *et seq.*

[33] See, *e.g.,* the discussion earlier in this chapter of the Texas River Basin authorities and the Gulf Coast Waste Disposal Authority.

of directors, or of its stockholder/members, neither appointed by nor responsible to the Federal Government. There is no history of federally chartered corporations in which majority control over their operations rests with participating States, either by themselves or in concert with one or more lesser governmental bodies of such States. But there does not appear to be any legal bar to Congress so providing.

It is hard to envision any major water resource problem which would not have a sufficient Federal interest or interstate effect to support Federal legislation.[34] Given such a Federal interest, a federally chartered corporation can be utilized as the administrative vehicle for carrying out these responsibilities. In addition, there is no legal inhibition in providing that a majority of the member/stockholders of the corporations, with majority control over the corporations' affairs, may consist of persons chosen by and responsible to the States or their subdivisions rather than to Federal officials or private parties as in the case of Comsat and the other corporations referred to above.

The possibility that the Federal Government or an agency thereof will be a member of the corporation or that the corporation might be classified as an agency of the Federal Government does not require a different conclusion. The legal problem here is essentially the same as that presented by the request for congressional approval of the Delaware River Basin Compact, where the Federal Government was to have only one-fifth of the voting strength of the Commission and could have been bound in a number of important respects by a majority vote of the State members. At that time, a detailed study was prepared of the power of the Federal Government to delegate its governmental responsibilities to such an entity.[35] The study concluded that the Congress had authority to commit the Federal Government to such a minority status.

While Federal legislation can authorize specified Federal officials to act with representatives of the States or their subdivisions to establish the corporations, additional implementing legislation by the participating States will be essential to provide for the participation at the State level. Even where broad home rule legislation already exists, it frequently will not extend to authorizing local participation in such federally created governmental units. To the extent that it might be advisable to provide for establishing any such corporation by means of an interstate compact, State action will be essential.

Status of the Corporations as Agencies of the Federal and State Governments: The participation of State or local governments in the corporation's organization and policy formation, even if such non-Federal representatives have voting control, would not preclude the Congress from endowing corporations with the status of an agency of the Federal Government any more than it precluded it from designating the Delaware and Susquehanna River Basin Commissions as Federal agencies for certain purposes. Designation as a Federal agency normally will not be dispositive of the powers which the corporations could be assigned to perform, but it could in some situations give them additional strength. Thus, such a classification might facilitate assumption by the corporations of Federal regulatory functions (including the developing and enforcement of comprehensive plans), and probably make their securities more easily marketable, whether or not such obligations were guaranteed by the Federal Government.

A more significant problem concerns the ability of a federally chartered corporation to exercise State governmental authority. Since an interstate compact is by definition an agency of the compacting States, whether or not the Federal Government is also a participant, it is in a position to exercise State governmental powers. The authority of the individual States to endow a federally chartered water resource corporation with State governmental powers is, however, primarily a matter of individual State constitutional law.

One answer to the question of endowing a federally chartered corporation with necessary State governmental powers could be to draft the Federal enabling legislation in terms of granting advance congressional consent to two or more participating States (together with the Federal Government) to enter into compacts to establish a corporation, or to become members in an already chartered corporation. Another possibility, discussed in greater detail below, is to provide by interstate compact that federally chartered corporations can be established directly by existing or future interstate or Federal-State compact organizations such as the Delaware and Susquehanna River Basin Commissions.

---

[34] Compare, *Federal Power Commission v. Union Electric Co.,* 381 U.S. 90 (1965).

[35] U.S. CONGRESS, Senate (1961). Delaware River Basin Compact, Senate Report No. 854, 87th Congress, 1st Session. U.S. Government Printing Office, Washington, D.C. pp. 36-48.

Financing Powers of Federally Chartered Water Resource Corporations: Where the functions of a water resource corporation can be self-sustaining through project revenues or user fees, financing problems would not appear to be serious. It is clear that such corporations can be granted authority to issue revenue bonds or any other securities resting on the credit or property of the corporation as contrasted with that of the Federal or a State government. It also seems clear that the Congress, if it wishes, can pledge the credit of the United States as a guarantor of the securities of a federally owned or chartered corporation utilized to achieve purposes for which Congress can appropriate money. Or, as in the case of the Federal National Mortgage Association, provision could be made for Federal purchase of the corporation's securities.[36]

Since some water resource operations may not be self-sufficient, or only partly self-sufficient, the question arises as to whether there is any other mechanism available to relieve them of dependency upon Federal or State grants or annual appropriations. The requirements of the United States Constitution, that direct Federal taxes be apportioned among the States and indirect taxes be uniform in their application, present serious if not insurmountable problems with respect to the availability of any Federal tax falling upon the local or regional beneficiaries of a particular water resource corporation. Even if it were to be determined that the legal authority existed, it seems most unlikely that the Congress would delegate any portion of its taxing authority to any corporation, particularly one in which the Federal Government would not have the controlling voice.

Can a federally chartered water resource corporation exercise State taxing authority? There is no simple answer to this question, even assuming that the States could and would designate the corporations as State instrumentalities. There are numerous State constitutional limitations on the exercise of State taxing authority by "municipal corporations" or other local or regional State bodies; to what extent they would apply to a particular water resource corporation will depend on the law of the particular States involved. Over and beyond such limitations, a question is presented as to how the taxing authority of each of the States involved can be simultaneously invoked by, or on behalf of, a multistate water resource corporation.

It is conceivable that the State legislation could provide that, with the consent of the State's representatives on the corporate board, the corporations would have limited authority to levy taxes within that portion of its area of operation lying within the State's boundaries, if concurrent action were taken to impose similar taxes upon the affected citizens of the other participating States. But in this situation the taxing authority for a region would be exercised by appointed officials with little or no political responsibility to the region. Alternatively, State legislation might provide for the simultaneous establishment of special taxing districts within each State. However, the corporations would then be dependent upon outside action for this part of their financing.

As a practical matter, operations of water resource corporations, or of any other type of water resource organization, which are not self-financing and self-supporting, may have to depend primarily upon grants. Where such grants are part of regular ongoing programs, and the Federal and State authorizing legislation for the corporations provide that the water resource corporations may be the beneficiaries of such grants, some of the worst features of the annual appropriation system may be mitigated.[37] If grants for water resource activities are made directly to the States with a minimum of Federal guidance, action at the State level will be required to provide the corporations with any assurance of continuing funds. And to the extent that the Federal or State grants call for matching funds by the ultimate recipient, it may be necessary to provide in the authorizing legislation that the corporation can raise such funds by contracting in advance with local governmental or private groups to purchase its services for the period necessary to pay off the corporate debt.

The Likelihood of Securing General Authorizing Legislation: There is no history of Federal legislation authorizing specified Federal and State officials to establish an indefinite number of corporations throughout the country to perform specified functions when and if they believe such action would serve congressional objectives. On the contrary, the

---

[36] See 12 USCA 1716b-1719.

[37] The grant program for the construction of treatment works authorized by Section 201(g)(1) of the Federal Water Pollution Control Act, P.L. 92-500, Oct. 18, 1972, 86 Stat. 816, 834, 33 USCA 1281(g)(1), provides for grants to interstate and intermunicipal agencies, as well as to States and municipalities, financed through an authorization of contract authority. Such grants could provide an adequate source of financing.

1945 Government Corporation Control Act[38] reflects the reluctance of the Congress to permit Federal officials to shield activities from congressional control and scrutiny by utilization of the corporate device. But the various situations in which Congress has granted advance consent, sometimes in fairly general terms, to the States entering into interstate compacts not yet negotiated, and without limitation upon the number or grouping of participating States, indicates that it might also be willing to give advance authority to the establishment of water resource corporations. Resort to general legislation would, initially at least, almost certainly carry with it a restriction on the scope of activities which could be performed by any federally chartered corporation established thereunder to those expressly specified in the authorizing legislation.[39] In addition, any general Federal legislation will be effective only if the constitutions and laws of the States involved authorize the States, or their local governmental units, to participate in such interstate organizations.

Functions to be Included in a Water Resource Corporation: Subject to the various considerations discussed above, there are no insurmountable legal barriers to legislation casting virtually all water resource agencies into the corporate mold. There appear to be practical or policy reasons, however, why some functions lend themselves more to the corporate form of administration than others.

Water resource activities can be said to fall into three broad categories: (1) comprehensive *planning;* (2) construction, *operation,* and maintenance of particular projects; and (3) *regulation* of various uses and users of waters. Most conventional thinking has considered that public authorities operating in corporate form best fit the second of these functional types and then, perhaps, only where such operations are self-supporting. Rigid limitation of the corporate role

to such self-supporting operations appears to be unduly restrictive.

Even where a water resource entity is dependent in whole or in part on grants or annual appropriations from the participating governmental bodies, a public corporation might well constitute a viable mechanism by which governmental units could act together to plan for and carry out one or more assigned operational tasks. The basic problem in both the planning and regulatory areas is whether a corporation's enhanced independence may not be at the expense of the essential political accountability and responsiveness of any entity clothed with governmental regulatory power. This problem could be enhanced substantially if a governmental agency responsible for comprehensive planning or regulation also is authorized to conduct some, but not all, of the operational functions within its area.

The problem of political accountability and responsiveness could be somewhat mitigated by providing that the directors of the corporation be chosen by and be accountable to the President and Governors of each State (or, to the extent lesser governmental entities of a State were directly represented, by the chief elected officials of such entity). But this remedy, or the more extreme one of having the corporate board members elected by the populace of the area they serve, not only will be at the expense of operational flexibility and continuity, but would be of doubtful utility unless such nominated or elected members of the board of the corporation devote full time to their activities as board members. If, instead, they perform the normal part-time role of corporate directors, it seems clear that the full-time corporate officers with only indirect political responsibility will normally become dominant.

Such considerations could lead to a decision to restrict the specific responsibilities of any water resource corporations to operational functions, including the internal planning necessary for such operations. Among possible types of operation, water supply and sewage treatment and disposal are obvious candidates since they can be self-supporting in whole or major part. And federally chartered corporations might play a useful role as sales or purchase agents, in the event there are major interbasin water transfers among private and public parties within a single basin but involving more than one State. Finally, other less self-sufficient functions related to water management such as recreational or fish and wildlife development or even the furnishing of flood control and navigational aids might fit the corporate mold, either as an

---

[38] P.L. 248, 79th Congress, Title III, December 6, 1945, 59 Stat. 602, 31 USCA 869.

[39] Thus, in giving its consent to the compact establishing the Bi-State Development Agency, in the St. Louis-East St. Louis area of Illinois and Missouri, the Congress added a proviso expressly requiring its approval before the Agency could assume any powers beyond those specifically provided for in the original charter. See P.L. 743, 81st Congress, August 31, 1950, 64 Stat. 571, 30 USCA 603. (The compact agreement as tendered to Congress had provided that the Agency could assume such new functions as might be conferred on it by concurrent legislation of the two States.)

adjunct to revenue-producing activities, or independently if the appropriate financial base could be established.

On the other hand, because of the problems of political accountability and responsiveness, two significant areas of water management, water pollution control and flood plain management, would appear to be particularly unsuited to the corporate form of agency organization. These areas are essentially regulatory in nature and are concerned primarily with imposing restraints and obligations on existing private entities in and around the waterway. For the same reasons, the corporate form seems unsuited to comprehensive river basin planning responsibilities where the approved plan must be adhered to by all public and private interests operating in the waterway.

The Federally Chartered Corporation as a Substitute for or Adjunct to a River Basin Authority Established by Interstate Compact

Does the federally chartered corporation have a role if the type of comprehensive river basin authority, exemplified by the Delaware and Susquehanna River Basin Commissions, is the optimum organizational device for waterway management? Such river basin commissions hitherto have been the product of Federal-interstate compacts adopted by the legislatures of the participating States after extensive periods of negotiation. The compacts then have been subjected to further intensive congressional study, and their subsequent ratification by the Federal Government in all cases has been accompanied by a large number of conditions and reservations, which could well result in future controversy and litigation.

Would any of these delays and ambiguities be avoided if the Federal Government were to take the lead in encouraging the establishment by such entities of federally chartered membership corporations in which the Federal and State governments would play essentially the same relative roles they do in the river basin commissions established by compact? A necessary corollary inquiry is whether use of the corporate device under such circumstances would create additional problems not inherent in the utilization of interstate compacts.

The first question, it seems clear, must be answered in the negative. The delays and ambiguities involved in Federal-interstate compacts would not be avoided by the alternative use of the corporate device. If the

executive and legislative branches of the Federal Government can be persuaded that they need have no fears of river basin compact commissions taking over control of waterway management at the expense of significant Federal interests, action to establish additional river basin compact commissions undoubtedly can be expedited. It does not appear, however, that the use of the corporate form of organization could significantly accelerate this process.

The corporate device might be useful as an organization ancillary to Federal-State interstate compacts. Thus, future compacts should be drafted to provide that the commissions established thereby could themselves establish either State or federally chartered corporations to perform discrete operational tasks *within their delegated powers* where the commission believes they could be more efficiently undertaken by a separate corporate agency. These subsidiary corporations should not be limited to the same member-participants as the commission itself. On the contrary, one of the principal advantages of authorizing the commissions to establish corporate offspring would be to permit local or municipal bodies along the waterway to assume direct responsibility for operational tasks which are not of immediate interest to all of the commission's participating States, or to the areas of the river basin remote from particular projects.

Prospects for Single or Limited Function Water Resource Corporations

Even if federally chartered corporations are not the optimum organization for broad-based water resource agencies covering an entire river basin, there may well be a place for such corporations to perform discrete operational functions for two or more governmental units in different States or where Federal and State interests in a particular problem are sufficiently great to require joint operational control.

While there might be exceptional situations where all Federal participation could be dispensed with, it seems clear that Federal enabling legislation will generally prove to be essential, at least to the securing of any debt financing required by the proposed agency. Some agreements between States do not require congressional approval under the compact clause,[40] and a number of operating "interstate compacts" have never received congressional

---

[40] See *Virginia v. Tennessee,* 148 U.S. 503 (1893).

approval.[41] But the touchstone for determining the validity of such extra-constitutional compacts is whether the subject matter of the agreement impinges on Federal or national interests. In the interstate water management area the Federal Government has long been recognized to have a direct and continuing interest, and it is difficult to envision that Congress in the foreseeable future would be prepared to withdraw completely from the field.

The need for Federal legislative authorization for a limited function interstate water agency does not also connote a need for direct Federal participation in the corporation. The Federal interest may be adequately protected by specific mandatory or prohibitory language written into the enabling statute. Conversely, State and local governmental bodies may be extremely reluctant to establish corporations for carrying out essentially local functions, if they can do so only at the expense of Federal participation in the management of the corporation. This inhibition on local participation would appear to be particularly strong if the Federal representative would exercise voting control or have a veto over the corporation's actions.

There are a number of federally chartered corporations, including Comsat and the Railroad Passenger Corporation, which have been organized to perform vital public functions in which the United States has an interest, which are not classified as Federal agencies and in which the Federal Government does not participate in a managerial capacity and appoints only a minority of "public" members to the controlling board. There is no existing situation, however, where a federally chartered corporation, established to perform important public functions, has no Federal nominees among its directors. It seems unlikely that the Congress would be prepared to charter any corporation as a Federal agency without at least some federally appointed directors. However, it might be willing in specific cases to authorize two or more localities in separate States to organize a federally chartered corporation, which would not be a Federal agency and over which it would exercise no continuing control, to perform discrete operations of a limited nature such as regional water supply and wastewater treatment functions.

Even if Congress is not prepared now to authorize a federally chartered corporation in the water management field without at least a minority Federal presence on the board, the availability of the corporate route may still be attractive in some situations. If the Federal authorizing legislation permits the local governmental bodies to act directly, without having to await the necessary State and Federal action required to effectuate an interstate compact, the necessity of accepting minority Federal nominees on the corporation's board of directors may be considered the lesser of two evils. This would be particularly true if the option afforded localities to join in creation of such a federally chartered corporation were tied either to a Federal grant of funds for capital investment, or to some other Federal benefit.

Conclusions on Federally Chartered Regional Corporations

There are no insurmountable legal barriers to the utilization of the federally chartered corporation as an administrative device for resolving water management problems involving joint efforts by two or more States (or the local governmental subdivisions of two or more States) in which the Federal Government also has a legitimate interest; however, unless the corporation is approved by, or itself stems from, an interstate compact, it may not be able to exercise some of the governmental powers of the participating States.

The corporate device, because of its flexibility and relative isolation from political control and responsibility, lends itself best to operational tasks rather than planning or regulatory activities intended to be binding upon outside parties.

Utilization of federally chartered corporations as a substitute for Federal-interstate compacts normally will not expedite materially the formation of broad-scope waterway agencies like the Delaware River Basin Commission. However, the federally chartered corporation, as an alternative method of organizing such agencies, might prove useful in isolated situations. Consideration should be given to authorizing river basin commissions, which have been or will be established by compact, to themselves establish subsidiary corporations. These could perform the discrete operational tasks which otherwise are likely to be subordinated to the river basin commission's planning and regulatory activities, and which the commissions may not be as well equipped to perform themselves as through subsidiary corporations established for the specific tasks.

Federally chartered corporations, with or without direct membership by respresentatives of the Federal

---

[41] See, e.g., the *Southern Regional Education Compact*, upheld, *McCready v. Byrd*, 195 Md. 131, 73 A.2d 8 (1950).

Government, can play an important role in facilitating joint efforts by the local governmental units of two or more States sharing a waterway to handle such limited functions as water treatment and supply. In view of the Federal interest in such waterways and the historical precedents in the water resources field, resort to reciprocal State legislation, without any Federal legislative input, would not generally appear to be feasible. There would appear to be some real hope in this more limited area for general Federal enabling legislation.

Recommendations on Federally Chartered Regional Corporations

11-22. Legislation should be enacted granting advance consent to two or more States to enter into a compact to establish a corporation to carry out limited water resources operation and management functions, such as water supply and wastewater management. Such legislation should spell out the terms and conditions under which such corporations may be established and operated.

11-23. Legislation should be enacted to enable two or more States, or two or more local governing bodies if at least one is located in a different State, to form corporations, or become a member of an existing corporation, for the purpose of carrying out discrete water resources operation and management functions. Such corporations could be chartered under either Federal or State law, with or without Federal membership. The congressional legislation should specify the terms and conditions under which such corporations may be established ånd may operate.

11-24. Legislation should be enacted to enable future or existing interstate or Federal-interstate water compact commissions, such as the Delaware or Susquehanna River Basin Commissions, to establish corporations, chartered under either Federal or State law, for the purpose of carrying out discrete water resources operation and management functions within the delegated powers of such commissions. These subsidiary corporations should not be limited to the same member-participants as the commission's member-participants. The States involved should also pass appropriate enabling legislation.

~~~~~~~~~~~~~~~~~~~~~~~~~~~~~~~~~~~~ *Section E*

The Great Lakes

The Great Lakes are a major natural resource of North America and of inestimable value to Canada and the United States. The Lakes, their connecting waters, and the St. Lawrence River provide a waterway of almost 2,000 miles extending into the heartland of the continent from the North Atlantic Ocean. The region is rich in extensive forests and farmlands and contains vast mineral deposits. The combination of a ready transportation route, vast resources, and an abundance of high-quality water favored early settlement of the region and the development of industries and large metropolitan areas.

The Lakes and the adjacent lands serve numerous, sometimes conflicting, uses: domestic and industrial water supply, transportation, waste disposal, power generation, fisheries (commercial and sports), recrea-tion, and sites for residences, parks, and industries.[42] Yet, these uses and the development and protection of the Lakes' resources are not subject to coordinated, basinwide management.

Various agencies of two nations, eight States, one Canadian province, 191 U.S. counties, and thousands of municipalities and other governmental units are concerned with decisions and activities affecting various components of the Great Lakes system. The Commission is concerned that the existing arrangements are needlessly overlapping and uncoordinated. There is no defined hierarchy or chain of command running through these agencies, nor could there be, considering the variety of governments, functions,

---

[42] Pollution problems of the Great Lakes are discussed in Chapter 4.

433

Soo Locks Complex of the U.S. Corps of Engineers facilitates navigation on the Great Lakes

goals, and constituencies involved. However, the Commission believes that basinwide management is needed, that existing programs affecting the Great Lakes can be better integrated, that needed new measures can be undertaken, and that the present overlap among agencies can be reduced, all without sacrificing representation of the diverse interests within the basin. Fundamental improvements are needed in two fields: institutional arrangements for managing the uses and quality of the Great Lakes, and analytical tools for predicting the full range of effects of different management measures.

INSTITUTIONS[43]

Existing International Arrangements

The *International Joint Commission* (IJC) was created pursuant to the Boundary Waters Treaty in 1909. It is empowered to make binding rulings on any "applications" brought before it concerning the use, diversion, or obstruction of flow of boundary waters by one nation which might affect the level or flow of boundary waters within the other nation. It also is authorized to investigate and make advisory recommendations on any problems referred to it by either of the Federal Governments. The IJC utilizes boards of technical advisors to investigate problems addressed to it and to oversee the operation of works constructed on its approval in response to an application.

The Boundary Waters Treaty provided that the boundary waters should not be polluted to the injury of those on the other side of the boundary. In order to implement this provision, the United States and Canada executed a *Great Lakes Water Quality Agreement* in 1972, after months of negotiation. This agreement specifies certain water quality objectives, such as desirable levels of dissolved oxygen for the Lakes, and describes pollution control measures which the two governments are to undertake. The IJC, assisted by a newly formed Water Quality Control Board of Canadian, U.S., State, and Provincial environmental officials, is currently undertaking its expanded programs to implement the objectives of the Agreement. It is responsible for collecting, analyzing, and disseminating water quality data and for recommending further water quality measures to the parties to the Agreement.

The International Joint Commission has been fairly successful in the missions which it has undertaken. It has been accepted by both nations, and has conducted its business in a sensitive manner. However, provided with only a skeleton staff and a minimum budget, it has had to rely almost entirely upon service contributions of State, provincial, Federal, and national agencies in making its investigations and discharging its operating responsibilities. Moreover, because of the limited authority it has been given, the IJC has had to pursue its objectives by patient negotiation, persuasion, and the building of a consensus.

The *Great Lakes Fisheries Commission,* established by the 1955 Convention on Great Lakes Fisheries, has the responsibilities of formulating and coordinating research programs on needed measures to produce maximum sustained productivity of certain fishes and a program of sea lamprey control. Therefore, it has a limited subject matter mandate.

Existing Arrangements Within the United States

The *Great Lakes Commission* (GLC) was created pursuant to a 1955 interstate compact among the Great Lakes States; congressional consent to the compact was granted in 1968, with certain reservations. The authority conferred upon the GLC by the Great Lakes Basin Compact is perhaps the most limited in the water resources field. The purposes of the compact include the promotion of "the orderly, integrated, and comprehensive development, use, and conservation of the water resources of the Great Lakes Basin" and planning "for the welfare and development of the water resources of the Basin as a whole as well as for those portions of the Basin which may have problems of special concern." However, the authority of the GLC is limited to considering problems and making recommendations. The compacting States (the Federal Government is not a party) agreed only to consider the GLC's recommendations.[44]

The Great Lakes Commission serves valuable functions in assembling data and information, in promoting the common interests of the member States, and in seeking assistance and cooperation from the Federal Government in overcoming obstacles to the proper development and conservation of the water resources of the basin. However, it is inadequately financed and staffed and, more importantly, lacks the necessary authority to act as a management entity itself or effectively to integrate the programs of other units of government. Furthermore, its membership is

---

[43] For general background, see KELNHOFER, Guy J Jr (1972). Preserving the Great Lakes, prepared for the National Water Commission. National Technical Information Service, Springfield, Va., Accession No. PB 211 442, and CRAINE, Lyle E (February 1972). Preliminary Draft of Final Report on Institutional Arrangements for the Great Lakes, A Report to the Great Lakes Basin Commission. Mimeo, Great Lakes Basin Commission, Ann Arbor, Mich.

[44] Great Lakes Basin Compact, 1955, pp. 177-183, in U.S. CONGRESS, House (1968). Documents on the Use and Control of the Waters of Interstate and International Streams, Compacts, Treaties, and Adjudications, 90th Congress, 2d Session, House Document No. 219. U.S. Government Printing Office, Washington, D.C.

limited to the States, so that the important Federal programs and interests are not directly represented.

The *Great Lakes Basin Commission* (GLBC) is a river basin commission established in 1967 pursuant to the Water Resources Planning Act. It has a Federal chairman and a number of Federal members, including the Department of State, representing agencies concerned with the basin, in addition to the State members. Membership of the Department of State establishes a relationship between GLBC and IJC. The Great Lakes Commission is also a member of the GLBC.

The GLBC has as its principal function the preparation and maintenance of a comprehensive, coordinated joint plan for Federal, State, interstate, local, and nongovernmental development of the water and related land resources of the basin. It currently is developing a comprehensive framework study. However, its planning is handicapped by the lack of clear policy guidelines, the absence of a regional policy body to which its planning might be related, and the rule of consensus which it respects for decisions. In its coordinating role, the GLBC is dealing with entities at different levels of government, not responsible to a single source of authority. It performs information, counseling, and persuasion activities, important in their own right, but lacks management authority.

The *Upper Great Lakes Regional Commission* was established following the designation of an area within Michigan, Wisconsin, and Minnesota as an economic development region under the Public Works and Economic Development Act of 1965. This Commission has one Federal member and three State members, the State Governors or their designees. Its major function is to promote the economic development of the region. Through a planned program of public investments, the Commission seeks to stimulate private investors to establish enterprises that will provide employment opportunities for the regional labor force.

There are a number of other significant institutional arrangements, either single government or intergovernmental, which bear upon the use and protection of the Great Lakes, but space does not permit a full description.[45]

Improving Institutional Arrangements

The Commission has concluded that existing entities, for the most part, are meeting their responsibilities adequately. The missing link seems to be a mechanism for providing overall policy guidance to integrate the things being done.

This conclusion does not mean that the solution to the problems of the Great Lakes is simply to superimpose upon or to supersede the existing complex of institutions with a new super agency given extensive management powers. The Commission believes that new arrangements should be structured so as to account for the diversity of Great Lakes basin problems and the local nature of many of them. Furthermore, new arrangements should recognize the existing institutional realities within the basin. The numerous governmental entities are independent in large measure from each other; many have and probably will retain a legitimate interest in aspects of Great Lakes problems. The decision rules which govern the dealings among the various entities are at least as important as the formal structure which may be designed.

Many different approaches have been suggested for dealing with the institutional problem of the Lakes. The proposals range from (1) intensifying coordination and information-exchange efforts of existing organizations; to (2) creating a Great Lakes Policy Council to formulate regional policy, which would be implemented in part by management agencies chartered by the Council for specific situations, or a Great Lakes Adjudication Council which would be analogous to a legislative court and make policy by its decisions in particular controversies;[46] to (3) establishing five separate councils to focus attention on each of the separate lakes and coordinating the work of these councils and of other organizations whose activities have broad impact through a Great Lakes Council on Environmental Management;[47] to (4) adopting a new Federal-interstate compact to establish a strong basinwide agency with extensive

---

[45] For a more complete description, see KELNHOFER, Guy J Jr (1972). Preserving the Great Lakes, prepared for the National Water Commission. National Technical Information Service, Springfield, Va., Accession No. PB 211 442.

[46] See CRAINE, Lyle E (February 1972). Preliminary Draft of Final Report on Institutional Arrangements for the Great Lakes, A Report to the Great Lakes Basin Commission. Mimeo, Great Lakes Basin Commission, Ann Arbor, Mich. Part IV.

[47] See KELNHOFER, Guy J Jr (1972). Preserving the Great Lakes, prepared for the National Water Commission. National Technical Information Service, Springfield, Va., Accession No. PB 211 442. pp. 56-61.

management powers within the United States' portion of the Great Lakes basin.[48]

The States and the Federal Government alike have strong interests in the uses, development, and protection of the Great Lakes. The Commission believes that the Federal-interstate compact is a flexible device to accommodate these interests and to provide both policy guidance for existing programs and a structure for new management arrangements where existing ones are insufficient. Accordingly, the Commission recommends that a joint Federal-State task force undertake the negotiation of an appropriate compact. If diversity of interests among the States would impede their initiating the task force, the Federal Government should take the lead.

The compact should create a basinwide agency with power to plan for the basin and to implement the planning by integrating and directing management. Such an agency likely would replace both the GLC and the GLBC, since its broader authority would encompass the present functions of the two existing agencies.

Beyond this point, the Commission believes that it is not appropriate to suggest the content of the compact or the structure of the resulting institutions. Clearly, it will not be sufficient simply to copy a structure adopted in another basin. The resulting arrangements should be a product of negotiations among the interested parties, responsive to the needs of their constituencies, and tailored to perform functions which are now unperformed, through realistic relationships and decision rules.

Without attempting to specify the details of any institutional arrangements which the task force should produce, the Commission does recommend that they include the following matters in their deliberations:

1. The proper jurisdiction of any entity which might provide policy guidance for the basin. Specifically, to what extent should such an entity concern itself with water-related land uses?

2. The functions of such an entity, considering such matters as the establishing of basic policy, development of a framework plan, promulgation of environmental standards, monitoring, the operation of a funding pool, chartering of subarea management agencies where needed for specific problems, and serving as a voice for common Great Lakes interests.

3. The decision rules which must govern the relationships of the existing entities with each other and with any new entities.

4. The questions of representation on any such entity: the types of interests that should be represented, the number of representatives, and the methods of selection.

5. The ways in which such a policy entity might implement policy, where necessary, itself or through new management entities responsible to the policy body.[49]

More than two-fifths of the Great Lakes basin lies in Canada. It is not practical, therefore, to make plans for the Great Lakes without considering how Canadian authorities will be brought into the planning. It is not practical, either, for the United States to attempt to define for Canada the role that country should play in these planning operations. Canada and the Province of Ontario have their own views about the proper use and development of the Great Lakes and about the conduct of Canadian-United States relationships.

The United States would be well advised, therefore, to pursue its own institutional arrangements for governing the development of its portion of the Lakes, but in such a way as to encourage eventual Canadian participation, perhaps through parallel organizations for its portion of the Great Lakes. This type of evolutionary approach seems to offer a more viable way to improve international cooperation on the Great Lakes than attempting a direct appeal for the establishment of a new binational arrangement.

MANAGEMENT

In making plans and assessing management strategies for the Great Lakes, there is a need for reliable and economical ways to test the effectiveness of alternative proposals before they are adopted. A cut-and-try approach is not workable in the Great Lakes; it takes so long for the volume of water currently in storage in the larger lakes to flow through, that as much as a hundred years might pass before the full effects of particular management

[48] See, for example, the draft compact developed by the Great Lakes Commission. SUBCOMMITTEE OF THE SPECIAL COMMITTEE ON GLC ACTIVITIES (1968). Proposed Federal-State Compact, Initial Draft of the Subcommittee of the Special Committee on GLC Activities as of July 1, 1968. Great Lakes Commission, Ann Arbor, Mich.

[49] Compare, CRAINE, Lyle E (January 1972). A Summary Report on Institutional Arrangements for the Great Lakes, A Report to the Great Lakes Basin Commission. Mimeo, Great Lakes Basin Commission, Ann Arbor, Mich.

policies could be demonstrated. Here is where it would be helpful to have models that would simulate the action of the Lakes and allow the responses, beneficial and adverse, to be traced through the Lakes system. These models would help planners and managers to predict the effects of alternative regulatory actions and development plans.

Hundreds of studies—research, data gathering, monitoring, predicting—have been conducted on the Great Lakes,[50] providing data which can be used in a modeling program. Moreover, a modeling program can channel future study by identifying matters on which more information is needed.

Several existing models suggest the promise of a broader modeling program as a management tool. A simple chemical budget model has been developed to investigate the response of the Lakes to alternative chemical loadings and to estimate how the Lakes will respond to the 80 percent reduction in phosphate loading that enforcement conferences have recommended for Lake Michigan and the lower Lakes. Working with the model, it was determined that, with the exception of Lake Ontario, 80 percent treatment is not sufficient to maintain a phosphorous concentration of 0.005 mg/liter, used in the study as a reasonable level to stabilize plant production in the Great Lakes.

...treatment levels must be in excess of 90 percent. With population growth, loss from uncontrollable sources, and release from the biota and sediment, even higher levels of treatment will be required.[51]

Two operating forms of a hydrologic balance model are in current use in the Great Lakes by the Corps of Engineers to predict lake levels for 6-month periods and to test various lake regulation alternatives. Models for indicator bacterial groups are being applied in the Great Lakes by the University of Michigan Sea Grant effort.

A Great Lakes Model — Understanding How the Lakes Function

The Great Lakes Basin Commission has turned to modeling techniques in its planning. In its framework planning study, the GLBC found that it was constrained in assessing planning alternatives by an incomplete and inconsistent data base, insufficient knowledge of interactions among the biota, water, and sediment, and the multiplicity of processes that must be considered. Finding no regional planning models interrelating the physical, chemical, and biological processes in the Lakes, several GLBC member agencies joined in undertaking a Limnological Systems Analysis in 1969 to investigate the level of mathematical simulation which might be most useful in evaluating the effects on the Great Lakes of alternative management strategies. The first phase, a combined feasibility and design study, was completed recently.[52] The second phase, which would be based on the findings of the first study, is projected to include modeling, data assembly, and the development of a water resources plan.

The GLBC's contractor for the first phase concluded that a broader, interrelated modeling program is feasible and has recommended the use of Great Lakes scale models to simulate the effects of consumptive use of the Lakes' waters and of increased fertilization. The contractor also recommends a eutrophication model, models to simulate water quality effects of discharges and runoff, and a food chain model on a lakewide or regional scale.

The Commission supports further steps toward increasing our understanding of how the Lakes function, to facilitate the choice of the best management strategies. The modeling techniques being developed by the Great Lakes Basin Commission show promise, and the Commission believes that they should be pursued. The GLBC has budgeted just over $3 million for Phase Two of its Limnological Systems Analysis, over 4 years, with $2 million to be spent on the development and use of models. Although it requested Federal funds in Fiscal Years 1972 and 1973, none were forthcoming. The State members of the GLBC have contributed $80,000 for the Limnological Systems Analysis through Fiscal Year 1973.[53]

Recommendations on the Great Lakes

11-25. **The President should work with the Governors of the Great Lakes States toward the creation of a Great Lakes task force to**

[50] See GREAT LAKES BASIN COMMISSION (1972). Great Lakes Environmental Planning Study, Preliminary Plan of Study. Great Lakes Basin Commission, Ann Arbor, Mich.

[51] UPCHURCH SB & ROBB DGN (April 1972). Mathematical Models: Planning Tools for the Great Lakes. Water Resources Bulletin 8(2):338-348.

[52] HYDROSCIENCE, INC., Westwood, N.J. (1972). Summary Report; Limnological Systems Analysis for the Great Lakes, prepared for the Great Lakes Basin Commission. Great Lakes Basin Commission, Ann Arbor, Mich.

[53] GREAT LAKES BASIN COMMISSION (1972). Great Lakes Environmental Planning Study, Preliminary Plan of Study. Great Lakes Basin Commission, Ann Arbor, Mich.

negotiate and obtain consent to a Federal-interstate compact especially designed to suit the unique circumstances of the Great Lakes Basin, including provisions for eventual cooperation with Canada on problems which transcend the international boundary.

11-26. Federal funds for research should be allocated to the Great Lakes Basin Commission or its successor over a period of at least 4 years to develop improved methods for analyzing the impact on the Lakes of alternative management strategies.

Water Problems
of Metropolitan Areas[1]

Most of the water problems discussed in this report—problems like water reuse, flood control, pricing, reservoir site preservation, pollution control, recreation, planning, and interbasin transfers—are problems which occur everywhere in the country, in humid areas and in arid ones, in areas where the economy thrives and in areas of poverty and unemployment, and in urban as well as in rural settings. Many of these problems, however, have special, as well as general, application. The solution of problems of providing water services for metropolitan areas affects so many people, involves so much water, and entails such large expenditures of money that it is one such special application that deserves separate recognition and treatment.

Seventy-five percent of the Nation's population now lives in metropolitan areas comprising less than 2 percent of its area.[2] Another 13 percent lives in nearby communities. By the year 2000, it is expected that the proportion of the population in metropolitan areas will have grown to 85 percent.[3] The most rapid

growth in recent years has been in communities of 25,000 to 100,000 persons on the fringe of existing large cities. Some metropolitan areas have emerged and others have expanded through coalescence of smaller communities or settlements. While in a few instances new towns and other unit developments are being built wherein residences, commercial establishments, utilities, and public facilities are planned together,[4] in too many instances growth has meant sprawl.

The water resources available to meet future metropolitan area needs are limited. The Nation's use of water has increased by two-thirds from daily withdrawals of just over 200 billion gallons in 1950 to an estimated 339 billion gallons in 1971.[5] Increasingly, cities are obliged to go outside their immediate metropolitan areas for sources of supply, even beyond the river basins in which such cities are located.

The costs of providing metropolitan water services are escalating rapidly. The replacement cost of existing urban systems to provide water services is in the vicinity of $175 billion and it is estimated that some $15 billion per year will be spent in the next few years for new construction.[6] Combined capital and other current expenditures in 38 of the Nation's

[1] As used in this chapter, the term "metropolitan area" refers to a geographic area in which there is at least one city of 50,000 or more inhabitants. The area includes the city and all adjacent areas having a population density of 1,000 or more persons per square mile. The term "urban" is used only in a general sense to mean nonrural. The term "water services" includes water supply and distribution for domestic, commercial, and industrial use, sewage collection and disposal, and urban storm water drainage.

[2] RIVKIN/CARSON, INC. (1971). Population Growth in Communities in Relation to Water Resources Policy, prepared for the National Water Commission. National Technical Information Service, Springfield, Va., Accession No. PB 205 248. p. 1.

[3] PICKARD, Jerome P (1967). Dimensions of Metropolitanism, Research Monograph 14. Urban Land Institute, Washington, D.C.

[4] RIVKIN/CARSON, INC. (1971). Population Growth in Communities in Relation to Water Resources Policy, prepared for the National Water Commission. National Technical Information Service, Springfield, Va., Accession No. PB 205 248.

[5] U.S. BUREAU OF THE CENSUS (1972). Statistical Abstract of the United States, 1972. [73rd edition] U.S. Government Printing Office, Washington, D.C. p. 173.

[6] AMERICAN SOCIETY OF CIVIL ENGINEERS (1968). Urban Water Resources Research. National Technical Information Service, Springfield, Va., Accession No. PB 184 318. Costs have been updated to 1971 using the Engineering News Record index.

Squaw Peak Water Treatment Plant serves burgeoning growth in the Phoenix, Arizona, area

SMSA's[7] in 1969 for water supply and waste collection and disposal were estimated at $30.50 per capita and represented 20 percent of total capital outlays and 4 percent of other current expenditures, respectively.[8] Both the amounts and percentages can be expected to rise dramatically in the future to achieve higher standards of water pollution control.

Urbanization creates drastic environmental changes. Landscapes are filled. Natural surfaces are dotted over with buildings and water-absorbing land is sealed with paving that accelerates and augments runoff. Some water flows are diverted, withdrawn, used, and discharged back to their watercourses as effluents. At the same time, people concentrated in high-density complexes desire the amenities of open space and water-related recreation. Water managers are going to be called increasingly to help furnish these amenities along with the basic water services they must provide to meet the demands of urban developments.

Against this background of increased demand for urban water services, rising costs, and competing claims for conserving and protecting the urban environment, the Commission has attempted to describe the most pressing metropolitan water management problems. Three basic water utility services are provided in metropolitan areas—water supply, wastewater collection and treatment, and storm water disposal. These services can often be improved through geographic consolidations and joint administration of different functions or tasks involved in supplying them. At the same time, good utility management can help improve the quality of the urban environment.

---

[7] Standard Metropolitan Statistical Areas (SMSA). The Nation's 247 SMSA's range in size from population concentrations of only 60,000 to over 10 million. SMSA's cover central cities, inner and outer suburbs and small communities in nearby rural surroundings. The SMSA's use county lines as minimum boundaries, and thus include large nonurban areas, and should be differentiated from the term "metropolitan area" as used in this report. RIVKIN/CARSON, INC. (1971). Population Growth in Communities in Relation to Water Resources Policy, prepared for the National Water Commission. National Technical Information Service, Springfield, Va., Accession No. PB 205 248. p. 30.

[8] RIVKIN/CARSON, INC. (1971). Population Growth in Communities in Relation to Water Resources Policy, prepared for the National Water Commission. National Technical Information Service, Springfield, Va., Accession No. PB 205 248. p. 45.

WATER MANAGEMENT PROBLEMS

The primary objectives of water management for metropolitan areas must be (1) to provide the three basic water services—water supply, wastewater collection and treatment, and storm water management—efficiently and effectively, (2) to make efficient use of scarce water resources, and (3) to lessen the disruptive and degrading effect of urban growth and development on the urban environment and water quality. In pursuing these objectives, metropolitan water planners and managers encounter numerous obstacles and problems which vary widely from area to area depending on the size of the population served, the geographic area involved, the source of water supply, topography, climate, natural drainage, political boundaries, and a host of other factors. The problems of most frequent occurrence are these:

1. Inadequate or unnecessarily costly service because too many different water agencies are operating within the same metropolitan area.

2. Poor integration of water supply, wastewater treatment and drainage services with each other and with planning for the use and occupancy of land.

3. Insufficient attention to the nonutility aspects of providing metropolitan water services—including neglect of recreational, esthetic, and environmental values.

4. Inadequate data, particularly on current water management practices in metropolitan areas.

5. Inability to finance future water needs of metropolitan areas.

6. Inadequate institutions for managing metropolitan water services and for determining and representing metropolitan viewpoints in Federal, State, regional, and multistate water resource management.

7. Water pollution, a substantial portion of which comes from nonpoint-sources outside current pollution control programs, particularly in growing communities.

8. The encroachment of urbanization upon watersheds and the resulting deterioration of the quality of water supplies.

Consolidating Fragmented Water Services

Providing each of the three basic water services—water supply, wastewater treatment, and storm water drainage—within a metropolitan area involves a number of tasks. For example, providing water supply may require collection, storage, transmission, treatment, and distribution of water to users. Storm water and wastewater management involves collection and interception of sanitary wastes and storm runoff, conveyance through combined or separate sewers, treatment, and discharge. Coordination of the major supply and disposal components serving different parts of a metropolitan area system is desirable to assure proper interconnections, capacities, pressures, and grade lines to avoid overdraft on sources of supply and to avoid overload on waste treatment plants.

Within a typical large metropolitan area there may be hundreds of local jurisdictions—cities, towns, counties, and special districts—that divide responsibility for management of the basic water services of the area among them. For example, the Chicago metropolitan area, comprising six counties and approximately 2,000 local units of government, has 349 separate water supply systems and 135 separate wastewater disposal systems. The City of Chicago treats and delivers water from Lake Michigan to the city and about 70 suburbs. The Metropolitan Sanitary District of Chicago provides main interceptors and waste treatment plants for Chicago and 105 suburbs.[9] Myriad park districts, forest preserves, and similar organizations have responsibilities for water-oriented recreation and for providing and maintaining open space.

In some instances, where several agencies are authorized to provide the same service to different parts of a metropolitan area, waste and inefficiency may result. Consolidation of the performance of one or more of the separate tasks in a single water service throughout a metropolitan area, or some significant portion of it, may yield economies of scale that have not heretofore been captured by individual cities or districts pursuing separate courses.

Economies may be realized through construction of larger facilities to serve larger areas. For example, in an area where the source of supply, the location of distribution lines, and the required pressure zones of individual localities permit it, a water treatment plant to supply 100 million gallons per day (m.g.d.) might be built and operated more economically than 10 plants to treat 10 m.g.d. each. Similarly, a 10-foot diameter supply line will cost less per cubic foot per second of flow capacity than a 5-foot diameter line of the same length. There are comparable economies in waste treatment plants, as is demonstrated by the following data on treatment costs for reuse:[10]

	Total cost (amortization and O&M) in cents per 1000 gallons for given capacity of plant		
	1 m.g.d.	10 m.g.d.	100 m.g.d.
Secondary treatment	19	11	6.5
Nutrient removal (including solids)	26.8	14	8.6
Removal of nutrients plus nonbiodegradable organics	58	24	15.6

Cost estimates made for construction of one-plant and three-plant designs to serve the Joliet, Illinois, area showed that the one-plant design would cost about two-thirds as much as the three-plant design.[11] Similar estimates for the Municipality of Metropolitan Seattle showed that a two-plant design for sewage treatment and disposal would cost significantly less than alternative designs for five plants and nine plants serving the same area.[12] Economies for operation and maintenance (O&M) of treatment plants are as impressive as those for construction costs. Unlike construction costs, O&M costs continue for the life of a facility and represent a relatively high proportion of total cost. Estimated O&M costs for the Joliet one-plant design for the period 1970-2005 were less than half the estimated O&M costs for the three-plant design for the same period.[13]

There are site-specific limits to the economy and efficiency that can be achieved through areawide consolidation. Both the degree of consolidation that may be efficient and the maximum size of a consolidated system are subject to these limits. For example, analyses of sewerage facilities for Niagara County, New York,[14] indicated that a regional plan involving 10 plants would result in capital costs practically equal to those of an 18-plant scheme. Moreover, when O&M costs were included, it was

---

Report of the Special Master at 75, *Wisconsin v. Illinois,* 388 U.S. 426 (1966).

Chapter 7, Section H, Table 7-5.

[11] NORTHEASTERN ILLINOIS PLANNING COMMISSION (1970). Wastewater Report for the Outer Area. Northeastern Illinois Planning Commission, Chicago. pp. 7-16.

[12] CORNELL, HOWLAND, HAYES & MERRYFIELD/HILL (1971). Reevaluation of Metro Comprehensive Sewerage Plan. Cornell, Howland, Hayes & Merryfield/Hill, Seattle, Wash.

[13] Costs for the one-plant and three-plant designs, respectively, were $1.6 million and $3.7 million with the present worth of future O&M costs escalated at 2-1/2 percent per year.

shown that while cumulative costs over a 50-year period for an 18-plant scheme would be $358 million; the same costs for the 10-plant design would be $340 million. Most interestingly, however, the study also showed that further consolidation from 10 plants to two plants would increase capital costs from $123 million to $173 million, and cumulative 50-year annual costs would increase from $340 million to $420 million.

Detailed analyses of a number of systems in the Dallas-Ft. Worth area indicated similar results.[15] While partial consolidation in several areas that are fully urbanized revealed savings of 3 to 10 percent, consolidation in suburban areas involving considerable open space would increase costs in some locations up to 25 percent. Another study has demonstrated that there are actually diseconomies of scale in facilities to transmit wastewater if they are designed to serve more than 100,000 people in a suburban setting.[16]

In addition to the distance that sewage is transported before treatment and disposal, there are other limits on economies of scale, such as topography, variations in the degree of treatment required at different discharge points, and variations in demands for reuse of treated water at different locations. For example, cost-savings of a two-plant design for the Seattle metropolitan area compared to an alternative five-plant design were shown to be dramatically greater where advantage was taken of topography to plan only for primary treatment for one plant and secondarily treatment for the other (one discharging effluents to the lower Duwamish River and the other discharging to deep salt water in Puget Sound) as opposed to providing necessary, advanced treatment for three additional plants where some effluent would have to be discharged to smaller receiving bodies, Lake Washington and Lake Sammamish.[17]

In addition to direct savings in costs of construction, operation, and maintenance, areawide water distribution system interconnections can improve operating efficiency and reliability. In some instances, lower pressures can be maintained for emergency peak demands. Damage or malfunction in one part of a system need not curtail service if that part can obtain supplies from other, unaffected parts of the system. Where several smaller treatment plants are placed under one management duplicated overhead can be avoided and more specialized management skills may be obtained than might be available to small, independent service agencies.

Unlike main water supply facilities and wastewater treatment plants, the consolidation of distribution systems (for water) and collection systems (for wastewater disposal) may not necessarily offer economies in scale. The distribution of water and collection of sewage may be more costly where the supply and collection lines must be longer for a consolidated system than for separate systems. Although there may be few economies of scale in construction of distribution and collection facilities, there can be economies in standardization of equipment, material purchases, specialization of crews, and higher quality supervision.

The settlement and urbanization of lands along watercourse alter the natural drainage and enlarge the risk of damage from floods. Flood control and flood plain management can be more effective on an areawide basis than if done by individual urban communities. In the Root River watershed in Southeast Wisconsin, 12 communities were affected by flooding; nine of these found it advantageous to adopt zoning ordinances in conformance with a plan to prevent flood plain encroachment; and three had such ordinances under preparation.[18] They found that certain elements of a coordinated flood plain regulation plan including parkway and open space would be in jeopardy unless all communities participated.

Areawide management of some functions is also likely to result in a better use of water resources. Uncoordinated management by many cities pumping ground water in a metropolitan area, for example, can result in unplanned depletion of ground water supplies. Similarly, complete treatment of wastewater b

[14] GREELEY & HANSEN (1970). Comprehensive Sewerage Study, Niagara County, State of New York, SPC-CS-172. Chicago, Ill.

[15] CAMP, DRESSER & McKEE (1970). Upper Trinity River–Comprehensive Sewerage Plan, vol. I. Camp, Dresser & McKee, Boston, Mass.

[16] DOWNING, Paul B (1969). The Economics of Urban Sewage Disposal. Frederick A. Praeger, Publishers, New York.

[17] CORNELL, HOWLAND, HAYES & MERRYFIELD/HILL (1971). Reevaluation of Metro Comprehensive Sewerage Plan. Cornell, Howland, Hayes & Merryfield/Hill, Seattle, Wash. p. V-2.

[18] SOUTHEAST WISCONSIN REGIONAL PLANNING COMMISSION (1966). A Comprehensive Plan for the Root River Watershed, Planning Report No. 9. Southeast Wisconsin Regional Planning Commission, Waukesha, W

ne city to attain quality standards is ineffective without the cooperation of other cities that discharge effluents into the same body of water.

Some cities, particularly those already providing local services efficiently and effectively, see few gains from areawide management to offset expected losses of local control over services which they view as essentially local in character and which affect land use and subdivision development. Pyramiding of management in an areawide organization may sacrifice the presumed economies of consolidation. Moreover, some real problems have to be met when areawide management of a service is implemented. Wastewater carried to a large downstream plant for treatment may change patterns of return flows in the intervening stretch of river to the detriment of some water rights holders.[19] Interconnections provided to meet emergencies, if carried too far, could negate economies of scale by increasing pump lifts.

Some cities, especially in the West, own their own water rights. Others have contracted debt for existing water and sewer systems. These assets and liabilities cannot be redistributed throughout larger metropolitan areas in which the cities are located without substantial adjustments, sometimes requiring changes in law.

Efficiency does not necessarily call for the consolidation of all the tasks of providing even a single water service for an entire metropolitan area. For example, the Metropolitan Water District of Southern California (MWD) provides main transmission facilities for water supply to the Los Angeles metropolitan area. Local distribution of treated water is left to individual cities. Similarly, areawide organizations in Chicago, Milwaukee, and Seattle provide sewage interceptors, treatment plants, and outfalls while some local organizations provide wastewater collection within their local service areas. The benefits of consolidation may thus sometimes be achieved by an arrangement in which the main transmission and treatment of water supply and the main interception and treatment of wastewater are brought under one areawide management, while local distribution of water and collection of wastewater remain under the management of individual local entities. Charges to customer agencies by wholesale suppliers should be based on cash requirements of the supplying utility rather than depreciation schedules which could per-

mit diversion of utility revenues to subsidize the general support of the areawide agency.

Improving Relationships Among Water Services and Land Use Through Coordinated Planning and Administration

Basic water services that are provided in metropolitan areas are often related to other kinds of urban services. The management of one service can frequently be integrated with and related to the management of other services that it affects or by which it is affected. Metropolitan land use planning and water facilities planning should be coordinated but not necessarily combined in the same agency. For example, plans for providing open spaces can be harmonized with plans to reserve floodways and regulate the occupancy of flood plains. Failure to reserve land or regulate its use can result in unsuitable development with attendant risk of loss in the event of floods.[20] Waste treatment plants can be located so that treated water that is stored for later discharge can be made available for swimming, fishing, boating, and esthetic uses.[21] However, the valid concerns of water facilities planners and land use planners are not always the same and the public interest may be better served by exposing and resolving such differences at a publicly visible level rather than submerging such differences in the internal decisionmaking process of a single agency. Water facilities planners and managers are primarily concerned with meeting the demands for service, with facility cost and technology and with the rates paid by users. Land use planners are primarily concerned with guiding population and activity allocation. Internal compromises of these different concerns could be made to serve bureaucratic or special interest influences unless an opportunity is provided for the public scrutiny which such issues warrant.

In addition to consolidating all elements of a single water service such as water supply throughout all or parts of a metropolitan area, the consolidation of different water services, such as water supply, wastewater treatment, flood control, flood plain management, and water-based recreation, may be related through joint administration of some or all of the

---

See, for example, *Metropolitan Denver Sewage Disposal District v. Farmers Reservoir & Irrigation Co.*, 499 P.2d 1190 (Colo. 1972).

[20] This subject is discussed in more detail in Chapter 10, Section B, Water Resources Planning.

[21] CORNELL, HOWLAND, HAYES & MERRYFIELD/HILL (1971). Reevaluation of Metro Comprehensive Sewerage Plan. Cornell, Howland, Hayes & Merryfield/Hill, Seattle, Wash. p. x.

Denver's Washington Park requires adequate water supply for its preservation

separate tasks involved in providing those services. For example, there is an important relationship between controlling water pollution through improved sewage treatment, and providing water supplies from municipal and industrial water use. By upgrading wastewater treatment, it may be possible to provide effluents which can be reused for industrial purposes, releasing for municipal use large quantities of high-quality water currently used by industry. At the same time, the volume of effluent to be discharged may be reduced.[22]

Joint administration can be achieved in a variety of ways. A single function such as planning may be combined in one office to deal with several services such as water supply, wastewater treatment, flood control, flood plain management, and water-related recreation. Similarly, planning for other kinds of urban services, such as transportation, parks, and recreation, may be combined with the planning of the

various water services. Ideally, land use planne[r] should provide the basic population and activi[ty] distribution base to guide the work of those who pla[n] for specific utilities and other services, and wat[er] facilities should be planned so as to be able to ada[pt] to changes in land use.

The Root River Basin Plan previously referred to [in] connection with areawide management is also a[n] example of integrating the planning of several wat[er] services with planning for land use. A coordinat[ed] watershed plan was developed in which the tradeo[ff] between flood-retarding structures, flood plain regu[la]tion, channel improvement, sewer grade lines, wildli[fe] needs, open space, and parkways were considered. [As] a result, the plan developed and now being impl[e]mented was satisfactory to all interests and involve[s a] relatively minor amount of construction. The integ[ra]tion of water management with land use, unfortu[n]ately, occurs too infrequently.

Some of the different functions (e.g., plannin[g,] design, construction, operation, and maintenanc[e]) involved in providing two or more services can b[e]

---

[22] See Chapter 7, Section H, Reuse of Municipal and Industrial Wastewater, for more detailed discussion of this subject.

ombined and administered jointly within one organization, as is sometimes done in water and sanitation
districts. In many instances, the management of
different services can be improved simply through
effective coordination of their operations without
resorting to joint administration of design, construction, and operation in one office. Good results are
most likely, however, where the different agencies are
guided by overall plans that include their separate,
but related, services.

Gains in efficiency to be had through joint
administration of different services were estimated in
the recent study summarized in Table 12-1; however,
the more important advantage is the better use of
resources that may be made possible.

In spite of growing advocacy,[2][3] the concept of
jointly administering different services is yet to be
fully implemented even though there has been significant progress on partial integration. A 1969 survey
indicates that 58 percent of the Nation's cities of over
50,000 population have combined water supply and
wastewater services under one administrative head,
but only about half of these included waste treatment
or water treatment (in other words, about half
confined joint administration only to the sanitary
collection system and the water distribution system)[24] and only one-fourth of them include the third
primary service, storm sewer systems. Few of the
joint administrations manage all water and water-
related services on an integrated basis for an entire
metropolitan area, although Philadelphia is an
example of a city that has combined water supply,
wastewater services, and storm sewer systems in one
department and supports them through service
charges.

The conditions that are found from metropolitan
area to metropolitan area are so different and the
potential number of formulas for combining the
performance of different tasks are so numerous that
the best arrangement for any particular metropolitan
area depends on the specific circumstances that exist
there. In many instances, combining the work forces
for administration, engineering, accounting, billing,
and O&M for water services can help improve

McPHERSON MB (1970). Prospects for Metropolitan
Water Management. American Society of Civil Engineers,
Urban Water Resources Council, U.S. Office of Water
Resources Research, New York. pp. 9-28.

AMERICAN WATER WORKS ASSOCIATION, Commit-
tee for Water and Wastewater Operations (April 4, 1971).
Joint administration water/wastewater works. Journal
American Water Works Association 63(4):199-202.

TABLE 12-1.—Estimated savings resulting from joint
administration of water supply and
waste disposal

	Percent of Total Separate Costs	
	Savings indicated by up to 69 percent of respondents	Savings indicated by 70 to 99 percent of respondents
Administration	36	7
Engineering and design	11	—
Construction	7	—
Operation and maintenance	13	—
Financial and collection	31	8
Overall savings	23	1

Source: AMERICAN WATER WORKS ASSOCIATION,
Committee for Water and Wastewater Operations
(April 4, 1971). Joint administration water/
wastewater works. Journal American Water Works
Association 63(4):199-202.

inadequately planned and fragmented water supply,
wastewater treatment, and drainage in metropolitan
areas. At the same time management of those services
should be related to planning for the use of land.
Gains in efficiency and economy like those demonstrated for areawide consolidation of a single water
service may be available if planning or administration
of different services are joined and extended over all
or parts of an entire metropolitan area.

Using Water Facilities to Improve the Quality of the Urban Environment

Urban development is often disruptive of the
natural environment. Urban water managers need to
explore ways in which water facilities can be used to
improve the quality of the urban environment. New
urban planning and design technologies may enable
them to utilize water as a means of better integrating
recreation areas and facilities into the total urban
environment. For example, natural watercourses can
be preserved as parks. In San Antonio, Texas, a
beautification plan for the San Antonio River front

improved an area that had become blighted.[25] The preservation of reservoir sites for storing water supply or storm flows may provide opportunities for their use as focal points in the design of new communities, parks, and recreation areas.

With the help of landscape architects, architects, recreation specialists, and urban planners, water facilities such as storage towers, treatment plants, and storm drainage channels can be made more esthetically pleasing. The design and location of water facilities can sometimes be made a part of plans for providing open space and recreation facilities, so long as skill and care are exercised to prevent unacceptable compromise of the quality of water supplies.

Basic Data and Research Needs[26]

Day-to-day operations of metropolitan water systems are likely to become increasingly complicated. The needs for data to operate them are greater than, for example, the general need for information in river basins which include large areas of less intensively developed land. Large metropolitan water systems require data of many kinds to allow water managers to make timely and efficient operating decisions throughout the system. Most metropolitan area water agencies are well aware of this need and some are moving to improve their information systems. In general, however, there has been a serious lack of analysis of existing data in developing techniques required for modern, urban water operating procedures.[27]

Data are still needed on some of the physical aspects of metropolitan water management including the quantity and quality of main storm and combined sewer flows and overflows. There is also a need for certain types of demographic and economic data such as population concentrations and property values that often are not readily available. Data are particularly limited for small systems, for factors influencing water utilization, and for factors affecting the condition of distribution systems.

Financing the Future Water Needs of Metropolitan Areas

The problem of financing future water facilities and services in the Nation's metropolitan areas involves determining how much it will cost to construct and operate the water facilities that will be required, and who is to pay the cost with what funds. These two questions are discussed in sections of the report dealing with capital demands for future water facilities[28] and with principles of cost-sharing.[29] The Commission has recommended that ultimately water services should be supported from their own revenues. If this recommendation is implemented, metropolitan areas themselves will face the necessity of covering most of the costs of providing the facilities needed by a growing number of metropolitan area residents. Local revenues raised within the metropolitan areas—taxes and user charges—will continue to be the major source of funds.

Metropolitan tax revenues increased from $130 to $229 per capita from 1962 to 1969.[30] Property taxes continued to make up the bulk of this revenue, although their proportion of the total has been decreasing.

Metropolitan areas have experienced a multitude of tax financing problems during the past 2 decades. The major problems include: (1) declining relative economic value of the central city as centers of production, trade, or consumption, (2) high income/low service population leaving the central city and low income/high service population moving to the city, (3) fixed boundaries of the central city preventing inclusion of suburban areas in the tax base, (4) increased Federal and State taxes causing city taxpayers to resist local tax increases, (5) mandated formulas by State and Federal governments committing large expenditures of local revenue, and (6) reliance on the property tax as the major source of revenue creating an inflexible revenue base. The problems of inflexible tax base and increased demands for services are critical and complicated. The administrative and political processes at the State level for evaluating new tax legislation, or often even for raising tax rates, are likely to require time.

When metropolitan services are financed through user charges government officials levy charges on the users of particular government goods and services as

[25] SAN ANTONIO RIVER AUTHORITY (1968). San Antonio River Study. San Antonio River Authority, San Antonio, Tex.

[26] The subject of basic data is more fully discussed in Chapter 17.

[27] ACKERMANN WC (1966). Research problems in hydrology and engineering, pp. 495-502 in KNEESE, Allen V & SMITH, Stephen C [editors], Water Research. The Johns Hopkins Press, Baltimore, Md.

[28] See Chapter 16.

[29] See Chapter 15.

[30] Derived from U.S. BUREAU OF THE CENSUS.

uch levels that the revenues from these charges equal he cost of supplying the goods and services. User harges not only ration government services and llocate the cost burden to the beneficiaries, but also rovide important information about the demand for articular services.

User charges for water and sewer service nearly oubled from $33 per capita in 1962 to $65 in 1969. evenue from these fees remained a constant 15 ercent of total urban revenues.

From 1962 to 1969, intergovernmental revenues to etropolitan areas more than doubled from $60 to 154 per capita. Intergovernmental revenues, most of hich came from State governments (less than 5 ercent came from the Federal Government) ncreased from 27 percent to 34 percent of total evenues for this 7-year period.[31] The pressure to crease intergovernmental revenues to metropolitan eas is intense. Cities face rising welfare costs, creased costs associated with crime and crime revention, rising costs of providing new and techni- lly more complicated facilities and equipment to eet rising standards of environmental protection, d a host of other demands on their fiscal capacities.

Total debt outstanding for all city governments ot SMSA's) has almost tripled from about $16 llion in 1955 to $43.8 billion in 1970.[32] During the me time, tax revenues have increased from just over 5.1 billion to $13.6 billion and the ratio of debt/tax venues has increased from 3.1 to 3.2. Over this riod, the ratio of long-term, full faith, and credit bt to tax revenue dropped from 2.1 to 1.6, while e ratio for nonguaranteed, revenue bond debt creased from .9 to 1.2. These debt/tax revenue tios reflect both an increased reliance on non- aranteed debt and a relatively stable capacity for w debt.

However, over the same period—from 1955 to 70—the ratio of debt to total revenues actually clined. While debt outstanding was increasing from 6 billion to $43.8 billion, total revenues, including tergovernmental revenues and user charges, were creasing from $10.2 billion to $32.7 billion, and the tio of debt to total revenues declined from 1.6 to 3. These ratios reflect the changes in makeup of tal revenues as a result of the increase of inter- vernmental revenues to cities. From 1955 to 1970, x revenues have declined from 50 percent of all city venues to 42 percent.

Thus, although there has been much speculation about the debt capacity of metropolitan areas to bear the capital costs of water facilities, there appears to be no indication of an immediate crisis as far as the relationship of debt to total revenues is concerned. Based on general financial trends established during the 1960's, metropolitan areas appear to be able to continue to make substantial contributions to capital costs and current expenditures for future water supply and sewage facilities, assuming that intergovernmental revenues, both from the States and Federal Government, to metropolitan areas are effectively spent where necessary to assist cities to catch up with federally imposed water quality requirements.

INSTITUTIONAL ARRANGEMENTS

The National Water Commission cannot invent or prescribe precise institutional arrangements for planning and managing water resources that would be appropriate for every one of the Nation's metropolitan areas. Metropolitan areas are too diverse in size, topography, climate, hydrology, political setting, and social characteristics to be analyzed and treated in a manner leading to prescription of uniform institutional arrangements. Arrangements prescribed for the Philadelphia-New Jersey-New York complex would necessarily differ from arrangements designed for Phoenix or for Portland-Vancouver. Each metropolitan area must fashion particular organizational arrangements suited to its own situation.

Governmental and private efforts to provide water supply in the United States generally have had an enviable record of delivery of safe water supplies for municipal use.[33] Treatment and disposal of wastewater has been done with less success. Water supply, wastewater treatment, and storm water removal today are still acute problems in some metropolitan areas. In some cases, existing local government institutional arrangements to provide these services are not working as well as they might, and State and Federal programs designed to give impetus and effect to these local efforts are not succeeding. There are few metropolitan areas showing fully satisfactory resolutions of water supply and wastewater treatment problems, although some, such as Seattle, Washington, and San Diego, California, have made impressive

---

bid.

See Table 12-2.

[33] Municipal and industrial water supply problems are discussed at greater length in Chapter 5, Section E.

Item	1955	1960	1965	1970
Total Revenue (millions)	$10,227	$14,915	$20,318	$32,704
Tax Revenue only (millions)	5,100	7,109	9,289	13,647
Percent of Total	50%	48%	46%	42%
Debt Outstanding (millions)	$15,973	$23,178	$31,862	$43,773
Long Term	15,302	21,904	29,280	38,870
Full Faith & Credit	10,864	14,473	18,477	22,005
Nonguaranteed	4,438	7,430	10,803	16,863
Short Term	671	1,274	2,582	4,903
Ratios of Debt/Total Revenue				
Debt Outstanding	1.6	1.6	1.6	1.3
Long Term	1.5	1.5	1.4	1.2
Full Faith & Credit	1.1	1.0	.9	.7
Nonguaranteed	.4	.5	.5	.5
Short Term	.1	.1	.1	.1
Ratio of Debt/Tax Revenue				
Debt Outstanding	3.1	3.3	3.5	3.2
Long Term	3.0	3.1	3.2	2.8
Full Faith & Credit	2.1	2.0	2.0	1.6
Nonguaranteed	.9	1.1	1.1	1.2
Short Term	.1	.2	.3	.4

Source: U.S. BUREAU OF THE CENSUS (1972). Statistical Abstract of the United States, 1972. [93rd edition]. U.S. Government Printing Office, Washington, D.C. p. 426.

gains through the use of metropolitan, areawide, and regional waste treatment systems.[34]

To the extent that revised institutional arrangements can contribute to the resolution of metropolitan water problems, the formation of new general-purpose metropolitan area governments would appear to be the most direct approach. It is, howev[er] one which though widely discussed has gained lit[tle] popular and political support. It does not, therefo[re] appear to be a realistic alternative for many met[ro]politan areas in the foreseeable future.

One can argue for the creation of a metropoli[tan] agency with a wide variety of related water mana[ge]ment functions which, over time, could become [the] precursor of a full-blown general-purpose met[ro]politan government. It is not the mission of t[he] Commission to develop the virtues of such [an] approach, but it is noted that when the purposes [of] special districts are too limited, their proliferati[on] may produce functional fragmentation that is [as] undesirable as the geographic fragmentation that [we]

[34]URBAN SYSTEMS RESEARCH & ENGINEERING, INC. (1971). Metropolitan Water Management, Case Studies and National Policy Implications, prepared for the National Water Commission. National Technical Information Service, Springfield, Va., Accession No. PB 199 493, and U.S. COUNCIL ON ENVIRONMENTAL QUALITY (1972). Environmental Quality, Third Annual Report of the Council on Environmental Quality. U.S. Government Printing Office, Washington, D.C. p. 204.

ntended to be corrected.[35] On the other hand, metropolitan water resource agencies which are too multipurpose in scope bring forth the opposition of stablished political interests to general-purpose reawide metropolitan government, and, depending on the form of their governing body, may bring the riticism of those who counsel in general terms gainst insulation of basic governmental services from olitical processes.

In some metropolitan areas the institutional answer nay be the formation of metropolitan area authorities to handle water supply, wastewater treatment, nd drainage. Such entities would be compatible with he familiar concept of a two-level approach to urban overnment, whereby areas may deal with some ervices on an areawide basis while leaving others to dministration at local and city levels.

The Advisory Commission on Intergovernmental elations and other organizations have recommended range of State and local governmental reforms to nable the metropolitan processes and institutions to vork more efficiently.[36] These recommendations nclude the preparation of State water resources plans hat account for metropolitan area needs; the use of xtraterritorial powers by cities to prevent the proferation of inefficient, unplanned, and nonintegrable vater systems serving developments just outside

municipal boundaries; the creation of areawide and multipurpose authorities to avoid the development of overlapping single-purpose authorities; authorizing interlocal contracting and joint exercise of local government powers; and providing State financial assistance to facilitate the planning and construction of areawide metropolitan capital improvements.[37] In many cases, existing institutional arrangements, strengthened by the adoption of these proposals, would be the best vehicles for solving metropolitan water problems.

Metropolitan agencies which have a statutory base, are created by election, and are governed by a reasonably representative council of local government officials can effectively contribute to the resolution of real metropolitan problems, including problems of water supply and wastewater treatment and may become effective metropolitan governments.

In contrast, the informally organized Councils of Government (COG), usually voluntary associations of cities and counties, act best as a planning agency and a forum for discussion. The earliest of these COG's dates back over 15 years, but it is only in the last 5 years that their numbers have increased significantly. There are more than 220 COG's now in operation and few were created by public election.

Although COG council members usually are individuals vested with political power and can exercise influence to implement COG-developed plans in their own jurisdictions, the informally organized, voluntary COG's themselves have a limited political basis on which to exercise their power to act as clearinghouses for Federal grant applications. Moreover, should Federal grants become a major source of local funds in the future, it would be inappropriate for voluntary COG's to become back-door governments by acting as a clearinghouse or screening agent for grants which are essential to the functioning of local government. Intervention by a multitude of Federal and State agencies administering grant programs for metropolitan water facilities can be an invitation to chaos. However, necessary procedures like those under OMB Circular A-95[38] for screening

[35] U.S. ADVISORY COMMISSION ON INTERGOVERN-MENTAL RELATIONS (1964). The Problems of Special Districts in American Governments, A-22. U.S. Government Printing Office, Washington, D.C. pp. 74-75. And HAGMAN D (1970). Regionalized-decentralism: A model for rapprochement in Los Angeles. Georgetown Law Journal 58:901-915.

[36] U.S. ADVISORY COMMISSION ON INTERGOVERN-MENTAL RELATIONS (1961). Organization and Planning in Metropolitan Areas, A-5. U.S. Government Printing Office, Washington, D.C. pp. 18-42. COMMITTEE FOR ECONOMIC DEVELOPMENT, Research and Policy Committee (1970). Reshaping Government in Metropolitan Areas. Committee for Economic Development, New York. COMMITTEE FOR ECONOMIC DEVELOPMENT (1966). Modernizing Local Government. Committee for Economic Development, New York. pp. 18-19. COMMITTEE FOR ECONOMIC DEVELOPMENT (1967). Modernizing State Government. Committee for Economic Development, New York. pp. 19-22. COUNCIL OF STATE GOVERNMENTS (1965, 1966). Suggested State Legislation, vol. 24, 25. Council of State Governments, Lexington, Ky. AMERICAN BAR ASSOCIATION (1967). Section of Local Government Law, Publications No. 5, 6, vol. 17. American Bar Association, New York. NATIONAL LEAGUE OF CITIES (1970). National Municipal Policy, Adopted at the 46th Annual Congress of Cities, December 1-4, 1969, San Diego. National League of Cities, Washington, D.C.

[37] U.S. ADVISORY COMMISSION ON INTERGOVERN-MENTAL RELATIONS (1969). 1970 Cumulative State Legislative Program, M-48. U.S. Government Printing Office, Washington, D.C. Sections 87-20-00; 31-31-00; 31-63-00; 31-69-00; 31-91-00; 31-91-30; 33-21-00.

[38] U.S. OFFICE OF MANAGEMENT AND BUDGET (1971). Evaluation, Review and Coordination of Federal Assistance Programs and Projects, Circular No. A-95, Revised July 26, 1971. Office of Management and Budget, Washington.

and reviewing local applications for Federal assistance should not be permitted to rest on discretionary decisions made by organizations that are not themselves duly constituted and locally politically accountable. This may occur where, as in the program of the Farmers Home Administration for grants for water and waste disposal systems, the approval of a "multijurisdictional substate areawide general purpose planning and development agency that has been officially designated as a clearinghouse agency" under OMB Circular A-95 is required for any grant to be made.[39] In other circumstances, Federal legislation has, in the Commission's view, unwisely dictated the creation of appointed local or regional agencies or planning groups having not only great discretionary authority over grant applications but also certain federally prescribed regulatory authority and powers that ordinarily are vested in formally constituted and elected units of local government, not in ad hoc collections of various elected officials.

For example, the 1972 Amendments to the Federal Water Pollution Control Act provide for a new "Areawide Waste Treatment Program."[40] That program calls for the Administrator of the Environmental Protection Agency to publish guidelines for the identification of certain areas which, as a result of urban-industrial concentrations or other factors, have substantial water quality control problems. After publication of the guidelines, the Governor of each State is called on to identify each area within his State which has such problems. The Governors, within an allotted time, are to designate for each area a "single representative organization, including elected officials from local governments or their designees, capable of developing effective areawide waste treatment management plans for such area."[41] If the Governors do not act within the given time, the "chief elected officials of local governments" within an area may by agreement designate the boundaries of the area and the "single representative organization."[42] Notwithstanding isolated declarations of intent that the development of management plans is to be based on technical, social, economic, and environmental considerations rather than political considerations,[43] the 1972 Amendments may imprudently place broad powers in organizations that are not required to be created by or accountable to either the States or any particular local electorate. For example, where the problem area covers parts of two or more States, the organization may be made up of elected officials of local governments from both States, or their designees, subject only to approval of the Administrator of EPA, who also has a veto power over designations by the Governors.[44]

The designated organization is to be capable of developing effective areawide waste treatment management plans. Within a year of its designation, the planning organization is to have a planning process in operation. Plans developed are to include alternatives for waste treatment management and are to be applicable to all wastes generated within the area. Plans are also to include, among other things, (1) the identification of treatment works necessary to meet anticipated municipal and industrial waste treatment needs of the area over a 20-year period; (2) the establishment of construction priorities and time schedules for such treatment works; and (3) the establishment of a regulatory program to implement the waste treatment management requirements of section 201(c) of the Act, to regulate the location, modification, and construction of any new facilities within the area that may result in any discharge in the area, and to assure that any industrial or commercial wastes discharged into any treatment works in the area meet applicable pretreatment requirements. The plan is also to include the identification of the agencies necessary to construct, operate, and maintain all facilities required by the plan, the identification of measures necessary to carry out the plan (including financing), the time and costs of doing so, the economic, social, and environmental impacts of carrying out the plan, and the processes to identify and control various sources of pollution within the area.

Plans are to be certified by the Governor to the Administrator for the latter's approval. All publicly owned treatment works in the area financed in part by grants under the Act must be in conformity with the plan.

[39] *Rural Development Act of 1972*, P.L. 92-419, Section 106, August 30, 1972, 86 Stat. 657, 658, 7 USCA 1926(a)(3).

[40] *Federal Water Pollution Control Act Amendments of 1972*, P.L. 92-500, Section 208, October 18, 1972, 86 Stat. 816, 839, 33 USCA 1288.

[41] *Ibid.*, Section 208(a)(2)(B), 86 Stat. 840, 33 USCA 1288(a)(2)(B).

[42] *Ibid.*, Section 208(a)(4)(A) and (B), 33 USCA 1288(a)(4)(A) and (B).

[43] ROE, Robert A (1972). Remarks of Representative Roe, Congressional Record 118 (158):H9132, October 4, 1972.

[44] P.L. 92-500, October 18, 1972, Section 208(a)(7), 86 Stat. 816, 840, 33 USCA 1288(a)(7).

In addition to planning agencies, the Governors are to designate one or more waste treatment management agencies for each problem area. Such management agencies may be existing or newly created local, regional, or State agencies or political subdivisions. They are to be the exclusive recipients of grants for publicly owned treatment works. Management agencies designated by the Governors must be found by the Administrator to have authority to carry out appropriate portions of the areawide waste treatment plan; to manage waste treatment works and related facilities; to design and construct new works; to operate and maintain new and existing works; to accept grants; to raise revenues, including waste treatment charges; to incur short- and long-term indebtedness; and to enforce community cost-sharing by participating communities.

FEDERAL-STATE-LOCAL COOPERATION

The State and local reforms already mentioned deal with water problems internal to the metropolitan area—those concerned with intercity and intracity coordination and with areawide consolidation of certain water services. Solution of these internal problems will require State and local action, perhaps with help from the Federal Government. Along with these internal problems is another class of external problems—those which require actions that are beyond the capabilities of State and local governments acting alone and which require Federal action, as well.

The need to secure additional water supply sources is an example of the type of external problem which many metropolitan areas are often, poorly equipped to solve on their own. Finding new sources of water supply for growing populations and industries in metropolitan areas, combined with the problems that arise from discharging increasing quantities of metropolitan wastewater into regional supply sources, are twin concerns that are placing unusual demands upon the institutional capabilities of both States and metropolitan areas. A Corps of Engineers official, discussing the situation in the Northeastern United States, made the following statements:

Current projections of well-established trends all point to a water-supply crisis of major proportions in the foreseeable future . . .

As the population increases and urban centers merge into supercities, the burden on existing water-supply systems will become intolerable. Localized response to the growing needs of independent municipalities will lead to ever-greater competition for the same relatively limited water sources and storage sites . . . Already competition for regional sources (and its attendant litigation) is growing rapidly . . . more and more, the problems of water supply are extending beyond local areas—often beyond states.[45]

Metropolitan areas in many parts of the country are finding it necessary to look well beyond their own jurisdictions to obtain the additional supplies they must have if they are to meet future demands. When those supply sources lie in another State, or when the metropolitan community is a multistate urban area, the kind of political and administrative problems involved in securing an equitable share of the regional water resources may be more than the State and local governments can cope with.

Examples of the extent and seriousness of this problem are not hard to find. Chicago was able to divert water for its use from Lake Michigan only after a lengthy court battle with other Great Lakes States. Growing requirements for water in the Chicago area may move that city within the near future to seek an additional diversion of water from the Lake. The Minneapolis-St. Paul metropolitan area is another example of a community that is looking for an additional supply source as its population and industry expand. It seeks ways to augment the low flow of the Mississippi River from which a large part of its water is being drawn. Two potential sources have been mentioned: the St. Croix River, which divides Minnesota from Wisconsin; and Lake Superior. It has been observed that such

—interbasin transfers are becoming an ever-more-prominent feature of metropolitan water systems. The Boston metropolitan region imports the bulk of its water from the Quabbin Reservoir, which is actually in the Connecticut River drainage basin. Plans to ease pollution in Lake Michigan from the Milwaukee region involve transfers of lake waters, in the form of sewer effluent, into rivers which ultimately empty into the Gulf of Mexico. Denver operates a diversion system across the Continental Divide from the headwaters of the Colorado River. The major water supply question in Lubbock, Texas,

---

[45] GROVES RH (May 1971). Northeastern US water supply study. Journal American Water Works Association 63(5):311-312.

is the possibility of long-distance water importation to satisfy future requirements. Houston, too, must consider this source before long.[46]

Congress has agreed that the major metropolitan areas of the country are indeed handicapped in their ability to solve unaided their large and complicated water supply problems. It stated its sense of the urgency of this problem in Title I of Public Law 89-298 when it said:

Congress hereby recognizes that assuring adequate supplies of water for the great metropolitan centers of the United States has become a problem of such magnitude that the welfare and prosperity of this country require the federal government to assist in the solution of water supply problems.[47]

In 1965, under the provision of that Act, it authorized the Corps of Engineers to undertake the Northeastern United States Water Supply Study (NEWS). Congress enacted the legislation in response to the drought of 1961-67 which reduced historic yields in the Northeast by 25 to 30 percent. The NEWS study encompassed a 200,000 square-mile area that included all or parts of 13 States and the District of Columbia. Five metropolitan regions were identified by the Corps as the Northeast's most critical supply areas: The Boston, Massachusetts, and Providence, Rhode Island, metropolitan areas; the Northern New Jersey-New York City-Western Connecticut metropolitan area; the York-Harrisburg-Lancaster area of Pennsylvania; metropolitan Baltimore; and the Washington, D.C., metropolitan area.[48] Sources of regional water supply under consideration for development in that study include such outlying bodies as the St. Lawrence River and Lake Ontario. Low-flow augmentation was one of the alternatives contemplated for the Hudson River basin, through such means as:

Diversion from the St. Lawrence River through Lake Champlain . . .

Diversion from Lake Francis in Canada through Lake Champlain.[49]

The solutions which are being studied would require the creation of new kinds of regional or interstate water institutions to plan, develop, and allocate water for groups of metropolitan areas throughout the northeastern United States. A Corps spokesman expressed the belief that:

Regionalization of water supply systems appears inevitable, and the process will be accelerated by the need to resolve environmental as well as economic problems—problems that are dealt with most effectively at the regional level.

Only supply systems of regional, state, or even interstate magnitude are likely to develop the quantities of water needed to meet estimated future demands.[50]

These types of regional organizations, with the capacity and the authority needed to make firm allocations of a regional water supply, do not yet exist. Without them, an increasing number of disputes can be expected among and between States and metropolitan areas as they begin to compete ever more actively for the water resources they must have to sustain their economies. It is totally inadequate to leave the resolution of such disputes among States to original actions in the U.S. Supreme Court. On the other hand, it is inappropriate and unnecessary for the Federal Government to intervene in the problems of water supply on the scale that has already occurred with respect to water quality and water pollution control.

Traditional interstate compact agreements have not to date proven sufficiently flexible or capable of being implemented quickly enough to solve metropolitan water problems, although deficiencies in the present use of compacts appear to be curable particularly through the device of advance congressional consent to compacts.[51] Interstate compact commissions, perhaps with the advice and assistance of Federal-State river basin planning agencies, may prove able not only to make allocations among areas but perhaps also among major uses within regions navigation, irrigation, power, municipal supply, recre-

---

[46] URBAN SYSTEMS RESEARCH & ENGINEERING, INC. (June 1971). Metropolitan Water Management, Case Studies and National Policy Implications, prepared for the National Water Commission. National Technical Information Service, Springfield, Va., Accession No. PB 199 493. pp. 69-70.

[47] P.L. 89-298, October 27, 1965, 79 Stat. 1073, 42 USCA 1962d-4(a).

[48] SCHWARTZ, Harry E (May 1971). Scope of the NEWS Study. Journal American Water Works Association 63(5):313.

[49] MONTANARI FW & KARATH EA (May 1971). N.Y. City Water Supply and Environmental Management. Journal American Water Works Association 63(5):319.

[50] GROVES RH (May 1971). Northeastern US water supply study. Journal American Water Works Association 63(5):311-312.

[51] See Chapter 11, Section C.

tion, and fish and wildlife propagation. Of course, these allocations would have to be conditioned by such related considerations as the amount of regional supplies already appropriated or allocated and not subject to reallocation from established uses, the effect of allocations on downstream users, and the effect of allocations on national objectives in power production, population distribution, food and fiber production, transportation, recreation, and so on.[52]

This regional allocation process, however it may be structured, will require metropolitan areas to play a more active role in basin affairs. The practice of having Federal-State bodies do the planning for river basins will not satisfy metropolitan interests when basin organizations are given the power to make determinations about water supply allocations. Many metropolitan areas extend into more than one State's jurisdiction. The State government and the metropolitan area are sometimes political and economic rivals. Faced with choices, State representatives to the basin planning bodies will tend to give priority to statewide interests. It will, therefore, not always be adequate to rely upon the State representative to define and defend the interests of the metropolitan area where competitive choices are being made on a regional level. Whatever body may be empowered to make allocations of a regional water supply, it is important that metropolitan areas be given a more direct voice than they have at present in the regional water planning processes.

CONCLUSIONS

In recent years, a number of different studies have resulted in recommendations that certain local government functions throughout entire metropolitan areas be consolidated. In many situations such an approach for selected functions of some water services will improve the physical and economic operation of metropolitan water systems.

While areawide consolidations may not everywhere necessary or desirable, in many instances they can result in economies of scale, improvements in efficiency and reliability, better coordination, and better overall use of the water resource. Where they are implemented, the anticipated loss of local control and legal and technological problems can usually be mitigated and offset by the advantages to be gained. There are, however, limits to what can be achieved through areawide consolidation. Efficiency gains are more dramatic in areas of high population density than in sparsely populated suburbs. Economies in construction of consolidated water supply, wastewater treatment plants, and drainage facilities do not necessarily extend to local water distribution and wastewater collection facilities, although in larger systems consolidation of distribution and collection also can yield economies in central purchasing, better equipment, specialization of crews, and higher-quality supervision.

Relationships among water services and between water services and other urban services need to be recognized. Placing the planning for different functions of basic water services under joint administration and coordinating the performances of other functions such as design, construction, operations, and maintenance can result in savings in the cost of providing services and enable the better use of metropolitan water resources. Land use planning and utility planning need to be coordinated. Planning for water should complement existing plans for the use of land. Water utility planners should design water systems which are complementary to land use goals but should anticipate and be prepared to accommodate to changes in land use plans that may come about in the future.

More attention by water planners and managers to esthetic, recreational, and environmental values can, within limitations imposed by other aspects of their duties such as maintaining the quality of water supplies, enable management of water utilities to help improve the urban environment.

Existing local governmental institutions which traditionally have delivered water supplies and handled wastewaters are in some cases being strained and are unable to meet the water supply and treatment demands being made of them. These existing institutions can and should be strengthened through State and local government reforms whereby (1) long-term State and river basin planning is made to account for metropolitan needs, (2) municipalities can exercise extraterritorial powers to prevent inefficient, unplanned water services from developing in their metropolitan areas, (3) areawide water management authorities are authorized and implemented, (4) interlocal contracting and the joint exercise of local government powers is encouraged, and (5) cities are not permitted to make excessive charges to water users served outside their corporate boundaries.

The Federal Government must assist the States and local governments in solving metropolitan problems of an external nature arising from the facts that

---

Chapter 7, Section F, discusses allocation of water in humid regions by a permit system.

(1) many metropolitan areas extend over two or more State boundaries, (2) many metropolitan areas must look beyond their jurisdictions to obtain supplies, and (3) their effluent discharges affect areas beyond their jursidictions. To date, interstate compact commissions have not been effective devices to solve such problems, but with improvements, they may prove able to make appropriate allocations of supplies and regulation of discharges for metropolitan areas. Metropolitan areas must be given a more direct voice than they have at present in the regional planning process.

Data on some aspects of urban hydrology are inadequate to meet the future needs of metropolitan area water management. Moreover, techniques for joint administration of some metropolitan water services on an areawide basis will create even greater demands for data and for analysis of the data that are available to enable water managers to make timely operating decisions throughout the system.

RECOMMENDATIONS

12-1. Municipalities, county governments, special districts, and other local government units should continue to explore the potential for consolidating separate tasks in providing water services to achieve economies of scale throughout all or significant portions of their metropolitan areas.

12-2. Municipalities, county governments, special districts, and other local government units responsible for providing basic water services in a metropolitan area should improve the efficiency and effectiveness of those services by coordinating the planning for water services with the planning for land use and occupancy. Consideration should also be given to combining other functions, such as engineering and design, construction, operation and maintenance, finance and collections, for different water services. Extension of such combined services should also be made to all or to significant portions of a metropolitan area where gains in efficiency and better use of resources can reasonably be expected to result.

12-3. In addition to reliance on hydrologists and engineers, water planners and managers should enlist the aid of landscape architects, architects, recreation specialists, and urban planners to help them make full use of whatever opportunities there may be to provide water services in ways that will also provide recreational and esthetic benefits to metropolitan area residents.

12-4. The following State and local government actions should be taken to improve metropolitan area water management.

a. States, with the cooperation of metropolitan areas, should prepare State water resources plans that account for metropolitan area needs and that require the head of the appropriate planning agency of the State government to encourage, assist, and advise metropolitan and local government agencies responsible for planning metropolitan area water program particularly with respect to preparation and updating of regional metropolitan water resources plans.

b. States should enact legislation authorizing new metropolitan management authorities, which may be created from and made up of existing local entities, to provide and coordinate specified public water services for particular areas including the main water supply, wastewater treatment, and storm drainage functions Accompanying the legislation authorize new management authorities should be additional legislation to establish procedures to insure that the activities of special authorities are coordinate with those of other government units and that the public is fully aware of the activities of special authorities operating within metropolitan areas.

c. States should permit local government units to cooperate with other localities providing services and facilities in accordance with geographic, economic, population, and other factors that influence the mutual needs and developments authorizing interlocal agreements and contracts for the joint use and exercise their powers, privileges, or authority.

d. States that have not done so should consider legislation to authorize cities exercise jurisdiction for planning and implementing water resources management, including zoning and subdivision regulation, in areas adjacent to or just beyond their corporate limits when a nexation of those areas is part of a State or county plan for city expansion. Such extraterritorial jurisdiction should not, however, be permitted to interfere with the exercise of lawful jurisdiction for the same areas for the same or similar purposes by counties, towns, special districts, or other units of local government.

e. States that have not already done so should consider legislation giving appropriate State and local authorities regulatory authority over individual wells and septic tank installations and directing the development of plans for metropolitan areawide water and sewerage systems that (1) provide for the orderly extension and expansion of metropolitan area water supply and sewerage system; (2) assure adequate sewage treatment facilities for safe and sanitary treatment of sewage and other liquid waste; (3) delineate portions of the metropolitan area which the systems may be expected to serve at projected dates in the future; and (4) set forth schedules and methods of acquiring necessary land and financing the construction and operation of the proposed system.

12-5. Congress should invite the formation of interstate compacts to solve water problems of multistate metropolitan areas by delineating the conditions under which it will give advance consent to compacts made for purposes of managing multistate metropolitan water systems.

12-6. Federal grant procedures should not be based on decisions made by local organizations that are not duly constituted under State law and politically accountable to their local electorate.

Federal-State Jurisdiction in the Law of Waters[1]

In a number of the regional conferences held by the Commission as it began its work, serious concern was expressed by government officials and private citizens about the relations between the Federal Government and the States and their citizens over water rights. State officials are troubled by the difficulties in coordinating Federal water claims and uses with State water law, administration, and planning. Owners of privately held water rights fear that Federal actions (based on recent court decisions) will impair or destroy their property without compensation. Adjudication of the conflicting claims is made difficult by uncertainties about the ability of a plaintiff to bring a law suit against the United States.

In the United States, water law has evolved under a system of dual sovereignty. Accordingly, it is separated into the Federal law of water on the one hand and 50 independent sets of State laws on the other. Each State has developed its own set of water laws and the Federal water law has been superimposed thereon. At one time it was thought that, apart from the navigation power of the United States, water law was exclusively State law. For example, the U.S. Bureau of Reclamation for many years developed its irrigation projects on the basis of water rights obtained in accordance with State laws and procedures. Now it is recognized that every owner of a water right can be, and often is, simultaneously and inconsistently affected both by State law and by Federal law.

Sometimes State and Federal water laws are compatible and work in harmony with one another. Other times they are incompatible. When conflict occurs, it is not impossible to strike a balance to insure effective and efficient performance of the economic system to optimize the yield which society derives from its scarce water resources. Neither jurisdiction, Federal nor State, need be subordinated absolutely to the other, particularly if the result is a reduction in social and economic efficiency. Effective compromises are constitutionally possible.

One expert has observed: "If [Federal law] fits with the state law into a single pattern it creates no problems. When it and state law clash, when gaps appear, when federal law upsets that which state law has set up, when federal law undoes the tenure security that states give to property rights, when federal rights override instead of mesh with private rights, then there is federal-state conflict in the field of water rights. There is confusion, uncertainty, bad feeling, jealousy and bitterness. To a substantial degree, this is what exists today."[2]

No law can be enacted to give an absolute and unqualified assurance as to the future. Virtually all property rights carry with them some uncertainties. But, to the extent that the law can be formulated to minimize future uncertainties, or at least compensate for them, it serves the socially useful purpose of encouraging long-range planning and development, both private and public, for optimum use of resources.

---

[1] This chapter is based in large measure on a study made for the Commission and reported on in TRELEASE, Frank J (1971). Federal-State Relations in Water Law, prepared for the National Water Commission. National Technical Information Service, Springfield, Va., Accession No. PB 203 600.

~~~~~~~~~~~~~~~~~~~~~~~

Supreme Court decisions form basis for conflict between Federal and State water laws

[2] TRELEASE, Frank J (1971). Federal-State Relations in Water Law, prepared for the National Water Commission. National Technical Information Service, Springfield, Va., Accession No. PB 203 600 p. 11.

THE PROBLEM

The issues in Federal-State relations in the law of water rights may be divided into three problem areas:[3]

1. Coordination of Federal water activities with State water administration;
2. Sovereign immunity as a bar to the adjudication of Federal water claims; and
3. Compensability of State-created water rights impaired by Federal activities.

A brief statement of background may help to explain the issues. It was observed earlier that during the formative period of State water law, Federal rights to the use of water were thought to be based on State law. Both the Bureau of Reclamation and the Forest Service explicitly adopted this concept and obtained rights by filings with State water law officials. In 1963, however, a very different concept of water rights was introduced by the U.S. Supreme Court's decisions in *City of Fresno v. California* and *Arizona v. California.*[4] The *Fresno* case rejected the city's claim under State law to area-of-origin protection, indicating that the 1902 Reclamation Act did not require compliance with State law but required only that compensation be paid for the taking of property interests recognized by State law. Since the city had no compensable property interest in area-of-origin protection, it received no protection at all. *Arizona v. California* similarly limited the operation of State law as applied to Federal reclamation projects.

Arizona v. California also created a new species of water right in the Federal Government, the reserved right for certain Federal establishments.[5] The Court held that water was reserved for a variety of Federal activities when public land was withdrawn for such purposes as national forests, parks, monuments, and wildlife refuges. A somewhat similar theory had been used in 1955 to justify a Federal Power Commission license for a private power dam on a nonnavigable river but on reserved Federal land.[6] The Supreme Court held the license could be issued to build the dam despite the fact that its construction violated State law.

An unrelated development occurred in the 1950's and 1960's. Since the days of Chief Justice John Marshall, the Commerce Clause of the Constitution has been construed to give the Federal Government *power* to regulate navigation. This power was extended in the 1930's to permit Federal development of navigable rivers with multipurpose projects, such as Hoover Dam.[7] The Commerce Clause was also construed to permit the United States to take certain property without compensation. The Court held that when the Government condemned land along a watercourse for navigation projects, it did not have to compensate the landowners for those values attributable to the navigable water, the "navigation servitude." Thus, the Government acquired dam sites and port sites at prices which did not take into account adjoining water.[8]

These decisions seemed to threaten established State procedures and vested private rights. In some instances, Federal officials refused to disclose their existing uses of water and were also claiming reserved rights to future uses of water in any amount necessary to serve the purposes of withdrawn Federal lands. These actions, seemingly validated by the Supreme Court, impaired planning, for neither present nor future water proposals could obtain satisfactory assurances of future prospects. First of all sovereign immunity was a bar to judicial definition of claims. And, since the priority date of reserved Federal rights is the date the Federal establishment was created—usually the turn of the century or earlier—a use commenced at any time by the Federal Government could wipe out water rights for other uses that may have been in effect for 70 years or longer, and without compensation. The reservation doctrine applied to both navigable and nonnavigable streams.

Throughout the Nation, owners of water rights and of real property, the values of which depended on water, were made vulnerable to uncompensated losses by development of a project on a navigable river or lake, and, in some cases, on a nonnavigable river or lake as well.

---

[3] Indian water rights are treated separately in Chapter 14.

[4] *City of Fresno v. California,* 372 U.S. 627 (1963), and *Arizona v. California,* 373 U.S. 546 (1963).

[5] This new species of water right originated in *Winters v. United States,* 207 U.S. 564 (1908), dealing with Indian water rights, which is discussed in Chapter 14. Prior to *Arizona v. California,* the *Winters* case was assumed by many to be limited to Indian Reservations. In *Arizona v. California* the concept was more broadly stated to apply to all Federal reservations.

[6] *Federal Power Commission v. Oregon,* 349 U.S. 435 (1955).

[7] *Arizona v. California,* 283 U.S. 423 (1931).

[8] *United States v. Rands,* 389 U.S. 121 (1967); *United States v. Twin City Power Co.,* 350 U.S. 222 (1956).

DISCUSSION

The Commission believes that the conflicts described above can be settled and the uncertainties they generate can be resolved by appropriate congressional action. Accordingly, it recommends the adoption of a proposed "National Water Rights Procedures Act," the principles of which are set forth hereafter in recommendations 13-1 through 13-9. The recommendations are designed to preserve Federal powers but to hold the Federal Government accountable in court for injury to individuals owning State-based water rights. The recommendations of this chapter also seek to integrate Federal water rights into State water rights administration, but they do not relate to Indian water rights, which are treated in the next chapter.

Although the principal effects of the proposed Act would occur in the West, where water rights are highly systematized, Eastern States would also be benefited by it. States with permit systems could include Federal uses in its records, and Eastern water officials and water rights owners would be entitled to sue the United States when water rights disputes arose, since the proposed Act would waive the defense of sovereign immunity. Moreover, Eastern water rights owners would be protected against noncompensable takings under the navigation servitude and would have the benefit of the proposed Act's eminent domain procedures in connection with Federal water resource development.

Conforming Federal Uses to State Procedures

Recommendation No. 13-1: The United States should adopt a policy of recognizing and utilizing the laws of the respective States relating to the creation, administration, and protection of water rights (1) by establishing, recording, and quantifying existing non-Indian Federal water uses in conformity with State laws, (2) by protecting non-Federal vested water rights held under State law through the elimination of the no-compensation features of the reservation doctrine and the navigation servitude, and (3) by providing new Federal procedures for the condemnation of water rights and the settlement of legal disputes.

Discussion — At the outset, the fundamental proposition that the United States must be able to exercise all of its constitutional powers and carry out all national policies, purposes, and programs free from State control must be acknowledged. The Constitution specifies the Nation's powers and the functions of the Congress. These cannot be abandoned. The United States has an interest in all of its territory and must manage its resources for the benefit of all of its people, not just those who live in the neighborhood in which a given issue arises.

The States, however, have a valid interest in protecting the rights of persons to use water and in the values associated with those rights. State water law and procedures are concerned with local conditions, with water rights held by individuals and organizations, with public water supplies for cities, and in general with promotion of State prosperity. Although State water laws are adapted to local conditions, they usually seek to create a system of secure water rights that will encourage investment yet provide the flexibility needed to accommodate change. In many States, water rights are quantified and recorded, withdrawals policed, uses regulated, and supplies rationed. This is the traditional sphere of State action.

There is no reason why federally-created water rights for Federal purposes cannot co-exist with State-created rights for private and public purposes. What is needed is a mechanism for insuring that they mesh smoothly.

For a time a sort of Federal-State partnership provided the machinery. The 1902 Reclamation Act directed that the Interior Department "shall proceed in conformity with [State] laws,"[9] and the assumption by other Federal agencies that their water rights stemmed from State law provided the needed impetus and unity. We now know that federally owned water rights may be created by Federal law, for if State water rights are not suitable for Federal purposes, the Federal Government must create its own, and has ample power to do so.[10]

No solution to the controversy is possible if the problem areas are regarded as arenas of conflict between State's rights and Federal supremacy, if the Federal attitude is one of haughty superiority or if

---

[9] *Reclamation Act of 1902*, P.L. 161, 57th Congress, June 17, 1902, Section 8, 32 Stat. 388, 390, 43 USCA 383.

[10] The United States, through the Bureau of Reclamation, administers the entire flow of the Colorado River below Lee Ferry in accordance with Federal law in the Mexican Water Treaty and the Boulder Canyon Project Act. No State filings were made by the United States for any of this water. *Arizona v. California*, 373 U.S. 546 (1963), indicates that both the water rights of the United States and those of the users are created and governed by Federal law.

States seek to control Federal powers and programs and put State interests above those of the Nation. A search must be made for the legitimate interests of each and for means to accommodate both.

There is a satisfactory solution at hand. The Federal Government must retain Federal control of Federal programs and the Federal water rights associated with those programs. The States, on the other hand, need stability of water rights and undisturbed State administration of water. Each objective can be achieved under the proposed National Water Rights Procedures Act. The Act would call for a revitalization of the concept of conformity—not Federal compliance with or submission to State law, but (1) the conforming of Federal water rights to the form of State law, (2) Federal use of those substantive State laws that advance the Federal purpose, and (3) Federal observance of those State procedures which do not impair the substance of the Federal right. The Act would establish a policy of compensation for the holders of State water rights if the Federal Government takes their water for its programs. It would provide improved procedures and remedies for the settlement of legal problems arising out of water rights.

Under this solution the Federal Government would surrender nothing of overriding importance. The Act would not permit a State to veto a Federal project or use, dictate the purpose of the use, or destroy a Federal water right.

Nor would the States lose anything of value. Protection of vested rights and orderly administration of water and water rights does not require control over the initiation and exercise of every right so protected and administered. The States would receive Federal water rights into their systems, record them, enforce them, protect them, and distribute water to them in accordance with their place in the whole scheme of rights. The laws that the States would not enforce against the United States are those they cannot enforce under the U.S. Constitution.

Pending in the 92nd Congress were two pertinent bills—the Moss and Hosmer bills, S. 28 and H.R. 2312, respectively. Both were word for word the Kuchel Bill, S. 1636, of the 89th Congress, which in turn was a modified version of S. 1275 of the 88th Congress. These were not bills that would subject the United States to the control of State governments. They were earnest attempts to propose workable solutions to the problems of (1) the reserved rights of non-Indians, (2) the navigation servitude, and (3) inverse condemnation (i.e., property taken by govern-mental action without prior payment of compensation). Nevertheless, these bills are now moribund, hopelessly terminal cases. Misunderstood, with the sins of predecessor proposals heaped upon them, they retain enough "State's rights" baggage to produce an automatic adverse reaction in the Federal departments, regardless of their real merits or their true faults. It is desirable to begin anew, and that is what the proposed National Water Rights Procedures Act proposes to do.

Recommendation No. 13-2: The United States, in making any use of water and in constructing, administering, and operating any program or project involving or effecting the use of water, should proceed in conformity with State laws and procedures relating to (1) the appropriation, diversion, and use of water and (2) the regulation, administration, and protection of water rights. This rule should be subject to two exceptions: (1) It should not apply to Indian water rights and (2) it should not apply where State law conflicts with the accomplishment of the purposes of a Federal program or project. In the second case the Federal official charged with administering the Act should be able to exercise his discretion in determining whether such inconsistency exists. If he concludes that there is a conflict or inconsistency, he should be obliged to hold a hearing on the question and thereafter set forth his conclusions in writing, which should be subject to judicial review.

Discussion — This recommendation proposes a procedural approach to most Federal-State water rights problems that should be satisfactory to both interests. If it were adopted, the Federal Government would retain all constitutional powers to deal with waters for Federal purposes, free from State control. Federal water rights and uses would not be subjected to those State regulations which impede the accomplishment of statutory purposes. For example, a State official could not deny a permit on the ground that the use was not in the public interest where Congress had decided the contrary by authorizing the use. Existing Federal water rights would merely be identified and quantified under the State system, and thereafter the bulk of them would, at least in that respect, be indistinguishable from water rights held under State law. They would be recorded on the same forms and in the same places and be administered and enforced in the same way.

The only requirement imposed on Federal officials is to cooperate with State officials; the only "surrender" is of the occasional autocratic refusal to adhere to State procedures. These refusals were inspired by fears that conformity and cooperation might constitute an acknowledgment of State power that could some day operate to the detriment of the United States. It is now clear that those fears were baseless. The States need only recognize the full effect of the supremacy clause and foreswear unconstitutional attempts to control Federal uses of water. It is clear that the States do not have the power to control Federal water uses, and they would not gain the power from a policy of Federal conformity to State procedures.

In the usual case, "compliance" with State laws would result from Federal conformity, since most State laws are consistent with and appropriate for most Federal objectives.[11] Federal conformity would mean obtaining a permit, constructing the works pursuant thereto, applying water to the project use, and eventually adjudicating or certifying the right. Thousands of Federal uses have been obtained in exactly this manner. The result of applying the policy of conformity would be the clear-cut identification of rights owned by the Federal Government and created by Federal law, but procedurally conformed to private rights owned by individuals which have been created by State law, so that both Federal and private rights will be interrelated and intermeshed into one system of administration and enforcement.

If the United States should encounter rejection of its applications, cancellation of its permits, or declarations that its rights were abandoned or forfeited, it need only assert its constitutional supremacy, announcing that it regards the permits as in force and the documents as evidence of the Federal water right. Judicial review of this assertion is provided for in Recommendation 13-9.[12]

Recommendation No. 13-3: Legislation should be enacted to provide:

a. that the United States may be joined as a party in proceedings for the adjudication of non-Indian water rights in any source of water, when the United States claims or is in the process of acquiring rights to water under the authority of an act of Congress, as owner, by appropriation under State law, by purchase, by exchange, or otherwise, and where those rights would, if owned or claimed by a private citizen, be included in and determined by such proceedings. "Proceedings for the adjudication of non-Indian water rights" means such proceedings as are provided by State law for the determination, adjudication, certification, and recording of water rights, excepting, however, Indian water rights;

b. that the United States shall be subject to all judgments, orders, and decrees of the court or agency conducting such proceedings;

c. that the United States shall have the right to judicial review of proceedings in which it has been joined as a party under these provisions before the U.S. Court of Appeals for the Circuit in which the State lies. The right to seek such review shall arise after a final judgment or order is entered by the State administrative agency or the State trial court, as the case may be, and when the case is ripe for consideration by the first State appellate court having jurisdiction. Findings of fact by the State tribunal shall be sustained if supported by substantial evidence.

Discussion — This recommendation is designed to restate and clarify existing Federal law (the McCarran Amendment)[13] and to carry out the principles announced in 1971 by the Supreme Court in the *Eagle County* and *Water Division No. 5* cases.[14] The

---

[1] A blanket claim by a Federal agency that compliance with any State procedures would be burdensome and thwart Federal objectives is not likely to succeed. A similar contention was made in *United States v. District Court for Water Division No. 5,* 401 U.S. 527 (1971), and was rejected, the Court indicating that compliance may be required as long as the United States has the same burdens as all other water users have.

[2] The question may be asked whether this procedure would lead to endless law suits and new Federal-State controversies over those laws which had to be conformed to and those which did not. A Supreme Court decision suggests an answer. In *First Iowa Hydro-Electric Coop. v. Federal*

Power Commission, 328 U.S. 152 (1946), the Supreme Court held that it was up to the FPC to determine which State laws were compatible with Federal objectives and which interfered therewith. Federal agencies at their discretion determine the necessity for exceptions, judicial review is triggered in the event of abuse of discretion, and negligible litigation has occurred since the Supreme Court rendered its decision.

[13] *McCarran Water Rights Suits Act (Federal Liability),* P.L. 495, 82d Congress, July 10, 1952, Section 208, 66 Stat. 549, 660, 43 USCA 666.

[14] *United States v. District Court in and for the County of Eagle,* 401 U.S. 520 (1971); *United States v. District Court in and for Water Division No. 5,* 401 U.S. 527 (1971).

recommended provision clarifies existing law by including all public proceedings designed to determine non-Indian water rights for regulatory and administrative purposes in any State, no matter where held, or what form the proceedings may take, or by whom initiated, or what sources of water are involved, so long as the States have found the proceedings to be appropriate for purposes of water administration.[15]

Proceedings being conducted at the present time in Colorado pursuant to the rulings in the *Eagle County* and *Water Division No. 5* cases illustrate the process. The Colorado law subordinates the priority of a private use for failure to appear in earlier adjudications. The United States cannot "comply with" this provision of Colorado law, but, as nearly as possible, the statements of United States' claims, the evidence presented, and other essential procedures are being "conformed to" the Colorado requirements. When these proceedings are complete, the rights of the United States to its water uses will be described and recorded in a manner that makes them indistinguishable from the water appropriations of Colorado water users.

Records of Federal water uses and claims would be conformed to State laws in all States, East or West, North or South, which have administrative procedures regulating water uses. If a State has no such procedures and puts no requirements on its own water users, the United States will be under no obligation to record its rights or notify any official or agency of its uses.

The Commission believes that the provisions on judicial review strike a satisfactory balance between the expertise and efficiency available to State proceedings and the natural preference of United States officials to have review of Federal water claims in a Federal court. At present, under the McCarran Amendment, the only chance of Federal court review is before the U.S. Supreme Court, usually in its discretionary *certiorari* (i.e., review) jurisdiction. By giving the United States a right of appeal from the State proceedings to the U.S. Circuit Court of Appeals, Federal court review is assured without sacrificing the potential contribution of those State administrative agencies charged with administering and adjudicating water rights.

---

[15] Neither the McCarran Amendment nor the *Eagle County* case is explicit on the adjudication of Indian Water rights. For reasons stated in Chapter 14, the Commission recommends their adjudication in Federal court.

Reserved Rights

Recommendations 13-4 through 13-6 deal with reserved rights for Federal establishments other than Indian Reservations. Before turning to the recommendations themselves, a brief discussion of the law may be helpful.

It has been held by the U.S. Supreme Court that the withdrawal of land from entry (by Congress or other lawful means) for Federal use (e.g., for military posts, national parks, forests, and wildlife refuges) may also result in the acquisition of a Federal right to use water on the reserved land.[16] Whether such reserved Federal water rights are created depends upon whether or not it was intended to create such water rights at the time the land was withdrawn. Such intent ordinarily must be based on implication, since withdrawal orders rarely mention water.

If a reserved Federal water right is determined to have been created, it has characteristics which are quite incompatible with State appropriation water law: (1) it may be created *without* diversion or beneficial use, (2) it is not lost by nonuse, (3) its priority dates from the time of the land withdrawal, and (4) the measure of the right is the amount of water reasonably necessary to satisfy the purposes for which the land has been withdrawn.

Reserved rights, which were not recognized until 1963 in *Arizona v. California,* create large uncertainties in the water budgets of Federal and State water resources planners and private investors. The privilege of the Federal Government to put to use in 1973 water attaching to land withdrawn in 1873, and thus cut off the supply of water which others had begun using during the intervening 100 years without notice of the Federal claim, creates substantial hardships.

In recognition of *existing* Federal uses based on the reserved rights doctrine and to prevent disruption of existing non-Federal uses by initiation of uses pursuant to non-Indian reserved rights claims, the Commission makes the following two recommendations:

Recommendation No. 13-4:

a. **If on the date the proposed National Water Rights Procedures Act becomes effective the United States is making use of water pursuant to an act of Congress or an Executive Order of the President, whether under the "reservation doctrine" on lands withdrawn from entry and reserved for Federal purposes, or on other lands pursuant to other authority, and the right to**

---

[16] *Arizona v. California,* 373 U.S. 546 (1963).

Instream values must be preserved

make such Federal use has not been filed with the State in conformity to State law, the Federal agency or officer in charge of such use should establish the quantity of such use and record the use by proceeding in conformity to State procedures for the acquisition and adjudication of water rights by other water users.

b. In the case of reserved lands of the United States, the priority of the water right should be the date the reserved land was withdrawn from entry; in the case of other lands owned by the United States, the priority of the water right should be the date the water use was initiated.

c. The proposed Act should also provide standards and procedures for establishing minimum flows in streams crossing Federal lands for the purpose of preserving instream values in such waters. The minimum streamflows should be limited to unappropriated water and should be recorded in the State water rights records as provided in (a) above.

Discussion – Where Federal uses have been initiated in reliance on the reserved rights theory, these rights should be brought into conformity to State law only in the sense that they be quantified and recorded. Thereafter it will be possible for resource planners and others to take them into account in the regulation of water resources. If Federal uses were required to comply with State law in the same way other uses are, many of the Federal uses would be forfeited or lose their priority for past failures of the United States to meet State requirements for permits or to appear in State adjudication proceedings. "Conformity to State procedures" means only application of State procedures to record these existing uses; it does not mean applying State law to forbid their continuation.

The procedural part of the recommendation, by removing ambiguities in the McCarran Amendment, is designed to make possible adjudication of existing Federal rights in all States. The United States should conform to the procedures of those States that have adjudicated early rights and that require new rights (1) to be initiated by permit and (2) to be separately proved, adjudicated, or licensed in proceedings initiated by the appropriator. If the use is of a stream which the State has not yet adjudicated, a permit application will serve as sufficient conformity and the Federal right can wait with other rights for its adjudication. In some instances the United States may see virtues in initiating such proceedings.

Recommendation 13-4 recognizes that Federal agencies may also have made some water uses that neither comply with State law nor can be justified under the reservation doctrine. The power of Federal agencies to make such uses cannot be denied under the Supremacy Clause, if the water has been taken through the exercise of constitutional power. Nevertheless, such Federal uses should also be subject to adjudication and recording so that the water rights records are complete and accurate. In this case, the priority date should be that customary under Western law, the date the use was initiated. Otherwise, prior established uses might be impaired without compensation. If a Federal agency needs more water than is available to it under its right, it can of course resort to eminent domain to acquire an additional supply.

The proposed Act recognizes the desirability of protecting instream values in unappropriated water on Federal lands and provides for the delegation of authority to Federal officials, under appropriate standards, for the establishment of minimum flows in streams crossing Federal lands, both reserved lands and acquired lands.[17] The minimum flow requirements should be filed in the State water records to provide notice to future water users; existing users would be protected by limiting the requirements to unappropriated water.

Recommendation No. 13-5: Any withdrawal, diversion, or use of water initiated by an agency or officer of the United States *after* the effective date of the proposed Act, for use on or in connection with any lands of the United States reserved or withdrawn at any time for any purpose other than for an Indian reservation, should be made in conformity to State law, as provided for in Recommendation 13-2, and the priority date of the water right for such use should be the date of the initiation of the use by application for permit or otherwise as determined by State law.

Discussion – This recommendation modifies the effect of the reservation doctrine by fixing the priority of future uses on reserved lands as the date the use is initiated as determined by State law. Thus, prior non-Federal uses are protected from uncompensated impairment.

---

[17] This recommendation to establish minimum flows for streams on Federal lands parallels the recommendations to the States in Chapter 7, Sections E and F, urging protection of instream values under State law.

The reservation doctrine is a financial doctrine only; it confers no power on the Federal Government that it does not otherwise enjoy. Anytime the United States needs water (or any other resource) to carry out a program authorized by the Constitution, it has ample power to acquire it. What the reservation doctrine does is to empower the taking of water without compensating prior established users for impairment of their supply.

The Commission believes that this aspect of the reservation doctrine should be eliminated. Uncompensated destruction of existing non-Federal uses places a disproportionate share of the burden of new Federal development upon a few. The loss will appear to them to be arbitrary and capricious. Other users in the same area but on another watershed will remain unaffected, though also subject to reserved rights. Moreover, since the reservation doctrine does not apply in Midwestern and Eastern States where there is comparatively little public land, its application in the West appears to be discriminatory. Finally, from the standpoint of economic efficiency, the United States should be required to cover the full costs of the resources it needs whether for exploring outer space, building a post office, or constructing a water project. Optimal resource allocation depends upon a proper accounting for the opportunity costs of foregone alternative uses. Paying for resources does just that by compensating sellers for their foregone opportunities. The traditional and most reliable means of determining those costs is by requiring the new user to purchase the resource in the open market or, in the case of the Government, requiring that it pay just compensation.

In addition to the adverse effects imposed on prior users, the reservation doctrine frustrates sound planning in the public and private sectors of the economy. The prospective claims of the Government are highly uncertain, as to time, manner, and quantity of use. Consequently, no planner or investor can establish a meaningful water budget. It is impossible to prove how many non-Federal projects were not undertaken because of these uncertainties, but statements to the Commission reveal profound concern on the part of State officials.

It is sometimes argued by Government attorneys that since no one has been hurt by the reservation doctrine since 1963, when it was first applied to non-Indian lands, there is no need to legislate at this time. There are two answers to this argument. First, we do not know how much investment has been held up which might otherwise have been undertaken and,

as a result, how much economic growth may have been lost. And second, while it is true that no prior user has yet been deprived of his supply by the invocation of reserved rights, the potential for harm is indisputable. It thus seems preferable to eliminate the threat to planning and investment and to existing users, in advance rather than to wait for injury to occur.

Eminent Domain — As a means of protecting private water users from exercise of Federal reserved rights, Recommendation No. 13-5 adopts the rule that new Federal uses on reserved land take their priority at the date the new use is initiated in accordance with State law.[18] This rule would operate to permit the United States to file on unappropriated water in the same manner as would any other prospective user. If, however, the supply of unappropriated water is insufficient to serve the new Federal use, the United States would acquire water through the eminent domain procedures set out in Recommendation 13-8. Prior users would thus be compensated when their water was taken for use on reserved land.

Quantification — The Public Land Law Review Commission, the U.S. Department of Justice, and the Dingell Bill (H. R. 659 of the 92d Cong.) have each proposed the quantification of non-Indian reserved rights as a solution to the problem of planning and investment. The Commission gave extended consideration to this proposal, but concluded that its disadvantages outweigh its advantages. In the first place, the quantification process would be expensive. The Dingell Bill would authorize appropriation of $10 million in the first year, $20 million in the second, and so on until the level of spending reached $50 million in the fifth year and in each year thereafter to keep the inventory up to date.

In the second place, Government officials would strenuously resist final, permanent quantification. The vagaries of the future combined with susceptibility to charges of "give away" naturally lead these officials to seek open-ended decrees which, after all the expense, settle nothing. Even if final quantification could be achieved, it would not satisfactorily solve the problem. Federal officials would be inclined to state their claims as broadly as possible, employing every faculty of the imagination to foresee every

---

[18] State law may give priority from the date of application for a permit or from some other date, but all States protect actual, existing uses.

conceivable future use in the largest quantities imaginable. The result would be the reservation of water on the basis of the grossest speculation with consequences for planning and development even more adverse than those produced by the present law. Efficient use of resources cannot be achieved when a resource is withdrawn from present use and stockpiled for possible future use, although no plans for such use exist and the purposes of the future use are mere speculative possibilities.

This is not to say that water should never be reserved for future use. Until definite plans exist for specific projects, water should not be withdrawn from other appropriations. When definite plans are formulated, however, water should be withdrawn for a sufficient period of time to permit perfection of the plans, securing of financing, and negotiation of water delivery contracts. Most States have procedures to accomplish this. However, to assure that the Federal interest is protected by Federal law, the Commission believes that Congress should enact legislation on the subject, as set forth in Recommendation 13-6 below.

Recommendation No. 13-6: In any State which requires a permit for the initiation of a use of water, or otherwise regulates the initiation of the use of water, the United States may apply for a permit or other permission to use water under State law, and, subject to vested rights, it should have the right to use such water from the date of its application if the following conditions are met:

1. **Congress authorizes the construction of the project for which the application was made within 5 years of the date of the application; and**
2. **Construction of the project commences within 5 years of the date of congressional authorization. Provided, however, that:**
   a. **Nothing in this recommendation is intended to deny the application of State law which allows longer periods of time for the initiation of water development projects; and**
   b. **Nothing in this or in Recommendation 13-5 above is intended to affect water rights for projects authorized by Congress prior to the effective date of the proposed Act. Specifically, any project authorized before the proposed Act takes effect, which project was designed to use reserved water rights appurtenant to withdrawn lands, shall be entitled to the amount of water and the priority date that obtained under Federal law prior to the enactment of the proposed Act.**

Discussion — This provision allows the United States to reserve water for a designated period of time for specific projects of sufficient importance to require congressional action. It would operate to allow a Federal agency with plans sufficiently developed for timely submission to Congress to obtain a State permit for water for the project. Thereafter, no intervening non-Federal use would be superior to the prospective Federal use until the time limit expires. The time period is geared to the authorization process and then to appropriation of funds and commencement of construction. The design is to strike a balance between the periods of time necessarily involved in moving projects through Congress and the desirability of averting undue postponement of other uses of water awaiting the congressional decision. Regardless of State law, proposed Federal uses will enjoy a minimum period of protection from competing uses. The State is free, however, to extend the period of protection for as long as its law allows.

Special provision for smaller Federal projects not requiring congressional authorization is unnecessary. The States are familiar with, and their laws accommodate, projects that require a few years to construct. A typical State procedure, applicable to the United States and other developers alike, would allow the project sponsor to apply for a permit on the basis of definite plans, fix a time period of completion of the project (based on duly diligent construction efforts) and, upon timely completion, fix the priority as of the date of the application.

The Navigation Servitude and the Rule of No Compensation

Recommendation No. 13-7: The proposed Act should provide that whenever the United States or a person acting under its authority takes, destroys, or impairs any right, acquired under the laws of a State, to the diversion, storage, or use of any water, in connection with or as the result of any Federal project for development of navigable or nonnavigable water or for altering its flow or level, the United States will pay to the owner the fair market value of such water right.

Discussion — This recommendation is directed solely at the no-compensation feature of the navigation servitude as applied to rights of use in water. The servitude also includes the historic public right of passage over navigable water, free from obstruction or monopolization by owners of the beds or banks, and this feature of the servitude is unaffected by the recommendation. The absolute powers of the United States to develop navigable waters also remain untouched.

What is aimed at here is the Federal taking, without compensation, of interests in water to further its own water development projects. Such uncompensated takings are subject to the same objections made against destruction of water rights under the reservation doctrine. The large number of cases of congressional disregard of the no-compensation rule merely heighten the inequities of enforcing it in other situations and places.

The major inroad on the rule was made by Section 111 of the 1970 River and Harbor and Flood Control Act,[19] which in effect provided for fair market value compensation of real property interests taken for a navigation project. This legislation overruled *United States v. Rands*[20] and similar cases, which held that port-site and dam-site values were not compensable when land was taken for navigation purposes. While Section 111 might be read by a court as similarly protecting the values created by water rights in navigable waters, it is desirable to clarify the matters in advance of litigation, giving equal protection to all property values, real property and water rights alike, impaired by Federal water works.

Apart from Section 111 of the 1970 Act, there is further precedent for congressional action of the sort proposed. In several cases the Supreme Court has construed Section 8 of the Reclamation Act of 1902 to require compensation for the taking of water rights.[21]

Eminent Domain Procedures

Recommendation No. 13-8: The proposed Act should provide that whenever the United States, in the construction and operation of a water resources project or in obtaining a supply of water for a use on Federal land or for a Federal purpose takes, destroys, or impairs existing water rights, the policies of Section 301 of the Uniform Relocation Assistance and Real Property Acquisition Act of 1970[22] shall specifically apply to such projects and uses, and the United States shall initiate proceedings to acquire, by negotiated purchase or condemnation, existing water rights so impaired or to acquire and use other water rights so as to avoid such impairment. It should be the policy of the United States to require its agencies and officials to proceed in conformity with State laws governing the acquisition of water rights by preferred users, and to acquire by purchase or condemnation specific water rights which will provide it with the needed quantity of water rather than taking the required amounts of water from the source and forcing the holders of water rights to prove injury and damage.

Discussion — Federal powers to take water are supreme, but supremacy does not require the disruption of systems of water rights and the damage and inconvenience to numerous persons under circumstances which may lead to confiscation. By simply seizing water, the United States leaves it to the prior users to sort out the damage and bring the suit. Since damage will depend on water shortages and who suffers them, the calculation of damage is both difficult and delayed. Considerations of fairness, accommodation, and comity require that the United States, wherever possible, acquire *water rights* and not just take water.

The declared policy of Congress for improved condemnation procedures expressed in the 1970 Relocation Act is obviously designed to apply to land acquisition for urban renewal and other purposes; it should be made clear that cases of water rights acquisition are also included. The major policy embodied in the 1970 Relocation Act is that no person should be displaced until he has the Government's money in hand; that is, the Government should not seize property and force the owner to sue. There are other policies as well, calling for efforts at fair negotiation for sale and for total acquisition if the owner would be left with an uneconomic remnant, and those are equally applicable in the water field. The latter might be especially needed, for 160 irrigated acres may be a fine farm but 160 desert acres only a poor pasture. In such cases the Government should condemn both land and water.

Sovereign Immunity: Suits by State Officials and Individuals

Recommendation No. 13-9: The proposed Act should provide that:

---

[19] *River and Harbor and Flood Control Act of 1970,* P.L. 91-611, December 31, 1970, 84 Stat. 1818, 33 USCA 595a.

[20] *United States v. Rands,* 389 U.S. 121 (1967).

[21] *Dugan v. Rank, 372 U.S. 609 (1963); United States v. Gerlach Live Stock Co.,* 339 U.S. 725 (1950).

[22] *Uniform Relocation Assistance and Real Property Acquisition Act of 1970,* P.L. 91-646, January 2, 1971, 84 Stat. 1894, 1904, 42 USCA 4651.

1. A person alleging an unlawful interference with his right to the diversion, storage, or use of water by the United States, its agents or officers, may bring an action in a District Court of the United States for appropriate relief.
2. A State official, acting in his official capacity, alleging that the United States, its agents or officers, have violated State law without justification under the law of the United States may bring an action in a District Court of the United States for appropriate relief.
3. Such actions shall not be dismissed nor relief denied on the ground that it is against the United States or that the United States is an indispensable party. The United States may be named as a defendant in any such action and a judgment or decree may be entered against the United States. Nothing in this provision is intended to affect other limitations on judicial review or on the power or duty of the court to permit any action or deny relief on any other appropriate legal or equitable grounds. The action may be brought against the United States, the Federal agency, or the appropriate Federal officer. Such an action may be brought in any judicial district in which (a) a defendant in the action resides, or (b) the cause of action arises, or (c) any real property or water right involved in the action is situated. Additional persons may be joined as parties to any such action in accordance with the Federal Rules of Civil Procedure without regard to other venue requirements.

Discussion — This recommendation proposes to abolish the defense of sovereign immunity, which allows the Federal Government to avoid judicial review of its actions in a number of instances. Just what those instances are is an exceedingly complex subject itself and the removal of the complexity is an independent reason for the recommendation. In making this recommendation, the Commission is following the lead of the Administrative Conference of the United States and the American Bar Association, both of which support S. 598, 92nd Congress, which provides for a general waiver of sovereign immunity.

With respect to use of water, Recommendation 13-2 would require Federal officials to conform to State law unless State law is inconsistent with the accomplishment of Federal purposes as established by Congress. Federal officials are given authority to determine what the statutory purposes are and whether they conflict with State law. Implementation of Recommendation 13-2 would require that sovereign immunity be waived in suits to determine whether a Federal official's refusal to conform to State law is an abuse of discretion. Judicial review of this determination requires waiver of sovereign immunity. Since the questions presented in the litigation are primarily questions of Federal law, exclusive jurisdiction is given to the Federal Courts. The question of remedies is left to the general law, as it now exists and as it may change in the future.

CONCLUSIONS

The Commission believes that existing law creates unnecessary friction between the Federal Government and the States, and poses threats of uncompensated taking of water rights held by private citizens under State law. These defects in present law can be remedied without impairment of Federal powers and Federal functions.

One source of friction is the failure of the Federal Government to proceed in conformity with State law when making use of water. As a consequence, adequate records of water use do not exist, impairing State and private planning and investment. All Federal uses of water, present and prospective, should be recorded with the State in accordance with State forms and procedures. Further, Federal water uses should comply with State law except in those cases where State law conflicts with the purposes of a Federal program or project authorized by Congress. The determination that a conflict exists should be the responsibility of the Federal program officer, subject to judicial review. The immunity of the United States from law suits should be waived so that such conflicts can be adjudicated. Sovereign immunity should also be waived so that Federal and State water rights can be determined and integrated into a single system of administration. Owners of State water rights should be able to sue the United States in Federal Courts for unlawful interference with the exercise of their rights.

Two legal doctrines enable the United States to take State created water rights without payment of compensation. The navigation servitude, created by the courts and already greatly modified by Congress, allowed the United States to take land and water without paying for water-dependent values in navigable streams. This doctrine should be changed and the United States required to proceed pursuant to the policies of Section 301 of the Uniform Relocation Assistance and Real Property Acquisition Act of 1970

The reserved rights doctrine as it applies to withdrawals of land for purposes other than Indian Reservations was first announced in 1963 and permits the creation of a water right by mere reservation of land for Federal use and without contemporaneous initiation of a water use. Many reservations were made between 70 and 100 years ago, but water has yet to be diverted onto the reserved land. Meanwhile, non-Federal uses have been made of the water supply, and these uses would be subject to divestment by future Federal action. In order to prevent such divestment without compensation, the non-Indian Federal reserved right to make use of water in the future should take its priority from the date the use is initiated, not from the date of the reservation. Minimum flows may be established using unappropriated water to protect instream values in waters on Federal lands.

RECOMMENDATIONS

13-10. To achieve the reforms which the Commission believes should be made with respect to Federal-State relations in the law of water rights, the provisions of Recommendations Nos. 13-1 through 13-9 should be enacted in a proposed "National Water Rights Procedures Act" covering the problems discussed in this chapter of:

a. conforming Federal water uses to State procedures;

b. future use of water on Federal reserved lands other than Indian Reservations;

c. the navigation servitude and the rule of no compensation;

d. eminent domain procedures; and

e. sovereign immunity.

Indian Water Rights

BACKGROUND

In the West, State law historically has provided for creation of water rights by diversion of water from a stream and its application to a beneficial use. The key attribute of an appropriative right created in this manner is its right to receive water in times of shortage before other rights similarly created later in time are served. As Western water law developed, statutory modifications required the filing of an application to appropriate water with a State official, and upon grant of the application, a permit was issued as evidence of the water right.

Indian water rights are created outside of this system of State law and exist independently of it.[1] An Indian water right arises under Federal law. In nearly all cases it comes into being when a Reservation is created, whether the act of creation is a treaty, an act of Congress, or an executive order, and it pertains to lands within the Reservation. Where the Reservation is located on lands aboriginally owned by the Indian tribe, their water rights may even be said to have existed from time immemorial.

No diversion of water and application to beneficial use is necessary for the creation of an Indian water right: The right arises no later than the date the Reservation is established, although the first use of the water is much later in time. Moreover, no application for a permit to appropriate water need be made to a State official in order to create an Indian water right because the right stems from Federal law. State regulations on initiation of use, purpose, place

and manner of use, and forfeiture of the right are inapplicable to Indian water rights. Finally, nor do the priority rules of appropriation law apply to Indian water rights. Ordinary appropriation rights date their priority from the time of use or from the date of permit; Indian water rights have priority at least from the date the Indian Reservation was established. Thus an Indian Reservation established in 1865 which commences its first use of water in 1965 has, in times of shortage, a right to receive water ahead of any non-Indian water right with a priority date after 1865. If an Indian Reservation is determined to have an aboriginal water right dating from time immemorial, it will, of course, be the first priority on the river.

The legal principles governing Indian water rights and the reasons behind them were established by the U.S. Supreme Court early in this century in the case of *Winters v. United States*.[2] That case remains the foundation on which the law of Indian water rights rests. The United States sued in behalf of the Indians of the Fort Belknap Reservation to enjoin upstream diversions that interfered with the flow of 120 cubic feet per second of water necessary for irrigating pasture and farmland on the Reservation. The defense was that the defendants had acquired a water right under State law by diverting and applying water to beneficial use prior to any use of water on the Reservation (excepting a small quantity not in issue). Accordingly, claimed the defendants, under Montana law and Western water law generally, the defendants were prior appropriators with the superior right. The Court rejected the argument, stating:[3]

> The power of the Government to reserve the waters and exempt them from appropriation under the state laws is not denied, and could not

---

[1] This chapter deals exclusively with the rights of Indians to use water from surface streams on Indian Reservations. It does not discuss Indian use of ground water, Indian rights off Reservations, or rights of Indian allottees.

~~~~~~~~~~~~~~~~~~~~~~~~~~~~

New techniques are being developed for irrigating the Navajo Irrigation Project in New Mexico

[2] *Winters v. United States*, 207 U.S. 564 (1908).

[3] *Ibid.*, at 577.

be. [Citations omitted.] That the Government did reserve them we have decided, and for a use which would be necessarily continued through the years. This was done May 1, 1888 [the date the Reservation was established by an agreement with the Indians] . . . .

Having disposed of the issue of the *power* of the Government to create a water right for an Indian Reservation, the Court was faced with the question of the exercise of the power. Did the Government *intend* to reserve water for the Fort Belknap Indian Reservation? This question was answered affirmatively, in language that has since become the Great Charter of Indian water rights.[4]

The case, as we view it, turns on the agreement of May, 1888, resulting in the creation of Fort Belknap Reservation. In the construction of this agreement there are certain elements to be considered that are prominent and significant. The reservation was a part of a very much larger tract which the Indians had the right to occupy and use and which was adequate for the habits and wants of a nomadic and uncivilized people. It was the policy of the Government, it was the desire of the Indians, to change those habits and to become a pastoral and civilized people. If they should become such the original tract was too extensive, but a smaller tract would be inadequate without a change of conditions. The lands were arid and, without irrigation, were practically valueless. And yet, it is contended, the means of irrigation were deliberately given up by the Indians and deliberately accepted by the Government. The lands ceded were, it is true, also arid; and some argument may be urged, and is urged, that with their cession there was the cession of the waters, without which they would be valueless, and "civilized communities could not be established thereon." And this, it is further contended, the Indians knew, and yet made no reservation of the waters. We realize that there is a conflict of implications, but that which makes for the retention of the waters is of greater force than that which makes for their cession. The Indians had command of the lands and the waters—command of all their beneficial use, whether kept for hunting, 'and grazing roving herds of stock,' or turned to agriculture and the arts of civilization. Did they give up all this? Did they reduce the area of their occupation and give up the waters which made it valuable or adequate? * * * If it were possible to believe affirmative answers, we might also believe that the Indians were awed by the power of the Government or deceived by its negotiators. Neither view is possible. The Government is asserting the right of the Indians. But extremes need not be taken into account. By a rule of interpretation of agreements and treaties with the Indians, ambiguities occurring will be resolved from the standpoint of the Indians. And the rule should certainly be applied to determine between two inferences, one of which would support the purpose of the agreement and the other impair or defeat it. On account of their relations to the Government, it cannot be supposed that the Indians were alert to exclude by formal words every inference which might militate against or defeat the declared purpose of themselves and the Government, even if it could be supposed that they had the intelligence to foresee the 'double sense' which might some time be urged against them.

Following *Winters*, more than 50 years elapsed before the Supreme Court again discussed significant aspects of Indian water rights.[5] During most of this 50-year period, the United States was pursuing a policy of encouraging the settlement of the West and the creation of family-sized farms on its arid lands. In retrospect, it can be seen that this policy was pursued with little or no regard for Indian water rights and the *Winters* doctrine. With the encouragement, or at least the cooperation, of the Secretary of the Interior—the very office entrusted with protection of all Indian rights—many large irrigation projects were con-

---

[4] *Ibid.*, at 575-77.

[5] The only Supreme Court opinion during the period was *United States v. Powers*, 305 U.S. 527 (1939), holding that allotted lands sold to non-Indians shared in the water supply reserved for the Reservation. The Court did not consider the nature and extent of Indian water rights, noting, "The present proceeding is not properly framed to that end." 305 U.S. at 533. However, the lower Federal courts did begin to refine the concepts underlying Indian water rights and struggled with the difficult question of admeasurement of the quantity of the entitlement. It is unnecessary to review the cases here. See *United States v. Ahtanum Irr. D.*, 236 F.2d 321 (9th Cir. 1956), on second appeal 330 F.2d 897 (9th Cir. 1964); *United States v. Walker River Irr. D.*, 104 F.2d 334 (9th Cir. 1939); *United States v. McIntire*, 101 F.2d 650 (9th Cir. 1939); *Skeem v. United States*, 273 Fed. 93 (9th Cir. 1921); *Conrad Investment Co. v. United States*, 161 Fed. 829 (9th Cir. 1908); *United States v. Hibner*, 27 F.2d 909 (D. Ida. 1928).

Some Indian tribes rely heavily on fishing for their food supply

tructed on streams that flowed through or bordered ndian Reservations, sometimes above and more often elow the Reservations. With few exceptions the rojects were planned and built by the Federal Jovernment without any attempt to define, let alone rotect, prior rights that Indian tribes might have had a the waters used for the projects. Before *Arizona v alifornia,* referred to hereinafter, actions involv- ig Indian water rights generally concerned then xisting uses by Indians and did not involve the full xtent of rights under the *Winters* doctrine. In the istory of the United States Government's treatment f Indian tribes, its failure to protect Indian water ghts for use on the Reservations it set aside for them one of the sorrier chapters.

There were, it should be said in fairness, some xtenuating circumstances. The full reach of the

Winters case was not readily apparent, though with hindsight it seems more obvious than the Department of the Interior perceived. To many Indian tribes, though not all, the confining way of life that goes along with intensive irrigation was not appealing. Their cultural values led them to prefer to pursue a livelihood as stockmen, hunters, and fishermen. For religious and esthetic reasons they often preferred to leave the waters of their Reservations undisturbed and free flowing. Indian Reservations often are located at high elevations with relatively short growing seasons and a paucity of fertile land, a circumstance that may reflect discredit on the Gov- ernment that located them there. Finally, it must be admitted that the physical task of quantifying the water rights of a Reservation is difficult, expensive, and time consuming—a consideration that leads this

Commission hereinafter to recommend that where tribes lack the means, the United States appropriate the necessary sums for the engineering, historical, and legal studies that should precede the institution of legal action to quantify and define tribal water rights.

In 1963, the Supreme Court of the United States addressed for the second time the question of the nature and extent of Indian water rights. In reaffirming the *Winters* doctrine in *Arizona v. California,*[6] the Supreme Court clarified substantially the question of quantification of Indian water rights. The Special Master had rejected both an open ended decree, which would have the vices of uncertainty and lack of finality, and final quantification based on projected water requirements on the Reservations, which would have the vice of all projections in granting too much or too little depending on the actuality of the future. Instead, the Master adopted as the full and final measure of water rights for the Reservations the amount of water necessary to irrigate the practically irrigable acreage on the Reservations. The Supreme Court affirmed this formula, stating:[7]

> We also agree with the Master's conclusion as to the quantity of water intended to be reserved. He found that the water was intended to satisfy the future as well as the present needs of the Indian reservations and ruled that enough water was reserved to irrigate all the practically irrigable acreage on the reservations. Arizona, on the other hand, contends that the quantity of water reserved should be measured by the Indians' 'reasonably foreseeable needs,' which, in fact, means by the number of Indians. How many Indians there will be and what their future uses will be can only be guessed. We have concluded, as did the Master, that the only feasible and fair way by which reserved water for the reservations can be measured is irrigable acreage. The various acreages of irrigable land which the Master found to be on the different reservations we find to be reasonable.

The amount of water adjudicated to the five Indian Reservations amounted to nearly 1 million acre-feet out of a supply estimated at the time to be between 6 and 7 million acre-feet. The five Reservations were for the most part sparsely inhabited and the priorities assigned to the Reservations generally antedated non-Indian priorities on the river, even though the latter went back to the late 19th century and consisted mostly of reclamation projects, planned, financed, and operated by the Federal Government, the same government that holds title to the Indian water rights as trustee for the tribes.

Although *Arizona v. California* indicates that "practically irrigable acreage" is the appropriate formula for measuring the quantity of Indian water rights for Reservations on which farming and ranching were expected to take place, other Indian Reservations created for other types of occupations may have water rights measured by different formulas. The general principle seems to be that stated in *Winters*, that the rule of interpretation of agreements with Indian Nations is that "which would support the purpose of the agreement."[8] Thus, the United States now seeks a decree on behalf of the Pyramid Lake Indians of sufficient water to maintain the Lake and its fisheries.[9]

Arizona v. California is a graphic illustration of the dilemma posed by the competition between Indian and non-Indian water rights. Most Indian Reservations were established before substantial water development was made by non Indians. Thus, Indian priorities are usually superior to non-Indian priorities. But for a variety of reasons, including some alluded to above, Indian irrigation lagged far behind other irrigation. The Nation is therefore confronted, in the decade of the 1970's—100 or more years after most Indian Reservations were established—with this dilemma: in the water-short West, billions of dollars have been invested, much of it by the Federal Government, in water resource projects benefiting non-Indians but using water in which the Indians have a priority of right if they choose to develop water projects of their own in the future. In short, the Nation faces a conflict between the right of Indians to develop their long-neglected water resources and the impairment of enormous capital investment already made by non-Indians in the same water supply. To resolve that conflict is not an easy task, but the Commission believes it must address the problem in a report which seeks to be comprehensive.

ACCEPTED PREMISES

In formulating its recommendations on Indian water rights, the Commission took as settled the following propositions:

---

[6] *Arizona v. California*, 373 U.S. 546 (1963), decree, 376 U.S. 340 (1964).

[7] 373 U.S. at 600-01.

[8] *Winters v. United States*, 207 U.S. at 577.

[9] *United States v. Nevada and California*, U.S. Supreme Court, No. 59 Original, 1972 Term.

1. The cases of *Winters v. United States* and *Arizona v. California* establish beyond dispute that water rights may attach to Indian Reservations upon creation of the Reservations by any lawful means (treaties, acts of Congress, executive orders, etc.).

2. The priority and quantity of these Indian water rights present questions of law which involve, at least in part, an interpretation of the documents creating each Reservation and may involve for some Reservations the question of aboriginal rights. These questions are judicial questions and legislation cannot determine them or adversely affect such rights without just compensation. The Indians, acting on their own behalf or in conjunction with the United States, may initiate litigation to determine their water rights.[10]

3. Indian water rights are different from Federal reserved rights for such lands as national parks and national forests, in that the United States is not the owner of the Indian rights but is a trustee for the benefit of the Indians. While the United States may sell, lease, quit claim, release, or otherwise convey its own Federal reserved water rights, its powers and duties regarding Indian water rights are constrained by its fiduciary duty to the Indian tribes who are beneficiaries of the trust.

4. The volume of water to which Indians have rights may be large, for it may be measured by irrigable acreage within a Reservation (i.e., land which is practically susceptible of being irrigated) and not by Indian population, present use, or projected future use. It may also be measured by other standards such as flows necessary to sustain a valuable species of fish relied upon by the tribe for sustenance.[11]

5. Development of supplies subject to Indian water rights was not illegal. Ordinarily, therefore, neither Indian tribes nor the United States as the trustee of their property can enjoin the use of water by others outside the Reservation prior to the time the Indians themselves need the water.

6. The future utilization of early Indian rights on fully appropriated streams will divest prior uses

initiated under both State and Federal law (and often financed with Federal funds) and will impose economic hardship, conceivably amounting in some cases to disaster for users with large investments made over long periods of time. The existence of unquantified Indian claims on streams not yet fully appropriated makes determination of legally available supply difficult and thus prevents satisfactory future planning and development.

7. The monetary value of unused Indian water rights is difficult but not impossible to determine. It should be possible on a case-by-case basis to establish a fair market value for unused Indian water rights. The problem of valuation is no more difficult than with other species of property that are not the subject of everyday commerce.

DISCUSSION AND RECOMMENDATIONS

Recommendation No. 14-1: At the request of any Indian tribe the Secretary of the Interior or such other Federal officer as the Congress may designate should conduct studies in cooperation with the Indian tribe of the water resources, the other natural resources, and the human resources available to its Reservation. An object of the studies should be to define and quantify Indian water rights in order to develop a general plan for the use of these rights in conjunction with other tribal resources. When warranted by the results of such studies, litigation should be instituted by the United States in behalf of the Indian tribe to adjudicate its water rights. Congress should appropriate funds to support the studies and the litigation.

Discussion — There is a need to make an inventory of the resources on Indian Reservations as part of the planning for the economic and social development of the reservations and their inhabitants. The Indians should have the major role in this planning, but Federal funds should be made available for its support. Irrigation is but one possible means of development; other activities contributing to economic and social growth should be considered. Indeed, it would be unfortunate if Indian tribes were to dedicate presently unused water rights to uneconomic irrigation projects in a hasty effort to find some use for the rights. If the other recommendations made hereinafter are adopted, tribes will suffer no prejudice from delaying use until valuable purposes are found for the water, since interim leasing to the United States is provided for.

---

[10] While the proposition that Indians alone may sue to adjudicate water rights has not yet been squarely adopted by the Supreme Court, it seems to be the congressional intent in 28 USCA 1362, and it seems to follow from other Indian litigation. See *Poafpybitty v. Skelly Oil Co.*, 390 U.S. 365 (1968); *United States v. Alpine Land and Reservoir Co.*, 431 F.2d 763 (9th Cir. 1970); *Great Lakes Inter-Tribal Council, Inc. v. Voight*, 309 F. Supp. 60 (D. Wis., 1970).

[11] See *United States v. California and Nevada*, No. 59 Original, 1972 Term, U.S. Supreme Court.

Because non-Indian water resource development tends to stifle water development on Indian Reservations, where both take from the same source of supply, a number of steps should be taken to quantify uses in such cases of potential competition.

Recommendation No. 14-2: Prior to the authorization of any federally assisted non-Indian water resource project, a final adjudication should be made of all Indian water rights which when exercised could substantially affect the water supply for the project.

Discussion — This recommendation has two objectives: (1) to force consideration of the supply of water available to a non-Indian project and (2) to protect Indian Reservations from the claim that their rights were indefinite when the non-Indian project was built. By forcing quantification of Indian water rights before a competing non-Indian Federal project is built, the amount of water available for the project can be determined and its feasibility (or lack thereof) can be established. If there is insufficient water for both Indian and non-Indian development, an agreement with the Indian water rights holders will have to be made if the non-Indian project is to be secure in its water supply.

Recommendation No. 14-3: Existing water uses on Indian Reservations, whether or not they have yet been adjudicated, should be quantified and recorded in State water rights records for the purpose of providing notice of such use. All adjudications or other binding determinations of Indian water rights whether heretofore or hereafter rendered similarly should be recorded. When requested to do so by a tribe, the Secretary of the Interior should also file notice of the existence of unquantified Indian water rights with the appropriate State official.

Discussion — This recommendation is in accord with the general belief of the Commission that State records should accurately reflect all actual and potential uses of water. Water resource planning, development, and administration depend upon accurate compilations of claims against supply. Quantification of existing uses should not require litigation but only a report by the Secretary of the Interior. Quantification and recording of Indian water rights with State officials would not—and could not under controlling law—affect in any way the special characteristics of the rights created and guaranteed by Federal law.

The recommendations so far have dealt primarily with quantification and recording of Indian water rights. It must be assumed that disagreements will arise between Indians and non-Indians over the priority dates and quantities of Indian water rights. Settlement of such disputes, whether actual or potential, requires action by some tribunal, and the question arises, what tribunal? Candidates for the nomination include (1) the State tribunals, employing State procedures, (2) existing Federal courts, or (3) a Federal tribunal especially created for the purpose. Even a Federal administrative agency could be designated as the initial forum, but judicial review would be required because of the many issues of law presented by Indian water rights litigation.

The present law is somewhat uncertain on the adjudication of Indian water rights. It is clear that the United States can initiate litigation in Federal district courts on behalf of Indians to adjudicate Indian water rights (as was done in the *Winters* case), and can intervene in other litigation for that purpose (as was done in *Arizona v. California*). It also seems highly probable, although there is no Supreme Court authority squarely on the question, that Indian tribes can themselves initiate litigation in Federal district court to adjudicate their water rights. What is less clear is whether non-Indian water users and State officials (or the States themselves) can sue the United States and the Indian tribes as defendants to obtain a water rights adjudication. The issue turns on the interpretation of the McCarran Amendment,[12] waiving sovereign immunity of the United States in certain water right adjudications. The only Supreme Court cases construing the McCarran Amendment, the *Eagle County*[13] and *Water Division No. 5*[14] cases, did not involve Indian water rights. With the law in this state of uncertainty, the Commission believes that new, clarifying legislation is desirable.

Recommendation No. 14-4: Jurisdiction of all actions affecting Indian water rights should be in the U.S. District Court for the district or districts in which lie the Indian Reservation and the water body to be adjudicated. Indian tribes may initiate such action and the United States and affected Indian tribes may

---

[12] *McCarran Water Rights Suits Act*, P.L. 495, Section 20 July 10, 1952, 82d Congress, 66 Stat. 549, 560, 43 USC 666.

[13] *United States v. District Court of Eagle County*, 401 U.S. 520 (1971).

[14] *United States v. District Court for Water Division No.* 401 U.S. 527 (1971).

be joined as parties in any such action. The jurisdiction of the Federal district court in such actions should be exclusive, except where Article III of the Constitution grants jurisdiction to the U.S. Supreme Court. In such actions, the United States should represent the Indian tribes whose water rights are in issue, unless the tribe itself becomes a party to the action and requests permission to represent itself. Any State in which the Reservation lies and any State having water users that might be affected by an Indian water rights adjudication may initiate an adjudication and may intervene in an adjudication commenced by others, including adjudications initiated by the United States and by Indian tribes. Upon such appearance by the State, the State may move to represent its non-Indian water users *parens patriae,* and the motion should be granted except as to non-Indian water users as to whom the State has a conflict of interest.

Discussion — Because of potential conflict between Indian and non-Indian water users and to avoid the suspicion of bias that might attend adjudication by elected State officials, the Commission recommends that Indian water rights be adjudicated in Federal court, the traditional forum for this kind of litigation. An effort should be made to simplify the litigation when numerous water users are affected, by allowing the State to represent them *parens patriae.* A final decree would be binding on all affected users in the State and the water supply would be administered in accordance with State-created priorities for non-Indians and the Federal adjudication of the Indian water rights. In effect, the Federal adjudication would be a supplementary adjudication for determining the amount of water available to the Indian Reservation and its place on the list of priorities.

A third alternative forum, in addition to State tribunals and Federal district courts, was also considered by the Commission. Several spokesmen for Indian interests suggested that a special Federal court be created for adjudicating Indian water claims. The advantages of specialized knowledge and more expeditious disposition of lawsuits were claimed to outweigh the disadvantages of increased litigation costs and the special court's lack of knowledge of local conditions. The Commission has been reluctant to recommend the creation of a special Federal court to adjudicate all Indian water rights. In the first place, not enough evidence now exists that such a court would keep occupied. While there are a large number of Indian Reservations with rights that have not yet been adjudicated, it is not clear that either Indians or non-Indians are about to launch litigation on all of

them, or even on a significant number. Until an adjudication is necessary to establish the supply available for further Indian or non-Indian development, or until an Indian or non-Indian use interferes with an existing use by the other, an adjudication may cost more than it is worth and hence will be avoided. If it should develop that Federal district courts are unduly burdened by Indian water rights cases, or that they are ill-adapted to adjudicate them, further attention can then be given to the establishment of a special court. For the present, the suggestion seems premature.

One further reason for establishing a special court has been advanced: the inability under existing law of *any* court other than the U.S. Supreme Court to adjudicate interstate stream disputes. No court in the Nation, short of the Supreme Court when States and the United States are parties, has power to adjudicate rights along a river in two or more States. State courts lack power to act outside of State boundaries; Federal district courts now lack the jurisdiction to do so, though they could be given it by Congress. These impediments to interstate stream adjudications have existed since the formation of the Union, and they have forced into the Supreme Court some troublesome litigation that might better have been handled in Federal district courts. But the Commission has insufficient evidence that interstate Indian water rights controversies are sufficiently numerous and incapable of settlement by other means to recommend either that jurisdiction of Federal district courts be extended or that a special Federal court be granted interstate jurisdiction.

Indian Water Rights Not Yet Utilized

Most Indian water rights have not yet been adjudicated and therefore the dates of the rights and their quantities are not yet fixed in judicial decrees. Even where the rights have been judicially determined, as in *Arizona v. California*, not all of the water set aside for Reservations has been put to use at the present time. As time goes on, increased utilization of the water reserved for Indians may be expected to occur, and as a result the water supply of some existing non-Indian projects is likely to be decreased. The injuries resulting from this collision between Indian and non-Indian uses may be mitigated in some instances by improved water practices in the affected projects,[15] but in other cases conflict will be unavoidable as demand for water will exceed the supply.

[15] See, for example, *Pyramid Lake Paiute Tribe v. Morton,* 4 E.R.C. 1714 (D.D.C. November 9, 1972).

This problem gives the Commission great concern and will become of increasing concern to the Nation. The Indians unquestionably should be encouraged to make use of water that is legally as well as morally theirs. Moreover the United States should offer financial assistance to Indian tribes which lack the funds to make economic use of their water. At the same time, efforts should be made to cushion the shock of those who have over decades made large investments in irrigation and municipal water supply and who accordingly have quite legitimate expectations of legal protection. In considering what advice to give the President and the Congress on the conflict between these two just causes, the Commission has explored three alternatives: (1) that nothing at all be done, leaving the situation as it now stands; (2) that the United States make a standing offer to acquire, in whole or in part, Indian water rights in fully appropriated streams, at the sole option of the Indian owners; or (3) that non-Indian users injured by subsequent Indian water development be compensated for the losses suffered. None of the alternatives is wholly satisfactory, but on balance the Commission has concluded that a combination of the second and third alternatives provides the greatest hope for a solution.

No Action: A recommendation that nothing be done might have the advantage of not stirring up trouble, although the growing awareness by the Indian tribes of the existence and value of their water rights makes this doubtful. It would also save the Federal Treasury some money, although the economy would be likely to suffer. But such a recommendation has the weakness of failing to face up to existing problems that almost certainly will become more pressing in the next 20 years. The costs of inaction are possible deprivation of benefits that rightly belong to Indian tribes, and more generally the social losses from impaired planning and deterred investment in both Indian and non-Indian uses on streams not fully appropriated and the disruption of existing uses on fully appropriated streams when presently unused Indian rights are subsequently utilized. Because of the concern of both Indians and non-Indians, the Commission believes that a do-nothing recommendation is an abdication of responsibility.

Standing Offer to Acquire Unused Indian Water Rights in Fully Appropriated Streams: A second alternative is for the United States to offer to acquire unused Indian water rights in fully appropriated streams, that is, in streams all of whose waters are being put to beneficial use. The Commission starts with the proposition that such acquisition must be made with the consent of the Indian water rights holders; eminent domain should not be employed as a tool to extinguish unused Indian water rights, for the promise to the Indians that there would be water available to the Reservation ought to be honored in kind if that is the Indians' desire.[16]

If, on the other hand, an Indian tribe should desire to lease some or all of its water, procedures should be established to make this possible. The Commission recommends that on fully appropriated streams the United States make a continuing, binding offer to lease any interest in Indian water that Indians care to tender, at a price fixed by fair market value for the interest tendered. Thus, Indians would have choices ranging from long-term leases of their water rights to the lease of their water from year to year under contracts renewable at the option of the Indians. No time limit should be placed on the right of the Indians to lease and the duty of the Federal Government to accept the offer, for the Indians should not be forced into untimely decisions on questions of great importance to them. Since the purpose of this recommendation is to reduce the conflict between potential Indian uses and existing non-Indian uses, it would apply to fully appropriated streams only. If there is unappropriated water available, the Indian use would not impair non-Indian uses, and *vice versa*.

Where an Indian tribe leases water to the United States, the Commission recommends that the lease payments be charged to those non-Indian users who had actual notice, or whose predecessors in title had actual notice of the prior Indian rights at the time they commenced their use. However, the Commission would not charge such lease payments to non-Indian water users who had no notice of the superior Indian water rights. As to such users, the Commission believes the United States itself should assume financial responsibility for the lease payments.

It is unnecessary and inadvisable to provide for quantification of all Indian water rights as a prerequisite to the operation of this lease arrangement. On many Indian Reservations there will be no desire to lease any water; on others, the quantity of the Indian entitlement will not be in dispute; and on still others

---

[16] An exception would be the taking by eminent domain of land and water incidental to the exercise by the United States of a sovereign power for a public purpose; for example, the construction of a flood control project, or public highway.

the quantity can be established by negotiation. Thus, to provide for mandatory quantification is wasteful of resources. Moreover, binding quantification must be accomplished by judicial action, for the priority and amount of Indian water rights present questions of law. Neither Congress nor an administrative agency can now declare the extent of Indian water rights, for those rights vested in the Indian tribes when the Reservations were established. Hence, rather than providing for blanket adjudication of Indian water rights, at great cost and for no purpose in many instances, the Commission recommends adjudications only when there is a genuine controversy. Procedures for such adjudications were set forth heretofore in Recommendation No. 14-4.

Recommendation No. 14-5: Congress should make available financial assistance to Indian tribes which lack the funds to make economic use of their water to permit them to make economic use of it. In addition, Congress should enact legislation providing that on fully appropriated streams the United States shall make a standing offer of indefinite duration to Indian tribes to lease for periods not to exceed 50 years any water or water rights tendered by the Indian owners at the fair market value of the interest tendered.

Compensation of Non-Indian Users

The preceding recommendation helps to solve the clash between Indian claims and earlier initiated non-Indian uses when Indians are prepared to accept the offer of the United States to acquire Indian water. But the problem still remains when the Indians wish to make use of their water and the use will impair a non-Indian use earlier in time though later in legal priority. In such cases, the Commission recommends that the United States provide a substitute water supply for the non-Indians users, or, if that is not feasible, compensate them for the impairment of existing values, unless the non-Indian users had notice of the Indian water rights at the time they commenced the development and had reason to believe that the water supply would be inadequate to serve both Indian and non-Indian uses.

For those who have made investments and are presently making use of water subject to divestment by the exercise of Indian rights, the provision of substitute water or the payment of compensation can be justified on the grounds of fairness. It has been the historic policy of the Federal Government to encourage development of water resources by others, even

though the supply was subject to Indian rights. For example, the United States entered into a contract with the Metropolitan Water District of Southern California in 1933 for the construction and operation of Parker Dam as the diversion point for the Colorado River Aqueduct, which was built by the District with a capacity of 1.3 million acre-feet per year at a cost to the District in excess of $200 million. The Parker Dam Project was authorized and the delivery contract confirmed by Congress in 1935.[17] At that time, as Congress knew well, a number of Indian Reservations had water rights in the mainstream of the Colorado River in an amount not yet quantified but with priority dates much earlier than the Aqueduct's. Those claims were later quantified at approximately 1 million acre-feet in *Arizona v. California* and if the water is ever fully utilized by the Indians, the supply for the Aqueduct will be substantially diminished. The Commission believes it is unfair to deprive users of their water supply without compensation when Congress has supported investments in projects whose supply was subject to unused Indian rights.

Not all water users subject to divestment by the exercise of Indian water rights are beneficiaries of Federal projects, but the Commission believes that these users should receive protection too. The Federal Government led the way in developing the West for non-Indian beneficiaries, and if private investors and State and local governments followed, the protection afforded Federal beneficiaries should be accorded to the others. The Federal Government was the trustee for the Indians and their water rights, yet by its actions in developing its own projects on streams subject to Indian claims it was indicating that such development was proper and that such investments would be secure. If that representation turns out to be wrong, those who suffer injury should receive protection whether or not they take their water from a Federal project.

It cannot be persuasively argued that in every development since 1908 investors have had adequate notice of the superior Indian water rights merely because of the decision in the *Winters* case. That decision gave little indication of the magnitude of Indian claims, and the quantity awarded in other cases thereafter remained relatively small until *Arizona v. California* adopted the irrigable acreage formula in 1963. Even that decision is not dispositive; the Court did not hold that the irrigable acreage formula is required as a matter of law, and it did not

---

[17]*Act of August 30, 1935*, P.L. 409, Section 2, 74th Congress, 49 Stat. 1028, 1039.

Main irrigation canal under construction on Colorado River Reservation in Arizona

set forth any standards for determining how much acreage is irrigable. In light of these circumstances, it cannot be fairly said that in the absence of a special showing of actual notice of conflicting Indian water rights non-Indian investors in water projects proceeded at their own risk before *Arizona v. California*.

There is precedent for the Federal Government assuming the financial responsibility for disruption occasioned by the implementation of Federal policies and programs. Section 202 of the Colorado River Basin Project Act declared the necessity of meeting the requirements of the U.S.-Mexican Water Treaty to be a national obligation to be satisfied by the nonreimbursable Federal importation of water into the basin rather than by reduction of the water rights

of existing users. The Commission endorses th approach and recommends that the cost of providir a substitute supply or paying compensation to no Indian users whose supply is impaired be treated nonreimbursable—a general obligation of the Natic as a whole—and not be charged to the Indian projec

Recommendation No. 14-6: Congress should ena legislation providing that whenever the constructi and operation of a water resource project on Indian Reservation shall take, destroy, or impair a water right valid under State law to the diversio storage, or use of water off the Reservation, whi right was initiated prior to the date of the decision *Arizona v. California* (June 3, 1963), the Unit

tates shall provide a substitute water supply or pay
st compensation to the owner of such right;
rovided, however, that:

   such owner shall not be entitled to a substitute
   supply or to compensation if prior to development of his right he had actual notice of
   conflicting Indian water rights claims that would
   render the water supply inadequate to serve the
   diversion requirements of himself and the Indian
   Reservation, and

   compensation shall not include values created by
   subsidies granted by the United States to such
   owner.

The cost of such compensation shall be recognized
 a prior national obligation and shall not be
imbursable by the beneficiaries of water resource
ojects on Indian reservations.

CONCLUSIONS

The Commission concludes that there is increasing
nger of conflict between Indian and non-Indian
es of water. The problem arises from the fact that
any non-Indian water resource projects rely on
pplies in which Indians have water rights with
rlier priorities. Indians wish to make use of their
ater, and the Commission, recognizing the legiti-
acy of this desire, believes that the Secretary of the
terior should conduct studies of the natural and
man resources available on Indian Reservations in
operation with the Indians for the purpose of
veloping plans for the utilization of the resources.
 the same time, it is important to obtain a
antification of existing uses on Indian Reservations
d to provide procedures for adjudicating Indian
hts to make new uses. These quantifications should
   filed for information purposes with the State
thorities who maintain records of non-Indian uses
thin the State, but such filings should not subject
dian water uses to State laws or State regulation.
ile adjudications are not necessary for all Indian

Reservations at this time, no new Federal water
resource project should go forward until an adjudication is had of Indian water rights that might
substantially affect the project's water supply.

The forum for adjudicating Indian water rights has
received the Commission's attention. At one time the
Commission proposed to adjudicate Indian water
rights in State tribunals according to State procedures
with an appeal to the Federal circuit court of appeals.
The Indian tribes objected to the proposal because of
controversies stretching back over the years between
State officials and Indians over water rights. It
seemed preferable, therefore, to place the litigation in
the Federal courts, the traditional forum for determining Indian water rights.

The most intractable problem the Commission
faced is the conflict between existing non-Indian uses
and newly initiated Indian withdrawals. While the
Indians often have legal superiority to make use of
water, a later initiated Indian use often would disrupt
preexisting non-Indian uses representing large Federal, State, and private investments. One means of
ameliorating the conflict is to provide for the Federal
Government to lease Indian water and water
rights in fully appropriated streams when the Indians
are of a mind to sell, but condemnation of unused
Indian water rights is not an acceptable solution to
the problem when Indians do not wish to sell. In that
event, the Commission recommends that a substitute
water supply be provided, or if that is not feasible
that compensation be granted to non-Indian water
rights holders whose supply is impaired by future
Indian development. This protection would be
afforded only for development undertaken before the
decision in *Arizona v. California* (June 3, 1963) and
in the absence of actual advance knowledge of the
existence of conflicting Indian water rights imperiling
the water supply of the non-Indian development. The
costs of the compensation would be a national
obligation not chargeable to Indian projects and the
compensation would not include those values generated by Federal subsidies to the non-Indian users.

Paying the Costs of Water Development Projects[1]

In this chapter the Commission deals with the subject of how the costs of water development projects are shared among various levels of government and the direct and indirect beneficiaries of the project.

Policies for cost-sharing are separate from, although closely related to, policies of economic valuation. The question of whether a project should be developed is not the same as the question of who should pay for it if it is developed. However, the question of who pays for a project will often determine the enthusiasm with which the project is supported and the prospects for its authorization.

Present policies governing Federal and non-Federal cost-sharing arrangements in the water resources field have been established over a long period of time by unrelated congressional actions on particular projects and programs and by similarly uncoordinated administrative determinations. As a result, these policies are now inconsistent among programs, among purposes, and among agencies. The situation causes widespread confusion, results in distorted development, encourages local interests to "shop around" among agencies to get the most favorable arrangement, and results in deviations from principles of equity which require that beneficiaries should bear an appropriate share of project costs.

The Commission believes that most past decisions on cost-sharing policies were wisely made given the circumstances of the time. However, circumstances have changed. The urgencies of such goals as developing the West and recovery from the Great Depression are no longer present. New national concerns, such as protection of the environment, are increasingly im-

The users of recreational facilities at irrigation project reservoirs should pay their appropriate share of the costs

portant. Furthermore, the Nation's water resources are now more highly used and the demands on them are so great that they are becoming increasingly valuable. New cost-sharing policies are needed to encourage improved management of water and related resources and to increase fairness in the distribution of financial burdens. Water shortages expected in the future will create an insistent demand that the users of water and water-related services pay in full for the benefits they receive.

The need for reform of cost-sharing policies has long been recognized, but numerous attempts by interdepartmental committees, most recently under sponsorship of the Water Resources Council, have met with little success. The supporters and beneficiaries of project construction, quite understandably, have resisted proposals for higher non-Federal shares as a threat to development programs and, in the case of beneficiaries, to their pocketbooks.

Reform of cost-sharing policies will require extensive attention by the Congress. The Commission believes the following analysis of present cost-sharing policies and of the principles which should be considered and its specific recommendations for reform will aid congressional consideration of the subject.

PRESENT FEDERAL COST-SHARING POLICIES

Present cost-sharing policies have been developed by the Congress and by administrative decisions. The Congress establishes general policy in two ways. The

[1] Background for this chapter is contained in a report prepared for the National Water Commission by the National Bureau of Standards: MARSHALL, Harold E & BROUSSALIAN, VL (January 1972). Federal Cost-Sharing Policies for Water Resources. National Technical Information Service, Springfield, Va., Accession No. PB 208 304.

first is through formal statements of cost-sharing policy contained in legislative acts covering broad programs such as flood control and water quality control. The second way is by Congress repeatedly authorizing Federal agencies to carry out specific programs or activities, and including cost-sharing arrangements in the authorizations. When this is done consistently over a period of time, it is usually considered that a firm congressional policy has thus been established.

Federal cost-sharing policies affect the "construction" agencies – the U.S. Army Corps of Engineers (Corps), the U.S. Bureau of Reclamation (Bureau), and the U.S. Soil Conservation Services (SCS) – and the "grant" agencies which help finance non-Federal water projects.[2]

In comparing the construction agencies with the Federal grant agencies, it may be observed that whereas the different construction agencies frequently have common developmental objectives, such as providing flood protection, recreation, or water supply benefits, the grant agencies are each charged with a different objective. The Environmental Protection Agency (EPA), for example, is a grant agency concerned with environmental improvement. The U.S. Department of Housing and Urban Development (HUD) furthers improved community development. The Farmers Home Administration (FHA) in the U.S. Department of Argiculture seeks development of rural areas. The Economic Development Administration (EDA) is the U.S. Department of Commerce attempts to increase incomes in depressed areas. Each grant agency pursues its independent objective, sometimes through programs of financial aid for provision of water and sewer services.

Since cost-sharing policy should be viewed as a means for accomplishing national objectives, one would expect consistent cost-sharing rules among the construction agencies dealing with the same purposes but not necessarily among the grant agencies. In fact, cost-sharing policies are inconsistent among both construction and grant agencies. The following discussion describes these cost-sharing policies by water development purposes.

Cost-Sharing for Waterway Navigation and Harbors

The Federal government generally bears all costs of constructing, operating, and maintaining waterway and channels for navigation purposes, including reservoir storage necessary to maintain minimum flow for navigation. Non-Federal interests provide necessary land, easements, and rights-of-way plus public terminals and port facilities and in some instances share in the construction costs in accordance with special or local benefits received.[3] Neither user charges nor tolls are collected for use of the improved harbor or waterway except on the St. Lawrence Seaway[4] and the Panama Canal.[5]

In a few instances, Congress has specifically authorized Federal funds for non-Federal projects providing navigation benefits.

Cost-Sharing for Irrigation

The general policy calls for project construction costs allocated to irrigation on Federal reclamation projects to be repaid without interest during 50-year period. However, under Section 9 the Reclamation Project Act of 1939,[6] and other legislation revenues from hydroelectric power and from other

---

[2] Technically, the SCS program is a grant program because construction is supposed to be contracted by local watershed organizations. The projects are usually designed and supervised by SCS personnel, and local organizations may request SCS to award the contracts for project construction. See 16 USCA 1005(2).

[3] Under the provisions of Section 2 of the River and Harbor Act of 1920 (P.L. 263, 66th Congress, 2d Session, June 5, 1920, 41 Stat. 1009, 1010, 33 USCA 547), the U.S. Army Corps of Engineers is required to include a statement in its reports on proposed navigation projects of the special or local benefits anticipated from the project and recommendations as to the local cooperation that should be required as a result of those benefits. During the Commission's New Orleans conference on the review draft of this report, the Executive Director of the Port of Houston Authority explained how the city had financed half the initial cost of the Houston Ship Channel in 1912. Similar

cost-sharing requirements were placed on the Port of Portland, Oregon, for the initial opening of the deepwater channel in the Columbia and Willamette Rivers from Portland to the sea early in the 20th century. More recently, efforts of the Corps of Engineers to require 5 percent cost-sharing on the deepening of the channel in the Delaware River above Philadelphia were rebuffed by the Congress. See House Document 358, 83rd Congress, and hearings on H.R. 9859, 83rd Congress, 2d Session, which became the River and Harbor Act of September 3, 195 P.L. 780, 83rd Congress.

[4] *Act of May 13, 1954*, P.L. 358, Sec. 12, 83rd Congress, Stat. 92, 96-97, as amended, 33 USCA 988.

[5] *Act of July 5, 1884*, c. 229, Sec. 4, 48th Congress, Session, 23 Stat. 133, 147, as amended, 33 USCA 5.

[6] P.L. 260, 76th Congress, 1st Session, August 4, 1939, Stat. 1187, 1193-1196, as amended, 43 USCA 485h.

ater users have been applied to repayment of the construction costs for irrigation facilities where irrigators do not have the ability to repay the interest-free irrigation cost allocation. Repayment of interest-free construction costs allocated to irrigation for all authorized projects is currently estimated to be about 0 percent from power revenues.[7] On many projects the irrigation water users will actually repay only about 10 to 15 percent of the total allocated irrigation construction costs, including interest. There has also been criticism that some of the allocations of multipurpose project costs to nonreimbursable features have been excessive and, therefore, some of the allocations to irrigation are unjustifiably low.[8]

The proportion of allocated irrigation construction costs designated for repayment by irrigators, on the basis of their capacity to pay, varies greatly among projects and project units. Among 21 units in the Missouri Basin Project, the proportion of allocated irrigation costs designated for repayment without interest ranged from zero to 72 percent.[9] In only two project units were irrigators designated to pay more than 40 percent of allocated construction costs.

Operation and maintenance costs are assessed against the irrigation districts served, except for irrigation water delivered under utility-type contracts where delivery prices include both repayment of construction costs, and operation and maintenance costs.

Irrigation cost-sharing policy for Soil Conservation Service small watershed projects (so-called P.L. 566 projects)[10] requires that non-Federal interests assume operation and maintenance costs and pay one-half of the allocated installation costs. Local interests may obtain interest-bearing loans for this purpose from the Farmers Home Administration.

On irrigation projects built by the Corps of Engineers in the Eastern States, cost-sharing policy varies from project to project, with the irrigators generally paying about half of the construction costs allocated to irrigation.[11]

Cost-Sharing for Flood Control

Flood control cost-sharing varies with the types of facilities constructed. With respect to major reservoirs, costs of flood control, including operation and maintenance, are borne entirely by the Federal Government.[12] With respect to minor reservoirs, the policy is the same except that the Corps of Engineers may recommend that non-Federal interests be required to provide land, easements, and rights-of-way if the reservoir is clearly in lieu of a local protection project.

The policy for local protection projects, including levees, flood walls, and channel improvements, requires non-Federal interests to provide land, easements, and rights-of-way, and to operate and maintain the projects after completion, except for a few projects authorized in the 1938 Flood Control Act or as a part of the Mississippi River and Tributaries Project. The non-Federal cost shares of these local protection projects average 20 percent of installation costs but have varied from 1 to 60 percent.

Hurricane protection projects under Corps policy require at least 30 percent local cost-sharing for construction and local assumption of all project operation costs. The policy for beach erosion control projects, protecting nonfederally owned shoreline, is for the Federal Government to assume up to 70 percent of construction costs depending on the degree of public ownership and public use. Protection of private property without public access receives no cost-sharing assistance. Operation, maintenance, and land rights costs are borne by non-Federal entities.

Under the P.L. 566 program, the Soil Conservation Service pays all construction costs allocated to flood control. Non-Federal interests provide land, easements, and rights-of-way, and operate and maintain the projects after completion.

In a few instances specifically authorized by Congress, Federal funds have been provided for State and local flood control projects in amounts not to exceed what the Federal flood control cost share would have been in a similar Federal project.

[7] U.S. BUREAU OF RECLAMATION (1969). Summary Report of the Commissioner, Statistical Appendix. U.S. Government Printing Office, Washington, D.C. Part II, p. 78.

[8] HOGAN, Harry (1972). The Acreage Limitation in the Federal Reclamation Program, prepared for the National Water Commission. National Technical Information Service, Springfield, Va., Accession No. PB 211 840. p. 231.

U.S. BUREAU OF RECLAMATION (1970). Summary Report of the Commissioner, Statistical and Financial Appendix. U.S. Government Printing Office, Washington, D.C. Part IV, pp. 159-227.

Watershed Protection and Flood Prevention Act of 1954, P.L. 566, 83rd Congress, August 4, 1954, 68 Stat. 666, as amended, 16 USCA 1001 et seq.

[11] For an example of how this is computed, see Chapter 5, Section C.

[12] Flood Control Act of 1938, P.L. 761, 75th Congress, June 28, 1938, 52 Stat. 1215, 33 USCA 701c-1.

Cost-Sharing for Drainage

Under Federal flood control acts,[13] the Corps of Engineers may undertake channelization of major tributaries providing outlets for non-Federal drainage enterprises. Administrative policy is to recommend that non-Federal interests assume one-half the costs allocated to land enhancement (increase in market value). Congress accepted these Corps recommendations for the Central and Southern Florida projects but in other cases it has not, particularly for Corps projects in the lower Mississippi Valley.

The SCS under the P.L. 566 program provides drainage for lands in agricultural production. Non-Federal interests are required to provide land, easements, and rights-of-way, and to bear up to 50 percent of the installation and operation and maintenance costs. No Federal cost-sharing assistance is provided for drainage in urban areas except as drainage conditions may be ameliorated by urban flood control projects.

Cost-Sharing for Hydroelectric Projects

Electric power generated by Corps of Engineers or Bureau of Reclamation projects is generally sold at prices sufficient to recover all project costs allocated to power, including interest. The power is generally marketed by agencies of the U.S. Department of the Interior. In several Western river basins that include both hydropower and irrigation water projects, consolidated "basin accounts" are used. On Federal Reclamation Projects power revenues in excess of those needed to repay costs allocated to power with interest are used to repay interest free costs allocated to irrigation. In many projects, power users have benefited from generous amounts of joint costs allocated to nonreimbursable purposes such as flood control or navigation.

The consolidated financial plan of the Bonneville Power Administration permits the use of revenues from older projects on which all reimbursable power costs have been paid, to pay power costs of new projects as well as some of the costs allocated to irrigation. The plan provides for paying all of the system power costs within 50 years after the last powerplant is completed.

Electric power produced by the Tennessee Valley Authority (TVA) is marketed by TVA. TVA now operates under a system of self-financing with respect to power production. It is required to repay to the Treasury from net power revenues the Federal investment in power facilities which earlier had been appropriated by Congress, plus a return on that investment. In addition, TVA pays approximately $25 million annually to State and local governments in lieu of taxes.

There is some dispute that the interest rate used for repayment of the Federal investment in hydroelectric facilities is artificially low, although in recent years it has been increased. Also, to the extent that most Federal power projects do not pay taxes, it is said that power consumers' rates do not cover all "costs." On the other hand, to the extent that power rates must cover some irrigation subsidies and to the extent that unrealistically short amortization periods are assigned to some Federal power facilities, power rates are higher than they might otherwise be.

Cost-Sharing for Recreation

The Federal Water Project Recreation Act of 1965[14] was intended to encourage the States and other non-Federal public entities to assume responsibility for the development of recreation potential created by Federal reservoirs. For any particular Federal water project, the responsible Federal agency is authorized to bear 50 percent of the "separable cost of providing recreational facilities and to make available Federal lands for the use of non-Federal entities agreeing to operate and maintain the facilities. All "joint" costs allocable to recreation are borne entirely by the Federal Government.[15]

Only a few non-Federal entities have taken advantage of the terms of the Act. If non-Federal interests do not accept responsibility for recreation development, the responsible Federal agency must bear the cost of developing "minimum facilities that are required for the public health and safety" and that are accessible by roads previously in existence or otherwise necessary for project construction. In certain cases, the Federal Government may bear the full cost of developing, operating, and maintaining reservoir recreation areas that are designated by the Congress as "National Recreation Areas."

The SCS assists non-Federal entities to develop recreation potentials created by P.L. 566 reservoirs and bears 50 percent of the construction cost thereof including land rights.

---

[13] *Flood Control Act of 1944,* P.L. 534, 78th Congress, 2d Session, December 22, 1944, Section 2, 58 Stat. 887, 889, 33 USCA 701a-1.

[14] *Federal Water Project Recreation Act of 1965,* P.L. 89-7 July 9, 1965, 79 Stat. 213, as amended, 16 USCA 460 *l-1 et seq.*

[15] See Glossary for definition of separable and joint costs.

At flood control and navigation projects other than reservoir projects the Corps encourages non-Federal development of recreation potentials by leasing lands without charge and by paying up to 50 percent of development costs if a non-Federal entity will agree to operate and maintain the development.

In the case of small boat harbor projects, the Corps requires non-Federal interests to (1) make cash contributions equal to 50 percent of those harbor costs allocable to recreation and (2) provide lands, easements, rights-of-way, spoil disposal areas, and onshore facilities.

Cost-Sharing for Fish and Wildlife Protection and Improvement

The cost of measures for preventing or offsetting damages to fish and wildlife under the Fish and Wildlife Coordination Act[16] are allocated to the various purposes served by a project and shared in by the Federal Government and others in accordance with the cost-sharing policies applicable to those respective purposes.

If costs are incurred to *improve* the fish and wildlife resource over what it would otherwise be without the project, and if the basic purpose of including measures for improvement is to create recreational benefits, the cost-sharing policy applied to these costs is that established by the Federal Water Project Recreation Act described above (i.e., the Federal Government pays 50 percent of separable costs and 100 percent of joint costs allocable to recreation).

The costs of those fish and wildlife facilities that remain under Federal administration, such as a national fish hatchery provided in connection with a Federal water project or a national wildlife refuge, are borne entirely by the Federal Government.

Cost-Sharing for Municipal and Industrial Water Supply

Both the Bureau of Reclamation and the U.S. Army Corps of Engineers may include storage capacity in reservoirs to make water available for municipal and industrial use. All the construction costs of storage for present or anticipated future demand must be repaid, with interest, by State or local interests. No payment for the costs of storage for future supply need be made until the supply is first used. An interest-free period of up to 10 years is

allowed on the costs of storage for future supply so long as that supply is not used. No more than 30 percent of the costs of the project may be allocated to storage for future supply.[17]

Capacity for water supply may also be included in reservoirs constructed under the P.L. 566 program of SCS. Non-Federal interests must repay all the costs of storage for future supply and at least one-half the costs of storage for present supply needs. Provision is made for postponement of the payment of the costs of storage for future supply and for an interest-free period of up to 10 years as above.[18]

The grant agencies also provide Federal cost-sharing for storage and conveyance of municipal and industrial water. HUD and FHA provide up to 50 percent of construction and land rights costs. EDA may supplement other grants up to a maximum of 80 percent of construction costs. Operation and maintenance, however, is a non-Federal responsibility under municipal and industrial water supply programs.

Cost-Sharing for Wastewater Collection

The grant agencies provide Federal cost-sharing for sewage collection projects. HUD may grant up to 50 percent of wastewater collection project costs or, under need criteria, up to 90 percent for communities of less than 10,000 people. FHA, limited to rural communities under 10,000 people, may grant up to 50 percent of sewage collection project costs. EDA may supplement other grants up to 80 percent (100 percent for Indians) in areas qualifying for economic development assistance.[19]

Cost-Sharing for Interceptor Sewers and Sewage Treatment Plants

The same policies that apply to HUD, FHA, and EDA for wastewater collection also apply for inter-

---

[16] *Fish and Wildlife Coordination Act,* P.L. 85-624, August 12, 1958, 72 Stat. 563, as amended, 16 USCA 661 *et seq.*

[17] *Water Supply Act of 1958,* P.L. 85-500, Title III, July 3, 1958, 72 Stat. 297, 319, as amended, 43 USCA 390b.

[18] *Rural Development Act of 1972,* P.L. 92-419, August 30, 1972, Sec. 201(f), 86 Stat. 657, 668 (amending the Watershed Protection and Flood Prevention Act of 1954), 16 USCA 1004.

[19] Under the Urban Growth and New Community Development Act of 1970, "new community assistance projects" including water and sewer facilities may receive 20 percent construction grants up to a total of 80 percent for all Federal funds. *Urban Growth and New Community Development Act of 1970,* P.L. 91-609, December 31, 1970, Sec. 781, 84 Stat. 1770, 1799, as amended, 45 USCA 4519.

ceptor sewers and sewage treatment. In addition, the Environmental Protection Agency (EPA) provides grants for up to 75 percent of such project cost.

Cost-Sharing for Water Quality Enhancement

Section 2 of the Federal Water Pollution Control Act Amendments of 1961[20] authorized the inclusion in Federal reservoirs of capacity to store water for release at times of low flow to improve water quality. The 1961 Act provided that the Federal Government shall pay all the costs of such additional storage where the benefits are "widespread or national in scope." The practical effect has been to provide for flow augmentation entirely at Federal expense. Congress has approved inclusion of this capacity in a few Corps of Engineers projects. It has disapproved inclusion of similar capacity in Bureau of Reclamation reservoirs. Authority was recently granted by amendments[21] to P.L. 566 for inclusion of similar capacity in SCS reservoirs under cost-sharing policies to be consistent with those adopted by the Water Resources Council.[22]

Maximum percentages for Federal cost shares are summarized in Tables 15-1 and 15-2.

APPRAISAL OF PRESENT COST-SHARING POLICIES

Planning a Federal or federally assisted water project involving cost-sharing sometimes leads to negotiations between the Federal and non-Federal interests over the kind of project, size of project, and the mix of project services. A loss in net benefits may result if, because of cost-sharing policies, non-Federal interests negotiate for an inferior project, but one that is desirable from a local financial standpoint. For example, the least-cost means of providing flood protection for a community may be a levee system. But, because local cost-sharing is required for levees

but not for reservoirs, the community may reje[ct] levees and bargain in favor of a more costly lar[ge] reservoir which provides the same protection.

Likewise, the least-cost means of irrigating a tra[ct] of land might call for a system of pumps an[d] sprinkler irrigation with high operating costs. Becau[se] Reclamation law provides a subsidy only for capit[al] costs and not operating expenses, the irrigators ma[y] select a high capital cost, water wasteful, gravi[ty] flow, flood irrigation system which has low operati[ng] expense.

Cost-sharing policies should provide incentives f[or] Federal and non-Federal interests to agree on projec[ts] that will be most desirable for both the Nation an[d] the local area. This does not imply that there is [a] single percentage of cost-sharing that will be suitab[le] in all circumstances. But, there is need to refor[m] cost-sharing policies to provide consistent incentiv[es] for bargaining to achieve selection of the mo[st] desirable projects from both national and loc[al] viewpoints. Present cost-sharing policies provi[de] inconsistent incentives in several major respec[ts:] (1) They are inconsistent among means. For exampl[e,] alternative means of achieving a particular purpo[se] such as flood reduction. (2) Policies differ amo[ng] agencies for similar purposes. (3) Policies diff[er] among purposes. (4) Policies for repayment of no[n-] Federal cost shares are not consistent among t[he] several major water development purposes.

Inconsistency Among Means

Present cost-sharing policies require different c[ost] shares for different means of accomplishing the sam[e] objectives. For example, an analysis of *local annu[al]* cost shares for 31 Corps of Engineers local flo[od] protection projects authorized in the 1968 Flo[od] Control Act revealed wide ranges both within an[d] among different means of flood control: For chann[el] improvements, the local cost share varied from 7[.?] percent to 54.3 percent; for diversion channels, 9[.?] percent to 53.7 percent; for levees, zero to 49[.?] percent; for small reservoirs, 33.9 percent to 42[.?] percent; and for one conduit project, 8.2 percent. Wide variation of cost shares within a particu[lar] means results from varying costs of land rights a[nd] other local contributions. A study of 462 Corps lo[cal]

[20] P.L. 87-88, July 20, 1961, 75 Stat. 204-205. Section 102(b) of the Federal Water Pollution Control Act Amendments of 1972, P.L. 92-500, Oct. 18, 1972, 86 Stat. 816, 817, contains similar provisions for storage capacity for water quality control.

[21] *Rural Development Act of 1972*, P.L. 92-419, August 30, 1972, Sec. 201(e), 86 Stat. 657, 668, 16 USCA 1004.

[22] The Water Resources Council has proposed that cost of reservoir capacity for low flow augmentation for water quality improvement should be shared on a matching basis. U.S. WATER RESOURCES COUNCIL (1971). Proposed principles and standards for planning water and related land resources. Federal Register 36(245):24144-24194, Part II. December 21, 1971.

[23] MARSHALL, Harold E & BROUSSALIAN VL, U[.S.] National Bureau of Standards (January 1972). Fede[ral] Cost-Sharing Policies for Water Resources, prepared for [the] National Water Commission. National Technical Inform[a-] tion Service, Springfield, Va., Accession No. PB 208 3[0?] p. 139.

TABLE 15-1.— Maximum Federal cost shares for construction agencies

Purpose	Agency[a]	Construction	Percentage of Costs Land, Easements and Rights-of-Way[b]	Operation, Maintenance and Replacement
FLOOD PROTECTION	Bureau	100	100	100
	SCS	100	0	0
[Local Flood Protection]	Corps	100	0	0
[Large Reservoir]	Corps	100	100	100
NAVIGATION	Bureau	100	100	100
	Corps	100	0[c]	100
[Recreation; small boat harbors]	Corps	50	0	100
HYDROELECTRIC POWER	Bureau	0[d]	0	0
	Corps	0[d]	0	0
MUNICIPAL AND INDUSTRIAL WATER SUPPLY	Bureau	0	0	0
	SCS	50	0	0
	Corps	0	0	0
IRRIGATION	Bureau	Variable	Variable	0
	SCS	50	0	0
	Corps	Variable	Variable	0
WATER QUALITY [Low flow augmentation]	Corps	100	100	100
RECREATION: FISH AND WILDLIFE ENHANCEMENT	Bureau	50 and 100[d]	50	0 and 100[e]
	SCS	50	50	0
	Corps	50 and 100[d]	50	0 and 100[e]
DRAINAGE	Bureau	Variable	Variable	0
	SCS	50	0	0
	Corps	50	50	0

[a] Bureau=Bureau of Reclamation, SCS=Soil Conservation Service, Corps=Army Corps of Engineers.

[b] When Federal lands are involved, they are provided to the project without charge.

[c] Costs of lands, easements, and rights-of-way for navigation reservoirs are borne by the Federal Government.

[d] Hydroelectric power users may have benefited from unwarranted allocation of joint construction costs to other project purposes and from repayment arrangements with low interest rates.

[e] The two percentages represent the maximum Federal shares of separable and joint costs, respectively.

TABLE 15-2.—Maximum Federal cost shares for grant agencies

Purpose	Type of Facility	Agency	Percentages of Costs		
			Construction	Land, Easements and Rights-of-Way	Operation, Maintenance and Replacement
Pollution Abatement	Collection Sewers	HUD	50-90	50-90	0
		FHA	50	50	0
		EDA	50-80[b]	50-80[b]	0
	Treatment Plants and Interceptor Sewers	EPA	75	0	0
		FHA	50	50	0
		EDA	50-80[b]	50-80[b]	0
Water Supply	Conveyance and Reservoir	HUD	50	50	0
		FHA	50	50	0
		EDA	50-80[b]	50-80[b]	0

[a] Cost share percentages shown in the Table are taken from the respective agencies' legislative acts.

[b] EDA can pay up to 100% of eligible costs on a project for American Indians.

flood protection projects indicated a weighted average local share of 18 percent of construction costs.[24]

There are instances where no Federal assistance is available to undertake the most efficient means in a given situation, such as relocation of residences in lieu of flood reduction or the use of instream aeration in lieu of low flow augmentation for water quality enhancement.

Inconsistency Among Agencies for Similar Purposes

In a number of instances, several construction agencies have different cost-sharing policies for the same or a similar purpose, such as flood reduction, irrigation, or recreation. This situation leads to unproductive competition between agencies and "shopping around" by local interests for the best deal.

For example, a study of the Papillion Creek project in Nebraska suggests that high local costs for land rights and for operation and maintenance induced local groups to choose a Corps project over the original proposal of a joint Corps-SCS project. The original project plan called for 21 reservoir sites, 13 to be undertaken by the SCS and eight by the Corps.

The Corps was ultimately authorized to build the 13 reservoirs allocated to the SCS in the original plan. As a result, all of the costs of land rights and operation and maintenance allocated to flood control and amounting to $4.7 million, will be borne by the Federal Government. Had the SCS built at the 13 sites, the $4.7 million would have been borne by the local interests. Unquestionably, the local interests (other things equal) chose the Corps project because it saved them money.[25]

Inconsistency Among Water Purposes

Existing cost-sharing policies for multiple-purpose projects provide for the Federal Government to assume large shares of the costs allocated to some purposes, such as flood reduction, and little or none of the costs allocated to other purposes, such as municipal water supply. This provides strong incentives for non-Federal interests to bargain for the formulation of projects where costs can be allocated to purposes requiring minimum or no local cost-sharing. If non-Federal interests are not required to

[24] *Ibid.*, p. 141.

[25] LOUGHLIN JC (April 1970). Cost-sharing for Federal water resources programs with emphasis on flood protection. Water Resources Research 6(2):374-378.

contribute significantly toward the costs for a particular water purpose, there is little incentive for the local interests to seek the most desirable project from the standpoint of the Nation. It follows that some non-Federal cost-sharing for all water purposes should be included in multiple-purpose projects.

Inconsistency Among Repayment Arrangements

Ideally, all parties to a cost-sharing agreement should provide their respective shares at the time project costs are incurred. This practice would help to insure that all members of each group fully understood their financial burden and it would reduce the Federal overhead now required to administer repayment arrangements.

Presently the Federal Government often advances funds for the full cost of building a project and permits repayment of the local cost share over a period of time. In effect, these are loans to the non-Federal entities and the terms of repayment are critical. Present policies for repayment of such non-Federal cost shares are inconsistent among agencies and among purposes.

Investments in water resource development projects are financed by diverting funds either from public and private consumption or from alternative investments. If reimbursement policy does not provide for repayment of the non-Federal cost share with interest comparable to the interest paid by the Federal Government on its borrowings, the interest foregone is an additional Federal contribution.

The Commission supports the use of Federal cost-sharing (subsidies) when it is the best way to obtain desirable social objectives. However, due to their complexity, current policies for reimbursement of cost shares are not easily understood and the subsidies inherent in them are not readily apparent. For example, if 6 percent interest is the cost of capital to the Government, project beneficiaries who begin immediate repayment of their cost shares in equal annual installments over 50 years, but with no charge for interest, pay an equivalent of only 32 percent rather than 100 percent of their real (i.e., with interest) cost share.

Interest costs during construction and during development periods following construction should properly be considered a part of the construction costs. A delay in repayment of 10 years, at 6 percent interest, increases the equivalent investment cost by 79 percent.

Congress has included interest rate formulas for repaying reimbursable costs of some projects in the legislation authorizing those projects, but it has been silent on the matter of repayment interest rates with respect to other projects. Except for the Water Supply Act of 1958, which established a rate formula for use in repaying costs associated with the supply of municipal and industrial water, Congress has not enacted general legislation covering the subject of repayment interest rates. The interest rate policy on reimbursable costs of projects for which repayment rate formulas have not been stipulated in the authorizing acts has been established primarily through agency administrative decisions.[26]

Repayment interest rates and formulas used for reimbursement of water project costs have varied among agencies and for different purposes of development. For example, reclamation law has provided for project cost shares associated with irrigation to be repaid *without* interest. Though a single consistent policy has not emerged for other purposes, in the past repayment interest rates have been based generally upon average interest rates paid (coupon rates) on outstanding long-term Federal bonds.

Currently, the repayment interest rate policy on new Federal power projects is tied closely to the Water Resources Council interest rate policy used for evaluating the economic feasibility of proposed projects. In effect, these policies are based not on the interest rate paid (coupon rate) by the Treasury on outstanding long-term U.S. Government bonds, but more or less on the average current market yield for such bonds. With current interest rates substantially higher than in the past, the new repayment interest rate, which is applicable only to new projects, is significantly higher than the old.[27]

There seems to be little logic and a large measure of inconsistency in the variety of repayment interest rates specified in different acts and developed administratively by agencies for water development purposes. Moreover, although cost-sharing policy may reflect the intent of Congress to favor one particular objective of water development over another, on the basis of sound economics, there seems to be a lack of logic in the difference that presently exists between

---

[26] HOGGAN DH (June 1970). Repayment interest rates for water projects. Water Resources Research 6(3):683-688.

[27] For example, a Government bond maturing 10 years from now, with a coupon rate of 3-1/4 percent, and originally issued at par, may now be selling on the market for a price of $80 for each $100 of par value. Accordingly, it would have a current market yield to maturity of approximately 6 percent compared with its coupon rate (the rate which the Treasury pays) of only 3-1/4 percent.

interest rates used for evaluation of proposed projects and the interest rates used for repayment of actual project costs. Unless a deliberate subsidy is intended to be injected by way of the repayment interest rate, it should be the same as the discount rate used in formulating the project. Otherwise, unintended subsidies will be bestowed.

CONCLUSIONS

The Commission believes that joint Federal and non-Federal financing of water development projects is a useful and appropriate procedure for accomplishing national objectives. However, the Commission has found what many other students of the subject have found and declared over many years – present cost-sharing policies are grossly inconsistent and lead to inefficiencies and inequities at both Federal and non-Federal levels.

There is a critical and long-recognized need for reform of cost-sharing policies. In the Commission's judgment, desirable reforms will not be forthcoming until cost-sharing policies receive extensive attention and review in the Congress. The Commission believes that the Congress should undertake such a review, looking toward enactment of cost-sharing legislation designed to remedy the deficiencies and to achieve the goals discussed in the following paragraphs.

Deficiencies in Present Cost-Sharing Policies

Cost-Sharing Policies Should be Consistent Among Alternative Means for Accomplishing the Same Purpose: Inconsistency in cost-sharing among different means for achieving a given purpose (such as flood control or water quality improvement) is a serious deficiency of present policies and leads to some means being inappropriately favored over others. To reduce these inconsistencies, (1) uniform cost-sharing policies should apply to all alternatives for a given purpose now available under agency authority and (2) the authorized scope of an agency's approaches to project development should be broadened to permit alternative means of producing desired ends, such as ground water pumping instead of dam building to augment periodic low streamflows, or relocation of people and property from hazard areas instead of levee building to protect against floods. To remedy this deficiency will probably require a broadening of the concept of a "project." For example, a flood control "project" might involve relocation of people away from a hazard area.

Cost-Sharing Policies Should be Consistent Among Federal Agencies for the Same Water Purpose: Present cost-sharing policies for specified water purposes are inconsistent among Federal agencies, which leads to considerable confusion and establishes incentives for distortion. Projects of some agencies are "pushed" more vigorously than similar or superior projects of other agencies. The grant agencies have established an interagency coordinating committee to channel applications to a single agency for negotiation, and thereby reduce or avoid the practice of "shopping around" by local groups. The Commission endorses this kind of coordination.

Cost-Sharing Policies Need Not Require a Uniform Percentage of Cost-Sharing for All Water Developments: Cost-sharing policies, varying among purposes and programs, cannot be improved simply by adopting a uniform cost-sharing formula. Variability among projects and shifting social preferences makes the adoption of a simple uniform percentage rule unwise.

Cost-Sharing Policies Should Require Uniform Terms for the Repayment of Non-Federal Cost Shares: The considered use of subsidies which result when direct beneficiaries are relieved of some of the costs of water projects may be a desirable means for the Federal Government to accomplish some public policy objectives. When subsidies are granted, however, it is desirable that they should be open and straightforward, so that considered and informed reviews may be carried out from time to time as objectives and conditions change. It is the Commission's position that the proportion of Federal financial assistance to non-Federal interests should be set forth in decisions on cost-sharing and not concealed in policies governing the terms of repayment. Present inconsistencies in this regard contribute to misallocations of the Nation's always-limited investment capital resources.

The use of a lower interest rate for repayment arrangements than the interest rate used for project evaluation purposes is one of several alternative ways to inject subsidies into water projects. But, unlike straightforward allocations of project costs to non reimbursable purposes, it tends to obscure the true magnitude of the subsidy. Hence, the Commission believes that unless it can be demonstrated as unsuitable, it is preferable that the interest rate used for project evaluation and for repayment arrangements should be comparable (assuming, of course, they realistically reflect the yield on long-term U.S.

Government securities).[28] In addition, the Commission believes that interest costs during construction and development should be included in the cost of projects and, where such costs are reimbursable, should be paid by beneficiaries.

Cost-Sharing Policies Should Promote Equity Among Project Beneficiaries and Taxpayers: Present cost-sharing policies tempt Federal water project beneficiaries to request projects that they would not be willing to pay for if their own money were involved. This leads to unwise development. For example, large Federal cost shares of flood control, drainage, and shoreline or hurricane protection projects have encouraged unwise economic developments in areas prone to periodic flooding and hurricane hazards. In some cases, large windfall gains have accrued to landowners and valuable open space and wetland areas have been destroyed. Likewise, availability of interest-free financing for irrigation projects has led to the construction of projects and facilities far in advance of need, and to the reclamation of lands at per acre costs far in excess of the value of the land after the project is completed.

Only by placing development of water projects for purposes that yield economic returns on a self-supporting basis can equity be promoted. The Commission believes that the best way to do this is for the identifiable users of project services insofar as is practicable and administratively feasible to bear their proportional share of development and operating costs of the projects through systems of pricing or beneficiary charges such as special assessments, taxes, and fees.

Cost-Sharing Policies Should Not Lead to Expansion of the Federal Role in Water Resources: Availability of Federal money under favorable cost-sharing arrangements has led in many instances to Federal construction of projects that could just as well have been built by non-Federal interests. Not only does this inequitably shift part of the cost of local benefits to Federal taxpayers, but it tends to move control over water resources to Washington officials and increase the size of the Federal payroll. To alleviate this situation, the Commission believes cost-sharing arrangements should be the same for projects that serve the national interest, whether they are built by Federal agencies or by non-Federal entities.

---

[28] See discussion of evaluation discount rate, Chapter 10, Section D.

The Role of Subsidies

The Commission does not disapprove of subsidies. But it believes that subsidies are only justified if they serve some compelling social purpose; where society benefits, but where conventional markets and pricing mechanisms cannot provide those benefits. The Commission believes that a general rule to follow is this: Direct beneficiaries of water projects who can be identified and reached should ordinarily be obliged to pay all project costs that are allocated to the services from which they benefit. Where water projects are to be subsidized because conventional markets and pricing mechanisms cannot be counted on to achieve socially desired benefits, such subsidized projects should be the most efficient way to achieve the purposes for which they are developed. It need scarcely be added that whatever cost-sharing arrangements are adopted should be financially sound and administratively feasible.

Goals of Cost-Sharing Policy

The initial step in the general review of cost-sharing policies should be to reconsider the goals that water development programs are designed to accomplish. The Commission believes that the general goals of water project development should be: (1) to provide adequate supplies of water and water-related services for the Nation developed at least-cost over time; (2) to promote the efficient use of water and water-related services by users; (3) to encourage improved management of land and other related resources in conjunction with water; and (4) to promote harmony of water developments with other national policies and programs. These national goals can best be achieved through complementary activities by Federal, State, and local governments and by private enterprise. Cost-sharing policies should be reshaped to promote achievement of these goals.

When direct beneficiaries share in the costs of Federal projects, costs are distributed more equitably and incentives are provided to improve water development projects. Such cost-sharing by non-Federal interests:

1. Provides incentives to require that Federal water projects harmonize with land and water management activities of regional, State, and local governments and of private interests as well.
2. Discourages uneconomic development to serve low-value uses or in advance of real need for project services.

495

Users should pay full costs of small boat harbors such as this one at Hastings, Minn.

3. Reduces unfair subsidization by promoting a more equitable distribution of costs.
4. Reduces windfall gains to landowners and others.

In summary, appropriate cost-sharing policies should provide incentives for the selection of efficient projects that will lead to progress toward water resources policies that are in harmony with othe national programs and policies. This requires project to be in the proper locations, at the proper time, t provide the proper services in the proper amounts Cost-sharing policies should be equitable, with projec beneficiaries bearing proportionate shares of projec costs. Adoption of the following recommendation will lead toward the achievement of these goals.

RECOMMENDATIONS

Legislation should be enacted to govern cost-sharing policy for Federal and federally assisted water developments, including arrangements for repayment over a period of time not beyond the useful life of projects of costs reimbursable to the Federal Government, and incorporating the principles stated below.

15-1. Insofar as is practicable and administratively feasible, the identifiable beneficiaries of project services should bear appropriate shares of development and operating costs through systems of pricing or user charges (e.g., special assessments, taxes, fees, etc.), as follows:

a. Municipal and Industrial Water Supply — Costs of Federal reservoir capacity allocated to municipal and industrial water supply should be completely recovered, with interest equal to prevailing yield rates for long-term U.S. Treasury bonds at the time of construction.

b. Irrigation Water Supply — All costs of new Federal irrigation facilities should be recovered from irrigators and other direct beneficiaries through contracting entities, with interest equal to prevailing yield rates for long-term U.S. Treasury bonds at the time of construction.

c. Inland Navigation — Costs incurred by the Federal Government for the operation, maintenance, and extension of the Nation's shallow-draft inland waterway system should be recovered as follows:

(1) Operation and Maintenance: By a combination of: (a) a uniform tax on all fuels used by commercial and recreational vessels when operating on the system; (b) lockage charges at Federal locks in amounts sufficient to repay the cost of operating and maintaining all of the locks within integral segments of the total system. The charges should be imposed gradually to allow the industry time to adapt over a 10-year period, after which the total amounts collected should be sufficient to recover the entire cost of operating and maintaining the total system.

(2) Extension of the System: Appropriate Federal or non-Federal entities should be required to reimburse the Federal Treasury, from charges assessed against the beneficiaries of the project over its useful life, for the entire first cost of each addition to the existing inland waterway system, with interest equal to prevailing yield rates for long-term U.S. Treasury bonds at the time of construction; provided that, if the Congress should determine that a part of the cost of any such addition is properly chargeable to national defense, it should authorize assumption of that part by the Federal Treasury.

d. Electric Power — All real costs of construction, operation, and maintenance of future Federal hydropower projects should be recovered through sale of power at rates based on the true economic costs of production and transmission. Appropriate payments from power revenues should be made to local governments in lieu of taxes. Any excess revenues after the project is paid out should be returned to the Treasury.

e. Water-Based Recreation — Recreation admission and user fees should be collected from all identifiable recreation users of Federal water projects where revenues can be expected to exceed the costs of collection. The goal should be to recover operation, maintenance, and replacement costs of recreation facilities, but charges should be related to fees charged for comparable nearby private facilities. If recreation and user fees are inadequate to offset the full recreation operation, maintenance, and replacement costs, consideration should be given to making up the deficit from other recreation-related revenue sources such as excise taxes on water-related recreation equipment. Where construction or operation of water development projects destroys, preempts, or degrades natural recreation opportunities, beneficiaries of the principal purposes of the project should pay, as part of the project's costs, for development and operation of substitute recreation facilities to compensate for lost recreation opportunities.

f. Municipal Waste Collection and Treatment — Costs of municipal waste collection and treatment should be recovered through charges based on the costs that users impose on the system; however, Federal grants will be required for a sufficient period to finance the massive investment programs now required to eliminate the backlog produced by generations of waste treatment neglect and meet higher standards now imposed. The Commission believes this period should be 10 years. Federal grants should be contingent on the adoption by the grantee of schedules of user charges that will recover all system costs exclusive of Federal and State grants.

g. Flood Control, Drainage, and Shoreline Protection, Including Hurricane Protection — Costs of Federal or federally assisted projects providing such benefits as protecting lands through flood control, drainage, and shoreline protection, including hurricane protection, should be recovered from identifiable beneficiaries through local units of government such as municipalities, flood control, drainage, or shoreline protection districts that have power to make assessments upon lands benefited by the projects, or through State governments because of their critical role in determining flood plain management, with interest equal to prevailing yield rates on long term U.S. Treasury bonds outstanding at the time of construction.

15-2. Enhancing Environmental Values

There should be heavy Federal financial involvement in the preservation and enhancement of nationally significant water-related environmental areas including wild and scenic rivers, such as the Salmon, Buffalo, Suwannee, or upper Delaware, or unique wetlands, such as the Everglades. There is a Federal responsibility for enhancement of migratory waterfowl and anadromous fish species and for the preservation of designated endangered wildlife species. However, the enhancement of common species of fish and wildlife should be primarily a non-Federal responsibility and should be financed by States or, possibly, by Federal-State grant programs for these purposes. Cost of enhancement of species which can safely be harvested should be borne by user charges such as special duck stamps or license fees.

15-3. Regional Development

Economic development benefits of water projects accruing only to one region may result in offsetting losses in other regions. This result may be desirable and intended, i.e., it may be national policy to develop one region, for example, Appalachia, without regard for other regions. However, the analysis of whether a water project is the best use of Federal funds for development of a particular region requires the expertise and judgment of agencies in addition to Federal water development agencies. In any particular region, Federal funds might be more effectively employed to achieve regional development by investing in transportation, education, or manpower training programs rather than in water projects.

Federal construction agencies should not be authorized to share in water project costs that are allocated to strictly regional development objectives. However, grants from other Federal agencies with regional economic objectives, such as EDA, should be eligible to meet such costs.

15-4. Low Flow Augmentation

Where practical, costs of low flow augmentation should be allocated and paid for in accordance with distribution of benefits. The beneficiaries of low flow augmentation are difficult to identify in a precise way, however, because release of stored water serves a number of purposes simultaneously. For example, low flow augmentation may benefit water supply, costs of which should be fully reimbursed. It may benefit navigation, costs of which should be paid for by user fees. It usually enhances fish and wildlife which should be paid for by the States involved unless national benefits are created. It also provides esthetic benefits which are of substantial regional or national value but not easily quantified or assigned to specific beneficiaries. Since it will be impossible to quantify all benefits and identify all beneficiaries, remaining unallocated costs should be assigned to water quality improvement and shared between Federal and non-Federal entities in the same proportion as grants-in-aid for waste treatment facilities. The cost share proportions, however, should be adjusted when necessary to reflect changes in the grant program for waste treatment.

15-5. Non-Federal Projects

Toward the end of providing financial incentives for the optimum design and operation of non-Federal multiple-purpose water projects, cost-sharing policies for Federal participation in such projects should be the same as for Federal water projects. Non-Federal projects also serve the national interest and Federal cost-sharing policies should fully recognize their contributions. For example, the river regulation purposes served by a hydroelectric power or water supply reservoir under State, local, or private ownership should be eligible for the same cost-sharing assistance as if the reservoir were under Federal control. In the case where water supply or low flow augmentation is needed, the additional reservoir capacity should be financed by the Federal Government where necessary and the costs subsequently recovered from the respective water users in accordance with recommendations for the purpose served.

15-6. Repayment Arrangements

Where the provision of initial excess capacity in water development projects is economically and environmentally superior to alternative piecemeal development of a series of smaller projects as each is needed, long-term Federal financing should be made available. This will be a definite advantage for project beneficiaries even where reimbursement requires full repayment with interest. Such long-term financing will facilitate development of large and complex projects serving various purposes where full capacity may not be utilized for several years. Repayment policies should provide for flexible repayment arrangements with provisions for deferred repayments and the capitalization of deferred interest charges.

Financing Water Programs

The successful achievement of water development goals depends upon the availability of adequate financial resources. The selection of realistic program goals depends upon assessments of the Nation's financial capability and the setting of priorities of expenditure to meet various national goals of which water development is only one.

This chapter presents various estimates of capital demands for water programs and discusses alternative means of raising the necessary financial resources. The capital demands presented are general estimates. They are included only to give a perspective on cost of meeting various water development goals. These estimates are not "needs" in any absolute sense. They must be related to the goals that might be adopted which will require very large capital expenditures in the next several years, particularly in the light of the recently stated congressional water quality program goal of no discharge of pollutants into navigable waters by 1985. The Commission, however, does not endorse the concept of "no discharge" on the grounds that such a goal is prohibitively costly and ignores the ultimate problem of waste disposal. If wastes cannot be recycled, they must be disposed of in air, water, or land disposal sites. Thus, the Commission's counsel is to thoroughly appraise the alternatives in each situation and to make reasoned judgments among them. These alternatives include alternative goals, alternative programs, alternative schedules for attaining selected goals, and alternative means of financing the investments.

It appears that revenues from available taxing sources will be barely adequate to meet projected demands for various programs at all levels of government over the next several years.[1] The Commission does not feel that water development programs are necessarily the place to economize in government expenditure, but is convinced that there is need for realistic reappraisals of the goals, programs and program schedules, and the means of financing governmental programs at all levels of government. The financial resources of the Nation are limited and judgments must be made as to national investment priorities in both the public and private sectors and among Federal, State, and local governments.

CAPITAL DEMANDS FOR WATER RESOURCES DEVELOPMENT

This section indicates the general magnitude of funding "demands" that may be expected for construction activities for water resources and closely related purposes. Estimates for water developments are based primarily on projections of past trends and project costs identified in comprehensive river basin plans. For water pollution control, cost estimates from various sources are presented to indicate the general order of magnitude of the differences in costs of meeting various goals for water quality programs. As such, the funding levels presented are intended for information and comparison purposes and should not be interpreted as amounts endorsed by the National Water Commission as needed to implement specific programs or policies.

Water pollution control activities are given special attention because current indications are that future expenditures in this category could greatly overshadow those in other water resource categories.

Historic Trends

Information published by the Office of Management and Budget in conjunction with the President's

---

Grand Coulee Dam, a key feature of $2 billion Columbia Basin project

[1] See SCHULTZE, Charles L et al. (1972). Setting National Priorities, The 1973 Budget. The Brookings Institution, Washington, D.C. Chapters 12 & 13.

TABLE 16-1.—Federal outlays by category and agency for water resources and related developments (in millions of dollars)				
Program and Agency	1971 Actual	1972 Actual	1973 Estimate	1974 Estimate
Flood control works:				
Agriculture: Soil Conservation Service (mostly grants)	65.5	71.2	90.7	75.3
Defense–Civil: Corps of Engineers	404.1	457.1	562.6	497.9
Interior: Bureau of Reclamation	2.4	1.8	2.5	2.4
State: International Boundary and Water Commission	1.8	2.9	7.8	12.3
Tennessee Valley Authority	0.4	.1	.9	.9
Total flood control works	474.2	533.1	664.5	588.8
Beach erosion control: Defense–Civil: Corps of Engineers	1.7	3.0	4.2	2.8
Irrigation and water conservation works:				
Agriculture: Soil Conservation Service (grants)	10.9	12.1	15.4	14.0
Interior:				
Bureau of Indian Affairs	6.9	11.7	13.0	15.0
Bureau of Reclamation (includes grants and loans)	64.6	84.3	147.6	122.5
Total irrigation works	82.4	108.1	176.0	151.5
Navigation facilities:				
Commerce: Economic Development Administration (mostly grants)		15.0	14.5	12.5
Defense–Civil:				
Corps of Engineers	220.0	233.3	259.3	218.7
Panama Canal Company		.1	1.8	1.0
Transportation: Saint Lawrence Seaway Corporation	0.1	.5	.6	1.7
Tennessee Valley Authority	0.3	2.2	4.9	.6
Total navigation facilities	220.4	251.1	281.1	234.5
Multiple-purpose dams and reservoirs with hydroelectric power facilities:				
Defense–Civil: Corps of Engineers	326.3	380.9	312.4	306.3
Interior: Bureau of Reclamation	119.2	144.7	181.3	149.5
Tennessee Valley Authority[1]	31.9	39.9	57.7	74.7
Total multiple-purpose facilities	477.4	565.5	551.4	530.5
Powerplants:				
Defense–Civil: Panama Canal Company			4.0	.3
Interior: Territorial Affairs (grants)	2.8	1.9	2.2	1.1
Tennessee Valley Authority	364.6	452.7	333.7	351.4
Total powerplants	367.4	454.6	339.9	352.8
Power transmission facilities:				
Defense–Civil: Panama Canal Company		1.2	.8	.2
Interior:				
Territorial Affairs (grants)		1.0	.8	.2
Bureau of Reclamation	10.8	6.9	8.8	16.9
Bonneville Power Administration	101.9	90.2	82.3	89.8
Southwestern Power Administration	2.4	2.6	1.7	.6
Tennessee Valley Authority	72.9	75.3	84.6	75.8
Total power transmission facilities	188.0	177.2	179.0	183.5
Water supply and waste disposal facilities:				
Agriculture:				
Farmers Home Administration (grants)	20.4	25.6	46.5	46.6
Forest Service	8.1	11.9	29.7	31.7
Commerce: Economic Development Administration and				
Regional Action Planning Commissions (primarily grants)	69.5	102.2	106.2	96.5
Health, Education, and Welfare: Health Services				
and Mental Health Administration	15.6	21.3	31.5	36.9
Housing and Urban Development: Grants and loans	163.4	148.2	145.2	144.1
Interior:				
National Park Service	5.6	24.3	20.0	22.1
Bureau of Reclamation	29.2	16.4	29.4	25.5
Environmental Protection Agency (grants)	478.4	413.4	727.0	1,600.0
Other agencies (mostly grants)	16.6	15.8	15.6	12.0
Total water supply and waste disposal	806.8	779.1	1,151.1	2,015.4
Total water resources and related developments	2,618.3	2,871.7	3,347.2	4,059.8

Source: U.S. OFFICE OF MANAGEMENT AND BUDGET (1972) and (1973). Special Analyses; Budget of the United States Government, Fiscal Years 1973 and 1974, U.S. Government Printing Office, Washington, D.C., pp. 267-8 and 239-40, respectively.

[1] Includes outlays for Racoon Mountain Pumped Storage Power Project (a single-purpose project) as follows: 1971, $16.2; 1972, $25.9; 1973 est., $40.0; 1974 est., $53.8.

TABLE 16-2.–Comparison of Federal outlays for water resources with those for other Federal civil public works and the total U.S. budget (billions of dollars)

| Year | Federal Civil Public Works | | | | Federal Water Resources Expenditures | | |
	Direct Civil Construction	Grants	Net Lending	Total	Total	% of Total Civil Works	% of Total Budget
1964	2.7	4.2	0.1	7.0	1.5	21	1.3
1965	2.8	4.6	0.2	7.6	1.5	20	1.3
1966	3.0	4.4	0.3	7.7	1.7	22	1.3
1967	2.8	4.7	0.4	7.9	1.7	22	1.1
1968	2.5	5.3	0.3	8.1	1.8	22	1.0
1969	2.2	5.5	0.3	8.0	1.8	22	1.0
1970	2.2	5.8	0.3	8.3	1.9	23	0.9
1971	2.6	6.4	0.2	9.2	2.6	28	1.2
1972	3.3	6.5	0.2	10.0	2.9	29	1.2
1973 est.	3.8	7.2	0.3	11.3	3.3	29	1.3
1974 est.	3.3	8.1	0.3	11.7	4.1	35	1.5

Source: Adapted from U.S. OFFICE OF MANAGEMENT AND BUDGET (1973). Special Analyses, Budget of the United States Government, 1974. U.S. Government Printing Office, Washington, D.C., p. 228.

Fiscal Years 1973 and 1974 budgets indicates actual and estimated Federal outlays for various water resources categories. This is presented in tabular and graphic form. Table 16-1 shows actual and projected water and related development outlays for grants and loans as well as for direct construction for Fiscal Years 1971, 1972, 1973, and 1974. It also serves to illustrate the degree of involvement of Federal agencies in various water and related activities. Figure 16-1 illustrates the trends in outlays for various water resources categories over the period 1965 to 1974. For example, it shows that "water supply and waste disposal" (primarily water pollution control) are responsible for most of the upturn since 1970.

Table 16-2 compares outlays for water resources from 1964 to 1974 with other Federal public works and with the total Federal budget. It shows that the proportion going towards water resources is increasing, primarily because of increases for water pollution control.

Table 16-3 is compiled from data contained in a report prepared for the Commission using information obtained directly from Federal water agencies and may not be on a comparable basis with the other tables. It indicates the growth, in constant dollars, of Federal expenditures since 1900 for water resources categories used in the Water Resources Council framework studies. There was little if any real growth in total expenditures in the 1950-1970 period.

It is extremely difficult to obtain similar data on how much is actually being spent on water resources development by entities other than Federal agencies because water resource development is an integral part of investment in traditional economic sectors, such as electric utilities and transportation, and because water resources development is carried out by hundreds of public agencies at all levels of government and by thousands of private firms. Expenditures on water facilities are not always separated from other expenditures on accounting records, and even if they were, the task of compiling these data would require a major effort. On the basis of the data available, the Commission staff estimates that current investment in water resources development by all entities is in excess of $11 billion annually, exclusive of thermal electric power generation and transmission line construction which are included in estimates of water and related resources investments in the Federal budget.

Table 16-4 presents generalized estimates of cumulative investments made for water resource developments by the Federal Government, by States and local entities, and by private interests. When municipal water supply, sanitary sewer, and storm and combined sewer facility costs are included, as well as those for wastewater treatment, State and local investments considerably exceed Federal and private expenditures.

503

FIGURE 16-1. 10-year trend in Federal water resources expenditures

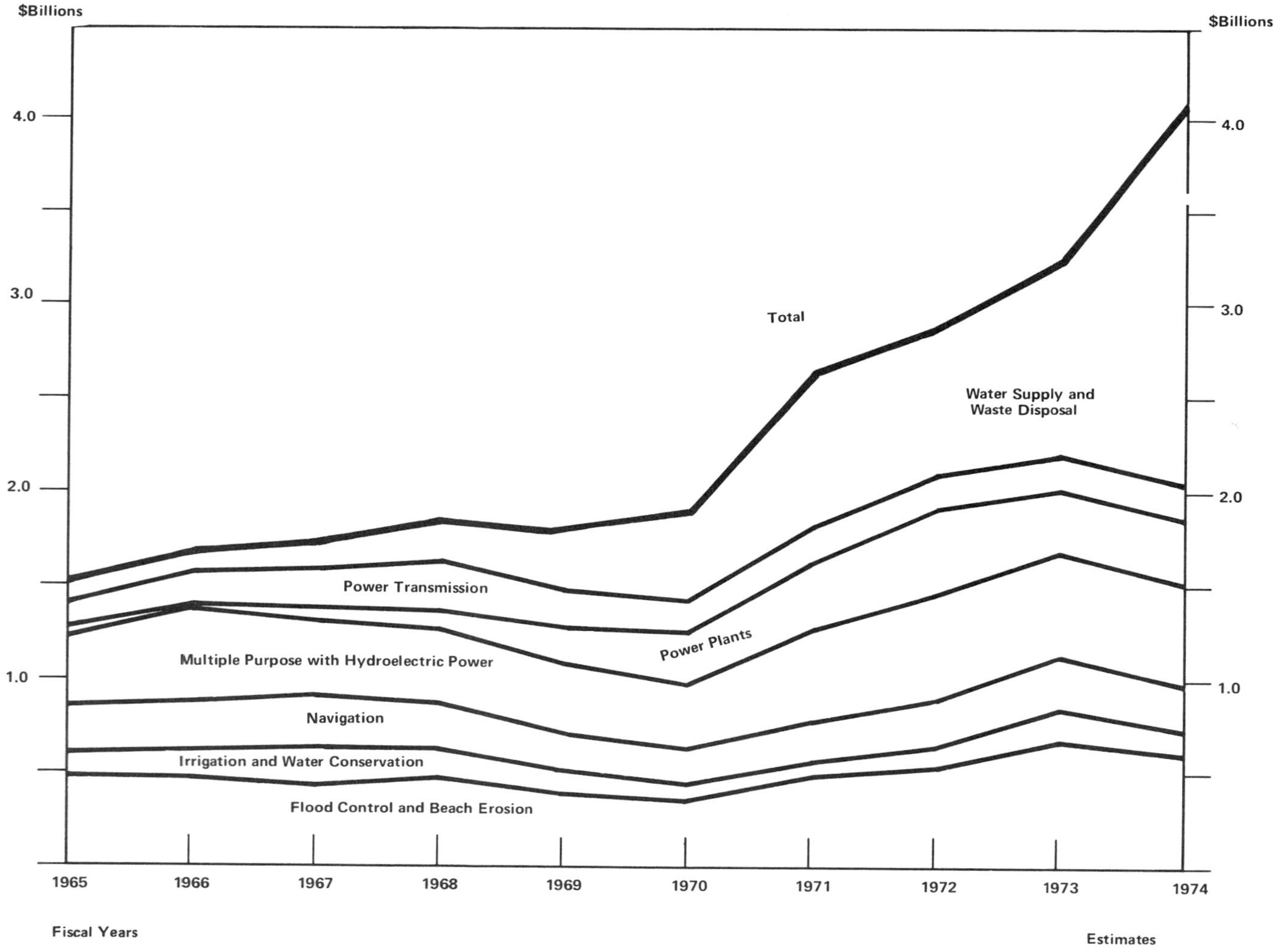

Source: U.S. OFFICE OF MANAGEMENT AND BUDGET (1973). Special Analyses; Budget of the United States Government, Fiscal Year 1974, U.S. Government Printing Office, Washington, D.C. p. 240.

504

TABLE 16-3.—Estimated historic Federal expenditures for water resources and related activities (billions of 1972 dollars)

	Indexing Factor	Navigation	Flood Control	Irrigation	Power	Water Supply & Pollution Control	Watershed Protection	Fisheries & Wildlife	Multiple Purpose	Total
1900	18.7	.35	—	—	—	—	—	—	—	.35
1905	18.6	.43	—	.09	—	—	—	—	—	.52
1910	17.5	.55	—	.14	—	—	—	—	—	.69
1915	18.2	.85	—	.18	—	—	—	—	—	1.03
1920	6.8	.28	.06	.04	—	—	—	—	—	.38
1925	8.1	.53	.12	.07	—	—	—	—	—	.72
1930	8.3	.66	.35	.07	.04	—	—	—	—	1.12
1935	8.6	1.48	.38	.18	.11	—	—	—	—	2.15
1940	7.0	1.02	.74	.24	.23	.01	—	—	.11	2.35
1945	5.5	.28	.40	.08	.14	—	—	—	.07	.97
1950	3.3	.44	.90	.48	.53	.03	.01	—	.84	3.23
1955	2.55	.29	.38	.19	.44	.02	.02	.01	.66	2.01
1960	2.03	.59	.69	.17	.46	.15	.03	.02	1.07	3.18
1965	1.73	.70	.92	.16	.61	.23	.06	.02	.49	3.19
1970	1.22	.23	.36	.11	.55	.56	.08	.02	.40	2.31

Note: Totals—without indexing factor—do not agree with amounts shown in Figure 16-1 due to differences in accounting procedures. The indexing factor is the multiplier used to convert current dollars to 1972 constant dollars.

Source: Adapted from LEGLER, John B et al., (1971). A Historical Study of Water Resources Policy of the Federal Government, 1900-1970, prepared for the National Water Commission. Mimeo, Washington University, St. Louis, Mo. pp. 397-398.

	Period of Estimate	Cumulative Expenditures			
		Federal Ownership or Financed	State & Local Ownership and Financed	Private Ownership and Financed	Total
		(billions of 1972 dollars)			
Instream Uses					
Hydro Power	Total to 1968	9.3	3.2	6.2	18.7
Flood Control	Total to 1969	25.3	2.0	1.3	28.6
Navigation	Total to 1969	16.8	1.6	–	18.4
Recreation	Total 1956–65	1.1	1.9	3.3	6.3
Fish & Wildlife				–	
Waste Treatment	Total to 1971 }	11.3[1]	62.8	no est. 4.6[2]	78.7
Sanitary Sewers	Total to 1971 }				
Storm & Combined Sewers	Total to 1971	–	36.3	3.2[2]	39.5
Out-of-Stream Uses					
Municipal Water	Total to 1971	6.6	78.5	9.3[2]	94.4
Industrial (except cooling water)	Total to 1965	6.6	4.6	13.3	24.5
Cooling Water	Total to 1969	.1	.1	1.4	1.6
Irrigation	Total to 1968	10.6	3.4	13.9	27.9
Total		87.7	194.4	56.5	338.6

[1] Includes $6.6 billion at Federal facilities.
[2] To 1966 only.

Source: NWC staff estimates.

Possible Future Expenditures

"Framework" planning studies undertaken by the Water Resources Council provide one measure of possible future capital demands. Drafts of such studies are available at present for 10 of the 20 water resource study areas used by the Water Resources Council for the United States. Studies are not available for the following river basins: Great Lakes, Lower Mississippi, Tennessee, Arkansas-White-Red, Texas-Gulf, Rio Grande, South Atlantic-Gulf Basin, Alaska, Hawaii, and Puerto Rico. The available studies cover 68 percent of the land area and 63 percent of the population of the 48 contiguous States.

Methods used in the various studies are not always consistent. For example, some only include estimates for hydroelectric power under the "power" category, while others include estimates for cooling water as well. Some include "needs" but not costs. Additionally, the estimates do not reflect comparable needs, costs, or program policies, particularly in the water pollution control category,[2] where water quality standards have been upgraded since they were originally required by the Water Quality Act of 1965.

Additional estimates of water quality needs were developed separately, primarily because of substantial changes in federally imposed treatment requirements under the Federal Water Pollution Control Act Amendments of 1972. However, for comparison purposes, the water pollution estimates in the framework studies are also shown in Table 16-5 with other

[2] Also commonly referred to as "water quality." In some cases (Fig. 16-1), it is also combined in the same category with water supply needs.

	(billions of 1972 dollars)							
	1970–1980			Percent of Total	1980–2020			Percent of Total
Category	Federal	Non-Federal	Total		Federal	Non-Federal	Total	
Municipal and Industrial Water Supply	0.4	13.7	14.1	7	6.7	32.2	38.9	7
Irrigation and Drainage	3.0	12.0	15.0	7	9.6	27.8	37.4	7
Power[1]	6.9	12.9	19.8	10	6.7	35.1	41.8	8
Flood Control	8.5	10.4	18.9	9	22.3	25.0	47.3	9
Recreation	9.4	9.3	18.7	9	24.4	24.4	48.8	9
Fish and Wildlife	2.4	1.8	4.2	2	6.9	5.2	12.1	2
Water Quality	31.0	50.5	81.5	40	116.0	111.0	227.0	42
Land Management	6.7	6.7	13.4	6	15.3	15.3	30.6	6
Navigation	10.8	3.1	13.9	6	25.5	7.6	33.1	6
Shoreline Protection and Development	2.8	2.8	5.6	3	7.8	7.9	15.7	3
Other	1.3	1.3	2.6	1	2.6	2.7	5.3	1
	83.2	124.5	207.7	100	243.8	294.2	538.0	100

[1] Primarily hydroelectric although cooling water facilities were included in some studies.

Source: National Water Commission staff compilation, adjustment, and extrapolation from framework planning studies undertaken by the Federal agencies and river basin commissions.

estimates from the framework studies. (In order to reflect roughly the policy change noted above, estimates in the framework studies for pollution control costs were increased by the following amounts: 1960, 100 percent; 1965, 50 percent; 1968, 25 percent.) Estimates for the 10 areas without studies were made by extrapolation, on the basis of area, population, type of development activity and character of water resources.

All of this data is combined in Table 16-5, which projects capital investment needs for Federal and non-Federal sectors for capital improvements for the 1970-1980 and 1980-2020 periods as developed by the Commission staff, based on data in framework studies for each of the water resource categories. These projections do not include any estimates for major interbasin water transfer projects.

Water Pollution Control Costs

Pollution Control Costs Under 1965 Act Standards: The information in Table 16-6 was compiled primarily from an unpublished study completed in 1970 by the former Federal Water Quality Administration (now a part of The Environmental Protection Agency). Estimated control costs are based on meeting water quality standards established under the 1965 Act.[3] These and the other data in Table 16-6 are illustrative of the relative magnitude of the various types of pollution problems.

Municipal Treatment Costs – The most thorough survey of municipal waste treatment needs conducted to date was made by the Environmental Protection Agency (EPA) in the fall of 1971 in cooperation with the States and cities involved.[4] All cities serving 10,000 or more persons were asked to indicate waste treatment construction measures planned through 1976 to meet water quality standards or related

[3] *Water Quality Act of 1965*, P.L. 89-234, 79 Stat. 903.

[4] U.S. ENVIRONMENTAL PROTECTION AGENCY (1972). The Economics of Clean Water, Summary of Analysis and volume I. Environmental Protection Agency, Washington, D.C.

TABLE 16-6.—Pollution control costs under standards established under the 1965 Federal Water Pollution Control Act

Pollution Sources	Relative Importance[a] (rank)	Control Priority[b] (rank)	Estimates of Capital Costs for Abatement[c] (billions of dollars)
Point sources:			
municipal sewage	1	1	14–18
industrial wastes	3	2	10–25
Other sources:			
storm and combined sewers	5	4	15–55
acid mine drainage	6	6	5–15
oil and hazardous spills	7	7	1–5
agricultural wastes	2	3	1–7
dredging spoil disposal; miscellaneous	4	5	1–2
			47–127

[a] Based on (1) the proportion of waste discharged by source to total of wastes discharges and (2) the population affected by such discharges.

[b] "Control priority" takes into account (1) the costs of control and (2) the availability of control technology.

[c] "Abatement" costs are the capital costs to meet water quality standards. (However, it should be noted (1) that abatement programs do not exist for all sources and (2) enforcement measures concentrate on municipal and industrial sources.) Estimates of costs have not been converted to 1972 dollars.

Source: U.S. FEDERAL WATER QUALITY ADMINISTRATION (1970). Unpublished information.

enforcement requirements.[5] These cost estimates total $18 billion when expanded to include the total sewered population, and they are shown in Table 16-7 for each State.

In addition to this survey, EPA made a study of probable expenditures for the same period and purposes, based on their projection of likely trends in actual construction costs and inflation. The study resulted in a reduced estimate of $14 billion of probable capital investment through 1976.

Industrial Waste Treatment Costs – EPA estimated that it will cost American manufacturers between $11 billion and $29 billion from 1968 to 1976 to meet the same pollution abatement requirements as the

cities.[6] The actual cost will depend on the abatement strategy used. Maximum application of processes conserve water and reduce liquid waste would result in lower costs; higher costs would result if additional treatment facilities were simply added to handle waste volumes generated under current production processes. Although some process changes will probably be employed to reduce waste treatment requirements, it is not likely that enough changes will be implemented to achieve a maximum reduction in treatment costs (the $11 billion level). Table 16 shows the estimated costs of meeting treatment requirements by industrial category for the anticipated median efficiency.

Time Schedule for Meeting Standards – The above cost estimates were based on the assumption that abatement facilities, municipal and industrial, co

[5] Federal policy, under the Federal Water Pollution Control Act, includes the following under "treatment facilities" as eligible for Federal cost-sharing: sewage treatment facilities, interceptor sewers, and related facilities such as pump stations. Normal sanitary sewers (or "collecting sewers") are *not* now included.

[6] See U.S. ENVIRONMENTAL PROTECTION AGENCY (1972). The Economics of Clean Water, volume I. Environmental Protection Agency, Washington, D.C.

TABLE 16-7.—Survey results of estimated construction cost of sewage treatment facilities planned for the period FY 1972–1976

	FY–1972	FY–1973[2]	FY–1974[2]	FY–1975	FY–1976[3]	Total
	(Millions of 1971 Dollars)[1]					
TOTALS	5,278.2	6,080.0	3,198.2	2,236.5	1,289.3	18,082.2
Alabama	33.5	9.6	9.5	7.9	5.1	65.6
Alaska	4.1	26.4	2.3	7.5	–	40.3
Arizona	10.7	8.9	–	6.2	1.4	27.2
Arkansas	12.5	27.7	11.3	10.0	–	61.5
California	280.4	930.9	218.4	369.0	340.8	2,139.5
Colorado	23.3	14.4	8.4	30.0	6.1	82.2
Connecticut	96.2	95.1	53.5	–	–	244.8
Delaware	7.8	8.8	79.0	2.5	5.6	103.7
District of Columbia	62.7	40.9	–	–	–	103.6
Florida	313.0	125.7	89.4	106.3	17.0	651.4
Georgia	36.3	89.6	15.8	–	12.6	154.3
Hawaii	15.0	28.5	4.6	24.1	–	72.2
Idaho	15.7	8.6	7.4	.3	.4	32.4
Illinois	336.7	332.5	240.8	382.9	38.7	1,331.6
Indiana	161.3	207.2	121.7	22.1	27.6	539.9
Iowa	16.8	78.8	72.7	21.8	7.2	197.3
Kansas	19.8	28.8	5.9	3.2	11.6	69.3
Kentucky	46.8	35.0	14.3	39.5	27.1	162.7
Louisiana	68.5	40.6	28.2	17.7	.1	155.1
Maine	25.4	100.5	15.0	35.4	25.0	201.3
Maryland	201.5	204.0	214.6	15.7	36.6	672.4
Massachusetts	206.5	190.8	149.9	80.0	–	627.2
Michigan	331.8	523.2	307.3	100.4	130.0	1,392.7
Minnestoa	142.3	112.1	41.5	30.8	12.9	339.6
Mississippi	32.5	17.4	7.4	14.5	18.2	90.0
Missouri	9.2	160.0	71.9	38.1	27.4	306.6
Montana	13.7	2.7	7.8	–	3.0	27.2
Nebraska	1.8	28.7	23.5	24.1	15.7	93.8
Nevada	.4	30.7	10.8	1.3	–	43.2
New Hampshire	21.3	36.9	62.8	58.5	10.5	190.0
New Jersey	461.9	554.4	105.6	299.6	6.3	1,427.8
New Mexico	17.8	12.8	.1	–	–	30.7
New York	1,047.1	422.4	140.8	102.0	167.2	1,879.5
North Carolina	36.6	66.5	31.3	18.2	1.1	153.7
North Dakota	1.4	3.7	1.7	–	.3	7.1
Ohio	277.2	250.3	313.3	62.7	156.8	1,060.3
Oklahoma	14.4	24.2	28.5	8.1	39.8	115.0
Oregon	41.5	72.3	9.9	13.0	12.6	149.3
Pennsylvania	187.2	343.3	259.0	105.8	1.2	896.5
Rhode Island	9.9	35.6	25.7	–	–	71.2
South Carolina	31.2	29.5	33.3	18.8	17.8	130.6
South Dakota	9.3	1.7	2.8	3.3	.9	18.0
Tennessee	120.6	31.0	17.4	11.9	7.8	188.7
Texas	127.5	165.5	110.3	34.4	11.5	449.2
Utah	14.5	3.5	2.5	1.4	5.5	27.4
Vermont	5.3	13.5	13.5	6.3	3.7	42.3
Virginia	100.0	243.3	81.1	11.0	61.5	496.9
Washington	38.1	67.8	23.8	52.6	5.8	188.1
West Virginia	38.2	32.5	2.1	23.0	–	95.8
Wisconsin	135.1	97.2	21.3	6.6	3.9	264.1
Wyoming	1.5	2.4	–	–	–	3.9
Guam	2.2	10.5	–	4.1	.7	17.5
Puerto Rico	4.2	48.6	76.0	.8	.5	130.1
Virgin Islands	8.0	2.5	2.5	3.1	3.8	19.9

[1] To convert to 1972 dollars multiply by 1.15.
[2] Separate costs for FY 1973 and FY 1974 estimated from FY 1972/1974 total.
[3] Estimates decline year by year because they relate only to facilities planned as of 1971.

Source: U.S. ENVIRONMENTAL PROTECTION AGENCY (1972). The Economics of Clean Water. Environmental Protection Agency, Washington, D.C. Volume I, p. 117.

Industry	Outlays for Construction, Interest, Operation, Maintenance, and Replacement 1968–1976. (billions of 1972 dollars)
Primary Metals	5.35
Chemical and Allied Products	4.26
Paper and Allied Products	4.13
Food and Kindred Products	3.28
Petroleum and Coal	2.37
Textiles	.87
Stone Clay and Glass	.62
Electrical Equipment	.48
Fabricated Metal Products	.47
Rubber and Plastics	.36
Lumber and Wood Products	.31
Transportation Equipment	.31
Leather	.30
Machinery	.28
Median Estimate Total	23.39[1]
Maximum Cost Total	29.04[2]
Minimum Cost Total	11.43[3]

[1] Totals do not account for publicly supplied waste treatment.
[2] Assumes little process improvement in water use in the plants involved.
[3] Assumes substantial process improvements in industrial water use.

Source: Adapted from U.S. ENVIRONMENTAL PROTECTION AGENCY (1972). The Economics of Clean Water–Summary Analysis. Environmental Protection Agency, Washington, D.C. p. 6, 1971 costs converted to 1972 costs using a factor of 1.15.

be under construction by 1976. This is probably not realistic. EPA estimates that the peak year effort to correct the known backlog could not be reached until 1977, even if the annual real growth in construction industry capacity is 25 percent.

In 1972, the Council on Environmental Quality (CEQ) published estimates of 1970 expenditures and of the capital and total annual costs required to meet then-existing water quality standards by 1980. Table 16-9 presents estimates of expenditures required to control major public and private point-sources of water pollution. The expenditures for State and local treatment systems include Federal grant assistance.

Effect of Recent Legislation: The Federal Water Pollution Control Act Amendments of 1972 impose considerably higher treatment requirements and extend Federal control to all discharges of waste material into the Nation's waters. EPA and CEQ have considered the cost implications of expanding current programs to actually achieve a goal of "no discharge" or "zero discharge" of pollutants.[7] They found that incremental costs rise very fast at higher levels of treatment and that incremental benefits as commonly measured rise more slowly.[8] Their findings are summarized in Table 16-10 which shows that 100 percent removal of pollutants from municipal and industrial wastewater (not including storm water flows) would cost five times as much as 85-90 percent

[7] *Ibid.*

[8] See Figure 4-1 for graphic presentation of this data.

TABLE 16-9.—Estimated water pollution control expenditures: Current levels and required to meet water quality standards established under the 1965 Act by 1980

(in billions of 1972 dollars)

Pollution Sources	1970 Capital Investment In Place	1970 Capital Investment Annual	1970 Annualized Cost[2]	1980 Capital Investment In Place	1980 Capital Investment Annual	1980 Annualized Cost[2]	Cumulative Requirements 1971–80 Capital Investment	+ Operating Costs	= Cash Flow Requirements
Public									
Federal installations	NA	NA	0.2	NA	*	0.3	1.4	3.1	4.5
State and local treatment systems[1]	20.9	1.5	2.6	33.8	1.8	4.3	21.8	27.1	48.9
Private									
Manufacturing	5.5	1.3	1.2	13.6	1.2	2.8	13.7	16.3	30.0
Utilities	0.3	0.1	0.1	4.4	0.3	0.9	5.2	4.8	10.0
Feedlots	–	–	–	.8	*	0.6	2.2	2.1	4.3
Construction Sediment	NA	*	*	NA	0.1	0.1	1.0	0.1	1.1
Vessels	–	–	–	0.3	*	0.2	1.0	0.6	1.6
Total	26.7	2.9	4.1	52.9	3.4	9.2	46.3	54.1	100.4

[1] Exclusive of collector or combined sewer system construction – includes Federal grants.
[2] Operating costs plus interest and depreciation on investments in environmental controls.

Source: U.S. COUNCIL ON ENVIRONMENTAL QUALITY (1972). Environmental Quality, The Third Annual Report of the Council on Environmental Quality. U.S. Government Printing Office, Washington, D.C: Table 1, p. 276. (Figures in table converted to 1972 price level by multiplying by 1.15.)

*indicates less than .05.

TABLE 16-10.—Index of pollution control investment costs related to level of abatement

Level of Removal	Gain from Previous Level	Cost Index (85 percent level of removal = 100)	Cost Index Increase per Percentage Point Gain
100 Percent	1	500	250
99	1	250	50
98	3	200	17
95	10	150	5
85	—	100	—

Source: U.S. ENVIRONMENTAL PROTECTION AGENCY (1972). The Economics of Clean Water – Summary Analysis. Environmental Protection Agency, Washington, D.C. p. 23

TABLE 16-11.—Total national costs for municipal and industrial treatment[1]
(dollars in billions)

Level of Removal	Ten-Year Capital Expenditures	20-25 Year Operating Costs	Total Expenditures	Annualized Cost in 1981
100 %	94.5	220.0	316.5	21.1
80 % @ 95–99% 20 % @ 100% }	47.2	110.1	157.3	12.4
95–99%	35.3	83.5	118.8	8.4
85–90%[2]	17.6	43.2	60.8	4.1

[1] Excludes $12.0 billion costs for intercepting sewers. (Also, no other sewer costs are included.)
[2] Roughly program to meet standards set under 1965 Act.

Source: U.S. ENVIRONMENTAL PROTECTION AGENCY (1972). The Economics of Clean Water. Environment Protection Agency, Washington, D.C. Volume I, p. 156.

removal generally required to meet standards under the 1965 Act.

Table 16-11 converts their findings into 10-year capital expenditures and operating costs over a 25-year period showing an increase from $61 billion contemplated under the current program to $316 billion at the zero discharge level, and an increase in annual costs in 1981 from $4.1 to $21.1.

The costs shown in Table 16-11 are rough estimates and do not include costs associated with control of the "other" pollution sources outlined in Table 16-6. The potential costs that may be required under the 1972 legislation to control pollution from such sources as storm and combined sewers, agricultural wastes, and other dispersed sources are not known but they could be tremendous.

Commission staff estimates (also rough) indica that control and treatment for the "first flush" storm-generated urban runoff would be disprop tionately costly in comparison with both the coll tion and treatment of municipal sewage wast Commission staff estimates of capital and operati costs for the collection and treatment of munici and industrial wastes and urban storm runoff to m water quality standards established under the 19 Act, and to use the "best known technology" shown in Table 16-12. Table 16-13 presents comp able estimates for treatment of municipal sewer and storm water runoff on an annual and per cap basis. The amounts shown in Tables 16-12 and 16 are similar to, but not the same as, the estimates EPA, due to differences in both estimating p

TABLE 16-12.–Estimated additional costs for municipal and industrial wastewater management
(billions of 1972 dollars)

Item	Capital Cost	Annual O&M in 1983	Cumulative O&M to 1983	Total Expenditures to 1983
To Achieve Water Quality Standards Established Under the 1965 Act				
Municipal Wastes				
Collector Systems	40	.04	0.3	40.3
Treatment	15	1.5	9.0	24.0
Storm Flows				
Combined Sewers	32	.40	2.0	34.0
Separate Storm Sewers	81	1.0	5.0	86.0
Industrial Wastes	10	1.7[1]	11.9[1]	21.9
Thermal Electric Cooling	4	NA	NA	>4.0
Total	182	4.64	28.2	210.2
To Achieve a "Best Known Technology"				
Municipal Wastes				
Collector Systems	40	.04	0.3	40.3
Treatment	40	3.3	23.1	63.1
Storm Flows				
Combined Sewers	54	.65	3.2	57.2
Separate Storm Sewers	180	2.2	11.0	191.0
Industrial Wastes	49	8.4[1]	59.0[1]	108.0
Thermal Electric Cooling	8	NA	NA	>8.0
Total	371	14.59	96.6	467.6

ncludes replacements costs.
– Not analyzed.
urce: NWC staff estimates.

ures and in the way costs are allocated between
te treatment and sewers.

mary of Cost Estimates: Capital requirements to
t different goals of water quality treatment have
been and probably cannot be estimated with any
ee of certainty except possibly with respect to
icipal sewage and industrial wastewater treat-
t. Many factors contribute to this uncertainty.
quantities of waste are unknown and the target
s of quality are poorly defined. Future tech-
gical advance can only be roughly estimated and
choices between alternative technologies cannot
effectively covered in a nationwide estimate.
ibly the most serious difficulty is our inability to
ict the continued escalation of costs.
ough estimates of the range of capital investment
ired to meet standards established under the

1965 Federal Water Pollution Control Act and a "no
discharge" policy are given in Table 16-14. The
reliability of available information appears inadequate
for policy and program decisions concerning the
billions of dollars of public and private moneys
involved.

Table 16-15 presents the Commission's estimates
of capital requirements for Federal and other governmental investments under three policy assumptions.
These are presented in terms of annual capital
investment for all water resource development.
Operation and maintenance costs are not included.

The Effect of Inflation on Construction Costs

The continued escalation of costs cannot be
reliably predicted. Since World War II, construction
costs have moved continually upward. Figure 16-2

513

	Capital Cost (billion $)	Annual Capital Cost[2] (billion $)	Per Capita Annual Capital Cost[3] ($)	Annual O&M Cost (billion $)	Per Capita Annual O&M Cost ($)	Total Annual Per Capita Cost ($)
A. To Achieve Water Quality Standards Established Under the 1965 Act						
Municipal Wastes						
Collector Systems	40	3.13	15.65	.04	.20	15.85
Treatment	15	1.17	5.85	1.50	7.50	13.35
Storm Flows						
Combined Sewers	32	2.50	12.50	.40	2.00	14.50
Separate Storm Sewers	81	6.34	31.70	1.00	5.00	36.70
Total	168	13.14	65.70	2.94	14.70	80.40
B. To Achieve a "Best Known Technology" Policy						
Municipal Wastes						
Collector Systems	40	3.13	15.65	.04	.20	15.85
Treatment	40	3.13	15.65	3.30	16.50	32.15
Storm Flows						
Combined Sewers	54	4.22	21.10	.65	3.25	24.35
Separate Storm Sewers	180	14.08	70.40	2.20	11.00	81.40
Total	314	24.56	122.80	6.19	30.95	153.75

[1] NWC staff estimates.
[2] Amortized annual capital cost, 25 years at 6 percent interest (.07823).
[3] Based on estimated 1983 sewered population of 200 million people.

presents the Engineering News-Record (ENR) Construction Cost Index for the past 70 years. The 1950-1970 period was characterized by a rather stable average annual increase of 4 percent. However, in the past 2 years there has been a sharp escalation. In 1971, EPA estimated an increase of 15 percent in construction costs for municipal waste treatment facilities.[9] While it is not likely that a 15 percent annual rate will continue for several years, it is important to recognize that such a rate would double the costs indicated here in less than 5 years.

[9] U.S. ENVIRONMENTAL PROTECTION AGENCY (1972). The Economics of Clean Water—Summary Analysis. Environmental Protection Agency, Washington, D.C. p. 10.

It is also obvious that sharply increasing the l[...] of expenditures for water pollution control [...] greatly increase the rate of inflation in water po[...] tion control costs. It appears that some investm[...] levels now being proposed will seriously escalate c[...] in waste treatment construction substantially bey[...] cost escalation associated with general inflation[...] trends in the economy.

Conclusions on Capital Demands

The Commission finds that the estimated dema[...] for capital at all levels of government for w[...] resources development might range from $23 to [...] billion annually in current dollars through 1[...]

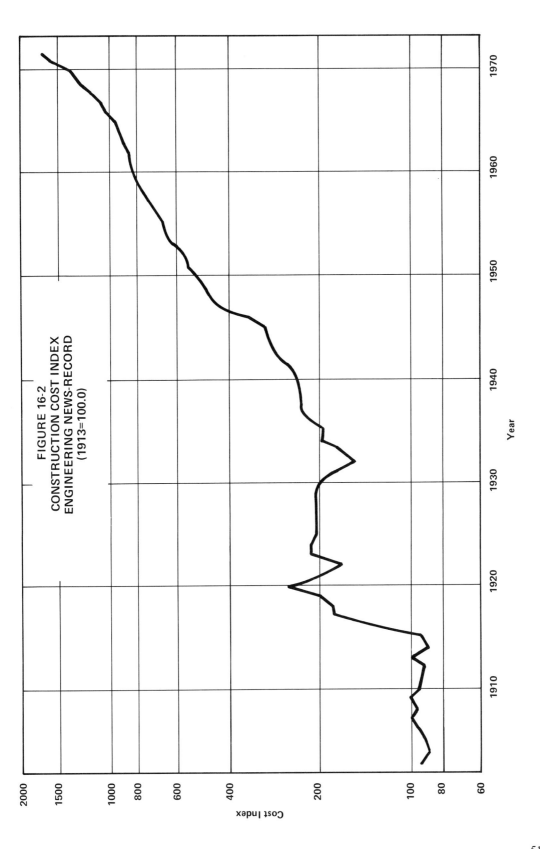

FIGURE 16-2
CONSTRUCTION COST INDEX
ENGINEERING NEWS-RECORD
(1913=100.0)

TABLE 16-14.—Estimated capital costs for water pollution control (billions of dollars)		
Source or Construction Aspect	To Meet Present Water Quality Standards	To Meet a "No Discharge" Policy
Treatment of Wastes:	18	95
(Municipal only)	(11)	(60)
(Industrial only)	(7)	(35)
Interceptor sewers:	12	12
Collecting sewers:	16	16
Storm and Combined sewers and other Urban Runoff:	15-55	54-180
Acid Mine Drainage:	5-15	10-30
Oil and Hazardous Spills:	1-5	2-10
Agricultural Wastes:	1-7	2-14
Dredging Spoil Disposal and Other:	1-2	2-4
Totals	69-130	193-361

Note: Cost estimates are to be considered as very rough. Ranges of costs are shown in some cases, where it is believed that there is little information to support detailed cost estimates. Costs have *not* been converted to the same base year.

Source: Environmental Protection Agency estimates.

under policies that are being considered for implementation by Federal agencies and the Congress. This compares with capital expenditures by Federal, State, and local governments for highways of about $12 billion in 1971 and 1972.[10]

The major factor in these capital estimates is construction for wastewater treatment. The cost of meeting either water quality standards under the 1965 Water Quality Act or "best known technology" by 1983 will require huge amounts of capital. In addition, costs for operation and maintenance of waste management facilities are relatively much higher than for other types of water projects.

The Commission does not necessarily endorse these indicated levels of expenditure or suggest that all the plans should be implemented. It has found the available information inadequate to make such a judgment. The estimates presented here are intended to give an indication of the magnitude of expenditures necessary to support traditional water development programs at planned levels while increasing the

level of investments in water pollution control faci ties. In each case the cost of going ahead with tl program must be weighed against the benefits to l gained before making a decision to proceed.

The Commission has not found it realistic attempt to independently estimate the costs meeting a "no discharge" goal of water quali management.[11] The "no discharge" concept could l construed to imply either the distillation of water prohibition of effluents from all point- and no point-sources of pollution. It is not clear whether th goal would apply to natural sources of pollutio such as salinity or organic debris. Furthermore, ev with implementation of policies to recycle us

[10] U.S. FEDERAL HIGHWAY ADMINISTRATION (December 3, 1971). News Release.

[11] New York State officials have developed an estimate f that State. The removal of 99 to 100 percent c biochemical oxygen demand is estimated to require capital cost of $150 billion and an annual operation ar maintenance cost of $1.35 billion. They also estimate th New York State constitutes 10 percent of the nation need. See METZLER DF & BOGEDAIN FO (1972). Tl Cost of Water Quality Goals, paper presented at th National Symposium of Costs of Water Pollution Contro Raleigh, North Carolina, April 6, 1972.

Policy	Average Annual Capital Expenditures 1974 to 1983 (billions of 1972 dollars)		
	Federal	State and Local Government	Total
1. "Needs" as visualized in Water Resources Council Framework Studies	10	13[1]	23[1]
2. Including environmental goal of attaining water quality standards established under the 1965 Act for municipal wastewater and stormflows by 1985[2]	15.0 (12.6)[3]	8.7 (4.2)[3]	23.7 (16.8)[3,4]
3. Including environmental goal of treatment with "best known technology" for municipal wastewater and stormflows by 1985[2]	26.0 (23.6)[3]	12.3 (7.8)[3]	38.3 (31.4)[3,5]

[1] Not strictly comparable because some private investment is included. Potential interbasin water transfers are not included in these estimates.
[2] Policies 2 and 3 assume that spending for water resources, other than for water quality, is as follows: Federal, $2.4 billion, including expenditure for thermal power and transmission lines; and State and local, $4.5 billion.
[3] Data in brackets are expenditures for water quality. Policies 2 and 3 assume a 75 percent cost share for municipal waste and stormflow facilities. (See Table 16-12.)
[4] $16.8 billion for 10 years is $168 billion. See Table 16-13.
[5] $31.4 billion for 10 years is $314 billion. See Table 16-13.

materials, some waste products will need to be disposed of in air, water, or land resources. It is clear that, in some cases, water resources are the most economic and environmentally least damaging media for disposal. Each situation should be judged on the actual merits involved. If no discharge were really adopted as a mandatory goal, it is very likely that the costs would be beyond the capacity of the Nation to finance without seriously neglecting other pressing needs.

There is presently not only inadequate information on the investments required to meet various levels of water pollution control but also a lack of adequate information on the relative effectiveness of investments to control various sources of water pollution. There is a definite need for a cost-effective strategy to control water pollution.

ALTERNATIVE METHODS OF FINANCING WATER DEVELOPMENTS

The Commission recognizes that adoption of the cost-sharing principles recommended in Chapter 15 will increase the financial burden of State and local governments. The purpose of this section is to consider alternative methods of financing governmental expenditures for future water resource developments.

Nature and Background of Public Finance Problems

It is not sufficient to look at water resource financing in isolation since water program expenditures must compete for funds with all public spending categories. An overview of total spending and revenue patterns is also useful in suggesting alternative sources for water resource expenditures, as well as in indicating potential problem areas that must be resolved to achieve effective water resource financing.

Over the past 20 years, total governmental revenues—Federal, State, and local—have increased from $67 billion in 1950 to $334 billion in 1970, a fivefold increase. During the same period, governmental expenditures increased by a like magnitude from $70 billion in 1950 to $333 billion in Fiscal

Year 1970.[12] The implication from these data is that there exists an endless cornucopia of funds in a growing U.S. economy to meet increasing needs for public expenditures.

As shown in Table 16-16, the rate of increase of total direct revenue collections for all levels of government nearly doubled during the last 5 years of the 1960's over the first 5 years. Collection of State revenues increased more rapidly during the decade than did the collection of Federal revenues. Such a rapid rate of increase in State and local expenditures is reflected by a concomitant increase in debt at all levels of government. While Federal Government debt increased by 30 percent during the decade of the 1960's, total State and local debt increased by 105 percent.

In summary, during the decade of the 1960's total government revenues increased by an annual average rate of over 8 percent compounded in comparison with an average annual increase during that same decade in gross national product (GNP) of 6.8 percent. GNP can be considered a crude index of capacity for generating revenues and it is clear that revenues have been increasing more rapidly than has GNP. At the State and local level, annual revenues have increased at an annual average of 9 percent during the 1960's, while total State direct expenditures have increased at an annual rate of nearly 12-1/2 percent during the period 1965-1970. At the same time, total governmental debt increased at an annual average rate of 3.7 percent during the decade 1960-1970, but State and local debt increased at an annual average rate of over 7-1/2 percent.

These data indicate the broad external dimensions of the aggregate public spending-revenue situation. They show that governmental spending, revenue, and State and local debt have grown at faster rates than GNP in the last decade. And they also make clear that the problem of funding new public expenditure increments must be considered in terms of all levels of government and in relation to total national output.

[12] U.S. BUREAU OF THE CENSUS (1972). Statistical Abstract of the United States, 1972. U.S. Government Printing Office, Washington, D.C. p. 406. And U.S. BUREAU OF THE CENSUS, Social and Economic Statistics Administration (May 1972). Guide to Recurrent and Special Governmental Statistics, State and Local Government Special Studies No. 62. U.S. Department of Commerce, Washington, D.C. pp. 16-17.

Alternative Sources of Revenue for Financing Water Resources Projects

A basic perspective of patterns of change for specific revenue sources at all levels of government for the period 1950-1970 is provided in Table 16-17. At the Federal level, general revenues increased at a slightly lower rate for the period 1950-1970 than did total governmental revenues. The growth in the personal income tax dominated tax collections by the Federal Government, accounting for nearly three fourths of the total increase in Federal tax revenue during the period 1965-1970. This indicates the tremendous response of the progressive personal income tax to increases in economic growth.

At the State level, growth of 13-1/2 percent per year in personal income taxes registered the greatest relative increase in tax revenues, but since personal income taxes started from a much lower base they accounted for only 19 percent of total State tax revenue in 1970. Although sales and gross receipts revenues increased at a compound annual rate of only 9.2 percent, they nonetheless continued to dominate State tax collections in 1970, accounting for 58 percent of total State tax collections.

For local government, the property tax has shown a strong resurgence in recent years. Property tax receipts accounted for 81 percent of the growth in local government revenues in the period 1965-1970. Revenues from user charges and miscellaneous fees also showed strong increases at both the local and State levels during this period.

In the following paragraphs, each existing and potential source of revenue for water resource project financing is briefly considered. The advantages and disadvantages of each source of revenue are pinpointed and the flexibility and potential of individual revenue sources for contributing increased revenues toward water resource financing are highlighted. Since many water resource projects are local in nature, the discussion begins with consideration of municipal, local, and State sources of revenue.

Debt: In 1970, State and local governments expended $29.6 billion for capital outlays of which $10.4 billion was for highways, $7.6 billion for education, and $2.4 billion for local utilities.[13] During the same year, as shown in Table 16-18, State and local

[13] MOODY'S INVESTORS SERVICE, INC (1972). Moody's Municipal and Government Manual. Moody's Investors Service, Inc., New York.

TABLE 16-16.—Government finances, revenue, direct expenditures, and debt 1960, 1965, 1970

(in billions of dollars)

	All Governments	Percent Increase	Federal	Percent Increase	State and Local	Percent Increase	State	Percent Increase	Local	Percent Increase
Revenue from own sources										
1960	153.1		99.8		53.3		26.1		27.2	
1965	202.6	32	125.8	26	76.7	44	38.5	48	38.2	41
1970	333.8	65	205.6	63	128.2	67	68.7	78	59.6	56
Direct expenditure										
1960	151.3		90.3		61.0		22.1		38.8	
1965	205.6	36	119.0	32	86.6	42	31.3	41	55.2	42
1970	333.0	62	184.9	55	148.1	71	56.2	79	91.9	67
Total expenditure, including inter-governmental										
1965	205.6		130.1		—		45.5		55.5	
1970	333.0	62	208.2	60	—		85.1	87	92.5	78
Debt outstanding										
1960	356.3		286.3		70.0		18.5		51.4	
1965	416.8	17	317.3	11	99.5	42	27.0	46	72.5	41
1970	514.5	23	370.9	17	143.6	44	42.0	55	101.6	40

Source: U.S. BUREAU OF THE CENSUS (1972). Statistical Abstract of the United States 1972. U.S. Government Printing Office, Washington, D.C. U.S. BUREAU OF THE CENSUS, Social and Economic Statistics Administration (May 1972). Guide to Recurrent and Special Governmental Statistics, State and Local Government Special Studies No. 62. U.S. Department of Commerce, Washington, D.C. and U.S. BUREAU OF THE CENSUS (1967). Governmental Finances in 1964-65. U.S. Department of Commerce, Washington, D.C.

TABLE 16-17.—Sources of revenue—Federal, State, and local governments

Source of Revenue	Fiscal Year 1970 Revenues by Level of Government				Annual Compound Rate of Growth — 1950-70			
	All	Federal	State	Local	All	Federal	State	Local
	(billions of dollars)				%	%	%	%
Total revenue from own sources	333.8	205.6	68.7	59.6	8.4	8.1	9.4	8.5
General revenue	272.5	163.6	57.5	51.4	8.0	7.3	9.8	8.8
Taxes	232.9	146.1	48.0	38.8	7.9	7.4	9.4	8.2
Individual income	101.2	90.4	9.2 }	1.6	9.5	9.1	13.5 }	17.6
Corporation income	36.6	32.8	3.7 }		6.2	5.9	9.7 }	
Sales, gross receipts, and customs	48.6	18.3	27.3	3.1	6.8	4.3	9.2	9.7
Property	34.1	–	1.1	33.0	8.0	–	6.6	8.0
Other	12.4	4.5	6.7	1.2	7.1	7.3	7.3	5.6
Charges and miscellaneous	39.6	17.5	9.5	12.6	8.8	6.6	12.5	10.8
Utility revenues	6.6	–	–	6.6	6.7	–	–	6.7
Liquor store revenues	2.0	–	1.7	.3	4.1	–	3.9	5.2
Insurance trust revenues	52.7	42.0	9.4	1.3	12.0	13.3	8.6	10.2

Source: U.S. DEPARTMENT OF COMMERCE, Bureau of the Census.

governments borrowed $12.8 billion for new long-term debt, retired $7.0 billion, and registered a total of $143.6 billion in total outstanding debt, including $12.2 billion in short-term debt.

Total new issue bond activity for calendar year 1971 included $16.2 billion for general obligation bonds and $8.1 billion for revenue bonds.[14] Historical growth patterns for various categories of State and local debt are shown in Table 16-19. Total State and local debt outstanding increased at an annual rate of 7.6 percent between 1965 and 1970—the long-term, full-faith-and-credit debt component increased by only 6.0 percent per year while nonguaranteed debt increased at an annual rate of 8.2 percent. As a generalization, approximately one-third of all capital outlays in recent years has been financed by new debt. As the authors of a Tax Foundation report have summarized:

> There are no universally accepted answers to questions concerning the propriety or sustainability of a given level of debt. For States and political subdivisions, the level of general obligation debt is limited by constitutional or statutory provisions. Other borrowing, however, is not so restricted and has been resorted to with increas-

ing frequency in the postwar period. Non-guaranteed debt has risen significantly in proportion to total debt, from 13.6 percent in 1950 to 38 percent in 1965 (39 percent in 1970). For practical purposes, it would thus appear that the existing strictures setting maximum limits to general obligation debt do not serve as a realistic guide to the future course of total debt.[15]

The principal issue with respect to continue financing of State and local capital outlays throug issuance of long-term debt is the constraints c statutory and constitutional limitations on the con position of State and local debt, not on the rate c growth in debt.[16] Although the extent of restrictiv ness in issuing debt differs by State, it is apparer that the principal effect of these limitations has bee

[14]Ibid.

[15]U.S. CONGRESS, Joint Economic Committee (Ju 1967). Revenue Sharing and Its Alternatives: What Futu for Fiscal Federalism? Volume III: Federal, State, Loc Fiscal Projections, prepared for the Subcommittee Fiscal Policy, 90th Congress, 1st Session. U.S. Governme Printing Office, Washington, D.C. p. 1316.

[16]HOGGAN, Daniel H (1971). State and Local Capability Share Financial Responsibility of Water Development wit the Federal Government. U.S. Water Resources Counc Washington, D.C. p. 13.

Item	Total	State Governments	Local Governments	Per Capita
		(billions of dollars)		
Debt outstanding, total	143.6	42.0	101.6	706.4
Long-term	131.4	38.9	92.5	646.6
Full faith and credit	75.3	17.7	57.6	370.7
Nonguaranteed	56.1	21.2	34.9	275.9
Short-term	12.2	3.1	9.1	59.8
Net long-term debt outstanding	121.7	34.5	87.3	599.0
Long-term debt by purpose:				
Local schools	31.5	3.0	28.6	155.1
Local utilities	19.6	–	19.6	96.4
All other	80.3	36.0	44.4	395.1
Long-term debt issued	12.8	3.9	8.9	63.2
Long-term debt retired	7.0	1.9	5.1	34.5

Source: U.S. BUREAU OF THE CENSUS (1971). Governmental Finances in 1969-70. U.S. Department of Commerce, Washington, D.C. p. 28.

expand reliance on revenue bonds which are not backed by the full faith and credit of the borrowing jurisdiction.

In addition to growth in revenue bond financing, there are two other principal methods of circumventing legal debt limitations. The first method is by shifting increased responsibility for debt financing from more restricted to less restricted governments. In some cases this shift is from State to local; in other cases the shift is from local to State levels.[17] The second method is through lease-purchase arrangements where the governmental jurisdiction requiring capital facilities leases such facilities and, in some cases, eventually purchases them.

Another means of facilitating acquisition of State and local capital facilities through debt expansion has been the creation of special districts, each with its own taxing and debt limitations. Although special districts are created for a variety of reasons, clearly one reason has been to circumvent local debt and property tax restrictions. In 1967, there were 21,264 special districts in the United States, excluding cities, counties, and school districts.[18] The pressure in recent years to decentralize government and bring it closer to the people has run head-on into the growing problem of fragmentation and overlapping of jurisdictions, tax bases, functions, and services.

State financing authorities have been created by several States to provide for purchase by the State of bonds issued by local governments. The State in turn issues its own bonds to provide the necessary funds. This method can effectively reduce local borrowing costs.

The use of State and local municipal bonds to finance pollution abatement facilities for private industries is growing rapidly. This low-cost financing affords an effective means of encouraging investment in pollution abatement facilities.

MITCHELL WE (October 1967). The effectiveness of debt limits on state and local government borrowing. The Bulletin [New York University, Graduate School of Business Administration, Institute of Finance] 45:19.

[18] U.S. BUREAU OF THE CENSUS (1967). 1967 Census of Governments, Governmental Organization, volume 1. U.S. Government Printing Office, Washington, D.C.

521

TABLE 16-19.–Gross outstanding debt of State and local governments[1] selected periods, 1950–1970

(billions of dollars)

Year	Total Debt Outstanding	Total	Long term Full Faith and Credit	Non-guaranteed	Short Term
1950	24.1	23.1	19.8	3.3	1.1
1955	44.3	42.3	30.5	11.7	2.0
1960	70.0	66.8	41.7	25.2	3.2
1965	99.5	94.2	56.4	37.8	5.3
1970	143.6	131.4	75.3	56.1	12.2

[1] Data represent debt for all functions, general and nongeneral.
[2] End of fiscal years.

Source: U.S. CONGRESS, Joint Economic Committee (July 1967). Revenue Sharing and Its Alternatives: What Future f[...] Fiscal Federalism?, Volume III, Federal, State, Local Fiscal Projections, prepared for the Subcommittee on Fisc[...] Policy, 90th Congress, 1st Session. U.S. Government Printing Office, Washington, D.C. p. 1316.

Federal Grants-in-Aid and Revenue Sharing: Federal payments to State and local governments totaled $24.2 billion on a checks-issued basis in Fiscal Year 1970 under 97 specific grants-in-aid programs and several miscellaneous programs.[19] Excluding duplicative transactions between levels of government, State governments received $19.2 billion from the Federal Government in intergovernmental revenues, while local governments received $2.6 billion from the Federal Government in intergovernmental revenues.[20] The estimated total 1972 grants-in-aid and shared revenues accruing to State and local governments from the Federal Government is $39.1 billion, up 258 percent from the total Federal aid to State and local governments in 1965 of $10.9 billion.[21]

A program of general revenue sharing was enacted into law in October 1972. Federal tax revenues are shared with States and localities with limited restrictions and controls. Quarterly general revenue sharing payments totaling $30.2 billion have been authoriz[...] over the period 1972 to 1977.

General revenue sharing funds are distribut[...] among the States by formula. Within the Sta[...] one-third of the funds go to State government a[...] two-thirds to local governments. The FY 1974 bud[...] estimates that $6.0 billion will be distributed to St[...] and local governments.[22]

The relative importance of Federal grants a[...] general revenue sharing in Federal intergovernmen[...] assistance is a subject of continuing debate. Howev[...] it is expected that the general revenue shar[...] program will ease somewhat the burden of financ[...] future State and local water projects by fund[...] competing services and reducing pressures to incre[...] taxes or issue debt to finance these services.

Property Tax: As indicated in Table 16-17, [...] property tax continues to be the bulwark of lc[...] finance. The future of the property tax, at least c[...] district-by-district basis, may be in some doubt a[...] result of a series of State supreme court decisi[...] declaring certain ways of financing schools under [...] property tax to be unconstitutional. However [...] U.S. Supreme Court, in *San Antonio Independ*[...] *School District v. Rodriguez*,[23] held that variation[...]

[19] U.S. DEPARTMENT OF THE TREASURY, Fiscal Service, Bureau of Accounts, Division of Government Financial Operations (1971). Federal Aid to States, Fiscal Year 1970. U.S. Government Printing Office, Washington, D.C. p. 20.

[20] U.S. BUREAU OF THE CENSUS (1971). Governmental Finances in 1969-70. U.S. Department of Commerce, Washington, D.C. p. 20.

[21] U.S. BUREAU OF THE CENSUS (1972). Statistical Abstract of the United States, 1972. U.S. Government Printing Office, Washington, D.C. p. 413.

[22] OFFICE OF MANAGEMENT AND BUDGET (1973). [...] Budget of the United States Government, Fiscal Y[...] 1974. U.S. Government Printing Office, Washington, D[...] pp. 162-163.

[23] 41 USLW 4407 (March 21, 1973).

Federal payments to State governments are increasing

State allocated tax base among Texas school districts did not violate the equal protection clause of the U.S. Constitution. If validity of the property tax is held by some States to depend on removal of inequities among geographic areas, among taxpayers, and among classes of property, the inevitable result will be greater State control over local assessments, if not direct State collection and redistribution to local governments.

Moreover, if the question of right of access by all citizens to some minimal standards of public services becomes extended beyond education to other public goods and services, such as water supply and sewer services, the pressures for overhauling the property tax will continue to increase. With a continued increase in new construction and with rapid acceleration of property values, it can be argued that State and local revenue growth will depend on basic property tax reform.

User Charges: The most straightforward method of public finance is to charge the users who benefit from the facility or services provided. With increased budget problems at all levels of government, increased attention has been given to user charges as noted earlier in this section.

The outlook is for continued expansion in both the volume and scope of application of user charges. Application of user charges requires that the service be priced in an understandable way and that payments be obtained from the direct beneficiaries. User charges can be readily implemented for financing many services of water resource projects, such as municipal water supply, sewers, irrigation, outdoor recreation, and electric power.

As water demands increase, use will press more heavily on natural supplies, costs of service will increase and competition among uses will increase. Financing water development projects through user charges would conserve water supplies, discourage premature investment in facilities and reduce financial burdens now borne by nonusers.

Environmental Financing Authority: The Environmental Financing Act of 1972[24] established the Environmental Financing Authority. The Authority is authorized to purchase, under certain conditions, debt issued by a State or local public body to finance the non-Federal share of the cost of any project for the construction of waste treatment works which the Administrator of the Environmental Protection Agency has determined to be eligible for Federal financial assistance. The operation of the Authority will ease the burden of water quality financing for States and local entities who experience difficulty in issuing bonds through conventional market channels.

Conclusions on Financing

An evaluation of State and local public facility needs and financing conducted in the mid-1960's for the Joint Economic Committee reached the conclusion:

> ... that sufficient funds would be available for requirements projected (but that) it is equally clear that this is only possible through heavy and growing reliance on commercial banks and to a lesser extent on two or three other specific sources of funds, e.g., personal trusts and fire and casualty companies.[25]

Numerous attempts have been made to project revenue availability from the existing tax structure along with potential expenditures in the next decade.[26] These fiscal surpluses, however, have a habit of disappearing just as cost overrides often swamp original construction estimates.

Realistically, it is concluded that the most likely sources of funding for new investments in water resource projects will come from incremental shifts in existing revenue structures. But the Commission believes that more reliance should be placed on user charge revenues.

Perhaps the most disturbing problem at the present time is that of persistent inflation. The problem of inflation is further aggravated at the local level because those goods and services purchased by local governments (school teachers, hospital services, construction, etc.) have risen in cost at a rate in excess of the general rate of inflation. Therefore, it is not sufficient to project average rates of inflation for

[24] *Federal Water Pollution Control Act Amendments of 1972*, P.L. 92-500, Section 12, 86 Stat. 816, 899, 33 USCA Section 1281 note.

[25] U.S. CONGRESS, Joint Economic Committee (December 1966). State and Local Public Facility Needs and Financing, Volume 2, Public Facility Financing, prepared for the Subcommittee on Economic Progress, 89th Congress, 2d Session. U.S. Government Printing Office, Washington D.C. p. iv.

[26] U.S. CONGRESS, Joint Economic Committee (July 1967). Revenue Sharing and Its Alternatives: What Future for Fiscal Federalism? Volume III: Federal, State, Local Fiscal Projections, prepared for the Subcommittee on Fiscal Policy, 90th Congress, 1st Session. U.S. Government Printing Office, Washington, D.C. p. 1256.

he economy as a whole in considering future outlay requirements for water resource projects at State and local levels.

A serious problem facing water resources financing is that of inflexibility for future commitments because of high fixed levels of current commitments for all public programs. This was well illustrated by the statement of former Under Secretary of the Treasury Charls E. Walker, who indicated that in Fiscal Year 1973 Federal programs with permanent mandatory spending will absorb $130 billion of total estimated outlays of $250 billion for that period.[27] In addition, mandatory increases are estimated to amount to $11 to $12 billion annually. Thus, requirements for fulfilling existing commitments provide a definite dampening effect on all new programs and this volume of committed expenditures must be taken into account when considering increases in future water resource expenditures.

RECOMMENDATIONS

6-1.   Since continued heavy reliance must be placed on debt financing of water resources projects of all types at the State and local levels, unrealistic legal barriers to efficient

[27] THE NEW YORK TIMES (June 11, 1972). Is Man the Master of His Budget?

debt acquisition and management should be removed in State and local constitutions, statutes, ordinances, and charters. These restrictions include debt and interest rate limitations that place local governments at a long-run cost and interest-rate disadvantage, and that ignore the fact that the bond markets themselves will reflect debt repayment capacity of local and State governments.

16-2.   In selling bonds to finance water resources projects, representatives of State and local governments should give increased attention to those factors and circumstances that will facilitate effective debt repayment, such as refunding provisions, implementation of user charges, and pooling of risks within the umbrella of larger more stable government jurisdictions.

16-3.   The increasing need for debt financing of water resource development by State and local governments, resulting from implementation of the Commission's recommendations on Federal cost-sharing policies, should not be impeded by repeal of the Federal tax exemption on State and local bond interest unless alternative provisions are made to assist these governments with increased interest cost burdens.

Basic Data and Research for Future Progress

Data collection is a long-standing activity in the Nation's water resources programs. Data are essential to the planning and evaluation of alternative courses of action. The Commission has looked at ongoing data collection programs in light of the broadening range of water problems and an expanding public interest in water and related environmental matters. While the main focus of water data collection in the past has been on the supply side with respect to quantity, future concerns will require more information on water quality and on the interrelationships between water and other aspects of the environment. The Commission's studies have indicated there are increased needs for data for impact analyses, to measure program effectiveness, and upon which to direct policy on such matters as flood damage reduction, water quality control, and water use.

Basic data collection is one thing; research is another. Research can expand man's ability to conserve resources and to attain social objectives more efficiently. The Commission foresees considerable "payoff" opportunity for research in evaluating the relation between (1) water, economic development, and the environment and (2) new techniques for the management of water.

BASIC DATA

Basic data on water and water-related matters provide a basis for evaluation, planning, and decision-making. A recent and still emerging need is for monitoring trends in water quality to improve selection of effective measures and for enforcement purposes. The need for data depends upon the analytical techniques, evaluation methods, planning objectives, and enforcement activities which are in

~~~~~~~~~~~~~~~~~~~~~~~~~~~~~~~~~~~~~~

Bonneville Power Administration's Control Center records telemetered data

effect. As these change, so does the need for basic data.

A good basic data program must include data collection, storage, retrieval, dissemination, and means for anticipating probable future needs. An especially important consideration in formulating a basic data program is insuring that potential users know what data are available so that they can obtain it when needed.

This section centers on the policy aspects of data collection. Specific data needs are identified in the various chapters throughout the Commission's report and are not recounted here.

The Problem

When first established, most water-data activity focused almost entirely upon water as a resource. The purpose of water data was to provide sound hydrologic information for water planning and development in their traditional senses. That purpose has been substantially broadened in recent years. Now water is not only regarded as a conventional resource but as a key aspect of man's environment. Hence the need to greatly expand the scope of data collection and dissemination.

Data on the biological and ecological aspects of water are now in demand by planners and administrators and the public. All types of water data are sought by economists, political scientists, environmentalists, and a wide range of interest groups. They want data in order to judge for themselves the merits of water projects and to develop, examine, and propose alternative ideas of their own. Diagnosis of water problems is a growing use to which water data are put. The National Environmental Policy Act (NEPA) with its requirements for environmental impact statements created a demand for much additional information and increased the importance of adequate retrieval and dissemination. Environmental data are sought by a much broader audience than hydrologic data ever were.

Future costs of deficiencies in water data are apt to be more subtle than the glaring examples of the past, such as reservoirs that do not fill,[1] levees that are overtopped, wells that run dry, or culverts that wash out. It is often difficult to establish the extent to which data inadequacies have adversely affected a design. More often than not, recognizing data inadequacies, designers tend to overdesign as a precaution. Therefore, while no physical failure may ever be evident, lack of data has resulted in excess cost. Adequate data are also of great importance in defining problems. For example, it is suggested that $110 billion be spent for treatment of urban storm water without knowing how often serious overflows occur or what quantity of pollutants are carried to the stream.[2]

The more diverse problems of data that lie ahead include such things as the avoidance of the costly consequences of delay and the need to assure efficiency of operation of increasingly complex water plant projects and technologies. Reservoirs, canals, and powerplants have become environmentally controversial. When or whether new facilities can be built will depend on understanding more completely their effects when in operation and the consequences of not having them available when needed.

The problem associated with basic data is the need to insure that the right kinds are available when needed and that potential users know and have ready access to what data are available. Since the ultimate use of basic data is to provide a sound base for decisionmaking, it is imperative that basic data needs be assessed in terms of the kinds of information needed for decisionmaking. It should also be remembered that basic data requirements change as the decisionmaking framework changes.

---

[1] As an example that has frequently been cited, the San Carlos Reservoir on the Gila River, Arizona, built in 1928 with a capacity of 1,200,000 acre-feet on the basis of a very short record of streamflow, has never been filled to capacity and is an outstanding instance of overdevelopment resulting from lack of basic data. For a discussion of the San Carlos Reservoir and other hydrologic problems caused by lack of or faulty analysis of basic data, see LANGBEIN, Walter B & HOYT, William G (1959). Water Facts for the Nation's Future. The Ronald Press Company, New York. Ch. 17.

[2] See Table 16-12.

The Existing Situation

Although quantitative data on surface water have been adequate in general, there are some deficiencies. For example, in stream gaging, the objective is rather modest—to be able to predict the character of flow of any stream with accuracy equivalent to a 10-year record. Studies show some inadequacies in coverage for small streams, incomplete information with respect to low flows, and no readily available information on flows at strategic points between gaging stations. There is need for continuous monitoring or at least daily sampling of both water quantity and quality at a substantial number of stations. The widespread practice of monthly samples is inadequate for many purposes.

Coverage of ground water, even at the level of "general inventory," is incomplete. Water quality data have fallen behind the pace of interest and demand. Climatological and hydrological programs, while generally adequate, have been inadequately coordinated. Recent developments promise a much improved coordination system with respect to water quantity and quality data, however.

Environmental data are only sketchily included in the ongoing water data collection program, and socioeconomic data remain spotty and are gathered largely in the absence of an understanding of needs. A national water quality monitoring network has been collecting water quality data for a number of years, but the quality of the data is poor, there are gaps in coverage, and neither the Environmental Protection Agency nor its predecessors have provided adequate interpretation of findings. The Commission's discussion of water quality data problems is contained in Chapter 4, and Recommendation 4-11 covers the Commission's proposed solution.

The Changing Scene: The problem of basic data is not one of developing a shopping list of specific data needs; it is the problem of achieving and maintaining relevant data to meet the changing needs of users and decisionmakers. This can best be understood by identifying some of the influences which must be dealt with in the future.

1. There will be an increase in the number of sectors of society concerned with water, water data, and water predictions. Water data will no longer be of concern only to specialists such as civil engineers, hydrologists, geologists, hydrometeorologists, etc.

2. There will be increased demand for hydrological-environmental integration; water quantity will

have to be closely related to water quality. The interrelations among precipitation, ground water, and streamflow, coupled with water quality, could be the first step in this integration process. Trends in water quality, whether improving or deteriorating, are essential in developing policy for water quality programs, and can be assessed only in conjunction with water quantity measures.

3. The scope of data will have to be expanded to include environmental information, such as the ecological and esthetic aspects of the surface water landscape and the monitoring of water quality.

4. The need for information on the potentials for using underground capacity for water storage and for combining underground and surface water systems will increase.

5. Demand for information on water costs, water use, and waste (residuals) discharge will also increase.

6. There will be greater emphasis on active rather than passive data storage whereby the data base can be subjected to routine statistical analysis to give prompt answers to queries.

7. Operations, management, and forecasting will require data which are recorded and reported practically simultaneously with the occurrence of the event. Examples include the continuous "real time" reporting of water data needed to operate a river system, such as in the Columbia River Basin. Continuous monitoring of water quality to provide a basis for detecting polluting discharges will also be required.

8. There will be greater use of remote sensing (aircraft and space satellites) for data collection and transmission.

9. Data systems will need to be designed to permit (1) feedback from monitoring, (2) analysis of requests for data at data centers, and (3) sensitivity analysis of water and environmental planning.

10. The demand for and importance of social and economic data related to water use will increase at a very rapid rate.

11. Multiobjective planning for water resources and plan implementation will require a much broader data base than in the past. For example, it was found early in the development of the Appalachian Water Resources Survey that there were very few data from which to determine regional socioeconomic impacts of water development. The same can be said for environmental impacts.

12. There will be an increasing need to develop social and environmental indicators (i.e., aggregate measures of data) to better judge program performance and to develop environmental baselines.

13. There will need to be an adequate and comprehensive program for collecting flood damage data to provide the basis for planning flood control works to more effectively reduce flood losses. A program, possibly centered in the Bureau of Census, should be developed on the pattern suggested by the Task Force on Flood Control Policy.[3]

14. There is an urgent need for more reliable information on the use of Federal water facilities for such purposes as navigation, recreation, irrigation, and water supply on a consistent basis to provide information for future planning.

Dissemination and Retrieval: A great amount of data are already available. Practically every Federal agency and many State and local agencies and private groups have data which are of interest and potential use to individuals concerned with water resources. The principal Federal water data agencies such as the U.S. Geological Survey (USGS), the National Oceanic and Atmospheric Administration (NOAA), and the U.S. Environmental Protection Agency (EPA) maintain catalogs of data in storage and available for retrieval. Unfortunately, owing in part to the pervasive nature of water resources and the wide range of interests involved, many people do not know what services are available and where, in what forms they are available, and how to get needed data. This situation could be corrected by establishing a referral center as to sources of water and water-related data. The reconstituted Water Resources Council (WRC)[4] is the logical agency for establishing such a center as it already provides a working forum and coordinating function for State and Federal agencies involved in water and water-related activities.

The primary purpose of a data referral center would be to maintain a continually updated reference system for water and water-related data indicating what kinds of data are available, in what forms, and where the data are available. Data would remain in existing storage systems rather than having WRC manage a master data storage and retrieval system. The WRC center would neither store data nor fill data

---

[3] TASK FORCE ON FLOOD CONTROL POLICY (August 1966). A Unified National Program for Managing Flood Losses, House Document No. 465, 89th Congress, 2d Session. U.S. Government Printing Office, Washington, D.C.

[4] See Chapter 11, Section B.

requests, but would direct requestors to appropriate agencies or data systems. The center would not replace the functions of the existing data services. Agencies such as the Office of Water Data Coordination, established as a result of Office of Management and Budget (OMB) Circular A-67, would be a major recipient of inquiries referred through the WRC referral center. The center should be publicized widely and its service should be available to all Federal, State, and local governmental agencies and private groups.

The WRC data center could also assist the data collection agencies in the development of flexible retrieval systems and more useful dissemination and retrieval formats. A desirable corollary to establishment of a water resources data referral center under the WRC would be publication of a periodically updated catalog of sources of water-related data which, if sufficiently complete and current, would obviate the need for many intermediate and time-consuming inquiries to the center.

Greater attention should also be focused on methods of data synthesis and transfer. For example, recent developments in data synthesis whereby non-existent data can be accurately imputed from other available data have resulted in satisfying increasing demands for data without significantly increasing the water quantity gaging network. Similar potentials exist for water quality.

Gaps in Data and Future Needs: As already indicated, a continuing problem is to insure that data collection and dissemination are relevant to present and probable future needs. There is not now a continuing broadly-based effort with this in mind except where individual agencies are identifying data needs which relate to their specific agency programs and objectives. The opportunity to mount such an effort is easily available, however.

The identification of specific gaps in the present data base should be a required part of planning and project studies, and of NEPA statements as well. This should not be confused with the unconvincing appeal for more and better data. Again, WRC is the logical candidate for assessing and identifying present and future water data needs. It reviews planning documents in a multiagency forum, is concerned with identifying possible future water problems, and is charged with preparing a biennial assessment of the Nation's water resources. WRC should also be able to work with the Council on Environmental Quality in determining data deficiencies related to water which are reported in NEPA statements.

In concert with its data referral center activities and its responsibilities under the Water Resources Planning Act, WRC should report periodically, perhaps once every 5 years, its recommendations for maintaining a program to insure that the proper kinds of data will be available when needed. The Council can provide the interagency forum to eliminate overlap and duplication among agencies, highlight common needs, and look to future problems not necessarily of concern in specific existing programs. Council efforts should include review of recent court decisions to assess where gaps in the data base were of significance.

In spite of the unquestioned value of learning from experience, water resources programs and activities have not always taken advantage of knowledge gained from past mistakes. Better information on cause and effect relationships in water project construction should be accumulated and made available to water planners. Most importantly, a continuing process of before-and-after-implementation studies would yield important information including cause and effect relationships and the adequacy of data.

Organizational Changes: The chief water data services of the Federal Government are presently divided between two agencies—the National Oceanic and Atmospheric Administration (NOAA) in the U.S. Department of Commerce and the Geological Survey (USGS) in the U.S. Department of the Interior. NOAA specializes in river stages, precipitation, and other hydrologic data; USGS specializes in data on river flow, the occurrence of ground water, and on the physical, chemical, and radioactive quality of water. The work of both agencies is coordinated with one another and with other agencies through the media of OMB Circulars A-62 (meteorological and climatic data) and A-67 (hydrologic data). Even though the coordination is cordial, active, and close, it can only go part way towards accomplishing economies of combination and scale. These potential economies can be achieved through joint design of precipitation and streamflow networks to take advantage of the natural relation between them, joint use of communication circuits, joint use of skills, complementary techniques of analysis, and the integration of data collection and processing services.

The hydrologists of NOAA and of the USGS have often attempted coordination in the collection of rainfall and streamflow data to take advantage of the elations between these two phenomena. However, such plans tend to flounder for at least two reasons. First, the budget of each organization encounters a different fate as it moves up through the departmental echelon and as different budgetary tradeoffs occur; and second, each organization has different sources of funds (NOAA data collection depends entirely on Federal funds and volunteer services; USGS depends on Federal funds and on funds provided by States and municipalities in a matching program).

Both organizations process, store, and publish water data. Both organizations release statements on current and prospective water conditions and outlooks. These services should be combined not only in the interest of economy but also to simplify public access to needed information. The two organizations, NOAA and USGS, interface as well in several other fields such as mapping, earthquakes, marine and tidal data, and geophysical investigations. For the above reasons, the Commission recommends that most of the functions of NOAA be merged with those of the USGS in the Department of the Interior.[5]

The merged organization should contain a bureau or service that combines the functions of the Environmental Data Service of NOAA and of the Water Resources Division of USGS as well as comparable data collection bureaus for the oceans, the atmosphere, and the earth's mineral resources. This merged data service could be strengthened further by transferring to it basic water data collection activities of other Federal agencies which are marginal to their primary missions. These include such programs as water quality data acquisition operated or funded by EPA (the prosecutor and the judge should not also be the expert witness) and the snow surveys and water supply forecasts of the U.S. Soil Conservation Service.

CONCLUSIONS ON BASIC DATA

. The adequacy of basic data to support evaluation, planning, and decisionmaking in water resources varies considerably. It is strongest with respect to the quantitative aspects. The areas of greatest need are in the water quality, environmental, socioeconomic, and water-use aspects, including improvement in the program of reporting flood damages.

. While great amounts of data are available, many potential data users do not know what data are available and where to go to get data. With the view to making better and more widespread use of available data, a well publicized referral system is needed.

3. There is a continuing need to identify gaps in the present data base as they become apparent through planning and evaluation studies and through a periodic assessment of the data program. One means of accomplishing this would be for planning and project study reports to regularly report data deficiencies. Such a regular reporting of data deficiencies should also be part of the Section 102 statements filed under NEPA.

4. Since planning and operational decisions are only as sound as the data base on which they rest, standards for gaging the accuracy of different types of data or the same kinds of data from different sources should be developed.

5. While data collection activities supportive of action programs or of a broad nature, such as the USGS gaging network and the Census, are continually reviewed for relevance, what is needed additionally is a focus on probable future data needs. This need is particularly apparent with respect to environmental data.

6. The water agencies should cooperate more extensively with general data collection and statistical agencies, such as the Census Bureau, to encourage collection of data useful for water resources planning and management. This may require transfers of funds.

7. The thrust of most past data collection activities has centered on the provision of raw statistics or elementary statistical relationships. While this is important and should be continued, future work should also focus on data which provide a general view of an entire system, and on data systems designed to provide information on routine cause and effect relationships.

8. A regularized process of before-and-after-implementation studies of water development projects would yield very valuable information.

9. It would be advantageous to combine the water data collection activities of the National Oceanic and Atmospheric Administration and the U.S. Geological Survey under one administration.

RECOMMENDATIONS

17-1. **The reconstituted Water Resources Council should:**

    a. **Establish a water resources data referral center and periodically publish an up-**

---

[5] See Chapter 11, Section C.

dated catalog of sources of water-related data.

   b. Identify gaps in the present water data base and identify the probable long-term basic data requirements which will be needed to support future planning and decisionmaking in water resources.

   c. Work more extensively with nonwater agencies to make their data collection more useful to water resources planning and management.

17-2. All water resources planning reports and environmental impact statements should contain an assessment of the deficiencies in the factual base. Such reports should indicate which decisions or findings are most sensitive to data deficiencies.

17-3. High priority should be given to research in developing methods for data synthesis and transfer.

17-4. Studies before and after project implementation should be conducted to ascertain the adequacy of the basic data used in planning and decisionmaking as well as cause and effect relationships.

17-5. Congress should enact legislation to merge the National Oceanic and Atmospheric Administration (with the exception of the fisheries and coastal zone management activities) and the U.S. Geological Survey into a single agency in the U.S. Department of the Interior.

RESEARCH

Research and development (R&D) is an integral component of the Nation's water resource management activities. The purpose of water resources R&D is to better understand, use, and manage the Nation's water resources. As water demands increase, R&D is needed to provide improved methods for making supplies available at reasonable costs and for disposing of wastewater in ways which are environmentally and economically acceptable. There is also an increasing need for R&D knowledge to reduce and, if possible, to eliminate adverse impact on the natural environment in the management of water resources. The Commission has not attempted to review in detail the performance of existing research agencies or to outline a total Federal research program in the field of water. Specific areas requiring additional R&D emphasis (e.g., precipitation modification, desalting, and environmental research) are discussed in

detail elsewhere in this report. The Commission's approach focuses primarily on organizational aspect of Federal water research activity.

The organization of R&D activities in water re sources and related fields is varied and complex While the Federal role in funding water resource R&D is predominant, actual R&D activities ar carried out by a variety of governmental agencies universities, industries, and independent researcl organizations. Rapidly changing social concerns an environmental problems require that research pro grams be relevant and responsive to real problems an issues. The Commission is concerned primarily wit the need to develop (1) closer ties between researcl and planning and (2) a more broadly-based an intensive research and development effort to increas usable water supplies and to handle growing volume of wastes.

The Problem

Water research should be looked upon as a important aid in the achievement of particular objec tives or the solving of water problems. The success o a water research program can be assessed in light o its contribution in assisting planners, designers, mana gers, and decision- and policymakers. The key ele ment in making such an assessment is a view of th future. The adequacy of the water resources researcl program in meeting past needs is relevant only to th extent that it provides a guide for developing research program that will help meet future needs.

Water R&D effort has been generally successful i meeting past needs. The existing reliance on agency R&D programs to support agency missions with a Office of Water Resources Research (OWRR) fillin the gaps as they become apparent should be main tained. Three aspects of the present situation concer the Commission. The first is whether fragmente research efforts of individual agencies will provide th needed capability to carry this Nation successfull through the latter part of the 20th century. Here reference is primarily to the major "big ticket" programs involving new technologies that will requir R&D effort beyond the capabilities of mission oriented agencies.

A second concern is whether planning and manage ment line agencies are reaping the most benefit from R&D efforts and whether R&D agencies are receivin worthwhile counsel and advice from those planner and managers on the "people-problem" end of th water resources spectrum.

A third source of concern is the natural tendency of any mission-oriented department having jurisdiction over a research agency to require the latter to devote its resources wholly, or largely, to solving the problems of that department. For example, there is a strong tendency for the Department of the Interior to look upon the Office of Water Resources Research as the research arm of that Department in the water field. It is difficult for a research agency placed in this position to maintain a broad outlook and strive to maximize the contribution of its program to the nation as a whole.

Need for Improvement

The Commission has not attempted to make a detailed review of water resources research under way, but has examined present water research programs in terms of major categories of research, who is doing what, which research activities appear to be serving their purposes well, the present priorities in and funding of research, the extent to which research is tied to planning, and the relationships between existing research organizations.

Present Research Program: At the Federal level, 21 agencies are actively involved in R&D activities in the water field. Most of the R&D in these agencies is carried out both in-house and by contract researchers, but largely in the context of agency missions. At the State level, water resources research and development is conducted on State-oriented problems and is often cooperatively funded by Federal agencies. At the university level, basic and applied water research is conducted on a broad spectrum from narrow single-interest points of view to interdisciplinary approaches.

A major contribution of the private-industrial sector to R&D progress has been in the context of solving industry problems, such as the development of equipment to improve water use efficiency and to cope with wasteproducts. For example, the steam electric power industry is conducting research directed toward more efficient cooling towers for recycling of cooling water. Private industry R&D has also been directed at marketable products or processes (instruments, treatment units, turbines, pumps, desalting plants, etc.). No data on private industrial expenditures on water resources R&D are available because of the proprietary nature of their activity and because developments in nonwater technology may have significant impact on water use. The

role of industrial R&D has been important and will very likely increase in importance as the hardware aspects of water management increase (e.g., recycling, process changes, etc.).

Present water resources research programs of the Federal Government include:

1. Agency mission research —
   Research undertaken or sponsored by action agencies, such as the U.S. Army Corps of Engineers, U.S. Department of Agriculture, and U.S. Environmental Protection Agency to improve their operations.

2. Earth-science research and surveys —
   Research by such agencies as the U.S. Geological Survey and the National Oceanic and Atmospheric Administration to advance the understanding of biospheric systems and processes. This research usually requires long and continued attack.

3. Research grant programs —
   These are the programs of the Office of Water Resources Research (OWRR) in the Department of the Interior and, to a lesser extent, of the National Science Foundation (NSF) to sponsor research, mainly in universities and on small projects, with considerable emphasis on the advancement of training and skills as an indirect result.

4. "Big-ticket" research to develop new technologies —
   The chief example is the Office of Saline Water (OSW) in the Department of the Interior which has had one job for many years. Another example is the weather modification program of the Bureau of Reclamation (USBR).

The first two research activities are oriented toward agency purposes. The second two research activities are those whose programs center on research itself and which are, therefore, subject to choice and redirection as may be desirable.

Generally, research under the first two categories has been good. Nevertheless, mission agency research should be subject to periodic review and redirection. Mission-oriented research has a tendency to focus on specific areas and to pursue these areas beyond the point of diminishing returns. Mission agencies are more likely to be open for criticism for what they do not do than for what they do. Mission agency research tends to be oriented toward the "hardware" aspects of the mission. Studies of environmental and social impact have, for example, been noticeably lacking. The final weakness of mission agency research is that it tends to be cut back whenever funds are tight. In other words, for most mission agencies, research is expendable–it is nice to have, but not at the expense of cuts elsewhere in the program.

Although researchers in the agencies can provide agency policymakers with ready access to competent scientific counseling on alternative policy positions, there is not much indication that policymakers take advantage of this. To a considerable degree, research is viewed as supportive of the engineering operations, not the policy areas. A much closer tie between the decisionmakers and the researchers is needed to accelerate application of research results.

The interagency Committee on Water Resources Research (COWRR) of the Federal Council for Science and Technology has provided a mechanism for the coordination of Federal water resources research activities. It has served to identify gaps and inadequacies in agency research programs, minimize duplication, and influence the scope and direction of future R&D programs. Since 1963, the Chairman of COWRR has been a member of the staff of the Office of Science and Technology (OST), and the Committee, while conducting its primary mission, has also served in an advisory capacity to OST which has been the R&D arm of the Executive Office of the President. Under Reorganization Plan No. 1 of 1973,[6] OST is abolished and its functions transferred to the National Science Foundation. This affords an opportunity to reassess the role of COWRR and improve its effectiveness in orienting the agency research programs toward meeting broad national needs. The Commission believes the effectiveness of COWRR could be improved if it were established as an arm of the Water Resources Council and given the strong role in water resources research that the Commission contemplates will be the role of the Water Resources Council in water resources planning when it is reconstituted as recommended in Chapter 11.[7]

The Office of Water Resources Research (OWRR) was established in the Department of the Interior to administer the Water Resources Research Act of 1964. The OWRR program includes (1) support of 53 State and territorial water resources research institutes, (2) contracts and grants for water resources research, and (3) the operation of a major informa-

tion system to disseminate water research results. Under the terms of the 1964 Act, OWRR has sponsored research related to a wide range of water resources topics.[8] The program has been of significant value to educational institutions in the establishment and development of water resources programs and has provided through research grants needed support for manpower training. It has also stimulated a good deal of thinking about new concepts of water use and management and has attracted funds from non-Federal sources. Title II of the Water Resources Research Act, however, requires that research undertaken under the Act, other than that performed at the State water resources research institutes created thereunder, be related to the mission of the Department of the Interior. This might prevent the agency from using the Title II program to fill in gaps left by the research programs of other agencies in the conduct of their mission-oriented research. If and when OWRR is made a part of the Office of Water Technology as recommended in Chapter 11[9] of this report, consideration should be given to removing this limitation, so that the Office of Water Technology can serve all agencies.

Research Priorities and Funding: At present, the Department of the Interior (mainly OSW, OWRR, USGS, and USBR) administers over one-third of the total Federal water resources research budget. The next two largest agency commitments to water resources R&D are those of the Environmental Protection Agency (approximately one-quarter) and the Department of Agriculture (approximately one-sixth), including the Agricultural Research Service and the Economic Research Service.

Approximately one-third of the total water resources research budget is allocated to advances in the area of water quality management and protection. The next three largest areas of water research emphasis include: (1) research into the processes and phenomena of the hydrologic cycle; (2) water supply augmentation and conservation, including desalting research, renovation and reuse of low-quality water, and the conservation of water (reduction of demand in municipal, industrial, and agricultural uses; and (3) water resources planning, including research on the market system, water law and institutions, non-

---

[6] Weekly Compilation of Presidential Documents (January 29, 1973). Vol. 9, No. 4, p. 75.

[7] Recommendations 11-1 and 11-2.

[8] *Water Resources Research Act of 1964*, P.L. 88-379, July 17, 1964, 78 Stat. 329, as amended, 42 USCA 1961, et seq.

[9] Recommendation 11-13.

Measuring salinity of stream helps assess adverse effects of mining operation

structural alternatives in water supply development, and the ecological impacts of all alternatives.

The identification of research needs is a never-ending job and a responsibility to some degree of all those involved in water resources. No two priorities lists are alike and priority ranking varies according to the views of those who prepare such lists. The major areas of needed research which appear to hold the greatest promise for payoff include:

1. The ecological, environmental, and socioeconomic impacts of water resources project development and management strategies.

2. The economic, social, and environmental costs and benefits of (a) various levels of wastewater

treatment, including the no discharge alternative, and (b) changes in water-using processes to reach alternative levels of water quality.

3. Relationships between energy production and water use and the effects of heat and consumptive use on local water resources.

4. The effects on water quality of nonpoint-sources of pollution, including investigations of alternative means of control and study of urban storm water control in relation to the quality of the Nation's water bodies.

5. Means of more efficient water use and extending the utility of existing supplies.

6. New and developing technologies in water, including such things as desalting, weather modification, wastewater reuse, and geothermal resources.

Of these, the first three are particularly important in the light of the current importance of environmental quality. With the likelihood of massive budgetary commitments for water quality control (item 2), it is especially important to insure the most cost-effective expenditure of these funds. Because steam electric powerplants presently constitute the largest and fastest growing withdrawal use of water, it is also important to increase research on relationships between energy production and cooling water (item 5).

Integrating Research and Planning: As stated earlier, one of the concerns of the Commission is the adequacy of the present R&D program to meet the needs of the future. Planning should not only consider future technological developments as possibilities but recommend the necessary research as well. Conversely, research should look to planning for a substantial part of its direction in identifying problem and priority areas. Recommendations along this line constituted five of the eight recommendations of the National Academy of Sciences Committee in its report to the Commission.[10]

There are steps which can be taken to encourage integration of planning and research. For example, Section 102 of the Water Resources Planning Act provides for study, assessment, and review of problems, plans, and programs, and Section 103 provides

for the establishment of principles, standards, an procedures for planning and project formulation WRC should consider technological impacts as part o its review of planning under Section 102, and unde Section 103 it should promulgate guidelines on how to reflect research in field planning. These guideline should also include directions to field plannin entities to highlight research needed to assist in th achievement of planning objectives and in the analysi of problems. Furthermore, river basin commission should be directed specifically to include in thei plans prepared under Section 204(3) of the Wate Resources Planning Act recommendations for th development of whatever research is needed to mee their objectives.

If these steps were implemented successfully, th Water Resources Council would be well equipped t prepare annually or biennially an assessment of neede research with specific priority recommendations t support the overall objectives of the Planning Ac Such an assessment should then be used as a genera guide for both mission and contract agency researc activities.

Organizational Relationships: The substance of re search is innovative exploration, which is whette most keenly in a competitive environment. Therefor the Commission makes no proposal for centra assembly of all water research; the several existin mission-oriented organizations have served their pu poses well within the limited fields in which the operate.

As a principle, however, research activities shoul serve broad objectives as well as fulfilling particula agency needs. For example, research into means o flood damage reduction is as proper an objective as research into various methods of designing or buildin dams to control floods. Unfortunately, research ofte becomes so involved in agency needs that it some times loses sight of more important broad objective The Commission believes that this loss of perspectiv has occurred, for example, with respect to the broa objectives of researching ways of increasing th supply of usable water.

The fragmented approach of establishing an Offic of Saline Water, a weather modification and geo thermal resources program in the Bureau of Reclama tion, research on surface and underground storage i the various action agencies, and research programs o EPA on wastewater reuse technology makes it diffi cult for anyone to develop a proper perspective particularly with respect to priorities and budgeting

[10] U.S. NATIONAL ACADEMY OF SCIENCES, Committee on Technologies and Water (June 1971). Potential Technological Advances and Their Impact on Anticipated Water Requirements, prepared for the National Water Commission. National Technical Information Service, Springfield, Va., Accession No. PB 204 053. pp. 5-8.

on the overall objective(s). Furthermore, single tool research organizations tend to persist in their studies beyond useful return. For this reason, there appears to be considerable merit to establishing an Office of Water Technology (OWT) in the Department of the Interior and giving it a broad objective (1) to assume these "fragmented" programs as well as the mission and functions of the Office of Water Resources Research and (2) to research such things as urban storm water control, underwater and offshore aqueducts, and other new areas.[11]

Such an Office of Water Technology should attack two other problems. First there is the tendency of research operations to perpetuate themselves, to push obsolete research, to proceed more or less independently without determining the extent to which other existing research projects would serve as well or better. Recognizing the reluctance of one government agency to criticize another, the new OWT should establish a special technical review board comprised of experts both from within and without the Government to evaluate existing water research operations and recommend whether those projects should be continued, modified, or dropped. A major contribution of such a special review board would be to identify areas in which there is unnecessary duplication of research.

Second, a number of water resources issues need to be more systematically assessed. Among these issues are (1) the quality of urban storm water runoff, (2) acid mine drainage, (3) lake eutrophication, and (4) urban sedimentation. The new OWT would make an important contribution to water resources research by undertaking a program of "problem assessments"—identifying and cataloging serious unsolved problems, carefully determining their nature and magnitude, assessing the potential consequences of failure to solve them, and recommending the kinds of economically feasible research efforts which are likely to result in solutions.

CONCLUSIONS ON RESEARCH

1. The presently diversified water resource research effort (i.e., mission agency research and grant agency research) has generally served the Nation well.

2. To assure continued success, steps should be taken to develop a closer tie between planning and research in order to reinforce the value and relevance of each.

3. If the Nation is aggressively to explore the research and development of new technologies in water resources and related fields, it is important that an agency or office charged with this mission be established.

RECOMMENDATIONS

17-6. The Water Resources Council should, through the exercise of authority granted to it under the Water Resources Planning Act:

a. Direct that water resources planning studies include an assessment of research needed to support planning objectives and a recommended research program to develop the scientific and technological base necessary to cope with future problems.

b. Review planning reports for needed research as part of the customary WRC review to aid the Council in preparing annually an assessment of needed research with specific priority recommendations to support the objectives of the Water Resources Planning Act.

c. Develop guidelines for field planning entities to assist in reflecting technological impacts in both short- and long-range water resources planning.

17-7. The research program of the Office of Saline Water, the weather modification activities of the National Oceanic and Atmospheric Administration, the weather modification and geothermal resources program of the Bureau of Reclamation, and research on wastewater reuse technology of the Environmental Protection Agency should be transferred to a new Office of Water Technology in the Department of the Interior. Additionally, this new office should absorb the functions of the Office of Water Resources Research and should maintain an up-to-date state-of-the-art assessment of new technologies to assist planners and decisionmakers in the development and evaluation of water management alternatives.

17-8. The Committee on Water Resources Research which has functioned as an arm of the Federal Council for Science and Technology should be reconstituted as a committee of the Water Resources Council.

---

[1] See Chapter 9, Section F, and Chapter 11, Section C.

The National Water Commission Act

Public Law 90-515
90th Congress, S. 20
September 26, 1968

An Act

82 STAT. 868

To provide for a comprehensive review of national water resource problems and programs, and for other purposes.

Be it enacted by the Senate and House of Representatives of the United States of America in Congress assembled, That this Act may be cited as the "National Water Commission Act".

National Water Commission Act.

THE NATIONAL WATER COMMISSION

SEC. 2. (a) There is established the National Water Commission (hereinafter referred to as the "Commission").

(b) The Commission shall be composed of seven members who shall be appointed by the President and serve at his pleasure. No member of the Commission shall, during his period of service on the Commission, hold any other position as an officer or employee of the United States, except as a retired officer or retired civilian employee of the United States.

Membership.

(c) The President shall designate a Chairman of the Commission (hereinafter referred to as the "Chairman") from among its members.

(d) Members of the Commission may each be compensated at the rate of $100 for each day such member is engaged in the actual performance of duties vested in the Commission. Each member shall be reimbursed for travel expenses, including per diem in lieu of subsistence, as authorized by 5 U.S.C., sec. 5703, for persons in the Government service employed intermittently.

Compensation.

Travel pay.

80 Stat. 499.

(e) The Commission shall have an Executive Director, who shall be appointed by the Chairman with the approval of the Commission and shall be compensated at the rate approved by the U.S. Civil Service Commissioners. The Executive Director shall have such duties and responsibilities as the Chairman may assign.

Executive Director.

DUTIES OF THE COMMISSION

SEC. 3. (a) The Commission shall (1) review present and anticipated national water resource problems, making such projections of water requirements as may be necessary and identifying alternative ways of meeting these requirements—giving consideration, among other things, to conservation and more efficient use of existing supplies, increased usability by reduction of pollution, innovations to encourage the highest economic use of water, interbasin transfers, and technological advances including, but not limited to, desalting, weather modification, and waste water purification and reuse; (2) consider economic and social consequences of water resource development, including, for example, the impact of water resource development on regional economic growth, on institutional arrangements, and on esthetic values affecting the quality of life of the American people; and (3) advise on such specific water resource matters as may be referred to it by the President and the Water Resources Council.

(b) The Commission shall consult with the Water Resources Council regarding its studies and shall furnish its proposed reports and recommendations to the Council for review and comment. The Commission shall submit simultaneously to the President and to the United States Congress such interim and final reports as it deems appropriate,

Reports to President and Congress.

and the Council shall submit simultaneously to the President and to the United States Congress its views on the Commission's reports. The President shall transmit the Commission's final report to the Congress together with such comments and recommendations for legislation as he deems appropriate.

82 STAT. 869

Termination date.

(c) The Commission shall terminate not later than five years from the effective date of this Act.

POWERS OF THE COMMISSION

SEC. 4. (a) The Commission may (1) hold such hearings, sit and act at such times and places, take such testimony, and receive such evidence as it may deem advisable; (2) acquire, furnish, and equip such office space as is necessary; (3) use the United States mails in the same manner and upon the same conditions as other departments and agencies of the United States; (4) without regard to the civil service laws and regulations and without regard to 5 U.S.C., ch. 51, employ and fix the compensation of such personnel as may be necessary to carry out the functions of the Commission; (5) procure services as authorized by 5 U.S.C., sec. 3109, at rates not to exceed $100 per diem for individuals; (6) purchase, hire, operate, and maintain passenger motor vehicles; (7) enter into contracts or agreements for studies and surveys with public and private organizations and transfer funds to Federal agencies and river basin commissions created pursuant to title II of the Water Resources Planning Act to carry out such aspects of the Commission's functions as the Commission determines can best be carried out in that manner; and (8) incur such necessary expenses and exercise such other powers as are consistent with and reasonably required to perform its functions under this title.

80 Stat. 443.
5 USC 5101-
5115.
80 Stat. 416.

79 Stat. 246.
42 USC 1962b-
1962b-6.

(b) Any member of the Commission is authorized to administer oaths when it is determined by a majority of the Commission that testimony shall be taken or evidence received under oath.

POWERS AND DUTIES OF THE CHAIRMAN

SEC. 5. (a) Subject to general policies adopted by the Commission, the Chairman shall be the chief executive of the Commission and shall exercise its executive and administrative powers as set forth in section 4(a)(2) through section 4(a)(8).

(b) The Chairman may make such provision as he shall deem appropriate authorizing the performance of any of his executive and administrative functions by the Executive Director or other personnel ·of the Commission.

OTHER FEDERAL AGENCIES

SEC. 6. (a) The Commission may, to the extent practicable, utilize the services of the Federal water resource agencies.

(b) Upon request of the Commission, the head of any Federal department or agency or river basin commission created pursuant to title II of the Water Resources Planning Act is authorized (1) to furnish to the Commission, to the extent permitted by law and within the limits of available funds, including funds transferred for that purpose pursuant to section 4(a)(7) of this Act, such information as may be necessary for carrying out its functions and as may be available to or procurable by such department or agency, and (2) to detail to temporary duty with this Commission on a reimbursable basis such personnel within his administrative jurisdiction as it may need or believe to be useful for carrying out its functions, each such detail to be without loss of seniority, pay, or other employee status.

Financial and administrative services by GSA.

(c) Financial and administrative services (including those related to budgeting, accounting, financial reporting, personnel, and procurement) shall be provided the Commission by the General Services Administration, for which payment shall be made in advance, or by

82 STAT. 870

reimbursement from funds of the Commission in such amounts as may be agreed upon by the Chairman of the Commission and the Administrator of General Services: *Provided*, That the regulations of the General Services Administration for the collection of indebtedness of personnel resulting from erroneous payments (5 U.S.C., sec. 5514) shall apply to the collection of erroneous payments made to or on behalf of a Commission employee, and regulations of said Administrator for the administrative control of funds (31 U.S.C. 665(g)) shall apply to appropriations of the Commission: *And provided further*, That the Commission shall not be required to prescribe such regulations.

80 Stat. 477.

APPROPRIATIONS

SEC. 7. There are hereby authorized to be appropriated not to exceed $5,000,000 to carry out the purposes of this Act.

Approved September 26, 1968.

LEGISLATIVE HISTORY:

HOUSE REPORTS: No. 376 (Comm. on Interior & Insular Affairs) and
              No. 1862 (Comm. of Conference).
SENATE REPORT No. 25 (Comm. on Interior & Insular Affairs).
CONGRESSIONAL RECORD:
    Vol. 113 (1967): Feb. 6, considered and passed Senate.
                     July 12, considered and passed House, amended.
    Vol. 114 (1968): Sept. 5, House agreed to conference report.
                     Sept. 12, Senate agreed to conference report.

Background Studies Undertaken for the
National Water Commission

Prior to the development of its recommendations and the preparation of its own report, the National Wate Commission undertook (1) to review the pertinent literature, (2) to analyze the relevant findings an recommendations of earlier water policy studies; (3) to consult with leading authorities; (4) to review th statements of State, local, and regional officials, private citizens, and representatives of groups interested i national water policy presented at the Commission's public conferences held in the summer and fall of 196⁹ (5) to obtain the views of the Federal water agencies; and (6) to carry out special studies in 22 fields of inquir in which the readily available material was insufficient, in the Commission's judgment, to provide an adequat basis for making policy recommendations. This Appendix describes and briefly summarizes the special studie undertaken for the Commission.

Altogether, 64 studies were undertaken ranging from simple state-of-the-art summarizations in several fielc to a massive summary digest of the water resources laws of the 50 States. Computer model studies wer undertaken to develop a possible range of future water demands for agriculture under certain assumptions.

The background studies were either commissioned under contract to universities, research organization consultant firms, and individual experts or were prepared by task forces or panels of consultants or by membei of the Commission's staff. In addition, a large number of staff studies were made in specific areas in which th Commission requested special information. Each report on a study or important phase of a study, upoi completion, was submitted to the Commissioners for use as background for the Commission's deliberatioi leading to the final report. In order to keep the general public and all those who had indicated their interest i the Commission's work informed on the progress, the Commission authorized release of the completed report through the National Technical Information Service (NTIS) of the U.S. Department of Commerce, and sei news releases to representatives of the press and others concerned. The reports were not necessarily approved b the Commission either as to conclusions drawn or as to the accuracy or completeness of data presented, bu were released without endorsement to stimulate public discussions of water resource policy issues. Readers c the reports were invited to give the Commission their comments and suggestions to give the Commissioi perspective in reaching its own conclusions and recommendations on the subjects covered.

Altogether, 62 background reports were released to the public and copies are available through NTIS. Th remaining two reports, summary-digests of Federal and State water laws, were deemed of sufficient interest ar lasting worth to warrant transmittal to the President and the Congress and are being published and sold throug the U.S. Government Printing Office.

There follows a list of the background study reports released through NTIS. The reports are grouped unde 10 broad fields of interest and each is described briefly, giving its NTIS accession number and the name(s) of it author(s).

	NTIS
Title and Description of Report	**Accession No.**

I. **Looking Ahead**

FUTURE WATER DEMANDS, Charles W. Howe, Clifford S. Russell, Robert A.   PB 197 877
Young, and William J. Vaughn, Resources for the Future, Inc.

This report summarizes three studies on water demands: (1) urban, (2) industrial, and (3) agricultural. It analyzes the effects of likely market trends, public policies, and technological change on water use and water pollution. Projections are given.

POTENTIAL TECHNOLOGICAL ADVANCES AND THEIR IMPACT ON ANTICI-   PB 204 053
PATED WATER REQUIREMENTS, Committee on Technologies and Water, National
Academy of Sciences.
This report evaluates potential technological advances and their effect on water supply
and demand in the future. It presents a directory of concepts to increase or decrease
future water demand, to increase usable supplies, and to extend usefulness of impure
water. In four scenarios of possible futures, technological concepts are applied to food
production, electric power generation, urban water supply, and municipal waste
disposal, with identification of political, social, and economic factors. The report
indicates research priorities and ways in which technological change should be given
greater emphasis in water planning.

FORECASTING WATER DEMANDS, Russell G. Thompson, M. Leon Hyatt, James   PB 206 491
W. McFarland, and H. Peyton Young.
This report explores the effects of policy and technology on the demand for water. It
describes models for forecasting water demands for agriculture, steam electric power
generation, petroleum refining, and residential use. Through use of a model developed
by Wollman and Bonem, alternative forecasts of relative levels of withdrawals and
losses of water in agriculture, mining, manufacturing, powerplant cooling, and
municipal purposes as well as use of water for waste disposal, are presented for the
years 1980, 2000, and 2020. The report shows how forecasts vary according to policy,
technology, population, the economy, and other basic variables. The different possible
directions are termed "alternative futures." The future water situation will depend on
options and policies chosen –rather than being a projection of the situation today.

AGRICULTURAL WATER DEMANDS, Earl O. Heady, Howard C. Madsen, Kenneth   PB 206 790
J. Nicol, and Stanley H. Hargrove, Center for Agricultural and Rural Development,
Iowa State University.
The primary objective of this study was to determine whether the Nation has enough
water and land to satisfy its future food and fiber needs under various assumptions as
to the future. Secondary objectives are to estimate agricultural demands for water, to
illustrate the substitutions between water and land, and to estimate levels of
commodity prices, value of water and land rents related to water use alternatives. The
study is based on a large-scale linear programing model of U.S. agriculture. The
analysis incorporates alternative sets of assumptions for (1) population, (2) water
prices, (3) technological advance, (4) exports, and (5) government supply control
programs. A general conclusion of the report is that projected domestic food and fiber
and export demands will not press against available water and land resources in 2000.
Present land surpluses can substitute for future water and irrigated land development
projects in agriculture.

ALTERNATIVE DEMANDS FOR WATER AND LAND FOR AGRICULTURAL   PB 211 444
PURPOSES, Howard C. Madsen, Earl O. Heady, Stanley H. Hargrove, and Kenneth J.
Nicol, Center for Agricultural and Rural Development, Iowa State University.
This report evaluates the impact on land and water needs and farm prices if either
(1) nitrogen fertilizer application in the year 2000 were restricted to (a) 110 pounds
per acre and (b) 50 pounds per acre or (2) per capita beef consumption were held at

present levels, and vegetable proteins used to meet increased demand for protein forecast in the year 2000. The study is based on the use of the large-scale linear programing model of U.S. agriculture referred to in the description of the Heady report. Results of the model studies show that if vegetable protein were to be accepted to meet the expected increased demand for protein in year 2000, productive capacity of U.S. agriculture would surpass any level previously experienced in this Nation. Results of the two fertilizer limitation policy models indicate that a mild restriction on the use of nitrogen fertilizer would not strain the productive capacity of U.S. agriculture. A severe restriction, however, would reduce the supply capacity of U.S. agriculture considerably.

II. Environmental Reports

ENVIRONMENTAL QUALITY AND WATER DEVELOPMENT, Charles R. Goldman, University of California, Davis, in two volumes.

PB 207 113
PB 207 114

This report brings together within a single report a number of individual monographs which together provide a basis for the author's evaluation of the causes of conflict between environmental quality and water-associated development in the United States. It includes surveys of the history of water development and the evolution of American values and attitudes toward the environment. Basic principles are identified for more realistic environmental planning and decisionmaking. The report suggests methods for balancing human values against cost-benefit analyses.

AN AESTHETIC OVERVIEW OF THE ROLE OF WATER IN THE LANDSCAPE, R. Burton Litton, Robert J. Tetlow, Jens Sorensen, and Russell A. Beatty, University of California, Berkeley.

PB 207 315

This report explores the contributions of water to recreation and the environment of everyday life. A classification framework is developed for native characteristics and these are considered together with manmade changes. Inventories of existing conditions as well as manmade elements and improvements are related to the characteristics of the units. The report suggests tangible ways in which water and its treatment can contribute to environmental quality.

CLASSIFYING WATER BODIES, Robert Aukerman and George I. Chesley, Colorado State University.

PB 208 667

This report determines the feasibility of classifying water bodies by potential use, and the desirability of designating certain water for specific use or uses. The report identifies criteria for a useful water classification system and evaluates existing natural resource classification systems. Weaknesses of predetermined categories and limited purpose classifications are explored. The authors suggest that satisfactory classification by potential optimum use requires a comprehensive planning process which identifies conflicts and is basically a decision system.

RECYCLING AND ECOSYSTEM RESPONSE, Harry K. Stevens, Thomas G. Bahr, and Richard A. Cole, Michigan State University.

PB 208 669

This report reviews the literature on ecosystem response to water manipulation, with emphasis on the need for recycling. Policy implications are discussed. Topics covered include (1) current ecosystem concepts, (2) the role of materials recycling in ecosystem functions, (3) North American watersheds, (4) ecosystem stability and human manipulation, and (5) the role of technology. The report includes management recommendations and identifies areas for future research.

LEGAL DEVICES FOR ACCOMMODATING WATER RESOURCES DEVELOP-
MENT AND ENVIRONMENTAL VALUES, William A. Hillhouse II and John L.
DeWeerdt.

This report deals with selected institutional and other legal devices which are used or
might be used to strike a balance among environmental and developmental values with
respect to water resource projects. Existing institutional arrangements are described
and procedures to improve the balancing of values and avoid unnecessary delay in
Federal and non-Federal water projects, and in licensing and permit proceedings are
recommended. The National Environmental Policy Act is assessed. Case studies
examining the Central Arizona Project, the Tocks Island Project, the Cross-Florida
Barge Canal, Zabel v. Tabb, the proposed Snake River dams below Hell's Canyon, the
Calvert Cliffs atomic powerplant, a proposed recreational lake in Wisconsin, and the
California Peripheral Canal are presented. Litigation as a device to resolve conflicts is
analyzed and other approaches under Federal or State law for balancing environmental
and developmental values are discussed.

PB 208 835

PRESERVING THE GREAT LAKES, Guy J. Kelnhofer, Jr.

This report describes the Great Lakes and how they are being used. Effects of the past
and present development practices on the Great Lakes environment are related. The
principal Great Lakes planning and management agencies are identified and their roles
are described briefly. An evaluation is made of the ability of the Great Lakes agencies,
using their authorized programs, to restore and preserve the environment of that basin.

PB 211 442

WATER USE AND MANAGEMENT ASPECTS OF STEAM ELECTRIC POWER
GENERATION, Consulting Panel on Waste Heat, Peter A. Krenkel, Chairman.

This report assesses the cause, magnitude, and possible effects of heat discharges to
water from steam electric power generation and related aspects of condenser cooling
system operation. Attention is focused on electrical energy growth and siting
requirements, means of more efficiently using electric energy, problems of concentrated heat release, the lack of an adequate environmental research program for
determining thermal effects and setting environmental standards, problems related to
increased consumptive use of water, the need to more fully consider aspects of steam
electric power generation in water resources planning, and the need to establish in
national policy a recognition of the waste assimilative capacity of water.

PB 210 355

4. Water Pollution Control

PUBLIC REGULATION OF WATER QUALITY IN THE UNITED STATES, N.
William Hines, University of Iowa.

This report explores public regulation of water quality in the United States. It
discusses the need for public regulation, inadequacies of private remedies, local and
State governmental efforts, interstate arrangements, the current Federal program, and
major legislative proposals pending in Congress. The study argues that the 1965
Federal Water Quality Act, which established a program of setting water quality
standards through a local, State, and Federal partnership, is a sound approach to
improving quality, and that current proposals to adopt a national goal of eliminating
all discharges to water would imperil rather than enhance the Nation's efforts for
water quality improvement.

PB 208 309

WATER POLLUTION CONTROL IN THE UNITED STATES, Consulting Panel on
Water Pollution Control, Dwight Metzler, Chairman.

This report provides perspective on water pollution control problems in the United
States. It analyzes responsibilities and roles of local, State, and Federal governments

PB 212 139

and regional organizations; the objectives and costs of present pollution abatement programs; and the effectiveness of these programs in reaching national goals. The report was produced by a panel of consultants, assisted by the staff of the National Water Commission, to assist the Commission in formulating its recommendations regarding pollution control. Recommendations are made with respect to goals and standards, workable programs of Federal assistance, public participation, enforcement and regulation, research, and policy formulation.

WASTEWATER MANAGEMENT PROJECT, MUSKEGON COUNTY, MICHIGAN, George W. Davis and Allison Dunham, Center for Urban Studies, University of Chicago.

PB 208 310

This report is a case study of the regional planning effort which led to adoption of a spray irrigation system for wastewater management in Muskegon County, Michigan. A general overview of the problems encountered by Muskegon County is given, describing past exploitation and the degradation which had taken place. Earlier attempts to provide areawide water resource management are described, and the recommended solution is explained, together with the steps leading to its implementation.

IV. Economics of Water Development

REGIONAL ECONOMIC DEVELOPMENT – THE ROLE OF WATER, W. Chris Lewis, Jay C. Anderson, Herbert H. Fullerton, and B. Delworth Gardner, Utah State University Foundation.

PB 206 372

This report analyzes the effectiveness of water resources development as a means of inducing economic development in subnational regions. It covers the economic rationale for using public works to achieve economic growth and provides a state-of-the-art analysis of the effects of alternative water development programs on economic development in various types of regions. Irrigation, navigation, hydropower, flood prevention, water supply, water quality, and recreation projects are considered.

POPULATION GROWTH IN COMMUNITIES IN RELATION TO WATER RESOURCES POLICY, Rivkin/Carson.

PB 205 248

This report examines the patterns of population growth in U.S. communities over the past two decades, with particular reference to the influence of water and water resources development on these patterns. Reviews are made of the experience of two types of Federal programs: those concerning local water, sewer, and allied facilities; and those directed towards stimulating economic and population growth in less developed areas.

PRICING AND EFFICIENCY IN WATER RESOURCE MANAGEMENT, George Washington University, Robert K. Davis, and Steve H. Hanke, The Johns Hopkins University.

PB 209 083

This report indicates that pricing has been long recognized as a potential mechanism to improve efficiencies in resource use but pricing of water resources for this purpose has not been widely employed in the United States. The study examines the potential for pricing various water resource services including municipal, industrial, and irrigation water supplies; sewage collection and treatment; control of losses from flooding; outdoor recreation; use of inland waterways; and hydroelectric power. The study concludes that efficiency in the use of water resource services can be improved through adopting policies of cost-based pricing although the potential varies among services.

| Title and Description of Report | NTIS
Accession No. |

ECONOMIC VALUE OF WATER: CONCEPTS AND EMPIRICAL ESTIMATES, Robert A. Young and S. Lee Gray, Colorado State University.

PB 210 356

This report examines a number of issues that must be taken into account in deriving valid estimates of the values of water, estimates which are essential for rational allocation of water among uses and users. The study also analyzes water values for various uses with attention to regional differences. The water uses considered are municipal, industrial, irrigation, waste assimilation, recreation, fish and wildlife, navigation, and hydroelectric production.

ECONOMIC VALUE OF WATER IN A SYSTEMS CONTEXT, Walter R. Butcher, Norman K. Whittlesey, and John F. Orsborn.

PB 210 357

This report shows that decisions about water allocation and investment in water resource developments can be improved by knowledge of the value of water in alternative uses. The interdependent system in which water resources occur and uses take place make it important to consider these water values in a systems context. Systems models provide the best approach to estimating these values but much can be learned through a careful description of effects that each use has not only on quantity of water but also on quality and time or place of availability.

Analyses of Policies

AUTHORIZATION OF FEDERAL WATER PROJECTS, Northcutt Ely.

PB 206 096

This report identifies the major Federal agencies involved in construction of water resource projects and examines the process by which projects come into being from the point of initial conception, through planning and review, to construction, including the role of the Office of Management and Budget and procedures used by Congress in authorizing water resource projects. It also examines the procedures of the primary agencies administering grant and loan programs for water resource development.

AUTHORIZATION AND APPROPRIATION PROCESSES FOR WATER RESOURCE DEVELOPMENT, David Allee and Helen Ingram, Cornell University.

PB 212 140

This report examines the complex procedural steps involved in getting water resources development projects and programs authorized and financed by the Federal Government on the basis of interviews with 160 people from Federal, State, and local governments and from organizations interested in water resource development. Emphasis is placed on what actually takes place, rather than official statements of procedures. The report discusses who is involved in the procedures, how they operate, and what is gained by their involvement. It concludes that decisionmaking capacity is a more limiting constraint than investment capital in water resource development. A number of possible recommendations are postulated and discussed, including proposals for reorganization of the structure and modus operandi of congressional committees and for reorganization of the executive branch of the Federal Government.

FEDERAL COST-SHARING POLICIES FOR WATER RESOURCES, Harold E. Marshall, National Bureau of Standards.

PB 208 304

This report examines Federal cost-sharing policies for water resources development with respect to their influence on decisions of local beneficiary groups. These influences are analyzed using criteria of efficiency, equity, administrative feasibility, and sound financial arrangements. Current cost-sharing policies are found to be deficient. Alternative cost-sharing rules are compared with existing Federal cost-sharing policies.

FEDERAL DECISIONMAKING FOR WATER RESOURCE DEVELOPMENT, A. Allan Schmid, Michigan State University.

PB 211 441

This report describes the important criteria for choice among decisionmaking organizations and assesses the impacts of a number of alternative structures. The pros and cons of movements toward consolidation of agencies are discussed. External bargaining rules are specified with respect to agency-clientele bargaining, interagency bargaining, State-Federal and State-State bargaining, and market bargaining. The conclusions are that detailed consideration must be given to organizational changes that affect negotiation rules and the rules that shape the kind of information available to various interested groups.

WATER RESOURCE POLICY IN WISCONSIN, Irving Fox, University of Wisconsin.

PB 204 928

This report provides a summary of three groups of studies pertaining to water resources management in the State of Wisconsin. One group is an integrated set of studies dealing with institutional design for water quality management in the Wisconsin River Basin. The second set deals with metropolitan water resources management, and focuses on the area of southeastern Wisconsin near Milwaukee. The third group consists of studies with implications for policy and institutional design.

VI. Analyses of Programs

INLAND WATERWAY TRANSPORT POLICY IN THE UNITED STATES, Dwight M. Blood, University of Wyoming.

PB 208 668

This report analyzes the role of inland waterway transport within the dual framework of national water policy and national transportation policy. A logical framework for identifying and evaluating the problem is developed as a basis for considering the future of inland waterway transport. A descriptive summary of the inland waterway system and industry is presented along with a review of the history and development of the system.

ACREAGE LIMITATION IN THE FEDERAL RECLAMATION PROGRAM, Harry J. Hogan.

PB 211 840

This report reviews the performance of the acreage limitation provisions of the Reclamation Act of 1902 limiting irrigable farm size to 160 acres on Reclamation project lands. The study explores congressional intent as to the role of the family farm in the Reclamation program from initiation to the present. It appraises the extent of family farms on Reclamation projects and how the acreage limitation on farm size has worked to fashion the present farming structure. Information is developed on the patterns of farm ownership and operation, including the size of farm units and the rental and leasing arrangements for farming operations. The extent and nature of the Federal subsidy in the Reclamation program are determined. Recommendations to reform the acreage limitation are reviewed and new recommendations are made.

ALTERNATIVE ADJUSTMENTS TO NATURAL HAZARDS, David G. Arey and Duane D. Baumann, University of Pittsburgh.

PB 211 922

This report reviews Federal water resources policies and programs for reduction of losses from floods, drought, and hurricanes and suggests changes. Federal flood control policy is reviewed. Response to the drought of the mid-1960's in Massachusetts is analyzed, showing that a pattern somewhat similar to the evolution of Federal programs for flood control is evolving, with Federal assumption of responsibility for finding solutions to water supply problems in the great metropolitan centers. The report shows that increasing damages from hurricanes has also led to increasing Federal responsibilities. Arguments are presented against single solutions, and emphasis is placed on the need for research on alternatives.

HYDROELECTRIC POWER POLICY, Truman Price.   PB 204 052

This report provides background and analysis of the more significant public policy issues related to hydroelectric power development. The historic issues examined include public vs. private development, preference clause, Federal transmission policy, Federal rates policy, headwater benefits, and partnership development. The emerging issues examined are environmental quality, project delay, and project relicensing or takeover.

RESEARCH AND DEVELOPMENT IN WATER RESOURCES, John S. Gladwell.   PB 210 823

This report reviews the role of water resources research with special emphasis on policy implications. It points out that although the actual dollar outlay has increased in water research, the relative effort with respect to other investments has indicated a decreasing emphasis on the water aspects of science. Yet, the general condition of Federal research (and water research in particular) is healthy. No single agency or group can be identified as having the "lead" in water research. The study points to the Office of Water Resources Research (OWRR) as having the greatest potential for this role, but notes that it is limited by present administrative arrangements. It recommends a National Institute for Water Resources Research responsive to all, yet not under the direction of any single agency. Such an institute would be a focal point of Federal and non-Federal interests in water resources research.

Preparation of Water Plans

WATER RESOURCE PLANNING, Consulting Panel on Water Resources, Harvey   PB 211 921
Banks, Chairman.

This report outlines the evolution of water planning, delineates roles of planning bodies, and notes the lack of coordination between river basin and urban planning. The report describes the interrelationships of water resources planning to other sectors of planning, to functions within the water resources sector, to jurisdictional areas, and to stages of planning. Institutional factors which inhibit good planning are discussed, including inadequate definition of goals, agency conflicts, financing constraints, inadequate public participation, and legal constraints. The Panel makes a number of recommendations, including changes in the Water Resources Council and reorganization at Federal, State, and regional levels.

SYSTEMS ANALYSIS IN WATER RESOURCES PLANNING, Meta Systems, Inc.   PB 204 374

This report describes the potential role of systems analysis in water resources planning processes. The fact that the systems approach is not limited to the analysis of formal mathematical models is emphasized. The history of and opportunity for the applications of the systems approach to water resource problems are discussed. A series of case discussions of systems studies are presented.

PUBLIC PARTICIPATION IN WATER RESOURCES PLANNING, Katharine P.   PB 204 245
Warner, University of Michigan.

This report reviews public participation activities and procedures that have been utilized in connection with governmental planning studies, particularly those dealing with water resources. Key problems and issues affecting participatory planning are discussed. These include securing adequate public involvement; appropriate responsibilities in the planning process; and resolution of conflicts between interests.

VIII. **Institutional Arrangements**

INTERSTATE WATER COMPACTS, Jerome C. Muys.   PB 202 998
This report explores the history, function, structure, and operations of interstate and
Federal-interstate water compacts, including water allocation, pollution control,
planning, flood control, and other kinds of compacts. The Federal-interstate compact
is recommended as the preferred, permanent institutional arrangement for regional
water planning and management.

THE FEDERAL-STATE REGIONAL CORPORATION, Richard A. Solomon.   PB 202 997
This report examines the political and legal aspects of federally chartered corporations
as arrangements or mechanisms for interstate water management that may be
alternatives to TVA-type Federal corporations and interstate or Federal-interstate
compact authorities. Problems of chartering and organizing corporations under Federal
law and non-Federal participation in the corporation together with the legal status of
the corporation as a Federal and as a State agency are examined.

INSTITUTIONS FOR WATER PLANNING, Gary W. Hart.   PB 204 244
This report describes and analyzes river basin commissions and Federal-State ad hoc
and interagency committees, evaluates their strengths and weaknesses, and makes
recommendations for improving these institutions.

THE NEW ENGLAND RIVER BASINS COMMISSION – A CASE STUDY, Helen   PB 204 375
Ingram.
This report addresses the key question "What difference do river basin commissions
make?" The New England River Basins Commission is the case study. The study
assumes a relationship between what an organization does and the inducements it
offers participants. Among participants, only the chairman and staff have a primary
stake in a commission and a commitment to make it work. The possibilities and
disabilities present in such organizations are reflected. The study concludes that river
basin commissions, with skilled leadership, serve a facilitating function which links
common interests.

INSTITUTIONAL ARRANGEMENTS FOR WATER RESOURCE DEVELOPMENT,   PB 207 314
Vincent Ostrom, University of Indiana.
This report examines the structural elements that have entered into the development
of the American water industry, with special reference to California. A variety of
public and private enterprises engaged in water resource development and the
rendering of water services are analyzed and evaluated in terms of the theory of
organization used by public administration and administrative analysts, and the
concepts of political economists.

THE WATER RESOURCES COUNCIL, Ernst Liebman.   PB 211 443
This report describes and evaluates the Water Resources Council, its activities, and
historical roots. Recommendations for improving the Council are made.

INTERGOVERNMENTAL RELATIONS IN WATER RESOURCES ACTIVITIES,   PB 210 358
Wendell and Schwan.
This report examines intergovernmental arrangements for public water activities within
their historical context. These arrangements are classified and analyzed in terms of
financial incentives, regulation, intergovernmental planning, technical assistance,
manpower training, project development, comprehensive management, legal rights to
water and development and dissemination of information. The efficacy of interagency

committees, interstate and Federal-interstate compacts, the Water Resources Planning Act, and other intergovernmental mechanisms is also assessed. Arrangements for improved environmental quality and solution of metropolitan problems are given particular emphasis.

METROPOLITAN WATER MANAGEMENT, Urban Systems Research and Engineering, Inc.
This report studied planning, decisionmaking, and program implementation practices with respect to urban water management in 12 metropolises, four of which –Boston, Lubbock, Milwaukee, and Seattle –were examined in detail onsite.

PB 199 493

METROPOLITAN WATER INSTITUTIONS, Orlando E. Delogu, University of Maine.
This report discusses existing water supply and wastewater treatment problems in metropolitan areas, and institutions dealing with them. New approaches for metropolitan water management are suggested, including the establishment of new metropolitan water quality control regions, massive Federal financial incentives, and direct Federal assumption of metropolitan water supply and wastewater treatment responsibilities.

PB 204 051

COURTS AND WATER, Grant P. Thompson, Environmental Law Institute.
This report is an essay examining the strengths and weaknesses of courts as institutions for resolving water conflicts. It finds that courts produce decisions, operate relatively quickly and impartially, are accessible, and are competent to deal with "technical" questions by isolating critical facts and the policy matters which underlie such questions. The study discusses the role of courts in water quality, including the effect of acts which permit an expanded judicial role in the setting, testing, and enforcement of standards, in reviewing whether water planning meets legal standards, particularly under NEPA, and in settlement negotiations.

PB 211 974

Special Studies in Water Law

FUNCTIONAL ANALYSIS OF APPROPRIATION LAW, Charles Meyers.
The origin and basic elements of the appropriation system in water law are explained. The analysis shows the economic objectives of the system. Weaknesses of the judicially created system are considered. The emergence of the permit system is described. Parallels and contrasts with the riparian system are noted. The relationship of Federal and State laws of water rights is explained. The reservation doctrine is treated. The monograph serves as an introduction to other legal studies conducted by the National Water Commission.

PB 202 617

MARKET TRANSFERS OF WATER RIGHTS, Charles Meyers and Richard Posner.
This study analyzes imperfections in law and institutions that interfere with market allocation of water resources, such as laws and policies that restrain transfers. Legislative remedies are suggested in both substantive law and procedure. Application of the market system to interbasin transfers is considered.

PB 202 620

ADMINISTRATIVE ALLOCATION OF WATER, Edward W. Clyde and Dallin W. Jensen.
This study defines the concept of administrative allocation of water and contrasts it with market allocation, noting that in the Western United States initial allocation of water and water rights is usually administrative and subsequent reallocation is usually made through market exchange. Current criteria for market allocation are examined and improvements are suggested. Allocation by the Bureau of Reclamation and the Corps of Engineers is discussed briefly as are conjunctive management programs.

PB 205 249

	NTIS
Title and Description of Report	**Accession No**

IMPROVEMENT OF STATE WATER RECORDS, Richard L. Dewsnup and Charles Meyers.

PB 202 618

This report describes defects in existing laws relating to water rights. These defects arise from inadequate records. The records are inadequate for three reasons: (1) Some water rights are not on record; (2) water rights on record are not accurately described; (3) water rights on record have lapsed. Recommendations to cure these defects are made; legislation is set forth. A proposal to quantify return flow from irrigation is set forth.

PUBLIC ACCESS RIGHTS IN WATERS AND SHORELANDS, Richard L. Dewsnup.

PB 205 247

This report surveys the historical development of legal doctrines which recognize rights of public access and use of waters for navigation and fishing and how such rights presently include general recreational use of waters and shorelands. The legal concept of navigability of waters is an important criterion for public use, but many States have found additional legal machinery for enhancing such public rights. This report discusses a number of alternative ways in which the States protect or enhance public rights in waters and shorelands, and several of those alternatives are recommended for further State action.

LEGAL PROTECTION OF INSTREAM WATER VALUES, Richard L. Dewsnup.

PB 205 003

This report examines State water law doctrines to determine the extent to which they provide for legal recognition of recreational, fish and wildlife, esthetic, environmental, and other instream uses of water. Historically, Western water law required water to be diverted from the watercourse before a water right could be acquired. Accordingly, there was virtually no protection for instream uses. Recently, however, many States have enacted statutes to provide ways of protecting instream water values. This report evaluates a number of these innovations as a basis for suggesting further legislative reforms to protect instream values.

LEGAL ASPECTS OF WATER SALVAGE, Richard L. Dewsnup.

PB 205 005

This report identifies the various ways in which water is lost to use through such processes as seepage, evaporation, and transpiration, and the extent to which State water law doctrines encourage or discourage salvage of such losses. In many respects legal reforms are needed in order to encourage salvage operations, and are proposed.

FEDERAL-STATE RELATIONS IN THE LAW OF WATER RIGHTS, Frank J. Trelease, University of Wyoming.

PB 203 600

This study describes the sources of conflict between the Federal Government and the States (and citizens claiming rights under State law); it presents a number of recommendations for resolving the conflicts. The study deals with (1) Federal reserved rights, (2) the navigation servitude, (3) sovereign immunity, and (4) eminent domain procedures. A National Water Rights Procedures Act dealing with those subjects is proposed.

RIPARIAN WATER LAW – A FUNCTIONAL ANALYSIS, Clifford Davis, University of Connecticut.

PB 205 004

This report describes allocation of water by the riparian water law system that obtains in the Eastern United States, from the standpoint of both textbook law and results in fact. The study is supplemented by several case studies and includes an examination of Eastern permit systems. Recommendations are included for an improved permit system.

Title and Description of Report	NTIS Accession No.

GROUND WATER LAW, MANAGEMENT AND ADMINISTRATION, Charles E. Corker, University of Washington.
This report describes ground water hydrology, emphasizing the importance of recognizing the interrelation of ground and surface water supplies. The legal doctrines applicable to the use of ground water are described and the differences among the States and the departure of law from scientific fact are noted. Major problems of ground water law are identified and solutions suggested. The problem of ground water mining is also dealt with.

PB 205 527

Means of Increasing Water Supplies

EXTENDING THE UTILITY OF NON-URBAN WATER SUPPLIES, Utah State University Foundation.
This report examines the concept of extending the utility of nonurban water supplies; considers the conditions for achieving greater utility; and discusses some of the things that might lead to better utilization from a regional or public viewpoint. Opportunities for extending the utility of a given water supply are outlined with consideration of institutional, legal, political, and economic constraints.

PB 207 115

LAW OF INTERBASIN TRANSFERS, Ralph W. Johnson, University of Washington.
This report investigates the legal and public policy aspects of major interbasin transfers of water. It contains recommendations for criteria to govern the authorization of interbasin projects and describes various kinds of protection devices for the area of origin. It also recommends consideration of environmental impacts of transfers.

PB 202 619

INTERBASIN WATER TRANSFERS – A POLITICAL AND INSTITUTIONAL ANALYSIS, Dean E. Mann.
This report analyzes interbasin transfers of water in terms of the institutional and political arrangements existing and potentially available in the American political system. The implications of ideology, size and place of diversion, costs, repayment policy, timing and staging of transfers, feasibility of institutional constraints, and the relationship of interbasin transfers to social goals are explored. Roles of planning institutions and Congress are analyzed and strategy recommended. Criteria for evaluation of interbasin transfers are stated and specific recommendations are made.

PB 208 303

DESALTING, Victor A. Koelzer.
This report evaluates the state of the art of desalting technology. It summarizes progress on desalting and describes applicability of distillation, crystallization, membrane, and chemical processes. In an attempt to evaluate the markets for desalted water, the report looks at water costs, economies of scale, and other marketing factors. Applications of desalting technology are considered for incremental supply, to improve quality of supply, for intermittent operations, in dual-purpose plants, to renovate water for reuse, and for agriculture.

PB 209 942

PRECIPITATION MODIFICATION, Jack D. Lackner.
This report evaluates the effectiveness of cloud seeding in increasing precipitation from different kinds of storm systems. The evaluation is based on conclusions of atmospheric scientists and on the results of well designed field tests. Primary interest centers on the leverage increased precipitation may exert in augmenting water supply. The nature of potential downwind precipitation effects and environmental side effects are identified.

PR 201 534

WASTEWATER REUSE, Jerome Gavis, The Johns Hopkins University.   PB 201 5

This report evaluates the potential for wastewater reuse through reclamation of municipal and industrial effluents from advanced wastewater treatment plants. Brief descriptions and references indicate the extent of such practice at the present time and likely possibilities for future developments. Comparison with desalting and interbasin transfer costs is suggested.

WATERSHED MANAGEMENT, William E. Sopper, Pennsylvania State University.   PB 206 37

This report surveys and analyzes the present state of knowledge regarding the extent to which water supplies can be augmented by vegetation management. Effects of total and partial vegetation removal on water quantity and quality are discussed in detail. Effects on streamflow are also considered. Special attention is given to snowpack management, phreatophyte vegetation management, and the potential for combining watershed management with weather modification to increase water yield.

GROUND WATER MANAGEMENT, Leslie E. Mack.   PB 201 53

This report provides a general summary of ground water management and makes recommendations for improving national water policies pertaining to ground water. The importance of ground water in the national water balance is outlined as are some principles of ground water-surface water relationships and some aspects of ground water hydrology and management.

As mentioned earlier, two of the background studies, comprising Summary-Digests of Federal and State l dealing with water resources, will be of lasting value and have sufficient public interest to warrant publicat through the U.S. Government Printing Office. The Commission has transmitted these reports to the Presid and the Congress with a recommendation that they be printed and that arrangements be made for keeping information contained in them up to date. A description of the two reports follows:

1. A SUMMARY-DIGEST OF THE FEDERAL WATER LAWS AND PROGRAMS, John L. DeWeerdt Philip M. Glick, Editors. This report briefly summarizes the water programs and the legislation authoriz water related activities of the 9 cabinet departments – Agriculture, Commerce, Defense, Health, Educat and Welfare, Housing and Urban Development, Interior, Justice, State, and Transportation – involved water resources matters. It covers also the water-related programs of the Atomic Energy Commissi Environmental Financing Authority, Environmental Protection Agency, Federal Power Commission, Sn Business Administration, and Tennessee Valley Authority; three agencies of the Executive Office of President – Council on Environmental Quality, Office of Emergency Preparedness, and Office Management and Budget; and the Water Resources Council. Three Federal-State regional commissions also covered–Appalachian Regional Commission, Delaware River Basin Commission, and Susqueha River Basin Commission.

2. A SUMMARY-DIGEST OF STATE WATER LAWS, Richard L. Dewsnup and Dallin W. Jensen, Edit and Robert W. Swenson, Associate Editor. The report is in two parts. Part I describes the water laws of States in general terms, covering their development over the years, the organizational structure of the St water and water law agencies, laws relating to surface and ground waters, and various miscellane provisions. Part II contains 50 individual chapters, each devoted to the laws of one of the States. Breakdo of the discussion of the laws follows the pattern of the general discussions in Part I.

The Commission Staff and Its Operations

The National Water Commission Act authorized the Commission to employ staff as needed to carry out its functions, including consultants on a when-actually-employed basis. In addition, the Commission engaged the services of a number of individuals, firms, research organizations, and universities under contract to develop some of the background needed for its work.

At the outset the staff was organized into three divisions—Engineering and Environmental Sciences, headed by Victor A. Koelzer; Social and Behavioral Sciences, headed by Lyle E. Craine; and Legal, under the direction of the Commission's Legal Counsel, Philip M. Glick. Executive direction and coordination was provided by the Executive Director, Theodore M. Schad, and the Deputy Director, Howard L. Cook. Liaison with other Federal agencies was carried on by Assistant Director Ralph E. Fuhrman, and administrative services were under the direction of Assistant Director Robert N. Baker. Working under the general direction of the Commission, which met about once a month throughout the entire life of the Commission, the staff formulated and revised the program of background studies and the general outline of the Commission's report, and arranged for and undertook the individual studies.

At the end of Dr. Craine's leave of absence from the University of Michigan, his place as chief of the Social and Behavioral Sciences Division was taken by Dean Mann, on leave from the University of California at Santa Barbara. Originally, the Commission attempted to collaborate with the Water Resources Council in making projections of future water requirements as called for in the National Water Commission Act, but when the Council was unable to secure appropriations sufficient to complete the second national assessment of water supply and demand in time to be available for the Commission's work, the Commission was forced to tackle this phase

of its activity on its own. A small, temporary Forecast Division was created for this purpose, directed by Russell Thompson who was on leave from the University of Texas. This group functioned from August of 1970 to October of 1971.

A large number of consultants was on call throughout the conduct of the Commission's work. The Commission's panel of eight general consultants was used in 1969 in the preparation of the Commission's tentative program of studies and its revision, and the members were called on frequently as individuals during the entire course of the Commission's work. Several of the group authored background studies for the Commission.

Seven other panels were created: The Panel on Ecology and the Environment advised the staff in the preparation of the Commission's program of environmental studies; the Panels on Institutional Arrangements and Forecast Procedures performed the same function in those fields, and members of all three also reviewed background studies and drafts of portions of the Commission's report in their special fields of interest. The Panels on Water Resources Planning, Water Pollution Control, and Waste Heat Disposal prepared three of the background studies in their respective fields, and also helped with review of drafts of the sections of the Commission's report dealing with these special areas. The final panel of consultants, on Federal Decisionmaking, met several times to critique a paper on that subject prepared for the Commission under contract.

In addition, the Commission utilized the services of a number of other consultants on its legal, economic, and forecasting studies.

As the background studies neared completion toward the end of 1971, the staff was reorganized into a number of interdisciplinary task forces, reporting to the Director of Report Preparation, an additional duty taken on by Howard L. Cook. The

555

work of the task forces was coordinated at the staff level by a Board of Coordination and Review chaired by the Director of Report Preparation and composed of the senior members of the staff. Each of the 48 task forces prepared a draft of a section of what was eventually to become the draft of the Commission's proposed report for review by the Commission during meetings held from August 1971 through August 1972. After the first review by the Commission changes were made as directed by the Commission to bring the section into consonance with the Commission's views, and the revised drafts were circulated to a large number of individuals, too numerous to list here, following which the Commission again considered the drafts, in the light of the comments received. In some instances, the process was repeated a second time, and the draft was brought back to the Commission a third time for review.

Finally in August of 1972, the drafts of all of the 48 sections were assembled by the staff, along with various ancillary materials, into the first draft of the proposed report, which was reviewed by the Commission at its September meeting. Further revisions were made after this meeting, and the Commission considered the second draft at its October meeting, following which the report, with the changes agreed on by the Commission, was released for review. By this time the staff was almost exhausted, but continued to work to revise and perfect the report in preparation for the Commission's final review during the spring of 1973, following the public conferences held by the Commission in January and February, and its consideration of the written comments received as a result of the circulation of the draft.

The maximum number of employees on the full time staff at any one time was 44 in the summer of 1971, but a total of 65 individuals served at one time or another as listed below. There were 68 consultants, some of whom served without compensation, or as part of their regular duties with other Federal agencies, and many of whom served in several capacities. They are listed on the following pages in such a way as to reflect their additional responsibilities.

Administrative and secretarial staffs performed valiantly against overwhelming odds to keep the Commission's offices operating smoothly and to maintain the flow of material to the Commissioner for review between meetings.

THE STAFF

Executive Director	Theodore M. Schad (Dec. '68-June '73)
Deputy Director	Howard L. Cook (Feb. '69-April '73)
Assistant Director-Programs	Ralph E. Fuhrman (June '69-Dec. '71)
Assistant Director-Administration	Robert N. Baker (April '69-June '73)
Assistant to the Director	Florence Broussard (Jan. '69-June '73)
Editor-in-Chief	Myron B. Katz (Mar. '72-Mar. '73)

Legal Division

Philip M. Glick, Legal Counsel (June '69-Feb. '73)

Charles J. Meyers, Asst. Legal Counsel (Jan. '70-March '73)

Ernst Liebman, Asst. Legal Counsel (Feb. '70-Jan. '73)

Olivia P. Adler (June '69-Feb. '71)

Henry Bernson (May '72-June '72)

John L. DeWeerdt (June '71-May '73)

Richard L. Dewsnup (Mar. '70-July '72)

Gary L. Greer (Oct. '70-Feb. '73)

William A. Hillhouse II (Jan. '72-Dec. '72)

Engineering and Environmental Sciences Division

Victor A. Koelzer, Chief (June '69-June '72)

Edwin B. Haycock, Asst. Chief (Feb. '70-Feb. '73)

Alexander Bigler (Jan. '70-Oct. '72)

Kenneth L. Bowden (Aug. '69-Sept. '71)

Jerome Gavis (June '69-Sept. '69)

John S. Gladwell (Sept. '70-Oct. '71)

Jack D. Lackner (June '69-Aug. '71)

Joseph Morgan (Dec. '69-May '70)

Linda Reybine (Apr. '70-Jan. '73)

Thomas Scott (Sept. '70-Oct. '71)

Richard Tucker (Mar. '70-Oct. '72)

Robert E. Vincent (Dec. '69-July '70)

Raymond H. Wilson (June '69-Oct. '69)

Social and Behavioral Sciences Division

Lyle E. Craine, Chief (June '69-Aug. '70)

Dean E. Mann, Chief (Sept. '70-Oct. '71)

Gary Taylor, Asst. Chief (Nov. '70-Mar. '73)

Frank Bollman (May '71-Jan. '73)

David S. Brookshire (July '71-Sept. '72)

Elizabeth M. Cleary (Mar. '70-Dec. '70)

James J. Furse (May '72-Aug. '72)

David Friedman (June '69-Sept. '69) (June '70-Oct. '70)

Helen Ingram (Dec. '70-Oct. '71)

Ray M. Johns (Dec. '70-Sept. '72)

Truman P. Price (June '69-Feb. '72)

Harry R. Seymour (Jan. '71-June '72)

John H. Stierna (Apr. '70-Oct. '72)

Henry J. Vaux, Jr. (Aug. '69-Sept. '70)

Ann Wilm (June '69-Sept. '71)

Forecast Division

Russell G. Thompson, Chief (Aug. '70-Sept. '71)

Richard W. Callen (June '71-Aug. '71)

M. Leon Hyatt (Nov. '70-Nov. '71)

James W. McFarland (Jan. '71-Aug. '71)

Lawrence C. Wolken (June '71-Aug. '71)

H. Peyton Young (Jan. '71-Sept. '71)

Administrative and Editorial

Harold D. Jefferson (Nov. '70-Jan. '71)

Rosa D. Keatts (May '69-May '73)

Jerome Horowitz (Sept. '70-June '71)

Arthur M. Stratton (Nov. '72-Mar. '73)

Janet Kline (Mar. '69-June '69)

Thomas E. Kaye (May '70-Jan. '73)

Secretarial

Dolores Anderson (June '69-May '73)

Bernice Ciaffone (Nov. '69-Sept. '72)

LaVon DuSold (July '70-July '72)

Lorraine Frederick (Dec. '69-June '73)

Patricia Hooper (June '69-Nov. '71)

Lena McAllister (Dec. '68-July '72)

Mary Quaintance (June '70-Aug. '71)

Dorothy Read (Nov. '71-June '73)

Elizabeth Tune (June '69-June '70)

Rebecca Waters (June '69-May '73)

CONSULTANTS

Principal Consultants

Edward A. Ackerman[1], Executive Officer, Carnegie Institution of Washington

Harvey O. Banks, Consulting Engineer, Belmont, California

Irving K. Fox, Director, Water Resources Centre, University of British Columbia, Vancouver

Maynard M. Hufschmidt, Professor of City and Regional Planning and Environmental Sciences and Engineering, University of North Carolina

Ralph W. Johnson, Professor of Law, University of Washington

Edward Weinberg[2], Attorney, Wyman, Bautzer, Rothman and Kuchel, Washington, D.C.

Gilbert F. White, Professor of Geography and Director, Institute of Behavioral Sciences, University of Colorado

Nathaniel Wollman, Dean, College of Arts and Sciences, University of New Mexico

Abel Wolman, Professor Emeritus, The Johns Hopkins University, Consulting Engineer, Baltimore, Maryland

Legal Consultants

Edward W. Clyde, Firm of Clyde, Mecham and Pratt, Salt Lake City

Charles E. Corker, Professor of Law, University of Washington

N. William Hines, Professor of Law, University of Iowa

Ralph W. Johnson, Professor of Law, University of Washington

Frank J. Trelease, Dean, College of Law, University of Wyoming

Economic Consultants

Walter R. Butcher, Professor of Agricultural Economics, Washington State University

Emery N. Castle, Head, Department of Agricultural Economics, Oregon State University

Charles L. Leven, Director of the Institute for Urban and Regional Studies, Washington University (St. Louis)

William B. Lord, Director of the Center for Resource Policy Studies, University of Wisconsin

Howard C. Madsen, Staff Economist, Iowa State University

Monroe Newman, Professor of Economics, Pennsylvania State University

Consultants on Forecasting

Melvin D. George, Dean, College of Arts and Sciences, University of Nebraska

Ronald R. Hocking, Professor of Statistics, Institute of Statistics, Texas A&M University

Charles W. Howe, Professor of Economics, University of Colorado

Michael S. Proctor, Assistant Professor of Economics, Purdue University

Nathaniel Wollman, Dean, College of Arts and Sciences, University of New Mexico

Consultant on Recreation

Edward Crafts,[3] Recreational Consultant, Washington, D.C.

---

[1] Dr. Ackerman died suddenly on March 8, 1973.
[2] Served without compensation.

[3] Served under contract.

PANELS

Panel on Ecology and the Environment

Bostwick H. Ketchum (Chairman), Associate Director, Woods Hole Oceanographic Institute

William J. Aron, Director of Ecology and Environmental Conservation, National Oceanic and Atmospheric Administration, Department of Commerce

Charles F. Cooper, Director, Center for Regional Environmental Studies, San Diego State College

David M. Gates, Professor of Botany, University of Michigan

George H. Lauff, Director, W. K. Kellogg Biological Station, Hickory Corners, Michigan

Edward C. Raney, Division of Biological Sciences, Section of Ecology and Systematics, Cornell University

Thomas G. Scott, Director, Wildlife Research Center, Department of the Interior, Denver

William C. Steere, President, New York Botanical Garden

George M. Woodwell, Department of Biology, Brookhaven National Laboratory

Panel on Institutional Arrangements

Dean E. Mann (Chairman), Chairman, Department of Political Science, University of California (Santa Barbara)

David J. Allee, Department of Agricultural Economics, Cornell University

Lyle E. Craine, Chairman, Department of Resource Planning and Conservation, School of Natural Resources, University of Michigan

Irving K. Fox, Water Resources Research Centre, University of British Columbia

N. William Hines, Professor, College of Law, University of Iowa

Vincent A. Ostrom, Professor of Political Science, Indiana University (Bloomington)

Panel on Water Resource Planning

Harvey O. Banks (Chairman), Consulting Engineer, Belmont, California (formerly Director, Division of Water Resources, State of California)

Kurt W. Bauer, Executive Director, Southeastern Wisconsin Regional Planning Commission

Hugh P. Dugan, Consulting Engineer, Walnut Creek, California (formerly Chief Project Development Engineer, and Regional Director, U.S. Bureau of Reclamation)

Irving K. Fox, Water Resources Research Centre, University of British Columbia

Charles W. Hodde, Consultant, Olympia, Washington (formerly Chairman, Pacific Northwest River Basins Commission)

Keith S. Krause, Executive Director, Kansas Water Resources Board

Harold O. Ogrosky, Consultant, Lake City, Minnesota (formerly Director, Watershed Planning Division, U.S. Soil Conservation Service)

Eugene W. Weber, Consulting Engineer, Washington, D.C. (formerly Deputy Director of Civil Works for Policy, U.S. Army Corps of Engineers)

Panel on Water Pollution Control

Dwight F. Metzler (Chairman), Deputy Commissioner, New York State Department of Environmental Conservation

Edward J. Cleary, Consultant, Ohio River Valley Sanitation Commission

Paul D. Haney, partner, Black & Veatch, Kansas City, Missouri

David H. Howells, Director, Water Resources Research Institute at North Carolina State University

Walter A. Lyon, Director, Bureau of Sanitary Engineering, Pennsylvania Department of Environmental Resources

John D. Parkhurst, Chief Engineer and General Manager, Sanitation Districts of Los Angeles County

Lloyd L. Smith, Jr., Department of Entomology, Fisheries, and Wildlife, University of Minnesota

Leon W. Weinberger, Leon W. Weinberger and Associates, Washington, D.C.

Panel on Waste Heat Disposal

Peter A. Krenkel (Chairman), Chairman, Department of Environmental and Water Resources Engineering, Vanderbilt University

Lawrence B. Bradley, Executive Director, Industrial Development Division, Washington Department of Commerce and Economic Development

V. Stevens Hastings, Director of Environmental Planning, Commonwealth Edison Company

Robert T. Jaske, Research Associate, Pacific Northwest Laboratories, Battelle Memorial Institute

Joseph A. Mihursky, Chairman, Department of Environmental Research, National Resources Institute, Chesapeake Biological Laboratory, University of Maryland

Floyd R. Smith, President, Gulf States Utilities Company, Beaumont, Texas

Peter M. Stern, Vice President for Regional and Environmental Planning, Northeast Utilities Service Company, Hartford, Connecticut

Gabriel O. Wessenauer, Consulting Engineer, Chattanooga, Tennessee (formerly Manager of Power, Tennessee Valley Authority)

James H. Wright, Director, Environmental Systems Department, Westinghouse Electric Corporation, Pittsburgh, Pennsylvania

Panel on Forecast Procedures

Robert M. Thrall (Chairman), Chairman, Department of Mathematical Sciences, Rice University, Houston, Texas

Blair Bower, Economist, Resources for the Future, Inc., Washington, D.C.

Hugh P. Dugan, Consulting Engineer, Walnut Creek, California (formerly Chief Project Development Engineer and Regional Director, U.S. Bureau of Reclamation)

Earl O. Heady, Professor of Economics, Iowa State University

Walter B. Langbein, Consultant on Hydrology, Arlington, Virginia (formerly Research Scientist, U.S. Geological Survey)

Panel on Federal Decisionmaking

Harry R. Seymour (Chairman), Staff of the National Water Commission

Edward A. Ackerman,[1] Executive Officer, Carnegie Institution of Washington

Daniel Dreyfus, Staff of the Senate Committee on Interior and Insular Affairs

William J. Duddleson, Director of Policy Studies, The Conservation Foundation

R. Frank Gregg, Chairman, New England River Basin Commission

Edwin T. Haefele, Resources for the Future, Inc.

Henry C. Hart, Professor of Political Science, University of Wisconsin

Guy J. Kelnhofer, Jr., Consultant, Roseville, Minnesota

S. E. Reynolds, State Engineer, State of New Mexico

A. Allan Schmid, Professor of Agricultural Economics, Michigan State University

---

[1] Deceased March 8, 1973

BIOGRAPHICAL SKETCHES
PROFESSIONAL STAFF

THEODORE M. SCHAD, Executive Director, B.E., The Johns Hopkins University, 1939. U.S. Army Corps of Engineers, 1939-40, 1942-46; U.S. Bureau of Reclamation 1940-42, 1946-54; Bureau of the Budget 1954-58; Legislative Reference Service, Library of Congress 1958-68; Staff Director, Senate Select Committee on National Water Resources 1959-61; Deputy Director, Legislative Reference Service 1967-68; National Water Commission 1968-73.

HOWARD L. COOK, Deputy Director. BSCE, State University of Iowa, 1929. Assistant to Robert E. Horton, Consulting Engineer 1929-34; Soil Erosion Service, U.S. Department of the Interior 1934-35; Soil Conservation Service, U.S. Department of Agriculture 1935-40; staff of the Secretary of Agriculture 1940-53; Office of the Chief of Engineers, U.S. Army Corps of Engineers 1953-69; National Water Commission 1969-73.

RALPH E. FUHRMAN, Assistant Director for Programs. BSCE, University of Kansas, 1930; MSSE,

Harvard University 1937; PhD., The Johns Hopkins University 1954. Missouri State Board of Health 1931-37; City of Springfield, Missouri 1931-36; District of Columbia 1937-54; Executive Director, Water Pollution Control Federation 1955-69; National Water Commission 1969-71.

ROBERT N. BAKER, Assistant Director for Administration. BA, Pennsylvania State University 1941. U.S. Army, U.S. Air Force (retired as Colonel) 1941-61; American Machine and Foundry Co. 1961-64; Office of Economic Opportunity 1964-69; National Water Commission 1969-73.

FLORENCE L. BROUSSARD, Assistant to the Director. BS, University of Southwestern Louisiana 1948. Headquarters, Fourth Army 1950-56; The Texas Company 1957-58; Southwest Research Institute 1958-60; Legislative Reference Service, Library of Congress 1960-61; Office of Science and Technology, Executive Office of the President 1961-64; Legislative Reference Service, Library of Congress 1964-67; National Council on Marine Resources and

560

ngineering Development, Executive Office of the President 1967-69; National Water Commission 1969-73.

MYRON B. KATZ, Editor-in-Chief. Ph.B., University of Wisconsin, 1947. Bonneville Power Administration, U.S. Department of the Interior 1951-53; J. Henry Helser & Co, Portland, Oregon 1953-57; Economic Consultant, Oregon Legislature 1957-59; staff member, office of U.S. Senator from Oregon, and Visiting Lecturer, Lewis and Clark College 1959-61; Economic Consultant, Oregon Legislature 1961; Consulting Economist 1959-61; Economist, Bonneville Power Administration, and Lecturer in Economics, Portland State University 1961-72; National Water Commission 1972-73.

Legal Division

PHILIP M. GLICK, Legal Counsel and Chief, Legal Division. Ph.B., University of Chicago 1928; J.D., University of Chicago Law School, 1930. Associated with private law firm 1931-33; General Counsel, Federal Subsistence Homestead Corporation, U.S. Department of the Interior 1933-34; Chief, Land Policy Division, Office of the Solicitor, U.S. Department of Agriculture 1934-42; Solicitor, War Relocation Authority 1942-44; U.S. Navy 1944-45; Deputy Director, War Relocation Authority 1945-46; General Counsel, Public Housing Administration 1946-48; General Counsel, Institute of Inter-American Affairs and Technical Cooperation Administration, U.S. Department of State 1948-53; Visiting Professor, University of Chicago 1953-55; Private practice of law, Washington, D.C. 1955-67; Assistant Director for Policy, Water Resources Council 1967-69; National Water Commission 1969-73.

CHARLES J. MEYERS, Assistant Legal Counsel, BA, Rice University, 1949; LLB, University of Texas, 1949; LLM Columbia University, 1953; SJD Columbia University, 1964. Assistant Professor of Law, University of Minnesota 1953-54; Professor of Law, Columbia University 1954-62; Professor of Law, Stanford University 1962-70; Assistant Legal Counsel, National Water Commission 1970-73.

ERNST LIEBMAN, Assistant Legal Counsel. BA, Harvard College, 1952; LLB, Harvard Law School, 1955. Private practice 1956-62; Federal Power Commission 1962-66; associated with private law firm 1966-68; Deputy Legal Advisor, U.S. Water Resources Council 1968; Legal Advisor, U.S. Water

Resources Council 1968-70; National Water Commission 1970-73.

OLIVIA P. ADLER, Attorney. AB, Radcliffe College, 1962; LLB, Harvard Law School, 1967. Central Intelligence Agency 1962-64; McKinsey and Co., Management Consultants 1967-69; National Water Commission 1969-71.

JOHN L. DeWEERDT, Attorney. BA, University of Washington, 1967; JD, University of Washington, 1970. Law clerk to the Honorable Frederick G. Hamley, U.S. Court of Appeals, Ninth Circuit, San Francisco, California 1970-71; National Water Commission 1971-73.

RICHARD L. DEWSNUP, Attorney. LLB, University of Utah, 1956. Teaching Fellow, University of Chicago 1956-57; Clyde and Mecham Law Firm 1957-62; Deputy Attorney General, State of Utah 1962-66; University of Utah Law School 1966-67; private practice 1967-70; Member, Utah State Board of Fish and Game 1969-73; National Water Commission 1970-72.

GARY L. GREER, Attorney. AB, Columbia College 1957; LLB University of Colorado, 1964. Law clerk to the Honorable Jean S. Breitenstein, U.S. Circuit Judge, Denver, Colorado 1964-65; associated with private law firm, Denver, Colorado 1965-70; National Water Commission 1970-73.

WILLIAM A. HILLHOUSE II, Attorney. AB, Stanford University, 1961; LLB, Stanford University Law School, 1964. Teaching Fellow, University of Chicago Law School 1964-65; Associated with private law firm, Denver, Colorado 1965-72; National Water Commission 1972-73.

Engineering and Environmental Sciences Division

VICTOR A. KOELZER, Chief, Engineering and Environmental Sciences Division. BSCE, University of Kansas, 1937; MS, University of Iowa, 1939. Hydraulic Engineer, U.S. Geological Survey 1938-40; Hydraulic Engineer, U.S. Army Corps of Engineers 1940-42; U.S. Navy 1942-46; Bureau of Reclamation (in various capacities at various localities in the Western United States) 1946-56; Harza Engineering Company (in various positions, advancing in 1968 to Vice President) 1956-69; National Water Commission 1969-72.

EDWIN B. HAYCOCK, Water Resources Planner. BS, Utah State Agricultural College, 1939; MS, Utah State University, 1963. Bureau of Reclamation (in

561

various capacities at various localities in the Western United States) 1939-58; California Department of Water Resources 1958-64; Planning Director, Utah Division of Water Resources 1964-70; National Water Commission 1970-73.

ALEXANDER B. BIGLER, Urban Planner. BA, Stanford University, 1958; MA, Sacramento State College, 1959. Placer County Planning Department 1959-61; Napa County Planning Department 1961-62; California State Office of Planning 1962-68; National Planning Association 1968-70; National Water Commission 1970-72.

KENNETH L. BOWDEN, Hydrologist. BS, Northern Illinois University, 1956; MS, Northern Illinois University 1957. Assistantship, University of Michigan, Department of Conservation 1958-61 (Ph.D. Candidate); Pacific Southwest Forest and Range Experiment Station, U.S. Forest Service 1961-64; Assistant Professor, Northern Illinois University 1964-69; National Water Commission 1969-71.

JOHN S. GLADWELL, Water Resources Research and Planning Engineer. BS, Texas A&M University, 1959; MS, Texas A&M University, 1961; Ph.D., University of Idaho, 1970. U.S. Forest Service 1959-61; Washington State University 1961-64; Assistant Professor, University of Maine 1964-65; Washington Water Research Center, Washington State University 1965-70; Associate Professor, Washington State University 1970; National Water Commission 1970-71.

JACK D. LACKNER, Civil Engineer. BS, California State College at Los Angeles, 1966; M.S., University of Wisconsin, 1967. Civil Engineer, Secretaria de Energia y Mineria 1967-69; National Water Commission 1969-71.

THOMAS G. SCOTT, Ecologist. BS, Iowa State University, 1935; MS, Iowa State University, 1937; Ph.D., Iowa State University, 1942. U.S. Bureau of Sport Fisheries and Wildlife 1938-48; U.S. Army 1942-46; J. V. Bailey Nursery 1948-49; Illinois Natural History Survey 1950-63; Oregon State University, Department of Fisheries and Wildlife, and Associate Director, Marine Science Center 1964-70; National Water Commission 1970-71.

RICHARD C. TUCKER, Water Resources Engineer. BCE, Georgia Institute of Technology, 1964; MSCE Georgia Institute of Technology, 1965. Project Engineer for two private engineering firms 1965-67;

U.S. Army Corps of Engineers, Baltimore District 1967-70; National Water Commission 1970-72.

ROBERT E. VINCENT, Ecologist. BS, Oregon State University, 1954; MS, Cornell University, 1959; Ph.D., University of Michigan, 1962. Alaska Department of Fish and Game 1954-57; Graduate Research Assistant 1957-59; Research Associate, University of Michigan 1960-62; Utah Cooperative Fishery Unit 1962-63; Bureau of Sport Fisheries and Wildlife, U.S. Department of the Interior 1963-69; National Water Commission 1969-70.

Social and Behavioral Sciences Division

LYLE E. CRAINE, Chief, Social and Behavioral Sciences Division. AB, Oberlin College, 1931; Ph.M University of Wisconsin, 1937; MPA, Syracuse University, 1952; Ph.D, University of Michigan, 1956. Teacher, American School, Japan 1935; Instructor Whitewater State College, Wisconsin 1936-37; Instructor, Northern State University, Michigan 1939; U.S. National Resources Committee 1934-44; U.S. War Production Board 1944-47; U.S. Bureau of the Budget 1947-49; Institute of Public Administration 1949-53; Program Planning Office, U.S. Department of the Interior 1955-56; Lecturer, University of Michigan 1956-61; Professor, Department of Conservation, Michigan University 1961-67; Chairman, Department of Conservation, University of Michigan 1967-69; National Water Commission 1969-70.

DEAN E. MANN, Chief, Social and Behavioral Sciences Division. AB, University of California, Berkeley, 1955; MA, University of California, Berkeley, 1954; Ph.D, University of California, Berkeley 1958. Instructor, University of Arizona 1955-57; American Political Science Association, Congressional Fellow 1957-58; Assistant Professor, University of Arizona 1958-60; Brookings Institution 1960-63; The Ford Foundation in Venezuela 1963-65; Professor, University of California at Santa Barbara 1965-70; National Water Commission 1970-71.

GARY C. TAYLOR, Economist. BS, Cornell University, 1952; MS, Cornell University, 1958; Ph.D University of California, Berkeley, 1964. U.S. Army 1952-56; Bureau of Land Management, U.S. Department of the Interior 1956; Research Assistant Cornell University 1956-58; Agricultural Economist Economic Research Service, U.S. Department of Agriculture 1958-59; Economic Research Service 1959-64; Leader, Research Unit, Economic Research Service 1964-65; Chief, Environmental Economics ranch, Economic Research Service 1965-70; Assistnt to the Director, Natural Resource Economics)ivision, Economic Research Service 1970; National Vater Commission 1970-73.

HARRY R. SEYMOUR, Political Scientist. AB, lamilton College; MA, Syracuse University, 1950; ʰh.D, Syracuse University, 1961. Bureau of Naval ʰersonnel 1951-55; Head, Program Development ;taff, Navy Management Office 1955-57; General ;ervices Administration 1958-59; Chief, Management)ffice, U.S. Department of Justice 1959-62; The 3rookings Institution, Advanced Study Program 960-66; The Ford Foundation, New Delhi, India 966-67; The Brookings Institution 1967-70; Direcor, Study Team on Reorganization of the Executive 3ranch, Puerto Rico 1970-71; National Water Commission 1971-72.

FRANK H. BOLLMAN, Economist. B Agr Sci, Jniversity of Queensland, 1952; B. Comm., Canberra Jniversity College, 1959; Ph.D, University of California at Berkeley, 1971. Commonwealth Employ-nent Service 1951-54; Bureau of Agricultural Eco-iomics, Canberra 1954-60; Postgraduate Research Agricultural Economist, University of California 960-64; Arthur D. Little, Inc. 1964; California)epartment of Agriculture 1964-65; Postgraduate Research Agricultural Economist, University of Cali-'ornia 1965-71; National Water Commission 1971-73.

HELEN M. INGRAM, Political Scientist. BA,)berlin College, 1959; Ph.D, Columbia University, 967. Assistant Professor, University of New Mexico 965-69; National Water Commission 1970-71. Asso-:iate Professor of Political Science, University of Arizona, 1972-.

RAY M. JOHNS, Economist. BS, University of Maryland, 1961; MS, University of Maryland, 1964; ʰh.D, University of Maryland, 1969. Agricultural ;tatistician, U.S. Department of Agriculture 1961-64; Resource Development Analyst, Extension Service, Jniversity of Maryland 1962-66; Economic Research ;ervice U.S. Department of Agriculture 1966-68; Calvert County Economic Development Corporation 968-70; National Water Commission 1970-72.

TRUMAN P. PRICE, Public Administration Specialist. BS, University of Washington, 1945. Public

Utility District, Washington State 1947-51; U.S. Navy 1951-53; Public Utility District 1953-57; Department of Conservation, State of Washington 1957-65; U.S. Department of the Interior, Office of the Secretary 1965-69; National Water Commission 1969-72.

JOHN H. STIERNA, Economist. BS, Michigan State University, 1965; MS, Michigan State University, 1970. Economic Research Service, U.S. Department of Agriculture 1966-67; Midwest Research Institute 1967-70; National Water Commission 1970-72.

HENRY J. VAUX, Jr., Economist. AB, University of California at Davis, 1962; MS, University of Michigan, 1964; MA, University of Michigan, 1968. Graduate Assistant, School of Natural Resources, University of Michigan, 1963-64; U.S. Bureau of the Budget 1964-66; U.S. Army Corps of Engineers 1967; National Water Commission 1969-70.

ANN S. WILM, Associate Behavioral Scientist. AB, Ohio Wesleyan University, 1966; MS, University of Michigan, 1967. Tennessee State Planning Commission 1968-69; National Water Commission 1969-71.

Forecast Division

RUSSELL G. THOMPSON, Operations Research Mathematician. BA, University of Minnesota 1957; Ph.D, University of Minnesota, 1962. U.S. Air Force 1952-55; Instructor, University of Minnesota 1958-61; Assistant Professor, Texas A&M University 1961-62; Associate Professor, University of Missouri 1962-65; Fellow, National Science Foundation 1965-66; National Advisory Commission on Food and Fiber 1966; Associate Professor, University of Missouri 1966-67; Associate Professor, Texas A&M University 1967-68; Professor, Institute of Statistics, Texas A&M University 1968-70, National Water Commission 1970-71.

M. LEON HYATT, Engineer and Hydrologist. BS, Utah State University, 1965; MS, Utah State University, 1965; Ph.D, Utah State University, 1969. Assistant to Consulting Engineer 1958-60; Research Engineer, Utah State University 1965-67; Graduate Research Assistant, Utah State University 1967-69; Hydrologist, Federal Water Quality Administration 1969-70; National Water Commission 1970-71.

ABEL WOLMAN, Consulting Engineer, Baltimore, Maryland. Dr. Wolman's achievements during sixty years of teaching and the practice of engineering have earned him an unsurpassed reputation as a learned, yet very practical, adviser on all aspects of the development, utilization, and management of the water resource. His counsel on problems of public health, in particular, is in great demand throughout the world. Among his many other accomplishments, Dr. Wolman served for seventeen years as Chief Engineer of the Maryland State Department of Health and for twenty years as Professor of Sanitary Engineering at The Johns Hopkins University with which he is still associated as Professor Emeritus. He has acted as adviser to the Government of the United States upon numerous occasions, and to many foreign governments and international organizations. He has been retained by commissions, States, major cities, and private enterprises. He is a member of the National Academy of Sciences, the National Academy of Engineers, and many professional organizations.

EDWARD A. ACKERMAN, Executive Officer, Carnegie Institution of Washington. The offices held by Dr. Ackerman during a long and illustrious career included: Professor of Geography, University of Chicago; staff member, First Hoover Commission; staff member of the President's Water Resources Policy Commission; Chief, Natural Resources and Civil Works Branch, U.S. Bureau of the Budget; Assistant General Manager, Tennessee Valley Authority; Director, Water Resources Program, Resources for the Future, Inc.; and, Executive Officer, Carnegie Institution of Washington. The experience he gained in these posts, his keen mind, and his unflagging concern for the national interest, made his counsel of great value to the Commission. Dr. Ackerman's untimely death on March 8, 1973 is a great loss to the Nation.

HARVEY O. BANKS, Consulting Engineer, Belmont, California. Mr. Banks was admirably prepared to advise the National Water Commission by four decades of intensive work in the water field. He has, among other things, served in the capacity of State Engineer and Director of Water Resources for the State of California, as Chairman of the Board of Directors of Leeds, Hill and Jewett, Inc., consulting engineers, and as a consultant to foreign nations, States, commissions, water districts, cities, and corporations.

IRVING K. FOX, Director, Water Resources Research Centre, University of British Columbia. For more than a quarter of a century, Dr. Fox has been engaged in water programs and in studies of water policies. He was on the staff of the First Hoover Commission, represented the Department of the Interior on the interagency committee established to formulate a comprehensive plan for the Arkansas, White, and Red River Basins, was Director of the Water Resources Program of Resources for the Future, Inc., and also served as Vice President of that organization. Subsequently, he became Chairman of the Department of Urban and Regional Planning and Professor of Regional Planning at the University of Wisconsin. He assumed his present position in 1971.

MAYNARD M. HUFSCHMIDT, Professor, City and Regional Planning and Environmental Sciences and Engineering, University of North Carolina at Chapel Hill. Dr. Hufschmidt's advice to the National Water Commission was based on more than thirty years of active participation in water programs and in intensive studies of water problems and policies. He served the Federal Government for fourteen years in the National Resources Planning Board, the U.S. Bureau of the Budget and the Office of the Secretary of the Interior. Thereafter he spent ten years at Harvard University in research on water resource planning and development. In 1965 he moved to his present position at the University of North Carolina. He has served as consultant to many Federal agencies, non-Federal public entities, and private companies.

RALPH W. JOHNSON, Professor of Law, University of Washington. Professor Johnson has distinguished himself by his studies in both natural resources law and international law. He is an acknowledged expert on the law of fisheries. He has served also as a consultant to the Committee on Interior and Insular Affairs, U.S. Senate, and to the National Academy of Sciences. He is widely recognized as an authority on the legal aspects of weather modification and interbasin water transfers, both of which were subjects of special interest to the National Water Commission.

EDWARD WEINBERG, Attorney with the firm of Wyman, Bautzer, Rothman and Kuchel. Mr. Weinberg was able to base his advice to the National Water Commission upon a long and distinguished career in the Department of the Interior; a career which culminated in his appointment as Solicitor for that Department. His knowledge of water law and of the egal problems that stem from resource development was held in the highest esteem by the members of the National Water Commission.

GILBERT F. WHITE, Professor of Geography and Director of Behavioral Science, University of Colorado. Dr. White has long been recognized as one of the Nation's leading authorities on the use, development and conservation of natural resources. Early in his career he gained a broad knowledge of resource problems and programs by serving with the National Resources Planning Board and the U.S. Bureau of the Budget. He has held three important educational posts: President of Haverford College; Professor of Geography at the University of Chicago, and his present post at the University of Colorado. Of particular value to the National Water Commission was the perspective he had gained as Vice Chairman of the President's Water Resources Policy Commission, Chairman of the United Nations Panel on Integrated River Development, Chairman of a Task Force on Federal Control Policy established by the Bureau of the Budget, and Chairman of the Committee on Water of the National Academy of Sciences. His studies of flood plain management are influencing fundamental changes in the nature of Federal flood control activities.

NATHANIEL WOLLMAN, Dean, College of Arts and Sciences, University of New Mexico. The value of Dr. Wollman's advice to the National Water Commission was greatly enhanced by the knowledge he had gained through the painstaking studies of national water requirements which he had carried out under the sponsorship of Resources for the Future, Inc., the results of which were published in "The Outlook for Water, Quality, Quantity, and National Growth." His counsel was also valued because of his study of the water problems of Chile, and his research and teaching experiences at Colorado College and the University of New Mexico.

Acknowledgements

This report would not be complete without acknowledging the support provided to the Commission by man Federal, State, and local agencies of government, universities, private organizations, professional association and individuals whose efforts made it possible for the Commission to complete its work on time and within th funds allotted for its work. Appendices II and III list the Commission's contractors, staff, and consultants. I this Appendix, the Executive Director has attempted to acknowledge the special efforts of those whos contributions to the Commission's work might not otherwise be recorded.

The Executive Director wishes first to express appreciation for the way in which the Commissione themselves carried out their work. Between November of 1969 and April 1973, a period of not quite 4-1/ years, the Commission held 53 meetings, or one each month. Attendance at the meetings averaged 6. Commissioners per meeting for an attendance rate of 87.1 percent. Each chapter of the report was reviewed a least five times by the Commissioners prior to final release of this report. The final report represents a dedicate effort on the part of each of the Commissioners, who collectively provided the staff with the leadership an direction which made it possible to complete the report on time.

While many individuals made significant contributions to the preparation and review of the drafts of each c the chapters in the report, and of the background studies, the work of Professor Charles Meyers of Stanfor University deserves special acknowledgement. Professor Meyers authored or co-authored three of th background legal studies, supervised the preparation of eight other background studies, and prepared the fir drafts of Chapters 7, 8, 13, and 14, and of Sections C and D of Chapter 5.

Special appreciation must also be expressed to the secretarial staff, Miss Dolores Anderson, Miss Florenc Broussard, Mrs. Lori Frederick, Mrs. Dorothy Read, and Mrs. Rebecca Waters, for their dedicated assistance i the preparation of innumerable drafts of the report, to Mr. Arthur Stratton for the almost impossible task c preparing an index to the report before it was completed, to Miss Linda Reybine for bringing uniformity to th footnotes, and to Mr. Robert Baker for taking charge of putting it all together into a completed report.

In the formative days of the Commission, November-December 1968, invaluable help was received from th Presidential Commissions Liaison Office of General Services Administration, the Office of the Solicitor, U.S Department of the Interior, the U.S. Civil Service Commission, and the Water Resources Council in getting th Commission's work under way. Mr. Robert W. Blakeley, detailed from the Corps of Engineers, handled th Commission's administrative functions in the early days of its existence, until the Commission's ow administrative staff was appointed in April of 1969.

In formulating the Commission's program of study, the Commission and its staff consulted on sever; occasions with knowledgeable staff members from several congressional committees, including Mr. Kenneth . Bousquet, formerly chief of the staff of the Senate Public Works Appropriations Subcommittee; Mr. Baile Guard, Minority Clerk, and Mr. Richard Royce, formerly Chief Clerk and Staff Director, of the Senat Committee on Public Works; Mr. Charles F. Cook, Jr., Minority Counsel, Mr. Daniel A. Dreyfus, Profession; Staff Member, Mr. William J. Van Ness, Jr., Counsel, and Mr. Jerry Verkler, Staff Director, of the Senat Committee on Interior and Insular Affairs; Mr. Eugene Wilhelm, chief of the staff of the House Public Work Appropriations Subcommittee; Mr. Richard Sullivan, Chief Counsel, and Mr. Clifton Enfield, Minority Counsel of th House Committee on Public Works; and Mr. Jim Casey, Consultant, Mr. Charles Leppert, Minority Counsel, and Mr Sidney L. McFarland, Staff Director, of the House Committee on Interior and Insular Affairs.

The Commission also acknowledges the assistance of the Western States Water Council which held a joir meeting with the Commission in Portland, Oregon, to help provide a greater understanding of western wate problems.

Field inspections of metropolitan problem areas were made through the courtesy of Vinton Bacon, the General Superintendent of the Metropolitan Sanitary District of Greater Chicago which provided transportatio and guidance for the Commission to view work in progress in the vicinity of Chicago and the southern tip c Lake Michigan.

The Mississippi River Commission and the Lower Mississippi Valley Division of the U.S. Corps of Engineers ovided the Commission with a briefing and tour of the New Orleans harbor, the lower Mississippi River levees d control works, and the destruction caused by Hurricane Camille in August 1969 in the Louisiana coastal eas. The Philadelphia District of the Corps later provided a survey boat for an inspection of the Delaware iver Port area at Philadelphia.

The Metropolitan Water District of Southern California provided an aerial inspection tour and explanation of e water supply and flood control works in the Los Angeles area. In Arizona the Commission viewed the Salt iver Irrigation Project; an experimental system for power production, desalting, and food production, at lerto Penasco on the Gulf of California; the Environmental Research Laboratory of the University of Arizona Tucson, and the Water Conservation Laboratory of the Agricultural Research Service in Phoenix, through the ourtesy of the Salt River Irrigation District and the Central Arizona Project Association.

In mid-June of 1970 the Tennessee Valley Authority provided a briefing and a field inspection of its ydropower, navigation, recreation, and regional development activities, including a tour of the area to be rved by rural water systems on Sand Mountain, Alabama, financed under the program of the Farmers Home dministration of the U.S. Department of Agriculture, which provided ground transportation at the site.

In early 1971 officials of the City of Philadelphia provided a briefing and tour of the City's water treatment ant. As a part of the same meeting, representatives of the Delaware River Basin Commission provided a riefing and answered questions on the organization, powers, and functions of that organization.

Bonneville Power Administration provided transportation from Portland to Sun River, Oregon, where the ommission met with the Oregon Water Resources Board and made an inspection of irrigation, recreation, and sh and wildlife conservation facilities along the Deschutes River.

In Texas the Commission was provided with information on their programs by State water agencies and the exas River Basin Authorities. The Texas Water Conservation Association and Water, Inc., of Lubbock, Texas, scorted the Commission on an aerial inspection of the Colorado River Basin and the Southern High Plains area. he Commission was also shown through the Texas Agricultural Research Station near Lubbock, operated by exas A&M University. This meeting was also participated in by representatives of the Governor of Texas, the ulf Coast Waste Disposal Authority, the Southwestern Public Services Company, High Plains Water onservation District #1, North High Plains Ground Water District, the West Texas Water Institute, Texas Tech niversity, and personnel of Texas A&M University Agriculture Research and Extension Center, all of whom rovided the Commission with valuable data and information.

The U.S. Coast Guard provided transportation for the Commission's meeting and inspection tour in the Puget ound area of Washington.

The National Science Foundation, the American Society of Civil Engineers, and the Engineering Foundation rovided support for a conference at Airlie House for discussion of national policy implications of urban water nanagement, and the American Bar Association held two conferences for discussion of legal aspects of the ommission's work. More than a hundred individuals gave freely of their time and paid their own expenses to articipate in these conferences, which provided valuable comments on the Commission's background studies.

The National Water Company Conference engaged the firm of Day and Zimmerman to provide the ommission with detailed information on the investor-owned water industry.

Numerous Federal agencies facilitated the Commission's work by meeting with the Commission near the utset of its work for discussion of water problems. Meeting rooms for the Commission's monthly meetings in nd around Washington, D.C., were provided by the Comptroller General of the United States, the Federal ower Commission, the General Services Administration, and the Smithsonian Institution, which made the acilities of the Belmont Conference Center available on numerous occasions. Special thanks are due to Mrs. Jo ugel and her competent staff at Belmont for the excellent attention given to the Commission's needs during everal meetings at that facility.

Photographic Credits

Photographic illustrations for the report were provided by a number of Federal agencies, private corporations, nd individuals, listed below by chapter. Where several photographs from a single source are used in the same hapter the source is mentioned only once.

FRONT MATERIAL, Bureau of Reclamation; General Services Administration. CHAPTER 1, Forest Service Soil Conservation Service. CHAPTER 2, Bureau of Reclamation; National Park Service; Bert Brandt and Associates, Bayou Preservation Association of Houston, Texas; Kentucky State Department of Fish and Wildlife Resources; Tennessee Game and Fish Commission. CHAPTER 3, Forest Service; Atomic Energy Commission Metropolitan Edison Company; National Park Service; Bureau of Reclamation. CHAPTER 4, Bureau of Reclamation; Bureau of Land Management; Forest Service; Federal Water Pollution Control Administration Bureau of Sport Fisheries and Wildlife; Federal Water Quality Administration; Corps of Engineers. CHAPTER 5, Bureau of Reclamation; Tennessee Valley Authority; Jim Mitchell; Portland General Electric Company; National Park Service; Forest Service. CHAPTER 6, Bureau of Reclamation; Bureau of Land Management; Portland General Electric Company. CHAPTER 7, Bureau of Reclamation; Soil Conservation Service; Forest Service; Environmental Protection Agency. CHAPTER 8, Bureau of Reclamation. CHAPTER 9, Office of Saline Water; E. I. DuPont de Nemours and Company; Bureau of Reclamation. CHAPTER 10, Washington Post; National Park Service; Bureau of Reclamation; Bert Brandt and Associates; Soil Conservation Service. CHAPTER 11, Bureau of Reclamation; Water Resources Council. Soil Conservation Service; Corps of Engineers. CHAPTER 12, Bureau of Reclamation. CHAPTER 13, General Services Administration; Bureau of Indian Affairs. CHAPTER 14, Bureau of Reclamation; Bureau of Indian Affairs. CHAPTER 15, Bureau of Reclamation; Corps of Engineers. CHAPTER 16, Bureau of Reclamation; National Park Service. CHAPTER 17, Bureau of Reclamation; Bonneville Power Administration; Forest Service.

Theodore M. Schad
Executive Director

Index

A

Abu Dhabi, Sheikdom of 343
Acid mine drainage 67
Acreage Limitation in Federal Reclamation
    Program 142-149
        Recommendations on 149
        Exceptions from 143
Administrative Allocation of Water Rights 292
Advisory Commission on Intergrovernmental
    Relations 423,451
Aesthetic (see Esthetic)
Agricultural chemicals, pollution
    from 66,103,184,187
Agricultural Stabilization and
    Conservation Service 122,185
Agriculture, U.S. Department of
        Food and Fiber Programs 122
        Forecasts of Land Availability, ... 140
        Recommendations on 413
Agriculture, use of water in 14,130-138
        (see also Irrigation, Drainage)
Air pollution, relation to water
    pollution 70,83,98
Algae, pollution from 69
        (see also Eutrophication)
Allocation of water by pricing 248
Allocation of water in periods of
    shortage 289-292
Altered flows, environmental effects of 24,34
Alternative Demands for Water and Land for
    Agricultural Purposes, Summary of
        Heady Reports 130-138
Alternative furrow irrigation 300
Alternative futures 3,11-17
        for agriculture 15,121,130-140
        for municipal water 14
Alternative plans 225,366
American Water Works Association 165,314
Animal wastes 65
Appalachian Regional Development
    Act of 1965 60,390
Appliances, household, water saving 303
Appropriation Doctrine of Water
    Law 260-270,271-279

Appropriations procedures 387,393-394
Aquaculture 72
Aquifer protection 236-238
Acquisition of land to control flood
    plain use 155,160
Area of origin protection 323
Arizona v. California 313,460,464,475,476,
                                479,481,483
Army, U.S. Department of
    (see Corps of Engineers)
Artificial ice fields 360
Ash Council 410
        (see also President's Advisory Council on
        Executive Organization)
Atmospheric, washout 64
Atomic Energy Commission 377
Augmenting fog drip 360
Authorization procedures 387-391
        Recommendations 394
Avalanching snow/ice to increase water
    yield 360-361

B

Background studies
        List and description 543-555
Backlog of authorized projects 393
Balancing environmental and developmental
    values 205-225
Barge operations on inland waterways 527-532
Basic data 114
        Flood Plains 161
        Ground water 245
        Metropolitan areas 448
        Recreation 198,199
        Referral center 529,531
        Water quality 94,108
Benefit-cost analysis 380-381
Biochemical Oxygen Demand (BOD) 68
Board of Review (proposed) . 220,329,333,406-409
Boats, recreational 8,118,120,489,491,497
Bolsa Island Desalting plant (proposed) 339
Bonneville Power Administration 488
Boulder, Colorado, sewer and water costs 258
Budget classifications for water resources 392

Budgeting procedures 387,391-393
Bureau of Indian Affairs 185
Bureau of Outdoor Recreation 189-190
Bureau of Reclamation . 126-130,153,162,191-196,
              372,389,410-413,486-490
    Acreage Limitations 142-149
    Flood coastal program 143
    Irrigation program 126-130
    Recommendations on future
       activities 413,539
    Recreation at reservoirs 191-196
    Cloud seeding programs 347-348
    Geothermal desalting program 339
Bureau of the Budget (see Office
  of Management and Budget)
Bureau of Sport Fisheries and Wildlife 192-196
Bureau of Water Hygiene (See Office
  of Water Programs)

C

Calvert Cliffs Project 207,216
Canalbank management to increase water
  supplies 353
Capital demands for water resources 501-518
Central and Southern Florida Project 125-126
Central Arizona Project 220
Central Valley Project, California 48
Change in point of diversion 268-269
Channelization 32-37,122-125
    Effect on downstream floods 34,159
    Recommendations on 37
Chicago, Illinois sewage treatment
  system 97-98
Chicago Sanitary Canal 105
Civil works program of the Corps of Engineers,
  Recommendations on 413
    See also Corps of Engineers
Cloud seeding 346-351
    See also precipitation augmentation
Coastal zones 28-32,100-102,368
Collapsible bladders for transport of
  liquids 361
Colorado River basin precipitation
  augmentation program 348
Colorado River Basin Project Act 324,482
Colorado River Compact 418
Commission on Food and Fiber 139-140
Commission on Intergovernmental
  Relations 407
Commission on Marine Science, Engineering,
  and Resources 28,113

Commission on Organization of the Executive Branc
  (2d Hoover Commission) 15
Commission on Population Growth and the
  American Future 50,6
Commission on Reorganization of the Executive
  Branch of the Government (1st Hoover
  Commission) 407,41
Commission on rural Poverty 14
Committee on Water Resources Research 53
Community response to flood threats 16
Compensation to areas of origin 327,33
Conflicting interests in land management 35
Congressional handling of water resources
  project authorizations 38
Conservation crusade 11
Consolidating licensing proceedings ... 217,224,37
Construction grants 390,39
    For municipal waste collection
      and treatment 77-80,89,90,107,10
    For water supply 16
Consumptive use of water ....
    Tabulations 7,9,11,12,13
    Under Florida Water Resources Act
      of 1972 29
    By cooling towers 17
Contract authority for grant programs 39
Cooling water 11,12,13,14,19,43
                101,171-18
Corps of Engineers . 372,389,409-413,454,486-49
    Bank protection programs 18
    Drainage programs 122-12
    Flood control programs 150-16
    Flood plain management 15
    Guidelines for assessment of social,
      economic, and environmental effects
      of civil works projects 38
    Inland waterways programs 113-12
    Irrigation programs 125-12
    Permits 37
    Recommendations on future activities ... 41
    Recreation programs 19
    Research 53
Cost allocations 12
Cost effectiveness
    Pollution abatement programs 98,108
Cost-sharing for water programs 485-49
    Channelization 3
    Deficiencies in present policies 494-49
    Drainage 488,498
    Environmental values 32,49
    Federal programs (table) 49

Fish and wildlife conservation and
   improvement 489,498
Flood control 487,498
Goals 495
Grants programs (table) 492
Hydroelctric power 488,497
Industrial water supply 489,497
Inland waterways 118,120,486,497
Irrigation 486,497
Municipal water supply 489,497
Pollution abatement 489,498
Recreation at reservoirs 488,497
Regional development 497
Sewage treatment plants 489,497
Water quality enhancement 490
ouncil of Representatives of the Water
Resources Council 399-404
ouncil on Environmental
Quality 68,219,220,221,510
ouncils of Government (COG's) 45,451
ross-Florida Barge Canal 48,217,220

D

ata, see basic data
eauthorization of projects 394
ebts, State and local 519-522
ecisionmaking in water management 365-394
eep-tunnel storage of storm water 73
eficiencies in water resources planning 366
elaware River Basin
Compact 372,406,421-426,432
epartment of Natural Resources 409,410
esalting 335-346
   Compact units for residential use 360
   Costs 336,340,343,344
   Environmental problems 342
   Markets 342
   Processes 336
   Prototype construction 344
   Research program 345
   Recommendations 346
evelopment procedures for resolving differences
over environmental values 205-225
   Recommendations on 224,225
ischarge permits 92-94
iscount rate (for project evaluation) 383-387
   Recommendation 387
issolved solids 4,5,67
ivision of Water Supply, Environmental
Protection Agency 165,166

Drainage
   Cost-sharing 488,498
   Corps of Engineers program 122-125
   Soil Conservation Service programs 122
Dredge spoil disposal 103
Drinking water standards 169,170
Dubos, Rene 17
Dual water supply systems,
   recommendations 315

E

Eagle County and Water Division
   No. 5 cases 463,464,478
Ecological principles and processes 20-24
Economic Development
   Administration 59,163,388,486,489
Economic dislocations resulting from pollution
   abatement programs 98
Economic inducements for pollution control . 77-80
Ecosystems 20-24
Effective demand principle 381
Efficiency in water use 299-306
Effluent charges 80
Electric power, effects on water
   resources 14,171-184
Emergency procedures
   For flood control 150,153
   For water supply 165
Eminent domain 466,468
Enforcement procedures (for pollution
   abatement) 94
Engineering News-Record Construction
   Cost Index (chart) 517
Environmental advocate 221
Environmental effects of water
   development 19-37,138
Environmental evaluation 381
Environmental financing authority 525
Environmental Protection Agency 69,76,99,
165,185,219,221,371,376,388,408,426,507,510,514
Environmental quality, urban 447
Environmental values
   Cost-sharing for 497
   Procedures for resolving differences
     with developmental values 205-225
   Recommendations on 224-225
Environmental veto over development
   projects 219
Erosion and sedimentation damage control . 184-187
Esthetic effects, of channelization 34
   Of reservoir development 25

Estuaries and coastal zones 100-103
Eutrophication 69
    In Great Lakes 104
Evaluation of alternatives 379
Evaluation procedures 379-387
    Inland waterways 117
    Recommendations on 386
    Recreation 276
Executive Order No. 11296 (flood damage
    prevention) 155,161
Executive Order No. 11508 (disposal of
    excess federal lands) 197,199
Expenditures for water resources development
    Federal 502,504,505
    Total 506

F

Family size farm 142-144
Farmers Home Administration 59,163,166,388,486,
                                  487,498
Farm management practices to save
    water 301,302
Farm price support programs 121,129,135
Federal expenditures for water programs
    Table 502
    Trend (graph) 504
Federal grant and loan programs 390,369
    Recommendations 394
Federal grants for planning 369
Federal Inter-Agency River Basin Committee .. 416
Federal-Interstate Compacts 418,421-423
    (Map, 419)
Federal Reclamation Act of 1902 111,142,267
Federal-State-Local cooperation 453-455
Federal-State jurisdiction over water 459-471
Federal Water Pollution Control Act
    of 1948 82
    1956 Amendments 82
    1961 Amendments 490
    1965 Amendments (Water Quality
    Act of 1965) 70,71,74,75,82,
              87,92,106,507,511,516
    1972 Amendments 69,74,84,87-89,
         93,99-102,107,108,207,371,
         376,390,391,506,510
Federal Water Project Recreation
    Act 187,192,190,489
Federally chartered corporations 427-433
Federal reclamation program
    (see Irrigation)
Feedlot wastes 65,73

Fertilizer (See agricultural chemicals)
Financing water programs .... 519-5?
    Metropolitan area water
        facilities .... 4?
    Pollution abatement .... ?
    Recommendations on .... 5?
    Recreational development .... 194,1?
    State and local .... 517-5?
First National Assessment (Water
    Resources Council) .... 9-?
Fish and Wildlife Coordination Act ... 200-203,4?
Fish and wildlife protection and
    improvement .... 200-2?
    Cost-sharing .... 489,4?
Fisheries, Great Lakes .... 1?
Five-year programs for water resources
    projects .... 3?
Fixtures and appliances to save water .... 3?
Flood control .... 149-1?
    Cost-sharing .... 487-4?
    Recommendations on .... 160-1?
Flood Control Act of 1936 ..... 111,150,151,1?
Flood Control Act of 1938
    Cost-sharing provisions of .... 4?
Flood Control Act of 1944 .... 125,389,4?
Flood Control Act of 1960 .... 151,154,1?
Flood Control Act of 1968 .... 125,4?
Flood Control Act of 1970 .... 1?
Flood Control Policy, Task Force on .... 1?
Flood damage reduction .... 149-1?
Flood emergency programs .... 1?
Flood forecasting .... 150-153,1?
Flood insurance .... 153,1?
Flood plain management .... 151,1?
    To increase water supplies .... 3?
Flood Plain mapping .... 1?
Florida Water Resources Act of 1972 ..... 294-2?
Fog drip .... 3?
Food and Fiber programs .... 121-1?
    Cost-sharing for .... 1?
Forest management to increase water
    supplies .... 353,3?
Forest Service .... 195,196,3?
Fort Chartres and Ivy Landing Drainage
    District No. 5, Illinois .... 1?
Framework plan for water resources
    development .... 168,5?
Frying Pan-Arkansas project, Colorado .... 3?

G

Geological Survey (see U.S. Geological Survey)
Geothermal Research and Development
    Program .... 339,3?

laciers, artificial 360
randfather rights to pollute 93
reat Lakes 433-439
   Dredge spoil disposal 103,108
   Environmental quality 103
   Institutions 435-437
   Interbasin transfers 322
   Management 437-439
   Pollution problems 103-107
   Recommendations on 438,439
reat Lakes Basin Commission 436
reat Lakes Commission 435
reat Lakes Fisheries Commission 435
round water management 230-247
round water mining 238
round water pollution 243-244,247
round water rights 293
ulf Coast Waste Authority 415

H

igh Plains of Texas 231,238-239,322
oover Commission (1st) 407,410
oover Commission (2nd) 157
ousing and Urban Development, U.S.
   Department of 155,157,162,163,372,
                    388,406,486,489
uman consumption of reused
   wastewaters 312-313
urricane Agnes 149,154
ydroelectric power, cost-sharing
   for 488,497
   Value of water for 45

I

ebergs, towing 361
dependent Board of Review
   (proposed) 220,329,333,406-409
dian water rights 473-483
cremental cost pricing 249,257
consistent cost-sharing policies 490-493
dustrial wastes 65
dustrial water supply 161-170
   Cost-sharing 489,497
   Potential for savings 304
   Storage in Federal reservoirs 162
   Value of water for 43
equities in cost-sharing policies 494-6
formal public participation in water
   resources planning 376
land waterways 113-121

Cost-sharing for 120,486,497
Deficiencies in program 115-117
Value of water for 45
As a part of National transportation
   system 120
Instream uses of water 6,8
Integrated grant application program 164
   Recommendation on 170
Integrated management of surface and ground
   water 233-236
Integrating research and planning 536
Interagency Committee on Water
   Resources 399,403,416
Inter-agency River Basin Committees 416
   (Map, 419)
Interbasin transfers of water 317-333
   Criteria for 330
   Recommendations 332-333
Interior, U.S. Department of
   Recommendations on 413,539
   (See also Bonneville Power Administration,
      Bureau of Reclamation, Bureau of
      Indian Affairs, etc.)
International Boundary and Water
   Commission 192
International Joint Commission 435
Interstate compacts 418-426
Interstate pollution control agencies . . . 90,418,420
Intrastate water planning 369
Investor-owned water utilities 165
Irrigation, Bureau of Reclamation program . 126-130
   Cost-sharing 486,497
   Corps of Engineers program 125
   Development in Western States graph 127
   Repayment, Missouri River Basin
      Project (Table) 146
   Soil Conservation Service program 122
   Value of water for 42-43
Irrigation Efficiency, improvement of 300
Irrigation use of sewage effluent 313
Islands, as recreational resources 197
   Recommendations on 199

J

Joint administration, water supply and
   waste disposal 445,447

K

L

Lake Erie 103-105

Lake Huron 104
Lake Michigan 105
Lake Ontario 105
Lake Superior 103
Land acquisition, for recreation 199
    For flood plain management 155,160
Land disposal (of sewage) 71
Land management to increase water supply   351-359

      Privately-owned lands 358
      Publicly-owned lands 359
      Recommendations 359
Land and Water Conservation Fund .. 156,189,278
Land use in relation to water resources 24,445
Land use planning 97,368
    Coordination with water resources
      planning 158,161,366
Land and Water Resources Council (proposed) . 368
Leak control programs 305
Legislative Reorganization Act of 1970 390
Legislative Reservation of Waters 272
Licensing non-Federal development 207
    Recommendations on 224-225
Licensing procedures for non-Federal projects
    Public participation 376-378
Lower Colorado River Authority, Texas 369

M

Magneto hydrodynamics 179
Manpower, for pollution abatement programs ... 99
Marginal costs of sewage collection and treatment in
    residential areas (Table) 250
Marine Protection, Research, and Sanctuaries
    Act of 1972 101
McCarran Amendment 463-464
Melting ice caps to create lakes 361
Metropolitan areas, water problems 441-457
    Institutions 449-453
    Planning 370
    Recommendations 456-457
Metropolitan Water District of Southern
    California 143,445
Mexican Water Treaty 482
Miami Conservancy District 159,414,415
Milorganite 98
Milwaukee, Wisconsin Sewage Treatment
    Plant 98
Mine drainage, pollution from 67
Minidoka Project, Idaho 52
Minimum stream flows, reservation
    of 273, 287-289, 465

Mississippi River and tributaries project
    Cost-sharing provisions of 48
Missouri River Basin Project
    Repayment provisions 146,48
Model (State) Water Use Act 28
Monomolecular films to reduce evaporation ... 30
Multiobjective planning 38
Municipal bonds, use of to finance water
    development 519,52
Municipal sewerage systems 6
Municipal water supply 161-17
    Cost-sharing 489,49
    Storage in Federal reservoirs 16
Municipal Water Use
    Influence of Meters on 25
    Influence of Pricing on 252-25
    Recommendations 25
    Value of water for 4
Muskegon, Michigan pollution abatement
    project 7

N

National Academy of Sciences
    Committee on Resources and Man 14
    Committee on Technologies and
      Water 359-36
    Report on Marine Environmental
      Quality 1C
    Report on Waste Management Concepts for
      Coastal Zone 1C
National Commissions
    Commission on Food and Fiber 139-14
    Commission on Intergovernmental
      Relations 4C
    Commission on Marine Science, Engineering,
      and Resources 28,1
    Commission on Organization of the Executive
      Branch of the Government (1955) (2d
      Hoover), ... 157,4C
    Commission on Reorganization of the Executiv
      Branch of the Government (1948) (1st
      Hoover) 407,4
    Commission on Population Growth and the
      American Future 50,6
    National Advisory Commission on Food and
      Fiber 139,14
    National Advisory Commission on Rural
      Poverty 14
    Presidential Advisory Committee on Water
      Resources Policy (1955) 385,4
    President's Advisory Council on Executive
      Organization (Ash Council) (1970) 4

President's Water Resources Policy Commission
(1950) 407
Public Land Law Review
Commission (1970) 466
Senate Select Committee on National Water
Resources (1961) 399,410
Task Force on Federal Flood Control
Policy (1965) 157-158
ational efficiency criteria 381
ational Environmental Policy
Act 200,206-211,215-225,390
ational Flood Insurance Act of 1968 157,372
ational Oceanic and Atmospheric
Administration 108,154,155,363,410,
413,531,534,537
Recommendations on 413,537
ational Park Service 195,196
ational Trails System 189
ational transportation system 120
ational Water Commission
Former members v
Members iv
Staff vii,557-567
ational Water Commission Act (text) 539-541
ational Water Rights Procedures Act
(proposed) 461-471
ational Wild and Scenic River System 189
ationwide Outdoor Recreation Plan 189
atural Resources, Department of 409,410
avigable waterways, see Inland navigation
avigation servitude 467
o-discharge goal for water pollution 69,70
onpoint-sources (of pollution) 65,74
ortheastern United States Water Supply
Study 163,372,454
utrients in wastewater 309

O

ak Ridge National Laboratory 343
BERS Projections 139
cean dumping 101
ffice of Civil Defense 165
ffice of Emergency Preparedness 156
ffice of Management and
Budget 164,391,404,407,501
ffice of Saline Water 336,337,339,341,
342,363,537
ffice of Science and Technology 534
ffice of Water Resources
Research 363,532,533,534
ffice of Water Technology
(proposed) 363,397,412,413,537

Offshore reservoirs 361
Ogllala Formation 221,238,239
Ohio River Valley Water Sanitation
Commission 78,406
Oil Spills 67
Omnibus (Reclamation) Adjustment Act
of 1926 143,267
One-stop licensing procedures 225
Onsite use of water 6
Orange County Water District 235,236
Osgood Project, Idaho, water
Savings on 305
Otsego, Michigan 255-256
Outdoor Recreation Resources Review
Commission 188-189
Overdrafts of ground water supplies 233

P

Papillion Creek Project (Nebraska) 492
Pathogens and viruses in wastewater 309
Permit system for riparian States 280-298
Recommendations on 293-294
Permits (for discharges) 92-94
Pesticides, see Agricultural chemicals
Philadelphia, Pennsylvania 256
Phreatophyte control 353
Planning 365-379
For metropolitan water management 370
For recreation 199
For water pollution abatement 83,84,371
To accomodate environmental values 217
Plant siting
Recommendations on 225
Plumbing codes, amendments to save water ... 305
Plumbing fixtures, water savings 303
Point-sources (of pollution) 64
Policies, Standards, and Procedures for the
Formulation, Evaluation, and Review of Plans for
Use and Development of Water and Related Land
Resources, Senate Document 97, 86th
Congress 399
Polluter pay principle 84-85
Pollution abatement 63-108
Cost-sharing 489,498
Regulation for 87,88
Pollution, definitions 69-70
From agricultural chemicals 66, 103
Of ground water 243-244,247
Population, effect of water policies and programs
on 50-51,59-61

Population Growth and the American Future,
    Commission on 50,60
Posten Bayou, Arkansas 124
Precipitation augmentation 346-351
    Costs 349
    Ecological effects 349
    Economic effects 349
    Environmental effects 349
    Legal implications 350
    Recommendations on 351
    Research on 347
Precipitation forecasting 360
Presidential Advisory Committee on Water
    Resources Policy (1955) 385
President's Advisory Council on Executive
    Organization (1970) 410
Pricing irrigation water 256
Pricing to motivate better water use 247-259
Pricing policies to conserve water 303
    Recommendations on 305
Pricing policy of water utilities (table) 254
Pricing sewerage services 80,81,255
Pricing system principles 249
Principles and Standards for Planning Water and
    Land Resources, Water Resources
    Council 156,382
Property tax as a source of revenues for water
    development 524
Protein substitutes
    Effect on demand for land and
    water 15,137,138
Public finance 519-525
Public Law 566 programs 122,184,196,
                              410,487,488,490
Public participation,
    In environmental decisionmaking 225
    In planning for non-Federal projects 377
    In water resources planning 372-379
Public relations programs to stress wise use
    of water 303-304
Public right to access to water bodies 274
Public rights in water 273
Public trust doctrine (in use of water
    bodies) 274,276,282,377
Public Works and Economic Development Act
    of 1965 60
Puerto Penasco, Sonora, Mexico,
    Multiple purpose desalting demonstration . 343
    Trickle irrigation 304,305
Pump taxes 240-241,251

Q

Quantification of Federal water rights 466

Quantification of water rights to increase
    efficiency of use 30
Quota restrictions (ground water) 241-24

R

Rainfall (see also Precipitation)
Rapid City, South Dakota, flood losses 149,15
Receiving water standards 82,91,10
Reclamation Act of 1902 111,142,267,46
Reclamation programs 121-14
    Bureau of Reclamation 126-13
    Corps of Engineers 122-12
    Cost-sharing for 142,148,149,486,49
    Department of Agriculture 12
    Relation to farm price supports 12
Reclamation Project Act of 1939 26
Recommendations on:
    Acreage limitation 14
    Appropriations procedures 39
    Authorization proceudres 39
    Basic data 52
    Board of Review 40
    Channelization 3
    Conflicts between Federal and State
        and Indian water rights 461,462,463
                              464,465,468,48
    Contract authority 39
    Cost-sharing 49
    Deauthorization of projects 39
    Desalting 34
    Discount rate for project evaluation 38
    Efficiency in water use 30
    Energy conservation 18
    Environmental values 22
    Erosion and sedimentation 18
    Estuaries and coastal zones 3
    Evaluation principles and standards 38
    Federal Agency Programs 413,532,53
    Financing by State and local governments . 52
    Fish and wildlife programs 20
    Flood plain management 16
    Food and fiber programs 14
    Government organizations 41
    Grant applications 170,40
    Great Lakes 43
    Ground water 233,234,235,236,238
                              242,243,244,245,246,247
    Independent Board of Review 40
    Indian water rights 477,478,481,48
    Inland waterways 12
    Integrated grant application program 17
    Interbasin transfers of water 33

Interstate compacts 418,424,425,426,457
Interstate planning 418
Intrastate organizations 415
Islands, as recreational resources 199
Land management to increase water yield . 359
Legal systems 233,261,269,278,293
Metropolitan water problems 456
Municipal and industrial water supply 170
Permit systems under riparian water law .. 293
Precipitation augmentation 351
Prelicense planning 224,377
Pricing of water 259
Public access to water bodies 279
Public participation in
  planning 374,375,376,378
Reclamation subsidies 148
Recreation at reservoirs 199
Reevaluation of projects before 394
  construction
Regional corporations 433
Research 537
Reuse of wastewater 314
Riparian permit systems 293
State water laws 262,263,264,278
State water records 261,262
Transfer of water rights 262,263,264,
                              265,266,267,268,269
Waste heat 183
Water pollution control 107
Water quality planning 107,372
Water recreation 199,279
Water Resources Council 160,161,203,
                              403,404,405,406
Water resources planning 369,370,371,
                              372,386,404,405
Water Rights Procedures Act 461,462,463,
                              464,465,467,468,471
Water Savings practices 305,306
ecreational boats 8,118,120,489,491,497
ecreational use of reclaimed wastewater 314
ecreation at reservoirs 187-199
  Cost-sharing for 195,488,497
  Statistics (Table) 193
ecreation, Value of Water for 45
ecycling (see Reuse)
eevaluation of projects 394
efuse Act of 1899 108,208,376
egional Development
  Cost-sharing for 497
egional economic development, effects of water
  development on 48-61
egulation by interstate compacts 421

Drinking water standards 169,170
Flood plain 155,160
Ground water withdrawals 233-242
To control pollution 82,85-86,87
Transportation rates 120,121
Water use to increase efficiency .. 299,300,305
Weather modification 350-351
Reimbursement (see Cost-sharing)
Repayment policy (see Cost-sharing)
Reports to Congress on public participation ... 375
Research 532-537
  Metropolitan areas 448
  On pollution abatement 86,87
  On water technology 362-363
  On wastewater reuse 314,315
Reserved rights of Federal government 464
Reserved rights of Indian Tribes 473
Residuals 4,97
Reuse of wastewater 306-315
  Costs 43,308-311
  Recommendations 314,315
Revenue sharing 522,524
Riparian Doctrine of Water Law .. 272,280-298,326
River and Harbor and Flood Control
  Act of 1970 123,468
River Basin Commissions 416
  Map 419
Root River Basin (Wisconsin) 444,446
Running Water Draw, Plainview, Texas 125
Runoff (Bar chart) 5
Rural Development Act of 1972 ... 59,162,163,489
Rural Environmental Assistance Program 185
Rural water supply programs 163,166

S

Sabine River and tributaries, Texas
  and Louisiana 124
Sale of water rights 260-270
Saline Water Conversion Act of 1971 344
San Carlos Reservoir, Arizona 530
Sea lamprey in the Great Lakes 103
Sedimentation 66,101
Selective cutting to increase water supplies 355
Senate Select Committee on National Water
  Resources 13,399
Sequencing uses to save water 303
Service charges for pollution abatement 80
Sewage treatment plants
  Cost-sharing 489,498
  Grants for construction of 77-80
Sheyenne River, North Dakota 124

Sludge disposal 97,102
Small Reclamation Projects Act of 1956 143
Snow/ice avalanching to increase water
    yield 360-361
Snowpack management to increase water
    supplies 354
Social values in water 271-279
Soil Conservation Service 32,122,151-153,157,
    162,184,196,389,409,410,411,486,487,490,492
Soil surface management to increase water
    supplies 355
Solid waste disposal 101
Souris River, North Dakota 125
Sovereign immunity 468
Springfield, Missouri 256
Sprinkler irrigation 301
State and local government financing of water
    development 517-524
State water laws
    Recommendations to provide recognition
        for social values 271-279
    (See also Federal-State jurisdiction over water)
State water rights records 261
    Recommendations for
        improvements 261-264,268,269
Steele Bayou, Yazoo River, Mississippi 124
Storm drainage in urban areas 158
Storm runoff in urban areas 158
Storm water pollution 65,73
Streambank management to increase water
    supplies 353
Streamflow 9
Stringtown Drainage and Levee District No. 4,
    Illinois 124
Subsidies
    To encourage pollution abatement 77
    In reclamation programs 142-149
    Recommendations on 148-149
    For water development 495

T

Task Force on Federal Flood Control
    Policy 157-158
Technological innovations to improve use of
    water 362-363
Technology and Water Development,
    Committee on 359-362
Tennessee River 53
Tennessee Valley Authority . 150,153,185,192,193,
    200,372,427,488
Texas River Authorities 414

Texas Water Plan . . . . 3[
Tocks Island Project . . . . 2[
Transfer of water rights 260-270,292-29
Trickle irrigation . . . . 3[
Tripartite Agreement . . . . 4[
Tucumcari Project, New Mexico . . . . [

U

Undersea aqueducts . . . . 3[
Unified National Program for Flood Plain Manageme
    Water Resources Council . . . . 1[
Unified National Program for Managing Flood Losse
    Task Force on Federal Flood Control Policy . 1[
Upper Great Lakes Regional Commission . . . . . 4[
Urban erosion and sedimentation problem . 184,18
U.S. Geological Survey 154,155,243,24
    246,247,410,53
User charges
    Inland waterways . . . . 1[
    Municipal water . . . . 2[
    Recreation facilities . . . . 190,194,1[
    Sewerage 80,52

V

Value of water 40-4
Variable pricing . . . .
    For pollution abatement 8
    Municipal water 25
Vegetable proteins (see protein substitutes)
Vegetal management to increase water
    supplies 35
Viruses in wastewater 30

W

Waste assimilation, value of water for 4
Waste heat 65,171-18
Wastewater reuse 306-31
    Costs 308-31
    Recommendations 314,31
Water meters 30
    Recommendation 25
Water pollution
    Definitions 69-7
    Sources of 64-6
Water pollution control costs 74-76,508-51
Water Quality Act of 1965, ... 70,71,74,75,8[
    87,92,106,51
Water Quality Enhancement
    Cost-sharing 49

ater quality management 63-108
    Planning for 83,84,372
ater Resources Council 160,161,202,203,
      218,369,370,371,372,374,382,383,385,
      398-406,485,493,506,531,537
ater resources planning 365-372
    Coordination with water quality
      planning 83,84,371,372
ater Resources Planning Act of 1965 112,161
      163,202,369,370,371,372,387,410,414,489

ater savings practices 253,299-304
    Recommendations 305-306
atershed Protection and Flood Prevention Act,
  PL 566 122,184,196,410,487,488,490
ater Supply Act of 1958 162,166,267,385
ater Supply Division, Environmental Protection
  Agency 166
eather Modification Reporting Act 350,351

Western Tennessee Tributaries, Tennessee and
  Kentucky 124
Westwide Study (Bureau of Reclamation) 372
Wild and scenic rivers 498
Wild and Scenic Rivers Act 25,189
Winters v. *United States* 473-476
Wisconsin Valley Improvement Company . . 369,427
Withdrawal charges for water 251
    Recommendations on 259
Withdrawal use of water 8
    Tabulations 7,9,11,12

X,Y

Z

Zero discharge goal (see no discharge goal)
Zoning 277

71020